The
ENCYCLOPEDIA
of DAYTIME
TELEVISION

The
ENCYCLOPEDIA
of DAYTIME
TELEVISION

Everything You Ever Wanted to Know About Daytime
TV But Didn't Know Where to Look! From *American
Bandstand*, *As the World Turns*, and *Bugs Bunny*, to *Meet
the Press*, *The Price is Right*, and *Wide World of Sports*,
the Rich History of Daytime Television in All Its Glory!

WESLEY HYATT

BILLBOARD BOOKS
An Imprint of Watson-Guptill Publications
New York

TO MY MOTHER AND FATHER, GAYLE AND RON HYATT,

AND MY SISTER, LUANN HYATT,

ALL OF WHOM WONDERED WHAT I WAS GOING TO GET OUT

OF WATCHING SO MUCH TELEVISION GROWING UP.

THIS IS THE ANSWER.

Senior Editor: Bob Nirkind
Edited by Sylvia Warren
Designed by Areta Buk
Production Manager: Ellen Greene

First published 1997 by Billboard Books,
an imprint of Watson-Guptill Publications,
a division of Billboard Productions, Inc.,
at 1515 Broadway, New York, NY 10036

Library of Congress Cataloging-in-Publication Data
Hyatt, Wesley.
    The encyclopedia of daytime television / Wesley Hyatt.
      p.   cm.
    ISBN 0-8230-8315-2
    1. Television programs—United States—History. 2. Television
broadcasting—United States—History. I. Title.
    PN1992.3.U5H93 1997
    791.45'75'097303—dc21   97-15658
                                              CIP

Manufactured in the United States

First printing, 1997

1 2 3 4 5 6 7 8 9 / 05 04 03 02 01 00 99 98 97

ACKNOWLEDGMENTS

Lily Tomlin once remarked that while a person who has finished many books is considered well read, a person who watches a lot of television is not necessarily well viewed. Well, I may not be "well viewed," but there must be an appropriate adjective to apply to a TV scholar like myself who has watched literally thousands of hours of shows to come up with the credits and story information included on daytime series in this book. Though sometimes a tedious process (anyone care to sit down and follow *Skeleton Warriors* with me?), overall it has been a labor of love, and I hope my entries on each show add details you may not know or have forgotten, or bring back fond memories. I have listed most data objectively, but in many cases have also included subjective comments that make clear what I think each program's place is in the history of daytime television.

Apart from the many books and periodicals I reviewed (which are listed in the bibliography), my principal source of information was the shows themselves. Some shows I watched on broadcast and satellite TV airings, and some I was able to rent on videotape or purchase locally. However, some relatively rare series were available to me only via mail order catalogs, so I salute the offerings from Outre Products of Evanston, Illinois; Stephen M. Russo of Boston, Massachusetts; Kevin Heumaneus of Flowery Branch, Georgia; Shokus Video of Chatsworth, California; and Don't Touch That Dial . . . of Mundelein, Illinois. Also providing some offbeat tapes and trivia on old shows was my old college buddy Joe Norrad, now program director for NBC affiliate WGBA, in Green Bay, Wisconsin.

I also contacted 15 fan clubs of daytime shows, and a few broadcasters groups, in my search for information; sad to report, only two representatives responded. (Maybe they are writing their own books about their shows' history for posterity.) In any event, I tip my hat to Jim Pierson of Dan Curtis Productions, Inc., who provided both helpful advice and a photograph of *Dark Shadows,* and to Sharon Kearns, president of the *Guiding Light* Fan Club.

Apart from *Dark Shadows,* all the great rare photos seen in this book are courtesy of Photofest in New York City.

Thank you, Ronald Mandelbaum, and your fine staff for wading through your files one dreary day in November 1995 to dig up shots I might want to include.

I started this project while working at Divers Alert Network, a scuba diving safety program affiliated with Duke University, in 1994. I wish to thank the entire staff there, particularly Renee Duncan Westerfield and John Rorem, for their encouragement and suggestions.

In 1995 I became coordinator of publicity for an act that guested on several series in this book, including *Mike Douglas, American Bandstand,* and even *Hollywood Squares—* KC and the Sunshine Band. I'd like to thank KC especially for his help and suggestions, which were definitely above and beyond the call of duty. Others in the association who contributed to the effort with advice and support were his backup singers Beverly Champion Foster and Maria DeCrescenzo, tour manager Barbara Stevens, road manager Rick Raymond, and business manager Mel Haber.

A special thanks is in order to the editor at Billboard Books who first approved the project, Paul Lukas. I appreciate his faith that a first-time author could do the job, his patience in answering my questions, and his willingness to solve the problems that arose as a result of my inexperience. The same hearty endorsement goes to my current editor, Bob Nirkind, who offered solid constructive criticism and brought general enthusiasm to a project that basically fell into his lap. And let me give a final nod to the copy editor, Sylvia Warren, whose input and questions concerning the manuscript were quite helpful.

I hope this final result wins approval from everyone listed above, as well as from all those who buy it. *The Encyclopedia of Daytime Television* may not be the last word on daytime television, but it is certainly the first encyclopedia on the subject, and is hopefully one that provides as much accurate information as it seemed feasible to include while being as entertaining as the best daytime TV series.

Wesley Hyatt
August 1997

CONTENTS

INTRODUCTION

Celebrating the 15th anniversary of As the World Turns *were these four original cast members: from left to right, Santos Ortega (who played Grandpa Hughes), Don MacLaughlin (Chris Hughes), Helen Wagner (Nancy Hughes), and William Johnstone (Judge Lowell).*

DO YOU REMEMBER the game show where a woman won only two cents on the debut? The talk show that had six movie Tarzans appear in loincloths? The cartoon for which Jesse White, Stubby Kaye, and other comedians auditioned unsuccessfully? The animal show on which Marlin Perkins was bitten by a rattlesnake? The two attempts to showcase professional football leagues in the spring rather than in autumn? If your answer to any of the above is "no," but you wish it were "yes," then you need to know the history of daytime television series.

Some shows going back near the start of it all 50 years ago are still with us—*Meet the Press, Today, As the World Turns, The Bugs Bunny Show, NFL Football*—and you may watch any or all of them. But do you remember who has appeared on those shows, when they ran, and what changes have occurred on them over the years? All that information—and more—is listed in *The Encyclopedia of Daytime TV,* up to date as of August 1, 1996.

There are probably several series in the alphabetical listings you will wish you had seen, and some you'll wish you hadn't. That's television for you. There are also appendices listing top-rated daytime shows and longest-running series and a bibliography.

This is the first book devoted specifically to *all* daytime series. It is written both for the TV scholar or fanatic, who will welcome this addition to a neglected field of knowledge, and for the casual viewer, who may care about only a few of the shows listed. For those in the latter category, and for the answers to the first few questions, go to the "How to Use This Book" section at the end of the introduction. For those wanting more background on what is to come, read on.

IN THE BEGINNING . . .

A successful daytime series requires a network of stations to show it, the backing of a network or sponsors to air a series daily or weekly, and enough viewers to support keeping the series on the air. The interrelationships among these elements developed over more than two decades.

The first working TV demonstrations were in 1925, when American Charles Francis Jenkins in Washington, D.C., and Scotsman John Baird in England conducted separate yet similar experiments. In 1928, the first regularly operating TV station opened in Schenectady, New York. More stations opened before the Wall Street crash in 1929 halted TV's growth. Network radio, in place since 1926 by the National Broadcasting Company (NBC) and since 1927 by the Columbia Broadcasting System (CBS), prospered instead in the 1930s.

But radio's success led to huge profits, some of which those companies invested in television development. NBC worked with a New York City station it opened in 1928, and CBS installed its own TV studio in Gotham in 1931. Broadcasting took place on both stations, but, due to limited audiences and overtime costs, most of it was experimental and not during daytime hours.

A major push for television occurred at the World's Fair in New York City, which opened on April 30, 1939. CBS and NBC lacked commercial licenses, and many technical problems needed to be resolved before series could be aired nationwide, but sets went on sale at the fair. Fewer than 1,000 sets sold in New York City that year, but the networks kept working with the medium. Joining them was electronics manufacturer Allen B. DuMont, who got a license for a New York station in 1940 and planned a network under his own name.

By 1941, NBC had a network of stations in New York, Schenectady, and Philadelphia that could relay shows from one station to another to air live at the same time, though no program ran regularly. On July 1, 1941, CBS's and NBC's New York stations got licenses for commercial use, but America's entry into World War II later that year virtually halted progress for a time. The biggest news in the early 1940s occurred after government regulators ruled that NBC's two branches, Red and Blue, constituted a monopoly. NBC gave up Blue. Blue became the American Broadcasting Company (ABC) in 1943, and had plans to be a TV network, too.

At the end of the war, in 1945, work on television picked up. But televising series before 6 p.m. remained infrequent. Sponsors preferred the larger nighttime audience, and with no financial support, broadcasters were skittish about such a risky scheduling proposition, although they did air some specials and sporting events. An exception was NBC's New York station WNBT, which debuted the *Radio City Matinee* variety show with Warren Hull in May 1946 on Mondays, Wednesdays, and Fridays from 1–2 p.m. A month later WNBT brought out *Your World,* an educational show airing from 2:30–3 p.m. daily. But advertisers avoided the shows. By July, *Billboard* noted, "what's left of them has been combined into one show on Friday evenings, as *For You and Yours.*"

While these efforts to mount series were occurring, so were attempts at networking. NBC and DuMont took the lead, and by October 1946 DuMont was relaying nighttime shows from its New York station WABD to WTTG in Washington, D.C. And WNBT aired some of its nightly series in Schenectady on August 19, 1946, and signed an agreement with WPTZ Philadelphia to relay shows on each other's stations in October. Those moves led to the earliest network daytime series listed in this book, *NCAA Football,* in November 1946.

A *Variety* article published the same month that *NCAA Football* debuted captured networks' stances on daytime television at the time. The magazine reported that when asked about merchants wanting daytime shows so that shoppers could see TV sets in action, NBC and DuMont cautiously agreed. NBC said it needed a second studio and a sponsor before it could air in daytime; DuMont said it lacked personnel but was hoping to have the necessary staff soon; CBS said it needed another mobile unit first. CBS was so convinced that outdoor studio work would dominate future schedules that it closed its New York studios in May 1947. The article did not mention ABC, because ABC had no TV stations until the spring of 1948. It was the last network to enter daytime.

Also not addressed by the article was how individual stations may have wanted to structure their daytime programming. The options remained stable through the 1990s. Stations could broadcast nothing (the option most often chosen during the 1940s and 1950s), put on their own local shows, or get series in syndication. (A *syndicated* show is one that is sold by producers to stations or groups of stations to air in lieu of airing over the networks.) Shows designed especially for syndication in daytime grew to major importance by the 1990s, as we shall see.

The star of Howdy Doody *stands between fellow puppets Phineas T. Bluster (left) and Dilly Dally.*

THE EXPERIMENTAL SERIES YEARS: 1947–50

The early daytime leader was NBC, which signed radio stars Tex and Jinx McCrary as host and hostess of *The Swift Home Service Club* on May 16, 1947 on WNBT Fridays from 1–1:30 p.m. By October, the show was airing in Washington, D.C.; *The Swift Home Service Club* expanded to other stations before ending, making it the first daytime network nonsports series. But other events in 1947 had greater impact on daytime television.

In October, CBS, NBC, and DuMont rotated airing seven games of baseball's World Series. *Variety* reported that the games had increased daytime sales in bars with TV sets by 500 percent. Then in December, NBC debuted a children's show which won glowing reviews and—more importantly—viewership as high as some nighttime shows. Retitled in honor of its star, *Howdy Doody* went from being a weekly to the first network daily series, and became the first hit daytime TV series.

Given these accomplishments, NBC added stations to its East Coast network (only four existed at the start of 1948). In March, *Billboard* reported that NBC asked affiliates to set aside 10 a.m.–1 p.m. and 3–6 p.m. daily for network series. But few shows aired before 6 p.m. until after the success of *American Forum of the Air* and *Hopalong Cassidy* on Sundays in mid-1949. Other efforts appeared weekdays, like *Judy Splinters,* and some shows popped up Sundays, such as *Zoo Parade* and *Meet the Press,* but NBC concentrated on selling nighttime slots over afternoon ones until the fall of 1950, when a slate of daily sponsored shows aired from 3–6 p.m. These programs included hits like *The Kate Smith Show* and helped NBC lead in daytime.

DuMont, which was already airing some series between New York and Washington, D.C. (e.g., *Rainbow House* and *Small Fry Club*), had added Pittsburgh and other locales by mid-1948. It then launched a full daily schedule of programs on its New York station WABD on November 1, 1948 starting at 7 a.m., and some of these shows had sponsors. *Billboard* gave DuMont an "A" for effort but judged most of the efforts cheap (a majority of the morning shows used the same background—a flowered drape). WABD shortened its schedule over the next few months and some programs went network, including *The Ted Steele Show* and *Okay Mother.* By the fall of 1950, DuMont led in daytime programming in quantity, if not quality.

Spurred by competitors, CBS reopened its New York studios and began connecting with affiliates in Philadelphia and Washington, D.C. Its first daytime series, *The Missus Goes A-Shopping,* aired Wednesdays at 1:30 p.m. To challenge NBC, it aired *The Chuck Wagon* daily at 5:30 p.m., opposite *Howdy Doody,* and by 1949 had mounted public affairs shows like *Lamp Unto My Feet* on Sunday afternoons to compete with *Hopalong Cassidy.* The results were lackluster. CBS took on DuMont in the fall of 1949 at 11 a.m. daily with *The U.N. General Assembly Sessions,* which led off a sporadic weekday lineup that included such shows as *Classified Column* and *Vanity Fair.* In 1950, CBS added *The Garry Moore Show,* but the lineup overall did not worry the competition.

ABC jumped into the fray last, offering *NFL Football* Sunday afternoons and the daily alternating *Cartoon Teletales* and *The Singing Lady* from 5:30–6 p.m. in the fall of 1948. When the latter two ended, so did daily programming on ABC until September 1950, when four 15-minute children's shows— *Mr. Magic, Paddy the Pelican, Hold 'Er Newt,* and *Space Patrol*—ran from 5–6 p.m. All but *Space Patrol* bombed. ABC did hit with *Super Circus* on Sundays in 1949. But that and NFL football was about all ABC had on weekends until *Animal Clinic* and *Acrobat Ranch* pioneered Saturday morning broadcasts from 11 a.m.–noon Eastern Time. ABC tried to use that time slot as a stepping-stone to better ratings, but it was more like a stumbling block over the next few years.

NBC AND CBS FIGHT, ABC AND DUMONT STRUGGLE: 1951–54

In 1951–52, NBC and CBS filled daytime with series as advertisers sold out their evenings. During this time, sponsors determined which shows would be aired and could change a program's content or time. CBS had seven New York City studios and used only a few "outside" shows, like *Art Linkletter's House Party* from Hollywood and *Quiz Kids* from Chicago. NBC's facilities were smaller and reserved for nighttime shows, so its daytime shows came from Philadelphia (*Miss Susan, Atom Squad*), Chicago (*Hawkins Falls, Ding Dong School*), and Cincinnati (*Midwestern Hayride, Breakfast Party*).

NBC led daytime through 1952, even though it did not start regular programming before 3 p.m. daily until the fall of 1951. *Kate Smith, Hawkins Falls, Gabby Hayes,* and *Howdy Doody* easily topped their CBS competition. NBC also showed faith in 1952 by backing a morning news/information show titled *Today.* After a few years, the latter became a hit too.

CBS tinkered patiently to see what would work. In 1951, it did some shows in experimental color, for example, *The Mel Torme Show,* and also tried soap operas, which NBC had not exploited. In 1951, CBS installed *Love of Life, Search for Tomorrow,* and *The Guiding Light,* all of which lasted over 25 years. A year later, the network added Arthur Godfrey to kick off the morning lineup, which had started a few months earlier with CBS's first pre-noon series, *Strike It Rich.* Almost all the shows won top ratings. CBS added other winners in 1953 (*The Big Payoff,* which it stole from NBC, and *The Bob Crosby Show*) and 1954 (*The Brighter Day, The Secret Storm*), which lasted through most of the 1950s and made further radical schedule shifts unnecessary.

Soon CBS was far ahead of the other networks in daytime ratings and sponsors. In 1954, *Billboard* noted that CBS expected to earn $20 million more in gross advertiser revenues that year than NBC. Nervous NBC tended to cancel shows quickly, particularly soap operas, which need time to attract faithful viewers. While it backed the ambitious *Home* for a few years, it canned *A Time to Live, Golden Windows,* and others after only a few months. By the start of 1955, NBC's only shows between *Today* and *Howdy Doody* over two years old were *Hawkins Falls* and *Ding Dong School.*

Hawkins Falls' *main couple was Lona Corey (played by Bernardine Flynn) and Floyd Corey (Maurice Copeland), seen here in 1954.*

Meanwhile, Sunday afternoons became "egghead ghettos" on CBS and NBC, where unsponsored quality shows aired. Some of the programs won substantial critical if not popular following, for example, *Youth Wants to Know* and *See It Now.* CBS and NBC confined sports to NCAA football and pro baseball on Saturday afternoons, and aired no more than two hours before noon Saturday and Sunday mornings through the end of 1954.

But 1951–54 took a toll on DuMont. While its daytime series were relatively successful, its nighttime programming did not fare so well, and financial losses mounted. Beaten by CBS and NBC in competition in the daily noon–1 p.m. slot in 1951–52, DuMont looked less desirable to sponsors. Weekend series virtually vanished to save money, with at most an hour of shows seen on Saturday or Sunday apart from its best asset, NFL football. In the fall of 1953, *The Paul Dixon Show* from 3–4 p.m. was the only weekday series on DuMont. It was to be the last.

By the start of 1955, DuMont had halved the number of stations on which it transmitted series, limiting itself to 20 stations in the Northeast. In April 1955, *All About Baby*, seen Thursdays, was one of only eight series on the network. While preparing its last turn to carry NFL football in the fall of 1955, DuMont's board of directors proposed formally dissolving the network in August. There was no fourth network in daytime until Fox, 35 years later.

ABC actually was in worse shape than DuMont in 1951–52. Its much-ballyhooed Saturday morning lineup for adults from 11 a.m.–1 p.m. (*Oh, Kay, A Date with Judy, Two Girls Named Smith, I Cover Times Square,* etc.) collapsed when 11 sponsors left by the spring of 1952. Between 1952 and 1954, ABC kept whittling down the number of programs it carried in this slot until it became for all practical purposes a one-hour slot, anchored by the half-hour *Space Patrol,* which aired from 11–11:30 a.m. From May 1955 through October 1958, ABC had no Saturday series before 4 p.m.

As for daily shows, in the fall of 1951 ABC unveiled *The Dennis James Show* at 11:30 a.m., which was followed by *The Frances Langford–Don Ameche Show* at noon. CBS killed them with *Strike It Rich, Love of Life,* and others, and between the fall of 1952 and October of 1955, ABC basically ended daily programming before 7 p.m. Exceptions included *Turn to a Friend* and *The Ern Westmore Show* in the fall of 1953 from 4–5 p.m., and a TV version of radio's *The Breakfast Club* at 9 a.m. in 1954. When sponsor Quaker Oats dropped the latter in 1955, ABC abandoned morning programming to try late afternoons instead.

ABC did have some Sunday shows, like *Faith for Today,* and a few sports, like NFL football and major league baseball, but its future was bleak until it merged with United Paramount Theaters in 1953. That made the difference. By April 1955, ABC was finally sold out in nighttime, in the black in operations, and ready for daytime television. With TV viewership, sales, and stations growing exponentially each year and television now topping radio in daytime audiences, ABC wanted a cut of the action, though it had a long way to go to get it.

ABC INCHES TOWARD THE OTHERS: 1955–58

ABC's big hope was *The Mickey Mouse Club,* which debuted in October 1955 from 5–6 p.m. daily and brought down the mighty *Howdy Doody.* ABC planned to work backward from *The Mickey Mouse Club* and sell each preceding period, but fumbled when in 1956 it put a British movie series, airing as *Afternoon Film Festival,* in the 3–5 p.m. slot before *The Mickey Mouse Club.* Trying again, ABC hit gold in August 1957 with *American Bandstand* from 3–4:30 p.m., followed by *Do You Trust Your Wife?* with Johnny Carson. Both shows beat the competition from NBC.

The biggest star of The Mickey Mouse Club *was Annette Funicello, seen here second from left. The other cast members with Annette are, from left, Mouseketeers Eileen Diamond and Cubby O'Brien, and "Big Mooseketeer" Roy Williams, a Disney animator.*

NBC daytime stayed chaotic during this time. It rid itself of 15-minute programs and added others in the previously unprogrammed 1–3 p.m. daily slots with so-so success. Its most innovative program was the dramatic anthology *Matinee Theater* from 3–4 p.m., but its most popular series were frenetic game shows like *The Price Is Right, It Could Be You, Truth or Consequences,* and *Queen for a Day.* Their successes led NBC to win daytime honors for a few months during this period. But model of decorum CBS made only minor adjustments when needed, and most of its new series in the era—such as *As the World Turns, The Edge of Night,* and *The Verdict Is Yours*—were huge hits and kept CBS at number one.

On weekends, ABC's scant resources allowed only a few shows, which aired on Sundays, ranging from the *John Hopkins File 7* to *The Paul Winchell Show.* NBC was top-rated Sunday afternoons with offerings like *Wide Wide World* and *Zoo Parade,* and aired NCAA football and pro baseball on Saturday afternoons. CBS programmed Sunday mornings with "cultural" offerings like *Look Up and Live* and *Camera Three,* but made its Sunday money every fall with the popular NFL football it had acquired from DuMont in 1956—and was to hold on to for 38 years, despite escalating rights costs. The real battlefield was Saturday mornings, when NBC's *Fury* and *Howdy Doody* fought for child viewers against CBS's *Mighty Mouse Playhouse* and *Captain Kangaroo.* The latter also successfully challenged *Today* at 8 a.m. weekdays, while CBS's other efforts, like *The Morning Show* and *The Jimmy Dean Show* at 7 a.m., flopped.

In the spring of 1958, ABC made the startling announcement that it would program shows from 11 a.m.–3 p.m. daily that fall. ABC President Oliver Treyz wrote in *Variety* that "lacking a full complement of daytime programs, ABC lost some after-dark advertisers. And for the same lack, we were at a disadvantage in building our station lineups. Let's face it, in a competitive situation a network has to be a network day and night." An emboldened ABC sales staff collected over $13 million in billings without even having its series ready.

Unfortunately, when "Operation Daybreak" dawned at 11 a.m. on October 13, 1958, the results were disastrous. Ratings were minuscule (CBS and NBC had three times ABC's audiences) and reviews were poor, and within six months *The Peter Lind Hayes Show, Mother's Day, The Liberace Show,* and *Chance for Romance* were gone. Obviously, ABC had much to learn before it could become a real factor in daytime programming.

In this 1959 picture, Captain Kangaroo *(Bob Keeshan) points to the face of Grandfather Clock while guest vocalist Betty Ann Grove watches him.*

THE BIG THREE'S COMPETITION TIGHTENS: 1959–65

Worried because it had promised advertisers 25 percent of all daytime sets in use yet was garnering ratings showing an audience only half that size, ABC dropped its morning hour to start at noon in 1959. Its new gimmick was to install reruns of nighttime shows like *The Restless Gun* and *The Gale Storm Show.* Its biggest winners—*Who Do You Trust?* and *American Bandstand*—remained in late afternoon. In 1961, the network moved its start-up time back to 11 a.m. and added more reruns and game shows like *About Faces* and *Camouflage;* despite these efforts, ABC remained a distant third.

ABC's first glimmer of hope came in 1963, with the debut of *General Hospital,* the network's first soap. Hoping to duplicate *General Hospital*'s success, ABC had chucked long-running but not really popular shows like

The core cast of the early years of General Hospital *consisted of, from left, Roy Thinnes as Phil Brewer, Emily McLaughlin as Nurse Jessie Brewer, and John Beradino as Dr. Steve Hardy.*

Day in Court and *Queen for a Day* to make room for more soaps by 1965. Unfortunately, *A Time for Us, The Young Marrieds, The Nurses,* and *Never Too Young* failed miserably, and ABC began 1966 just as unsuccessful as it had been seven years earlier.

The network did improve substantially in two areas. It returned to Saturday mornings in the fall of 1962 with a nearly all-cartoon lineup including *Bugs Bunny, Casper,* and *Beany and Cecil;* the cartoon slots expanded to start at 10:30 a.m. in 1963 and 9:30 a.m. in 1964, nearly equalling the number of shows CBS and NBC were airing Saturday mornings. Victory was achieved in the fall of 1965, when *The Beatles* cartoon hit number one and led ABC to the top on Saturday mornings for the 1965–66 season, marking the network's first lead in any part of the broadcasting schedule where the three networks competed.

ABC's other successes were in sports. It helped the American Football League establish itself as a viable option to the NFL in Sunday games from the fall of 1960 through 1965, when NBC brought the property for a substantial fee, and also got a few airings of NCAA football and basketball. But ABC really hit it big in 1961 with the anthology *ABC's Wide World of Sports* and in 1962 with *Pro Bowlers Tour,* both of which ran more than 30 years.

CBS and NBC had sports too, but neither approached the field with ABC's energy and dedication, and ABC was the preeminent sports network for decades. CBS and NBC did compete directly Saturdays with major league baseball until ABC bought all the rights in 1965. Golf series proliferated in this period too (*All Star Golf, Celebrity Golf,* etc.). The results were that weekend afternoons were heavy with sports, and news and entertainment appeared generally before 2 p.m. and after 5 p.m. Some developed long runs in the late-afternoon period, such as *The Original Amateur Hour, Wild Kingdom,* and *G.E. College Bowl.* And there were some cultural series, like *Do You Know?, Exploring,* and *Science All-Stars.* But in general, weekend television was looking a lot more commercial than it had in the 1950s.

In the daily battle, CBS's lead increased. After enduring several disappointments in the morning hours and at the 2–2:30 p.m. slot, it hit the jackpot in the fall of 1962 by putting mostly nighttime sitcom reruns (*I Love Lucy, The Real McCoys*) in the mornings and *Password* at 2 p.m. These shows, along with the soaps from the 1950s, gave CBS almost all the top-ranked daytime series, and changes occurred only among shows being rerun.

The setup in the early 1960s made CBS's lead look insurmountable. However, at the time NBC daytime programmers were taking chances on developing audiences by sticking with slow-building shows like *The Doctors, Another World,* and *Days of Our Lives.* The strategy paid off a few years later and made NBC number one in daytime—almost.

THE GLORY YEARS OF DAYTIME SHOWS: 1966–69

Daytime television arguably peaked in the late 1960s. Soaps dealt with formerly taboo subjects like racism and rape, game shows were wilder and wackier than ever (e.g., *Supermarket Sweep*), and at the same time, networks were trying new formats, such as variety (*Swingin' Country, Where the Action Is*) and talk (*Pat Boone, Dick Cavett*). By 1969, all shows were in color as well. Many of the best-remembered daytime shows either were on or started in this era, among them *Dark Shadows, The Hollywood Squares,* and *One Life to Live.*

Creativity was so plentiful at ABC and NBC that by mid-1967, CBS found its hammerlock on the daily top 10 broken by shows on both networks. A year later, NBC tied CBS, which forced it to drop *To Tell the Truth, Password,* and *Art Linkletter's House Party* and rethink its daytime strategy.

NBC looked ready to be champion until it dropped one of its best performers, *Let's Make a Deal,* at the end of 1968. ABC picked that show up and found itself the new number two, thanks to respectable performances by games like *The Dating Game* and by its soap operas. ABC made another wise move by moving its starting time forward from 10:30 a.m., which had been established in 1967, to noon to cut losses and improve ratings. From this point forward, the claim for first place in daytime switched hands often during the 1970s.

On Saturday mornings, the story was one network and one man: CBS and its daytime programming head Fred Silverman. Stung by the loss to ABC in 1965–66, Silverman requested and got $8 million to use to develop series for the network's Saturday morning lineup in the fall of 1966. He first developed a cartoon superhero lineup that included *Space Ghost* and *The Lone Ranger* and led to CBS claiming all the top slots on Saturdays. In 1968–69, Silverman cleverly switched the emphasis away from superheroes, airing cartoons like *The Archies* and *Scooby Doo,* offerings which featured comedy, rock music, and teenagers. That combination was influential and oft-imitated in the 1970s, and it helped CBS stay number one and make millions through 1970.

ABC and NBC went cartoon crazy as well, scoring a few hits with *The Banana Splits Adventure Hour* and *The Pink Panther* on NBC and *Spider-Man* and *George of the Jungle* on ABC. ABC also used Sunday mornings for cartoons from 9:30–11:30 a.m. Otherwise, weekend programming looked much as it had before, only with more sports, including abortive stabs at hockey and soccer. The latter unimaginative programming approach unfortunately foreshadowed what would happen throughout daytime in the early 1970s.

Those fangs and that wolf's-head cane could mean only one person in daytime television—Barnabas Collins (played by Jonathan Frid) of Dark Shadows. *(Courtesy Dan Curtis Productions.)*

CAUTION, THEN CHANGEOVER AMONG THE NETWORKS: 1970–73

On March 30, 1970, three new soap operas hit the air—*The Best of Everything* and *A World Apart* on ABC and *Somerset* on NBC—for an unprecedented total of 19 daytime serials. Broadcasters were so sure that soaps were the ticket to success that soaps glutted the daytime roster. Little else was tried in 1970–71, with the only new shows with promise being ABC's well-written *All My Children* and NBC's enjoyable chatfest *Dinah's Place.*

Perhaps responding to the melodrama overdose, *The Hollywood Squares* hit number one in daytime in early 1972. Seeing this development, CBS ended reruns and added *Gambit, The Price Is Right,* and *The $10,000 Pyramid* to the lineup in 1972–73. The games did fine, as did a soap called *The Young and the Restless* and a *Squares*-type celebrity game show, *Match Game,* both in 1973. Meanwhile, NBC chucked such stalwarts as *Concentration* and *Sale of the Century* for flashier games like *Baffle* and *The Wizard of Odds.* ABC remained unadventurous, adding just a revived *Password,* plus *Split Second* and *The Girl in My Life.* The lead in daytime kept changing, and the three networks were sometimes in a dead heat.

Saturday mornings were full of cartoons with rock music or live-action sitcoms with rock music like *The Bugaloos* and *Lidsville.* The shows were

In 1974 George C. Scott and his then-wife Trish Van Devere (right) made their debut on The Hollywood Squares *to the delight of host Peter Marshall (left).*

more derivative than they had been in the late 1960s, with cartoons based on stars (*The Harlem Globetrotters, The Jackson Five*), TV shows (*The Brady Kids, The Addams Family*), and even 1960s cartoon characters (*Yogi's Gang, Pebbles and Bamm Bamm*). CBS stayed number one. Given the minute number of new programs, the rest of the weekend became virtually all sports after 1 p.m.

THE LAST YEARS OF DAYTIME'S GOLDEN AGE: 1974–79

The mid-1970s brought a huge burst of activity on weekdays, with new shows arriving almost every four months. Game shows dominated for a time, with the saturation level in May 1975 equaling the 19 total set by soaps five years earlier. One could watch the networks from 10 a.m. to 4 p.m. and see nothing but games, but because they were spread out on each schedule and usually faced at least one soap or rerun, they didn't seem quite as all-pervasive as the soaps had earlier. A few big hits debuted (*Wheel of Fortune, Family Feud, The Gong Show*), and there were some moderate successes as well (*Celebrity Sweepstakes, High Rollers, Tattletales*), but the bombs (*Showoffs, Spin-off, Stumpers,* etc.) far outnumbered the triumphs.

A few new soaps got shots—for example, *How to Survive a Marriage; For Richer, For Poorer;* and *Ryan's Hope* (the only hit)—but the main event was NBC's expansion in 1975 of the top-rated *Another World* to an hour, where it continued to do well. Other soaps followed, including *Days of Our Lives, As the World Turns,* and *All My Children,* as broadcasters got timid again and thought that increased air time for a hit was the only way to fill a schedule. Indeed, programmers at NBC, which led daytime in the mid-1970s but had become a weak third by the late 1970s, basically admitted that they had stretched *Another World* to 90 minutes daily in 1979 because they couldn't come up with a better idea.

By that time a more ominous trend was developing. In 1978, NBC found that affiliates no longer wanted to carry shows from 4–4:30 p.m. weekdays due to the low ratings garnered by shows in that slot. And top-rated ABC found its stations did not want it to air programs earlier than 11 a.m. even though NBC and CBS began at 10 a.m. Daily network schedules began to close ever so slightly.

Weekends got loaded with pseudo-sports competitions, and such shows as *The Superstars* and *Challenge of the Sexes* joined baseball, basketball, and football. Pregame shows like *The NFL Today* and *NFL '77* received attention too. As for Sunday mornings, in 1979 CBS gave pink slips to veterans *Camera Three, Lamp Unto My Feet,* and *Look Up and Live* to make room for *Sunday Morning,* a news and feature program that led its time slot.

Saturday morning series in this era displayed a tendency toward greater length, if nothing else. The champion was the two-hour *Scooby's All-Star Laff-A-Lympics* on ABC in 1977–78, but several others went to 90 minutes, including perennial favorite *Bugs Bunny.* As had happened with the daily shows, NBC's mid-1970s Saturday morning lead had disappeared by 1979; ABC was the new leader. Casualties were high each season, with the NBC lineups of 1976–79 particularly vulnerable, as the only returning shows those years were *The Pink Panther* and *Godzilla.*

These failures caused NBC to give serious thought in 1979 to airing a Saturday morning edition of *Today.* The huge hit *The Smurfs* stopped that talk in 1981, and in any event, NBC was soon faced with a strong upsurge in the competitive strength of ABC's *Good Morning America,* which had started in 1975 and was growing bigger each year. Also competing was *The CBS Morning News,* but that beleaguered show stayed last in the pack, as it would during the 1980s and 1990s. Indeed, the loser status of *The CBS Morning News* was one of the few "givens" on daytime television over the next several volatile years.

OUT WITH THE OLD, IN WITH A FEW HITS: 1980–87

From 1980–87, many long-running series died: *Love of Life* and *Hollywood Squares* in 1980, *The Doctors* in 1982, *Captain Kangaroo* and *The Edge of Night* in 1984, *Family Feud* in 1985, *Search for Tomorrow* in 1986, and *American Bandstand* in 1987. Unfortunately, few daily series the networks came up with after the demise of those shows could match their long-term success. True, *Loving, Scrabble, Santa Barbara,* and a revised *Concentration* ran into the 1990s, but none generated audiences large enough to beat established shows like *The Price Is Right* or *General Hospital.* The top news was that ABC and CBS lost their ability to program 4–4:30 p.m. daily due to lack of station support, a pattern that was to escalate in the 1990s.

To get a feel for the entire Saturday morning lineup, one had to look at only two shows: *The Smurfs* and *Saturday Supercade.* The former became such a huge success that "cute" tiny cartoon creatures took over the airwaves, with the best and most successful being those on *Alvin and the Chipmunks* and *Jim Henson's Muppet Babies.* The latter was representative of a discouraging wave of cartoons based on arcade or video games like *Pac-Man, Pole Position,* and *LazerTag Academy,* and most of them lasted only a year as the fad for the game they were based on died down.

In sports, CBS got a piece of the NCAA football action from ABC in 1984 due to a dispute by NCAA member universities who felt they, rather than the NCAA, should set their own TV contracts. The courts agreed, allowing CBS to air some college football games. ABC took a chance on professional football in the spring, but *USFL Football* (and in the 1990s, *WLAF Football*) proved not to be a big audience attraction. Apart from sports, the main element of Sunday programming was *This Week with David Brinkley,* a newsmaker interview show that became a hit and forced longtime panel shows *Face the Nation* on CBS and *Meet the Press* on NBC to copy some of its conventions.

This Week with David Brinkley featured the formidable trio of (from left) George Will, David Brinkley, and Sam Donaldson.

WHERE DO WE GO FROM HERE? 1988–98

The current decade has seen the most unimaginative programming in the history of daytime television. Consider this: The networks' daily lineup from 12:30–4 p.m. in 1996 was almost the same as in 1988. The only difference was that by 1993 perennial loser NBC, forced by lack of affiliate support, had stopped programming from 12:30–1 p.m. (where the soap *Generations* and talk show *A Closer Look* were the last contenders) and from 3–4 p.m. (home to *Santa Barbara*). By the fall of 1995, the network was in such dreadful shape that it added a rerun of the NBC talk show *Leeza* to its lineup, which meant that after *Today,* the network provided a grand total of three hours of original programs daily—an original *Leeza* at 11 a.m. (*Leeza* repeats aired earlier, at 10 a.m.), *Days of Our Lives* at 1 p.m., and *Another World* at 2 p.m. This tally meant that NBC was airing the lowest number of daytime shows since 1951—and it was still a poor daytime third. The network's clinging to *Another World* seemed particularly desperate because, despite the soap's declining popularity, NBC had nothing else with a chance of beating *As the World Turns* on CBS or *One Life to Live* on ABC.

NBC tried several series in its 10 a.m.–noon slots, but with the end of *Concentration* and *Wheel of Fortune,* among others, it had no other hit game shows, and alternative programs, such as *TrialWatch,* were bores. At least NBC was making *some* effort; ABC somehow kept *The Home Show* from 11 a.m.–noon for over five years despite its horrible ratings against stalwart *The Price Is Right* on CBS. ABC finally replaced *The Home Show* in 1994 with the unimpressive *Mike & Maty* talk show, which lasted for two years of lousy ratings. By 1991, the network had also stopped programming from noon–12:30 p.m. due to—what else?—affiliate defections. It was, however, content to let its lowest-rated soap, *Loving,* stumble along in the 12:30–1 p.m. slot until 1995. Then, when stations looked ready to drop *Loving* altogether, ABC revamped the show and named it *The City,* but in 1996 that fared only marginally better than its predecessor.

CBS saw its 1988 revival of *Family Feud* become a hit, but in 1993 had to cancel the hour-long version of the show because few affiliates were willing to clear the 10–11 a.m. slot. CBS then stopped airing shows in that time slot. Indeed, with stations receiving a welter of syndicated talk shows to add in the 1990s (for example, *Maury Povich, Jerry Springer,* and *Rosie O'Donnell),* the networks found that many stations were even shifting their afternoon soaps to other slots. Perhaps the networks' unwillingness to make innovative changes was partially a reaction to this trend. If affiliates were going to use the cancellation of a long-time series as a excuse to put one of their own programs in that slot, it made some sense for the networks to keep the old show where it was.

Affiliate pressures also impacted Saturday mornings. NBC, appalled by its poor showing in 1991–92, dropped all cartoons and added a two-hour version of *Today* and series with adolescent appeal like *Saved by the Bell* and *California Dreams.* The moves picked up their ratings and left the juvenile field to ABC, CBS, and Fox. Fox? Yes, the network that had started up in 1987 first mounted a Saturday morning lineup in 1990, and by 1992, after an indifferent first season, was beating NBC. By cultivating such popular hits as *X-Men, Mighty Morphin Power Rangers,* and *The Tick,* Fox had catapulted to number one on Saturday mornings by 1994. CBS and ABC scrambled rather ineffectively to take on the upstart network, but the best they could do were the ever-popular *Teenage Mutant Ninja Turtles* on CBS and the hardy *Bugs Bunny* on ABC. Those networks also suffered some affiliate defections in their noon–1 p.m. slot, which aired "educational" shows like *CBS Storybreak* and *The ABC Weekend Special,* but as of 1996 both series were still on the air.

Fox wreaked even more havoc in the world of TV sports, flooring CBS by outbidding for NFL football in 1994, then getting pro hockey and pro baseball in 1995. Also in 1995, two more newcomers—both movie company networks, The WB from Warner Brothers and UPN from Paramount—started and added a few shows of their own to daytime (for example, WB's *Earthworm Jim* and UPN's *Teknoman).* Will all six networks survive into the 21st century? What kind of programming will their rivalry produce? Can game shows make a comeback? As broadcasters like to say, keep watching.

In 1995, NFL Sunday *on Fox featured, from left, Jim Brown, Terry Bradshaw, Howie Long, and Jimmy Johnson.*

HOW TO USE THIS BOOK

THIS BOOK LISTS alphabetically by title all series known to have been aired on a network on a regular basis before 6 p.m. A series must have run at least a month for inclusion, or have been planned to run at least that long. Each listing gives in order the program's genre, viewing format (black-and-white, color, or, in the case of long-running shows, both), first and last air dates on a network, network running times and dates, on-air personnel and their tenures, and a synopsis of what appeared on screen. The emphasis in each entry is on what the average viewer saw, which is why production credits are limited. But pertinent information about the development before, during, or after the show's run is included where judged necessary, including details on cable, syndicated, or nighttime network runs.

A series is listed under its best-known title, with cross-references given for other titles. Whenever possible, the title is given as it was seen on the screen and not necessarily as it appeared in printed program listings. For sports, some series are listed with the generic term first (for example, boxing programs are all listed with *Boxing* first, like *Boxing Live from Madison Square Garden,* and soccer programs are all discussed under the single heading *Soccer*), and some are an overall title for events which ran on the networks in various incarnations, like *NBA Basketball.* Running times are Eastern Time as transmitted by the network, but any of these programs, particularly recorded shows, may have aired at different times locally.

The star of The Oprah Winfrey Show *as she looked in the late 1980s.*

The impact of such syndicated offerings as *The Oprah Winfrey Show* and *Bozo the Clown* on daytime programming cannot be discounted, so 50 selected series in this category are included. That number could easily be 10 times that amount, especially if the genres of animated cartoons and religious shows were included, so the syndicated series listed are only a sampling and not a full collection of what has been produced for individual stations in daytime. The recent explosion in talk shows has perhaps resulted in their being overrepresented as a genre in syndication, but series of all types are included, dating all the way from the early 1950s.

Not listed are special events which ran several weeks in daytime (e.g., the Army-McCarthy hearings in 1954 and the O. J. Simpson murder trial in 1995), and the times when they preempted regular series are not listed within those series' listings. Also excluded are shows not airing on a regular weekly, biweekly, or monthly basis, such as *Young People's Concerts* and *The ABC Afterschool Special,* and shows which ran less than five minutes, such as *In the News* and *Schoolhouse Rock.* Finally, shows produced for nighttime network or syndicated airing which had daytime network repeats, such as *I Love Lucy, The Adventures of Superman,* and *NBC News Encore,* are listed in an appendix, by title only, because they were not designed originally for daytime viewing. Series that ran original episodes in daytime before being repeated there on a network, such as *Sky King* and *Tales of the Texas Rangers,* are included in the main body along with the times and dates they ran in repeats. Also in the main text are nighttime or syndicated cartoons repeated in daytime, since they are best remembered as daytime shows (*The Flintstones, The Jetsons, Deputy Dawg,* etc.).

Program information was culled from articles, reviews, and listings in *TV Guide, Variety,* and *Billboard;* from articles in assorted periodicals from 1948–1996; and from reference books (see Bibliography, page 492). An • appearing in front of the series title indicates that I have verified information by actually viewing at least one show of the series, either during its original run, in repeats, or on videocassette. Doing this whenever possible has helped correct misinformation perpetuated by the casual use of inaccurate press release information by some of the works consulted. For example, despite at least four books saying otherwise, the female superheroine on the second half of *Birdman and the Galaxy Trio* is named *Gravity* Girl, not Galaxy Girl. But errors can be made by even the most careful researcher, and since many programs were out of reach to an author born in 1965, any additional data or corrections are welcome and can be sent in care of the publisher.

Oh, and the answers to the first paragraph's questions are, in order, *For Love or Money, The Mike Douglas Show, Top Cat, Zoo Parade,* and *USFL Football* and *WLAF Football.* Of course, I could have asked about what Olympic champ hosted *AAU Track and Field,* but that leads us to page 1 . . . .

AAU TRACK AND FIELD
Sports; Color
May 18, 1969–August 27, 1972

CBS Sun. 3:30–4:30 p.m. (5/18/69–8/31/69)
CBS Sun. 3:30–4:30 p.m. (5/17/70–9/6/70)
CBS Sun. 3:30–5 p.m. (5/23/71–9/5/71)
CBS Sun. 3–4:30 p.m. (4/30/72–8/27/72)

Announcers: *Jack Whitaker, Ralph Boston, Dick Bank (1969–1970), Bill Toomey (1971–72)*

With the failure of soccer, CBS filled the void of summer sports coverage with this series of amateur contests taped at various spots around the world, from Oslo, Norway, to Warsaw, Poland. American talent from the Amateur Athletic Union (AAU) competed against international entries in running, swimming, and other outdoor sports. In the last two seasons, former Olympic decathlon winner Bill Toomey was part of the trio of announcers covering the event.

ABC CHILDREN'S NOVELS FOR TELEVISION—See *ABC Weekend Special, The.*

ABC MIDDAY REPORT
News; B&W and Color
March 5, 1961–March 1, 1968

ABC Mon.–Fri. 1:25–1:30 p.m. (3/5/61–6/29/62)
ABC Mon.–Fri. 12:55–1 p.m. (7/2/62–12/16/62)
ABC Mon.–Fri. 2:25–2:30 p.m. (12/19/62–9/6/63)
ABC Mon.–Fri. 2:55–3 p.m. (9/9/63–12/29/67)
ABC Mon.–Fri. 11:25–11:30 a.m. (1/1/68–3/1/68)

Anchors/Writers: *Al Mann (1961), Alex Dreier (10/2/61–9/6/63), Lisa Howard (9/9/63–10/2/64), Marlene Sanders (10/5/64–3/1/68)*

ABC News was the perennial runner-up to CBS and NBC in ratings and respect in the 1960s, so it is not surprising that its daily news show was the last among the networks to debut and the first to leave. The five-minute updates, coming from New York except for a time in Chicago under Alex Dreier, aired after *About Faces* in 1961, *Day in Court* in 1961 and 1962–65, *Camouflage* in 1962, *A Time for Us* in 1965–66, *Dream Girl of '67* in 1967, and *Temptation* in 1968.

There is a sad tale about the fate of the show's third anchor. Lisa Howard was an actress (a regular on *Guiding Light* in the 1950s) who joined ABC News in the early 1960s. In honor of her being the first female to host a daily network TV newscast, the show also was known as *Lisa Howard with the News* and *Lisa Howard and the Woman's Touch.* Controversy hit in 1964, when she worked for a group of Democrats supporting Republican Kenneth Keating of New York for the U.S. Senate. ABC considered the move a conflict of interest and fired her, although she remained on salary under contract

through 1965. After unsuccessfully suing ABC for $2 million in damages, and reportedly depressed after a miscarriage, Howard bought sleeping pills at a pharmacy on Independence Day 1965 and died of an overdose while in the store's parking lot. She was 35 years old.

ABC NEWS THIS MORNING—See *ABC World News This Morning.*

ABC PRESENTS MAJOR LEAGUE CHAMPIONSHIP BASEBALL
Sports; B&W and Color
April 16, 1960–June 29, 1986

ABC Sat. 2:55–5:30 p.m./Conclusion (4/16/60–9/17/60)
ABC Sat. 2 p.m.–Conclusion (4/17/65–10/2/65)
ABC Sun. 2–4:30 p.m. or 3–5:30 p.m. (8/17/80–10/3/81, August–October only each year)
ABC Sun. 3–6 p.m. (4/13/86–6/29/86)

Announcers included: *Jack Buck (1960), Carl Erskine (1960), Howard Cosell (1965), Leo Durocher (1965), Merle Harmon (1965), Tommy Heinrich (1965), Keith Jackson (1965), Jackie Robinson (1965), Chris Schenkel (1965), Al Michaels (1986), Jim Palmer (1986), Don Drysdale (1986), Johnny Bench (1986)*

After pioneering network daytime baseball in 1953–54 (see *Game of the Week, The*), ABC found itself frozen out in the field before getting the rights to air a game in 1960 two hours after CBS and NBC's games already were underway, with Jack Buck doing play-by-play and Carl Erskine commentary. Most games were from San Francisco or Kansas City and drew unimpressive ratings. Five years later, ABC outbid NBC for rights for major league baseball and used three coverage teams—Robinson-Harmon, Durocher-Schenkel, and Heinrich-Jackson—each consisting respectively of an analyst and play-by-play man, to handle one of the day's regional contests. Howard Cosell did pregame interviews.

Distinguishing ABC's coverage in 1965 was its extensive use of cameras isolated on all bases and instant replay. Leo "the Lip" Durocher was the most talkative and opinionated commentator, although even he seemed terse on the May 1965 show, where Vice President Hubert Humphrey outgabbed him in the booth during a Washington Senators–N.Y. Yankees game (one Humphrey quip was "Waiting on a 3–2 pitch is like waiting for the last precinct to come in."). But the network could not offer a competing price against NBC for baseball rights, so ABC would not have another daytime baseball series for 15 years.

In 1979 *ABC Sunday Afternoon Baseball* aired as three specials, following three years of summer shows on Monday nights. It became a series in 1980, but ABC was not interested in carrying baseball on Sundays, and from 1982–85 only a few playoff games aired there, usually each September. ABC carried more baseball in 1986, with Al Michaels at play-by-play and Jim Palmer at analysis for the lead team, but only for three months. *ABC Sunday Afternoon Baseball* was not a success, however. It was not an exclusive package, and local stations that could get bigger ratings by airing games with their home teams didn't carry the show.

With a new baseball contract in 1994, ABC got an exclusive package and planned to cover regular games on Saturdays, but the baseball strike in 1994 left it with an abbreviated first season, so no games aired. Saturday baseball did return in 1996; see *Fox Baseball.*

•ABC SATURDAY SUPERSTAR MOVIE, THE
Cartoon Anthology; Color
September 9, 1972–August 31, 1974

ABC Sat. 9:30–10:30 a.m. (9/9/72–9/1/73)
ABC Sat. Noon–1 p.m. (9/8/73–8/31/74)

This was the first anthology of original cartoons designed for network airing. It contained a mixture from various producers of both series pilots (including failed adaptations of live-action nighttime 1960s hits *Bewitched, Lost in Space,* and *The Munsters)* and original productions. Among the latter group was a two-part adaptation of *Oliver Twist* and *Willie Mays and the Say-Hey Kid,* with the baseball great in the title providing his voice. A few shows did appear elsewhere on the ABC Saturday morning schedule. The debut "The Brady Kids on Mysterious Island" aired a week before *The Brady Kids* premiered in the time slot after the series. "Yogi's Ark Lark" was the pilot for *Yogi's Gang,* and "Lassie and the Spirit of Thunder Mountain" later aired on *Lassie's Rescue Rangers* as a two-part show (see individual titles for more details).

In September 1973 the show was titled *The New Saturday Superstar Movie,* even though only three new shows aired in the mix. One of these was a second adaptation of ABC's nighttime sitcom *Nanny and the Professor,* with the original cast including leads Juliet Mills and Richard Long providing the voices.

ABC SUNDAY AFTERNOON BASEBALL—See *ABC Presents Major League Championship Baseball.*

•ABC WEEKEND SPECIAL, THE
Children's Anthology; Color
January 29, 1977–

ABC Sat. Noon–12:30 p.m. (1/29/77–9/5/87; off summers of 1978 and 1979)
ABC Sat. 12:30–1 p.m. (9/12/87–; off some fall months)

Host: *Michael Young (1979–81), Willie Tyler and his dummy Lester (1981–84)*

Starting as a monthly item through August 1977, *The ABC Weekend Special* offered some original live-action and cartoon productions and some repeats of ABC's irregularly scheduled *ABC Short Story Special* and *ABC Afterschool Specials.* Most of its stars were at best in the second rank of the business (e.g., Noah Beery Jr., Jack Elam, Lou Jacobi), and the stories were largely unexceptional comedies or light dramatic fare. By 1985 the emphasis switched to animated

fare, including some pilots for series like *The Puppy's Further Adventures,* and a few more familiar voices participated, such as Michael York and Samantha Eggar. An animated character, feline Cap'n O. G. Readmore, became a recurring element with his versions of children's tales like "Jack and the Beanstalk." The series also was known by its subtitle from 1977–79, *The ABC Children's Novels for Television.*

•ABC WORLD NEWS THIS MORNING
News; Color
July 5, 1982–

ABC Mon.–Fri. 6–7 a.m. (7/5/82–)

Anchor: *Steve Bell (1982–87), Kathleen Sullivan (1982–85), Jeanne Meserve (1985–87), Jed Duvall (1987–88), Edie Magnus (1987–89), Paula Zahn (1989–90), Forrest Sawyer (1989), Mike Schneider (1989–93)*

ABC surprised the other networks in 1982 when it announced it would start a daily news hour before *Good Morning America,* prompting them to do the same within the year. Though available for a full hour to stations, most took only a half hour or even just 15 minutes of the show each day, as the show was set up to deliver news, sports, and weather within quarter-hour segments. Some stations even cut out part of the 15-minute segments to deliver their own 5-minute local reports.

Good Morning America's news anchor Steve Bell co-anchored the new program with Kathleen Sullivan until May 1985, when Jeanne Meserve replaced her. At the start of 1987 Jed Duvall replaced the duo as sole anchor, but in June Edie Magnus joined him to do news, and then Forrest Sawyer replaced Duvall. By mid-1989 Magnus left the show to do the flop nighttime syndicated series *USA Today—The Television Show,* and Paula Zahn replaced her. Sawyer lasted until September 1989, when Mike Schneider replaced him. Schneider became the sole anchor when Zahn left in February 1990 to do *The CBS Morning News;* then a variety of ABC news reporters assumed duties for the show.

The show's original title was *ABC News This Morning;* it was changed in 1983.

ABC'S WIDE WORLD OF SPORTS
Sports; B&W and Color
April 29, 1961–

ABC Sat. 5–7 p.m. (4/29/61–9/9/61)
ABC Sun. 5–6:30 p.m. (1/20/62–9/2/62)
ABC Sat. 5–6:30 p.m. (9/8/62–)
ABC Sun. 4–5:30 p.m., 4–6 p.m., or 4:30–6 p.m. (1/6/74–; off fall months)

Host: *Jim McKay (1961–86), Frank Gifford (1987–93), Becky Dixon (1987), John Saunders (1993), Julie Moran (1994–95), Robin Roberts (1996–)*

Executive Producer: *Roone Arledge*

ABC's longest-running series is one which gave the network an identity at a time it desperately needed one. *ABC's Wide World of Sports* began "spanning the globe" for "the thrill of victory and the agony of defeat," as its memorable opening put it, in 1961 as a temporary effort to replace the loss of baseball on the network. But the anthology proved to have staying power and led ABC to become the top name in sports coverage, thanks to the effort of an ambitious staff led by a visionary producer named Roone Arledge.

Arledge had made his name at ABC in his twenties as producer of *NCAA Football,* where his use of five cameras to allow viewers to get intimate sideline shots of fans, cheerleaders, and players was a hit and revolutionized TV's coverage of the game. Arledge's *Wide World of Sports* concoction showed an assortment of competitions that had limited appeal as events in their own right, but with the right amount of pacing would prove to be entertaining to the public.

The show achieved its ambitions quickly. On July 15–16, 1961, for example, it received praise when it went to Moscow to videotape a track meet between the United States and the Soviet Union. Other early highlights from abroad were a skating show from Czechoslovakia, the Grand Prix from South Africa, and a fishing tournament in Argentina. Many ABC sportscasters covered events, but Jim McKay was seen most frequently. By 1966, *Wide World of Sports* had showcased more than 80 sports.

On May 21, 1966, the show aired the first boxing match telecast live in the United States from overseas, featuring American Cassius Clay versus Briton Henry Cooper in London. On August 6, 1966, the show again covered Clay fighting in London, but by then the boxer was using his new name, Muhammad Ali. Bill Flemming did not use the pugilist's Muslim moniker, but Howard Cosell did and defended doing so, prompting some intolerant sports fans to denounce Ali and Cosell. Nonetheless, both men appeared often on the show over the next few years and received publicity from their odd relationship, which vacillated between Cosell's respect for Ali (and vice versa) and Ali's deflating Cosell's tendency toward pomposity. Ali appeared on the show more than 60 times through 1991, a record number for an athlete.

Another memorable event from the first decade of *Wide World of Sports* was a ski jumping contest in Germany in 1970, where Vinko Bogataj of Yugoslavia spun off the ramp. He survived, and so did the film clip, appearing in the show's opening montage as representing "the agony of defeat." On the show's 30th anniversary special, Bogataj was said to be doing well as a painter in his homeland.

A big audience draw in the 1970s was daredevil motorcyclist Evel Knieval. In February 1974 his jump over 11 trucks in Dallas broke the show's record for viewership at that time. On September 10, 1974, Knieval made an unsuccessful attempt to jump Snake River Canyon in Idaho, and four days later the show had footage of the event. This too was a ratings smash, as were Knieval's jumps over 13 buses in London and over 15 buses in Ohio in 1975. But injuries sustained in these events and bad publicity caused Knieval's stardom to fade by the late 1970s, and *Wide World of Sports* went back to focusing on more traditional sports.

In 1974 the show added a Sunday version for eight months each year. As it headed into the 1980s it boasted of having visited some 40 countries on six continents. It also found itself facing competitors galore, from the *CBS Sports Spectacular* to *Sportsworld* on NBC. But by this time, ABC had become the acknowledged leader in sports coverage from techniques developed on this series, and knockoffs of the show never matched it in prestige or ratings.

On its 35th anniversary, *ABC's Wide World of Sports* had its first black female host, Robin Roberts (who followed McKay's first successor Frank Gifford, who had occasional co-hosts, and then the thirtyish and also female Julie Moran), and offered a new weekly feature called "Women in the Game," examining females in athletics. At this writing, the show remains as solid as ever, having won Emmies for best sports programming at least 15 times since 1966, and it appears that *Wide World of Sports* will easily remain ABC's longest-running show into the 21st century.

AFL FOOTBALL
Sports; B&W and Color
September 11, 1960–December 14, 1969

ABC Sun. 3:30–6:30 p.m. (9/11/60–12/20/64, September–December only)
NBC Sun. 1–4 p.m. or 2–5 p.m. (9/12/65–12/31/67, September–December only)
NBC Sun. 1:30–7 p.m. (9/8/68–12/14/69, September–December only)

Announcers included: *Bob Neal (at least 1961), Curt Gowdy (play-by-play; at least 1961–69), Paul Christman (analyst; at least 1961–67), Jack Buck (play-by-play; at least 1963), George Ratterman (analyst; at least 1963–64 & 1966), Charlie Jones (play-by-play; 1964–69), Jim Simpson (play-by-play; 1967–69), Kyle Rote (analyst; 1967–69), Al DeRogatis (analyst; 1968–69)*

If anyone doubts how much power television has in the sports world, then consider the story of the American Football League. Begun as an upstart competitor of the National Football League on the upstart network of ABC, it found itself almost a decade later showing two games a day nationally and planning to be a partner with its once-mighty competition. The league emerged when ultra-rich Lamar Hunt, denied by the NFL a chance to own the Dallas franchise, contacted some other well-to-do football friends of his and formed a new eight-team league. They found they needed TV exposure and offered it to the networks. Program-hungry ABC eagerly accepted it with a five-year, $10 million contract. However, during the ABC years the AFL remained far behind the NFL in terms of numbers of franchises and ratings appeal.

When NBC signed a five-year, $36 million deal for TV rights starting in 1965 (not far from the two-year, $43.6 million CBS signed with the NFL at about the same time), it went all out to build up its stature to beat CBS. For example, Carl Lindemann Jr., then head of

NBC's sports programming, wrote a letter to top college football players saying, "Your future undoubtedly would be best served in the American Football League." But real swaying of the players came with the competitive salaries AFL teams now offered, with each franchise being guaranteed $750,000 a year by NBC's deal. That gave them the ability to offer fat contracts to draft choices, and so talented athletes like quarterback Joe Namath began joining the AFL over the NFL, making names and money for themselves in the process.

NBC also took the unprecedented step in 1968 of airing two games back to back each Sunday. The main announcing teams were Curt Gowdy and Al DeRogatis (Paul Christman, Gowdy's main announcing partner since the ABC days, left in 1968 to cover NFL football on CBS), and Jim Simpson and Kyle Rote. Charlie Jones occasionally replaced Gowdy, as did some other announcers over the years.

But what really put the AFL over the top was the first playing of the league's top winner against the NFL champion in the Super Bowl in 1967. The excitement and high ratings generated by the annual contest, along with a general consensus about the parity between the leagues, led to talks on merger and an eventual realignment of the parties by 1970. For details on the results, see *NFL Football (NBC)*.

AFL HIGHLIGHTS

Sports; B&W and Color
September 7, 1963–December 17, 1966

ABC Sat. 4:30–5 p.m. (9/7/63–12/21/63)
NBC Sat. 5:30–6 p.m. (10/1/66–12/17/66)

Hosts: *Curt Gowdy, Paul Christman (1963)*

Two different seasons and networks presented this wrap-up of the previous Saturday's AFL matches and a look ahead to the next day's contests. On NBC the show's title was *AFL Report*, and Curt Gowdy handled the chores without broadcasting buddy Paul Christman.

•A. J.'S TIME TRAVELERS

Children's; Color
December 3, 1994–December 31, 1994

Fox Sat. 11:30 a.m.–Noon (12/3/94–12/31/94)

Cast:
A. J. Malloy   John Patrick White

Beaming up from Earth, space cadet adolescent A. J. Malloy led a rather comic band of crewmen on the ship *Kyros* on voyages to locate visitors from Earth's past, such as pioneering printer Johann Gutenberg in the 1400s, scientist Sir Isaac Newton in the 1600s, and the Tuskegee Airmen in the 1940s. Then he returned to his family on Earth to review what he learned and do a quick comic bit. The result was like a cross between *Beakman's World* and *Where on Earth is Carmen Sandiego?* Though Fox aired only four episodes of this educational series, it did run in syndication as part of a package titled *Amazin! Adventures*.

ALF

Cartoon; Color
September 26, 1987–August 25, 1990

NBC Sat. 11–11:30 a.m. (9/26/87–11/14/87)
NBC Sat. 10–10:30 a.m. (11/21/87–9/3/88)
NBC Sat. 10–11 a.m. (9/10/88–10/15/88)
NBC Sat. 10:30–11:30 a.m. (10/22/88–9/2/89)
NBC Sat. 8–8:30 a.m. and Noon–12:30 p.m.
   (9/16/89–3/3/90)
NBC Sat. Noon–1 p.m. (3/10/90–8/25/90)

Voices:

ALF (Gordon Shumway)	*Paul Fusco*
Augie/Rhoda	*Paulina Gillis*
Bob/Larson Petty	*Thick Wilson*
Curtis (1987–89)	*Michael Fantini*
Flo	*Peggy Mahon*
Harry (1987–89)	*Stephen McMulkin*
Skip	*Rob Cowan*
Sloop	*Dan Hennessey*
Sgt. Staff/Cantfayl (1987–89)	*Len Carlson*
Stella	*Ellen-Ray Hennessey*

ALF stood for Alien Life Form, as any prepubescent (and probably many postpubescents) could tell you in the late 1980s. This animated entry was based on the NBC Monday night sitcom of the same name, which began on September 22, 1986. Here the adolescent days of ALF, when the diminutive hairball with an attitude was a mere 193 years old, were dramatized with his parents Bob and Flo, his brother Curtis, and his sister Augie, plus assorted pals at the restaurant on the planet Melmac.

In 1988 it became an hour and added "ALF Tales," which employed the cast in takeoffs of fairy tales. On September 16, 1989, *ALF Tales* became a series at 8 a.m., while *ALF* aired at noon. Six months later, *ALF* moved to 12:30 p.m. and followed its spin-off. The nighttime sitcom ended on June 18, 1990, two months before both cartoons died.

Believe it or not, this cartoon generated controversy when a Long Island, New York viewer announced that a subliminal shot of the Statue of Liberty came up during an explosion in a first-season episode. The president of Studio Korumi, a Japanese firm handling the animation, acknowledged that the graphic appeared on one frame as a joke, since it was an American product. Luckily the incident did not lead to any hysteria about other possible subliminal shots in the show or their effects on the viewer, as had been the case among some movies in the 1950s, and *ALF* managed to have a decent three-year run.

A.M. AMERICA

News/Information; Color
January 6, 1975–October 31, 1975

ABC Mon.–Fri. 7–9 a.m. (1/6/75–10/31/75)

Regulars: *Bill Beutel, Stephanie Edwards (January–May), Peter Jennings*

The precursor to *Good Morning America* was this inaugural, belated challenge by ABC to NBC's *Today Show*. Bill Beutel, anchor of *Eyewitness News* of WABC-TV in New York City, and Stephanie Edwards, hostess of a Los Angeles morning show, took the reins as the equivalents of Hugh Downs and Barbara Walters, and Peter Jennings delivered news updates every half hour. The series was fraught with difficulties from the start. Chicago morning personality Bob Kennedy, who had been slated to do features segments, died of cancer on November 6, 1974. Then Edwards quit after four months to get married and was replaced in the summer by such weekly guest hostesses as Candice Bergen, Barbara Howar, and Lynn Redgrave. Sensing the problems, ABC overhauled the show with mostly new personnel; the result was *Good Morning America* (q.v.).

ABOUT FACES
Game; B&W
January 4, 1960–June 30, 1961

ABC Mon.–Fri. 1–1:30 p.m. (1/4/60–3/2/61)
ABC Mon.–Fri. 1–1:25 p.m. (3/5/61–6/30/61)

Host: *Ben Alexander*

About Faces, a potpourri of games about fame in general, had been tested by NBC for its daytime lineup a year before ABC added it. (The program was not related to *All About Faces*, a 1971 syndicated game show hosted by Richard Hayes.) Each show, which came live from Hollywood, began with a celebrity guessing the identity of a face from his or her past (on the debut, the celeb was Zsa Zsa Gabor and the face was her milkman). Following that was a mystery guest in the audience, then a mini *This Is Your Life* tribute to a celebrity, with family and friends reminiscing about the person's past in a manner similar to the long-running NBC nighttime show. *About Faces* had nothing to fear in terms of lawsuits for the latter segment, for it and *This Is Your Life* were both Ralph Edwards Productions.

By November 1960, the show had added a game where three audience members competed to identify a star whose incomplete face hid behind a jigsaw puzzle. If the first player failed, more of the celebrity face appeared until one player guessed correctly. The game did not keep the show from being canceled within the year.

ACCENT
Documentary; B&W
February 26, 1961–June 3, 1962

CBS Sun. 12:30–1 p.m. (2/26/61–6/11/61)
CBS Sun. 5–5:30 p.m. (6/18/61–9/17/61)
CBS Sat. 1–1:30 p.m. (9/23/61–9/30/61)
CBS Sat. 1:30–2 p.m. (10/7/61–4/28/62)
CBS Sat. 1–1:30 p.m. (5/5/62–6/3/62)

Hosts: *James Fleming (1961), John Ciardi (mid-1961, 10/21/61–6/3/62), Alexander Kendrick (7/9/61–10/14/61), Winston Burdett (7/9/61–10/14/61)*

One of several early 1960s cultural series spawned after FCC Chairman Newton Minow claimed that television had become a "vast wasteland," *Accent* offered viewers a heady brew of highbrow events. The debut, a tribute to poet Robert Frost, featured no less than President John Kennedy as a guest, and Kennedy's wife Jacqueline appeared three weeks later on a tour of the National Gallery of Art. Other shows were devoted to subjects both living (e.g., choreographer George Balanchine) and dead (writer D. H. Lawrence), trends affecting the arts (two-part discussions on such topics as blacks in culture since Emancipation and the British "angry young man" school of writing), and traditional documentaries, some using actors such as Donald Pleasance and Robert Shaw to portray participants in the stories being told.

Not all was serious, though. One show featured sketches and interviews with Dudley Moore, Peter Cook, Jonathan Miller, and Alan Bennett of the hit Broadway show "Beyond the Fringe." All this activity was accomplished in a taping schedule of only three days, with no editing allowed by CBS, a feat that led *Newsweek* to write that *Accent* was "the best new show to go on the air this year."

Host James Fleming was replaced after a few months by John Ciardi, a poet recommended for the job by a former student of his, *Accent*'s associate producer James Perrin. In the summer of 1961, CBS News foreign correspondents Alexander Kendrick and Winston Burdett led a taped tour of Europe until Ciardi returned. The show aired on CBS nighttime from June 7–September 6, 1962 under the title *Accent on an American Summer* before ending.

•ACE VENTURA, PET DETECTIVE
Cartoon; Color
January 20, 1996–

CBS Sat. 10:30–11 a.m. (1/20/96–)

Voice:
Ace Ventura   *Michael Hall*

Ace Ventura, Pet Detective was the last of three network Saturday morning cartoons based on a Jim Carrey movie to arrive in the 1995–96 season, even though the 1994 film of the same title on which it was based was the first hit for the comedian. Airing after the Carrey-inspired *The Mask*, the series stayed true to the movie and its 1995 sequel *Ace Ventura: When Nature Calls*, featuring a demented detective sporting a loud Hawaiian print shirt, who fought against evildoers attempting to harm animals in some way. And as in the PG-13 movies, the character got involved in a few tasteless comic bits, including squeezing his butt cheeks to pretend he was talking to someone. Ace's base was Miami, and his sidekick was Spike, his pet monkey.

ACROBAT RANCH
Children's Variety; B&W
August 19, 1950–May 12, 1951

ABC Sat. 11:30 a.m.–Noon (8/19/50–2/10/51)
ABC Sat. 10:45–11 a.m. (2/17/51–5/12/51)

Cast:

Flying Flo	*Valerie Alberts*
Tumbling Tim	*Billy Alberts*
Uncle Jim	*Jack Stilwell*

One of ABC's first two shows to air on Saturday mornings (the other was *Animal Clinic*), *Acrobat Ranch* featured cowboy host Uncle Jim introducing acts with a circus theme, including young gymnasts Tumbling Tim and Flying Flo. The live Chicago-based show had the General Shoe Corporation as sponsor on behalf of its Acrobat Shoe Division.

ACROSS THE BOARD
Game; B&W
June 1, 1959–October 9, 1959

ABC Mon.–Fri. Noon–12:30 p.m. (6/1/59–10/9/59)

Host: *Ted Brown*

This live offering from New York had contestants receive clues from questions and cartoons to words in a large crossword puzzle they had to solve. Players received one point per letter for each right answer, and the one with the most points at the game's end won prizes. This vanished soon against *Love of Life* on CBS and *Tic Tac Dough* on NBC.

•ACTION IN THE AFTERNOON
Western; B&W
February 2, 1953–January 29, 1954

CBS Mon.–Fri. 4–4:30 p.m. (2/2/53–5/8/53)
CBS Mon.–Fri. 3:30–4 p.m. (5/11/53–9/11/53)
CBS Mon.–Fri. 4–4:30 p.m. (9/14/53–1/29/54)

Cast:

Ace Bancroft	*Barry Cassell*
Ozzie Matthews	*Harriss Forrest*
Jack Valentine	*Himself*
The Coroner	*John Zacherley*
Kate	*Mary Elaine Watts*
Narrator	*Blake Ritter*

Other regulars: *Chris Keegan, Sam Kressen, Creighton Stewart, the Tommy Ferguson Trio*

TV's oddest western was this daily live production in which the outskirts of Philadelphia served as the 1890 setting for fictional Huberle, Montana (altitude 2,291 feet, population 486). The hero was singing cowboy Jack Valentine, backed by the Tommy Ferguson Trio, and supported by Sheriff Ace Bancroft. Their pal Kate was editor and publisher of *The Huberle Record*, and Ozzie was Jack's dense sidekick. Other regulars played various local citizens. Many characters passed through the rough-and-tumble town in this violent oater, which notched up one dead and one wounded on the premiere.

CBS tried earnestly to make this program work. The set included a general store, bank, blacksmith shop, six stagecoaches, and even a saloon called the Copper Cup Bar. It had the largest technical staff ever gathered for a live show

The sheriff of TV's only live outdoor western was Ace Bancroft, played by Barry Cassell, on Action in the Afternoon.

at the time, with two camera crews covering the drama. But for all the effort, no one really explained why CBS was staging a live cowboy show, given the difficulties of working with horses, outdoor noises, and the like, although they did claim that Philly was chosen because its climate mimicked that of Montana. There were sound problems galore for the performers (hitching posts usually hid microphones), not to mention the anachronism of planes zooming around, and exasperated viewers gave up on the challenge of following the shoot-'em-up within a year.

Among the curiosities of this production was the question of the town's bizarre name: why Huberle (pronounced "hubber-lee")? That's easy; it came from the names of CBS programming vice president *Hubbell* Robinson Jr. and his chief associate Harry *Ommerle*.

ACTION '73/'74—See *Where the Action Is.*

•ADDAMS FAMILY, THE
Cartoon; Color
September 8, 1973–January 7, 1995

NBC Sat. 9–9:30 a.m. (9/8/73–12/29/73)
NBC Sat. 8:30–9 a.m. (1/5/74–8/31/74)
NBC Sat. 8–8:30 a.m. (9/7/74–8/30/75)
ABC Sat. 10:30–11 a.m. (9/12/92–1/30/93)
ABC Sat. 9:30–10 a.m. (2/6/93–9/3/94)
ABC Sat. 10:30–11 a.m. (12/10/94–1/7/95)

Voices:

Gomez Addams (1973–75)	*Lennie Weinrib*
Gomez Addams (1992–95)	*John Astin*
Morticia Addams/Granny	
(1973–75)	*Janet Waldo*

Morticia Addams (1992–95)	Nancy Linari
Pugsley Addams (1973–75)	Jodie Foster
Pugsley Addams (1992–95)	Jeannie Elias
Wednesday Addams (1973–75)	Cindy Henderson
Wednesday Addams (1992–95)	Debi Derryberry
Uncle Fester (1973–75)	Jackie Coogan
Uncle Fester (1992–95)	Rip Taylor
Granny (1992–95)	Carol Channing
Cousin Itt (1992–95)	Pat Fraley
Lurch (1973–75)	Ted Cassidy
Lurch (1992–95)	Jim Cummings
Mr. Normanmeyer (1992–95)	Rob Paulsen
Mrs. Normanmeyer (1992–95)	Edie McClurg
N. J. Normanmeyer (1992–95)	Dick Beals

Charles Addams's ghoulish cartoons for *The New Yorker* magazine became a surprising source for several TV shows and movies in the latter half of the 20th century. The first was a well-remembered though short-lived (1964–66) live-action ABC nighttime series starring John Astin as the laid-back Gomez and Carolyn Jones as his alluring wife, Morticia. Seven years later, the concept revived in two forms. The first was a failed 1973 syndicated pilot called *The Addams Family Fun House,* with Jack Riley as Gomez and Liz Torres as Morticia. (Ironically, also appearing was Butch Patrick, who was Eddie on *The Munsters,* the other "monster comedy" which ran in nighttime from 1964–66, like the first *Addams Family.)* The show set the characters in a musical comedy format. A *Variety* review said, "It couldn't have been worse if they'd done it in blackface."

The second Addams try in 1973 fared a little better. Now the eerie clan appeared in cartoon form as they drove a haunted camper with a moat, bats, and dark clouds overhead across America on an extended vacation. Joining Gomez and Morticia were their fat son Pugsley, enterprising daughter Wednesday, gnomelike Uncle Fester, potion-making Granny, and lumbering servant Lurch, not to mention a disembodied hand from a box they called Thing. Jackie Coogan and Ted Cassidy voiced the same characters they had on the earlier show, but the real surprise was child actress Jodie Foster doing the voice of the male Pugsley.

After the NBC cartoon ended, the property languished until a live-action *Addams Family* movie appeared in 1991 with Raul Julia as Gomez and Anjelica Huston as Morticia. Its success prompted a cartoon revival on ABC with the original Gomez, John Astin, voicing his role, and another girl actress voicing Pugsley, now cast as Wednesday's older brother. The Addams now lived in Happydale Heights and their kooky next-door neighbors were the Normanmeyers, whose avocations were weird enough that they sometimes made the oddities of the Addamses seem virtually normal. The 1994–95 shows were repeats.

ADLAI STEVENSON REPORTS
Public Affairs; B&W
October 1, 1961–May 26, 1963

ABC Sun. 3–3:30 p.m. (10/1/61–12/24/61)
ABC Sun. 3:30–4 p.m. (1/21/62–5/27/62)
ABC Sun. 2:30–3 p.m. (9/30/62–1/6/63)
ABC Sun. Various half hours between 1–3:30 p.m. (1/20/63–5/26/63)

Regulars: *Arnold Michaelis, Adlai Stevenson, John MacVane*

Seen on alternate Sundays, *Adlai Stevenson Reports* gave viewers a perspective on global concerns from Adlai Stevenson, the Illinois Democrat serving as America's representative in the United Nations during the Kennedy administration. Reporter John MacVane gave a brief news update at the start of each show, and host Arnold Michaelis, who co-produced the show, discussed current events with Stevenson and guests who were divided roughly equally among American officials, U.N. employees and representatives, and foreign leaders. A notable guest was U Thant on October 29, 1961; he would become acting U.N. secretary general following Dag Hammarskjold's death at the end of that year.

Stevenson told *TV Guide* he enjoyed the forum this show allowed him. "There is no doubt in my mind that television at its best can add a dimension to the appreciation of almost any subject," he said. "And it's for this reason that I am grateful for the opportunity to do this series, which I believe can substantially contribute to the never-ending job of bringing government and the people into harmony through mutual understanding of the great issues of our day." Stevenson died in 1965, not long after the series went off the air.

ADVENTURE
Documentary; B&W
May 10, 1953–July 8, 1956

CBS Sun. 5–6 p.m. (5/10/53–6/21/53)
CBS Sun. 4:30–5 p.m. (10/11/53–3/28/54)
CBS Sun. 5–6 p.m. (4/4/54–6/27/54)
CBS Sun. 3:30–4:30 p.m. (9/26/54–4/10/55)
CBS Sun. 5–6 p.m. (4/17/55–4/24/55)
CBS Sun. 5:30–6 p.m. (5/8/55–6/19/55)
CBS Sun. 3:30–4 p.m. (10/9/55–1/1/56)
CBS Sun. 2:30–3 p.m. (1/8/56–4/8/56)
CBS Sun. 4:30–5 p.m. (4/15/56–7/8/56)

Regulars: *Charles Collingwood (1953–55), Mike Wallace, Robert Northshield*

Three CBS reporters, led by host Charles Collingwood, talked on camera with scientists in this educational series for children produced in cooperation with the American Museum of Natural History in New York City. Typically, two or three topics came into discussion during the early shows, including "Dance and Trance with Bali" with anthropologist Dr. Margaret Mead on May 24, 1953. Later shows featured one topic, such as Mike Wallace making his first solo flight, and personnel not associated with the museum (e.g., Supreme Court Justice William O. Douglas discussing films shot in Tibet by Nazis fleeing the British in the 1940s, architect Frank Lloyd Wright commenting on the Mayan civilization's influence on contemporary design, and comedian Henry Morgan describing the human body). The series also aired on CBS nighttime from June 28–September 27, 1953.

ADVENTURES OF AQUAMAN—See *Aquaman.*

ADVENTURES OF BATMAN—See *Batman.*

ADVENTURES OF CAPTAIN HARTZ—See *Captain Hartz.*

ADVENTURES OF GULLIVER, THE
Cartoon; Color
September 14, 1968–September 5, 1970

ABC Sat. 9:30–10 a.m. (9/14/68–8/30/69)
ABC Sat. 11:30 a.m.–Noon (9/6/69–12/27/69)
ABC Sat. 8–8:30 a.m. (1/3/70–9/5/70)

Voices:

Flirtacia	Ginny Tyler
Glum/Eager	Don Messick
Gary Gulliver	Jerry Dexter
Bunko	Allan Melvin
King Pomp/Captain Leech	John Stephenson
Shag	Herb Vigran

Jonathan Swift's classic novel of 1726 became a Saturday morning cartoon with virtually all its satire drained and replaced by tired adventure plots. Here Gary Gulliver, accompanied by his dog Shag, attempted to locate his father, Thomas, who disappeared in the land of Lilliput. Lilliput was a land of six-inch people led by King Pomp, and Gary's miniature pals Flirtacia (Pomp's daughter), Eager, Glum, and Bunko tried to help him find his dad while avoiding Captain Leech, who wanted Gary's treasure map.

ADVENTURES OF GUMMI BEARS—See *Gummi Bears.*

ADVENTURES OF HOPPITY HOOPER, THE
Cartoon; Color
September 26, 1964–September 2, 1967

ABC Sat. 12:30–1 p.m. (9/26/64–10/2/65)
ABC Sat. 1–1:30 p.m. (10/9/65–9/2/67)

Voices:

"Cousin" Fillmore	Bill Scott
"Uncle" Waldo Wigglesworth	Hans Conreid
Hoppity Hooper	Chris Allen
Narrator	Paul Frees

Hoppity Hooper was a talking frog living in Foggybog, Wisconsin, who found himself befriended by con artist Professor Wigglesworth, a fox who took it upon himself to announce he was Hoppity's uncle and join him in various misadventures. Waldo's stooge, Fillmore the bear, fell in line with his boss and became Hoppity's cousin. Each show included two episodes of a four-part adventure, along with

repeated segments of "Fractured Fairy Tales" and "Peabody's Improbable History" from *The Bullwinkle Show* and "Commander McBragg" from *Tennessee Tuxedo and His Tales.* The series aired in syndication as *Uncle Waldo and His Friends.*

•ADVENTURES OF HYPERMAN, THE
Cartoon; Color
October 14, 1995–

CBS Sat. 8–8:30 a.m. (10/14/95–2/10/96)
CBS Sat. 11:30 a.m.–Noon (5/18/96–)

Voices: *Max Casella, Steve Mackall*

Another 1990s superhero spoof à la *The Tick, The Adventures of Hyperman* had an "intergalactic sheriff" in red tights attempting to save Earth from the evil green ogreish Entrobe, who used material for his own benefit without regard to others. Blue midget blob Studd Puppy and brilliant 13-year-old scientist Emma C. Squared joined Hyperman in his unintentionally comic efforts (due to his inability to understand Earth's physical properties) to thwart Entrope and the latter's Peter Lorre–like sidekick, Kid Chaos.

•ADVENTURES OF RAGGEDY ANN AND ANDY, THE
Cartoon; Color
September 17, 1988–August 31, 1991

CBS Sat. 8–8:30 a.m (9/17/88–9/9/89)
CBS Sat. Noon–12:30 p.m. (9/16/89–9/1/90)
CBS Sat. 11:30 a.m.–Noon (7/27/91–8/31/91)

Voices:

Raggedy Ann	Christina Lange
Raggedy Andy	Josh Rodine
Raggedy Cat	Kath Soucie
Raggedy Dog	Dana Hill
Grouchy Bear	Charlie Adler
Sunny Bunny	Katie Leigh
The Camel with Wrinkled Knees	Ken Mars
Marcella	Tracy Rowe

Raggedy Ann and Andy had just celebrated their 70th anniversary as pop culture characters when this cartoon debuted. The dolls with the red, stringy hair and their assorted stuffed pals left the bedroom of human child Marcella, seen only from the shoulders down and accompanied by her dog Fido, for various excursions into Raggedyland in fanciful stories designed to appeal to younger children. Among the other dolls, Raggedy Cat and Dog spoke, and Grouchy Bear was the resident grump who reluctantly participated in the adventures. The series had a brief round of repeats in 1991, hastily added to cover the abrupt cancellation of *Pee Wee's Playhouse* (q.v.).

ADVENTURES OF SONIC THE HEDGEHOG—See *Sonic the Hedgehog.*

ADVENTURES OF SUPERMAN—See *Superman.*

ADVENTURES OF WALDO KITTY—See *Secret Lives of Waldo Kitty*.

AFTERNOON FILM FESTIVAL
Films; B&W
January 16, 1956–August 2, 1957

ABC Mon.–Fri. 3–5 p.m. (1/16/56–10/26/56)
ABC Mon.–Fri. 3–4:30 p.m. (10/29/56–8/2/57)

Hosts: *Allyn Edwards (early to mid-1956), Donald Woods (mid- to late 1956), Don Gardner (1957)*

ABC presented the first—and likely only—daily network presentation of feature films as its inaugural effort to expand its virtually nonexistent daytime lineup at the time. In November 1955 it purchased 100 films never seen on American television from Great Britain's J. Arthur Rank company for $1.5 million, including the 1948 Oscar-winning movie version of *Hamlet* by Sir Laurence Olivier and Alfred Hitchcock's *The Lady Vanishes*, for the afternoon slot. To fill out the running time, the network installed Allyn Edwards, then hosting a similar series of English features on ABC Sunday nights called *Famous Film Festival*, to serve as host, narrator of plot points when needed, and reporter of news highlights during breaks in the day's film. Two others succeeded him as host.

After more than a year of unsuccessfully challenging CBS and NBC, ABC replaced this with a much more productive venture. See *American Bandstand*.

AL PEARCE SHOW, THE
Variety; B&W
February 11, 1952–September 26, 1952

CBS Mon.–Fri. 10:45–11:30 a.m. (2/11/52–4/1/52)
CBS Mon.–Fri. 11–11:30 a.m. (4/4/52–5/9/52)
CBS Mon.–Thu. 10:45–11:15 a.m.; Fri 10:30–11 a.m.
  (6/30/52–9/26/52)

Host: *Al Pearce*

Comic Al Pearce, a moderate success on radio from 1934–46 on NBC, CBS, and ABC, tried video in 1952 with his act of jokes and characters, including Elmer Blurt, a clumsy salesman whose catch phrase was "Nobody's home, I hope, I hope." The program aired live from Hollywood at 7:45 a.m. Western Time from February to May. CBS offered free coffee and donuts for potential in-studio audiences, but refused to make kinescopes (it would have cost $1,000 per show to do so), so no one in Los Angeles got to see the production. In late June Pearce relocated his show to New York, but it did not last beyond the fall due to high costs and no sponsors.

Pearce returned to daytime with a daily local TV show in Los Angeles in 1954. He died in 1961.

•ALADDIN'S ARABIAN ADVENTURES
Cartoon; Color
September 17, 1994–

CBS Sat. 9–9:30 a.m. (9/17/94–)

Voices:

Aladdin	*Scott Weinger*
The Genie	*Dan Castellaneta*
Iago	*Gilbert Gottfried*
Princess Jasmine	*Linda Larkin*
The Monkey	*Frank Welker*

The popular Disney 1992 animated musical comedy movie *Aladdin* became a Saturday morning cartoon a few years later with most of its appealing ingredients intact, including spectacular artwork, most of the original voices, and humorous and engaging story lines. Missing, however, was the voice of Robin Williams as the joke-spewing Genie; Dan Castellaneta made a serviceable if less inspiredly wacky substitute. (It's hard to imagine anyone equaling Williams's rapid-fire, off-the-wall improvisations.) Also gone was the Oscar-winning score by Alan Menken, Tim Rice, and the late Howard Ashman, but the cartoon did use a title theme written by Ashman and Menken.

The series dealt mainly with the perils faced in ancient Arabia by cocky but gullible young Aladdin, his levelheaded girlfriend Princess Jasmine, their pet monkey, and the omnipotent if offbeat blue Genie which protected them all, as did a magic carpet used for transportation. Iago the parrot, a cohort to the villainous Jafar in the movie, became a cranky commentator on the troupe and their sometimes inept efforts to see that good triumphed over dangerous foes. He had the best lines in the show along with the Genie, whose supposed ability to travel through time gave him the opportunity to pepper the adventures with modern shapes and asides, as when he transformed himself into an aerosol can to repel a deadly locust and then told viewers, "Don't worry, it's ozone-friendly."

The overall result was a breezy program which both adults and children could easily enjoy. This series also debuted in daily syndication on September 5, 1994.

•ALIENS IN THE FAMILY
Sitcom; Color
July 27, 1996–

ABC Sat. 11:30 a.m.–Noon (7/27/96–)

Cast:

Adam	*Chris Marquette*
Bobut (voice only)	*John Kennedy*
Doug Brody	*John Bedford Lloyd*
Cookie	*Margaret Trigg*

Under normal circumstances, *Aliens in the Family* would be listed in this book's daytime reruns appendix. But this series lasted only two episodes during its disastrous run from March 15–22, 1996, on ABC Fridays at 9 p.m., so it actually aired some "new" shows not seen in nighttime. The scenario had single dad Doug Brody marrying Cookie, a humanoid alien who abducted him, and claiming her three hairless, bug-eyed progeny as his own along with his existing three children. The setup and house design gave definite echoes of *The Brady Bunch*, as Doug's children Sally, Heather, and Adam, in descending age order, coexisted uneasily with Cookie's alien kids Spit, Snizzy, and Bobut the infant (Bobut causing considerable havoc with a rattle with magical powers). Unfortunately, the humor and situations were tiresome and laden with an obnoxious laugh track, not something one would expect from Henson Productions. ALF had nothing to worry about.

ALL ABOARD
Children's Variety; B&W
October 19, 1952–January 11, 1953

CBS Sun. 12:15–12:30 p.m. (10/19/52–1/11/53)

Regulars: *Skeets Minton, Junie Keegan*

Ventriloquist Skeets Minton and his dummy Jimmy Morton, teenage singer Junie Keegan, and guests provided entertainment in this short-lived program. The show's title was a reference to its sponsor, Lionel Trains.

ALL ABOUT BABY
Informational; B&W
October 15, 1954–July 1, 1955

DuMont Fri 2–2:15 p.m. (10/15/54–1/7/55)
DuMont Thu./Fri. 2–2:15 p.m. (1/13/55–4/8/55)
DuMont Thu./Fri. 1:45–2 p.m. (4/14/55–7/1/55)

Hostess: *Ruth Crowley, R.N.*

This was the last show on DuMont to air on a weekday before 6 p.m. (*NFL Football* on Sundays was the network's last daytime show). Nurse Ruth Crowley offered her professional wisdom to viewing mothers on how to care for infants. It began in 1952 on WNBQ, NBC's Chicago station, as a local Wednesday morning show with Crowley. In 1953 it became a daily show on ABC's Chicago affiliate WBKB. ABC did not pick it up due to its short length and the fact that a limited number of affiliates were able to show it live at the time, so DuMont took the program by default. By April 1955 DuMont got it carried on 11 stations for two days a week, three of them carrying it live, which in retrospect seems like a high point for the rapidly disintegrating network. In fact, sponsorship from the Swift Company kept it as one of only eight shows on DuMont at the time. It went off the network three months later.

ALL AROUND THE TOWN
Variety; B&W and Color
June 18, 1951–November 2, 1951

CBS Mon/Wed/Fri 3:30–4 p.m. (6/18/51–11/2/51)

Regulars: *Mike Wallace, Buff Cobb*

The town was New York City, and going all around it three times a week were Mike Wallace and his then-wife Buff Cobb. They ventured to hangouts like Times Square to interview people and discuss the area and what was happening there. After a few months, this series went onto early evening Saturdays on CBS from November 10, 1951–June 7, 1952.

•ALL MY CHILDREN
Soap Opera; Color
January 5, 1970–

ABC Mon.–Fri. 1–1:30 p.m. (1/5/70–7/4/75)
ABC Mon.–Fri. 12:30–1 p.m. (7/7/75–12/31/76)
ABC Mon.–Fri. 1–1:30 p.m. (1/3/77–4/22/77)
ABC Mon.–Fri. 1–2 p.m. (4/25/77–)

Cast:

Phoebe Tyler	*Ruth Warrick*
Dr. Charles Tyler (1970–83, 1985)	*Hugh Franklin*
Lincoln Tyler (1970)	*James Karen*
Lincoln Tyler (1970–71)	*Paul Dumont*
Lincoln Tyler (1971)	*Nicholas Pryor*
Lincoln Tyler (1974–81, 1984, 1986)	*Peter White*
Ann Tyler (1970)	*Diana De Vegh*
Ann Tyler (1970–71)	*Joanna Miles*
Ann Tyler (1971–77)	*Judith Barcroft*
Ann Tyler (1979–81)	*Gwyn Gilliss*
Chuck Tyler (1970–72)	*Jack Stauffer*
Chuck Tyler (1972–73)	*Gregory Chase*
Chuck Tyler (1973–75)	*Chris Hubbell*
Chuck Tyler (1975–84, 1986, 1989–92)	*Richard Van Vleet*
Nick Davis (1970–78, 1983–84, 1988, 1991, 1993–94)	*Lawrence Keith*
Erica Kane	*Susan Lucci*
Mona Kane (1970–94)	*Frances Heflin*
Ruth Brent Martin (1970–96)	*Mary Fickett*
Ruth Brent Martin (1996–)	*Lee Meriwether*
Dr. Joseph Martin	*Ray MacDonnell*
Tara Martin (1970–74, 1976–77, 1995)	*Karen Lynn Gorney*
Tara Martin (1974–76)	*Stephanie Braxton*
Tara Martin (1977–79, 1985)	*Nancy Frangione*
Tara Martin (1979–80)	*Mary Lynn Blanks*
Dr. Jeff Martin (1970)	*Christopher Wines*
Dr. Jeff Martin (1970–75, 1988)	*Charles Frank*
Dr. Jeff Martin (1976–77)	*Robert Perault*
Dr. Jeff Martin (1977–79)	*James O'Sullivan*
Dr. Jeff Martin (1986–87)	*Jeffrey Byron*
Phillip Brent (1970–72)	*Richard Hatch*
Phillip Brent (1973–79, 1988)	*Nicholas Benedict*
Kate Martin (1970)	*Kate Harrington*
Kate Martin (1970)	*Christine Thomas*
Kate Martin (1970–85)	*Kay Campbell*
Paul Martin (1970–72)	*Ken Rabat*
Paul Martin (1972–82, 1984–85)	*William Mooney*
Amy Tyler (1970)	*Rosemary Prinz*
Ted Brent (1970)	*Mark Dawson*
Mary Kennicott (1971)	*Jacqueline Boslow*
Mary Kennicott (1971–75)	*Susan Blanchard*
Kitty Shea (1972–77)/Kelly Cole (1978–86)	*Francesca James*

Character	Actor
Phillip Jr. "Charlie" Brent (1972–76)	Ian Washam
Phillip Jr. "Charlie" Brent (1976–79)	Brian Lima
Charlie Brent (1985)	Josh Hamilton
Charlie Brent (1985–88)	Ross Duncan McNeill
Charlie Brent (1990–91)	Charles Van Eman
Charlie Brent (1992–)	Christopher Lawford
Dr. Frank Grant (1972)	Don Blakely
Dr. Frank Grant (1972–82)	John Danelle
Margo Flax (1972–76)	Eileen Letchworth
Jason Maxwell (1972)	Tom Rosqui
Jason Maxwell (1972–73)	John Devlin
Tad Gardner Martin (1973–77)	Matthew Anton
Tad Gardner Martin (1978–81)	John E. Dunn
Tad Gardner Martin (1982–86, 1988–90, 1992–)	Michael Knight
Tad Gardner Martin (1990)	Terrell Anthony
Nancy Grant (1973–84)	Lisa Wilkinson
Caroline Murray (1975–79)	Patricia Dixon
Claudette Montgomery (1975)	Paulette Breen
Claudette Montgomery (1977–80)	Susan Plantt-Winston
Myrtle Lum Fargate (1976–)	Eileen Hurlie
Brooke English (1976)	Elissa Leeds
Brooke English (1976–81, 1982–)	Julia Barr
Brooke English (1981)	Harriet Hall
Donna Beck Tyler (1976)	Francesca Poston
Donna Beck Tyler (1976–93)	Candice Earley
Benny Sago (1976–79)	Larry Fleischman
Benny Sago (1980–90)	Vasili Bogazianos
Dr. Christina Karras (1976–79)	Robin Strasser
Dan Kennicott (1976–79)	Daren Kelly
Dr. David Thornton (1976–78)	Paul Gleason
Nigel Fargate (1976)	Sidney Armus
Nigel Fargate (1976–77)	Alexander Scourby
Tom Cudahy (1977–)	Richard Shoberg
Mark Dalton (1977–89, 1994)	Mark LaMura
Ellen Shepherd (1977–89)	Kathleen Noone
Father Tierney (1977–)	Mel Boudrot
Billy Clyde Tuggle (1977–80, 1984–90)	Matthew Cowles
Edna Thornton (1977–80, 1983–86)	Sandy Gabriel
Devon Shepherd (1977–81, 1983–84)	Tricia Pursley
Harlan Tucker (1977–81, 1983)	William Griffis
Dottie Thornton (1977–80)	Dawn Marie Boyle
Dottie Thornton (1983–86)	Tasia Valenza
Carl Blair (1977–79)	John K. Carroll
Carl Blair (1979–84)	Steven James
Ray Gardner (1977–79, 1982, 1993–94)	Gil Rogers
Marestella LaTour (1977–82)	Kathleen Denzina
Wally McFadden (1978–80)	Jack Magee
Wally McFadden (1980)	Nigel Reed
Wally McFadden (1980–81)	Patrick Skelton

Character	Actor
Dr. Russ Anderson (1978–79)	David Pendleton
Dr. Russ Anderson (1979–80)	Charles Brown
Eddie Dorrance (1978)	Ross Petty
Eddie Dorrance (1978–79)	Warren Burton
Palmer Cortlandt (1979–)	James Mitchell
Langley Wallingford (1979–)	Louis Edmonds
Myra Murdoch (1979–92)	Elizabeth Lawrence
Dr. Cliff Warner (1979–87, 1988–89)	Peter Bergman
Nina Cortlandt (1979–84, 1986–89)	Taylor Miller
Nina Cortlandt (1984–85)	Heather Stanford
Nina Cortlandt (1985–86)	Barbara Kearns
Sean Cudahy (1979–81, 1988–91)	Alan Dysert
Betsy Kennicott (1979–82)	Carla Dragoni
Sybil Thorne (1979–81)	Linda Gibboney
Lettie Jean (1979–80)	Judith Roberts
Lettie Jean (1980)	Delphi Harrington
Daisy Cortlandt (1980–87, 1989, 1990, 1995)	Gillian Spencer
Carrie Sanders (1980–83)	Andrea Moar
Brandon Kingsley (1980–82, 1988)	Michael Minor
Sara Kingsley (1980–82)	Tudi Wiggins
Pamela Kingsley (1980–82)	Kathleen Kamhi
Peg English (1980–81)	Patricia Barry
Kurt Sanders (1980–81)	William Ferriter
Leora Sanders (1980–81)	Lizbeth MacKay
Jim Jefferson (1980–81)	Paul Falzone
Jesse Hubbard (1981–88)	Darnell Williams
Enid Nelson (1981–86, 1991)	Natalie Ross
Opal Gardner (1981–83)	Dorothy Lyman
Opal Gardner (1989–)	Jill Larson
Greg Nelson (1981–85)	Laurence Lau
Greg Nelson (1986)	Jack Armstrong
Liza Colby (1981–84, 1995–)	Marcy Walker
Liza Colby (1984)	Alice Haining
Jenny Gardner (1981–84)	Kim Delaney
Candy Brown (1981–85)	Elizabeth Forsyth
Rick Kincaid (1981–82)	Stephen Parr
Melanie Sawyer (1981–82)	Carol McCluer
Olga Svenson (1982–)	Peg Murray
Jasper Sloane (1982–92)	Ronald Drake
Angie Baxter (1982–90)	Debbi Morgan
Angie Baxter (1990–91)	Saundra Quarterman
Pat Baxter (1982–91)	Lee Chamberlain
Les Baxter/"Mr. Big" (1982–83, 1987)	Antonio Fargas
Lars Bogard (1982)	William Blankenship
Lars Bogard (1982–83)	Robert Milli
Lars Bogard (1983)	Jack Betts
Kent Bogard (1982)	Michael Woods
Kent Bogard (1982)	Lee Godart
Amanda Cousins (1982–84)	Amanda Bearse
Sam Brady (1982–84)	Jason Kincaid

Character	Actor
Silver Kane (1982–83)	Deborah Goodrich
Silver Kane, a.k.a. Noelle Keaton (1987)	
Silver Kane (1988)	Rosalind Ingledew
Steve Jacobi (1982–83)	Claire Beckman
Adam Chandler/Stuart Chandler (1983–)	Dack Rambo
Ross Chandler (1983–89)	David Canary
Marian Colby (1983–85, 1989, 1995–)	Robert Gentry
Joey Martin (1983–88)	Jennifer Bassey
Joey Martin (1989–91, 1994)	Michael Scaleri
Alfred Vanderpoole (1983–86, 1989)	Michael Brainard
Mike Roy (1983–84, 1988)	Bill Timoney
Mike Roy (1984–85)	Nicolas Surovy
Joanna Yaeger (1983–84, 1987)	Hugo Napier
Larry Colby (1983–84)	Meg Myles
Tony Barclay (1983–84)	Joseph Warren
Judy Barclay (1983–84)	Brent Barrett
Laura Cudahy (1984–88)	Maia Danziger
Laura Cudahy (1989)	Ann Delahanty
Hillary Wilson (1984–88)	Kyndra Joy Casper
June Hagen (1984–86)	Carmen Thomas
Cynthia Preston (1984–86)	Carole Shelley
Andrew Preston (1984–86)	Jane Elliot
Yvonne Caldwell (1984–85, 1987)	Steve Caffrey
Zack Grayson (1984–85)	Vanessa Bell
Linda Warner (1984–85)	Robert LuPone
Eugene Hubbard (1984–85)	Melissa Leo
Bob Georgia (1984–85)	Tom Wright
Sheila Thomas (1984–85)	Peter Strong
Jeremy Hunter (1985–92)	Cynthia Sullivan
Natalie Hunter (1985–92)	Jean LeClerc
Natalie Hunter (1992–93)	Kate Collins
Dr. Tim Gould (1985–90)	Melody Anderson
Dr. Tim Gould (1993)	Tim Van Pelt
Julie Chandler (1985–86)	Michael Levin
Julie Chandler (1986–89)	Stephanie Winters
Wilma Marlowe (1985–86)	Lauren Holly
Wilma Marlowe (1986–87)	Jo Henderson
Wilma Marlowe (1994–95)	Ruby Holbrook
Robin McCall (1985–87)	Dena Dietrich
Skye Patterson (1986–87)	Deborah Morehart
Skye Patterson (1987–91)	Antoinette Byron
Gilles St. Clair (1985–86)	Robin Christopher
Bryan Sanders (1985–86)	Gilles Kohler
Frankie Hubbard (1986–91)	Curt May
Cecily Davidson (1986–89, 1995–)	Z Wright
Matt Connolly (1986–88)	Rosa Langschwadt Nevin
Matt Connolly (1989)	Michael Tylo
Victor Borelli (1986–87)	Steve Fletcher
Michael LaGuardia (1986–87)	Antony Ponzini
Wade Matthews (1986)	Josh Dubinsky
	Christopher Holder

Character	Actor
Travis Montgomery (1987–91)	Larkin Malloy
Travis Montgomery (1993–94)	Daniel Hugh Kelly
Barbara Montgomery (1987–91)	Susan Pratt
Cindy Parker (1987–89)/Karen Parker (1989–90)	Ellen Wheeler
Nico Kelly (1987–89)	Maurice Benard
Mitch Beck (1987–88)	Brian Fitzpatrick
Elizabeth Carlyle (1987–88)	Lisa Eichhorn
Dixie Cooney (1988)	Kari Gibson
Dixie Cooney (1989–)	Cady McClain
Bianca Montgomery (1988–91)	Jessica Leigh Falborn
Bianca Montgomery (1991)	Caroline Wilde
Bianca Montgomery (1993)	Lacey Chabert
Bianca Montgomery (1993–)	Gina Gallagher
Will Cooney Cortlandt (1988–89)	Lonnie Quinn
Will Cooney Cortlandt (1989–92)	James Patrick Stuart
Stan Ulatowski (1988–91)	Eugene Anthony
Scott Chandler (1988–91)	Philip Amelio
Scott Chandler (1995–)	Shane McDermott
Emily Ann Sago (1988)	Amber Barretto
Emily Ann Sago (1988–91)	Liz Vassey
Steven Andrews (1988–89)	Nicholas Coster
Bitsy Davidson (1988–89)	Ann Flood
Creed Kelly (1988–89)	James Horan
Josh Waleski (1988–89)	Stan Albers
John "Remy" Remington (1988–89)	Eddie Earl Hatch
Jackson Montgomery (1989–)	Walt Willey
Trevor Dillon (1989–)	James Kiberd
Timmy Dillon (1989–91)	Michael Shulman
Timmy Dillon (1991–)	Tommy Michaels
Melanie Cortlandt (1989–91)	Paige Turco
David Rampal (1989–91)	Trent Bushey
Cal Cummings (1989–91)	Count Stovall
Eric Kane (1989–90)	Albert Stratton
Trask Bodine (1989–90)	Matt Servitto
Hayley Vaughan (1990–)	Kelly Ripa
Dr. Anna Tolan (1990–92)	Courtney Sherman
Dr. Anna Tolan (1992–)	Lois Robbins
Janet Green (1990–92)	Kate Collins
Janet Green (1994–)	Robin Mattson
Arlene Vaughan (1990–93)	Phyllis Lyons
Brian Bodine (1990–91)	Gregory Gordon
Brian Bodine (1991–93, 1996)	Matt Borlenghi
Brian Bodine (1993–94)	Brian Green
Ceara Connor (1990–92)	Genie Francis
Katie Kennicott (1990–91)	Greta Lind
Dimitri Marick (1991–)	Michael Nader
Derek Frye (1991–)	William Christian
Livia Frye (1991–)	Tonya Pinkins
Terrence Frye (1991)	Akili Prince
Terrence Frye (1991–95)	Dondre T. Whitfield
Gloria Marsh Chandler (1991–)	Teresa Blake
Mimi Reed (1991–95)	Shari Headley
Dr. Stephen Hamill (1991–93)	Andrew Jackson
An-Li Chen (1991)	Irene Ng
An-Li Chen (1991–93)	Lindsey Price

Craig Lawson (1991–92)	Scott Thompson Baker
Helga (1991–92)	Susan Willis
Edmund Grey (1992–)	John Callahan
Peggy Moody (1992–)	Anne Meara
Taylor Roxbury Cannon	
(1992–95)	Ingrid Rogers
Corvina Lang (1992–95)	Margaret Sophie Stein
Laurel Banning (1992–93)	Kristen Jensen
Laurel Banning (1993–)	Felicity LaFortune
Lucas Barnes (1992–94)	Richard Lawson
Nola Orsini (1992–94)	Barbara Rush
Angelique Marick (1992–94)	Season Hubley
Galen Henderson (1992)	Courtney Eplin
Galen Henderson (1992–93)	Karen Person
Jamal Wilson (1993)	James Wiggins
Jamal Wilson (1993–95)	Amir Jamal Williams
Julia Santos (1993–)	Sydney Penny
Dr. Maria Santos (1993–)	Eva LaRue
Hector Santos (1993–)	Raul Davila
Anton Lang (1993–)	Rudolf Martin
Kendall Hart (1993–95)	Sarah Michelle Gellar
Alec McIntyre (1993–95)	Grant Aleksander
Noah Keefer (1994–)	Keith Hamilton Cobb
Grace Keefer (1994–)	Lynn Thigpen
Del Henry (1994–95)	Winsor Harmon
Mateo Santos (1995–)	Mark Conseulos
Michael Delaney (1995–)	Chris Bruno
Dr. Jonathan Kinder (1995–96)	Michael Sabatino
Pierce Riley (1995–96)	James A. Fitzpatrick

In the early 1960s Agnes Nixon, then head writer for *Guiding Light,* tried to sell a property called *All My Children* to NBC, then CBS, then NBC again through the auspices of sponsor Procter & Gamble. Despite her *Guiding Light* success and sponsor support, it was not until the start of 1970 that her brainchild finally aired. After a slow start, *All My Children* rose to the top of the ratings in 1978 and has remained near there ever since.

Set in the town of Pine Valley (though initially the state was not revealed, by the 1990s it was said to be in the state of Pennsylvania), the initial drama centered around the well-to-do Tyler family headed by Charles, a doctor, his spoiled wife Phoebe, their grown children Ann and Lincoln, and grandson Chuck, whose father, Charles Tyler II, had died years earlier. Their lives were spun off track by the arrival of charmer Nick Davis. Nick had had an affair previously with Lincoln's wife Amy, which resulted in the birth of a boy, Phillip Brent, who was being pawned off as Amy's nephew (Amy's sister Ruth and Ruth's husband Ted Brent were raising the child.) When the truth was disclosed, everyone handled it in different ways. Amy left town in disgrace, Phillip ended his relationship with Tara Martin and went off to fight in the Vietnam War, where he was presumed dead, and Phoebe became a lush when Nick decided to marry her daughter Ann.

While Phil was gone, Tara married Chuck Tyler, even though she was pregnant by Phil. Her father, widower Dr.

Joseph Martin, wed Ruth Brent after Ted died in a car crash following an argument with Nick. Joe and Ruth became the most stable couple in Pine Valley for the next two decades, although she was briefly tempted by David Thornton. But for Tara, the revelation that Phil was alive meant not a reunion for her but a usurpation of their romance by the one and only Erica Kane.

Erica, Erica—to the legions of *All My Children* fans, she has been the quintessential vixen of fiction. Her first victim of seduction was Joe's son and Tara's brother Jeff Martin, whose child she aborted in favor of her pursuit of a modeling career. She asked Jeff for a divorce when she got involved with agent Jason Maxwell, but Maxwell's death, which resulted in a high-profile murder case in which Jeff was charged and exonerated, left her with a bad reputation. That's when she pounced on Phil, with whom she had a miscarriage that resulted in a mental breakdown. By the time she recovered, Erica found that Phil wanted a divorce so he could marry the newly free Tara and reclaim his natural son Phillip Jr., which eventually happened. (When Phil died in a plane crash in 1979, Tara wed Jim Jefferson and left town with Phil Jr.) Erica could forget about getting Jeff, too, as he found bliss with nurse Mary Kennicott until her murder prompted him to leave town for a time. Jeff returned later and had an unsatisfactory marriage to Dr. Christine Karras. But Erica had *plenty* of suitors in her future.

Erica's mother Mona, who had accidentally killed Jason Maxwell, was ashamed of her daughter's antics, but saw little wrong in seeing Charles Tyler, who was weary of Phoebe's actions. Ann Tyler had an even more problematic relationship. Nick asked her for a divorce, fearing that he was sterile and unable to be a good husband for her, which led Ann to marry Joe Martin's lawyer brother Paul while being pregnant with the unknowing Nick's child. Nick then married fellow dancing instructor Kitty Shea and had a child by her even though he still wanted Ann. When Ann was left mute by an accident, Nick claimed that she was planning to divorce Paul, which convinced the latter to do so and wed Erica's modeling pal Margo Flax. But Ann's pregnancy by Paul prior to the divorce, and Margo's desperate attempts to keep Paul, including a secret face-lift (which actress Eileen Letchworth had in real life, letting the show tape postoperative scenes), eventually led to Paul going back to Ann in a pleasant union until she died from a bomb planted to kill Paul.

In the meantime, Kitty Shea left Paul for Lincoln Tyler, and Nick now had no one to use. Kitty and Lincoln's marriage faced much opposition from Phoebe, who thought her son wed beneath his class, and Phoebe hired Myrtle Lum to play Kitty's long-lost mother. But Myrtle ended up having maternal feelings for Kitty, especially when they learned Kitty was dying. After Kitty passed away, Lincoln's grief disappeared when he met Kitty's twin, Kelly Cole, whom he wed after she was cleared of murdering her cruel manager Eddie Dorrance, a deed actually confessed to by Margo Flax's daughter Claudette Montgomery on her deathbed. Linc and Kelly left Pine Valley a very happy couple.

Another contented duo was Dr. Charles Tyler and his new wife, Mona Kane, although their marriage left Phoebe Tyler aghast and alcoholic. So did Chuck's marriage to teenage hooker Donna Beck and the romances of Phoebe's niece Brooke English with both Mary Kennicott's brother Dan and criminal-type Benny Sago. Brooke found happiness with neither, so Benny wed ditzy Edna Thornton, whose ex-husband David tried to kill her after she returned to town with their daughter Dottie. The Benny-Edna coupling failed because Benny carried a torch for Donna's sister ex-whore Estelle La Tour and wed her after Estelle divorced her trashy pimp, Billy Clyde Tuggle. Estelle later died and Benny raised their adopted daughter Emily Ann.

But the most elaborate romantic entanglements on the show in the late 1970s involved—who else?—Erica Kane. After an engagement to Nick Davis, who got cold feet and left town for a while, she wed ex-football player Tom Cudahy and saw her modeling career hit high gear. One fan was cosmetics executive Brandon Kingsley, who made her his new love after Tom, disgusted by her favoring work over family life, left her. Brandon's wife Sara and daughter Pamela were not thrilled by this development, but had nothing to worry about, as ever-ambitious Erica found a new lover in Kent Bogard, whose father Lars owned a larger rival firm. However, Erica did not walk down the aisle with Kent.

In this early 1970 shot from All My Children, *Amy Tyler (at left, played by Rosemary Prinz) comforts her "nephew" Phil Brent (Richard Hatch), who was really her son, while Phil's love Tara Martin (Karen Gorney) watches.*

Erica's ex-husband Tom had a devious brother named Sean who was the lover of Devon Shepherd, the daughter of nervous divorcee Ellen Shepherd. Devon survived the affair and relocated to St. Louis with her rather colorless husband, Wally McFadden. But Ellen had a tougher relationship with Mark Dalton, a man 10 years younger than she who was an ex-fling of Erica's (she left him when she discovered he was her half-brother on her dad's side). Ellen's insecurities led him to sleep with Brooke English, who ended up marrying Tom Cudahy.

The 1970s ended on several happy notes. Ruth and Joe Martin become parents of Joey Martin, while reassuring a boy they adopted named Tad that he would be just as loved as the new addition to the family. Tad's seedy natural father Ray Gardner earlier had been a nasty thorn in the Martinses' side, having raped Ruth and demanded sole custody of Tad, but he was arrested and, a few years later, died in a bomb blast. And even Phoebe found a new husband when con man Langley Wallingford found to his surprise he loved the cantankerous matriarch.

Another new addition in 1979 was the arrival of aristocratic Palmer Cortlandt, his somewhat creepy housekeeper Myra Murdoch, and his overprotected daughter Nina, who, to Palmer's chagrin, caught the fancy of Dr. Cliff Warner. Palmer broke up Nina's marriage by having Cliff's past flame, nurse Sybil Thorne, confront him about fathering her son Bobby, but this was temporary, because Sybil was murdered by Sean Cudahy. During the murder trial, Nina was astonished to learn that her mother, Daisy Cortlandt, whom she believed

The upper crust of All My Children—*from left to right, Palmer Cortlandt (played by James Mitchell), Nina Cortlandt (Taylor Miller), Phoebe Tyler (Ruth Warrick), and Dr. Cliff Warner (Peter Bergman)—gathered in 1982 to play croquet at Nina and Cliff's second wedding anniversary.*

to be dead, was in fact alive and living in Pine Valley. To complete everyone's shock, Myra acknowledged that Daisy was her daughter.

Around the same time, Palmer successfully wooed Donna Tyler from her husband Chuck, leaving the latter to wed Carrie Sanders, whose dad Kurt was being treated for beating his wife Leora. But Donna and Chuck had a one-night fling, and when Chuck learned of his being the birth father of the child, called Palmer John Cortlandt, he and Donna reunited briefly while the senior Palmer suffered amnesia, then tried to win back Daisy's love.

The early 1980s saw an influx of new young characters. One was Jesse Hubbard, who was the nephew of longtime local couple Dr. Frank Grant and his wife Nancy. (The couple playing Frank and Nancy, John Danelle and Lisa Wilkinson, were married in real life.) His pal was Jenny Gardner, who was the daughter of blowsy, outrageously behaving Opal Gardner and the natural sister of Tad Martin. Jenny fell in love with clean-cut Greg Nelson, son of Enid Nelson, while Jesse took up with Angie Baxter. Along with scheming Liza Colby, who tried to thwart Jenny and Greg, and Tony Barclay, a male model who became obsessed with Jenny, these youngsters' star-crossed romances made up the show's core stories for a few years, with Jenny and Jesse eventually dying in their lovers' arms.

In 1982 other Pine Valley residents seemed to suffer major calamities. The marriages of Ellen Shepherd to Mark Dalton and Nina to Cliff were on shaky ground, the former due to Mark's affair with Pamela Kingsley and the latter to Nina's obsession with Steve Jacobi. Ellen and Mark divorced following her miscarriage and his subsequent drug addiction. Mark wed Brooke English, then left her as she began seeing

bon vivant Gilles St. Clair. Nina and Cliff split for a time, with the latter dating Devon Shepherd briefly, but the real kicker came when a deranged Nina tried to shoot Donna Beck as the latter wed Benny Sago. Nina became institutionalized, leading to another divorce and later a second remarriage for her and Cliff.

As for old good-time girl Erica, she had to deal with the arrival of Silver Kane, a somewhat homely girl who was Erica's half-sister and eventual nemesis as she tried to steal Erica's current boy toy Kent Bogard. Erica fought Silver, then went undercover as a nun (!) when charged with Kent's murder before Silver was found to be an impostor and sent back to California. She then left modeling, started her own cosmetics business, and collaborated in more ways than one with writer Mike Roy on her autobiography, *Raising Kane.* One wonders if and how they got everything in one installment!

Erica did not settle down with Mike Roy but did give matrimony another shot with movie producer Adam Chandler, who maneuvered Mike out of her life. Several developments emerged after Erica lived with Adam on his estate, among them the existence of Adam's retarded twin brother Stuart, Ellen wedding Adam's nephew Ross Chandler, and the emergence of the family feud with Palmer Cortlandt, who was the natural father of Ross. Palmer, finding himself in financial straits, was desperate enough to work for Adam in 1984, then married Cynthia Preston the next year in a disastrous union which made him realize Daisy was the only woman for him.

Also in the early 1980s, Tad Martin became a major character, albeit a flawed one. Tad "the Cad" slept with both Liza Colby and her amorous mother Marian. An enraged Liza took up with Cliff while her mother dated Zack Grayson, a quack who became the enemy of most of the town due to his blackmailing ways and ended up slain by Marian Colby in self-defense in 1985. As for Tad, he got his just deserts by marrying Dottie Thornton, only to learn that Dottie was not carrying his child. His new true love, Langley Wallingford's daughter Hillary Wilson, wed Bob Georgia until learning he was not terminally ill, as she had been led to believe. She and Tad finally wed in 1986. Unfortunately, that same year Tad condoned shyster Wade Matthews's elaborate plan to rob and even kill Hillary's stepmother Phoebe (he was stopped as he tried to catch an airplane out of town dressed in drag), and Hillary, horrified to learn of Tad's complicity, divorced him. He left town to "find himself," but later returned.

By this time Erica's hyperactive love life had gone into overdrive. When Adam faked his death to see how faithful Erica would remain to him, she got re-engaged to Mike Roy and dismissed Adam after he revealed his cheap tactic. But Mike was killed, and when Erica strewed his ashes in Tibet, a monk named Jeremy Hunter whom Mike had saved years earlier followed her back to Pine Valley to woo her. It worked, but Jeremy's ex-girlfriend Natalie arrived in town wanting him back and made him think he impregnated her. That was disproved, but when Jeremy, imprisoned wrongly for a murder, refused to escape from jail with Erica's help, she lost interest in him and went after self-made millionaire Travis Montgomery, who wed Erica when he learned she was pregnant with his child. But Erica nearly died giving birth to Bianca in 1988, and it was not until she went through a retrospective of her ex-lovers on her sickbed, including Jeff Martin, Nick Davis, Brandon Kingsley, Mike Roy, Jeremy Hunter, Adam Chandler, and Tom Cudahy, that she was able to return to consciousness and become a mother for her first time.

Jeremy found that Natalie did not want him on the rebound from Erica, finding more interest in her new job as nurse for Palmer while spying on him for Adam. She began an affair with Ross Chandler which she felt would not lead to marriage, so when Palmer proposed to her, she accepted. Then when Ross's wife Ellen learned of the trysts and left Ross, he went wild and raped Natalie. He later confessed to the crime and went into treatment. Ross's adopted daughter Julie heard Natalie's screams and skedaddled to New York City, leaving behind boyfriend Charlie Brent. In Gotham Julie met criminal Creed Kelly and his nephew Nico Kelly, becoming entranced with the latter, while Charlie took up with Phoebe's goddaughter Cecily Davidson. Julie and Nico married, Charlie and Cecily did not.

Julie's natural parents were Elizabeth Carlyle and Mark Dalton. The latter had a hellish year in 1987 when his cocaine abuse required friends and family to confront him until he went into treatment. Then Mark worried he contracted AIDS from the late Fred Parker, a man with whom he shared needles. Mark turned out HIV-negative, but Fred's widow Cindy contracted the disease and tried to make plans for her son Scott while wedding mentally challenged Stuart Chandler. Cindy did die, but Mark found himself remarrying Ellen Shepherd and reconnecting with his daughter Julie.

Some in Pine Valley had prejudices against Cindy for having AIDS, chief among them Adam Chandler's daughter Skye, wed to Tom Cudahy, who nearly killed Cindy in a fire. A repentant Skye then saved Cindy from the destruction but went into a coma, and Tom fell in love with Travis Montgomery's ex-wife Barbara. Skye came out of the coma and tried to kill Barbara before being caught and shipped off to the asylum. As Tom married Barbara, his brother Sean came out of jail and dated Cecily, over her mother Bitsy's objections. They planned to marry, but when Cecily overheard Sean and Bitsy talk suggestively, she wed instead Nico Kelly, who was a free man when his wedding to Julie was found to be invalid. After a rough initial period, Nico and Cecily's romance blossomed, and they eventually left Pine Valley as a happy couple.

Not doing as well as a duo were Erica and Travis. Floundering in debts and a takeover attempt from his ambitious brother Jack and Adam Chandler, Travis faked kidnapping Bianca. When the plot came to light, Erica, very much disturbed, took Bianca to Sea City, where Erica disguised herself as a diner waitress. When Travis saved Erica's life there, she was ready to forgive him, but he became an amnesiac and romanced his ex-wife Barbara before she wed Tom. The fact that Barbara was pregnant with Travis's baby was known and accepted by Tom.

Meanwhile, Erica's real half-sister Silver Kane came to Pine Valley and entranced Jeremy. But Natalie's attraction to Jeremy, and vice versa, soon emerged, and an enraged Silver died after a struggle with Natalie. Natalie's ex-husband Palmer tried to blackmail her into marriage by covering up the incident, but Natalie was exonerated anyway and wed Jeremy in 1988. Their bliss was short-lived, though; another ex-love of Jeremy's, Marissa Rampal, arrived with their teenage son David, ready to stake a claim on him.

Their difficulties were nothing next to what Palmer faced in 1989. His ex-wife Daisy firmly rebuffed his last marriage proposal and left for France. His daughter Nina, who in 1987 wed Matt Connelly after the two looked unsuccessfully for her missing husband Cliff in South America, decided to get together with Cliff for a third remarriage after he learned her son Michael was his and not Matt's, and they left town as well. Then Palmer unwittingly hired his niece Dixie Cooney as his maid, and she left his employ to work as nanny for his rival Adam Chandler. Dixie fell in love with Adam and prompted a bitter divorce between him and Brooke.

However, Dixie and Adam did not wed even though she gave birth to his child. She fell instead for the returning Tad Martin, who saw her on the rebound after being dropped by Barbara Montgomery during her separation from Tom Cudahy. Yet another niece of Palmer's, Melanie Cortlandt, arrived and fell for David Rampal until he was emotionally destroyed by his mother's death following a spat with Natalie. Melanie then dated Trask Bodine and later Charlie Brent, the son of Phillip Brent, while David dated Ceara Connor, a niece of Myrtle Fargate's who was a victim of incest. However, David's dad Jeremy was the one who ended up marrying Ceara, while David and Melanie wed instead.

By the start of 1990, Palmer finally got the upper hand. He surprised Adam by announcing he owned the latter's business, causing Adam to have a stroke. Then Palmer found a successful love life by wedding Opal Gardner and managed to break up Dixie's marriage to Tad, whom he hated. Tad slept with Brooke, resulting in a son named Jamie, while Dixie took up with scummy old Billy Clyde Tuggle, who returned to town to start a relationship with Emily Ann, his daughter by Donna Beck. Emily Ann's discovery that she was Billy's daughter led to her marriage with Joey Martin going on the rocks. But Billy did far worse damage by trying to rape Dixie. Tad eventually fought Billy to the latter's death on a railroad bridge, but Tad's fall left him with amnesia and he left town.

Meanwhile, Erica was as active as ever. She planned to wed Jackson Montgomery, but Bianca wanted her mom to stay with her father, Jackson's brother Travis, which Erica did until news about Travis's affair with ex-wife Barbara reached Erica and she began seeing Jackson again. Travis found out and sued for custody of Bianca in his divorce of Erica, which he got. Feeling that Jackson had let her down, Erica went after Charlie Brent, who was the son and grandson of two of her former boyfriends! Charlie's grandfather Nick Davis came to the wedding and convinced Erica she did not love his descendent. Instead, Erica made an even worse decision by wedding ex-husband Adam Chandler.

Prior to this reunion, Adam was in a love triangle with Natalie and new police detective Trevor Dillon. He and Natalie wed after she had an argument with Trevor, a decision they both regretted. After their divorce, Adam wanted to get back with ex-wife Brooke, but she now dated Jackson. Even worse, the latter two nearly died in a car wreck with Arlene Vaughan and her daughter Hayley. Arlene, who was drunk when behind the wheel, was Adam's old flame, and Hayley was the product of their affair. All parties survived, and Hayley learned to love her newfound father while dating Trask Bodine's brother Brian.

As for Natalie, she and Trevor faced more trouble when her estranged sister Janet "From Another Planet" Green came to town and made efforts to seduce Trevor. When that failed, she imprisoned Natalie at the bottom of a well and imitated her in an effort to fool Trevor up to their wedding day. A rich man named Dimitri Marick saved Natalie, and Janet was arrested. But that did not mean Trevor and Natalie were ready to reunite, for Janet revealed in her jail cell she was pregnant with Trevor's child, while Natalie felt compassion for Dimitri for saving her life. Natalie and Dimitri got engaged, but unfortunately, Dimitri's mother-in-law and housekeeper Helga found his long-missing wife Angelique and brought her home.

Angelique was not the only unexpected arrival in Pine Valley in 1992. Tad Martin returned, although he had been convinced by Napa Valley vineyard owner Nola Orsini that he was her missing son. When he regained his memory, he found that Dixie had been married twice in his absence. The first was to con artist Craig Lawson, whose plans went awry when his ex-girlfriend Gloria Marsh blackmailed him. (He did, however, get Dixie's brother Will to engage in crimes against him, which led Palmer to disown his nephew). The second was to Brian Bodine, who offered to help raise her son Adam Jr. For his son Jamie's sake, Tad wed Brooke, but a miscarriage led to their divorce. Tad and Dixie remarried.

By this time Erica had yet another man in her life— Dimitri Marick! As he attempted to take over her business, love flowered between the two, but he still felt he had an obligation to Angelique. Complicating matters was the arrival of famed reporter Edmund Grey, who learned that he was Dimitri's brother. Helga tried to put a stop to Grey's claims, even to the point of imprisoning Erica in a crypt before Helga herself died. Edmund helped his brother gain the confidence to wed Erica, while having his love life undergo stress by wedding Dr. Maria Santos in 1994 while still carrying a torch for Brooke English. Adding to the complications, Maria found herself pregnant by ex-boyfriend Del Henry, who also turned out to be Dixie Martin's brother!

But while Erica's new marriage should have put her at ease, her life was anything but smooth. A young girl named Kendall Hart showed up in Pine Valley and stunned everyone by announcing she was Erica's daughter, whom Erica put up for adoption at age 14 after a rape. Erica felt a whirlwind of emotions as Kendall tried to find her birth father as well, culminating in Erica's temporary insanity, a rape flashback, during which she attacked Dimitri, in part because Kendall had said she was similarly assaulted by Dimitri's ward Anton Lang, who was in fact Dimitri's son. Then Kendall became vicious toward Erica, writing an exposé on her and even perjuring herself during Erica's trial for stabbing Dimitri, to suggest that her mother meant to kill him. Worst of all, Erica's beloved mother Mona died in 1994 (actress Frances Heflin had died in real life). The death hit Erica so hard that she jumped onto her mother's casket. Kendall, who had been jailed for perjury, later got out of jail and left town.

Other story lines in the early 1990s revolved around despicable Will Cortlandt, who raped Gloria Marsh and wed Hayley after she fought with Brian and he wed Chinese immigrant An Li to keep the latter from being deported. When Will was found dead in 1992, Brian went to court and was defended by Livia Frye, whose teenage son Terrence had been through an earlier trial of two Caucasians who beat him brutally in a racial attack. The real murderer turned out to be Janet Green, who had left the hospital before delivering her baby, planning to kill Will in the belief it would somehow win Trevor over. She went back to jail, where she gave birth to Amanda, whom her sister Natalie claimed as a ward as she and Trevor wed. Sadly, Natalie died in 1993 from a car accident, spurring her son Timmy into drug addiction.

The other passenger in Natalie's car during the crash was Adam Chandler. He was going with Natalie to confront Laurel Banning, a woman in love with Jackson Montgomery who had been embezzling from the community center where Natalie worked. Paralyzed from the waist down after the wreck, Adam brought in Alec McIntyre as his business operator, but Alec wanted control of all of Chandler Enterprises, including Adam's wife Gloria. Alec fathered a boy who grew up to be Tom and Livia Cudahy's foster son Jamal, who sued to stay with the Cudahys rather than be with Alec. But Alec did seem to be winning over Gloria, who planned to divorce Adam until she learned she was pregnant with his child.

In 1994 Tad Martin, injured in a tornado that destroyed the Martin home, had a near-death out-of-body experience, seeing his dead sister Jenny, deceased pal Jesse, and his evil father Ray Gardner. He emerged stronger than ever in his business life as a producer of Erica's new talk show on WRCW, only to find complications in 1995 when ex-flame Liza Colby returned as his superior at work and temptress of his soul. Also returning to Pine Valley was Brian Bodine, in an effort to drive a wedge between his old love Hayley and her new boyfriend and eventual husband Mateo Santos, and Janet Green, in a face remade by plastic surgery. Alas, the physical change did not alter her devious mind-set.

The front-burner story in 1995 was the love affair of Julia and her tall, dreadlocked boyfriend Noah Keefer, whom she met in a shelter following the tornado. Raped there by a junkie, she had an abortion and passed an HIV-test scare, while Noah stood by her. They wed in 1996. Another, more controversial story line that year was the revelation by teacher

Michael Delaney to his class that he was gay, prompting a possible expulsion of him and much dissension within his family, especially from his homophobic brother-in-law Trevor.

For true *All My Children* addicts, however, the big event of 1995–96 was probably what happened to Erica. Her new role as a local talk show hostess went downhill when her drug dependence, exacerbated by the careless medical treatment of Dr. Jonathan Kinder, made her into an addict who, supported by Dimitri and Bianca, needed treatment at the Betty Ford Center. Susan Lucci was splendid in her pre- and posttreatment scenes, and pundits predicted she finally would win a long-desired Emmy for her work. But she did not, incredibly for a record 16th nomination with no victories. Who says long-running soap operas occur only on television?

ALL-NEW BEAT THE CLOCK, THE—See *Beat the Clock*

ALL-NEW BOZO THE CLOWN, THE—See *Bozo the Clown.*

ALL-NEW DENNIS THE MENACE, THE—See *Dennis the Menace.*

ALL-NEW EWOKS, THE—See *Ewoks, The.*

ALL-NEW PINK PANTHER SHOW, THE—See *Pink Panther Show, The.*

ALL-NEW POPEYE HOUR, THE
Cartoon; Color
September 9, 1978–September 10, 1983

CBS Sat. 8–9 a.m. (9/9/78–9/1/79)
CBS Sat. 10:30–11:30 a.m. (9/8/79–3/7/81)
CBS Sat. 11 a.m.–Noon (3/14/81–6/13/81)
CBS Sat. 10–11 a.m. (6/20/81–9/5/81)
CBS Sat. 10:30–11 a.m. (9/12/81–11/28/81)
CBS Sat. 8–8:30 a.m. (12/5/81–9/11/82)
CBS Sat. Noon–12:30 p.m (9/18/82–11/27/82)
CBS Sat. 8–8:30 a.m. (2/5/83–9/10/83)

Voices:

Sgt. Blast (1981–82)	*Joanne Worley*
Col. Crumb (1981–82)	*Hal Smith*
Bluto	*Allan Melvin*
Dinky	*Frank Welker*
Uncle Dudley	*Frank Nelson*
Monica	*Julie Bennett*
Olive Oyl/The Evil Sea Hag	*Marilyn Schreffler*
Popeye	*Jack Mercer*
Sandy	*Jackie Joseph*
Wimpy	*Daws Butler*

One of the most enduring comic creations of the 20th century was Popeye the Sailor Man. The pipe-smoking Navy man who gulped spinach to activate massive strength in his oversized forearms and lower legs popped up first in 1928 in a newspaper comic strip drawn by E. C. Segar called *The Thimble Theater.* Olive Oyl, Popeye's skinny, jittery girlfriend, was already a regular in the strip, along with her brother Castor Oyl, who spotted Popeye on a dock. The character's popularity grew, and soon his sayings like "I yam what I yam!" and "Well, blow me down!" became a hit with the younger set, leading in short time to having the character adapted for the movies, first in a 1931 Betty Boop short. The character also starred in a radio series heard briefly on NBC in 1935–36 and CBS in 1936.

In 1958 Paramount Pictures released 234 *Popeye* theatrical cartoon shorts to local television stations, where they proved to be very successful. Two years later, King Features Syndicate, which had syndicated the Popeye comic strips for newspapers, went into its first TV production with a new version, supposedly because it was not getting residuals from the video screenings of the movie cartoons. As with the Paramount shorts, Mercer voiced Popeye and Mae Questel was Olive Oyl. Bluto, the movie villain, was replaced by the similar looking and sounding Brutus, voiced by Jackson Beck. But after 1962, no Popeye cartoons were produced until this series.

The 1978 Popeye show had him with the old crew, including Sweetpea the infant and Wimpy the rotund burger enthusiast, in various adventures, plus the stories of "Dinky Dog," a large canine in the care of Uncle Dudley and his nieces Sandy and Monica. In 1979 "Popeye's Sports Parade" became a regular element, as did "Prehistoric Popeye" with the crew in Neanderthal motif in 1980. In 1981, the show went down to a half hour and was retitled *The Popeye and Olive Comedy Show* with the addition of a segment called "Private Olive Oyl" with Sgt. Blast and Col. Crumb.

As in previous versions, Popeye and/or Olive were threatened constantly by Bluto and his cruel plots, which Popeye foiled when he became strong. But here the violence quotient was markedly deemphasized—to the point where Popeye could not even roll up his sleeves to show off his massive biceps, much less make a threatening gesture. And to make sure everyone was educated and not incited by the show's content, the short "Popeye's Safety Tips" also received airing, using Popeye's miniature look-alike nephews Peepeye, Pupeye, and Pipeye.

The latter concept got a reworking in the next TV incarnation of the sailor man in 1987. For more details, see *Popeye and Son.*

ALL-NEW POUND PUPPIES, THE—See *Pound Puppies, The.*

ALL-NEW SUPERFRIENDS, THE—See *SuperFriends, The.*

ALL-STAR BAFFLE—See *Baffle*

ALL-STAR BEAT THE CLOCK—See *Beat the Clock.*

•ALL STAR BLITZ

Game; Color
April 8, 1985–December 20, 1985

ABC Mon.–Fri. 11–11:30 a.m. (4/8/85–6/14/85)
ABC Mon.–Fri. 11:30 a.m.–Noon (6/17/85–12/20/85)

Host: *Peter Marshall*

With Peter Marshall as host to four wisecracking celebrities, *All Star Blitz* came off as something like *Hollywood Squares Jr.* The format had the celebrities underneath a grid of 12 vertices connected to make two rows of three video boxes which contained hidden parts of a phrase or title. Two competing contestants alternated in stopping the vertices from flashing, and the point which the contestant landed on indicated which adjacent celebrities could be called on to win it and reveal any box which had its lines connected to other captured vertices. As with *Squares,* the contestants had to agree whether the celebrity was giving a correct answer or bluffing in order to win a vertex.

The first player to solve the puzzle won a game, and the first to win two games got to play the "Blitz Bonanza," where he or she spun a wheel four times to reveal some of the six boxes with another mystery phrase. Making it difficult for the contestant was that each time a box was revealed, it still remained in contention on the wheel, meaning that it was possible for a player to spin four times and get only one box revealed. The celebrities helped out by giving their guesses to the contestant, which were worth $250 for each correct one, but in order to win the top prize of $10,000, the contestant alone had to guess the puzzle. There were no regular celebrities on the panel.

ALL STAR GOLF

Sports; B&W
October 12, 1957–March 23, 1963

ABC Sat. 4–5 p.m. (10/12/57–4/12/58)
ABC Sat. 5–6 p.m. (10/11/58–4/29/61; summers off)
NBC Sat. 5–6 p.m. (10/14/61–3/23/63; summers off)

Host: *Jim Britt (1957–58), Dick Danehe (1958–59), Jimmy Demaret (1959–61)*

All Star Golf employed some of the sport's top names, including Sam Snead, Gene Littler, Jimmy Demaret, and Arnold Palmer, in annual two-man contests of 26 rounds of golf on 10 courses. The host followed the action around one 18-hole course each week. Winners got a guaranteed $3,000, $2,000 of which was for winning that day's game and $1,000 to compete in a subsequent match.

The victor for 1957–58 was Billy Casper, who took $12,000 for six victories plus a $500 bonus for scoring an eagle on one hole. (Anyone who made a hole-in-one netted a whopping $10,000.) The top winner in 1958–59 was Snead, who won 13 games for a total of $27,000 before falling to Gary Player in the 1959 fall opener.

ABC reran the series Mondays at 9:30 p.m. from April 6–September 28, 1959 under the title *Top Pro Golf,* the same one used when the show's repeats went into syndication.

All Star Golf continued on ABC through 1961, then switched to NBC for its last two years.

•ALL STAR SECRETS

Game; Color
January 8, 1979–August 10, 1979

NBC Mon.–Fri. 10:30–11 a.m. (1/8/79–8/10/79)

Host: *Bob Eubanks*

All Star Secrets was the first of a short-lived venture in game show production by host Bob Eubanks and his partner Michael Hill (their other major creation was the 1979 syndicated nighttime series *The Guinness Game*). Three contestants competed in guessing which one out of five guest celebrities had an avocation, opinion, or other matter which until then had been unpublicized. To help contestants, Eubanks called on one celebrity who did not have the secret to offer his or her opinion on which one of the remaining four it might be. The contestants revealed their picks, and money was split none, one, two or three ways depending on their choice. Each contestant took a turn in electronically stopping a money machine to determine the amount at large, with each potential amount divisible by two and three to allow for possible ties. Money in the first round went from $120 to $300, in the second from $360 to $600, and in the final round, where contestants had to guess with no help from a celebrity, the amount was a flat $1,500.

While basically an enjoyable game, *All Star Secrets* was limited by the fact that hardly anyone could return on the panel, since a week's worth of interrogations used up most of their interesting facts. Up for the first week of revelations was the unlikely quintet of Pat Boone, Phyllis Diller, Mary Ann Mobley, Greg Morris, and McLean Stevenson.

ALMOST ANYTHING GOES—See *Junior Almost Anything Goes.*

ALUMNI FUN

Game; B&W
January 20, 1963–May 1, 1966

ABC Sun. 4:30–5 p.m. (1/20/63–4/28/63)
CBS Sun. 5–5:30 p.m. (1/12/64–4/4/64)
CBS Sun. 4–4:30 p.m. (1/10/65–3/28/65)
CBS Sun. 4–4:30 p.m. (1/23/66–5/1/66)

Hosts: *John K. M. McCaffery (1963), Clifton Fadiman (1964), Peter Lind Hayes (1965–66)*

Some of the most unlikely trios of graduates from major colleges appeared head-to-head on this show to answer questions and try to win as much as possible for their alma maters. Where else could one find such surprising match-ups as baseball pitcher Sandy Koufax, actor Lee Bowman, and Admiral Edward Kenney (they represented the University of Cincinnati)? Other celebrities included Jackie Robinson and Lloyd Bridges for UCLA, Rip Torn for the University of Texas, and David Susskind for the University of Wisconsin.

Begun on ABC in 1963, *Alumni Fun* switched to CBS the following year. Ironically, the show aired on CBS immediately before *G.E. College Bowl* on NBC. *G.E. College Bowl*, the obvious inspiration for *Alumni Fun* right down to the pace and bonus questions, had been on CBS the previous year before switching networks.

•ALVIN SHOW, THE

Cartoon; Color
September 29, 1962–September 7, 1991

CBS Sat. 10–10:30 a.m. (9/29/62–9/21/63)
CBS Sat. 9–9:30 a.m. (9/28/63–9/18/65)
NBC Sat. 8–8:30 a.m. (3/17/79–9/1/79)
NBC Sat. 10:30–11 a.m. (9/17/83–9/7/85)
NBC Sat. 11–11:30 a.m. (9/14/85–10/18/86)
NBC Sat. 10:30–11 a.m. (10/25/86–9/3/88)
NBC Sat. 11–11:30 a.m. (9/10/88–10/15/88)
NBC Sat. 10–10:30 a.m. (10/22/88–9/2/89)
NBC Sat. 11–11:30 a.m. (9/9/89–9/1/90)
NBC Sat. 10:30–11 a.m. (9/8/90–9/7/91)

Voices:
Alvin/Simon/Theodore/David
 Seville (1962–65)   Ross Bagdasarian
Alvin/Simon/Theodore/David
 Seville (1983–91)   Ross Bagdasarian Jr.
Brittany/Eleanor/Jeanette
 (1983–90)   Janice Karman
Clyde Crashcup (1962–65)   Sheperd Menken

Various (1983–91): *Frank Welker, Dody Goodman, Thom Watkins*

Creators/Executive Producers: *Ross Bagdasarian Jr., Janice Karman*

Here's a show featuring one musical act whose broadcasting career arguably was more successful than its record sales—and its members never really existed. Alvin, Simon, and Theodore were supposedly singing chipmunks when introduced in the Grammy-winning 1958 Yuletide million seller "The Christmas Song" ("Christmas, Christmas time is here . . ."), but as any pop culture fan can tell you, they were really just the voice of singer Ross Bagdasarian electronically sped up and multitracked. Bagdasarian, who also recorded as novelty singer David Seville, managed to extend the concept longer than some expected on albums into the 1960s, prompting a cartoon titled *The Alvin Show* to run on CBS Wednesdays at 7:30–8 p.m. from October 4, 1961–September 5, 1962. While it fared poorly against *Wagon Train* on NBC then, it did better in repeats for three years on CBS Saturdays.

On the cartoon all the Chipmunks wore full-body sweaters and lived with David Seville, their manager. Alvin wore a cap and a big "A" on his chest, Simon sported glasses, and Theodore was the small, chubby one. Between musical numbers, including "The Christmas Song," of course, the animal trio and Seville engaged in short comic misadventures, typically sparked by Alvin's impulsive behavior. A separate

segment featured somewhat egotistical scientist Clyde Crashcup lecturing viewers on his latest creations, which turned out not to be as great as he thought they were.

After leaving CBS for syndicated reruns in 1965, the Chipmunks' recording career went into low gear as well. Bagdasarian died in 1972. Then in 1979, a desperate NBC reran the original show for a few months, and in 1980 a new album titled *Chipmunk Punk* featuring high-pitched versions of "Call Me" and other songs emerged. Recorded by Ross Bagsdasarian's son, the album became a surprise hit, leading to a few follow-ups and a new series called *Alvin and the Chipmunks*. The 1980s rendition was rather reminiscent of the early show, although Dave looked somewhat younger than his previous counterpart and the Chipmunks had frillier hairstyles. While they lacked Clyde Crashcup, Alvin, Simon, and Theodore now did have big-name guest visitors such as Dolly Parton, as well as wilder comedy premises. The biggest change came in September 1988, when the show became titled simply *The Chipmunks* and the three originals hung around with their female counterparts Brittany, Eleanor, and Jeannette, who made up the singing trio the Chipettes, and their dog Lily.

In its final season, the show was retitled *The Chipmunks Go to the Movies* as the trio spoofed such film favorites as *Jaws* and *Star Wars*. The best of these for longtime fans had to be "Back to Alvin's Future," where their old buddy Clyde Crashcup drove a time-machine car to tell the present-day Chipmunks that they must go back in time because Alvin in 1957 is now thinking about quitting his dreams of a musical career. Arriving there prompted ribbing about their old house's artwork in comparison to the vivid colors of the later show ("Everything looks so flat," sighed Simon). Things really got chaotic as the two groups switched time zones, but by the end of the show all was corrected.

Beside providing some voices, Thom Watkins was a coordinating producer and one of the recording supervisors of the 1980s show. Janice Karman also provided various voices and served multiple functions, including that of co-creator, co–executive producer, co–executive story editor and sole color consultant. The person with whom she shared these duties was Ross Bagdasarian Jr., who just happened to be her husband.

In all, Alvin and company aired on two networks for 13 seasons, including the initial nighttime run, and "The Christmas Song" continued to get Yuletide airplay during and after the runs—not too shabby accomplishments for a novelty act.

AMANDA

Musical Variety; B&W
January 12, 1949–November 4, 1949

DuMont Mon.–Fri. Noon–12:15 p.m., later 10:45–11 a.m.
 (1/12/49–11/4/49)

Hostess: *Amanda Randolph*

Actress Amanda Randolph was the first black woman to host a network daytime series. Here she sang spiritual and boogie-woogie tunes. "The gal is by far the most entertaining part of the early stretch," noted a *Billboard* reviewer when her show debuted as part of WABD's pioneer daytime lineup in New York City November 1, 1948, from 9:40–9:55 a.m.

AMATEUR'S GUIDE TO LOVE, THE
Game; Color
March 27, 1972–June 23, 1972

CBS Mon.–Fri. 4–4:30 p.m. (3/27/72–6/23/72)

Host: *Gene Rayburn*

This short-lived entry had a celebrity trio ("The Guidebook Experts") give their opinions on the wisest way to handle a *Candid Camera*–type film segment involving other celebrities and unwitting participants in an situation with amorous implications. Contestants seen in the segments won prizes if the panel, which did not see the end of each film, correctly predicted how they had reacted. The show first aired in a somewhat different format as a CBS nighttime special on August 8, 1971, titled *An Amateur's Guide to Love,* and hosted by Joe Flynn.

AMAZIN! ADVENTURES—An umbrella title for a syndicated package of TV series, including *A.J.'s Time Travelers* (q.v.).

•AMAZING CHAN AND THE CHAN CLAN, THE
Cartoon; Color
September 9, 1972–September 1, 1974

CBS Sat. 9–9:30 a.m. (9/9/72–9/1/73)
CBS Sun. 9:30–10 a.m. (9/9/73–9/1/74)

Voices:

Alan Chan	*Brian Tochi*
Anne Chan (1972)	*Leslie Kumamota*
Anne Chan (1972–74)	*Jodie Foster*
Charlie Chan	*Keye Luke*
Flip Chan (1972)	*Jay Jay Jue*
Flip Chan (1972–74)	*Gene Andrusco*
Henry Chan	*Bob Ito*
Mimi Chan (1972)	*Leslie Juwai*
Nancy Chan (1972)	*Debbie Jue*
Nancy Chan (1972–74)	*Beverly Kushida*
Scooter Chan (1972)	*Robin Toma*
Scooter Chan (1972–74)	*Michael Morgan*
Stanley Chan (1972)	*Steven Wong*
Stanley Chan (1972–74)	*Lennie Weinrib*
Suzie Chan (1972)	*Virginia Ann Lee*
Suzie Chan/Mimi Chan	
(both 1972–74)	*Cherylene Lee*
Tom Chan (1972)	*Michael Takamoto*
Tom Chan (1972–74)	*John Gunn*
Chu-Chu	*Don Messick*

Producers/Directors: *William Hanna and Joseph Barbera*

Keye Luke, who portrayed the Number One son in Charlie Chan movies of the 1940s, got the opportunity to at least voice Chan himself in this innocuous cartoon. The Chan clan consisted of 10 kids of Mr. Chan's, with Henry and Stanley the eldest and generally the leaders of each mystery/search story line involving the family in some American locale. Henry and Stanley drove a van which could change into various vehicles, plus they led the family's rock group. Despite his children's often fumbling work, Charlie Chan usually managed to nail the suspect in each show. Chu-Chu was the family dog.

Except for the characters of Henry and Alan, the show replaced most of the children's voices immediately as their dialects were judged too thick to be understood by an Occidental audience. The second season consisted of repeats only.

AMAZING LIVE SEA MONKEYS, THE
Children's; Color
September 19, 1992–August 28, 1993

CBS Sat. Noon–12:30 p.m. (9/19/92–8/28/93)

Regular: *Howie Mandel*

Remember the ads in comic books for "amazing live sea monkeys" that would grow in your aquarium? Well, this series told their stories. Comedian Howie Mandel, who also created the program, played the professor who enlarged a trio of microscopic beings into web-footed, fish-faced characters named Aquarius, Bill, and Dave, causing much havoc. This show was a late addition to the CBS lineup due to more money being required than first budgeted for the special effects.

•AMERICA ALIVE
Talk; Color
July 24, 1978–January 4, 1979

NBC Mon.–Fri. Noon–1 p.m. (7/24/78–1/4/79)

Regulars: *Virginia Graham (1978), David Horowitz, Bruce Jenner, Janet Langhart, Jack Linkletter, [Dr. William H.] Masters and [Virginia] Johnson, Pat Mitchell, Dick Orkin and Bert Berdis, David Sheehan*

The daytime disaster of 1978 was *America Alive,* originating "live from New York," as debut guest Chevy Chase would say. Like many other TV failures, the hype was much greater than the sum of its parts. Its much-vaunted screen that let people talk back and forth with one another, for example, was nothing more than the same process producer Woody Fraser used when he started *Good Morning America.* Host Jack Linkletter was fine, but the show had Bruce Jenner, Pat Mitchell, and Janet Langhart, the latter a co-host of the daily *Good Day* series on WCVB Boston, file choppy reports outside the studio that often set an uneasy pace. Also awkwardly mixed were segments on shopping advice by David Horowitz, sex talk from Masters and Johnson, comic bits from Orkin and Berdis, and entertainment news and reviews from David Sheehan in Hollywood.

Three months after its debut, *America Alive* had terrible ratings (a 13 share of the audience versus a 20 share for its predecessor in the time slot, *The Gong Show*), and it cost an

Jack Linkletter hosted his third daytime show in 1978, this one called America Alive.

average of $35,000 more than most other daytime shows. To make it more appealing, Virginia Graham's "Gossip Check" and the "People Comedy" segment vanished and longer stories ran to give the show a harder edge. But ABC and CBS were faring much better with *The $20,000 Pyramid, Ryan's Hope, The Young and the Restless,* and *Search for Tomorrow,* so NBC had to drop its somewhat pricey experiment after six months.

AMERICA SPEAKS
Informational; B&W
July 2, 1951–August 24, 1951

NBC Mon.–Fri. 3:30–4 p.m. (7/2/51–8/24/51)

Host: *Robert Trout*

America Speaks used government and industrial films plus in-studio guests to discuss topics related to "the American story." It was the summer replacement for *The Bert Parks Show.*

•AMERICAN BANDSTAND
Music; B&W and Color
August 5, 1957–September 5, 1987

ABC Mon.–Fri. 3–4:30 p.m. (8/5/57–11/15/57)
ABC Mon.–Fri. 3–3:30 and 4–5 p.m. (11/18/57–9/26/58)
ABC Mon.–Fri. 4–5:30 p.m. (9/29/58–9/29/61)
ABC Mon.–Fri. 4–4:50 p.m. (10/2/61–9/28/62)
ABC Mon.–Fri. 4–4:55 p.m. (10/1/62–8/30/63)
ABC Sat. Various hours between 12:30 and 2:30 p.m.
  (9/7/63–8/17/74)
ABC Sat. 12:30–1:30 p.m. (9/6/74–9/6/86)
ABC Sat. 1–1:30 p.m. (9/13/86–9/5/87)

Host: *Dick Clark*

Network TV's longest-running music show was *American Bandstand,* which also was ABC's longest-running show until *ABC's Wide World of Sports* surpassed it in 1991 (it was the only 1950s ABC daytime series to survive into the 1970s as well). It began on October 13, 1952 in Philadelphia, but Dick Clark did not host it until 1956. Within a few months after Clark started, *American Bandstand* became the highest-rated local daytime show in Philadelphia, a fact not lost on ABC officials looking to set up their daytime lineup in 1957.

The show's format was simple and remained basically unchanged for the next 30 years. Clark introduced records and their artists, then cameras caught a swarm of teenagers dancing to the songs. Clark joined the adolescents after a few tunes to introduce one or two guest artists who appeared in the studio to lip sync to a hit or two. A couple of selected dancers got to play "Rate a Record," where they heard two songs and graded them on a scale of 35 to 98 (the range, according to Clark, reflecting the notion that no song is all bad or perfect). Other occasional features were the displaying of the week's top 10 records, and the yearly dance contest.

Shortly after its debut, *American Bandstand* impressed ABC well enough to try a version Mondays from 7:30–8 p.m. from October 7–December 30, 1957. The daytime show aired throughout most of the 1950s for 90 minutes on the network and two hours locally due to sponsor requests (thus, Philadelphia missed seeing its hometown announcer Ed McMahon on *Who Do You Trust?* those years, as ABC aired it daily at 3:30 p.m.). It went to nearly an hour daily in the early 1960s, with the last 5 or 10 minutes filled by *American Newsstand* (q.v.). In the fall of 1963 it went to Saturday afternoons only, and shortly thereafter the home base moved from Philadelphia to Los Angeles.

The weekday run was so successful that it made Clark into a sizable presence in both television and music. He received some 200 new records a week to use on the show, and he set aside noon to 1 p.m. every day to meet with people who wanted to promote a record. He joked to *TV Guide* about the insane desire of some promoters to get a tune on *American Bandstand,* saying, "I'm the Number One plug in the country." But he was not laughing when a Senate subcommittee interrogated him in 1959 to see if he was being paid money to play songs on the air. He sold his interests in a few record companies to come clean during the investigation. Clark survived the pressure, but came out somewhat chastened as a result.

Clark moved more into TV and movie production in the 1960s, plus occasional acting and hosting jobs. He still remained a force in the music industry, as did his show, even when it went to Saturdays, and nearly every major and plenty of minor recording acts stopped to do at least one show, with the notable exceptions of Elvis Presley and the Beatles. In fact, *American Bandstand* lasted longer than most of the recording careers of the artists featured, and lived through all the genres of popular music into the 1980s, from the English invasion to punk rock.

American Bandstand died not due to a lack of ratings but rather ABC's frequent preemptions or shortenings of the show due to *NCAA Football*, plus the network's insistence by 1986 that the show run only a half hour. After three decades, a new hour show went into syndication from 1987–89. The USA cable network then accepted the show with a new host, twenty-something David Hirsch, but it ran only from April 8–October 7, 1989.

Despite its cancellation, the series maintained a foothold in American pop culture. ABC granted the show a "40th Anniversary Special" on April 13, 1992, and the VH-1 cable network started daily and nightly edited half-hour repeats of the series in 1995. Additionally, several cities now have Dick Clark's American Bandstand Grill restaurants displaying old clips and memorabilia from the series, ensuring that the program's legacy will not be forgotten soon.

AMERICAN FORUM OF THE AIR, THE
Public Affairs ; B&W
May 22, 1949–September 15, 1957

NBC Sun. Various half-hours between 1 and 5:30 p.m.
(5/22/49–9/15/57; off summers 1950–53)

Moderator: *Theodore Granik (1949–53), Stephen McCormick (1953–57)*

The American Forum of the Air started in the early days of radio in 1928 and joined the Mutual radio broadcasting system in 1934 as *The Mutual Forum Hour*. The name had been changed at the end of the decade, and the show switched to NBC in 1949 before becoming a TV attraction. By that time, on the program's 21st anniversary in January 1949, Sen. Edwin C. Johnson (D-Colorado) publicly praised the program in *Broadcasting* magazine by saying, "It is one of the best examples of democracy at work that we have."

Three months later, the venerable show made its TV bow from Washington, D.C. with the national committee chairmen of the Democratic and Republican parties (Sen. J. Howard McGrath and Sen. Hugh Scott, respectively). As with the radio show, which occasionally was simulcast with the TV show, the format had two opposing guests present their opinions on a topic at hand, followed by at least 10 minutes for the audience to ask questions of the guests. The moderator also directed a few questions of his own to the interviewees.

The show's producer Theodore Granik hosted the show for its first four years. In its last season it alternated weekly with another Granik-produced, McCormick-hosted series, *Youth Wants to Know*. When it was off daytime during the summers of 1950–53, NBC aired it on Saturday or Sunday evenings.

Three years after the NBC run, in 1960, the show aired in cooperation with Ted Granik on TV stations owned by Westinghouse.

AMERICAN INVENTORY
Documentary; B&W
September 9, 1951–December 25, 1955

NBC Sun. 1:30–2 p.m. (9/9/51–5/25/52)
NBC Sun. 2–2:30 p.m. (9/14/52–4/4/54; off summers)
NBC Sun. 12:30–1 p.m. (11/7/54–3/27/55)
NBC Sun. 2–2:30 p.m. (9/18/55–12/25/55)

Host: *Ray Morgan (1951–52)*

American Inventory was a widely varied collection of live and filmed telecasts about the state of the United States. Among the topics covered through news reports or dramas were a look at peaceful uses of atomic energy (November 11, 1951); a performance of Kukla, Fran, and Ollie (February 17, 1952); a biography of George Washington Carver, played by Canada Lee (April 13, 1952); the heart machine at Harper Hospital in Detroit, which pumped blood to patients during surgery (February 15, 1953); a discussion by hotel mogul Conrad Hilton and actress Peggy Wood on how they overcame handicaps to obtain success (March 7, 1954); and aptitude tests (October 16, 1955).

The program debuted on NBC Sundays at 8 p.m. on July 1, 1951. After two months in that slot, it moved to Sunday afternoons, except for a brief run Saturdays at 7:30 p.m. in the summer of 1952. The series was produced under a grant from the Alfred P. Sloan Foundation.

AMERICAN NEWSSTAND
News; B&W
October 2, 1961–August 30, 1963

ABC Mon.–Fri. 4:50–5 p.m. (10/2/61–9/28/62)
ABC Mon.–Fri. 4:55–5 p.m. (10/1/62–8/30/63)

Regulars: *Roger Sharp, David Jayne, Bill Lord*

American Newsstand offered a daily youthful slant on the news, both in its coverage of items of interest to teenagers and in its use of on-air talent. Regular correspondents David Jayne and Bill Lord were both 24 and recent journalism graduates who filed stories. The somewhat more seasoned Roger Sharp (if you call 26 years old experienced) served as anchor. Interestingly, Jayne became a news item himself on the show on April 23, 1962, when he got married. Fittingly, this show aired after *American Bandstand*.

•AMERICAN SPORTSMAN, THE
Sports/Documentary; B&W and Color
January 31, 1965–June 24, 1984

ABC Sun. Various hours between 2:30 and 6 p.m., except
  Sat. 2:30–3:30 in winters of 1979 and 1980
  (1/31/65–6/24/84; January–April only 1965–76,
  summer months 1977–78 and 1981–84)

Host: *Curt Gowdy*

Narrator (1960s at least): *Joe Foss*

The American Sportsman was TV's most controversial sports show. It underwent a dramatic change in its nearly two-decade run, from shooting at animals with guns to shooting some of the same species with cameras to detail efforts to preserve them.

The first four shows aired monthly, including one with Robert Stack joining Curt Gowdy on an African safari. The following year, as the series appeared in the winter months on a fairly regular schedule, actors Mike Connors, Phil Harris, David Jansen, John Saxon, and Craig Stevens, among other celebrities, took part in animal hunts on treks that cost $100,000 per outing and covered 150,000 miles a year. For those offended by the sight of a defenseless tiger or elephant being felled by a gunman, the show warned them with this original introduction: "*The American Sportsman* is a series dedicated to the adventurous life of the out-of-doors. If you are among those who do not enjoy the challenge of the stalk, the strike, or the lure of the wild, then this is not the show for you."

One definitely not enjoying "the challenge of the stalk" was *TV Guide* critic Cleveland Amory, who also was president of the Fund for Animals Inc. He considered *American Sportsman* the worst show on the air and wrote in 1967, "If the men who run ABC find enjoyment in such 'sport,' it is sad news." He chastised the series especially for showing people hunting animals nearing extinction, such as an archer who killed a polar bear even though an international conference had requested that hunting the beasts be abolished.

Other viewers expressed similar sentiments, and by 1971 public pressure had caused the series to modify its focus. This led to some interesting turnabouts by repeat guests. Bing Crosby, first seen shooting quail in 1968, described preservation efforts for ducks in Canada. And Jimmy Dean, who appeared in 1967 bagging a moose in Alaska, turned up to narrate the slaughtering of the mustang. To explain the series' new philosophy, producer Bud Morgan told *TV Guide*, "We are not anti-hunting. We believe the hunter serves a useful purpose and that areas should be kept open for game. But we do concentrate more now on educating the viewers on wildlife and exciting them with adventure that doesn't involve a lot of shooting."

Later shows included Robert Redford narrating "Following the Tundra Wolf" in 1975, model Cheryl Tiegs looking at efforts to prevent the extinction of the whooping crane in 1979, Sir Edmund Hillary and an American climbing team going up the last unscaled face of Mount Everest in 1982, and former president Jimmy Carter and his wife Rosalynn observing salmon in Quebec in 1983.

By the end of the 1970s, the show was devoting almost all of its broadcasts to animal studies or nonkilling sports and very little to hunting and fishing. This slant disturbed host Curt Gowdy, who thought hunters and fishers did a great favor in paying fees for their activities that are used to preserve the outdoors for everyone to use. But the real reasons for the show's cancellation probably were its rising costs and increasingly irregular appearances in the 1980s, when it often popped up for brief, unpublicized periods. Still, its run of over 19 years assures its place among the top 50 longest-running daytime shows ever.

AMERICAN TAILS—See *Fievel's American Tails.*

AMERICAN WEEK, THE
News; B&W
October 17, 1954–June 19, 1955
CBS Sun. 4–4:30 p.m. (10/17/54–4/24/55)
CBS Sun. 5–5:30 p.m. (5/1/55–6/19/55)
Anchor: *Eric Sevareid*

Eric Sevareid both reported and analyzed the week's news in this recap first seen on CBS Sundays at 6 p.m. from April 4–October 10, 1954. During that period, the show went from airing from New York City at its debut to Sevareid's home base of Washington, D.C. by September 1954. It moved back to the afternoon in 1954–55 to make room for *Omnibus*.

AMERICAN YOUTH FORUM—See *Youth Wants to Know.*

ANDY'S GANG—See *Smilin' Ed McConnell and His Buster Brown Gang.*

ANIMAL CLINIC
Informational; B&W
August 19, 1950–January 13, 1951
ABC Sat. 11–11:30 a.m. (8/19/50–9/16/50)
ABC Sat. 12:15–12:45 p.m. (9/23/50–1/13/51)
Regulars: *Don Carroll, Oscar Frazen, Dr. Wesley A. Young*

Veterinarian Dr. Wesley Young, director of the Chicago Anti-Cruelty Society, hosted this series examining living creatures and their habits. It was seen as early as May 1950 from 4:15–4:30 p.m. Saturdays locally on WENR Chicago. On ABC, dog trainer Oscar Frazen provided obedience lessons, while Don Carroll provided unnecessary comic relief as a bungling handyman. There was a nurse on hand offstage in case any animals acted improperly before the cameras. The show was produced by Gail Compton, who hosted a similar series on DuMont in prime time from 1951–53 called *Pet Shop*.

•ANIMAL CRACK-UPS
Game; Color
September 12, 1987–September 1, 1990
ABC Sat. Noon–12:30 p.m. (9/12/87–12/30/89)
ABC Sat. Noon–12:30 p.m. (6/2/90–9/1/90)
Host: *Alan Thicke*

Using video clips supplied by the Tokyo Broadcasting System and narration from Alan Thicke as background, four celebrities tried to guess the correct answer about habits and curiosities of the entity being profiled. A right guess won him or her a stuffed monkey, and the player with the most stuffed monkeys at the end of the game won $2,500 for his or her charity. This setup was the same for the show's Saturday night version, which debuted a month prior to the daytime show and ran from August 8–September 12, 1987.

Most of the competing celebrities were adults, including multiple appearances by Scott Baio, JM J. Bullock, John Byner, Zsa Zsa Gabor, and that game show perennial, Betty White. Interestingly, Alan Thicke hosted the "family" of his hit nighttime sitcom for a few shows beginning October 3, 1987 as *Growing Pains* regulars Joanna Kerns, Kirk Cameron, Tracey Gold, and Jeremy Miller competed.

ANIMAL SECRETS
Documentary; Color
October 15, 1966–May 19, 1968

NBC Sat. 1–1:30 p.m. (10/15/66–4/8/67)
NBC Sun. 4:30–5 p.m. (5/5/68–5/19/68)

Host: *Dr. Loren Eiseley*

Narrator: *Mel Brandt*

Filmed in cooperation with New York's Museum of Natural History, *Animal Secrets* investigated one behavioral curiosity of a species per show and explained it via films, with its target audience being children. In addition to the listed times, the series aired in repeats on NBC Sundays from 7 p.m. from July 2–August 27, 1967.

ANIMAL TIME
Children's; B&W
October 17, 1953–April 17, 1954

ABC Sat. 9:45–10 a.m. (10/17/53–1/30/54)
ABC Sat. 10:15–10:30 a.m. (2/6/54–4/17/54)

This little-known informational show about assorted creatures of the world ran as part of ABC's abortive attempt to program Saturday mornings. For an earlier example, see *Scouting in Action.*

ANIMAL WORLD
Documentary; Color
September 1, 1968–September 17, 1972

CBS Sun. 5–5:30 p.m. (9/1/68–10/27/68)
CBS Sun. 5:30–6 p.m. (1/3/71–7/4/71)
CBS Sun. 5:30–6 p.m. (1/23/72–9/17/72)

Host/Producer: *Bill Burrud*

The only producer who could give Marlin Perkins a run for his money on TV nature documentaries was Bill Burrud, and *Animal World* was his most successful effort. *Animal World* showed excellent footage of creatures and their lifestyles in both natural and manmade habitats, with the former naturally being more problematic to cover. The production company researched areas considerably before doing fieldwork, but despite the best preparations some difficulties hit during filming. Three of the show's crews were involved in plane crashes, one of them fatal. During one shoot, a 13,000-pound bull elephant charged at technicians, who barely managed to escape.

The series toured the networks in nighttime airings during the summers of 1968–71, on NBC in 1968 (where it began on June 16), on CBS in 1969 and 1971, and on ABC in

Host and producer Bill Burrud poses with a half-and-half Bengal and Siberian tiger he included in one of his shows on Animal World.

1970. It went into syndication after its network run, airing in some versions under the title *Wildlife Adventures.* It stayed in production through 1979.

•ANIMALS, ANIMALS, ANIMALS
Documentary; Color
September 12, 1976–November 8, 1981

ABC Sun. 11:30 a.m.–Noon (9/12/76–11/8/81)

Regulars: *Hal Linden, Lynn Kellogg, Roger Caras*

While starring on the ABC nighttime sitcom *Barney Miller*, actor Hal Linden hosted this pleasant designed-for-children informational series about creatures living outdoors. Lynn Kellogg penned and sang folk songs about the animals profiled, while ABC news correspondent Roger Caras filed veterinary care tips. It lasted until ABC took it off to make room for the hour-long *This Week with David Brinkley.*

•ANIMANIACS
Cartoon; Color
September 20, 1993–

Fox Mon.–Fri. Various half-hours (9/20/93–9/18/95)
Fox Sat. 9–9:30 a.m. (9/10/94–3/11/95)
Fox Sat. 8–8:30 a.m. (3/18/95–9/2/95)
The WB Sun. 9–9:30 a.m. (9/20/95–)

Voices:

Yakko/Pinky	Rob Paulsen
Dot Warner	Tress MacNeille
Wakko Warner	Jess Harnell
The Brain	Maurice LaMarche

This successful spin-off of *Tiny Toon Adventures* continued mining the latter's brand of wacky comedy. Looking like demented versions of Mickey Mouse, the Animaniacs were a trio of characters supposedly trapped in the Warner Brothers water tower back in the 1930s, considered to be too weird for the general public, until they were freed accidentally 60 years later. Dot Warner was the cute one, Yakko was a blabbermouth, and Wakko wore a hat and talked like Paul McCartney. Bubbly and fun-loving, they left chaos in their wake, all the while lampooning virtually every aspect of popular culture, including their own cartoon world. (One episode ended with the Warners questioning themselves about what moral they learned from the day's episode of mayhem.)

A large variety of supporting characters rotated appearances on the show, with the most frequent and memorable being "Pinky and the Brain," about a duo of lab rats, one a goon (Pinky) and the other a Vincent Price clone hell-bent on taking over the world. They were spun off in their own nighttime show in 1995. When *Animaniacs* went from Fox to The WB in 1995, the show had a regular time slot on Saturdays plus a daily slot where stations could run it at their discretion.

•ANOTHER WORLD

Soap Opera; B&W and Color
May 4, 1964–

NBC Mon.–Fri. 3–3:30 p.m. (5/4/64–1/3/75)
NBC Mon.–Fri. 3–4 p.m. (1/6/75–3/2/79)
NBC Mon.–Fri. 2:30–4 p.m. (3/5/79–8/1/80)
NBC Mon.–Fri. 2–3 p.m. (8/4/80–)

Cast:

Jim Matthews (1964)	John Beal
Jim Matthews (1964–65)	Leon Janney
Jim Matthews (1965–69)	Shepperd Strudwick
Jim Matthews (1969–82)	Hugh Marlowe
Mary Matthews (1964–75)	Virginia Dwyer
Pat Matthews (1964–66)	Susan Trustman
Pat Matthews (1967–82)	Beverly Penberthy
Russ Matthews (1964)	Joey Trent
Russ Matthews (1966–71)	Sam Groom
Russ Matthews (1971–72)	Robert Hover
Russ Matthews (1973–81)	David Bailey
Alice Matthews (1964–75, 1984–85, 1989)	Jacqueline Courtney
Alice Matthews (1976–79)	Susan Harney
Alice Matthews (1979)	Wesley Ann Pfenning
Alice Matthews (1981)	Vana Tribbey
Alice Matthews (1981–82)	Linda Borgeson
Liz Matthews (1964)	Sara Cunningham
Liz Matthews (1964–69)	Audra Lindley
Liz Matthews (1969–71)	Nancy Wickwire
Liz Matthews (1973–86, 1987–88)	Irene Dailey
Susan Matthews (1964)	Fran Sharon
Susan Matthews (1964)	Roni Dengel
Susan Matthews (1969–71)	Lisa Cameron
Susan Matthews (1978–79, 1982–83)	Lynn Milgram
Bill Matthews (1964–68)	Joe Gallison
Janet Matthews (1964–65)	Liza Chapman
Grandma Matthews (1964)	Vera Allen
John Randolph (1964–79)	Michael M. Ryan
Lee Randolph (1964–67)	Gaye Huston
Lee Randolph (1967–69)	Barbara Rodell
Missy Palmer (1964–70)	Carol Roux
Ken Baxter (1964–65)	William Prince
Laura Baxter (1964–65)	Augusta Dabney
Tom Baxter (1964)	Nicholas Pryor
Fred Douglas (1964–70)	Charles Baxter
Katherine Corning (1965–66)	Ann Sheridan
Lenore Moore (1966–71)	Judith Barcroft
Lenore Moore (1971–76)	Susan Sullivan
Helen Moore (1966–75)	Murial Williams
Peggy Harris Nolan (1966–73)	Micki Grant
Danny Fargo (1966–67)	Antony Ponzini
Madge Murray (1966–67)	Doris Belack
Flo Murray (1966–67)	Marcella Martin
Michael Bauer (1966–67)/ Raymond Gordon (1977)	Gary Pillar [Carpenter]
Hope Bauer (1966)	Elissa Leeds
David Thornton (1966)	Colgate Salisbury
Alex Gregory (c. 1966)	James Congdon
Karen Gregory (c. 1966)	Ellen Watson
Dr. Ernest Gregory (c. 1966)	Mark Lenard
Rachel Davis (1967–71, 1972)	Robin Strasser
Rachel Davis (1971)	Margaret Impert
Rachel Davis (1972–)/Justine (1995)	Victoria Wyndham
Ada Hobson (1967–92)	Constance Ford
Walter Curtin (1967–72)	Val Dufour
Sam Lucas (1967–70, 1974)	Jordan Charney
Lahoma Vane Lucas (1967–70)	Ann Wedgeworth
Lefty Burns (1967–68)	Lawrence Keith
Steve Frame (1968–75, 1989)	George Reinholt
Steve Frame (1981–83)	David Canary
Ernie Downs (1968–70 at least)	Harry Bellaver
Michael Randolph (1972–73)	Tom Ruger
Michael Randolph (1975–79)	Lionel Johnston
Marianne Randolph (1972–73)	Loriann Ruger
Marianne Randolph (1973–74)	Jill Turnball
Marianne Randolph (1974–75)	Tiberia Mitri
Marianne Randolph (1975–77)	Ariane Munker
Marianne Randolph (1977–79)	Adrienne Wallace
Marianne Randolph (1980–81)	Beth Collins
Dr. Dan Shearer (1970–71)	John Cunningham
Dr. Dan Shearer (1978–79)	Brian Murray
Cindy Clark (1970–72)	Leonie Norton
Caroline Johnson (1970–71)	Rue McClanahan

Wayne Addison (1970–71)
Ted Clark (1971–73)
Jamie Frame (1972–73)
Jamie Frame (1975–78)
Jamie Frame (1978–79)
Jamie Frame (1979–83)
Jamie Frame (1983–85)
Jamie Frame (1986–87 at least)
Jamie Frame (at least 1990–92)
Iris Cory (1972–80)
Iris Cory (at least 1992)
Louise Goddard (1972–82)
Gil McGowan (1972)
Gil McGowan (1972–77)
Robert Delaney (1972–76, 1980, 1989)
Janice Frame (1972–74)
Janice Frame (1978–80)
Dennis Carrington (1972–78)
Dennis Carrington (1978–80)
Eliot Carrington (1972)
Eliot Carrington (1972–74)
Gerald Davis (1972–73)
Mackenzie Cory (1973)
Mackenzie Cory (1974–89)
Tim McGowan (1973–74)
Vic Hastings (1974–82)/
Reginald Love (1986–87 at least)
Nancy McGowan (1974–83)
Nancy McGowan (1984–87)
Dr. Dave Gilchrist (1974–77)
Carol Lamonte (1974–76)
Neil Johnson (1974–75)
Sally Frame (1975–78)
Sally Frame (1979–80)
Sally Frame (1981–83)
Sally Frame (1983)
Sally Frame (1983–85)
Sally Frame (1985–86)
Clarice Hobson (1975–86)
Molly Ordway (1975–78)
Sharlene Frame (1975–77)
Beatrice Gordon (1975–77)
Raymond Gordon (1975–77)
Rocky Olsen (1975–77)
Philip Wainwright (1975)
Olive Gordon (1976–79)
Emmy Ordway (1976–79)
Evan Webster (1976–77)
Brian Bancroft (1977–85)
Ted Bancroft (1977)
Ted Bancroft (1979)
Ted Bancroft (1983–84)
Elena de Poulignac (1977–79)
Elena de Poulignac (1981–82)
Leonard Brooks (1977–78)

Robert Milli
Stephen Bolster
Aiden McNulty
Bobby Doran
Tim Holcomb
Richard Bekins
Stephen Yates
Laurence Lau
Russell Todd
Beverlee McKinsey
Carmen Duncan
Anne Meacham
Charles Durning
Dolph Sweet

Nicolas Coster
Victoria Thompson
Christine Jones
Mike Hammett
Jim Poyner
Joe Hannahan
James Douglas
Walter Matthews
Robert Emhardt
Douglass Watson
Christopher Allport

John Considine
Danielle Burns
Jane Cameron
David Ackroyd
Jeanne Lange
John Getz
Cathy Greene
Julie Philips
Jennifer Runyon
Dawn Benz
Mary Page Keller
Taylor Miller
Gail Brown
Rolanda Mendels
Laurie Heineman
Jacqueline Brookes
Ted Shackelford
John Braden
James Luisi
Jennifer Leak
Tresa Hughes
Barry Jenner
Paul Stevens
Eric Roberts
Richard Backus
Luke Reilly
Christina Pickles
Maeve McGuire
John Horton

Leonard Brooks (1978–82)
Charlie Hobson (1977–81)
Jeff Stone (1977–79)
Burt McGowan (1977–78)
Burt McGowan (1978)
Sven Petersen (1977–78)
Helga Lindeman (1977–78)
Regine Lindeman (1977–78)
Joan Barnard (1977–78)
Greg Barnard (1977–78)
Larry Ewing (1978–86)
Blaine Ewing (1978–84)
Blaine Ewing (1984–85)
Vivien Gorrow (1978–80, 1983–84)
Buzz Winslow (1978–80, 1982)
Joey Perrini (1978)
Joey Perrini (1978–81)
Rose Perrini (1978–80)
Vince Frame (1978–79)
Eileen Simpson (1978–79)
Sylvie Kosloff (1978–79)
Mitch Blake (1979–82, 1986–88 at least)
Cecile de Poulignac (1979–81)
Cecile de Poulignac (1981–84, 1986)
Jerry Grove (1979–80)
Jerry Grove (1980–81)
Jerry Grove (1981–82)
Philip Lyons (1979–81)
Kirk Laverty (1979)
Dr. Rick Holloway (1980–82)
Jason Dunlap (1980–82)
Melissa Needham (1980–82)
Miranda Bishop (1980–81)
Zachary Colton (1980–81)
Jordan Scott (1980–81)
Dr. Oliva Delaney (1980–81)
Alexander "Sandy" Cory (1981–85)
R.J. Morgan (1981–83)
Diane Frame Shea (1981–82)
Pete Shea (1981–82)
Harry Shea (1981–82)
Denny Hobson (1981–82)
Ilsa Fredericks (1981–82)
Anne Whitelaw (1981–82)
Cass Winthrop (1982–)
Peter Love (1982–84)
Peter Love (1985)
Peter Love (1985–)
Maisie Watkins (1982–87)
Quinn Harding (1982–87)
Thomasina Harding (1982–83)
Thomasina Harding (1984–87)
Henrietta Morgan (1982–84)

John Tillinger
Fred J. Scollay
Dan Hamilton
Joseph Hindy
William Russ
Roberts Blossom
Helen Stenborg
Barbara Eda-Young
Patricia Estrin
Ned Schmidtke
Richard J. Porter
Laura Malone
Judy Dewey

Gretchen Oehler
Eric Conger
Paul Perri
Ray Liotta
Kathleen Widdoes
Jay Morran
Vicky Dawson
Leora Dana

William Gray Espy
Susan Keith

Nancy Frangione
Michael Garfield
Kevin Conroy
Paul Tinder
Robert Gentry
Charles Cioffi
Tony Cummings
Warren Burton
Taro Meyer
Judith McConnell
Curt Dawson
J. Kenneth Campbell
Tina Sloan
Christopher Rich
Reggie Rock Blythewood
Anne Rose Brooks
Christopher Marcantel
Ed Power
James Horan
Gwyda DonHowe
Mary Joan Negro
Stephen Schnetzer
John Hutton
Christopher Holder
Marcus Smythe
Patricia Hodges
Petronia Paley
Shelia Spencer
Pamela G. Kay
Michelle Shay

Julia Shearer (1982–83)	Kyra Sedgwick
Julia Shearer (1983)	Jonna Leigh
Julia Shearer (1983–84)	Faith Ford
Roy Bingham (1982–84)	Morgan Freeman
Stacey Winthrop (1982–83)	Terry Davis
Alma Rudder (1982–83)	Elizabeth Franz
Jeanne Ewing (1982–83)	Melissa Luciano
Louis St. George (1982–83)	Jack Betts
Ella Fitz (1982–83)	Lois Smith
Ed Harding (1982)	Howard E. Rollins Jr.
Felicia Gallant (1983–)	Linda Dano
Carl Hutchins (1983–86, 1991–)	Charles Keating
Donna Love (1983–86, 1989–92)	Anna Stuart
Donna Love (1987–88, 1992–)	Philece Sampler
Nicole Love (1983–84)	Kim Morgan Greene
Nicole Love (1986–87)	Laurie Landry
Lily Mason (1983–86)	Jackee Harry
Perry Hutchins (1983–85)	David Oliver
Mark Singleton (1983–85)	Robin Thomas
Dr. Abel Marsh/Leo Marsh	
(1983–84)	Joe Morton
Gil Fenton (1983–84)	Tom Wiggin
David Thatcher (1983–84)	Lewis Arlt
Miss Devon (1983–84)	Evalyn Baron
Dr. Royal Dunning (1983–84)	Michael Minor
Marley Love/Victoria Love	
(1984–86)	Ellen Wheeler
Victoria Love (1986–87)	Rhonda Lewin
Marley Love/Victoria Love	
(1987–91)	Ann Heche
Victoria Love (1991–)	Jensen Buchanan
Vince McKinnon (1984–85)	Jack Ryland
Vince McKinnon (1986)	Duke Stroud
Vince McKinnon (1987–88	
at least)	Robert Hogan
Wallingford (1984–88)	Brent Collins
Catlin Ewing (1984–87)	Thomas Ian Griffith
M.J. McKinnon (1984–86)	Kathleen Layman
M.J. McKinnon (1986–87)	Sally Spencer
Tony "the Tuna" Jones (1984–87)	George Pentecost
Kathleen McKinnon (1984–86)	Julie Osburn
Carter Todd (1984–86)	Russell Curry
Ben McKinnon (1984–85)	Richard Steen
Grant Todd (1984–85)	John Dewey-Carter
Nurse Emily Benson (1984–85)	Alex (Dianne) Neil
Hunter Bradshaw (1984–85)	Robert Sedgwick
Jake McKinnon (1985–)	Tom Eplin
Bridget Connell (1985–)	Barbara Berjer
Brittany Peterson (1985–87)	Sharon Gabet
Zane Lindquist (1985–86)	Patrick Tovatt
Edward Gerald (1985–86)	John Saxon
Dr. Chris Chapin (1985–86)	Don Scardino
Neal Cory (1985–86)	Robert LuPone
Daniel Gabriel (1985–86)	Peter Lochran
Michael Hudson (1986–88 at	
least, 1993–)	Kale Brown

Adam Cory (1986–87 at least)	Ed Fry
Zack Edwards (1986–87 at least)	James Pickens, Jr.
Peggy Lazaras (1986–87 at least)	Rebecca Hollen
Chad Rollo (1986–87 at least)	Richard Burgi
Cheryl McKinnon (1986–87	
at least)	Kristen Marie
Scott LaSalle (1986–87 at least)	Hank Cheyne
Sara Montaigne (1986–87)	Missy Hughes
Rose Livingston (1986–87)	Ann Flood
Tony Carlise (1986–87)	John H. Brennan
Greg Houston (1986–87)	Christopher Cousins
John Hudson (1987–)	David Forsyth
Amanda Cory (1987–88 at least)	Sandi Ferguson
Lisa Grady (1987–88 at least)	Joanna Going
Barbara Van Arkdale (at least	
1987)	Carla Borelli
Jason Frame (1987–88 at least)	Chris Robinson
Sam Fowler (1987–90 at least)	Robert Kelker-Kelly
Dawn Rollo (c. 1988)	Barbara Bush
Matt Cory (at least 1988–)	Matt Crane
Sharlene Hudson (1989–)	Anna Holbrook
Reuben (1989–90 at least)	Clayton Prince
Derek (at least 1989–90)	Kevin Carrington
Lucas (1989–92)	John Aprea
Frankie Frame (1989–96)	Alice Barrett
Paulina McKinnon (at least	
1990–91)	Cali Timmins
Paulina McKinnon (1991–)	Judi Evans
Zack Richards (1990 at least)	Terry Alexander
Dean Frame (1990–93 at least)	Ricky Paull Goldin
Sen. Grant Harrison (1991)	Dack Rambo
Sen. Grant Harrison (1991–)	Mark Pinter
Byron Pierce, paraplegic lawyer	
(1991–)	Mitch Long
Lorna Devon, rape victim (at least	
1992–93)	Alicia Coppola
Lorna Devon (at least 1995–)	Robin Christopher
Christy Carson (1992–93 at least)	Patti D'Arbanville
Dennis Wheeler (1992 at least)	Chris Bruno
Maggie Cory (1993–95)	Robyn Griggs
Brett Gardner (1993–at least 1994)	Colleen Dion
Marshall Lincoln Kramer III	
(1994–)	Randy Brooks
Ian (1994)	Julian McMahon
Tomas Rivera (1994–)	Diego Serrano
Captain Gabe McNamara	
(at least 1996–)	John Bolger

In the pressure-cooker atmosphere of daily soap operas, it's not surprising that almost all of them have backstage incidents as chaotic as what appears on the screen. But *Another World* towers over all comers in this respect in having its seams show publicly. Consider the following: In more than 30 years on the air, the show virtually wrote out its entire core family not once but twice; became the first daily soap to run 60 minutes and then, temporarily, 90 minutes; became the first soap to have both a daytime spin-off (*Somerset*) and a second spin-off (*Texas*); caused one head writer to pen a book about his ordeals doing the show (*Eight Years in Another World* by Harding Lemay, who ironically returned in 1988 and 1995 as a consultant); and went from near cancellation in the mid-1960s to NBC's top attraction of the mid- to late 1970s, only to fall back in the pack as a low-rated offering in the 1980s and 1990s. So if you want to hear its full story, to paraphrase Bette Davis, fasten your seat belts, it's going to be a bumpy read.

Another World was so titled because its creator, Irna Phillips, was referring to her pet creation *As the World Turns*. This soap, however, emphasized melodrama over characterization, and did so from the start, both on and off screen. Members of the Matthews family had to deal with the death of William, whose survivors were his rich wife Liz and children Susan and Bill, plus William's middle-class brother Jim, his wife Mary, and their children Pat, Russ, and Alice, and William's sister Janet and mom Grandma Matthews. Janet and Grandma Matthews disappeared shortly after the show began and virtually no reference was made to them, while offstage an anxious Irna, for no reason whatsoever, canned John Beal as Jim after the first show and Sarah Cunningham as Liz after the first week. These were the initial indications of what was to be a pattern during the show's first two decades.

Pat Matthews had the main action during the show's first year, as she became pregnant by Tom Baxter, was forced by him into having an abortion, and was traumatized to the point of hearing babies scream. She killed Tom while temporarily insane, saying, "You love me, you love me," and when lawyer John Randolph successfully defended her, she fell in love with and married him. But John's daughter Lee tried to kill herself faced with this situation, then felt guilt when she ended up crippling him in an auto accident, and called a truce with Pat.

The truce broke off when the two of them fell in love with, of all people, Lee's new law partner Michael Bauer, on leave from *The Guiding Light*. (Apparently Irna had enough power to have CBS let this character go onto the NBC show for a time. Wow!) When Michael decided that he and his daughter Hope should return to Springfield rather than wreck the Randolph family, a distraught Lee got involved with shady Lefty Burns, who hooked her on drugs. In 1968, having tripped on LSD contained in a spiked drink, she worried that the child she was carrying by ex-convict Sam Lucas would be deformed. That concern was rendered moot when Lee, under the influence of LSD in 1969, crashed her car and died, leaving Pat and John to face more trouble on their own in the 1970s.

Meanwhile, Bill Matthews found himself attracted to Missy Palmer, an orphan (coincidentally, so was actress Carol Roux). Missy was a recovering schizophrenic who, when she found out she was illegitimate via Bill's conniving mother Liz who had invited Missy's natural mother Cathryn Corning to town, went insane and left Bay City for Chicago. There scummy criminal Danny Fargo forced Missy into marriage and raped her. Bill found Missy being tried for Danny's murder; battling Bay City district attorney Walter Curtin, he

proved that Danny's ex-girlfriend Flo Murray had killed him accidentally. Missy and Bill wed, but sadly in 1968 Bill drowned in an accident. His sister Susan had problems with their mom, too, in the romance department, as they fought over the affections of lawyer Fred Douglas before Susan wed him (she later divorced him and married Dr. Dan Shearer).

After the first year, Irna Phillips left the series, and new head writer James Lipton introduced the Gregory family while demoting or writing out most of the Matthewses. Before the whole family disappeared along with the lousy ratings, Agnes Nixon, former *Guiding Light* head writer, took over in 1967 and killed off the Gregories. She hit paydirt with what dominated the story line in the late 1960s and early 1970s and became known as the Alice-Steven-Rachel triangle.

Russ Matthews wed hellion Rachel Davis, daughter of beautician Ada Davis, who would be widowed four times. Rachel was a demanding dame who complained about the lack of income from Russ due to his work as a hospital intern. She found solace in a tryst with businessman Steven Frame, who unfortunately had a romance going at the same time with Russ's sister Alice. She had a baby by Steven named Jamie, but despite using all her wiles, and despite Alice's dismay over the situation, Alice and Steven married in 1971, while Russ divorced Rachel when he learned he was not Jamie's father. Romantic maneuvers in these relationships deepened when Russ starting dating nurse Cindy Clark while Rachel wed Cindy's brother Ted. Not much came of either relationship, particularly when Rachel convinced Alice that Steven still loved her, which led to Alice and Steven divorcing and Rachel marrying Steven. For a time, Rachel had the upper hand.

Rachel's mother Ada also had her hand in a few of the plots during these years. The sister of con man Sam Lucas, Lee Randolph's old fling, Ada wed Ernie Downs. When Lee died, Sam wed Lahoma Vane, and the two of them along with Missy Palmer left town for Somerset, the title of the soap's first spin-off, in 1970. A few years later, Ada's ex-husband Gerald Davis came to town from Somerset to stay for a spell, and Ada got a new husband in policeman Gil McGowan, with Ada giving birth to their child.

Also in the thick of things was socialite Lenore Moore, who tried to split up Missy and Bill before wedding Walter Curtin. To provide for spoiled Lenore, Walter quit his job as district attorney and went into cahoots with Wayne Addison, who romanced Liz Matthews. Liz, while friendly with Lenore's mother Helen, hated Lenore and tried to pin Wayne's murder on her, a crime that had actually been committed by Walter. Walter died in a car accident in 1972 while on his way to confess his crime, and Lenore eventually got over her grief to marry architect Robert Delaney, a rare character crossover from *Somerset*, in 1974. Robert had an affair with Carol Lamonte, who blackmailed Lenore, hinting she knew what atrocity her late husband had done. A fearful Lenore left town, and an equally unhappy Robert ended his affair with Carol.

Amid all this, the Alice-Steven-Rachel triangle still dominated, as Alice tried in 1973 to forget Steven by being a governess to Dennis Carrington while the child's father Eliot fell in love with her. This did not thrill Eliot's estranged wife Iris, who tried to reunite with him before divorcing. Then, learning that she could never bear children, Alice went into deep depression, and Steven, informed of her situation, nursed her to health and reclaimed her. In a special one-hour episode on May 3, 1974, a day shy of its 10th anniversary, Allison finally married Steven. The format and plot point both served as hints of things to come.

Over the next year, Rachel, now finding herself with few friends in Bay City, found a new, true love in a man several years her senior, Iris Corrington's rich father Mackenzie "Mac" Cory. Iris objected to this new couple, and their conflicts formed the core activities of *Another World* in the mid- to late 1970s. First Iris almost convinced her dad that Rachel slept with bon vivante Philip Wainwright, until Philip's old flame Clarice Hobson revealed the truth. When even her fiancé Russ Matthews avoided her following this deception, Iris went for revenge by stealing Clarice's current flame Robert Delaney and marrying him, even though Clarice was carrying Delaney's child. That fact eventually came out too, and all parties ended up alone and unsatisfied, although Iris did have the support of her secretary and listening ear Louise Goddard.

These goings-on, most of which happened in 1975, were nothing to what was going on offstage. First, the show's packager, Procter & Gamble, endorsed an expansion to an

hour, with the new 30 minutes coming from the cancellation of *How to Survive a Marriage*. At the start of 1975 it become the first soap to run 60 minutes daily. At the same time, the ongoing conflict between head writer Harding Lemay, who joined the show in 1971 and led it to the top of the ratings, and several actors whose performances he loathed, escalated. Chief among these actors were Virginia Dwyer (Mary), George Reinholt (Steven), and Jacqueline Courtney (Alice). All played popular characters, but Lemay felt they fell far short of professionalism. He accused Dwyer of relying on cue cards heavily and hardly learning her lines at all, Reinholt of being egotistical, and Courtney of simply being a bad actress. So he had Mary die of a coronary attack, Steven announced dead in a helicopter crash in Australia, and Courtney replaced by another actress. These changes represented as drastic a cast changeover as had ever been seen in a serial, but since the emphasis now was on Mac, Rachel, and Iris, its impact in the ratings was fairly minimal, even though Courtney and Reinholt appeared shortly thereafter as regulars on rival soap *One Life to Live*.

With the new hour format came a few other stories, of course. Pat and John Randolph, who each had endured a few separations and bouts with the bottle, finally divorced in 1976, much to their fraternal twins Michael and Marianne's dismay. Pat fell in love with Dr. Dave Gilchrist, while John wed hot-to-trot Olive Gordon, who promptly cheated on him with architect Evan Webster. Evan died in a fight with John, who had a mental breakdown afterward before recovering and divorcing Olive. (Surprisingly, Pat also found herself a murder defendant in the death of her daughter Marianne's

The longest-running characters and occasional adversaries on Another World *were Liz Matthews (played by Irene Dailey, left) and Rachel Frame (Victoria Wyndham), here both seen in a 1974 photo.*

fiancé Greg Bernard, who tried to rape Pat.) Sadly, there would be no reunion for Pat and John, as the latter died in 1979 from a fire Olive set to try to kill Alice, who had announced her engagement to Dan Shearer during his separation from Susan. Dan and Susan reconciled and left Bay City for a second time.

Alice had several suitors after Steven's death besides Dan. The first was Steve's scheming brother Willis Frame, who used Alice to gain control of Frame Enterprises while really seeing Carol Lamonte. Protecting her from his plot were lawyer Vic Hastings and Raymond Gordon, the son of Rachel and Mac's housekeeper Beatrice Gordon and ex-husband of aforementioned Olive Gordon. When Raymond and Alice got engaged, Beatrice shocked them by announcing she was the grandmother of Sally, Alice's newly adopted daughter, and temporarily kidnapped the child, fearing Ray unfit to be a father. She returned Sally and left town but proved to be right, as Ray's business and marriage to Alice crumbled. Alice got engaged to Dan Shearer after a final fling with Willis, who dated Angie Perrini after finishing with Carol. (Coincidentally, teenager Sally was in love with Angie's sister Joey, and her efforts to stop him from loving Eileen Simpson drove a wedge between her and her mom Alice.)

Willis was the first of a host of Frame relatives who showed up in the late 1970s, all either brothers or sisters to the supposedly late Steve. There was Emma Ordway, whose daughter Molly wed Michael Randolph while seeing Cliff Tanner on the side; Sharlene Watts, whose marriage to Russ Matthews went bust once her prior life as a hooker came to light; Vince Frame, who wed Angie Perrini after her love with Willis died; and Janice Frame, who caused Mac to divorce Rachel for her while really trying to get his money with the help of her boyfriend Mitch Blake. Mitch decided to mend his ways and help Rachel stop Janice from killing Mac, allowing Rachel and Mac to remarry.

The latter was not the first conflict faced by Rachel and Mac in the late 1970s. Iris tried to prevent Rachel from having a child by Mac. Then Iris hired the rather eerie Sven Peterson as the duo's new butler. Sven went off on his own tangent; he drugged Mac and Sven's daughter Regine and put them in a bed, thereby convincing them that they had had sex. Regine's baby actually had been sired by Cliff Tanner, a fact uncovered after Sven was captured for dismembering Mac's chauffeur Rocky Olsen, who found out about the plot. Rachel and Mac then got together and finally had a child named Amanda while trying to deal with the restless nature of Rachel's now grown child Jamie. Jamie had a wife named Blaine Ewing, whom Rachel disapproved of, and Rachel encouraged Blaine's ex-boyfriend Buzz Winslow to try and win back his old flame's affections. Rifts like this between mother and son cropped up frequently into the 1980s.

Other members of Rachel and Mac's family had similarly rocky relationships. Ada became a widow after Gil McGowan died, then made Charlie Hobson her fourth husband. Charlie was Clarice Hobson's father, and she wed policeman Larry Ewing, Blaine's brother, after a failed union with Burt

McGowan, the late Gil's son. Mac's daughter Iris stewed over the fact that her teenage son Dennis was having a tryst with Countess Elena de Poulignac, who earlier had been in a love triangle with Russ Matthews and Gwen Parrish. Then Iris was mortified to learn she was adopted, which caused her to separate from husband Brian Bancroft as she searched for her natural mother. Iris found her in the person of somewhat earthy New York clothes designer Sylvie Kosloff, who relocated to Bay City along with her partner Kirk Laverty. Kirk and Iris had a fling until his lawyer Jeff Stone murdered her, and she went back to Brian for a time.

In 1979, as *Another World*'s top ratings began to falter, the show became the first soap to stretch to 90 minutes daily in an attempt to revive NBC's anemic daytime performance. The show's personnel prepared five months for the event and devised a system whereby there were separate casts for morning and afternoon sessions of shooting. The show also added eight new characters and increased the main plots from three to five. To those doubting the viability of the effort, Pete Lemay told *TV Guide*, "I always say, it's not more difficult than doing an hour, which is much easier than 30 minutes."

Lemay ended up eating his words, as he found the constrictions and time pressures of the new format untenable, like having to allow Douglass Watson (Mac), Victoria Wyndham (Rachel), and Beverlee McKinsey (Iris) to work only three days each week per their contracts. He left the show shortly after the change to write his highly opinionated history of his work in the 1981 book *Eight Years in Another World*, but loved the series enough to return later as a consultant. His successors had just as much difficulty in handling the show, and after a year the series went back to an hour, with Iris leaving her husband Brian Bancroft to find romance with Alex Wheeler in *Texas* (q.v.).

Some new characters in the 90-minute show were nurse Kit Farrell, who pursued a rocky love with Joey Perrini while trying to conceal her identity as a rich woman; her brother Dr. Rick Halloway, who wed Marianne Randolph despite her interest in Jamie Frame; Jerry Grove, a lawyer who wed Jamie's ex-wife Blaine Ewing until the latter was blackmailed by the mob into divorcing him and marrying their leader Jordan Scott; and Cecile de Poulignac, Elena's niece (actually daughter, as it turned out), who fought with Pat Randolph for the love of Cory Publications editor Philip Lyons. Cecile was a central villainess the next few years, particularly when she wed Jamie Frame and got him hooked on drugs while two-timing him with ex-gigolo Sandy Alexander, the latter Mac's illegitimate son, whom she married and with whom she had a child.

Family relations were a big hassle for Mac and Rachel by the early 1980s, when the show shrank back to a more reasonable hour daily format. They broke up when Rachel, found guilty of the supposed murder of Mitch Blake thanks to the strong prosecutorial work of D.A. Zachary Colton, had to admit that she was pregnant from her fling with Mitch. Colton later was found guilty of murdering Jordan Scott. Rachel escaped from prison to look for Mitch, whom she found alive with amnesia, then gave birth to their son Matthew. Mac in the meantime won custody of Amanda, his daughter with Rachel.

Meanwhile, the Matthews clan nearly vanished from the show, with only Aunt Liz and Alice surviving. Russ Matthews left town after his wife Tracy De Witt was knocked off accidentally by her manager Jason Dunlap and his cohort Ilsa Fredericks in an explosion meant for Russ. In 1982 his father Jim died of a heart attack out of town (actor Hugh Marlowe had in fact passed away that year). And Jim's daughter Pat left town and her fiancé Brian Bancroft when she learned Jamie had written a *roman à clef* that included her troubles in its narrative. When Beverly Penberthy, the actress playing Pat, was fired from the show in January 1982, she summed up its deficiencies astutely for *TV Guide:* "You used to have characters that people believed in and were very familiar with—who became their friends. Now I see very short episodes with very young people who quickly fade away. And getting more people into bed or beaten up seems to be [the producers'] only idea of how to get ratings up. Older viewers are so unhappy, they come up to me and sob."

The changes did not help ratings either, so several well-intentioned approaches took place in 1982–83, though their execution often came up short. The old Steven-Rachel-Alice triangle reactivated when Steven was found alive with amnesia after his helicopter accident. Steven's reappearance meant a bitter breakup between Mitch and Rachel, and a dissolution of the engagement between Mac and Alice as the latter went back to trying to win Steve. But the updated version of the triangle had new actors playing Steven and Alice, who failed to supply the resonance of the old days, and when Steven died for real in a car accident after confessing he loved Rachel the most, probably the most truly tragic ramification was that Alice left the show, which meant that the Matthews family basically was gone. Rachel, blinded temporarily in the crash, was won over again by Mac, and had a double wedding with Mac's son Sandy and Blaine Ewing after Sandy left Cecile. By 1986 Sandy and Blaine had left town.

Another nice idea with meager results was the concious effort to integrate Bay City through the Hardings, featuring Vietnam veteran Ed Harding and his sister Quinn, who was fond of Lt. Bob Morgan until his death. In 1983 Quinn dated Dr. Abel Marsh, who was gun-shy of marriage, and then D.A. Adam Banks. But the black character who made the most impact could be considered a stereotypical one, except that Lily Mason the hooker was played with such verve by Jackee Harry that the actress later had an Emmy Award–winning career in nighttime sitcoms.

As with other soaps of the time, the other defining trend of the early 1980s on *Another World* involved youth stories. Alice's daughter Sally wed Clarice Hobson's brother Denny Hobson, who was a murderer. Sandy's ex, Cecile, hired Blaine Ewing's old boyfriend Buzz Winslow and his sister Alma Rudder to woo Blaine and let Cecile get Sandy back, but Buzz went nuts and died while kidnapping Blaine, and Alma later was murdered while trying to blackmail Cecile over her

new lover Cass Winthrop. Cass also was seeing novelist Felicia Gallant at the time, and the two flamboyant characters became a mainstay on the show over the next decade. Incidentally, in 1984 a book supposedly written by Felicia was released into stores by Harlequin Enterprises (actress Linda Dano said she really was involved in the writing of it).

Steve Frame brought his daughter Diana Frame into the scene, and she romanced Pete Shea. Steve's other child Jamie became a busy boy, having flings with Marianne Randolph, who left him for her husband Rick Halloway after the publication of Jamie's novel on Bay City upset her; Susan Shearer, who returned to her estranged husband Dan; Julia Shearer, Susan's daughter; and attorney Stacey Winthrop.

The youthful stories remained strong into 1985 when Sally and handsome Catlin Ewing, after two postponements, finally married, and a depressed Nancy McGowan got hooked on the drug Ecstasy while Larry Ewing attempted to find the pushers at the Plains Motel nightclub. Weirdest of all that year, Donna Love found out she gave birth to two daughters and not one, as the second occurred when she was sedated during labor! The brightest addition to the show turned out to be the arrival of a suave but driven newcomer, as Terrence Rafferty noted in *Film Comment* magazine.

"For a few months, the character of Carl Hutchins seemed to transform *Another World* into something resembling a Victorian novel, in which every scheme and dark secret is the trace of a past catastrophe: in this case, the suicide of Hutchins's father years before in England, an act precipitated by Mac Cory's takeover of the Hutchins family business," wrote Rafferty. "Carl's obsession, revealed in flashbacks and dream sequences, was to right the old accounts by ruining Mac's business and destroying his family." Hutchins did so with increasingly treacherous schemes culminating in a shootout which wounded Rachel and left her with temporary amnesia.

As engrossing as that was, Rafferty noted, after the denouement "the show seemed to unravel, the remaining characters left hanging by little dangling threads of story." Mac and Rachel went to being listening boards for other characters, and characters like ex-hooker Lily Mason and punk debutante Dee did little of note before disappearing. The show tried such trendy additions as a teenage diner hangout called Smiley's and a beauty shop called Le Soleil, plus bizarre adventures that did little to further the show. Among the latter were lovers Nancy McGowan and Chris Chapin facing danger in Africa and cliffs in Monument Valley, and Hutchins returning from prison "on furlough" not to terrorize the Corys as before but rather to unearth a collection of ancient Egyptian art stowed under Le Soleil.

On February 14, 1986, Felicia married fisherman Zane Lindquist in a rented $12,000 Chantilly-lace gown, with Liberace (in his last TV acting appearance) playing the piano. That same year, Chris Chapin served as a guinea pig for an experimental antidote to a mysterious poison dust which killed two people and started to afflict Mac and Rachel. (Carl Hutchins led Chris Chapin and his girlfriend to the dust, which was contained in an Egyptian treasure hidden in Arizona.)

And Mac's nephew Neal Cory was involved both with Victoria Love and a foreign extremist who was terrorizing the town. Offstage, Tom Eplin and Ellen Wheeler wed in real life.

The most showy event of 1986, however, had to be the trial of Brittany Love for the murder of her husband Peter after months of arguments, where viewers decided whether she would be innocent or guilty. Also that year, Crystal Gayle appeared as herself in March at the new nightclub Tops to sing "You Take Me Away to Another World," which lasted nearly a decade as the show's theme song.

In 1987 Nicole Love wed Cass after wife Kathleen died (Nicole also was upset that Barbara Van Arkdale had stolen her designs). Cass had returned after a seven-month "extended world honeymoon" without Kathleen. Amanda Cory returned from boarding school as an adult fighting for a piece of the family's publishing business, and the "Sin Stalker" killed at least five people before being pursued by psychic Lisa Grady. Also, Donna Love and Michael Hudson tracked down Michael's long-lost brother John Hudson.

In 1988 another Cory Publishing takeover threat occurred along with a love triangle between Jamie, Victoria Love, and Lisa. A pregnant Amanda Cory wed blue-collar guy Sam Fowler. Also, AIDS patient Dawn Rollo went to Italy to die.

The show continued to slog along in 1989, when the main highlights among generally tiresome activities, such as the machinations of an art theft ring, were the arrival of Lucas, who began an intense romance with Felicia until he died in 1992, and a week of shows celebrating the soap's 25th anniversary where Steven Frame was seen in a dream sequence by Rachel. Sadly, actor Douglass Watson died around the time these shows aired on May 1, 1989, and his character Mac was said to have died too, making Rachel a widow. In 1995 she remarried once more, this time to a reformed Carl Hutchins.

Not long after Mac's death, in 1993, Ada died too (actress Constance Ford made her last appearance as the character three months before her own death in 1992). That same year, Felicia Gallant became an alcoholic and then had an affair with her black publisher Marshall Lincoln Kramer III. Also, Frankie wed Cass, and in a dream sequence Frankie revisited his ex-flames Kathleen (Julie Osburn), Nicole (Anne Howard), and Cecile (Nancy Frangione) on his honeymoon!

Among other story lines of the early 1990s, Jake was shot during an affair with Paulina in 1990, and twins Vicky and Marley thought the other one did it, and Dean Frame was a teen delinquent seen romancing several young women. In 1992 there was an attempted assassination of Sen. Grant Harrison, while Christy Carson arrived as a man-stealing murderess. Felicia was kidnapped by a nutty fan in 1994, and then she and Cass opened a bookstore named Wallingford's in honor of their old pal. Jake and Paulina, after splitting up when she went with boring Ian, got back together. And orderly Tomas Rivera had a fling with Maggie Cory.

In 1995 came the rather ludicrous Justine story: Justine, an old flame of Rachel's new husband Carl Hutchins, came to reclaim him by disguising herself as Rachel. Inanity continued in 1996 with pseudo-vampires attacking people,

and Jake donning drag (!). More normally, police Captain McNamara romanced nervous Lorna Devon, while Felicia decided to date her pal John Hudson.

But the show seemed as desperate as ever, especially as a town stalker graphically killed Frankie Winthrop in August, and intimations of black magic abounded. Clearly NBC had faith in the show, giving it another contract extension into 1998. But given its continual shortcomings in ratings and quality, one wonders how long the network's patience will last, or if the show will go to another world of canceled serials.

ANSWERS FOR AMERICANS
Public Affairs; B&W
March 7, 1954–June 27, 1954
ABC Sun. 1–1:30 p.m. (3/7/54–6/27/54)

Regulars: *Hardy Burt, Devin Garrity, Dr. Charles Hodges, Brig. General Frank Howley, John K. Norton*

Begun as a Mutual radio show on January 25, 1953, *Answers for Americans* came onto ABC Wednesdays at 8:30 p.m. from November 11, 1953–February 24, 1954 before moving to Sunday afternoons. A panel of four people, led by moderator Hardy Burt, debated a question about current interest or opinions. Most of the panelists were from universities.

•AQUAMAN
Cartoon; Color
September 14, 1968–September 7, 1969
CBS Sun. 9:30–10 a.m. (9/14/68–9/7/69)

Voices:

Aquaman/Others	*Marvin Miller*
Narrator	*Ted Knight*

Aquaman, "King of the Seven Seas," came to television after years as a comic book character with cartoons first seen in 1967–68 as segments of *Superman* (q.v.) before being repeated the following season in his own series, officially titled *The Adventures of Aquaman*. Able to live underwater, he communicated via brain waves, represented by circles from his head, with clams, sharks, and other sea creatures who helped him fight criminals. His own fighting style consisted mainly of throwing balls of water against baddies. And like a cowboy, he rode a seahorse named Storm. Occasionally seen was his wife Mera and son Aqualad, also known as Tadpole, who had a sea pony named Imp and a comical pet named Tusky.

•ARCHIES, THE
Cartoon; Color
September 14, 1968–February 4, 1989

CBS Sat. 10–10:30 a.m. (9/14/68–9/6/69)
CBS Sat. 11 a.m.–Noon (9/13/69–9/4/71)
CBS Sat. 10:30–11 a.m. (9/11/71–9/2/72)
CBS Sat. Noon–12:30 p.m. and Sun. 9–9:30 a.m. (9/9/72–9/2/73)
CBS Sat. Noon–12:30 p.m. (9/8/73–1/26/74)
CBS Sat. Noon–12:30 p.m. (9/7/74–1/11/75)

CBS Sun. 9–9:30 a.m. (1/18/75–9/5/76)
NBC Sat. 8:30–9:30 a.m. (9/10/77–11/19/77)
NBC Sat. 10–10:30 a.m. (11/26/77–1/28/78)
NBC Sat. 11:30 a.m.–Noon (9/12/87–9/3/88)
NBC Sat. 12:30–1 p.m. (10/29/88–2/4/89)

Voices (1968–78):

Archie Andrews/Mr. Weatherbee	Dallas McKennon
Betty Cooper/Veronica Lodge/Big	
Ethel/Jughead Jones/Big	
Moose/Hot Dog	Howard Morris
Reggie Mantle	John Erwin
Sabrina the Teenage Witch	
(1969–70)	Jane Webb

Musical supervisor (1968–78): *Don Kirschner*

Voices (1987–88):

Amani	Karen Burthwright
Archie Andrews	J. Michael Roncetti
Betty Cooper	Lisa Coristine
Big Ethel	Jazzmin Lausanne
Big Moose	Victor E. Erdos
Coach	Greg Swanson
Eugene	Colin Waterman
Jughead Jones	Michael Fantini
Miss Grundy	Linda Sorenson
Mr. Weatherbee	Marvin Goldhar
Reggie Mantle	Sunny Besen Thrasher
Veronica Lodge	Alyson Court

The number one cartoon of 1968–69 by a huge margin, *The Archies* had success beyond its ratings: it revived interest in the Archie character, which had been seen in comic books since 1941; it showed the appeal of silly jokes, teenagers, and music to the Saturday morning audience, a mix which would be much copied in the 1970s; and it even generated an international single.

The show's format changed considerably over the years, but most incarnations featured amiable Archie Andrews as nominal leader of a clique in fictional Riverdale High, where Mr. Weatherbee was the principal. His cohorts were vain, rich Veronica, who had an exaggerated Southern drawl in the cartoon; egocentric Reggie, who often fought Archie for the attention of Veronica; down-to-earth blonde Betty, whom Archie should have been pursuing; Jughead, the skinny yet always hungry sidekick of Archie's; and Hot Dog, the group mutt. They rode around in Archie's jalopy and hung out at Pop's Chok'lit Shoppe.

In the first two seasons (titled officially *The Archie Show* in 1968–69 and then *The Archie Comedy Hour* in 1969–70), interspersed between brief sketches involving the gang were musical numbers with flashy color backgrounds having the characters show off the "Dance of the Week" and sing new songs. (A character introduced here got her own show in 1970; see *Sabrina, the Teenage Witch.)* More significantly, for the first time, there was a concerted effort to make some of the show's tunes hits on *Billboard's* Hot 100 singles chart. While the first try, "Bang-Shang-a-Lang," did moderately

well, hitting #22, the real monster was "Sugar Sugar," a #1 hit in 1969 in America and many other countries. That song stands as perhaps the most successful example of "bubblegum music," a form of rock 'n' roll designed to appeal to prepubescents with its juvenile lyrics and catchy music. Singing on these singles as Archie was Ron Dante.

The singing career of the Archies (as the musical group was called) had vanished by the 1970–71 season, but the show continued anew with *Archie's Funhouse,* which had Archie and company supposedly performing a TV variety show complete with shots of a live cheering juvenile audience, "Lightning Bolt" blackouts, and jokes told as characters ran on top of a huge spinning record. Then came *Archie's TV Funnies* from 1971–73, where the gang introduced comic strip characters in supposed cartoons airing on a TV station they ran. Included in that mix were "Nancy," "Dick Tracy," "The Katzenjammer Kids," "Broom Hilda," "Moon Mullins," "Smokey Stover," and others, all voiced by the show's cast members. That was followed by *Everything's Archie* in 1973–74, which repeated the first two seasons of shows.

But the series took an unexpected plunge in popularity with *The U.S. of Archie* in 1974. Designed as a mingling of history with entertainment, it found the gang going back in time in such plots as working with Harriet Tubman on the Underground Railroad for slaves during the 1800s. Such serious concerns were off-kilter for the normally light series, and it disappeared from Saturday mornings in 1975. Its last season on CBS consisted of *U.S. of Archie* repeats. NBC tried repeats of earlier shows in 1977 under the title *The Bang-Shang Lalapalooza Show,* but it flopped too.

Nearly a decade later, NBC gave the property another try under the title *The New Archies.* The characters became prepubescents in this installment, with a few modifications made for the properties to accommodate the 1980s. Some were substantial (Eugene the egghead and Amani the nice girl finally integrated previously lily white Riverside), others were subtle (Pop's Chok'lit Shoppe was now Pop's Video Cafe). Even Hot Dog became an English terrier. The emphasis remained on jokes and hijinks, but without the music and peppy atmosphere, this edition looked decidedly inferior to the earlier cartoon. There were two stories used in each show, and the 1988–89 season consisted of repeats.

Besides the comic book and cartoons, there was a radio sitcom titled *Archie Andrews* on Mutual from 1943–44 and NBC from 1946–53. Additionally, ABC commissioned unsold sitcom pilots for the show in 1962 and 1976, and there was a lousy live-action NBC TV movie in 1990 titled *Archie: To Riverdale and Back Again,* starring Christopher Rich as Archie, in which the characters appeared in middle age.

•ARK II
Drama; Color
September 11, 1976–August 25, 1979
CBS Sat. 11–11:30 a.m. (9/11/76–10/30/76)
CBS Sat. 11:30 a.m.–Noon (11/6/76–2/5/77)

CBS Sat. 12:30–1 p.m. (2/12/77–8/27/77)
CBS Sun. 9:30–10 a.m. (9/11/77–11/13/77)
CBS Sat. 1–1:30 a.m. (9/16/78–8/25/79)

Cast:

Jonah	Terry Lester
Ruth	Jean Marie Hon
Samuel	Jose Flores

Set in the year 2476, *Ark II* concerned three humans who rode in a white, camper-like Land Rover with a lab contained inside it known as Ark II and their efforts to restore civilization to Earth following nuclear war. Jonah was the bearded blond hero who had a jet rocket to propel him into some areas, Ruth was the scientific expert, and Samuel was an assistant. Adam was a trained chimp who accompanied them. Typical shows combined sci-fi adventure with environmental educational information, such as the episode where Jim Backus played a businessman who unknowingly threatened to poison a village with contaminated materials. The episodes seen from 1978–79 were repeats.

ARLENE DAHL'S BEAUTY SPOT
Informational; Color
March 28, 1966–June 24, 1966

ABC Mon.–Fri. 4:25–4:30 p.m. (3/28/66–6/24/66)

Hostess: *Arlene Dahl*

Glamorous movie star redhead Arlene Dahl dispensed grooming tips on this short daily following *Never Too Young*. It aired from Hollywood on tape with Clairol as the sponsor.

ARLENE FRANCIS SHOW, THE
Variety; B&W
August 12, 1957–February 21, 1958

NBC Mon.–Fri. 10–10:30 a.m. (8/12/57–2/21/58)

Regulars: *Arlene Francis, Hugh Downs, the Foursome, the Norman Paris Trio*

Imagine a less ambitious version of *Home* and the result probably would have been *The Arlene Francis Show*. *Home* veteran Francis and her assistant Hugh Downs presided over this standard 1950s variety show which took over their old show's time slot. It had guest interviews, a word game called "Cross My Heart" in which the studio audience participated, and music from the Norman Paris Trio and the Foursome, the latter a male singing quartet. After six months on air, Francis asked NBC to take this show off the air, no doubt realizing that this was an unexceptional effort, in contrast to *Home*, which strove for the best entertainment and information daytime television could offer.

ARMED FORCES HOUR, THE
Documentary; B&W
October 30, 1949–June 11, 1950

NBC Sun. 5–5:30 p.m. (10/30/49–6/11/50)

Announcers: *Lt. Cass Bielski, USAF, Ensign Jack Siegal, USN*

Yes, *The Armed Forces Hour* actually ran half an hour. It was the first TV series from the U.S. Department of Defense. Based in Washington, D.C., the 39 episodes used some of the department's 500 million feet of film to illustrate how unified the efforts of the Army, Navy, Air Force, and Marines were to protect the country and to promote recruiting in all branches. It aired live with announcers, graphics, and guest appearances on the premiere by the assistant secretaries of the Army, Navy, and Air Force. Despite the show's professed intentions, a *Billboard* reviewer wrote in regard to the secretaries' speeches, "It sounded as though the boys were carrying their competitive feud right onto the program." Presumably such differences were downplayed during the rest of the run. The series was revived on DuMont Sundays from 8–9 p.m. (now a real hour) from February 4–May 6, 1951.

AROUND THE WORLD IN 80 DAYS
Cartoon; Color
September 9, 1972–September 1, 1973

NBC Sat. Noon–12:30 p.m. (9/9/72–9/1/73)

Voices:

Phineas Fogg	Alistair Duncan
Jean Passepartout	Ross Higgins
Mr. Fix	Max Obinstein

The first Australian-produced cartoon seen on American network TV was based on the classic 19th-century novel by Frenchman Jules Verne about an ambitious Briton. To prove himself worthy of the hand of Lord Maze's niece Belinda in marriage, Phineas Fogg announced that he would circumnavigate the globe within 12 weeks. Intrigued by the notion of doing so given the conditions of the time (the story was set in 1872), Maze upped the ante to betting 20,000 pounds, but did not tell Fogg that he had hired Mr. Fix to spoil his efforts. For 16 shows Fogg and his partner Jean Passepartout crossed many nations by boat, balloon, and other means of transportation to meet their goal while coping with Fix's machinations.

A knockoff of the concept, called "Around the World in 79 Days," had aired a year earlier Sunday mornings on ABC as part of *Cattanooga Cats* (q.v.). Viewers in 1972 also could see another animated version in a syndicated special airing as part of the *Festival of Family Classics* series. A more ambitious TV adaptation of the novel aired as a nighttime miniseries on NBC from April 16–18, 1989.

•ART LINKLETTER'S HOUSE PARTY
Variety; B&W and Color
September 1, 1952–September 25, 1970

CBS Mon.–Fri. 2:45–3:15 p.m. (9/1/52–1/30/53)
CBS Mon.–Fri. 2:30–3 p.m. (2/1/53–9/6/68)
CBS Mon.–Fri. 4–4:25 p.m. (9/9/68–2/21/69)
CBS Mon.–Fri. 4–4:30 p.m. (2/24/69–9/5/69)
NBC Mon.–Fri. 1:30–2 p.m. (12/29/69–9/25/70)

Host: *Art Linkletter*

Co-Hosts: *Diane Linkletter (1969), Jack Linkletter (1969–70)*

Art Linkletter's House Party began as a CBS radio program on January 15, 1945 and ran there until October 13, 1967, with the last few years using a tape of the TV audio portion aired daily from 3:15–3:40 p.m. When it arrived on television, it became the first CBS daily series produced live from Hollywood, where it soon became a fixture at the 2:30 p.m. daily time slot. In 1955 it won the very first Emmy for Best Daytime Program. Thanks mainly to its long broadcasting run, Art Linkletter, who developed and split ownership of the show with producer John Guedel, became a millionaire.

Each show usually opened with a few jokes by Art, then a simple quiz for a woman in his audience. Then Art interviewed a guest expert who also answered some questions from his audience (those asking questions got gifts). Among the experts who appeared occasionally were actor Adolphe Menjou as permanent "fashion authority" in 1957; Dr. James A. Peterson, marriage counselor at the University of South Carolina and host of *For Better or Worse*, with bridal advice in 1959; and Hollywood fashion designer Edith Head.

But the highlight of the show for most viewers was the daily 10-minute segment where Linkletter interviewed four children. The children generally ranged in age from 5 to 10, and their spontaneous comments were priceless. One time a 5-year-old girl, asked if she had any siblings, replied, "No, I'm single." And following Linkletter's perpetual question to the group if they knew what a pedigree is, one boy said, "I think she lost her pedigree last week." Some of the kids who said the "darndest things" grew up to be celebrated adults, such as 4-year-old Mark Harmon, who appeared in 1955.

By 1964 regular features included Bonnie Prudden's exercise tips for women, bloopers from CBS series, and interviews with former movie stars. On the show's 20th anniversary in broadcasting on January 22, 1965, Ralph Edwards did a *This Is Your Life* tribute on Linkletter. The following year, the series added a feature on unclaimed estates which netted heirs a total of more than $1 million before the program's cancellation.

In the fall of 1968, with its ratings sinking against *The Doctors* on NBC, CBS moved the show to 4 p.m. and retitled it *The Art Linkletter Show*. Linkletter's daughter Diane joined him as a regular, and the format became a more standard talk show. This effort caused the ratings to drop further, and the show went off the network in 1969 after an impressive 17-year run. Sadly, on one of the last shows Art and Diane did a performance of their narrative record "We Love You, Call Collect," about parents' plea to their troubled daughter. Shortly thereafter—on October 4, 1969—Diane leapt to her death under the influence of drugs, an act which led Art to become a strong antidrug crusader.

Near the start of 1970, NBC revived the property under the name its nighttime NBC version from 1950–52 used, *Life with Linkletter*, with Art's son Jack co-hosting the talk show. It fared poorly against *As the World Turns* and *Let's Make a Deal* and went off within a year. Both Linkletters appeared only occasionally on television after this show.

Art Linkletter's House Party *had a special guest in 1968 when the host (left) taped an interview with President-elect Richard M. Nixon for the program.*

In 1990 *House Party*, with Steve Doocy serving as host, received a brief revival in syndication as a daily hour series.

•ARTHUR GODFREY TIME

Variety; B&W
January 7, 1952–April 24, 1959

CBS Mon.–Thu. Various times and lengths between 10 and 11:30 a.m. (1/7/52–7/2/54)
CBS Mon.–Thu. 10:30–11:30 a.m. (7/5/54–3/28/58)
CBS Mon.–Fri. 11–11:30 a.m. (3/31/58–1/2/59)
CBS Mon.–Fri. 10:30–11 a.m. (1/5/59–4/24/59)

Regulars: *Arthur Godfrey, Tony Marvin, Janette Davis (1952–57), the McGuire Sisters (1952–57), Frank Parker (1952–56), Haleloke (1952–55), Marion Marlowe (1952–55), the Mariners (1952–55), LuAnn Simms (1952–55), Julius LaRosa (1952–53), the Chordettes (1952–53), Carmel Quinn (1954–57), Pat Boone (1955–57), the Toppers (1955–57), Anita Bryant (1958 at least), Johnny Nash (1958 at least), Louise O'Brien (1958 at least), Alan Copeland (1958 at least), Ilene Woods (1958 at least), the Honeydreamers (1958 at least), the Archie Bleyer Orchestra (1952–54), the Bert Farber Orchestra (1955–58 at least), the Will Roland Orchestra (1955–57 at least), the Dick Hyman Orchestra (1959 at least)*

Personable Arthur Godfrey, "the old redhead," debuted his morning show as a CBS radio attraction on April 30, 1945. It soon became a top attraction for the network, and when Godfrey brought his nighttime series onto television in the late 1940s with great success, CBS was increasingly interested in adding his morning program whenever a schedule for it could be developed. A measure of how popular Godfrey was came in a report by *Variety* in June 1950 stating that the performer generated sales of $10.5 million annually for CBS, about a sixth of the network's total annual revenue.

A special 20-minute broadcast featuring him and singer Janette Davis on CBS's color system aired November 20, 1950, and a kinescope of his 90-minute morning extravaganza was made on February 22, 1951. A year later, he finally simulcast his morning radio show on television. Joining him were Davis, and a horde of little-known (till they joined Godfrey) singers like Julius LaRosa, Frank Parker, and Marian Marlowe, plus two fine female vocal groups, the Chordettes quartet and the McGuire Sisters trio, and the racially integrated male singing and dancing quartet the Mariners. Godfrey typically delivered some light patter and commercials between introducing his regulars and their performances, and maybe strummed his ukelele or sang a little if he felt like it. The atmosphere was one of easygoing entertainment, although "easygoing" was hardly the right adjective for the way Godfrey ran his show when it was off the air.

Godfrey's daytime run began as a daily 15-minute segment first, then went anywhere from 30 up to 75 minutes a day in the first two years before settling down to an hour each day by 1954. His Friday radio show did not appear on television for most of its run because Godfrey broadcast that day from his farm in Leesburg, Virginia while the other acts performed from New York City. During its last year Godfrey agreed to do the TV show daily, but only for a half hour each time.

Such unusual scheduling was allowed because Godfrey was seen by CBS as a special talent. By 1953, for example, Godfrey generated an estimated $15 million in billings on radio and television, and CBS considered expanding his morning show to Saturdays. But one Monday show on October 19 that year dramatically reduced his drawing power and appeal and would haunt Godfrey for the rest of his broadcasting career.

Godfrey brought Julius LaRosa on to do a number, then ended it by telling the audience, "That, folks, was Julie's swan song." Godfrey's unceremonious and humiliating firing of LaRosa was made to look even worse by Godfrey saying he did it because the increasingly popular LaRosa lacked "humility," while many believed that Godfrey was the one who was acting conceited. This belief was reinforced when Godfrey started firing more acts on the show, beginning with Archie Bleyer, whose running of his own recording company (Cadence) and dating Chordette member Janet Ertel apparently upset Godfrey, and snowballed over the next two years. Among the disappearing acts, the Chordettes said they felt their days were numbered when the similar McGuire Sisters came on board (reportedly Godfrey did not fire them directly but had a CBS executive tell them, "We don't need you anymore"), while Haleloke, the Mariners, and Marion Marlowe, all dropped on the same Friday in April 1955, had no idea why they were dismissed.

Godfrey explained his rationale for the banishments in 1955 when he told *TV Guide*, "In choosing folks, I look for the ones who will grow on people—and get rid of them when they stop growing on people." He defended his firing of LaRosa by saying, "When a person reaches the LaRosa stage, there is no place for him on our stage anymore. It wouldn't be fair to tie him down. There are two ways you can do this thing—either stay with us and take advantage of chances to do outside work, or go on your own." But he became increasingly testy about having to defend his actions,

for by the end of 1955, asked by *Billboard* about his dismissal of LuAnn Simms, he growled, "Do I have to give reasons? I'm running this job and if I can't fire and hire people to suit myself, I'm going to quit myself."

If it was sympathy Godfrey was expecting in response to these and similar statements, he surely did not get it. What might have kept his show going was the addition of some fairly popular new talent, including Pat Boone, and the enduring appeal of the Chordettes. Significantly, both of these acts were ones which left Godfrey on their own to pursue highly successful independent careers. Still, ratings began to lower from their early 1950s highs due to competition from *The Price Is Right* on NBC starting in 1957, and the rate of change accelerated.

By 1958 virtually all of Godfrey's "Friends" had been fired or resigned, and Godfrey used a rotating flow of some 15 to 20 young performers on his show, with singers Anita Bryant, Alan Copeland, Johnny Nash, and Louise O'Brien the most prominent among them. He still had some appeal left in him, like the well-received week of talks with Jackie Gleason (November 3–7, 1958) that drew raves for its comedy and insight. But mostly the old fire was gone, especially with many of the shows in 1957–58 being on tape without a studio audience. He left in 1959 officially to undergo lung surgery.

After his successful recovery, Godfrey announced he would be returning to TV that same year, but did only three nighttime specials. In 1962 it was reported he was ready to have a daytime TV series soon, but for whatever reason it did not happen. However, *Arthur Godfrey Time* did continue on radio until April 30, 1972, ending exactly 27 years on CBS.

•AS THE WORLD TURNS
Soap Opera; B&W and Color
April 2, 1956–

CBS Mon.–Fri. 1:30–2 p.m. (4/2/56–11/28/75)
CBS Mon.–Fri. 1:30–2:30 p.m. (12/1/75–2/1/80)
CBS Mon.–Fri. 2–3 p.m. (2/4/80–6/5/81)
CBS Mon.–Fri. 1:30–2:30 p.m. (6/8/81–3/20/87)
CBS Mon.–Fri. 2–3 p.m. (3/23/87–)

Cast:

Nancy Hughes	Helen Wagner
Chris Hughes (1956–86)	Don MacLaughlin
Bob Hughes (1956–58)	Bobby Alford
Bob Hughes (1958–60)	Ronnie Welch
Bob Hughes (1960–)	Don Hastings
Penny Hughes (1956–68, 1985, 1986–87, 1993)	Rosemary Prinz
Penny Hughes (1971)	Phoebe Dorin
Donald Hughes (1956)	Hal Studer
Donald Hughes (1956–62)	Richard Holland
Donald Hughes (1962)	James Noble
Donald Hughes (1966–72)	Peter Brandon
Donald Hughes (1977–78)	Martin West
Donald Hughes (1978–81, 1985, 1986, 1993)	Conard Fowkes

Grandpa Hughes (1956)	William Lee	Dr. Al Suker (1964–66)	Michael Ingram
Grandpa Hughes (1956–76)	Santos Ortega	Sylvia Hill (1964–66)	Millette Alexander
Aunt Edith Hughes (1956–60,		Dr. Jerry Stevens (1964–65)	Roy Poole
1963)	Ruth Warrick	Sara Fuller (1965–67)	Gloria DeHaven
Ellen Lowell (1956–60)	Wendy Drew	Dr. Susan Burke (1966–67)	Connie Scott
Ellen Lowell (1960–95)	Pat Bruder	Dr. Susan Burke (1967)	Diana Walker
Judge James Lowell (1956–79)	William Johnstone	Dr. Susan Burke (1967–68)	Jada Rowland
Claire Lowell (1956–59)	Anne Burr	Dr. Susan Burke (1968)	Leslie Perkins
Claire Lowell (1960)	Gertrude Warner	Dr. Susan Burke (1968–73,	
Claire Lowell (1960–64)	Nancy Wickwire	1974–79, 1986–)	Marie Masters
Claire Lowell (1964–65)	Joan Allison	Dr. Susan Burke (1978,	
Claire Lowell (1965–71)	Barbara Berjer	temporary replacement)	Judith Barcroft
Dr. Doug Cassen (1956–67)	Nat Polen	Dick Martin (1966)	Joe Maross
Jeff Baker (1956–62)	Mark Rydell	Dick Martin (1966–70,	
Jim Lowell (1956–57)	Les Damon	1975–78)	Edward Kemmer
Janice Turner (1956–57)	Joyce Van Patten	Sandy McGuire (1966–71)	Dagne Crane
Janice Turner (1962)	Virginia Dwyer	Sandy McGuire (1968,	
Dr. Tim Cole (1958)	William Redfield	temporary replacement)	Jill Andre
Louise Cole (1958)	Mary K. Wells	Sandy McGuire (1975)	Ronnie Carrol
Lisa Miller (1960–65, 1967–83,		Sandy McGuire (1975–79)	Barbara Rucker
1984–)	Eileen Fulton	Carl Wilson (1966–71)	Martin Rudy
Lisa Miller (1964, temporary		Martha Wilson (1966–70)	Anna Minot
replacement)	Pamela King	Amanda Holmes (1966–70)	Deborah Steinberg
Lisa Miller (1983–84)	Betsy von Furstenberg	Soloman	
Alma Miller (1963–77)	Ethel Remey	Dr. Michael Shea (1966–68)	Jay Lanin
Alma Miller (1978)	Dorothy Blackburn	Dr. Michael Shea (1968–70)	Roy Shuman
Dr. David Stewart (1960–90)	Henderson Forsythe	John Eldridge (1966)/Eduardo	
Betty Stewart (1960–62)	Patricia Benoit	Grimaldi (1993–95)	Nicolas Coster
Dan Stewart (1962–63)	Paul O'Keefe	John Eldridge (1991–92)	Michael Levin
Dan Stewart (1964)	Doug Chapin	Roy McGuire (1966–68)/Grant	
Dan Stewart (1966)	Jeffrey Rowland	Colman (1973–74)	Konrad Matthaei
Dan Stewart (1966–73,		Otto Martin (1966–68)	Allen Nourse
1976–79)	John Colenback	Ann Holmes (1966–67)	Augusta Dabney
Dan Stewart (1974–76)	John Reilly	Bill Holmes (1966–67)	William Prince
Dr. Paul Stewart (1962–64)	Alan Howard	Joan Rogers (1966–67)/Greta	
Dr. Paul Stewart (1964–66)	Edmund Gaynes	Aldrin (1983)	Joan Copeland
Dr. Paul Stewart (1966–68)	Steven Mines	Ted Rogers (1966–67)	Clifford Carpenter
Dr. Paul Stewart (1968–69)	Michael Hawkins	Julia Burke (1968–75)	Fran Carlon
Dr. Paul Stewart (1969–70)	Marco St. John	Nurse Karen Adams (1968–70)	Doe Lang
Dr. Paul Stewart (1970–72)	Dean Santoro	Dr. John Dixon (1969–)	Larry Bryggman
Dr. Neil Wade (1962–67)	Michael Lipton	Carol Ann "Annie" Stewart	
Alice Whipple (1962)	Jean McClintock	(1969–70)/Dawn "Dee"	
Alice Whipple (1966)	Leslie Charleson	Stewart (1972–73)	Jean Mazza
Franny Brennan, Ellen's maid		Carol Ann "Annie" Stewart	
(1963–65)	Toni Darnay	(1970–71)	Barbara Jean Ehrhardt
Mary Mitchell (1963–65)	Joan Anderson	Carol Ann "Annie" Stewart	
Tom Hughes (1964–66)	Frankie Michaels	(1972–73)	Ariane Munker
Tom Hughes (1966–67)	Richard Thomas	Carol Ann "Annie" Stewart	
Tom Hughes (1967–68)	Paul O'Keefe	(1973–74)	Shelly Spurlock
Tom Hughes (1969–73)	Peter Galman	Carol Ann "Annie" Stewart	
Tom Hughes (1974–78)	C. David Colson	(1976–79)	Martina Deignan
Tom Hughes (1979–80)	Tom Tammi	Carol Ann "Annie" Stewart	
Tom Hughes (1981–84)	Justin Deas	(1980–82)	Julie Ridley
Tom Hughes (1984–87)	Gregg Marx	Carol Ann "Annie" Stewart (1982)	Randall Edwards
Tom Hughes (1987–)	Scott Holmes	Carol Ann "Annie" Stewart	
Judith Wade (1964–67)	Connie Lembcke	(1982–84)	Mary Lynn Blanks

Elizabeth Talbot (1969–72) Jane House
Elizabeth Talbot (1972–73) Judith McGilligan
Carol Deming (1970–81) Rita McLaughlin Walter
Meredith Halliday (1970–71) Nina Hart
Hank Barton (1970) Gary Sandy
Barbara Ryan (1971–72) Donna Wandrey
Barbara Ryan (1978–) Colleen Zenk Pinter
Dawn "Dee" Stewart (1971) Simone Schachter
Dawn "Dee" Stewart (1973)/Margo
   Montgomery (1993–94) Glynnis O'Connor
Dawn "Dee" Stewart (1976–78) Marcia McClain
Dawn "Dee" Stewart (1979–82) Jacqueline Schultz
Dawn "Dee" Stewart (1980) Heather Cunningham
Dawn "Dee" Stewart (1982–83,
   1986) Vicky Dawson
Jennifer Reynolds Ryan (1971–72) Geraldine Court
Jennifer Reynolds Ryan (1972–75) Gillian Spencer
Kim Reynolds (1972–) Kathryn Hays
Kim Reynolds (1975–76,
   temporary replacement) Patty McCormack
Betsy Stewart (1972–80) Suzanne Davidson
Betsy Stewart (1981–82) Lisa Denton
Betsy Stewart (1982–84) Meg Ryan
Betsy Stewart (1984–88) Lindsay Frost
Dr. Rick Ryan (1972–73,
   1986–87) Con Roche
Dr. Rick Ryan (1978) Gary Hudson
Dr. Bruce Baxter (1972) Steve Harmon
Dr. Bruce Baxter (1972–73) Ben Hayes
Grant Colman (1974–81, 1986,
   1988, 1995) James Douglas
Jay Stallings (1973–80) Dennis Cooney
Amy Lin Hughes (1973–74) Irene Yaah-Ling Sun
Amy Lin Hughes (1986–87) Una Kim
Joyce Colman (1974–81) Barbara Rodell
Mark Galloway (1974) Stephen Bolster
Mark Galloway (1974–75)/James
   Stenbeck (1980–83, 1986–87,
   1989, 1996) Anthony Herrera
Emmy "Emily" Stewart (1975–79) Jenny Harris
Emmy "Emily" Stewart (1986–87) Colleen McDermott
Emmy "Emily" Stewart (1987–90) Melanie Smith
Emmy "Emily" Stewart (1992–) Kelley Menighan
Frannie Hughes (1975–78) Maura Gilligan
Frannie Hughes (1980) Tracy O'Neil
Frannie Hughes (1983) Helene Udy
Frannie Hughes (1983–84) Terri VandenBosch
Frannie Hughes (1985–88)/
   Sabrina Hughes (1986–88) Julianne Moore
Frannie Hughes (1989–92) Mary Ellen Stuart
Sabrina Hughes (1990–92) Claire Beckman
Mary Ellison (1975–80) Kelly Wood
Natalie Bannon (1975–78) Judith Chapman
Natalie Bannon (1981) Janet Zarish
Valerie Reynolds Conway
   (1976–79) Judith McConnell

Marion Connelly (1976–78) Clarice Blackburn
Kevin Thompson (1976–78) Michael Nader
Kevin Thompson (1978) Max Brown
Pat Holland Dixon (1976–77) Melinda Peterson
Ralph Mitchell (1977–79) Keith Charles
Dr. Alex Keith (1977–79) John Cypher
Jane Spencer (1977–79) Georgann Johnson
Beau Spencer (1977–79) Wayne Hudgins
Dr. Jeff Ward (1978–84) Robert Lipton
Karen Peters (1978)/Carolyn
   Crawford (1990–91) Leslie Denniston
Ian McFarland (1979–80) Peter Simon
Lyla Montgomery (1980) Veleka Gray
Lyla Montgomery (1981–94) Anne Sward
Steve Andropoulos (1980–86) Frank Runyeon
Nick Andropoulos (1980–82) Michael Forest
Nels Anderson (1980–84) Einar Perry Scott
Brad Hollister (1980–81) Peter Brouwer
Eric Hollister (1980–81) Peter Reckell
Margo Montgomery (1981–83) Margaret Colin
Margo Montgomery (1983–90) Hillary Bailey Smith
Margo Montgomery (1990–93,
   1994–) Ellen Dolan
Cricket Montgomery (1981–83) Lisa Loring
Maggie Crawford (1981–85) Mary Linda Rapeleye
Karen Haines (1981–84) Kathy McNeil
Cynthia Haines (1981–82) Linda Dano
Miranda Marlowe (1981–82) Elaine Princi
Stan Holden (1981–82) W.T. Martin
Dr. Matt Butler (1981–82) Robin Thomas
Craig Montgomery (1982–87,
   1990–94) Scott Bryce
Ariel Aldrin (1982–85) Judith Blazer
Tucker Foster (1982–85) Eddie Earl Hatch
Gunnar St. Clair Stenbeck
   (1982–85) Hugo Napier
Whit McColl (1982–84) Robert Horton
Brian McColl (1982) Robert Burton
Brian McColl (1983–84) Frank Telfer
Brian McColl (1984–87) Mark Pinter
Ernie Ross (1982–83) Marshall Watson
Paul Stenbeck (1983–84) Danny Pintauro
Paul Stenbeck (1985–86) C.B. Barnes
Paul Stenbeck (1986) Damion Scheller
Paul Stenbeck (1986–91) Andrew Kavovit
Paul Stenbeck (1996–) John Howard
Dustin "Dusty" Donovan
   (1983–88) Brian Bloom
Jay Connors (1983–86) Breck Jamison
Frank Andropoulos (1983–85) Jacques Perreault
Marcy Thompson (1983–85) Marisa Tomei
Kirk McColl (1983–85) Christian J. LeBlanc
Diana McColl (1983–85) Kim Ulrich
Charmane McColl (1983–84) Lee Meredith
Lucinda Walsh (1984–) Elizabeth Hubbard
Lily Walsh (1984–85) Lucy Deakins

Character	Actor
Lily Walsh (1985–90, 1993–)	*Martha Byrne*
Lily Walsh (1990–92)	*Heather Rattray*
Lt. Dan McCloskey (1984–96)	*Dan Frazer*
Andy Dixon (1984–95)	*Scott DeFreitas*
Heather Dalton (1984–86)	*Tonya Pinkins*
Michael Christopher (1984–85)	*Harris Yulin*
Dorothy Connors (1984–85)	*Nancy Pinkerton*
Peggy Thompson (1984–85)	*Cheryl Gianni*
Beverly Taylor (1984–85)	*Wendy Edmead*
Dr. Russ Elliot (1984–85)/Carl Eldridge (1991–92)	*Richard Backus*
Cal Randolph (1984–85)	*Luke Reilly*
Detective Hal Munson (1985–)	*Benjamin Hendrickson*
Emma Snyder (1985–)	*Kathleen Widdoes*
Holden Snyder (1985–95)	*Jon Hensley*
Iva Snyder (1985–93)	*Lisa Brown*
Shannon O'Hara (1985–90, 1994–95)	*Margaret Reed*
Harriet Corbman (1985–91)	*Sloane Shelton*
Roy Franklin (1985–89)	*Count Stovall*
Sierra Esteban (1985–88)	*Finn Carter*
Kevin Gibson (1985–86)	*Steven Weber*
Douglas Cummings (1985–86)	*John Wesley Shipp*
Marsha Talbot (1985–86)	*Giulia Pagano*
Ken Wayne (1985–86)	*Jared Holmes*
Jerry Halpern (1985–86)	*Harry Spillman*
Duncan McKechnie (1986–95)	*Michael Swan*
Tonio Reyes (1986–91)	*Peter Boynton*
Dr. Casey Peretti (1986–90)	*Bill Shanks*
Meg Snyder (1986–89)	*Jennifer Ashe*
Seth Snyder (1986–88, 1991–94)	*Steve Bassett*
Earl Mitchell (1986–87)	*Farley Granger*
Beatrice McKechnie (1986–87)	*Ashley Crow*
Charles Pierson (1986–88)	*Ben George*
Monica Lawrence (1986–88)	*Julianne Lowry*
Monica Lawrence (1992)	*Juliet Pritner*
Nick Costello (1986–88)	*Rick Giolito*
Jessica Griffin (1987–95)	*Tamara Tunie*
Jessica Griffin (1995–)	*Joanna Rhinehart*
Rod Landry a.k.a. Josh Snyder (1987–89)	*William Fichtner*
Pamela Wagner (1987–89)	*Robin Morse*
Kathy Evans (1987–88)	*Catherine Kellner*
Kirk Anderson (1988–)	*Tom Wiggin*
Cal Stricklyn (1988–)	*Patrick Tovatt*
Caleb Snyder (1988–92)	*Michael David Morrison*
Caleb Snyder (1992–95)	*Graham Winton*
Ellie Snyder (1988–92)	*Renee Props*
Angel Lange (1988–94)	*Alice Haining*
Henry Lange (1988–91)	*James Rebhorn*
Barclay Lange (1988–91)	*John Ottavino*
Lien Hughes (1988–91)	*Ming-Na Wen*
Hank Elliot (1988–89)	*Brian Starcher*
Beau Farrell (1988–89)	*Neil Maffin*
Glenn Harrington (1988–89)	*Richard Burgi*
Julie Wendall (1989–95)	*Susan Marie Snyder*

Character	Actor
Jason Benedict (1989–94)	*Jonathan Hogan*
Bianca Marquez Walsh (1989–94)	*Karina Arroyave*
Fred Greer (1989–94)	*William Bogart*
Sean Baxter (1989–91)	*Burke Moses*
Sean Baxter (1992)	*Mark Lewis*
Ian "Duke" Kramer (1989–91)	*Michael Loudon*
Sawyer (1989–91)	*Barry Cullison*
Bill Harper (1989–90)	*John Dossett*
Bill Harper (1991)	*Wayne Maugans*
Brock Lombard (1989–90)	*Gregory Beecroft*
Marjorie Lombard (1989–90)	*Mary Ann Urbano*
Philip Lombard (1989–90)	*David Cryer*
Connie Lombard (1989–90)	*Barbara Caruso*
Derek Mason (1989–90)	*Thomas Gibson*
Niles Mason (1989–90)	*Charles Keating*
Trish Mason (1989–90)	*Sherry Ramsey*
Blake Stevens (1989–90)	*Peter Francis James*
Connor Jamison Walsh (1990–)	*Allyson Rice-Taylor*
Larry McDermott (1990–95)	*Ed Fry*
Courtney Baxter (1990–94)	*Hayley Barr*
Linc Lafferty (1990–92)	*James Wlcek*
Linc Lafferty (1993)	*Lonnie McCullough*
Darryl Crawford (1990–92)	*Rex Smith*
Gavin Kruger (1990)	*Joris Stuyck*
Gavin Kruger (1990–92)	*Mark Tymchyshyn*
Jade Sullivan (1990–92)	*Laura Baler*
Frank Wendall (1990–91)	*Keith Douglas Pruitt*
Colin Crowley (1990–91)	*Christopher Cousins*
Virgil Cartwright (1990–91)	*Steve Deighan*
Dr. Henry Matthews (1990–91)	*David Brand*
James Evan Walsh III (1991–95)	*Greg Watkins*
Aaron Snyder (1991–95)	*Mason Boccardo*
Joel Higgins (1991–95)	*Damian Leake*
Hannah Lafferty (1991–94)	*Lee Bryant*
Ron Gillette (1991–94)	*Tony Carlin*
Ron Gillette (1994)	*Malcolm Gets*
Alexander "Hutch" Hutchinson (1991–95)	*Judson Mills*
Woody Hutchinson (1991–93)	*Dan Ziskie*
Marcy Breen (1991)	*Kathleen McNenny*
Marcy Breen (1991–92, 1994)	*Jill Powell*
Tess Shelby (1991–92)	*Parker Posey*
Dana Lambert (1991–92)	*Louise Roberts*
Billy Lambert (1991–92)	*Michael Lord*
Anthony Harper (1991–92)	*Michael Hammond*
Vicki Harper (1991–92)	*Donna Mitchell*
Arthur Clayborne (1991–92)	*Bill Tatum*
Rosanna Cabot (1992–96)	*Yvonne Perry*
Alexander Cabot (1992–95)	*Paul Hecht*
Edwina Walsh (1992–95)	*Rita Lloyd*
Dawn Wheeler (1992–93)	*Lisa Emory*
Dawn Wheeler (1993–95)	*Alexandria Neil*
Scott Eldridge (1992–93)	*Joe Breen*
Scott Eldridge (1995–96)	*Doug Wert*
Ned Simon (1992–94)	*Frank Converse*
Valerie Simon (1992–94)	*Sigrunn Omark*

Royce Keller (1992–94)	Terry Lester
Neal Keller (1992–93)	Mary Kay Adams
Debbie Simon (1992–93)	Sharon Case
Ruth Mansfield (1992–93)	Ann Flood
Cynthia Linders (1992–93)	Linda Cook
Leslie Bordeau (1992–93)	Kim Snyder
Simone Bordeau (1992–93)	Kimberly Norris
Elroy Nevins (1992–93)	Cliff Weissman
Dr. Marsha McKay (1992–93)	Justine Miceli
Steve Hennessy (1992)	James Carroll
Steve Hennessy (1992–93)	Robert Mackey
Damian Grimaldi (1993–96)	Paolo Seganti
Janice Maxwell (1993–95)	Holly Cate
Patricia Kingsley (1993–94)	Rebecca Holden
Gregory Varner (1993–94)	Mark Kevin Lewis
Renata Minardi (1993–94)	Elizabeth Satre
Lexi Funk (1993–94)	Annie Meisels
Mike Kasnoff (1994–)	Shawn Christian
Dani Andropoulos (1994)	Kristanna Loken
Dani Andropoulos (1994–)	Ashley Williams
Samantha Markham (1994–96)	Brooke Alexander
Orlena Grimaldi (1994–95)	Claire Bloom
Orlena Grimaldi (1995)	Lynn Milgram
Jef Hamlin (1994–95)	Christopher Fuller
Tracey Donely (1994–95)	Sarah Knowlton
R. J. Donely (1994–95)	Dane Leach
Pete Wendall (1994–95)	Jason Biggs
Helen Wendall (1994–95)	Elizabeth Franz
Jack Devere (1994–95)	Darnell Williams
Dr. Tony Cook (1994–95)	Jeffrey Donovan
Mark Kasnoff (1995–)	Alexander Walters
Nikki Graves (1995–)	Jordana Brewster
Carly Tenney (1995–96)	Maura West

TV's first half-hour soap opera has always been one of its top-rated attractions, and in 1996 became the second soap opera to run 40 years, after *Guiding Light*. Unlike the tumultuous runs of some others in its genre, its focus has remained constantly on the middle-class Hughes family of Oakdale, identified as being in Illinois by the 1980s, and the audience has connected with its longer-running characters so strongly that attempts to recast them, particularly heroine Penny and so-bad-she's-good Lisa, have met with much disfavor and ended quickly. (The show in fact does hold the record with the most number of actors being regulars in their roles for at least a decade.) Oddly, despite the show's reputation as being conservative, it was the first soap to have a regular character bear an illegitimate child (Ellen in 1958), and to feature an acknowledged gay male character as a regular (Hank Elliot, Barbara's dress designer colleague, in 1988).

The debut opened with a good-morning greeting between lawyer Chris Hughes and his wife Nancy, who could be domineering when it came to raising her children Don, an 18-year-old in love with Janice Turner, and Don's younger sister Penny and brother Bob. Grandpa Hughes also lived with his son Chris and family, and his other child Edith was

nearby. She was the primary cause of discomfort for the family during its first year due to her affair with rich Jim Lowell, who lived with his father Judge Lowell, wife Claire, and daughter Ellen. When Jim died, Edith survived in 1958 by serving as Doug Cassen's compassionate office technician, but Doug ended up wedding Jim's widow Claire. Edith found romance with Dr. George Frye in 1959 and left town as his wife, but the other principals remained in the thick of the drama.

Nancy found herself butting heads with all of her children's love interests. She persuaded Janice Turner to marry Carl Whipple rather than Don in 1957, but when Janice came back a widow in 1962, Don became her husband over Nancy's objections and moved to Texas with her and her wild daughter Alice for a few years. After Janice died, Don dated Ellen briefly, but became more interested in Amanda Holmes, daughter of Ann and Bill Holmes. Bill actually fathered Amanda with fashion designer Sara Fuller, and after his death Sara and Amanda fought for Don's hand. He planned to wed Sara but she died falling down a flight of stairs following a spat with Amanda, and once she knew a dejected Don would not marry her, Amanda left too. Don would not marry again until the 1970s.

Nancy also wanted Penny to marry Tom Pope, Chris's assistant, over the trouble-prone Jeff Baker, even though Chris thought Jeff was all right. But Penny and Jeff proved to be a devoted pair, and they remarried on Christmas Eve 1959 after their first wedding was annulled by Nancy and Chris. Jeff later became an alcoholic, a murder suspect, and a deserter of his marriage before he died in a car crash on August 23, 1962, just as he and Penny were about to adopt a baby. The death occurred because actor Mark Rydell refused to sign a long-term contract with the show. Fan reaction was immediate and deafening, with one woman writing 97 irate letters to the show. Penny then spent much of the 1960s in luckless romances, the biggest being Dr. Neil Wade, who accidentally shot his natural father Doug Cassen, who had an affair with Neil's mother Judith years earlier. Neil avoided serious jail time, only to die in a car accident, leaving Penny husbandless again.

The other big story of the 1950s involved Ellen Lowell, who loved the married Dr. Tim Cole and had his child but gave it up for adoption. Dr. Cole eventually divorced his wife, and Ellen married him when she learned he had a terminal illness. After his death, Ellen still felt guilt over her romance and ended it by leaving town temporarily. Wendy Drew left her role as Ellen in August 1960 after she got married in real life, and Pat Bruder took her place when the character returned in late September. Bruder stayed on the show for 35 years.

Two other pivotal changes took place in 1960, as Don Hastings assumed the role of now-adult Bob Hughes and Eileen Fulton arrived as the devilishly charming Lisa Miller from Rockford, Illinois. Audiences went ballistic as Lisa wheedled her way into seducing Bob into eloping with her. But before Nancy and Chris could plan to annul the union, the way they did with Penny and Jeff on their first marriage, Lisa announced she was pregnant. Her son Tom became the pride and joy of the family, but Lisa's chicanery irritated her in-laws, and later she had no qualms about divorcing Bob for a lover. Then when Bob fell in love with Sylvia Hill, a nurse with a terminal form of lupus, Lisa tried to break them up and win Bob back. She succeeded only in engineering the breakup.

Meanwhile, Eileen Fulton got into a spat backstage and found herself replaced as Lisa went on a cross-country trek where she was beaten and attacked by various and sundry shady types, then was revealed as having a new look in the person of actress Pamela King. Viewer response was extremely negative to the cast change, and Eileen returned to the role, only to leave it within a year to star in the first, and unsuccessful, nighttime spin-off of a daytime soap called *Our Private World,* which aired on CBS Wednesday and Friday nights from May 5–September 10, 1965. On that show, her character left for Chicago to wed John Eldridge and played second fiddle to the various activities of other Eldridges. Lisa did return to *As the World Turns* briefly to finish her story line, then came back in 1967 with nary a word about her divorce from John Eldridge—or the fact that she had a child named Scott by him, which would be revealed nearly a quarter century later after Eldridge's death!

Despite the children's screwed-up marriages, the Hughes clan remained basically a happy, supportive clan with whom the home audience empathized. In 1963, for example, viewers sent approximately 150,000 cards wishing Grandpa Hughes a happy 70th birthday, and even Aunt Edith returned for four shows to take part in the activities. The same could not

Veteran members of the Hughes clan on As the World Turns *by the 1970s included, from left, Nancy (played by Helen Wagner), Chris (Don MacLaughlin), Bob (Don Hastings), and Grandpa (Santos Ortega).*

be said about the Lowells. After overcoming the news about Doug's affair, Claire found herself a widow when he died from a concussion. Meanwhile, Ellen fought for custody of her illegitimate son Dan against Dr. David Stewart and his wife Betty, who already had another son named Paul. When Betty died, David became attracted to Ellen, but his vicious nanny Franny Brennan tried to cause discord and estrange Ellen from his children.

In 1964 an ad in *Variety* by CBS boasted that *As the World Turns* attracted a larger audience than 40 percent of all nighttime programs on ABC. This may have prompted ABC to bring out its big guns by putting reruns of the nighttime drama *Ben Casey* against the soap in 1965, but it failed miserably. Series creator and headwriter Irna Phillips, sensing the challenge, had Dr. David Stewart propose to Ellen Lowell the Friday before the reruns began, and *As the World Turns* continued its hold on number one, just as David and Ellen continued as a couple for the next 25 years on the show after Ellen served jail time for the accidental death of Franny, with Ellen giving birth to their daughters Annie and Dee.

While Ellen and David went on to a happy union, her mother could not claim the same. Though Claire was courted by Judge Lowell's new partner Dick Martin, she fell for the charms of younger heel Dr. Michael Shea instead, only to find herself competing for him against Lisa, now divorced from John Eldridge. Lisa first tried to go back to Bob until he wed model Sandy McGuire in a difficult union that at one point had her parents Martha and Carl Wilson fight Bob for custody of her child Jimmy while she was being treated for depression, and she and Bob later divorced. Sandy's ex-husband Roy wed Penny and she took care of Jimmy temporarily, but their marriage was annulled, and

Penny left Oakdale, eventually moving to England to adopt an Asian girl named Amy and wed Anton Cunningham, a French racing driver. As for Claire and Lisa, their situation grew more complicated when Claire wed Michael, but he had a child named Chuckie with Lisa. Claire divorced him and he wed Lisa, but continued to blackmail both women until he was murdered. Sadly, Claire died shortly thereafter from a car crash.

Lisa's son Tom Hughes did not bear his parents' travails lightly. At age 17, he was smoking pot under the encouragement of Hank Barton, a dope pusher. He was also in Vietnam for a brief stint, then became the prime suspect in Michael Shea's death and was in a car crash which caused Chuckie's death. He also dated nurse Karen Adams and Meredith Halliday before wedding Carol Deming, only to find himself attracted shortly thereafter to Natalie Bannon, the initial client in his law practice.

Tom was not the only maturing child on the show. David and Ellen's son Dan learned of his parentage while wed to aspiring doctor Susan Burke, and also lusted after his brother Paul's wife Liz Talbot. Susan manipulated Dan when she learned he had fathered Liz's illegitimate child Betsy. Helping her was a scheming protégé of Michael Shea's who would be featured more in the future—Dr. John Dixon.

Assessing that story line and others in 1969 for *TV Guide,* a stunned Cleveland Amory claimed that Oakdale "makes *Peyton Place* look like a morality play." But it was a popular setup, and two years later, Amory's magazine put the cast of *As the World Turns* on its cover, the first for any soap opera. However, by that time, *As the World Turns* was one of only two soaps still airing live rather than on videotape, and its supremacy at the top was beginning to wear thin, thanks to dubious plots.

The trouble began in 1971 with Lisa thinking she was pregnant but not knowing how it could have happened (the "pregnancy" turned out to be an ovarian cyst, but Eileen Fulton thought it was the worst story she ever had to play on the show). Things got worse the next year when Irna Phillips returned to write the show and made major blunders. One was having longtime romantic lead Bob Hughes, now married to widow Jennifer Ryan, callously cheat on her with her free-spirited sister Kim. Irna planned to have the pregnant Kim raise the child on her own, but negative audience reaction led to Bob and Jennifer staying together and having a daughter Franny to add to Jennifer's children Barbara and Rick, while Kim married John Dixon to give her baby a name, only to lose the child at birth, or so she thought at the time.

Another unsuccesful plot line involved Irna's treatment of the Stewarts. Even after Susan and Dan had their own child, Emily, Dan still worshipped Liz and their daughter Betsy. Something about this story and/or its actors upset Irna to the point where she decimated it within a few weeks. She first had Paul die and David tell Ellen about it in a ludicrous scene by getting her drunk and having her react too calmly. Then Susan and Dan split up, and Dan wed Liz until she died by falling *up* a staircase, causing her liver to rupture! To top it

off, Susan wed Dr. Bruce Baxter, only to have it annulled when it turned out that he was impotent. Given those changes, it is surprising in retrospect that the show did not lose more of an audience than it did.

There were some productive developments that survived this upheaval. Dan went on to a long-lasting affair with Kim while John tried to keep her wed to him at every turn, including fathering her child Andy, and Susan did the same with Dan over custody of Emily despite flings with Mark Galloway and Kevin Thompson. Bob and Jennifer maintained a relatively happy marriage until her death in 1975. And Lisa found the most exciting romance of her life with Chris's new law partner Grant Colman, though that had its own complications.

Grant, you see, had an ex-wife Joyce who caused constant grief for Lisa and others in Oakdale. She threw him off by announcing, after their divorce, that they had a child which she had put up for adoption. It came out that Mary and Brian Ellison were the parents seeking custody of little Teddy, but Grant felt the child should be with them and not him or Joyce. The whole situation left Lisa so disgusted with Grant's involvement that she saw an ex-lover, lawyer Dick Martin, briefly while the drama played out, including Brian's death, Joyce's marriage to Don Hughes while having an affair with Ralph Mitchell, and then Mary's marriage to Don. Eventually, despite Joyce's efforts, which went so far that she faked her own death, Mary and Don left town with Teddy, Joyce disappeared, and Lisa and Grant had a marriage that later disintegrated, though the two remained friends long after he left town.

Lisa's son Tom was not doing much better, divorcing Carol to wed Natalie Bannon and leaving Carol to wed Jay Stallings. Then Natalie slept with her old boyfriend Jay, leading Tom to divorce her. Carol withstood the affair until Jay died in a mine explosion, and after another failed marriage with Steve Andropolous, she left town. Meanwhile, Tom ventured into dating his stepsister Barbara Ryan, but she left him at the altar for her old flame James Stenbeck and their son Paul, a decision she would come to regret.

As the world turned into the late 1970s, Bob's ex-wife Sandy McGuire returned and wed Kevin Thompson until he died from a car crash, prompting her to leave town again. Playgirl Valerie Conway, after pining unsuccessfully for Dan Stewart, moved out after marrying Dr. Alex Keith. Grown-up sisters Annie and Dee competed for the love of Beau Spencer, with Annie winning, only to give up after the smothering competition from his disapproving mother Jane and his vixenish lover Melinda Gray, who claimed to be the late Jennifer Ryan's illegitimate daughter and later died. Susan took Emily out of town after overcoming her alcoholism. Dan and Kim finally got together and lived with Betsy, who learned he was really her father and not her uncle, until Dan died.

The early 1980s was marked by the shenanigans of two men, John Dixon and James Stenbeck. The former rebounded from a marriage to the late nurse Pat Holland to wed Dee Stewart, to her parents' horror. Dee went for John because he knew her affair with composer Ian McFarland ended when he died having sex with her, leaving her unable to deal with the love of geologist Brad Hollister, who married her sister Annie instead. John also found out that Lyla Montgomery, a new nurse in Oakdale dating Bob, actually had a daughter by him named Margo in addition to her horny daughter Cricket and troubled son Craig.

Dee pressed rape charges against John because, as she later admitted, she thought she was making love to Brad, resulted in multiple ramifications. Brad left town, leaving Annie to wed Dr. Jeff Ward and have Oakdale's first quadruplets before departing too. News of Lyla and John's earlier affair ended Lyla's relationship with Bob. Lyla's sister Maggie ended her relationship with Tom Hughes after they represented opposite sides in the conflict (Tom for Dee, Maggie for John). And before the trial's verdict was rendered, John became a victim of a hit-and-run accident. Many thought it was Dee's dad David who had done the deed, since he disappeared during that time, but he actually had amnesia and lived with widow Cynthia Haines and her daughter Karen before recuperating. Karen dated Jeff Ward before seeing James Stenbeck, the person who actually hit John Dixon, fearing John would tell Barbara about his ongoing affair with Margo Montgomery.

Margo got over James, trained to be a cop, and wed Tom Hughes, but the enmity between John and James only grew stronger. After divorcing Dee, John wed Ariel Aldrin, whose mother Greta had been James's nanny and actually his mother, having switched him with the true heir of the Stenbeck fortune, a man named Gunnar St. Clair. Incredibly, Gunnar arrived in Oakdale and became affectionate with Barbara. James tried everything to end the attraction, including releasing a bull in a ring in Spain to charge at Barbara. When John learned the truth about James and Gunnar's lineage, James tried to kill him, but John faked his own death using Dee as a suspect in his "murder" to haunt James. Dee, upset at being used as a pawn in the scheme, departed Oakdale, but John and James remained a battling duo.

James did surrender Barbara and custody of his son Paul to Gunnar, while the ambitious Karen Haines became infuriated that her new love James gave up on getting the Stenbeck fortune, now believed to be held by Paul. Karen was just as deceitful as James, though, and when she learned a boy named Dusty Donovan may have been the illegitimate child of Gunnar's and thus the real Stenbeck heir, she fought for custody of the boy. As it turned out, Ariel Aldrin had actually wed Dusty's father Burke before he died, but Burke named Karen as Dusty's guardian. As Karen wed John Dixon and they learned that Dusty was the true heir, James tried to kill them and Gunnar on a plane as Gunnar learned on a trip that Dusty was his son. Gunnar threw James out of the plane to his apparent death, then later contracted a fatal disease that forced him to leave Barbara and Paul. Dusty went to live with John and Karen until she divorced him in 1984, leaving Dusty in his care.

John's ex-loves were hardly dormant during this period. Kim wed Nick Andropolous, but he died on her, while her stepdaughter Betsy had the hots for Nick's brother Steve. Continuing on this vaguely incestuous theme, Betsy instead wed lying louse Craig Montgomery while having a child Dani by

Celebrating the 15th anniversary of As the World Turns *were these four original cast members: from left to right, Santos Ortega (who played Grandpa Hughes), Don MacLaughlin (Chris Hughes), Helen Wagner (Nancy Hughes), and William Johnstone (Judge Lowell).*

Steve (she later divorced Craig and wed Steve), and Craig's mom Lyla and aunt Maggie vied for the love of Steve's cousin Frank. Craig and Steve earlier had been in joint pursuit of Diana McColl, whose father Whit became Lisa's fifth husband. Whit's playboy son Kirk had his own love quadrangle going with Franny Hughes, Marcy Thompson, and Jay Connors.

An important new arrival in 1984 was Lucinda Walsh, a rich bitch with an earlier crush on John Dixon who held Whit McColl responsible for her husband's death. When Whit died, Lisa blamed it on Lucinda, but it was actually done by Whit's housekeeper Dorothy Connors, who also was Jay's mother and, as it turned out, was Kirk's mother too due to a fling with Whit. Lucinda's daughter Lily pursued a relationship with Dusty Donovan, while Lisa still bore a grudge toward Lucinda as they competed in business interests. Lucinda's new love was ambitious Craig Montgomery, but he also fell for Sierra Esteban, the daughter Lucinda gave up for adoption. Though Sierra wed her crafty oldtime friend Tonio Reyes, Craig impregnated her and they eventually wed and left to live in the fictional Latin American country of Montega.

There was a happy event in 1985. Bob, coming off a loser marriage to ex-con Miranda Marlowe, finally decided it was time to declare his love for Kim and wed her in a beautiful ceremony, with Don and even Penny returning for it (Chris and Nancy, who were written out for a few years, had come back full force as regulars by this time too). It was the fifth marriage for each, but it proved to be solid. Kim became a loving mother to Franny to the point of lying on the stand when Franny was accused in the death of Doug Cummings, a young man obsessed with Kim. Both women were exonerated, as the real killer was Marsha Talbot, but unfortunately Franny's latest boyfriend Kevin Gibson was killed by Doug during the standoff.

Kim's niece and now stepdaughter Barbara got married to down-to-earth policeman Hal Munson and had a daughter by him, but their relationship was complicated in part by her own mischieviousness. When she claimed a drunken Tom slept with her, in time it led to Margo separating from Tom and sleeping with Hal. She thought she was unable to have children based on a previous miscarriage, but in fact she gave birth to Hal's child Adam while it came out that Barbara had lied. Barbara's marriage to Hal was complicated by such shows of duplicity, while Tom and Margo stuck together despite facing greater hardships.

One of Barbara's worst problems emerged earlier when she stopped the marriage of her old boyfriend Brian McColl to mysterious newcomer Shannon O'Hara by having her legal husband Duncan McKechnie arrive in Oakdale. Setting up operations in the castle he had moved piece by piece to town, Duncan stayed in town and managed to convince Shannon to remain his wife, but Brian did not go back to Barbara but wed instead Duncan's sister Beatrice, who actually turned out to be his daughter! That was not the half of it; Duncan had business dealings with a mystery man who was revealed to be James Stenbeck. He had survived his fall from a plane by grabbing a parachute before leaving the plane (which had not been shown went he first "died"), and somehow he was exonerated for attempting to kill John Dixon. Naturally Lucinda found him fascinating and began sleeping with him, only to regret it when he used her as he had many others. Meanwhile James was carrying on with Emily Stewart, Susan's daughter, but his evil acts caught up with him: in 1989 his son Paul shot him to death and changed his last name back to Ryan to absolve himself of the Stenbeck stain. Paul also embarked on an affair with Emily before leaving town.

James was not the only one to make a comeback. When the show reached 30 years old in 1986, many former regulars returned to celebrate Chris and Nancy's 50th anniversary (longtime viewers must have had doubts about the chronology, since the duo had celebrated 40 years of bliss back in 1972). The event was a melancholy one, as Don MacLaughlin, who played Chris, was ill at the time and died later that year. Nancy later married police Lt. Dan McCloskey, and Bob and Kim named their child Chris in honor of the late man.

The nostalgia kick continued in 1986–87 when Franny went to England to stay with her aunt Penny and cousin Amy but became intrigued with a look-alike woman she saw there. It turned out that the woman, named Sabrina, resembled Franny because she was the product of Bob and Kim's affair. John had told Kim the baby had died in the hospital, when in fact he had the child switched with a dead infant with the help of Rick Ryan, who had constantly undermined Bob's work while working as an intern years earlier. Rick had returned to Oakdale to work at the hospital but left the country in haste after everyone learned about the situation. The wildest outcome, though, had to involve John. Exonerated for his

part in the act by an impassioned plea from Lucinda Walsh, he and Lucinda stunned everyone by getting married.

Relatives of many characters also popped up in the late 1980s. There was Earl Mitchell, Shannon's uncle who wed Lisa before dying; Pamela Wagner, John's niece who dated longhaired blond Beau Farrell; Ian "Duke" Kramer, John's illegitimate son; Bianca Marquez, a Montegan girl adopted by Lucinda; and, most shockingly, Lien Hughes, a child Tom had when in Vietnam who dated both Andy and Paul before leaving town.

But most characters found themselves interacting with the Snyder family, a farming clan who dominated many story lines in the late 1980s and early 1990s. John dated widowed matriarch Emma for a time, and Franny dated oldest son Seth until Sabrina seduced him by pretending to be her near-twin sister one dark night. But the family had the strongest impact on Lucinda Walsh. She learned that Lily, her adopted daughter, was actually the product of her cousin Rod Landry's rape of Seth's sister Iva. That revelation nearly ruined Lily's love for hunky Holden Snyder, but Emma explained that Iva was adopted herself, meaning that Lily and Holden were not related. In a somewhat kinky resolution, Holden's sister Meg wed Rod, who also was not directly related to the family, after her affair with Dusty Donovan petered out and he moved overseas.

Lily and Holden's relationship was fraught with trauma. When she learned that he knew about her parentage but had not told her what he knew, they separated, with Holden marrying Emily briefly. Then his brother Caleb, newly arrived from Chicago, envied him, and Caleb's erstwhile fling Angel Lange made passes at Holden, leading Lily to see Caleb. Then shyster Derek Mason eloped with Lily before dying in an explosion designed to kill her. In 1991 the two finally wed, but there was gloom in store for them as neither knew at first that a one-night stand Holden had with Caleb's then-wife Julie Wendall had produced a son, Aaron. When what had happened sunk in to Holden, he suffered amnesia, and in the meantime Lily miscarried. Not knowing who he really was anymore, Holden lost interest in Lily, and she wed millionaire playboy Damian Grimaldi in 1993.

The other Snyder to see action was Emma's fifth child Ellie, who clamored for Craig for a while, then went after Lucinda's seemingly suspicious executive employee Kirk Anderson, with whom she had a pregnancy she ended by having an abortion. Indeed, it seemed like no one in the Snyders had a happy time in Oakdale. Iva had a child with John Dixon but did not marry him, moving out instead with Jason Benedict. Julie and Caleb departed after a second wedding and the arrival of her illegitimate son Pete. Seth also hit the trail when he wed Angel Lange after it was revealed her father Henry sexually abused her and killed himself. And luckless Emma struck out with Cal Stricklyn, who later started seeing Lyla, then wed Connor Jamison, and then Ned Simon, who killed Linc Lafferty, the half-brother of "Hutch" Hutchinson who had been sleeping with Ned's daughter Debbie.

For the longtime characters, life in the 1990s was no piece of cake either. Nancy had to cope with Mac's Alzheimer's disease, which affected him until his death in 1996. Lyla's great marriage to young Dr. Casey Peretti ended with his premature death. Kim's son Andy Dixon got over his alcoholism with an assist from bulemic Courtney Baxter, but their marriage unraveled and he got involved with Janice Maxwell, who tried to kill his mother. Andy went to Paris at the end of 1995 to pursue a photography career. Franny dated Courtney's brother Sean, then wed Darryl Crawford but left him because she feared (erroneously) that he had killed his first wife Carolyn. She and her sister Sabrina moved to work at a clinic in Montega. Barbara, thinking Hal was having an affair with Margo, disappeared briefly but returned to give birth to a girl named Jennifer, whose father was Darryl Crawford even though she claimed it was Gavin Kruger. Hal forgave her and they remarried in 1993, but her continued chicanery and deceit, such as seeing Evan Walsh, led to their marriage dissolving two years later. And Susan, wed to Dr. Larry McDermott, had her daughter Emily carry their child via in vitro fertilization, then saw Larry transferred to another hospital and leave her.

Even Margo had her share of calamities in the 1990s as she was raped by an AIDS-infected man. Despite her worries, she did not test positive, but she befriended Dawn Wheeler, another victim of the rapist who did die of the disease. Husband Tom also dealt with the arrival of his previously unannounced half-brother Scott Eldridge, who arrived after his dad John's death and made peace with Lisa before leaving.

And as always, Lucinda appeared to occupy her own rarefied world of incidents. There was her breakup with John; the loss of her company to Connor Jamison Walsh and her brother Evan Walsh, relatives of Lucinda's late husband's family; the establishment of a new company, WorldWide, with her aide Marcy Breen; and the discovery of not one but three siblings— her sister Neal, who dated Scott; her brother Royce, who dated Emily until it was learned his alternate personality had killed Neal and he left town; and her sister Samantha, who first dated Craig during a temporary separation from Sierra, then wed Kirk after the two pretended to be in love to con Lucinda.

The wave of characters and seeming lack of focus on the show resulted in a streamlining of the cast in 1995 that basically removed the Snyders and focused on Lisa's marriage to Eduardo Grimaldi (husband number seven, for those keeping count). He was murdered in the hospital by his aunt Orlena, disturbed mother of Lily's husband Damian, but Lisa blamed Eduardo's attending physician John Dixon for his death and sued him successfully for malpractice. Family and friends of both took opposite sides in Lisa's lawsuit, but when Orlena confessed to the crime later that year before dying, John was exonerated. That was not enough for him, however; he tricked Lisa into thinking he wanted to marry her, only to denounce her at their engagement party in early 1996.

Damian was dead by this time too from a plane crash which Lily, who had a son Luke with Damian, investigated to find the true murderers. Helping Lily search was ex-convict Mike Kasnoff, who had already had unsatisfactory relationships with Rosanna Cabot and her half-sister Carly Tenney. Mike's brother Mark had his own dilemma; he desired Connor Jamison, who married Cal Stricklyn.

Not all was despair at this time. As the series celebrated 40 years on air, a montage of old scenes ran on the anniversary. Shortly thereafter, the story line added Bob's adopted nephew Teddy, Don and Mary's son now calling himself Ryder, in the center of a love triangle with Nikki Graves, Hal's unknown teenage daughter from a marriage before seeing Barbara, and Dani Andropolous, Betsy's daughter staying with her aunt Susan. That meant a Hughes was seeing a Lowell, something that had not happened since the start of the show with Aunt Edith and Jim Lowell. What comes around goes around, even as the world turns.

ASK WASHINGTON
Informational; B&W
January 11, 1954–March 10, 1962

NBC Mon.–Fri. 11–11:30 a.m. (1/11/54–2/26/54)
NBC Sun. 4–4:30 p.m. (11/29/59–3/27/60)
NBC Sun. 4:30–5 p.m. (1/22/61–4/9/61)
NBC Sat. 3:30–4 p.m. or 4:30–5 p.m. (10/21/61–3/10/62)

Moderators: *Bryson Rash (1959–60, 1961–62), Russ Ward (early 1961)*

Regular Panelist: *Esther Van Wagoner Tufty (1959–60)*

This public affairs show initially filled in the time between the cancellation of NBC's morning soaps *The Bennetts* and *Follow Your Heart* and the start of *Home*. Viewers sent questions about current affairs to a panel of reporters based in America's capital who then discussed them. More than five years after the daily show ended, NBC revived the property to air at the end of *NBA Basketball* games for three seasons. Besides a regular moderator overseeing three reporters, the new version was marked by the occasional need to shorten the program if the basketball games ran long.

AT ISSUE
Public Affairs; B&W
March 7, 1954–June 27, 1954

ABC Sun. 3:45–4 p.m. (3/7/54–6/27/54)

Host: *Martin Agronsky*

Originally seen on ABC nighttime from July 12, 1953–February 24, 1954, *At Issue* ended its run on Sunday afternoons following *Elmer Davis*. Reporter Martin Agronsky discussed current affairs with a newsworthy guest each week.

ATOM ANT/SECRET SQUIRREL SHOW, THE
Cartoon; Color
October 2, 1965–August 31, 1968

NBC Sat. 9:30–10:30 a.m. (10/2/65–12/31/66)
NBC Sat. 9:30–10 a.m. and 11–11:30 a.m. (1/7/67–9/2/67)
NBC Sat. 11:30 p.m.–Noon (9/9/67–8/31/68)

Voices:

Atom Ant	*Howard Morris*
Atom Ant (later)/Precious Pupp/Shag Rugg	*Don Messick*
Maw Rugg/Floral Rugg/Winsome Witch	*Jean VanderPyl*
Morocco Mole/Squiddly Diddly	*Paul Frees*
Paw Rugg	*Henry Corden*
Secret Squirrel (Agent 000)	*Mel Blanc*

Originally two cartoons which aired back to back, Atom Ant and Secret Squirrel split and then combined again in 1967 as one show. The title characters of each were comic figures. Atom Ant was an insect who gained super powers when he sported a pair of atomized glasses. He read "The Crook Book" to get background on his prospective foes and went into action by yelling "Up and at 'em!" (get it?). Secret Squirrel was a trenchcoat-wearing spoof of James Bond who worked in England under boss Double Q and along with fez-wearing sidekick Morocco Mole. Two adventures of Atom Ant and Secret Squirrel appeared on each show.

Supporting elements were "The Hillbilly Bears," a knockoff of *The Beverly Hillbillies* with Paw (the hunched-over, muttering one), Maw, Floral, and Shag Rugg living the backwoods life; "Precious Pupp," a conniving dog who tries to convince his owner Granny that he is an honorable canine; "Squiddly Diddly," a hopeful performer who happened to be a squid; and the good-hearted "Winsome Witch," whose calling card was "Have Broom, Will Travel."

The series had a nighttime NBC hour-long preview on September 12, 1965 titled "The World of Secret Squirrel and Atom Ant." In January 1967 *Atom Ant* aired 90 minutes before *Secret Squirrel,* then combined back as one in the fall of 1967 for a year. More than 25 years after his cancellation, Secret Squirrel came back as a recurring character on the Cartoon Network cable channel series *Two Stupid Dogs,* and Morocco Mole and his Peter Lorre-ish voice popped up in a few commercials and special events on the channel for at least three years.

ATOM SQUAD
Science Fiction; B&W
July 6, 1953–January 22, 1954

NBC Mon.–Fri. 5–5:15 p.m. (7/6/53–1/22/54)

Cast:

Steve Elliot	*Bob Hastings*
Dave	*Bob Courtleigh*
Another assistant	*Bram Nossen*

The Atom Squad was a New York-based security group that stopped foreign spies during the Cold War. The first installment involved Steve Elliott and his two aides fighting a demented scientist who stole a vital radioactive element from various atomic plants. This series was replaced by *The Pinky Lee Show.*

•ATTACK OF THE KILLER TOMATOES
Cartoon; Color
September 8, 1990–

Fox Sat. 9:30–10 a.m. (9/8/90–4/13/91)
Fox Sat. 10–10:30 a.m. (4/20/91–8/3/91)
Fox Sat. 10:30–11 a.m. (8/10/91–8/31/91)
Fox Sat. 8–8:30 a.m. (9/7/91–9/5/92)
Fox Sat. 9:30–10 a.m. (4/20/96–)

Voices:

Dr. Putrid T. Gangreen	*John Astin*

Also: *Thom Bray, S. Scott Bullock, Cam Clarke, Chris Guzer, Maurice LaMarche, Chuck McCann, Rob Paulsen, Neil Ross, Susan Silo, Kath Soucie*

Based loosely on the 1978 cult live-action movie of the same name, *Attack of the Killer Tomatoes* told how Dr. Putrid T. Gangreen and his assistant Igor Smith stimulated tomatoes in the town of San Zucchini into being instruments of terror. Leading the fight against them were Tara Boumdeay, an ex-Gangreen experiment who looked like a teenage girl but was really a tomato who reverted if salt was sprayed on her; mutant "Friendly Tomato" (F.T.), who pretended to be a dog; and 10-year-old John Finletter, the only one who knew what Tara and F.T. really were. Pizza-loving John had his pals work with him at his Uncle Wilbur's restaurant while they attempted to nullify Putrid's doings. Also seen was egotistical reporter Whitley White of KRUD-TV, who informed the populace of San Zucchini of the current status of the battle against the vegetables (or is it fruits?).

The show was one of the first to use computer-generated animation. The episodes seen in 1996 were repeats.

BABY GAME, THE
Game; Color
January 1, 1968–July 12, 1968

ABC Mon.–Fri. 2:30–2:55 p.m. (1/1/68–7/12/68)

Host: *Richard Hayes*

Three couples guessed how infants would react in filmed situations shown to them in this short-lived show. The highest-scoring duo won merchandise. First produced for NBC, *The Baby Game* was bought by ABC on the basis of the enthusiasm of sponsor Procter & Gamble, who thought it would sell a lot of products for tots. (There *was* a series with an apt title in the next time slot; see *Children's Doctor.*)

•BACK TO THE FUTURE
Cartoon; Color
September 14, 1991–August 14, 1993

CBS Sat. 11–11:30 a.m. (9/14/91–3/20/93)
CBS Sat. 12:30–1 p.m. (3/27/93–8/14/93)

Voices:

Biff	*Thomas F. Wilson*
Clara Brown	*Mary Steenburgen*
Doc Brown	*Dan Castellaneta*
Jules Brown	*Josh Wiener*
Verne Brown	*Troy Davidson*
Marty McFly	*David Kaufman*

Regulars (live action): *Christopher Lloyd (as Doc Brown), Bill Nye the Science Guy (as himself)*

A hit film trilogy from 1985–91, *Back to the Future* came to Saturday morning cartoons using the basic characters from the second sequel as its basis. Doc Brown was an eccentric but brilliant white-haired scientist who lived in Hill Valley in the early 1990s with his wife Clara, sons Jules and Verne (get it?), and pet dog Einstein. His preoccupation with time travel led him to develop a floating De Lorean sports car that could go to the past or future. Joining him in these sojourns was Marty McFly, a teenage kid who loved to use his hovercraft skateboard when danger threatened during these trips, which was often. Biff, Marty's nemesis in the movies, became on the cartoon a recurring villain, depending on the time period. For example, he was the Christmas-hating Ebiffnezer Tannen when the gang went back to England in 1845, and the terrorizing Bifficus Antanneni during a trek to Rome in 36 A.D. Biff's other appearance was at the end of the show to tell a corny joke for which he received, shall we say, animation retribution.

Though a comedy, there was a concerted effort in this cartoon to be as realistic as possible in the time travel, with Doc Brown using "clothing conversion coordinates" to create outfits appropriate to the era visited and a "universal linguistic translator" to understand ancient or foreign tongues. Continuing with this theme, the show had the movie Doc Brown, Christopher Lloyd, impart scientific facts to home viewers in live-action bits, with Bill Nye the Science Guy demonstrating the discussion as "video scientist/technical advisor." *Bill Nye the Science Guy* later became a highly successful syndicated educational series in 1993 that continued through 1996.

The other movie actors repeating their roles in the cartoon were Thomas F. Wilson as Biff and Mary Steenburgen as Doc's wife, seen in the third movie. Michael J. Fox, Marty McFly on film, did not turn up, nor did musical group Huey Lewis and the News, who scored a *Billboard* number one hit in 1985 with the movie theme "The Power of Love." However, another top 10 hit by the News for the movie series "Back in Time" was used in the cartoon but not sung by the group.

BACKGROUND
News; B&W
October 10, 1954–June 26, 1955

NBC Sun. 5:30–6 p.m. (10/10/54–2/6/55)
NBC Sun. 3–3:30 p.m. (2/20/55–3/27/55)
NBC Sun. 4–4:30 p.m. (4/3/55–6/26/55)

Hosts: *Joseph C. Harsch (10/10/54–3/20/55), Dave Garroway (3/27/55–6/26/55)*

Background examined one topic per show in detail with special film reports, such as the Detroit auto industry leaders, Communism in Italy, or the challenges facing the mining town of Elizabethtown, Illinois. Joseph C. Harsch served as the show's producer as well as host. NBC News reporter John Chancellor contributed to roughly a fourth of all the telecasts. The series ran on NBC Mondays at 8:30 p.m. from August 16–September 6, 1954 before moving to Sunday afternoons, where it appeared two or three Sundays per month.

•BAFFLE
Game; Color
March 26, 1973–March 29, 1974

NBC Mon.–Fri. 10:30–11 a.m. (3/26/73–1/4/74)
NBC Mon.–Fri. 12:30–12:55 p.m. (1/7/74–3/29/74)

Host: *Dick Enberg*

Based on the successful nightly syndicated game *PDQ* (1965–69) hosted by Dennis James, *Baffle* had two pairs each of a celebrity and a civilian contestant who competed to see who could identify a phrase in the least amount of time. One member of each team received a phrase and put three oversized letters on a rack in the hopes of inducing his or her partner to come up with the right words. They got to add other letters after the first try. After the answer was revealed, the other team (which was in an isolation booth) came out and tried to solve the same phrase in less time. The team that identified the phrase in the least amount of time in each game won that round. Four wins by a team led to a bonus game, where the noncelebrity contestant had to identify words from three letters to win a new automobile.

When it aired as *PDQ*, the show used three celebrities and one contestant as its two competing pairs. It became a game using celebrities only when its title changed to *All-Star Baffle* on September 29, 1973.

•BAGGY PANTS AND THE NITWITS
Cartoon; Color
September 10, 1977–October 28, 1978

NBC Sat. Noon–12:30 p.m. (9/10/77–1/21/78)
NBC Sat. 11–11:30 a.m. (2/4/78–9/2/78)
NBC Sat. 12:30–1 p.m. (9/9/78–10/28/78)

Voices:

Gladys Ormphby	*Ruth Buzzi*
Tyrone	*Arte Johnson*

Two top comic routines of the 20th century found themselves reduced to caricature in this cartoon. The first part of the title referred to a Charles Chaplinesque walking cat called Baggy Pants, who never talked. The humor here was weak and nowhere near as inventive as Chaplin's film work, and the lack of a laugh track, while appropriate in spirit, only made the segments duller to watch.

The other element was "the Nitwits," cartoon versions of characters performed by Arte Johnson and Ruth Buzzi on the NBC nighttime variety hit *Laugh-In* in the late 1960s.

The recurring gag had dumpy codger Tyrone spy the homely, hairnet-wearing Gladys Ormphby sitting on a bench and then join her to make some suggestive comment that prompted Gladys to hit him with her purse. (A typical routine had Tyrone ask, "Do you believe in the hereafter?" When Gladys matter-of-factly responded, "Yes," Tyrone quipped, "Then you know what I'm here after!") In the cartoon the two put aside their differences to become crime fighters. Tyrone, whose code name was Agony Nine, was able to fly with the help of his cane Elmo, which could bounce like a coil, but Gladys usually saved the day. It was a cute idea, but it was funnier on *Laugh-In*.

•BAILEY'S COMETS
Cartoon; Color
September 8, 1973–August 31, 1975

CBS Sat. 8:30–9 a.m. (9/8/73–1/26/74)
CBS Sun. 9–9:30 a.m. (2/3/74–9/1/74)
CBS Sun. 9:30–10 a.m. (9/8/74–8/31/75)

Voices:

Barnaby Bailey	Carl Esser
Bunny	Sarah Kennedy
Candy	Karen Smith
Dooter Roo	Daws Butler
Dude	Bob Holt
Gabby	Don Messick
Pudge	Frank Welker
Sarge	Kathi Gori
Wheelie	Jim Begg

A team of six adolescents, called the Comets, competed in a $1 million treasure hunt in a roller skate competition against teams like the Dr. Jekyll/Hydes (whose members could transform from good to evil types in a puff of smoke involuntarily) and the Yo Ho Hos (pirates). The teams, except the Comets, often plotted against each other in their worldwide chase, which spanned from Tokyo to Transylvania to Australia, in two episodes per show. Each episode ended with one team being the first to find rhyming clues about the next destination, and the Comets always arrived first in the last episode of each show. Gabby, flying in a helicopter piloted by Dooter Roo, reported on the race. The second season was all repeats.

•BANANA SPLITS ADVENTURE HOUR, THE
Children's; Color
September 7, 1968–September 5, 1970

NBC Sat. 10:30–11:30 a.m. (9/7/68–9/5/70)

Voices:

Athos	Jonathan Harris
Bez	Henry Corden
Bingo	Daws Butler
Constance/The Queen	Julie Bennett
D'Artagnan	Bruce Watson
Drooper	Allan Melvin
Evil Vangore	Paul Frees
Fariik/Bakaar	John Stephenson
Fleegle	Paul Winchell
Jill Carter	Patsy Garrett
Mike Carter	Tommy Cook
Porthos	Barney Phillips
Prince Turhan	Jay North
Princess Nidor	Shari Lewis
Raseem	Frank Gerstle
Snorky/Professor Carter/Aramis	Don Messick
Toolie	Teddy Eccles

Cast ("Mystery Island" segment):

Chongo	Kahana
Chu	Rodrigo Arrendondo
Professor Irwin Hayden	Frank Aletter
Leslie Hayden	Ronnie Troup
Luke Simmons	Jan-Michael Vincent
Morgan	Rockne Tarkington
Mu-tan	Victor Eberg

Narrator: *Gary Owens*

The Banana Splits Adventure Hour was the most expensive Saturday morning show up to that time, costing $135,000 per hour to produce. It also was also Hanna Barbera's first show to contain live action. Though it ran only two years, it was an influential project in many ways and holds up splendidly as an example of creative entertainment for children.

The show had a roughly even mix of animated and live-action segments. Falling into the latter category were the appearances of its nominal hosts, four people in costumes voiced by others. They were Bingo the smiling gorilla, Drooper the lion, Fleegle the lisping dog, and Snorky the honking elephant. The quartet joked and sang both on location and on an odd set which had a wisecracking cuckoo clock. A regular feature was the mock advice column spot "Dear Drooper." Two things of note about the Bananas were (1) the show featured the first costumes made for television by Sid and Marty Krofft, who later set up shop on their own and created such "costumed adult" hits as *H.R. Pufnstuf* and *Land of the Lost*, and (2) their theme, "The Tra La La Song (One Banana, Two Banana)," managed to crack the *Billboard* Hot 100 singles chart, albeit briefly at the lower rungs, and inspired a host of other singing Saturday morning characters, including the Archies.

Among the animated segments, "Micro Venture" was the most erudite. Professor Carter employed a "Micro-Reducer" that allowed him and his kids to view the world, both indoors and outdoors, on a smaller scale and pass a few scientific facts along the way. At the other end, "The Three Musketeers" was a somewhat loose adaptation of the Alexandre Dumas novel, as Athos, Porthos and Aramis, plus their new addition of D'Artagnan, got a blonde kid helper named Toolie to fight for the Queen's honor. Another cartoon, "Arabian Knights," had Bez, Fariik, and Raseem protect Princess Nida and Prince Turhan from Bakaar and the Evil Vangore. The final component, "The Hillbilly Bears," consisted of repeats from when the cartoon ran as part of *The Atom Ant/Secret Squirrel Show*.

"Tra la la . . ." TV's first costumed rock group, which hosted The Banana Splits Adventure Hour, *consisted of, clockwise from top, Snorky the elephant, Fleegle the dog, Drooper the lion, and Bingo the gorilla.*

The one live-action continuing adventure was "Danger Island," wherein bearded Dr. Irwin Hayden and his daughter Leslie, shipwrecked on a strange land, found assistance from hunky Luke Simmons, mute Chongo, and Morgan the black castaway and confidante. Villains Mu-Tan and Chu wanted the scientists for reasons never quite clear, but the quick location-centered action made "Danger Island" a memorable part of the show, and it stood out dramatically from everything else on Saturday mornings.

The Banana Splits Adventure Hour was a welcome relief from the violent superhero craze that was responsible for a lot of Saturday morning fare from 1966 through 1968. It excelled as the only non-CBS series in the top 10 for Saturday morning shows in 1968–69, but declined greatly in its second year when *Scooby-Doo* debuted on CBS. Ironically, a series which developed a trend for comedy-oriented cartoons on Saturday mornings managed to be superseded by one.

BANANA SPLITS AND FRIENDS—A syndicated title for a packaged show containing *Adventures of Gulliver, The; Atom Ant/Secret Squirrel Show, The; Banana Splits Adventure Hour, The;* and *New Adventures of Huckleberry Finn, The* (the latter was a nighttime NBC series from 1968–69).

BANDSTAND—See American Bandstand; NBC Bandstand.

BANDWAGON '56
News/Public Affairs; B&W
July 15, 1956–November 4, 1956
CBS Sun. 4:30–5 p.m. (7/5/56–9/2/56)
CBS Sun. 5:30–6 p.m. (9/16/56–11/4/56)
Host: *Robert Trout*

Using live and filmed reports, this series profiled the 1956 Presidential campaigns of incumbent Republican Dwight Eisenhower and Democrat Adlai Stevenson. The program began with a review of the national primaries and ended with predictions from leaders in both parties about the results of the election. Pollster Elmo Roper summarized survey results on a few shows, and on two programs singer Dylan Todd gave an offbeat touch with his report on past campaign tunes. CBS reporters Walter Cronkite, Charles Collingwood, Doug Edwards, and Eric Sevareid also contributed stories.

BANG-SHANG LALAPALOOZA SHOW, THE—See Archie Show, The.

BARBARA DEANGELIS
Informational; Color
January 14, 1991–April 26, 1991
CBS Mon.–Fri. 10–10:30 a.m. (1/14/91–4/26/91)
Host: *Dr. Barbara DeAngelis*

Former syndicated radio therapist Dr. Barbera DeAngelis brought her advice and pleasant brunette looks to CBS briefly as a replacement for *Wheel of Fortune*. This series failed due to frequent preemptions for coverage of the Persian Gulf War and that fact that fewer than 70 percent of CBS affiliates carried the show. After cancellation, DeAngelis did infomercials.

•BARGAIN HUNTERS
Game; Color
July 6, 1987–September 4, 1987
ABC Mon.–Fri. 11:30 a.m.–Noon (7/6/87–9/4/87)
Host: *Peter Tomarken*

An ungodly combination of game show flash and home shopping trash, *Bargain Hunters* had six contestants play various shopping games involving the costs of items à la *The Price Is Right* to determine the three top competitors for the day's final round. That round, titled "Super Savers," required them to identify three out of seven prizes they felt offered the best bargains. The winner received those items. What made the show really unbearable was the constant hawking of each item on display for home viewers to buy, with slavish attention to details that might entice the audience to buy this show's goods via a toll-free number. Apparently most viewers were not enticed, as *Bargain Hunters* vanished off the shelves of ABC within 13 weeks.

BARKER BILL'S CARTOONS
Cartoon; B&W
November 18, 1953–November 25, 1956

CBS Wed/Fri 5–5:15 p.m. (11/18/53–11/25/56)

One of network television's earliest showcases for animated theatrical shorts, *Barker Bill's Cartoons* typically aired two cartoons of six to eight minutes in length per show, with an unidentified offstage announcer providing the voice for a drawing of Barker Bill and introducing the segments. The shorts were the Terrytoons series from the 1930s, including such continuing characters as Farmer Al Falfa and Puddy the Pup. Surprisingly, the show did few reruns (by February 1955, for example, nearly 150 of the more than 600 Terrytoons had aired on the show). The series actually gave *Howdy Doody* a run for the money in the ratings until *Mickey Mouse Club* came onto ABC in late 1955.

BARKLEYS, THE
Cartoon; Color
September 9, 1972–September 1, 1973

NBC Sat. 10:30–11 a.m. (9/9/72–9/1/73)

Voices:

Arnie Barkley	Henry Corden
Agnes Barkley	Joan Gerber
Terri Barkley	Julie McWhirter
Chester Barkley	Steve Lewis
Roger Barkley	Gene Andrusco

What nighttime series was so popular in the early 1970s that it spawned not one but two cartoon ripoffs in 1972? The fairly obvious answer is the CBS sitcom *All in the Family*, which ran from 1971–79. The copy seen in nighttime syndication was *Wait Till Your Father Gets Home* from Hanna-Barbera, using a human family, while producers David H. DePatie and Friz Freleng gave Saturday morning viewers a pooch for a lead bigot in *The Barkleys*. Ironically, actress Joan Gerber provided the voice of the mother (who sounded something like Edith Bunker) for both cartoons.

For this entry, Archie Bunker became Arnie Barkley, espousing his opinions freely no matter how ignorant they were. His wife was Agnes, who frequently sided with their children Terri, Chester, and Roger over various topical concerns of the time, including women's liberation. However, TV tykes preferred the feline *Josie and the Pussycats* on CBS over the canine Barkleys. Adult viewers were none too impressed either, with *Variety* terming the show "stupefying beyond belief." With no real enthusiasm from any quarter, the show disappeared from the airwaves after 1973.

BARRIER REEF
Drama; Color
September 11, 1971–September 2, 1972

NBC Sat. 10–10:30 a.m. (9/11/71–12/25/71)
NBC Sat. 10:30–11 a.m. (1/8/72–9/2/72)

Cast:

Tracey Deane	Rowena Wallace
Joe Francis, marine biologist	Richard Melkle
Steve Goba	Harold Hopkins
Dr. Elizabeth Hanna	Ihab Nafa
Kip King, Ted's son	Ken James
Jack Meuranki	George Assana
Diana Parker	Ellie Maclure
Captain Ted King	Joe Jones

The Great Barrier Reef is a 350,000-square-kilometer site in the South Pacific Ocean consisting of 2,900 individual reefs serving as home to 1,500 different species of fish. In this Australian-produced adventure, Ted King was captain of the *Endeavor,* a 220-ton windjammer patrolling the Great Barrier Reef, and Tracey Deane was a scientist on board who used the Minus 5 Computer to calculate data. First mate Jack Meuranki did the dives, while Diana Parker was the computer operator. Dr. Hanna was a research scientist and Steve was a crew member.

In this sea of no-name cast members (to American audiences, at least), the real star was cinematographer Ron Taylor, who did the impressive underwater footage for the series. But this series was one of the biggest disasters in what was NBC's huge failure on Saturday mornings in the 1971–72 season, garnering a mere 15 share of the available audience in the early going.

BASEBALL GAME OF THE WEEK
Sports; B&W and Color
May 6, 1957–October 9, 1993

NBC Sat. 2 p.m.–Conclusion (5/6/57–10/10/64; April or May–September or October only)
NBC Sat. 1 or 2 p.m.–Conclusion (4/16/66–9/30/89; April–September only)
CBS Sat. 1, 2, or 3 p.m.–Conclusion (6/16/90–10/9/93; summers only)

Regulars: *Lindsey Nelson (1957–61), Leo Durocher (1957–59), Fred Haney (1960), Joe Garagiola (1961–64, at least 1975–88), Bob Wolff (1962–64), Curt Gowdy (1966–75), Pee Wee Reese (1966–68), Sandy Koufax (1967–72), Jim Simpson (at least 1967–70), Tony Kubek (at least 1967–89), Maury Wills (1973–74 at least), Jack Buck (at least 1976, 1990–91), Merle Harmon (1980–81), Dick Enberg (at least 1982), Bob Costas (1982–89), Vin Scully (1983–89), Tom Seaver (at least 1989), Tim McCarver (1990–93), Sean McDonough (1992–93)*

After noticing the big ratings CBS racked up with its *Game of the Week,* NBC jumped into the fray in 1957 with its own major league baseball coverage of teams not under CBS's control, with Lindsey Nelson as announcer and Leo Durocher as commentator. Leo the Lip lasted three seasons before being replaced by former Pittsburgh Pirates and Milwaukee Braves manager Fred Haney, followed after one summer by former St. Louis Cardinal Joe Garagiola. Nelson left to cover the New York Mets locally in 1962, so Garagiola paired up with

Bob Wolff in 1962 for three seasons until ABC acquired NBC's baseball TV rights temporarily in 1965.

The games on CBS always had better ratings than those on NBC, so in 1966 NBC put its resources together and bought up all the rights to cover major league baseball, leaving CBS and ABC in the dust for a decade. Leading off its main team was Curt Gowdy with commentator Pee Wee Reese, fresh from *Game of the Week* on CBS. Pitcher Sandy Koufax split analyst duties with Reese the following year, with Koufax handling the pregame show. Jim Simpson and Tony Kubek served as the principal backup team. In 1969 Reese was fired and Kubek replaced him as Gowdy's partner, while Koufax teamed with Simpson in backup. When Koufax left in 1972, Maury Wills became the new analyst with Simpson. In 1973, Garagiola replaced Dick Schaap as host of the pregame show.

The next big change came in 1975, when Gowdy alternated with Joe Garagiola doing play-by-play with Kubek as commentator. Then from 1976–82, Garagiola and Kubek alone became the lead team. Jack Buck and Maury Wills were the backup team.

In 1983 Garagiola went from play-by-play to color when Vin Scully joined the announcing staff. Kubek went to backup commentator with Bob Costas, who had joined a year earlier to replace Merle Harmon on play-by-play. The Garagiola-Scully and Costas-Kubek teams remained intact until 1989, when Tom Seaver replaced Garagiola.

In 1990 CBS won control of all major league baseball events for four years for an unprecedented—and wildly overpriced—total of $1 billion. Former player Tim McCarver was the lead analyst during this period, teamed first by Jack Buck and then Sean McDonough. The high costs made the network skittish about scheduling many games, and coverage of them was spotty and variable through 1993.

In 1994–95, the games went to NBC and ABC, as CBS felt it had been burned by its overpayment, but a strike affected these seasons, and there were no regularly scheduled weekend games. Then Fox got rights in 1996 and reinstalled Saturday games. For more details, see *Fox Baseball.*

•BATMAN
Cartoon; Color
September 14, 1968–

CBS Sat. 10:30–11:30 a.m. (9/14/68–9/6/69)
CBS Sun. 9:30–10 a.m. (9/14/69–9/6/70)
CBS Sat. 10:30–11 a.m. (2/12/77–9/3/77)
CBS Sat. 11 a.m.–Noon (9/10/77–11/12/77)
CBS Sat. 10:30–11:30 a.m. (11/19/77–9/2/78)
NBC Sat. 11 a.m.–Noon (9/27/80–5/16/81)
NBC Sat. 9:30–10:30 a.m. (5/23/81–9/5/81)
Fox Sat. 10–10:30 a.m. (9/5/92–9/12/92)
Fox Mon.–Fri. Various times (9/7/92–)
Fox Sat. 10–10:30 a.m. (9/10/94–1/28/95)
Fox Sat. 11:30 a.m.–Noon (2/4/95–3/11/95)
Fox Sat. 9:30–10 a.m. (3/18/95–9/2/95)

Voices:
Narrator (1968–70) — Jackson Beck
Batmite (1977–81) — Lennie Weinrib
Dick Grayson (Robin) (1968–70) — Casey Kasem
Dick Grayson (1977–81) — Burt Ward
Dick Grayson (Robin) (1992–) — Loren Lester
Alfred Pennyworth (1992–) — Efrem Zimbalist, Jr.
Bruce Wayne (Batman)/Alfred Pennyworth (1968–70) — Olan Soule
Bruce Wayne (Batman) (1977–81) — Adam West
Bruce Wayne (Batman) (1992–) — Kevin Conroy

The Caped Crusader of comics made his biggest splash on television with the wonderfully campy *Batman* series on ABC nighttime from Jan. 12, 1966–March 14, 1968. The success of the ABC series led CBS to add Batman to its Saturday morning schedule of superheroes. The first season was titled *The Batman/Superman Hour;* the second-year repeats, in half-hour form, were titled *The Batman Show.* Unlike the nighttime version, the first cartoon was played in a straight adventure format.

In early 1977 CBS unveiled *The New Adventures of Batman.* In the fall of 1977 it became *The Batman/Tarzan Adventure Hour,* and in 1978–80 Batman became just one of the elements of *Tarzan and the Super Seven* (q.v.). In 1980–81 NBC reran the series as *Batman and the Super Seven.* This incarnation installed a spritelike midget alien called Batmite, who assisted the Dynamic Duo in mostly comic fashion, but as before, the adventures had little hint of camp to them, unless you count the voices of Adam West and Burt Ward from the ABC 1960s show.

After a decade's absence, Fox began running the 65 shows daily, which later aired briefly on Sunday nights. These efforts were more along the line of the hit 1989 *Batman* movie, emphasizing an Art Deco look with big-name celebrities serving as the voices of villains, including Roddy McDowall, Ed Asner, and Michael York, among others. Alfred the butler returned to assist Batman and Robin, the only one who knew their regular identities. The crime fighters also appeared on *Super Friends* (q.v.).

BATTLE REPORT
Public Affairs; B&W
September 17, 1950–April 20, 1952

NBC Sun. 3–3:30 p.m. (9/17/50–7/1/51)
NBC Sun. 2–2:30 p.m. (11/4/51–4/20/52)

Host: *Robert McCormick*

A patriotic effort to show the U.S. Department of Defense's efforts to promote American democracy throughout the world, *Battle Report* concentrated on the work being done in the Korean War using live and filmed reports. It debuted on NBC Sunday at 8 p.m. August 13, 1950, where it ran for a month, and it also returned to nighttime briefly from June–August 1951. The program ended after 86 consecutive Sunday shows with presidential assistant John R. Steelman serving as guest host following several appearances as a speaker.

•BATTLESTARS
Game; Color
October 26, 1981–July 1, 1983

NBC Mon.–Fri. 11:30 a.m.–Noon (10/26/81–4/23/82)
NBC Mon.–Fri. Noon–12:30 p.m. (4/4/83–7/1/83)

Host: *Alex Trebek*

Mix the largely comic questions and celebrities' bluffs of *Hollywood Squares* with *Match Game*'s blue-red set design of two tiers each with three stars and you had *Battlestars*. Two contestants faced six celebrities enclosed on all sides by individual yet interconnected triangles, three pointing up and three pointing down. At each vertex there was a number from 1 to 10, and a flashing light bounced around, lighting the 10 numbers one at a time. The first contestant (the returning champion) would stop the light and could pick any celebrity adjacent to the stopped light to answer a question posed by Trebek. A monitor (unseen by the contestant) showed two answers to the celebrity, one correct and one incorrect, and the celebrity would say which was correct. The contestant had to say if he or she agreed or disagreed with the celebrity's answer. If the contestant was right, that light went out, and the other lights started flashing again. If the contestant was wrong, the light still went out, but it became the other contestant's chance to play. When all the lights around a celebrity were out, that celebrity was "captured." To win the game, a contestant had to "capture" three celebrities.

The winner of the game played a bonus round consisting of a closeup photograph of a celebrity (not on the panel) beneath 16 numbered squares. The contestant picked two cards with a number encoded on them and gave an extra number of his or her choice to reveal three squares. The contestant then could guess the mystery face or have a celebrity make a choice. A correct guess won $5,000; if incorrect, the contestant could win $500 after an identification with another box removed, or $300 with another box revealed.

Though it lasted only half a season, NBC decided to bring the series back a year after cancellation under the title *The New Battlestars* with a few alterations. Now contestants could call out numbers for the rest of their turns after the first flashed vertex was captured, and the bonus game included a jackpot of prizes which increased each day it was not cracked. The bonus game now consisted of the contestant correctly agreeing or disagreeing on three questions with one of the celebrities he or she "captured" in the regular games. Contestants answering the three questions the right way won the jackpot, or received $1,000 for two correct answers or $500 for one right.

Though there were no regulars, Nell Carter, Stuart Damon, Dody Goodman, Jenilee Harrison, Tom Poston, Skip Stephenson, Rip Taylor, and Betty White all made at least five appearances on the show's initial 25-week run. For the second run, the only celebrities seen more than three weeks were JM J. Bullock and Charles Nelson Reilly, each on six of the show's 13 final weeks.

BAY CITY ROLLERS SHOW, THE
Variety; Color
September 9, 1978–January 27, 1979

NBC Sat. 11 a.m.–Noon (9/9/78–10/28/78)
NBC Sat. 12:30–1 p.m. (11/4/78–1/27/79)

Regulars: *The Bay City Rollers (Eric Faulkner, Alan Longmuir, Derek Longmuir, Leslie McKeown, and Stuart Wood), Billie Hayes (as Witchiepoo), Jay Robinson (as Dr. Shrinker), Billy Barty (as Hugo), Paul Gale (as Whoo Doo), Sharon Baird, Patty Maloney*

Originally titled *The Krofft Superstar Hour* (for its first two months), this series signaled the dying popularity of both the teenybopper music group the Bay City Rollers and the Sid and Marty Krofft production company. The five Scottish lads who made up the Bay City Rollers uneasily served as hosts and actors in sketches with characters from previous Sid and Marty Krofft productions, like Witchiepoo from *H. R. Pufnstuf*, Whoo Doo from *Lidsville*, and Dr. Shrinker and Hugo from *The Krofft Supershow*. All of these were done by the original actors except for Whoo Doo, whom Charles Nelson Reilly portrayed on *Lidsville*. The setting for some of the comedy was a lobby in Horror Hotel, in which the Rollers seemed to be mildly uncomfortable. Noticing the disastrous ratings, NBC had a stronger reaction than the Rollers, and pared the show down to 30 minutes on November 4, 1978 before canning it two months later.

BEAGLES, THE
Cartoon; Color
September 10, 1966–September 7, 1968

CBS Sat. 12:30–1 p.m. (9/10/66–9/2/67)
ABC Sun. 4–4:30 p.m. (9/17/67–9/7/68)

The Beagles consisted of the misadventures of two rock musician pups, Stringer and Tubby, who actually acted more like a comedy team. Though it was promoted as featuring rocking pooches, it was not a spoof of the similarly named rock group the Beatles. After this program finished in the top 10 for Saturday mornings in 1966–67, easily beating *Magilla Gorilla* on ABC and *The Smithsonian* on NBC, CBS somewhat surprisingly did not renew it, and the series went into repeats on ABC the following season, ironically preceding *Magilla Gorilla* reruns.

•BEAKMAN'S WORLD
Children's; Color
September 18, 1993–

CBS Sat. Noon–12:30 p.m. (9/18/93–)

Cast:
Beakman	Paul Zaloom
Eliza	Eliza Schneider
Lester	Mark Ritts

Voices of the penguins: *Alan Barzman, Bert Bertis*

Performance artist Paul Zaloom brought a touch of wackiness to the normally dry presentation of science-oriented education on television. Adapted from the Universal Press Syndicate comic strip "You Can with Beakman" by John Church, *Beakman's World* took viewers' questions about various phenomena and answered them factually but humorously too. (Could you imagine Miss Frances on *Ding Dong School* singing a doo-wop tune about the workings of the kidneys?) Beakman was a scientist with a big brunette hairdo, Eliza his eager assistant, and Lester the humanoid laboratory rat (actually an actor in a rodent suit). Bookending the activities were two penguin puppets, Don and Herb, supposedly watching the show, who dryly commented on what was happening.

The series was syndicated in the fall of 1992, then went onto CBS on Saturdays a year later while running concurrently on cable's The Learning Channel on Wednesday nights starting September 30, 1993. It also aired in 50 countries overseas.

•BEANY AND CECIL
Cartoon; Color
January 5, 1963–October 8, 1988

ABC Sat. 11:30 a.m.–Noon (1/5/63–12/19/64)
ABC Sun. 10:30–11 a.m. (12/26/64–4/25/65)
ABC Sun. 11–11:30 a.m. (5/2/65–9/19/65)
ABC Sun. 10:30–11 a.m. (9/26/65–12/26/65)
ABC Sun. 10–10:30 a.m. (1/2/66–12/25/66)
ABC Sun. 9:30–10 a.m. (1/1/67–9/3/67)
ABC Sat. 8–8:30 a.m. (9/10/88–10/8/88)

Voices:

Beany Boy (1963–67)/Captain Huffenpuff	Jim McGeorge
Beany Boy (1988)	Mark Hildreth
Cecil/Dishonest John (both 1963–67)	Irv Shoemaker
Cecil (1988)	Billy West
Dishonest John (1988)	Maurice La Marche

Beany and Cecil first appeared on television as a Emmy-winning syndicated puppet show from Los Angeles in the 1950s titled *Time for Beany*, with Daws Butler and Stan Freberg providing the voices. It maintained its basic format when it first appeared in cartoon form on January 6, 1962 as part of the nighttime *Matty's Funday Funnies* (q.v.), where it became its own series a few months later before shifting to Saturday mornings in 1963. The principals were the ever-smiling Beany, who wore a cap, as his name implied; his uncle Huffenpuff, who was captain of their boat the Leakin' Lena; Beany's pet Cecil, who was a seasick serpent; and Dishonest John, who was their conniving nemesis in a trench coat. There were puns galore in the four adventures per show, such as the time our heroes met Davy Crickett. The episode parodied not only the character seen in 1950s episodes of the nighttime *Disneyland* show, but also gave a dead-on spoof of the sappy "Ballad of Davy Crockett" theme used on the series. As for Davy, his parting words of advice were "Remember the Al-imony!" Ex–Warner Brothers cartoon director Bob Clampett created the characters and produced all 78 cartoons.

In 1988 the series had a short-lived revival without the participation of Bob Clampett, who died in 1984. Only Jim McGeorge returned from the first cartoon, and he no longer did Beany Boy. The new voices, animation, and early time slot probably deterred anyone but the most die-hard fan from seeing the two episodes per show, and the new "Beany and Cecil" vanished after five programs.

•BEAT THE CLOCK
Game; B&W and Color
September 16, 1957–February 1, 1980

CBS Mon.–Fri. 2–2:30 p.m. (9/16/57–9/12/58)
ABC Mon.–Fri. 3–3:30 p.m. (10/13/58–1/27/61)
CBS Mon.–Fri. 10–10:30 a.m. (9/17/79–2/1/80)

Host: *Clayton "Bud" Collyer (1957–61), Monty Hall (1979–80)*

One of TV's best remembered stunt shows, *Beat the Clock* had contestants picked from the studio audience do wacky tasks usually involving balloons, pies, water, crockery, and other devices within various time frames, typically under 60 seconds. Agility and dexterity, plus some luck, were the keys to winning the game. An example of the show's difficult challenges was the daytime version's bonus stunt. For a car and a cash amount that began at $100 and increased $100 each day the stunt was not accomplished, a player had to stand 10 feet from a narrow inclined ramp leading to a flat surface 18 inches square and roll three balls up the ramp onto the surface in order to win the prize. At one point it was 161 days before a contestant managed to complete the stunt and collect the by-then-impressive prize of $16,100.

Beat the Clock began on radio with Collyer hosting as *Time's A Wastin'* in 1948; it changed its name on January 5,

Bud Collyer tells the audience of Beat the Clock *his show will move to 3 p.m. on ABC daily.*

1949, then joined the CBS nighttime TV lineup from March 23, 1950–February 16, 1958. Five months before the nighttime series was canned, CBS started a simultaneous afternoon version (the first time CBS did so with a game show), which ran a year before transferring to ABC as part of the latter's initial full schedule of daily shows in 1958. Collyer also served as co-producer.

Following its cancellation in 1961, the series returned eight years later as a syndicated nightly series from Montreal hosted by Jack Narz from 1969–72 and then Gene Wood (formerly the announcer under Narz) from 1972–74. Five years later, CBS aired a version titled *The All-New Beat the Clock*, with Monty Hall as host and, ironically, Jack Narz as announcer and associate producer. In the 1979–80 revival, two pairs of contestants competed until November 5, 1979, when celebrity couples played for members of the studio audience and the show was retitled *All-Star Beat the Clock*. A new addition was a shuffleboard game with cash amounts on each space that all four contestants played to see who did the final stunt of the day. The changes were not enough to prevent the revival from ending three months later.

•BEATLES, THE
Cartoon; Color
September 25, 1965–April 20, 1969

ABC Sat. 10:30–11 a.m. (9/25/65–9/2/67)
ABC Sat. Noon–12:30 p.m. (9/9/67–9/7/68)
ABC Sun. 9:30–10 a.m. (9/15/68–4/20/69)

Voices:

John Lennon/George Harrison   *Paul Frees*
Paul McCartney/Ringo Starr   *Lance Percival*

When the histories of the 20th century are written, the influence of the rock music group the Beatles will no doubt merit a mention in any serious retrospective. The Beatles phenomenon affected virtually every facet of culture in the mid- to late 1960s, and the group's achievements in music remain astounding both for their sound and for their popularity. Beatlemania was still in full force with "Help!" and "Yesterday" hitting #1 when the Fab Four became the first living individuals adapted as regular cartoon characters on a network TV series (Alvin and the Chipmunks don't count, wise guy!).

The episodes were nothing much visually or thematically. The bare-bones story lines shoehorned in at least two songs in sort of a primitive music video, with words to the song shown at the bottom of the screen for youngsters who wanted to sing along. Virtually the whole Beatles record catalogue up through 1966 went through this adaptation, including their German version of "I Want to Hold Your Hand." The rest of the time the four lads from Liverpool cracked jokes and engaged in general nonsense in the spirit of their 1964 movie romp *A Hard Day's Night*. Other than providing their voices from the records, John, Paul, George, and Ringo did not participate in the series. Englishman Lance Percival and American Paul Frees did their voices (Frees went to England

to tape the first 17 cartoons), and the animation was done in the United Kingdom and Australia.

A massive hit in its first season, *The Beatles* took a severe beating in 1966–67 when *Space Ghost* on CBS topped it. ABC moved the show and changed the title to *The New Beatles* in 1967, but the series actually used only reruns starting then and the ratings kept slipping. It went to Sundays in 1968, where it ended up flopping rather badly and was replaced by *Dudley Do-Right* before the end of the season. The Beatles themselves broke up not long thereafter.

A final note: Even though the animation on the series was the typical, unexceptional limited variety, it was enough to get its producers, King Features, a deal with United Artists to do the 1968 animated feature film *Yellow Submarine*. Looking at the elaborate visuals and plot of *Yellow Submarine*, it's hard to believe the film had anything to do with ABC's one-time hit.

•BEETHOVEN
Cartoon; Color
September 17, 1994–September 2, 1995

CBS Sat. 8:30–9 a.m. (9/17/94–9/2/95)

Voices:

George Phineas Newton   *Dean Jones*
Ryce Newton   *Nicholle Tom*

Also: *J. D. Daniels, Bill Faggerbakke, Brian George, Maurice LaMarche, Tress MacNeille, Joel Murray, Joe Pantoliano, Kath Soucie, Francesca Marie Smith*

Beethoven was a slobbering, headstrong St. Bernard who caused much unintended grief for his owner George Newton. George's family, consisting of his wife Alice and children Ted, Ryce, and young daughter Emily, had more tolerance for Beethoven's actions and worked as a buffer between the two whenever George reached the breaking point after Beethoven had made a particularly horrendous mess. For his part, Beethoven had only unconditional love of his master, a situation which perplexed his fellow talking dog pals—Caesar, the stupid one, Ginger, the wise one, and Sparky, the energetic one. Mr. Huggs was the Newtons' family guinea pig. All characters lived in the town of Valley Vista. Each show contained two separate episodes.

The show derived from the 1992 live-action movie of the same name and its 1993 sequel *Beethoven's 2nd,* wherein the pooch became a father of a litter of pups. Dean Jones, the voice of George in the cartoon, was the villain in the first movie, which starred Charles Grodin as George and Bonnie Bedelia as his wife. The only other cast member from either movie to be in the cartoon was Nicholle Tom, who played the older sister. Ivan Reitman produced both movies and the TV show.

•BEETLEJUICE
Cartoon; Color
September 9, 1989–September 5, 1992

ABC Sat. 10:30–11 a.m. (9/9/89–9/1/90)
ABC Sat. 10–10:30 a.m. (9/8/90–8/31/91)
ABC Sat. 9:30–10 a.m. (9/7/91–9/5/92)

Voices:

Beetlejuice	Stephen Ouimette
Charles Deetz	Roger Dunn
Delia Deetz	Elizabeth Hanna
Lydia Deetz	Alyson Court

Lydia Deetz was a ponytailed prepubescent girl living with her average suburban parents Charles and Delia in an average suburban house when she hooked up with Beetlejuice, a bizarre fellow from the afterlife. Dressed in a garish stripped shirt and sporting some of the most crooked green teeth seen on television, Beetlejuice acted as a protector to Lydia in various scrapes once she conjured him up by saying his name three times fast. His solutions typically involved him going along with an intrigued Lydia to his home the Neitherworld, where even more bizarre creatures, most of them parodies of pop culture, either befriended or bedeviled them.

The series was based on the 1988 film of the same name which starred Michael Keaton as Beetlejuice and Winona Ryder as Lydia. Toward the end of its run the show also included Doomie the Car, who liked to chase dogs. It went into repeats on the Nickelodeon cable channel.

BEFORE HOURS
News; Color
March 2, 1987–September 16, 1988

NBC Mon.–Fri. 6–6:15 a.m. (3/2/87–9/16/88)

Host: *Bob Jamieson*

Commentator: *Donald T. Regan*

This early morning business news update aired live before *NBC News at Sunrise,* but stations were free to program it anytime before *Today* at 7 a.m. It included a "market outlook" done in association with *The Wall Street Journal,* which produced the series, and commentary by ex-Treasury Secretary and White House Chief of Staff (under Ronald Reagan) Donald T. Regan. As only 149 of 212 NBC affiliates carried it, the network decided after a year and a half to absorb the show's elements, but not regulars, into *NBC News at Sunrise.*

BEHIND THE NEWS WITH HOWARD K. SMITH
News/Public Affairs; B&W
January 11, 1959–March 29, 1959

CBS Sun. 4:30–5 p.m. (1/11/59–3/29/59)

Host: *Howard K. Smith*

Howard K. Smith, who had been doing news analysis on *The CBS Evening News with Douglas Edwards* since 1957, expanded his activities on this series. Here he lectured from a podium as he and other CBS correspondents examined a single issue per show, incorporating interviews, animation, and other visual aids to make points. A recurring topic was the Cold War, as the debut dealt with a visit of the USSR first Deputy Premier Arasias Mikoyan, and the last two shows on daytime covered "The Berlin Crisis." In April 1959 the show went into the Sunday 6 p.m. slot, but CBS felt that Smith's

analysis of the news on this evening show was more personal opinion than impartial reporting, and canceled the series on September 20, 1959. Smith continued his work on *The CBS Evening News* until a dispute with the network in 1961, after which he moved to ABC for nearly two decades.

BEHOLD WONDROUS THINGS—See *Lamp Unto My Feet.*

BEN JERROD
Soap Opera; Color
April 1, 1963–June 28, 1963

NBC Mon.–Fri. 2–2:30 p.m. (4/1/63–6/28/63)

Cast:

John P. Abbott	Addison Richards
Agnes Abbott	Jeanne Baird
Lieutenant Choates	Lyle Talbot
Janet Donelli	Regina Gleason
Ben Jerrod	Michael M. Ryan
D.A. Dan Joplin	John Napier
Jim O'Hara	Ken Scott
Pete Morrison	Peter Hansen
Lil Morrison	Martine Bartlett

Attorney Ben Jerrod found himself only 13 weeks of overheated conflicts in this failed melodrama from Hollywood. After he teamed up with ex-judge John Abbott in a law practice in the town of Indian Hill, Rhode Island, they were retained by Janet Donelli, charged with murdering her husband. Janet had some strikes against her, notably affairs with Jim O'Hara and married pharmacist Pete Morrison, the latter of whom died in her home on April 22. D.A. Joplin and Lt. Choates were sure Donelli killed Morrison, but Jerrod and crew thought O'Hara seemed a likely suspect, and even Abbott's daughter Agnes searched for clues about the murder as the trial began on June 17. Most viewers could have cared less about the whole mess. Ben Jerrod's practice closed shop quickly due to drawing lower ratings than the program it replaced, *The Merv Griffin Show.*

•BENJI, ZAX AND THE ALIEN PRINCE
Children's; Color
September 17, 1983–August 25, 1984

CBS Sat. 11–11:30 a.m. (9/17/83–2/4/84)
CBS Sat. 12:30–1 p.m. (2/11/84–8/25/84)

Cast:

Prince Yubi	Chris Burton
Zax (voice only)	Rig Spiegel

Taped in Dallas, this odd science fiction/adventure offering had the alien child Rubi and his robot bodyguard Zax the talking disk seek comfort on Earth with Benji the dog as various stooges for the mean ruler of their home planet tried to reclaim them. None succeeded during this show's short run.

The original Benji was a mixed breed cocker, poodle, and schnauzer found at a Burbank animal shelter in the 1960s. He played Higgins on the 1960s CBS nighttime sitcom *Petticoat Junction,* but gained real fame in 1974 in a movie named after himself. He became the second animal named to the Animal Actors Hall of Fame after Lassie. This series starred Benji's daughter, who in 1978 headlined a prime time TV special on ABC titled "The Phenomenon of Benji," the first of four Benji specials before this show. For some strange reason, this Benji even did a layout for *Playgirl* magazine.

•BENNETTS, THE
Soap Opera; B&W
July 6, 1953–January 8, 1954

NBC Mon.–Fri. 11:15–11:30 a.m. (7/6/53–1/8/54)

Cast:

Wayne Bennett	Don Gibson
Nancy Bennett (early episodes)	Paula Houston
Nancy Bennett (later episodes)	Eloise Kummer
Blaney Cobb	Jack Lester
Meg Cobb	Beverly Younger
Speedy Winters	Vi Berwick

Attorney Wayne Bennett and his wife Nancy, residents of the small town of Kingsport, found themselves constantly entangled with their friends' dilemmas in this live melodrama from Chicago. Among their friends were their next-door neighbors Blaney and Meg, who planned to adopt an 8-year-old girl named Hope, and Wayne's old buddy Bert Wells, whom Wayne cleared of theft only to learn later that Wells had really done the deed. Bert added to Wayne's distress by announcing he would divorce Ellie, his wife of 15 months, in order to wed his secretary Helen Meade during this serial's short run.

•BERENSTAIN BEARS, THE
Cartoon; Color
September 14, 1985–September 5, 1987

CBS Sat. 8–8:30 a.m. (9/14/85–4/19/86)
CBS Sat. 8:30–9 a.m. (4/26/86–9/6/86)
CBS Sat. 8–8:30 a.m. (9/13/86–9/5/87)

Voices:

Brother Bear	David Mendenhall
Mama Bear	Ruth Buzzi
Papa Q. Bear	Jim Cummings
Raffish Ralph	Frank Welker
Sister Bear	Christina Lange

"This way to Bear Country, you'll know when you're there, as soon as you enter, you'll feel like a bear." Thus began each episode of *The Berenstain Bears,* which led into a tune which sounded like "Stars and Stripes Forever," followed by an enjoyable if tame adventure about a family of four bears—Mamma, Papa, 8-year-old Brother, and 6-year-old Sister—who lived in a split-level tree. They congregated with other types like Mayor Bear and Honeybear. The recurring threat, albeit a mild one, was Raffish Ralph, who often nearly bankrupted the Bears with his moneymaking plans.

Stan and Jan Berenstain created the books on which this program was based and served as producers of the TV cartoon as well as story and teleplay writers for it. The first TV adaption was a NBC nighttime special, "The Berenstain Bears' Christmas Tree," on December 3, 1979, followed by several others through 1984 before this show debuted.

BERT PARKS SHOW, THE
Variety; B&W
November 1, 1950–June 26, 1952

NBC Mon./Wed./Fri. 3:30–4 p.m. (11/1/50–1/11/52; off summer 1951)
CBS Mon./Wed./Fri. 3:30–4 p.m. (1/14/52–6/26/52)

Regulars: Bert Parks, Betty Ann Grove, Harold Lang, Bobby Sherwood, the Heathertones

The Bert Parks Show came confidently onto NBC's burgeoning daytime schedule in 1950, thanks to more than $1 million in sponsor money promised by General Foods (ironically, CBS auditioned the show for sponsors on March 28, 1950). Bert was his usual booming, overpowering self, while Betty Ann Grove was a vocalist, Harold Lang was a dancer, and the Heathertones were an all-female singing quintet (a trio by 1952).

In 1952 the series left NBC after advertiser General Foods argued with the network about its sponsorship of the Sunday night sitcom *Young Mr. Bobbin,* which NBC felt was a drag on its lineup, and some other concessions. NBC's tiff with General Foods cost the network an estimated $1 million in revenues. But the show had so much station clearance trouble on CBS that the network took the then-rare step of offering some ad spots for sale to local stations to get better exposure Wednesdays and Fridays. The effort did not work, and Bert went back to hosting game shows.

BEST OF EVERYTHING, THE
Soap Opera; Color
March 30, 1970–September 25, 1970

ABC Mon.–Fri. Noon–12:30 p.m. (3/30/70–9/25/70)

Cast:

Anne Carter	Diane Kagan
Mike Carter	Jean-Pierre Stewart
Kate Farrow/Mrs. Bang	M'El Dowd
Kim Jordan	Katherine Glass
Violet Jordan	Geraldine Fitzgerald
Joshua Jordan (first)	John Rust
Joshua Jordan (second)	Peter Harris
Amanda Key	Gale Sondergaard
Dexter Key	James Davidson
Joanna Key	Bonnie Bee Buzzard
Ken Lamont	Barry Ford
Barbara Lamont	Rochelle Oliver
Johnny Lamont	Stephen Grover
Gwen Mitchell	Ginnie Curtis
April Morrison (first)	Julie Mannix

April Morrison (second)	Susan Sullivan
Dr. Ed Perrone	Victor Arnold
Linda Warren	Patty McCormack
Randy Wilson	Ted LePlat

April Morrison was a "dewy-eyed innocent" from Maine befriended by fellow stenographer Linda and Kim and Kim's parents Violet and Joshua, who were teachers, when she arrived to work at the Key Publishing Company in New York City. She found that life there could be brutal to an aspiring woman, such as when Kim Jordan was left for dead after someone mixed LSD using her chemistry lab equipment and stabbed her seven times. Training April in the ways of the world was her boss, the once-cordial but now hard-bitten Amanda Key. Among the other characters seen were Gwen Mitchell, another stenographer, and Anne and Mike Carter, a troubled couple. The basis for all stories was a novel by Rona Jaffe that became a movie in 1959 starring Joan Crawford.

The Best of Everything had the worst of everything in terms of timing. It came on the air the same day as *Somerset* and *A World Apart* to bring the total number of daily soaps on the air to 19 series. All that competition more than sated viewers' appetite for serials, and the show generated a minuscule 1.8 rating, guaranteeing its cancellation after only six months.

BEST OF SCOOBY-DOO, THE—See *Scooby-Doo, Where Are You?*

BETTER LIVING TV THEATRE
Documentary; B&W
June 21, 1953–August 16, 1953

ABC Sun. 1:30–2 p.m. (6/21/53–8/16/53)

Host/Narrator: *Peter Roberts*

This collection of industrial films ran briefly on ABC before returning a year later on DuMont's nighttime schedule from April 21–August 28, 1954 with Fischer Black as host.

BETTER SEX, THE
Game; Color
July 18, 1977–January 13, 1978

ABC Mon.–Fri. Noon–12:30 p.m. (7/18/77–1/13/78)

Host: *Bill Anderson*
Hostess: *Sarah Purcell*

Two sexually segregated teams of six members competed daily on this series to determine which was "the better sex." A person on one team received a question and gave either a right answer or a bluff. The first two contestants on the other team had to agree whether it was the answer or a bluff. If they were right, two members of the opposing team went out of competition, but if they were wrong, two members of their team were eliminated. The game continued until one team was completely eliminated. The winning team then faced 30 studio audience members of the opposite sex in a bonus contest using six questions in the same game, with studio

audience contestants using green lights to indicate agreement and red lights to signal opposition. If the team defeated the 30 audience members, the six split $5,000; if not, the surviving audience members split $500 among themselves.

BETTY CROCKER SHOW, THE
Instructional; B&W
November 9, 1950–April 26, 1952

CBS Thu. 3:30–4 p.m. (11/9/50–12/28/50)
CBS Tue./Thu. 3:30–4 p.m. (1/2/51–5/31/51)
ABC Sat. Noon–12:30 p.m. (11/3/51–4/26/52)

Hostess: *Adelaide Hawley (as Betty Crocker)*

Perhaps the most famous woman created through advertising in the 20th century (how many people know she has never existed?), "Betty Crocker" came to early television to promote General Mills products in an extended commercial. In the 1950 filmed premiere, Betty told a teenage girl who wrote to her how to cook for the family while her mother was gone, and this bit was followed by a dramatization about a Thanksgiving dinner where Betty entered the home, and the girl followed Betty's instructions to the point where Betty's family liked her pies better than mom's! Actress Adelaide Hawley did fine as Betty, as she had played her character in a similar radio series in the 1940s.

The first try was a ratings disaster for CBS, and ABC gave it a second shot as *The Betty Crocker Star Matinee*, a talk show hosted by "Betty." The series promised "three stars" per show, with the first being a famous actor doing a scene (Thomas Mitchell and Basil Rathbone did the first two shows), the second a "food star" with a recipe using the sponsor's products, and the third a "field of service star" to women, like a florist. The second version was no more successful than the first, so Betty went back to being a product symbol.

BETTY WHITE SHOW, THE
Variety; B&W
February 8, 1954–December 31, 1954

NBC Mon.–Fri. 12:30–1 p.m. (2/8/54–7/2/54)
NBC Mon.–Fri. 4:30–5 p.m. (7/5/54–9/10/54)
NBC Mon.–Fri. Noon–12:30 p.m. (9/13/54–12/31/54)

Regulars: *Betty White, the Four Jokers, the Frank DeVol Orchestra*

In her first regular network TV series, Los Angeles native Betty White presided over an easy-to-take daily half-hour of talking with guests like comic Jack Carson, singing upbeat songs like "Getting to Know You," and clowning with bandleader Frank DeVol. The Four Jokers was a singing quartet.

•BIG JOHN, LITTLE JOHN
Sitcom; Color
September 11, 1976–September 3, 1977

NBC Sat. 11:30 a.m.–Noon (9/11/76–9/3/77)

Cast:

"Big" John Martin	*Herb Edelman*
"Little" John Martin	*Robbie Rist*
Marjorie Martin	*Joyce Bulifant*
Ricky Martin	*Mike Darnell*
Miss Bertha Bottomly	*Olive Dunbar*

Schoolteacher John Martin found himself in the dicey situation of going from a middle-aged guy to a 12-year-old, thanks to his discovery of the fountain of youth in Florida. As a result of the fountain's unusual powers, John found that whenever he was doused with water, he changed into an owlish prepubescent. His wife Marjorie and son Ricky knew of his dilemma and covered for the inopportune alterations using various stratagems, including claiming that "Little John" was actually John's nephew. Several co-workers, including Miss Bottomly the principal, and other observers got suspicious, but they never learned the truth.

Created by Sherwood Schwartz, the guy responsible for *Gilligan's Island,* this show was quite a respectable sitcom, especially when compared with the usual offerings for the Saturday morning children's market. It even had one show where John attempted to confess to the outside world what had happened (the attempt failed). But kids preferred a different kind of magic with *Superfriends* on ABC, so the show lasted just one season.

BIG PAYOFF, THE
Game; B&W
December 31, 1951–October 16, 1959

NBC Mon.–Fri. 3–3:30 p.m. (12/31/51–3/27/53)
CBS Mon.–Fri. 3–3:30 p.m. (3/30/53–10/16/59)

Regulars: *Randy Merriman (12/31/51–12/31/57), Bobby Sherwood, Robert Paige (12/30/57–9/25/59), Bert Parks (9/28/59–10/16/59), Bess Myerson, Betty Ann Grove (12/31/51–3/22/57), Denise Lor, Susan Sayers, Judy Lynn (3/25/57–7/22/59), Dori Anne Gray (7/27/59–10/16/59), the Burt Buhrman Trio (1959 at least)*

In *The Big Payoff* men used their intelligence, rather than battle prowess, to honor their wives. The men had to answer three rather challenging questions correctly to win a small bounty of prizes. If they could answer a fourth one as well, they won the Big Payoff, consisting of a mink coat (modeled by Bess Myerson) for the wife, a new car for the man, and a free plane trip for the couple. Among the show's other contests were "Knight in Shining Armor" and "Little Big Payoff."

Bess Myerson became a household name thanks to her hosting work on this series. Her co-host for the first six years was Randy Merriman, who left at the start of 1958 to return to his native Minneapolis, Minnesota to do a local daytime TV series. As Merriman headed out, Robert Paige was introduced as his successor. Paige lasted for all but the last month of the run, when Bert Parks replaced him. Betty Ann Grove, Denise Lor, Susan Sayers, Judy Lynn, and Dori Anne Gray (the name presumably was a pseudonym; get it?) served as featured singers at various points during the show's run.

The gifts on the show were among the most lavish on daytime in the 1950s. After three years, the show had dispensed 104 mink coats, 104 European trips, 62 automobiles, and close to $1 million in merchandise. For its fourth anniversary celebration in late 1955, it held a six-week contest where contestants had to guess how many sequins were on a bathing suit, with the right answer netting a car, a trip to Europe, a diamond ring, and a mink coat.

After six months in daytime, *The Big Payoff* went onto NBC nighttime Sundays from 8–9 p.m. in the summers of 1952 and 1953. Before the second summer run, the daytime show switched networks to CBS in March 1953. The show proved to be lethal competition for most series NBC tried against it in the 1950s until the quiz show scandals broke. *The Big Payoff* had been living up to its name, and to quell any suspicions that the show's large winnings may have been fixed in the volatile atmosphere of the time, CBS canceled the show. In 1962 it ran in daily syndication with Robert Paige as host.

BIG QUESTION, THE
Discussion; B&W
November 11, 1951–April 13, 1952

CBS Sun. 2:30–3 p.m. (11/11/51–4/13/52)

Host: *Charles Collingwood*

People involved in a current issue took part in discussing "the big question" each week on this live Washington, D.C.–based series. It first ran on CBS Sundays at 6 p.m. from September 9–October 21, 1951 before moving for a few months to the midafternoon slot.

•BIG SHOWDOWN, THE
Game; Color
December 23, 1974–July 4, 1975

ABC Mon.–Fri. 2:30–3 p.m. (12/23/74–7/4/75)

Host: *Jim Peck*

The Big Showdown, taped in New York City, was an uneasy combination of skill and luck—a hard quiz which ended with the roll of a pair of dice. The quiz portion had three contestants try to answer questions on six subjects, each represented by the face of a die. The number on that die awarded the points for the question. Players aimed to be the first to answer each question to claim the points on their way to reach a target score in two rounds. The top two finishers played "Final Showdown," where they tried to be the first to reach seven points in categories represented by one, two, or three points of a die. The winner at this point claimed $250 and then learned he or she had to go gambling following their display of knowledge.

The winner went to a table to roll two oversized dice whose six-dot sides were replace by "Show" on one and "Down" on the other. The object was to roll both of the sides up in the first toss of the dice to claim $10,000. Unfortunately for the show and its viewers, no one ever did it, though several did win a rather anticlimactic $5,000 for rolling the two faces within a 30-second time limit following the first toss.

BIG 10 BASKETBALL—See *College Basketball*.

BIG 3 GOLF
Sports; Color
February 20, 1965–March 27, 1965
NBC Sat. 5–6 p.m. (2/20/65–3/27/65)
Regulars: *Jack Nicklaus, Arnold Palmer, Gary Player*

A trio of golf's greatest professionals played against each other every week on this series. If nothing else, *Big 3 Golf* showed the swift ascension in popularity and success for Jack Nicklaus, who only a few years earlier was an upstart taking on Arnold Palmer and Gary Player in their series *Challenge Golf* (q.v.).

•BIG TOP
Children's; B&W
January 27, 1951–September 21, 1957
CBS Sat. Noon–1 p.m. (1/27/51–9/21/57)
Regulars: *Jack Sterling, Ed McMahon, Dan Lurie (as Circus Dan the Muscle Man), Joe Basile the Brass King and His Band*

Arguably a knockoff of *Super Circus*, *Big Top* presented five or six guest artists like acrobats and gymnasts performing in a three-ring circus live from the Brass Armory in Philadelphia and introduced by ringmaster Jack Sterling. Between acts, future *Tonight Show* sidekick Ed McMahon appeared as one of many clowns seen in greasepaint on the show, while Dan Lurie displayed his beefy physique. CBS first aired the show Saturday evenings from July 1, 1950–January 6, 1951 before moving it to an earlier slot. The network canceled the show because they wanted a "more adult" program on Saturdays at noon and because longtime sponsor Sealtest had decided to stop advertising with *Big Top*.

Ringleader Jack Sterling, left, and bandleader Joe Basile provided the entertainment on Big Top.

BIGFOOT AND WILDBOY
Adventure; Color
June 2, 1979–August 19, 1979
ABC Sat. 11:30 a.m.–Noon (6/2/79–8/19/79)
Cast:

Bigfoot	*Ray Young*
Cindy	*Yvonne Regalado*
Suzie	*Monica Ramirez*
Wildboy	*Joe Butcher*

Originally a segment of *The Krofft Supershow* in 1977–78, *Bigfoot and Wildboy* aired in repeats briefly in the summer of 1979. Bigfoot, the hairy beast of legend in the U.S. Northwest and also known as Sasquatch, was cast as sort of an alien being who acted as guardian and foster parent to Wildboy, a human orphan. Assisting them in their adventures against various foes were Cindy and then Suzie, both young ladies.

BIL BAIRD SHOW, THE
Puppets; B&W
August 4, 1953–October 29, 1953
CBS Tue./Thu. 11:15–11:30 a.m (8/4/53–10/29/53)
Puppeteers/Voices: *Bil Baird, Cora Baird, Franz Fazakas, Frank Sullivan*

Bil and his wife Cora Baird were two of the most frequently working puppeteers on daytime television in the 1950s, appearing regularly on *The Morning Show, Washington Square,* and *The Whistling Wizard,* among others. For this program, the puppet stars were Groovy, a floppy-eared rabbit, as the resident disc jockey who talked to the Bairds (seen occasionally on camera) and Slugger Ryan, the droopy-eyed barrelhouse piano player. Other puppets pantomimed routines to the music. The series alternated daily with *Arthur Godfrey Time* and, on Fridays, an expanded version of its lead-in *I'll Buy That.*

BILL AND TED'S EXCELLENT ADVENTURES
Cartoon; Color
September 15, 1990–September 5, 1992
CBS Sat. 11–11:30 a.m. (9/15/90–8/31/91)
Fox Sat. 10:30–11 a.m. (9/14/91–10/19/91)
Fox Sat. 10–10:30 a.m. (10/26/91–9/5/92)
Voices:

Bill (1990–91)	*Alex Winter*
Rufus (1990–91)	*George Carlin*
Ted (1990–91)	*Keanu Reeves*

Based on the 1989 movie *Bill & Ted's Excellent Adventure,* this cartoon featured two amateur musicians and generally brain-dead teenagers from California befriended by Rufus, a man from the future who needed the two of them to pass high school in order to fulfill their destiny of becoming a top rock band which would entertain and inspire future generations. As in the movie, the trio went through various periods in time to make sure past events took place as planned. This was the first daytime series to switch from one of the "Big Three" networks (ABC, CBS, and NBC) to Fox.

BILL CULLEN SHOW, THE
Variety; B&W
February 12, 1953–May 14, 1953
CBS Thu. 11:15–11:30 a.m. (2/12/53–5/14/53)
Regulars: *Bill Cullen, Betty Brewer, the Milton DeLugg Trio*

This oddly scheduled program (it replaced the last 15 minutes of *There's One in Every Family* on Thursdays, normally a daily half-hour show) deserves note as the first variety show hosted by game show moderator Bill Cullen. The ever-busy Cullen also could be seen Thursday nights on CBS at the same time as a panelist on *I've Got a Secret*.

BILL GOODWIN SHOW, THE
Variety; B&W
September 11, 1951–March 27, 1952
NBC Tue./Thu. 3:30–4 p.m. (9/11/51–3/27/52)
Regulars: *Bill Goodwin, Eileen Barton, Roger Dann, the Joe Bushkin Trio*

This variety show alternated daily with *The Bert Parks Show* in 1951. Ironically, the idea for the series came when Goodwin, then the announcer and "neighbor" on *The George Burns and Gracie Allen Show,* substituted for Parks during the previous season. As with Parks's series, the emphasis was on music.

BILL NYE THE SCIENCE GUY—See *Back to the Future.*

•BIRDMAN AND THE GALAXY TRIO
Cartoon; Color
September 9, 1967–December 28, 1968
NBC Sat. 11–11:30 a.m. (9/9/67–8/31/68)
NBC Sat. Noon–12:30 p.m. (9/7/68–12/28/68)
Voices:
Birdman (Ray Randall)	Keith Andes
Falcon 7/Vapor Man	Don Messick
Gravity Girl	Virginia Eiler
Meteor Man	Ted Cassidy

Rex Randall, saved from a fiery death by the Egyptian sun-god Ra, found that he now possessed super strengths imparted to him by sunlight, such as the ability to shoot "solar ray beams" from his fists to melt objects. Inspired, Rex dubbed himself Birdman; decked himself out in blue wings, a solar shield, and cowl and cape with a bird crest on the hood; and established himself in a volcano hideaway replete with electronic devices. Falcon 7, who resembled the Arrow T-shirt man wearing an eyepatch and smoking a pipe, communicated with Birdman via a TV screen, which gave him his missions. After receiving his assignment, Birdman yelled his name while soaring away from his hideaway, then engaged in somewhat violent combat with his enemies. His eagle companion was Avenger.

In separate adventures, the Galaxy Trio traveled the universe on their spaceship Condor One to protect other aliens as part of Intergalactic Security. They were comprised of Gravity Girl, who defied the laws of nature by being able to lift heavy objects with her rays, Meteor Man, a pointy-eared strongman whose fists grew to enormous proportions when fighting, and Vapor Man, an aqua-green being who could become various gases. As with *Star Trek*, the trio could "beam down" to other planets rather than have to land their ship. The Galaxy Trio appeared once in each show, while Birdman had two adventures in every episode.

BISHOP PIKE—See *James Pike.*

BISKITTS, THE
Cartoon; Color
September 17, 1983–September 7, 1985
CBS Sat. 8–8:30 a.m. (9/17/83–2/4/84)
CBS Sat. Noon–12:30 p.m. (2/11/84–9/1/84)
CBS Sat. 8–8:30 a.m. (3/30/85–9/7/85)
Voices:
Downer	Henry Gibson
King Max/Snarl/Fetch	Kenneth Mars
Mooch	Marshall Efron
Scat	Dick Beals
Scratch/Fang/Dog Foot	Peter Culen
Shecky	Kip King
Shiner	Jerry Houser
Spinner/Bump/Flip	Bob Holt
Sweets	Kathleen Helppie
Lady	B. J. Ward
Waggs	Darryl Hickman
Wiggle	Jennifer Darling

On the land of Biskitt Island, a group of miniature dogs led by Waggs protected their late king's jewels from the king's evil brother Max, king of the nearby Lower Suburbia. But Max, accompanied by his jester Shecky and mean dogs Snarl and Fang, was not the only nemesis for the Biskitts, as a wildcat named Scratch tried to eat them all as well. As befit the show's theme, the Biskitts all wore hoods, recalling Robin Hood's band in their efforts to benefit all rather than the rich and powerful. Repeats of the shows were aired in 1985.

BLACK STALLION—A syndicated title for *Fury* (q.v.).

•BLACKOUT
Game; Color
January 4, 1988–April 1, 1988
CBS Mon.–Fri. 10–10:30 a.m. (1/4/88–4/1/88)
Host: *Bob Goen*

This short-lived effort was CBS's brief replacement for the venerable *$25,000 Pyramid*. Two celebrity-contestant pairs tried to fill in four missing words in a phrase. The returning champion team played first, and one member had 20 seconds to give clues about the first word to his partner, who had been listening to music when the word was given. The clues were recorded on a tape. The catch was that a member of the other team could hear the description being given. When the tape was played to the partner who had to guess the word from the clues, one of the opposing team could "black out" up to seven seconds of the description by pressing a button. The object for the opponent was to prevent the player from hearing enough information to guess the word. A successful identification by a player from his teammate's "blacked out" tape placed that word in the phrase and let that pair guess the puzzle. A wrong solution let the other team have a shot at guessing the puzzle. The game continued until the phrase was guessed. The first team to solve two puzzles correctly got to play a bonus round, where one member of a team selected clues to enable the partner to guess five items within 70 seconds. Doing so won the team $10,000.

•BLACKSTAR
Cartoon; Color
September 12, 1981–September 11, 1982
CBS Sat. 11–11:30 a.m. (9/12/81–11/28/81)
CBS Sat. 11:30 a.m.–Noon (12/5/81–9/11/82)
Voices:
John Blackstar
Balkar/Terra/Klone
Gossamear/Burble/Rif
Mara
Overlord/Carpo
George DiCenzo
Pat Pinney
Frank Welker
Linda Gary
Alan Oppenheimer

Imagine a hybrid of the movies *Star Wars* and *Snow White and the Seven Dwarfs* with the *Smurfs* cartoon and you roughly have *Blackstar*. Astronaut John Blackstar went through a black hole in space and ended on a planet called Sagar. A tyrant named the Overlord ruled the ancient world there by the might of the Power Star, but when Blackstar arrived, that source had been split into the Power Sword, which the Overlord possessed, and the Star Sword, which Blackstar received. Astride a beast named Warlock, the Adonis-like Blackstar wielded his Power Sword in the continuing battle to get the Power Star and defeat the Overlord. Joining Blackstar in his efforts were his sometimes comical rescuers the Trobbits, a group of seven tiny humanoids, and Mara the sorceress.

•BLANK CHECK
Game; Color
January 6, 1975–July 4, 1975
NBC Mon.–Fri. 12:30–12:55 p.m. (1/6/75–7/4/75)
Host: *Art James*

Six contestants played, with one the designated "check writer." The five other contestants tried to be the first to answer a word game riddle correctly in order to guess a digit selected. If the first three digits were incorrectly guessed by the contestants and became part of the check, a studio audience member was selected to guess which of the two remaining

digits had been chosen by the contestant. If wrong, the contestant received the check amount. At the end of the week, the contestant with the highest check written during the competition received a bonus prize.

•BLANKETY BLANKS
Game; Color
April 21, 1975–June 27, 1975
ABC Mon.–Fri. 11:30 a.m.–Noon (4/21/75–6/27/75)
Host: *Bill Cullen*

Two pairs, each with one celebrity, alternated in answering riddles for amounts ranging from $10 to $100, which could be doubled by answering another riddle. The object was to be the first team to earn $2,000. This attraction failed so miserably that the show it replaced, reruns of *The Brady Bunch*, in turn succeeded it on the ABC schedule.

•BLOCKBUSTERS
Game; Color
October 27, 1980–May 1, 1987
NBC Mon.–Fri. 10:30–11 a.m. (10/27/80–4/23/82)
NBC Mon.–Fri. 10:30–11 a.m. (1/5/87–5/1/87)
Host: *Bill Cullen (1980–82), Bill Rafferty (1987)*

Originally promoted as the game show which attempted to learn if two heads are better than one, *Blockbusters* ran for a year and a half in its original format, then returned five years later with a straight one-on-one competition. In both versions one side used white hexagons (the two family members in the first incarnation) and the other red hexagons. The object for each side was to connect their colors from one end to the other on a board of 20 hexagons, with the whites working horizontally and the reds vertically. Each hexagon contained a letter which started the answer to the question read by the host. A correct guess won the letter for a competitor. The first team to have adjacent hexagons from one end to the other won a game, and two-game winners played the "Gold Rush" bonus game for a possible $5,000. Here one player had to join the polygons horizontally within 60 seconds by answering questions using the initials contained in each hexagon as a clue to the answer. An incorrect or failed response removed the polygon from the board and made it into a block. A contestant failing to achieve the goal still won $100 for every correct answer.

BOB CONSIDINE SHOW, THE—See *On the Line with Considine*.

BOB CROSBY SHOW, THE
Musical Variety; B&W and Color
September 14, 1953–August 30, 1957
CBS Sat. 3:30–4 p.m. (9/14/53–8/30/57)
Regulars: *Bob Crosby, Joan O'Brien, Alan Copeland (1954 at least), Steve Dunne, Jack Narz, Cathy Crosby (1955), Carol Richards (1956 at least), the Modernaires*

Bob Crosby, who like it or not always will be best remembered as Bing Crosby's brother, became the only bandleader to make a successful transition to daytime television when he brought his band and a few other singers to the CBS in 1953. The emphasis always was on music, but it came across as more of a family affair during later years. Bob had his 16-year-old daughter Cathy as a regular three times a week during the summer of 1955 to replace singer Joan O'Brien on leave, and his nephew Gary Crosby also appeared roughly once a week during that period. Steve Dunne served as announcer and host of a game segment involving the audience.

Crosby's series ended after four years, but not due to ratings. He wanted to put his daytime show on nighttime, but CBS declined. Crosby then claimed to have spent $30,000 to buy out his contract with the network and leave the show, but the best he could do with his increasingly out-of-fashion music style was to get a similarly titled Saturday evening show on NBC from June 14-September 6, 1958. Rarely seen on television after the show ended, Crosby died in 1993 at age 79.

BOB SMITH SHOW, THE
Variety; B&W
July 5, 1954–October 1, 1954

NBC Mon.–Fri. Noon–12:30 p.m. (7/5/54–9/10/54)
NBC Mon.–Fri. 4–4:30 p.m. (9/13/54–10/1/54)

Regulars: *Bob Smith (7/5/54–9/3/54), Skitch Henderson (9/8/54–10/1/54), Clark Dennis, the Honeydreamers, the Bob Nicholson Orchestra*

"Buffalo" Bob Smith of *Howdy Doody* fame increased his TV exposure with this series, using the cast of his daily NBC radio 10–10:45 a.m. show. Between his patter were a "Memory Quiz" with studio audience members and songs by tenor Clark Dennis and the Honeydreamers, a three-man, two-woman vocal group led by Lew Anderson, later to be Clarabell on *Howdy Doody.* Smith's heart attack on September 5, 1954 led to bandleader Skitch Henderson substituting for him and NBC switching the slot, but the show held little appeal without Buffalo Bob at the helm and folded within a month.

•BOBBY'S WORLD
Cartoon; Color
September 8, 1990–

Fox Sat. 8–8:30 a.m. (9/8/90–10/6/90)
Fox Sat. 8:30–9 a.m. (10/13/90–9/5/92)
Fox Sat. 8–8:30 a.m. (9/12/92–10/3/92)
Fox Sat. 8:30–9 a.m. (10/10/92–10/30/93)
Fox Sat. 9–9:30 a.m. (11/6/93–5/7/94)
Fox Sat. 8:30–9 a.m. (5/14/94–9/3/94)
Fox Sat. 8:30–9 a.m. (6/15/96–)

Voices:

Bobby Generic/Howie Generic	*Howie Mandel*

Also: *Benny Grant, Tino Insana, Charity James, Gail Matthius, Susan Tolsky, Frank Welker*

Comic Howie Mandel created, did voices, and even appeared as "himself" on this inaugural cartoon for the Fox network. He opened and closed each show by transforming himself into the cartoon form of Howie Generic, the pompadoured father of the show's title character. Bobby Generic (pronounced "GEN er ick") was an oval-headed child who had an imaginative mind which helped him escape the slightly hostile family with which he lived. Besides his dad, his relatives included his mother Martha, who had a slight Irish brogue; his obnoxious older brother Derek, who wore an appropriate zero on his shirt; and his self-obsessed older sister Kelly. The only one who seemed to encourage Bobby to fantasize movie scenes and dramatize figures of speech was his irrepressible Uncle Ted, the traveling salesman brother of Bobby's mother and lover of loud, oversized print shirts. Others joining in the weekly adventures were Bobby's sheepdog Roger and pet toy spider Webley.

BODY LANGUAGE
Game; Color
June 4, 1984–January 3, 1986

CBS Mon.–Fri. 4–4:30 p.m. (6/4/84–1/3/86)

Host: *Tom Kennedy*

A semirevival of *Showoffs, Body Language* had a similar format: A contestant had a 60-second time limit in which to identify charades of words acted out by his or her partner as the aforementioned series, but here every correct answer went into a descriptive clue with seven blanks which had to be answered correctly to win at least $100. Each competing pair had one celebrity who alternated as guesser and "actor." The goal was to be the first to reach $500. The winning duo then played a bonus game where they had to identify up to 10 clues in a minute with one partner doing charades. Each correct clue netted $100, and the total amount generated from this segment was increased 10 times if a partner could convey three more charades within 20 extra seconds. Lucille Ball, who made her TV debut on *Pantomime Quiz* when it was a local show in Los Angeles in the late 1940s, made several appearances on this series.

•BOING BOING SHOW, THE
Cartoon; Color
December 16, 1956–March 24, 1957

CBS Sun. 5:30–6 p.m. (12/16/56–3/24/57)

Narrator: *Bill Goodwin*

Gerald McBoingBoing (his actual last name was McCloy, according to *Newsweek)* was a 6-year-old with huge saucerlike eyes and a beanie on his curly head who was created by none other than Dr. Seuss (real name Theodore Geisel). Gerald did not speak words to communicate; he made metallic "Boing!" sounds or other noises, like a train whistle, drum roll, car crash, or dynamite blast. He was on six minutes per show to introduce United Productions of America (UPA) cartoons. More than half the shorts had appeared previously in theaters (as did Gerald, who first popped up in 1951 in an Academy Award–winning Best Short Subject and ended his run three cartoons later in 1956 in another Oscar-winning Best Short). Others were new, and some were continuing ones, such as "The Twirliger Twins," two identical girls who sang in unison but acted in disharmony, and "Dusty of the Circus," about a boy's adventures under the big top. The emphasis in most cartoons was gentle whimsy, though the inserts ran the gamut from a faithful adaptation of the British puppet show "Punch and Judy" to the informational bits "Meet the Artist" and "Meet the Inventor." Among the vocal talent heard often on the show were Daws Butler, Stan Freberg, and Marvin Miller.

CBS helped create this visual treat when it bought 25 percent of UPA's stock and commissioned 26 episodes. *Time* magazine raved that "*The Boing Boing Show* probably makes the most artful use of color yet seen in television; the reason is that the palette is in the hands of artists." Yet CBS had trouble finding a sponsor for the costly series ($60,000 per episode), and it went off after three months, returning briefly in repeats on CBS Friday nights from May 30–October 3, 1958. Ironically, Bill Goodwin, who "talked" with Gerald off-screen, died shortly before this last run on May 6, 1958.

•BOLD AND THE BEAUTIFUL, THE
Soap Opera; Color
March 23, 1987–

CBS Mon.–Fri. 1:30–2 p.m. (3/23/87–)

Cast:

Eric Forrester	John McCook
Stephanie Forrester	Susan Flannery
Ridge Forrester	Ronn Moss
Thorne Forrester (1987–89)	Clayton Norcross
Thorne Forrester (1989–)	Jeff Trachta
Kristen Forrester (1987–90, 1992–94)	Teri Ann Linn
Beth Logan (1987)	Judith Baldwin
Beth Logan (1987–90, 1994, 1996)	Nancy Burnett
Storm Logan (1987–88, 1994)	Ethan Wayne
Storm Logan (1990–91)	Brian Patrick Clarke
Brooke Logan	Katherine Kelly Lang
Donna Logan (1987–91, 1995–)	Carrie Mitchum
Katie Logan (1987–88, 1995–)	Nancy Sloan
Grandma Logan (1987–89)	Lesley Woods
William Spencer (1987–94)	James Storm
Caroline "Karen" Spencer (1987–90)	Joanna Johnson
Margo Lynley (1987–93)	Lauren Koslow
Clarke Garrison (1987–92, 1996)	Daniel McVicar
Tommy Bayland (1987–90)	Tim Choate
Rocco Carner (1987–88)	Bryan Genesse
Steve Logan (1988, 1994, 1996)	Robert Pine
Nick Preston (1988–89)	Allan Hayes
Angela Forrester (1988–89)	Judith Borne
Dr. Todd Powell (1988–89)	Cal Bartlett
Dr. Todd Powell (1989)	Joseph Rainer
Sally Spectra (1989–)	Darlene Conley
Macy Spectra (1989–)	Bobbie Eakes
Darla Einstein (1989–)	Schae Harrison
Saul Feinberg (1989–96)	Michael Fox
Mick Savage (1989–90)	Jeff Conaway
Lt. Burke (1989–95)	Jeff Allin
Jake MacLaine (1989–92)	Todd McKee
Taylor Hayes (1990–)	Hunter Tylo
Julie Delorean (1990–92)	Jane Rogers
Felicia Forrester (1990–92)	Colleen Dion
Pierre Jourdan (1990–92)	Robert Clary
Faith Roberts/Karen Spencer (1991–94)	Joanna Johnson
Bonnie Roberts (1991–92, 1994)	Dorothy Lyman
Ruthanne Owens (1991–93, 1995)	Michelle Davison
Blake Hayes (1991–93)	Peter Brown
Sheila Carter (1992–)	Kimberlin Brown
Irving "Sly" Donovan (1992–)	Brent Jasmer
Jack Hamilton (1992–95)	Chris Robinson
Molly Carter (1992–94)	Marilyn Alex
Dr. Jay Garvin (1992–93)	Brett Stimely
Dr. Tracy Peters (1992–93)	Marnie Mosiman
James Warwick (1993–)	Ian Buchanan
Mike Guthrie (1993–96)	Ken Hanes
Keith Anderson (1993–95)	Ken LaRon
Kevin Anderson (1993–95)	Keith Jones
Connor Davis (1993–95)	Scott Thompson Baker
Anthony Armando, (1993–95)	Michael Sabatino
Damon Warwick (1993–94, 1996)	James Doohan
Dylan Shaw (1994–)	Dylan Neal
Jessica Forrester (1994–)	Maitland Ward
Prince Omar Rashid (1994–95)	Kabir Bedi
Ivana Vanderveld (1994–95)	Monika Schnarre
Teresa Emerson (1994–95)	Olivia Virgil White
Gordon (1994–95)	Marc Andrews Gones
Lauren Fenmore (1995–)	Tracey Bregman
Maggie Forrester (1995–)	Barbara Crampton
Jasmine Malone (1995–)	Lark Voorhies
Michael Lai (1995–)	Lindsay Price
Psychiatrist Brian Carey (1995–96)	Ken Shriner
Ramone (1995–96)	Joel Gretsch
Samantha (1995–96)	Tamara Olson
Dr. Benson (1995–96)	Richard Kline
Megan (1995–96)	Maeve Quinlan
Vince (1996–)	Scott Layne
Grant Chambers (1996–)	Charles Grant

CBS replaced its okay-performing soap *Capitol* with this, the second creation for the network by William J. Bell and his wife Lee Phillip, the duo behind *The Young and the Restless*. In the initial cast, Eric Forrester was president of Los Angeles–based fashion firm Forrester Creations, Ridge was his son and vice president, Thorne was his dejected second son, and Stephanie was his unhappy wife. Beth Logan was the head of her family, which was poorer than the Forresters and included law student Storm and his sisters Brooke, Donna, and Katie. The other main family was the Spencers, with Caroline Spencer, who was overprotected by her dad William, planning to wed Ridge.

The main early activity had Caroline marry Thorne, thinking that Ridge no longer loved her, while her pal Brooke became obsessed with Ridge. Their parents Eric and Beth started an adulterous affair, while Brooke's kid sisters Donna and Katie fought over Rocco Carner, with Katie emerging as the victor while Donna became a model for shady Tommy Bayland's agency. Stepping into this muddle during a return home was Kristen Forrester, Eric and Stephanie's daughter, who wed conniving competing designer Clarke Garrison.

In 1988 Ridge made love to a drunk Caroline, which he thought was a cute prank but left Caroline unable to have sex with Thorne. When Thorne found out about the indiscretion, he shot Ridge and Stephanie tried to cover it up, telling Lt. Burke she accidentally shot her son. Ridge recovered and proposed to Brooke. But various complications ensued, including Caroline blackmailing Brooke, Brooke miscarrying, and Caroline divorcing Thorne, with the final result being Ridge marrying Caroline in 1989 in a ceremony producing real shocks. Eric and Stephanie's youngest daughter Felicia returned home, while Eric told Stephanie he wanted to divorce her to marry another—not longtime girlfriend Beth Logan, but Brooke, whom he consoled after she had lost Ridge.

Her family's sexual peccadillos were not the only woes which beset Stephanie. She confessed to hiding Angela, her 25-year-old microcephalic daughter, from the rest of the family in a special room in the house. Her appearance gave the soap a sense of social concern it never exhibited previously, but it was a false front: "Angela Forrester" was actually a decoy out for revenge with a new face courtesy of plastic surgery from Dr. Todd Powell, her pretend physician. They blackmailed Stephanie for $150,000 but ended up presumed dead following a car crash. Then in 1989, "Angela" emerged as a burn victim from the crash and called herself Deveney Dickson. In her second incarnation, she conned Thorne out of money for plastic surgery.

Stephanie also had to endure her daughter Kristen's marriage to Clarke Garrison being a sham due to his impregnating designer Margo Lynley (Margo told Kristen Storm that Logan was the child's father). Worse for her family, Clarke began stealing Forrester fashion designs and giving them to vampy Sally Spectra, his former boss. Sally and her company, including fashion cutter Saul Feinberg and assistant Darla Einstein, became the main competition for the Forresters in the 1990s.

Margo went on to wed Bill Spencer, who earlier had been so infuriated with the relationship between his pornography magazine head Nick Preston and model Donna Logan that he printed nude photos of her in one of his magazines. Nick got even by printing nude photos of Bill, taken unknown to him at a gym. (Donna hated Nick's tactics and left him for Thorne, but that relationship never panned out.) Bill and Margo's marriage eventually deteriorated, with him having an affair with his assistant Julie Delorean and she doing the same with Blake Hayes, and she left town. Bill then dated Darla Einstein, but that never led to matrimony, and he went on to pursue business interests outside town.

Darla's co-workers at Sally Spectra's had several passion plays of their own. Photographer Mick Savage resumed an earlier affair with Kristen, and they left town. Her ex-husband Clarke wed Sally in 1991 and she gave birth to their baby boy. Around the same time, Julie Delorean fell in love with Clarke while spying on him for Bill Spencer. When Sally learned of their fling, she fired him and installed Felicia Forrester as her main designer, to the consternation of Felicia's dad Eric. But Felicia's line failed and Clarke feigned interest in Sally again, so they reunited temporarily. Sally later tired of Clarke's shenanigans and dated Jack Hamilton until she lost him to Stephanie.

Sally's estranged daughter Macy arrived and generated much attention. She fell in love with Thorne, but after one spat started dating Jake Maclaine, Margo's younger brother who had been abused sexually by his uncle and had been unable to make love initially with his first girlfriend, Felicia. When Thorne found out, he attacked Jake and rejected Macy. Macy and Jake did not make it as a couple, though. He lied about stealing Forrester designs for Spectra to divert suspicion from Macy, then left town with Margo.

Meanwhile, Caroline Spencer's death had multiple reverberations. Her husband Ridge became the object of affection of her psychiatrist Taylor Hayes, who dated him after fiddling with Storm Logan. Also, Brooke thought about returning to Ridge rather than marrying his dad Eric, but she gave birth to his son Eric Jr. and then wed him. Stephanie gained some sympathy from ex-husband Eric after she got amnesia and lived in a car with homeless Ruthanne Owens, but he was disgusted to learn that she had continued to fake her condition, even after her memory returned, in an effort to hold onto him. However, by that time Brooke had started seeing her old flame Ridge on the sly, and their affair blossomed to the point where Ridge and Brooke planned to be wed.

During the same period, Taylor's ex-husband Blake tried to win her back, but his affair with Margo Spencer and her devotion to Ridge defeated this effort. Finding himself an unwanted man, he went to Texas and discovered a waitress named Faith living with her presumed mother Bonnie Roberts. Blake knew the real truth about Faith—that she was in reality the late Caroline Spencer's identical twin Karen who had been kidnapped at birth! Blake's diabolic plan was to have Ridge transfer his love of Caroline onto Karen. But Ridge was now back with Taylor after seeing how much Brooke still cared for Eric, and Karen felt uncomfortable trying to live up to Caroline's image, so the two became friends instead. A disgusted Blake left town, while Thorne became entranced with the newcomer and favored her over Macy, who in turn dated Sly Donovan, a server at the Bikini Bar in Malibu. About the only persons having a fairly stable relationship during this time was Sly's pal Zach Hamilton, who was Taylor's brother, and Felicia Forrester, and the two later left town.

In 1992 a certain interplay between this show and *The Young and the Restless* began. In one incident, Lauren Fenmore attended a Forrester fashion show because her late father Neil had been friends with Eric. Ironically, actor James Storm had played Neil before joining *The Bold and the Beautiful* as Eric's rival Bill Spencer. In 1995 Lauren became a regular. But another cast member had come over before her, and boy, did she have an impact.

Sheila Carter had stolen Lauren's baby, among other crimes, in Genoa City before deciding to leave for greener pastures in Los Angeles. She wormed her way into becoming Eric Jr.'s nanny, then into his heart as he grew estranged from Brooke. Sheila brought her timid mother Molly Carter into town as she schemed to win Eric over, no matter what the consequences. Convincing hospital security guard Mike Guthrie to give her access, Sheila attempted to make Brooke's paternity test show Ridge, not Eric, as the father of Brooke's baby, but she could not be sure her plan had worked. Nevertheless, Dr. Tracy Peters announced that Ridge was the father of Bridget, so Eric divorced Brooke and planned to wed Sheila. Lauren learned about the engagement during a visit, but could not reveal Sheila's past to him, as the latter threatened to reveal Lauren's adulterous affair with Brad Carlton to her husband Scott.

Brooke wanted to get back with Ridge after her divorce, but he now was committed to Taylor. To irk him, she dated his old high school rival Connor Davis. Then, in a surprise announcement, Brooke assumed control of Forrester Creations with Sheila as her aide. But when Karen started dating Connor, Brooke remained drawn to Ridge while Taylor went to Scotland to treat her old teacher, Dr. James Warwick. Warwick was suffering from memories of abuse from his dad Damon, played by ex-*Star Trek* Scotty James Doohan, but overcame his problem with Taylor's help (he lost his virginity to her), although Taylor remained attached to Ridge. James then began dating Brooke, but all were devastated to learn that Taylor had been declared dead in a plane crash in Cairo.

Sheila's working for Brooke made Eric plan to divorce her, but Eric stayed when he saw Brooke's compassion for Lauren's dying husband Scott, whom Sheila convinced to make Lauren stop threatening her. Still, Eric kept a distance from Brooke. Thinking a baby would create a bond, Brooke made love with Connor and told Eric she was pregnant by him, only to learn that he had had a vasectomy. Connor fared no better, as his relationship with Karen collapsed. Sheila, however, went back to her psychotic mode and imprisoned James, her psychiatrist, in a torture chamber with the help of Mike Guthrie. James eventually escaped, but Sheila, realizing her past would be revealed by James and Lauren, held them and the Forresters at gunpoint before ending up in an insane aylum. But that was hardly the last of Sheila.

Eric's son Thorne watched Macy become a drunk, a predicament manipulated by Sly, which kindled his love for her anew. Unfortunately, Spectra's newest designer Anthony Armando made strong moves on Macy, which irritated Thorne to the point of divorcing Macy. Sally became enamored with Anthony, who at the same time continued his moves on both Macy and Spectra co-worker Darla. Then Macy and Thorne started singing professionally as a duo, and he became attracted to her again, partially because she was battling throat cancer. Anthony and Thorne's new love interest Ivana Vanderveld hated the rekindled relationship between Macy and Thorne, and they both threatened Macy anonymously until, worried about their scheme being discovered, Anthony killed Ivana and pinned her death on Thorne. When Macy found out, Anthony tried to kill her but shot Sally instead. Anthony was arrested, and Thorne and Macy remarried.

Things were dicier for Thorne's brother Ridge. He wed Brooke in 1994, not knowing that Taylor was alive and in Casablanca. Taylor, suffering from amnesia, had wed Prince Omar, who had held her as a hostage. When Taylor's memory came back and she saw how happy Ridge and Brooke were, she planned to stay with Omar in a loveless marriage until James discovered her whereabouts and convinced her to return home. Eventually Taylor revealed herself and Ridge, after much soul searching, decided to stay with Brooke and end his marriage to Taylor.

As that situation played out, Thorne's cousin Jessica Forrester had her own romantic ordeals when she came to live with her uncle Eric. She slept with Dylan Shaw, an intern with Forrester Fashions, at age 17, enraging Eric and resulting in Dylan's being put on trial for statutory rape, of which he was found not guilty. Then Jessica's just-divorced mother Maggie arrived and Dylan started seeing her too, not knowing her connection to Jessica. When he found out, he started seeing his roommate Michael Lai (a woman) instead, but remained enamored of Jessica, who now was the target of affection of the aptly named Sly. He planned to get her drunk and impregnate her by using a condom with a hole in it. But Sly passed out before completing the act. A vengeful Jessica said that they had slept together and that she was pregnant. Much to Sly's chagrin, she forced him to act like a father, right down to carrying around and caring for a doll that was supposed to be the baby. The only bright spot in his life was his love for Jasmine Malone, a former designer at Spectra Fashions now working as a waitress. Dylan stayed true to Jessica, although he hid from her the fact that he was a male stripper to make money on the side.

As *The Bold and the Beautiful* neared its 10th anniversary, Ridge and Brooke's renewal of vows went awry when it was discovered her daughter Bridget's real father was Eric, not Ridge. A shattered Brooke became mentally unstable in Barbados, but she was rescued by Ridge, accompanied by new flame Lauren. Fashion designer Grant Chambers joined Forrester Creations while Ridge searched for Brooke, and he ended up in a romantic triangle with Brooke and Ridge after making moves on Michael and Taylor. Taylor, frustrated that Ridge apparently did not want to resume their affair, left town. Meanwhile, Sheila, released from the asylum by a parole board, slipped Stephanie mercury pills, which nearly killed her.

The '90s story with perhaps the most impact of all was part of the Spectra Fashions story line. No, it was not Sally

reluctantly letting her ex-husband Clarke Garrison return as
her designer and befriending their son C. J., or Clarke making
moves on co-worker Darla. It was the death of Saul Feinberg,
as actor Michael Fox passed away in the summer of 1996.
He was the only character who apparently had a happy love
life, albeit one implied and not shown. As the show heads
into its second decade, it seems unlikely that any other
character will be so blessed.

BONKERS—See *Marsupilami.*

BOTH SIDES
Discussion; B&W
March 15, 1953– June 7, 1953

ABC Sun. 1:30–2 p.m. (3/15/53–6/7/53)

Host: *Quincy Howe*

Presented as a public service series by the American Federation
of Labor, *Both Sides* had two legislators discuss opposite
opinions of an issue every week. In an unusual scheduling
move, the Washington, D.C.–based series also aired on ABC
later each Sunday from 10:30–11 p.m.

BOWLING STARS
Sports; B&W
January 5, 1958–May 6, 1961

ABC Sun. 4–4:30 p.m. (1/5/58–3/16/58)
ABC Sun. 4:30–5 p.m. (10/5/58–3/29/59)
NBC Sat. 4:30–5 p.m. (10/15/60–5/6/61)

Host/Announcer: *"Whispering" Joe Wilson (1958–59), Bud
Palmer (1960–61)*

Bowling Stars began its life as *National Bowling Champions*
on NBC Sunday nights from April 1956–March 1957.
Then both its format and its host, Joe Wilson, returned in
September 1957 on ABC Sunday nights for three months
before transferring to Sunday afternoons. Twenty-six bowling
games, each between two professional players and filmed as
far back as June 1957, ran on the first season in daytime.
Included among these were three perfect 300 games, each of
which netted the winner $10,000. The show ended in early
1959, only to be revived again on NBC in the fall of 1960.
Its new host Bud Palmer co-hosted a similarly themed hour-
long weekly syndicated program called *Bowling Time* with
Sam Levene from 1955–57. All versions were from Chicago.

BOXING
Sports; Color
February 9, 1986–April 6, 1986

ABC Sun. 3–4 p.m. or 3:30–4:30 p.m. (2/9/86–4/6/86)

Announcers: *Al Trautwig, Alex Wallau*

This edition of sparring matches featured various divisions
in contests at locales ranging from Indianapolis to Reno.
Among the fighters was future heavyweight champion
Evander Holyfield.

BOXING LIVE FROM MADISON SQUARE GARDEN
Sports; Color
July 7, 1973–September 1, 1973

ABC Sat. 4–5 p.m. (7/7/73–9/1/73)

Trying to capitalize on the popularity of pugilists during
their appearances on *ABC's Wild World of Sports*, the network
offered this weekly card of two bouts, a preliminary and a
main event, for viewers just before that program.

•BOZO THE CLOWN
Children's; B&W and Color
1949–50; 1956–

Syndicated 30 and 60 minutes daily beginning 1949.

TV's longest running children's show—indeed, perhaps TV's
longest-running entertainment character—is *Bozo the Clown.*
Although not as widely seen now as during his heyday, Bozo
nonetheless remains familiar to many Americans (remember
how many times you or someone else called a jerk a "Bozo"?),
and his rise to stardom is one of the great tales of American
popular culture.

Capitol Records introduced the character on a 1946
record for children titled *Bozo at the Circus,* which spent
more than 200 weeks on *Billboard's* Best Selling Children's
Records chart. In 1949 Capitol began licensing the character,
and that same year KTTV Los Angeles brought *Bozo the
Clown* to television starring Pinto Colvig, Bozo's voice on
records, in a half-hour circus show which was kinescoped.
By 1950 Capitol Records had filmed 390 minutes of *Bozo's
Circus* for $400,000, enough for 26 weeks of original shows.
Nonetheless, the program did not catch on immediately

In 1956 Larry Harmon received the TV rights for the
clown with the white face, red nose, and tufts of red hair,
which by this time had generated $20 million in children's
records sales for Capitol Records. Harmon came up with the
idea of a daily half-hour show with a live Bozo doing activities
with kids in the studio along with 260 five-minute Bozo
cartoons produced in 1958 and 1960 to break the action.
The show's success was limited until it really blew open in
1959. Los Angeles started a new version in January, and
New York City had its own by October.

Harmon soon trained 100 Bozos in the United States,
plus several in Germany, France, and Japan. Besides learning
the basics about handling overactive children, these trainees
had to learn such sayings as "What are you doodly-do-doing?"
and "You're kazowee!" as part of their repertoire. Harmon's
best-known graduate was future *Today* weathercaster Willard
Scott, who played Bozo in Washington, D.C., but Harmon's
personal favorite was Frank Avruch of Boston. In 1965 he
tried to syndicate Avruch as the only Bozo, but stations with
their own local Bozos (about half the lineup in America)
objected to the idea, and the show, known in some markets
as *Bozo's Big Top,* did not replace their homegrown clown
hosts. Around that time, Harmon was making 5 percent off
the annual $150 million gross sales of Bozo merchandise.

After the 1960s, there were few format changes. Even the ancient cartoons stayed. There was, in 1977, the emergence of *The All-New Bozo Show*, 130 half-hour shows available for syndication, which fared poorly. Harmon did unveil annually his "Bozo" awards, given to people he felt were doing stupid things, keeping the name alive among adults who had grown up with the character.

Bozo's biggest and best-known successes were based on the version seen on WGN Chicago, which debuted in September 1961. The show there was wildly popular and always sold out years in advance, and on September 7, 1986, WGN aired "The Bozo 25th Anniversary Special" featuring a host of guests. In 1995 the station renewed the program for another five years, or into the start of the 21st century. That is not too bad for a guy with poor coloring and big red shoes.

•BRADY KIDS, THE

Cartoon; Color
September 16, 1972–August 31, 1974

ABC Sat. 10:30–11 a.m. (9/16/72–9/1/73)
ABC Sat. 11–11:30 a.m. (9/8/73–8/31/74)

Voices:

Bobby Brady	Mike Lookinland
Cindy Brady	Susan Olsen
Greg Brady	Barry Williams
Jan Brady	Eve Plumb
Marcia Brady	Maureen McCormick
Marlon/Ping/Pong	Larry Storch
Peter Brady	Christopher Knight

Like executive producer Sherwood Schwartz's *Gilligan's Island*, *The Brady Bunch* was a moderately popular sitcom begun in the 1960s which gained familiarity with young viewers in reruns in the 1970s, then became an object of camp affection by the 1980s, spinning off several revivals along the way. This cartoon was an adjunct to the then-running series, minus parents Mike and Carol, played respectively by Robert Reed and Florence Henderson, and nutty maid Alice, played by Ann B. Nelson. The squeaky-clean youngsters, three blonde girls and three brunette boys in a "blended" family, got into various misadventures interrupted occasionally by a song from their rock combo the Bradys. The latter resembled *The Archies* (q.v.), with Bobby on drums, Marcia on tambourine, Jan on keyboards, and the rest on stringed instruments (maybe they forgot the sitcom episode where they sang on a talent show as the Silver Platters?). Others seen were Marlon, a wisecracking black myna bird with a twirling tail and a wizard's cap; Ping and Pong, comical twin pandas from China; and a dog called Mop Top, who in keeping with the Archies theme resembled a tan version of Hot Dog. (On the sitcom the family pooch was Tiger, who disappeared after the first year.)

The voices and singing came from nighttime cast members excepting Larry Storch, with Greg, the oldest male, the nominal group leader. The show's pilot aired a week before the series debuted on *The ABC Saturday Superstar Movie* (q.v.).

BRAINS AND BRAWN

Game; Color
July 10, 1993–October 16, 1993

NBC Sat. 12:30–1 p.m. (7/10/93–9/4/93)
NBC Sat. Noon–12:30 p.m. (9/11/93–10/16/93)

Hosts: *Mark-Paul Gosselaar, Danielle Harris, Tatyana Ali*

This game show had no connection to the 1958 NBC nighttime series of the same name. Two trios of teens, each led by a celebrity, competed in six games, two of which tested their intellect and four of which tested their agility, to win an assortment of prizes. The last few shows employed all-celebrity teams from shows like *California Dreams* and *Saved by the Bell*, the latter of which had host Mark-Paul Gosselaar as a regular. Alternating co-hosts Danielle Harris and Tatyana Ali were regulars on the nighttime sitcoms *Roseanne* and *The Fresh Prince of Bel Air* respectively.

BRAUN & CO.—See *Ruth Lyons' 50 Club.*

BRAVE STALLION—The syndicated title for *Fury.*

•BREAK THE BANK

Game; B&W
March 30, 1953–July 23, 1976

NBC Mon.–Fri. 3–3:30 p.m. (3/30/53–9/18/53)
ABC Mon.–Fri. 2:30–3 p.m. (4/12/76–7/23/76)

Host: *Bud Collyer (1953), Tom Kennedy (1976)*

Break the Bank, the game show that gave Bert Parks his first hosting job, aired on radio on Mutual from 1945–46, ABC from 1946–49, and NBC from 1949–50. It ran on television in the evenings from October 22, 1948–September, 23, 1949 on ABC, October 5, 1949–January 9, 1952 on NBC, and January 27, 1952–February 1, 1953 on CBS before beginning its daytime run on NBC. Bud Collyer, who had co-hosted the nighttime TV entries with Parks, was the sole host in daytime.

The format was a question-and-answer session, with contestants called from the studio audience having to give correct responses to queries under one category. Only one wrong answer out of eight questions was allowed for a person to continue and try to "break the bank" with a right response to the ninth poser. The bank consisted of how much other contestants had earned before having to forfeit their winnings by answering two questions wrong. The bank typically went into the thousands of dollars, a sizable amount by 1950s standards. It was said that the TV versions had given away at least $3.5 million in cash and prizes by the start of 1965.

Break the Bank in daytime was somewhat of a last-minute replacement for NBC when the network lost *The Big Payoff* to CBS. It flopped against *Payoff* and ended its daytime run two weeks after the cancellation of a summer run on NBC Tuesdays 8:30–9 p.m. which had begun while the daytime show was running on June 23, 1953. The series continued in the nighttime on ABC from January 31, 1954–June 20, 1956, and on NBC from October 9, 1956–January 15, 1957.

Nearly 20 years later, the game was brought out of mothballs in title only by producers Jack Barry and Dan Enright, who brought in a panel of nine celebrities to sit on the left and top side of a large board with four rows of five boxes. Contestants chose a box, and the two celebrities on the same line of the box on the left and on the top gave different responses to a question, only one of which was right. The contestant picked which contestant was correct and won the box and the amount hidden underneath it if he or she was right. Winning a box meant a contestant could continue to play until winning three boxes of the same amount scattered on the board (amounts were $100, $200, and $300). Giving an incorrect guess or winning a box with a blank amount led to the other contestant having a turn. One could "break the bank" by winning the three boxes with dollar signs on the board. One contestant made approximately $17,000 by doing this twice in the show's first week. The end game consisted of a contestant trying to avoid picking the "marked" celebrity out of a panel of nine, who, if picked, would prevent the player from winning a cash bonus.

Although no celebrities in 1976's 15-week run were listed as regulars, Jan Murray and Liz Torres were in more than half of the shows. Others on more than one week were astronaut Buzz Aldrin, Joan Collins, Dick Gautier, Alice Ghostley, Dody Goodman, Marilyn Michaels, Jaye P. Morgan, Avery Schrieber, Lonnie Shorr, Rip Taylor, Abe Vigoda, Jimmie Walker, and Anson Williams.

Following the network run, Jack Barry hosted a syndicated version from 1976–77. Nearly a decade later, in September 1985, a new syndicated version of *Break the Bank* hit the airwaves with yet another format, this time a combination of question-and-answer periods with a puzzle consisting of one-word clues à la *Password Plus* (q.v.). Richard Kline, who had directed the 1976 version, did the same here and assumed the role of executive producer from Barry and Enright. Gene Rayburn hosted the first three months, then Joe Farago took over through the summer of 1986.

BREAKFAST CLUB, THE
Variety; B&W
February 22, 1954–February 25, 1955

ABC Mon.–Fri. 9–10 a.m. (2/22/54–2/25/55)

Regulars: *Don McNeill, Fran Allison, Sam Cowling, Johnny Desmond, Eileen Parker, the Eddie Ballantine Orchestra*

The Breakfast Club was a radio institution, airing from June 23, 1933–December 27, 1968, first on NBC and then ABC when the latter spun off as a separate radio network. It pioneered entertainment on national morning radio shows and made McNeill the top money earner for ABC in the late 1940s and early 1950s, yet it failed on television due to a variety of obstacles.

The first TV adaptation aired as a local special on WBKB Chicago on September 27, 1946 at 8 p.m. (it was titled *Don McNeill's Dinner Club* due to the broadcast hour). A second special occurred May 12, 1948 on a New York–Philadelphia–

Baltimore–Washington, D.C. station hookup from 9–10 a.m., which was the first daytime show networked simultaneously on radio and television. Still, ABC was cautious about developing programming before 6 p.m. weekdays, and it decided to air *The Don McNeill TV Club* Wednesday nights from September 13, 1950–December 19, 1951. More than two years after that, ABC finally decided to telecast the morning radio show from its base in Chicago.

When it arrived in 1954, most of the cast were veterans who had been with McNeill for several years. The one exception was singer Eileen Parker, who had replaced Patsy Lee a year earlier. Fran Allison was perhaps the best-known member of the troupe, not just for her work on *Kukla, Fran and Ollie* but already for her character on this show, gossiping Aunt Fanny. Rotund Sam Cowling dispensed jokes, while Johnny Desmond crooned tunes. McNeill reigned over all the segments. The one big change for television was the inclusion of live commercials while taped ones ran on the radio version.

The program did well in the ratings, but sponsors did not bite for the TV version and ABC could not afford to sustain the series, so it ended after a year. Don McNeill blamed it on the scheduling. He told *Billboard,* "There was no network programming around us, which made it very difficult to come up with the supposed ratings which advertisers and agencies seem to insist on." In fact, ABC was so lacking in sponsor support in those days that it was not until the fall of 1958 that the network had a show on any day of the week to air before 1 p.m. McNeill remained on radio a decade after that, but the only other TV show he did was *Take Two* (q.v.) in 1963. He died in 1996.

Don McNeill and "Aunt Fanny" (Fran Allison) got dressed up to do the 1954 video version of their longtime radio favorite The Breakfast Club.

BREAKFAST IN HOLLYWOOD
Talk/Informational; B&W
January 11, 1954–February 5, 1954
NBC Mon.–Fri. 10:30–11 a.m. (1/11/54–2/5/54)

Host: *Johnny Dugan*

Assistant: *Jeff Donnell*

Breakfast in Hollywood was based on a radio show of the same name that ran on NBC and ABC from 1941–49, initially under the title *Breakfast at Sardi's.* The radio program's host was Tom Breneman until his sudden death in 1948, when Garry Moore replaced him for the last year. On television Johnny Dugan interviewed guests at the Hotel Ambassador swimming pool in Los Angeles, not during breakfast but lunchtime (it aired on kinescope). This version flopped immediately and went off after four weeks. The series was revived in 1958 on KTLA Los Angeles with Harry Babbitt as host.

BREAKFAST PARTY
Variety; B&W
January 7, 1952–May 23, 1952
NBC Mon.–Fri. 10–10:30 a.m. (1/7/52–5/23/52)

Host: *Mel Martin, Larry Downing, Eileen Martin, the Bel-Aires (Bruce Brownfield, accordion; Larry Downs, guitar; Mel Horner, bass)*

Breakfast Party aired on WLW-TV Cincinnati in 1951 Mondays through Saturdays from 9:30–10:30 a.m. with singer Eileen Martin and the Bel-Aires musical trio, plus comedy segments. When it came to NBC, Mel Martin was host and Larry Downing was another singer. After May 1952, the show reverted to its local status. Its biggest event there was on April 10, 1953, when 38-year-old Mel Martin surprised everyone by saying he was leaving the show to become an evangelical preacher.

•BRIDE AND GROOM
Wedding; B&W and Color
January 25, 1951–January 10, 1958

CBS Mon.–Fri. 3:15–3:30 p.m. (1/25/51–2/9/51)
CBS Tue./Thu. 2:45–3 p.m. or 3:15–3:30 p.m. (2/13/51–11/1/51)
CBS Mon.–Fri. 2:45–3 p.m. (11/5/51–2/1/52)
CBS Mon.–Fri. 10:30–11 a.m. (4/4/52–5/23/52)
CBS Mon.–Thu. 11:15–11:30 a.m. & Fri 11–11:30 a.m. (5/26/52–9/26/52)
CBS Mon.–Fri. Noon–12:15 p.m. (9/29/52–10/9/53)
NBC Mon.–Fri. Noon–12:15 p.m. (12/7/53–8/27/54)
NBC Mon.–Fri. 2:30–3 p.m. (7/1/57–1/10/58)

Host: *John Nelson (1951–54), Robert Paige (1957–58), Frank Parker (July 1957), Byron Palmer (1957–58)*

Couples who married on this show received one of the most lavish weddings one could have in the 1950s. They got their own formal outfits from the show, as well as clothes for their attendants and music from an organist, a harpist, and a solo

singer. The host(s) interviewed the couples to learn about their romance before the ceremony, and after the wedding the lucky pair got about $2,000 worth of gifts at their reception, all elaborately plugged, plus a free weeklong honeymoon and a Pontiac car on loan for a week. In the early years, the show rotated roughly 30 ministers to officiate the ceremonies.

When it came to TV after an ABC radio run from 1945–1950, the series received more than 70,000 letters from prospective couples wanting to be on it, according to *Time* magazine. Automatically restricted from the series were weddings by Roman Catholics (the religion's doctrine required weddings to take place only in a church) and divorcées, according to *Newsweek* magazine. However, the show did accept couples from outside the United States, and weddings occurred for people ranging in age from their late teens to mid-eighties. Before the end of its run, more than 2,500 couples had been married on the series (including the radio days), and they generated more than 1,000 children.

It wasn't always bliss after the show, however. The Amateur Athletic Union (AAU) suspended Olympic track and field star Lee Calhoun for the 1958 season after his *Bride and Groom* wedding because he received gifts which were judged to be in violation of the terms of his amateur status. (*Time* reported that boxing great Jackie Robinson congratulated him on the show.) Undaunted, Calhoun returned to competition, won his second gold medal in the 110-meter hurdles in the 1960 Olympics, and even stayed married.

Original host John Nelson came from the radio version and even saw his sister get married on the show. When NBC revived it in 1957 it had two hosts, Robert Paige and Frank Parker, with the latter singing a song to the newlyweds. Because of other commitments, Parker left within a month and was replaced by Byron Palmer, who also sang.

Bride and Groom deserves note for winning what was on paper the largest judgment rendered in broadcasting history up to that time. In July 1951 producers John Masterson, John Reddy, and John Nelson (yes, the host) won $800,000 from a jury who believed their claim that a local Hollywood show titled *Wedding Bells* was a ripoff of *Bride and Groom.* However, that amount had shrunk to $50,000 within a month, and by September the "three Johns" said all they really wanted was to win in principle, and they settled for an $800 cocktail party for all sides instead of the settlement! Wonder what their lawyer thought of that?

BRIGHT PROMISE
Soap Opera; Color
September 29, 1969–March 31, 1972
NBC Mon.–Fri. 3:30–4 p.m. (9/29/69–3/31/72)

Cast:

Thomas Boswell (1969–70)	Dana Andrews
Martha Ferguson	Susan Brown
William Ferguson (1969–71)	Paul Lukather
William Ferguson (1970)	John Napier
Dean Henry Pierce (1969)	Tod Andrews

Dean Henry Pierce (1969–72)	David Lewis
Sandra Jones Pierce (1969–70)	Susannah Darrow
Sandra Jones Pierce (1970–72)	Pamela Murphy
Ann Boyd Jones (1969–70)	Coleen Gray
Ann Boyd Jones (1970–72)	Gail Kobe
Stuart Pierce	Peter Ratray
Professor Mitchell	Ivor Francis
Red Wilson	Richard Eastham
Jennifer Matthews (1969–70)	Nancy Stephens
Chet Matthews (1969–70)	Gary Pillar
Howard Jones (1971–72)	Mark Miller
Isabel Jones (1971–72)	Lesley Woods
Dr. Tracy Graham (1971–72)	Dabney Coleman
Dr. Brian Walsh (1971–72)	John Considine
David Lockhart (1971–72)	Anthony Geary
Jody Harper (1971–72)	Sherry Alberoni
Dr. Amanda Winninger (1971–72)	June Vincent
Sylvia Bancroft (first, 1971)	Anne Jeffreys
Sylvia Bancroft (second, 1971)	Regina Gleason
Elaine Bancroft (1971)	Jennifer Leak
Charles Diedrich (1971)	Anthony Eisley

Set in the midwestern town of Bancroft, *Bright Promise* told of the romantic trials and tribulations of students and faculty at Bancroft College. Thomas Boswell, a widower, was president of the institution and lead character. But despite the marquee value of film star Dana Andrews as Boswell, the show's producers decided after six months to concentrate on the conflicts faced by the Jones and Pierce families. The most spirited of these characters was Sandy Jones, who dropped out of school, wed and then cheated on Stuart Pierce, and then found herself accused of murder. Yet no story line could pull this serial out of third place behind its competition, *The Edge of Night* on CBS and *One Life to Live* on ABC, so it ended after a run of 2¹/₂ years. A note for trivia enthusiasts: Besides acting on the soap, Dabney Coleman wrote at least two scripts for the show in 1972.

BRIGHTER DAY, THE

Soap Opera; B&W
January 4, 1954–September 28, 1962

CBS Mon.–Fri. 1–1:15 p.m. (1/4/54–5/15/54)
CBS Mon.–Fri. 4–4:15 p.m. (7/5/54–6/15/62)
CBS Mon.–Fri. 11:30–11:55 a.m. (6/18/62–9/28/62)

Regulars:

Rev. Richard Dennis (1954–56)	William Smith
Rev. Richard Dennis (1956–62)	Blair Davies
Emily Potter	Mona Bruns
Althea Dennis (1954–55)	Brooke Byron
Althea Dennis (1956)	Jayne Heller
Althea Dennis (1960)	Maggie O'Neill
Althea Dennis (1960–61)	Anne Meacham
Grayling Dennis (1954–59)	Hal Holbrook
Grayling Dennis (1959–60)	James Noble
Grayling Dennis (1961–62)	Forrest Compton
Patsy Dennis Hamilton (1954–57)	Lois Nettleton

Patsy Dennis Hamilton (1961–62)	June Dayton
Barbara "Babby" Dennis (1954–59)	Mary Linn Beller
Barbara "Babby" Dennis (1959–60)	Nancy Malone
Dr. Randy Hamilton (1954–57)	Larry Ward
Sandra Talbot Dennis (1956)	Diane Gentner
Sandra Talbot Dennis (1957–59)	Gloria Hoye
Sandra Talbot Dennis (1960–61)	Mary K. Wells
Sandra Talbot Dennis (1961–62)	Nancy Rennick
Rev. Max Canfield (1956–58)	Herb Nelson
Lydia Harrick Canfield (1956–58)	Murial Williams
Lenore Bradley (1956–58)	Lori March
Donald Harrick (1956–58)	Walter Brooke
Robert Ralston (c. 1957)	Mark Daniels
Ellen Williams Dennis (1958–59)	Patty Duke
Ellen Williams Dennis (1960–61)	Lanna Saunders
Steven Markley (1958)	Peter Donat
Tom Bradley (1958)	Robert Webber
Crystal Carpenter (c. 1958)	Vivian Dorsett
Peter Nino (1959–61)	Joe Sirola
Eliot Clark (1959)	Lawrence Weber
Eliot Clark (1960)	Ernest Graves
Bud Clark (1959)	Charles Taylor
Diane Clark (1959)	Lin Pierson
Lois Williams, R.N. (1960–61)	Marian Winters
Adolph McClure (1960)	Frank Thomas
Dr. Charles Fuller (1961–62)	Dean Harens
Chris Hamilton (1961–62)	Mike Barton
Uncle Walter Dennis (1962)	Paul Langton
Toby Ballard (1962)	Don Penny
Judith Potter (1962)	Bennye Gatteys
Maggie Quincy (1962)	Patsy Garrett
Dean Wilbur (1962)	Perry Ivins
Mort Barrows (1962)	Benny Rubin

The Brighter Day began on NBC radio on October 11, 1948 as a replacement of Irna Phillips's soap *Joyce Jordan, M.D.* and ran there until 1956. The character of Liz Dennis had been introduced on the latter show a few weeks earlier, and the new series, created by Irna Phillips, emphasized the Dennis family. Liz was happily married and rarely seen by the time the series came to television on CBS in 1954, but the others arrived intact, including patriarch widow the Rev. Richard Dennis, his daughters Althea, Patsy, and Babby, and his son Grayling. The main change on the show was its locale, which went from the town of Three Rivers to New Hope, Pennsylvania on television due to a flood which forced the Dennises to leave (later in the 1950s, the Dennises moved to Columbus, a college town).

Althea, the second oldest daughter, was the focal point during much of the show's early run. Her husband Bruce Bigsby died in the Korean War, and she found herself going insane. After being ineffectually treated by Dr. Blake Hamilton, her psychiatrist brother-in-law (he was Patsy's husband), she left to pursue an acting career in New York City. By the late 1950s Grayling had taken center stage, with his business and romantic life getting a thorough airing.

On the work front, Grayling was a partner with reverend-turned-reporter Max Canfield for the struggling *New Hope Herald*, a newspaper which included a regular column by Aunt Emily Potter, a family housekeeper and surrogate mother to the Dennises. Grayling had an earlier business partner named Robert Ralston who had been connected to newcomer Sandra Talbot, a shady character indeed (she was once a murder trial suspect). Sandra had married Grayling by 1958, and later had a breakdown when it appeared she could never conceive a child. Grayling, a weak-willed alcoholic, then had a fling with Sandra's nurse when Sandra finally did get pregnant.

Also seen in the late '50s were Lydia Harrick, Max Canfield's wife, who was involved with 21-year-old Ted Blake in 1958 (Babby had a crush on Ted at the same time); Lenore Bradley, Lydia's socialite sister who eventually lost her snobbish ways toward the Dennises; Steven Markley, a young minister whom the Rev. Dennis wanted Babby to marry; Ellen Williams, a girl who was a Dennis family friend; and members of the Clark family.

Throughout the 1950s, *The Brighter Day,* like the other CBS soaps, had good ratings, though it usually ranked last

The initial Dennis family on The Brighter Day *on television included, from left, the kneeling Babby (Mary Linn Beller), Grayling (Hal Holbrook), Reverend Richard (Bill Smith) and Patsy (Lois Nettleton).*

in the bunch. But in 1961, as Rev. Dennis tried to persuade a French teacher to have an operation to restore her eyesight and Babby married one-time gambler Peter Nino, the series took a serious blow when production shifted from New York to CBS's studios in Hollywood. The switch on July 3, 1961 meant that Peter and Babby suddenly disappeared during a big business deal (Joe Sirola went to play a doctor briefly on *As the World Turns,* while Nancy Malone starred in the prime-time ABC police drama *Naked City),* as did Sandra and Grayling after learning they were going to have a child. Also disappearing without warning were Ellen Williams, her mother Nurse Lois Williams, and her boyfriend.

The dropping of these characters, some of which occurred without explanation on air, led to audience erosion, which only increased when the series went from the afternoon to the late morning in early 1962 (typically soap operas perform poorly before noon). That year there was an influx of new characters and stories, including the introduction of Walter and Emily's hapless brother Dennis and the return of Patsy following the death of her husband Dr. Randy Hamilton. In August the show's producers announced the hiring of the first black regular on a soap opera, an actor named Rex Ingram, but he had little to do, as the series vanished a month later, ending its eight-year run.

•BRUCE FORSYTH'S HOT STREAK
Game; Color
January 6, 1986–April 4, 1986
ABC Mon.–Fri. 11–11:30 a.m. (1/6/86–4/4/86)
Host: *Bruce Forsyth*

A rare game show in that the host's name was in the title, *Bruce Forsyth's Hot Streak* used a longtime United Kingdom game show host to lead a game that was rarely jolly. The cumbersome format had two sexually segregated quintets compete individually in describing a subject within 40 seconds among group members. The team captain received the word or phrase while his or her four other partners wore headsets playing music. After starting the 40-second countdown, the captain tapped the partner behind him or her on the shoulder, and as the partner removed the headset the captain gave clues to the item. After the partner identified it, he or she in turn tapped the next player to give clues while having to keep in mind not to repeat any major words used by the captain. This routine continued until all four headset-wearing partners identified the word or one accidentally repeated a clue. Unfortunately, the latter happened so often that a viewer seldom got to enjoy a clean sweep by one team.

Each correct identification was worth $100 in the first two rounds and $200 in the third. The team with the most cash after round three got to keep their earnings and play a bonus game in which the captain gave four words associated with a subject and had his or her partners rejoin him on stage to guess the words, with each getting five seconds to try it. This was done twice, with $200 per correct guess the first time and $300 the second. The whole team then competed to identify four words associated with a subject to win five times the amount already earned in the bonus games. All earnings were divided equally among team members.

BUCK BRADLEY'S RODEO
Children's; B&W
October 22, 1950–December 3, 1950
ABC Sun. 4:30–5 p.m. (10/22/50–12/3/50)
Host: *Buck Bradley*

This obscure show, seen live in Los Angeles but on kinescope in other parts of the country, employed a western theme.

BUFFALO BILLY SHOW, THE
Children's; B&W
October 22, 1950–January 14, 1951
CBS Sun. 4–4:30 p.m. (10/22/50–1/14/51)
Puppeteer: *Bob Clampett*
Voices: *Don Messick, Joan Gardner, Chris Allen, Jim McGeorge, Erv Shoemaker*

Created and co-written (with Don Messick and Joan Gardner) by Bob Clampett of *Beany and Cecil* fame, *The Buffalo Billy Show* had puppets Buffalo Billy (named after his hometown), his aunt Ima Hag, old cowpoke Pop Gunn, Billy's horse Blunderhead, Dilly the armadillo, and others on a trek westward in search of gold. Four unidentified puppeteers handled the action while others did the voices. The show aired live in Los Angeles and on kinescope on the network.

•BUFORD AND THE GALLOPING GHOST
Cartoon; Color
February 3, 1979–September 1, 1979
NBC Sat. Noon–12:30 p.m. (2/3/79–9/1/79)
Voices:

Buford/Nugget Nose	*Frank Welker*
Cindy Mae/Rita	*Pat Parris*
Deputy Goofer	*Roger Peltz*
Fuddy Duddy	*Hal Peary*
Sheriff Dupres	*Henry Corden*
Wendy	*Marilyn Schreffler*
Woody	*David Landsberg*

This spin-off of *Yogi's Space Race* consisted of two segments from that series, "The Buford Files" and "The Galloping Ghost." "Buford" took place in Pendike County (viewers could tell it was in the south by the bad drawls and the fact that Buford wore a Confederate cap), and featured the bloodhound Buford, whose nose turned red when he and investigative teenagers Cindy Mae and Woody were getting a clue. Hampering their work was Buford's inherent laziness and the bungling efforts of Sheriff Dupres and his Deputy Goofer, the latter an obvious Gomer Pyle soundalike.

The other segment's "Galloping Ghost" was Nugget Nose, the spirit of a feisty, diminutive prospector who was summoned by Wendy by rubbing on a gold nugget whenever she and co-worker Rita needed assistance on the Fuddy Duddy Dude Ranch. The resort's stuffy namesake was Nugget's perpetual if unintentional comic foe. Like Buford, Nugget Nose had a strong sense of smell, only in his case he sniffed for gold. Too bad none of the characters could smell a dog when they were in one, as the series vanished in less than a season.

•BUGALOOS, THE
Sitcom; Color
September 12, 1970–September 2, 1972
NBC Sat. 9:30–10 a.m. (9/12/70–9/4/71)
NBC Sat. 11:30 a.m.–Noon (9/11/71–12/25/71)
NBC Sat. 12:30–1 p.m. (1/8/72–9/2/72)
Cast:

Benita Bizarre	*Martha Raye*
Courage	*John Philpott*
Flunky Rat (in costume)	*Sharon Baird*
Harmony	*Wayne Laryea*
IQ	*John McIndoe*
Joy	*Caroline Ellis*
Sparky (in costume)	*Billy Barty*
Tweeter (in costume)	*Van Snowden*
Woofer (in costume)	*Joy Campbell*

Sid and Marty Krofft's production company outdid themselves just coming up with the set for this show, probably the most psychedelic set design to appear on a Saturday morning show. Amid the swirling Day-Glo colors on videotape were the Bugaloos, four human-appearing insects with wings on their backs, English dialects on their tongues, and gooey monikers like Joy, Harmony, IQ, and Courage. They liked to sing insistently upbeat tunes like their theme song ("The Bug-a-loos, the Bug-a-loos, we're in the air and everywhere . . .") and hang out with their friend Sparky, who looked much more like a typical fly. Unfortunately, Sparky had a tendency to get in trouble and be manipulated by the group's main nemesis, Benita Bizarre.

Ah, Benita, what a gal. She was a tone-deaf witch who lived in a jukebox and liked to sing, much to the distress of her henchmen Woofer and Tweeter and Nazi-ish chauffeur Flunky Rat. Her outrageous, gaudy costumes replete with feather boa were so showy they might have given Phyllis Diller pause. Add to that comedienne Martha Raye's usual wild theatrics, and you get the idea that this was anything but a subtle comedy. A typical episode had Benita trying to capture the Bugaloos so she could have their sweet sounds, but despite her best efforts she never managed to outwit the group from Tranquility Forest.

Believe it or not, Capitol Records actually signed the Bugaloos as a musical act, but they failed to make the *Billboard* record charts. As for their show, the second season consisted of repeats.

•BUGS BUNNY SHOW, THE
Cartoon; Color
April 7, 1962–

ABC Sat. Noon–12:30 p.m. (4/7/62–9/2/67)
ABC Sun. 10:30–11 a.m. (12/31/67–9/8/68)
CBS Sat. 8:30–9:30 a.m. (9/14/68–9/5/70)
CBS Sat. 8–9 a.m. (9/12/70–9/4/71)
CBS Sat. 8–8:30 a.m. (9/11/71–9/1/73)
ABC Sat. 8–8:30 a.m. (9/8/73–8/31/74)
ABC Sat. 8:30–9 a.m. (9/7/74–8/30/75)
CBS Sat. 8:30–9:30 a.m. (9/6/75–10/30/76)
CBS Sat. 9–10 a.m. (11/6/76–9/3/77)
CBS Sat. 8–9 a.m. or 8:30–9:30 a.m. (9/19/77–11/12/77)
CBS Sat. 9–10:30 a.m. (11/19/77–2/28/81)
CBS Sat. 8:30–10 a.m. (3/7/81–9/5/81)
CBS Sat. 9–10:30 a.m. (9/12/81–11/28/81)
CBS Sat. 9:30–11:30 a.m. (12/5/81–9/11/82)
CBS Sat. 9:30–10:30 a.m. (9/18/82–10/23/82)
CBS Sat. 9:30–11:30 a.m. (10/30/82–1/29/83)
CBS Sat. 9:30–10:30 a.m. and 11 a.m.–Noon (2/5/83–9/10/83)
CBS Sat. 11:30 a.m.–Noon (9/17/83–2/4/84)
CBS Sat. 10:30 a.m.–Noon (2/11/84–9/8/84)
CBS Sat. Noon–12:30 p.m. (12/22/84–12/29/84)
CBS Sat. 10–11:30 a.m. (1/5/85–6/1/85)
CBS Sat. 10–11 a.m. and Noon–1:30 p.m. (6/8/85–9/7/85)
ABC Sat. 8–9 a.m. (9/7/85–10/26/85)
ABC Sat. 8:30–9:30 a.m. (11/2/85–2/22/86)
ABC Sat. 9–10 a.m. (3/1/86–9/6/86)
ABC Sat. 11 a.m.–Noon (9/13/86–9/5/87)
ABC Sat. 11:30 a.m.–Noon (9/12/87–1/23/88)
ABC Sat. 11–11:30 a.m. (1/30/88–7/16/88)
ABC Sat. 11 a.m.–Noon (7/23/88–1/30/93)
ABC Sat. 10–11 a.m. (2/6/93–5/22/93)
ABC Sat. 10:30–11:30 a.m. (5/29/93–4/30/94)
ABC Sat. 8–9 a.m. (5/7/94–9/3/94)
ABC Sat. 11 a.m.–Noon (9/10/94–7/15/95)
ABC Sat. 11:30 a.m.-12:30 p.m. (7/29/95–9/2/95)
ABC Sat. 11 a.m.–Noon (9/9/95–5/4/96)
ABC Sat. 10–11 a.m. (5/11/96–)

Voice Characterizations: *Mel Blanc, June Foray*

Ever since Warner Brothers released its *Looney Tunes* cartoon shorts to television in 1955, the medium and "wascally wabbit" Bugs Bunny have had a long-lasting love affair. The success of the old animation for local stations in evening slots was so striking that ABC installed a nighttime version on October 11, 1960 Tuesdays at 7:30–8 p.m. There *The Bugs Bunny Show* was composed mostly of cartoons seen in movie theaters after 1948, along with 4$^{1}/_{2}$ minutes each week of new comic introductions shot specifically for the series. That incarnation lasted through September 25, 1962, by which time ABC had installed it as a cornerstone for its long-delayed Saturday morning children's lineup.

The star of it all was Bugs Bunny, a wisecracking hare whose greeting to any new foe was "Eh, what's up, doc?" His nemeses included easily confused, bulb-headed hunter Elmer Fudd; diminutive, gruff-voiced cowpoke Yosemite Sam; a whirling Tasmanian devil; and even Marvin the Martian, an alien hell-bent on destroying earth. Bugs responded to their threats with some of the greatest animated slapstick and wordplay ever put on film, and the tightly drawn and directed films with their incisive plots and dialogue held up wonderfully.

The same could be said of the segments featuring a memorable supporting cast. There was stuttering Porky Pig; insufferably vain Daffy Duck; slurring Sylvester the Cat and his prey the yellow Tweety Bird, whose protector was the kindly Granny; and self-proclaimed genius Wile E. Coyote and his prey the Road Runner. All of them headlined their own network Saturday morning series at one time, but none fared as well as this show. Various one-shot animated shorts also ran on some episodes. Doing most of the voices was Mel Blanc, who said Bugs was his favorite character. Granny and most females were from the talented mouth of June Foray, later Rocky on *The Bullwinkle Show*.

After the show had been going more than five years on Saturdays, ABC started a Sunday run. Bugs Bunny fan Fred Silverman, no doubt feeling Bugs's potential was being wasted and feeling heat over his network CBS's violence-laden Saturday morning schedule of 1967–68, moved the show to his base and gave it a new title, *The Bugs Bunny/Road Runner Hour,* under which it ran through 1973. ABC had the show back to a half hour for two years as *The Bugs Bunny Show,* then it returned to CBS, where it went up to an hour again with its previous title, then 90 minutes from 1977–81, and even to a whopping 2½ hours by 1985. The series was titled *The Bugs Bunny/Road Runner Show* from 1977–85, then moved to ABC and was known for a season as *The Bugs Bunny/Looney Tunes Comedy Hour.* It was retitled *The Bugs Bunny & Tweety Show* on September 13, 1986 and lasted as an hour show for the next decade, during which time it became the network's most popular cartoon, with a surprisingly large portion of its audience being adult viewers.

Besides this show, several Bugs Bunny nighttime specials aired on CBS from 1976 into the 1990s, featuring some new but mostly vintage material. The network also aired *The Bugs Bunny/Road Runner Show* on Tuesdays at 8 a.m. from April 27–June 1, 1976. As for the evergreen *Looney Tunes,* those cartoons were a daily staple of the cable channel Nickelodeon in 1996 following decades of popularity on local stations.

•BULLWINKLE SHOW, THE

Cartoon; Color
November 19, 1959–July 24, 1982

ABC Thu. 5:30–6 p.m. (11/19/59–3/3/60)
ABC Tue./Thu. 5:30–6 p.m. (3/8/60–9/21/61; Thursdays
    only September–December 1960)
ABC Sun. 12:30–1 p.m. (9/25/60–12/18/60)
ABC Sun. 5:30–6 p.m. (12/25/60–9/3/61)
NBC Sun. 5:30–6 p.m. (9/23/62–9/15/63)
NBC Sat. 12:30–1 p.m. (9/21/63–9/5/64)
ABC Sun. 11–11:30 a.m. (9/20/64–4/25/65)
ABC Sun. 11:30 a.m.–Noon (5/2/65–9/19/65)
ABC Sun. 11–11:30 a.m. (9/26/65–9/2/73)
NBC Sat. 12:30–1 p.m. (9/12/81–7/24/82)

Voices:

Bullwinkle J. Moose/Mr. Peabody/	
Dudley Doright	*Bill Scott*
Rocky Squirrel/Natasha Fatale	*June Foray*
Aesop	*Charles Ruggles*
Aesop Jr.	*Daws Butler*
Boris Badenov/Inspector Fenwick	*Paul Frees*
Sherman	*Walter Tetley*
Snidely Whiplash	*Hans Conreid*

Narrators:

"Bullwinkle"	*William Conrad*
"Fractured Fairy Tales"	*Edward Everett Horton*

The most unconventional cartoon for television in the 1950s, and arguably for all time, was the pun-laden, satirical *Bullwinkle Show.* Bullwinkle was a dim-witted moose from Frostbite Falls, Minnesota whose diminutive pal Rocky was a flying squirrel with an aviator's cap. The unlikely duo faced another twosome of Cold War combatants, trench coat–clad Boris and husky-voiced Natasha, whose sole mission was to "kill moose and squirrel." They never succeeded, with thanks due in varying proportions to Boris's stupidity, Rocky's quick

thinking, and interactions with other odd types, including aliens from outer space, robots, demented bureaucrats, and much more. Topping it off was a narrator whose comments brought occasional responses in support or opposition from the participants, ending it all by telling viewers to "tune in to our next episode" and giving two jokey titles for the next serialized adventure. The result was a concoction that appealed to both adults and children.

One supporting segment later had its own spin-off (see *Dudley Doright).* Another was "Fractured Fairy Tales," the title segment of which featured a hapless fairy opening the first pages of a volume of fairy tales, then getting snapped up by the suddenly closing book. Following was an off-the-wall rendition of *Cinderella, Sleeping Beauty, Rapunzel,* and other well-known classics, plus a narrator who, as in the main show, talked with the characters. "Peabody's Improbable History" had a bespectacled pooch take his pet boy Sherman back in time via his Waybac machine and make dry comments about circumstances that did not square with what history said had happened. The "Mr. Know-It-All" segment featured Bullwinkle's helpful but bumbling attempts to answer viewers' questions. And "Aesop and Son" featured a young-looking, curly-haired Aesop telling his tunic-wearing offspring so-called parables with such characters as a lion who caught cold every time he roared because he really wanted to sing. The moral of that one was "Psychiatrists are good, but they've never cured the common cold."

The cartoon was the only original series in ABC's late afternoon lineup in 1959, airing under the title *Rocky and His Friends.* Its success prompted ABC to air adventures twice a week within five months. In 1960–61 ABC added repeats of the show on Sundays before canceling the series. It then

Getting ready to smile before moon men Cloyd and Gidney are, clockwise from top left, Bullwinkle Moose, Natasha Fatale, Sherman, Peabody, Boris Badenov, and Rocky Squirrel from The Bullwinkle Show.

went onto NBC Sundays at 7 p.m. from September 24, 1961–September 16, 1962 with new episodes and the new *Bullwinkle* title before returning to daytime.

Series creator Jay Ward's offscreen antics involving this cartoon rate a mention. He sold the series by a promotion he called "Operation Loudmouth," whereby he tickled the network brass by offering such gimmicks as the Jay Ward Pyramid Club (if your name reached the top, you would get 2,458 series for the price of one). However, NBC was not amused by on-air jabs at them and the show's freewheeling promotions (once in New York, Ward had a woman dressed as a Salvation Army missionary wearing a sign that said, "Repent! Watch *The Bullwinkle Show!"),* and moved it out of the nighttime lineup into a late afternoon slot. Ward reaped his own revenge with a press release stating, "It is with great ennui and professional personal apathy that the National Broadcasting Company announces the renewal of *The Bullwinkle Show* for the 1962–63 TV season. *The Bullwinkle Show* will air at 5:30 p.m. on Sundays, a time slot once occupied by *Omnibus.* Oh, well, it's in color."

From 1963–73 the show aired on network weekends in repeats, and there was a final network run in 1981–82. Though barren of network exposure afterward, the reputation of Bullwinkle and company grew even stronger in the 1990s. The home video release of the cartoons received much favorable publicity, and even public television granted a special retrospective on the series on March 12, 1991 titled "Of Moose and Men: The Rocky and Bullwinkle Story." There was also an odd live-action film titled *Boris and Natasha* with Dave Thomas and Sally Kellerman as the leads, which was to go into theatrical release but ended up debuting on the Showtime cable network on April 17, 1992 instead.

•BUMP IN THE NIGHT
Cartoon; Color
September 10, 1994–

ABC Sat. 10–10:30 a.m. (9/10/94–7/15/95)
ABC Sat. 8:30–9:30 a.m. (two shows; 7/29/95–9/2/95)
ABC Sat. 9:30–10 a.m. (9/9/95–2/24/96)
ABC Sat. 9–9:30 a.m. (3/2/96–5/4/96)
ABC Sat. 9:30–10 a.m. (5/11/96–)

Voices:

Bumpy	*Jim Cummings*
Molly Coddle	*Gail Matthius*
Squishy	*Rob Paulsen*

Gumby looked positively plebeian next to the star of this Claymation-style cartoon. Bumpy, a froglike, buggy-eyed creature, took pigtailed Molly and worrywart blue blob Squishy (also known as Squishington) on new adventures each week using household objects found inside a 10-year-old boy's room. The show had a nifty theme song reminiscent both in style and performance of Bette Midler and her Harlettes doing "Boogie Woogie Bugle Boy," and in fact, each show closed with a visit to "Mr. Bumpy's Karaoke Cafe," where one or more of the regulars mouthed a popular tune.

BUNCH, THE
Variety; B&W
January 7, 1952–February 23, 1952

NBC Mon.–Fri. 12:30–1 p.m. (1/7/52–2/23/52)

Regulars: *Hugh Downs, Bette Chapel, the Art Van Damme musical group*

Stately Hugh Downs singing? That was one of the attractions of this sponsorless Chicago-based entry, along with music from Bette Chapel. This was Downs's first network TV on-camera work.

•BUSINESS WORLD
News; Color
October 6, 1986–March 28, 1993

ABC Sun. Various half hours between 9:30 a.m. and 1 p.m. (10/6/86–3/28/93)

Host: *Sander Vanocur (1986–92), Stephen Aug (1992–93)*

This straightforward weekend wrap-up of features on the financial field was available for ABC affiliates to program either before or after *This Week with David Brinkley.* When Sander Vanocur retired from ABC News in 1992, business news editor Stephen Aug, a frequent reporter for *Good Morning America,* replaced him as anchor for the last of its seven seasons on air.

•BUTCH CASSIDY AND THE SUNDANCE KIDS
Cartoon; Color
September 8, 1973–August 31, 1974

NBC Sat. 10–10:30 a.m. (9/8/73–12/29/73)
NBC Sat. 11:30 a.m.–Noon (1/5/74–8/31/74)

Voices:

Butch Cassidy	*Lucas "Chip" Hand III*
Elvis	*Frank Welker*
Harvey	*Mickey Dolenz*
Merilee	*Judy Strangis*
Mr. Socrates	*John Stephenson*
Steffy	*Tina Holland*

No relation to the similarly titled 1969 movie starring Paul Newman and Robert Redford, *Butch Cassidy and the Sundance Kids* consisted of a quartet of teenage undercover agents posing as a rock group. Butch Cassidy (who actually resembled *David* Cassidy of the Partridge Family) was the dreamboat lead singer and guitarist who was summoned to get information from Mr. Socrates on his missions via a beeper on his ring. Mr. Socrates was a computer voice who was the boss of the World-Wide Talent Agency, and he dictated spying assignments to the bell-bottomed boys and go-go outfitted girls. Harvey was the screeching comic relief, Merilee the commonsense blond, and Steffy the brunette. Elvis was the group's comical dog. With tired references to other pop culture icons (which extended to ex-Monkee Mickey Dolenz participating as a voice), and derivative touches from other cartoons, this came across as one of Hanna-Barbera's most insipid shows.

BYLINE—See *News Gal.*

C

•CB BEARS

Cartoon; Color
September 10, 1977–January 28, 1978
NBC Sat. 8–9 a.m. (9/10/77–1/28/78)

Voices:

Hustle/Undercover Elephant/	
Big Duke/Stick	*Daws Butler*
Bump	*Henry Corden*
Boogie/Blubber	*Chuck McCann*
Charlie	*Susan Davis*
The King/Yukayuka/Rattle	*Lennie Weinrib*
Loud Mouse	*Bob Hastings*
Big H	*Sheldon Allman*
Clyde	*Don Messick*
Skids	*Marvin Kaplan*
Zelda	*Susan Silo*
Sheena	*Ginny McSwain*
Sheriff	*Bill Woodson*
Shake	*Paul Winchell*
Roll	*Joe E. Ross*
Sidney Merciless	*Alan Oppenheimer*

This incredibly varied cartoon presentation starred the CB Bears, a trio who fought criminals from a broken-down, gadget-laden garbage truck and got messages via citizens band (CB) radio from an unseen purring female named Charlie, à la *Charlie's Angels.* Hustle was the Phil Silver–ish leader, Bump was a moron who resembled Scooby-Doo and wore a garbage can lid as a hat, and Boogie was a clone of Boo-Boo Bear (see *Yogi's Gang*).

A host of other cartoons appeared to fill out the running time. "Undercover Elephant" had Loud Mouse as his partner in investigating crimes. "Shake, Rattle and Roll" involved a trio of ghosts running a hotel against the wishes of its operator, Sidney Merciless. "Hey, It's the King" had a city cat meet with Big H the hippopotamus, Clyde the ape, Skids the alligator, Yukayuka the mole, Zelda the ostrich, and Sheena the lioness. "Blastoff Buzzard and Crazy Legs" featured a no-dialogue desert chase with a bird pursuing a snake. "Posse Impossible" involved a quartet of bumbling cowboys led by the strong-willed Sheriff with his deputies Big Duke, a little person with a John Wayne drawl; Blubber, a fat man prone to crying; and Stick the hillbilly. They defended justice in the Old West town of Saddlesore.

On February 4, 1978, the series was absorbed into the two-hour *Go Go Globetrotters* (see *The Harlem Globetrotters*), where it ran through September 3, 1978.

•CBS CHILDREN'S FILM FESTIVAL, THE

Films; Color
February 5, 1967–August 25, 1979

CBS Sun. 4–5 p.m. (2/5/67–3/26/67)
CBS Sun. 4:30–5:30 p.m. (2/4/68–3/3/68)
CBS Sun. 1:30–2:30 p.m. (1/26/69–4/6/69)
CBS Sun. 4:30–5:30 p.m. (1/31/71–3/7/71)
CBS Sat. 1–2 p.m. (9/11/71–2/5/77)
CBS Sat. 1:30–2 p.m. (2/12/77–4/2/77)
CBS Sat. 1–2 p.m. (4/9/77–8/27/77)
CBS Sat. 1:30–2 p.m. (9/17/77–8/25/79)

Hosts: *Burr Tillstrom (as Kukla and Ollie; 1967–77), Fran Allison (1967–77)*

Who says foreign films can't attract a wide audience? *The CBS Children's Film Festival* drew a sizable number of viewers for more than a decade's worth of presenting movies from overseas. What's more, many of them made their American TV debuts, including the award-winning French film *The Red Balloon* in 1967. To top it off, introducing the films and commenting afterward were TV's favorite puppets, Kukla, Fran, and Ollie. No wonder one-time CBS programming chief Fred Silverman always pointed with pride to this show whenever critics accused him of going after ratings only on Saturday mornings.

In 1977 CBS dropped Kukla, Fran, and Ollie as the show went to half an hour and retitled the series *CBS Saturday Film Festival.* A year later, the show ran monthly as a replacement for *30 Minutes* before disappearing after a 12-year run.

•CBS EARLY MORNING NEWS

News; Color
October 4, 1982–1996

CBS Mon.–Fri. 6–6:30 or 6:30–7 a.m. (10/4/82–1/9/87)
CBS Mon.–Fri. 6–7:30 a.m. (1/12/87–11/27/87)
CBS Mon.–Fri. 6–7 a.m. (11/30/87–)

Anchors: *Diane Sawyer (1982–84), Bill Kurtis (1982–85), Jane Wallace (1984), Faith Daniels (1985–90), Forrest Sawyer (1985–87), Charles Osgood (1987–92), Victoria Corderi (1990–91), Giselle Fernandez (1991–92), Meredith Viera (1992–93), John Roberts (1992–94), Monica Gayle (1993–95), Jane Robelot (1995–96), Troy Roberts (1995–96)*

Like its adjacent program *The CBS Morning News,* this series underwent many changes of anchor without making much of a dent in the ratings. CBS had to launch the show when the other networks decided to add a pre–7 a.m. show for their affiliates, and as with NBC's *Early Today* it was decided to use the anchors of the morning news show for the early edition as well. Bill Kurtis and Diane Sawyer remained intact for nearly two years, until Sawyer left. Jane Wallace replaced Sawyer for a few months, then Kurtis was the sole anchor until Faith Daniels succeeded him in March 1985. Forrest Sawyer joined her as co-anchor in the summer of 1985 and stayed with her off and on through the next 2½ years.

In January 1987, CBS expanded the show to be an 1½-hour lead-in to its new morning show, and in the process renamed this series *The CBS Morning News.* The changeover was a ratings bomb, and when the show shrank down to an hour in the fall, Sawyer departed and Charles Osgood became co-anchor with Daniels. Daniels left in 1990 to take over *NBC News at Sunrise,* and Victoria Corderi replaced her, followed by Giselle Fernandez in 1991. By mid-1992, John Roberts and Meredith Vieira were the anchors. Roberts went solo for a time until Monica Gayle joined him; when Roberts left, in 1994, Gayle worked alone until the team of Jane Robelot and Troy Roberts succeeded her.

CBS EYE ON SPORTS—See CBS Sports Illustrated and, for the 1990s version, CBS Sports Spectacular.

CBS GOLF CLASSIC
Sports; B&W and Color
December 28, 1963–June 29, 1974

CBS Sat. 4–5 p.m. (12/28/63–6/29/74; December–January through April–June each year only)

Hosts: *Tommy Armour (1963–64 at least), Chris Schenkel (1963–64 at least), Jack Whitaker (at least 1971–74), Ken Venturi (1971–74)*

The *CBS Golf Classic* had all major pro golfers compete in a tournament for $150,000. By 1967, the tournament prize had been reduced to $50,000, but it still generated interest among 32 pros yearly, enough to keep it going another seven years. Among its announcers, former U.S. Open champion Ken Venturi called the action with veteran announcer Jack Whitaker in 1971.

In the early years Arnold Palmer and Gary Player were the two notable no-shows on the series. The reason was that they had their own show on ABC at the time, *Challenge Golf.* Ironically, Dan Curtis, the creator of *CBS Golf Classic* (and later *Dark Shadows*), developed the format for *Challenge Golf* (q.v.). This series won an Emmy in 1966 for Achievements in Sports Programs. In its last season, the show was retitled *CBS Golf Championship.*

•CBS MORNING NEWS, THE
News/Informational; B&W and Color
September 2, 1963–

CBS Mon.–Fri. 10–10:30 a.m. (9/2/63–8/13/65)
CBS Mon.–Fri. 7:05–7:30 a.m. (8/16/65–3/28/69)
CBS Mon.–Fri. 7–8 a.m. (3/31/69–9/25/81)
CBS Mon.–Fri. 7:30–9 a.m. (9/25/81–1/15/82)
CBS Mon.–Fri. 7–9 a.m. (1/18/82–1/9/87)
CBS Mon.–Fri. 7:30–9 a.m. (1/12/87–11/27/87)
CBS Mon.–Fri. 7–9 a.m. (11/30/87–)

Regulars: *Mike Wallace (1963–66), Joseph Benti (1966–8/28/70), Hughes Rudd (at least 1969–77), John Hart (1969–73), Bernard Kalb (1970–71 at least), Nelson Benton (at least 1972), Sally Quinn (8/6/73–2/1/74), Marshall Efron (1973 at least), Ray Gandolf (sports; 1974 at least–82), Bruce Morton (1974–77), Lesley Stahl (10/3/77–1/26/78), Richard Threlkeld (11/77–1/26/79), Bob Schieffer (1/29/79–1980, 1985), Jane Bryant Quinn (business; 1979–85), Charles Kuralt (1980–81), Jeff Greenfield (TV criticism; at least 1981), Gordon Barnes (weatherman; at least 1981), Diane Sawyer (9/28/81–8/84), Bill Kurtis (3/82–6/84), Jim Kelly (Philadelphia sportscaster;*

1982 at least), Warner Wolf (1982–85), John Madden (sports; at least 1982), Pat Collins (entertainment; 1982–85 at least), Ray Brady (business; 1982–83 at least), Dr. Holly Atkinson (health; 1983 at least), Jane Wallace (7/84–9/84), Phyllis George (10/1/84–9/4/85), Steve Baskerville (weatherman; at least 1985–86), Ken Prewitt (finance; at least 1985–86), Dr. Bob Arnot (health; 1985–94), Robert Krulwich (business; 1985–93), Terence Smith (D.C. correspondent; at least 1985–86), Phil Boyer (media critic; at least 1985–), Faith Daniels (hostess 1986; newscaster 1987–89 at least), Forrest Sawyer (1985–86), Maria Shriver (1985–86), Bruce Morton (1986), Mariette Hartley (1986–87), Rolland Smith (1986–87), Harry Smith (1987–96), Kathleen Sullivan (1987–90), Jim Lampley (sports; at least 1988), Paula Zahn (1990–96), Steve Kmetko (Hollywood news; at least 1989–90), Gene Siskel (movie reviews; 1990–), Greg Gumbel (sports; at least 1990), Victoria Corderi (newsreader; at least 1990–91), Charles Osgood (newsreader; at least 1990–91), Hattie Kaufman (consumer affairs; 1991–), Jane Robelot (newsreader; March 1995–)

Despite its reputation, *The CBS Morning News* was not always a ratings also-ran. When it started in 1963 as a replacement for the midmorning series *Calendar,* it actually improved upon the latter's ratings enough that CBS felt confident to move it against NBC's *Today* after two years. But the show's schizophrenic approach—hard news during one period and trivial entertainment the next—attracted few regular viewers, and the many cast overhauls during the show's run of 30-plus years didn't help.

From the beginning, *The CBS Morning News* filmed news reports and interviews, many of which were designed to appeal to women. (Mike Wallace interviewed Rose Kennedy on October 30, 1963, less than a month before her son John was assassinated.) But in general the show gave Wallace back his reputation as a hard-edged journalist, and when the opportunity to do even more in-depth reporting came his way at CBS in 1966, he left the show. Joseph Benti then became host of the program, which graduated to becoming a full hour lead-in to *Captain Kangaroo* in early 1969. Around this time, John Hart gave the news from Washington, D.C., and Hughes Rudd became an occasional contributor.

Hart took over the helm from Benti on August 31, 1970, with Bernard Kalb assuming his post. Kalb served in the Washington, D.C. anchor spot until 1972, when Nelson Benton assumed it and Kalb became a roving reporter for the series. During this period the show had special series on such topics as J. Edgar Hoover and "Hunger in America," and Benton and Kalb occasionally substituted for Hart as host. Also, from 1971–74, the show had a thrice-weekly segment called "Spectrum" in which various commentators from all political persuasions gave their opinions on the news.

Then on August 6, 1973, in an effort to emulate *Today,* CBS debuted the unforgettable team of Sally Quinn and Hughes Rudd in what turned out to be the show's first major disaster. Ex–*Washington Post* reporter Quinn, who had never reported news on television before, collapsed with the flu an

One of several editions of The CBS Morning News *the network probably would like to forget was this 1987 combination of, from top clockwise, Bob Saget, Rolland Smith, Mariette Hartley, and Mark McEwen.*

hour and a half before the premiere was to air, and made it through the program only through valiant effort. The next day, Hughes Rudd's mother died. Amid this chaos, Quinn's awkward banter during the first week virtually destroyed any credibility the show might have generated. For example, *Newsweek* noted that after a film aired about the horrors which juvenile California migrant workers endure, Quinn glibly quipped that child labor "was how I felt when my mother and father made me clean up my room." While Quinn supplied some unintentional if grotesque amusement, Marshall Efron did the occasional intended comedy spots.

Mercifully, Hughes Rudd became a solo anchor in early 1974, joined by sports reporter Ray Gandolf and by Bruce Morton as Washington, D.C. anchor (Charles Osgood was doing feature stories by 1975). Lesley Stahl replaced Morton in 1977, and a month later Richard Threlkeld replaced Rudd, who gave up his chair voluntarily to do features for the show. Ironically, Stahl had rejected the co-hosting role with Rudd back in 1974, paving the way for Sally Quinn. The Stahl-Threlkeld pairing did little to boost the ratings, so Bob Schieffer became the new anchor near the start of 1979; Hughes Rudd stayed around to do features until leaving for ABC that summer.

Under Schieffer's anchorship, the show was retitled according to what day it was (e.g. *Monday Morning, Tuesday Morning,* etc.), and used the same set as its more successful weekend counterpart *Sunday Morning* (q.v.). Then it became simply *Morning* in 1980. *Sunday Morning*'s host Charles Kuralt assumed anchorship, but ratings still did not budge. The following year CBS enlarged the program to 90 minutes and in the process started the reduction of time for *Captain Kangaroo,* something CBS programmers had long considered in the 1960s and 1970s but rejected in the face of potential reaction from outraged parents. Ex–Nixon aide Diane Sawyer joined Kuralt as co-host in this change.

Just four months later, at the start of 1982, the show went to two hours, knocking *Captain Kangaroo* back to 6:30 a.m. daily, and saw Chicago newscaster Bill Kurtis assume co-host duties from Charles Kuralt within two months of the change. Kurtis and Sawyer at one point brought the show within throwing distance of being the top-rated morning show, ranking ahead of *Today* and closing in on *Good Morning America* for several weeks before it dropped again. Sawyer, who said she was tired of the early morning hours, left in July 1984 to report for the CBS nighttime newsmagazine *60 Minutes.*

Jane Wallace replaced Sawyer temporarily, and Sawyer's permanent replacement was ex–*NFL Today* hostess Phyllis George. Unfortunately, George brought with her an on-air sloppiness and lack of television news experience not seen since the Sally Quinn tenure. Her most shocking faux pas came at the end of an interview on May 14, 1985 with a woman named Cathleen Webb and the imprisoned man Webb had falsely accused of rape in 1977 named Gary Dotson. George asked the two to hug, a request they declined with more grace than might be expected, given the outrageous nature of George's proposal. She was out by September. An obviously unhappy Kurtis left in July 1985, and Bob Scheiffer returned as his temporary replacement.

CBS next tried the team of Forrest Sawyer and Maria Shriver in the fall of 1985, then Bruce Morton and Faith Daniels a year later. The latter duo was an interim one, as the network turned over the program from its news to its entertainment division, added a studio audience, and had actress Mariette Hartley co-host with New York reporter Rolland Smith in front of a studio audience, supplemented by young comedian Bob Saget for humor spots on "This Day in History." The show, retitled *The Morning Program,* aired for 90 minutes behind an enlarged *CBS Early Morning News* (q.v.), which confusingly now was titled *CBS Morning News.* In any event, *The Morning Program* became the joke of the industry with its mix of news and trivial entertainment features (*TV Guide* said it was "hardly worthy of the network that brought us *Me and the Chimp*"), and CBS fell further behind its morning competition, slumping one week to its lowest ratings in five years.

Despite all the public scorn and damning reviews, the show went back to CBS News control on November 30, 1987, when it debuted as *CBS This Morning.* Reporters Harry Smith (no relation to Rolland Smith) and Kathleen Sullivan helmed the show until Paula Zahn assumed her job on February 26, 1990. This co-anchor duo was the longest the program ever had. By March 1991 Smith and Zahn were doing the news summaries as well, leaving Charles Osgood and Victoria Corderi to do the honors on *CBS Early Morning News* only. Among the new regular contributors were Greg Gumbel on sports and Gene Siskel on movie news and reviews.

On October 26, 1991, CBS gave its affiliates 12 minutes per hour to use for local news rather than the typical 4 minutes near the end of the first half hour that the other morning programs gave. It was designed to keep affiliates carrying the show, but in response, the competitors soon let affiliates expand their local news reports for nearly 12 minutes as well.

Ratings remained stubbornly in third place, even with the addition in 1995 of a studio audience to perk up viewer interest, so in 1996 CBS announced that the show's newsreader Jane Robelot and chubby weatherman Mark McEwen would become hosts of the latest incarnation, with more input from local stations.

CBS MORNING NEWS (1950s)—See *Morning News.*

CBS NEWS
News; B&W and Color
May 28, 1956–May 30, 1980

CBS Mon.–Fri. 1–1:10 p.m. (5/28/56–4/5/57)
CBS Mon.–Fri. 7:45–8 a.m., 8:45–9 a.m. and periodically
    from 1–10 p.m. (4/8/57–12/12/57)
CBS Mon.–Fri. 8:45–9 a.m. and 1–1:05 p.m. or 1:25–1:30
    p.m. (12/15/57–3/13/59)
CBS Mon.–Fri. 8–8:15 a.m. and 1–1:05 p.m.
    (3/16/59–9/29/61)
CBS Mon.–Fri. 11:55 a.m.–Noon and 3:55–4 p.m.
    (10/2/61–9/28/62)
CBS Mon.–Fri. 12:25–12:30 p.m. and 3:55–4 p.m.
    (10/1/62–9/6/68)
CBS Mon.–Fri. 12:25–12:30 p.m. and 4:25–4:30 p.m.
    (9/9/68–2/21/69)
CBS Mon.–Fri. 12:25–12:30 p.m. (2/24/69–3/23/73)
CBS Mon.–Fri. 11:55 a.m.–Noon (3/26/73–4/26/79)
CBS Mon.–Fri. 10:55–11 a.m. (4/29/79–5/30/80)

Hosts: *Charles Collingwood (1956, 1961–62 at least), Walter Cronkite (late 1956–57 at least), Richard Hottelot (1957–61 at least), Ron Cochran (1960–61), Harry Reasoner (1961–62 at least), Douglas Edwards (1961–64 at least), Robert Trout (1964 at least)*

Veteran reporter Charles Collingwood first hosted CBS's numerous daily newscasts of the 1950s and 1960s. His 10-minute show featured a roundup of headlines, commentary with film clips and a humorous closing story. After a year, during which time Walter Cronkite replaced Collingwood, CBS added two 15-minute news casts following *The Jimmy Dean Show* and *Captain Kangaroo* in early morning. After a year the 7:45–8 a.m. portion was discontinued, and the afternoon 10-minute report went to five minutes.

Richard Hottelot handled the early morning news by the fall of 1958. That report first followed *Captain Kangaroo,* then preceded it until CBS expanded the children's show to a full hour daily in 1961. Then Harry Reasoner handled the mid-morning reports and Douglas Edwards the afternoon ones in 1961, following the end of a five-minute report Ron Cochran had been giving. Edwards remained the daytime anchor while Robert Trout assumed morning duties by 1964.

CBS SATURDAY FILM FESTIVAL—See *CBS Children's Film Festival.*

CBS SATURDAY NEWS, THE
News; B&W and Color
April 4, 1959–December 25, 1965

CBS Sat. Noon–12:30 p.m. (4/4/59–9/26/59)
CBS Sat. 12:30–1 p.m. (10/3/59–12/31/60)
CBS Sat. 1–1:30 p.m. (1/7/61–4/25/64; aired Sat. 12:30–1
    p.m. during summer months)
CBS Sat. 1:30–2 p.m. (5/2/64–12/25/65; off summer of
    1965)

Anchor: *Robert Trout (1959–62 at least), Martin Agronsky (1964–65), Charles Kuralt (1965)*

CBS was the only network to program a half-hour newscast on Saturdays before 1965. However, few stations aired it then (in 1960, for example, only 63 of 199 CBS affiliates carried the series). In fact, when it debuted in 1959, it aired in New York City an hour later at 1 p.m., even though it originated from that city! After six years of spotty coverage, it moved to the early evening slot of 6:30 p.m. in January 1966 with Roger Mudd at the helm to get higher clearances, and it has remained at that time slot to this day. Harry Reasoner also hosted the show briefly in 1959.

CBS SPORTS ILLUSTRATED
Sports; Color
January 28, 1973–May 12, 1974

CBS Sun. 5:30–6 p.m. (1/28/73–9/9/73)
CBS Sun. 5–5:30 p.m. (1/27/74–5/12/74)

Host: *Jack Whitaker*

The popular weekly magazine *Sports Illustrated* had been in publication since 1954 when it came to television initially in September 1971 as a syndicated series titled *The World of Sports Illustrated* with Tom Brookshier as host. A year and a half later, CBS brought the show to its Sunday afternoon lineup as a replacement for professional hockey. As with the syndicated version, the series concentrated on interviews with top athletes and related types plus stories about the big sports news of the week, with the CBS edition changing only the host and adding more immediacy.

In 1974 the show returned without a *Sports Illustrated* connection as *CBS Eye on Sports.* The show later ran for a time as part of *CBS Sports Spectacular* (q.v.). *Sports Illustrated* had a sketchy relationship with television in later years, including four syndicated specials airing in 1982 under the title *Sports Illustrated: A Series for Television,* and the announcement of a cable channel joint venture with Cable News Network (CNN) to be called CNN/SI and set for launching in late 1996.

CBS SPORTS PRESENTS—See *CBS Sports Spectacular.*

•CBS SPORTS SPECTACULAR
Sports; B&W and Color
January 3, 1960–

CBS Sun. 3–4:30 p.m (1/3/60–4/17/60)
CBS Sun. Various lengths and times (1/8/61–4/30/67; not seen fall months)
CBS Sun. Various lengths and times (1/28/73–; not seen fall months)
CBS Sat. Various lengths and times (9/14/74–; not seen fall months)

Hosts: *Bud Palmer (1960–61), Jack Whitaker (1962–63, 1965–67), Chris Schenkel (1964), Brent Musburger (1973–81 at least, 1984), John Tesh (as commentator; 1981–86), Pat O'Brien (at least 1981–86), Sandy Hill (at least 1981–84), Tim Ryan (1987–88 at least), Greg Gumbel (1994–95), Andrea Joyce (1994–)*

CBS Sports Spectacular is that network's long-running sports anthology series, first airing as a filler between the network's pro football and baseball coverage on Sundays. It actually predated *ABC's Wide World of Sports,* but the latter's emphasis on live events gave it an edge and immediacy that this entry, which used taped and filmed events for its first five years, lacked. Begun as *Sunday Sports Spectacular,* a title it used through 1963, its debut covered pro basketball (the Harlem Globetrotters versus the Baltimore Rockets) and women's tennis (Karol Fageros versus Althea Gibson). The show also aired on CBS Thursdays from 7:30–8:30 p.m. from April 27–September 28, 1961 as *The Summer Sports Spectacular* with Bud Palmer as host.

Later shows dealt with karate, water polo, billiards, auto races, rodeos, ice skating, sumo wrestling, and other nonheadlining events, with the oddest probably being Jackie Gleason playing Arnold Palmer in a round of golf. A noteworthy show was the July 5, 1964 edition, where Philadelphia Phillies Manager Gene Mauch wore a cordless microphone from a pregame meeting with his players to a night game versus the Cardinals, and the show aired his edited comments from the dugout during the game. During that season the show went from its 90-minute format to a 30-minute entry, following baseball in the summer.

The show expanded to two hours in 1965 under the title *CBS Sports Presents.* Then in 1966 the series reverted to the old title and became a studio show with host Jack Whitaker doing live interviews and introducing taped events. That same year professional golfer Ken Venturi gave a weekly report on the PGA tour. But after another year, CBS gave up on the show for seven years as the network aired soccer and hockey during the summer months.

In 1973 *CBS Sports Spectacular* came back. Pointedly, the series started carrying some matches of the World Hockey Association for a few years after losing control of the *NHL Game of the Week* to NBC. But despite these and other events, it never challenged veteran *ABC's Wide World of Sports* in terms of ratings and prestige, so in 1981 the show was retitled *CBS Sports Saturday/Sunday* to emphasis its transformation from using taped "trash sports" to more pertinent sporting news and coverage of live events. John Tesh, Pat O'Brien, and Sandy Hill contributed news and features for the program.

On April 17, 1994 CBS retitled the anthology again to *CBS Eye on Sports.* What the series eyed most were boxing matches and ice skating competitions, the latter of which appeared several Sundays against the NFL football games CBS lost to Fox, and performed quite well in the ratings.

•CBS STORYBREAK
Children's; Color
March 30, 1985–August 26, 1995

CBS Sat. 1:30–2 p.m. (3/30/85–6/1/85)
CBS Sat. 11–11:30 a.m. (6/8/85–1/4/86)
CBS Sat. 11:30 a.m.–Noon (1/3/87–6/6/87)
CBS Sat. 12:30–1 p.m. (6/13/87–8/29/87)
CBS Sat. Noon–12:30 p.m. (9/19/87–12/26/87)
CBS Sat. 12:30–1 p.m. (10/ /88–10/26/91)
CBS Sat. 12:30–1 p.m. (9/18/93–8/26/95)

Host: *Bob Keeshan*

This long-running anthology series presented animated versions of children's books hosted by Bob Keeshan, formerly Captain Kangaroo, who appeared on a painted set to introduce the week's show. Initial offerings came from Hanna-Barbera Productions and included such adaptations as *Hank the Cowboy, Chocolate Fever,* and *How to Eat Fried Worms.* Keeshan returned at the end of each show to tell viewers about other books for children, similar to the story just aired and recommended by the Library of Congress.

•CBS SUNDAY AFTERNOON SHOWCASE
Movies; Color
September 25, 1994–November 13, 1994

CBS Sun. 4–6 p.m. (9/25/94–11/13/94)

In an unprecedented move, CBS presented network television's first daytime weekend movie series following the network's loss of NFL football to Fox after 38 years of coverage. The TV movies were video versions of Harlequin romance novels geared for women viewers. They starred largely unknown actors, with the most familiar names in the debut "Treacherous Beauties" being Emma Samms, Tippi Hedren, and Catherine Oxenberg. Others seen included Justine Bateman, Rick Springfield, Mel Harris, Ellen Burstyn, and Meg Tilley. After less than two months of indifferent audiences, CBS replaced this with the much more successful *CBS Eye on Sports* (q.v.).

CBS SUNDAY NEWS

News; B&W

October 7, 1951–December 22, 1957

CBS Sun. 5:30–5:45 p.m. (10/7/51–12/16/51)
CBS Sun. 3:30–4 p.m. (1/8/56–4/8/56)
CBS Sun. 5:30–6 p.m. (4/15/56–9/9/56)
CBS Sun. 4:45–5 p.m. (9/16/56–12/23/56)
CBS Sun. 5:30–6 p.m. (1/5/57–8/25/57)
CBS Sun. 4:45–5 p.m. (9/8/57–12/22/57)

Anchor: *Eric Sevareid (1/8/56–7/21/57), Bob Trout (7/28/57–12/22/57)*

CBS tried two Sunday afternoon newscasts in the 1950s. The first was a quarter-hour affair which lasted three months. After a five-year hiatus, Eric Sevareid anchored a half-hour version in 1956 which appeared in several time slots during the day. In January 1957 the series returned under the title *World News Roundup*, with a slight twist. The angle was that its films and live reports, including two-way remotes, centered on global events in such countries as France, Poland, and Israel. The show had no sponsor.

CBS TELEVISION WORKSHOP

Dramatic Anthology; B&W

January 13, 1952–December 25, 1960

CBS Sun. 4–4:30 p.m. (1/13/52–4/13/52)
CBS Sun. Noon–12:55 p.m. (1/24/60–12/25/60; off summer months)

CBS Television Workshop received two go-rounds, with neither doing particularly well. The 1952 version debuted with *Don Quixote* directed by Sidney Lumet and starring Boris Karloff and Grace Kelly, but despite the talent involved, *Variety* noted, "the production itself emerged as almost amateurish." Later productions included a jazz fantasy called "Careless Love" featuring Conrad Janis and his Tailgate Jazz Five and productions of *Tom Sawyer* and H. G. Wells's *The Time Machine*. Audrey Hepburn made an early and rare TV acting appearance on this show.

Eight years later, the series reemerged with new producer Albert McCleery, formerly producer of *Matinee Theater*. McCleery promised viewers a fresh and different approach in drama by focusing on closeups—in other words, the same thing done on *Matinee Theater*. Despite this emphasis, and a lack of general acclaim for most of the shows, the show did manage to mix a nice share of rising talent (Ozzie Davis and Cicely Tyson in an all-black production on April 24, 1960) with a few more established performers (Maureen Stapleton, Margaret Truman, and even Morey Amsterdam). But as only 52 stations carried it (roughly a quarter of the CBS affiliate lineup), its ratings were never good, and it went off on Christmas Day 1960 after nearly a year.

There also was a *CBS Radio Workshop* which ran from January 27, 1956–September 22, 1957. Apart from its format, it had little to do with the TV series.

CBS TENNIS CLASSIC

Sports; Color

May 21, 1972–August 24, 1975

CBS Sun. 4:30–5 p.m. (5/21/72–8/19/73; summers only)
CBS Sun. 2:30–3:30 p.m. (5/19/74–8/25/74)
CBS Sun. 4:30–5:30 p.m. (6/1/75–8/24/75)

Commentators: *Bud Collins (1972), Pat Summerall (1973–74), Vin Scully (1975), Tony Trabert (1975)*

Billionaire Lamar Hunt oversaw this weekly tournament, which in its first year featured 16 tennis professionals competing in games taped at Sea Pines Plantation at Hilton Head Island in South Carolina. Each entrant got $1,000 for participating, with the top finisher getting $7,500. By 1974 the contest took place in Austin, Texas, for a top prize of $10,000. The next year Puerto Rico hosted the event, and Arthur Ashe competed against Rod Laver for $12,000. Also new in 1975 was the use of two announcers, including ex-pro Tony Trabert, and "pressure point" action by two female players.

CBS THIS MORNING—See *CBS Morning News.*

CBS WASHINGTON REPORT

News; B&W

September 23, 1962–September 8, 1963

CBS Sun. 12:30–12:55 p.m. (9/23/62–9/8/63)

Hosts: *David Schoenbrun (9/62–2/63), Roger Mudd (3/63–9/63)*
Reporter: *Paul Niven*

District of Columbia correspondent David Schoenbrun hosted this news update, with Paul Niven giving a five-minute summary of the latest events at the start of the show, followed by Schoenbrun giving a review of the week's top activities. On the debut Schoenbrun talked with President John F. Kennedy about the latter's foreign aid appropriations bill.

Longtime D.C. correspondent Roger Mudd took Schoenbrun's place as host in March 1963 when CBS transferred Schoenbrun back to his old assignment as European news chief, which he had held for 18 years before this show began. That reversal, and CBS denying him another hosting job, led Schoenbrun to resign from the network by July 1963. Shortly thereafter, this show was replaced by the venerable *Face the Nation*.

CBS-TV COLOR FOOTBALL—See *NCAA Football.*

COPS—See *Cyber COPS.*

•CADILLACS AND DINOSAURS

Cartoon; Color

September 18, 1993–March 26, 1994

CBS Sat. 11:30 a.m.–Noon (9/18/93–3/26/94)

Voices:

Hannah Dundee	*Susan Roman*
Grith (Hobb)	*Don Francks*

Mustapha	*Bruce Tubbe*
Noc	*Don Dickinson*
Wilhelmina Scharnhorst	*Dawn Greenhaigh*
Jack Tenrec	*David Keeley*
Hammer Terhune	*Tedd Dillon*
Vice Terhune	*Frank Pellegrino*
Wrench Terhune	*Colin O'Meara*
Toulouse	*Philip Williams*

"In the 26th century, mankind faces an epic struggle for survival. The forces of nature have spun wildly out of control. Mighty cities have crumbled and the dinosaurs have returned to reclaim the earth. In this savage land, one man stands alone—Jack Tenrec, defending humanity in a world gone mad, a world where only the strong survive. A world of Cadillacs and dinosaurs."

Purple prose aside, this opening narration of this cartoon, based on the comic book *Xenozoic Tales* by Mark Schultz, gave a fairly accurate setup for each show, but it was incomplete. The only Cadillacs driven were the 1950s models owned by Tenrec, a member of the Old Blood Mechanics, an ecological group whose motto was "The Machinery of Life is a balance, and we have to maintain it." Thus, Jack defended the dinosaurs now roaming the planet, claiming that the fear humans had of them went both ways. Helping him in his cause was Hannah Dundee, a scientist serving as ambassador to people dealing with the dinosaurs; Mustapha, a bandana-wearing muscular assistant who oversaw Jack's Cadillac fleet in a garage; and even Hermes, Jack's pet dinosaur whom he raised when poachers killed the latter's mother.

Their biggest foes were not dinosaurs but humans, chiefly Wilhelmina Scharnhorst, an imposingly built woman who did not care one whit about what would happen to the earth's environment if the dinosaurs became extinct again. She campaigned vigorously against all of Jack's advice and actions and enlisted the militaristic Hammer Terhune and his brothers Wrench and Vice to put Jack and his group out of business. Toulouse was a member of the Council of Governors who constantly weighed Scharnhorst's and Jack's positions in his decisions. Noc was Scharnhorst's lackey. Grith was a wise ancient adviser seen by Jack in flashbacks, allowing him to recall bits of knowledge along the way.

This cartoon was one of the most ambitiously plotted action yarns put on Saturday mornings, or on all of television for that matter. But the use of such coinages as "City by the Sea" (for New York City) and "Chevattes" (for dinosaurs) made the show a challenge for young and casual viewers to watch, and it lasted only a season.

•CAESARS CHALLENGE
Game; Color
June 14, 1993–January 14, 1994

NBC Mon.–Fri. 12:30–1 p.m. (6/14/93–12/31/93)
NBC Mon.–Fri. Noon–1 p.m. (two shows;
   1/3/94–1/14/94)

Host: *Ahmad Rashad*

Assistant ("Centurion"): *Dan Doherty*

Having failed with *Las Vegas Gambit* in 1981, NBC decided to give the Nevada gambling town another shot at hosting a game show. This time, legendary Caesars Palace served as the taping site for three contestants who tried to solve words whose letters were scrambled. Muscular, tall (6-foot 6-inch) "centurion" Dan Doherty pulled the lever to spin the letters for each game. After three rounds, the top winner got to play another letter-unscrambling game. As of this writing, this was the last daytime game show to air on NBC.

•CALENDAR
Informational; B&W
October 2, 1961–August 30, 1963

CBS Mon.–Fri. 10–10:30 a.m. (10/2/61–8/30/63)

Hosts: *Mary Fickett, Harry Reasoner*

This live-from-New-York entry was a CBS News production which intentionally strove to avoid strictly "feminine" topics, even though it was a daily morning show. Features ranged from a native bazaar in Vietnam to political discussions with the likes of West Berlin Mayor Willy Brandt. Between reports, newsman Harry Reasoner managed to do a few essays and use his wry sense of humor occasionally with the help of co-host Mary Fickett (later an Emmy winner on *All My Children*). A typical example came on the debut, when after Reasoner said, "We will remain as we are," he followed it with "Goodnight, David," and Fickett said, "Goodnight, Chet," à la the closer used by NBC's nightly news team of Huntley and Brinkley.

CBS made a reasonable effort to promote this show, even giving it an hour special in nighttime in July 1962, but to no avail. The final show ended with a review of the guests who had been on the show (Reasoner enjoyed Peter Ustinov but hated Peter O'Toole). All in all, it was an effort that deserved better from viewers.

The hosts of Calendar, *Harry Reasoner and Mary Fickett, made a rare excursion outside the studio for this publicity shot.*

•CALIFORNIA DREAMS

Sitcom; Color
September 12, 1992–

NBC Sat. 10:30–11 a.m. (9/12/92–9/3/94)
NBC Sat. 11:30 a.m.–Noon (9/10/94–)

Cast:

Lorena Costa (1994–)	Diana Uribe
Matt Garrison (1992–94)	Brent Gore
Jenny Garrison (1992–93)	Heidi Lenhart
Melody Garrison (1992–93)	Gail Ramsey
Richard Garrison (1992–93)	Michael Cutt
Dennis Garrison (1992–93)	Ryan O'Neill
Tiffany Smith	Kelly Packard
Jake Sommers (1993–)	Jay Anthony Franke
Michael Sylvester "Sly" Winkle	
(1992–)	Michael Cade
Tony Wickes	William James Jones
Mark Winkle (1994–)	Aaron Jackson
Samantha "Sam" Wu (1993–)	Jennie Kwan

California Dreams was the title of a teenage bubblegum rock combo formed at Pacific Coast High School in Redondo Beach, California. When the show began, Matt Garrison and his sister Jenny led the group, with Matt its lead singer and Jenny its keyboardist. Joining them were guitarist Tiffany, a stereotypical dumb blonde, and Tony on drums. They rehearsed at Matt and Jenny's home at 128 Ocean Drive and had occasional interplay with Mr. and Mrs. Garrison and their other child Dennis. There was also the inevitable music video per show designed to promote the group on the music charts in real life, though nothing MCA Records released became a hit. Sly was the Garrisons' next-door neighbor, group manager, resident stud (or at least thought he was!), and Matt's best friend.

In the second season Jake Sommers and Samantha Wu joined the band as guitarist and singer respectively, while Jenny and the rest of Matt's family disappeared. The next season Matt and his family moved to New York, and Sam, previously a boarder of the Garrisons, found a new home courtesy of Lorena Costa, Jake's girlfriend. Also joining the group as a singer and keyboardist was Sly's nicer cousin Mark Winkle. Through all the changes, Sharkey's remained the group's favorite hangout, and Earl Boen appeared occasionally as goofy Pacific Coast High principal Mr. Blumford.

CALIFORNIA RAISINS SHOW, THE

Cartoon; Color
September 16, 1989–September 1, 1990

CBS Sat. 10–10:30 a.m. (9/16/89–12/30/89)
CBS Sat. 8–8:30 a.m. (1/6/90–9/1/90)

Voices: Cam Clarke, Brian Cummings, Jim Cummings, Dorian Harewood, Gailee Heideman, Michelle Marianna, Brian Mitchell, Cree Summers, Rebecca Summers, Todd Tolces

First seen in commercials in 1986 by Will Vinton Productions, the California Raisins were animated clay models promoting their fruit by singing and dancing to a new recording of the Motown classic "I Heard it Through the Grapevine." The ads became a hit, prompting increased consumption of raisins, and the record made the lower reaches of Billboard's Hot 100 singles chart for a few weeks in early 1988, with Buddy Miles supplying the lead vocal. After a few nighttime cartoon specials on CBS in 1988, the characters got their own regular show. It featured a quartet of raisins—Stretch, Beebop, A.C., and Red—in misadventures on the road and in their penthouse above their recording studios.

CALL MY BLUFF

Game; Color
March 29, 1965–September 24, 1965

NBC Mon.–Fri. Noon–12:30 p.m. (3/29/65–9/24/65)

Host: Bill Leyden

Imagine To Tell the Truth using words instead of people and you will have a good idea of what Call My Bluff was about. Two trios, each with one celebrity guest, alternated play with one team receiving an obscure word and having to guess who on the other side provided the right definition along with the others' bluffs. Celebrity captains on the first week were game show regulars Orson Bean and Peggy Cass. The concept was revived more than 20 years later (see Wordplay).

CAMEO THEATRE—A syndicated title for Matinee Theatre.

CAMERA HEADLINES

News; B&W
January 12, 1949–May 28, 1949

DuMont Mon.–Fri. 12:30–12:45 p.m. (1/12/49–1/28/49)
DuMont Mon.–Fri. 10:15–10:30 a.m. and 12:30–12:45 p.m. (1/31/49–2/11/49)
DuMont Mon.–Fri. 12:30–12:45 p.m. (2/14/49–4/28/49)

This primitive newscast debuted on the inaugural WABD daytime schedule November 1, 1948 from 7–7:15 a.m. with Jack Rayel reading stories from reports by the International News Service (INS) while headlines were typed on a sheet of paper and displayed on camera. Camera Headlines then aired between WABD shows all morning long. It ran some multiple daily telecasts when it joined the DuMont daily lineup in early 1949, and the show also aired on DuMont nightly from 7:30–7:45 p.m. from January 1948–January 1949.

•CAMERA THREE

Various; B&W and Color
January 22, 1956–January 21, 1979

CBS Sun. 11:30 a.m.–Noon (1/22/56–8/27/61)
CBS Sun. 11–11:30 a.m. (9/3/61–1/21/79)

Host: James MacAndrew (1956–66 at least)

Starting in May 1953 as a local series produced by the public affairs department of WCBS New York City in conjunction with the New York State Education Department, Camera

Three lasted some 23 years, with perhaps the most variety of any long-running TV series. The show began as an experiment in Saturday afternoon programming with a starting weekly budget of $1,400 and no advertising (the latter feature remained into the 1970s). Airing originally as *It's Worth Knowing,* it employed poetry readings, one-act operas, and dramatizations of classic works—virtually anything connected to literature, music, and the arts—with plain sets in the background. Three years later it was on CBS with a new title which came, not surprisingly, from the number of TV cameras used on the show.

On CBS, *Camera Three* thrived by letting artists do largely what they wanted to do. Earle Hyman became the first black actor to play Hamlet on television. In 1961 Richard Burton read some Dylan Thomas poetry, and such talent as Sir John Gielgud, Agnes Moorehead, and Christopher Plummer also popped up. Newcomers also got early guest shots on *Camera Three,* such as William Shatner in a three-part series in November 1957 dramatizing pre–World War II culture in Germany. There also were talks by famed writers S. J. Perelman and Thornton Wilder, special dance performances by the likes of Twyla Tharp, and tributes to such luminaries as William Faulkner and Billie Holiday following their deaths. One noteworthy example of the latter was Lotte Lenya singing songs written by her late husband Kurt Weill on June 29, 1958.

Other programs dealt with the Sacco-Vanzetti case, the history of the Fifth Amendment, food critic Craig Claiborne at a clambake, and a discussion of Dylan Thomas and his poetry. One show compared the comic strip character Krazy Kat to Samuel Beckett's play *Waiting for Godot!* And like all good art, the show had its share of controversy, notably in a sketch where a Caucasian male and African-American woman danced around a bed.

Perhaps the most star-studded event was a two-part salute to New York's Circle in the Square theater on March 13 and 20, 1977. For these programs, actors Colleen Dewhurst, Dustin Hoffman, James Earl Jones, Vanessa Redgrave, and George C. Scott made guest appearances.

The series won much acclaim, including an Emmy in 1966 for Achievement in Daytime Programming. The shows "seem miraculously to leap out of the TV tube like conjurer's rabbits out of a hat," said critic Faubion Bowers in *Saturday Review* in 1972. The host of *Camera Three* in the early years was James MacAndrew, director of broadcasting for the New York City Board of Education. It finally went off, with *Lamp Unto My Feet* and *Look Up and Live,* in 1979 when CBS replaced them with *Sunday Morning.*

CAMOUFLAGE

Game; B&W
January 9, 1961–November 16, 1962

ABC Mon.–Fri. Noon–12:30 p.m. (1/9/61–6/29/62)
ABC Mon.–Fri. 12:30–12:55 p.m. (7/2/62–11/16/62)

Host: *Don Morrow*
Organist: *Paul Taubman*

After seeing an elaborate etching which hid an unknown object within it, two contestants tried to be the first to buzz in and answer a true-false question, with a right response causing a part of the picture camouflage to disappear. To help the contestants, organist Paul Taubman plunked a few musical clues. A contestant had to trace the hidden object to win.

Despite a rather unimpressive run of less than two years, this game enjoyed a brief weekly revival in syndication in 1980 by Chuck Barris Productions, of all things. Hosted by Tom Campbell, it gave players $50 for each correct answer before removing a portion of the puzzle, and the contestant with the most money got to try to solve a final puzzle, with the top prize being a new automobile.

•CAMP CANDY

Cartoon; Color
September 9, 1989–September 7, 1991

NBC Sat. 8:30–9 a.m. (9/9/89–9/1/90)
NBC Sat. 8–8:30 a.m. (9/8/90–9/7/91)

Voices:

John Candy	*Himself*
Alex	*Chiara Zanni*
Binky	*Tony Ail*
Chester	*Danny Mann*
Iggy	*Tom Davidson*
Nurse Molly	*Valri Bromfield*
Rex de Forrest III	*Lewis Arquette*
Rick	*Andrew Seebarin*
Robin	*Danielle Ferrandes*
Vanessa	*Willow Johnson*

Chubby comedian John Candy played chief counselor at a summer camp at Lake Cacciatore in this routine cartoon. A nature lover but far from a genius, Candy found himself fighting the plots of Rex de Forrest (get it?) and his dimwit aide Chester to condemn the camp so the land could be used for condos. Assisting his efforts were Nurse Molly, who had the hots for Candy, and his young campers Rick the party kid, Robin the sane one, Binky the youngest boy, Vanessa the little princess, Iggy the nerd, and Alex.

The series returned in daily syndication in 1992, with a reemphasis on its ecological themes via new live-action introductions by Candy in some of his last professional work (he died in 1994). Candy also helped to develop the cartoon and sang the theme song with its writer, Harry Nilsson.

CAMPAIGN AND THE CANDIDATES, THE

Documentary; Color
July 14, 1968–September 1, 1968

NBC Sun. 5–5:30 p.m. (7/14/68–9/1/68)

Host/Narrator: *Elie Abel*

The men, issues, and public opinion surrounding the 1968 presidential campaign received a weekly summary here. The debut featured reports on plans to get to the Oval Office by Gov. George Wallace and Gov. Nelson Rockefeller. Elie

Abel was the diplomatic correspondent for NBC News. A similar show with the same title aired earlier from September 17–November 5, 1960, on NBC Saturday nights.

CAMPAIGN ROUNDUP

News; B&W
July 15, 1956–March 26, 1961

ABC Sun. 4–4:30 p.m. (7/15/56–8/19/56)
ABC Sun. 3:30–4 p.m. (4/10/60–6/26/60)
ABC Sun. 3:30–4 p.m. (1/9/61–3/26/61)

Anchors: *Quincy Howe (1956), Ernest K. Lindley (1956), Bill Shadel (1960–61)*

Campaign Roundup began with eight reporters, four each from ABC and *Newsweek* magazine, giving regional reports on the 1956 campaign. Ernest K. Lindley represented the magazine and co-hosted the show in Washington, D.C. with ABC reporter Quincy Howe, who was based in New York. Four years later, a new version appeared. In 1961 it aired as *Roundup USA,* with Bill Shadel checking with various correspondents about the latest news in their regions, plus some news analysis and taped interviews with current headline personalities. Some of the reporters seen in this incarnation, including Howe, Paul Harvey, and Edward P. Morgan, had also worked on the earlier show.

A version of *Campaign Roundup* anchored by Quincy Howe also aired from May 12–June 9, 1958, on ABC Mondays at 8 p.m., covering that year's congressional races.

CAN WE SHOP?—See *Joan Rivers Show, The.*

•CANADIAN FOOTBALL

Sports; B&W and Color
August 28, 1954–October 10, 1982

NBC Sat. 1:45 p.m.–Conclusion (8/28/54–11/27/54)
NBC Sun. 1–7 p.m. (9/26/82–10/10/82)

Announcers: *James Harold "Sleepy Jim" Crowley (analyst; 1954), Lindsey Nelson (play-by-play; 1954), Don Criqui (analyst; 1982), John Brodie (play-by-play; 1982), Merlin Olsen (analyst; 1982), Dick Enberg (play-by-play; 1982)*

One sport that has proved several times to be a nondraw on U.S. television is the Canadian version of American football. Canadian football has a longer playing field, one extra player on each side, and three rather than four downs, plus different bonus points, all of which make it somewhat difficult for a sports fan in the States to follow teams like the Ottawa Rough Riders and Toronto Argos. The first effort to air Canadian football came in 1954, when NBC tried to draw an audience away from *NCAA Football* on ABC and failed miserably. Nearly 30 years later, when the NFL endured a players' strike, NBC gave Canadian football another go with weekly doubleheaders. But with even less viewer interest, the network canned the show after three weeks, despite the fact that the strike went on for five more weeks. Another effort to telecast the event below the border by a network seems unlikely, at least in this century.

CANDY CARNIVAL—See *Grand Chance Roundup.*

•CAPITOL

Soap Opera; Color
March 26, 1982–March 20, 1987

CBS Mon.–Fri. 2:30–3 p.m. (3/26/82–3/20/87)

Cast:

Myrna Clegg (1982–83)	Carolyn Jones
Myrna Clegg (1983)	Marla Adams
Myrna Clegg (1983–87)	Marj Dusay
Sam Clegg (1982)	Robert Sampson
Sam Clegg (1982–87)	Richard Egan
Sam "Trey" Clegg III	Nicholas Walker
Jordy Clegg	Todd Curtis
Julie Clegg (1982–83)	Kimberly Beck
Julie Clegg (1983–87)/Jenny Diamond (1985–86)	Catherine Hickland
Brenda Clegg (1982–84)	Leslie Graves
Brenda Clegg (1985)	Ashley Laurence
Brenda Clegg (1985–87)	Karen Kelly
Clarissa McCandless	Constance Towers
Wally McCandless	Bill Beyers
Tyler McCandless (1982–85)	David Mason-Daniels
Tyler McCandless (1985–86)	Dane Witherspoon
Dr. Thomas McCandless (1982–83)	Brian Robert Taylor
Dr. Thomas McCandless (1983–87)	Michael Catlin
Matt McCandless (1982)	Shea Farrell
Matt McCandless (1982–84)	Christopher Durham
Matt McCandless (1987)	Rod Stryker
Sen. Mark Denning	Ed Nelson
Sloane Denning	Deborah Mullowney
Judson Tyler	Rory Calhoun
Shelly Granger/Kelly Harper (1982–83)	Jane Daly
Shelly Granger/Kelly Harper (1984–87)	Jess Walton
Lizbeth Bachman (1982–86)	Tonja Walker
Maggie Brady (1982–85)	Julie Parrish
Lawrence Barrington (1982–83)	Jeff Chamberlain
Jeff Johnson (1982–83)	Rodney Saulsberry
Gillian McCandless (1982)	Kelly Palzis
Paula Denning (1983–87)	Julie Adams
Zed Diamond (1983–87)	Bradley Lockerman
Veronica Angelo (1983–85)	Dawn Parrish
Danny Donato (1983)	Victor Brant
Danny Donato (1984)	Eddie Zammitt
Detective Keyes (1983–84)	John Colenback
Fran Burke (1983)	Lana Wood
Amy Burke (1983)	Kimberly Ross
Ricky Driscoll (1984–85)	Billy Warlock
Hal Dayton (1984–85)	Arthur Malet
Cheetah (1984–85)	Becca C. Ashley
Chip Landry (1984–85)	Lindsey Richardson

Jarrett Morgan/Baxter
  McCandless (1985–87)   Ron Harper
Dylan Ross (1985–87)   Mitch Brown
Leanne Foster (1985–87)   Christine Kellogg
Linda Vandenberg (1985–86)   Lara Parker
Vera Sweet (1985–86)   Valarie Reynolds
Megan Belvoir (1985)   Devon Ericson
Prince Ali (1986–87)   Peter Lochran
Jeffrey Martin Sahim (1986–87)   Michael Evans
Darlene Stankowski (1986–87)   Tammy Wynette
Meredith Ross (1986–87)   Tawny Kitaen
Kate Wells (1986–87)   Cheryl-Ann Wilson
Angelica Stimac Clegg (1986–87)   Terri Hatcher
D. J. Phillips (1986)   Grant Aleksander
Tracy Harris (1987)   Sachi Parker
Laureen Clegg (1987)   Janis Paige
Scotty Harper (1987)   Malachi Pearson

What was *Capitol?* Well, the CBS press release announcing this routine soap was almost as lurid and florid as some of the show's dialogue, to wit: "Against the socially and politically charged backdrop of today's Washington [D.C.], two lovers yearn to cut through the barriers that have traditionally divided their families, only to find themselves caught in a dangerous web of power, passion and revenge." A *TV Guide* reviewer gave a more realistic assessment: "This new serial might be subtitled 'Romeo and Juliet Go to Washington,' though 'Blabscam' would be a good second choice."

The two warring families were the superpowerful Cleggs and the ambitious McCandlesses, with the two young lovers being university student Julie Clegg and Air Force hero Tyler McCandless. Their screwed-up clans included Julie's politician father Sam, her meddling socialite mother Myrna, their children Jordy and Brenda, and Sam's son Trey (a member of the House of Representatives) on the Clegg side, and Tyler's mom Clarissa, his collegiate brothers Wally and Matt and doctor brother Thomas, and his sister Gillian, an adoptee, on the McCandless side. The animosity between the families stemmed from Myrna, who destroyed the career of Clarissa's father Judson Tyler in the 1950s by pegging him as a Communist sympathizer. Myrna also hated Clarissa for marrying Baxter McCandless, Myrna's one-time passion who now was presumed dead.

Myrna was none too thrilled about Julie's planned nuptials, and neither was Trey, who viewed it as a liability in his effort to get ultimately elected President. Lucky for them, Julie developed amnesia, so crafty Myrna planned for her aide Lawrence Barrington to wed Julie and convinced the unknowing girl to do so. But Myrna did not know that Lawrence's real identity was that of Gordon Hull, a schemer. Tyler interrupted that marriage after he and TV news reporter Sloane Denning, the daughter of Sen. Mark Denning and his wife Paula, had been war criminals together in the fictitious land of N'shoba. Senator Denning had wanted Sloane to get together with Tyler, but Tyler still loved Julie and married her in 1983, while Sloane preferred the more ambitious Trey,

even though Tyler decided to run against Trey for Congress. Senator Denning also had a yearning for Clarissa to be his wife, even though he was wed to Paula.

The other children in the families exhibited some dysfunctional behaviors, such as Jordy Clegg's drinking problem and mooching off his parents. Jordy's problems were later exacerbated when he was scarred in an automobile accident (actor Todd Curtis was scarred by an accident in real life). Other situations involved Wally McCandless's gambling difficulties, which led to loan shark Danny Donato blackmailing Wally's football hero brother Matt, and Dr. Thomas McCandless, who seemed to be overcoming his worries about his walking disability with a love for Lizbeth Bachman, who actually had the hots for Jordy.

Meanwhile, Myrna and her operatives tried to destroy Tyler's run against Trey by making it appear that he had leaked government secrets from a top-secret committee. They blackmailed another committee member using prostitute Shelley Granger, but when Shelley learned of their plot she changed her name to Kelly Harper and went to work for Trey. The two of them fell in love, but the affair came to an end when she confessed her past and left town.

Following several more failed romances and intrigue among the lead characters, *Capitol* went into plot overdrive in 1986. That year Clarissa, thinking herself a widow, and Senator Denning were about to marry until Clarissa's very much alive first husband Baxter, now calling himself Jarrett Morgan, arrived. Then Denning turned out to be a traitor working for foreign interests against the United States. Another person believed dead, Prince Ali of the fictional Mideast country Baracq, told Matt McCandless he was his real father and wed Sloane Denning. Trey got word that Sam was his child Scotty's father and got married to Angelica Stimec. Sam's first wife Laureen, a disguised escapee from the insane asylum, became Scotty's nanny. D. J. Phillips got Kelly Harper hooked on drugs and sexually harassed his employee Brenda Clegg, who dated Dylan Ross, and most dramatic of all, a firing squad in Baracq prepared to shoot at Sloane on the last show!

CBS launched this show with great fanfare on a nighttime special which aired March 26, 1982. The show also engaged in some stunt casting, such as country music great Tammy Wynette playing nightclub singer Darlene Stankowski and Sachi Parker, Shirley MacLaine's daughter, playing a recovering drug addict who befriended Kelly Harper. But despite fairly respectable ratings, CBS believed the show could do better and replaced it with *The Bold and the Beautiful* and a switch in the time slot for *As the World Turns.*

CAPITOL CLOAKROOM
Public Affairs; B&W
September 17, 1950–December 31, 1950
CBS Sun. 5–5:30 p.m. (9/17/50–12/31/50)

This political discussion series originally ran from October 14, 1949–September 8, 1950 on CBS Fridays from 10:30–11 p.m., simulcast with the radio series, which began March 29,

1948. When the network dropped the simulcasting, the radio version stayed put and the TV *Capitol Cloakroom* ran on Sundays separately for three months. The radio version ran at least through 1972, with the overwhelming number of guests being U.S. Senators interviewed by various CBS correspondents.

•CAPTAIN CAVEMAN AND THE TEEN ANGELS
Cartoon; Color
March 8, 1980–June 21, 1980

ABC Sat. 11:30 a.m.–Noon (3/8/80–6/21/80)

Voices:

Captain Caveman	Mel Blanc
Brenda Chance	Marilyn Schreffler
Taffy Dare	Laurel Page
Dee Dee Sykes	Vernee Watson

"No redeeming values" concluded a 1980 *TV Guide* survey by 11 experts about this series, placing it at the bottom of 27 children's series studied. Some kids might have disagreed. A hairy, prehistoric lump of a man nicknamed "Cavey" was melted out of his suspended animation by the Teen Angels (Brenda Chance the brain, Dee Dee Sykes the worrywart, and Taffy Dare the fraidycat). He helped them with his powerful club, which could open and reveal a light or other device, and with the shout of "Captain Cave-maaan!" Cave Bird was his feathered assistant. The cartoons originally aired as part of *Scooby's All-Star Laff-a-Lympics* in 1977, and Cavey later popped up on *The Flintstones* and *The Flintstone Kids* (see all titles for more details).

•CAPTAIN GALLANT OF THE FOREIGN LEGION
Adventure; B&W
February 13, 1955–December 21, 1963

NBC Sun. 5:30–6 p.m. (2/13/55–3/24/57)
NBC Sat. 11:30 a.m.–Noon (3/30/57–12/7/57)
ABC Mon 5:30–6 p.m. (6/6/60–1/2/61)
NBC Sat. 5–5:30 p.m. (10/1/60–4/1/61)
NBC Sat. 5:30–6 p.m. (4/8/61–12/21/63)

Cast:

Captain Michael Gallant	Buster Crabbe
Pvt. Fuzzy Knight	Fuzzy Knight
Cuffy Sanders	Cullen "Cuffy" Crabbe

For kids weary of cowboys, *Captain Gallant of the Foreign Legion* at least offered a change in scenery. Now the heroes rode camels instead of horses and fought evil Arabs, instead of Native Americans, on the perimeter of the Sahara Desert. Leading them was noble Captain Gallant, who adopted Cuffy Sanders after Cuffy's father, a fellow Legionnaire and Michael's brother, died. Fuzzy was the comic sidekick orderly, just like in any western. As with other 1950s kiddie shows, the series offered premiums for viewers, though this one had an odd albeit appropriate one—a sundial!

Buster Crabbe started filming the show in November 1953 in Rabat, French Morocco, with a French TV crew.

He thought a TV show with a Legionnaire and a boy helping him defend justice would be a success, so he filmed 39 episodes in nine months despite several sandstorms and a flash flood that wiped out the crew's hotel. Recalling once when he and Cuffy (his son in real life) got lost in the desert, Buster told *TV Guide*, "We weren't in any danger, but we were surrounded by sand, and all I could think about was how nice it would be back in New York on my old [local] TV show, teaching housewives how to take off weight."

In 1955, production moved to Libya, Tripoli, and Italy due to friendlier political climates there. The producer was Harry Saltzman, who did the same chores for James Bond movies from 1962–1989. Interestingly, in 1955 the program held back 14 shows filmed in Morocco and used them in 1956–57 along with 26 new shows filmed in Rome. The show's credits thanked the French Minister of National Defense, the Commander General of French troops in Morocco, and officers and men at outposts in Rabat, Zagora, Marrakech, Taroudant, and Agadir who played themselves.

Three years after its final show on NBC, *Captain Gallant* turned up in reruns on ABC, followed four months later by a separate slate of reruns airing concurrently on NBC on a different day. This rare situation ended at the start of 1961, at which time NBC alone aired the reruns for nearly three more years. In syndication, the reruns aired as *Foreign Legionnaire*.

CAPTAIN HARTZ AND PETS
Children; B&W
October 3, 1954–January 1, 1956

NBC Sun. Noon–12:15 p.m. (10/3/54–1/1/56; off summer of 1955)

Cast:

Captain Hartz (1954–55)	Tom Mercein
Captain Hartz (Feb. 1955–1956)	Ned Locke
Captain Hartz's pal (1954 at least)	Jerry Garvey
Captain Hartz's pal (by Mar. 1955)	Pat Crane
Captain Hartz's pal (1955–56)	Darlene Conley
Captain Hartz's pal (1955–56)	Bruce Podewell

Captain Hartz and Pets began as a local show in Chicago in 1953 which aired March 15, 1954 from 7:45–8 a.m. on WABD New York City. Sponsored by Hartz Mountain Products, it had the old pipe-smoking captain, then played by Philip Lord, tell tales illustrated with stock footage to a young man played by Bruce Lindgren. On the network version, teenager Jerry Garvey replaced Lindgren as the captain narrated film footage about animals like dogs and raccoons. A new boy and girl alternated weekly as his pal, but the show ended at the start of 1956.

A year after its debut, *Captain Hartz* was the only network daytime show from Chicago, a dramatic dropoff for network shows from the Windy City since its early 1950s heyday.

CAPTAIN INVENTORY—A title for a syndicated package of the following series: *Birdman and the Galaxy Trio; The Fantastic Four; Frankenstein Jr. and the Impossibles; The Herculoids; Moby Dick and the Mighty Mightor;* and *Space Ghost and Dino Boy.*

•CAPTAIN KANGAROO

Children's; B&W and Color
October 3, 1955–December 8, 1984

CBS Mon.–Fri. 8–9 a.m. (10/3/55–4/5/57)
CBS Mon.–Fri. 8–8:45 a.m. (4/8/57–3/13/59)
CBS Mon.–Fri. 8:15–9 a.m. (3/16/59–9/29/61)
CBS Mon.–Fri. 8–9 a.m. (10/2/61–9/25/81)
CBS Sat. 9:30–10:30 a.m. (8/4/56–9/26/59)
CBS Sat. 8–9 a.m. (10/3/59–9/24/60)
CBS Sat. 10–11 a.m. (10/1/60–4/8/61)
CBS Sat. 9:30–10:30 a.m. (4/15/61–9/23/61)
CBS Sat. 9–10 a.m. (9/30/61–9/21/63)
CBS Sat. 8–9 a.m. (9/28/63–9/19/64)
CBS Sat. 8–9 a.m. (9/25/65–9/7/68)
CBS Mon.–Fri. 7–7:30 a.m. (9/28/81–1/15/82)
CBS Mon.–Fri. 6:30–7 a.m. (1/18/82–9/17/82)
CBS Sat. 7–8 a.m. and Sun. 8–9 a.m. (9/18/82–9/8/84)
CBS Sat. 7:30–8 a.m. (9/15/84–12/8/84)

Regulars: *Bob Keeshan (as Captain Kangaroo), Cosmo "Gus" Allegretti, Hugh "Lumpy" Brannum (as Mr. Green Jeans), James Wall (as Mr. Baxter; 1975 at least), Debbie Weems (1973–75 at least)*

Television's longest-running daily series for children—indeed, virtually the only kind of its type for most of the 1960s through 1980s—was the beloved *Captain Kangaroo*, which ran for nearly 30 years under essentially the same format. Host Bob Keeshan had previous experience in the field, having played

In this 1959 picture, Captain Kangaroo (Bob Keeshan) points to the face of Grandfather Clock while guest vocalist Betty Ann Grove watches him.

Clarabell the clown from 1948–1952 on *Howdy Doody* (q.v.), then getting his own local shows on WABC New York City as Corny the Clown on *Time for Fun* and *Tinker's Workshop*. Due to the popularity of *Tinker's Workshop*, which beat NBC's *Today* and CBS's *Morning Show* in local ratings, CBS gave him the chance to do his own network morning show.

The original concept of *Captain Kangaroo* was that Keeshan would play a guard at a museum, but subsequently it was decided that he would be the captain of the Treasure House. "Then we decided that he should have those big pockets," Keeshan told *TV Guide*. "When an artist drew the character as we described him, somebody said, 'Hey, he looks like a kangaroo.' Hence Captain Kangaroo."

Joining the captain as a regular was Mr. Green Jeans, a farmer type played by Fred Waring and the Pennsylvanians member Hugh Brannum. Mr. Green Jeans typically introduced the captain and home viewers to farm animals and told of their habits, but he was not averse to doing some dancing and acting in sketches. Others in recurring sketches were Mr. Bunny Rabbit, a bespectacled hare who always stole the carrots laid out by the captain; Mr. Moose, who liked to snicker after dropping colored ping-pong balls on the captain; Grandfather Clock, who spoke in rhymes and had a tendency to get sleepy; and the Dancing Bear. All of these were done at least in voice or costume by Cosmo Allegretti, who appeared as Dennis the eager but hapless handyman. Keeshan also played a regular character called the Town Clown, who was mute in silent comic episodes.

Filling out the program were various animated shorts. The first batch of these were some 500 Terrytoon cartoons CBS purchased for use on the series. The most memorable and longest-lasting of these was Tom Terrific, a simply drawn segment about a young boy with a funnel on his curly head who could transform himself into anything and who was accompanied by his sidekick Mighty Manfred the Wonder Dog. Later, in 1972–73, the series carried the first project financed by the U.S. federal government to air on a commercial network: a series of 50 animated 3½-minute cartoons from the Department of Health, Education, and Welfare about the importance of health and happiness, titled "The Most Important Person." In 1977, 20 four-minute animated segments promoting dental hygiene, titled "The Toothbrush Family," were added.

Within a year after the debut, the show added a sixth day to its schedule, which lasted through 1968 (during the 1964–65 season, Keeshan starred in the Saturday 8–9 a.m. period with the unsuccessful *Mr. Mayor*). Karen Waters, a young girl, did sketches on the Saturday edition in 1957. This extra day of work had been eliminated by 1959, when the show went to videotape instead of live broadcasts. By 1962 all shows were taped, and by the end of the 1960s the series was in color.

In the 1970s more guest stars appeared, including Pearl Bailey, Jack Gilford, Celeste Holm, Dick Shawn, and Andy Williams. In June 1971 Bob Keeshan dropped the Treasure House and had the Captain go casual in blazers and slacks.

A few new characters popped up, including the youthful Debby and friendly Mr. Baxter, but the casual, relaxed tone of entertainment and education stayed.

From almost day one, *Captain Kangaroo* faced constant threats from CBS to be canceled or reduced in length due to the reluctance of advertisers to spend money on a show reaching basically a preschool audience. Intense parental pressure through the years kept this from happening. But by 1981, CBS felt more pressure than ever from its affiliates to come up with a viable competitor to *Good Morning America* on ABC and *Today* on NBC, so it shortened the show to a half-hour daily and retitled it *Wake Up with the Captain*. At the start of 1982, the show relocated to the very early hour of 6:30 a.m. daily. In the fall of 1982, CBS installed it as a weekend-only hour offering, and two years later, in fall 1984, the show became a Saturday half-hour entry.

Tired of CBS's constant reductions of his show, Keeshan left *Captain Kangaroo* when his contract with the network ended in December 1984, just nine months shy of the show's 30th anniversary. He returned the next year as host of *CBS StoryBreak*, and by 1987 repeats of *Captain Kangaroo* were airing daily on many public television stations. These appearances, plus some occasional guest shots, kept the image of the Captain alive despite a lack of new shows.

But truth be told, network television lost some intangible greatness when *Captain Kangaroo* stopped airing daily. There has been nothing else quite like it on video, and most likely there never will be.

Captain Kangaroo, *played by Bob Keeshan, looks away while Bunny Rabbit adjust his glasses in the lower left corner.*

•CAPTAIN MIDNIGHT
Adventure; B&W
September 4, 1954–April 28, 1956

CBS Sat. 11–11:30 a.m. (9/4/54–2/26/55)
CBS Sat. 11:30 a.m.–Noon (3/5/55–8/27/55)
CBS Sat. 11–11:30 a.m. (10/1/55–12/10/55)
CBS Sat. 1:30–2 p.m. (12/17/55–4/28/56)

Cast:

Captain Midnight/Jim Albright ("SQ-1")	Richard Webb
Professor Ichabod "Ikky" Mudd ("SQ-2")	Sid Melton
Aristotle Jones ("Tut")	Olan Soule

"On a mountaintop high above a large city stands the headquarters of a man devoted to the cause of freedom and justice, a war hero who has never stopped fighting against his country's enemies, a private citizen who is dedicating his life to the struggle against evil men everywhere—*Captain Midnight!*"

As with most children's series openings, a few caveats are in order. After running on Mutual radio from September 30, 1940 to December 15, 1949 with Ed Prentiss in the lead, *Captain Midnight* came to television as head of the crime-fighting organization the Secret Squadron, whose members included the somewhat dense co-pilot and general assistant Ikky and the bespectacled lab scientist Tut. Captain Midnight, whose real name was Jim Albright, and Ikky had to leave their base via jet to stop assorted spies and saboteurs in the Cold War of the 1950s, and Tut gave them advanced scientific knowledge to help their efforts. The captain's motto was "Justice Through Strength and Courage."

The series' sponsor Ovaltine made a mint by offering viewers a decoder badge and membership to the Secret Squadron if they mailed in a waxed paper disk from a jar of the product. Richard Webb appeared in character in commercials giving home viewer members a special numerical message they could translate into a phrase by using their badges, and other members of the "Secret Squadron Hall of Fame," like athletes Elroy "Crazy Legs" Hirsch and Duke Snider, pitched Ovaltine as well.

Before the series hit the air, its production company Screen Gems set up a deal to syndicate the property as *Jet Jackson, Flying Commando* for approximately 130 markets that did not get the network version, as Ovaltine owned the rights to the *Captain Midnight* title. This odd switch (why use such a different name as Jet Jackson, with one less syllable than *Captain Midnight?*) affected all 39 series episodes. Webb tried unsuccessfully to revive the series in the 1970s and 1980s.

CAPTAIN N AND THE ADVENTURES OF SUPER MARIO BROS.
Cartoon; Color
September 9, 1989–July 25, 1992

NBC Sat. 9–9:30 a.m. (9/9/89–9/1/90)
NBC Sat. 8:30–9:30 a.m. (9/8/90–11/17/90)
NBC Sat. 9–9:30 a.m. (11/24/90–1/19/91)

NBC Sat. 8:30–9:30 a.m. (1/26/91–9/7/91)
NBC Sat. 9–9:30 a.m. (9/14/91–7/25/92)

Voices:

Kevin Keene (live action)	Dorian Barag
Captain N/Narrator	Matt Hill
Princess Lana	Venus Terzo
Simon Belmont	Andrew Kavadas
Dr. Wiley	Ian James Corlett
Megaman	Doug Parker
Kid Icarus	Alessandro Juliani
Motherbrain	Levi Stubbs Jr.
King Hippo	Gary Chalk
Duke the dog	Tomm Wright
Mario (1990–91)	Captain Lou Albano
Mario (1991–92)	Tony Rosato
Luigi (1991–92)	Danny Wells
Princess Toadstool (1990–92)	Jeannie Elias
King Koopa (1990–92)	Harvey Atkin
Toad (1990–92)	John Stocker

NBC's tribute to Nintendo home video games was this series, which incorporated more of them every year before its cancellation. The initial adventure had a boy named Kevin Keene become Captain N when he and his dog Duke went through a video screen into an animated world run by a "sun stone." His new cohorts included Dr. Wiley, Simon Belmont, Kid Icarus, and Megaman the robot. They all became part of the N-Team, led by Captain N, whose job was to protect Princess Lana, and they all fought the vicious Motherbrain and her helpers, including King Hippo.

On September 8, 1990, the show was retitled *Captain N and the Adventures of Super Mario Bros.,* adding the characters previously seen in daily syndication in 1989 in *The Super Mario Bros. Super Show!* Mario and Luigi were two plumber brothers who traveled in a mobile bathtub in the Mushroom Kingdom. They acted as protectors for Princess Toadstool and her aide Toad, the latter of whom actually resembled a toadstool. Their constant nemesis was the overgrown reptile King Koopa. The cartoons came to network television minus the live-action segments from the syndicated show where Captain Lou Albano and Danny Wells actually appeared as Mario and Luigi.

On September 14, 1991, the show had its final season as *Captain N and the New Super Mario World,* where it added a cartoon based on the Gameboy, Link, and Zelda video home games. After this final season, the show went into repeats in syndication, without the Mario Brothers segments, under the title *Captain N and the Video Game Masters.*

CAPTAIN VIDEO
Adventure; B&W
September 5, 1953–May 29, 1954

DuMont Sat. 11:30 a.m.–Noon (9/5/53–5/29/54)

Cast:

Captain Video	Al Hodge
The Ranger	Don Hastings

Captain Video spent most of its TV life as a nightly entry on DuMont from June 27, 1949–April 1, 1955, but it did surface on DuMont's abortive Saturday morning schedule. The adventures were separate from the nighttime ones, but they were set in the same futuristic era and featured the same mission for Captain Video and his young partner the Ranger: to save Earth from all kinds of peril. The first daytime story had the two work with a scientist played by Werner Klemperer to crack a "dome force" threatening to engulf a city, and the second had the duo fight a corps of unmanned light tanks controlled by a Univac calculating machine that commanded them to attack while sending teletyped calls for surrender to the U.S. President.

The official title of the Saturday edition was *The Secret Files of Captain Video.* It alternated weekly with what was once its competition, *Tom Corbett, Space Cadet.* After the nighttime show ended, Hodge returned as the Captain to host a cartoon show on WABD New York City from 1955–57.

•CARD SHARKS
Game; Color
April 24, 1978–March 31, 1989

NBC Mon.–Fri. 10–10:30 a.m. (4/24/78–6/20/80)
NBC Mon.–Fri. Noon–12:30 p.m. (6/23/80–10/23/81)
CBS Mon.–Fri. 10:30–11 a.m. (1/6/86–3/31/89)

Hosts: *Jim Perry (1978–81), Bob Eubanks (1986–89)*

Card Sharks was the first Mark Goodson–Bill Todman Production seen on NBC since *Match Game* went off in 1969. The show used the inverse of that company's *Family Feud* as its main game. Here two contestants learned the highest vote-getting answer to a question among 100 people polled, but one of them had to guess the number of people who answered that way, and the other said whether they thought the number was higher or lower than what the first contestant said. Whoever made the correct prediction won the right to play the show's card game (if the number was higher but the second contestant guessed it would be lower or vice versa, the first contestant won). The winning contestant received a card on a standard deck, no jokers with aces high, and predicted whether the next card would be higher or lower than that card's face value. (If he or she did not like the first card unveiled, the contestant could try another card, but that one had to be played.) With a correct prediction, the process could continue or the contestant could "freeze" at that point to try and continue further following a correct call on the next question. Any contestant who called the cards successfully four times in a row won a game, but a miss anywhere along the way put the contestant back at the original starting point, and his or her opponent got a free turn.

The first player to win two games got the chance to play a bonus round where he or she received $200 and a card to keep or discard for a second, must-play card for the same predicting strategy as in the main game, with the addition of having to bet any or all of that $200. Contestants played three hands on the bottom row, then moved to the middle to receive an additional $200 and play three more hands, having the option again of changing the first card when receiving the $200 (they got to go to the second level even if they lost everything on the first). If they succeeded in their calls on the second row to have any money left over, they went to the top row and had to bet half the amount earned to that point. The result of that final card turn determined the money won by a player.

After a three-year run on NBC, repeats of the show's last year were syndicated in the fall of 1982 in hopes of reviving the property. *Card Sharks* did return in 1986 with new host Bob Eubanks (Jim Perry was handling *Sale of the Century* on NBC at the time). There also was a new version airing in syndication in 1986–87, hosted by Bill Rafferty.

•CARE BEARS FAMILY, THE
Cartoon; Color
September 13, 1986–January 23, 1988

ABC Sat. 8:30–9 a.m. (9/13/86–9/5/87)
ABC Sat. 8–8:30 a.m. (9/12/87–1/23/88)

Voices:

Mr. Beastley	John Stocker
Birthday Bear	Melany Brown
Cozy Heart Penguin/Treat	
Heart Pig	Pauline Renny
Funshine Bear	Jane Eastwood
Gentle Heart Lamb/Lotsa	
Heart Elephant	Luba Goy
Good Luck Bear/Brave Heart	
Lion/Loyal Heart Dog	Dan Hennessey
Grumpy Bear	Bobby Dermie
Tenderheart Bear	Billie Mae Richard

Coming to Earth from the cloud world of Care-a-Lot via rainbows, the Care Bears sought to promote morals and decent behavior among all creatures, especially among young children, the show's target audience. The pint-sized cuddly, colorful ones used magic if needed to right wrongs in addition to delivering some low-key advice. Their recurring nemesis, although that seems to be too strong a word, was Mr. Beastley, who provided more humor than harm in the episodes. Other animals seen on this show were relatives of the Care Bears who lived in the Forest of Feelings. As ought to be painfully obvious from the summary, this series was practically too cute and precious for anyone older than kindergarten age to watch.

The cartoon was based on a line of characters created in 1981 for American Greeting Cards. Prior to coming to television, the characters appeared in *The Care Bears Movie*, released to theaters in 1985, as well as its sequels, the 1986 *Care Bears Movie II: A New Generation* and the 1987 *The Care Bears Adventure in Wonderland*.

CARTOON FUN—See *Topper Cartoon Fun.*

CARTOON TELETALES
Children's; B&W
August 11, 1948–November 2, 1948

ABC Mon./Wed. 5:30–6 p.m. (8/11/48–11/2/48)

Cartoonist: *Chuck Luchsinger*

Narrator: *Jack Luchsinger*

Apparently ABC's first daytime series, *Cartoon Teletales* alternated with *The Singing Lady* in the fall of 1948 before transferring to nighttime. Brothers Chuck and Jack Luchsinger entertained tykes via Jack's music and characters drawn by Chuck, like Mimi the Mole and Cletus the Caterpillar. Kids were encouraged to do artwork too and send it to the series, and the show got more than 3,700 drawings to display on air by February 1949 (they showed only 17 each week, with those seen winning a set of drawing pencils). That was pretty impressive, considering that the show at its peak aired on only 10 stations. After three months, the show ran Sundays at 6 p.m. from November 14, 1948–September 24, 1950.

•CARTOONIES
Cartoon; Color
April 6, 1963–September 28, 1963

ABC Sat. 11–11:30 a.m. (4/6/63–9/28/63)

Host: *Paul Winchell (with his dummy Jerry Mahoney)*

Debuting under the title *Cartoonsville*, *Cartoonies* featured a variety of animated shorts released by Paramount Pictures to theaters in the 1940s and 1950s. Among them were the Modern Madcaps, Noveltoons, and Screen Songs shorts, the latter featuring a bouncing ball for viewers to follow so they could sing along with the featured song. But the Noveltoons, narrated by Frank Gallop and featuring such characters as Casper the Friendly Ghost, Herman the Mouse, Blackie the Lamb, Baby Huey the Duck, and Little Audrey, predominated, with Casper being seen most frequently. This series was replaced by a new batch of original cartoons involving the latter (see *Casper the Friendly Ghost*). The show ran in syndication in 1974 under the title *Casper the Friendly Ghost and Company.*

•CARYL & MARILYN: REAL FRIENDS
Talk; Color
June 10, 1996–

ABC Mon.–Fri. 11 a.m.–Noon (6/10/96–)

Hosts: *Caryl Kristensen, Marilyn Kentz*

Despite failing with their NBC nighttime sitcom *The Mommies* twice from 1994–95, ABC was impressed enough with the comic duo of Caryl Kristensen (the blonde one) and Marilyn Kentz (the brunette) to try them as hosts of their latest effort to program a morning show against *The Price Is Right* on CBS. Like previous entries *The Home Show* and *Mike & Maty*, it was taped in Los Angeles on a living room set. Although most of the guests were "informational/lifestyle" types, such as doctors, advice columnists, and the like, there was room for segments like the kid who was the chuckling champion of Texas.

•CASPER

Cartoon; Color
February 24, 1996–

Fox Sat. 8:30–9 a.m. (2/24/96–4/13/96)
Fox Sat. 10–10:30 a.m. (4/20/96-)

Voices: *Joe Alaskey, Dan Castellaneta, Miriam Flynn, Brad Garrett, Tress MacNeille, Joe Nipote, Rob Paulsen, Malachi Pearson, Kath Soucie*

There was no confusing this Casper with the previous editions. Inspired by the surprise hit 1995 live-action movie of the same name, the benevolent ghost found himself the object of much ridicule and harassment by the Ghastly Trio, which consisted of his uncles Stretch, Stinky, and lamebrained Fatso. Aiding Casper in his fight to be good was his human pal Kat Harvey, a teenage girl whose father Dr. James Harvey was a "ghost therapist" who valiantly but vainly worked on curing the Ghastley Trio's love of mischief. They all lived in Whipstaff Manor, and occasionally were visited by tough tyke ghost Spooky, who wore freckles and a derby, and his girl Pearl, or "goil Poil," as he called her. There were two segments, both laced liberally with popular culture jokes, per show.

•CASPER AND THE ANGELS

Cartoon; Color
September 22, 1979–May 3, 1980

NBC Sat. 8:30–9 a.m. (9/22/79–12/1/79)
NBC Sat. 11–11:30 a.m. (12/8/79–4/5/80)
NBC Sat. 8:30–9 a.m. (4/12/80–5/3/80)

Voices:
Casper	Julie McWhirter
Maxie	Diane McCannon
Minnie	Laurel Page
Harry Scary/Commander	John Stephenson

There was no way this horrid revival of everyone's favorite friendly ghost could be confused with the original item (see following entry). Despite the title billing, here Casper played fourth to the antics of African-American Maxie and redhead Minnie, two cops for the Space Police who were dubbed familiarly as Angels by their Commander, à la the nighttime hit *Charlie's Angels*, and their buffoonish pal Harry Scary, a raggedy-looking ghost who sounded like Bert Lahr. They all tried to maintain justice and fairness in the year 2179 amid drawings that resembled leftovers from *The Jetsons*. Casper had a rather minor role in most of the stories, which ran two per show.

The dismal quality of this cartoon left Casper without an animated revival until 1996, when *Casper* (q.v.) appeared, a cartoon series based on an elaborate and somewhat controversial (because of a few adult jokes) live action plus special effects film with the same title.

•CASPER, THE FRIENDLY GHOST

Cartoon; Color
October 5, 1963–December 27, 1969

ABC Sat. 11–11:30 a.m. (10/5/63–9/2/67)
ABC Sat. 9–9:30 a.m. (9/9/67–8/30/69)
ABC Sat. 8–8:30 a.m. (9/6/69–12/27/69)

Voice:
Casper	Ginny Tyler

After old Paramount cartoons of Casper aired on ABC on *Matty's Funday Funnies* and *Cartoonies*, the amiable spirit got himself his own program. The afterlife of a young child, Casper spent much of his time trying to convince humans and other living creatures that he only wanted to play and have fun and not haunt them. Joining him occasionally were Wendy the good witch and the naughty Ghastly Trio. There were three cartoons per show.

The official title of the series was *The New Casper Cartoon Show* until September 1969, when it was retitled *The New Adventures of Casper* for its abbreviated last season. Casper retreated for a time back to comic books but was not forgotten, as evidenced by the fact that on April 16, 1972, his name was used for the command ship on the Apollo 16 mission. He reappeared on Saturday mornings in 1979 (see *Casper and the Angels)* and again in 1996 (see *Casper*).

CASPER THE FRIENDLY GHOST AND COMPANY—
See *Cartoonies.*

CATHOLIC HOUR, THE—See *NBC-TV Religious Program.*

•CATTANOOGA CATS

Cartoon; Color
September 6, 1969–September 5, 1971

ABC Sat. 9–10 a.m. (9/6/69–9/5/70)
ABC Sun. 10:30–11 a.m. (9/13/70–9/5/71)

Voices:
Auto Cat	Marty Ingels
Bumbler/Bristol Hound	Allan Melvin
Country	Bill Callaway
Crumden/Lambsy	Daws Butler
Groovey	Casey Kasem
Hoppy/Smirky	Don Messick
Jenny Trent	Janet Waldo
Kitty Jo	Julie Bennett
Mildew Wolf	Paul Lynde
Motor Mouse	Dick Curtis
Phileas Fogg Jr.	Bruce Watson
Scoots	Jim Begg

The Cattanooga Cats were a feline rock 'n' roll quartet who served as comic and musical relief for several elements seen within this series, a cross between *The Archies* and *The Banana Splits*. The cartoon combo included lead singer and dancer Kitty Jo, drummer Groovey, guitarist Country, and cellist Scoots. All participated in short humorous blackouts between other segments and commercials.

As for the supporting acts, "Around the World in 79 Days" was a very loose modern adaptation of the classic Jules Verne novel, with adolescents Phileas Fogg Jr., Jenny, and rotund Happy trying to win a million pounds by traversing the globe. Putting obstacles in their way were Crumden, his loser lackey Bumbler, and their pet monkey Smirky. For information on the other segments, see *Motor Mouse and Auto Cat,* a 1970 spin-off which left *Cattanooga Cats* only a half hour long in its last season.

CELEBRITY BOWLING
Game; Color
1971–1978, 1987–1988

Syndicated 30 minutes weekly beginning 1971

Host: *Jed Allan*

Celebrity Bowling was what its name implied, with pairs of stars competing in a 10-frame game to win money for members of the studio audience. In its first year it taped the season's 26 shows over a three-day weekend, with stars ranging from Cesar [Romero] to [Sid] Caesar playing, and similar vigorous shooting schedules were reported in later seasons. After a near-decade hiatus, the show returned briefly as *The New Celebrity Bowling,* with Jed Allan back at the helm and 26 shows that had been taped over a five-day period.

CELEBRITY DOUBLE TALK—See *Double Talk.*

CELEBRITY GOLF
Sports; B&W
September 25, 1960–May 21, 1961
NBC Sun. 5–5:30 p.m. (9/25/60–5/21/61)

Regular Player: *Sam Snead*
Commentator: *Harry Von Zell*

For those who ever wondered how golfing great Sam Snead would fare using his clubs against, say, Jerry Lewis, *Celebrity Golf* provided the answer. Each week Snead challenged a star at the latter's home course in a nine-hole game, with the performer receiving his usual handicap. Among those brave or, depending on your position, stupid enough to take up this challenge were familiar golfer Bob Hope on the opener, followed by such unlikelies as Randolph Scott, Ray Bolger, Mickey Rooney, Perry Como, and Dale Robertson. The series, which was interrupted roughly once a month by an *Omnibus* episode, later had its 26 shows syndicated.

CELEBRITY FAMILY FEUD—See *Family Feud.*

CELEBRITY HOT POTATO—See *Hot Potato.*

•CELEBRITY SWEEPSTAKES
Game; Color
April 1, 1974–October 1, 1976
NBC Mon.–Fri. 12:30–12:55 p.m. (4/1/74–1/3/75)
NBC Mon.–Fri. 10–10:30 a.m. (1/6/75–6/11/76)
NBC Mon.–Fri. 10:30–11 a.m. (6/14/76–10/1/76)

Regulars: *Jim McKrell, Joey Bishop (9/74–12/75), Carol Wayne (8/74–10/76)*

Celebrity Sweepstakes was one of several game shows of the 1970s designed to capitalize on the success of the star-laden

Seen in this shot from a week in 1974 on Celebrity Sweepstakes *are, from left, host Jim McKrell and panelists John Astin, Luci Arnaz, Ted Knight, Patty Duke, Dean Jones, and Jane Withers.*

Hollywood Squares, with the approach being to see who was the smartest, and who was the dumbest, famous personality. A sextet of celebrities sat in cubicles resembling the starting gate of a horse race (ergo the "sweepstakes" in the title) as host Jim McKrell read them a question. The studio audience entered into a computer who they thought among the six stars would be able to answer the question right, then the machine tabulated the results and posted odds based on the audience response. The two contestants each picked one star they thought could answer, with the payoff for a correct response depending on the posted odds. For the day's final question, the computer posted odds for each celebrity based on the celebrity's number of correct answers that day, and players bid amounts earned so far using those odds. The results of this contest could sometime be humbling to a celebrity ego, like the time the odds that Jimmie Walker would be able to answer a question were 99-to-1!

Comedian Joey Bishop and Carol Wayne were listed as regulars for the show, although Bishop did not start showing up on a fairly consistent every-other-week basis until the fall of 1974. Wayne, the "Tea Time Lady" in the Johnny Carson Art Fern sketches on *The Tonight Show* in the 1970s, had an advantage in that her then-husband was *Celebrity Sweepstakes* co-producer Burt Sugarman. Jacqueline Susann and "Mama" Cass Elliot each made one of their last TV appearances on the show—in April and May 1974, respectively.

Others seen fairly often (at least 10 weeks on the show) were Adrienne Barbeau, James Darren, Clifton Davis, James Farentino, Buddy Hackett, George Hamilton, Gabriel Kaplan, Dick Martin, Anne Meara, Leslie Neilsen, and Dan Rowan. (Rowan and Martin appeared on separate weeks, not as a team.) A syndicated version of the show hosted by McKrell aired from 1974–77.

CELEBRITY WHEW—See *Whew*.

CHAIN LETTER
Game; Color
July 4, 1966–October 14, 1966
NBC Mon.–Fri. 11–11:30 a.m. (7/4/66–10/14/66)
Host: *Jan Murray*

The last of three daytime game shows hosted by Jan Murray after *Treasure Hunt* and *The Jan Murray Show, Chain Letter* was notable in that it was the only one not handled by his production company (Stefan Hatos produced it in partnership with Monty Hall). Murray revealed a category, and two pairs of teams, each with one celebrity, alternated in giving items pertaining to the topic, with the catch that the last letter of each answer had to be the first letter in the next answer. The first player unable to provide an appropriate answer within 10 seconds was eliminated, and two more rounds were played until one remained. Game show perennials Hans Conreid and Betty White were guests the first week.

•CHAIN REACTION
Game; Color
January 14, 1980–June 20, 1980
NBC Mon.–Fri. Noon–12:30 a.m. (1/14/80–6/20/80)
Host: *Bill Cullen*

Two trios, each with two celebrities and a contestant, attempted to link words on a board with eight blank horizontal lines in the main game. The words on the top and bottom lines were revealed, and the first player up could ask for a letter in a line either directly below the top or above the bottom. Using that first letter and the word adjacent to it as clues, the contestant had to guess the missing word. An incorrect answer switched control to a player on the other team to ask for another missing first letter in either slot. A correct answer gave a team points based on the number of letters in the word, and two lines were usually "double score" ones, where words were worth twice their number of letters. The first team to make at least 50 points won.

The winners played a bonus game where the celebrities alternated in saying words to form a question serving as a clue to a subject seen by the celebrities and audience on a monitor. The team's effort was disqualified if they used a phrase that was not a question, used part of the word, or had one celebrity say two or more words. Contestants had to identify 10 subjects in 90 seconds to win the top prize of $10,000 in the bonus round; any amount less than that awarded the contestant $100 per correct answer. The dollar amounts used to reach $10,000 changed twice during the series' brief run; only the third setup has been described. Players continued until defeated.

There were no regular celebrities among the two men and two women who appeared weekly, but Brian Patrick Clarke, Anita Gillette, Jay Johnson, Vicki Lawrence, Robert Mandan, Richard Paul, and Nipsey Russell were seen most frequently, each appearing in at least 4 out of 22 weeks of shows.

From September 29, 1986–December 27, 1991, the USA cable channel ran a revised version of this series hosted by Geoff Edwards and taped in Canada.

CHALLENGE GOLF
Sports; B&W and Color
January 5, 1963–April 5, 1964
ABC Sat. 2:30–3:30 p.m. and Sun. Noon–1 p.m.
 (1/5/63–4/5/64; off summer 1963)
Host: *Bill Flemming*
Participants/Commentators: *Arnold Palmer, Gary Player*

Jumping into the wave of specialty golf shows dominating the network weekends in the early 1960s (e.g. *All Star Golf* and *Wonderful World of Golf*), ABC gave golf lovers two installments of *Challenge Golf,* with the Sunday show repeating the previous day's game. The first matches were filmed in California in the summer and autumn of 1962, with Arnold Palmer and Gary Player taking on two other professionals in match-play best-ball (the lower score of the partners on each hole is used as the team score). Each competition began with the players deciding to play from one to four matches of nine holes each. Challengers could get $6,000 for winning one match, $15,000 for two wins, $25,000 for three wins, and $50,000 for four wins, while Palmer and Player always divided $5,000 for each match they won. A loss of any match eliminated challengers from further contesting the duo during the season, with consolation prizes being anywhere from $1,000 to $10,000. First up were up-and-coming professionals Phil Rodgers and 23-year-old Jack Nicklaus.

Palmer, the top PGA money earner in 1960 and 1962, had a special reason for wanting to win on every show. The series was partially owned by World Wide Productions, in which he was a shareholder, so every loss he posted cost his production company money and reduced his dividends.

Despite its surefire talent and ample coverage, the run for *Challenge Golf* was short. The reason might be explained by a *TV Guide* review which bemoaned the lack of decent shots of swings and even putts and added, "Camera work so far has been deplorable. So has the commentary by Palmer and Player, two fine gentlemen and wonderful golfers and miserable commentators."

•CHALLENGE OF THE SEXES
Sports; Color
January 10, 1976–April 15, 1979

CBS Sat. 1–1:45 p.m. (1/10/76–4/15/79; January–April each year only)

In the early 1970s Beverly Hills promoters Shelly Saltman and Tommy Cook approached the networks with the concept of a "Decathalon of the Sexes" series featuring 10 men versus 10 women in 10 events. It did not sell. Then came the pretentious, heavily promoted tennis matchup of Billie Jean King versus Bobby Riggs in a two-hour nighttime extravaganza on ABC on September 20, 1973. The entire project was more hoopla than gamesmanship, but the match (which King won) drew huge ratings, and soon rival network CBS decided it would take a second look at the Saltman-Cook proposal. *Challenge of the Sexes* was the result.

The show first appeared on January 10, 1975 as part of *CBS Sports Spectacular* with Vin Scully and Suzy Chaffee as hosts. CBS then installed it as a regular feature before *NBA Basketball* for four years. Additionally, on Tuesday nights from January 31–February 28, 1978 CBS ran *Celebrity Challenge of the Sexes* with Tom Brookshier as host and McLean Stevenson and Barbara Rhoades as the alleged "coaches" for their sexes.

CHALLENGE OF THE SUPER FRIENDS—See *Super Friends*.

CHAMPIONSHIP BOWLING
Sports; B&W and Color
1953–1970

Syndicated 60 minutes weekly beginning 1954

Announcer: *Fred Wolf, Jack Drees (at least 1966–67), Bud Palmer (1968–70), Bill Burnetta (1968–70)*

This long-running sports show first aired on WNBQ Chicago in a late-night slot on November 15, 1953, but most stations played it on weekend afternoons. It used match elimination play. The biggest change on the show occurred in 1968, when it went from film to videotape and employed a pair of announcers, with Bud Palmer hosting and Bill Burnetta adding commentary. The show also was known as *All Star Bowling*. Walter Schwimmer, the creative force behind this series, was responsible for a few other efforts, including *Championship Bridge* (q.v.).

CHAMPIONSHIP BRIDGE WITH CHARLES GOREN
Sports; B&W
October 18, 1959–April 9, 1961

ABC Sun. 3:30–4 p.m. (10/18/59–4/10/60)
ABC Sun. 3–3:30 p.m. (10/16/60–1/1/61)
ABC Sun. 4–4:30 p.m. (1/8/61–4/9/61)

Regulars: *Charles Goren, Alex Dreier*

Championship Bridge had two pairs of Life Masters bridge players compete to gain the most points during each show, with cash prizes and other bonuses awarded for little and grand slams. Generally a total of eight rounds of cards, or 32 hands, were dealt. Bridge expert Charles Goren, who by 1960 had earned more Master points and money than any other bridge player in the world, presorted all the hands himself to prevent having unbiddable hands. Goren also handled play analysis, while Alex Dreier served as commentator for the program, which was filmed in Chicago by the same production company that did *Championship Bowling*.

The show received terrible ratings yet returned for a second season because its sponsor, North American Van Lines, had research that men who moved often were usually bridge players. There was an effort to try to boost the ratings by adding celebrities, but the sight of the likes of Chico Marx losing at bridge did not attract bigger audiences, and ABC canceled it in 1961. The series continued to produce 26 original weekly shows for syndication through 1962.

CHAMPIONSHIP DEBATE
Game; B&W
February 3, 1962–May 19, 1962

NBC Sat. 12:30–1 p.m. (2/3/62–5/19/62)

Moderator: *Dr. James McBath*

Two college teams argued pro and con opinions on a selected question each week before a three-judge panel on this New York–based contest. It used the Oregon University method where teams could cross-examine each other after opening affirmative and negative statements. Dr. James McBath, associate professor of speech at the University of Southern California, called time between the statements and rebuttals.

The American Forensic Association, of which Dr. McBath was president, picked the 16 competing colleges, and surprisingly many of the smaller ones beat the bigger names, including Southwest Missouri over Notre Dame and

Kings College of Wilkes-Barres, Pennsylvania, over Fordham. Among the provocative statements debated were "Resolved, that the Peace Corps be abolished," and "Resolved, that labor unions should be governed by anti-trust laws."

The show's early demise may have been due to the finale, which pitted two national winners from North Texas State University against a duo from the U.K.'s Oxford University and which turned out to be a fiasco. North Texas State had to argue "Resolved, that the decline and fall of western civilization are at hand," but found themselves flustered by the Englishmen's flip comments and tried in vain to copy that style toward the end of the show. To make matters worse, the judges of the debate (two American, one British) voted along national lines to determine the champ. *Saturday Review* critic Robert Lewis Shayon, who had been an enthusiastic supporter of the series, strongly criticized the whole affair, and this and other bad press may have left a sour enough taste in NBC's mouth to keep the network from renewing the program.

CHAMPIONSHIP WRESTLING FROM HOLLYWOOD
Sports; B&W
February 6, 1954–May 1, 1954
CBS Sat. 4–5 p.m. (2/6/54–5/1/54)

Although wrestling was a top attraction in the late 1940s and early 1950s on television, it surprisingly received little daytime airing by the networks. *Championship Wrestling from Hollywood* was one of the rare exceptions. Five cameras filmed the action in Legion Stadium in Los Angeles, with such names as Baron Leone and Mr. Moto competing. Highlights of the matches were edited to fit the weekly half-hour slot.

In 1955, 39 shows were syndicated under this name. The series should not be confused with another show titled *Championship Wrestling*, which ran in syndication from 1963–67 and took place at Buffalo Auditorium in New York.

CHANCE FOR ROMANCE
Game; B&W
October 13, 1958–December 5, 1958
ABC Mon.–Fri. 2–2:30 p.m. (10/13/58–12/5/58)
Host: *John Cameron Swayze*

Chance for Romance was one of the programs included in ABC's 1958 "Operation Daybreak" to offer daily series to affiliates before 3 p.m., and by most accounts the New York–based show was the weakest. John Cameron Swayze, fresh from hosting NBC's nightly news, found himself awkwardly watching a trio of psychologists pick three potential dates for a man or woman contestant, with the latter then making the final choice. Despite weak competition (*The Jimmy Dean Show* on CBS and *Truth or Consequences* on NBC), ABC canceled the show after just eight weeks.

CHANCE TO SHOW, A
Variety; B&W
January 4, 1953–January 25, 1953
NBC Sun. 5:30–5:45 p.m. (1/4/53–1/25/53)

A Chance to Show was a showcase for developing comedians to audition and polish their material, with some songs between the routines. Apparently they needed to do a lot more rehearsal before hitting the air, for after only four programs no comic had a chance to show anything in this time slot as *Meet the Veep* took it over.

CHARGE ACCOUNT—See *Jan Murray Show, The.*

CHARLES COLLINGWOOD WITH THE NEWS—See *CBS News.*

•CHARLIE BROWN AND SNOOPY SHOW, THE
Cartoon; Color
September 17, 1983–December 21, 1985
CBS Sat. 10:30–11 a.m. (9/17/83–2/4/84)
CBS Sat. 8–8:30 a.m. (2/11/84–9/8/84)
CBS Sat. 1:30–2 p.m. (9/15/84–6/8/85)
CBS Sat. 12:30–1 p.m. (9/14/85–12/21/85)

Voices:

Charlie Brown (1983–84)	*Brian Kersten*
Charlie Brown (1984–85)	*Bret Johnson*
Snoopy	*Bill Melendez*
Lucy Van Pelt (1983–84)	*Angela Lee*
Lucy Van Pelt (1984–85)	*Heather Stoneman*
Linus Van Pelt	*Jeremy Schoenberg*
Peppermint Patty (1983–84)	*Victoria Hodges*
Peppermint Patty (1984–85)	*Gini Holtzman*
Schroeder (1983–84)	*Kevin Brando*
Schroeder (1984–85)	*Danny Colby*
Marcie (1983–84)	*Michael Dockery*
Marcie (1984–85)	*Keri Holtzman*
Rerun	*Jason Muller (Mendelson)*
Franklin	*Carl Steven*

Peanuts, the comic strip featuring a menagerie of children with pithy comments on everyday life, debuted in the early 1950s but experienced its greatest popularity during the 1960s and 1970s, when the characters appeared in a variety of animated specials on CBS, including the first, 1965's annually repeated *A Charlie Brown Christmas*. In 1983, after turning down years of offers, creator Charles Schultz and his TV special co-producers Bill Melendez and Lee Mendelson added their characters and gentle yet insightful humor to the mixed bag that was Saturday morning television. The featured players were Charlie Brown, life's habitual loser who nonetheless tried always to see the good in others, and his free-spirited dog Snoopy, a mischievous beagle who lived in a fantasy world with his diminutive pal, the yellow bird Woodstock (Melendez voiced Snoopy's yelps and laughs, as he had in the specials). Charlie's perpetual adversary was Lucy Van Pelt, who could always con him into trying to kick a football which she would snatch away at the last moment. She never conquered her distaste or fear of Snoopy, however, who always seemed to get the better of her.

Others seen were Linus, Lucy's kid brother and Charlie's best friend, a frequently sage dispenser of advice whose main quirks were carrying a blanket and sucking his thumb; Schroeder, who played classical music on a toy piano and for whom Lucy unsuccessfully carried a torch; Peppermint Patty, a down-to-earth tomboy who called Charlie "Chuck"; Marcie, Peppermint's bespectacled, rather quiet tagalong pal; Franklin, the black kid; and Rerun, Linus and Lucy's baby brother who made comments from the back bike seat he rode. Adults appeared infrequently in the cartoons, and when they did invariably they made a hornlike sound which went something like "Mmwah mmwah mmwah mmwah mmwah." The emphasis was on the children and their unique outlook on the human condition.

Typically, four playlets involving the characters ran each show. The series produced original episodes the first two years before running all repeats in its final season.

CHESTER THE PUP
Children's; B&W
October 7, 1950–September 30, 1951

ABC Sat. Noon–12:15 p.m. (10/7/50–1/13/51)
ABC Sun. 12:15–12:30 p.m. (1/21/51–9/30/51)
Narrator/Announcer: *Art Whitfield*
Cartoon Creator: *George O'Halloran*
Cartoonist: *Sid Stone*

Chester the Pup was a standard-issue early 1950s cartoon show, which meant that the drawings were done on the spot by the prompting of a narrator and the story line. The star characters were Chester, a mutt, and his master Drizzlepuss. The Chicago-based show's sponsor was Mason Candies.

CHET HUNTLEY REPORTING—See *Outlook.*

CHICAGO FOOTBALL—See *NFL Football.*

CHICAGO SYMPHONY
Music; B&W
October 11, 1953–December 27, 1953

DuMont Sun. 5–6 p.m. (10/11/53–12/27/53)
Orchestra Conductor: *Dr. Fritz Reiner*
Commentator: *Fran Coughlin*

The Chicago Symphony began appearing regularly locally on WGN in 1951 with Ken Nordine announcing the selections being played. ABC carried the show Tuesday nights from September 25, 1951–March 18, 1952. When it went to DuMont in 1953, Nordine continued doing local broadcasts Wednesday nights while Fran Coughlin assumed his role on the network's Sunday kinescopes of earlier shows. By January 6, 1954, the show was aired only on Wednesday

nights, with George Kuyper as commentator. It ended around the time DuMont began to crumble, on April 6, 1955.

•CHILD'S PLAY
Game; Color
September 20, 1982–September 16, 1983
CBS Mon.–Fri. 10:30–11 a.m. (9/20/82–9/16/83)
Host: *Bill Cullen*

A game determined to prove Art Linkletter's maxim that kids really do say the darndest things, *Child's Play* required two contestants to identify words or phrases from descriptions given to them on videotape by various 6-to 9-year-olds. An incorrect guess by one contestant gave the other a chance to hear another child's definition and take a shot at it, with four guesses the most allowed for each topic. There were two rounds of this game, and each correct guess netted a point. The third round was "Fast Play," in which a player had to be the first to buzz in during a kid's definition to win two points. The player with the most points after three rounds played a bonus game for a top prize of $5,000, which initially involved having to guess seven topics in 45 seconds from definitions given by children. By early 1983, however, the setup altered so that the contestant had 45 seconds to give clues to seven words to five children seen on stage. If the kids succeeded, there were the invariable group hugs, smiles, and kisses all around. Can you say, "Too cute for words?"

CHILDREN'S CORNER, THE
Children's; B&W
August 20, 1955–April 28, 1956
NBC Sat. 10:30–11 a.m. (8/20/55–9/10/55)
NBC Sat. 10–10:30 a.m. (12/24/55–4/28/56)
Regulars: *Fred Rogers, Josie Carey*

Fred Rogers, better known to TV fans as the soft-spoken, sweater-wearing "Mister Rogers" of public television fame, created and wrote this series, his first and only network TV show. He started it on WQED Pittsburgh in 1953 following a stint as a floor manager for NBC. Josie Carey joined him as co-host and singer, and it ran for seven years locally (1954–1961) in addition to the network run. Asked by *TV Guide* why he did the program, he said, "I guess I went into it because I didn't like [children's programs]. I wanted to see what I could do." What he could do was a gentle series featuring puppets—like timid Daniel Striped Tiger, stuffily regal King Friday XIII, and vain Lady Elaine Fairchilde—interacting with him and Josie in low-key yet entertaining and educational playlets. Nonetheless, it was easily swamped in the ratings by *Mighty Mouse Playhouse* on CBS and stayed on NBC less than a year.

Rogers went to Canada in 1963 following the show's run to do another children's series. In 1965 he returned to WQED to do *Mister Rogers' Neighborhood*. It went national on public television in 1967, and ever since that time he has been doing a few shows a year in addition to many pretaped ones while touring the country, always to promote children's education.

CHILDREN'S DOCTOR, THE
Informational; Color
April 3, 1967–June 27, 1969

ABC Mon.–Fri. 10:55–11 a.m. (4/3/67–12/29/67)
ABC Mon.–Fri. 2:55–3 p.m. (1/1/68–7/12/68)
ABC Mon.–Fri. 1:30–2 p.m. (7/15/68–12/27/68)
ABC Mon.–Fri. 12:55–1 p.m. (12/30/68–6/27/69)

Host: *Lendon Smith, M.D.*

Dr. Lendon Smith, a 16-year veteran practitioner from
Portland, Oregon, offered mothers advice on care for their
toddlers on this short program, typically taped in 10-show
sittings in two hours. *Time* magazine endorsed the physician's
video-side manner by noting, "Dr. Smith's easygoing
competence makes it hard to decide whether he is the Julia
Child of medicine or the Dr. Spock of television."
  The series followed *Dateline: Hollywood* in 1967, *The Baby
Game* and *It's Happening* in 1968, and *Funny You Should Ask*
in 1968–69. It had a strange odyssey onto the ABC lineup,
as it began as a daily show on NBC affiliate KGW in Portland
in 1966 before it got the attention of CBS Films, which in
turn sold the series to ABC.

CHILDREN'S SKETCH BOOK
Children's; B&W
March 12, 1949–December 31, 1949

NBC Sat. 5:30–6 p.m. (3/12/49–12/31/49)

Regulars: *Edith Skinner, Lisl Weil, Merrill E. Joels*

Juvenile viewers got a story each week told by Edith Skinner
while artist Lisl Weil (pronounced "LEE-zul while") drew
pictures and Merrill E. Joels made sounds to accompany the
tale. On January 7, 1950 the show moved up to a 7 p.m.
start, where it aired for five weeks before disappearing.

CHIP & PEPPER'S CARTOON MADNESS
Children's; Color
September 14, 1991–July 25, 1992

NBC Sat. 8–8:30 a.m. (9/14/91–10/12/91)
NBC Sat. 10:30–11 a.m. (10/19/91–7/25/92)

Hosts: *Chip Foster, Pepper Foster*

Chip and Pepper Foster, twins from Canada, hosted this
mélange of comedy sketches, interviews, and repeats of classic
cartoon shorts like Popeye. It was one of the last cartoon-based
entries seen on NBC Saturday mornings.

CHIPMUNKS GO TO THE MOVIES, THE—See *Alvin and the Chipmunks.*

CHOOSE UP SIDES
Game; B&W
January 7, 1956–March 31, 1956

NBC Sat. Noon–12:30 p.m. (1/7/56–2/25/56)
NBC Sat. 12:30–1 p.m. (3/3/56–3/31/56)

Host: *Gene Rayburn*

A rare Saturday morning game show from Mark Goodson–
Bill Todman Productions, *Choose Up Sides* had two teams
of four kids in New York do time-limited stunts. The teams
were the "Bronco Busters," headed by Tommy Tompkins,
versus the "Space Pilots," led by Roger Peterson, and they
competed in such events as sack races in an attempt to be
the first to amass 200 points. The losing team did get a
chance to earn 100 points for an easily accomplished task.
Also part of the mix was a home viewer contest where the
contestants selected postcards mailed by viewers and won
prizes for the latter if the players completed their stunt. The
show ended after 13 weeks due to lack of a sponsor. The
show started locally on November 2, 1953 on WCBS New
York with Dean Miller as host.

CHRISTOPHERS, THE
Religious; B&W and Color
1949–1987

Syndicated 15 and 30 minutes beginning 1951

Hosts: *Father James Keller (1951–1969), Father Richard
Armstrong (1970–1987)*

In 1945 the Rev. James Keller started the Christophers
religious movement for the purpose of fostering a sense of
moral and spiritual responsibility. Its TV show in the 1950s
and 1960s had top names donate their time to promote the
organization's works and beliefs. Such stars as James Cagney,
Ann Blyth, Jeanne Crain, Bing Crosby, and even Harpo
Marx acted in playlets on the show, while the likes of Celeste
Holm, Rosalind Russell, and Danny Thomas read Biblical
verses and history lessons. The group's first film was shot in
Jack Benny's living room by famed director Leo McCarey in
1949 for clubs, schools, and church groups. Then in 1951,
fifty-two 15-minute films went into syndication, and the
show remained fairly consistent in its format for the next
two decades, with the exception of its expansion to 30
minutes in 1954.
  In 1969 the Rev. Keller stepped down as host due to the
effects of Parkinson's disease (he died in 1977). Father Richard
Armstrong replaced him in the fall of 1970, when the show
expanded to 30 minutes and became an interview show under
the title *The Christopher Closeup.*

CHUCK WAGON, THE
Children's; B&W
February 22, 1949–March 29, 1951

CBS Mon.–Fri. Various times between 5–7 p.m., usually
  5:30–6:30 p.m. (2/22/49–3/29/51)

Host: *"Sheriff" Bob Dixon*

This series of western films was one of CBS's first daytime
series, not to mention a rather cheap and obscure competitor
to *Howdy Doody* on NBC. Beginning on May 29, 1949,
it aired a sixth day of shows Sundays from 6–7 p.m. for a
time. Bob Dixon introduced the movies, and occasionally
interviewed guests, such as a Native American called Little

Grey Wolf who came to give the history of Little Big Horn, and even Edward R. Murrow (on November 9, 1949). By August 1950 Dixon had added a quiz feature for children. By then, the show was doing well enough for Dixon to market his own line of western apparel.

However, one commercial tie-in to this short-lived show backfired badly. *Variety* reported in February 1951 that Avon Periodicals filed a lawsuit against CBS because Avon expected the series to be carried on the full network in order to promote its comic book based on the program. Avon blamed the incomplete national airing for the company's being stuck with 250,000 unsold comic books. The show was canceled a month later, before a settlement had been reached and, for that matter, before a second issue of the comic book. Dixon continued in a local daily show on CBS in 1951.

CITY HOSPITAL
Drama; B&W
November 3, 1951–April 19, 1952
ABC Sat. 12:30–1 p.m. (11/3/51–4/19/52)

Cast:

Dr. Barton Crane	Melville Ruick
Dr. Kate Morrow	Anne Burr

City Hospital made one of the quickest radio-to-television transfers ever. It debuted on CBS radio Saturdays at 1:30 p.m. on October 6, 1951, with Santos Ortega and Anne Burr, then came onto ABC television a month later, airing an hour earlier than the radio version, with Melville Ruick assuming Ortega's role. On its TV debut the doctors, one a female, treated a child suffering from psychosomatic paralysis due to the latter's bickering parents. The show alternated weekly with *Personal Appearance Theater.* Before its daytime run ended, the show went to CBS nighttime from March 25, 1952–October 1, 1953.

CITYKIDS
Drama; Color
September 18, 1993–September 3, 1994
ABC Sat. 11:30 a.m.–Noon (9/18/93–1/1/94)
ABC Sat. Noon–12:30 p.m. (1/8/94–9/3/94)

Cast:

Angelica	Cyndi Cartagena
Chris	Hassan Elgendi
David	Brad Stoll
John	Dule Hill
Nikki	Diana Smith
Tito	Renoly Santiago

The CityKids Foundation was a real-life nonprofit group based in New York City which provided artistic programs for low-income urban youth. On this show six children involved in CityKids participated in live-action playlets and music videos shot mostly in the Big Apple. The show also had some guest appearances by the Muppets, not surprising in that it came from Henson Productions. In fact, some Muppets made

their first appearance on *CityKids,* such as Trish and Toya, the gossiping Dirt Sisters. The show first aired as a special on Saturday, January 30, 1992 from 12:30–1 p.m.

Though *CityKids* ran for only one unsuccessful year, during which few affiliates carried it, ABC was not quite through with the organization. On April 20, 1996 from 8–9 p.m. it aired a special called *CityKids All Star Celebration,* hosted by Demi Moore with performances by comedians like Sinbad and music acts like Salt-N-Pepa. Moore, at the time national spokeswoman for CityKids, told *TV Guide* she hoped to create a movie about the group because "with all the negative coverage we get on young people, it would be wonderful to show kids who are coming together to create unity, love, and healing."

CLASSIC CONCENTRATION—See *Concentration.*

CLASSIFIED COLUMN
Informational; B&W
July 25, 1949–January 13, 1950
CBS Mon.–Fri. 5:15–5:30 p.m. or 2:45–3 p.m. (7/25/49–12/9/49)
CBS Mon.–Fri. 3:45–4 p.m. (12/12/49–1/13/50)

Host: *Paul de Fur*

Another in early TV's endless parade of homemaker advice shows, *Classified Column* featured demonstrations of new products designed to help in doing chores, such as a hanger for belts, a garlic controller, and even a homemade beer can funnel. Viewers were to submit their own ideas to use on the show, with those used on air earning the writer a Gruen watch.

CLEAR HORIZON, THE
Soap Opera; B&W
July 11, 1960–June 11, 1962
CBS Mon.–Fri. 11:30 a.m.–Noon (7/11/60–3/11/61)
CBS Mon.–Fri. 11:30–11:55 a.m. (2/26/62–6/11/62)

Cast:

Roy Selby	Edward Kemmer
Anne Selby	Phyllis Avery
Ricky Selby (1960–61)	Jimmy Carter
Ricky Selby (1962)	Charles Herbert
Greg Selby (1960 at least)	Craig Curtis
Sgt. Harry Moseby	Rusty Lane
Frances Moseby	Eve McVeagh
Lt. Sig Levy	Michael Fox
Lois Adams (1960 at least)	Denise Alexander
Col. Theodore Adams (1960 at least)	William Roerick
Frank (1960 at least)	William Allyn
Mitchell Corbin (1962)	Richard Coogan
Major Allen (1962 at least)	Tom Brown
Airman Davis (1962 at least)	James Edwards

On this show's debut, Army Signal Corps officer Roy Selby had just been transferred from an Alaskan post to the Pentagon in Washington, D.C. when he received yet another offer that

The Clear Horizon *starred Ed Kemmer as Roy Selby and Phyllis Avery as his wife Anne.*

would require a move to Cape Canaveral, Florida. His wife Anne was none too eager to leave Arlington, Virginia, but eventually complied, wearily noting that "I don't think there's one of us Army wives who hasn't been bitter about where we're stationed." They and their rambunctious 10-year-old son Ricky, who used such exclamations as "Hot pajamas!" (and was not played by the later U.S. President of the same name), found themselves embroiled in the lives of other military types with problems on the home front. For example, Colonel Adams, who depended on his unwed daughter Lois, had to deal with her romantic complications as she went from planning to marry Frank to having a fling with Greg, another Selby family member. Then there was Anne meeting Julian at the officers' club, causing tongues to wag as she eventually became romantically involved with him. Julian tracked her down as she went to her parents' house in New Haven, Connecticut, when the series ended its first run in 1961.

The show returned for an abbreviated and rare (for soap operas) second try a year later, when Roy disappeared while the Russians planned a "spy swap." Roy and pal Lt. Levy were caught during the transfer. They escaped, but the nervous activity at the base continued with Airman Davis being court-martialed for illegal activities actually performed by the innocent-seeming Sgt. Moseby and his wife, the main carryovers from the earlier run. Roy and Anne also got back together after a brief parting, but by then the series had been canceled.

•CLOSER LOOK, A
News/Interview; Color
January 28, 1991–March 19, 1993
NBC Mon.–Fri. 12:30–1 p.m. (1/28/91–6/12/92)
NBC Mon.–Fri. 11:30 a.m.–Noon (6/15/92–3/19/93)
Host: *Faith Daniels*

On *A Closer Look,* NBC News reporter and *Today* anchor Faith Daniels examined one current issue of interest each day, interviewing the people involved or people who might have an informed opinion on the topic. Most stories examined serious concerns such as drug addiction, though some trivia did pop up on occasion (e.g., Is pop singer Madonna a bad influence on our culture?). Unfortunately, NBC lost its faith in viewers taking a chance on studying hard news, and by February 1992 had transformed the show into a standard-issue talk show with a studio audience and such topics as an update on 1970s nostalgia. By October 1992 the show had been retitled *Faith Daniels,* and Daniels grimaced her way through the new version, having left her *Today* job to concentrate full time on the hosting job. It was, however, hopeless and the show was canceled after two years.

CLOSE-UP
Talk; B&W
February 18, 1957–January 31, 1958
NBC Mon.–Fri. 1–1:30 p.m. (2/18/57–1/31/58)
Hosts: *Tex McCrary, Jinx Falkenberg*

Tex McCrary and his wife Jinx Falkenberg teamed together initially for a New York radio show in 1945 which went network over NBC two years later. Around the same time they became hosts of *Swift's Home Service Club* (q.v.) on NBC television, then did a few nighttime TV series for NBC and CBS from 1947–49. They then appeared mostly locally in New York during the 1950s until this series debuted. Its emphasis was on discussions with guests on current topics of interest like Hollywood's Production Code and how it handled sex and violence in films.

Originally just seven affiliates ran the series, but within five weeks 62 stations were carrying it. Nevertheless, ratings were never good, so NBC canned the show just before it had been on for a year. On February 3, 1958, the show became *Tex and Jinx Jury,* which aired from 1–2 p.m. daily on WRCA New York for a few months following the cancellation of the original show and its leadout *Club 60.*

CLUB 60
Musical Variety; Color
February 18, 1957–January 10, 1958
NBC Mon.–Fri. 1:30–2:30 p.m. (2/18/57–1/10/58)
Regulars: *Dennis James (3/13/57–8/16/57), Howard Miller (8/19/57–1/10/58), Mike Douglas, Nancy Wright (1957), Barbara Becker (8/19/57–1/10/58), the Mellolarks, Art Vanne Damme Quartet, Joe Gallichio's Orchestra*

This Chicago-based tunefest got off to a rocky start when its scheduled host, San Francisco personality Don Sherwood, did not show up and comedian Mort Sahl, of all people, was corralled to guest-host the first week. After four weeks it settled down with old pro Dennis James introducing singers Mike Douglas, Nancy Wright, and the Mellolarks, and with the Art Van Damme instrumental quartet, among others, providing music. On September 23, 1957, the show was retitled *The Howard Miller Show* following that Chicago disk jockey's assumption of the hosting role. At the same time, Barbara Becker replaced Nancy Wright. The changes did little to improve the ratings against *As the World Turns* on CBS, however. With the series' cancellation, NBC returned its 1–2 p.m. block back to affiliates and did not program there again until *Let's Make a Deal* in 1964. Miller's show continued as a local program in Chicago through at least the late 1950s.

•CLUE CLUB
Cartoon; Color
August 14, 1976–January 21, 1979

CBS Sat. 9:30–10 a.m. (8/14/76–9/4/76)
CBS Sat. 11:30 a.m.–Noon (9/11/76–10/30/76)
CBS Sat. 8:30–9 a.m. (11/6/76–9/3/77)
CBS Sun. 9:30–10 a.m. (9/10/78–1/21/79)

Voices:

D.D.	Bob Hastings
Dotty	Tara Talboy
Larry	David Joliffe
Pepper	Patricia Stich
Wimper	Jim McGeorge
Woofer	Paul Winchell

The Clue Club consisted of a quartet of adolescent criminal investigators joined by their mascot bloodhounds Woofer and Wimper. Dotty was the 13-year-old genius of the group, which, in classic 1970s style, kept in contact via CB radio. However, most of the humor came from the dogs, who found themselves occasionally scared of the weird villains they met. Any resemblance to *Scooby-Doo* (and there were many) was purely intentional, since this too was a Hanna-Barbera Production.

After cancellation, the series aired in edited, hard-to-follow repeats in 1977–78 on *The Skatebirds* as a segment titled "Woofer and Wimper, Dog Detectives." CBS then installed full shows for repeats briefly on Sundays in 1978.

COLLEGE BASKETBALL—See *NCAA Basketball*.

COLLEGE BOWL—See *G.E. College Bowl*.

COLLEGE FOOTBALL—See *NCAA Football*.

COLLEGE NEWS/PRESS CONFERENCE—See *Junior Press Conference*.

COLUMBIA FOOTBALL—See *NCAA Football*.

COLUMBIA UNIVERSITY SEMINAR
Instructional; B&W
February 1, 1953–May 24, 1953

ABC Sun. 1–1:30 p.m. (2/1/53–5/24/53)

Moderator: Donald N. Bigelow

The idea of auditing a lecture on American civilization every week may not sound appealing to you, but that is what ABC offered in this series. Columbia University Assistant Professor of History Donald N. Bigelow presided over the half hour, and some of his students participated in the discussion. This series, which was also known as *Seminar*, first aired on Saturdays at 6:30 p.m. from October 4, 1952–January 3, 1953.

•COMMANDO CODY—SKY MARSHALL OF THE UNIVERSE
Adventure; B&W
July 16, 1955–October 8, 1955

NBC Sat. 11–11:30 a.m. (7/16/55–10/8/55)

Cast:

Commando Cody	*Judd Holdren*
Joan Gilbert	*Aline Towne*
Ted Richards (7/16/55–7/30/55)	*William Schallert*
Dick Preston (8/7/55–10/8/55)	*Richard Crane*
The Ruler	*Gregory Gay*
Mr. Henderson	*Craig Kelly*

The last and to some least of the 1950s live-action sci-fi dramas for children, *Commando Cody* began filming for Republic Pictures in 1952 for theatrical release as a serial two years later. Done on the cheap, it recycled a rocket backpack and helmet costume and footage from 1940s Republic films. Hero Commando Cody, who flew with the backpack and helmet, led efforts to save Earth from the Ruler, a humanoid based on various planets who looked and acted like an imperious pharaoh with a Russian accent and hatched schemes involving co-conspirators on Earth. Commando's work was so secret that he wore a mask around his boss Mr. Henderson and scientists Ted Richards and Joan Gilbert. The latter two developed a rocket ship with atomic power to assist Cody on his missions. Cody, Ted, and Joan communicated via two-way radios disguised as badges.

After three episodes Dick Preston replaced Ted, who transferred to another unit. Later, NBC replaced *Commando Cody* with the more popular animal adventure *Fury* (q.v.) rather than showing all 39 filmed episodes.

COMMENT
News; B&W
April 24, 1954–August 31, 1958

NBC Sun. 4–4:30 p.m. (4/24/54–6/5/54)
NBC Sun. 3:30–4 p.m. (8/29/54–9/26/54)
NBC Sun. 4–4:30 p.m. (4/24/55–6/19/55)
NBC Sun. 2:30–3 p.m. (4/13/58–6/8/58)
NBC Sun. 5:30–6 p.m. (7/6/58–8/31/58)

On each *Comment* show NBC reporters based in Washington, D.C. gave background reports on an issue under examination, while other reporters not affiliated with the network gave their opinions on the topic at hand. One notable guest was author Aldous Huxley, who took part in a discussion of "The Brave New World of 1958" and what the year promised in politics, economics, and space exploration. NBC aired this in prime time from June–August 1954 between its biweekly afternoon runs in 1954 and in a 15-minute version concurrent with the daytime series from January–August 1958.

•COMPLETELY MENTAL MISADVENTURES OF ED GRIMLEY, THE
Cartoon; Color
September 10, 1988–September 2, 1989

NBC Sat. 11:30 a.m.–Noon (9/10/88–2/4/89)
NBC Sat. 12:30–1 p.m. (2/11/89–9/2/89)

Voices:

Ed Grimley	Martin Short
Mr. Leo Freebus/Roger Gustav	Jonathan Winters
Miss Malone	Catherine O'Hara
Mrs. Deidre Freebus	Andrea Martin
Sheldon	Frank Welker
Wendell Gustav	Danny Cooksey
Count Floyd (live-action character)	Joe Flaherty

When comic actor Martin Short transplanted his Ed Grimley creation from *Saturday Night Live* to Saturday morning cartoons, he was joined by many of his former cohorts from his previous TV variety show of the early 1980s, *Second City TV*. Grimley was one of *Saturday Night Live*'s most memorable oddballs—a Pat Sajak fan resembling Alfalfa of *The Little Rascals* with his huge cowlick along with a jutting jaw and squinty eyes. He talked in a quavering voice peppered with odd exclamations such as "I must say!" His object of affection was blonde dingbat Miss Malone, and his landlord was the short-tempered, toupee-wearing Mr. Freebus, whose wife Deidre was excessively proper. Living with Ed in his apartment were a sharklike pet goldfish named Moby and a pet rat named Sheldon.

The plot tangents of this show were bizarre enough, but somehow each episode included an interruption by the Amazing Gustav Brothers, dissimilar-looking identical twins who constantly failed in getting to the science lesson they were to teach about a particular scene in the show. Another intrusion in the action was the appearance of a live segment featuring Count Floyd, who tried to instill fear in a studio audience of cranky children with his monotonous "scary movies." Count Floyd was a creation actor Joe Flaherty first did on *Second City TV.*

Besides Short, Flaherty, O'Hara, and Martin, another SCTV alumnus working often on the show was Dave Thomas, who in one episode voiced an uproarious on-target spoof of Bob Hope, complete with the comedian cracking a stream of lame jokes for which his team of writers faked laughter. This and other scattershot attacks on popular culture, including

the time when Miss Malone kept repeating vacuously, "When a bell rings, an angel gets his wings" à la endless TV repeats of the 1946 movie classic *It's a Wonderful Life*, gave the series more appeal to hip adults than to children. Though it lasted only one year, the show became a staple of the Cartoon Network cable channel's late-night lineup in 1996.

CONAN AND THE YOUNG WARRIORS
Cartoon; Color
March 5, 1994–September 3, 1994

CBS Sat. 10–10:30 a.m. (3/5/94–3/26/94)
CBS Sat. 11:30 a.m.–Noon (4/2/94–9/3/94)

The hero of this short-lived cartoon was better known to comic-book fans as Conan the Barbarian, but by the time he hit Saturday mornings he was no longer a sword-wielding savage but acted as mentor to three children in their fight against evil. This series was a quasi-spin-off from a 1992 syndicated animated series titled *Conan the Adventurer.*

•CONCENTRATION
Game; B&W and Color
August 25, 1958–December 31, 1993

NBC Mon.–Fri. 11:30 a.m.–Noon (8/25/58–9/6/63)
NBC Mon.–Fri. 11–11:30 a.m. (9/9/63–9/24/65)
NBC Mon.–Fri. 10:30–11 a.m. (9/27/65–3/23/73)
NBC Mon.–Fri. 10:30–11 a.m. or 11:30 a.m.–Noon (5/4/87–11/1/91)
NBC Mon.–Fri. 11–11:30 a.m. (11/4/91–6/11/93)
NBC Mon.–Fri. Noon–12:30 p.m. (6/14/93–12/31/93)

Hosts: *Hugh Downs (8/25/58–1/3/69), Bob Clayton (1/6/69–3/28/69, 9/29/69–3/23/73), Ed McMahon (3/31/69–9/26/69), Alex Trebek (1987–93)*

NBC's longest-running game show was *Concentration,* based on the popular child's game of the same name but with a catch. As with the child's version, two players alternated in picking two tiles out of a board of 30 in an attempt to make a match. If that occurred, a player got to keep the prize named on the tile and see the portions of a rebus hidden behind the tiles. The player had to guess the rebus correctly to win the game and claim the prize. If not, he or she got to try again to pick another two to match and repeat the process. Failure to come up with a match turned control over to the other player. The first one to identify the rebus won the game and any prizes accumulated.

That bare-bones description may make the game sound humdrum, but it was anything but. To enhance game activity, there were also wild cards, which allowed a player to claim the prize of whatever other card he or she picked during that turn; and forfeit and take cards, which when matched caused a prize to shift from one player's control to another. There also were a few gag prizes, like bottles of mustard, but this eventually backfired. One player demanded that a "gag" prize brick wall actually be built on his property. After that incident, the show made sure that contestants knew that all such prizes were worth only $1 each. Contestants played up to 20 games or until they were defeated.

The show's original host was Hugh Downs, who found himself on perhaps the most grueling on-camera hosting job ever in the 1960s as he helmed the *Today* show for two hours daily followed by this half-hour daily offering. Downs also hosted a prime-time version of the game on NBC from April 17–September 18, 1961. Jack Barry hosted an earlier NBC nighttime version from October 30–November 20, 1958, when it was an emergency substitute for *Twenty-One*.

When Downs left early in 1969, Bob Clayton, who had been the show's announcer since January 1964, assumed hosting chores for a few weeks as he had done several times during Downs's absences. NBC then decided to use Ed McMahon as host to promote the sidekick of *The Tonight Show* (as NBC did for several other game shows in the 1960s) before giving the job back to Clayton. When NBC canceled the show four years later, Mark Goodson–Bill Todman Productions bought the rights to make it a syndicated series hosted by Jack Narz with the addition of a bonus round where a winner in the regular game could claim a car by deciphering two rebuses in 10 seconds. This version lasted until 1978.

Nearly a decade later, Mark Goodson Productions (Bill Todman had died) brought out *Classic Concentration.* It was essentially the same game, with a few changes. The board now had only 25 squares and was laid out on a video screen rather than on a wall. Those who won a regular game played a bonus round where they had to match seven pairs of car names hidden under 15 squares in 35 seconds, with a winner claiming the car whose brand was the last matched on the board. When it ended in 1993, it marked an impressive 21 years of *Concentration* on NBC.

Anyone interested in more details about the show and other fascinating facts about game shows up to the mid-1970s should get *The TV Game Shows* (1975, Pyramid), written by Norman Blumenthal, a co-producer of *Concentration* from 1958–73 who created all of the more than 7,000 rebuses used on the show during that period.

CONCERNING MISS MARLOWE
Soap Opera; B&W
July 5, 1954–July 1, 1955
NBC Mon.–Fri. 3:45–4 p.m. (7/5/54–7/1/55)

Cast:

Margaret "Maggie" Marlowe (1954–55)	*Louise Allbritton*
Margaret "Maggie" Marlowe (by April 1955)	*Helen Shields*
Jim Gavin	*Efrem Zimbalist, Jr.*
Barbara Gavin	*Sarah Burton*
Mrs. Gavin ("Belle Mere")	*Kathleen Comegys*
Harriet the Hat	*Jane Seymour*
Kit Christy	*Chris White*
Ralph (1954)	*David Buka*
Bojalian	*Ross Martin*
Mike Donovan	*Byron Sanders*

Maggie Marlowe was a stage actress who preferred being a housewife, as she freely confided to her friend Harriet the Hat. Unfortunately, as she returned from England to New York City with plans to retire and raise a family, she learned that her fiancé had died four days earlier, forcing her to go back to treading the boards. Things got worse when she learned that her long-lost daughter was none other than her professional rival Kit Christy, the eager ingenue in the play in which Maggie was starring. Maggie began an uneasy relationship with Kit and her boyfriend Ralph while romancing the married successful attorney Jim Gavin, whose mother, referred to commonly as Belle Mere, seemed more angry about the situation than his wife Barbara.

In 1955 Bojalian, a stage director, made some advances toward Kit which she accepted with an eye toward career advancement. Meanwhile, Maggie and Jim broke up temporarily while Maggie considered a film offer, then reunited after Barbara died from an overdose of sleeping pills in suspicious circumstances, leading the police to suspect Jim killed her. Eventually Barbara's boyfriend-on-the-side Mike Donovan admitted he had done the dirty deed, but before the story could progress much further, the show was canceled.

CONFIDENTIAL FOR WOMEN
Dramatic Anthology; Color
March 28, 1966–July 8, 1966
ABC Mon.–Fri. 2–2:30 p.m. (3/28/66–7/8/66)

Hostess: *Jane Wyatt*

Commentator: *Dr. Theodore Isaac Rubin*

Confidential for Women offered a week-long melodrama with observations on the playlet and its implications from best-selling psychiatrist-author Dr. Rubin, whose case files provided the germ for the stories. The opener dealt with a couple whose marriage was failing. Guest actors were a mix of newcomers and old pros, such as Barbara Barrie, Joe Campanella, Kim Hunter, Darren McGavin, Sheree North, and Arthur O'Connell. Despite the presence of genial Jane Wyatt as hostess (whose sitcom *Father Knows Best* aired in repeats daily on ABC 90 minutes before this show began), the serial had such little promise that ABC began a month of reruns starting June 13, 1966 until its cancellation after 13 weeks. ABC replaced it with an arguably more accurate picture of domestic life (see *The Newlywed Game*).

CONGRESSIONAL REPORT
Public Affairs; Color
April 13, 1969–June 1, 1969
NBC Sun. 5–5:30 p.m. (4/13/69–6/1/69)

Host: *Bill Monroe*

In this series a quartet of U.S. Congress members discussed current events. Following its daytime run, the show aired Sundays at 6 p.m. from June 15–August 31, 1969.

CONQUEST
Public Affairs; B&W
November 1, 1959–April 3, 1960
CBS Sun. 5–5:30 p.m. (11/1/59–4/3/60)
Host: *Charles Collingwood*

Conquest was the natural follow-up to six International Geophysical Year specials seen on CBS Sundays from 5–6 p.m. from December 1, 1957 through December 14, 1958. The shows, hosted by Eric Sevareid and produced by CBS News with the National Academy of Sciences and the American Association for the Advancement of Sciences, were designed to showcase recent scientific advances. Several of them were repeated in half-hour form on Sunday evenings in the summer of 1959 before a new series of regularly scheduled shows emerged in the fall. The debut discussed the emotional bond between mother animals and their offspring. Topics for later shows predominantly involved university scientists, including Harvard psychologist B. F. Skinner in a March 1960 story on human learning patterns.

CONTEST CARNIVAL—See *Grand Chance Roundup.*

CONTINENTAL CLASSROOM
Informational; Color
October 6, 1958–December 18, 1964
NBC Mon.–Fri. 6–7 or 6:30–7 a.m. (10/6/58–12/18/64)

Produced by NBC in cooperation with the American Association of Colleges for Teacher Education, *Continental Classroom* was really a learn-at-home program where viewers could earn college credits. Its first classes had Dr. Harvey E. White, on leave as vice chairman of the physics department at the University of California at Berkeley, teaching basic physics. But though NBC Director of Public Affairs Edward Stanley claimed the program was a means of teaching college students, twice a week classes on the show were designed to inform teachers how to instruct in such areas as statistics or chemistry, with one subject being taught per semester.

Approximately 300 universities had teachers participate in the series, which at one point aired on 172 stations, including some ABC, CBS, and public television affiliates. But the similar and competing *Sunrise Semester* on CBS fared much better, at least in terms of participation, so after a little more than six years *Continental Classroom*'s school was out. In its last season, which started in the fall of 1963, the show was retitled *Education Exchange.*

CONVERSATIONS WITH ELDER WISE MEN—See *Wisdom.*

COOL McCOOL
Cartoon; Color
September 10, 1966–August 30, 1969
NBC Sat. 11–11:30 a.m. (9/10/66–12/30/66)
NBC Sat. Noon–12:30 p.m. (1/7/67–9/2/67)

NBC Sat. 12:30–1 p.m. (9/9/67–8/31/68)
NBC Sat. Noon–12:30 p.m. (9/7/68–8/31/68)
NBC Sat. 9:30–10 a.m. (5/17/69–8/30/69)
Voices:

Cool McCool/Harry McCool	*Bob McFadden*
Number One	*Chuck McCann*
Friday	*Carol Corbett*

The trench-coated Cool McCool, who was sort of a cross between Robert Goulet and Peter Sellers as his Inspector Clouseau character, used a transistorized mustache among his weapons to fight such foes as Gretta Ghoul. He took orders from his boss Number One, who never appeared on screen, probably to hide his embarrassment at the way Cool bumbled his way through each crime investigation. Friday was Number One's secretary. Cool's dad Harry, a policeman, had his own slapstick segment on the show.

Bob Kane, creator of Batman, also created this series. Ironically, Jerry Seigel, co-creator of *Superman,* wrote a few scripts for this show while it ran unsuccessfully against the *Superman* cartoon. Its last two years consisted only of repeats.

COUNTDOWN TO KICKOFF—See *NFL Countdown to Kickoff.*

COUNTY FAIR
Game; B&W
September 22, 1958–September 25, 1959
NBC Mon.–Fri. 4:30–5 p.m. (9/22/58–9/25/59)
Host: *Bert Parks*
Musicians: *Bill Gale and his Fairgrounds Philharmonic*

Joining Bert Parks on County Fair *here in 1958 is Christie Logan, one of the weekly "Miss County Fairs" gracing the program as a temporary assistant.*

County Fair was a carnival-flavor game show where players punched their way out of a paper bag—literally. For the centerpiece stunt, celebrities such as Frank Gifford and Gene Barry used their fists to bust through a 205-pound life-size paper sack. The rest of the show consisted of *Truth or Consequences/Beat the Clock* gags, like the woman who had to throw pies at a man who sang while sticking his head through a hole. But few laughed on April 7, 1959 when a male contestant ran offstage in flames after a prop malfunctioned and had to be hospitalized with burns on his hands and face. Despite the incident, the series ran five more months, though it never really challenged *American Bandstand* on ABC or *The Edge of Night* on CBS. *County Fair* had started out in 1945 as a CBS radio show with Win Elliot and Jack Bailey as hosts.

COURT OF HUMAN RELATIONS, THE
Informational; B&W
June 22, 1959–August 14, 1959

NBC Mon.–Fri. 2:30–3 p.m. (6/22/59–8/14/59)

Host/Producer/Creator: *A. L. Alexander*

A. L. Alexander hosted an NBC radio show in 1936 titled *Goodwill Court* in which persons told their troubles on air in exchange for getting free legal advice. But when the New York Supreme Court ruled that attorneys and judges could not appear on the show, it died. Undaunted, Alexander started a similar local radio program on WOR New York City in 1937 titled *A. L. Alexander's Mediation Board,* where sociologists and educators dispensed their opinions. It ran on the Mutual radio network from 1943–1950.

Nine years later, Alexander revived the concept for television. *The Court of Human Relations* had him and four guest panelists (50 rotating supposed "experts" in their fields, including Pearl Buck and Fannie Hurst) offer advice to persons dealing with tragedies such as adulterous spouses, juvenile delinquents, and so on. The concept provoked some harsh reviews ("This daytimer is a study in commercial perversion," opined *Variety*), and NBC replaced it after eight weeks with reruns of the nighttime sitcom *Blondie.* Alexander died in 1967.

COVER TO COVER
Informational; Color
June 29, 1991–October 25, 1991

NBC Mon.–Fri. 10–10:30 a.m. (6/29/91–9/6/91)
NBC Mon.–Fri. 11:30 a.m.–Noon (9/9/91–10/25/91)

Hosts: *Gayle King, Robin Wagner*

Cover to Cover offered news and features gleaned from articles seen in such female-oriented publications as *Ladies Home Journal* and *Glamour,* with whose partnership the show was produced. The hosts, Gayle King of Hartford, Connecticut, and Robin Wagner of Cleveland, were both former local news anchors.

COWBOY PLAYHOUSE
Films; B&W
July 22, 1951–August 31, 1951

NBC Mon.–Fri. 5:15–5:30 p.m. (7/22/51–8/31/51)

This summer replacement for *The Gabby Hayes Show* was a series of various western shorts.

COWBOY THEATER
Films; B&W
September 15, 1956–March 9, 1957

NBC Sat. Noon–1 p.m. (9/15/56–11/24/56)
NBC Sat. 11:30 a.m.-12:30 p.m. (12/1/56–3/9/57)

Host: *Monty Hall*

This series was the first regular American TV hosting job for Canadian Monty Hall, and used 78 westerns from Columbia Pictures which NBC purchased specifically for this program. After its daytime run it appeared Sundays at 6:30 p.m. on NBC from June 9–September 15, 1957.

CREATIVE COOKERY
Informational; B&W
October 10, 1953–February 25, 1955

NBC Sat. 11 a.m.–Noon (10/10/53–4/3/54)
ABC Mon.–Fri. 11 a.m.–Noon (8/30/54–2/25/55)

Regulars: *François Pope, Frank Pope*

Creative Cookery was one of Chicago's longest-running daily series, running from June 4, 1951 through at least 1962. Chefs François and Frank Pope hosted the series from its local start, with François (Frank's dad) also serving as director of the Antoinette Pope School of Fancy Cookery in Chicago. After the show had run two years locally, NBC programmed it, oddly enough, as the network's only Saturday morning show in 1953–54, airing opposite *Space Patrol* on ABC and *Winky Dink and You* on CBS.

In the fall of 1954 the series came onto ABC's threadbare daytime lineup (the network's only other daily program was *Breakfast Club)* in an unusual manner. When ABC merged with United Paramount Theatres in 1953, WBKB Chicago, the station from which the series aired, had to become a CBS affiliate. However, the program stayed at the station, where it had been sold out for sponsors for two years, while airing on ABC. It remained on WBKB through the rest of its local run.

•CRO
Cartoon; Color
September 18, 1993–July 15, 1995

ABC Sat. 8–8:30 a.m. (9/18/93–4/30/94)
ABC Sat. Noon–12:30 p.m. (5/7/94–9/3/94)
ABC Sat. 8–8:30 a.m. (9/10/94–12/3/94)
ABC Sat. Noon–12:30 p.m. (12/10/94–7/15/95)

Voices:

Cro Magnon	*Max Casella*
Nandy	*Ruth Buzzi*

Also: *Charlie Adler, Jim Cummings, Tress MacNeille, Candy Milo, Laurie O'Brien, April Ortiz, Jane Singer, Jussie Smollet, Frank Welker*

After revolutionizing children's programming with public TV's long-running *Sesame Street* in 1969, the Children's Television Workshop finally made this, its first commercial TV series. Each show began with Phil, a woolly mammoth revived in the modern day, recounting an adventure applicable to a dilemma faced by his saviors, scientist Dr. C and her teenage trainee aide Mike. A flashback to the Ice Age showed Phil's 11-year-old pal Cro, a member of the slow-witted Neanderthal family consisting of Nandy, Gogg, and Ogg, and their animal pal Bob the monkey, working out a similar problem using scientific theories or mechanical principles with the help of woolly mammoths Pakka and her mom Ivana. By the closeout, Phil, Dr. C, and Mike had applied what they had learned, like the aerodynamics of flying, to their situation. Also seen were Earl and Mojo, woolly mammoths conniving against the Neanderthals; Selene, a saber-toothed tiger and occasional menace; and in 1994–95 Sooli, a female buddy of Cro's.

According to *Variety, Cro* took 18 months of planning before reaching the air. Its principle source of background was David Macaulay's 1988 book *The Way Things Work*. Test groups of grammar school children reviewed audio tapes of scripts and initial drawings of characters and then completed shows before being tried on their comprehension of the story lines and the scientific messages being presented. While the National Science Foundation was impressed enough that it gave money to the enterprise, other viewers were less enthusiastic, so *Cro* ended after two seasons.

CUBHOUSE
Children's; Color
October 3, 1994–

Fox Mon.–Fri. 8–8:30 a.m. (10/3/94–)

Cubhouse was the umbrella title for several shows designed to teach preschoolers good manners and behavior as well as some prekindergarten alphabet and number skills. The first year's schedule was made up of *Jim Henson's Animal Show with Stinky and Jake,* on Mondays and Fridays, which featured a skunk and included educational nature films; *Johnson and Friends,* seen Tuesdays and Thursdays, which featured a large pink elephant and his toy-box pals Squeaky, Alfred, McDuff, Diesel, and Victoria who taught lessons in living; and *Rimba's Island,* seen Wednesdays, which was inhabited by a multicultural gorilla plus a giraffe, elephant, lion, and rhino and was designed to teach the alphabet, numbers, and other educational basics.

On September 12, 1995, Fox added *The Magic Adventures of Mumfie* to the mix. Airing Tuesdays, this musical cartoon featured a small pink elephant named Mumfie, who was befriended by others, including the Scarecrow and Pinky the pig, who helped the pint-sized pachyderm overcome life's difficulties. But the splashiest entrant had to be *Budgie the Little Helicopter,* an animated British import about the smallest chopper in the fleet. *Budgie,* based on a line of children's books by Sarah Ferguson, the Duchess of York and wife of Prince Andrew of England, debuted November 2, 1995, slotted for Thursdays.

Fox announced in early 1996 they would drop the program due to increased competition for viewers in syndicated and cable programming.

CURIOSITY SHOP
Children's; Color
September 11, 1971–September 2, 1973

ABC Sat. 11 a.m.–Noon (9/11/71–9/2/72)
ABC Sun. 10–11 a.m. (9/10/72–9/2/73)

Cast:

Pam	*Pamelyn Ferdin*
Cindy	*Jerrelyn Fields*
Gerrard	*John Levin*
Ralph	*Kerry MacLane*
Gittel the Bumbling Witch	*Barbara Minkus*
Mr. Jones (voice only)	*Chuck Jones*

Other Voices for Animation: *Mel Blanc, June Foray, Bob Holt, Don Messick, Les Tremayne*

Puppets: *The Bob Baker Marionettes*

Curiosity Shop might have failed simply because it tried to cover too much in terms of both education and entertainment. Its "sneak preview," an ABC nighttime special on September 2, 1971, set the stage, presenting the regular cast of four children who would investigate an ambitious topic each week (on the special, the theme involved music and dance), along with such animals as Darwin the chimp and Eunice the seal, on a set containing elements like an "elevator to everywhere" and a talking computer. But wait, there was more.

The series also employed such human-sized puppets as Flippo the Hippo, Hudson the Talking Rock, and Oogle the large mute creature, and a wall of hand puppets including Eeek A Mouse, Nostalgia the Elephant, Hermione Giraffe, and Woodrow the Groundhog. And then there was Baron Balthazar, a costumed man who could talk to animals. Away from the set came old films and new cartoons. "Granny TV" featured clips of black-and-white comedy shorts, while the comic strips appearing in new animated versions were Hank Ketcham's "Dennis the Menace," Mel Lazarus's "Miss Peach," and John Hart's "B.C."

Additionally, Ray Bradbury contributed to some scripts, and Henry Mancini provided background music. ABC also bought seven shorts from the National Film Board of Canada to use as well. And if that wasn't enough, series creator and producer Chuck Jones, the cartoonist for several top *Bugs Bunny* shows, lent his voice to "Mr. Jones Answering Service" (Mr. Jones was also the proprietor of a shop).

All this top talent was supposed to appeal to and enlighten children. But the components were so diverse and extensive that they created a cluttered atmosphere that stunted rather than enhanced the series' entertainment and educational values, and kids in 1971–72 flocked instead to *Sabrina, the Teenage Witch* and *Josie and the Pussycats* (which at least were less confusing) on CBS. The last season consisted entirely of reruns.

•CYBER COPS

Cartoon; Color
March 27, 1993–September 4, 1993

CBS Sat. 11–11:30 a.m. (3/27/93–9/4/93)

Voices:

Agent Baldwin P. ("Bulletproof") Vess	Ken Ryan
Brandon Babel (The Big Boss)/Colt "Mace" Howard	Len Carlson
David E. "Highway" Harlson/Stan "Barricade" Hide	Ray James
Buttons McBoom Boom/Rex "Bowzer" Pointer	Nick Nichols
Hugh "Bullseye" Forward	Peter Keleghan
Suzy "Mirage" Young	Elizabeth Hanna
Sgt. P. J. "Longarm" O'Malley	John Stocker
Officer Tina "Mainframe" Cassidy	Mary Long
Officer "Hardtop" Brooks	Darren Baker

COPS (Central Organization of Police Specialists) maintained law and order in Empire City's 647th Precinct in the year 2020 as a unit of computer-assisted crime fighters led by FBI agent "Bulletproof" Vess. The force, recruited from across America, used their talents indicated by their nicknames against the evil, corpulent Big Boss. Highway, for example, was an "ace cycle trooper" from the California Highway Patrol, and Bowser was a Chicago cop who handled the cyborg police dog Blitz. Longarm, Hardtop, and Mainframe the computer whiz were Empire City cops who joined the force. This show consisted of repeats of a 1988 daily syndicated cartoon titled *COPS*.

D

•DAFFY DUCK SHOW, THE

Cartoon; Color
November 4, 1978–September 11, 1982

NBC Sat. 10:30–11 a.m. (11/4/78–9/1/79)
NBC Sat. 8–8:30 a.m. (9/8/79–12/1/79)
NBC Sat. 10:30–11 a.m. (12/8/79–9/5/81)
NBC Sat. Noon–12:30 p.m. (9/12/81–9/11/82)

Voice Characterizations: *Mel Blanc*

Loud, lisping Daffy Duck, the perpetual second banana in the long-running *Bugs Bunny Show*, finally got a chance to star in his own show in 1978 when NBC's fall schedule went south in

the ratings. Besides Bugs, the other character seen most often with Daffy in these theatrical repeats of the 1950s and 1960s was Porky Pig as his simple-minded unintentional stooge. Cannily (or ingenuously, depending on one's viewpoint), NBC ran this show immediately following *The Bugs Bunny/Road Runner Show* on CBS for most of 1978–81. In the fall of 1981 the show was moved and retitled *The Daffy/Speedy Show* for including Speedy Gonzales cartoons.

•DARK SHADOWS

Soap Opera; B&W and Color
June 27, 1966–April 2, 1971

ABC Mon.–Fri. 4–4:30 p.m. (6/27/66–3/31/67)
ABC Mon.–Fri. 3:30–4 p.m. (4/2/67–7/12/68)
ABC Mon.–Fri. 4–4:30 p.m. (7/15/68–4/2/71)

Cast:

Elizabeth Collins Stoddard	Joan Bennett
Roger Collins	Louis Edmonds
Carolyn Stoddard Hawkes (1966–70)	Nancy Barrett
Maggie Evans (1966–70)/Josette DuPres (1967–70)	Kathryn Leigh Scott
David Collins (1966–70)	David Henesy
Mrs. Sarah Johnson (1966–70)	Clarice Blackburn
Joe Haskell (1966–69)	Joel Crothers
Victoria Winters (1966–68)	Alexandre Moltke
Sam Evans (1966–68)	David Ford
Burke Devlin (1966–67)	Mitchell Ryan
Burke Devlin (1967)	Anthony George
Sheriff George Patterson (1966–67)	Dana Elcar
Laura Collins (1966–67)	Diana Millay
Matthew Morgan (1966)/Professor Timothy Eliot Stokes (1968–71)	David Thayer
Bob Rooney (Andy; 1966–67, 1970)	Bob O'Connell
Barnabas Collins (1967–71)	Jonathan Frid
Dr. Julia Hoffman (1967–71)	Grayson Hall
Willie Loomis (1967–70)	John Karlen
Tony Peterson (1967–68)/Rev. Trask (1968)/Gregory Trask (1968–69)/Lamar Trask (1971)	Jerry Lacy
Jason McGuire (1967)/Paul Stoddard (1969–70)	Dennis Patrick
Dr. Peter Guthrie (1967)	John Lasell
Sarah Collins (1967)	Sharon Smyth
Quentin Collins (1968–71)	David Selby
Angelique (1968–70)/Catherine Harridge Collins (1971)	Lara Parker
Amy Jennings (1968–70)	Denise Nickerson
Nicholas Blair (1968–70)	Humbert Allen Astredo
Tom Jennings (1968)/Chris Jennings (1968–70)	Donald Briscoe
Eve (1968)/Megan Todd (1969–70)	Marie Wallace
Adam (1968)	Richard Rodan
Jeff Clark (1968)/Ned Stuart (1969)	Roger Davis
Dr. Eric Lang (1968)	Addison Powell

Philip Todd (1969–70)	*Chris Bernau*
Sabrina Stuart (1969–70)	*Lisa Richards*
Amanda Harris (Olivia Corey;	
1969–70)	*Donna McKechnie*
Daphne Herridge (1970–71)	*Kate Jackson*
Gerard Stiles (1970–71)	*James Storm*
Jeb Hawkes (1970)/Gabriel Collins	
(1970–71)	*Christopher Pennock*
Samantha Drew Collins (1970)	*Virginia Vestoff*
Hallie Stokes (1970)	*Kathy Cody*
Bruno (1970)	*Michael Stroka*
Morgan Collins (1971)	*Keith Prentice*

Even viewers who claim to despise soap operas find a soft spot in their hearts for *Dark Shadows,* TV's first, unequaled great "ghost" opera. In part, this soap had others beat because

On Dark Shadows *in 1967, Barnabas Collins (played by Jonathan Frid) found himself obsessed with Maggie Evans (Kathryn Leigh Scott), who reminded him of an earlier love. (Courtesy Dan Curtis Productions.)*

if a character did die, there was no need to concoct a lengthy explanation to justify his or her return—he or she just came back as a ghoul, vampire, or whatever creature the writers wanted. The series took full advantage of its supernatural milieu during its five-year run, having werewolves, a monstrous couple, and characters traveling back in time or "parallel time" at various periods. Along the way, it spawned a hit song, a successful line of books and comic books, and a cult following which was still holding conventions with members of the cast 30 years after the show began. How many soap operas can claim such distinctions?

Despite later claims to the contrary, ABC and Dan Curtis knew the show was going to be about ghosts and goblins from the start, and promoted it that way among the trade press. The eerie mood certainly was set in the opening episode, when Victoria Winters arrived as a governess for young David Collins at the coastal town of Collinsport, Maine. Waitress Maggie Evans frankly told Victoria she was a "jerk-J-E-R-K!" for working for the family, warning Victoria of the mysterious reputations of David's father Roger, his older sister Elizabeth, Elizabeth's daughter Carolyn, and Mrs. Johnson the housekeeper, all of whom lived in the gloomy manor of Collinwood. The more sedate Maggie lived with her widowed father Sam and had a boyfriend in Joe Haskell. Adding to the intrigue was beefy Burke Devlin, who became Victoria's fiancé as he vowed vengeance on Roger Collins for supposedly framing him and sending him to jail years earlier.

Then the macabre events began. Collinwood caretaker Matthew Morgan kidnapped Victoria when she learned he had killed a man. Morgan was planning to do the same to Victoria until he saw the ghost of Collins ancestor Josette DuPres and died. Then the ghost of Roger's dead wife Laura Collins tried to possess her son David and make him walk into flames to join her in the afterlife. As for the other dead Collins member, Elizabeth's late husband Paul Stoddard, it was believed that he had been killed accidentally by Elizabeth, and as a result she planned to wed her blackmailer Jason McGuire to shut him up. McGuire, however, turned up murdered. At about the same time, Jason's former lackey Willie Loomis, who was entranced by the portrait of a Collins ancestor, accidentally freed from his crypt the man who would put many of the future plots in motion.

On April 14, 1967, Barnabas Collins arrived at Collinwood to live in the adjacent Old House on the property, and in the process propelled *Dark Shadows* into a ratings success. Barnabas was a vampire who abducted Maggie because he reminded her of his wife in the 1700s, Josette DuPres. With the help of Willie, now his servant, Barnabas kidnapped Maggie and planned to wed her before she escaped to Windcliff Sanitarium. A doctor there, Julia Hoffman, became intrigued with her story and went to Collinwood to investigate its validity. She would spend the rest of her run in a tangled effort to undo the curse on Barnabas while coping with her growing affection for the man. At first she was not successful, and Barnabas stopped his reign of terror (for a few episodes anyway) only when he saw the ghost of his little sister Sarah Collins.

Then a seance held at Collinwood transported Victoria Winters back to 1795, where she learned of how Barnabas had lost Josette due to a hex from Angelique, an envious witch. Angelique then "died," and Victoria was tried as a witch by the cruel Rev. Trask. When she returned to the present, Victoria was haunted by her memories and eventually went insane. Maggie assumed the governess role, but the events of the past had implications for the present, as Collinsport in 1968 found itself swarming with creatures of the night.

Angelique arrived at Collinwood disguised as Roger's new wife Cassandra to hound Barnabas, who was now being treated for his vampirism by Dr. Hoffman and Dr. Eric Lang. The latter created an artificial man named Adam before dying. Adam got a mate named Eve courtesy of the influence of warlock Nicholas Blair, but eventually killed her. Blair, on the other hand, transformed Angelique into a vampire to menace Barnabas. To round out the year, Amy Jennings came to live at Collinwood and brought her werewolf brother Chris, whose twin brother Tom became a vampire thanks to Angelique. Amy and Chris used a disconnected telephone to summon Quentin Collins from 1897, who arrived in town in late 1968 after an unsuccessful attempt to possess his descendent David.

Quentin merited his own story the following year, when Barnabas went back to 1897, learning how Quentin became a werewolf, as well as other details about his family's past. This was the first of several sequences that took place during *Dark Shadows*'s final two years, in which the Barnabas either traveled back through time or the characters experienced "parallel time." The parallel-time sequences depicted what would have happened to characters had different choices been made. For example, Barnabas and Julia saw a parallel 1995, and realized how dreary Collinwood would be if they did not change the past, and in an 1840–41 sequence, Barnabas fought Angelique one last time and had his son Bramwell fall in love with Catherine Harridge, with the latter being able to break the curse of the supernatural in the Collins family. During these sequences, actors on *Dark Shadows* usually played the ancestors of their characters, their ghosts, or whatever the plot required of them. The cast list above records only the most frequently seen characters played by the actors. Thayer David, for example, also turned up as Ben Stokes, Sandor Rakosi, Count Petofi, Mordecai Grimes, and more.

Nothing in the bare plot synopsis indicates the notable effects this series had on popular culture during its run. In 1968 "Quentin's Theme," a light instrumental featuring a celeste piano recorded by the Charles Randolph Greane Sound, became a surprise hit, cracking *Billboard*'s Top 20 singles chart, the first for a song from a soap opera. Another first was two feature film spinoffs, *House of Dark Shadows* in 1970 and *Night of Dark Shadows* in 1971. The show also became the first daytime soap to be revived in nighttime when NBC tried a belated recreation with the same title Fridays from 9–10 p.m. from January 13–March 22, 1991.

And then there was the show's reputation for bloopers, the on-camera gaffes that seemed to blossom on this soap more than on others, even though *Dark Shadows* was videotaped

Those fangs and that wolf's-head cane could mean only one person in daytime television—Barnabas Collins (played by Jonathan Frid) of Dark Shadows. *(Courtesy Dan Curtis Productions.)*

while many others were live. This was in part due to ABC's attempt to cut costs by refusing to do retakes, and in part to the extensive special effects used on the show, which added to an already hectic pace. Whatever the reasons, there are so many shots of microphones entering the shot, props going awry, and scenery falling apart that there actually is a videotape on the market composed exclusively of the show's mistakes.

The mystique of *Dark Shadows* that attracted so many dedicated viewers remained powerful right up to the end, even though the show's younger watchers were showing a preference for *Gomer Pyle* reruns on CBS, which led to the soap's replacement by a revival of *Password*. One writer to *TV Guide,* Margaret Feehan of Thomaston, Maine, summed up her feelings with the following heartfelt if obsessive letter: "Our television set is turned off this 4 p.m. in mourning for the passing of the most fabulously innovative afternoon program ever to have graced TV—*Dark Shadows,* that exquisitely mounted and star-adorned daily feast for the eyes. We are bereft. . . . I am grateful to ABC for the beauty (some scenes were Rembrandts in motion) and the fantasy (a delightful way to unwind after battle with a prosaic world) and the inspired casting. *Password* indeed!"

Feehan was not alone in her passion for the show. Julie Hoover, manager of Audience Information at ABC, told *TV Guide* that phones rang constantly at the network for several days after the series was canned. "We thought we'd go mad!" she said. *TV Guide* also found that many readers were seriously interested in the unresolved story lines, so it allowed head writer Sam Hall to write an article on how he had planned to wrap them up. Among the developments, Hall wrote he would have had Elizabeth Collins remarry and David Collins take over the estate; Angelique kill Roger Collins, who then would become a ghost haunting the home; Carolyn Stoddard left a widow by Jeb Hawkes; Quentin treated for being a werewolf; Maggie Evans return from a divorce from Philip Todd to marry Joe Haskell, who would have recuperated in the Windcliff Sanitarium with no memories of what had driven him crazy; Chris Jennings become a werewolf, kill Sabrina Stuart, and then commit suicide; and Julia find Adam and cure Barnabas so that she and the latter could marry and leave Collinsport. In other words, a ghost story with a happily-ever-after ending.

After its cancellation, *Dark Shadows* aired sporadically in syndicated reruns during the 1970s and 1980s, the first network soap opera to air in that format. In 1989 the show had the first of its 1,245 episodes released on videotape on MPI home video (with the February 25, 1971 show being recreated via stills and an audio recording because the video portion was lost). It also was the first show to be purchased by cable's Sci-Fi Channel and started running on that network daily beginning September 25, 1992. Books on the series and its history proliferated as well, with perhaps the best being *Dark Shadows Almanac*, edited by Kathryn Leigh Scott and Jim Pierson and published in 1995 by Pomegrante Press, Ltd., of Los Angeles. And the fan club is still going strong. Just like its characters, *Dark Shadows* is enjoying life after death.

DARK WATER—See *Pirates of Dark Water*.

•DARKWING DUCK
Cartoon; Color
September 7, 1991–September 4, 1993

ABC Sat. 9–9:30 a.m. (9/7/91–9/5/92)
ABC Sat. 9:30–10 a.m. (9/12/92–1/30/93)
ABC Sat. 11:30 a.m.–Noon (2/6/93–9/4/93)

Voices:

Darkwing Duck (Drake Mallard)	Jim Cummings
Gosalyn Mallard	Christine Cavanaugh
Launchpad McQuack	Terry McGovern
Honker Muddlefoot	Katie Leigh

Darkwing Duck, a rather hapless superhero fowl, searched for foes in the town of St. Canard along with his pal Launchpad McQuack. "L.P.," as Darkwing called him, wore an aviator's outfit with goggles and flowing scarf, while Darkwing ("D.W." to Launchpad) settled for the standard eye mask and cape. In civilian life Darkwing was simply Drake Mallard, the father of the adopted Gosalyn, who arguably was the show's real star. A resourceful girl who knew her father's alter ego, she and her prodigy pal Honker, who had a stuffed nose, often used their combined intelligence to defeat the incredible

villains in this cartoon. Darkwing's catch phrase was "Let's get dangerous!"

This cartoon first aired on cable's Disney Channel on April 6, 1991. While on ABC, 65 other episodes aired in daily syndication. After two years, the property went back to the Disney Channel.

•DASTARDLY AND MUTTLEY IN THEIR FLYING MACHINES
Cartoon; Color
September 13, 1969–September 3, 1971

CBS Sat. 9:30–10 a.m. (9/13/69–9/5/70)
CBS Sat. 1–1:30 p.m. (9/12/70–9/3/71)

Voices:

Dick Dastardly/the General	Paul Winchell
Muttley/Klunk/Zilly	Don Messick

With its humorous old-fashioned chases and ragtime theme song which sounded suspiciously like "Hold That Tiger," *Dastardly and Muttley* was a rather enjoyable change from the superhero cartoons that had dominated most of Saturday mornings in the late 1960s. The title characters drove all sorts of modified biplanes in order to fulfill their orders from the General and stop American carrier pigeon Yankee Doodle from successfully crossing enemy lines (it was never explained what foreign country the pigeon was supposed to be invading, and since all participants spoke English, who could tell?). The efforts of Muttley and tall, conniving, mustachioed Dastardly were hampered by two worthless mechanics, the dull-witted Klunk and timid Zilly. Between the action sequences were brief segments involving the characters alone, including a fantasy sequence titled "The Magnificent Muttley" and centering on the snickering dog. Both Dastardly and Muttley had previously appeared as participants in *Wacky Races* in 1968–69.

DATE WITH JUDY, A
Sitcom; B&W
June 2, 1951–February 23, 1952

ABC Sat. 11:30 a.m.–Noon (6/2/51–2/23/52)

Cast:

Judy Foster	Pat Crowley
Melvin Foster	Gene O'Donnell
Dora Foster	Anna Lee
Randolph Foster	Judson Rees
Oogie Pringle	Jimmy Sommers

A Date with Judy ran on radio from 1941–49 on NBC and 1949–50 on ABC before coming to television in 1951, when it aired on a then-impressive 56 stations. The live "teencom" focused on the activities of Judy Foster, who bewildered boyfriend Oogie and parents Melvin and Dora with her antics, although Judy herself thought the real troublemaker in the family was her impish younger brother Randolph. The series ran on ABC nighttime with a new cast from July 10, 1952–September 30, 1953.

DATE WITH LIFE, A
Dramatic Anthology; B&W
October 10, 1955–June 29, 1956
NBC Mon.–Fri. 4–4:15 p.m. (10/10/55–6/29/56)
Cast:

Jim Bradley (1955)	*Logan Field*
Tom Bradley (1956)	*Mark Roberts*

A Date with Life was similar to the series it replaced, *Way of the World,* in that it had stories run at least a week and an actor serve as narrator in a character role. In this case, the character was initially newspaper editor Jim Bradley, later replaced by his supposed brother Tom. The major adjustment was that there was more of an attempt to link the melodramas by setting them in the fictional town of Bay City in Anywhere, U.S.A., and having characters overlap between changes in stories. Most of the actors were unknowns who appeared mainly in various soap operas, such as Georgann Johnson (*As the World Turns*) and Pat Sully (*A Time to Live*). The latter appeared near the end of the run (June 25, 1956) as the bride in a wedding. *A Date with Life* was beaten in the ratings by CBS's *The Brighter Day,* and NBC replaced it with *Queen for a Day.*

DATELINE: HOLLYWOOD
Informational; B&W
April 3, 1967–September 29, 1967
ABC Mon.–Fri. 10:30–10:55 a.m. (4/3/67–9/29/67)
Hostess: *Joanna Barnes, Rona Barrett (by September 1967)*

This celebrity news and interview show was chiefly notable as being the first network series hosted by Los Angeles gossip columnist Rona Barrett, who replaced Joanna Barnes when the latter left the series to act in a movie.

DATELINE: U.N.—See U.N. in Action, The.

•DATING GAME, THE
Game; B&W and Color
December 20, 1965–July 6, 1973
ABC Mon.–Fri. 11:30 a.m.–Noon (12/20/65–3/29/67)
ABC Mon.–Fri. 4–4:30 p.m. (4/2/67–7/12/68)
ABC Mon.–Fri. 2:30–3 p.m. (7/15/68–7/6/73)
Host: *Jim Lange*
Executive Producer: *Chuck Barris*

The series that for better or worse gave Chuck Barris his start as the king of bad taste game shows, *The Dating Game* featured one contestant interviewing three members of the opposite sex whom he or she could not see and selecting one of them based on a round of questioning. Host Jim Lange gave a brief background description of each of the three potential mates to the audience, then the contestant emerged and posed questions, often of a sexual or suggestive nature, to the bachelors or bachelorettes. After a break for a commercial, the contestant then revealed his or her pick and learned what vacation spot (usually in the United States)

would be the setting for the pair's date. Although the double entendre nature of the questioning suggested that some real hanky panky would occur on the dates, the producers made sure that all *Dating Game* dates had chaperones. The show ended with the two couples of the day joining with Lange to blow a kiss to the home audience, usually accompanied by a cutesy phrase like "Wet Kiss."

Sometimes the show used a panel of celebrities as potential dates (in one such contest Ronald Reagan's son Michael won out over Sal Mineo and UCLA football star Norman Dow), and occasionally celebrities, like Robert Vaughn or Sally Field, did the picking. One who auditioned to be a contestant but failed to make the grade was TV screenwriter and critic Harlan Ellison, who wrote about his amusing experience in the *Los Angeles Free Press.*

Despite the frothy nature of the contest, *The Dating Game* could boast of some successful matchmaking. By March 1968 the show had already resulted in five marriages (one of which ended in divorce). When it ended in 1973, the final tally was more than 4,000 dates, over 2,000 appearances by celebrities, and 12 marriages. Despite the show's infamous set, which was strewn with brightly colored daisy petals and had drab folding chairs for the three possible dates, *The Dating Game* inspired enough popularity at the time to cause ABC to run it at night from October 6, 1966–January 17, 1970.

After its daytime run ended, Lange hosted two syndicated versions of *The Dating Game,* one from 1973–74 and another from 1978–80. Reruns of shows with celebrities in them were syndicated in 1985; then a syndicated revival called *The All New Dating Game* ran from 1986–89 with Elaine Joyce as host the first season and Jeff MacGregor succeeding her from 1987 to 1989. The series reappeared in syndication in the fall of 1996 in conjunction with *The Newlywed Game* (q.v.).

DAVE AND CHARLEY
Variety; B&W
January 7, 1952–March 28, 1952
NBC Mon.–Fri. 11:30–11:45 a.m. (1/7/52–3/28/52)
Regulars/Writers/Producers: *Cliff Arquette, Dave Willock*

Comics Dave Willock and Cliff Arquette, the latter appearing as his character Charley Weaver, starred in sketches for this weak comedy series airing live from Hollywood at 8:30 a.m. Pacific Time.

DAVID BRINKLEY'S NEWSROOM
News; B&W
November 21, 1954–December 26, 1954
NBC Sun. 12:15–12:30 p.m. (11/21/54–12/26/54)
Host/Anchor: *David Brinkley*

Two years before he joined Chet Huntley on NBC's nighttime news, reporter David Brinkley helmed this live Washington, D.C.–based commentary on the latest happenings. The show contained man-on-the-street reactions to an issue of the week, a live or filmed interview, and an offbeat feature or two.

DAVID FROST SHOW, THE—See *Merv Griffin Show, The.*

•DAVID LETTERMAN SHOW, THE
Talk/Comedy; Color
June 23, 1980–October 24, 1980

NBC Mon.–Fri. 10–11:30 a.m. (6/23/80–8/1/80)
NBC Mon.–Fri. 10–11 a.m. (8/4/80–10/24/80)

Regulars: *David Letterman, Valri Bromfield, Mark Goldstein, Edie McClurg, Edwin Newman, Paul Raley, Bob Sarlatte, Wil Shriner*

Long before he became a hit on late-night television, David Letterman had as his first TV series this live mock talk show from New York City. It was unlike anything seen on daytime nationally in 1980, with Letterman doing a comic opening monologue, followed by interviews with guests both real and phony. Among the latter were Edie McClurg as "Mrs. Marv Mendenhall," a homemaker who recommended old fish and garlic to freshen up a stale room in her hints to viewers. Even supposedly straight interviews could be strange. On the debut Bill Murray answered questions from supposed "members of the audience" (you could never tell on a Letterman show) that included one query about his opinions on strip mining! To add to the quirky mix, some NBC executive forced the show to include a news break from Edwin Newman in the middle of each telecast. Thankfully, Newman warmed to the audience and started playing to them in his deliveries, making it one of the best spots on the show.

Other regulars doing comic bits were writer-comedians Valri Bromfield (as spacey teenager "Debbie Smith"), Paul Raley (as paranoid ex-FBI agent "P. J. Rails"), Wil Shriner, and Mark Goldstein, who did "on the road" sketches. Four rotating contributors—former senator William Proxmire, psychotherapist Karen Blaker, columnist Jimmy Breslin, and soap opera writer Jon-Michael Reed—were also slated to appear regularly, but their comments fared badly next to Dave's smart-alecky humor and they didn't last long.

The assessment by *Newsweek*—"The result is a laudable, if somewhat erratic, TV departure"—was perhaps the best summation of the show. Some sketches bombed badly, including one interminable five-minute sequence where Letterman forced a woman to handle his show alone. To make the show more cohesive, it went from 90 to 60 minutes daily within two months, with a few regulars leaving. However, by October the show was such a ratings loser that 12 affiliates dropped it, and an anxious NBC, eager to retain its outlets, canned the series. The show went on to win Emmies for Outstanding Host and Outstanding Writing for a Variety Series in 1981.

Letterman's reputation survived this debacle, and NBC and Johnny Carson had enough confidence in him in the aftermath to give him the nightly 12:30–1:30 a.m. slot with *Late Night with David Letterman* on February 2, 1982. Letterman admitted to the press at the time that he thought scheduling affected his first show, saying that the main

difference with his new show was that "we'll be in the right time period." He stayed there until 1993, leaving for CBS when NBC decided to favor Jay Leno to succeed Carson on *The Tonight Show.* Dave was an immediate hit for CBS when *The Late Show with David Letterman* debuted on August 30, 1993.

DAY IN COURT
Dramatic Anthology; B&W
October 13, 1958–June 24, 1965

ABC Mon.–Fri. 11–11:30 a.m. (10/13/58–12/19/58)
ABC Mon.–Fri. 2–2:30 p.m. (12/22/58–9/29/61)
ABC Mon.–Fri. 11–11:30 a.m. (10/10/60–5/12/61)
ABC Mon.–Fri. 1–1:25 p.m. (10/2/61–6/29/62)
ABC Mon.–Fri. 2–2:30 p.m. (7/2/62–11/23/62)
ABC Mon.–Fri. 2–2:25 p.m. (11/26/62–9/6/63)
ABC Mon.–Fri. 2:30–2:55 p.m. (9/9/63–6/24/65)

Regulars: *Edgar Allan Jones Jr. (as the judge), William Gwinn (1960–61), Georgianna Hardy (1960–61)*

Day in Court, ABC's first daily program to air before 3 p.m. since *The Breakfast Club* in 1954, can be considered that network's equivalent to CBS's *The Verdict Is Yours.* Like the latter series, *Day in Court* stressed realism in its trial dramas, using actual lawyers, clerks of court, and probation officers as well as actors. Some 65 to 80 actors per week acted as plaintiffs, defendants, and witnesses. Most were unknowns, but by 1963 several veteran movie character actors had guested, among them Mae Clarke, Neil Hamilton, and Benny Rubin. The Hollywood-based series had several cases per show, with the debut featuring indecent exposure, drunkenness, and property damage.

As for stories, six UCLA law students scoured trial transcripts and legal journals for ideas the writers could use. There was room for ad-libbing, however, and on one show an attorney's failure to question one witness as planned gave the opposing counsel three minutes of airtime to destroy the former's case and made the judge reverse the originally scripted ending!

From December 10, 1958–September 30, 1959, the show also aired on ABC Wednesdays at 9:30 p.m. under the title *Accused,* with the same cast. In 1960 ABC tried a second version at 11 a.m. titled *Morning Court* with a different cast; it lasted seven months. Although never a ratings winner, *Day in Court* did well enough to last an impressive seven seasons.

•DAYS OF OUR LIVES
Soap; Color
November 8, 1965–

NBC Mon.–Fri. 2–2:30 p.m. (11/8/65–4/18/75)
NBC Mon.–Fri. 1:30–2:30 p.m. (4/21/75–3/2/79)
NBC Mon.–Fri. 1–2 p.m. (3/5/79–)

Cast:
Tom Horton (1965–94) .... *Macdonald Carey*
Alice Horton .... *Frances Reid*
Mickey Horton .... *John Clarke*

Bill Horton (1965–66)
Bill Horton (1966–80, 1991,
    1992)
Bill Horton (1987–88, 1994)
Marie Horton (1965–68,
    1970–73, 1994)
Marie Horton (1977)
Marie Horton (1979–85)
Addie Horton (1965–66)
Addie Horton (1971–74)
Julie Olson (1965–66)
Julie Olson (1967)
Julie Olson (1967–68)
Julie Olson (1968–84, 1990–93,
    1994)
Steve Olson (1965)
Steve Olson (1972)
Steve Olson (1978–80)
Tony Merritt (1965–66)
Tony Merritt (1966)
Tony Merritt (1966–67)
Diane Hunter (1965–66)
Diane Hunter (1967–68)
Ben Olson (1965)
Laura Spencer Horton (1966)
Laura Spencer Horton (1966–75)
Laura Spencer Horton (1975–76)
Laura Spencer Horton (1976–80)
Laura Spencer Horton (1993–)
Susan Hunter (1966–73)
Susan Hunter (1973–76)
John Martin (1966)
John Martin (1966–71)
Helen Martin (1966–67, 1969)
Richard Hunter (1966–68)
Tommy Horton (1967–72,
    1975–79)
Kitty Horton (1967–69)
Sandy Horton (1967)
Sandy Horton (1967–71)
Sandy Horton (1982)
Sandy Horton (1983–84)
David Banning (1968–70)
David Banning (1970–73)
David Banning (1975)
David Banning (1975–81)
David Banning (1981–83)
Scott Banning (1968)
Scott Banning (1968–70)
Scott Banning (1970–71)
Scott Banning (1971–73)
Michael Horton (1968–69)
Michael Horton (1970–71)
Michael Horton (1971–73)
Michael Horton (1974–81)
Michael Horton (1981–82)

Paul Carr

Edward Mallory
Christopher Stone

Marie Cheatham
Kate Woodville
Lanna Sanders
Patricia Huston
Patricia Barry
Carla Doherty
Catherine Dunn
Catherine Ferrar

Susan Seaforth Hayes
Flip Mark
James Carroll Jordan
Stephen Schnetzer
Richard Colla
Don Briscoe
Ron Husmann
Jane Kean
Coleen Gray
Robert Knapp
Floy Dean
Susan Flannery
Susan Oliver
Rosemary Forsyth
Jaime Lyn Bauer
Denise Alexander
Bennye Gatteys
Ed Prentiss
Robert Brubaker
K.T. Stevens
Terry O'Sullivan

John Lupton
Regina Gleason
Astrid Warner
Heather North
Martha Smith
Pamela Roylance
Chad Barstad
Jeffrey Williams
Steve Doubet
Richard Guthrie
Gregg Marx
Robert Carraway
Mike Farrell
Robert Hogan
Ryan MacDonald
Kyle Puerner
Alan Decker
John Amour
Wesley Eure
Paul Coufos

Michael Horton (1985–90)
Michael Horton (1994–)
Janet Banning (1968–69)
Peter Larkin (1968–69)
Claire Larkin (1968–69)
Mel Bailey (1968–69)
Janene Whitney (1969)
Janene Whitney (1969)
Janene Whitney (1969–70)
Doug Williams (1970–84,
    1985–87, 1994)
Linda Phillips (1970–71,
    1975–80, 1982)
Linda Phillips (1984–85)
Eric Peters (1971)
Eric Peters (1972–76)
Kim Williams (1971–72,
    1976–77)
Jim Phillips (1971, 1974–75)
Robert LeClair (1972–73,
    1975–80, 1981–83, 1986)
Bob Anderson (1972–80)
Bob Anderson (1978)
Mary Anderson (1972)
Mary Anderson (1972–75)
Mary Anderson (1975)
Mary Anderson (1975)
Mary Anderson (1975–81)
Mary Anderson (1980)
Mary Anderson (1981–82)
Phyllis Anderson Curtis (1972–73)
Phyllis Anderson Curtis (1973–82)
Greg Peters (1972–79)
Phil Peters (1972–75)
Anne Peters (1972–75)
Annie Peters (1972–73)
Annie Peters (1974)
Annie Peters (1975–76)
Neil Curtis (1973)
Neil Curtis (1974–91)
Maggie Simmons Horton (1974–)
Hope Williams (1974)
Hope Williams (1974–75)
Hope Williams (1975–80)
Hope Williams (1981)
Hope Williams (1983–87,
    1990–91, 1994–)
Trish Clayton (1974–82)
Amanda Howard (1974–79)
Jeri Clayton (1974–79)
Jack Clayton (1974–77)
Don Craig (1975–85)
Valerie Grant (1975–77)
Valerie Grant (1977–78)
Valerie Grant (1981–82)
Danny Grant (1975–78)

Michael Weiss
Roark Critchlow
Joyce Easton
Gene Peterson
Catherine McLeod
Richard McMurray
Mary Wilcox
Pat Hornung
Joan Van Ark

Bill Hayes

Margaret Mason
Elaine Princi
John Lombardo
Stanley Kamel

Helen Funai
Victor Holchak

Robert Clary
Mark Tapscott
Dick Gittings
Brigid Bazlen
Karin Wolfe
Nancy Stephens
Carla Borelli
Barbara Stanger
Susan Keller
Melinda Fee
Nancy Wickwire
Corinne Conley
Peter Brown
Herb Nelson
Jeanne Bates
Andreana Marie Chutuk
Lisa Lynch
Elizabeth Hoy
Ben Archibek
Joseph Gallison
Suzanne Rogers
Kristina Osterhaut
Kimberly Joy Weber
Natasha Ryan
Tammy Taylor

Kristian Alfonso
Patty Weaver
Mary Frann
Kaye Stevens
Jack Denbo
Jed Allan
Tina Andrews
Rose Fonseca
Diane Sommerfield
Michael Dwight-Smith

Danny Grant (1976)
Danny Grant (1981–85)
Brooke Hamilton (1975–77)
Brooke Hamilton/Stephanie
  Woodruff (1978–80)
Rebecca North (1975–77)
Johnny Collins (1975–77)
Helen Grant (1975–77)
Paul Grant (1975–76)
Nathan Curtis (1975–76)
Adele Winston Hamilton
  (1975–76)
Dr. Marlena Evans (1976–87,
  1991–)
Melissa Anderson (1976)
Melissa Anderson (1978–80,
  1982)
Melissa Anderson (1982–88)
Melissa Anderson (1990–91)
Jennifer Rose Horton (1976–77)
Jennifer Rose Horton (1977–78)
Jennifer Rose Horton (1985–96)
Jennifer Rose Horton (1996–)
Rosie Carlson (1976–79)
Janice Barnes (1976–77)
Janice Barnes (1987)
Jim Stanhope (1976–77)
Kay Stanhope (1976)
Kay Stanhope (1976–77)
Chris Kositchek (1977–87)
Samantha Evans (1977–80,
  1982)
Margo Anderman Horton
  (1977–80)
Larry Atwood (1977–78)
Scotty Banning (1978–80)
Scotty Banning (1981–83)
Scotty Banning (1989–90)
Donna Temple (1978–80)
Amelia Craig (1978–79)
Amy Kositchek (1978–79)
Tony Johnson (1978–79)
Pete Curtis (1978–79)
Alex Marshall (1979–87)
Lee Dumonde (1979–82)
Dougie LeClair (1979–80)
Joanne Barnes (1979–80)
Jordan Barr (1979–80)
Liz Chandler (1980–86)
Tod Chandler (1980)
Tod Chandler (1980–81)
Tod Chandler (1985–86)
Renee Dumonde Banning
  (1980–84)
Jessica Blake Fallon (1980–82)
Joshua Fallon (1980–81)

Hazzan Shaheed
Roger Aaron Brown
Adrienne LaRussa

Eileen Barnett
Brooke Bundy
Paul Henry Itkin
Ketty Lester
Lawrence Cook
Tom Brown

Dee Carroll

Deidre Hall
Kim Durso

Debbie Lytton
Lisa Trusel
Camilla Scott
Maren Stephenson
Jennifer Petersen
Melissa Brennan Reeves
Stephanie Cameron
Fran Ryan
Martha Nix
Elizabeth Storm
William Traylor
Doris Singleton
Sandy Balson
Josh Taylor

Andrea Hall

Suzanne Zenor
Fred Beir
Erick Petersen
Dick Billingsley
David Hearst
Tracy Bregman
Loretta Fury
Robin Pohle
Chip Fields
Meegan King
Quinn Redeker
Brenda Benet
Mikey Martin
Corinne Michaels
George McDaniel
Gloria Loring
Brett Williams
Paul Keenan
David Wallace

Philece Sampler
Jean Bruce Scott
Stephen Brooks

Joshua Fallon (1981–82)
Maxwell Jarvis (1980–81)
Kellam Chandler (1980–81)
Cassie Burns (1980–81)
Leslie James (1980)
Leslie James (1980–81)
Brent Cavanaugh (1980–81)
Brent Cavanaugh (1981)
Kyle McCullough (1980–81)
Abe Carver (1981–)
Count Antony DiMera
  (1981–85, 1993–95)
Roman Brady (1981–84,
  1991–94)
John Black/"Roman Brady"
  (1986–)
Nick Corelli (1981, 1984,
  1986–90)
Evan Whyland (1981–82)
Jake Kositchek (1981)
Jake Kositchek (1981–82)
Stefano DiMera (1982–85,
  1988, 1993–)
Carrie Brady (1982–86)
Carrie Brady (1986–90, 1992–)
Carrie Brady (1991–92)
Kayla Brady (1982–83)
Kayla Brady (1986–92)
Anna Brady DiMera (1982–86)
Eugene Bradford (1982–86, 1989)
Gwen Davies (1982–85)
Daphne DiMera (1982–84)
Delia Abernathy (1982–84)
Nikki Wade (1982–83)
Mitzi Matuso (1982–83)
Woody King (1982–83)
Oliver Martin (1982–83)
Bo Brady (1983–87, 1990–91,
  1995–)
Bo Brady (1992–95)
Caroline Brady (1983, 1985–)
Caroline Brady (1984)
Caroline Brady (1984–85)
Shawn Brady (1983, 1985–)
Shawn Brady (1984–85)
Shawn Brady (1989–90)
Pete Jannings (1983–86)
Howie Hofstedder (1983–86)
Larry Welch (1983–85)
Speed Selejko (1983–85)
Speed Selejko (1985)
Noel Curtis (1983)
Noel Curtis (1984–86, 1988)
Diane Parker (1983–84)
Diane Parker (1984)
Diane Parker (1984)

Scott Palmer
Charles Bateman
Bill Joyce
Deborah Dalton
Dianne Harper
Pamela Bowen
Perry Bullington
Frank Ashmore
Richard Hill
James Reynolds

Thaao Penghlis

Wayne Northrop

Drake Hogestyn

George Jenesky
Lane Davies
Rene Lamart
Jack Coleman

Joseph Mascolo
Andrea Barber
Christine Clark
Tracy Middendorf
Catherine Mary Stewart
Mary Beth Evans
Leann Hunley
John de Lancie
Ann-Marie Martin
Madlyn Rhue
Shirley DeBurgh
Renee Jones
Livia Ginise
Lane Caudell
Shawn Stevens

Peter Reckell
Robert Kelker-Kelly
Peggy McCay
Jody Carter
Barbara Beckley
Frank Parker
Lew Brown
Frank MacLean
Michael Leon
Stanley Brock
Andrew Massett
Robert Romanus
Tom Everett
Christina Maisano
Samantha Barrows
Dana Kimmel
Cindy Fisher
DeAnna Robbins

Samantha "Sami" Brady (1984)
Samantha "Sami" Brady (1985)
Samantha "Sami" Brady
  (1985–86)
Samantha "Sami" Brady
  (1990–92)
Samantha "Sami" Brady (1992–)
Eric Brady (1984)
Eric Brady (1985–86)
Eric Brady (1986–92)
Kimberly Brady Donovan
  (1984–90, 1991–92, 1994)
Kimberly Brady Donovan
  (1990, 1991)
Kimberly Brady Donovan
  (1992–93)
Shane Donovan (1984–92)
Calliope Jones Bradford
  (1984–90, 1992)
Mabel (1984–85)
Mabel (1988–89)
Nurse Kate Honeycutt (1984–86)
Ivy Selejko Jannings (1984–86)
Carlo Forenza (1984–85)
Officer McBride (1984–85)
Dr. Kate Winograd (1984–85)
Megan Hathaway (1984–85)
Jasmine (1984–85)
Zack Parker (1984–85)
Victor Kiriakis (1985–)
Livinia Peach (1985–86)
Livinia Peach (1986–91)
Stephen "Patch" Johnson
  (1985–90)
Sarah Horton (1985–89)
Robin Jacobs (1985–87, 1989)
Emma Donovan Marshall
  (1985–87)
Savannah Wilder (1985–86)
Richard Cates (1985–86)
Maid Janet (1985–86)
Jake Sellers (1985–86)
Brother Francis (1985–86)
Ian Griffith (1985)
Ian Griffith (1985–86)
Simmons (1986–92)
Andrew Donovan (1986–88)
Andrew Donovan (1988–89)
Andrew Donovan (1989–90)
Andrew Donovan (1990–91)
Andrew Donovan (1991–92)
Adrienne Johnson Kiriakis
  (1986–91)
Frankie Brady (1986–88,
  1990–91)
Eli Jacobs (1986–87, 1989)

Ronit Arnoff
Lauren Ann Bundy

Jessica Davis

Christina Wagoner
Alison Sweeney
Rory Beauregard
Jesse Davis
Bradley Hallock

Patsy Pease

Anne Howard

Ariana Chase
Charles Shaughnessy

Arleen Sorkin
Kathryn Fuller
Lieux Dressler
Elinor Donahue
Holly Gagnier
Don Diamont
Terrance Goodman
Elaine Princi
Cheryl-Ann Wilson
Jolina Collins
Brian Autenrieth
John Aniston
Diane Webster
Pamela Kosh

Stephen Nichols
Lisa Brinegar
Derya Ruggles

Jane Windsor
Shannon Tweed
Rod Arrants
Dale Kristien
Gregory Wagrowski
Brian Matthews
Harrison Douglas
Darby Hinton
Gerry Gibson
Robert Elliott Canko
Brian Amber
Justin Page
Bradley Pierce
Brian Davila

Judi Evans

Billy Warlock
S. Marc Jordon

Tamara Price (1986–87)
Lars England (1986–87)
Glenn Gallagher (1986–87)
Silvie Gallagher (1986–87)
Olivia Reed (1986–87)
Gillian Forrester (1986–87)/
  Grace Forrester (1987)
Orpheus (1986–87)
Derek (1986–87)
Barbara Stewart (1986–87)
Paul Stewart (1986)
Paul Stewart (1986–87)
Sasha Roberts (1986)
Sasha Roberts (1987)
Sasha Roberts (1987)
Jack Devereaux (1987)
Jack Devereaux (1987)
Jack Devereaux (1987–93)
Jack Devereaux (1994–)
Jo Johnson (1987–93)
Jo Johnson (1993)
Jonah Carver (1987–89)
Jonah Carver (1993–)
Marcus Hunter (1987–92)
Harper Devereaux (1987–88,
  1990–92)
Justin Kiriakis (1987–91)
Eve Donovan (1987–91)
Anjelica Devereaux (1987–89)
Anjelica Devereaux (1989)
Anjelica Devereaux (1989–90)
Duke Johnson (1987, 1990–92)
Max Brady (1987–88, 1990–92)
Diana Colville (1987–89)
Serena Colville (1987–88)
Gabrielle Pascal (1987–88)
Ethan Reilly (1987–88)
Vern Scofield (1988–93)
Chief Tarrington (1988–92)
Nico (1988–91)
April Ramirez (1988–91)
Emilio Ramirez (1988–90)
Benjy DiMera (1988–90)
Julio Ramirez (1988–89)
Isabella Toscano Black (1989–92,
  1995)
Alexander Kiriakis (1989–91)
Cal Winters (1989–90)
Cal Winters (1991)
Grace Jeffries (1989–90)
Monty Dolan (1989–90)
Faith Taylor (1989–90)
Hank Tobin (1989)
Hank Tobin (1989)/Jimmy
  Porterfield (1984–85)
Hank Tobin (1989–90)

Marilyn McCoo
Ken Jezek
Rob Estes
Belinda Montgomery
Amy Yasbeck

Camilla More
George Deloy
Brian Cole
Elizabeth Burr
Gregory Mortensen
Robert S. Woods
Julie Jeter
Danielle Brisebois
Yvette Napier
Joseph Adams
James Acheson
Matthew Ashford
Mark Valley
Joy Garrett
Marilyn McIntyre
Bumper Robinson
Thyme Lewis
Richard Biggs

Joseph Campanella
Wally Kurth
Charlotte Ross
Jane Elliot
Shelly Taylor Morgan
Judith Chapman
James Luisi
Ryan Brennan
Genie Francis
Valerie Karasek
Karen Moncrieff
Joe Colligan
Wayne Heffley
Ron Barker
Lorenzo Caccialanza
Lisa Howard
Billy Hufsey
Darrell Utley
Michael Bays

Staci Greason
Jonathan Thornton
Wortham Krimmer
Joseph Bottoms
Sandra Canning
Jay Robinson
Mindy Clarke
John Lavachielli

Ron Kuhlman
Rick Porter

Marina Toscano Johnson (1989–90)	Hunter Tylo
Col. Jericho (1989–90)	Steve Eastin
Arthur Downey (1989–90)	John Calvin
Rebecca Downey (1989–90)	Tracy Kolis
J. J. Bagwood (1989–90)	Patti Johns
Simon Prescott (1989–90)	Dominick Allen
Shawn-Douglas Brady (1990–95)	Scott Groff
Shawn-Douglas Brady (1995–)	Collin O'Donnell
Carly Manning (1990–93)	Crystal Chappell
Lawrence Alamain (1990–93)	Michael Sabatino
Dan Ryan (1990–92)	David Ruprecht
Madeline Armstrong (1990–92)	Lynn Clark
Tanner Scofield (1990–92)	Micheal Easton
Brian Scofield (1990–92)	Robert Mailhouse
Cassie Scofield (1990–91)	Melissa Baum
Glynnis Turner (1990–91)	Felicia Bell
Emmy Borden (1990–91)	Susan Diol
Jill Bailey (1990–91)	Deborah Hobart
Johnny Corelli (1990–91)	Antony Alda
Craig Norris (1990–91)	Robb Curtis-Brown
Ivan Marais (1991–)	Ivan G'Vera
Fernando Torres (1991–92)	Dan Zukovic
Rafi Torres (1991–92)	David Ciminello
Desiree (1991–92)	Charlayne Woodard
Danielle Stevens (1991–92)	Deborah Moore
Chip Lakin (1991–92)	Jay Pickett
Molly Brinker (1991–92)	Shannon Sturges
Howard Alston Hawkins (1991–92)	
Howark Hawk Hawkins (1991–92)	Ray Stricklyn
Gaby (1991–92)	J. Eddie Peck
Rob Stemkowski (1991–92)	Karen Racicot
Ginger Dawson (1991–92)	Charley Lang
Vivian Alamain (1992–93)	Roberta Leighton
Vivian Alamain (1993–)	Marj Dusay
Austin Reed (1992–95)	Louise Sorel
Austin Reed (1995–)	Patrick Muldoon
Nicholas Alamain (1992–93)	Austin Peck
Rebecca Morrison (1992–93)	Erik Von Detten
Taylor McCall (1992–93)	Dani Minnick
Gus (1992–93)	J. Cynthia Brooks
Cash (1992–93)	Leonard Kelly Young
Kristen Blake (1993–)	John Marlo
Lucas Roberts (1993–)	Eileen Davidson
Jamie Caldwell (1993–)	Bryan Datillo
Pat Hamilton (1993–)	Miriam Parrish
Marie (1993–)	Catherine MacNeal
Wendy Reardon (1993–94)	Harris Kendall
Wendy Reardon (1994–)	Lark Voorhees
Peter Blake (1993–96)	Tammy Townsend
Billie Reed (1993–95)	Jason Brooks
Kate Roberts (1993–95)	Lisa Rinna
Alan Harris (1993–95)	Deborah Adair
Ann Goldberg (1993–94)	Paul Kerse
	Lee Kessler

Fr. Kyle (1993–94)	Gordon Paddison
Nurse Jackson (1993–94)	Nancy Parsons
Fr. Timothy Jansen (1994–)	Michael O'Neill
Celeste (1994–)	Tanya Boyd
Daniel Scott (1994–95)	Stan Ivar
Father Francis (1994–95)	Charles Welch
Father Francis (1995)	Eric Christmas
Gabe the Angel (1994–95)	Mark Colson
Dr. Perkins (1994–95)	Janice Kent
Olga (1994–95)	Diane Delano
Dr. Hunt (1994–95)	Robert Gentry
Lynn (1994–95)	Marie Alise Recasner

It seems appropriate that *Days of Our Lives* came to television after NBC considered, then rejected, a video update of *One Man's Family* (q.v.) for its time slot, for, like the latter, the stories on this long-running serial were centered around an extended family for more than 30 years. In *Days'* case, that family was the Hortons of the town of Salem, somewhere in the Midwest. The pleasant heads of household were Tom, a doctor, and Alice Horton, who in the opener were planning their daughter Marie's marriage to neighbor Tony Merritt. Joining them were Tom and Alice's sons Mickey, a lawyer, and Bill, a doctor who like Mickey was a bachelor, and their daughter Addie, wed to Ben Olson. The only shadow on the wedding preparations involved Addie's daughter Julie, who was charged with shoplifting. Julie, whose brother was Steven, was an untamed teenager who cared little about the bad consequences of her actions and who would cause much more trouble over the next 15 years.

Marie's wedding came to naught as Tony, facing a terminal illness, called it off. Undaunted and uninformed of the reason, she wed Tony's dad Craig Merritt instead. Then Craig learned of Tony's situation and told Marie he would divorce her, though not giving a reason why. But the newly free Marie did not cotton to returning to Tony, preferring to bury herself in work as a research assistant at the hospital. There she found love in the form of Mark Brooks, only it turned to horror when she and everyone else learned he was really Tom and Alice's amnesiac first son Tommy, believed to have died in the Korean War. A distraught Marie left town and became a nun, while Tommy tried, with disastrous results, to rebuild his life with his legal wife Kitty and her daughter Sandy.

Other Hortons had problematic romantic entanglements as well. Julie went after David Martin, but he cheated on her with Susan Hunter and had to marry her once she became pregnant. Sadly, the child died, and David ended up murdered by a temporarily crazed Susan while impregnating Julie before he died. Julie gave up her child for adoption, prompting further complications when she met the adoptive parents Janet and Scott Banning. Janet was terminally ill, and Julie's old rival Susan aided the family during this difficult period and fell in love with Scott. Then after Janet's death Julie learned her son David had indeed been adopted by the Bannings, so she wed Scott mainly to thwart Susan from becoming her natural son's mother. More conflicts with Susan followed.

In less initially traumatic fashion, Mickey dated Susan's sister Diane, while his brother Dr. Bill saw Dr. Laura Spencer. But Laura fell in love with Mickey, who had needed her expert advice when he was defending Susan, so they wed. A jealous, intoxicated Bill raped Laura, and she gave birth to his child Michael. At first only Laura and Tom knew the truth (Mickey was sterile), and when Bill found out he joined in keeping the information from Mickey. Tommy's now ex-wife Kitty learned the truth as well, but she died in 1969 after trying to blackmail Bill with the information. Bill continued to desire Laura despite interest from model Janene Whitley and disinterest from Laura herself, who desperately wanted her marriage to work. Matters were not improved by Mickey's fling with Linda Patterson and Linda's disappointment to learn her child Melissa was not Mickey's but the product of her romp with ex-husband Jim Phillips, with whom she reunited.

Bill went to jail on a charge of involuntary manslaughter in Kitty's case. His cell mate Doug Williams played a pivotal role with the Hortons once he got out of prison. The con artist tried his wiles on Susan, but she wised up to his motives and sent him to Julie. To Doug's surprise, he began to feel true romantic urges toward Julie. Complicating their relationship was the growing closeness of David to his adoptive father, and the arrival of Julie's estranged, worldly mother Addie, back in Salem from Paris. Julie's rival Susan, having been raped, was also faring badly, although she had decided to keep her child, with the caring assistance of Dr. Greg Peters. As these stories progressed in November 1971, the show topped *As the World Turns* for a week to be #1 in daytime, the first NBC show with that honor in more than a decade.

As 1972 dawned, Laura learned of how Kitty tried to blackmail Bill and grew more fond of him. Yet when she began to express her feelings to him one night, their son Michael, overhearing them, ran out in traffic and nearly died after being hit by a car. While that put the kibosh on that affair, Julie discovered that her rendezvous with Doug had run afoul of Addie's sudden interest in him. He impetuously wed Addie after a fight with Julie over having to deal with David. Addie bought him a club and renamed it Doug's Place, allowing him to croon tunes with ex-Frenchman Robert LeClair, while Julie turned to pretending to be Scott's devoted wife and befriending his employer Bob Anderson and Bob's wife Phyllis and daughter Mary. Scott's death and Addie's pregnancy by Doug in 1973 changed the dynamics of Julie's life considerably.

Meanwhile, Susan learned her rapist was Eric Peters, the brother of her boyfriend Greg. Eric nearly succeeded in confusing Susan into thinking the attack was consensual. Her psychiatrist Laura Horton confronted Eric about what he had done (he had stirred repressed memories in her that made her think he was David Martin). Then Eric realized his novel *In My Brother's Shadow* included a dramatization of his situation. When Greg read it and figured out what Eric had done, he beat Eric senseless, causing a concerned Susan to visit him in the hospital. Slowly, all three reached a level of understanding, and Susan wed Greg despite his mother Annie's fears.

Amid all this, the situation involving Mickey, Laura, and Bill worsened as Mickey lost his memory over the stress he had caused Michael. Calling himself Marty Hansen, he met farmer Maggie Simmons and fell in love with her. But when the Hortons found the newlyweds, there were mixed emotions as Mickey had no recognition of them. He did, however, give Laura a divorce so that she could and did marry Bill in 1974, followed by her pregnancy the following year and eventual birth of daughter Jennifer. But the return of Linda Patterson and her daughter Melissa started stirring Mickey's memories. Things came to a head when Michael needed a blood transfusion and Mickey found out he was not his son's type, which led to the revelation that Bill had been the boy's father and remembrance of all the past lies. Mickey accidentally shot Bill in a rage, and later hospitalized, he blurted to Michael the truth about his parentage, leading to more distress among the involved parties.

In the meantime, Julie dated Don Craig and Bob Anderson, causing the latter to divorce Phyllis and wed Julie. That marriage prompted Phyllis to try to kill Julie, but she ended up harming her daughter Mary instead. That threat was the least of Julie's problems, as her mother gave birth to Hope and then died from a car accident. Julie now had to act as mother to her half-sister while knowing that her true love was free to wed and that her marriage to Bob was a sexless one.

Also now in Salem were Amanda Howard, who had an affair with Dr. Neil Curtis while her husband was alive; nightclub singer Jeri Clayton, whose daughter Trish was the object of sexual aggression by her new husband Jack; Brooke Hamilton, girlfriend of Julie's now-grown son David Banning; and Rebecca North, who became a surrogate mother for Doug when he donated his sperm to her to have a baby brother for Hope. Dr. Greg Peters found himself drawn to Amanda while his brother Eric renewed his interest in Susan, making a spurned Neil wed Phyllis Anderson. Then complications after brain surgery left Phyllis confused as to whether she loved Greg or Neil. At the same time, Trish found solace in teenager Michael Horton and vice versa due to their family complications, which included Trish meeting her birth father James Stanhope.

Time passed. David left Brooke in a rage after she brought up questions about Julie's relationship to Doug while still wed to Bob. David left town and moved in with an African-American family, the Grants, falling in love with their daughter Valerie. Doug also began romancing Julie full time again once she divorced Bob, and so he dropped his claim on Rebecca's baby Dougie as fellow singer Robert LeClair wed her, even though Rebecca's old boyfriend Johnny Collins said he wanted her to stay a part of his life. While Doug's dropping his claim on the child seemed to clear the way for Doug and Julie to marry, the arrival of Kim Douglas, who claimed to have never divorced Doug, spoiled it until she admitted she had lied. Finally, after six years of romance, Doug and Julie had a beautiful, lavish wedding in 1976.

Julie's ex-husband Bob was not to be alone for long, however. He learned from the dying Adele Hamilton that Brooke was their daughter. And Linda Patterson started dating him when she learned that Mickey and Maggie, who had adopted a girl named Janice, were one family that was not going to separate. They wed in 1978. Unfortunately for Bob's ex-wife Phyllis, her husband Neil was now seeing her daughter Mary behind her back after Amanda decided to wed Greg, and the two later left for Chicago (Greg's ex-wife Susan divorced him to live with his brother Eric in California).

Another former love of Julie's, Don Craig, was now dating psychiatrist Dr. Marlena Evans, who arrived on the show during the interim in 1976 when the show was looking for a new Laura Horton to replace Susan Oliver. In mid-1977 Marlena's (and Deidre Hall's) twin sister came to Salem. Samantha Evans was a drug-addicted actress who assumed her sister's place and even put Marlena in a sanitarium. After Don discovered what had happened and Samantha went into treatment, Marlena and Don resumed dating until his ex-girlfriend Lorraine Temple arrived with Donna in tow, the daughter that Don did not know he had fathered. Lorraine later left but Donna stayed with Don, causing friction with her new stepmother-to-be for a time before Marlena and Don wed in 1979.

Trish Clayton had her own grief to deal with in the late 1970s. She slept with David Banning after a spat he had with Valerie Grant. That enraged Trish's envious stepfather Jack, whom she accidentally murdered during a struggle. Trish became a split personality in the aftermath, then recovered, wed David, and gave birth to a child named Scotty. Mike Horton, upset by these developments, wed Margo Anderman in 1978, but she died of leukemia two years later. Trish and David had a rocky relationship, with problems including battles over how to raise Scotty, and David dated vixen Stephanie Woodruff for a time during the period 1978–79. Later, David's espionage work for Kellam Chandler made him realize he was endangering Trish and Scotty, so he left with his Scotty. Trish tracked them down and divorced David, and he went to jail on an assault charge. David later wed scheming Renee Dumonde, but divorced her before she died. He and Scotty left town, as did Michael when he realized that he and Trish had no chance of getting back together.

Several other marriages went through strains in the late 1970s. Bill and Laura locked horns over his affair with Dr. Kate Winograd, after which she lost her mind and was confined to a sanitarium. Bereft over the loss of his true love, Bill left town, leaving Tom and Alice to raise his and Laura's daughter Jennifer. Mickey and Maggie had a custody fight with Joanne Barnes, mother of their adopted daughter Janice. Maggie turned into an alcoholic during the struggle, and eventually Joanne got Janice while Mickey and Maggie tried to salvage their marriage. Linda saw Neil Curtis while Bob Anderson was hospitalized. When Bob found out, she pretended to be pregnant to win him over. When he died in 1980, he left her a settlement valid only if she and her daughter Melissa left town, which they did. Even Julie and

Doug's relationship disintegrated. After Julie was raped by Larry Atwood, a man who also tried to frame Doug on drug charges, temptress Lee Dumonde seduced him and he wed her in 1979 to Julie's dismay.

Following his own winding path of romantic tribulations in Salem during this time was Chris Kositchek, a foreman at Bob Anderson's company. He first dated Bob's daughter Mary, then found himself being chased by Stephanie Woodruff, who turned out to be Bob's now-presumed-dead other daughter Brooke. Chris proposed to Mary, but Mary's indecision led him to see Amanda for a time after she divorced Greg, then found out she no longer wanted him after she miscarried following her pregnancy with Chris. Stephanie began seeing Alex Marshall, who cheated on her with Mary, of all people. Alex, who later wed Mary, had a big secret in that he had been seeing Marie Horton, now a practicing nun, who returned in 1979 not knowing he was in town too.

By 1980, the show's ratings were horrible. New head writer Nina Laemmle said that to win back viewers, the show needed get rid of repetitive story lines and characters she felt were old and, in the case of most of the men, emasculated. Her work resulted in a major cast shakeup. Series producer Al Rabin, who summoned actors into his office to fire them during this period, told *TV Guide* that the traditional cake and champagne sendoff for departing actors ended at this time. "It would have been like a bad joke. Every week for 10 weeks, you would have had a party," he said.

Laemmle's scripts resulted in a tumultuous year. Stephanie/Brooke died in a car crash not long after her dad Bob passed away. Bill Horton, Robert LeClair and Dougie, Phyllis Anderson, Samantha Evans, and Donna Craig all left Salem. Taking up the slack were the Chandler clan, consisting of patriarch Kellam, his wife Sunny, their singing daughter Liz, and sons Tod and Joshua Fallon. Tod and Joshua dated respectively Cassie Burns and Jessica Blake, the latter the daughter Marie Horton gave up for adoption after Alex Marshall impregnated her. When Alex learned this and told Jessica, she slowly developed split personalities but finally regained her senses and returned to Joshua. Sunny and Kellam later died, the latter after a fight with Tod led to an accidental shooting. Liz dated and then wed Neil Curtis, followed by Don Craig when his marriage to Marlena went south.

As these developments played out, they fared poorly with viewers, and the show imported Pat Falken Smith and six other writers from *General Hospital* to shore up the series in 1981 as it dropped to 15th place in daytime. That year, Julie and Doug remarried after he learned how duplicitous Lee Dumonde had been to him. Lee's sister Renee arrived and fell in love with Tony DiMera, the son of powerful mobster Stefano DiMera and ex-husband of Liz Chandler (they could not wed, as Renee really was Lee's daughter by Stefano, plus it turned out that Liz was still married to Tony). Maggie decided to become a surrogate mother, which Mickey reluctantly approved, and Dr. Evan Whyland was named as the sperm donor of the baby, which Maggie named Sarah.

Days of Our Lives *celebrated its 4,000th taping in 1981 with, from front left to right, Lane Davies, Tammy Taylor, Deidre Hall, Macdonald Carey, executive producer Betty Corday, Frances Reid, and Gregg Marx, and, from back left to right, John Clarke, Gloria Loring, Melinda Fee, Philece Sampler, Brenda Benet, Suzanne Rogers, Joe Gallison, and Stephen Brooks.*

But the real excitement came from the "Salem Strangler," a murderer who called Marlena repeatedly between trying to choke Renee and killing a few others like Mary Anderson and Samantha Evans. The latter's death really shocked fans and brought up the ratings, as viewers thought it was Marlena whom the Strangler killed. The killer turned out to be Jake Kositchek, Chris's brother and onetime love of Jessica Blake. He was slain by policeman Roman Brady, who became Marlena's new love. Their bliss ended temporarily when his missing wife Anna and daughter Carrie surfaced, but Anna agreed to a divorce and Roman tried to wed Marlena despite attempts on his life by Stefano.

Stefano was the nexus of plenty of activity in 1982–83. He had Alex and Anna work for him and managed to get Mickey out of town when Mickey started looking into

Stefano's activities. Stefano made it appear Mickey was dead, although he had actually only escaped Stafano's clutches, leading Maggie to date Don Craig. Stefano's son Tony insisted to Liz they remain married, then raped her as she tried to leave him. He went on to learn that his dad had lied about Renee being his sister and tried unsuccessfully to stop her marriage to David Banning, then agreed to divorce Liz, only to be drugged and forced into marrying Anna Brady.

In other sequences, Dr. Evan Whyland romanced Dr. Sandy Horton, the daughter of Tommy and Kitty from the 1960s, until Alex caused his death. Neil, still loved by Liz, went to Marie Horton and wed her while Liz gave birth to his baby. Liz later accidentally shot Marie. Liz was sent to jail, got amnesia, and escaped, thinking she was Don's wife. Eugene Bradford, an eccentric scientist, dated Gwen Davies while having time for several amusing comic scenes with his robot SICO. But Eugene's real honey was nutty Calliope Jones, the gal with Salem's wildest fashion sense.

As his war against Stefano continued, Roman Brady's family gained prominence in 1983. Besides his parents Shawn and Caroline, there were Roman's sister Kayla, who dated Chris, and his younger brother Bo, who wed Doug's daughter Hope and, like Roman, was a lawman, though he worked undercover for Howie Hofstedder. Roman had to go into hiding when framed for murder while a slasher attacked various townfolk including Renee, all these events being orchestrated by Stefano under the alias "the Phoenix." When Anna and Tony, now a couple, found who was behind all the trouble, they were imprisoned but managed to escape. Finally tailed by police, Stefano escaped town and disappeared, though Salem had by no means seen the last of him.

After Stefan's temporary disappearance, things settled down for a while. For example, Roman and Marlena had twin babies Eric and Samantha (later called Sami), Liz regained her memory and wed Neil, and Maggie left Don and eventually went back to Mickey. But not everything went well. Mickey's old flame Linda Patterson returned to do dirty work with Alex. Her nice daughter Melissa, in love with male stripper Pete Jannings, did not find out about her mom's plots until almost too late.

Stefano returned, and after a struggle between him and Roman, Roman was reported dead. His brother Bo planned to avenge the loss, while his sister Kimberly Brady rejoined the rest of the clan and took up with agent Shane Donovan. Demented Megan Hathaway tried to stop Bo, whom she loved, while Stefano came back to haunt Marlena. Bo and his wife Hope became international spies, together with Shane, to try to stop Stefano and crew, but the appearance of a new local enemy signaled a new set of tribulations.

Tycoon Victor Kiriakis hit Salem in 1985 with a bang. He intimidated Caroline Brady by telling her that he was Bo's father, while masterminding vice crimes like narcotics peddling and production of pornography with Savannah Wilder and Alex Marshall. He even had a fling with Kimberly, which made her worry temporarily that her child Andrew was his. Another of his henchmen was Steve "Patch" Johnson, so nicknamed because he wore an eyepatch, who reformed his ways as Kayla became attached to him. Bedeviling Victor's operations was an amnesiac known as John Black, who was believed to be Roman Brady after undergoing plastic surgery (he really was not). John and Marlena got together until a criminal known as Orpheus double-crossed Victor and supposedly killed Marlena.

Not all events in the mid-1980s were related to mystery and intrigue, however. Mike Horton came back to be a doctor and dated Robin Jacobs, a niece of Robert LeClair's who, Mike later learned, had given birth to their child Jeremy. His sister Jennifer dated Glenn Gallagher. Liz managed to have a hit duet with Carl Anderson called "Friends and Lovers," which was Shane and Kimberly's song, but Liz's emphasis on her career led Neil to divorce her and led her to leave Salem. ("Friends and Lovers" became a hit in real life too, peaking at #2 on *Billboard*'s Hot 100 chart in 1985.)

As Bo left town with Hope, Frank and Caroline adopted Jennifer Horton's new boyfriend Frankie and his brother Max. Patch reunited with his sister Adrienne, who wed Victor's nephew Justin, and his mother Jo, who had been abused by

their dad Duke Johnson. Melissa lost Frankie and then her dancing partner Lars as lovers, while Mike and Robin split up. Mike's college friend Diana Colville dated John Black, but despite numerous worldwide adventures, she never wed. Shane and Kimberly adjusted to living with hooker Eve Baron, who claimed to be Shane's daughter, but eventually broke up. Shane then dated Kimberly's sister Kayla until the trio left town separately.

But the new family making the most impact in the late 1980s was the Deverauxs—Senator Harper, his wife Anjelica, and their "son" Jack, who actually was the son of Jo Johnson. Patch, learning of Jack's true parentage, let his sick brother wed Kayla. Harper poisoned Kayla because he thought she had Jack's adoption papers. Then Jack raped Kayla and Patch saved her, leading to a divorce, and Jack began dating Melissa Horton. Anjelica turned to Justin when Adrienne rejected him for staying in his uncle's shady business and ended up giving birth to his son Alexander. She did not wed Justin, however, but Dr. Neil Curtis, though she remained fond of Justin even when Justin returned to Adrienne. Eventually her desire for Justin grew to the point that she threatened to wed his uncle Victor, then tried to kill Adrienne, before leaving town. As for Harper, he was revealed to be the "Riverfront Knifer" who had killed Janice Barnes and a few others.

Some minor-league crime players in Salem did reform, like attempted robbers April Ramirez and her brother Emilio. April dated Mike Horton after his flings with Robin Jacobs and Janice Barnes fell through, but wed ex-pimp Nick Corelli. Mike ended up leaving town again with no woman with him, while April also departed after being cleared of suspicion in Nick's murder (which had been committed by a temporarily insane Jo Johnson). Emilio slept with Adrienne, then became Jennifer's boyfriend when Frankie left Salem. Then Jennifer could not decide between Emilio and Jack until the former fell to his death.

As the 1980s drew to a close, Shane was presumed dead, but was actually alive with no memory of his past (sound familiar?); Scotty Banning, David's son, returned to Salem and bought a club where Faith Taylor became the resident singer as well as Scotty's lover; and Isabella Toscano found her family's hidden treasure, which had long been sought by many Salemites. Though she accidentally killed her sister Marina, Isabella managed to stay free due to the efforts of Victor, who was her real father. She wed John Black before dying. In the midst of these exotic stories, the show also planned to remove six middle-aged actors as regulars in 1989 (Frank Parker, James Reynolds, Peggy McCay, Suzanne Rogers, Joy Garrett, and Jay Robinson), but following public outcry, the show reinstated virtually all of them.

The early 1990s had several Hortons in the mix. Returning were Julie and Melissa, who warned Jennifer about Jack while falling in love with Emilio. Melissa left in 1992 along with Sarah Horton, Maggie's surrogate daughter, who learned to her horror that her birth father was not the late Dr. Evan Whyland as first stated, but Neil Curtis, whom Maggie now saw while back with Mickey. Jennifer wed Jack after testifying against her rapist Lawrence Alamain, who killed Patch Johnson. Not all Hortons made it back home, though. Hope was believed to be killed in an explosion, leaving Bo a grieving widower.

Bo fell in love with Dr. Carly Manning, but she ended up treating and then marrying Victor, thinking, due to Victor's tricks, that Bo no longer loved her. She eventually found Victor out and planned to marry Bo instead, but a freed Lawrence Alamain stopped the wedding with the news that he had fathered her child Nikki, the foster child of Lawrence's nutty sister Vivian. Vivian paralyzed Carly with a potion that caused the latter to be buried alive, then went on to kill several of Carly's patients while assuming a variety of disguises. Carly survived all this and, after a bout with amnesia, left town with Lawrence and Nikki. Bo began dating drug addict Billie Reed.

Also popping up in the early 1990s were believed-dead Marlena, who reunited with the real Roman Brady (not John Black), but Roman left her when he learned that her child Belle, whom their daughter Sami had tried to sell to a black-market ring, was not his but John Black's. She did not go back to John, though, who favored perpetual damsel in distress Kristen Blake instead.

But Marlena's love life was nothing compared to that of newspaper magnate Kate Roberts. Kate wed Victor but found herself harassed by Vivian, who stole Kate's embryo and impregnated herself with it. And if that wasn't enough, she had to contend with a trashy ex-husband, Curtis Reed; the revelation that two children she thought were dead, Austin and Billie Reed, were in fact alive; and an estranged son, Lucas Roberts, who turned out to be Bill Horton's illegitimate son and the reason why Laura Horton had gone nuts nearly 15 years earlier! Laura became sane after facing the truth of the past events and reunited with her children Mike and Jennifer.

All this intrigue paled in mid-1994, when actor MacDonald Carey died and the decision was made to have his character Tom Horton pass away as well. A host of Hortons returned to pay tribute to the beloved doctor. And though Tom was dead, his presence remained on the show via the taped introduction that had been read by Carey at the start of each show since the 1970s: "Like sand through the hourglass, so are the days of our lives."

Whatever warmth that device was good for was partially dissipated in late 1994 through 1995 as the show came up with a story line that became the laughingstock of the industry. Marlena was under Satanic possession! She spoke in a bellowing bass voice, levitated, the whole works, until John Black and some priests managed to defeat the devil. What's more, Marlena decided to move in with Stefano after the exorcism.

Yet the show gained renewed popularity at the same time due to many young love conflicts. Half-sisters Carrie and Sami Brady became rivals for Billie's brother Austin, with Sami and Lucas conning Austin into thinking Lucas was sleeping with Carrie to break up that couple temporarily, followed by Sami drugging Austin into making love with her under the

pretense of thinking she was Carrie, then forcing Austin to wed her when she said she had given birth to his child. Jack and Jennifer separated, and Jennifer went after Peter Blake, Stefano's foster son. And amnesiac Gina, learning that she really was Hope Brady, was reunited with Bo. She went to live with them and their natural son from a few years earlier, Shawn-Douglas.

Shawn-Douglas was a Horton descendant as well. For the record, matriarch Alice Horton could claim in 1996 to be the mother of five, the grandmother of 11 (counting Mickey and Maggie's adoption of Melissa and their temporary custody of Janice), great-grandmother of four, including Shawn-Douglas, and great-great-grandmother of one (Scotty Banning). One shudders to think how many more may arrive in the next 30 years!

DEAR ALEX AND ANNIE—See *Kids Are People Too.*

DENNIS JAMES SHOW, THE
Variety; B&W
September 24, 1951–February 15, 1952
ABC Mon.–Fri. 11:30 a.m.–Noon (9/24/51–2/15/52)
Regulars: *Dennis James, Julia Meade*

Following his three-year run on DuMont with *Okay Mother* (q.v.), Dennis James went to ABC's fledgling daily lineup with this series featuring sketches and activities designed to highlight the needs of motherhood. He did several giveaways as part of the show, with Julia Meade helping in various guises, like being a crew member giving away merchandise on the SS *Okay Mother.*

•DENNIS THE MENACE
Cartoon; Color
January 2, 1988–September 10, 1994
CBS Sat. 11:30 a.m.–Noon (1/2/88–9/10/88)
CBS Sat. 10–10:30 a.m. (9/11/93–11/20/93)
CBS Sat. 11–11:30 a.m. (11/27/93–2/26/94)
CBS Sat. 11–11:30 a.m. (4/2/94–8/27/94)
CBS Sat. Various (9/3/94–9/10/94)

Voices (1988):

Dennis the Menace	*Brennan Thicke*
Henry Mitchell/Ruff	*Phil Hartman*
Joey/Margaret/Tommy	*Jeannie Elias*
Mr. (George) Wilson	*Maurice LaMarche*
Alice Mitchell/Martha Wilson	*Marilyn Lightstone*

Also: *Brian George, Sharon Noble, Riva Spier, Louise Vallance*

Voices (1993–94):

Dennis the Menace	*Adam Wylie*
Mr. Wilson	*Greg Burson*
Mrs. Wilson	*June Foray*
Alice Mitchell	*Jeannie Elias*

Hank Ketcham's comic strip character Dennis (Mitchell) the Menace had been in existence for eight years when CBS adapted it as a nighttime sitcom in 1959 for a four-year run starring Jay North. Despite being fairly faithful to the cartoon, it was said that Ketcham would have preferred to have seen his creation in animated form on television. Dennis showed up that way from 1971 to 1973 as a segment on *Curiosity Shop* (q.v.), but he did not get his own cartoon series until one debuted first in daily syndication in 1985 and then on CBS briefly in 1988.

In the program, Dennis's mischievous antics terrorized his well-meaning parents Henry and Alice as much as they did arch-antagonist Mr. Wilson and various others. Dennis did such things as surf on a tray cart on a plane and press various buttons he was not supposed to touch. Joey, Tommy, and Margaret were his neighborhood pals. Ruff, a shaggy dog and pet for Dennis, could talk, about the only detail that made the TV show different from the comic strip.

Five years after its first run, *The All-New Dennis the Menace* came on CBS, prompted no doubt by a feature film release that year based on the comic strip and starring Walter Matthau as Mr. Wilson. Dennis was just as aggravating as ever, but the series did not fare as well as the early version, which remained popular in syndication in repeats.

•DEPUTY DAWG

Cartoon; Color
September 11, 1971–September 2, 1972

NBC Sat. 9–9:30 a.m. (9/11/71–1/1/72)
NBC Sat. 8:30–9 a.m. (1/8/72–9/2/72)

Voice Characterizations: *Dayton Allen*

Deputy Dawg was the friendly but not too smart defender of law and order in the small town of Creek Mud, Mississippi. Deputy Dawg's efforts were often thwarted by local pranksters Vince Van Gopher, who wore a beret, and Ty Coon, a raccoon with a Southern drawl. But every time he tried to retaliate he found himself halted by the old mustachioed Sheriff, who unwittingly supported the other animals and told Deputy Dawg to keep himself in line. About all Deputy Dawg could do was defend himself and mutter, in his slurred speech, about revenge on Vince and Ty. This cartoon first aired in syndication in 1960, and each episode lasted about six minutes.

DEVLIN

Cartoon; Color
September 7, 1974–February 15, 1976

ABC Sat. 10–10:30 a.m. (9/7/74–8/30/75)
ABC Sun. 10:30–11 a.m. (9/7/75–2/15/76)

Voices:

Ernie Devlin	*Mike Bell*
Tod Devlin	*Mickey Dolenz*
Sandy Devlin	*Michele Robinson*
Hank	*Norman Alden*

The Devlins were a trio of orphans who supported themselves through their daredevil motorcycle act. Twenty-year-old Ernie

drove the car during the stunts, while teenager Tod oversaw the mechanical work and designed routines and eleven-year-old Sandy provided assistance whenever she was needed. Hank, the owner of the circus in which they worked, served as the father figure. Interspersed with the stunts and interpersonal dramas were tips on motorcycle safety to let young viewers know the Devlins' occupation had plenty of risks. The Sunday shows were all repeats.

DICK CAVETT SHOW, THE

Talk; Color
March 4, 1968–January 29, 1969

ABC Mon.–Fri. 10:30 a.m.–Noon (3/4/68–1/29/69)

Host: *Dick Cavett*

Of all the talk show hosts, Dick Cavett has had the oddest long-running career, with series on nearly all the networks for more than 25 years without ever being a significant ratings draw. This daytime entry was his first show. Debuting under the title *This Morning*, Cavett's show had an eclectic taste in guests (Buckminster Fuller, Patricia Neal, and Jack Albertson on the premiere), and his talks with them could rarely be confused with the groveling occasionally dispensed by other talk show types like Mike Douglas and Merv Griffin. For example, *Newsweek* reported that when Harvard professor Timothy Leary said the Old Testament was written "by a bunch of nuts on a bad trip," Cavett shot back, "Dr. Leary, you're full of crap." By May 1968 the show was retitled in his name.

The series had great reviews but poor ratings, a characteristic all his shows would share. Cavett presented highlights of his daytime show on a nighttime ABC special on June 14, 1968 with Groucho Marx and Dionne Warwick, but even this did not boost ratings substantially. Neither did winning the Emmy for Outstanding Achievement in Daytime Programming in 1969, by which time ABC had canceled the show and stopped programming before noon daily for about a year in order to cut costs.

Cavett went on to do a thrice-nightly hour series on ABC from May–September 1969, then a late night show on ABC from December 1969–December 1972, continuing as an occasional offering through January 1975. In the summer of 1975 he had a variety show replacing *The Carol Burnett Show* on CBS, then went to public television from 1977–1981. In 1985 he did another chat show on the USA cable channel, then returned to ABC for another late-night talk show in the fall of 1986. His final go-round was yet another nightly talk show on the CNBC cable channel from 1989–95.

DINAH'S PLACE

Talk; Color
August 3, 1970–July 26, 1974

NBC Mon.–Fri. 10–10:30 a.m. (8/3/70–7/26/74)

Host: *Dinah Shore*

After spending much of the 1950s and 1960s as one of nighttime TV's top personalities, singer Dinah Shore came to daytime television in 1970 in a talk show and made it her home for the rest of the decade. She had a great deal of top-name guests doing the most unlikely activities. Among others, Burt Lancaster whipped up some spaghetti sauce, Joanne Woodward did needlepoint, and Ethel Kennedy played the piano. But the best-remembered guest had to have been Burt Reynolds, who met Dinah for the first time at *Dinah's Place.* The two of them embarked on a romance that lasted through the mid-1970s, but they never married.

Dinah taped an entire week of shows in two days, plus an extra one if she wanted a day off. In 1973 the series won an Emmy for Outstanding Program Achievement in Daytime, but neither the Emmy nor the respectable ratings stopped NBC from unexpectedly canceling the show the following year.

Undaunted, Shore returned to the airwaves in a similar syndicated talk show titled *Dinah!* in October 1974. The

impressive guest roster on the debut included Jack Benny (in one of his last TV appearances), Sammy Davis Jr., Rock Hudson, Mary Tyler Moore, the Pointer Sisters, and Senator Edward Kennedy. The show was available to stations daily for 90 or 60 minutes until its cancellation in 1980. In its last season, the producers tried unsuccessfully to woo viewers by retitling it *Dinah & Friends* and rotating as weekly co-hosts Fernando Lamas, Don Meredith, Charles Nelson Reilly, and Paul Williams.

•DING DONG SCHOOL

Children's; B&W and Color
November 24, 1952–December 31, 1956
NBC Mon.–Fri. 10–10:30 a.m. (11/24/52–12/31/56)
Hostess: *Dr. Frances Horwich*

Ding Dong School began locally on WNBQ Chicago on October 3, 1952 before going on NBC. It starred Dr. Frances Horwich, a plump 44-year-old Chicago school supervisor who sat on a hassock and sang the show's theme song before beginning the instructional segments. She

Dr. Frances Horwich, better known to her fans as "Miss Frances," presided over Ding Dong School.

encouraged children to paint, draw, count, and even plant food with the help of Raggedy Andy dolls, puppets Lucky the rabbit and Jocko the monkey, and live goldfish Wynken, Blynken, and Nod. All materials were wheeled back and forth in front of Dr. Horwich on a cart for each segment. After completing each exercise, she asked, "Wasn't that fun?" or "What did you think of that?" and paused as if having a conversation with them. Horwich also told parents at the end of the show what the children learned that day.

Conceived by WNBQ program director (and future NBC children's programmer) George Heinemann, *Ding Dong School* was a well-intentioned program whose most memorable elements came about by accident. According to *Newsweek*, the show interviewed actresses to host the series when Horwich, then head of the educational department at Chicago's Roosevelt College, accidentally got an audition because it was thought she was another actress looking for the job. Another bit of serendipity was the program's name. Director Reinald Werrenrath Jr.'s son overheard his father and mother discussing the opening shot of a ringing school bell, and piped in with the idea that the show should be called "Ding Dong School."

Ding Dong School reaped a bounty of awards as it was the only type of home teaching tool seen daily for much of its run (*Captain Kangaroo* came in late 1955). Then after four years and 1,105 consecutive telecasts led by Horwich, NBC suddenly pulled the plug despite the objections of at least 11,000 letters of protest and the fact the series was doing well enough in the ratings and cost the network little to produce. *Saturday Review* columnist Robert Lewis Shayon claimed that the real reason for the cancellation was Horwich's picking only 30 out of 700 potential sponsors to advertise for the show. Horwich had said she would endorse only inexpensive items her young viewers could reuse.

After leaving NBC, *Ding Dong School* returned as a local Chicago show on WGN on October 22, 1957 (Horwich had moved the show to New York in May 1955). Two years later, it ran as a nationally syndicated daily half-hour show, both taped and filmed in Hollywood, which lasted 130 shows.

DINK, THE LITTLE DINOSAUR
Cartoon; Color
September 16, 1989–August 24, 1991

CBS Sat. 8–8:30 a.m. (9/16/89–9/8/90)
CBS Sat. Noon–12:30 p.m. (9/15/90–8/24/91)

Voices:

Dink	*R. J. Williams*
Amber	*Anndi McAfee*
Shyler	*Ben Granger*
Flapper	*S. Scott Bullock*
Scar/Crusty	*Frank Welker*

Dink was a brontosaurus who led his pals, all of whom were dinosaurs except for old sea turtle Crusty, in various adventures in Dinosaur Valley in this unremarkable cartoon.

DIRECTIONS
Religious; B&W and Color
November 13, 1960–March 25, 1984

ABC Sun. 1–1:30 p.m. (11/13/60–5/7/61)
ABC Sun. Noon–12:30 p.m. (5/14/61–10/22/61; off summer)
ABC Sun. 1–1:30 p.m. (10/29/61–12/31/61)
ABC Sun. 3–3:30 p.m. (1/7/62–6/17/62)
ABC Sun. 2–2:30 p.m. (10/7/62–4/14/63)
ABC Sun. 1–1:30 p.m. (10/6/63–12/22/63)
ABC Sun. 2–2:30 p.m. (12/29/63–6/28/64)
ABC Sun. 1–1:30 p.m. (10/4/64–12/29/75; off summers)
ABC Sun. 12:30–1 p.m. or 1–1:30 p.m. (1/11/76–3/25/84)

Hosts (1960–61): *John Alcorn, Theodore Bikel, George Hicks*

Directions was ABC's knockoff of the *NBC Television Religious Program.* Like that series, it featured material designed for three religious groups, with programs for each rotated weekly. Also in the first year, each denomination had a host for its segments—John Alcorn for Catholics, Theodore Bikel for Jews, and George Hicks for Protestants. But after using Eli Wallach as host for a few shows in October 1961, the show had no regular for the rest of its run. Dramas and some musicals predominated during the first two years, with several annual productions of "The Rag Tent," an hour-long Christmas special on migrant farm workers first staged in 1960. In 1965 a new opera commissioned especially for the series called "The Final Ingredient" ran annually into the 1970s.

In 1962 documentaries began to seep into the lineup. ABC newsman Bill Shadel narrated a four-part series on Communism that year, and the following year a five-part look at Israel's archeology aired. An unusual offering was "The Ruling Gods" on May 7, 1967, with sportscaster Jim McKay showing the relationship between sports and religion. There still were some occasional dramas on the show throughout the 1960s, but during its last 15 years or so, *Directions* spent most of its time doing news and discussion with religious figures.

DISCOVERY '62–'71
Children's; B&W and Color
October 1, 1962–September 5, 1971

ABC Mon.–Fri. 4:30–4:55 p.m. (10/1/62–8/30/63)
ABC Sun. 12:30–1 p.m. (9/6/63–12/22/63)
ABC Sun. 1–1:30 p.m. (12/29/63–9/13/64)
ABC Sun. 11:30 a.m.–Noon (9/20/64–9/5/71)

Hosts: *Veronica Gibson, Frank Buxton (1962–66), Bill Owen (1966–71)*

Discovery came about when FCC Chairman Newton Minow, following his 1961 speech characterizing television as "a vast wasteland," suggested that all the networks rotate a daily educational program for children. CBS and NBC balked at the idea, and ABC decided to brave it alone. It was to debut in the fall of 1961 but was called off just six days before the first scheduled show because not enough affiliates planned to carry the program (it was to take the last 30 minutes of *American Bandstand)* and no sponsor could be found. When *Discovery* managed to get on the air, during its first season it did shows on subjects ranging from the Bronx Zoo's animal hospital to dinosaurs to Indians and presented programs recorded in Italy and England. But sponsor problems continued, and the show became a Sunday-only offering in the fall of 1963, doing 26 shows a season.

Later offerings included the U.S. TV debut of Leslie Caron during a two-part tour of London (December 8, 1963); a rare tour of Moscow with two Soviet children as guides to such attractions as Lenin's tomb and the Kremlin (February 22 and 29, 1964); ex-President Dwight Eisenhower talking to children about the U.S. political system (July 12, 1964); Margaret Hamilton, famous for her role as the Wicked Witch of the West in *The Wizard of Oz,* appearing in "The Weird World of Witchcraft" (October 25, 1964); and a reciprocal visit from Russia by two Soviet children on the show (January 1965). By 1964 the show had its own mascot, a bloodhound named Corpuscle.

Native American painter Dave Paladin displayed his "Nativity" piece to Bill Owen (left) and Virginia Gibson on Discovery *in 1970.*

In 1966 the show left its New York studios to do color film exclusively on location. That same year Bill Owen, formerly the show's announcer, replaced the departing Frank Buxton (incidentally, Owen and Buxton were co-authors of the first—1966—edition of *The Big Broadcast 1920–1950,* a book that was used for researching radio shows for this book). The 1967–68 season marked another first, with all that season's shows dedicated to the theme of American history.

The show went to at least 17 different countries and recommended three books on each week's subject based on suggestions from the American Library Association. Its efforts won it an Emmy for Outstanding Program Achievement in the Field of Children's Programming in 1964, but despite that and a nine-year run, it was never a huge audience attraction.

DISNEY'S ALADDIN'S ARABIAN ADVENTURE—See *Aladdin's Arabian Adventure.*

DISNEY'S GOOF TROOP—See *Goof Troop.*

DISNEY'S GUMMI BEARS—See *Gummi Bears.*

DISNEY'S LITTLE MERMAID—See *Little Mermaid.*

DISNEY'S MARSUPILAMI—See *Marsupilami.*

•DIVORCE COURT
Drama; B&W and Color
1958–1969; 1984–1991; 1993

Syndicated weekly and daily 60 and 30 minutes beginning
1959

Regular Judge: *Voltaire Perkins (1962–69), William B. Keene
(1984–1991)*

The first incarnation of *Divorce Court* aired on KTTV Los
Angeles as a live show starting January 1958 before going
into mainly nighttime syndication the following year. Each
episode dramatized a couple being interrogated by attorneys
about the reasons for their wanting to separate legally, followed
by a judge giving his final verdict. It should not be confused
with the similarly titled *Divorce Hearing,* which first appeared
in 1958 with Dr. Paul Popenoe, director of the American
Institute of Family Relations, helping real-life couples.

By 1962 *Divorce Court* had 130 shows available for daily
showing, one of the first of its kind in syndication. It reemerged
in production with a regular judge named Voltaire Perkins,
a practicing attorney for 25 years, and the number of actors
used during the new run topped 5,500!

Divorce Court was nowhere to be seen during the 1970s, as
daytime programmers concentrated more on talk shows, game
shows, and soap operas. Then in 1984, 15 years after leaving
the airwaves, a new version emerged as a half-hour daily with
new stories, often badly acted and loaded with lurid revelations
concerning such topics as adultery and sexual dysfunction. The
new regular judge was William B. Keene, who was a justice of
the peace for 20 years in California before stepping down from
his post in Los Angeles County Superior Court in January
1984 to preside over the show. The crew taped four shows per
day for 45 days a year. As in the 1960s, Judge Keene made
his own decisions using information provided on each show.

The series returned as a half-hour daily show in January
1993 under the title *The New Divorce Court,* but this last
go-round was not a success, and the show did not last past
the year. Nonetheless, the earlier success of the series should
not be forgotten, as it created numerous syndicated imitations.
(For some examples, see *The Judge* and *Superior Court.*)

DO YOU KNOW?
Children; B&W
October 12, 1963–April 25, 1964

CBS Sat. 12:30–1 p.m. (10/12/63–4/25/64)

Host: *Robert Maxwell*

Do You Know? was the TV equivalent of a book report by
children. Two teams of grade-schoolers ages 9 to 12 answered
questions about a work they had read for that week's show
(for the debut, the book was Rachel Carson's ecological tome
The Sea Around Us). The emphasis was on education, so the
kids got no prizes for correct answers. The series was taped
in New York City.

DO YOU TRUST YOUR WIFE?—See *Who Do You Trust?*

DR. DEAN
Informational; Color
June 15, 1992–December 11, 1992

NBC Mon.–Fri. 12:30–1 p.m. (6/15/92–12/11/92)

Host: *Dr. Dean Edell*

Psychologist Dr. Dean Edell got his start in the broadcasting
world as a syndicated radio host before entering television
with a syndicated half-hour weekly program titled *Dr. Edell's
Medical Journal,* which ran from 1989 until the start of this
show. His counseling of guests, including some stars, on one
topic per show fared poorly on the network, and this version
lasted only six months.

DR. DOLITTLE—See *Further Adventures of Dr.
Dolittle, The.*

DR. EDELL'S MEDICAL JOURNAL—See *Dr. Dean.*

DR. SPOCK
Informational; B&W
October 9, 1955–August 9, 1956

NBC Sun. 3–3:30 p.m. (10/9/55–8/9/56)

Host: *Dr. Benjamin Spock*

Dr. Spock's tome *Baby and Child Care* had sold more
than 7 million copies when NBC entered this show in the
Sunday afternoon lineup. Spock discussed infant rearing
with two sets of parents each week in this filmed series from
Cleveland, where the doctor taught child development at
Western Reserve University.

•DOCTORS, THE
Anthology/Soap Opera; B&W and Color
April 1, 1963–December 31, 1982

NBC Mon.–Fri. 2:30–3 p.m. (4/1/63–3/2/79)
NBC Mon.–Fri. 2–2:30 p.m. (3/5/79–8/1/80)
NBC Mon.–Fri. 12:30–1 p.m. (8/4/80–3/26/82)
NBC Mon.–Fri. Noon–12:30 p.m. (3/29/82–12/31/82)

Cast:

Dr. William Scott (1963–64)	Jock Gaynor
Dr. Jerry Chandler (1963–64)	Richard Roat
Dr. Elizabeth Hayes (1963–64)	Margot Moser
Rev. Samuel Shafer (1963–64)	Fred J. Scollay
Dr. Matt Powers	James Pritchett
Dr. Maggie Powers (1964–65)	Ann Williams
Dr. Maggie Powers (1965–68)	Bethel Leslie
Dr. Maggie Powers (1968–82)	Lydia Bruce
Dr. Althea Davis (1964–69, 1970–82)	Elizabeth Hubbard
Dr. Althea Davis (1969–70)	Virginia Vestoff
Kurt Van Alen (1964–66)	Byron Sanders
Nurse Brown (1964–66)	Dorothy Fielding

Character	Actor
Dr. Steve Lloyd (1964–65)	Craig Huebing
Peter Banas (1965 at least)	Gerald S. O'Loughlin
Brock Hayden (1965 at least)	Adam Kennedy
Theodora Van Alen (1966)	Carmen Matthews
Theodora Van Alen (1966)	Clarice Blackburn
Theodora Van Alen (1980–81)	Augusta Dabney
Liz Wilson (1966–70)	Pamela Toll
Keith Wilson (1966–67)	Morgan Sterne
Harriet Wilson (1966–67)	Meg Myles
Dr. Steve Aldrich (1967–82)	David O'Brien
Carolee Aldrich (1967–76)	Carolee Campbell
Carolee Aldrich (1976–82)	Jada Rowland
Dr. Karen Werner (1967–69, 1971–75)	Laryssa Lauret
Dr. John Rice (1967–69)	Terry Kiser
Martha Allen (1968–77)	Sally Gracie
Nurse Nancy Bennett (1968–69)	Nancy Donohue
Anna Ford (1968 at least)	Zeida Coles
Dr. Simon Harris (1968 at least)	Conrad Roberts
Paul Bennett (1969)	James Shannon
Billy Allison Aldrich (1970–71)	Mark Kearney
Billy Allison Aldrich (1971–72)	Bobby Hennessey
Billy Allison Aldrich (1973–77)	David Elliott
Billy Allison Aldrich (1977–79)	Shawn Campbell
Billy Allison Aldrich (1980–82)	Alec Baldwin
Dr. John Morrison (1970–74)	Patrick Horgan
Kathy Ryker (1970–71)	Carol Pfander
Kathy Ryker (1971–72)	Nancy Barrett
Kathy Ryker (1972–73)	Holly Peters
Dr. Rico Bellini (1970–71)	Richard Niles
Dr. Rico Bellini (1975–76)	Chandler Hill Harben
Toni Ferra Powers (1971–77)	Anna Stuart
Dr. Hank Iverson (1971–76)	Palmer Deane
Dr. Dan Allison (1971)	Richard Higgs
Mona Aldrich Croft (1972–82)	Meg Mundy
Barbara Ferra (1972)	Nancy Franklin
Dr. Vito McCray (1972 at least)	Paul Henry Itkin
Emma Simpson (1972)	Katherine Squire
Dr. Ann Larimer (1973–74, 1976–77)	Geraldine Court
Margo Stewart (1973–74)	Mary Denham
Dr. Alan Stewart (1974–76)	Gil Gerard
Mary Jane "M. J." Match (1975–78)	Lauren White
Mary Jane "M. J." Match (1978)	Carla Dragoni
Mary Jane "M. J." Match (1978–81)	Katherine Glass
Mary Jane "M. J." Match (1981–82)	Amy Ingersoll
Stacy Wells (1975–77)	Leslie Ray
Eleanor Conrad (1975–77)	Lois Smith
Andy Anderson (1975)	Lloyd Bremseth
Dr. Kevin MacIntyre (1975 at least)	Dino Narizzano
Luke Dancy (1976–82)	Frank Telfer
Nola Dancy Aldrich (1976–78)	Kathryn Harrold

Character	Actor
Nola Dancy Aldrich (1978–79)	Kathleen Turner
Nola Dancy Aldrich (1979–82)	Kim Zimmer
Jason Aldrich (1976–81)	Glenn Corbett
Doreen Aldrich (1976–77)	Jennifer Wood
Doreen Aldrich (1977–79)	Pamela Lincoln
Dr. Jerry Dancy (1976–77)	Jonathan Hogan
Dr. Jerry Dancy (1981)	Terry O'Quinn
Virginia Dancy (1976–78)	Elizabeth Lawrence
Sara Dancy Powers (1976–77)	Antionette Panneck
Sara Dancy Powers (1977–78)	Dorothy Fielding
Virginia Dancy (1976–78)	Elizabeth Lawrence
Joan Dancy (1976)	Peggy Whitton
Dr. Paul Summers (c. 1976)	Paul Carr
Stephanie Aldrich (1977–79)	Bridget Breen
Stephanie Aldrich (1980)	Gloria Mattioli
Stephanie Aldrich (1981–82)	Renee Pearl
Stephanie Aldrich (1982)	Anne Rose Brooks
Barney Dancy (1977–79)	Lawrence Weber
Tom Carroll (1977)	James Rebhorn
Tom Carroll (1977–78)	Jonathan Frakes
Missy Roberts Dancy (1978–80)	Dorian LoPinto
Dr. Colin Wakefield (1978–79)	Philip English
H. Swenney (1978–79)	Peggy Cass
Viveca Strand (1979–81)	Nancy Pinkerton
Dr. John Bennett (1979–81)	Franc Luz
Ashley Bennett (1979–81)	Valarie Mahaffey
Dr. Jack Garner (1979–81)	Ben Thomas
Calvin Barnes (1980–82)	Larry Riley
Natalie Bell (1980–81)	Laurie Klatscher
Natalie Bell (1981–82)	Jane Badler
Brad Huntington (1980–81)	Nicholas Walker
Darcy Collins (1980–81)	Nana Tucker
Alan Ross (1980–81)	Richard Borg
Theo Whitney (1981–82)	Tuck Milligan
Katy Whitney (1981–82)	Maia Danziger
Danny Martin (1981–82)	John Pankow
Dr. Jeff Manning (1981–82)	Michael J. Stark
Philip Manning (1981)	Alvin Epstein
Philip Manning (1982)	James Douglas
Adrienne Hunt (1982)	Nancy Stafford
Kit McCormick (1982)	Hillary Bailey

The Doctors deserves note as the only TV anthology series to transform itself into a soap opera. It premiered with daily stories whose leads alternated between serious surgeon Dr. William Scott, happy-go-lucky internist Dr. Jerry Chandler, female pediatrician Dr. Elizabeth Hayes, and hospital chaplain the Rev. Samuel Shafer. After three months, on July 9, 1963, the show added Dr. Matt Powers to the lineup and used continuing dramas that lasted a week, a pattern which continued through February 28, 1964. A few other regulars popped up during this period, including Matt's teenage son Mike, his unhappily married colleague Dr. Maggie Fielding, and her husband Alec.

On March 2, 1964, *The Doctors* became a full-fledged serial. Dr. Chandler and Rev. Shafer remained for a time but found themselves overshadowed by the Powers and Fieldings. The featured story had Dr. Powers as the head of Hope Memorial Hospital in the town of Madison falling in love with Maggie despite her marital status. Matt nobly treated Alec Fielding for his impotence, which was causing problems for the Fielding marriage, but Alec died in an accident after the operation. Despite this convenient development for the lovers, Matt found that his love for Maggie was hampered by haunting memories of his late wife Grace, whose suicide he blamed on his dedication to work.

Maggie, smarting from Matt's inexplicable disinterest in her, found herself being romanced by cattle tycoon Brock Hayden and Kurt Van Allen. She wed the latter, which proved to be a bad choice as he mistreated her and then left her pregnant. After Maggie gave birth to a daughter, Greta, and learned that Kurt had been reported dead after a fight in the South Seas, she went after Matt again. The Matt-Maggie nuptials finally took place in 1968 after Maggie won a bitter custody battle for Greta against Kurt's sister Theodora Rostand.

Other medical personnel took center stage in the hospital-based drama, including Dr. Kate Bartok, hospital custodian Pete Banas, and Dr. Steve Lloyd, and Banas and Lloyd got married (actors Craig Huebing and Joan Anderson, who played the roles, were married in real life and left the series for Hollywood in 1965). But the most important of these was Dr. Althea Hamilton Davis, a divorcée and mother of Penny and Buddy Davis, who had been engaged to Matt Powers before he decided to go for Maggie. When the rather proper head of Hope Memorial's outpatient clinic met rough-hewn brain surgeon Dr. Nick Bellini, sparks began to fly, and they wed in 1968. Family difficulties hampered their happiness, however. Buddy died following an attack of spinal meningitis, which triggered a temporary breakup. Then, when Nick and Althea found that their temperaments clashed and got divorced, Penny blamed her mother for the marriage's dissolution and went to live with her natural father, Dave Davis, in California.

In 1966 (the same year Dr. Benjamin Spock told *TV Guide* that *The Doctors* was the only TV show he watched regularly), the show began to spotlight the younger generation, when Liz Wilson arrived to romance aspiring doctor Mike Powers. Liz had problems first with her neurotic, overprotective mother Harriet, whom her father Keith eventually spirited away, then nearly killed herself when she ingested an experimental psychedelic drug Mike created. Dr. Greg Rice took an interest in her as well, but Liz ended up leaving in 1968 without either Greg or Mike.

Mike branched out in 1969, first dating Nancy Bennett, a physical rehabilitation nurse who left Mike when her presumed dead husband Paul returned, and then Julie Forrest, Maggie's distant cousin who died after a fall. He finally found a steady relationship and marriage with Toni Ferra in 1972. Toni's mother Barbara redeemed her shady past by preventing Dr. Vito McCray from breaking up Mike and Toni. Complications abounded in 1974, when a pregnant Toni, thinking Mike dead after he deserted her due to professional fears about an addiction to amphetamines, fell in love with Mike's cousin Dr. Alan Stewart, whose wife Margo had also died recently. When Mike reentered her life, the newly married Toni first fought with him for custody of their son Michael Paul, then reconciled with him, then left him finally to care for her ill mother in California.

The other big romantic lead on the show was Dr. Steve Aldrich, who sparked a series of star-crossed entanglements in the late 1960s and early 1970s. He first impregnated and then wed Dr. Karen Werner. Karen, an unbalanced woman who had tried to break up Matt and Maggie's marriage, attempted suicide while wed to Steve. Dr. Aldrich, stressed out by his wife's behavior, divorced her and had a fling with nurse Carolee Simpson, who left him and wed Dr. Dan Allison even though she was carrying Steve's child. The vengeful and fatally ill Dr. Allison committed suicide, but rigged it to look as though Steve had killed him. His son Billy exonerated Steve at the last moment, and Steve married Carolee in 1972. That same year, *The Doctors* became the first winner of an Emmy for Outstanding Achievement in Daytime Drama.

The early 1970s saw a rash of psychologically challenged characters. One was Althea's new husband John Morrison, a psychiatrist who detested her ex-husband Nick so much that he went to elaborate lengths to keep them apart, including

The Powers family of The Doctors *in 1980 included, clockwise from top left, Mike (played by Jim Storm), Matt (James Pritchett), Greta (holding child; Jennifer Houlton), Maggie (Lydia Bruce), and Paul (John Downes).*

The Doctors hit its 5,000th telecast in May 1982 (it ended seven months later). Shown here, from top left clockwise, are longtime cast members David O'Brien, James Pritchett, Jada Rowland, Lydia Bruce, and Elizabeth Hubbard.

brainwashing nurse Kathy Ryker into pretending that Nick made her pregnant. Kathy later killed herself and Nick was murdered. And then there was Mona Aldrich, Steve's overbearing mother who interfered with his marriage to Carolee, of whom Mona disapproved. Even Maggie began functioning unstably due to a brain tumor. About the only "normal" regulars were Dr. Hank Iverson and his girlfriend and eventual wife Lauri James, a singer turned nurse.

The up-and-down relationships of the longtime regulars dominated the mid-1970s story lines. Nick had a difficult relationship with Dr. Ann Larimer, who could not have sex with him because she was suffering from Obonda fever. She recovered, returned to town, and proceeded to wreck Steve and Carolee's marriage by causing Carolee to break down mentally so that she had to be institutionalized. Actress Jada Rowland may have had the weirdest acting task of any soap opera regular during this period, as her character Carolee was catatonic for her first eight months on the show. Finally,

in March 1977, she spoke, crying out "Steve!" but she found he had married the manipulative Dr. Larimer. Steve and Dr. Larimar eventually divorced, and Steve remarried Carolee.

About this time Penny Davis returned to forge an uneasy bond with her mom Althea and endure a romantic triangle involving herself, artist Stacy Wells, and singer Andy Anderson. Penny's roommate and friend M. J. Match, Carolee's cousin, proved similarly luckless in her failed romances with Dr. Alan Stewart, Dr. Kevin MacIntyre, and even Dr. Matt Powers during a strain in his marriage to Maggie. (She did, however, marry Tom Carroll at one point.)

The dominant family toward the end of the run was the Dancy dynasty, whose members touched the lives of all the other characters in some way. For example, Mike Powers wed Sara Dancy on the rebound from her affair with Dr. Colin Wakefield. Their relationship was one in which each seemed to take the other for granted until they faced death (Sara died from cancer with Mike at her bedside). Sara's drug addict sister Joan died under treatment by Dr. Matt Powers, whose lawyer Jason Aldrich, Steve's newly arrived brother, cleared Matt's name and fingered the real culprit, Dr. Paul Summers. Jerry, Sara and Joan's brother, wed Penny in an abrasive marriage which ended in the latter leaving and then dying.

The other Dancy brother and sister, Luke and Nola, were involved in even more complicated machinations. Luke dated not one but two older socialites before settling with Missy Palmer, a rape victim. Their love was harmed by hospital medical inspector Viveca Strand's attempts to worm her way into Luke's life, but the closer was Missy ending up being kidnapped by a cult leader and shot to death. Moving right along, Nola Dancy managed to win over Jason Aldrich after the latter divorced his wife Doreen only to have—you guessed it—a difficult relationship with Jason which got even more involved with various claims of paternity of and custody for Nola's daughter Jessica, culminating with Jason's murder by an angry ex-girlfriend.

During much of the late 1960s through mid-1970s, *The Doctors* performed near the top of the ratings, as did the other soap opera which shared the show's debut date, *General Hospital.* But toward the end of the 1970s the show's appeal waned, with time shifts perhaps hastening its demise. The program continued some of the old plot lines (teenagers Billy Allison and Greta Van Alen had a child and a tumultuous relationship as Greta's aunt Theodora Rostand returned with her inheritance, leading Greta to marry Theo Whitney and the money-hungry Billy to end up a murder victim), while adding some plot devices that were outlandish even for the world of soap operas (the most bizarre had to be a series of grave robberies which resulted in a plague which claimed Mona Aldrich's life, and a potion which turned haughty, rich, sixty-something newcomer Adrienne Hunt into a vivacious twenty-something lady).

But viewers in 1982 much preferred *Family Feud* on ABC, so NBC pulled the plug on *The Doctors* on New Year's Eve just three months shy of its 20th anniversary. All turned out well in the end, with Mike planning to take Kit McCormick as his third wife, and Matt and Maggie deciding to remarry.

•DOG CITY
Cartoon; Color
September 26, 1992–January 28, 1995

Fox Sat. 8:30–9 a.m. (9/26/92–10/3/92)
Fox Sat. 8–8:30 a.m. (10/10/92–1/28/95)

Voices (Animated Segments):

Ace Heart	Ron White
Chief Rosie O'Gravy	Elizabeth Hanna
Eddie	Stuart Stone
Bugsy Vile	John Stocker
Frisky	James Rankin
Bruiser	Howard Jerome
Kitty	Paulina Gillis
Maddog	Stephen Ouimette

Voices (Muppet Segments):

Eliot Shag	Kevin Clash
Colleen	Fran Brill
Artie	Joey Mazzarino
Bruno	Brian Meehl
Bowser	David Rudman

Dog City combined a private-eye cartoon spoof with short sketches by the Muppets, all involving canine characters. Eliot Shag was a Muppet dog who used his pals' habits and situations as the basis for stories involving animated alter ego Ace Heart. They included neighbor boy Artie, who became Eddie the newspup, who sold the *Dog City Howler* and helped Ace solve mysteries; Eliot's girlfriend Colleen, who became Ace's competitor as sleuthing police chief O'Gravy; and construction worker Bruno and his idiot assistant Bowser, who became part of a gang that engaged Ace in recurring fights. The gang consisted of the bulldog Bugsy Vile, the "Dogfather" of Dog City, his gun moll Kitty, and his henchmen Bruiser, Maddog, and Frisky. Bridging these two worlds were conversations between Eliot and Ace about plot developments and any extra dog puns they could conceive for the tails—er, tales. Beside providing Eliot's voice, Kevin Clash also served as Muppet coordinator for the show.

DON HO SHOW, THE
Variety; Color
October 25, 1976–March 4, 1977

ABC Mon.–Fri. Noon–12:30 p.m. (10/25/76–3/4/77)

Host: *Don Ho*

Hawaiian native Don Ho made a name for himself, and promoted his homeland, in the 1960s crooning such easy-listening tunes as "Tiny Bubbles (in the Wine)" which found favor with older, non-rock-music fans. For some reason, ABC thought he would be a top attraction if he hosted a series taped at the Cinerama Reef Hotel in Honolulu with celebrity guests. They were wrong; viewers favored *The Young and the Restless* on CBS by a wide margin, and *The Don Ho Show*

became the last daily variety show seen on a network, the previous being *Art Linkletter's House Party* in 1969.

DON MCNEILL'S BREAKFAST CLUB—See *Breakfast Club, The*.

•DONAHUE
Talk; Color
1967–1996

Syndicated 60 minutes daily beginning 1969

Host: *Phil Donahue*

No host revolutionized the daytime talk show world so much as did Phil Donahue. Unlike the celebrity-oriented shows of Mike Douglas and Merv Griffin, Donahue's series concentrated on serious topics or one guest, and it was the first to have its audience members ask questions as well as the host. After *Donahue's* success, the talk field proliferated steadily, and, by the 1990s, had degenerated into a name-calling free-for-all rather than an intelligent forum for discussion. Left trailing behind this type of programming, Donahue was forced into cancellation after nearly 30 years on air.

Originally titled *The Phil Donahue Show* (it became *Donahue* by 1977), the series debuted on KYW Cleveland beginning November 7, 1967 with its basic format in place. Its first guest was a solo—atheist Madalyn Murray O'Hair. Later shows would have several guests addressing one topic, but the emphasis remained on relevant subjects no matter how many people were on stage.

Controversial guests within its first few years included actress Jane Fonda defending her visit to North Vietnam, segregation advocate Governor George Wallace of Alabama, and representatives of then-rarely-seen groups such as prostitutes and homosexuals. *Newsweek* reported that radical activist Jerry Rubin gave Donahue a difficult time in 1970, calling the host "Mr. Plastic Man" and asking him, "You got an anal problem?" Talk like that was radical for daytime television, and at first the show had rough going in syndication (just 16 markets in 1971), but through perseverance, critical acclaim, and a move to Chicago in 1974, *Donahue* gradually gained strength, with a big breakthrough coming when the all-important New York City market took the show in 1977.

One thing that might have limited his appeal was Donahue's unabashedly liberal views on many of the topics discussed, which he felt free to add. Not all viewers wanted to hear this, for as Donahue told *TV Guide* in 1972, "A lot of people call me a radical fink. They say I'm destroying the fabric of America." Also, virtually no other program on daytime television seemed to be addressing the issues Phil raised or treating its audience as an interested, intelligent entity, which some stations no doubt thought was a risky proposition.

Controversies did abound on Donahue's shows. There was the 1976 flap where an appearance by the Reverend Richard Ginder, who condoned premarital sex and masturbation and claimed that a third of all Catholic priests were gay, prompted a demand for equal time to respond by Father Leo McKenzie, head of the Delaware Valley Catholic Office for Radio and Television. Then there was a 1977 segment on natural childbirth which at least four stations rejected. In 1981 the Coalition for Better Television issued a press release stating that two out of every week's *Donahue* shows dealt with sex, but the Reverend Donald Wildmon, president of the Coalition, later apologized, although he refused to back down totally, adding that he believed that the show did have a "flagrant use of some areas of sex."

Donahue also loved putting strong opponents up against one another, such as Ralph Nader head to head with General Motors president Ed Cole or Equal Rights Amendment (ERA) opponent Phyllis Schlafly against National Organization for Women President Eleanor Smeal. But there were lighter shows to leaven the heaviness, the best remembered being with Marlo Thomas in 1977. "You are a very loving and generous man, and whoever is the woman in your life is very lucky," cooed the actress to the flustered host at the end of their taping. The two of them later married.

The show's popularity grew in the late 1970s, and Donahue began branching out into nighttime specials on NBC, regular spots on *Today* from 1979–1982, and other shows. In January 1985 the program moved to New York and began airing live daily via satellite feed from 9–10 a.m. on the East Coast. In February 1987 Donahue became the first American talk show host to tape shows in Russia, and other hard-hitting shows appeared over the next few years. Oddly, the one show which caused the most controversy was one in 1988, in which he wore a skirt during a discussion of fashion.

When his show hit its 25th year on the air, Donahue mounted a two-hour nighttime anniversary special on NBC November 16, 1992, recounting favorite moments and guests seen over the years. Many of his rival talk show hosts appeared to salute him, including Oprah Winfrey, Sally Jesse Raphael, and Joan Rivers. Given that and his well-received interviews with the 1992 presidential candidates, it looked as if his show would run until the day Phil died.

But as he continued his thoughtful presentation of issues, tackier, trashier entries like *Jerry Springer* and *Jenny Jones* began to pass him in the ratings, and in 1995 the show suffered a near-fatal blow: New York City, where he still did the show, dropped him. It thus came as no surprise when he announced a few months later that he was ending his reign. Donahue taped his last show in May 1996 with his production staff as guests. His legacy remains, though, and it is doubtful that any of the hosts now currently popular will establish as respected and envied a long run (it lasted almost three decades) as Donahue did.

DOTTO

Game; B&W
January 6, 1958–August 15, 1958
CBS Mon.–Fri. 11:30 a.m.–Noon (1/6/58–8/15/58)
Host: *Jack Narz*

On *Dotto* two contestants vied to be first to identify a line drawing of a celebrity's face. Jack Narz stood on a podium between the players, while each had their own electronic screen hiding the celebrity face. Narz asked a question worth 5, 8, or 10 dots, depending on its difficulty, and a correct response by a player connected the lines between that number of dots for that player's screen. The lines and up to three cryptic clues (the first given after 25 dots were connected) shown individually helped players in identifying the star, and the first to do so won $20 for each unconnected dot on his or her screen. There also was a puzzle for home viewers to play via mail, and the show boasted of receiving nearly 1.2 million postcards in a single day.

Dotto was doing fine as a daytime entry, even hitting #1 in February 1958, when a potential contestant named Edward Hilgemeier Jr. notified the Attorney General's Office of New York that he had found a player's notebook containing answers to questions which she was asked on the show. When Hilgemeier complained to legal representatives despite having been given $1,500 by the show to keep quiet, he started a chain reaction that affected TV's big-money game shows. The fallout included the cancellation of *Dotto* and its nighttime version, which had been running on NBC from July 1–August 12, 1958.

DOUBLE DARE

Game; Color
December 13, 1976–April 29, 1977
CBS Mon.–Fri. 11–11:30 a.m. (12/13/76–4/29/77)
Host: *Alex Trebek*

Having the right answer first on *Double Dare* meant that you won $50 and could challenge your opponent, locked in a soundproof room, to receive another clue for a mystery topic which was worth $50 more if it stumped your competitor. If he or she guessed correctly, however, the competitor won $100. To sweeten the pot, the show offered contestants the right to "double dare" an opponent who had missed the $50 clue by showing another clue and winning another $100 if the double-dared contestant failed (if the competitor did guess correctly, he or she won $200). The first to win $500 faced "the Spoilers," three Ph.D.s whom the winner had to give 5 out of 10 preselected clues about a mystery topic. Failure by any of the Ph.D.s to guess the topic won the bonus.

DOUBLE EXPOSURE

Game; B&W
March 13, 1961–September 29, 1961
CBS Mon.–Fri. 11–11:30 a.m. (3/13/61–9/29/61)
Host: *Steve Dunne*

Two contestants had their own 12-piece puzzle under which lay a celebrity's picture. In order to pick up a piece, a player spun a wheel with amounts ranging from $10 to $60 and added that figure to his or her tally while calling out the number of a piece to remove (the face under each puzzle was the same, but the numbering system was not). That piece also had a dollar amount or prize under it, which was added to the bank. A player who tallied $100 or more had to identify the person from what was showing under the pieces he or she had already removed or risk losing the game by giving the other contestant a chance for a free guess.

DOUBLE OR NOTHING
Game; B&W
October 6, 1952–July 2, 1954

CBS Mon./Wed./Fri. 2–2:30 p.m. (10/6/52–7/2/54)
CBS Tue./Thu. 2–2:30 p.m. (7/6/54–7/2/54)

Host: *Bert Parks*

Announcer/Commercial Spokesman: *Bob Williams*

Double or Nothing began on radio, where it ran from 1940–47 on Mutual, CBS in 1947, and then NBC for the rest of its run until 1952. Walter Compton, John Reed King, Todd Russell, and Walter O'Keefe served as hosts. On television it had five contestants compete in being the first with three correct answers to play for a jackpot worth, appropriately, double or nothing. If the answer on the jackpot question was correct, the contestant won $140.

The series also ran on NBC Fridays at 9:30 p.m. from June 5–July 3, 1953. On daytime it alternated daily with *Everywhere I Go* in 1952, *Freedom Rings* and *I'll Buy That* in 1953, and *The Robert Q. Lewis Show* in 1954.

DOUBLE PLAY WITH DUROCHER AND DAY—See *Laraine Day Show, The.*

•DOUBLE TALK
Game; Color
August 18, 1986–December 19, 1986

ABC Mon.–Fri. 11:30 a.m.–Noon (8/18/86–12/19/86)

Host: *Henry Polic II*

Double Talk had two pairs, each with a celebrity and a contestant, compete in a contest involving synonyms. Each pair had one partner decipher the first part of the phrase read by the host and the other the second part. For example, to decode "Chew the Pellet" correctly, one partner had to say "Bite . . ." and the other say ". . . the Bullet." Each correct answer allowed the pair to continue to try to solve three other hidden phrases on the board for a prize of $1,000 (few teams won the $1,000, as one of the phrases was always particularly obscure). Teams alternated through four boards, and the one with the highest score at the end (10 points per correct answer in the first three rounds, then 20 points in the final round) got to play a bonus. In the bonus game, one partner saw only a pair of initials while the other gave an incomplete sentence serving as a clue to what the letters stood for. The first partner had to solve 10 phrases hidden by initials to claim $10,000.

On September 29, 1986, the series was retitled *Celebrity Double Talk.* Host Henry Polic II also acted on the ABC prime-time sitcom *Webster* when this series aired, and, ironically, reruns of that show assumed the time slot when *Double Talk* went off the air.

DOUBLE UP
Game; Color
September 5, 1992–October 17, 1992

NBC Sat. Noon–12:30 p.m. (9/5/92–10/17/92)

Host: *J. D. Roth*

Ex-*Fox Fun House* host J. D. Roth got another, even less successful shot at Saturday morning stardom with this teen-oriented contest where a pair of siblings (brother and sister) served as matchmakers to each other. Each of them got to quiz three potential dates and then try to chose the same one the audience picked in order to win prizes that winners on the chintzy *Dating Game* could only dream of, like limousine service, $500 in spending money, and rock concert tickets. And keeping it somewhat respectable, the siblings went on a double date if both made matches.

DOUGH RE MI
Game; B&W
February 29, 1958–December 30, 1960

NBC Mon.–Fri. 10–10:30 a.m. (2/29/58–12/30/60)

Host: *Gene Rayburn*

Music: *The Paul Taubman Orchestra*

A trio of players tried to be the first to identify a tune after hearing three notes. Past that point, each could buy another note for $200 in an attempt to gain more money. A player who failed after hearing the fourth note could challenge one of the other contestants to guess. The person with the correct answer won the amount bid. There were three rounds of songs worth at least $100, $200, and finally $400 per identification.

Toward the end of the show's run, three celebrities played for home viewers. And in an unusual switch, NBC went from doing the show on tape to live from New York by the summer of 1960.

DRAGON'S LAIR
Cartoon; Color
September 8, 1984–April 20, 1985

ABC Sat. 10–10:30 a.m. (9/8/84–4/20/85)

Voices:

Dirk the Daring	*Bob Sarlatte*
Princess Daphne	*Ellen Gerstell*
King Ethelred	*Fred Travalena*
Cinge the Dragon	*Arthur Burghardt*
Sir Timothy	*Michael Mish*
Bertram	*Peter Cullen*
Storyteller	*Clive Revill*

Based on the video game of the same name, *Dragon's Lair* featured the somewhat befuddled-looking Dirk the Daring, who with his horse Bertram (also known as Bert) served under King Ethelred. Dirk's main duty each week was to save Princess Daphne from assorted baddies and the vicious Cinge the Dragon. ABC aired this an hour ahead of the similarly themed *Dungeons and Dragons* on CBS, but it lasted only one season.

DRAK PACK
Cartoon; Color
September 6, 1980–September 5, 1981

CBS Sat. 11:30 a.m.–Noon (9/6/80–2/28/81)
CBS Sat. 12:30–1 p.m. (3/7/81–9/5/81)

Voices:

Drak Jr.	*Jerry Dexter*
Frankie/Howler	*Bill Callaway*
Dracula	*Alan Oppenheimer*
Dr. Dred	*Hans Conried*
Vampira	*Julie McWhirter*
Mummy Man	*Chuck McCann*
Toad/Fly	*Don Messick*

In 1976 NBC gave Saturday morning viewers monsters fighting for the forces of good in the sitcom *The Monster Squad*. Four years later CBS gave them the same thing, only with the teenage offspring of the original monsters. Drak Jr., Frankie, and Howler, the latter related to the Werewolf, used their "Drak Wack" power, made by holding their right hands together and saying "Wacko," to become crime fighters serving under the direction of Dracula, Drak Jr.'s great-grandfather. The leader of their main adversary, O.G.R.E. (Organization of Generally Rotten Endeavors), was Dr. Dred. Headquarted on Skull Island, O.G.R.E. members Vampira, Mummy Man, Toad, and Fly all tried fruitlessly to stop the Drak Pack.

DRAW WITH ME—See *You Are an Artist.*

DRAWING POWER
Children's; Color
October 11, 1980–May 16, 1981

NBC Sat. 12:30–1 p.m. (10/11/80–5/16/81)

Regulars: *Bob Kaliban (as Pop), Kari Page, Lenny Schultz*

This feature-packed offering could not disguise the fact that its supposed "entertainment" of live action and cartoons was actually educational matter for younger viewers. Among its features, "Superperson U." had a superhero enact a moral on the day's subject; "Bus Stop" highlighted people with common elements; "What Do You Do, Dad/Mom?" explored careers; "The Book Report" had character Dewey Decimal work with other characters from children's novels; "Professor Rutabaga" talked about health and nutrition; "It's a Wacky World" discussed animals; and "Turkey of the Week" awarded a Golden Gobbler to kids with bad habits.

DREAM GIRL OF '67
Game; B&W and Color
December 19, 1966–December 29, 1967

ABC Mon.–Fri. 2:30–2:55 a.m. (12/19/66–12/29/67)

Host: *Dick Stewart (12/19/66–6/23/67), Wink Martindale (6/26/67–9/67), Paul Peterson (9/67–12/67)*

The concept of having a year-long beauty contest may appall some, but that's what Chuck Barris Productions offered in this game show which went through three hosts in nine months. A quartet of ladies competed daily in evening gown, questioning, and personality contests—just like the festivities in the long-running Miss America pageant (an annual TV special since 1954). The Monday through Thursday winners competed on Friday to become "Dream Girl of the Week," and those making it to that stage returned in December 1967 to become the first "Dream Girl of '67." Doing the judging and asking contestants questions were three guest male celebrities, who in the first week were Troy Donahue, Ross Martin, and future host Paul Peterson.

An interesting footnote is that Candy Howard, a winner on the show, was also a contestant on the first *Dating Game*, but she had to withdraw from competition to get married to the man she met on *The Dating Game*.

•DREAM HOUSE
Game; Color
April 1, 1968–June 29, 1984

ABC Mon.–Fri. 1–1:30 p.m. (4/1/68–1/2/70)
NBC Mon.–Fri. 11:30 a.m.–Noon (4/4/83–6/29/84)

Regulars: *Mike Darrow (1968–70), Bob Eubanks (1983–84), Debbie Bartlett (1983–84)*

The first incarnation of *Dream House* debuted on ABC Wednesdays 8:30–9 p.m. on March 27, 1968, five days before the first daytime installment. Both shows had Mike Darrow ask two competing newlywed couples general-interest questions for points, and after several rounds the couple with the most points earned a room. In the daytime version, a couple had to win seven "rooms" to have the show buy them their "dream house." (For the nighttime version, which ran until September 19, 1968, only four rooms were needed.)

The 1968–70 contestants chose from styles ranging from French colonial homes to ranches. Couples received a $40,000 home plus $7,000 to purchase land for it. The income taxes on this investment or the need to borrow more money to cover costs scared many winners into taking a cash payoff over the house. For those who did pursue a home, the action was anything but a dream. As of June 1969, 24 houses had been won on the game, but only five were being built and none was complete.

Despite this bad publicity and so-so ratings, NBC decided to revise the property in 1983, with Bob Eubanks as host and Debbie Bartlett as his newly added assistant-model. Homes now were furnished by the U.S. Home

Mike Darrow shows a couple a model of the home they could win in the 1968–70 version of Dream House.

Company and cost more than twice what those on the earlier show had cost. Here couples who won a room after several rounds of questioning could bypass the seven-room win rule by matching with the code on a computer the right number on each row of four rows with four numbers each. Each day a couple won, some numbers would be removed to increase their chances of winning, with the system set up so that a couple automatically won the house if they were victorious for six days.

DROIDS: THE ADVENTURES OF R2D2 AND C3PO
Cartoon; Color
September 7, 1985–February 22, 1986

ABC Sat. 9:30–10 a.m. (9/7/85–10/26/85)
ABC Sat. 10–10:30 a.m. (11/2/85–2/22/86)

Voices:

C3PO	Graham Haley
Electronic sounds	Anthony Daniels

R2D2 (the bright white cylinder resembling a fancy trash can and communicating via an assortment of burps and chirps) and C3PO (the gilded, pragmatic humanoid robot with a nervous, effeminate speaking style) made an impact as comic relief on the *Star Wars* movie trilogy (the first film was released in 1977, the third in 1983), and belatedly got a chance to star on their own in this series of continuing adventures. The program combined with *The Ewoks* (q.v.) in March 1986, where it stayed till the end of the season.

DROOPY, MASTER DETECTIVE
Cartoon; Color
October 2, 1993–January 1, 1994

Fox Sat. 11:30 a.m.–Noon (10/2/93)
Fox Sat. 9–9:30 a.m. (10/9/93–10/30/93)
Fox Sat. 8:30–9 a.m. (11/6/93–1/1/94)

Officially *Droopy, Master Detective* was a spinoff of *Tom and Jerry Kids*, but the lead character went back to several MGM cartoon theatrical shorts of the 1940s. A miniature basset hound with a voice that sounded like someone with a cold inhaling helium, Droopy outwitted his physically domineering challengers with miles of guile. Here he and his similar son Dripple played private eyes in their weekly adventures, which were interspersed with the escapades of Screwball Squirrel. "Screwy" also was a 1940s MGM cartoon character, and here he fought public park attendant Dweeble and his Grappley.

•DUDLEY DO-RIGHT SHOW, THE

Cartoon; Color

April 27, 1969–September 6, 1970

ABC Sun. 9:30–10 a.m. (4/27/69–9/6/70)

Voices:

Dudley Do-Right	Bill Scott
Nell Fenwick	June Foray
Snidely Whiplash	Hans Conreid
Inspector Ray Fenwick/Narrator	Paul Frees

With a jutting jaw, wavy blond hair, and a tight, high, modulated voice, Dudley Do-Right was one Canadian Mountie who did not fit the mold. Nevertheless, he served faithfully under Inspector Fenwick, but found that the task he most often faced was freeing the latter's pigtailed daughter Nell from the clutches of menacing Snidely ("Heh heh!") Whiplash. Alas, although Dudley unfailingly accomplished this duty each show, Nell had eyes only for Dudley's hat- and suit-wearing steed Horse. The result was a delicious sendup of both *Perils of Pauline* and Canadian Mountie movies.

Bill Scott helped create as well as voice the lead character, who first appeared as a segment on *The Bullwinkle Show* in 1961. These cartoons were repeats of those shows, and included some supporting components from *Bullwinkle* as well. When it went off in 1970, Dudley and company went back to appearing in *Bullwinkle* reruns as well as this series, which had its repeats syndicated under the title *Dudley Do-Right and His Friends*.

DUKES, THE

Cartoon; Color

February 5, 1983–November 5, 1983

CBS Sat. 10:30–11 a.m. (2/5/83–9/10/83)

CBS Sat. 10–10:30 a.m. (9/17/83–11/5/83)

Voices:

Bo Duke	John Schneider
Luke Duke	Tom Wopat
Boss Hogg	Sorrell Booke
Sheriff Rosco P. Coltrane	James Best
Vance Duke	Christopher Mayer
Daisy Duke	Catherine Bach
Uncle Jesse	Denver Pyle
Flash/Smokey/General Lee	Frank Welker

The hugely popular, hugely moronic CBS Friday night series *The Dukes of Hazzard* had been a top hit since its debut on January 26, 1979, especially with children, so it was not too surprising that CBS took a chance with an animated version. Like the original, it featured Bo and Luke Duke, two brothers in the fictional Hazzard County of the Southeast, who made a mockery of top politico Boss Hogg's efforts to dominate various enterprises in the county via illegal means. Sheriff Coltrane was his bumbling servant who constantly chased the Dukes unsuccessfully as they fled in their revved-up "General Lee," a red 1969 Dodge

Charger. The main difference between the live-action show and the cartoon was that the cartoon chases took place all over the world, with Coltrane and the Dukes spinning their wheels across Scotland, Morocco, Spain, Vienna, and other continental locales.

Other characters in the show were the Dukes' cousin Daisy, who wore some rather provocative skimpy outfits; their sage Uncle Jesse; and Vance Duke, another cousin who was a holdover from the period in the 1982–83 nighttime season when John Schneider and Tom Wopat left the show in a salary dispute and were replaced with similar-looking actors as their relatives until their return late that season (Vance was the Bo equivalent). In fact, *The Dukes* was to debut in the fall of 1982, but the leads' dispute pushed back its premiere. With the exception of Frank Welker, who also voiced the Duke boys' pet dog Flash, cast members from the nighttime show provided all the voiceovers.

DUMB AND DUMBER

Cartoon; Color

October 28, 1995–February 24, 1996

ABC Sat. 9–9:30 a.m. (10/28/95–2/24/96)

This short-lived cartoon adapted comedian Jim Carrey's hit 1995 movie of the same name, albeit without the abundant scatalogical humor. It told of the comic misadventures of the moronic pair Lloyd (Carrey's character) and Harry (Jeff Daniels in the film), who traveled to assorted spots across America in a vehicle with a sheepdog. For more successful adaptations of Carrey's films (both on CBS), see *Ace Ventura Pet Detective* and *The Mask.*

•DUNGEONS & DRAGONS

Cartoon; Color

September 17, 1983–June 2, 1990

CBS Sat. 9:30–10 a.m. (9/17/83–9/8/84)

CBS Sat. 11–11:30 a.m. (9/15/84–10/27/84)

CBS Sat. 9:30–10 a.m. (11/3/84–9/7/85)

CBS Sat. 11:30 a.m.–Noon (9/14/85–8/30/86)

CBS Sat. 11–11:30 a.m. (6/20/87–9/5/87)

CBS Sat. 11:30 a.m.–Noon (1/6/90–6/2/90)

Voices:

Hank	Willie Aames
Eric	Donny Most
Presto	Adam Rich
Sheila	Katie Leigh
Diana	Tony Gayle Smith
Bobby	Ted Field III
Dungeon Master	Sidney Miller
Venger	Peter Cullen
Uni	Frank Welker

A sextet of teenagers riding a park attraction called Dungeons & Dragons found themselves transported into a medieval fantasy world in which they received new identities by the monklike Dungeon Master, "the protector of all that is good," to fight winged humanoid Venger, "the ultimate source of evil." Hank became an archer, Presto a magician, Diana an acrobat, Sheila a girl with a cloak that allowed her to become invisible, and Sheila's younger brother Bobby, a boy with a club. As for Eric, he became a cavalier both in person and in attitude, often endangering the group with his stubbornness. Uni was the kids' white unicorn, one of many incredible animals seen on the show.

Midway during the show's run in 1985, a group called the National Coalition on Television Violence, based in Champaign, Illinois, named this program the most violent show on television, claiming that it had some 65 acts of violence per hour. The coalition's chairman, Dr. Thomas Radecki of the University of Illinois, went further in telling *Variety* that the board game on which the series was based, which began in 1974, had played a part in 45 suicides and murders at that time. Anyone who asked for the proof of that assertion probably laughed off the study's data (as CBS apparently did, airing another season of new shows before repeating it in the summer of 1987 and in 1990). It did nothing for the coalition's credibility when the same study claimed that the cartoon tying *Dungeons & Dragons* for mind-altering violence was—*The Bugs Bunny Show!*

DYNAMIC DUOS
Sports; Color
January 22, 1978–February 26, 1978

NBC Sun. 2–2:30 p.m. (1/22/78–2/26/78)

Host: *John Brodie*

Two-man teams of athletes from the same sport competed in a regular game of bowling, of all things, in this short-lived entry. The debut had pro baseball's Johnny Bench and Tom Seaver take on the NFL's Dick Butkus and Ray Nitschke.

•DYNOMUTT, DOG WONDER
Cartoon; Color
June 3, 1978–September 2, 1978

ABC Sat. Noon–12:30 p.m. (6/3/78–7/1/78)
ABC Sat. 8–8:30 a.m. (7/8/78–9/2/78)

Voices:

The Blue Falcon (Bradley Crown)	Gary Owens
Dynomutt	Frank Welker
The Mayor	Larry McCormick

ABC took repeats of the latter section of *The Scooby-Doo/Dynomutt Show* from 1976–77 to use as a 1978 summer series (for information about the former, see *Scooby-Doo*). The Blue Falcon, the alias for millionaire Bradley Crown, spoke with a pompous, modulated voice and piloted an airplane, perhaps reminding older viewers of the lead character in *Space Ghost*, who had a similar voice and occupation. The Blue Falcon's partner in fighting crime in Big City was

Dynomutt, a numbskull of a dog who just happened to be a robot. The mechanical nature of Dynomutt was a blessing and a curse, as some of his special talents backfired on him and the Falcon in their crime-fighting adventures, while others saved his life (that is, would have saved his life if Dynomutt had been alive). The duo reported to the mayor, who somehow kept faith in them despite Dynomutt's obvious clumsiness.

Following this run, Dynomutt returned in repeats again in 1980 (see *Godzilla*).

EARLY TODAY
News/Information; Color
July 5, 1982–July 29, 1983

NBC Mon.–Fri. 6–7 a.m. (7/5/82–7/29/83)

Regulars: *Bryant Gumbel, Jane Pauley, Willard Scott*

More than three decades after pioneering early morning network TV programming with *Today*, NBC added a separate hour in front of the daily offering using the regulars of the parent show. The format was similar to *Today*, with the show being designed so affiliates could use only a half hour of it if desired. After a year, NBC tried a different program in the slot (see *NBC News at Sunrise*).

From left, Jane Pauley, Willard Scott, and Bryant Gumbel of Early Today, *who seem somewhat pensive but may be just tired, as this show meant they had to wake up an hour earlier.*

•EARTHWORM JIM
Cartoon; Color
September 9, 1995–

The WB Sat. or Sun. 10:30–11 a.m. (9/9/95–)

Voice:

Earthworm Jim	*Dan Castellaneta*

Superhero Earthworm Jim acted as the guardian of goodness along with his companion Peter Puppy on this offbeat animated action comedy. Wearing an indestructible super suit which fell from the sky one day and gave him his powers, and sporting a ray gun which also converted into a hovercraft, Jim staved off such recurring nasties as Queen Slug-for-a-Butt and Psy-Crow in this effort which owed more than a little inspiration to *The Tick* (q.v.). The series was based on a video game.

ED GRIMLEY—See Completely Mental Misadventures of Ed Grimley, The.

EDDIE ALBERT SHOW, THE
Variety; B&W
March 2, 1953–May 8, 1953

CBS Mon.–Fri. 3:30–4 p.m. (3/2/53–5/8/53)

Regulars: *Eddie Albert, Ellen Hanley, the Norman Paris Trio*

Frequent TV actor Eddie Albert seemed to want to become another Art Linkletter in this short-lived daytime show. Eddie did a monologue, interviewed guests, and sang, joined by vocalist Ellen Hanley and the Norman Paris Trio. Albert reappeared as a variety host two months after the daytime show was canceled, in the NBC nighttime series *Nothing But the Best* (July 7–September 13, 1953).

•EDGE OF NIGHT, THE
Soap Opera; B&W and Color
April 2, 1956–December 28, 1984

CBS Mon.–Fri. 4:30–5 p.m. (4/2/56–6/28/63)
CBS Mon.–Fri. 3:30–4 p.m. (7/1/63–9/1/72)
CBS Mon.–Fri. 2:30–3 p.m. (9/4/72–11/28/75)
ABC Mon.–Fri. 4–4:30 p.m. (12/1/75–12/28/84)

Cast:

Mike Karr (1956–61)	*John Larkin*
Mike Karr (1962–71)	*Laurence Hugo*
Mike Karr (1971–84)	*Forrest Compton*
Sara Lane Karr (1956–61)	*Teal Ames*
Jack Lane (1956–60)	*Don Hastings*
Uncle Harry Lane (1956–59)	*Lauren Gilbert*
Cora Lane (1956–59)	*Sara Burton*
Winston Grimsley (1956–73)	*Walter Greaza*
Mattie Lane Grimsley (1956)	*Betty Garde*
Mattie Lane Grimsley (1956–66)	*Peggy Allenby*
Mattie Lane Grimsley (1969–71)	*Katherine Meskill*
Louise Grimsley Capice (1956–60)	*Lisa Howard*
Louise Grimsley Capice (1960–70)	*Mary K. Wells*
Phil Capice (1956–57)	*Robert Webber*
Phil Capice (1957)	*Earl Hammond*
Phil Capice (1961–69)	*Ray MacDonnell*
Det. Willie Bryan (1956–61)	*Ed Holmes*
Martin Spode (at least 1956)	*Eric Dressler*
Martin Spode (at least 1957)	*Henderson Forsythe*
Hester Spode (1956–58)	*Helen Shields*
Grace O'Keefe (Police Department secretary) (1956)	*Maxine Stuart*
Detective Sergeant Charlie Brooks (1956)	*Ian Martin*
Walt Johnson (1956)	*Mark Rydell*
Rose LaTour (1956)	*Henrietta Moore*
Betty Jean Battle Lane (c. 1957–58)	*Mary Moor*
Gail Armstrong (1958–59)	*Millette Alexander*
Dr. Hugh Campbell (1958–59)	*Wesley Addy*
D.A. Peter Dalton (1958 at least)	*George Petrie*
Sybil Gordon (c. 1958)	*Doris Belack*
Bill Marceau (1959–79)	*Mandel Kramer*
Dick Appleman (1959)	*Michael Strong*
Mary Appleman (1959)	*Joan Copeland*
Big Frankie Dubeck (1960)	*Michael Conrad*
Laurie Ann Karr (1961)	*Victoria Larkin*
Laurie Ann Karr (196?)	*Kathleen Bracken*
Laurie Ann Karr (1967–68)	*Kathy Cody*
Laurie Ann Karr (1968–73)	*Emily Prager*
Laurie Ann Karr (1973–75)	*Jeanne Ruskin*
Laurie Ann Karr (1975–77, 1984)	*Linda Cook*
Judy Marceau (1961–63)	*Joan Harvey*
Ed Gibson (1961–63)	*Larry Hagman*
Sara Capice (1961–63)	*Mary Breen*
Sara Capice (1968–70)	*Christopher Norris*
Sally Smith (1961)/Katherine Lovell (1967–68)	*Mary Fickett*
Victor Carlson (at least 1961)	*Byron Sanders*
Nancy Pollack Karr (1962–84)	*Ann Flood*
Rose Pollock (1962–63)	*Ruth Matteson*
Rose Pollock (1964)	*Frances Reid*
Rose Pollock (1965–68)	*Kay Campbell*
Rose Pollock (1973–79)	*Virginia Kaye*
Joe Pollock (1962–71)	*John Gibson*
Roy Cameron (1965–66)/Joe Pollock (1973–79)	*Allen Nourse*
Cookie Pollock (1962)	*June Carter*
Cookie Pollock (1962–72)	*Fran Sharon*
Lee Pollock (1962–64)	*Ronnie Welch*
Lee Pollock (1964)	*Sam Groom*
Lee Pollock (1965–67)	*Tony Roberts*
Austin Johnson (1962–63)	*Lawrence Weber*
Constance Johnson (1962–63)	*Elizabeth Lawrence*
Toby Marshall (1962–63)	*Rita Lloyd*
Lyn Wilkins Warren (1962–63)	*Gillian Spencer*
Beth Anderson Barnes (1963–67)	*Nancy Pinkerton*
John Paul Anderson (1963)/Steve Prentiss (1967–68)	*Conard Fowkes*

Carol Kramer (1963)
Emory Warren (1963)
Martha Marceau (1964–75)
Gerry McGrath Pollock (1964)
Gerry McGrath Pollock (1964–65)
Gerry McGrath Pollock (1966)
Elizabeth McGrath (1964–66)
Elizabeth McGrath (1967)
John Barnes (1964–65)
Eve Morris (1964–65)
Evelyn Dark (at least 1964)
Phoebe Smith (1965–67)
Phoebe Smith (late 1960s)
Phoebe Smith (late 1960s)
Phoebe Smith (1973–76)
Malcolm Thomas (c. 1965)
Andre Lazar (1965–66)
Tony Wyatt (1965–66)
Abby Cameron (1965–66)
Orin Hillyer (1966–68,
    1972–73)
Liz Hillyer (1966–74)
Laura Hillyer (1966)/Julie
    Jamison (1967–68)
Rick Oliver (1966)
David Gideon (1966–67)
Adam Drake (1967–77)
Harry Constable (1967–68)
Nicole Travis (1968–74,
    1975–77)
Nicole Travis (1978–81)
Nicole Travis (1981–83)
Ben Travis (1968–69)
Ben Travis (1974)
Ron Christopher (c. 1968–72)
Vic Lamont (1969–75)
Dr. Jim Fields (1969–74)
Susan Forbes (1969–70)
Stephanie Martin (1969–70)
Pamela Stewart (1969–70)
Duane Stewart (1970)
Geraldine Whitney (1970–71,
    1973–84)
Tiffany Whitney (1970–71,
    1973–76)
Gordon Whitney (1970–71)
Sen. Colin Whitney (1970–71)
Keith Whitney (1970–71)
Trudy the maid (1970–78)
John the butler (1970–78)
Kevin Jamison (1972–75)
Kevin Jamison (1975–78)
Elly Jo Jamison (1972–73)
Lt. Luke Chandler (1973–78)
Johnny Dallas (1973–77)
Danny Micelli (1973–77)

Elizabeth Hubbard
Philip Abbott
Teri Keane
Penny Fuller
Joanna Miles
Millee Taggart
Ludi Claire
Nancy Coleman
Barry Newman
Constance Ford
Leslie Woods
Heidi Vaughn
Renne Jarrett
Laurie Kennedy
Johanna Leister
Edward Kemmer
Val Dufour
Antony Ponzini
Margaret DePriest

Lester Rawlins
Alberta Grant

Millette Alexander
Keith Charles
John Cullum
Donald May
Dolph Sweet

Maeve McGuire
Jayne Bentzen
Lisa Sloan
William Prince
Cec Linder
Burt Douglas
Ted Tinling
Alan Feinstein
Bibi Besch
Alice Hirson
Irene Dailey
Richard Clarke

Lois Kibbee

Lucy Martin
Alan Gifford
Anthony Call
Bruce Martin
Mary Hayden
George Hall
Richard Shoberg
John Driver
Dorothy Lyman
Herb Davis
John LaGoia
Lou Criscuolo

Taffy Simms (1973–74)
Babs Micelli (1973–74)
Tracy Dallas (1974–77)
Brandy Henderson (1974–76)
Kaye Reynolds (c. 1974–75)
Walter Le Page (c. 1974–75)
Morlock Sevingy (c. 1974–75)
Noel Douglas (c. 1975)
Dr. Clay Jordan (c. 1975)
Draper Scott (1975–81)
Gilbert Darcy/Claude Revenant
    (c. 1975–76)
Serena/Josie Faraday (1975–76)
Timmy Faraday (1975–76)
Mark Faraday (1975)
Raven Alexander (1976–77)
Raven Alexander (1977–84)
Nadine Alexander (1976–77,
    1980)
Deborah Saxon (1976–81)
Steve Guthrie (1976–80)
Tony Saxon (1976–80)
Ansel Scott (1976–77)
Beau Richardson (1976–77)
Dr. Miles Cavanaugh (1977–84)
April Cavanaugh (1977–81)
Denise Cavanaugh (1977–78)
Dr. Gus Norwood (1977–78)
Logan Swift (1977–81)
Logan Swift (1984)
Cliff Nelson (1978–84)
Calvin Stoner (1978–84)
Star Stoner (1978–82)
Margo Huntington (1978–80)
"Rev." Eliot Dorn (1978–80)
Winter Austen (1978–79)
Winter Austen (1979)
Derek Mallory (1979–84)
Nola Madison/Martha Cory
    (1979–80)
Owen Madison (1979–80)
Brian Madison (1979–80)
Paige Madison (1979–80)
Schyler Whitney (1980–84)
Jody Travis (1980–83)
Jody Travis (1983–84)
Gavin Wylie (1980–83)
Kelly McGrath (1980)
Kelly McGrath (1980–82)
Martine Duval (1980–81)
Emily Michaels (1980–81)
Molly Sherwood (1980)
Molly Sherwood (1980–81)
Mitzi Martin (1981–84)
Spencer Varney (1981–83)
Gunther Wagner (1981–83)

Mari Gorman
Leslie Ray
Pat Conwell
Dixie Carter
Elizabeth Farley
William Post, Jr.
Jay Gregory
Dick Latessa
Niles McMaster
Tony Craig

Scott McKay
Louise Shaffer
Doug McKeon
Bernie McInerney
Juanin Clay
Sharon Gabet

Dorothy Stinnette
Frances Fisher
Denny Albee
Louis Turenne
Patrick Hogan
David Gale
Joel Crothers
Terry Davis
Holland Taylor
Wyman Pendleton
Joe Lambie
Tom Tammi
Ernest Townsend
Irving Lee
Yahee
Ann Williams
Lee Godart
Lori Cardille
Stephanie Braxton
Dennis Parker

Kim Hunter
Bruce Gray
Stephen McNaughton
Margaret Colin
Larkin Malloy
Lori Loughlin
Karrie Emerson
Mark Arnold
Joey Alan Phipps
Allen Fawcett
Sonia Petrovna
Margo McKenna
Jane Hoffman
Laurinda Barrett
Lela Ivey
Richard Borg
David Froman

Damian Tyler (1981–83)	Christopher Jarrett
Valerie Bryson (1981–83)	Leah Ayres
Jinx Avery Mallory (1981)	Kate Capshaw
Jinx Avery Mallory (1981–82)	Susan MacDonald
Nora Fulton (1981–82)	Catherine Bruno
Jim Diedrickson (1981–82)	David Allen Brooks
Smiley Wilson (1981–82)	Frank Gorshin
Hector Wilson (1981–82)	John Rensenhouse
Johnny Gentry (1981–82)	Craig Augustine
Beth Bryson (1981)	Doris Belack
Dr. Kenneth Bryson (1981)	James Hawthorne
Didi Bannister (1982–84)	Mariann Aalda
Poppy Johnson (1982–83)	Karen Needle
David Cameron (1982–83)	Norman Parker
Ian Devereaux (1982–83)	Alan Coates
Dwight Endicott (1982)	Alfred Drake
John "Preacher" Emerson	
(1983–84)	Charles Flohe
Del Emerson (1983–84)	Robert Gerringer
Louis Van Dine (1983–84)	Jerry Zaks
Alicia Van Dine (1983–84)	Chris Weatherfield
Shelley Franklyn (1983–84)	Pamela Shoemaker
Detective Chris Egan (1983–84)	Jennifer Taylor
Dr. Beth Corell (1983–84)	Sandy Faison
Camilla Devereaux (1983)	Mary Layne
Robbie Hamlin (1983)	Willie Aames
Moe Everhardt (1983)	Dick Cavett
Liz Corell (1984)	Marcia Cross
Jeremy Rhodes (1984)	Michael Conforti
Mark Hamilton (1984)	Christopher Holder
Dr. Juliana Stanhower (1984)	Amanda Blake

Had it been up to the network, there would have been a *Perry Mason* a year before the debut of the well-known nighttime lawyer series of that name. Erle Stanley Gardner, the author of a series of books about fictional attorney Perry Mason, had approved a CBS radio series from 1943–55 based on his creation. But when Procter & Gamble wanted to make it a daily 30-minute series (the first soap opera that length along with *As the World Turns,* which debuted the same day), Gardner refused permission. Undaunted, the head writer of the radio series Irving Vendig refashioned the show slightly and hired its star John Larkin to come up with *The Edge of Night.*

Some similarities to Gardner's approach could be seen from the start. Monticello (a fictional city) assistant district attorney Mike Karr's gung-ho, unorthodox approach to catching crooks in ways that sometimes skirted illegality mirrored the manner of Mason. But there were differences too, such as more action than the nighttime show, much of it realistically set. For example, *Variety* reviewed a December 1956 episode in which two policemen were clobbered and one lieutenant was shot. And remember, this was a *live* show until 1975.

Another difference was that Mike's sweetheart Sara Lane had a more overt romantic involvement with her boss than

Della Street did. Sara also had a heck of a vicious family, with her brother Jack being pressured to join the illicit activities of their Uncle Harry. Harry's wife Cora objected to her husband's work, while his equally conniving secretary tried to drive her insane. Jack eventually went straight and married Betty Jean Battle in 1958, by which time Mike and Sara were wed as well.

Sara felt maternal instincts then for Bebe Spode (played by several actresses), the daughter of the troubled Martin and Hester Spode. Martin, a ne'er-do-well from the beginning, went to jail from 1956–57 and later was murdered, while good-hearted Hester wound up in a sanitarium. Sara and Mike did not adopt Bebe, but had a beautiful daughter named Laurie Ann instead. Alas, their joy with her was to be short-lived.

On February 17, 1961, a bus hit Sara as she tried to save her 2-year-old daughter, who had wandered out into the street. Sara died on February 22, 1961. The events prompted a huge outcry—a flood of calls to the network offices and at least 2,500 protest letters in one week. (One writer tried to intimidate the sponsor by sending a missive containing the heart-breaking information that she "had baked a Pet-Ritz cherry pie, but . . . could hardly eat it for supper after that terrible episode.") Due to the response, the day after her "death," actress Teal Ames faced the camera and said she was fine in real life but had left the show for other career options.

Mike's private life may have had its troubles, but his work life was downright dangerous. Framed by district attorney Peter Dalton in the spring of 1958, he left his post as assistant D.A. in Monticello, but continued to fight crime. Winston Grimsley, a prominent citizen who married Sara's mother Mattie, hired Mike privately to expose underworld boss J. H. Phillips, which Mike did before becoming the D.A. again. (Grimsley remained loyal to Mike through 1973, when actor Walter Greaza died.) A year later, Monticello police chief Bill Marceau teamed up with Mike and remained on the show as a defender of justice for the next two decades.

There also were a number of deaths among baddies, including the D.A.'s conniving secretary Sybil Gordon, Big Frankie the sadistic multiple strangler, and suave racketeer Victor Carlson. Social worker Judith Marceau, Bill's daughter, was on trial for killing the latter in 1961, who used a fake justice to "marry" her. She was cleared and really wed lawyer Ed Gibson, who assumed lead status on the show for a few months when Mike went to the state capitol to organize a crime commission on October 10, 1961. In reality, actor John Larkin left his role to work in Hollywood, and Larry Hugo replaced him as Mike in 1962. Ironically, in 1963 Larry Hagman also left for Hollywood, so his character Ed and wife Judy were written off the show.

Other highlights from the early 1960s were Mike's assistance from businessman Phil Capice, who married Winston Grimsley's daughter Louise and had a daughter named Sara, and the marriage of Bill Marceau to his secretary Martha Spears, followed by their adoption of troubled 15-year-old Phoebe Smith. But the biggest development was Mike's romance and marriage (on April 22, 1963) with newspaper reporter Nancy Pollock, which spurred plot lines involving Nancy's parents Rose and Joe, the latter a newspaper owner; her brother Lee, who married Gerry McGrath; and her sister Cookie, who wed Malcolm Thomas and then Ron Christopher after Malcolm's murder.

A measure of the series' success was a 1963 review of the genre in *TV Guide* by writer Marya Mannes, who judged *The Edge of Night* the best daytime soap opera. "The serial is loaded with action, suspense and emotion but (except for a grotesquely lurid interlude about plastic surgery and mixed identities last summer) is logically worked out, cleverly contrived and written with some sophistication," wrote Mannes. "It is refreshing to find the sentiment occasionally leavened with humor, and some indication that the American female exists outside the kitchen."

A few years later, Mike finally found a permanent law partner in the person of Adam Drake, who followed Ed Gibson and John Barnes. His decade-long run on the show revolved chiefly around his romantic complications with Nicole Travis, whom he defended on the charge of murdering Stephanie Martin (Pamela Stewart, the vengeful wife of Nicole's ex-husband Duane, did the deed, mistaking Stephanie for Nicole). Nicole supposedly died at the hands of the mob in 1974 amid a convoluted story line, which involved her ex-convict father Ben Travis as a mob plant trying but failing to dissuade Adam from running for senator, after which Ben's caretaker Morlock Sevingy killed Ben because of the failure and then blew up a boat that Nicole was on. A grieving Adam found solace with assistant district attorney Brandy Henderson. He then learned Nicole was alive, and reconciled

with her, but the syndicate was still after him, and one of the ring shot Adam in the back, leaving Nicole in mourning.

Other story lines in the late 1960s predominantly revolved around the rich Hillyer family. Patriarch Olin Hillyer learned that his wife Laura had committed a crime of passion by killing Rick Oliver, who loved the younger Phoebe Smith rather than herself. Laura killed herself, but her look-alike Julie Jamison emerged a few months later to romance and wed Olin and face a separate murder trial, in which Adam was her defender. Julie and Olin left town after the trial, while Olin's daughter Liz Hillyer went through a failed romance with lawyer Vic Lamont and then a marriage to Steve Prentiss which ended when he disappeared without a trace. (The same happened to Susan Forbes, Nicole's pal and co-worker at a dress shop, who left in 1970 for an extended vacation in Florida and never returned.) Liz's second marriage to Jim Fields in the early 1970s proved happier, although psychotic Elly Jo Jamison, a relative of the now-deceased Julie Jamison, died in her effort to kill Liz to get hold of Olin's money.

In 1971 Mike Karr was on leave of absence when actor Laurence Hugo toured in a play. He never reprised the role, as Forrest Compton became the new Mike. Around then the show featured Laurie Ann Karr, Mike's grown-up daughter by Sara Lane, who lived as a hippie before having a flopped marriage with lawyer Vic Lamont. An affair and then marriage with Johnny Dallas, an ex-convict who ran the New Moon Cafe where she worked, produced a child by

The veteran crew on The Edge of Night *in the 1970s included, from left, Bill Marceau (played by Mandel Kramer), Mike Karr (Forrest Compton), Nancy Karr (Ann Flood), and Adam Drake (Donald May).*

him and Laurie called John Victor, and for a while it seemed that their marriage would work. But there were complications, which would come to a head over the next few years.

Despite Johnny's record, he was actually working to stop the mob, and its henchmen often found their way into his and Laurie's lives. In 1974 they killed Babs, a waitress at his cafe married to bartender Danny Micelli, and then Laurie's ex-husband Vic Lamont, who married Kaye Reynolds but unfortunately did not know her father Walter Le Page was the head of the syndicate and told Walter about Johnny's antimob activities. Learning that Johnny's life was in danger because of what he had told Walter, Vic took the bullet meant for Johnny in 1975. Both mob hits were ordered by Morlock Sevingy, who confessed while dying after a shoot-out. The 1974 arrival of Johnny's sister Tracy, an ex-hooker who later wed Danny, added more stress to Laurie and Johnny's world.

But the topper came in 1977–78 from Laurie's parents Mike and Nancy. A few years earlier, a woman named Serena Faraday had attracted local attention during a bitter divorce from her husband Mark, who accused her of being promiscuous. Her slutty look-alike sister Josie appeared on the scene sounding more like Mark's description of Serena, and when Serena or Josie killed Mark at the courthouse, Adam Drake figured out that Serena/Josie was a split personality and the homicidal Josie personality was in control. The Karrs' involvement here was the adoption of the Faradays' son Timmy following Serena's institutionalization. Mobster Beau Richardson abducted Timmy and told Nancy he would kill Timmy unless she gave him Mike's files on the mob. Given this impossible situation, Nancy left Mike to save him, but he thought she was having an affair with Beau. When another syndicate member killed Beau, the duo finally got back together and had a brief reunion with Timmy before he left for boarding school. But the effect of all the trauma on Laurie was a mental breakdown, and Johnny left town with their son.

Interspersed with Laurie's, Adam's, and Nicole's troubles, the other top story in the early to mid–1970s involved the rich Whitney family: former senator Gordon Whitney; his bitchy wife Geraldine; and their sons Colin, also a senator, and Keith, another split personality whose alter ego, Jonah Lockwood, was a psychotic murdering hippie who died during an attempt on Laurie's life. Meanwhile, Colin's wife Tiffany cheated on him with Ron Christopher, Cookie Pollock's husband. Cookie went kooky but recovered and reunited with Ron, and they left town. Gordon and Colin later died in an accident.

Geraldine and Tiffany remained in town, with the latter marrying Noel Douglas, who turned the tables on Tiffany by sleeping with Tracy Dallas. Noel pushed Geraldine down a flight of stairs after she threatened to reveal his tryst to her ex-daughter-in-law, and Geraldine went into a coma. Reporter and friend Kevin Jamison went to Paris to try to find a cure and located Dr. Clay Jordan, who coincidentally had found the amnesiac Nicole. Meanwhile, Tiffany, who

was planning to divorce Noel for his philandering, died after being pushed out of a window by Jordan, with the help of his mob partner Gilbert Darcy. Meanwhile, Geraldine recovered and stayed with the show for the rest of its run.

Though the story lines make it sound seamless, *The Edge of Night* actually went through a somewhat troubled time in the 1970s. One of the top-rated soaps since its start, it stumbled and became CBS's lowest-rated show following a move to 2 p.m. which had been requested by production company Procter & Gamble and which cost the show much of its audience. CBS canceled the show in 1975, but ABC picked it up for the 4 p.m. slot, although some affiliates aired it on a delayed basis and others, increasingly in the 1980s, did not carry it at all.

After nearly a decade of mob-related intricacies, including the blackmailing of Chief Marceau, who had, unwittingly, adopted a daughter in a black-market scheme, and the framing of his wife Martha in the staged death of the daughter's natural mother Taffy Sims, whom the mob later really killed, the syndicate's activities wound down, and at the end of the 1970s, top boss Tony Saxon was killed in a hail of gunfire. The new emphasis was on whacked-out families. First case in point were the Cavanaughs. Dr. Miles Cavanaugh oversaw Nicole's birth of the late Adam Drake's son, and his dying wife Denise noted a growing fondness between the two on which she intended to put the kibosh. She staged her death so that Miles's sister April would be accused of giving her a poisonous injection, and her plan seemed to be working until Denise's dad Dr. Gus Norwood confessed his part in the plot. Miles and Nicole became a happy new lead couple on the show until Nicole's bizarre death from putting on poisoned makeup while doing a TV news program in 1983.

April, on the other hand, found her romance with prosecuting attorney Draper Scott jeopardized by the discovery that hard-driving Margo Huntington, the owner of the local TV station WMON, was her and Miles's real mother. April was thrown off by Margo, who married one-time cult leader Eliot Dorn and interfered with April's marriage to Draper. When Margo died, Draper became a suspect and was convicted of the crime. Then, hours before his exoneration, the plane taking him back to prison crashed and he lost his memory. Emily Michaels and her maid Molly Sherwood found him, and Emily's delusions made her think he was her missing husband Kirk. Her mad obsession with Draper even after he remembered his past soon overwhelmed Molly, and she killed Geraldine Whitney's pal Nadine Alexander and Eliot Dorn when they inadvertently stumbled onto her plots to kill April. Molly fell to her death before succeeding, and Draper and April moved to Europe to investigate the connections of Dr. Kenneth Bryson, the mental clinic head who had let Emily run free.

Margo's real killer was Nola Madison, a real nut case. Nola was an actress playing witch Martha Cory in a horror film whose macabre alter ego was taking over her personality. Still in love with her estranged husband Owen, although having an affair with Eliot Dorn, she plotted to kill his new lover Deborah Saxon, a police officer with the shame of having been the daughter of crime boss Tony Saxon. She drugged Miles into a semicrazed state and presided over a household where her children Brian and Paige fell in love even though they believed they were half-brother and sister. (When Brian learned that Owen was not his father, they were free to marry and did so.) Policeman Steve Guthrie fingered Nola as Margo's killer and went on to romance Deborah.

Other major plot lines in the late 1970s revolved around temptress Raven Alexander, Nadine's daughter. Kevin Jamison, who was married to Phoebe Smith until her mob-related death in 1976, then married Raven, but Kevin died in 1978. Logan Swift, an up-and-coming star in the D.A.'s office, was Raven's adulterous lover and then husband after Kevin's death, and then ex-husband after she had a fling with Eliot Dorn (however, Logan had an affair with Winter Austen, an ex-hooker who murdered Wade Meecham when the latter threatened to expose her). Lawyer Ansel Scott had a fling with Raven before marrying her mom. And Derek Mallory, who replaced Bill Marceau as police chief, also had a go at Raven.

The show apparently was on a "youth kick" in 1979, because it got rid of not only Bill Marceau but also Nancy's parents Joe and Rose. The trend continued in the 1980s with the arrival of Nancy Karr's curly-haired nephew Kelly McGrath; his girlfriend Jody Travis; Nicole's half-sister, Gavin Wylie, a dance teacher with whom Jody fell in love; and Valerie Bryson, Kelly's new girlfriend and the daughter of the late Dr. Bryson. After her time with Kelly, Valerie went with Jim Diedrickson, who used actor brothers Hector and Smiley Wilson in a con game to make Raven think she had killed actress Jinx Avery. The Wilsons were killed, and Jinx died from a fatal illness a few days after marrying Derek Mallory, thus keeping his record of luckless romances intact.

Derek's former squeeze Raven found herself entangled in the most intriguing mystery of all, involving Geraldine Whitney's nephew "Sky" Schuyler, whom she romanced and wed before learning he was an imposter who was blackmailing dancer Martine Duval about her theft of jewels in Europe and who had a bald sidekick, Gunther Wagner, who was responsible for some dirty deeds of his own. Raven fell in love with both the real and fake Skys (some surprise), but eventually the real one won out—as did the real Gunther, whose brother Bruno impersonated him for a time as well!

Sky went on to purchase WMON-TV and brought his assistant Spencer Varney to Monticello to join him. Gunther became the object of an unlikely love triangle between Mitzi Martin, a spacey waitress once involved with lawyer Cliff Nelson, and Nora Fulton, whose boss Camilla Devereaux was an ex-lover of Spencer's and had a brother Ian who was in love with Raven. Nora tried to murder Mitzi, but the attempt failed when spy David Cameron killed her instead. Later, Sky recovered $40 million worth of diamonds that Spencer had stolen from his family, and Spencer was revealed as the thief.

On other fronts, Jody allowed herself to be used in a plot by mobster Dwight Endicott, but Mike, Derek, and cop Damian Tyler destroyed Dwight's plans. Her relationship with Gavin Wylie went downhill, and he left to become a director. Another relationship, with John "Preacher" Emerson, also failed, but Preacher hooked up with Liz Corell, and Jody found love with Jeremy Rhodes.

Meanwhile, the audience share of *The Edge of Night* was heading south, toward single digits. In 1983 ABC installed Lee Sheldon as head writer to replace Henry Slesar, who had held the position since 1968 and won an Emmy for his work. Needless to say, this change made many cast members "edgy." But Sheldon showed he had quite a few surprises in store for viewers, like returning Logan Swift only to have him be killed alone in a locked room. Nonetheless, ratings did not improve, so ABC killed the show by the end of 1984.

The final weeks wrapped up most story lines. Widower Miles Cavanaugh married radio psychologist Beth Corell. After a kidnapping by Mark Hamilton, Raven gave birth to a girl. Calvin Stoner and Didi Bannister, Calvin's second wife after nightclub singer Star, were expecting. And, after an eight-year absence, a sane Laurie Ann visited the Karrs. Even Geraldine Whitney was happy at the wrap-up New Year's Eve party, though the goodwill in evidence at the party was quite a switch from the mayhem seen over the previous 28 years.

After the cancellation, ABC turned over the 4–4:30 p.m. time slot to local stations to program. *The Edge of Night* was not quite over, however. The USA cable network ran repeats of the series nightly after midnight E.S.T. for several years starting August 5, 1985, beginning with episodes from June 1980 on. And *One Life to Live* had several *Edge* alumni in its cast in 1988, including Mark Arnold, Sharon Gabet, and Lois Kibbee.

EDITOR'S CHOICE
Public Affairs; B&W
January 14, 1962–December 30, 1962
ABC Sun. 3:30–4 p.m. (1/14/62–9/23/62)
ABC Sun. 2:30–3 p.m. (10/7/62–12/30/62)
Host: *Fendall Yerxa*

On *Editor's Choice* one topic per week received in-depth treatment with reports, interviews, or a combination of both. Programs covered events ranging from the 50th anniversary of the Girl Scouts to the admission of black student James Meredith into the all-white University of Mississippi in Oxford. Host Fendall Yerxa did fit the show's title, as he was a former metropolitan editor for *The New York Tribune*. He left ABC News in June 1963 to become news editor of *The New York Times*'s Washington, D.C. bureau.

Editor's Choice alternated weekly with *Adlai Stevenson Presents* except in the summer, when it ran weekly. The series aired on ABC Sundays at 10:30 p.m. from June 18–September 24, 1961 before its afternoon run.

EDUCATION EXCHANGE—See *Continental Classroom.*

•EEK! THE CAT
Cartoon; Color
September 19, 1992–

Fox Sat. 10:30–11 a.m. (9/19/92–10/14/92)
Fox Sat. 9:30–10 a.m. (10/21/92–6/25/94)
Fox Sat. 8:30–9 a.m. (7/2/94–7/30/94)
Fox Sat. 9:30–10 a.m. (8/6/94–3/11/95)
Fox Sat. 9–9:30 a.m. (3/18/95–9/2/95)
Fox Sat. 9:30–10 a.m. (9/9/95–10/28/95)
Fox Sat. 8:30–9 a.m. (11/4/95–1/17/96)
Fox Mon.–Fri. Various half hours (1/29/96–)

Voices:

Eek	*Bill Kopp*
Wendy Elizabeth	*E.G. Daily*
Annabelle	*Tawny Kitean*

Also: *Savage Steve Holland, Gary Owens*

Purple tubby tabby Eek was unlike any feline seen on television. An easily befuddled type with slurred speech, Eek had misadventures both with his obnoxious obese owners J.B. and his sister Wendy Elizabeth and their out-to-lunch mother; his next-door neighbor and unrequited love interest Annabelle, a *really* stout cat who weighed 800 pounds; and Annabelle's vicious pet Sharky the Sharkdog. Other characters in the two weekly segments included the Squishy Bearz, a saccharine takeoff on *The Care Bears* (q.v.). Some of them could be as unconventional as what had been seen on Warner Brothers cartoons, such as the episode where Eek went to visit his cartoon creators at the Fox network (depicted as a rundown structure) and found them frantically trying to finish the episode. Coincidentally, Bill Kopp was both a creator and supervising producer of the series as well as Eek's voice.

On November 20, 1993, the series was retitled *Eek! and the Terrible Thunderlizards* with the introduction of a segment involving three dinosaurs named "Doc" Tari, the leader of the gang, Day Z. Cutter, and Bo "Diddley" Squatt, the group imbecile, fighting Neanderthals Bill and Scooter. Two weeks later, the *Eek! the Cat Christmas Special* aired on Fox nighttime on December 5, 1993. In September 1995, when it ran in reruns daily on Fox as well as on Saturdays, the show was retitled *Eek!stravaganza.*

EGG AND I, THE
Soap Opera; B&W
September 3, 1951–August 1, 1952

CBS Mon.–Fri. Noon–12:15 p.m. (9/3/51–8/1/52)

Cast:

Betty MacDonald (1951–52)	*Pat Kirkland*
Betty MacDonald	
(3/10/52–8/1/52)	*Betty Lynn*
Bob MacDonald	*John Craven*
Ma Kettle	*Doris Rich*
Pa Kettle	*Frank Twedell*
Jed Simmons	*Grady Sutton*
Lisa Schumacher	*Ingeborg Theek*
Paula French	*Karen Hale*

The Egg and I began as a best-selling book in 1945 by Betty MacDonald in which she recounted her humorous misadventures in trying to adapt to farm life. It became a hit movie in 1947 with Claudette Colbert as Betty and Fred MacMurray as her husband Bob, then had several sequels starting in 1949 focusing on their wacky neighbors Ma and Pa Kettle, played by Marjorie Main and Percy Kilbride. CBS bought the rights to the property in 1951, and a pilot for a weekly half-hour show was filmed that summer starring William Prince and Diana Lynn. It emerged that fall as a daily 15-minute serial.

The TV show followed the book and movie story lines, with the MacDonalds running a chicken farm in the Northeast after moving from the city. The Kettles helped them get accustomed to rural life, as did Jed Simmons, their handyman, and others. The tone of *The Egg and I*, unlike that of most soap operas, emphasized light comedy rather than drama. When Pat Kirkland left to have a baby in early 1952, Betty Lynn replaced her.

The Egg and I led all daily network shows before 5 p.m. in the ratings by early 1952, but the only sponsor it had by late February 1952 was Procter & Gamble on Tuesdays and Thursdays. It remained near the top of the ratings through 1952. But when Procter & Gamble inexplicably ended its sponsorship in June, no other advertisers replaced them, perhaps because at the time radio soap operas had larger audiences than TV serials. In any case, *The Egg and I* became past history within a year of its premiere.

EICHMANN ON TRIAL
Public Affairs; B&W
April 16, 1961–August 20, 1961

ABC Sun. 4–4:30 p.m. (4/16/61–8/20/61)

Regulars: *Bill Shadel, Quincy Howe, Martin Levin, Yale Newman*

Karl Adolf Eichmann was a Nazi leader who had been one of the primary architects of Germany's extermination program during the Holocaust. Eichmann, who had escaped to Argentina, was captured in 1960 and tried in Israel for war crimes and murder. This series examined the trial and reactions to it. Bill Shadel was host, while three other ABC News reporters filed film reports from overseas. Two weeks prior to the show's debut, ABC aired specials Sunday afternoon about the trial.

ELECTIONS '66
Public Affairs; B&W
October 2, 1966–November 6, 1966

ABC Sun. 1–1:30 p.m. (10/2/66–11/6/66)

Various ABC reporters filed updates on state governorship and Congressional races for this short-run series, with one show examining the Vietnam War's impact on contests. Though not regulars, Bill Lawrence and Howard K. Smith appeared on three shows.

ELMER DAVIS
Commentary; B&W
February 21, 1954–May 2, 1954

ABC Sun. 3:30–3:45 p.m. (2/21/54–5/2/54)

Commentator: *Elmer Davis*

Liberal commentator Elmer Davis, who began doing radio reports on CBS in the 1930s, gave his opinions each week about politics and other concerns in this New York–based attraction. The first show aired at 1 p.m. before going to 3:30 the following week. ABC also aired the program on radio Sunday nights using a tape of the TV show. Illness forced Davis off the air in the spring, and he died in 1958 without doing another TV series.

EMERGENCY + 4
Cartoon; Color
September 8, 1973–September 4, 1976

NBC Sat. 9:30–10 a.m. (9/8/73–12/29/73)
NBC Sat. 9–9:30 a.m. (1/5/74–8/30/75)
NBC Sat. 8–8:30 a.m. (9/6/75–9/4/76)

Voices:

Roy DeSoto	Kevin Tighe
John Gage	Randolph Mantooth
Sally/Carol Harper	Sarah Kennedy
Matthew Harper	David Joliffe
Jason Phillips	Donald Fullilove
Randy Aldrich	Peter Haas

The first part of this series' title referred to paramedics Roy DeSoto and John Gage, who initially appeared in the NBC Saturday night drama *Emergency* from 1972–77. Here they teamed with four youngsters—Jason, Randy, Matthew, and Matthew's sister Sally (later renamed Carol)—plus Flash the dog, Charlemagne the mynah bird, and Bananas the monkey to avert disasters in Los Angeles County. The last season consisted of reruns.

ERN WESTMORE SHOW, THE
Women's; B&W
October 5, 1953–December 9, 1955

ABC Mon.–Fri. 4:30–5 p.m. (10/5/53–12/31/53)
NBC Mon.–Fri. 10:30–11 a.m. (9/12/55–12/9/55)

Regulars: *Ern Westmore, Betty Westmore, Dick Hyde (1953)*

Programs featuring beauty tips from leading Hollywood makeup artist Ern Westmore popped up a few times in the 1950s. On his ABC series, he began the program by introducing a woman with a makeover to demonstrate the proper techniques for "getting pretty," then went into the studio audience to find the best-looking female. Ern sometimes criticized individual women harshly before selecting "the loveliest lady in the audience." He then asked the audience to choose candidates for beauty makeovers on the next day's show. His wife Betty handed out gifts to selected audience members, and Dick Hyde doubled as vocalist and announcer.

The series aired in local tryouts in Miami, Cincinnati, and Birmingham, Alabama, before becoming one of ABC's few daily shows of the early 1950s airing before 7 p.m. Prior to the debut, Ern threatened to sue NBC's morning show *Glamour Girl*, claiming that show had been his idea. It did not matter; ABC canned his show before the start of 1954 due to lack of a sponsor, and *Glamour Girl* went off a week later.

In the summer of 1955 Ern had a daily show similar to the first one, with Betty joining him on WABD New York. On August 7, 1955, Ern returned to network television with the nighttime ABC show *Hollywood Backstage*. A day after that show ended, he went back to daytime on NBC with a series called *The Search for Beauty*, which had a similar format to that of his earlier daytime show and, like that prior effort, lasted less than three months.

ERNIE KOVACS SHOW, THE
Comedy; B&W
May 14, 1951–July 27, 1956

NBC Mon.–Fri. 3:15–3:30 p.m. (5/14/51–6/29/51)
NBC Mon.–Fri. 11–11:30 a.m. (1/4/52–3/28/52)
NBC Mon.–Fri. 10:30–11 a.m. (12/12/55–7/27/56)

Regulars: *Ernie Kovacs, Edie Adams (1952, 1955–56), the Harry Sosnick Orchestra (1951), Peter Boyle (1952), the Dave Appell Trio (1952), Matt Dennis (1955–56), Trigger Lund (1955–56), Barbara Loden (1955–56), the Archie Koty Orchestra (1955–56)*

Comedian Ernie Kovacs's highly technical visual slapstick and innovations (he is credited with pioneering comic skits done before the main titles) had a major influence on later shows like *Laugh-In* and *The David Letterman Show*. He got his start on daytime television on WPTZ Philadelphia in 1950 with three daily shows (including *Three to Get Ready*, a 7–9 a.m. offering whose rating success inspired NBC to program *The Today Show* in that time period). His local popularity led to a new series in 1951, his first network series.

It's Time for Ernie was billed as "the shortest 15 minutes in TV—it just seems long." Ernie hosted, wrote, and produced, as he would in later shows. Comic segments included a burlesque of a Chinese submarine and a film where Ernie played all positions in a baseball game. It followed the maudlin *Miss Susan* serial, and the offbeat humor coming from the brawny, mustachioed, cigar-smoking Kovacs must have left holdover viewers bewildered. The show died within two months.

NBC then gave Kovacs a nighttime series called *Ernie in Kovacsland* from July 2–August 24, 1951. In 1952 the network gave him another daytime series, albeit more structured and elaborate than the first one. Called *Kovacs on the Corner*, it had a studio audience who got to play such stunts as "Yoo Hoo Time" (a camera would focus on one audience member and let her or him wave frantically to acquaintances supposedly watching at home) while watching odd features like a swap of useless items. The show's mascot was Tondelayo, a cat said to be visible only to Ernie and children. There was also a theme of sorts with Ernie visiting some regular players on a "corner neighborhood" of the set. Actor Peter Boyle, then a WPTZ staff member, played an Irish cop, and the Dave Appell Trio sported street cleaner outfits while providing music. Edie Adams, who became Ernie's wife in 1955, sang a few times. This was the last Kovacs show to come from Philadelphia.

The Kovacs shows of 1951–52 only hinted at Ernie's wild, nutty humor. After stints on other network series as a regular, including *I'll Buy That* (q.v.), Ernie came back better than ever with his third and final daytime show, this time based in New York City. Among other elements, it starred "Howard the Strongest Ant in the World," whom Ernie regularly "interviewed." An enthusiastic home audience showered Howard with an average of 1,800 gifts a week. Then there were the openings. One February 1956 show began with a shot of two goldfish named Henry and Alice to whom Ernie and Edie lent their voices in an imaginary conversation. For daytime viewers used to more conventional entries like news updates, Ernie gave them Kovacs's Pathetic News, "The Eye, Ear, Nose and Throat of the World." By this time, Ernie also had developed a cast of recurring characters he played, the most familiar being the goggle-eyed, mincing, martini-drinking poet Percy Dovetonsils.

Kovacs went to Hollywood in 1957 for an ultimately unsatisfying movie career and a few more series. His last TV work consisted of some brilliant videotaped monthly specials on ABC from 1961–62 which featured elaborate visual stunts like the one in which a woman is enjoying a bubble bath while all sorts of people emerge from the tub's drain with nary a drop on them. Kovacs died in a car crash on January 13, 1962 at the age of 42.

ETERNAL LIGHT, THE—See NBC Religious Television Program.

EVERYBODY'S TALKING
Game; B&W
February 6, 1967–December 29, 1967
ABC Mon.–Fri. Noon–12:30 p.m. (2/6/67–12/29/67)
Host: *Lloyd Thaxton*

Three players (celebrities by the end of the run) viewed film clips of people speaking on camera and tried to determine the mystery person, place, or item about which "everybody's talking" in the clips. Home viewers could have cared less, as the show wilted against *Jeopardy* on NBC and *Love of Life* on CBS. Jack Barry created this series but got no screen credit due to lingering concerns about his involvements in the 1950s quiz show scandals.

EVERYDAY
Talk/Variety; Color
1978–79
Syndicated 30 minutes daily beginning September 1978
Hosts: *John Bennett Perry, Stephanie Edwards*
Regulars: *Anne Bloom, Tom Chapin, Robert Corff, Judy Gibson, Murray Langston*

A mishmash of information and entertainment, *Everyday* featured John Bennett Perry and Stephanie Edwards as hosts of a wide range of features, from interviews with guests to comedy and songs from a regular troupe. The show was a production of the Group W organization, and after it flopped, Group W asked women what type of information they wanted from a daily TV show, discovering that much of what they wanted—such as tips on health, money, child care, and other issues—was *not* what *Everyday* had offered. Using the results of the survey, Group W came up with one of the biggest hits of the 1980s—see *Hour Magazine*.

•EVERYDAY WITH JOAN LUNDEN
Talk; Color
1989–91
Syndicated daily 30 or 60 minutes beginning September 1989
Hostess: *Joan Lunden*

While hosting *Good Morning America*, Joan Lunden did this easygoing show with celebrity guests and informational spots. The result was not unlike a second helping of *Good Morning America* without the news. Taped for hour slots in New York, some stations ran it for 30 minutes. Helping produce the series was Lunden's husband Michael Krauss, whom she divorced not long after its final show in a bitter, much publicized split.

EVERYTHING'S ARCHIE—See Archie Show, The.

EVERYWHERE I GO
Talk; B&W
October 7, 1952–January 6, 1953
CBS Tue./Thu. 2–2:30 p.m. (10/7/52–1/6/53)
Regulars: *Dan Seymour, the Sammy Spear Orchestra*

This series made extensive use of rear projection to make host Dan Seymour look like he was piloting a flying saucer to "visit" the guests he interviewed, like a royal couple from Uganda and a family living on a Chinese junk in New Rochelle, New York. Seymour performed a similar task, without the special effects, on the nighttime NBC show *We, the People* from 1950–52. The show alternated daily with *Double or Nothing*.

EWOKS, THE
Cartoon; Color
September 7, 1985–September 5, 1987

ABC Sat. 9–9:30 a.m. (9/7/85–10/26/85)
ABC Sat. 9:30–10 a.m. (11/2/85–2/22/86)
ABC Sat. 10:30–11:30 a.m. (3/1/86–9/6/86)
ABC Sat. 11:30 a.m.–Noon (9/13/86–9/5/87)

Voices:

Wicket (1985–86)	*Jim Henshaw*
Wicket (1986–87)	*Denny Delk*
Widdle (1985–86)	*John Stocker*
Weechee (1985–86)	*Greg Swanson*
Princess Kneesaa (1985–86)	*Cree Summer Francks*
Latara (1985–86)	*Taborah Johnson*
Latara (1986–87)	*Sue Murphy*
Teebo (1986–87)	*Jim Cranna*
Shodu (1986–87)	*Esther Scott*
Logray (1986–87)	*Rick Cimino*

The Ewoks were teddy bear–like creatures who waddled their way into movie viewers' hearts in 1983 when they assisted Luke Skywalker and company in defeating the Empire in *Return of the Jedi.* Two years later the Ewoks arrived in animated form as teenagers in their own adventures. Wicket was the group's scout leader, Widdle was his younger brother, and Weechee was his older brother. They lived on the distant moon of Endor in thatched houses with their humanoid pals Princess Kneesaa and impish Latara, engaging in adventures in which they met other creatures and, as with any Saturday morning cartoon, learned a lesson in the process.

At the end of February 1986 this series merged with *Droids: The Adventures of R2D2 and C3PO* (q.v.) to become *The Ewoks and Star Wars Droids Adventure Hour.* In the fall of 1986 that ended, and *The All-New Ewoks* debuted with a largely new crew of Ewoks, but it did not draw bigger audiences than the first edition and went off after a season.

EXCURSION
Children's; B&W
September 13, 1953–March 21, 1954

NBC Sun. 3:30–4 p.m. (9/13/53–12/10/53)
NBC Sun. 4–4:30 p.m. (12/20/53–3/21/54)

Host: *Burgess Meredith*

Known within the industry as "Junior *Omnibus*," *Excursion* was geared to give children education and information about such high-minded topics as culture and politics. Its host was veteran actor Burgess Meredith, in his first regular job on television. The debut was a dramatization of Mark Twain's classic *Huckleberry Finn,* with Clifford Tatum as Huck, boxer Sugar Ray Robinson as Jim (his first TV acting role), Eddie Albert as the Duke, and Thomas Mitchell as the Dauphin. The following week, former president Harry Truman appeared for a brief chat, as did ex-president Herbert Hoover on October 21.

Other shows were similarly ambitious. For example, the February 28, 1954 telecast on the history of jazz was broadcast in color. But *Excursion* was expensive to produce and audiences were small, so after six months it took a trip to the world of canceled TV shows.

EXPECT A MIRACLE—See *Oral Roberts.*

EXPERIMENT IN TELEVISION
Various; Color
February 19, 1967–March 7, 1971

NBC Sun. 4–5 p.m. (2/19/67–4/30/67)
NBC Sun. 3–4 p.m. (2/18/68–4/28/68)
NBC Sun. 4:30–5:30 p.m. (2/16/69–4/20/69)
NBC Sun. 5–6 p.m. (2/15/70–4/19/70)
NBC Sun. 5–6 p.m. (1/24/71–3/7/71)

Officially titled *NBC Experiment in Television,* this was an eclectic assortment of programs on which anything and anyone could appear—and often did. For example, the debut was an original play, "Losers Weepers" by Harry Dolan. A month later, the March 19, 1967 presentation was "This Is Marshall McLuhan," in which social commentator McLuhan discussed his belief that for now, "the medium is the message." The following week was "We Interrupt This Season," a series of satirical sketches on the TV business with a cast of unknown actors. Later shows included a review of English music styles, ranging from the Beatles recording "Hey Jude" to Yehudi Menuhin conducting the Bath Festival Orchestra in a Benjamin Britten music march (February 22, 1970), and an examination of the life of engineer and architect Buckminster Fuller (February 7, 1971).

EXPLORING
Children's; Color
October 13, 1962–April 9, 1966

NBC Sat. 12:30–1:30 p.m. (10/13/62–5/25/63)
NBC Sat. 1–2 p.m. (10/12/63–4/10/65; off summer 1964)
NBC Sat. 12:30–1 p.m. (10/16/65–4/9/66)

Regulars: *Dr. Albert Hibbs, the Ritts Puppets, the Gus Soloman Dancers*

The regulars and guest stars on *Exploring* tried to teach children about the world around them, in cooperation with many school systems. Participating schools received advanced information on each week's topic, and some programs were available for use by schools and libraries on 16mm film. The show used puppetry (regular characters were Magnolia the Ostrich, Albert the Chipmunk, and Sir Godfrey Turtle), dancing, and some unusual linking devices to get points across. Host Dr. Albert Hibbs was a physicist with the California Institute of Technology.

EXPLORING GOD'S WORLD
Religious; B&W
July 4, 1954–September 26, 1954

CBS Sun. 10:30–11 a.m. (7/4/54–9/26/54)

Regulars: *Carrie McCord, Lydia Jean Shaffer, Glenn Walken*

Presented in cooperation with the Connecticut Council of Churches, *Exploring God's World* offered games and Biblical readings designed to appeal to children. Juvenile actors Lydia

Jean Shaffer and Glenn Walken joined hostess Carrie McCord in the activities in this summer replacement for *Look Up and Live.*

EYE GUESS
Game; Color
January 3, 1966–September 26, 1969

NBC Mon.–Fri. 10–10:25 a.m. (1/3/66–12/30/66)
NBC Mon.–Fri. 12:30–12:55 p.m. (1/2/67–9/26/69)
Host: *Bill Cullen*

Two contestants had eight seconds to examine eight answers on a board before they were concealed at the start of *Eye Guess.* The host asked a question and the first player to respond had to pick which box on the board had the right answer. The game consisted of two rounds (10 points in round one, 20 points in round two). The first player to score 100 played a bonus game in which the object was to avoid the hidden "Stop" underneath one of eight squares (others had "Go").

In 1969 players received prizes for correct matches rather than points, and seven prizes led to a bonus game. Viewers who stayed with NBC a half-hour longer after the show ended in the summer of 1969 could get a double dose of host Bill Cullen, as he also appeared as a regular on *You're Putting Me On* (q.v.).

EYE ON NEW YORK
Interview; B&W
January 22, 1956–September 6, 1959

CBS Sun. 11–11:30 a.m. (1/22/56–11/4/56)
CBS Sun. 11–11:30 a.m. (6/9/57–9/1/57)
CBS Sun. 11–11:30 a.m. (3/2/58–8/31/58)
CBS Sun. 11–11:30 a.m. (12/28/58–9/6/59)
Host: *Bill Leonard*

Eye on New York was one of the Big Apple's longest-running local series, airing from at least July 1953 on WCBS through at least the 1970s. When it was a network show during the mid- to late 1950s, it focused on discussions with guests about all aspects of New York (nightclubs, educational TV, etc.). The August 10, 1958 telecast saluted the 1,000th performance of the Broadway musical *My Fair Lady,* with cast members Edward Mulhare as Professor Henry Higgins and Lola Fisher as Eliza Doolittle performing a few scenes.

The series ran sporadically on Sunday mornings, with *The U.N. in Action* (q.v.) often running in its time slot on its days off. Bill Leonard joined the show in its local days on August 9, 1953, replacing original host Larry LeSueur. After the CBS run the show had several different hosts locally, including Mike Wallace in 1963.

EYES HAVE IT, THE
Game; B&W
January 28, 1949–June 19, 1949

NBC Sun. 4–4:30 p.m. (1/28/49–6/19/49)
Host: *Ralph McNair*

One of the first game shows to move from prime time (where it began on NBC November 20, 1948) to daytime, *The Eyes Have It* was a Washington, D.C.–based quiz where contestants had to name a celebrity or famous site using a photo altered in some way to obscure the view. The show began as a local offering on September 25, 1948.

F.Y.I.
Public Affairs; B&W
January 3, 1960–May 29, 1960

CBS Sun. 11–11:30 a.m. (1/3/60–5/29/60)
Host: *Douglas Edwards*

Using taped and filmed discussions and reports, this public affairs series spent each show addressing a controversial issue such as anti-Semitism in New York, civil rights, and juvenile delinquency. A special departure occurred in March and April 1960 with a three-part look at the Wisconsin primary and its impact, with reporter Blaine Littell as moderator. The show moved to CBS Sundays at 6 p.m. in June before ending its run on September 25, 1960.

F.Y.I. (or the spelled-out version, "For Your Information") also appeared as the title for several public affairs shows at local stations plus one DuMont series (*For Your Information,* q.v.), for a series of minute-long inserts on lifestyle advice which aired weekdays on ABC daytime from 1979–84 with Hal Linden as host, and as the name of the TV newsmagazine on the CBS nighttime sitcom *Murphy Brown* (1988–).

FABULOUS FUNNIES, THE
Cartoons; Color
September 9, 1978–September 1, 1979

NBC Sat. Noon–12:30 p.m. (9/9/78–1/27/79)
NBC Sat. 12:30–1 p.m. (2/3/79–9/1/79)
Voices:

Broom Hilda/Sluggo/Oola/Hans and Fritz Katzenjammer	*June Foray*
King Guzzle/Der Inspector	*Alan Oppenheimer*
Alley Oop/Der Captain Katzenjammer	*Bob Holt*
Nancy/Emmy Lou	*Jayne Hamil*

A potpourri of some well-known and obscure comic strip characters involved in separate adventures made up *The Fabulous Funnies.* The more recognized ones (to adults, at least) were Alley Oop, a caveman who had been around on the funny pages since 1933 with his romantic interest Oola living under the rule of King Guzzle in the ancient Kingdom of Moo; Nancy, who since 1940 had been hanging out with her tough-looking pal Sluggo; and the ancestor of them all, the Katzenjammer Kids, who since 1897 had terrorized the Captain with their mischievous antics. The Johnny-come-lately to the bunch was Broom Hilda, an inept 1,500-year-old witch with somewhat rusty powers who had been a comic character only since 1970, and a rather minor one at that. The goal of all of them was to be educational as well as entertaining for children.

Interestingly, a special by the same name aired on NBC prime time on February 11, 1968 with Carl Reiner as host. While it had a different production company, the special did feature Ernie Bushmiller, the creator of the Nancy comic character.

FACE THE FACTS
Game; B&W
March 13, 1961–September 29, 1961

CBS Mon.–Fri. 2–2:30 p.m. (3/13/61–9/29/61)

Host: *Red Rowe*

Running opposite *Day in Court* on ABC, this game show took its competition's format of using actors as plaintiffs and defendants for three hypothetical cases per show. Four contestants watched and then bet part of the 500 points they had received at the start of the show on their prediction of the judgment for each case presented. Correct guesses earned points, and the contestant with the most points at the end of the show won merchandise. Some cases on the debut were a beauty operator sued for improper work and a writer sued for libel by a wrestler. Unable to match the ratings set by its lead-in, *As the World Turns,* this show went off to be replaced by *Password.*

•FACE THE NATION
Public Affairs; B&W and Color
November 7, 1954–

CBS Sun. Various half hours between 11:30 a.m. and
   6 p.m., except for 1–1:45 p.m. 9/29/57–12/22/57
   (11/7/54–9/25/60)
CBS Sun. 12:30–1 p.m. (9/15/63–9/8/68)
CBS Sun. 11:30 a.m.–Noon (9/15/68–9/11/83)
CBS Sun. 10:30–11 a.m. (9/18/83–)

Host: *Ted Koop (11/7/54–8/14/55), Stuart Novins (8/21/55–9/25/60), Paul Niven (9/15/63–1965), Martin Agronsky (1965–69), George Herman (1969–9/11/83), Leslie Stahl (9/18/83–1991), Bob Schieffer (1991–)*

CBS had a few interview shows in which journalists asked newsmakers about current events, in the manner of NBC's long-running *Meet the Press,* but none was as venerable as *Face the Nation.* Its basic format remained unchanged for nearly 30 years, with three reporters (usually one affiliated with CBS News) and the host doing the questioning of one guest in Washington, D.C. Senator Joseph McCarthy appeared on the premiere to discuss what eventually was a censure of him by the U.S. Senate (on the show, he compared the action to a lynching).

Due to its Sunday time slot (another similarity with *Meet the Press),* the show often provided newspapers with

information to fill up the rather slow Monday papers. Sometimes the events from the show were so dramatic that they would have made news no matter what day they had been aired. For example, on June 2, 1957, the show scored a coup by filming an hour interview with Communist Party head Nikita Khrushchev at the Kremlin, something even Russian journalists had been unable to accomplish. This was Khrushchev's first American TV interview, and his comments were so inflammatory that President Dwight Eisenhower received offers from all three networks to have a full hour of air time to respond to them. He declined, but *Face the Nation* did another special hour show the following week to review the event.

Another headline-making show aired on July 30, 1972, when Missouri senator Thomas Eagleton, then the Democratic candidate for vice president, tried to recover from the negative publicity generated by the revelation that he had undergone electroshock treatment for depression by explaining his circumstances on the show. It didn't work; the grilling Eagleton received by George Herman and columnist Jack Anderson about his past made him visibly nervous, and he was dropped from the ticket soon afterward. "He left the impression of a man clinging to a life raft in very stormy waters," noted a *Variety* reviewer.

While the show's content was solid, its scheduling was not. CBS bounced it around 25 times on Sunday afternoons and even expanded it to 45 minutes briefly in 1957 before moving it into prime time from October 2, 1960–April 6, 1961 (Howard Smith succeeded Stuart Novins as host on November 1960). It returned in 1963 in a more stable time period, and by the end of the 1960s it had found a host, George Herman, whose tenure lasted longer than all his predecessors' combined.

When Leslie Stahl succeeded Herman in 1983, the show revamped itself much in the mold of its direct competition on ABC, *This Week with David Brinkley:* The panel of reporters was dropped in favor of Stahl interviewing one or several guests per show, and only an occasional guest reporter joined her in asking questions. Bob Schieffer maintained that format in the 1990s, by which time *Face the Nation* had become the longest-running daytime TV show produced by CBS News.

FACTS WE FACE, THE—See *Open Hearing.*

FAIRMEADOWS, U.S.A.
Soap Opera; B&W
November 4, 1951–April 27, 1952

NBC Sun. 3–3:30 p.m. (11/4/51–4/27/52)

Cast:
John Olcott	Howard St. John
Alice Olcott	Ruth Matteson
Evie Olcott	Mimi Strongin

The only network soap opera to air on Sundays, centered around general store owner John Olcott, his wife Alice, and their daughter Evie, who had just relocated from an unspecified big city to the small town of Fairmeadows when the show started. The reason for their move was a melancholy one; John's business partner had killed himself after borrowing $250,000 of their firm's money and losing it all in a craps game. John hoped that he and his family would be able to start afresh in Fairmeadows, but since the Olcotts resided in a soap opera, they did not find their new home a paradise, to say the least.

In March the sponsor of *Fairmeadows, U.S.A.* announced that it was canceling the show. In September 1952 the show reappeared as a segment titled "The House in the Garden" on *The Kate Smith Hour.* Matteson and Strongin continued to play Alice and Evie, Lauren Gilbert replaced Howard St. John as John, Tom Taylor played John and Alice's son, and Monica Lovett played an older daughter. On the debut Lovett's character was in love with a minister played by James Vickery. The segment lasted less than a season on the show.

FAITH BALDWIN THEATRE OF ROMANCE, THE
Dramatic Anthology; B&W
January 20, 1951–October 20, 1951

ABC Sat. 11–11:30 a.m. (1/20/51–4/28/51)
ABC Sat. 12:30–1 p.m. (5/5/51–10/20/51)

Hostess/Narrator: *Faith Baldwin*

Producers: *Jack Barry, Dan Enright, Geoffrey Jones*

The first live dramatic anthology to air on a network Saturday mornings was *The Faith Baldwin Theatre of Romance,* featuring the famous author doing introductions and narrations for each production from New York. The first was "To My Beloved Wife," a light comedy starring Walter Abel as a father who, while making out his will, reviews the past, expressing doubts about how he has provided for his family. Other famous performers who appeared were Constance Bennett, John Carradine, Nancy Carroll, Nina Foch, and Luise Rainer (in a rare TV acting appearance). After three weeks on the air, the show alternated weekly with *Oh, Kay!* through April and *I Cover Times Square* until October.

FAITH DANIELS—See *Closer Look, A.*

FAITH FOR TODAY
Religious; B&W
May 21, 1950–December 25, 1955

ABC Sun. 12:30–1 p.m. (5/21/50–12/25/55)

Host: *Rev. William A. Fagal*

The Rev. William A. Fagal of the Washington Avenue Church in Brooklyn, New York, hosted this long-running inspirational series. Produced in cooperation with his denomination, the Seventh Day Adventist Church, *Faith for Today* began by having Fagal simply give religious advice and quote Biblical scripture, but expanded by having him act out a few lessons on the show. This trend continued once the show left ABC for syndication and gained more prominence by the mid-1970s, when it aired in many

markets under the title of *Westbrook Hospital* and became a religious drama with continuing characters in which Fagal played a hospital chaplain. When Fagal died in 1981, the series ended.

FAME, FORTUNE AND ROMANCE—See *Lifestyles of the Rich and Famous.*

•FAMILY FEUD
Game; Color
July 12, 1976–September 3, 1993

ABC Mon.–Fri. 1:30–2 p.m. (7/12/76–4/22/77)
ABC Mon.–Fri. 11:30 a.m.–Noon (4/25/77–6/27/80)
ABC Mon.–Fri. Noon–12:30 p.m. (6/30/80–7/23/84)
ABC Mon.–Fri. 11–11:30 a.m. and Noon–12:30 p.m. (8/13/84–10/5/84)
ABC Mon.–Fri. 11:30 a.m.–Noon (10/8/84–6/14/85)
CBS Mon.–Fri. 10–10:30 a.m. (7/4/88–1/11/91)
CBS Mon.–Fri. 10:30–11 a.m. (1/14/91–4/26/91)
CBS Mon.–Fri. 10–11 a.m. (4/29/91–5/24/91)
CBS Mon.–Fri. 10:30–11 a.m. (5/27/91–6/26/92)
CBS Mon.–Fri. 10–11 a.m. (6/29/92–9/3/93)

Hosts: *Richard Dawson (1976–85), Ray Combs (1988–93)*

ABC's longest-running daytime game show was *Family Feud,* a show which was an immediate success once it hit the air and had a successful revival a few years later. Original host Richard Dawson, who was a regular panelist on *The Match Game* when the show debuted, reprised the light, congenial style he displayed there. His distinctive approach (he had a habit of kissing the female contestants, and spent the first several minutes of the show bantering with players and the audience) helped set *Family Feud* apart from other game shows, and game show hosts, at the time.

The simple, fast-paced show did have its own appeal, which was no accident: Producer Mark Goodson had spent two years developing the concept. Two teams of five family members, related either by blood or marriage, competed in rounds to be the first to score 300 (later 400) points. Each round had one member of each family in a "face-off," where the two tried to be the first to hit a buzzer and give the most popular answer to a question asked of 100 people in a survey, such as "Name something that happens every four years." If the response given by the contestant who had buzzed in first was the number one answer, that family would be given the chance to list the rest of the survey answers (generally anywhere from 3 to 12). If the response was not the number one response, the other team got a chance to answer, and the team whose answer was higher on the list got to play on. The family attempting to give all the survey's answers lost the opportunity if it had three strikes, with each strike representing a wrong guess by a player. If the family failed to name all the survey's elements, the opposing team could win the round and the points accumulated by the other family by guessing one of the remaining unknown responses. Otherwise, the first family got the money. After two rounds, point values for each answer in succeeding rounds doubled and then tripled to allow for a family to win and play "Fast Money."

In "Fast Money," one family member tried to give the most popular answers (again, according to a survey of 100 people) to five questions in 15 seconds. If that player could not reach a total of 200 points with his or her answers, another family member held in isolation without knowing the previous answers had 20 seconds to offer different answers to the five questions, with a buzzer sounding if that contestant repeated a previous answer. Families failing to reach 200 points received $5 for every point, for a possible total of $995. But if the 200-point goal was met or surpassed, the family won $5,000.

Adding to the entertainment value of the game were the opening of each show, in which family members posed in frozen motion while announcer Gene Wood read their names, then came to life and moved to their podium to play; the shots of the opposing team trying to come up with potential responses the playing team members had missed; and the bizarre answers players came up with in desperation, which inevitably led their fellow family members to shout out the show's catch phrase, "Good answer!" to each other, even when it clearly wasn't. (Once, when asked to "Name a famous Mickey," a contestant replied, "The Mickey Way.")

Family Feud's popularity was wide-ranging. In 1978 the show started doing special nighttime celebrity shows on ABC which continued into the early 1980s. A year after it became a daytime hit, the show went into syndication at nighttime where the only difference was that $10,000 was the top prize in the Fast Money segment. It went from daily to nightly airings by 1980 and was very popular with local stations until *Wheel of Fortune* began to beat it decisively in the 1983–84 season. Around the same time the daytime network show began to sag, and both versions went off in 1985.

When *Family Feud* returned in 1988, it had a new host, a wisecracking blond imp named Ray Combs who took much the same approach as Dawson had toward contestants. It remained essentially the same game until 1992, when an opening "Bullseye" round let families increase the $5,000 up for grabs for a few additional thousand dollars if they could give the most popular answer for a question. Money was won in five quick face-offs between two contestants from each family, with each family member competing once. That same year, under the umbrella title *The New Family Feud Challenge,* the show aired twice daily, something done briefly in 1984 on ABC (with *Celebrity Family Feud* airing an hour earlier than the regular show and consisting of repeats of special weeks where casts of soap operas or old TV shows competed), and in 1991 on CBS. When it ended in 1993, CBS turned the 10–11 a.m. slot over to its affiliates to program, which many had been already been filling on their own.

"Bullseye" was also on the new syndicated version of the show, which Combs hosted from 1988 until September 1994. Then, when Dawson expressed a wish to come out of retirement and host *Family Feud* again, the producers dropped Combs unceremoniously and Dawson was host for the show's last year. A year later, on June 2, 1996, Combs committed suicide.

FAMILY GAME, THE
Game; B&W
June 19, 1967–December 29, 1967
ABC Mon.–Fri. 11:30 a.m.–Noon (6/19/67–12/29/67)
Host: *Bob Barker*

The format of this short-lived Chuck Barris production had surface similarities to that company's *The Newlywed Game,* only with the kids included, but its tone was different. The questions were nowhere near as suggestive as those on the latter, which may, oddly enough, explain why it did not catch on. Three teams, each composed of a husband, wife, and two kids, competed with the adults trying to predict their children's responses to questions. Despite the simple format, the show died against *The Hollywood Squares* on NBC and *The Dick Van Dyke Show* reruns on CBS. However, *The Family Game* did become the only daytime game show Bob Barker hosted between his two much bigger successes, *Truth or Consequences* from 1956–65 and *The Price Is Right* starting in 1972.

FAMILY SECRETS
Game; Color
March 22, 1993–June 11, 1993
NBC Mon.–Fri. 10:30–11 a.m. (3/22/93–6/11/93)
Host: *Bob Eubanks*

Produced at Disney/MGM Studios in Orlando, Florida, *Family Secrets* was similar to *Family Game.* Two competing family teams (consisting of husband, wife, and child) tried to guess each others' responses to questions about their respective members. Each correct answer netted at least $100 for the team. The team with the most money after three rounds of questions played for a family vacation, which they won if the mother or father answered three questions correctly.

•FANGFACE
Cartoon; Color
September 9, 1978–September 8, 1979
ABC Sat. 8:30–9 a.m. (9/9/78–10/28/78)
ABC Sat. 11–11:30 a.m. (11/4/78–5/26/79)
ABC Sat. 8–8:30 a.m. (6/2/79–9/8/79)
Voices:

Sherman Fangsworth (Fangface)	*Jerry Dexter*
Biff	*Frank Welker*
Puggsy	*Bart Braverman*
Kim	*Susan Blu*

With an unofficial nod to the 1957 cult horror movie *I Was a Teen-Age Werewolf, Fangface* told the story of a quartet of pubescent kids whose friendship was complicated by the fact that one of them could turn into a beast with one large arrow-pointed incisor sticking out from his mouth. Under the circumstances, Sherman Fangsworth (whose hairy alter ego was known as Fangface), his two male buddies, and Kim, a woman of Eurasian extraction, did pretty well. Riding in Fangface's Wolf Buggy vehicle, they helped fight crime successfully, sometimes despite themselves, since they had to contend not only with Fangsworth's condition but with the lamebrained antics of Fangface and Puggsy.

After a season's run, the character of Fangface appeared in the 1979 fall season as part of a longer cartoon series. See *The Plasticman Comedy Adventure Show.*

FANTASTIC FOUR, THE
Cartoon; Color
September 9, 1967–September 1, 1979

ABC Sat. 9:30–10 a.m. (9/9/67–9/7/68)
ABC Sat. 11:30–Noon (9/14/68–8/30/69)
ABC Sun. 10:30–11 a.m. (9/6/69–3/15/70)
NBC Sat. 10:30–11 a.m. (9/9/78–10/28/78)
NBC Sat. 8:30–9 a.m. (11/4/78–9/1/79)

Voices:

Mr. Fantastic (Reed Richards) (1967–70)	Gerald Mohr
Mr. Fantastic (Reed Richards) (1978–79)	Mike Road
The Invisible Girl (Sue Richards) (1967–70)	Jo Ann Pflug
The Invisible Girl (Sue Richards) (1978–79)	Ginny Tyler
The Thing (Ben Grimm) (1967–70)	Paul Frees
The Thing (Ben Grimm) (1978–79)	Ted Cassidy
The Human Torch (Johnny Storm) (1967–70)	Jack Flounders
H.E.R.B. (1978–79)	Frank Welker

Based on characters which made their debut in Marvel Comics in 1961, *The Fantastic Four* appeared in two different cartoon incarnations. Although the two versions were nearly a decade apart, three of the foursome remained pretty much the same, as did the characters' inability to conquer their human hang-ups despite their superheroic powers. The original group had scientists Reed Richards, his wife Sue, her brother Ben, and Johnny Storm bombarded unexpectedly by odd cosmic rays during the test flight of a rocket ship. The effects of the radiation left Reed a pliable mass whose body could be pulled and stretched to a seemingly limitless extent; Sue a woman with powers of invisibility; Ben a granitelike being reminiscent of the Incredible Hulk both in power and looks (except he was not green); and Johnny a man who could become a streaking flame. They used their new abilities to fight evildoers such as the Mole Men and Dr. Doom and donned circus tights with a stylized "4" emblazoned on their chests to make sure the bad guys knew who they were up against. The show's second and third seasons were repeats.

The Fantastic Four went into action again in 1978, but with a robot named H.E.R.B. (pronounced "Herbie") taking the place of the Human Torch. The new version also featured more gimmicks, such as the gang's U-Car of the original being superseded by the Fantisticar, which had nearly as many incredible abilities as its passengers.

Surprisingly, three weeks after the second show's cancellation, the Thing made his third network cartoon appearance with none other than Fred Flintstone in quite a different format (see *The Flintstones Comedy Show*).

FANTASTIC VOYAGE
Cartoon; Color
September 14, 1968–September 9, 1970

ABC Sat. 10:30–11 a.m. (9/14/68–8/30/69)
ABC Sat. Noon–12:30 a.m. (9/7/69–12/27/69)
ABC Sun. 10–10:30 a.m. (1/3/70–9/6/70)

Voices:

Commander Jonathan Kidd/ Professor Carter	Ted Knight
Dr. Erica Stone	Jane Webb
Dr. Cosby Birdwell	Marvin Miller

Based on the Oscar-winning (for special effects) 1966 feature film with Stephen Boyd and Raquel Welch, which in turn was based on a novel by Isaac Asimov, *Fantastic Voyage* detailed the exploits of scientists working for the Combined Miniature Defense Force. The CMDF had Kidd, Dr. Stone, and the mute, mystical Guru enter the Voyager, a vessel the CMDF had the ability to shrink and inject into the body of a researcher from the Soviet bloc who had sustained a head injury and needed the work of the miniaturized doctors to save his life. (In the movie, the ship was called the Proteus.) Inside the Voyager, the scientists explored the biological functions of the researcher's body while trying to complete their mission. The second season consisted of repeats.

FANTASY
Game; Color
September 13, 1982–October 28, 1983

NBC Mon.–Fri. 3–4 p.m. (9/13/82–10/28/83)

Regulars: *Peter Marshall, Leslie Uggams, Chris Lemmon, Meredith MacRae*

This update of such old tearjerkers as *Queen for a Day* and *Strike It Rich* was notable only in that it was a rare hour-long game show and the first game show with a black co-hostess. Leslie Uggams shared emceeing duties with Peter Marshall, who formerly served as the host asking Uggams questions when she was an occasional guest on *The Hollywood Squares* from 1972–80. (Ironically, a revival of that game show would replace *Fantasy*—see *The Match Game/Hollywood Squares Hour.*) The duo gave contestants in the studio audience new products or services suggested by their family or friends. Segments designed to project an image of largesse featured videotapes of actors—"roving reporters" Chris Lemmon and Meredith MacRae—who roamed across America bestowing unexpected gifts on selected "lucky" folk.

If *Fantasy* accomplished anything at all, it reinforced the notion left by its predecessors that Americans' fantasies most often involve a desire for money. The show received a reported 85,000 letters of request weekly, with the most desired item being money for food, medical bills, and electrical bills. However, the large amount of correspondence did not manifest itself in big ratings against *General Hospital* and *Guiding Light,* so *Fantasy* had to face the reality of cancellation shortly after a year's run.

•FAR OUT SPACE NUTS
Sitcom; Color
September 6, 1975–September 4, 1977

CBS Sat. 11–11:30 a.m. (9/6/75–9/4/76)
CBS Sun. 9:30–10 a.m. (9/12/76–9/4/77)

Cast:

Junior	*Bob Denver*
Barney	*Chuck McCann*
Honk	*Patty Maloney*

Two of TV's favorite bumblers, Bob Denver and Chuck McCann (McCann also co-wrote some of the scripts), combined forces in this slapstick-oriented Saturday morning entry. While serving as dockworkers for NASA, Junior and Barney routinely went about loading meals onto a rocket set for outer space. All went well until Junior absentmindedly thought Barney said "Launch" instead of "Lunch" and pressed a button blasting the ship into space. When they arrived on an unknown planet, a native creature who resembled a shaggy white dog with a horn for its snout befriended the hapless duo, and Junior named it Honk. Barney showed more concern than Junior did over getting back home, but despite several opportunities they never seemed to make it, thanks largely to Junior. For example, the best Junior could do when he received the power to wish for anything he wanted in the world was to conjure up a pie to hit Barney in the face with. And then there was the episode when a device transported them back in time to the scene of the accidental launching, and Barney tried to repeat their routine without making the same mistake, but Junior . . . well, you can guess the rest. The second season consisted of repeats.

FASHION MAGIC
Women's; B&W
November 10, 1950–September 29, 1951

CBS Mon/Fri 3:30–4 p.m. (11/10/50–6/1/51)
CBS Tue./Fri. 3:30–4 p.m. (6/5/51–6/15/51)
CBS Sat. 11–11:30 a.m. (6/23/51–9/29/51)

Hostess: *Ilka Chase (11/10/50–4/20/51), Arlene Francis (4/23/51–9/29/51)*

Discussions with industry leaders and models on wardrobe and accessories, with the accent on the feminine side, was the focus of this series. Sponsor International Latex Corporation made sure no one forgot its involvement in the fashion. A *Billboard* review of the November 24, 1950 show noted that Ilka Chase interviewed guests with the sponsor's undergarments surrounding them on the set.

Chase left the show after five months due to a heavy lecture schedule, and fellow New York socialite Arlene Francis replaced her. It did not matter, however; the show was a ratings disaster, scoring an overall minuscule 1.3 while airing in 20 cities, and it went off in the fall of 1951.

•FAT ALBERT AND THE COSBY KIDS
Cartoon; Color
September 9, 1972–September 2, 1989

CBS Sat. 12:30–1 p.m. (9/9/72–8/28/76)
CBS Sat. Noon–12:30 p.m. (9/11/76–8/27/77)
CBS Sat. 12:30–1 p.m. (9/17/77–1/21/78)
CBS Sat. Noon–12:30 p.m. (1/28/78–9/2/78)
CBS Sat. 12:30–1 p.m. (9/16/78–9/1/79)
CBS Sat. 11:30 a.m.–Noon (9/8/79–8/30/80)
CBS Sat. Noon–12:30 p.m. (9/16/80–9/5/81)
CBS Sat. 12:30–1 p.m. (9/19/81–11/28/81)
CBS Sat. 12:30–1 p.m. (9/18/82–8/20/83)
CBS Sat. 1–1:30 p.m. (11/19/83–8/25/84)
NBC Sat. 12:30–1 p.m. (1/14/89–2/4/89)
NBC Sat. 11:30 a.m.–Noon (2/11/89–9/2/89)

Voices:

Fat Albert/Mushmouth/Mudfoot/	
Dumb Donald/the Brown	
Hornet (1979–80)	*Bill Cosby*
Russell/Bucky	*Jan Crawford*
Weird Harold	*Gerald Edwards*
Rudy/Devery	*Eric Suter*

No other Saturday morning cartoon of the 1970s succeeded as well as *Fat Albert and the Cosby Kids* in combining entertaining story lines with thought-provoking messages for young viewers. The concept for the show sprang from comedian Bill Cosby's early stand-up routines where he reminisced about his days growing up in Philadelphia. This led to a nighttime NBC cartoon special, "Hey, Hey, Hey, It's Fat Albert," on November 12, 1969, which formed the basis of this series. Fat Albert was the unofficial leader of a coterie of kids who hung out in some unspecified junkyard in a big city. With his deep voice, stocky build, and friendly demeanor, he won the respect of such offbeat types as Rudy, a well-to-do and occasionally conniving sort; Weird Harold, who besides living up to his name was tall and gangly; Mushmouth, who as his name implied had a garbled manner of speaking; and Russell, the nasal-voiced youngest member of the group (he was based on Cosby's real-life little brother). Their parents rarely appeared. The show dealt with the boys' recreational activities, their insights into general social issues like relating to the physically challenged, and the ways in which they

Hey hey hey! It's Fat Albert and the Cosby Kids, *who were part of a series named by* TV Guide *in 1993 as the best cartoon of the 1970s.*

came to terms with their own emotions, which was often a rocky process.

Bill Cosby came on camera during parts of the show to comment with or about the characters and what they learned during the episode. But it was not at all preachy, with much of the cartoon devoted to comic interludes that did not detract from the message, plus a song at the end of each show reinforcing the information with a peppy tune in which the characters sang and made music with materials from their landfill hangout.

From 1972–74 and 1975–77, several variations aired. In September 1979, the series assumed the title *The New Fat Albert Show*, but it was similar to prior episodes with the exception of a new character, the Brown Hornet, whose animated adventures in outer space as a dashing, hammy superhero were watched by the gang on their TV set in their club shack midway through each episode. After 1980, all shows seen were reruns. However, 50 new half-hour shows had been made for syndication by 1984.

FEARLESS FOSDICK
Children's; B&W
June 15, 1952–July 6, 1952
NBC Sun. 4–4:30 p.m. (6/15/52–7/6/52)
Voices: *Jean Carson, John Griggs, Gilbert Mack*
Regulars: *Mary Chase Marionettes*

Fearless Fosdick was a parody of the Dick Tracy cartoon character who first appeared in Al Capp's "Li'l Abner" newspaper cartoon. On this TV series, Fosdick and the rest

of the troupe were marionettes. Joining the derby-wearing Fosdick in his struggle against nefarious forces were his sidekick Schmoozer (Junior in Dick Tracy's world) and their boss, the Chief. The series moved into the early evening before ending on September 28, 1952.

FEATHER YOUR NEST
Game; B&W
October 4, 1954–July 27, 1956
NBC Mon.–Fri. 12:30–1 p.m. (10/4/54–7/27/56)
Regulars: *Bud Collyer, Lou Prentiss (10/4/54–10/8/54), Jeanne Williams (10/11/54–10/22/54), Janis Carter (10/25/54–7/27/56)*

In this game show, two competing couples tried to win the chance to furnish a room in their apartment or home each day. To reach that goal, one member of each couple had a minute to find hidden feathers with questions attached to merchandise on display in that day's "room." After completing that task, his or her spouse had to answer each question correctly to claim that prize. Contestants had a chance to win all the furniture on display in every show.

The show weathered some initial shakeups involving the role of the female assistant who displayed the furniture. After going through two of them in the first three weeks, it finally settled with former 1940s film star Janis Carter, who handled the duties for the rest of its 21-month run. Assisting her was the show's unlikely mascot, a dachshund named Miss Liebchen, who sported ermine necklaces.

FELIX THE CAT—See *Twisted Tales of Felix the Cat, The.*

•FIEVEL'S AMERICAN TAILS
Cartoon; Color
September 12, 1992–September 11, 1993
CBS Sat. 8–8:30 a.m. (9/12/92–9/11/93)
Voices:

Fievel Mousekewitz	*Philip Glasser*
Tiger	*Dom DeLuise*
Cat R. Waul ("Boss")	*Gerrit Graham*
Chula	*Dan Castellaneta*
Mr. Bernie Mousekewitz ("Poppa")	*Lloyd Battista*
Mrs. Mousekewitz ("Momma")	*Susan Silo*
Tanya Mousekewitz	*Cathy Cavadini*

Fievel Mousekewitz was a cowboy in training living in the Old West town of Green River. The twist was that he and other residents were rodents trying to avoid the hungry mouth of shifty Cat R. Waul, a dapper feline dandy who had an English accent and sported a monocle. Cat's occasionally gullible accomplice was Chula the tarantula, and the two of them plotted their deeds in the Morton Walton Funerals building. Keeping Fievel in check and out of danger was his big pal Tiger the cat with the walrus mustache, who nonetheless could be timid and childlike himself. Fievel's family included his immigrant parents, who ran a violin shop, his sister Tanya, and his baby sister Tasha. The mouse town was laid out under a general merchandise store in the human world.

The emphasis of *Fievel's American Tails* was on friendship and respect for one another, with Fievel often setting the example for others to follow. To its credit, the program did not downplay the Mousekewitz's Jewish heritage, and in fact Poppa often spoke with a Yiddish accent, a rarity among the WASPy leads dominating TV cartoons.

Fievel's American Tails top-billed Dom DeLuise in its official cast list, and even credited him for "special oohs and aahs." The series was a spin-off of two theatrical cartoons, *An American Tail* (1986) and *An American Tail: Fievel Goes West* (1991), with DeLuise and Philip Glasser voicing their same characters.

50 CLUB—See *Ruth Lyons' 50 Club.*

50 GRAND SLAM
Game; Color
October 4, 1976–December 31, 1976
NBC Mon.–Fri. Noon–12:30 p.m. (10/4/76–12/31/76)

Host: *Tom Kennedy*

The networks banished "big money" game shows in the late 1950s following testimony that nighttime shows *Twenty-One* and *The $64,000 Question,* among others, were rigged to allow some contestants to know answers ahead of time. But thanks to the passage of time and the increased competition of game shows by the mid-1970s, *50 Grand Slam* became the first daytime network show in more than 15 years to allow winnings of up to $50,000. In this format, four players in various fields of knowledge attempted to answer questions about their areas of expertise by competing one-on-one starting at a round worth $200. The winner there could stop or try for $500. He or she faced similar decisions in six subsequent rounds which paid $1,000, $2,000, $5,000, $10,000, $20,000, and $50,000, with the risk being that anyone trying for the higher amounts who lost forfeited all money earned to that point.

The show did have one clever visual aspect, a set with the isolation booth located inside the zero of a large "50" seen on stage. But viewers preferred the melodramatic suspense of *The Young and the Restless* on CBS instead, so *50 Grand Slam* collapsed after a 13-week run.

•FIGHT BACK! WITH DAVID HOROWITZ
Informational; Color
1980–92
Syndicated 30 minutes weekly beginning September 1980

Host: *David Horowitz*

Los Angeles–based consumer expert David Horowitz hosted this entry, which began as a local offering on the NBC affiliate, in which he offered buying tips in a sprightly, fast-paced format. He began each show with its highlight, the "Fight Back! Commercial Challenge," in which he, and sometimes audience members as well, tested the claims of an actual advertisement. Included in one test were the notorious claims and counterclaims between soft drink giants Coke and Pepsi in commercials in the 1980s over whose cola beverage consumers preferred (neither emerged with a substantial victory). Other elements included some in-studio information and taped on-location reports about various shopping issues, such as whether to use paper or plastic shopping bags.

Horowitz's approach prompted some critics to say he was more concerned with the promotions of products and services than with the quality of the goods and duties themselves. (For example, one observer charged that he cared only whether a can of soup contained exactly what the label said it contained, and not how the soup tasted.) Others objected to the fact that he contacted the companies used in the challenge to ask how they tested their claims before trying to do so himself, with some experts believing this compromised the integrity of the experiment. But this did not stop Horowitz from using his version of on-air testing not only on *Fight Back!* but also on other talk shows on which he was a guest, such as *The Tonight Show* (where Johnny Carson parodied him as "David Howitzer"). And even skeptics had to admit that Horowitz's catchy theme song, with its prominent "Fight Back!" hook line, worked to get viewers into the consumer spirit. So did Horowitz's closing bit where, after asking viewers what they should do if they felt they were being ripped off, he and the audience yelled—you guessed it—"Fight Back!"

After the show ended production, Horowitz continued doing his program as a daily syndicated radio show.

•FIREBALL XL-5
Children's Sci-Fi; B&W
October 5, 1963–September 25, 1965
NBC Sat. 10:30–11 a.m. (10/5/63–9/25/65)

Voices:

Col. Steve Zodiac	Paul Maxwell
Venus	Sylvia Anderson
Robert the Robot	Gerry Anderson
Lt. Ninety	David Graham
Commander Zero	John Bluthal

Creators/Executive Producers: *Gerry and Sylvia Anderson*

A rare British import on the networks' Saturday morning lineup, *Fireball XL-5* was filmed in 1961, shown on England's Associated Television by 1962, and came to America a year later. It was the first show to use "Supermarionation," a process developed by Gerry and Sylvia Anderson, where a puppeteer could manipulate parts of a marionette with electronics in addition to strings to make them seem more lifelike. It was a solid effort to make the characters look more realistic, although there was one glitch in the initial outing: The heads of the marionettes were too big for their small bodies.

From left, Venus, the Professor, and Steve Zodiac fly to a new adventure in Fireball XL-5.

Nonetheless, *Fireball XL-5* garnered good reviews and a decent audience during its 39-show run. Its title referred to a spaceship about 100 years in the future. Colonel Zodiac was its pilot, and Venus, his girlfriend, was its co-pilot. Along with eccentric science whiz Professor Matic and occasional pilot Robert the Robot, they protected Space City from aliens as part of World Space Patrol under the orders of Commander Zero and Lt. Ninety. Their adventures were distinguished by a variety of futuristic gadgets like hovering motorcycles and oxygen pills that let characters float in space without a suit.

Other Supermarionation series seen in America in syndication were *Supercar* (1962, whose success led NBC to try *Fireball XL-5*), *Stingray* (1965), *Captain Scarlet and the Mysterons* (1967), and *Joe 90* (1968). It was not until 1994 that another show in this field aired on a U.S. network (see *Thunderbirds*). The Andersons also produced several science fiction series with live actors syndicated in America, including *Space 1999* (1975–77) and *Space Precinct* (1994–95).

FIRST 100 YEARS, THE
Soap Opera; B&W
December 4, 1950–June 27, 1952
CBS Mon.–Fri. 2:30–2:45 p.m. (12/4/50–6/27/52)
Cast:

Chris Thayer	James Lydon
Connie Martin Thayer	
(1950–January 1952)	Olive Stacey
Connie Martin Thayer	
(January–June 1952)	Anne Sargent
Mr. Thayer	Don Tobin
Mrs. Thayer	Valerie Cossart
Mr. Martin	Robert Armstrong
Mrs. Martin	Nana Bryant
Margy Martin	Nancy Malone

The first CBS soap opera was *The First 100 Years,* based on an obscure ABC radio show which aired in the summer of 1948. In early 1950, the CBS nighttime anthology series *Silver Theater* ran a TV adaptation with Jimmy Lydon and William Frawley. Then the giant consumer company Procter & Gamble decided to make its first sponsorship in daytime TV with the property, and it was announced that both Lydon and Frawley would repeat their roles. There has been no confirmation, however, that Frawley actually took part in the daytime show before beginning his biggest role in the fall of 1951 as Fred Mertz of *I Love Lucy.*

Lydon did make the series, though, playing a man getting married on the first week of the show and then moving his new wife into a decrepit three-story Victorian mansion. The couple's problems with their living quarters, their meddling in-laws, including Connie's sister Margy, and the typical problems any newlyweds face gave credence to the show's title, a reference to the old saying that "the first 100 years of marriage are the hardest."

For a 15-minute daily show, *The First 100 Years* represented quite an undertaking for television. The cast rehearsed four hours a day for each episode on a special stage in New York City's Liederkranz Hall, which contained a permanent house set. To retain small-town flavor, cameramen went to villas in Long Island and Westchester County in New York to film authentic backgrounds which were used on the show. But the show's most notable achievement was technical: Its debut also saw the first commercial use of the Teleprompter, a machine which cues actors on their lines and which is now used routinely throughout the medium.

The show, which emphasized light, sometimes comic conflicts, did fairly well in its 2½ years on the air. In the spring of 1952 the show ranked among the top 10 daily daytime series. But Procter & Gamble officials reportedly felt that it was not drawing quite the audience the company desired, so they replaced it with another soap opera which might actually last 100 years—see *The Guiding Light.*

FIRST LOOK, THE

Children's; B&W

October 16, 1965–April 9, 1966

NBC Sat. Noon–12:30 p.m. (10/16/65–4/9/66)

Regulars: *Oscar Brand, Neil Jones, Sally Sheffield, Jackie Washington*

Subtitled "Wonders of the World," this live New York studio show starred folk singer Oscar Brand, who each week led the exploration of an educational issue, such as the use of language, the debut's theme. Accompanying Brand in examining the topic at hand were three talented youngsters—Jackie and Sally, both singers, and Neil, a dancer. The inspiration for the series was a group of books by Jeanne Bendick. It died opposite the more entertaining *Bugs Bunny Show* on ABC.

FIRST LOVE

Soap Opera; B&W

July 5, 1954–December 30, 1955

NBC Mon.–Fri. 3:30–3:45 p.m. (7/5/54–8/27/54)

NBC Mon.–Fri. 4:15–4:30 p.m. (8/30/54–12/30/55)

Cast:

Zach James (7/5/54–4/8/55)	*Val Dufour*
Zach James (4/11/55–12/30/55)	*Tod Andrews*
Laurie Kennedy James	*Patricia Barry*
Chris (1954)	*Frankie Thomas*
Amy	*Rosemary Prinz*
Paul Kennedy	*Melvin Ruick*
Doris Kennedy	*Peggy Allenby*
Judge Kennedy	*Howard Smith*
Mike Kennedy	*John Dutra*
Wallace Grant	*Henry Stanton*
Ruth Taylor (1954)	*Scotty MacGregor*
Sam Morrison (1954)	*Hal Currier*
Priscilla "Petey" Cummings	
(1954–55)	*Rita Fredericks*
David (early 1955)	*Bob Courtleigh*
David (May 1955–)	*Dean Harens*
Quentin Andrews (1955)	*Frederick Downs*
Tony Morgan (1955)	*Peter Cookson*
Bruce McKee (1955)	*Jay Barney*
Jenny (1955)	*Barbara Myers*
Matthew James (8/15/55–12/55)	*Paul McGrath*
Leona (late 1955)	*Nancy Pollock*
Jack Doyle (late 1955)	*Court Benson*

NBC's ex-head of daytime programming Adrian Samish produced this live serial from Philadelphia for the network. It examined the tumultuous marriage of the Jameses, a pair of young lovers, and their relationships with others, chiefly Chris and Amy, another married couple, and Laurie's family, including her parents Paul and Doris. Weak-willed Zach had difficulties at home and at work at a jet engine plant, where his nemesis was scheming Wallace Grant. Wallace eagerly seized the chance to aggravate Zach when

he caught wind of an affair between the latter and Petey. This news upset Laurie, and in early 1955 she and Zach separated.

Laurie moved from the fictional town of Harrison when she accepted a job offer from Washington, D.C. While Zach confided his sad situation to sympathetic friend and co-worker Quentin Andrews, Laurie began seeing David, an attorney, in the nation's capital, but circumstances eventually brought her back to Harrison and her husband. Tony Morgan, a newcomer, had a fling with Petey and was planning to leave with her until she turned up murdered. Zach, who collapsed in her apartment, became investigator Bruce McKee's prime suspect. Laurie was sure of her husband's innocence, and with the help of David they searched the apartment and found proof that exonerated him, generating suspicions that Grant may have been the real killer. Meanwhile, tragedy struck Amy in late 1954 when her pilot husband Chris died in a test flight, leaving Grant to make a move on the widow. She put the kibosh on his attempt and moved out of town briefly, then returned and married Bruce McKee before the show ended, even though he had to cope with the possibility that a recently arrived girl in Harrison named Jenny might be his biological daughter.

As for the newly reunited Laurie and Zach, she went to work at a dress shop, and he came back to the jet engine plant following Andrews's recommendation. Zach's father Matthew arrived in town and started working at the plant too while wooing Leona. Yet Matthew's world was shattered dramatically in the last major story line as conniving Jack Doyle broke into the plant and wounded him fatally. Zach survived the onslaught and saw Doyle arrested, and on the show's last episode could at least be hopeful that he and Laurie might be heading for a less eventful new year.

FIVE STAR COMEDY—See *Popsicle Five Star Comedy.*

FLAME IN THE WIND—See *A Time For Us.*

FLASH GORDON—See *The New Adventures of Flash Gordon.*

FLINTSTONE FUNNIES, THE—See *The Flintstones Comedy Show.*

•FLINTSTONE KIDS, THE

Cartoon; Color

September 13, 1986–May 26, 1990

ABC Sat. 9–10 a.m. (9/13/86–9/19/87)

ABC Sat. 11–11:30 a.m. (9/26/87–1/23/88)

ABC Sat. 11:30 a.m.–Noon (1/30/88–7/16/88)

ABC Sat. 9:30–10 a.m. (7/23/88–9/3/88)

ABC Sat. 8–8:30 a.m. (10/22/88–9/2/89)

ABC Sat. Noon–12:30 a.m. (1/6/90–5/26/90)

Voices:

Freddy Flintstone (1986–87)	Lennie Weinrib
Freddy Flintstone (1987–90)	Scott Menville
Barney Rubble/Cragmire/Flab Slab	Hamilton Camp
Wilma Flintstone (1986–87)	Julie Dees
Wilma Flintstone (1987–90)	Elizabeth Lyn Fraser
Betty Rubble/Miss Rockbottom	B. J. Ward
Ed Flintstone/Edna Flintstone	Henry Corden
Robert Rubble/Dino the	
Dinosaur (1986–88)/	
Captain Caveman	Mel Blanc
Nate Slate/Dino the Dinosaur	
(1988–90)	Frank Welker
Rocky Ratrock	Marilyn Schreffler
Dreamchip Gemstone	Susan Blu
Philo Quartz	Bumper Robinson
Cavey Jr.	Charles Adler
Narrator	Kenneth Mars

After having spent four years in reruns on NBC, two years in new shows on CBS, and six more years in new shows on NBC, the Flintstone characters returned to the network they had left 20 years earlier in prime time in a "prequel" of their later selves. The 10-year-old versions of Fred, Barney, Wilma, and Betty had to contend with their "puppy" Dino, their parents Ed and Edna Flintstone, and Robert Rubble (voiced by the same actors who did the adult Fred and Barney), and plenty of new faces, the most prominent of which were the bully Rocky Ratrock, future debutante Dreamchip Gemstone, junior detective Philo Quartz, and budding entrepreneur Nate Slate. Between stories involving these personalities there were sketches like "Captain Caveman and Son," featuring the prehistoric crime fighter and his offspring (see *Captain Caveman and the Teen Angels*); "Flintstone Funnies," not to be confused with the earlier series of the same name, where the four main characters got to enact their dreams; and "Dino's Dilemma," a spot showing baby Dino handling certain situations by himself.

On September 15, 1988, the show aired on ABC nighttime with "*The Flintstones Kids* 'Just Say No' Special," in which First Lady Nancy Reagan appeared after the cartoon to promote nationwide "Just Say No" clubs designed to prevent drug abuse among the young. The show had its last full run that season, coming back in repeats in 1990. For more details, see *The Flintstones*.

•FLINTSTONES, THE

Cartoon; Color
January 17, 1967–September 5, 1970

NBC Sat. 10–10:30 a.m. (1/17/67–8/30/69)
NBC Sat. Noon–12:30 p.m. (9/6/69–12/20/69)
NBC Sat. 11:30 a.m.–Noon (12/27/69–9/5/70)

Cast:

Fred Flintstone	Alan Reed
Wilma Flintstone/Pebbles	
Flintstone (1962–66)	Jean VanderPyl

Barney Rubble/Dino the Dinosaur	Mel Blanc
Betty Jean McBricker Rubble	
(1960–64)	Bea Benaderet
Betty Jean McBricker Rubble	
(1964–66)	Gerry Johnson
Bamm Bamm (1963–66)	Don Messick

Other Regular Voices: Howard Morris, Doug Young

Co-Producers: William Hanna, Joseph Barbera

The only network TV cartoon show to last more than two nighttime seasons before *The Simpsons* in 1989, *The Flintstones* and their spin-offs represent the longest-running and most successful cartoon characters made for television. Fred, Barney, Wilma, Betty, and their children and pets are among the most recognizable figures in modern American popular culture, which makes it somewhat surprising to learn that when the show debuted on ABC nighttime on September 30, 1960, few insiders predicted it would last the season, much less become an institution.

The premise was simple—a prehistoric version of *The Honeymooners* characters created on Jackie Gleason's nighttime TV program of the 1950s, with loudmouth, grumbling Fred replacing Ralph Kramden and goofy, occasionally cowering Barney doing the same for Ed Norton. The difference of course was the cleverly exploited prehistoric angle, which saw elements of modern-day life transposed to the Stone Age, such as a telephone with a ram's horn for a receiver, a dishwasher using a mammoth woolly elephant's trunk as a nozzle, and staircases made of stationary dinosaurs and their serrated fins. The most often seen device was Fred's automobile, which sported steamroller wheels and an animal skin top and back.

The Flintstones and Rubbles lived on Cobblestone Lane in the town of Bedrock (population 2,500), located 250 feet below sea level. Fred worked for Mr. Slately at a quarry company which had a variety of titles, but most of his misadventures happened back home in the suburbs with next-door neighbor Barney. Like Kramden and Norton, the duo brought out each other's worst tendencies to do the wrong thing. Their wives learned to laugh about and forgive many of their schemes, though Wilma, like Alice Kramden on *The Honeymooners*, could be rather stern when she was upset by her hubby. In turn, Fred was sometimes exasperated by Wilma, but he usually hid his anger from her. On the other hand, he did not hold back at all when Barney noticed something at Fred's expense and chuckled, "Ah-hee-hee-hee!" at him. There was no doubt in anyone's mind when Fred was happy—he let out a gleeful "Yabba-dabba-doo," his (and the series') best-known catch phrase.

Although Fred and Wilma had put up with their yammering, affectionate pet Dino, a Snorkasaurus, since the start of the show, both couples remained childless until February 22, 1963, when Wilma gave birth to a daughter named Pebbles (on the show, Pebbles's birth year was given as 10,000 B.C.). That same day, the Ideal Toy Company distributed 250,000 Pebbles dolls to stores. The next season, the Rubbles adopted a strong blond infant named Bamm-Bamm, who liked to say his name while hitting his club to the ground, and both added to the often tumultuous mix at their parents' houses.

Guests on the show included some recognizable stars who voiced caricatures of themselves, such as two visits by Tony Curtis (as "Stony Curtis"), and Elizabeth Montgomery and Dick York as Samantha and Darrin from *Bewitched*. Those who wonder how much emphasis the producers placed on having distinctive voices for the show should know that Hanna and Barbera threw out the soundtrack for the first five shows because they did not like the way Fred and Barney sounded.

One voice the show nearly lost was that of Mel Blanc, who came close to dying following a car crash on Dead Man's Curve in California in 1962. While he recuperated, he and the cast recorded their lines from his bedroom. During this time Daws Butler replaced Blanc for a few episodes, and it is hard not to miss—Butler's Barney sounds much more higher-pitched and nasal than Blanc's.

Somehow the cast made it more or less intact until its final nighttime show of September 2, 1966 (Bea Benadaret left in 1964 to star in the nighttime sitcom *Petticoat Junction*). After repeats aired on NBC Saturdays for nearly four years, the show began a long run in syndication among juvenile viewers—somewhat of a surprise, as the original promotion for *The Flintstones* was as a cartoon for adults.

One thing viewers will not find in repeats are commercials during the prime time run for sponsor Winston Cigarettes where Fred and Barney were shown having a few smokes while trying to avoid house chores from their wives. That image stands in stark contrast to the successful Flintstone chewable vitamin line which began in the 1970s and sported the imprints of all the characters except Betty. Flintstone characters also have fared well since the 1970s on a line of cereals featuring their names (e.g., Cocoa Pebbles) and on rides bearing their names on amusement parks such as King's Island in Cincinnati, Ohio, and King's Dominion in Virginia.

There have been numerous other well-received offshoots from the show, including some later network incarnations (see *The Flintstone Kids, The Flintstones Comedy Hour,* and *The Flintstones Comedy Show*). In 1994 the show became a hit live-action feature film with John Goodman as Fred and Elizabeth Taylor as Wilma's mother.

•FLINTSTONES COMEDY HOUR, THE
Cartoon; Color
September 9, 1972–January 26, 1974

CBS Sat. 11 a.m.–Noon (9/9/72–9/1/73)
CBS Sat. 8–8:30 a.m. (9/8/73–1/26/74)

Voices:

Fred Flintstone	Alan Reed
Wilma Flintstone	Jean VanderPyl
Barney Rubble/Zonk/Stub	Mel Blanc
Betty Rubble/Wiggy/Cindy	Gay Hartwig

Pebbles Flintstone	Mickey Stevens
Bamm-Bamm Rubble	Jay North
Moonrock	Lennie Weinrib
Penny	Mitzi McCall
Fabian	Carl Esser
Noodles	John Stephenson
Schleprock	Don Messick

After CBS gave the Flintstone offspring a show in 1971–72 (see *Pebbles and Bamm-Bamm*), the network approved the return of their elders on their first Saturday morning series since the 1960s repeats ended. Betty had a new voice, but the situations were similar to what the Flintstones and Rubbleses had faced before, only now Fred and Barney meddled more in the affairs of their grown-up children and their friends. The latter group included the same members seen on *Pebbles and Bamm-Bamm,* such as Moonrock, who participated in drag races with buddy Bamm-Bamm in their Cave Buggy against the bad Bronto Bunch (Zonk, Stub, and Noodles), and Schleprock, a walking, whining purple lump of a man whose full face was hidden from view by an oversized hat. The series ran a half hour less in its short-lived second season and sported the new title *The Flintstones Show.*

By the way, Pebbles and Bamm-Bamm did get married, though not on this show. It occurred on a nighttime ABC two-hour special on February 7, 1993 titled "I Yabba-Dabba Doo!"

•FLINTSTONES COMEDY SHOW, THE
Cartoon; Color
February 3, 1979–September 8, 1984

NBC Sat. 11–11:30 a.m. (2/3/79–9/15/79)
NBC Sat. 9–10 a.m. (9/22/79–12/1/79)
NBC Sat. 9–10:30 a.m. (12/8/79–9/5/81)
NBC Sat. 8–8:30 a.m. (9/12/81–9/8/84)

Voices:

Fred Flintstone	Henry Corden
Wilma Flintstone/Pebbles Flintstone (1979–80)	Jean VanderPyl
Barney Rubble/Dino/Captain Caveman (1980–81)/Chester (1980–81)	Mel Blanc
Betty Rubble	Gay Autterson
Pebbles Flintstone (1980–82)	Russi Taylor
Bamm-Bamm (1979–80)	Don Messick
Bamm-Bamm (1980–82)/Turkey (1979–80)	Michael Sheehan
Benjamin "Benjy" Grimm (1979–80)	Wayne Morton
The Thing (1979–80)	Joe Baker
Kelly (1979–80)	Noelle North
Betty (1979–80)/Miss Twilly (1979–80)	Marilyn Schreffler
Spike (1979–80)	Art Metrano
Stretch (1979–80)	John Stephenson
Ronald Redford (1979–80)	John Erwin

The Schmoo (1979–80)/Rockjaw
   (1980–82) — Frank Welker
Nita (1979–80) — Dolores Cantu-Primo
Billy Joe (1979–80) — Chuck McCann
Mickey (1979–80) — Bill Edelson
Frank Frankenstone (1980–82) — Charles Nelson Reilly
Hidea Frankenstone (1980–82) — Ruta Lee
Atrocia Frankenstone (1980–82) — Zelda Rubinstein
Freaky Frankenstone (1980–82) — Paul Reubens
Lou Granite (1980–82) — Ken Mars

Five years after leaving CBS, Fred, Wilma, Barney, Betty, and the rest returned to Saturday mornings on NBC under an array of titles and different formats. First up was *The New Fred and Barney Show* (February 3–September 15, 1979), basically a rehash of *The Flintstones*. From September to December it became *Fred and Barney Meet the Thing*, in which the character from *The Fantastic Four* (q.v.) became a separate installment of the Bedrock group (Fred and Barney did not meet the Thing physically on the show). Here the Thing and his "normal" high school alter ego Benjy were voiced by two actors, whereas one actor handled both on *The Fantastic Four*. Benjy hung out with his cohorts Kelly, Betty, and Ronald at Centerville High School but was ready to transform himself at any time into the Thing by connecting two halves of a ring together and saying "Thing Ring, do your thing!" The sight of the Thing usually kept the Yancey Street Gang, a mean group on choppers consisting of Spike the leader and Turkey and Stretch, at bay.

In mid-December 1979 came *Fred and Barney Meet the Schmoo*, in which cartoons from *The New Schmoo* (q.v.) joined the existing show to form a 90-minute extravaganza (and no, Fred and Barney did not meet the Schmoo, either). The following season, on November 22, 1980, the Thing and Schmoo segments vanished and the show became *The Flintstones Comedy Show*. The show retained its hour and a half length for the first season, but several new elements were added. For returning characters, Dino had his own adventures, and Pebbles and Bamm-Bamm became sleuths with Dino in another segment. The biggest transformation came for Betty and Wilma, who in one segment became reporters for the Bedrock Daily News under publisher Lou Granite and found themselves involved in predicaments requiring the help of Captain Caveman (see *Captain Caveman and the Teen Angels)* and the paper's bespectacled copyboy Chester. All new to the cast were Fred and Barney's monstrous neighbors the Frankenstones, their children Atrocia and Freaky, and their tough pet Rockjaw. All segments had original episodes in both the 1980–81 and 1981–82 seasons, something of a rarity for the Saturday morning cartoon world, especially since the second season had the show shrink 60 minutes, down to a half-hour presentation.

The Flintstone Funnies was the September 1982 incarnation of the show, with the main four characters dealing with outer space creatures in new adventures. "The Flintstones have joined the sci-fi caravan and managed to lose much of the show's earlier humor in the process," moaned a *Variety* reviewer. Nevertheless, the format lasted the longest of any of them tried by NBC during the Flintstones' nearly six-year run at the network. The characters returned yet again two years later as *The Flintstone Kids* (q.v.).

FLINTSTONES SHOW, THE—See *Flintstones Comedy Show, The*.

FLIP!
Children's; Color
September 17, 1988–October 22, 1988
CBS Sat. 11:30 a.m.–Noon (9/17/88–10/22/88)

This short-lived variety show designed for youths ages 8–13, which featured music videos and comic sketches by unknown actors, had no host or regulars.

FLYING TIGERS—See *Major Dell Conway of the Flying Tigers*.

FOLLOW YOUR HEART
Soap Opera; B&W
August 3, 1953–January 8, 1954
NBC Mon.–Fri. 11:45 a.m.–Noon (8/3/53–1/8/54)
Cast:
Julie Fielding — Sallie Brophy
Peter Davis — Grant Richards
Samuel Tilden Fielding — John Seymour
Mrs. Fielding — Nancy Sheridan
Jocelyn Fielding — Laura Weber
Harry Phillips — Howard Erskine

Elaine Carrington created several successful radio soap operas in the 1930s and 1940s, but this was her only TV series effort. The show was an adaptation of her radio series *When a Girl Marries* (1939–58), though listeners of the version which aired on ABC radio from 1951–58 would have had trouble identifying the connection, as the television show was quite dissimilar. Carrington altered not only the title but also names and locations in the show, and none of the radio actors appeared on the TV rendition.

The main action took place at the Worthington House in Philadelphia's Ardmore district, where 19-year-old Julie Fielding lived with her mom and younger teenaged sister Jocelyn. Her father Sam, who ran a one-man scientific research lab, had what one might consider an open marriage, having lived apart from his family in a hotel for 15 years. She confessed that she had doubts over her engagement to her high-society neighbor Harry Phillips and asked her dad how one knows if he or she is in love. "Just follow your heart," he told her.

Coincidentally, during her engagement party Julie met Peter Davis, a man going for a job interview with her father as a research assistant. Going on instinct, she announced that she would not marry Harry. This upset her iron-willed mother, who blamed her estranged husband for the situation and encouraged Harry to continue his wedding plans. Peter eventually confessed his love for Julie but admitted that her upper-class lifestyle scared him. This did not dampen her passion for him, and so she took a job at the country club library to show she could be like "common folk," while telling Harry that the engagement really was off and trying to convince her mom that Peter was honorable.

But Peter felt Julie's move was a superficial one, and he had other concerns on his hands. A gangster tried to blackmail him into spying on Sam's work with the threat of revealing that Peter had been fired from his last job under the suspicion of stealing drugs. This prompted Peter to leave town, but Julie caught up with him before he left and convinced him to stay. The story line then degenerated into a whirl of minor shady characters who threatened Peter into becoming a double agent or tried to seduce Julie, or both, all of which hastened the show's demise. Viewers preferred *Strike It Rich* over a plot which veered from young love to adventure, and *Follow Your Heart* joined *The Bennetts* as one of two soap operas NBC axed in early 1954 after a six-month run.

•FONZ AND THE HAPPY DAYS GANG
Cartoon; Color
November 12, 1980–September 18, 1982

ABC Sat. 9–9:30 a.m. (11/12/80–2/6/82)
ABC Sat. 11–11:30 a.m. (2/13/82–9/18/82)

Voices:

Arthur Fonzarelli (a.k.a. "Fonzie" or "the Fonz")	Henry Winkler
Richie Cunningham	Ron Howard
Ralph Malph	Donny Most
Cupcake	Didi Conn
Mr. Cool	Frank Welker

Some members of the popular gang from the ABC nighttime sitcom *Happy Days* (1974–83) took part in this animated counterpart to the series. Encountering a time machine craft piloted by a girl from the future named Cupcake, the Fonz, Richie, and Ralph decided to board the machine and leave 1950s Milwaukee behind for the chance to observe history in the making. The crew went everywhere, from the ancient Arab world to America's Wild West. Mr. Cool was Fonzie's dog, who came along for the ride and idolized his master to the point of aping his "Ayyy!" thumbs-up routine (in Mr. Cool's case, it was more like paws-up).

Donny Most, who had left *Happy Days* by the fall of 1980 to "pursue other career options," as they say in Hollywood, somehow found time to recreate his character in vocal form for original episodes both in the 1980–81 and 1981–82 seasons. He and the rest of the outfit, except Fonzie and Mr. Cool, vanished in the fall of 1982, with Fonzie and his pet going onto *Laverne and Shirley* (q.v.).

FOOD FOR THOUGHT—See *Girl Talk*.

•FOODINI THE GREAT
Children's; B&W
August 25, 1951–December 29, 1951

ABC Sat. 11–11:30 a.m. (8/25/51–12/29/51)

Cast:

Foodini (voice and puppeteer)	Morey Bunin
Pinhead (voice and puppeteer)	Hope Bunin
Ellen Parker	Herself

When ABC won the rights to the CBS puppet show *Lucky Pup* (q.v.), the network renamed it *Foodini the Great* in honor of its true star, the bearded, mystical magician Foodini. Unfortunately for him, his old *Lucky Pup* sidekick, teenage stooge Pinhead, kept bungling Foodini's grandiose albeit unethical plans due to Pinhead's gullible susceptibility to such types as con artist Phineas T. Pitch. Ellen Parker served as hostess on this filmed production, while the Bunins, a married couple, created, produced, and directed the show. A nice touch had Foodini burn the opening titles with his wand.

•FOOFUR
Cartoon; Color
September 13, 1986–September 3, 1988

NBC Sat. 11:30 a.m.–Noon (9/13/86–10/25/86)
NBC Sat. 11–11:30 a.m. (11/1/86–9/19/87)
NBC Sat. Noon–12:30 p.m. (9/26/87–9/3/88)

Voices:

Foofur	Frank Welker
Hazel	Pat Carroll
Louis	Dick Gautier
Rocki	Christina Lange
Fritz-Carlos	Jonathan Schmock
Annabell	Susan Tolsky
Fencer	Eugene Williams
Mrs. Escrow	Susan Silo
Pepe	Don Messick

Foofur was a blue hound dog whose late owner bequeathed to him a mansion in his will. Foofur then spirited some of his fellow four-legged friends from the Bowser Buster dog pound truck to join him at the manor. They included Hazel, a *grand dame;* Fritz-Carlos, her Fernando Lamas–sounding husband with a handlebar mustache; Louis, a bulldog with a gruff Brooklynese dialect; and Annabell, a sheepdog in love with Louis. Fencer, a black alley cat with a samurai headband and yen for karate, and Rocki, Foofur's niece, also became tenants. The residents found that their luxurious lifestyle did not prevent them from being targets of crimes by greedy humans and even cats and rats. Their most persistent nemesis was Mrs. Escrow, who checked up on Foofur from time to time to make sure he followed the letter of his master's will. Her pet chihuahua Pepe knew of the illegal existence of the other pooches, but his plans to expose them to his mistress always failed. The series ran two seasons of original episodes, with each show containing two separate stories.

FOOTBALL—For college football, see *Notre Dame Football* and *NCAA College Football*. For professional football, see *NFL Football* (1947–55); *Canadian Football; NFL Football* (CBS and Fox); *AFL Football; NFL Football* (NBC); *USFL Football;* and *WLAF Football.*

FOOTBALL FORECAST
Sports; B&W
1955–56

Syndicated 15 minutes weekly beginning September 1955

Host: *Frank Leahy*

Ex–Notre Dame football coach Frank Leahy spent two successive fall seasons in the mid-1950s giving his predictions on the outcomes for each week's college football games. This show usually aired before network sports shows on Saturday afternoons.

FOOTBALL ROUNDUP
Sports; B&W
October 6, 1956–November 24, 1956

CBS Sat. 2–5:30 p.m. (10/6/56–10/20/56)
CBS Sat. 2:30–5 p.m. (10/27/56–11/24/56)

Regulars: *Jack Drees, Herman Hickman, Johnny Lujack, Jim McKay, Kyle Rote, Chris Schenkel, Bryan Field*

In an effort to compete with NBC's *NCAA Football,* CBS came up with this 3½-hour extravaganza of footage of previous games, predictions of upcoming games, updates of college games being played that day, interviews—just about everything they could do related to college football *except* a live game, which they could not air due to NCAA restrictions. Officially titled *Collegiate Football Roundup,* this potpourri required three producers, six sportscasters, and 40 other crew members at a New York studio to make this live show seem competitive despite its lack of live competition on the football field. Jack Drees anchored the festivities as "city editor" by "assigning rewrites" to his colleagues of reports of 50 games being played each week and covered for the show by college students. For example, Chris Schenkel translated write-ups of games played in the East, while Johnny Lujack oversaw the Big Ten activity. The only exception among the regulars was Herman Hickman, who offered his veteran insight and anecdotes. The closest thing to a "real game" on the show was the use of special effects to recreate plays from that day's games.

All the frenetic activity failed to overcome the fact that viewers preferred watching a game to being told about several different ones. By November, the show had shrunk an hour and Bryan Field was calling a horse race in Philadelphia to add some spark, but it was hopeless. CBS tried other sports but failed in giving NBC a run in the ratings in the late 1950s opposite college football on Saturdays.

FOR BETTER OR WORSE
Soap Opera Anthology; B&W
June 29, 1959–June 24, 1960

CBS Mon.–Fri. 2–2:30 p.m. (6/29/59–6/24/60)

Host/Announcer: *Jim Bannon*

Regular: *Dr. James A. Peterson*

Before the start of each day's drama, the host asked Dr. James A. Peterson, associate professor of psychology at the University of Southern California, a few questions regarding the scenario's dilemma. Following that discussion, a dramatization took place, ranging from "The Case of the Childish Bride" on the debut, with Dyan Cannon as a happy-go-lucky gal who marries a man in spite of her parents' opposition and her inexperience, to "The Case of Mike and Linda" at the end, where William Redfield and Peggy McCay portrayed a childless couple. The show had not been originally slated for CBS; NBC paid for the pilot in 1958 and dropped its option, then ABC paid for a new script but dropped its option as well. The Hollywood production was one of the first daytime TV shows to be videotaped.

FOR LOVE OR MONEY
Game; B&W
June 30, 1958–January 30, 1959

CBS Mon.–Fri. 10–10:30 a.m. (6/30/58–1/30/59)

Host: *Bill Nimmo*

Producer: *Walt Framer*

This game show may hold the record for giving out the cheapest prize ever—a measly two cents to one unfortunate woman on the premiere. The format in retrospect comes off as a test run for *Let's Make a Deal.* Each of three contestants chose whether to try for prizes on view, like dresses and oil paintings, or take a stab at "The Money Machine," which could give them up to $10,000. The woman who got two cents from the machine, for example, took the chance after being offered a prize worth $239. On the same show a competitor nixed a $65 prize and collected $650 instead. Home viewers had the advantage of seeing the hidden amount on "The Money Machine" on screen, and the show had a gimmick of calling people at home to ask if they knew what that amount was, with a correct answer winning a prize.

What canceled *For Love or Money* was not bad ratings but its modified money machine, which after the premiere could win a contestant anywhere from 25 cents to $2,500, depending on where the decimal point landed. CBS believed that the machine was rigged and removed the show from the lineup over Walt Framer's protestations. Despite running only half a year, this game was revived in Great Britain in 1960, where it ran under the same title on that country's ABC-TV.

FOR OUR TIMES
Religious; Color
April 29, 1979–December 25, 1988

CBS Sun. 10:30–11 a.m. or 7:30–8 a.m.
(4/29/79–12/25/88)

Host: *Douglas Edwards*

In early 1979 CBS combined its long-running religious series *Look Up and Live* and *Lamp Unto My Feet*, both produced by Pamela Ilott, into this informational nondenominational effort, which followed *Sunday Morning*. It was done in cooperation with the New York Board of Rabbis, the U.S. Catholic Conference, and the National Council of Churches, and Ilott stayed on as producer until her retirement in 1986. The show carried no advertising, and only 44 of 210 CBS affiliates were carrying it by 1988. Veteran CBS reporter Douglas Edwards was host, and the show went off shortly after he retired from the network on April 1, 1988.

•FOR RICHER, FOR POORER
Soap Opera; Color
January 3, 1977–September 29, 1978

NBC Mon.–Fri. 12:30–1 p.m. (1/3/77–5/6/77)
NBC Mon.–Fri. 1–1:30 p.m. (12/6/77–9/29/78)

Cast:

Rhett Saxton (1977)	Bob Purvey
Rhett Saxton (1977)	David Ramsey
Bill Saxton (1977–78)	Tom Happer
Megan Cushing (1977)	Patricia Estrin
Megan Cushing Saxton (1977–78)	Darlene Parks
Lester Saxton (1977)	John Heffernan
Lester Saxton (1977–78)	Albert Stratton
Josie Saxton	Patricia Englund
Jason Saxton	Richard Backus
Bentley Saxton	David Abbott
Tessa Saxton (1977)	Vicky Dawson
Tessa Saxton (1977–78)	Breon Gorman
Austin Cushing	Rod Arrants
Richard Cushing (1977)	Ron Randell
Edith Cushing (1977)	Nancy Marchand
Edith Cushing (1977–78)	Laurinda Barrett
Connie Ferguson (1977)	Susan Foster
Connie Ferguson (1977–78)	Cynthia Bostick
Amy Gifford Cushing	Christine Jones
Eleanor Saxton Kimball	Flora Plumb
George Kimball	Stephen Joyce
Sophie Slocum (1977)	Margaret Barker
Viola Brewster (1977–78)	Patricia Barry
Laura Brewster (1977–78)	Julia MacKenzie
Lee Ferguson (1977–78)	Robert Burton
Ira Ferguson (1977–78)	Roy Poole
Desmond Hamilton (1977–78)	David Knapp
Sgt. Frank Damico (1977–78)	Stephen Burleigh
Colleen Griffin (1977–78)	Nancy Snyder

NBC took two shots at doing this soap opera created by Harding Lemay, who was doing well at the time as head writer for that network's top-rated soap *Another World*. The first version, titled *Lovers and Friends*, emphasized the conflicts between the struggling Saxtons and well-to-do Cushings, connected by a romance between Rhett (renamed Bill in the second incarnation) and Megan. Megan's family consisted of her brother Austin, her mother Edith, and her father Richard, while Rhett's family included his younger brothers Jason and Bentley, sisters Eleanor and Tessa, and parents Lester and Josie. Others living in the Chicago suburb of Point Clair, Illinois, were Amy Gifford, Austin's girlfriend; George Kimball, Eleanor's husband; and Connie Ferguson, Rhett's ex-girlfriend.

The show emphasized character portraits over plot development, and its slow pace did nothing to grab any viewers away from the competition, *Ryan's Hope* on ABC and *Search for Tomorrow* on CBS. NBC shut the show down after just four months, then overhauled it for a second try in late 1977. The Cushings no longer had a father, Amy married Austin, and Lester and Josie Saxton found that their youngest children Bentley and Tessa were now college students. Finally, the Saxtons made room in their social world for another well-off family, Viola Brewster and her daughter Laura. Conflicts included Megan's revelation on her wedding day that her husband-to-be Bill had impregnated his ex-girlfriend Connie, plus the usual alcoholism- and addiction-related story lines.

Although Harding Lemay still was listed as the show's creator and head writer, as he was in *Lovers and Friends*, he claimed in his book *Eight Years in Another World* that for the 1977–78 show he served only as consultant to head writer Tom King in an uneasy working relationship where he reviewed King's plans. "He seldom called me and I hesitated to offer criticisms of his outlines and scripts, assuming, from my own experience, that he was already barraged with criticisms from the producers and sponsors," Lemay wrote. Lemay claimed that he was virtually shut out from the show even though he owned 60 percent of it, blaming the situation on the battle of wills in which he and producer Paul Rauch were engaged at the time, both on this show and *Another World*.

Audiences were even less impressed than Lemay by the melodramatic tales of white slavery, kidnapping, and street gang violence which cropped up during the run. These activities may have been prompted by early reviews suggesting that the show was stodgy. Adding to the soap's difficulties was the time slot: NBC programmed it for a time where the network had rarely broadcast any series to its affiliates before 1977, making its success problematic from the start, as some chose not to take it and others aired it at another period. All these factors combined to cancel *For Richer, For Poorer* before it had celebrated its first birthday.

FOR WOMEN ONLY
Women's; B&W
1952–53

Syndicated 15 minutes daily beginning January 1953
Hostess/Narrator: *Amy Sedell*

This obscure filmed women's magazine show (apparently the first of its kind in TV syndication) should not be confused with a similarly titled show in the 1970s with Barbara Walters as host (see *Not For Women Only*).

FOR YOUR INFORMATION
Women's; B&W
May 7, 1951–November 16, 1951

DuMont Mon.–Fri. 12:15–12:30 p.m. (5/7/51–9/7/51)
DuMont Mon.–Fri. Noon–12:15 p.m. (9/10/51–11/16/51)
Hostess: *Helen Faith Keane*

The angle on this interview show was that Helen Faith Keane asked guests questions purportedly sent to the show by viewers in addition to her own queries. Jerry Wexler, several years before becoming a major record producer, reviewed Keane's program harshly in *Billboard*. "Her debut program is a 15-minute essay in futility," he wrote. Nonetheless, it managed to run six months on DuMont, not as short a time as some of that network's other lesser daytime entries. *For Your Information* should not be confused with a later CBS series (see *F.Y.I.*).

FOREIGN LEGIONNAIRE—See *Captain Gallant of the Foreign Legion.*

•FOX BASEBALL
Sports; Color
June 1, 1996–

Fox Sat. 1 p.m.–Conclusion (6/1/96–)
Announcers: *Joe Buck, Tim McCarver, Thom Brennaman, Bob Brenly, John Rooney, Jeff Torborg, Josh Lewin, Ken Singleton*

After a three-year absence, the former *Baseball Game of the Week* (q.v.) came back to network television via regular doubleheaders on Fox in 1996. The lead announcing team had play-by-play from Joe Buck and analysis from Tim McCarver. (Interestingly, McCarver had announced games with Joe's father Jack Buck on *Baseball Game of the Week* on CBS from 1990–91.) The other announcers covered various regional games.

FOX FUN HOUSE—See *Fun House.*

FOX NFL FOOTBALL—See *NFL* (CBS and Fox).

•FOX NEWS SUNDAY
Public Affairs; Color
April 28, 1996–

Fox Sun. 9–10 a.m. (4/28/96–)
Host: *Tony Snow*

This series was the first attempt of the Fox network to do an interview show like *Meet the Press* with politicians and other newsmakers from Washington, D.C. It was also Fox's first Sunday morning series. Host Tony Snow also served as a conservative columnist for the *USA Today* and *Detroit News* daily newspapers.

•FOX SATURDAY BASEBALL
Sports; Color
June 1, 1996–

Fox Sat. 12:30–1 p.m. (6/1/96–)
Regulars: *Chip Caray, Dave Winfield, Steve Lyons*

Airing from the same Hollywood studio used for *Fox NFL Sunday* (q.v.), this program was the lead-in for the major league baseball games acquired by Fox as part of its ongoing commitment to sports coverage in the mid-1990s. Chip Caray, formerly an announcer on the WTBS cable channel for the Atlanta Braves and grandson of legendary Chicago Cub announcer Harry Caray, hosted the event, with Dave Winfield and Steve Lyons providing opinions and analysis of previous games and that day's actions.

FRACTURED PHRASES
Game; Color
September 27, 1965–December 31, 1965

NBC Mon.–Fri. 10–10:30 a.m. (9/27/65–12/31/65)
Host: *Art James*

Another one of several *Password* knockoffs of the 1960s and 1970s, *Fractured Phrases* had two duos competing, each composed of a celebrity and a contestant, with each member alternating in giving phonetic pronunciations of familiar slogans and titles. Those who guessed correctly won points for their team and got to play a bonus round to identify "fractured" names (e.g., "Jose . . ." instead of "Oh, Say [can you see]"), winning $25 for each correct identification.

FRAGGLE ROCK
Cartoon; Color
September 12, 1987–September 3, 1988

NBC Sat. 10–10:30 a.m. (9/12/87–11/14/87)
NBC Sat. 11–11:30 a.m. (11/21/87–2/27/88)
NBC Sat. 8–8:30 a.m. (3/5/88–3/26/88)
NBC Sat. 11–11:30 a.m. (4/2/88–9/3/88)
Voices:

Doc/Philo/Gunge	*John Stephenson*
Pa Gorge/Travelling Matt/Flange	*Pat Pinney*
Gobo/Architect/Wrench	*Townsend Coleman*
Red/Wingnut	*Barbara Goodson*
Mokey/Cotterpin	*Mona Marshall*
Ma Gorge	*Patti Paris*
Wembley	*Bob Bergen*

| Boober/Sprocket | Rob Paulsen |
| The Storyteller | Stu Rosen |

Jim Henson, creator of the Muppets, expanded his repertoire of unique characters when he created a new puppet series for the cable channel HBO called *Fraggle Rock* from 1983 to 1988. This network cartoon used the same characters and setup as that show. Doc, a scientist, had a house under which lived a subterranean society composed of three species: the playful Fraggles; the miniature Doozers, who liked to build towers; and the Gorges, the giants of the underground village. Their lighthearted adventures usually focused on one character per show (for example, one episode featured Wembley in a voyage to outer space), and some shows were two-part episodes.

Fraggle Rock was designed for international consumption, and some segments were specifically produced to appeal to foreign countries. For example, a tinkerer in the U.S. version became a retired chef in France and a lighthouse keeper in the United Kingdom. In America, the cartoon managed to avoid being scheduled opposite *Muppet Babies* on CBS, another cartoon based on Henson's creations, despite the show's four time-slot changes in its single season on NBC.

FRANCES LANGFORD-DON AMECHE SHOW, THE
Variety; B&W
September 10, 1951–March 14, 1952

ABC Mon.–Fri. Noon–1 p.m. (9/10/51–3/14/52)

Regulars: *Frances Langford, Don Ameche, Neil Hamilton, Fran Lee (as "Mrs. Fix-It"), Tony Romano and His Orchestra*

Billed as "The Biggest Show in Daytime Television," this outing actually proved to be a ratings disaster that discouraged ABC from daytime programming for several years. ABC promised the moon in early ads, saying the program would have a multimillion-dollar budget, nighttime stars and production values, and audience participation and dramatic scenes. What emerged, though not quite up to its advance press, was still impressive, with Frances Langford and Don Ameche displaying the rapport they had on the hit radio sitcom *The Bickersons,* actor Neil Hamilton hosting an informal quiz, and actress Fran Lee giving out household hints for 10-minute segments Tuesdays and Thursdays. Angel, a 9-year-old ventriloquist, delivered the commercials for sponsor Cliquot Club. The studio audience at the debut got to cut and eat a "premiere cake."

The show's problem was that timing and scheduling were all wrong. The noon–1 p.m. slot on the East Coast was the only daily period in 1951 where all four networks competed directly against each other, plus there were some local established favorites with which the show had to contend. By October, the report from Chicago was that a local show named *Creative Cookery* (q.v.) had topped it in the ratings. Four months later, a ratings update found the CBS soaps *The Egg and I, Love of Life,* and *Search for Tomorrow* well ahead of the competition, and even *Ruth Lyons' 50 Club* on NBC had a larger audience. Those

numbers left ABC unable to sell more than a third of the time period to sponsors, and this, combined with a staggering weekly production budget in the neighborhood of $40,000, led to a $1 million shortfall for ABC by March of 1952. ABC canceled the show the same month, replacing it briefly with *The Paul Dixon Show* (q.v.), but when that show went to DuMont in the summer of 1952, ABC didn't program another show at noontime for six years.

FRANK MCGEE REPORTS
News; Color
January 7, 1968–June 8, 1969

NBC Sun. 5:30–6 p.m. (1/7/68–6/11/68)
NBC Sun. 5:30–6 p.m. (12/28/68–6/8/69)

Host/Anchor: *Frank McGee*

NBC News correspondent Frank McGee functioned mainly as a newsreader of current events in this series, which was essentially the same as NBC's late afternoon/early evening news on Sundays, which began in nighttime September 5, 1965. However, the show did usually examine one topic in depth per show, using filmed reports and contributions from various reporters. Following its brief late-afternoon runs, the show returned to the 6–6:30 p.m. slot permanently in the summer of 1969. A year later, McGee departed to host *Today,* and the series title changed to *The NBC Nightly News,* which it has kept to this day through a variety of hosts over the last quarter century.

•FRANKENSTEIN JR. AND THE IMPOSSIBLES
Cartoon; Color
September 10, 1966–September 7, 1968

CBS Sat. 10–10:30 a.m. (9/10/66–9/2/67)
CBS Sat. 9–9:30 a.m. (9/9/67–9/7/68)

Voices:

Frankenstein Jr.	Ted Cassidy
Buzz Conroy	Dick Beals
Dr. Conroy	John Stephenson
Coil Man	Hal Smith
Fluid Man	Paul Frees
Multi Man	Don Messick

One of the "monster superhero" shows which dominated Saturday mornings from 1966–68, this show consisted of two different sorts of strange leaders. Frankenstein Jr. was a gigantic talking robot at least 10 yards tall created by Buzz Conroy, the son of a scientist, to defend attacks from such provocative enemies as "the Colossal Junk Monster" and "the Alien Brain from Outer Space." Buzz activated the robot's powers with a ring. Among Frankenstein Jr.'s abilities were speech, underwater swimming, flying, and shooting stun rays at baddies.

The Impossibles were three secret agents with incredible powers posing as a rock band. Their villains were just as outlandish as those faced by Frankenstein Jr. (for example, Smogula and Fero the Fiendish Fiddler), and so were their abilities. Coil Man bounced and stretched himself almost anywhere, Fluid Man went from solid to liquid to turn the tables on those confronting him, and Multi Man made duplicate copies of himself to confound evildoers.

The show ended in 1968 following protests from parents about the violence depicted in this and other children's cartoons. It reappeared in reruns in 1976–77. See *Space Ghost* for more details.

•FREAKAZOID!

Cartoon; Color
September 9, 1995–

The WB Sat. or Sun. 10–10:30 a.m. (9/9/95–)

Voice:

Dexter Douglas/Freakazoid   *Paul Rugg*

Much in the manner of *The Tick* (q.v.), *Freakazoid!* was a superhero cartoon where the main character was more weird and humorous than valiant. Originally a calm teenager named Dexter Douglas by day, as Freakazoid he wore a red suit with an "F!" on it and had black hair with a white streak in it à la Cruella De Vil plus a blue face with eyes lined with black makeup. He fought equally bizarre criminals, such as Arms Akimbo, a former model whose arms were frozen in place like hooks, in two episodes per show. Cosgrove, his contact on the police force, gave him deadpan advice. The show's executive producer was Steven Spielberg.

FRED AND BARNEY MEET THE SCHMOO/THING— See *The Flintstones Comedy Show.*

FRED FLINTSTONE AND FRIENDS—A syndicated title for a package of Hanna-Barbera cartoons. See *The Flintstones Comedy Hour, Goober and the Ghost Chasers, Jeannie, Partridge Family: 2200* A.D., and *Yogi's Gang.*

FRED WARING SHOW, THE

Music; B&W
July 22, 1957–August 30, 1957

CBS Mon.–Thu. 10–10:30 a.m. and Fri. 10–11:30 a.m. (7/22/57–8/30/57)

Regulars: *Fred Waring and His Pennsylvanians*

Fred Waring, a bandleader successful on records in the 1920s (including his group's theme, "Sleep") and on radio from 1932–50, appeared on TV as early as January 1944 on a special on DuMont's New York City station and had a nighttime series on CBS from 1949–54 before coming to daytime a few years later as a summer replacement for *The Garry Moore Show.* Airing live from Shawnee-on-the-Delaware, Waring's country club in Pennsylvania, his musicians continued their unique approach of singing the music as well as playing it. This show marked the last regular appearance of Fred Waring and his group, whose music style fell out of favor in the late 1950s and left Waring to do only infrequent TV guest shots before his death in 1984.

•FREE WILLY

Cartoon; Color
September 24, 1994–

ABC Sat. 9–9:30 a.m. (9/24/94–12/3/94)
ABC Sat. 8:30–9 a.m. (12/10/94–6/3/95)
ABC Sat. 8–9 a.m. (two shows; 6/10/95–7/22/95)
ABC Sat. 8–8:30 a.m. (7/29/95–9/2/95)
ABC Sat. 8:30–9 a.m. (9/9/95–)

Voice:

Jesse   *Zachary Bennett*

Based on the hit 1993 film of the same name, *Free Willy* was an oh-so-cute tale of a 12-year-old boy named Jesse and his friendship with a killer whale. The whale, named Free Willy, was a remarkably humanlike creature, able to toss balls back to Jesse and even speak to the youngster (in the cartoon at least). Another talking animal and pal of Jesse's was Lucille the sea lion, whose thinking, like Jesse's, was not as mature as Willy's, and who often got into trouble inadvertently as a result. Also featured were Jesse's cohorts on the boat the *Eco-Ranger II*, sea experts Randolph and Marlene. Pro-social responsibility or pro-ecology messages were written in to many of the adventures, but no show was complete without having at least one shot of Jesse riding Free Willy. One of the executive producers of the series was veteran director Richard Donner.

FREEDOM RINGS

Game; B&W
March 2, 1953–August 27, 1953

CBS Tue./Thu. 2–2:30 p.m. (3/2/53–8/27/53)

Host: *John Beal (3/2/53–5/28/53), Rex Marshall (6/2/53–8/27/53)*

Regulars: *Malcolm Broderick, Alice Ghostley, Joy Hilton, Chuck Taylor, Ted Tiller, the Ben Ludlow Orchestra*

Three contestants from the studio audience played games involving five actors and an orchestra on this twice-weekly live offering from New York, with the initial prize being bonds worth $50 and $100. Between games, the host called home viewers who won the grand prize of $2,500 worth of appliances from Westinghouse, the show's sponsor, if they answered a difficult question. Westingho use offered clue sheets for viewers interested in participating in this contest.

Westinghouse's support was so critical that when the company decided to sponsor DuMont's pro football lineup in the fall of 1953 and pulled its money out of the show, the result was that *Freedom Rings* rang for the last time in late August.

FROM THESE ROOTS

Soap Opera; B&W
June 30, 1958–December 29, 1961

NBC Mon.–Fri. 3:30–4 p.m. (6/30/58–12/29/61)

Cast:

Liz Fraser Allen	Ann Flood
Liz Fraser (temporary replacement, 1959)	Susan Brown
Ben Fraser Sr. (1958)	Grant Code
Ben Fraser Sr. (1958–61)	Rod Hendrickson
Ben Fraser Sr. (1961)	Joseph Macauley
Emily Fraser Benson	Helen Shields
Jim Benson (1958–60)	Henderson Forsythe
Lyddy Benson	Sarah Hardy
Tim Benson	John Stewart
Ben Fraser Jr. (1958–60)	Frank Marth
Rose Carelli Fraser (1958–60)	Julie Bovasso
Rose Carelli Fraser (1960–61)	Tresa Hughes
Dan Fraser (1958–60)	Dan White
Kass	Vera Allen
Bruce Crawford (1958–59)	Byron Sanders
Enid Chambers Allen (1958–59)	Mary Alice Moore
Dr. Buck Weaver	Len Wayland
Maggie Barker Weaver	Billie Lou Watt
David Allen (1959–61)	Robert Mandan
Lynn Franklin (1959–61)	Barbara Berjer
Tom Jennings (1959–61)	Craig Huebing
Lance (1959–61)	David Daniels
Luisa Corelli (1959–60)	Dolores Sutton
Artie Corelli (1959–60)	Frank Campanella
Jimmy Hull (1960–61)	John Colenback
Frank Teton (1960–61)	George Smith
Gloria Saxon (1961)	Millette Alexander
Hilda Furman (1961)	Charlotte Rae
Richard (1961)	Richard Thomas

One of the rare NBC soap operas of the 1950s to last more than a year and a half, *From These Roots* stayed on the air more because of the faith its sponsor Procter & Gamble had in the show than because of high ratings (it never fared well against *The Verdict Is Yours* on CBS and *Who Do You Trust?* on ABC). In fact, many of its cast members later enjoyed success as regulars on other Procter & Gamble soaps, and the show has a following among some soap fanatics, who thought that its acting and production approach made it a lost treasure, one that should have been a hit but failed instead.

The story commenced with Liz Fraser coming back to her hometown in New England following the heart attack of her dad Ben, the editor, publisher, and owner of *The Strathfield Record,* the town's newspaper. Ben recuperated but fretted about his advancing age (he was 65), and his large but discordant family, which besides Liz included his daughter Emily, married to Jim Benson, a mill foreman, with daughter Lyddy and son Tim, and Ben Jr., husband to the colorful Sicilian Rose Corelli and father to their children Dan, Sarah, and Robin, the latter two of whom remained more or less minor characters during the show's run. The youngest generation complained early in the run that their elders did not understand them, but it was Ben Sr.'s children and not his grandchildren who dominated the story line over the next 3¹/₂ years.

From These Roots starred Robert Mandan as David Allen and Ann Flood as his wife Liz Fraser.

Liz had the most complicated romantic entanglements. Engaged to Bruce Crawford, who was starting a magazine back in Washington, D.C., where Liz had lived before returning to Strathfield, she found herself competing for his affections with his long-standing rich rival Enid Chambers, who cannily offered to back Bruce's periodical. Ultimately neither woman won that contest. The next year, in 1959, erratic playwright David Allen married Enid for a short period while Liz caught up with an old flame from her teenage years, Dr. Buck Weaver. After the Allen marriage dissolved, the playwright then vied with Dr. Weaver for Liz's affections and won, marrying her on February 18, 1960. The marriage lasted through the rest of the show's run despite attempts to woo Allen by Lynn Franklin, an actress married to theatrical director Tom Jennings, who had a weakness for booze. Liz's former flame Buck found happiness when he wed his secretary Maggie.

Liz's sister Emily found her domestic tranquility shattered in 1959 with the revelation that her husband Jim had maintained an affair with Luisa, a relative of her sister-in-law's. She tried to save her marriage unsuccessfully. Her daughter Lyddy had better luck, marrying Lance and announcing on the last show that she was expecting a child. Emily's brother Ben Jr.'s love life seemed like a piece of cake compared to the romances of Emily and Liz, but he had his problems, like trying to keep the family farm going after his dad's heart attack and keeping a watchful eye on his son Dan and Dan's friends.

From These Roots came to an end in late 1961 after 915 shows with good news for almost everyone. Ben, now mayor of the town, and the district attorney knocked some racketeers out of business, the Fraser family maid Kass received a $200,000 check from her late husband's estate, and David and Liz were at peace with each other. NBC replaced it with an even less successful soap (see Our Five Daughters).

FRONT ROW CENTER
Dramatic Anthology; B&W
January 8, 1956–April 22, 1956

CBS Sun. 4–5 p.m. (1/8/56–4/22/56)

Host: Robert Sterling

Two rarities among 1950s dramatic anthologies popped up in this series. One was that it was telecast live from Hollywood rather than New York, and the other was its placement in daytime rather than nighttime. Front Row Center in fact started on June 1, 1955 on CBS Wednesday nights and ran there through September 21, 1955 before returning four months later with presentations ranging from James Arness (then starring on the nighttime Gunsmoke) in a western about a lynch mob to John Carradine and Rita Gam in a melodrama involving love and murder in the African jungle, plus a few comedies. But none of the offerings enticed a sponsor, so after three months of sustaining it, CBS drew the curtain on Front Row Center.

Most of the stories were unmemorable, but the acting talent was impressive, with some veteran performers and then-rising stars. Besides those already mentioned, recognizable guests included Eddie Bracken, Beulah Bondi, Lilia Skala, James Daly, Sidney Blackmer, Betsy Palmer, Ellen Corby, and Lloyd Bridges in January; Piper Laurie, Anthony Perkins, and Jim Backus in February; Dean Stockwell, Margaret O'Brien, Beverly Garland, Howard Duff, and Lee Marvin in March; and Jan Sterling, Kevin McCarthy, Angela Lansbury, and Mercedes McCambridge in April.

FRONTIERS OF FAITH—See NBC Television Religious Program.

•FUDGE
Sitcom; Color
January 14, 1995–

ABC Sat. 10:30–11 a.m. (1/14/95–7/15/95)
ABC Sat. 10:30–11:30 a.m. (two shows; 7/29/95–9/2/95)
ABC Sat. 10–10:30 a.m. (9/9/95–2/24/96)

ABC Sat. 9:30–10 a.m. (3/2/96–5/4/96)
ABC Sat. 9–9:30 and 11–11:30 a.m. (two shows; 5/11/96–)

Cast:

Farley Drexel "Fudge" Hatcher	Luke Tarsitano
Peter Hatcher	Jake Richardson
Ann Hatcher	Eve Plumb
Warren Hatcher	Forrest Witt
Sheila Tubman	Nassira Nicola

Despite the title, Fudge centered not on the imp of the Hatcher family, played adorably by Luke Tarsitano at age 4 on the debut, but on his 9-year-old brother Peter. Peter talked directly to the camera in detailing the weekly woes caused by those he saw as conspiring against him, who beside Fudge included his parents Ann and Warren, who he thought favored Fudge, and his dreaded playmate Sheila Tubman, "the queen of cooties." This sitcom created a nice balance in being cute but not corny, and the characters came off as fairly realistic, unusual for any Saturday morning show.

The series actually debuted as an ABC nighttime two-hour TV movie titled Fudge-A-Mania on January 7, 1995, where the in-joke for older viewers was that actress Florence Henderson, playing Ann's mom, had acted a similar role 25 years earlier when Eve Plumb was Jan to Florence's Carol on The Brady Bunch. Another note for fans of 1970s trivia was that Anson Williams, who played Potsie on Happy Days, directed 11 episodes. The program, a production of Steven Spielberg's Amblin Television, was based on a series of best-selling Fudge books by Judy Blume.

FULL CIRCLE
Soap Opera; B&W
June 27, 1960–March 10, 1961

CBS Mon.–Fri. 2–2:30 p.m. (6/27/60–3/10/61)

Cast:

Gary Donovan	Robert Fortier
Lisa Linda Crowder	Dyan Cannon
Loyal Crowder	John McNamara
Dr. Kit Aldrich	Jean Byron
Virgil Denker	Michael Ross
Ellen Denker	Nancy Millard
Ray Pollard	Andrew Colmar
David Talton	Bill Lundmark
Chris Talton (fall 1960–61)	Ann Daniels
Parker Hill (fall 1960)	Gene Lyons
Carter Talton, David's dad (1960)	Byron Foulger
The Deputy (1960)	Sam Edwards
Beth Perce (1960)	Amzie Strickland

"Meet Gary Donovan, restless wanderer. His only companions are romance and adventure," purred the ads for this, the first network serial to air live from Hollywood. The tag line was true. Donovan did find both "companions" in Crowder, Virginia, where, in the show's debut, he settled down and met Lisa Linda Crowder, a young woman unhappily married to Loyal, an older descendent of the town's founder, and Dr.

Kit Aldrich, who fell in love with him. As he dealt with his attraction to the medic, he also developed an interest in unraveling the mystery behind the death of Lisa's first husband while working at Loyal's mill along with Virgil Denker.

Donovan did not have to wait long for the murder investigation to produce results. A deputy arrested Loyal for the crime, and although he did not go to jail, Lisa divorced him anyway and went after the affections first of Gary, during a period when he and Kit were on the outs, and then of musician David Talton, who decided to marry Chris instead. Both the married Chris and David and the dating Kit and Gary had rocky on-and-off romances for months. A slew of other characters worked their way into the action, though they added very little to the plot in comparison with the principals. Busybody Beth Perce made sure to pry her way into hearing about all of these details for a time.

In 1961, shortly before the show was canceled, life became more pleasant for the citizens of Crowder. David and Chris were expecting a child, Lisa had married again, this time to a minor character named Tony, and even Loyal, who had managed to keep running his mill following his arrest, looked to be developing a romantic image. As for the restless wanderer, the *TV Guide* write-up of the finale said, "The future looks bright for Kit and Gary." Maybe that meant they got to leave town?

•FUN FACTORY, THE
Game; Color
June 14, 1976–October 1, 1976

NBC Mon.–Fri. Noon–12:30 p.m. (6/14/76–10/1/76)

Regulars: *Bobby Van, Marty Barris, Rhonda Bates, Dick Blasucci, Buddy Douglas, Deborah Harmon, Doug Steckler, Betty Thomas*

Bobby Van served as emcee and performer in this game show where a troupe of actors appeared in comic sketches designed to entertain and serve as questions for members of the studio audience. Van selected audience members and asked them questions during or following a skit. The characters in the sketches often were bizarre, such as the woman whose head consisted of a huge pair of lips (don't ask). But Van always managed to keep the audience relaxed with a song or two during the festivities.

At the end of each show, the three top candidates competed in a contest to total three unknown amounts suggested by clues from the actors (for example, the number of pages contained in the issue of the *New York Times* that had been the largest Sunday paper ever printed). The contestant with the closest guess, without going over, won merchandise, and any contestant within 10 points of the correct answer received a new automobile. The show used new players each day.

FUN FAIR
Children's Game; B&W
December 30, 1950–March 10, 1951

ABC Sat. 10:30–11 a.m. (12/30/50–2/10/51)
ABC Sat. 10:15–10:45 a.m. (2/17/51–3/10/51)

Host/Producer: *Jay Stewart*

A game show with children and occasionally parents doing a stunt, *Fun Fair* began in Hollywood on December 3, 1950 and came to ABC on delayed kinescopes in the East before the start of 1951. In addition to the stunt activity, Jay Stewart spent a little time interviewing his contestants. This show was slated to move in March to Sundays at 4 p.m., to air before the new *Your Pet Parade*, but its network run ended prior to the planned change.

FUN HOUSE
Game; Color
September 10, 1990–August 3, 1991

Fox Sat. 10:30–11 a.m. (9/10/90–4/13/91)
Fox Sat. 10:30–11 a.m. (5/25/91–8/3/91)

Host: *J. D. Roth*

"Cheerleaders": *Jacqueline and Samantha Forrest*

Fun House was a daily series that had run in syndication since the fall of 1988 before being picked up by Fox as part of that network's initial Saturday morning lineup. In both versions twentyish J. D. Roth presided over two pairs of prepubescents competing in answering questions and performing stunts, the latter often involving food and other slimy materials. After several rounds plus a race around the "Fun House Grand Prix" track, the winning team got two minutes to try for the big grand prize vacation by finding hidden tags in the show's "Fun House" set. The Forrests were two youthful gals rah-rahhing both sides to do their best.

FUN WORLD OF HANNA-BARBERA, THE—A title for
a syndicated package of cartoons from the Hanna-Barbera production company; see *The Amazing Chan and the Chan Clan, Dastardly and Muttley, The Funky Phantom, The Perils of Pauline Pitstop,* and *Wacky Races.*

•FUNKY PHANTOM, THE
Cartoon; Color
September 11, 1971–September 1, 1973

ABC Sat. 9–9:30 p.m. (9/11/71–9/2/72)
ABC Sat. Noon–12:30 p.m. (9/9/72–9/1/73)

Voices:

Jonathan Wellington "Muggsey"	
Muddlemore	Daws Butler
April Stewart	Tina Holland
Skip	Mickey Dolenz
Augie	Tommy Cook

Producers/Directors: *William Hanna and Joseph Barbera*

A cowardly New Englander hiding from the British in 1776 in his mansion's grandfather clock found the spirit of himself and his cat Boo freed almost 200 years later, thanks to an accident. A trio of teenagers taking refuge from a storm one night reset the clock to the proper time of midnight. This released the still-nervous ghost of Jonathan Muddlemore, known by all as "Muggsey," who joined them in their Looney Duney dune buggy as they traveled across America and fought evildoers. Some major difficulties were caused by Muggsey and Boo, who typically became invisible whenever any sort of fear struck them. The teenagers had their own pet, a bulldog named Elmo.

The second season consisted of repeats of the first season's 17 cartoons. The gang returned to Saturday morning briefly in 1980 (see *The Godzilla Show*).

FUNNY BONERS
Children's Game; B&W
November 27, 1954–July 9, 1955

NBC Sat. 11–11:30 a.m. (11/27/54–7/9/55)

Host: *Jimmy Weldon*

Executive Producer Ralph Edwards gave the world *Truth or Consequences,* and this 1954 entry by him played as a kiddie version of that show, which coincidentally NBC aired on Thursday nights during this period. Ventriloquist Jimmy Weldon interacted with his dummies Webster Webfoot (a duck given to braggadocio) and Easy Marvin in asking contestants questions and having them do embarrassing penalty stunts. Ironically, the show followed another hosted by a famous ventriloquist, *The Paul Winchell–Jerry Mahoney Show,* but the latter returned on NBC in the fall of 1955, whereas *Funny Boners* became history that summer.

FUNNY YOU SHOULD ASK
Game; Color
October 28, 1968–June 27, 1969

ABC Mon.–Fri. 1:30–2 p.m. (10/28/68–12/27/68)
ABC Mon.–Fri. 12:30–1 p.m. (12/30/68–6/27/69)

Host: *Lloyd Thaxton*

Semiregulars: *Stu Gilliam, Jan Murray*

Heatter-Quigley Productions, the packager of *The Hollywood Squares,* offered ABC this similar comedy game show which premiered two years after *Squares* debuted. Taped in Hollywood, this offering had five celebrities answer questions prior to air time on topics like "What one item would you take with you to a nudist camp?" Two contestants tried to match the stars with their answers, which usually were on the humorous side. The one with the most matches won valuable prizes.

Though there were no regulars, comics Stu Gilliam and Jan Murray appeared in nearly half the shows. Other frequent guests were Rose Marie (12 weeks) and Marty Allen (9 weeks). All four also were familiar faces on—you guessed it—*The Hollywood Squares.*

FUNTASTIC WORLD OF HANNA-BARBERA, THE—
An umbrella title for a syndicated package of Hanna-Barbera cartoons airing back-to-back daily from 1985–93, some of

them original. For repeated network series which ran here, see the following titles: *Flintstone Kids; Jonny Quest; Paw Paws; Pirates of Dark Water; Richie Rich; Snorks;* and *Yo, Yogi.*

FURTHER ADVENTURES OF DR. DOLITTLE, THE
Cartoon; Color
September 12, 1970–September 2, 1972

NBC Sat. 10–10:30 a.m (9/12/70–9/4/71)
NBC Sat. 8–8:30 a.m. (9/11/71–9/2/72)

Voices:

Dr. John Dolittle	*Bob Holt*
Tommy Stubbins	*Hal Smith*
Sam Scurvy the Pirate	*Lennie Weinrib*
Mooncats, other animals	*Don Messick, Barbara Towers*
The Grasshoppers	*Ronnie Fallon, Colin Julian, and Annabell*

Hugh Lofting wrote a successful series of children's novels from 1920–52 about Dr. Dolittle, a veterinarian who could talk to the animals, but the character's appeal has yet to survive transfer to other media. An early try was an obscure 1932 children's radio series on NBC. In 1967 a musical movie with Rex Harrison as the doctor was a major box office flop despite several Academy Award nominations, including an undeserved Best Picture, given to shore up its appeal. Three years later the doctor came to Saturday mornings and finished far behind its competition of *Josie and the Pussycats* in its first season and *The Bugs Bunny Show* in its second. The cartoon had Dolittle, joined by his 14-year-old aide Tommy Stubbins and other creatures with whom he communicated, battle the skullduggery of Scurvy the Pirate. Hippos, bears, snails, and other beings teamed up with the doctor on occasion, as did an unlikely rock group known as the Grasshoppers. The show's second season consisted of repeats.

FURY
Children's Adventure; B&W
October 15, 1955–September 3, 1966

NBC Sat. 11–11:30 a.m. (10/15/55–9/28/63)
NBC Sat. 11:30 a.m.–Noon (10/5/63–9/3/66)

Cast:

Jim Newton	*Peter Graves*
Joey Newton	*Bobby Diamond*
Pete	*William Fawcett*
Rodney "Pee Wee" Jenkins (1955–58)	*Jimmy Baird*
Packey Lambert (1958–60)	*Roger Mobley*

This popular children's adventure show was in production for five years and ran incessantly in reruns both on the network and in syndication, with the latter shows usually under the title *Black Stallion.* It told of the friendship and conflicts shared by bachelor Jim Newton, his adopted son Joey, and their horse Fury, played by a stallion called Gypsy.

Jim claimed Joey as his own when police in Capitol City, located somewhere in the Southwest, charged the boy for breaking the window of a house while playing baseball with some kids. He was innocent, but before he had a chance to tell his side of the story, Jim offered to take the orphan home if Joey's name was cleared. Joey did go with Jim to his home, the spacious Broken Wheel Ranch, where Joey interacted with Jim, a friendly trainer named Pete, and a horse named Fury. He later enjoyed the company of two other young male equestrians, Packey, who rode Pokey, and Pee Wee, who rode Lucky. Appearing occasionally were his teachers Helen Watkins, played in early seasons by Ann Robinson, and later Jim's sister Harriet Newton, played by Nan Leslie.

When not, pardon the pun, horsing around, Joey was gaining liberal helpings of knowledge through everyday life at the ranch. Of course, an assortment of dubious or evil characters were part of the story lines, and one con artist in the first season even tried to pass himself off as Joey's natural father. But good always triumphed, and Jim,

Joey, and crew learned a moral from each story which thankfully did not get in the way of exciting action scenes and crisp cinematography.

Fury was one of only two new NBC shows in 1955 to be filmed (the other was the nighttime anthology *Frontier*). Peter Graves thought it was going to be a nighttime entry and became upset when he learned it was not, but he stuck with the series for five seasons as it racked up ratings higher than some prime-time shows. An announcement in the fall of 1959, when Graves began work on the syndicated nighttime series *Whiplash* in Australia, claimed that actor John Compton had signed a five-year contract to replace Graves on the show in 1960, but it went into repeats instead. When *Fury* went off in 1966, Saturday morning network television stopped airing any live adventure shows until the fall of 1974.

The horse named Fury *co-starred with, from left, actors Peter Graves (as Jim Newton), Bobby Diamond (Joey Newton), and William Fawcett (Pete).*

G.E. COLLEGE BOWL
Game; B&W and Color
January 4, 1959–December 23, 1967

CBS Sun. 5–5:30 p.m. (1/4/59–4/26/59)
CBS Sun. 5:30–6 p.m. (5/3/59–6/16/63; summers off)
NBC Sun. 5:30–6 p.m. (9/22/63–6/4/67; summers off)
NBC Sat. 5:30–6 p.m. (9/23/67–12/23/67)

Host: *Allen Ludden (1959–61), Robert Earle (1962–67)*

This well-remembered brainy, intense quizzer engendered a fanaticism among some viewers in the 1960s, who cheered their home colleges to victory almost as strongly as they would in an athletic event. It started on NBC radio on October 10, 1953 as *College Quiz Bowl,* and much of the basic format was intact when the show came to television six years later. Two universities or colleges sent four representatives apiece to answer rapid-fire questions from the host, almost all of which were more difficult than any others heard on television. The teams got a break in action at "halftime," during which members briefly discussed their postgraduate plans. Apart from that moment, it was all questions waiting for answers until the day's game ended and the team with the most answers won (correct answers garnered at least five points, and some questions were worth bonus points). A $1,500 grant went to the scholarship fund of the winning school and a $500 grant to the losing one, upped to $3,000 and $1,000 respectively at the end of the run.

Among the typical head scratchers viewers heard were "What are meleagridea?" (turkeys) and "What two countries in South America have no coastlines?" (Bolivia and Paraguay). The show's chief writer was Nancy Fobes, a Fulbright scholar who authenticated answers with the *Encyclopedia Britannica.*

Allen Ludden, host since the show started in radio on 1953, received a briefing of all the questions three hours in advance so that he would not be stumped by the answers. Ludden, who was a Phi Beta Kappa graduate with an M.A. in English from the University of Texas, defended the show's intense pace in *Newsweek.* "Some adults think I go too fast and don't give the kids enough time," he said. "But the students don't think so. . . . It's always the viewing adults who are slower." Not all viewers complained about the format; reportedly some quick-thinking contestants were recruited heavily by leaders in intellectual and artistic fields.

The early winner in the first two years was Purdue University, which defeated four other challengers. The show was broadcast from various points until the October 2, 1960 season opener when it made New York City its permanent home. That broadcast also featured one of the most lopsided victories ever, as the University of Illinois thrashed the University of Iowa 270 to 5. Two years later, Ludden left the series to host *Password.* General Electric employee Robert Earle got the nod to replace Ludden over veteran announcers

Win Elliot and Dick Stark due to an ingenious audition tape, in which he edited himself in, in place of Ludden, and to a live audition where students responded to him well. The fact that Earle resembled Ludden with his sandy hair and horn-rimmed glasses didn't hurt either.

In 1963 the show switched to NBC and announced that it had awarded more than $352,000 in scholarship money to 175 different schools since it began. It continued on the network until June 14, 1970, spending its last three years airing early Sunday evenings on NBC. It ended at that time because General Electric decided to stop its sponsorship.

The show had a few revivals over the years, including a 1978 syndicated special hosted by Art Fleming, a CBS radio series also hosted by Fleming in the late 1970s, a NBC nighttime special in 1984 hosted by Pat Sajak (with Robert Earle as "color commentator"), and a 1987 revival on the Disney cable channel hosted by Dick Cavett.

•GABBY HAYES SHOW, THE
Children's; B&W
October 1, 1950–July 14, 1956

NBC Sun. 5–5:30 p.m. (10/1/50–12/30/51)
NBC Mon./Wed./Fri. 5:15–5:30 p.m. (12/11/50–7/19/51)
NBC Mon.–Fri. 5:15–5:30 (9/2/51–1/1/54)
ABC Sat. 5:30–6 p.m. (5/12/56–7/14/56)

Host: *Gabby Hayes*

Bewhiskered Western sidekick Gabby Hayes gained newfound popularity in the 1950s with his own children's show from New York City which aired most of its run before *Howdy Doody.* Guests on the debut were none other than his old boss Roy Rogers and his wife Dale Evans. Gabby then introduced the first of many films made specifically for his show, with his initial tale being a reenactment of the Lewis and Clark expedition.

Gabby wrote some for his 1950–54 series, which after two months aired more than once a week and had its Thursday broadcast titled *The Double Bar M Ranch* for no particular reason. Later the show was officially titled *The Quaker Oats Show Starring Gabby Hayes,* and viewers could see Aunt Jemima products in the background of a Western town where Gabby talked to two children about the day's filmed story (these introductions were filmed too). Gabby also did the commercials. The adventures starred generally obscure players, some of whom later became famous, like Andrew Duggan and John Randolph, and used a few aspiring playwrights who later did well also, such as Horton Foote.

In 1954, after four years and a few crossover appearances on *Howdy Doody,* NBC replaced Gabby with an even more popular child host, Pinky Lee (according to *Billboard,* it was because executives thought Lee would appeal to more women viewers!). Gabby rode the airwaves briefly again in a 1956 edition which was far less ambitious. The show opened with the host saying, "This is your old pal Gabby Hayes, coming at ya with a rip-roarin' Western," then ran old films of cowpokes Tex Ritter, Hoot Gibson, Bob Steele, and

Beef Bonk	John Stephenson
Flat Freddy/Gilda Gossip	Nancy Cartwright
Reggie Unicycle/Ollie Oilslick	Gino Conforti
Earl Ecch	Gary Christopher
Booey Bubblehead/Wendy Garbo	Jennifer Darling
Coach Frogface/Sludge	Pat Fraley
Doyle's Locker/Aimee's Locker	Henry Gibson

The Archies were never this wild. Teenage aliens attending Galaxy High School on the asteroid Flutor in an unspecified time zone came from throughout the universe to study the basic subjects. The first students from the planet Earth were Doyle Cleverlobe, a handsome jock, and Aimee Brightower, an introverted, quiet, brainy girl. Joining them in studies were various odd types whose names were keyed in some way to their looks. For example, Milo DeVenus, the class president, had six arms (get it?). Perhaps the most unusual of the group was the Creep, who resembled a cross between a blob and a penguin. Faculty members included Professor Icenstein, a blue-hued scientific genius, and Miss McBrain, the principal.

The large cast of characters with their weird names and talents probably made the show a bit too complicated for young children, although in its favor were the futuristic artwork, which was a cut above the typical Saturday morning herky-jerky style for outer space, and a nicely electronic vocal theme composed and performed by Don Felder. The episodes seen in 1988 were repeats.

•GALLOPING GOURMET, THE
Cooking; Color
1968–1971

Syndicated daily 30 minutes beginning January 1969

Host: *Graham Kerr*

The most refreshing face to hit daytime television in the late 1960s was Graham Kerr (pronounced "care"), a lighthearted chef whose how-to cooking approach relied on a heavy dose of comedy and just a pinch of traditional recipe explanations. The tall (6 feet 4 inches) 35-year-old gave such unconventional instructions to viewers as "sloshing" some liquid into the mixture, and sometimes appeared not to know exactly what he was doing. Nevertheless, he always invited a member of the appreciative studio audience in Ottawa, Canada, where the show was taped, to join him in a candlelit dinner to taste the final result, which she usually approved.

Kerr honed his cooking with comedy skills while in the New Zealand Air Force in the late 1950s. Eventually his success there led to a hit series in New Zealand and Australia, followed by this very popular series syndicated in America, the Philippines, Hong Kong, and other countries. Taping of that series stopped while Kerr struggled to recover from a near fatal auto accident. He returned in a five-minute daily syndicated series in January 1975 called *Take Kerr* (get it?). Neither that nor a 1990 daily syndicated revival of his original series called *Graham Kerr* managed to hold the

Gabby Hayes, host of the 1950s children's program The Gabby Hayes Show, *used tall tales to make his points to guest children like Clifford Sales (left) and Lee Graham.*

others in which he played a supporting role. Gabby supplied any needed narration between scenes while whittling in front of a frontier cabin set. After that, his TV appearances were relatively few until his death in 1969.

GALAXY GOOF-UPS, THE—See *Yogi's Space Race.*

•GALAXY HIGH SCHOOL
Cartoon; Color
September 13, 1986–August 27, 1988

CBS Sat. 10–10:30 a.m. (9/13/86–10/11/86)
CBS Sat. 11–11:30 a.m. (10/18/86–6/6/87)
CBS Sat. Noon–12:30 p.m. (6/13/87–9/5/87)
CBS Sat. 12:30–1 p.m. (1/9/88–8/27/88)

Voices:

Doyle Cleverlobe	Hal Rayle
Aimee Brightower	Susan Blu
Miss Biddy McBrain/Katrina	Pat Carroll
Milo DeVenus	David L. Lander
The Creep	Danny Mann
Professor Icenstein/Luigi LaBounci	Howard Morris

masses the way the first version did, possibly because Kerr seemed to have more interest in his newfound Christianity than in freewheeling food preparation.

•GAMBIT
Game; Color
September 4, 1972–November 27, 1981

CBS Mon.–Fri. 11–11:30 a.m. (9/4/72–3/28/74)
CBS Mon.–Fri. 10:30–11 a.m. (4/1/74–8/15/75)
CBS Mon.–Fri. 11–11:30 a.m. (8/18/75–12/10/76)
NBC Mon.–Fri. 10–10:30 a.m. (10/27/80–11/27/81)

Regulars: *Wink Martindale, Elaine Stewart (1972–76), Beverly Maudlin (1980–81), Lee Menning (1981)*

Two married couples played blackjack on this enjoyable game show, which began with a female dealer showing the first card at play. As Wink Martindale asked a question, each couple tried to be the first to buzz in and give the correct answer. Doing so meant they could either keep the card or pass it to their opponents, but a wrong answer gave the other couple control of that card. The rest of the game continued in like fashion, with the hitch that the couple in control after a question did not know what the next card would be. The ultimate object was to get to 21, where a couple could win at least $500 (the booty increased by $500 more for each game in which 21 was not made). However, a couple who received a card and stayed close to but below 21 could freeze at that point, forcing their opponents to try to answer questions to earn cards totaling more than the cards held by the "frozen" couple. If the second couple went over 21, the frozen couple won.

The first couple to win two games played a bonus round by choosing from 21 cards on a board. Each card had a prize hidden underneath it, and to reveal it a couple had to take a playing card before calling out the number. Again, the object here was to come at or near 21 without going over in order to claim the prizes. Any combination of 21 during this round won a couple a new car. The most distinctive prize offered in the 1970s was $100 worth of free groceries, which most contestants said they would use at Ralph's, a large supermarket chain in California.

Dealing all the oversized cards was Elaine Stewart, an actress who was a pinup queen of the 1950s and who may have landed the job because she was married to the show's co-creator, Merrill Heatter.

In 1980 the show returned as *Las Vegas Gambit,* with the big change being that it was now taped in Vegas's Tropicana Hotel. Among the minor wrinkles were that Martindale had a new assistant in Beverly Maudlin (replaced by Lee Menning by May 1981), and the bonus game had 18 rather than 21 boxes to select. By June 1981 the bonus game had also changed: couples had to remove the numbers one through nine off a board by rolling a pair of dice—the same bonus used in *High Rollers* (q.v.). Not surprisingly, both games were from Heatter-Quigley Productions.

GAME OF THE WEEK, THE
Sports; B&W and Color
May 30, 1953–August 14, 1965

ABC Sat. 1–3:30 p.m. (5/30/53–9/25/54; summers only)
CBS Sat. 2–5 p.m. (4/2/55–8/14/65; summers only)

Announcers: *Dizzy Dean, Buddy Blattner (1953–59), Pee Wee Reese (1960–65)*

TV's premiere showcase for professional baseball, *The Game of the Week* brought games into regions where the sport had previously been largely inaccessible. Its main attraction was its commentator, ex–St. Louis Cardinal Jerome H. "Dizzy" Dean, who had been the Yankees announcer on local television in New York for three years prior to this series. Dean's garbled grammar (pitchers "throwed" the ball and runners "slud" into bases, for example) horrified teachers but amused viewers, and his inimitable delivery, along with his laid-back approach, worked to keep the show on the air for more than a decade. Joining him at play-by-play was Buddy Blattner, later replaced by former Brooklyn Dodgers shortstop Pee Wee Reese. A pregame show was also added, and was hosted by Dean for a time (see also *George Kell*).

The success of *The Game of the Week* was especially impressive because the series was "blacked out" (not shown) in major markets with baseball teams such as New York, Chicago, Washington, D.C., and Philadelphia, or in sites within 50 miles of the game, all to encourage fans to attend local home games. Nonetheless, the program cultivated a strong, devoted following in areas not having a major league team nearby. ABC dropped the event after two years, not because of poor ratings but because sponsor Falstaff Beer wanted the program at a price at which the network felt it would not benefit financially from a deal. After CBS picked up the show, it remained popular for the next decade.

The series had one major change in 1965 when it covered the New York Yankees exclusively, CBS having bought the Yankees in a failed hope for increased revenue (it sold the team within a few years). In 1966 NBC outbid CBS for control of major league games and ran the series for more than two decades with new personnel (see *Baseball Game of the Week*).

•GARFIELD AND FRIENDS
Cartoon; Color
September 17, 1988–October 7, 1995

CBS Sat. 10:30–11 a.m. (9/17/88–9/9/89)
CBS Sat. 10:30–11:30 a.m. (9/16/89–9/1/90)
CBS Sat. 9–10 a.m. (9/8/90–9/10/94)
CBS Sat. 11 a.m.–Noon (9/17/94–2/4/95)
CBS Sat. 10–11 a.m. (2/11/95–8/5/95)
CBS Sat. 10:30–11 a.m. (8/12/95–9/9/95)
CBS Sat. 8–8:30 a.m. (9/16/95–10/7/95)

Voices:

Garfield	Lorenzo Music
Jon Arbuckle/Binky/Roy	Thom Huge
Odie/Orson	Gregg Berger

Wade	Howard Morris
Sheldon/Booker/Bo	Frank Welker
Liz/Lanolin	Julie Payne
Nermal	Desiree Goyette

Jim Davis probably had no idea when he created his newspaper comic strip "Garfield" in 1978 that the main character would go on to become the hottest animated cat ever seen on television. The persnickety feline got his first CBS special on October 25, 1982 (titled *Here Comes Garfield*), and almost annually thereafter a new special appeared before the network gave him a series six years later. The annual prime-time specials continued into the 1990s, by which time Garfield was a top cat on Saturday mornings as well.

Garfield's appeal to viewers was obvious: His bad habits were comically exaggerated reflections of the poor habits of human beings. The tabby loved lasagna to the point of gluttony, made an art out of being lazy, barely tolerated the goofy ideas of his geeky owner Jon Arbuckle, and actively despised Jon's other pet Odie, a big-eyed dog with a perpetual grin and a dangling, slobbering tongue. Speaking in voice-over thoughts, viewers learned Garfield's distaste for anything too precious, like fellow cat Nermal, or too tacky, like Jon's invariably loud and ignorant relatives or his attempts to score with the opposite sex. Garfield typically came out on top or at least even in the end of each playlet, but not without undergoing some sort of mild torture for him, which usually meant walking or trying to be friendly. Lorenzo Music, which provided Garfield's sarcastic tone, did the same for the inebriated and unseen Carlton the Doorman on the CBS nighttime sitcom *Rhoda* from 1974 to 1978.

Between Garfield's exploits was a component called "U.S. Acres," also a comic strip from Jim Davis. Orson the pig was the leader of a coterie of rather quirky farm animals, including Wade, a nervous duck who wore an inflated tube around his waist should he get into the water; Roy, the confident rooster; Sheldon, a baby chick who refused to come out of the eggshell, save for its legs; Booker, another baby chick who loved to hunt for worms; and Lanolin, a lamb with an occasional attitude. Typically there was one song punctuating the action in this segment as the creatures attempted to live in relative harmony with one another.

After an impressive seven-year run, *Garfield and Friends* went into reruns on the Cartoon Network cable channel.

•GARRY MOORE SHOW, THE

Variety; B&W
October 16, 1950–June 27, 1958

CBS Mon.–Fri. 1:30–2:30 p.m. (10/16/50–10/3/52)
CBS Mon.–Fri. 1:30–2 p.m. (10/6/52–7/2/54)
CBS Mon.–Thu. 10–10:30 a.m. & Fri 10–11:30 a.m.
  (7/5/54–3/28/58; off summers of 1956–57)
CBS Mon.–Thu. 10–10:30 a.m. & Fri 10–11 a.m.
  (3/31/58–6/27/58)

Regulars: *Garry Moore, Durwood Kirby, Ken Carson, Denise Lor, Ivan Sanderson (1952–55), Ray Malone (1952–53)*

Garry Moore began in radio as a comedy writer in Baltimore, Maryland, in 1935. By 1943 he had moved to headlining a show with Jimmy Durante, which lasted for five years, and starting on September 12, 1949, he had his own self-titled show on radio. The latter lasted only one season, but Garry's tenure on television proved to be much longer, with CBS giving him an exclusive seven-year deal in March 1950. The network gave him a nightly 7 p.m. slot beginning June 26, 1950, then moved him into the daytime in the fall, where he became one of CBS's biggest daytime successes of the 1950s.

The daytime show's accent was on comedy. It opened with a two-minute monologue from Garry, followed by a seven-minute comedy piece, a song, or just banter by Garry and his regulars. Sidekick Durward Kirby often was the foil in the sketches and mimicked everyone from Rudy Vallee to Edward R. Murrow. He and Garry frequently played Martha and Jenny, two gossiping old ladies. Garry was willing to do all kinds of slapstick in an effort to be entertaining. He allowed his clothes to be ripped off and soaked by water, and he even kissed monkeys and climbed chandeliers.

Other regulars included singers Ken Carson and Denise Lor, and for a time dancer Ray Malone. British zoologist Ivan Sanderson made weekly appearances with wild animals. There were some notable guests interviewed too, such as Carl Sandburg.

There was also room for talent auditions on air every Friday, particularly when the Friday show moved to the morning hours in 1954 and expanded to 90 minutes to replace *Arthur Godfrey Time* (Godfrey did his radio show from his Virginia farm on Fridays). Such upcoming stars as George Gobel (30 times from 1951–54) and Arte Johnson appeared. But the biggest find was Carol Burnett, who had done only small parts on TV for about a year when she debuted in October 1956 and hit with a funny monologue about vocalists' different styles during auditions. Her name became closely associated with Moore's over the next decade as they worked together in both daytime and nighttime television.

In 1955 Garry added "The Five-Cent Question," not a takeoff on giveaway shows then dominating the airwaves, but rather a test of viewers' generosity. He had already found out how giving they could be on September 10, 1954, when he told viewers to mail an envelope with a nickel in it just for kicks to a Mrs. Margaret Deibel from Mt. Pleasant, Michigan in his audience. Before the month was out, the woman had received more than 137,000 letters with nickels in them, for a total haul of close to $7,000.

The series had a slow start in the ratings and some sponsor trouble, not to mention poor reviews. (Jack Gould, TV critic for *The New York Times*, was referring to the five-year contract Moore signed with CBS before coming to television when he wrote, "I trust we won't have five more years of this trash.") But once Procter & Gamble decided to sponsor the show in early 1951, it managed to run in all 61 TV market areas then available, ensuring its popularity. It ended in 1958, after 2,070 shows, for three reasons, according to Moore in a *TV Guide* article. One, he wanted to do something new; two, he was sick of the overcommercialization of daytime television, having to do commercials now for about 30 products versus 4 in the beginning; and three, he was pooped.

Moore returned in a popular CBS nighttime variety series from September 30, 1958–June 14, 1964, then spent another long run hosting the syndicated *To Tell the Truth* from 1969–77. He retired to Hilton Head, South Carolina, where he lived until his death in 1993 at age 78.

GARY COLEMAN SHOW, THE
Cartoon; Color
September 18, 1982–September 10, 1983

NBC Sat. 10:30–11 a.m. (9/18/82–9/10/83)

Voices:

Andy LeBeau	Gary Coleman
Angelica	Jennifer Darling
Hornswoggle	Sidney Miller
Spence	Calvin Mason
Tina	LaShanda Dendy
Bartholomew	Jerry Houser
Chris	Lauren Anders
Lydia	Julie McWhirter Dees
Mack	Steve Schatzberg
Haggle	Jeff Gordon

The 1982 NBC TV movie *The Kid with the Broken Halo* served as the basis for this animated creation featuring the then-star of NBC's nighttime hit sitcom *Diff'rent Strokes*. Andy LeBeau was an angel-to-be who had to right wrongs on Earth to satisfy Angelica, his long-suffering evaluator. Tempting him along the way was Hornswoggle, an emissary from Down Below. Two episodes ran per show. An interesting oddity concerning this series, according to information in producer Bill Hanna's 1996 autobiography *A Cast of Friends,* was that a new animation unit in Mexico unfamiliar with Coleman drew him as a Caucasian rather than an African-American, forcing major alterations at the last minute.

GAYELORD HAUSER SHOW, THE
Talk; B&W
October 31, 1951–April 25, 1952

ABC Wed./Fri. 1–1:15 p.m. (10/31/51–4/25/52)

Regulars: *Gayelord Hauser, Ona Munson*

Health and nutrition expert Gayelord Hauser, author of the 1950 book *Stay Younger, Live Longer* ("a best seller in 16 languages," he reminded his audience on the show's debut) interviewed mainly female celebrities like Margaret O'Brien and Anita Loos in this short, and short-lived, talk show from New York City. Ona Munson served as his assistant.

GENERAL ELECTRIC COLLEGE BOWL—See *G.E. College Bowl.*

•GENERAL HOSPITAL
Soap Opera; B&W and Color
April 1, 1963–

ABC Mon.–Fri. 1–1:30 p.m. (4/1/63–12/27/63)
ABC Mon.–Fri. 3–3:30 p.m. (12/30/63–7/23/76)
ABC Mon.–Fri. 3:15–4 p.m. (7/26/76–1/13/78)
ABC Mon.–Fri. 3–4 p.m. (1/16/78–)

Cast:

Nurse Jessie Brewer (1963–91)	Emily McLaughlin
Dr. Steve Baldwin (1963–96)	John Beradino
Dr. Phil Brewer (1963–64, 1965–66)	Roy Thinnes
Dr. Phil Brewer (1966)	Robert Hogan
Dr. Phil Brewer (1966)/Dr. Peter Taylor (1969–79)	Craig Huebing
Dr. Phil Brewer (1967–75)	Martin West
Nurse Lucille March (1963–76, 1982)	Lucille Wall
Lee Baldwin (1963–65)	Ross Elliott
Lee Baldwin (1965–85)	Peter Hansen
Al Weeks (1963–65, 1970–74)	Tom Brown
Lenore Weeks (1963–65)	Lenore Kingston
Eddie Weeks (1963–64)	Craig Curtis
Eddie Weeks (1965)	Doug Lambert
Angie Costello Weeks (1963–65)	Jana Taylor
Peggy Mercer (1963–65)	K. T. Stevens
Priscilla Longworth (1963–64)	Allison Hayes
Nurse Audrey March (1964–)	Rachel Ames
Nurse Judy Clampett (1964–74)	Robin Blake
Dr. John Prentice (1964–67)	Barry Atwater
Meg Baldwin (1965–69)	Patricia Breslin
Meg Baldwin (1969–70, 1972–73)	Elizabeth MacRae
Scotty Baldwin (1965)	Johnny Whittaker
Scotty Baldwin (1966)	Teddy Quinn
Scotty Baldwin (1967–72)	Tony Campo
Scotty Baldwin (1973–74)	Don Clarke
Scotty Baldwin (1974–75)	Johnny Jensen
Scotty Baldwin (1977–83, 1987–93)	Kin Shriner
Brooke Clinton (1965–69)	Adrienne Hayes
Brooke Clinton (1970–73)	Indus Arthur
Nurse Sharon Pinkham (1965–73)	Sharon DeBord
Polly Prentice (1965–66)	Catherine Ferrar
Polly Prentice (1966–67)	Jennifer Billingsley
D.A. Chase Murdock (1966–67, 1971–73, 1977)	Ivan Bonar
Dr. Tom Baldwin (1967–72)	Paul Savior
Dr. Tom Baldwin (1976–77)	Don Chastain
Iris Fairchild (1967–70)	Peggy McCay
Howie Dawson (1968–74)	Ray Girardin
Nurse Jane Dawson (1968–75)	Shelby Hiatt

Mrs. Dawson (1968–70)	Maxine Stuart	Lamont Corbin (1977)	George E. Carey
Mrs. Dawson (1970–75)	Phyllis Hill	Lamont Corbin (1978)	Wiliam Bryant
Dr. Peter Taylor (1969)	Paul Carr	Kathryn Corbin (1977–78)	Maggie Sullivan
Nurse Diana Taylor (1969–73)	Valerie Starrett	David Hamilton (1977–78)	Jerry Ayres
Nurse Diana Taylor (1973–76)	Brooke Bundy	Lila Quartermaine (1978–)	Anna Lee
Dr. Henry Pinkham (1969–75)	Peter Kilman	Edward Quartermaine	
Dr. Tracy Adams (1969–70)	Kim Hamilton	(1978–88, 1991–93)	David Lewis
Nurse Mary Briggs (1971–73)	Anne Helm	Edward Quartermaine (1988–91)	Les Tremayne
Caroline Murray (1972–73)	Anne Wyndham	Edward Quartermaine (1993–)	John Ingle
Kent Murray (1972–73)	Mark Hamill	Luke Spencer (1978–84, 1993–)/	
Teddy Holmes (1972)	James Westmoreland	Bill Eckert (1991–93)	Anthony Geary
Teddy Holmes (1972–73)	John Gabriel	Dan Rooney (1978–)	Frank Maxwell
Dr. Lesley Williams Webber		Claudia Phillips (1978–)	Bianca Ferguson
(1973–84)	Denise Alexander	Bryan Phillips (1978–87)	Todd Davis
Dr. James Hobart (1973–76)	James B. Sikking	Tracy Quartermaine (1978–80,	
Nurse Augusta McLeod (1973–75)	Judith McConnell	1989–93, 1996)	Jane Eliot
Gordon Gray (1973–74)	Howard Sherman	Susan Moore (1978–83)	Gail Rae Carlson
Gordon Gray (1974)	Eric Server	Nurse Anne Logan (1978–82)	Susan Pratt
Dr. Joel Stratton (1974)	Barry Coe	Jeremy Logan (1978–82)	Philip Tanzini
Dr. Joel Stratton (1974–75)	Rod McCary	Howard Lansing (1978–81)	Richard Sarradet
Kira Faulkner (1974–75)	Victoria Shaw	Roy DiLucca (1978–79)	Asher Brauner
Samantha Chandler (1975)	Kimberly Beck	Ruby Anderson (1979–)	Norma Connolly
Samantha Chandler (1976–79)	Marla Pennington	Captain Burt Ramsey (1979–86)	Bob Hastings
Laura Vining Spencer (1975–76)	Stacey Baldwin	Joe Kelly (1979–82)	Douglas Sheehan
Laura Vining Spencer (1976–81,		Richard Simmons (1979–81)	Himself
1983–84, 1993–)	Genie Francis	Mitch Williams (1979–80)	Christopher Pennock
Barbara Vining (1975–76, 1978)	Judy Lewis	Stella Fields (1980–88)	Jeff Donnell
Carolyn Chandler (1975–76)	Augusta Dabney	Mike Webber (1980–86)	David Mendenhall
Bobby Chandler (1975–76)	Ted Eccles	Rose Kelly (1980–84)	Loanne Bishop
Cameron Faulkner (1975–76)	Don Matheson	Alexandria Quartermaine	
Beth Maynard (1975–76)	Michele Conaway	(1980–81)	Renee Anderson
Dr. Kyle Bradley (1975–76)	Daniel Black	Jefferson Smith "Hutch"	
Dr. Monica Webber		Hutchinson (1980–81)	Rick Moses
Quartermaine (1976–77)	Patsy Rahn	Sarah Abbott (1980–81)	Eileen Dietz
Dr. Monica Webber		Tiffany Hill (1981–83, 1986–95)	Sharon Wyatt
Quartermaine (1977–)	Leslie Charleson	Robert Scorpio (1981–85,	
Heather Grant Webber (1976–77)	Georgeanne LaPiere	1986–92)	Tristan Rogers
Heather Grant Webber (1977–79)	Mary O'Brien	Dr. Tom Hardy (1981–82)	Bradley Green
Heather Grant Webber (1980–83)	Robin Mattson	Dr. Tom Hardy (1982–84)	David Walker
Alice Grant (1976–77)	Camila Ashland	Dr. Tom Hardy (1987–)	David Wallace
Alice Grant (1978–83)	Lieux Dressler	Emma Lutz (1981–84)	Merrie Lynn Ross
Dr. Mark Dante (1976–78,		Dr. Noah Drake (1981–83)	Rick Springfield
1982–83)	Gerald Gordon	Slick Jones (1981–83)	Eddie Ryder
Mary Ellen Dante (1976–77)	Lee Warrick	Mickey Miller (1981–82)	Milton Berle
Terri Webber Arnett (1976–77)	Bobbi Jordan	Mikkos Cassadine (1981)	John Colicos
Dr. Adam Streeter (1976–77)	Brett Halsey	Holly Sutton (1982–85, 1992–93)	Emma Samms
Dr. Alan Quartermaine (1977–)	Stuart Damon	Blackie Parrish (1982–84)	John Stamos
Nurse Barbara Jean "Bobbie"		Jackie Templeton (1982–83)	Demi Moore
Spencer (1977–)	Jacklyn Zeman	Laura Templeton (1982–83)	Janine Turner
Dr. Gail Adamson Baldwin		Jake Meyer (1983–)	Sam Behrens
(1977–85)	Susan Brown	Frisco Jones (1983–87, 1989–91)	Jack P. Wagner
Nurse Dorrie Fleming (1977–80)	Angela Cheyne	Dr. Grant Andrews/Putnam	
Dr. Gina Dante (1977–78)	Anna Stuart	(1983–85, 1988)	Brian Patrick Clarke
Dr. Gina Dante (1978)	Brenda Scott	Celia Quartermaine (1983–86)	Sherilyn Wolter
Dr. Gina Dante (1978–79)	Donna Bacakka	Jimmy Lee Holt (1983–86)	Steve Bond
Dr. Gary Lansing (1977–79)	Steve Carlson	D. L. Brock (1983–85)	David Groh

Louisa "Lou" Swenson (1983–84)
Dr. Anthony Jones (1984–)
Terry Brock (1984–89)
Sean Donely (1984–95)
Felicia Cummings (1984–88)
Tanya Roskov (1984–87)
Maria Rameriz (1984–86)
D.A./Mayor Ken Morgan
    (1984–86)
Amanda Barrington (1984–86)
Derek Barrington (1984–86)
Lorena Sharpe (1984–86)
Ginny Blake (1984–86)
Josh Clayton (1984–85)
Jack Slater (1984–85)
Leo Russell (1984–85)
Sylvia Whitby (1984–85)
Robin Soltini (1985–)
Patrick O'Connor (1985–)
Kevin O'Connor (1985–86)
Jade Soong (1985–87)
Anna Devane (1985–92)
Dr. Yank Se Chung (1985–87)
Ted Holmes (1985–87)
Buzz Stryker (1985–87)
Brett Madison (1985–87)
Lucy Coe (1986–92, 1993–)
Duke Lavery (1986–89)
Duke Lavery (1990–)
Sandy Stryker (1986–87)
Dr. Simone Ravelle Hardy
    (1987–89)
Dr. Simone Ravelle Hardy
    (1990–93)
Dr. Simone Ravelle Hardy
    (1993–)
Autumn Clayton (1987–)
Nancy Becker Kennedy (1988–)
Colton Shore (1988–)
Olivia St. John Jerome (1988–)
Prunella Witherspoon (1988–)
Gregory Howard (1988–)
Katherine Delafield (1989–)
Ned Ashton (1989–92)
Ned Ashton (1992–)
Domino (1989–)
Dominique Taub (1990–91)
Dominique Taub (1991–92)
Mac Scorpio (1991–)
Jason Quartermaine (1991–)
Sly Eckert (1991–93)
Angela Eckert (1991–92)
Mayor Richmond (1991–92)
Madalyn Richmond (1991–92)
A. J. Quartermaine (1992–93)
A. J. Quartermaine (1993–)

Danielle von Zerneck
Brad Maule
Robyn Bernard
John Reilly
Kristina Malandro
Hilary Edson
June Lockhart

Lloyd Haines
Anne Jeffreys
Mark Goddard
Shelley Taylor Morgan
Judith Chapman
James McNichol
Randall England
John Callahan
Linda Borgeson
Kimberly McCullough
Guy Mack
Kevin Bernhardt
Tia Carrere
Finola Hughes
Patrick Bishop
David Doyle
Don Galloway
James Horan
Lynn Herring
Ian Buchanan
Gregory Beecroft
Yvette Nipar

Laura Carrington

Stephanie Williams

Felecia Bell
Linda Sanders
Martha McKee
Scott Thompson Baker
Tonja Walker
Chantal Contouri
Alan Feinstein
Edie Lehmann
Kurt Robin McKinney
Wally Kurth
Joe Mascolo
Tawny Fere Ellis
Shell Danielson
John J. York
Steve Burton
Glenn Walker Harris Jr.
Carol Lawrence
Frank Aletter
Sheila MacRae
Gerald Hopkins
Sean Kanan

Brenda Barrett (1992–)
Jagger Cates (1992–94)
Karen Wexler (1992–94)
Sonny Corinthos (1993–)
Lois Cerullo Ashton (1993–)
Stone Cates (1993–95)
Jon Hanley (1994–96)
Mary Mae Ward (1994–95)
Miguel Morez (1994–)

Vanessa Marcil
Antonio Sabato Jr.
Cari Shayne
Maurice Benard
Rena Sofer
Michael Sutton
Lee Mathis
Rosalind Cash
Ricky Martin

The format of General Hospital, ABC's longest-running daily show and soap opera, has been through a strange odyssey over the years. In its first decade it was set largely in one health care facility and concentrated virtually only on the hospital staff. By the mid-1970s ratings had fallen, and subsequently the show had several influxes of new characters and story lines as it expanded to cover the fictional city of Port Charles, which by 1992 was said to be near Buffalo, New York. In the 1980s international sites, location studios, and exotic, crime-driven stories figured prominently, as General Hospital gained and held first place in the ratings (wait, Luke and Laura fans, we'll get there!), but by the end of that decade the glow had faded and, as ratings sank, domestic dramas at the hospital once again took center stage. By then there was a new crew at the helm, so let's get a little background, shall we?

Lead characters in the 1960s and 1970s were Dr. Steve Hardy, chief of the internal medicine department at General Hospital, and his pal Nurse Jessie Brewer. Though many fans expected the two to get together romantically, they never did, preferring instead to support each other throughout their troubled ordeals. Steve, for instance, found that his devotion to work cost him chances at marriage to Peggy Mercer and Priscilla Longworth. But when free spirit Audrey March joined the hospital as a nurse, he found the right woman to balance his work and personal life, and the two wed in 1965. However, Audrey became frustrated by her inability to give Steve a child, so she left him to work in Vietnam; she then returned and wed Dr. Tom Baldwin, but their marriage was rocky. Audrey planned to leave Tom, only to find she was carrying his child. After many efforts by Audrey to extricate herself from this situation, Tom eventually kidnapped their son Tommy, but died of a heart attack in Mexico. Tommy returned needing the help of heart surgeon Dr. Jim Hobart, and when he saved Tommy's life, a grateful Audrey married him. Unfortunately, Steve was helpless to stop his true love's latest irrational decision.

Jessie foolishly involved herself with the younger Dr. Phil Brewer, whose carousing ways kept her threatening to divorce him until two pregnancies by him—the first a miscarriage, the second a child who died shortly after birth—kept him with her. Dr. Lee Baldwin offered to marry her when pregnant the second time, but she went into labor before their ceremony, prompting an unhappy Lee to wed widow Meg Bentley and become father to her son Scotty and rebellious 17-year-old stepdaughter Brooke Clinton. After

The core cast of the early years of General Hospital *consisted of, from left, Roy Thinnes as Phil Brewer, Emily McLaughlin as Nurse Jessie Brewer, and John Beradino as Dr. Steve Hardy.*

her child's death, Jessie divorced Phil and wed obstetrician Dr. John Prentice, who died in 1967 shortly after their marriage. John's envious daughter Polly accused Jessie of killing him, which led to Jessie being put in jail, but Polly later confessed to Phil that her dad had committed suicide. A gullible Jessie showed Phil too much appreciation by remarrying him even though he was carrying on with Polly, but when his car crashed with Polly in it, Phil thought he would be charged with murder and left town. Jessie then wed the more stable Dr. Peter Taylor, unaware that she had not seen the last of Phil.

Other characters seen in the 1960s included Steve's first patient Angie Costello, whose face was damaged after an accident involving her drunk boyfriend Eddie Weeks. Eddie got Angie pregnant in 1964, and through Steve and Jessie's encouragement they ended up marrying each other. Eddie's dad Al later became a widower who fell in love with feisty senior nurse Lucille March, Audrey's sister. Unlikely love also blossomed between meek intern Henry Pinkham and perky nurse Sharon McGillis, until she left him in 1973. Her colleague Jane Harland became his new squeeze after she rid herself of her lecherous bum of a husband Howie Dawson, who was a murder suspect at one point in the case of his girl on the side, Brooke Clinton. Meanwhile, the hospital staff became integrated with the arrival of black female kidney specialist Dr. Tracy Adams.

But Jessie and Steve remained the focus of the show in the early 1970s, as Phil Brewer had amnesia and forgot he was married to Jessie when he impregnated waitress Diana Maynard. He realized who he was before he had to undergo brain surgery, during which a horrified Jessie recognized him and realized her marriage to Peter Taylor was invalid. As she went back to Phil again, Diana married the now free and equally crestfallen Peter to give her baby a home. But Diana lost the baby, and Phil and Jessie were at odds once again and divorced, while Phil suffered from temporary impotence. Then Phil raped Diana, but she kept it a secret and Phil went to Africa. Peter found out and had a fling with nurse Augusta McLeod before reconciling with Diana.

Phil, however, returned to town as more of a louse than ever, giving a number of characters strong motives to murder him. Jessie, Diana, Peter, Augusta, and even Audrey's husband Jim Hobart, who thought Phil was trying to sabotage his career, all became suspects when Steve found Jessie sobbing over Phil's body on December 6, 1974. (The show taped five denouements with the characters, none of whom knew who the murderer was until three months later.) Amid fake confessions and false leads, it emerged that Augusta had killed Phil after he threatened to tell Diana that she was pregnant from her affair with Peter. Augusta went to jail and gave birth, while Peter and Diana resolved their differences. Jim and Audrey disintegrated as a couple due to his continued drinking and their lack of sexual relations.

As for Jessie, she found herself used by Teddy Holmes, who flirted with her but left town with her niece Caroline Murray. She fared better as a suspect in Phil's trial, as Lee Baldwin rekindled their flame following Meg's death (Meg first went insane, then died of a stroke). But Lee found more romance in the arms of widow Caroline Chandler, whom he wed. Her son Bobby, a medical student, married Samantha, a nurse. Then Bobby developed the "nearly always fatal" fictional Malenkov's disease, and he, Caroline, Samantha, and Lee disappeared suddenly in 1976, the year the show made radical changes in its format as the ratings fell to the bottom of the scale. One of these, sadly, was the diminishment of Jessie's story line, with the character having only minor scenes and a brief live-in relationship with hospital administrator Dan Rooney before actress Emily McLaughlin died in 1991.

There were developments aplenty in 1976. Dr. Lesley Williams finally got custody of her 12-year-old daughter Laura, whom a nurse had switched with the body of a dead child when Lesley gave birth after an affair with Professor Gordon Grey and who had been living in the family of Barbara Vining and Barbara's 10-year-old daughter Amy. Lesley by this time was wed to millionaire Cameron Faulkner after having dated Joel Stratton, but Cameron resented the attention Lesley lavished on her newfound daughter, and he died in a car crash after trying to persuade Lesley that Laura was not her real child.

Eventually Lesley and Laura established a mother-daughter relationship when Lesley married Dr. Rick Webber. Rick earlier had been part of the dominant love triangle on the show in 1976, when he returned from the Vietnam War only to find that his girlfriend Monica, told that he was reported dead in Vietnam, had wed his brother Jeff, also a doctor. A confused Monica loved both men, but neither stayed with her. Jeff eventually divorced Monica to wed unstable Heather Grant. As for Rick and Lesley, they let Rick's old pal David Hamilton live with them, but he turned out to be a pure cad, trying to seduce Lesley and Laura until the latter accidentally killed him. Laura found herself befriended by a now grown-up Scotty Baldwin.

Scotty returned to town in 1977 with his dad Lee Baldwin, who said he and wife Caroline had moved to Florida for his stepson Bobby's health. He was planning to move Caroline back up to Port Charles with him when an announcement came saying that a boating accident had blown up both her and Bobby. He barely had time to console himself as Dr. Gail Adamson started making an overture for Lee's love.

The return of Lee came at a time when *General Hospital* was near the bottom of the ratings, having expanded to 45 minutes unproductively in 1976–77 with many new characters and story lines which did not grip viewers, such as Dr. Mark Dante trying to prevent his crazy wife Mary Ellen from killing his admirer, Terri Webber, who was Rick and Jeff's sister. Bringing Lee back did not help much either, so many changes in personnel took place backstage. The most telling addition proved to the hiring of Gloria Monty as the new producer.

Monty, a long-time director on *The Secret Storm,* was hired in early 1978 as the show got a last chance to prove itself in a new, hour-long version. She threw out dozens of scripts, hired new actors, writers, set designers, and technicians, and reportedly worked 15-hour days seven days a week to get the series to the top of the ratings within a year, which she achieved. She knew exactly what audience she wanted, and it wasn't the one watching *General Hospital.* "We didn't go after ladies behind their ironing boards, or the ones in the rockers," she told *TV Guide.* "We wanted to get the kids."

The key element in Monty's plan, storywise, was pushing Laura as the show's top dramatic lead. She fought with ambitious young nurse Bobbie Spencer for the affections of Scotty Baldwin, whom she eventually married. Then, in a very controversial move, Laura was raped by Bobbie's brother Luke Spencer in October 1979, recuperated from the ordeal, and then became attracted to her attacker. Scotty (who later became a lawyer) found himself odd man out. While experts on rape loathed the implicit message that the attraction between Luke and Laura was sending, the duo became the hot couple of the soaps in the early 1980s. The show wrapped most of its story lines around Luke and Laura, and most of them were centered on working against the mob. A number of plot lines converged—ridiculously, some said—in drawn-out sequences in 1981 that had Luke and Laura saving Port Charles and the rest of the world from being frozen to death via a lunatic plan concocted by Miklos Cassadine.

Finally, on November 16 and 17, 1981, the show aired Luke and Laura's wedding. Sixteen million people watched at least some of the wedding episodes, the highest number ever to watch a daytime soap opera. No doubt adding to the tally was the appearance of Elizabeth Taylor as Helena Cassadine, Miklos's widow, who put a curse on the nuptials. Helena's brief appearance did actually serve a purpose beyond the marquee value of Taylor's name, her curse being the plot justification for Laura's mysterious disappearance in a fog a few weeks later, as actress Genie Francis decided to leave the show. Efforts to pair Luke with newly arrived sisters Laura and Jackie Templeton both flopped with viewers, but a hit was made when Luke found himself smitten with Holly Sutton and tried to win her over from his former best friend, Robert Scorpio. In 1983 the old Laura returned briefly, then left, Luke in hand, for almost a decade, save for a short visit by the couple in 1984.

Other characters assisted in giving the soap a trendy appeal in the late 1970s and early 1980s. Fitness guru Richard Simmons appeared as himself leading a weight and exercise class at the Campus Disco club, and emerging rock star Rick Springfield played heartthrob Dr. Noah Drake. Bobbie Spencer loved Drake, but her faking blindness to gain his attention backfired and he left her. The show even made hunks out of Josh Clayton, a singing bellhop, and Joe Kelly, a bagpipe-playing detective who fell in love with his stepmother!

But as it turned out, the characters from that period who were to become mainstays were the rich, wackily dysfunctional Quartermaines, who dominated story lines for the next two decades. Monica Webber had become part of the family by marrying the emotional Dr. Alan Quartermaine, but Alan's devious sister Tracy hated her and proved that Monica had been pregnant by her old boyfriend Rick Webber. Although that did not lead Alan to divorce Monica, it did set the tone of mistrust between the duo that began with Alan cheating on Monica with Susan Moore. Tracy had little to gloat about herself. She refused to give her dying father Edward pills for his heart condition until he said he would include her in his will, but her greedy cruelty backfired. Edward had faked his condition to test Tracy's loyalty, and he banished her from the house, after which she was seen only for only brief returns. Edward did, however, have a fan in his longtime love, wife Lila.

Celia Quartermaine, a distant relative of the family, added to the drama when she arrived in town and attracted the attentions of both Jimmy Lee Holt (who first claimed he was Edward's illegitimate son) and Dr. Grant Putnam, who for a time was impersonated by a look-alike and involved in a few spy stories. Grant and Robert Scorpio shared the spotlight as the leading men on the show in the early to mid-1980s as they fought international criminals and endured romantic entanglements. Scorpio's biggest headache came in 1986, when he returned to town from a sabbatical with his daughter Robin Soltini, only to find his ex-wife and now Port Charles Police Commissioner Anna Devane dating ex-waterfront boss Duke Lavery. Duke and Anna ended up marrying in 1987, but plenty of obstacles remained. One was Duke's past, which at one point required him to leave Anna as part of the federal witness protection program. After a few flings with others, including pianist Katherine Delafield, Scorpio successfully wooed Anna back, and they wed in 1991, the same year his brother Mac arrived in town and became a leading hero over the next few years. (In 1996, he even went undercover disguised as a woman.)

Other couples who dominated the story lines in the 1980s were secret agent Sean Donely and ex-actress Tiffany Hill, who wed in 1988; policeman Frisco Jones and Felicia Cummings, who wed in 1986; and Dr. Kevin O'Connor and Terry Brock, who wed in 1985 without Terry knowing that Kevin had killed several people, including her own grandmother! And Dr. Steve Hardy's son Tom, also a doctor, gave the show its first interracial marriage in 1988 when he wed Simon Ravelle in a relationship marked by numerous breakups and makeups.

But the most well-traveled in marriage in the 1980s had to be nurse Bobbie Spencer and Dr. Anthony Jones. Bobbie's first marriage, to D. L. Brock in 1983, ended with his death, and her second husband, Jake Meyer, had an affair with Lucy Coe. Lucy, incidentally, was quite a gal. She went from being the town slut to author of *Lust for Death,* a best-seller about her sex life with a mass murderer, then became operator of the hospital's day care center, and married Alan Quartermaine for a brief period in 1990 after he divorced Monica. Lucy was also the second wife of Dr. Jones, but Bobbie overlooked that when she became his third wife in 1989. Their marriage faced its biggest challenge in 1994 when their child B. J. died and Bobbie cheated on Tony. In a touching sequence, B. J.'s heart was transplanted to save the life of his cousin Maxie, the child of Tony's brother Frisco and his wife Felicia.

In 1991, with the series no longer leading in the ratings as it had most of the previous decade, Gloria Monty returned as executive producer (she had left in 1986.) But this time she could work no magic; the show began to descend in the ratings as she replaced several regulars and emphasized her new creation, the lower-class Eckert family headed by Bill, played by Tony Geary. Bill was nowhere near as appealing as Geary's earlier Luke Spencer, and realizing the mistake, ABC forced Monty out and negotiated with Genie Francis to return as Laura. In October 1993, Luke and Laura returned as a couple on the show as Bill Eckert was killed by criminals believing him to be Luke. This time around, things were rockier as the two tried to adapt to married life and Laura struggled to come to terms with her mother Lesley's death in a car crash back in 1984.

Others who took prominence in the 1990s were Alan and Monica Quartermaine's hunky sons Jason and A. J.; their foxy cousin Ned Ashton, who was the son of Tracy Quartermaine; one-time mob princess Brenda Barrett; mobster Sonny Corinthos; and sultry stud Jagger Cates, who romanced Karen Wexler.

It was Jagger's brother Stone who took part in the show's boldest story line in 1995 when Stone learned he had AIDS, which he had contracted because of his promiscuous lifestyle, and his girlfriend Robin realized they had had unprotected sex. Stone died in December, but Robin survived. ABC shortly thereafter issued a real book, titled *Robin's Diary*, which told the history of Robin and Stone's relationship. AIDS claimed another character in 1996, when longtime patient Jon Hanley succumbed to the disease (as did actor Lee Mathis in real life in May that year).

But another actor's death that year hit the series hard too—that of John Beradino, who had been playing everybody's favorite, Dr. Steve Hardy, since the first day of the show. His passing meant the end of an era both on and off the show. In fact, while Audrey and Tom Hardy were seen on-screen regrouping from the tragedy and figuring out how to handle hospital activities (Audrey was now an administrator), ABC executives finally put an end to speculation that had been going on for years by announcing that there would be a spin-off from *General Hospital*, this time set to air in 1997 under the title of *Port Charles.*

GENERAL SPORTS TIME

Sports; B&W

October 9, 1954–November 14, 1954

DuMont Sun. 1:45–2 p.m. (10/9/54–11/14/54)

Host/Narrator: *Harry Wismer*

General Sports Time was the title DuMont used when it put the syndicated *This Week in Sports* series on its network before Sunday football games in 1954. The program began in 1950 as a 15-minute weekly program with Tommy Heinrich, the "Old Reliable" of the New York Yankees, narrating filmed highlights of both amateur and professional sporting events, and this format lasted for the first four years. By the time it arrived on DuMont, sportscaster Harry Wismer was presiding over the series, which was retitled in honor of its sponsor, General Tire and Rubber Company.

The DuMont tenure was short-lived because the network, banking on the appeal of the NFL games it aired on Sundays, promised General Tire that 101 stations would carry the show, but ended up getting only 55. Even worse was the fact that the series continued in syndication in some markets, including New York City, where independent station WOR aired the 1954 season debut on September 30, more than a week in advance of the DuMont airing. After leaving its unrewarding network run, the series continued through the 1950s in syndication under its original title. In 1957 sportscaster Marty Glickman took over hosting chores from Wismer.

•GENERATIONS

Soap; Color

March 27, 1989–January 25, 1991

NBC Mon.–Fri. 12:30–1 a.m. (3/27/89–1/25/91)

Cast:

Vivian Potter	*Lynn Hamilton*
Ruth Marshall	*Joan Pringle*
Henry Marshall (1989)	*Taureen Blaque*
Henry Marshall (1990–91)	*James Reynolds*
Rebecca Whitmore (1989)	*Pat Crowley*
Rebecca Whitmore (1990–91)	*Dorothy Lyman*
Jason Gardner	*Anthony Addabbo*
Monique McCallum	*Nancy Sorel*
Doreen Jackson	*Jonelle Allen*
Sam Whitmore	*Kelly Rutherford*
Chantal Marshall (1989)	*Sharon Brown*
Chantal Marshall (1990–91)	*Debbi Morgan*
Trevor McCallum (1989)	*Andrew Masset*
Dr. Daniel Reubens (1990–91)	*Richard Roundtree*
Eric Royal (1990 at least)	*Randy Brooks*
Martin Jackson (1990 at least)	*Rick Fitts*
Kyle Masters (1990 at least)	*Robert Torti*
Jordan Hale (at least 1990–91)	*Robert Gentry*

NBC initially boasted that this in-house production was the first to feature an African-American family, but the achievement was unfortunately undercut by somewhat tasteless ads using that angle which promoted the series as "Black and White—In Color." Set in Chicago, it started with the Whitmores with their naughty girl Sam, who slept with her college biology professor (George Deloy). Vivian had once worked for the Whitmores as a maid, and Adam was her grandson (and Henry and Ruth's son). Ruth resented the family's history with the Whitmores, feeling it was demeaning. Rebecca was an attorney who was rich until her ex-husband wasted the family fortune.

By the fall Jason was cheating on Monique with Sam, and Adam was in jail. In order to spice up unimpressive ratings, Doreen gave birth to a child with sickle cell anemia.

Nonetheless, the show had lost its major star, veteran Pat Crowley, by the end of the year (she had been getting few lines, and her departure was by mutual consent). It started 1990 by introducing veteran actor Richard Roundtree as a doctor who was accused of a murder that had taken place 15 years earlier. Later arrivals included Eric Royal, who while being prosecuted by Assistant D.A. Chantal Marshall for the accidental death of a woman, fell in love with her (she ended up trying to get him out of jail), and Martin, who made a revelation destroying Doreen and Ruth's friendship. Yet the couple getting the most airtime was, ironically, Caucasians Sam and Kyle.

On the last week of the show Doreen and Ruth clashed while Vivian and Henry nixed Ruth singing at the local club, Kyle visited Sean in prison, and Jessica tried to discredit Sam. NBC Chairman Brandon Tartikoff made a cameo as a waiter on the last show, which had virtually no airtime at all in the East and Midwest owing to updates of the Persian Gulf War.

After the show ended its run, the Black Entertainment Television (BET) cable channel bought rerun rights for all

470 episodes and began repeating them in the nighttime in the fall of 1991; the repeats went on for a few years.

GEORGE HAMILTON IV SHOW, THE

Musical Variety; B&W
September 6, 1958–May 29, 1959

CBS Sat. Noon–1 p.m. (9/6/58–9/27/58)
ABC Mon.–Fri. Noon–12:30 p.m. (4/13/59–5/29/59)

Regulars: *George Hamilton IV, Mary Glick, Jan Crockett (1958), Jo Davis (1958), the Country Lads (1958), the Tennessee Wildcats (1958), Clint Miller (1959), Roy Clark (1959), Buck Ryan (1959), Smitty Idwin (1959), Alec Houston (May 1959), Jack French (1959)*

George Hamilton IV, the "international ambassador for country music," made two brief stops as host on network television in the late 1950s when he was a college student in his early twenties in Washington, D.C.. His first show replaced *The Jimmy Dean Show*, and though it used the same talent Dean had, it failed so miserably that CBS gave the noon–1 p.m. Saturday time slots back to its affiliates for a year. A few months later ABC gave Hamilton another chance with a new lineup consisting of singer Clint Miller, fiddlers Roy Clark and Buck Ryan, banjoist Smitty Idwin, ventriloquist Alec Houston, and musical director Jack French, along with holdover singer Mary Glick, but that effort flopped too.

GEORGE KELL

Sports; B&W
April 12, 1958–September 20, 1958

CBS Sat. 12:45–12:55 p.m. (4/12/58–9/20/58)

Host: *George Kell*

George Kell was a 15-year veteran American League third baseman who stopped playing for the Baltimore Orioles to do this biweekly interview show with CBS. Here Kell interviewed famed athletes like Stan Musial, Willie Mays, and Casey Stengel, the Yankees manager who on the debut talked nearly nonstop through the show about the history of baseball.

•GEORGE OF THE JUNGLE

Cartoon; Color
September 9, 1967–October 21, 1995

ABC Sat. 11:30 a.m.–Noon (9/9/67–9/7/68)
ABC Sat. Noon–12:30 p.m. (9/14/68–8/31/69)
ABC Sun. 10–10:30 a.m. (9/7/69–12/26/69)
ABC Sat. 11:30 a.m.–Noon (1/3/70–9/5/70)
Fox Sat. 11:30 a.m.–Noon (9/19/92–10/24/92)
ABC Sat. 9–9:30 a.m. (9/9/95–10/21/95)

Voices:

George/Super Chicken/Tom Slick/Gertie	*Bill Scott*
Ape/Fred/Narrator	*Paul Frees*
Ursula/Marigold	*June Foray*

"George, George, George of the Jungle, look out for that tree!" With that memorable opening punctuated by drums and followed by an anguished "AAAAHH!" from the Adonis-like apeman as he hit the tree, one could tell that George of the Jungle was no Tarzan. Poor George seemed to have spent more time developing the muscles in his body than the circuits in his head, as he spoke halting English in a strange voice, often forgot that his wife Ursula was a woman, and believed that his pet elephant Shep was a dog. His main savior was an erudite Ape, who with the others chipped in to help George come up a winner when confronted by visitors from the outside world or other hazards in Imgwee Gwee Valley in Africa.

A supporting segment on the cartoon featured "Super Chicken," a mild-mannered fowl whose pronunciation of the word *power* sounded like a battle infantry cry with clucks substituted instead of "Charge!" His sidekick was Fred the lion, and they flew in the Supercoupe, a mobile craft not unlike the Jetsons' bubble car. The scripts were often quite witty, as the duo tracked down criminals like the Oyster, who had to serve jail time in months with the letter "R" in them.

The other component was "Tom Slick," a race driver with a weird, off-center grin and lantern jaw who raced against competitors like the Teutonic Baron Otto Matic, who often hit his henchman Clutcher (who sounded like Deputy Dawg) with a wrench after one of their innumerable attempts to stop Tom Slick had failed. Cheering him on in various contests was his faithful girlfriend Marigold and spunky grandmother Gertie.

Sad to say, this was the last TV series created by Jay Ward, who gave the networks such top cartoon characters as Bullwinkle and Dudley Do-Right. But *George of the Jungle* obviously made an impact on viewers who later became TV programmers in the 1990s, coming back in repeats on Fox in 1992 as a stop-gap replacement for the late debut of *X-Men* and on ABC in 1995 to fill time before *Dumb and Dumber* debuted. Unfortunately, many of the principals, including Ward, Paul Frees, and co-performer and co-executive producer Bill Scott, were dead by that time, so a George revival, in cartoon form at least, appears unlikely.

GERALD MCBOING-BOING—See *Boing Boing Show, The.*

GERALD JOHNSON

News Commentary; B&W
September 6, 1953–January 10, 1954

ABC Sun. 1–1:15 p.m. (9/6/53–1/10/54)

Commentator: *Gerald Johnson*

ABC's low-budget attempt to emulate Edward R. Murrow and *See It Now* was this quarter hour of opinions on current affairs from newsman Gerald Johnson. The network replaced him after four months with a more acclaimed reporter (see *Elmer Davis*).

•GERALDO
Talk; Color
1986–

Syndicated daily 60 minutes beginning September 1986
Host: *Geraldo Rivera*

Geraldo Rivera was the first daytime talk show host to emphasis sleazy subjects as his main selling point, and as such can be credited, if that's the word, for pioneering a form that became extremely popular in the 1990s. An ABC News reporter since the early 1970s, he did the show after leaving the nighttime newsmagazine *20/20* on December 1985 when ABC News President Roone Arledge killed his piece on Marilyn Monroe's death and her relationship with the Kennedys. Free of network control, his tendencies toward overstatement and exploitation flowered fully when he went into daytime, and his bombastic techniques became fodder for comic routines and a regular target for critics.

The most outrageous early incident was a wild chair-throwing fight on a November 11, 1988 show on supremacists, which landed him and his broken nose on the cover of *Newsweek*. Geraldo kept the tawdriness going by disrobing for a show taped at a nudist camp on February 2, 1989, a show that was followed less than a year later by a visit to a topless donut shop in Fort Collins, Colorado. Rivera toned down his format following negative reactions to these shows, but he could not keep himself in check for long. Indeed, when O. J. Simpson was under suspicion for the murders of his wife and her friend Ron Goldman in 1994, Rivera's shows let everyone know he considered the football player guilty, even before the trial began, and he constantly hammered away at this theme during and after the trial.

By 1996 Rivera had a nightly show on the cable channel CNBC and announced he planned to end his talk show before the start of the 21st century to concentrate on other ventures (he also retitled his daily show *The Geraldo Rivera Show* and sat in a redesigned, spacious set). But while his series may disappear, its impact on daytime television, detrimental as it may be, will long be felt.

GET ALONG GANG, THE
Cartoon; Color
September 15, 1984–June 28, 1986

CBS Sat. 8:30–9 a.m. (9/15/84–9/7/85)
CBS Sat. 12:30–1 p.m. (1/4/86–6/28/86)

Voices: *Bettina Bush, Donovan S. Freberg, Timothy Gibbs, Eva Marie Hesse, Georgi Irene, Nick Katt, Robbie Lee, Sherry Lynn, Sparky Marcus, Chuck McCann, Scott Menville, Don Messick, Frank Welker*

The Get Along Gang dealt with six animals living in the Clubhouse Caboose in the village of Greenmeadow who acted like children. Their leader and best athlete was Montgomery "Good News" Moose, commonly called Monty. Joining him in weekly lessons of living in harmony with other species and dealing with their own shortcomings were health enthusiast

Zipper Cat, social trendsetter Portia Porcupine, prima donna Woolma Lamb, smart cheerleader Dottie Dog, and mischievous Bingo "Bet It All" Beaver.

The scenario was based on a line of greeting cards from American Greetings Corporation and books from Scholastic. Its pilot aired as a special on the Nickelodeon cable channel on May 6 and 19, 1984, and then in syndication on broadcast TV stations the next month. The second season was all repeats.

GET IT TOGETHER
Musical Variety; Color
January 3, 1970–September 5, 1970

ABC Sat. Noon–12:30 p.m. (1/3/70–9/5/70)

Hosts: *Sam Riddle, Cass Elliot*

Imagine *American Bandstand* with a little more pandering to the youth and no dancing by the audience, and you've got *Get It Together*, which preceded the former show. Guests on the debut were currently hot acts Three Dog Night and Credence Clearwater Revival. Ironically, this series was beaten in the ratings by reruns of that "old" pop group *The Monkees* on CBS.

GET THE MESSAGE
Game; B&W
March 30, 1964–December 25, 1964

ABC Mon.–Fri. 11–11:30 a.m. (3/30/64–12/25/64)

Host: *Frank Buxton (3/30/64–9/25/64), Robert Q. Lewis (9/28/64–12/25/64)*

The old boys-versus-girls motif cropped up on *Get the Message*, where a trio of each, with two celebrities included, tried to identify mystery subjects or phrases using one-word clues from their fellow members. The first team to score three times won the game and claimed $100. All three networks received proposals for the show, but only ABC took it for a modest run.

•GHOST BUSTERS, THE
Sitcom; Color
September 6, 1975–September 3, 1978

CBS Sat. 11:30 a.m.–Noon (9/6/75–9/4/76)
CBS Sun. 9–9:30 a.m. (9/11/77–9/3/78)

Cast:

Eddie Spenser	Larry Storch
Tracy	Forrest Tucker
Kong (costume character)	Bob Burns

Mimic Larry Storch and actor Forrest Tucker were a winning team on the ABC nighttime sitcom *F Troop* (1965–67), and nearly a decade later their comic chemistry remained strong as they played unlikely gumshoes with an ape sidekick on the prowl for new ghoulish duos haunting a local manor on the outskirts of an unnamed town. Much of the comedy used puns and slapstick, with Tucker as the level-headed, vest-wearing Tracy, and Storch the wisecracking, zoot-suited

Spenser. Among the monsters showing up were a dense Dracula and his bloodsucking wife, and Dr. Jekyll and his idiotic other self Mr. Hyde. All of the latter were dispatched by the Ghost Busters via a device that looked like a TV camera called a "dematerializer" which vanished them into oblivion. The 1977–78 shows were repeats.

In 1986 the series was revived as a cartoon, with the sons of the first version said to be working with TV reporter Jessica and sorceress Futura. None of the 1975–76 cast was used. The series used the same title, which no doubt confused kids who thought it was a spinoff of the 1984 movie of the same name. There was a cartoon version of the latter, however (see *The Real Ghostbusters*).

•GILLIGAN'S PLANET
Cartoon; Color
September 18, 1982–September 3, 1983

CBS Sat. 10:30–11 a.m. (9/18/82–1/29/83)
CBS Sat. Noon–12:30 p.m. (2/5/83–9/3/83)

Voices:

Gilligan	Bob Denver
The Skipper (Jonas Grumby)	Alan Hale Jr.
Thurston Howell III	Jim Backus
Lovey Howell	Natalie Shafer
Ginger/Mary Anne	Dawn Wells
The Professor (Roy Hinkley)	Russell Johnson

To the chagrin of most critics, and probably quite a few viewers, the networks kept on recycling the amazingly successful, and silly, nighttime CBS sitcom *Gilligan's Island* (1964–67) in new forms in the 1970s and 1980s. This was actually the second try in cartoon form (for the first, see *The New Adventures of Gilligan*). Here the "seven stranded castaways" found themselves adrift from civilization in another galaxy, rather than an island, courtesy of a rocket ship the Professor created (and he couldn't make them a boat in all those years?). Joining them was Gilligan's buddy Thumper, a knee-high alien who giggled a lot and resembled a green dinosaur with a human baby face, and a robot at his beck and call. Interestingly, Dawn Wells, the original Mary Anne, here also provided the voice of Ginger. She and Tina Louise, the original Ginger, did not join their fellow former castmates for the first cartoon, which was handled by the same production company which did *Gilligan's Planet*.

GIRL IN MY LIFE, THE
Testimonial; Color
July 9, 1973–December 20, 1974

ABC Mon.–Fri. 2:30–3 p.m. (7/9/73–12/20/74)

Host: *Fred Holliday*

A cornball throwback to the 1950s, *The Girl in My Life* typically had a man appear before a studio audience to tell them what good deed or noble sacrifice a female he knew had been responsible for, and this introduction was followed by the show, which honored that woman with a prize. This concoction, which replaced *The Dating Game*, generated little competition for *The Doctors* on NBC and *The Edge of Night* on CBS.

GIRL TALK
Talk; B&W and Color
1962–1970

Syndicated daily 30 minutes beginning May 1963

Hostess: *Virginia Graham (1962–69), Betsy Palmer (1969–70)*

Seen on this edition of Girl Talk *were, from left, Lee Remick, Peggy Hoffman, Florence Henderson, and hostess Virginia Graham.*

If any TV show of the 1960s deserved to be called a "bitch session," *Girl Talk* was it. It was nothing more than three celebrity women, led by opinionated Virginia Graham, expressing their feelings about life, current events, and most often, their thoughts about each other. This was the show where put-downs seemed to be the order of the day both onstage *(Time* magazine reported that actress Natalie Schafer told columnist Sheilah Graham, "Oh, I'm so glad to meet you. You were the cause of my divorce") and offstage (supposedly Jayne Mansfield was nonplussed when rotund comedienne Totie Fields told her, "People are constantly telling me how much alike you and I are"). Guests the caliber of Bette Davis, Joan Crawford, and Joan Fontaine felt free to let the fur fly. As Monty Morgan, the show's creator/producer/director, told *TV Guide,* "If Clare Boothe Luce ever should decide to write a sequel to her funny play 'The Women,' all she'd have to do is hang around here. She would come up with all the female cattiness she could ever need."

Not all the talk consisted of backbiting. For example, in 1966 actress Jean Muir discussed how she had been blacklisted in 1950 from the nighttime NBC sitcom *The Aldrich Family* 1950 following accusations that she was a Communist. The program proved to be rather uninformative to watch, for censors bleeped out not only the show, network, and sponsor (General Foods) involved in the matter, but even the man to whom Muir appealed her dismissal.

Cackling, somewhat loudmouthed Virginia Graham got her start as a syndicated talk show hostess with *Food for Thought,* an unspectacular effort, in the late 1950s after a run as a local New York show in 1953 on WABD. A contract dispute led Graham to do her own hour-long daily syndicated talk show (*The Virginia Graham Show,* 1970–72), while Betsy Palmer became hostess and the show adapted a more informational tone which included some men as guests. In other words, it became like every other daytime talk show, and shortly after it lost its distinctive edge, it went off the air.

GIVE AND TAKE
Game; B&W
March 20, 1952–June 12, 1952
CBS Thu. 3:30–4 p.m. (3/20/52–6/12/52)
Co-Hosts: *Bill Cullen, John Reed King*

Give and Take began on CBS radio in 1945 with John Reed King as host. Joined by Bill Cullen, he popped up again in this video adaptation. Here a quintet of contestants competed in answering questions, with any miss resulting in elimination. The surviving player won a bonanza of prizes. The show aired weekly in the same time slot shared by *The Bert Parks Show* and *The Mel Torme Show.*

GIVE-N-TAKE
Game; Color
September 8, 1975–November 26, 1975
CBS Mon.–Fri. 10–10:30 a.m. (9/8/75–11/26/75)
Host: *Jim Lange*

Somewhat reminiscent of *The Price Is Right,* which replaced it, this game show had four players each start with a different expensive prize. The contestants sat in a circle, and the audience was in a theater-in-the-round setting. The object was to amass prizes without going over a $5,000 total limit. The first round started when the contestant who answered a question correctly got to spin a giant wheel (which an overhead camera looked down on). When the wheel stopped, the contestant to whom the arrow was pointing had to decide whether to keep the prize indicated by the wheel, adding its value to the value of the one they had started with, or pass it on to another contestant. The player who came the closest to $5,000 without going over played for the final jackpot, which was worth at least $15,000.

Jim Lange moved from hosting *Spin-Off* in this time slot to hosting this game.

GLAMOUR GIRL
Game; B&W
July 6, 1953–January 8, 1954
NBC Mon.–Fri. 10:30–11 a.m. (7/6/53–1/8/54)
Regulars: *Harry Babbitt (7/6/53–10/5/53), Jack McCoy (10/8/53–1/8/54), Gaylelord Carter*

This filmed-in-Hollywood series had four women contestants who wanted a beauty makeover replete with new wardrobe. Audience applause determined who got it, and the transformed lady came back for inspection the following day (she also won a holiday trip). The show typically dispensed more than $4,000 worth of gifts each day. Musician-composer Gaylelord Carter supplied live music. Jack McCoy, the show's executive producer, succeeded Harry Babbitt as host midway through its run.

GO
Children's; Color
September 8, 1973–September 4, 1976
NBC Sat. 12:30–1 p.m. (9/8/73–9/4/76)

Go was an educational anthology series for children. The debut featured a day on the job with the police at New York City's 20th Precinct. Later that year, Rod Serling narrated a segment on the life of John Carr, the son of Skylab IV astronaut Lt. Col. Gerald P. Carr, and NBC News anchor John Chancellor also hosted and narrated a show on February 8, 1975. Perhaps the most interesting program was the November 2, 1974 installment, where animator Friz Freleng demonstrated how his *Pink Panther* cartoons were created.

In the fall of 1975 the show was retitled *Go-USA,* and featured stories related to the Revolutionary War to celebrate America's upcoming Bicentennial. The change failed to improve the ratings, however, and the series continued to finish last behind *American Bandstand* on ABC and *Fat Albert and the Cosby Kids* on CBS, and the show went off in 1976.

•GO
Game; Color
October 3, 1983–January 20, 1984
NBC Mon.–Fri. Noon–12:30 p.m. (10/3/83–1/20/84)
Host: *Kevin O'Connell*

Go made the bonus used in *Chain Reaction* (q.v.) its
central game. Two quintets, each led by a celebrity captain,
competed one at a time to answer five questions as quickly
as possible. Four players sat in chairs as one player stood
between the first two players in a podium designed to move
back and forth between two players. Each duo alternated
saying one word at a time to make a question for the subject
they saw on the monitor that the standing player had to
guess. When he or she answered correctly, the contestant
moved on to the next duo, which included one of the previous
contestants, for another constructed question. This process
continued until the contestant returned to the first duo after
answering five questions. The time taken by the first team
to complete the task was the one the other quintet had to
beat in order to win that round. It took 1,500 points to win
a game. Winning the first round netted 250 points, the
second 500 points, the third 750 points, and the fourth (if
needed) 1,250 points.

The bonus game had one contestant try to provide seven
answers, in one-minute, to questions again constructed by
his or her teammates, but this time the process was one of
elimination followed by addition. That is, all four players
were used to make the first question, then after a correct
answer only three did so, then two, then one, then two, then
three and finally all four. Getting seven answers won a team
$10,000 or $20,000 if they prevented their opponents from
winning a round. Teams competed all week long, with all
earnings split among contestants.

Host Kevin O'Connell also served at the time as an on-
air personality on NBC's Los Angeles affiliate KNBC.

GO GO GLOBETROTTERS—See *Harlem Globetrotters, The.*

•GO GO GOPHERS, THE
Cartoon; Color
September 14, 1968–September 6, 1969
CBS Sat. 8–8:30 a.m. (9/14/68–9/6/69)
Voices:

Ruffled Feather/Sgt. Hokey Loma	Sandy Becker
Running Board	George S. Irving
Col. Kit Coyote	Kenny Delmar

A spin-off from *Underdog*, *The Go Go Gophers*, a rare series
where the Indians always beat the cowboys, featured two
gopherish Native Americans, the virtually indecipherable
Ruffled Feather and his interpreter Running Board, who
masterminded their schemes. They fought to keep from
being the last two natives run out of their territory by the
bullheaded Col. Kit Coyote and his reluctant subordinate

Sgt. Hokey Loma, who always questioned the colonel's plans
while serving him at Fort Gopher. Also featured were the
adventures of Klondike Kat, a slow-on-the-uptake mountie
whose belt was on too tight, causing his clothes to ride up.
He took orders from Major Minor to chase a mouse named
Savoir Faire, whom he always captured at the end of the
cartoon. It too was a segment from *Underdog*.

GO-U.S.A.—See *Go.*

•GODZILLA POWER HOUR, THE
Cartoon; Color
September 9, 1978–September 5, 1981
NBC Sat. 9:30–10:30 a.m. (9/9/78–10/28/78)
NBC Sat. 9–10:30 a.m. (11/4/78–9/1/79)
NBC Sat. 11:30 a.m.–Noon (9/8/79–11/3/79)
NBC Sat. 8–9 a.m. (11/10/79–4/5/80)
NBC Sat. 8–9 a.m. and Noon–12:30 p.m. (two shows;
    4/12/80–9/20/80)
NBC Sat. 8–9 a.m. (9/27/80–5/16/81)
NBC Sat. 9–9:30 a.m. (5/23/81–9/5/81)
Voices:

Capt. Carl Majors	Jeff David
Godzilla/Montaro (1978–79)	Ted Cassidy
Dr. Quinn Darien	Brenda Thompson
Pete	Al Eisenman
Brock	Hilly Hicks
Jana (1978–79)	B.J. Ward
Dr. Ben Cooper (1978–79)	Mike Bell

The Godzilla Power Hour originally consisted of two
main separate elements. The first was of course Godzilla,
a humongous lizardlike being who starred in countless
Japanese horror films during the 1950s. Godzilla actually
played a rather minor role on this series, appearing only
when summoned from the depths of the ocean with a hand
buzzer by Capt. Carl Majors. Majors navigated the *Calico*, a
research ship which traveled to unknown lands. Aboard with
Majors was scientist Dr. Quinn Darien, her peppy nephew
Pete, and Brock, Carl's mate. They always got entangled
with some creature or villain who required them to fetch
Godzilla, described in the opening narration as 30 stories
high and sporting a green skin, fiery breath, and laser eyes.
Along for the adventure was Godzooky ("Zooky" to Pete),
Godzilla's nephew, who had wings to fly but basically served
as comic relief while Godzilla performed the final rescues.

The other element, seen the first season only, was Jana
of the jungle. Jana, a blonde girl whose pets were Tiko, a
coatimundi, and Ghost, a jaguar, grew up in South America
as an orphan under the eye of Indian chief Montaro. She
and Montaro, who had a magical "staff of power," looked
for her long-lost father who had disappeared in the Amazon
accompanied by Dr. Ben Cooper from America.

Within two months after its debut, the series became
Godzilla Super 90, with reruns of *Jonny Quest* (q.v.) added
to fill out the hour and a half show. In the fall of 1979 it

contracted to 30 minutes under the title *Godzilla* and ended its run that way. However, from December 1979–April 1980 it became *The Godzilla/Globetrotters Adventure Hour*, with the latter referring to reruns of *The Super Globetrotters* (q.v.), followed by five months where the shows ran twice on NBC's then impoverished Saturday morning schedule. Then from September–November 1980 it got new repeats and became *The Godzilla/Dynomutt Hour with the Funky Phantom* (see *Dynomutt* and *Funky Phantom* for more details), and then *The Godzilla/Hong Kong Phooey Hour* (see *Hong Kong Phooey*) with the latter's repeats running with the main show through May 15, 1981. All of which proves that Hanna-Barbera and the networks could be every bit as good at exploiting the success of the TV Godzilla as Japan's Toho Studios had been with Godzilla in the movies.

GOING BANANAS
Sitcom; Color
September 15, 1984–December 1, 1984
NBC Sat. Noon–12:30 p.m. (9/15/84–10/20/84)
NBC Sat. 12:30–1 p.m. (10/27/84–12/1/84)
Cast:

James Cole	Tim Topper
Louise Cole	Emily Moultrie
Hubert	Bill Saluga
Hank	James Avery

It's hard to believe that Margaret Loesch, executive producer of this loser comedy, would a decade later be president of the top-ranked Fox Children's Network on Saturday mornings. But, as the saying goes, everybody's got to start someplace, and this was her trial by fire. The show had Louise and her brother James serving as protectors for Roxanna Banana the orangutan. The latter faced repeated attempted captures by hapless baddies Hubert and Hank. The audience cared so little about Roxanna's plight that before three months were out she and the rest had disappeared permanently.

GOING PLACES
Variety; B&W
June 3, 1956–August 26, 1956
ABC Sun. 5–6 p.m. (6/3/56–8/26/56)
Host: *Jack Gregson, Merv Griffin*

A summer replacement for *Super Circus, Going Places* was a variety show seen live from various locales in Florida and hosted by Jack Gregson. It was seen on location from Miami's Seaquarium on the debut. Merv Griffin had replaced Gregson by July 1956.

GOLDEN WINDOWS
Soap Opera; B&W
July 5, 1954–April 1, 1955
NBC Mon.–Fri. 3:15–3:30 p.m. (7/5/54–4/1/55)

Cast:

Juliet Goodwin	Leila Martin
Charles Goodwin	Eric Dressler
John Brandon (1954 at least)	Grant Sullivan
Tom Anderson	Herbert Patterson
Ann Summers (1954 at least)	Sonny Adams
Ruth Brandon (1954 at least)	Harriet MacGibbon
Ellen Stockwell (1954 at least)	Millicent Brower
Hazel, Juliet's pal (1954 at least)	Barbara Cook
Carl Grant (1955)	Joe De Santis
Otto (1955)	Martin Kosleck
Dr. Paul Anderson (1955)	Philip Pine

Twenty-one-year-old Leila Martin starred in this soaper as Juliet Goodwin, a native of Capstan Island, Maine, who left her hometown to pursue a singing career in New York City. Her move appalled her foster father Charles and her boyfriend John Brandon, both of whom wanted her back on the Maine coast, but she did not care, as she found a new love interest in Tom Anderson. Unfortunately for her, Tom faced indictment for a crime, and she and her father could be charged as accomplices. As for Juliet's ex-fiancé John, he partied with his new girlfriend and later bride Ann Summers, even having his mother Ruth throw them a bash at Ruth's residence, Gray Gables.

Meanwhile, as 1955 began, Tom had been sentenced, but Juliet vowed to clear his name and, with the help of Carl Grant, found the real criminal, a man named Fred Stanton. Tom celebrated his release from jail by behaving badly toward Juliet—he accepted a job with an oil firm which took him away from Gotham. To add to Juliet's woes, Charles suddenly became ill, and Juliet had to care for him in New York. Plus, Carl Grant and his fellow conspirator Otto decided to do a little more dirty work by kidnapping Juliet! Luckily, our poor heroine had a new love interest in Dr. Anderson, who confessed his amour for her in time for her to be saved from Carl and Otto. Unfortunately for them, it was also just in time for the series to be canceled.

GOLDIE GOLD AND ACTION JACK
Cartoon; Color
September 12, 1981–September 18, 1982
ABC Sat. 11–11:30 a.m. (9/12/81–2/6/82)
ABC Sat. 9–9:30 a.m. (2/13/82–9/18/82)
Voices:

Goldie Gold	Judy Strangis
"Action" Jack Travis	Sonny Melendez
Sam Gritt	Booker Bradshaw

Eighteen-year-old Goldie was the richest girl in the world, so it must have been a sense of boredom which prompted her to join Action Jack, the top reporter for the publication she owned, *The Gold Street Journal*, on exotic, skullduggery-filled excursions around the world. Sam Gritt was Goldie's editor, and Nugget was her Labrador.

GOLF CLASSIC—See *CBS Golf Classic*.

GOLF WITH SAM SNEAD
Sports; Color
March 26, 1966–August 26, 1967

NBC Sat. 5:30–6 p.m. (3/26/66–6/25/66)
ABC Sat. 4:30–5 p.m. (4/29/67–8/26/67)

Regulars: *Sam Snead, Jerry Healey*

"Slamming" Sam Snead taught sportscaster Jerry Healey lessons in becoming a top golfer in this series filmed at Firestone Country Club in Akron, Ohio. The shows on ABC in 1967 were reruns.

•GONG SHOW, THE
Game; Color
June 14, 1976–July 21, 1978

NBC Mon.–Fri. 12:30–12:55 p.m. (7/14/76–12/31/76)
NBC Mon.–Fri. 4–4:30 p.m. (1/3/77–12/2/77)
NBC Mon.–Fri. 12:30–1 p.m. (12/5/77–7/21/78)

Host/Creator: *Chuck Barris*

Regulars: *Sivi Aberg, Jerry Maren, Jaye P. Morgan, Rex Reed, Arte Johnson*

Could it be more than coincidence that Ted Mack, host of *The Original Amateur Hour* (q.v.), died within a month after the premiere of this tacky yet briefly successful burlesque of his show's concept? *The Gong Show* was only technically a talent contest, with nonprofessionals receiving at least 45 seconds to do their act before a rowdy audience and panel of three celebrities. Members of the latter trio could decide at any time during the act to hit a huge gong on stage, indicating their displeasure and ending the performance. The show and its viewers thrived on the gonging, and it sometimes seemed that series personnel had scheduled as many lousy acts as possible per show to prevent anyone from winning the daily grand prize of a check for $516.32 and a golden gong. Those who were not gonged received a score from 1 to 10 from each judge for their performance; thus the highest score one could receive was 30.

Despite the potential indignities one could suffer on the show, there were more than 3,000 people willing to audition for it within its first year alone. Fat people making obscene body noises or gestures, off-key singers, and unfunny comedians got more than their fair share of airtime. However, a few acts were too weird even to be put on the show, such as the exotic dancer with a fondness for tarantulas. As far as the celebrity panel was concerned, the emphasis was on acerbic sarcasm. (Jaye P. Morgan, a moderately successful 1950s pop singer, gained something of a cult following for supplying often obscenity-laced opinions of acts which NBC had to censor.)

Los Angeles film critic John Barbour was originally slated to host the series, but NBC reportedly gonged him just before taping the debut with Chuck Barris instead. The curly-haired, diminutive Barris became known to his fans as "Chucky Baby." Audiences loved his casual, sometimes incoherent hosting style and his clowning with statuesque model Sivi Aberg, who displayed scores, and Jerry Maren, the little person who threw confetti at the day's acts at the end of each show. It was Barris who came up with the idea for the show. In 1975 he was carping to Chris Bearde, another producer, about the bad talent trying out for a TV show, and Bearde asked him why he didn't showcase the poor acts. Barris followed up on the idea. Eventually Barris grew so fond of the show (or obsessed, if you are a detractor) that by 1977 he had bought out Bearde's participation in the series and replaced Gary Owens as host of the nighttime syndicated version of the show, which began in 1976.

The series became popular enough that it was incorporated into episodes of such nighttime series as *Sanford and Son, What's Happening!* and *The Carol Burnett Show.* The latter employed perhaps the most artful critique of the show's appeal in a sketch where southern belle Eunice, played by Burnett, got gonged after working her heart out to sing "Feelings" on the series. The skit ended with a shot of an obviously dejected and hurt Eunice fading into a dot on the TV screen. It was far more classy than the show it spoofed, or anything Barris produced for that matter.

The Gong Show was still hot in 1978 when NBC decided to cancel it in favor of the more adventurous (and respectable) *America Alive* (q.v.). It continued in syndication through 1980, the same year of theatrical release for the flop R-rated *Gong Show Movie*, which used some censored material from the series. A failed syndicated revival in 1988 had Don Bleu as host.

GOOBER AND THE GHOST CHASERS
Cartoon; Color
September 8, 1973–August 31, 1975

ABC Sat. 10:30–11 a.m. (9/8/73–8/31/74)
ABC Sun. 11–11:30 a.m. (9/8/74–8/31/75)

Voices:

Goober	*Paul Winchell*
Gilly	*Ronnie Schell*
Ted	*Jerry Dexter*
Tina	*Jo Ann Harris*

Goober was a cowardly dog who whenever scared turned invisible, although his stocking cap did not disappear. He found a lot of occasions to fade away on this show, as his owners Gilly, Ted, and Tina worked for *Ghost Chasers* magazine and brought him along in their investigations of singing spirits, mummies, and the like, though almost all of them turned out to be natural villains rather than paranormal beings. Occasionally seen as guest stars and giving their voices were members of the ABC nighttime sitcom *The Partridge Family,* including Laurie (Susan Dey), Danny (Danny Bonaduce), Tracy (Suzanne Crough), and Chris (Brian Foster). The second season was all repeats.

GOOD MORNING—See _Morning Show, The._

•GOOD MORNING AMERICA
Informational; Color
November 3, 1975–

ABC Mon.–Fri. 7–9 a.m. (11/3/75–)
ABC Sun. 8–9 a.m. (1/3/93–)

Hosts: _David Hartman (11/75–2/87), Nancy Dussault (11/3/75–4/22/77), Sandy Hill (4/25/77–80), Joan Lunden (1980–), Charles Gibson (1987–)_

Newscasters: _Steve Bell (1975–87), Margaret Osmer (1975–79 at least), Forrest Sawyer (at least 1988), Mike Schneider (at least 1989–93), Morton Dean (1993–96), Elizabeth Vargas (1996–)_

Weathermen: _John Coleman (1976–83), Spencer Christian (1983–)_

Regulars: _Erma Bombeck (1975–86), Rona Barrett (1975–80), Jack Anderson (1975–80 at least), Geraldo Rivera (1975–78 at least), John Lindsay (1975–76), Helen Gurley Brown (1975–76 at least), Jonathan Winters (1975–76), Dr. Tim Johnson (1976–), F. Lee Bailey (1976–77 at least), Sylvia Porter (1977–78 at least), Ruth Batchelor (1981), Pat Collins (1981), Joel Siegal (1981–), Chantal [Westerman] (1986–), Linda Ellerbee (1986–87), Dr. Nancy Snyderman (1987–), Harm de Bli (1989–), Paula Lyons (1990–94)_

David Hartman and Sandy Hill hosted Good Morning America _in the late 1970s._

Sunday Hosts: _Dana King (1993), Bill Ritter (1993–94), Willow Bay (1994–), Antonio Mora (1994–95), Kevin Newman (1996–)_

ABC carved its own very successful niche in morning news/information shows with _Good Morning America,_ the replacement for the ill-fated _A.M. America_ (q.v.). Owing much to an excellent production job and on- and off-air difficulties at the competing _Today Show,_ this series managed to corral more than a quarter of the morning audience within four years and became the leader in its time period for most of the 1980s and 1990s, winning several Emmys along the way.

　Good Morning America began in much the same vein as _Today,_ with news updates originally handled alternately by Steve Bell and Margaret Osmer at the start of every half hour, followed by interviews with newsmakers, advice givers, and celebrities; demonstrations, reports, or light segments from regulars; and so on. What stood out was the intricate use of TV monitors on the show to allow original hosts David Hartman and Nancy Dussault (who was replaced by Sandy Hill within two years) to at least look like they were talking to the interviewee, who appeared on a monitor shown on-screen. The cutting from the New York studios to various locales worked beautifully, whether it was to Steve Bell in Washington, D.C., John Coleman in Chicago, or Rona Barrett from Los Angeles in a segment taped the previous day. Incidentally, Rona's three-quarter face profile shot and "I'm Rona Barrett. Keep thinking good thoughts"

The longest-running regular cast on Good Morning America *consisted of, from left, Charles Gibson, Joan Lunden, and Spencer Christian.*

sign-off provoked almost as much derision among comics at the time as her nasal delivery of Hollywood gossip.

Among other early regulars were Jonathan Winters and newspaper humorist Erma Bombeck doing comic monologues (Bombeck's were taped), Jack Anderson from Washington with some muckraking news, Helen Gurley Brown with a segment titled "Men/Women," Sylvia Porter with financial advice, and Geraldo Rivera and John Lindsay with various reports. There also was a "Face Off" debate between people on the opposite side of a current issue, and a man-on-the-street portion called "Talk Back."

There was some turnover in the co-host department, however. Sandy Hill left in 1980 to become a special correspondent for the series for a time, saying that she was fed up with her limited role in the studio. Her successor Joan Lunden had been doing "People in the News" and new products and safety ideas segments for the show since 1977 before being promoted to the co-host level. But despite these changes, *Good Morning America* steadily increased in audience size; by early 1979 it was challenging longtime leader *Today,* by 1980 it was out in front.

A fair number of changes took place in the early 1980s. When Rona Barrett left, her show business news replacements

were, in Hollywood, Ruth Bachelor, who left in June 1981 after six months of backstage arguments with ABC executives and was replaced by Chantal, and, in New York, Pat Collins, who also was replaced in 1981 by movie critic Joel Siegal. John Coleman got the ax as weathercaster the same week in August 1983 he was forced out of his job as chairman and president of cable's Weather Channel, and pun-loving Spencer Christian, previously a special correspondent since 1979, replaced him.

By April 1987 Charles Gibson, an ABC Washington, D.C. correspondent since 1981 who had substituted for Hartman for a few years, took over as host, and his arrival meant that longtime co-host Joan Lunden had greater latitude in what segments she could do on air than she had with Hartman. Around the same time the budget-crunching management at Capital Cities Broadcasting, which took over ABC, removed Linda Ellerbee's "T.G.I.F. (Thank God It's Friday)" end-of-each-week humorous recap of odd stories, which Ellerbee had been doing on rival *Today.* The main new correspondents who joined during Gibson's tenure were medical correspondent Dr. Nancy Snyderman, who occasionally substituted for Lunden; geography expert Harm de Bli; and consumer reporter Paula Lyons.

When the show started a Sunday edition in 1993 to challenge a similar spinoff by *Today,* it ran nearly a year with Dana King and Bill Ritter as its first hosts. King left toward the end of 1993, and Ritter disappeared shortly thereafter. The new team of Antonio Mora and Willow Bay took over, but Kevin Newman later replaced Mora. However, this edition placed third behind *Today* and *Sunday Morning,* and there was some doubt as to whether ABC would keep it on the air into the 20th century.

Meanwhile in 1996, the daily show got a slightly revamped set with the arrival of former *Today* newscaster Elizabeth Vargas as anchor. She was the first reporter to do the news at the New York set rather than in Washington, and her presence even extended to appearing on the couch with Charles and Joan, spurring rumors she was being groomed to replace Lunden. Lunden's signing of a long-term contract later that year squelched those stories for the time being.

•GOOF TROOP
Cartoon; Color
September 12, 1992–September 11, 1993
ABC Sat. 10–10:30 a.m. (9/12/92–1/30/93)
ABC Sat. 9–9:30 a.m. (2/6/93–9/11/93)
Voices:

Max	Dana Hill
Peg	April Winchell
Pistol	Nancy Cartwright

Also: *Jim Cummings, Bill Farmer, Rob Paulsen, Frank Welker*

Disney's ever-popular talking dog Goofy celebrated his 60th anniversary by starring in this, his first TV cartoon series. Goofy played a happy-go-lucky though not always bright father-figure to 11-year-old Maximus, known commonly as

Max. Max hung out with his next-door neighbor P.J., a rotund, somewhat slow child, though P.J. was nowhere near as out of it as Goofy was. Max's notions set in motion much of each week's plot, and P.J. and Goofy were usually inadvertently corralled into trouble. But Pete, P.J.'s rather mean father, always emerged as the real idiot. Watching the men generally act like jerks in the town of Spoonerville were Pete's nice wife Peg and their daughter Pistol.

Goof Troop was officially titled *Disney's Goof Troop* and started its run in daily syndication in the spring of 1992. It kept airing concurrently with the network version that fall. Goofy and Max reappeared in 1995 with the theatrical release *A Goofy Movie*.

GOOSEBUMPS
Horror Anthology; Color
November 3, 1995–

Fox Fri 4:30–5 p.m. (11/3/95–)
Fox Sat. 10:30–11 a.m. (7/13/96–)

A supernatural live-action series for children? Sounds odd, but *Goosebumps*, based on R. L. Stine's scary book series with the same name, received surprisingly favorable reviews for its emphasis on literate horror, if that's the right term, for kids ages 7 and up. Its special hour-long prime-time debut on October 27, 1995 was typical. A girl who finds that donning a creepy mask unnerves her classmates puts it on so often that her face ends up looking like the mask. Shades of *The Twilight Zone*, to say the least. Prior to its move to Saturday mornings, the show also aired a few times as nighttime specials on Fox.

•GORDON ELLIOTT
Talk; Color
1994–

Syndicated 60 minutes daily beginning September 1994

Host: *Gordon Elliott*

Tall (6 feet 7 inches), casual Gordon Elliott had been a regular on the Down Under TV series *Good Morning, Australia* for five years when he left his native country for America in the early 1990s, going to the New York Fox affiliate WNYW for *Good Morning, New York* and then *The CBS Morning News* as a wacky visitor to people's houses to wake them up. He kept his sly sense of humor intact when he moved into talk shows, despite the fact that the talk show format meant that he had to deal with people in "relationship problems" and the usual gamut of "trash television" topics. This series was an unusual joint production effort by CBS and 20th Century Television, the latter a sister company to the Fox network.

GRAHAM KERR—See *Galloping Gourmet, The.*

GRAND CHANCE ROUNDUP
Children's; B&W
January 27, 1951–December 18, 1955

CBS Sun. 11:30 a.m.–Noon (1/27/51–8/4/51)
CBS Sun. 12:30–1 p.m. (1/6/52–6/28/53)
CBS Sun. 12:30–1 p.m. (1/3/54–9/18/55)
CBS Sun. 11:30 a.m.–Noon (9/25/55–12/18/55)

Regulars: *Gene Crane, the Dave Stephens Orchestra, Tommy Ferguson (1951), George Hamid (1952–55), Barry Cassell (as "Major Merriweather"; 1952 at least), Don Lenox (1952 at least), Bill Bailey (1952 at least), Harry Levan (as "Carny"; 1953), Phil Sheridan (as "Kernel"; 1953), Joan Coale (as "Puff"; 1953)*

Grand Chance Roundup was the first title of three similar 1950s Philadelphia talent shows hosted by Gene Crane that let children under 18 compete for government bond prizes. For the initial series, which had a frontier milieu, Crane wore chaps and a sombrero, and three judges grading talent sat on hay bales. The finalists, after 13 weeks of competition, tried to win a week's engagement at George Hamid's Steel Pier in Atlantic City, the same top prize awarded on later versions.

The concept turned up in a slicker version officially titled *The M & M Candy Carnival* in 1952. This time there was a circus setting, with Crane as a carnival barker, Barry Cassell as the ringmaster and owner of the show, and Don Lenox and Bill Bailey as clowns (Lenox was also a writer for the series). George Hamid himself appeared to judge the talent, while two TV editors from various newspapers across the United States also phoned in their opinions of the acts. Also in this version, the Dave Stephens Orchestra became the Dave Stephens Carnival Band.

The final version in 1954–55 was titled *Contest Carnival.* Here the circus atmosphere continued, and two men and one woman with names designed to plug sponsor Quaker Oats cereals played clowns. Crane, Hamid, and the Carnival Band all returned doing their previous jobs.

GRANDSTAND
Sports Anthology; Color
September 21, 1975–October 1, 1977

NBC Sun. 12:30–1 p.m. fall months, then Sat. and Sun. various times rest of year (9/21/75–10/1/77)

Host: *Jack Buck (1975–76), Bryant Gumbel (1976–77), Lee Leonard (3/5/76–10/1/77)*

Grandstand was NBC's effort to distinguish itself in overall network sports coverage. Named after a BBC show which had started almost 20 years earlier, it debuted with some footage from that United Kingdom series plus live updates and recorded investigative reports from America. Originally Jack Buck, play-by-play announcer for the St. Louis Cardinals baseball team since 1954, hosted regional pickups on the day's top football games and current sports news as the show aired pregame to an NFL matchup, then reappeared at halftime and briefly at postgame.

After the 1975 NFL season ended, the show became situated in New York City and Buck was joined by Bryant

Gumbel as co-host. But the pressures of being sports director of nightly shows in St. Louis and working the weekend job proved too much for Buck, and Lee Leonard took his place (Buck remained a special reporter for the series). The series went back to NFL updates in the fall of 1976 and then floated alone again in various slots in 1977, but NBC replaced it with *SportsWorld* in 1978.

GRAVEDALE HIGH—See *Rick Moranis in Gravedale High.*

GREAT CHALLENGE, THE
Public Affairs; B&W
February 3, 1963–March 3, 1963
CBS Sun. 4–5 p.m. (2/3/63–3/3/63)
Host: *Eric Sevareid*

This program's premise was that America had "the great challenge" to meet its goals in the future for arts, individual freedoms, the economy, science, and education. It devoted five symposiums from the Caspery Auditorium at the Rockefeller Institute in New York City to reviewing and discussing each of those topics in 1963, usually with some top government officials as guests. Previously the series aired in specials or two- to three-week spurts on Sunday afternoons from February 23, 1958–April 5, 1962. Eric Sevareid hosted the specials in 1959, while Howard K. Smith did the same in 1958 and 1960–62.

GREAT GAME OF POLITICS, THE
Documentary; B&W
September 25, 1958–November 9, 1958
CBS Sun. 5–5:30 p.m. (9/28/58–11/9/58)
Narrator: *Eric Sevareid*

Veteran CBS correspondent Eric Sevareid guided viewers through a tour of American politics in 1958, from upcoming contests to campaign financing, with taped reports. The last show reviewed results of the mid-term elections and forecast what might happen politically 10 years down the road.

GREAT GRAPE APE SHOW, THE
Cartoon; Color
September 11, 1977–September 3, 1978
ABC Sat. 11–11:30 a.m. (9/11/77–9/3/78)
Voices:

Grape Ape	*Bob Holt*
Beegle Beagle	*Marty Ingles*

The Grape Ape was a 30-foot-tall purple chimp with fast-talking pal Beegle Beagle (Beegily Beagily to the ape, who often said, "Grape Ape, Grape Ape") who unintentionally upset people in an unspecified city by his very existence, a situation he often tried to rectify with usually comic results. He first appeared on *Tom and Jerry* from 1975–77 and got his own show for one season.

•GREAT SPACE COASTER, THE
Children's; Color
1980–1986
Syndicated 30 minutes daily beginning January 1981
Cast:

Francine	*Emily Bindiger*
Danny	*Chris Gifford*
Roy	*Ray Stephens*
Knock-Knock/Edison the	
Elephant (voice only)	*John Lovelady*
Gary Gnu/M. T. Promises	
(voice only)	*Jim Martin*
Baxter, a kid (voice only)	*Francis Keane*
Speed Reader (voice only)	*Ken Myles*

Francine, Danny, and Roy were the human teenagers who led this successful syndicated videotaped concoction for kids, which included animated features and puppets like Knock-Knock the woodpecker and banana-loving Goriddle Gorilla, who participated in educational and entertaining skits with some well-known guests like Carol Channing, Marvin Hamlisch, Sugar Ray Leonard, and Sally Struthers. The series won a Peabody Award for an episode filmed on location in 1983 at a riding camp for handicapped children. Between 30 and 40 shows were taped annually, and more than 250 were produced. CBS had an option on the series for a year and a half before dropping it.

GREATEST FOOTBALL PLAYS OF THE WEEK
Sports; B&W
October 9, 1954–December 11, 1954
DuMont Sat. 5–5:30 p.m. (10/9/54–11/27/54)
DuMont Sat. 4:30–5 p.m. (12/4/54–12/11/54)

The top three to four minutes of each of the preceding week's National Professional Football League games were highlighted on this entry. This was the last DuMont show seen Saturdays before 8 p.m.

GREATEST GIFT, THE
Soap Opera; B&W
August 30, 1954–July 1, 1955
NBC Mon.–Fri. 3–3:15 p.m. (8/30/54–4/1/55)
NBC Mon.–Fri. 3:30–3:45 p.m. (4/4/55–7/1/55)
Cast:

Dr. Eve Allen	*Anne Burr*
Dr. Phil Stone	*Philip Foster*
Betty Matthews	*Athena Lorde*
Harold "Hal" Matthews (first)	*Martin Balsam*
Harold "Hal" Matthews (second)	*Will Hare*
Ned Blackman (c. 1955)	*Ward Costello*
Ned Blackman (c. 1955)	*Gene Peterson*
Jim Hanson (1954 at least)	*Jack Klugman*
Lee Connor (1954 at least)	*Marian Russell*
Fran Allen (1955)	*Janet Ward*
Harriet (1955 at least)	*Anne Meara*

When her uncle died, Dr. Eve Allen decided she would take over his small-town practice in Ridgeton, Connecticut. Story lines focused on her sometimes tempestuous love affair with fellow physician Phil Stone and her involvement in the private lives of her patients and friends, such as Jim Hanson, who faced tough business decisions, and Harriet, who may have been related to Betty and Hal Matthews. After a few months, much of the drama concerned Ned Blackman, a dealer in the baby black market who narrowly avoided problems with police and a suspicious Dr. Stone through his good works, such as saving Eve from an accidental hotel fire which threatened Eve and her troubled sister Fran. The show was canceled not long after it began to focus on the ordeal of a couple who adopted a black-market baby.

GRIMMY—See *Mother Goose and Grimm.*

•GROOVIE GOOLIES, THE
Cartoon; Color
September 12, 1971–September 5, 1976

CBS Sun. 9:30–10 a.m. (9/12/71–9/3/72)
ABC Sat. 10:30–11 a.m. (10/25/75–2/14/76)
ABC Sun. 10:30–11 a.m. (2/22/76–9/5/76)

Voices:

Frankie/Wolfie/Orville Mummy/	
Ghoulihand	*Howard Morris*
Tom Drac/Fatso	*Larry Storch*
Hagatha/Broom Hilda/Sabrina	*Jane Webb*
Dr. Jekyll-Hyde/Batso/Boneapart	*Larry Mann*

Also: *John Erwin, Dallas McKennon, Don Messick*

After being a supporting act on *Sabrina the Teenage Witch, The Groovie Goolies* spun off a year later as kind of a comic rapid-fire ghoul revue. The thin story line had a group of monsters—the Groovie Goolies—who resided at Horrible Hall as boarders of Tom Drac the vampire; his wife Hagatha, who had a cat (Salem) and a mischievous broom (Broom Hilda); and their son Frankie, who resembled Dr. Frankenstein's monster and had a pet dinosaur named Rover. Among the joke-spewing renters were Wolfie the wolfman, the Thing Eating Plant, Orville Mummy, Dr. Jekyll-Hyde the two-headed doctor, Fatso and Batso the vampire kids, the disembodied Ghoulihand, Bella La Ghostly the switchboard operator, the Ask It Casket, Boneapart the collapsing skeleton, and various other rocking ghosts. It concluded with a *Laugh-In*-type joke wall segment, just one aspect of the series that was influenced by that NBC nighttime variety show which ran from 1968–73.

A little-known fact about this show is that in 1971 one of its backstage personnel, a man named Dick Monda, recorded a top 10 novelty hit, "Chick-A-Boom (Don't Ya Jes' Love It)," with a studio group which was released under the name of Daddy Dewdrop. After a year's run, the series ran in repeats in 1975 as a stopgap replacement after *Uncle Croc's Block* failed.

GROOVIE GOOLIES AND FRIENDS—An overall title for a syndicated package of *The Groovie Goolies, Lassie's Rescue Rangers, My Favorite Martians, The New Adventures of Gilligan, The Secret World of Waldo Kitty,* and *Uncle Croc's Block* (cartoon segments only).

GUEST IN YOUR HOUSE, A
Variety; B&W
March 5, 1951–March 30, 1951

NBC Mon.–Fri. 3:15–3:30 p.m. (3/5/51–3/30/51)

Regulars: *Edgar Guest, Rachel Stevenson*

Poet Edgar Guest sat at a table talking about his life experiences, and those segments were interspersed with occasional verses and a few guest appearances (the guests were usually female), in this short-lived Chicago-based series. Rachel Stevenson served as his sidekick.

GUIDELINE—See *NBC Television Religious Program.*

•GUIDING LIGHT
Soap Opera; B&W and Color
June 30, 1952–

CBS Mon.–Fri. 2:30–2:45 p.m. (6/30/52–12/26/52)
CBS Mon.–Fri. 12:45–1 p.m. (12/29/52–9/6/68)
CBS Mon.–Fri. 2:30–3 p.m. (9/9/68–9/1/72)
CBS Mon.–Fri. 2–2:30 p.m. (9/4/72–11/28/75)
CBS Mon.–Fri. 2:30–3 p.m. (12/1/75–11/4/77)
CBS Mon.–Fri. 2:30–3:30 p.m. (11/7/77–2/1/80)
CBS Mon.–Fri. 3–4 p.m. (2/4/80–)

Cast:

Bert Bauer (1952–84)	*Charita Bauer*
Bill Bauer (1952–59)	*Lyle Sudrow*
Bill Bauer (1959–63, 1965–69,	
1977–78, 1983)	*Ed Bryce*
Bill Bauer (1964)	*Eugene Smith*
Papa Bauer (1952–72)	*Theo Getz*
Meta Bauer (1952)	*Jone Allison*
Meta Bauer (1953–74)	*Ellen Demming*
Kathy Roberts Holden (1952–58)	*Susan Douglas*
Joe Roberts (1952–55)	*Herb Nelson*
Joey Roberts (1952–53)	*Tarry Green*
Joey Roberts (1953)	*Richard Holland*
Trudy Bauer (1952)	*Helen Wagner*
Trudy Bauer (1957–58)	*Lisa Howard*
Dr. Dick Grant (1952–62)	*James Lipton*
Rev. Dr. Paul Keeler (1952)	*Ed Begley*
Rev. Dr. Paul Keeler (1952–54)	*Melville Ruick*
Sid Harper (1952–54)	*Philip Sterling*
Gloria LaRue Harper (1952–54)	*Anne Burr*
Laura Grant (1953)	*Katherine Anderson*
Laura Grant (1953–62)	*Alice Yourman*
Janet Johnson, R.N. (1953–54)	*Ruth Warrick*
Janet Johnson, R.N. (1954–58)	*Lois Wheeler*

Mike Bauer (1954–56)
Mike Bauer (1959–62)
Mike Bauer (1962)
Mike Bauer (1962–66)
Mike Bauer (1968)
Mike Bauer (1968–84)
Marie Wallace (1954)
Marie Wallace (1955–62)
Lila Taylor (1954–55)
Lila Taylor (1957)
Dr. Jim Kelly (1954–55)
Mark Holden (1955–59)
Dr. Paul Fletcher (1956)
Dr. Paul Fletcher (1956–70)
Dr. Bruce Banning (1956–60)
Dr. Bruce Banning (1961–66)
Dr. Bruce Banning (1970–71)
Dr. Bruce Banning (1974)/
Henry Chamberlain (1980–96)
Anne Benedict Fletcher
   (1956–62)
Anne Benedict Fletcher (1962)
Robin Lang Holden (1956–58)
Robin Lang Holden (1959–60)
Robin Lang Holden (1960–61)
Robin Lang Holden (1961–63)
Robin Lang Holden (1963–64)
Robin Lang Holden (1964–67)
Alice Holden (1956)
Alice Holden (1956–58)
Alice Holden (1958–60)
Elsie Miller Franklin (1956–57)
Helene Benedict (1957–64)
Henry Benedict (1959–62)
Henry Benedict (1962–66)
Henry Benedict (1967)
Henry Benedict (1967)
Ruth Jannings Holden (1958)
Ruth Jannings Holden
   (1958–59)
Ruth Jannings Holden
   (1959–60)
Karl Jannings (1959–60)
Joe Turino (1959–60)
Alex Bowden (1960–66)
Philip Collins (1960–61)
Jane Fletcher Hayes (1961–63)
Jane Fletcher Hayes (1963–68)
Doris Crandall (1961–63)
Hope Bauer (1962–65)
Hope Bauer (1968)
Hope Bauer (1968–73)
Hope Bauer (1975–76)
Hope Bauer (1976–77)
Hope Bauer (1977)
Hope Bauer (1979–83)

Glenn Walken
Michael Allen
Paul Prokop
Gary Pillar
Robert Pickering
Don Stewart
Joyce Holden
Lynne Rogers
Nancy Wickwire
Teri Keane
Paul Potter
Whitfield Connor
Michael Kane
Bernard Grant
Les Damon
Barnard Hughes
Sydney Walker

William Roerick

Joan Gray
Elizabeth Hubbard
Zina Bethune
Judy Robinson
Abigail Kellogg
Nancy Malone
Ellen Weston
Gillian Spencer
Sandy Dennis
Diane Gentner
Lin Pierson
Ethel Remey
Kay Campbell
John Gibson
John Boruff
Lester Rawlins
Paul McGrath
Irja Jensen

Louise Platt

Virginia Dwyer
Richard Morse
Joseph Campanella
Ernest Graves
Carson Woods
Pamela King
Chase Crosley
Barbara Becker
Jennifer Kirschner
Paula Schwartz
Elissa Leeds
Tisch Raye
Robin Mattson
Katherine Justice
Elvera Roussel

Johnny Fletcher (1962)
Johnny Fletcher (1963–64)
Johnny Fletcher (1965)
Johnny Fletcher (1965–67)
Johnny Fletcher (1967–71)
Julie Conrad Bauer (1962–65)
George Hayes (1963–68)
Dr. Peter Nelson (1963–64)
Dr. Stephen Jackson (1965–81)
Peggy Scott, R.N. (1965–79)
Maggie Scott (1965–68)
Ben Scott (1965–68)
Jason Weber (1965–66)
Dr. Ed Bauer (1966–69)
Dr. Ed Bauer (1969–81)
Dr. Ed Bauer (1981–84,
   1986–96)
Dr. Ed Bauer (1984–86)
Leslie Jackson (1966–71,
   1973–76)
Leslie Jackson (1971)
Leslie Jackson (1971–73)
Dr. Joe Werner (1966–67)
Dr. Joe Werner (1967–72)
Dr. Joe Werner (1972)
Dr. Joe Werner (1972–76)
Dr. Sara McIntyre (1967–68)
Dr. Sara McIntyre (1968)
Dr. Sara McIntyre (1969–82)
Charlotte Waring/Tracy Delmar
   (1967–70)
Charlotte Waring/Tracy Delmar
   (1970–73)
Marty Dillman (1968)
Marty Dillman (1968–69)
Claudia Dillman (1968–69)
Flip Malone (1968–69)
Janet Mason Norris (1969–75)
Ellen Mason (1969–73)
Peter Wexler (1969)
Peter Wexler (1969–71)
Deborah Mehren (1969–71)
Lee Gantry (1969–71)
Mildred Foss (1969–70)
Tom Halverson (1969–70)
Grove Mason (1969–70)
Dusty McGuire (1969–70)
Tyler Meade (1969–70)
Frederick (Freddie) Bauer
   (1970–71)
Frederick (Freddie) Bauer
   (1972–76)
Frederick (Freddie) Bauer
   (1976–78)
Frederick (Rick) Bauer
   (1982–83)

Sheldon Golomb
Donald Melvin
Daniel Fortas
Don Scardino
Erik Howell
Sandra Smith
Phil Sterling
Gene Rupert
Stefan Schnabel
Fran Myers
June Graham
Bernard Kates
Marc O'Daniels
Robert Gentry
Mart Hulswit

Peter Simon
Richard Van Vleet

Lynne Adams
Kathryn Hays
Barbara Rodell
Ben Hayes
Ed Zimmerman
Berkeley Harris
Anthony Call
Patricia Roe
Jill Andre
Millette Alexander

Victoria Wyndham

Melinda Fee
Robert Lawson
Christopher Wines
Grace Matthews
Paul Carpinelli
Caroline McWilliams
Jeanne Arnold
Leon Russom
Michael Durrell
Olivia Cole
Ray Fulmer
Jan Sterling
Chris Sarandon
Vince O'Brien
Jamie Donnelly
Paul Collins

Albert Zungalo III

Gary Hannoch

Robbie Berridge

Phil MacGregor

Frederick (Rick) Bauer
  (1983–91, 1995–)   Michael O'Leary
Holly Norris (1970–76)   Lynn Deerfield
Holly Norris (1976–80, 1988–)   Maureen Garrett
Barbara Norris Thorpe (1970)   Augusta Dabney
Barbara Norris Thorpe
  (1971–81, 1995–)   Barbara Berjer
Billy Fletcher (1970–73)   James Long
Billy Fletcher (1973)   Matthew Schlossberg
Billy Fletcher (1973–76)   Shane Nickerson
Billy Fletcher (1976)   Dai Stockton
Ken Norris (1970–75)   Roger Newman
Kit Vested (1970–74)   Nancy Addison
David Vested (1970–71)   Peter D. Greene
David Vested (1971)   Dan Hamilton
Christie Rogers (1970–71)/
Christine Valere (1986–87)   Ariana Munker
Stanley Norris (1970)   Michael Higgins
Stanley Norris (1971)   William Smithers
Gil Mehren (1970–71)   David Pendleton
Gil Mehren (1971)   James A. Preston
Dinah Buckley (1970–71)   Courtney Sherman
Roger Thorpe (1971–80, 1989–)   Michael Zaslow
Betty Eiler (1971–72)   Madeline Sherwood
Charles Eiler (1971–72)   Graham Jarvis
Karen Martin (1971–72)   Trudi Wiggins
Adam Thorpe (1972)   Robert Gerringer
Adam Thorpe (1972–81,
  1989, 1994)   Robert Milli
Dr. Dick Carey (1972)   Paul Nesbit
Dr. Dick Carey (1972–73)   Roger Morden
Emma Earnest (1972–73)   Agnes Young
Victoria Ballenger (1973–74)   Carol Teitel
Dr. Wilson Frost (1973–74)   Jack Betts
Tim Werner (1974–76)   T. J. Hargrave
Tim Werner (1980–81)   Kevin Bacon
Tim Werner (1981)   Christopher Marcantel
Tim Werner (1981–82)   Nigel Reed
Dr. Tim Ryan (1974–76)/Billy
  Lewis II (1982–94)   Jordan Clarke
Billy Lewis II (1994)   Geoffrey Scott
Pam Chandler (1974–76)   Maureen Silliman
Rita Stapleton (1975–81)   Lenore Kasdorf
Viola Stapleton (1975)   Sudie Bond
Viola Stapleton (1975–81)   Kate Wilkinson
Ann Jeffers (1975–80)   Maureen Mooney
Chad Richards (1975–76)   Everett McGill
Eve Stapleton (1976–83)   Janet Grey
Dr. Justin Marler (1976–83,
  1987)   Tom O'Rourke
Dr. Justin Marler (1990–91)   Christopher Pennock
Jackie Scott Marler (1976–80)   Cindy Pickett
Jackie Scott Marler (1980–82)   Carrie Mowrey
Ben McFarren (1976–82)   Stephen Yates
Dr. Emmet Scott (1976)   Kenneth Harvey
Dr. Emmet Scott (1976–79)   Frank Latimore

Dr. Emmet Scott (1982)   Peter Turgeon
Alan Spaulding (1977–88)   Christopher Bernau
Alan Spaulding (1988–89)   Daniel Pilon
Alan Spaulding (1994–)   Ron Raines
Phillip Spaulding (1977–81)   Jarrod Ross
Phillip Spaulding (1982–84,
  1987–90, 1996–)   Grant Aleksander
Phillip Spaulding (1985–86)   John Bolger
Katie Parker, R.N. (1977–85)   Denise Pence
Hillary Kincaid Bauer
  (1977–78)   Linda McCullough
Hillary Kincaid Bauer
  (1978–84)   Marsha Clark
Elizabeth Spaulding Marler
  (1977–81)   Lezlie Dalton
Diane Ballard (1977–81)   Sofia Landon
Brandy Shellooe (1977)   Sandy Faison
Brandy Shellooe (1977–81)   JoBeth Williams
Dean Blackford (1977–79)   Gordon Rigsby
Simone Kincaid (1977–78)   Laryssa Lauret
Amanda Wexler Spaulding
  (1978–83, 1987)   Kathleen Cullen
Lucille Wexler (1978–80)   Rita Lloyd
Carmen Monvales (1978)   Julie Carmen
Carmen Monvales (1978–80)   Blancha Camacho
Dr. Peter Chapman (1978–80)   Curt Dawson
Dr. Mark Hamilton (1978–79)   Burton Cooper
Gordon Middleton (1978–79)   Marcus Smythe
Ross Marler (1979–)   Jerry verDorn
Lt. Larry Wyatt (1979–82,
  1987–91, 1994)   Joe Ponazecki
Clarence Bailey (1979)   Philip Bosco
Clarence Bailey (1982–85,
  1987–90)   Lawrence Weber
Floyd Parker (1979–85)   Tom Nielsen
Dr. Renee DuBois (1979–80)/
  Ivy Pierce (1982–83)   Deborah May
Neil Blake (1979–80, 1982)   Patrick Horgan
Dr. Greg Fairbanks (1979–80)   David Greenan
Lainie Marler Bowden
  (1979–80)   Kathleen Kellaigh
Dr. Paul LaCrosse (1979–80)   Jacques Roux
Vanessa Chamberlain (1980–)   Maeve Kinkead
Nola Reardon (1980–85,
  1995–)   Lisa Brown
Trish Lewis Norris (1980–85)   Rebecca Hollen
Dr. Kelly Nelson (1980–84)   John Wesley Shipp
Jennifer Richards (1980–83)   Geraldine Court
Morgan Richards (1980–81)   Kristen Vigard
Morgan Richards (1981–83)   Jennifer Cook
Derek Colby (1980–82)   Harley Venton
Duke Lafferty (1980–81)   Gary Phillips
Chet Stafford (1980–81)   Bill Herndon
Logan Stafford (1980–81)   Richard Hamilton
Trudy Wilson (1980–81)   Amy Steel
Joe Bradley (1980–81)   Michael J. Stark

Josh Lewis (1981–90, 1993–)
Bea Reardon (1981–87, 1990)
Tony Reardon (1981–85)
Quinton McCord Chamberlain
    (1981–85)
Leslie Ann Monroe, R.N.
    (1981–84)
Silas Crocker (1981–83)
Mark Evans (1981–83)
Helena Manzini (1981–83)
Mrs. Violet Renfield (1981–83)
Gracie Middleton (1981–83)
Wayne Jennings (1981–82)
Maureen Reardon (1982–86)
Maureen Reardon (1986–93)
Helen Tynan (1982–84)
Clay Tynan (1982–83)
Rebecca Cartwright (1982–83)
Dr. Matt Davenport (1982–83)
Brian Lister (1982–83)
Lillian Raines, R.N. (1983–)
Beth Raines (1983–86)
Beth Raines (1989–91)
Reva Shayne (1983–90, 1995–)
Mindy Lewis (1983–90)
Mindy Lewis (1990–92)
Mindy Lewis (1992–93)
Mindy Lewis (1993–95)
Lujack (1983–85)/Nick
    McHenry (1991–96)
Lionel Harris (1983–89)
H. B. Lewis (1983–88)
Warren Andrews (1983–87)
Dr. Louis Darnell (1983–86)
Dr. Jim Reardon (1983–85)
Annabelle Sims (1983–85)
Eli Sims (1983)
Fletcher Reade (1984–)
Alexandra Spaulding
    (1984–92)
Alexandra Spaulding (1993–)
India von Halkein (1984–87,
    1990)
Sally Gleason (1984–87)
Kyle Sampson (1984–87)
Martin Wilson ("I.Q.")
    (1984–86)
Jonathan Brooks (1984–85)
Gina Daniels (1984–85)
Andy Ferris (1984–85)
Nancy Ferris (1984–85)
Jane Hogan (1984–85)
David Preston (1984–85)
Johnny "Dub" Taylor (1984–85)
Hawk Shayne (1985–90,
    1995–)

Robert Newman
Lee Lawson
Gregory Beecroft

Michael Tylo

Carolyn Ann Clark
Benjamin Hendrickson
Mark Pinter
Rose Alaio
Beulah Garrick
Lori Shelle
Roger Baron
Ellen Dolan
Ellen Parker
Micki Grant
Giancarlo Esposito
Leslie O'Hara
James Carroll
Richard Clarke
Tina Sloan
Judi Evans
Beth Chamberlin
Kim Zimmer
Krista Tesreau
Kimberley Simms
Ann Hamilton
Barbara Crampton

Vincent Irizarry
Jack White
Larry Gates
Warren Burton
Eric Brooks
Michael Woods
Harley Jane Kozak
Stephen Joyce
Jay Hammer

Beverlee McKinsey
Marj Dusay

Mary Kay Adams
Patricia Barry
Larkin Malloy

Jaison Walker
Damon Scheller
Annabelle Gurwitch
Victor Slezak
J. Smith-Cameron
Mary Pat Gleason
John Martinuzzi
Maarko Maglich

Gil Rogers

Wanda M. Hite (1985–90)
Maeve Stoddard (1985–88)
Simon Hall (1985–87)
Jackson Freemont (1985–87)
Calla Matthews (1985–86)
Jesse Matthews (1985–86)
Kurt Corday (1985–86)
Trevor (1985, 1991–92)
Chelsea Reardon (1986–91)
Johnny Bauer (1986–90)
Dinah Morgan (1986–87)
Dinah Morgan (1987–89)
Dinah Morgan (1995–)
Rusty Shayne (1986–89)
Cameron Stewart (1986–88)
Cat Brixton (1986–87)
Dorie Smith von Halkein
    (1986–87)
Julia Stoddard (1986, 1988)
Alan-Michael Spaulding
    (1987–89)
Alan-Michael Spaulding
    (1990–96)
Alan-Michael Spaulding (1996–)
Frank Cooper (1987–)
Harley Davidson Cooper
    (1987–93)
Sarah Shayne (1987–91)
Sonni/Solita Lewis (1987–89)
Dr. Will Jeffries (1987–89)
Dr. Meredith Reade (1987–89)
Dr. Eileen Lyndon (1987–89)
Rose McLaren (1987–89)
Jenny Holmes (1987–88)
George Stewart (1987–88)
Nick Sutton (1987–88)
Blake Lindsey (Christina Thorpe)
    (1988–89)
Blake Lindsey (1989–92)
Blake Lindsey (1992–)
Samantha Marler (1988–92)
Anita Ybarra (1988–89)
Gilly Grant Speakes (1989–96)
Michelle Bauer (1989–95)
Michelle Bauer (1995–)
Marah Shayne (1989–91)
Marah Shayne (1995–)
Nadine Cooper (1989–95)
Hampton "Hamp" Speakes
    (1989–95)
Dylan Shayne Lewis (1989–94)
"Pops" Cooper (1989–90)
Neil Everest (1989–90)
Dana Jones (1989–90)
Gary Swanson (1989–90)
Rae Rooney (1989–90)

Carey Cromelin
Leslie Denniston
Shawn Thompson
Michael Wilding Jr.
Lisby Larson
Rebecca Staab
Mark Lewis
Norman Snow
Kassie Wesley
James Goodwin
Jennifer Gatti
Paige Turco
Wendy Moniz
Terrell Anthony
Ian Ziering
Don Fisher

Kimi Parks
Meg Mundy

Carl Evans

Rick Hearst
Michael Dietz
Frank Dicopoulos

Beth Ehlers
Audrey Peters
Michelle Forbes
Joseph Breen
Nicolette Goulet
Cynthia Hayden
Alexandra Neil
Mary Ellen Stuart
Joe Lambie
W. T. Martin

Elizabeth Dennehy
Sherry Stringfield
Elizabeth Keifer
Susan Cote
Carla Pinza
Amelia Marshall
Rachel Miner
Rebecca Budig
Ashley Peldon
Kimberly J. Brown
Jean Carol

Vince Williams
Morgan Englund
Vince O'Brien
Patrick O'Connell
Katell Plevin
William Bell Sullivan
Allison Daugherty

A. C. Mallet (1990–93)	Mark Derwin
Dr. Daniel St. John (1990–92)	David Bishins
Eleni Andros (1991–94)	Melina Kanakaredes
Eleni Andros (1994, 1995–)	Jennifer Roszell
Eleni Andros (1994–95)	Wendy Kaplan
Katherine "Kat" Speakes	
(1991–94)	Nia Long
Julie Camaletti (1991–94)	Jocelyn Seagrave
Bridget Reardon (1991–)	Melissa Hayden
Dr. Charles Grant (1991–95)	Ron Foster
Dr. Charles Grant (1995–)	David Wolos-Fonteno
Hart Jessup (1991–92)	Jeff Phillips
Hart Jessup (1993)	Leonard Stabb
Hart Jessup (1996)	Marshall Hilliard
Hart Jessup (1996–)	Frank Grillo
David Grant (1992–)	Monti Sharp
Frank Cooper Sr. (1992–)	Justin Deas
Jenna Bradshaw (1992–)	Fiona Hutchison
Vivian Grant (1992–)	Petronia Paley
David Grant (1992–95)	Monti Sharp
David Grant (1995–)	Russell Curry
Dr. Eve Guthrie (1992–95)	Hilary Edson
Ari Andros (1992–94)	John Syragakisari
Jory Andros (1992–94)	James M. Gregory
Ya Ya Andros (1992–94)	Irma St. Paul
Grady (1992–93)	Eddie Mekka
Jim Haggerty (1992–93)	Nick Gregory
Lucy Cooper Spaulding (1993–)	Sonia Satra
Shayne Lewis (1993–)	Brett Cooper
Tangie Hill (1993–95)	Marcy Walker
Bess Lowell (1993–94)	Elizabeth Lawrence
Matt Reardon (1994–)	Kurt McKinney
Sid Dickerson (1994–95)	Kelly Neal
Gabriella Lopez (1994–95)	Veronica Cruz
Carroll O'Malley (1994–95)	Will Lyman
Detective Patrick Cutter	
(1993–95)	Scott Hoxby
Brent Lawrence/Marian Crane	
(1995–)	Frank Beaty
Marcus Williams (1995–)	Kevin Mambo
Susan Bates (1995–96)	Nancy Bell

The longest-running dramatic series in TV (and broadcasting) history, *The Guiding Light* began on radio on NBC on January 25, 1937 telling the story of the Rev. John Ruthledge, pastor of the small town of Five Points. By the time the series transferred to CBS in 1947, Ruthledge had been superseded as the lead character by Dr. Charles Matthews, pastor of the Church of the Good Samaritan. Five years later, when it debuted on television, the Bauer family took center stage and remained the focal family for the next 30 years.

The TV debut provided little background for those unfamiliar with the radio series. The central conflict had Meta Bauer separated from Joe Roberts due to his grown-up daughter Kathy hating her new stepmother (his other child, Joey, liked Meta). Reacting to this dilemma on Meta's side

were her compassionate Papa Bauer, who dispensed wisdom to all; her sister Trudy Bauer, who remained a minor character and had been forgotten by the 1960s; and her weak-willed brother Bill and his domineering wife Bert, whose mother Elsie Miller lived near them for a time a few years later. Actors Jone Allison, Charita Bauer, Susan Douglas, Theo Geotz, Tarry Green, and Herb Nelson had been with the radio series for at least two years each when they went on television to play their characters.

Kathy had the pivotal action in the early years of the show. While still hating Meta, she became pregnant in 1953 while married to Dr. Dick Grant but learned the father of her baby daughter Robin actually was her deceased first husband, leading to her marriage being annulled. Dr. Grant soon found himself plagued by the ardent pursuit of Nurse Janet Johnson, whose passion he did not reciprocate; by personal and professional jealousy over Dr. Jim Kelly, who went after Kathy; and by interference from his snooty mother Laura in his marriage to artist Marie Wallace, whom he met on a sabbatical to New York City. He and Marie, unable to have children, adopted Phillip Collins and left town.

Meanwhile, when Joe Roberts died, his widow Meta had to compete with Kathy for the affections of Mark Holden, Bill Bauer's business colleague. Kathy won the contest and wed Holden but ended up dying of complications from injuries sustained in a car accident. Her temperamental daughter Robin then took center stage in major story lines of the late 1950s and early 1960s, while Meta eventually found happiness after marrying Dr. Bruce Banning. Robin became the object of desire of both Bill and Bert's oldest son Mike and Karl Jannings, the son of maid Ruth Jannings, who married Robin's stepfather Mark Holden. Mike accidentally killed Karl and then wed Robin, but an irate Bert made them annul their union. Robin subsequently married middle-aged cad Alex Bowden, who later divorced and left her, and then wed Dr. Paul Fletcher. Fletcher had his own woes. He had accidentally killed his true love Anne Benedict, the daughter of snooty Henry and Helene Benedict, and now found his half-sister Jane trying to turn his son Johnny against Robin. Jane stopped trying to interfere in Paul's affairs after marrying George Hayes, the man who defended Mike against murder charges in Karl's death.

Mike and his brother Ed developed their own headaches as adults in the 1960s. After getting over Robin, Mike wed George's secretary Julie Conrad, but she was unstable and ended up killing herself in a mental institution. For a time Mike took Hope, his daughter by Julie, out of town to Bay City (see *Another World* for more details). When he returned to the show to practice law, his family and many friends had relocated from Selby Flats to Springfield, a town located somewhere in the Midwest. He also discovered he was in love with Leslie Jackson. Unfortunately for him, Leslie was married to Ed, now an aspiring medical student who idolized Leslie's father, Cedar Hospital's Chief of Surgery Dr. Stephen

Seen in this 1953 shot from The Guiding Light *are, from left, Herb Nelson (as Joe Roberts), James Lipton (Dr. Dick Grant), Susan Douglas (Kathy Roberts), and Ellen Demming (Meta Bauer).*

Jackson. Dr. Jackson was confident and successful, two traits which Ed and Mike's father Bill clearly lacked. In fact, Bill's alcoholism worsened, and he cheated on Bert with his secretary Maggie Scott, who was unhappily married to Ben Scott. Their daughter Peggy dated Johnny Fletcher, and when her parents died and Bill and Bert patched up their marriage, Peggy was adopted as part of the Bauer household. Unfortunately, not long thereafter, Bill was declared dead in a plane crash.

Toward the end of the 1960s, Robin was hit by a truck and died, after which her widower Paul Fletcher began a romance with Dr. Sara McIntyre. That affair went nowhere, and Sara went on to be romanced by devious Lee Gantry,

who with his maid Mildred Foss planned to murder her for her money. Lee and Mildred were killed, however, and Sara wed Dr. Joe Werner. Joe and Sara adopted T.J., also known as Tim, but were stalked by the obsessive Kit Vested, who loved Joe and wanted to break up his marriage. As for Paul, he moved to Washington, D.C., after his son Johnny dropped Peggy in favor of Tracy Delmar, who claimed to be Sara's long-lost niece. She actually was a con artist named Charlotte Waring, who later married Mike Bauer, much to his regret, but Charlotte got her just deserts because Kit Vested, discovering that Charlotte had romantic feelings for Joe Werner, murdered her. Johnny eventually wound up in a mental hospital after having reunited with Peggy, who had been accused of murdering her husband Marty Dillman (his criminal cohort Flip Malone was the true guilty party).

As the 1970s dawned, the Bauers became involved with members of the Thorpe and Norris families. After having slept with Janet Mason and then returning to Leslie, Ed was divorced by Leslie because she and Mike were still in love, even though she gave birth to a son by Ed, Frederick, who was later nicknamed Freddie or Rick. Leslie then wed rich Stanley Norris, father of Ken and Holly Norris and ex-husband of Barbara Norris. Ken wed Janet Mason, while Holly began her long, tempestuous relationship with ne'er-do-well Roger Thorpe, who also romanced Holly's sister-in-law Janet. Roger's brother Adam became part of the Norris-Thorpe-Bauer nexus when he dated Barbara. After Stanley was murdered, Leslie was considered a chief suspect until her old love Mike proved she did not do it. (The real killer was Marion Conway, the mother of Stanley's secretary.) Mike and Leslie finally wed, while Ed found himself conned into marrying Holly, who was upset by Roger's philandering ways. Ed's relationship with Holly was plagued by trouble at every point. Holly slept with Roger again and give birth to their child Christina while claiming that Ed was the father, and Ken went psychotic and tried to kill Ed but only succeeded in paralyzing the nerves in Ed's left hand, preventing him from doing surgery. Ed went into an institution and Janet left town.

When Ed learned that Christina was not his child, he left Holly for nurse Rita Stapleton, who had been wooed unsuccessfully by Dr. Tim Ryan, who was in turn chased by Pam Chandler. Despite learning from Ed of Roger's behavior, Peggy Fletcher decided to take a chance on Roger, and they were married until Peggy decided to divorce him. Holly, now divorced from Ed, tried to win him back, and it came out that Rita had dated Roger previously. Feeling rejected, Roger raped Rita before she married Ed, but Rita did not mention the attack to Ed. Holly, seeing that she was not going to get Ed or Dr. Peter Chapman (another beau) down the aisle, wed Roger despite her mother Barbara's warnings. (Barbara had in fact divorced Roger's dad Adam after Adam refused to blame his son for his indiscretions.) Roger's continued his unscrupulous ways, and even sexually assaulted Holly at one point. Unlike Rita, she took him to court, where he was found guilty of marital rape. Roger became a fugitive and had an affair with a French plastic surgeon, Dr. Renee Dubois, whom he later murdered as he began to nurse increasingly insane notions about how to get his daughter Christina away from Holly. In 1980 Ed and Mike finally located Roger in the Caribbean, and Roger fell from a mountain, presumably to his death. Holly left town with Christina in tow.

Assisting Roger in his escape from town was Alan Spaulding, an amoral businessman who had emerged as a

leading character when *The Guiding Light* became just *Guiding Light* in 1977 and went to an hour. The boss of huge conglomerate Spaulding Enterprises, Alan was married to Elizabeth Spaulding, but their son Phillip was actually the child of Dr. Justin Marler and his wife Jackie, who had given him up for adoption years earlier. The couples ended up switching partners due to their unhappy marriages and to Jackie's desire to be closer to Phillip, despite the fact that Jackie loved Mike Bauer, whose wife Leslie died in a car accident. When Jackie died, Alan appalled many when he went on to make Mike's daughter Hope his third wife. Hope was always attracted to the wrong kind of man—for a time she dated ex-con Ben McFarren, who also had failed relationships with Rita Stapleton's sister Eve and Alan's illegitimate daughter Amanda Wexler—and even after Alan and Hope had a son, Alan-Michael, Alan continued his philandering ways. All this caused Hope to abuse alcohol, but she managed to stop drinking and leave town with Alan-Michael. Meanwhile, Alan uneasily tried to establish both professional and personal ties to Phillip when the latter learned of his parentage. Sensing he was unwanted, Dr. Marler also left Springfield with his daughter Samantha.

The other big plot line in the late 1970s involved the return of Bill Bauer, who had in fact survived his plane crash and established a new life that included being the father of Hillary Bauer, a nurse at Cedars Hospital. Bill and Bert found themselves unable to reconcile, so he returned to his new life in Chicago, but Hillary stayed and became attracted to Ed's hunky godson, intern Kelly Nelson. But Kelly's true love was young Morgan Richards, and they entered into an ill-fated marriage. Among other problems, Nola Reardon, a poor girl with big ambitions, tried her best to break Kelly and Morgan up by claiming that Kelly had impregnated her one night when he was drunk. When that charge proved to be false, Nola tried to marry her admirer Floyd Parker, but called it off at the last minute. Her salvation was dashing archaeologist Quint McCord, who after defeating his nemesis Silas Crocker had a romantic wedding with Nola and announced that he was the illegitimate son of wealthy, Henry Chamberlain. That revelation made Henry's spoiled daughter Vanessa very unhappy, since she detested Nola even though she had dated Nola's earthy brother Tony for a while.

In the early 1980s Tony and Nola's older sister Maureen, also known as Mo, eventually became Ed's third wife, which helped cement the Reardons' position (Bea Reardon was the trio's mother) as a major family in Springfield. Another important family was the Lewises, who challenged the Spauldings for dominance in the local business scene. Grizzled, down-home H.B. was the patriarch of the clan, which also included his daughter Trish and sons Josh and Billy. Billy later married Vanessa Chamberlain, and their rocky romance lasted into the mid-1990s. Also becoming prominent during those years were Ed's son Rick, who loved Billy's self-obsessed daughter Mindy even though she wanted the now grown-up Phillip Spaulding; Beth Raines, Phillip's true love, who survived a rape attack by her stepfather and as Marler pursued a variety of women. Marler eventually became Springfield's district attorney and exhibited more noble behavior.

The year 1983 was an adventurous one in Springfield. Actors James Farentino, Ben Murphy, and Lauren Hutton turned up in the cast briefly as characters in *The Cradle Will Fall*, a TV movie that aired in May on CBS with Charita Bauer, Carolyn Ann Clark, Joe Ponazecki, Elvera Roussel, Peter Simon, and Jerry verDorn recreating their parts. The major story line on the daytime show that year involved Bert Bauer's boarder Annabelle Sims, who learned from a mysterious photograph involving some of Springfield's oldest citizens that her father Eli had drowned his wife in the lake and killed Bea Reardon's husband years before. After Eli had been arrested for the murders of several people, including Bill Bauer, one of the men who knew about Eli's crimes, Annabelle wed Tony Reardon and they left town.

But over the next few years things took a turn for the worse, both backstage and on the show. Management made some bad decisions, and in the mid-1980s the story lines were weak. Mike Bauer was written out in 1984 (he supposedly left town on an assignment), and Bert had to undergo surgery to amputate a leg (actress Charita Bauer had the same thing done in real life, but remained ill and died in early 1985 a few months after her last appearance on the show). Oh, and let's not forget the death of Hillary, who along with gullible nurse Lesley Ann Monroe, girlfriend to the hospital's slimy administrator Warren Andrews, succumbed to the dread Central American "Dreaming Death" disease. Some events stretched credibility even for a soap opera. Alan Spaulding's father Brandon, who had been clearly shown onscreen to be dead in 1979, was resurrected without explanation, and Floyd Parker confessed to Beth Raines—out of nowhere—that he had accidentally blinded Beth as part of a plan to win her love.

The creative indecision crippling the show at the time was typified by what happened with the character of Dr. Claire Ramsey. Clare had been brought in as a strong character who would be a romantic interest for Kelly Nelson, but when Kelly left town, Claire degenerated into a petty, scheming woman who had an affair with Ed Bauer when Maureen was out of town, bitched endlessly during her pregnancy, and tried to sabotage Rick Bauer's career as a doctor. Adding to the inconsistency, Clare suddenly had a change of heart in 1986 and gave custody of her daughter Michelle to Ed and Maureen, then left by Christmas with the help of loving Dr. Mark Jarrett. As actress Susan Pratt later told *TV Guide*, "Three weeks after I started shooting, they told me, 'Oh, by the way, we forgot—Claire has a limp! So add a limp!' I figured that was a sign they didn't exactly have a clear understanding of who she was."

Not surprisingly given these happenings, the show's ratings dropped considerably toward the end of the 1980s, but not all that aired was hopeless. The series found two splendid leading ladies in Alan's sister Alexandra Spaulding, whose estranged son Lujack managed to entice Beth away

In 1977 the Bauers of The Guiding Light *included, clockwise from top left, Ed (played by Mart Hulswit), Mike (Don Stewart), and their mother Bert (Charita Bauer).*

indecisive action from her mom Lillian, a nurse at Cedars; and Andrew Norris, Barbara's unscrupulous son, whose blackmailing of several Springfield citizens in return for information on his book on Alan Spaulding led her and Rita to leave town. Surprisingly, the longest-running character of the period turned out to be Ross Marler. Marler, the shady attorney brother of Justin, was married to Carrie, who had a split personality and was later institutionalized from Phillip before he died in an accident, and Reva Shayne, the most consummate vixen ever created on the show. Reva had been wed to Billy Lewis and left a lasting impression on his brother Josh before she and Billy divorced, then she came back into both men's lives and tempted not only them but their father H.B. and Kyle Sampson, H.B.'s illegitimate son by Sally Gleason. Reva's truest passion was Josh, however, and they wed before she went crazy and drove off a bridge into the Florida Keys in 1990 (Reva's body was never found). The rest of the Shayne family—father Hawk, mother Sarah, sister Roxie, and brother Rusty—also enmeshed themselves with the Springfield regulars.

Others showing up in the mid- to late 1980s were Josh's old pal from South America, psychiatrist Dr. Will Jeffries, who along with Sonni Lewis, impersonating her dead twin sister Solita, tried unsuccessfully to kill Josh; Johnny Bauer, a distant relative from a brother of Papa Bauer's side of the family who claimed that he rid himself of cancer in 1988 through the power of faith in God; newspaper reporter Fletcher Reade, who after a fling with Nurse Ramsey had more serious relationships with Maeve Stoddard and Alexandra Spaulding; and Alan-Michael, who was last seen with his mom in 1983 as a preschooler but became a college student in Springfield four years later. He and Phillip often argued over business and personal decisions.

In late June 1987, the show celebrated its 35th year on television and 50th year in broadcasting by airing five days of clips from the past voted the best by the fans. The oldest clip showed Roger Thorpe's fall off the cliff in 1980. Given that immense popularity of the character, it was no surprise when the show brought Roger back in 1989. Roger was said to have been living on a remote island off Venezuela tending to his power base before returning to Springfield, where Alan Spaulding tried to kill him. That act put Alan behind bars while Roger worked on renewing the relationship with his daughter Christina, who had come back to town a few months earlier calling herself Blake Lindsey. Also back was his ex-wife Holly, who still hated Roger even as she attempted to start a new life which included, by 1995, marriage to Fletcher and their becoming parents of a Down's syndrome child. Everybody connected to either Roger or Alexandra was stunned when in 1990 they wed and she made him president of the company she owned.

Roger, Holly, Alexandra, and Blake, the latter of which later had a torrid affair with Ross Marler, remained the central characters in the early to mid-1990s, but others did have their moments in the sun. Chelsea Reardon, Bea's youngest child, returned home to pursue a singing career and marry her fiancé, but when he died following a car crash she sued his doctor Rick Bauer. Naturally, the two of them eventually became lovers for a while. Another Reardon, Bridget, had a baby out of wedlock with Hart Jessup, who was none other than Roger Thorpe's son. And story lines involving members of the Speakes and Grant families, minority clans who finally integrated Springfield

successfully, featured enjoyable romances and intrigue. The event that upset fans the most, however, was when in late 1992 Ed Bauer had an affair with longtime pal and working colleague Lillian Raines, and his wife Maureen, after getting word of the event, died in a car crash. With Rick gone out of town to pursue his doctoring career, that meant that only two characters had the Bauer surname, Ed and his growing daughter Michelle. This was the low point for the "Bauer power," as some fans called it, that had fueled the popularity of the show since the 1950s.

But *Guiding Light* could slump still further, as was shown in 1994 with such loser concepts as an evil double for Ross; a wasted role for veteran soap actress Marcy Walker as Tangie Hill, who bothered Josh for no apparent reason; Vanessa's fear of letting anyone know about her love for handsome Matt because he was—horrors!—younger than she was; and other, similarly lame, plots. As viewer interest sagged and the show headed to its lowest ratings ever, producers decided to bring back some old favorites, including Rick, Alan, and Reva. The returns, however, were often badly done, straining credibility. Alan, for example, got out of jail on an early prison release, yet no one seemed to know how to locate him. And Reva first returned as a ghost to haunt Josh's new love, nurse Annie Dutton, then finally came to town to fight against Annie for real after Alan found she had been living in an Amish community.

At least no one could accuse the writers of not taking risks. This was especially true in 1995, when psycho Brent Lawrence terrorized the amiable Coopers, a working-class family. Brent pretended to be dead, dressed as a woman calling herself Marian Crane, killed the unfortunate, wackily lovable matriarch Nadine Cooper, raped Nadine's daughter Lucy, and then switched Lucy's HIV test results so that Lucy thought she had AIDS as a result of the rape. Helping to save Lucy from Brent's clutches was her half-brother Frank, who had become a rookie cop after serving as a restaurant worker previously. When captured, a delirious Brent insisted he was Marian Crane. Whew!

But the events that made the biggest news on the show at the time involved longtime cast members. Avuncular, well-liked Henry Chamberlain was lost after 15 years on the show when actor William Roerick died in real life on November 30, 1995, and Ed Bauer (who had been played by a succession of actors) announced he was leaving to go to Africa to do medical work. The loss of these characters was a huge blow to those who remembered the heritage of the show, causing them to wonder where *Guiding Light* would shine next.

Despite all of its failings and questionable calls, the show endures and continues to have a strong, devoted fan base, many of whom either have watched it for decades or are children of those who did. No other radio soap prospered so well on television. No other TV serial managed to go from 15 to 30 to 60 minutes in length over the years. And no other dramatic series on radio or television can boast of having aired for so long—now at over 12,000 hours and still counting.

In 1954, a negative review of the show in *TV Guide* ended with the comment, "This is television?" In truth, for nearly 60 years the show has transcended the medium to become a part of millions of American's lives.

GULLIVER—See *Adventures of Gulliver, The.*

•GUMBY SHOW, THE
Children's; Color
March 16, 1957–November 16, 1957

NBC Sat. 10:30–11 a.m. (3/16/57–11/16/57)

Regulars: *Bobby Nicholson (as Scotty McKee; 3/16/57–5/29/57), Buffalo Bob Smith (commercial announcer), Pinky Lee (6/5/57–11/16/57)*

Voices:

Gumby	*Dallas McKennon*
Pokey/Various	*Art Clokey*

Take some green clay, shape into a standing male figure with a sloping hairline, stumplike lower legs, and bulging eyes, and you have Gumby, a character whose appeal lasted much longer than its network run suggests. Created by artist Art Clokey and activated through the technique of stop-action animation, Gumby and his most frequently seen companion, his pet horse Pokey, moved and changed shapes endlessly during each show, though most individual segments lasted no more than six minutes. NBC had *Howdy Doody* regular Bobby Nicholson, whose show preceded Gumby on Saturday mornings, serve as initial host, followed by the network's former late-afternoon star Pinky Lee.

More segments were added to the package from a new production in syndication in 1966. Then Eddie Murphy revived the character on *Saturday Night Live* in the early 1980s as a grumpy Jewish senior citizen ("My name is Gumby, dammit!"). Though a spoof, it brought a wave of new merchandising and renewed interest in the character, and Clokey revived his property in a 1988 syndicated series titled *The All-New Gumby.* This was followed in 1995 by the theatrical release *Gumby: The Movie,* with Clokey directing. All of which shows that it's hard to keep a good cartoon character down.

•GUMMI BEARS, THE
Cartoon; Color
September 14, 1985–September 1, 1990

NBC Sat. 8:30–9 a.m. (9/14/85–9/5/87)
NBC Sat. 8–8:30 a.m. (9/12/87–2/20/88)
NBC Sat. 11–11:30 a.m. (2/27/88–3/26/88)
NBC Sat. 8–8:30 a.m. (4/2/88–9/3/88)
NBC Sat. 8:30–9 a.m. (9/10/88–9/2/89)
ABC Sat. 8:30–9:30 a.m. (9/9/89–9/1/90)

Voices:

Cubbi Gummi/Princess Calla	*Noelle North*
Grammi Gummi	*June Foray*
Gruffi Gummi (1985–86)	*Bill Scott*
Gruffi Gummi (1986–90)	*Corey Burton*
Sunni Gummi	*Katie Leigh*
Tummi Gummi	*Lorenzo Music*
Zummi Gummi (1985–88)	*Paul Winchell*
Zummi Gummi (1988–90)	*Jim Cummings*
Cavin (1985–86)	*Christian Jacobs*
Cavin (1986–87)	*Brett Johnson*
Cavin (1987–88)	*David Faustino*
Cavin (1988–90)	*Jason Marsden*
Duke Igthorn	*Michael Rye*

As any child of the 1980s could tell you, Gummi Bears in reality were translucent, artificially colored and flavored chewy, licorice-like snacks. For this cartoon, officially titled *Disney's Adventures of the Gummi Bears,* the edible animals assumed new identities in a fantasy story line. Six Gummis, specifically Cubbi, Grammi, Gruffi, Sunni, Tummi, and Zummi, protected humans Princess Calla and Cavin the 11-year-old page in the mythical kingdom of Dunwyn. Grammi Gummi's own Gummiberry Juice gave them the strength to combat a variety of foes ranging from trolls to evil nobles (e.g., Duke Igthorn), while keeping the Gummis their own adorable selves. A sense of sly humor permeated each adventure and helped keep the show from the saccharine excesses of its probable inspiration, *The Smurfs.*

The Gummi Bears series deserves note as the first cartoons Disney Studios produced for television on a regular basis, a path that led to increasing success over the next decade with such follow-ups as *The Little Mermaid* and *The Lion King's Timon and Pumbaa.* On September 9, 1989, the show added a new half hour of Winnie the Pooh segments, was retitled *Disney's Gummi Bears/Winnie the Pooh Hour,* and moved to ABC. It ended its run there after one season.

•GUYS NEXT DOOR, THE
Sitcom; Color
August 27, 1990–May 25, 1991

NBC Sat. 11:30 a.m.–Noon (8/27/90–5/25/91)

Regulars: *Patrick Dancy, Eddie Garcia, Bobby Leslie, Damon Sharpe, Chris Wolf*

Nearly a quarter century after NBC created its own knockoff of the Beatles with the nighttime hit *The Monkees,* the network showcased another artificially assembled group in this in-house production which featured a quintet obviously designed to be another New Kids on the Block. But while the handsome actors may have been near-clones of the latter, the format of the show reminded one more of *The Monkees,* what with its comic blackouts, occasional songs, and loosely constructed plot lines. But there was no laugh track and no really talented musicians among the bunch, which may be why the Guys, whom *TV Guide* mockingly termed the Prefab Five, ended up forgotten even more quickly than the New Kids.

•H. R. PUFNSTUF
Sitcom; Color
September 6, 1969–September 1, 1974

NBC Sat. 10–10:30 a.m. (9/6/69–9/5/70)
NBC Sat. 11–11:30 a.m. (9/12/70–9/4/71)
ABC Sat. 8–8:30 a.m. (9/16/72–9/1/73)
ABC Sun. 11–11:30 a.m. (9/9/73–9/1/74)

Cast:

Jimmy	*Jack Wild*
Witchiepoo	*Billie Hayes*
Freddy Flute (voice only)	*Joan Gerber*

Other Voices: *Walker Edmiston, Lennie Weinrib*

Costumed Actors: *Buddy Douglas, Jerry Landon, John Linton, Angelo Rosetti, Felix Silla, Hommy Stewart*

A memorable fantasy that was the first of several Sid and Marty Krofft Productions for Saturday morning, *H. R. Pufnstuf* had all the standard tricks associated with the production

Who's your friend when things get rough? H. R. Pufnstuf, of course, seen here on the right with Jimmy (played by Jack Wild) and his magic flute.

company, including fantastic costumes, brightly colored sets, and noisy comedy. The action centered on prepubescent Jimmy, the only human seen on the show, who set sail one day with his talking flute Freddy in his shirt pocket. The evil and ugly Witchiepoo, however, who coveted the magic flute, put a spell on Jimmy's boat, causing it to crash on Living Island. Once there, Jimmy was rescued by the island's leading citizen, an amiable dragon named H. R. Pufnstuf, and adopted by the other adorable denizens of the island, including Blinky the wise owl, Cling and Clang the midget cops, and Four Winds, a breeze with a human visage. All worked to keep Jimmy and his high-pitched, nervous flute out of Witchiepoo's clutches.

Witchiepoo's plans constantly ran afoul of her incompetent help. On the plus side was her Vroom-Broom, a gaudy contraption featuring an umbrella-shaded seat for the witch and a bathtub sidecar for her goofy vulture sidekick Orson. Unfortunately, Orson was part of Witchiepoo's problem, as were Seymour the yellow spider and Stupid Bat. The fearsome looking Evil Trees and the Mushrooms were supposed to be the scary part of the show.

Only the first season had original episodes. During that time, *H. R. Pufnstuf* scored higher ratings than shows airing in the same slot on ABC and CBS, the only NBC Saturday morning series beside *Pink Panther* to do so in 1969–70.

HAGGIS BAGGIS

Game; Color

June 30, 1958–June 19, 1959

NBC Mon.–Fri. 2:30–3 p.m. (6/30/58–6/19/59)

Host: *Fred Robbins (6/30/58–2/6/59), Dennis James (2/9/59–6/19/59)*

On *Haggis Baggis* four players faced a board of 25 squares, with rows represented by categories and columns by letters. The players were asked questions, and giving a correct answer "won" that player a square, which meant seeing what piece of a celebrity's face was underneath. The first to identify the celebrity won the game and got to chose whether he or she wanted the "haggis" merchandise (fancy items) or the "baggis" items (the essentials). The closest runner-up in correct answers tried to guess what items the winner did not pick in order to win the latter (a match gave the runner-up nothing).

Haggis Baggis first aired on NBC Monday nights from June 20–September 29, 1958. Nighttime host Jack Linkletter rejected doing the daytime version because it ran against his dad's show *Art Linkletter's House Party.* Disk jockey Fred Robbins took the job initially instead. Although it ran less than a year, by the time the show expired, it had its own home game available for viewers to purchase.

HAIL THE CHAMP

Children's; B&W

December 27, 1952–June 20, 1953

ABC Sat. 11:30 a.m.–Noon (12/27/52–6/20/53)

Host: *Howard Roberts*

Assistant: *Angel Casey*

Six kids played in pairs in three contests to be "Champ of the Week" on *Hail the Champ,* which aired from Chicago and alternated weekly with *Sky King.* The show began on KLAC Hollywood in 1948 with Herb Allen as the host and a partner in production. It started airing on three ABC Midwest stations September 22, 1951 from WENR Chicago early Saturday evenings and ran there until June 14, 1952, still with Allen as host. Before the last network run ended, the sponsor of *Hail the Champ,* Powerhouse Candy Bar, had franchised the format to local stations.

HAL IN HOLLYWOOD—See *Sawyer Views Hollywood.*

HALF-PINT PARTY

Children's; B&W

February 14, 1951–May 11, 1951

ABC Mon.–Fri. 4:45–5 p.m. (2/14/51–5/11/51)

Host: *Al Gannaway*

Al Gannaway's pet Mexican chihuahua Half-Pint served as mascot and namesake of this show for kids featuring games, songs, and fairy tales for the audience. From March 8–May

10, 1952, it aired Saturdays from 1:15–2 p.m. on WCBS New York under the title *Al Gannaway's Half-Pint Party.*

•HALLMARK HALL OF FAME

Interview/Dramatic Anthology; B&W and Color

October 8, 1951–May 6, 1956

CBS Sun. 5:45–6 p.m. (10/8/51–12/30/51)

NBC Sun. 3:30–4 p.m. (1/6/52–3/16/52)

NBC Sun. 4:30–5 p.m. (3/23/52–11/16/52)

NBC Sun. 5–5:30 p.m., occasionally 5–6 p.m. (11/23/52–6/26/55)

NBC Sun. 4–5:30 p.m. (10/23/55–5/6/56)

Host: *Sarah Churchill (1951–55), Maurice Evans (1955–56)*

Hallmark Hall of Fame was long the most prestigious series of specials on network television, but its initial offerings were not the classy, splashy presentations that critics and select audiences loved. Its first series was *Hallmark Presents Sarah Churchill,* with the famed actress interviewing guests like Eleanor Roosevelt and Antony Beauchamp, Churchill's photographer husband, in a 15-minute late Sunday afternoon offering on CBS. The shows were not exceptional, but NBC saw enough to convince the sponsor and Churchill to move over at the start of 1952.

Probably the event most responsible for getting things off the ground was the December 24, 1951 presentation of *Amahl and the Night Visitors,* sponsored by Hallmark Cards founder Joyce Hall when no one else would. He used the show as a vehicle to thank viewers for sending his company's Christmas cards during that season, then let the play begin. That started an illustrious 40-plus year involvement with the medium, not to mention an annual airing of *Amahl . . .* through the 1960s. (On radio, Hallmark sponsored a CBS show titled *Hallmark Playhouse,* which ran from 1948–55. In 1953 it changed its name to *The Hallmark Hall of Fame,* but it never gained the prestige or popularity of its video counterpart.)

Two weeks after *Amahl and the Night Visitors, Hallmark Television Theatre* debuted with Churchill hosting and occasionally acting in a weekly drama. The opener, Jean Holloway's *Dr. Serocold* with a no-name cast, got such lousy reviews that the show was retitled *Hallmark Hall of Fame* on its second telecast. The shows improved, and viewers marveled at such offerings as *Joan of Arc* on December 7, 1952 with Churchill and E. G. Marshall. But the show that really attracted audience attention and at the same time garnered excellent critical notices was a lavish, special two-hour *Hamlet* on April 26, 1953, with Maurice Evans as Hamlet in his American TV debut.

The following year, the series tried another extended show with *MacBeth* on November 28, 1954. It drew an impressive Nielsen rating of 25.5, meaning nearly 6$\frac{1}{2}$ million homes watched, and won Dame Judith Anderson an Emmy for Best Actress in a Single Performance for her Lady MacBeth, the first of many Emmy wins for the series. Sensing the appeal of its longer productions, Hallmark expanded the series to become a monthly offering on

October 23, 1955, presenting *Alice in Wonderland* with Eva LeGallienne, puppeteer Burr Tillstrom, and 14-year-old Gillian Barber in the title role. That show marked Maurice Evans's debut as host and producer, and in his honor the series was retitled *Maurice Evans Presents.*

During the 1955–56 season, Evans narrated Molner's "The Good Fairy" on February 5, 1956 with Julie Harris, Walter Slezak, Paul Lynde, and Roddy McDowall, and starred in *The Taming of the Shrew* with Lilli Palmer on March 18, 1956. A production of *The Corn Is Green* starring James Dean was scheduled, but the actor died before the presentation. The show ended its Sunday afternoon run with Judith Anderson starring in *The Cradle Song.*

Evans's Broadway commitments kept him from producing and hosting the show the following season, but the show continued as nighttime specials on NBC under the *Hallmark Hall of Fame* title. In 1960 the show went to tape or film presentations, then in 1980 they became all filmed, with most of the dramas now airing on CBS. By the 1990s, *Hallmark Hall of Fame* movies were airing on NBC, ABC, and CBS, and invariably the productions dominated the Emmy nominations, if not the ratings.

The emphasis on quality over ratings has always been the overriding concern for the show's advertiser. "I'll never sponsor a western, a private eye or a situation comedy glamorizing idiots," Joyce Hall told *TV Guide* in 1961. "I can't get a kick out of copying what 40 other fellows have done. I want to be able to look people in the eye without cringing the day after the show." His company's search for excellence in television programming continues to this day and lives up to the famous Hallmark Cards motto: "When you care enough to send the very best."

HAMMERMAN
Cartoon; Color
September 7, 1991–September 5, 1992

ABC Sat. 10–10:30 a.m. (9/7/91–11/30/91)
ABC Sat. Noon–12:30 p.m. (12/7/91–9/5/92)

Voice:
Stanley Kirk Burrell/Hammerman   *Hammer*

In 1990 the former Stanley Burrell burst onto the music scene as M. C. Hammer, singing the big hits "U Can't Touch This" and "Pray," songs that used tracks from previous hits by Rick James and Prince. By 1991, the singer's brand of pop rap had declined in popularity, and he became simply Hammer, a childhood nickname bestowed on him because of his resemblance to baseball slugger Hank "the Hammer" Aaron. He also joined the cartoon world to provide music and voices for a semiautobiographical series. Set in the slums of mythical Oaktown, *Hammerman* featured the exploits of Stanley Burrell, an employee at the local recreation center for children who found that a pair of Magic Dancin' Shoes transformed him into superhero Hammerman, savior of the neighborhood. His main foe was the evil Boss Grindenheimer, a convict whose contacts on the outside world did his bidding.

During and after the one-year run of this personality-driven cartoon, Hammer's popularity kept declining, and the show was rarely seen in reruns. In 1996, it was announced that Hammer was bankrupt, and it's unlikely this show will get a revival any time soon.

•HANG TIME
Sitcom; Color
September 9, 1995–

NBC Sat. 10:30–11 a.m. (9/9/95–)

Cast:

Chris Atwater	David Hanson
Julie Connor	Daniella Deutscher
Danny Mellon	Chad Gabriel
Mary Beth Pepperton	Megan Parlen
Earl Hatfield	Robert Michael Ryan
Michael Maxwell	Christian Belnavis
Samantha Morgan	Hillary Tuck
Coach Fuller	Reggie Theus

The Deering Tornados boys high school basketball team in the small town of Dover, Indiana, was infused with new life when female transfer Julie Connor joined the team along with brash freshman Michael Maxwell. Their arrivals brought a host of changes to the other team members in their interactions on and off the court. Among them were team captain Chris, who romanced head cheerleader Mary Beth, farm boy Earl, jokester Danny, and team manager Samantha. Guiding them through their occasional disagreements and difficulties was Coach Fuller, played by Reggie Theus, who was a former NBA All-Star before going into acting.

HANNA-BARBERA'S WORLD OF SUPER ADVENTURE—
An umbrella title in syndication for the following series in the package: *Birdman and the Galaxy Trio; Fantastic Four; Frankenstein Jr. and the Impossibles; Herculoids; Moby Dick and the Mighty Mightor; Shazzan!;* and *Space Ghost.*

HANSON BALDWIN'S WAR NEWS DIGEST
News; B&W
July 31, 1950–October 29, 1950

NBC Mon.–Fri. 5:15–5:30 (7/31/50–9/8/50)
NBC Sun. 2:45–3 p.m. (9/17/50–10/29/50)

Host: *Hanson Baldwin*

This was a daily and later weekly update of the Korean War situation. When it moved to Sundays in the fall of 1950 it was retitled *Hanson Baldwin's Weekly War Room.*

HAPPENING '68–'69—See *It's Happening.*

HAPPY FELTON'S SPOTLIGHT GANG
Children's; B&W
November 20, 1954–February 26, 1955

NBC Sat. 10–10:30 a.m. (11/20/54–2/26/55)

Host: *Happy Felton*

As early as 1950, former vaudevillian and bandleader Happy Felton had a local New York show with his "Knothole Gang" that aired for several seasons before Brooklyn Dodgers baseball games. In 1954 he moved to network television with a mix of his comedy and contests involving clips of European vaudeville acts from the NBC film vault. Kids on stage attempted to answer questions about the films, and correct answers won a player (and a home viewer whose postcard was drawn by the player) prizes like bicycles. Happy's closing line to viewers was "Tell Five," which meant, "Let a quintet of your friends know you're watching the show and get them to watch it too."

Due to scheduling conflicts, this series did not air on NBC's flagship station WRCA New York until a week later on kinescope in the 11:30 a.m.–noon slot.

HAPPY'S PARTY
Children's; B&W
September 6, 1952–May 9, 1953
DuMont Sat. 11–11:30 a.m. (9/6/52–5/9/53)
Hostess: *Ida Mae Maher*

The first network show to come from Pittsburgh, *Happy's Party* involved a puppet named Happy, who promoted educational ideas. The Pittsburgh school system worked on the scripts and provided production assistance. The show aired in front of DuMont's only other Saturday morning show in 1952–53, *Kids and Company.*

HARDY BOYS, THE
Cartoon; Color
September 6, 1969–September 4, 1971
ABC Sat. 10:30–11 a.m. (9/6/69–9/5/70)
ABC Sat. Noon–12:30 p.m. (9/12/70–12/26/70)
ABC Sat. 12:30–1 p.m. (1/2/71–9/4/71)
Voices:

Joe Hardy/Pete Jones/Fenton Hardy	Byron Kane
Frank Hardy/Chubby Morton	Dal McKennon
Wanda Kay Breckenridge/Aunt Gertrude Hardy	Jane Webb

Apart from their book series written in the early 1900s under the pseudonym "Franklin W. Dixon," the Hardy Boys are best known for two TV appearances—as a serial on *The Mickey Mouse Club* (q.v.), and as an ABC nighttime series from January 30, 1977–August 26, 1979 with Shaun Cassidy as Joe and Parker Stevenson as his brother Frank. Often forgotten are the hour adventure pilot that aired on NBC nighttime September 8, 1967, with Rick Gates and Tim Matheson in the leads; another live-action series syndicated in 1995; and this cartoon. Here they became rock stars touring the world in concerts, with the opportunity to solve crimes. Joining them in the band were their pals Pete, Chubby, and Wanda, leading it to be called the Hardy Boys Plus Three. Fenton was their detective father.

As unlikely as it may seem, an album featuring the singing voices of this group titled *Here Come the Hardy Boys* actually made *Billboard*'s Top 200 Albums Chart briefly in 1969 (the singing voices were not the same as the cartoon voices). However, the leadoff single "Love and Let Love" failed to crack the Hot 100, so any hopes of emulating the Archies as a recording entity ended quite fast, and the Hardy Boys returned to being mere fictional teenage detectives.

•HARLEM GLOBETROTTERS, THE
Cartoon; Color
September 12, 1970–September 2, 1978
CBS Sat. 10:30–11 a.m. (9/12/70–9/4/71)
CBS Sat. 9–9:30 a.m. (9/11/71–9/2/72)
CBS Sun. 9:30–10 a.m. (9/10/72–5/20/73)
NBC Sat. 8:30–10:30 a.m. (2/4/78–9/2/78)
Voices:

Meadowlark Lemon	Scatman Crothers
Freddie "Curly" Neal	Stu Gilliam
Bobby Joe "B.J." Mason	Eddie Anderson
Geese Ausbie	Johnny Williams
Gip Gipson	Richard Elkins
Pabs "Pablo" Robertson	Robert Do Qui
Granny	Nancy Wible

The Harlem Globetrotters, arguably the best-known professional basketball team in the world, was organized in 1927 by Abe Saperstein in Chicago rather than the famous uptown New York City neighborhood that gave the team its name. The all–African American team grew in fame over the next few decades, and got excellent exposure on 1960s TV sports series like *The CBS Sports Spectacular,* which no doubt led to this animated adaptation. As befits their name, the Globetrotters traversed the world to play various opponents in locales from hillbilly country in the United States to snowy European mountains. Granny, the only Caucasian on board, drove the team bus, and Dribbles the dog accompanied the group as sort of a team mascot.

The group also did its own album for Don Kirshner in 1970, but even he could not make them emulate the success of his protégés, the Archies. *The Harlem Globetrotters* returned in repeats titled *Go Go Globetrotters* in 1978, which also contained repeats of *The Herculoids* and *C.B. Bears.* In 1978 the team returned in a new animated incarnation (see *Super Globetrotters*).

•HARLEM GLOBETROTTERS POPCORN MACHINE, THE
Comedy Variety; Color
September 7, 1974–September 5, 1976
CBS Sat. 11–11:30 a.m. (9/7/74–1/11/75)
CBS Sat. Noon–12:30 a.m. (1/18/75–8/30/75)
CBS Sun. 9:30–10 a.m. (9/7/75–9/5/76)

Regulars: *The Harlem Globetrotters (Meadowlark Lemon, Freddie "Curly" Neal, Geese Ausbie, Nate Brown, Tex Harrison, Marquis Haynes, Theodis Lee, Bobby Joe "B. J." Mason, John Smith), Rodney Allen Rippy, Avery Schreiber (as Mr. Evil)*

Following the cancellation of the first series featuring the famous basketball team (see above), the Harlem Globetrotters did an hour-long nighttime special aired as a pilot under the series title on CBS December 13, 1972, with several guest stars. As a series, it became a revue featuring social messages mixed with jokes and songs. Meadowlark Lemon was the ostensible host, and Curly Neal (the bald one) was the main comic relief. In keeping with the title, the program's recurring graphic used basketballs appearing to "pop" in a machine before and after commercials. The second season was all repeats.

HATS IN THE RING
Political; B&W
May 4, 1952–July 13, 1952

NBC Sun. 2–2:30 p.m. (5/4/52–7/13/52)

For those who think hard-hitting tactics by politicians on television represent a relatively new phenomenon, consider the premiere of *Hats in the Ring*. The Republicans took advantage of this donation of NBC's time for "legally qualified Presidential candidates of the major parties" by offering a filmed dramatization called "The Case for a Republican Congress." The courtroom setting featured three senators (including Richard Nixon) and five representatives, all GOP members, who took the stand, with a "prosecuting attorney," played by Wilfred Lytell, acting in support of the party's charges. Henry Hamilton played the "defense counsel" for the Truman administration, and responded either weakly or contemptuously to GOP claims. Critics slammed the work as biased, but then participants did not intend to be even-handed, but to win over voters.

The next week's broadcast was less "show-bizzy," with Democratic senators Blair Moody and Mike Monroney and representatives Richard Bolling and Henry Jackson engaging in an informal table discussion about their party. This was followed by a plea by Citizens for Eisenhower on May 18, although the general made no direct pitch on camera himself. Neither of those shows aroused controversy, nor did the other programs aired during the next two months.

•HAWKINS FALLS
Soap Opera; B&W
April 2, 1951–July 1, 1955

NBC Mon.–Fri. 5–5:15 p.m. (4/2/51–7/3/53)
NBC Mon.–Fri. 11–11:15 a.m. (7/6/53–1/8/54)
NBC Mon.–Fri. 12:15–12:30 p.m. (1/11/54–7/2/54)
NBC Mon.–Fri. 4–4:15 p.m. (7/5/54–7/1/55)

Cast:

Knap Drewer (1951–53 at least)	Frank Dane
Lona Drewer Corey	Bernadine Flynn
Mrs. Belinda Catherwood	
(at least 1951–52)	Hope Summers
Dr. Floyd Corey	Michael Golda
Dr. Floyd Corey (at least 1953–55)	Maurice Copeland
Roy Bettert Corey	Bruce Dane

Laif Flagle (1951–53 at least)	Win Stracke
Millie Flagle (at least 1953–54)	Ros Twohey
The Judge (1951 at least)	Phil Lord
Mitch Fredericks (at least 1954–55)	Jim Bannon
Calvin Sperry (at least 1954–55)	Art Van Harvey
Sheriff Boylan (at least 1954)	Doug Chandler
Dr. Glen Bowden (at least 1954)	Lee Henry
Elmira Cleebe (1953 at least)	Elmira Roessler
Spec Bassett (1953 at least)	Russ Reed
Toby Winfield (1953 at least)	Tom Poston

Also: *Marie Engstrand-Brady (at least 1951), Bev Younger (at least 1952–53), Arthur Peterson (at least 1952), Carlton Kadell (at least 1953), Bill Griskey (at least 1953), Richard Clary (at least 1953), Jackie Berkey (at least 1953), Peter Donat (at least 1953), Will Hussing (at least 1953)*

Airing live from Chicago, with outdoor scenes filmed in Woodstock, Illinois, and with Hugh Downs as the announcer, *Hawkins Falls* was NBC's only serial of the 1950s to last more than two years until *From These Roots*, which debuted in 1958. The show began as a sitcom on NBC nighttime June 17–October 12, 1950 with the subtitle "Pop. 6,200" before heading to daytime with continuing characters but only occasional humor. Actors Frank Dane, Hope Summers, Phil Lord, and Win Stracke were seen in both versions, although Dane played a different character in the nighttime program.

On the afternoon debut, ill, bedridden Knap Drewer befriended runaway Roy Bettert, and he and his wife Lona adopted Roy, stirring up much talk among local gossips, including busybody Mrs. Catherwood. Later developments included the standard soap opera story lines—divorces, murders, affairs, etc.—and the show lived up to its new subtitle, "A Television Novel." The Drewers mainly reacted to various subplots throughout the run, although Knap died when Frank Dane was judged too difficult to handle off the set, letting Lona wed Dr. Corey.

Other characters were Toby Winfield and his wife April, who was expecting a baby; Laif Flagle, the town bum; Millie Flagle, Laif's one-time wife who received a marriage proposal from Sheriff Boylan in 1954; Mitch Fredericks, a local reporter who fended off the advances of young Jenny Karns; and Dr. Glen Bowdon, who became Dr. Corey's assistant. Interestingly, Art Van Harvey, who played crusty soda-shop proprietor Calvin Sperry, had worked with castmate Bernadine Flynn earlier on radio; they were the stars of *Vic and Sade*.

The emphasis in *Hawkins Falls* was on representing small-town life, and on this level it did fine, right down to a theme song based on "Skip to My Lou, My Darling." But by 1955 the show's down-home scenes had fallen from favor. The show lost audience share to the family-based drama on the competition, CBS's *A Brighter Day*, and NBC dropped the series. Nonetheless, *Hawkins Falls* was one of the longest-running network shows from Chicago during the Windy City's national programming heyday.

Hawkins Falls' *main couple was Lona Corey (played by Bernardine Flynn) and Floyd Corey (Maurice Copeland), seen here in 1954.*

HEADLINE CLUES

News/Game; B&W
July 4, 1949–May 4, 1951

DuMont Mon.–Fri. Noon–12:30 p.m. (7/4/49–5/4/51)

Host: *George F. Putnam (1949–51), Don Russell (1951)*

One of only two game shows seen in the daytime on DuMont (the other was *It's in the Bag* in 1952), *Headline Clues* had reports on the news from the International News Service (INS), accompanied by a few background stills, followed by quizzes to home viewers about the stories. Those called at

home who gave correct answers were given the chance to win prizes like gas ranges if they could identify a city shown on screen while the host gave a hint about it.

Headline Clues debuted in daytime 16 days before a nighttime version appeared. That incarnation, which became known as *Broadway to Hollywood Headline Clues* on October 21, 1949, changed into a news/talk show once the daytime counterpart had left the air, with Putnam followed as host by Bill Slater (1951–53) and Conrad Nagel (1953–54). It continued on DuMont nighttime until July 15, 1954.

•HEALTH SHOW, THE

News; Color
January 17, 1987–November 4, 1990

ABC Sat. 12:30–1 p.m. (1/17/87–9/3/88)
ABC Sun. Various half hours (9/11/88–11/4/90)

Host: *Kathleen Sullivan (1987), Paula Zahn (1988)*

Airing from the ABC News Washington, D.C. bureau, *The Health Show* reported on the latest advances in medical developments. Original anchor Kathleen Sullivan left after nine months to host *The CBS Morning News*, leaving the show without a permanent anchor until Paula Zahn, a former newscaster on the CBS Los Angeles affiliate KCBS, took over in early 1988. Zahn's departure a few months later to take over *ABC World News This Morning* spurred another round of interim hosts, including Karen Stone and Hilary Bowker. In the fall of 1988, only 165 of 215 affiliates were carrying the show (with major markets like Miami, Baltimore, Phoenix, and Cincinnati declining to do so). Betting that this low clearance was in part due to the show's time slot, which followed cartoons for children, ABC moved *The Health Show* to Sunday mornings, where it ended two years later.

HEATHCLIFF AND DINGBAT/HEATHCLIFF AND MARMADUKE

Cartoon; Color
October 4, 1980–September 18, 1982

ABC Sat. 11–11:30 a.m. (10/4/80–9/5/81)
ABC Sat. 8:30–9 a.m. (9/12/81–9/18/82)

Voices:

Heathcliff/Spike/Mr. Schultz/Iggy	*Mel Blanc*
Sonja/Crazy Shirley/Grandma/Marcy	*June Foray*
Clem/Digby/Dogsnatcher	*Henry Corden*
Dingbat	*Frank Welker*
Nobody/Sparerib	*Don Messick*
Marmaduke/Phil Winslow (both 1981–82)	*Paul Winchell*
Dottie Winslow/Barbie Winslow/Billy Winslow/ Missy (both 1981–82)	*Russi Taylor*

Heathcliff, created in a comic strip by George Gately in 1973, was a bon vivant type, slightly rough around the edges, who liked to fight Spike the bulldog, romance his lovely tabby Sonja, and irritate meat market owner Mr. Schultz by stealing his food. He did all this in two segments per show, all the while trying to avoid dog snatchers and other hazards. His co-headliner during the first season was Dingbat, a dog who was a vampire. His pals "the Creeps" were Nobody, a pumpkin with a baseball cap, and Sparerib, a skeleton. They worked as temps for Odd Jobs Inc.

Heathcliff, Dingbat, and company returned in the show's second season, but now the other titled dog was a newcomer, albeit a regular feature in newspaper comic strips. Marmaduke, a large Great Dane who belonged to the Winslows (Phil and Dottie and their two kids Barbie and Billy), regularly wreaked comic havoc due to his size. Marmaduke also did a few segments involving riddles and letters about other funny dogs.

Two years after the network series ended, *Heathcliff* returned in daily syndication in 1984 under a different production company, but still using Mel Blanc as Heathcliff's voice.

HEAVYWEIGHT CHAMPIONSHIP OF TENNIS
Sports; Color
February 15, 1975–March 8, 1975

CBS Sat. 3:30–5 p.m. (2/15/75–3/8/75)

Host: *Don Criqui*

This made-for-television competition of tennis pros is of note chiefly because the FCC investigated the series for promoting a winner-take-all format when in fact both players were paid (for example, once John Newcombe made $280,000 even though he lost), and for plugging hotels hosting the events without saying on air that the endorsements were paid promotions. It aired on CBS in specials through 1977 before the government crackdown ended it.

HECKLE AND JECKLE CARTOON SHOW, THE
Cartoon; Color
October 14, 1956–September 7, 1971

CBS Sun. 1–1:30 p.m. (10/14/56–9/22/57)
CBS Sat. 11–11:30 a.m. (1/25/58–4/26/58)
CBS Sat. 10–10:30 a.m. (5/30/58–8/30/58)
CBS Sat. 11–11:30 a.m. (9/6/58–9/26/59)
CBS Sat. 10–10:30 a.m. (10/3/59–9/24/60)
CBS Sat. 9–9:30 a.m. (9/25/65–9/3/66)
NBC Sat. 8–9 a.m. (9/6/69–9/5/70)
NBC Sat. 8–8:30 a.m. (9/12/70–1/9/71)
NBC Sat. 8:30–9 a.m. (1/16/71–9/4/71)

Voices:

Heckle/Jeckle	*Dayton Allen*
Little Roquefort/Percy the Cat	*Tom Morrison*
Gandy Goose/Sourpuss	*Arthur Kay*

Heckle and Jeckle were the most popular animated characters from Terrytoon productions behind the unforgettable Mighty Mouse, and they appeared in sporadic network runs during a 15-year period. The featured duo was a pair of identical magpies who favored comic harassment as a way of handling their opponents. Other Terrytoon characters

appeared too, including Gandy Goose and his scrappy feline friend Sourpuss, Little Roquefort the mouse and his enemy Percy the Cat, and Dinky Duck. All the cartoons were screened first in movie theaters before running on television, some going back to the 1930s.

Besides the daytime run, Heckle, Jeckle, and the rest were also on the *CBS Cartoon Theatre*, a nighttime series which ran from June 13–September 5, 1956 with Dick Van Dyke as host. The main characters returned as a supporting act in 1979 (see *Mighty Mouse Playhouse*).

•HECTOR HEATHCOTE SHOW, THE
Cartoon; Color
October 5, 1963–September 25, 1965

NBC Sat. 10–10:30 a.m. (10/5/63–9/26/64)
NBC Sat. 9:30–10 a.m. (10/3/64–9/25/65)

Voices:

Hector Heathcote/Hashimoto/	
Hanako/Saburo/Yuriko	*John Myhers*
Sidney/Stanley/Cleo	*Dayton Allen*

Though billed in various press releases as a "time travelling scientist," the lead character in this cartoon actually just appeared in various time frames as a person of the period and not a bona fide time traveler, à la Sherman and Peabody on *The Bullwinkle Show*. Hector Heathcote was a diminutive, eager, and clumsy American patriot whose misadventures typically though not exclusively took place during the Revolutionary War. Wearing a hat and usually playing a drum, Hector usually found himself helping his country in some unlikely comic fashion. His pet dog's name was Winston.

Other components of the series were two previously released theatrical animated shorts of the early 1960s (as was Hector), "Hashimoto" and "Sidney the Elephant." Hashimoto concerned a somewhat stereotyped Japanese mouse telling tales about his wife Hanako and their children Yuriko and Saburo to American G.I. Joe. Sidney was a middle-aged pachyderm who acted like a panicky child and who had to be handled with care by his pals Stanley the lion and Cleo the giraffe. In some of the Sidney shorts, the lead character was voiced by Lionel Wilson.

In what surely was one of TV's odder transactions, CBS Films' Terrytoons division sold this cartoon to rival network NBC for a two-year run. Ironically, the series aired just before Terrytoons' biggest hit, *Mighty Mouse Playhouse* on CBS, during its first season.

HELLO KITTY'S FURRY TALE THEATER
Cartoon; Color
September 19, 1987–September 10, 1988

CBS Sat. 8–8:30 a.m. (9/19/87–9/10/88)

Voices:

Hello Kitty	*Tara Charendoff*
Tuxedo Sam	*Sean Roberge*
Chip	*Noam Zylberman*

My Melody	Maron Bennett
Grandpa Kitty	Carl Banas
Grandma Kitty/Mama Kitty	Elizabeth Hanna
Papa Kitty	Len Carlson
Catnip	Cree Summer Francks
Grinder	Greg Morton
Fangora	Denise Pidgeon

The gist of *Hello Kitty's Furry Tale Theater* was that a feline repertory company presented two adaptations of children's stories each week, with Hello Kitty hosting and starring in each. Friends and family members played supporting roles, although some appeared typecast, like Catnip and Grinder, who inevitably received villainous parts. (Catnip, for example, played the title character in "How Schrinchnip Stole Christmas.") Among the sources of the adaptations were Grimm's fairy tales ("Rumpeldogskin"), horror novels ("Frankencat"), and movies ("K.T.—The Kitty Terrestial").

HELLO PEAPICKERS—See *Tennessee Ernie Ford Show, The.*

•HELP! IT'S THE HAIR BEAR BUNCH
Cartoon; Color
September 11, 1971–August 31, 1974

CBS Sat. 9:30–10 a.m. (9/11/71–9/2/72)
CBS Sun. 9–9:30 a.m. (9/9/73–8/31/74)

Voices:

Hair Bear	Daws Butler
Square Bear	Bill Callaway
Bubi Bear	Paul Winchell
Mr. Peevely	John Stephenson
Botch	Joe E. Ross

Bearing a certain resemblance to the venerable Hanna-Barbera characters Yogi Bear and friends, the Hair Bear Bunch were three cousins who lived in Cave Block #9 at Wonderland Zoo but regularly made their escape to the outside world, usually at night, to see what action they were missing. Their leader was Hair Bear, who sported a frizzy Afro-style head of hair. Square Bear was a tall, goony bear in a cap, and Bubi Bear was the rough equivalent of Boo Boo Bear. Chasing them constantly on their excursions were the zoo curator Mr. Peevely and his chubby right-hand man Botch, whose catch phrase was "Ooo, ooo!"

The Sunday shows were repeats. The series went into syndication under the title *The Yo Yo Bears.*

•HERCULOIDS, THE
Cartoon; Color
September 9, 1967–September 6, 1969

CBS Sat. 9:30–10 a.m. (9/9/67–9/7/68)
CBS Sat. 11:30 a.m.–Noon (9/14/68–9/6/69)

Voices:

Zandor/Tundro/Igoo/Zok	Mike Road
Tara	Virginia Gregg
Dorno	Ted Eccles
Gloop/Gleep	Don Messick

The distant planet Quasar was under the rule of King Zandor, his wife Tara, and son Dorno. The trio, handsome by human standards (mom and dad dressed like Amazons, and Dorno sported a nifty blond page-boy haircut), found themselves constantly defending their world from alien invaders in adventures that always required the talents of a quintet of animals. There was Tundro, a 10-legged, winged rhinoceros ridden by Dorno; Igoo, a King Kong–like gorilla made of petrified rock; Zok, a flying mechanical dragon; and Gloop and Gleep, two shapeless ectoplasmic ghosts who mumbled a lot. They successfully fought for their home each week against such bizarre attackers as the Faceless People, the Beaked People, and the Mutoids.

Segments of the show appeared in repeats on *The Harlem Globetrotters* in 1978. A new version, featuring the same voices except for Ted Eccles, was a segment on *Space Stars* in 1981.

HERE COME THE DOUBLEDECKERS
Children's; Color
September 12, 1970–September 3, 1972

ABC Sat. 10:30–11 a.m. (9/12/70–9/4/71)
ABC Sun. 10:30–11 a.m. (9/12/71–9/3/72)

Cast:

Scooper	Peter Firth
Brains	Michael Auderson
Billie	Gillian Bailey
Sticks	Bruce Clark
Spring	Brinsley Forde
Tiger	Debbie Russ
Doughnut	Douglas Simmonds
Albert	Melvyn Hayes

This show featured a septet that met in a London Bus clubhouse, a sort of Limey update of the Little Rascals film troupe. Scooper was the unofficial leader of the occasionally mischievous gang, while Albert was the only regular adult in the cast. *Variety* said of the show, "It is low farce, but very substantial fare against the one-dimensional characterizations of the cartoons. It also has a uniquely refreshing score—no rock." This rare Saturday morning British import ran repeats for its second season.

HERE COMES THE GRUMP
Cartoon; Color
September 6, 1969–September 4, 1971

NBC Sat. 9–9:30 a.m. (9/6/69–9/5/70)
NBC Sat. 11:30 a.m.–Noon (9/12/70–9/4/71)

Voices:

Terry Dexter	Jay North
Princess Dawn	Stefanianna Christopher
The Grump	Rip Taylor

"A pallid imitation of the great Beatles film *Yellow Submarine*" was *Newsweek*'s assessment of this rather elaborate fantasy. American Terry Dexter arrived in a distant, unspecified country where Princess Dawn and her dog Bib tried to avoid the Grump, a diminutive, pink, wizardlike entity who rode the flying Jolly Green Dragon. The Grump (actually a rather comic figure striving for success), placed a curse of gloom on the princess, which could be unlocked by the Crystal Key located in the Cave of the Whispering Orchids. Terry assisted Dawn and Bib in efforts to locate the key while they met such unlikely people as the Eenie Meenie Miners, the Bloony Woonies, and the Cork Men along the way. The second season consisted solely of repeats.

HERE'S ARCHER
Musical Variety; B&W
March 1, 1949–July 14, 1949

NBC Tue./Thu. 5–5:15 p.m. (3/1/49–7/14/49)

Host: *Gene Archer*

Singer Gene Archer belted out a few tunes in this early NBC entry, a twice-weekly show from Washington, D.C.

HERE'S HOLLYWOOD
Interview; B&W
September 26, 1960–December 28, 1962

NBC Mon.–Fri. 4:30–5 p.m. (9/26/60–9/29/61)
NBC Mon.–Fri. 4:30–4:55 p.m. (10/2/61–12/28/62)

Regulars: *Joanne Jordan (1960–61), Helen O'Connell (1961–62), Dean Miller (1960–61), Jack Linkletter (1961–62)*

Here's Hollywood videotaped on-the-spot talks with celebrities, usually at their homes, studios, or favorite Los Angeles hangouts. Among the guests on the first week were Tab Hunter, Martha Hyer, Juliet Prowse, and Barry Sullivan. The hosts ended shows by answering viewers' questions from a parked convertible ostensibly used by them to meet the stars. Actress Joanne Jordan left in mid-1961 and was replaced by singer Helen O'Connell, and original co-host Dean Miller left in October of that year to pursue business interests involving radio stations in the Midwest.

HERE'S LOOKING AT YOU
Women's; B&W
October 8, 1951–December 28, 1951

NBC Mon.–Fri. 3:15–3:30 p.m. (10/8/51–12/28/51)

Host/Producer: *Richard Willis*

This beauty hints show starred makeup artist Richard Willis and followed the short-lived *Miss Susan* soap opera. After the NBC run, it aired with Willis's advice daily from 1:30–2 p.m. on WNBT New York through February 15, 1957.

HERE'S TO YOUR HEALTH
Informational; B&W
February 10, 1952–December 7, 1952

NBC Sun. 5:30–6 p.m. monthly (2/10/52–12/7/52)

This entry told viewers about the prevention and treatment of various diseases via filmed reports and live dramatizations and discussions. On the debut, the New York County Medical Society, which did the show in cooperation with NBC, orchestrated a discussion of polio, using both doctors and patients.

HEY VERN, IT'S ERNEST!
Sitcom; Color
September 17, 1988–September 2, 1989

CBS Sat. 11–11:30 a.m. (9/17/88–10/15/88)
CBS Sat. Noon–12:30 p.m. (10/22/88–12/31/88)
CBS Sat. 11–11:30 a.m. (1/7/89–9/2/89)

Cast: *Jim Varney (as Ernest P. Worrell and others), Denice Hicks, Mark Goldman, Gailard Sartain*

Jim Varney, who believe it or not built his professional acting career on Shakespearean parts, gained prominence with TV viewers in the 1980s in a plethora of commercials playing good ole boy Ernest P. Worrell pitching regional products to his unseen pal Vern, and usually ending up a comical victim by fadeout. Here he built on that gimmick, playing the Worrell character and others (including a baby!) in comic sketches designed to teach kids a few lessons in life as well as generate a few laughs. The title came from the catch phrase he used at the start of each of the commercials. Though the series did not last long, the character did surface in several films in the 1990s, including *Ernest Goes to Jail* and *Ernest Scared Stupid*.

HIDDEN FACES
Soap Opera; Color
December 30, 1968–June 27, 1969

NBC Mon.–Fri. 1:30–2 p.m. (12/30/68–6/27/69)

Cast:

Arthur Adams	Conard Fowkes
Dr. Katherine Logan	Gretchen Walther
Martha Logan	Louise Shaffer
Mark Utley	Stephen Joyce
Nick Capello Turner	Tony LoBianco
Earl Harriman	Nat Polen
Sen. Robert Jaffe	Joseph Daly
Mimi Jaffe	Rita Gam
Allyn Jaffe	Linda Blair
Wilbur Ensley	John Towley
Grace Ensley	Ludi Claire

When *Let's Make a Deal* left NBC daytime for ABC in the same time slot, this show was chosen as its replacement and ultimately unsuccessful competition. Its lead was Arthur Adams, a pipe-smoking, ex-military, "rugged 35-year-old lawyer" (*Variety*'s words) whose background gave him international contacts for worldwide troubleshooting. He found that he needed this asset as he served as legal counsel to former surgeon Dr. Katherine Logan, charged with the accidental death of a patient. You get only one guess as to whether these two fell in love. Rounding out the cast during its half-year run were devious white collar criminal Earl Harriman; Mark Utley and Nick Turner, two suspicious types with whom Arthur consulted; and the Jaffes—the senator, his wife Mimi, and their daughter Allyn. A failure throughout its run, *Hidden Faces* was the first of a number of NBC shows that flopped against *Let's Make a Deal* and *As the World Turns*. (NBC didn't mount a successful competitor until *Days of Our Lives* expanded to an hour in 1975.)

•HIGH ROLLERS
Game; Color
July 1, 1974–June 20, 1980

NBC Mon.–Fri. 11–11:30 a.m. (7/1/74–11/28/75)
NBC Mon.–Fri. 10:30–11 a.m. (1/19/76–6/11/76)
NBC Mon.–Fri. 11–11:30 a.m. (4/24/78–6/20/80)

Regulars: *Alex Trebek, Ruta Lee (1974–76)*

In its 1974–76 incarnation, *High Rollers* featured a game board of consisting of numbers, with each digit connected to a prize. A simple question was read, and the first of two competing contestants to sound a buzzer during or after the reading and answer the question correctly got control of play (a wrong answer gave the opponent control). The controlling player could elect to roll a pair of dice to match a digit on the board and claim the prize attached to it. However, once a number was rolled, it disappeared from the board, and a future roll of it during the round caused a contestant to lose that round and any prizes accumulated to that point. The first contestant to win two rounds got to play a bonus round just involving rolling the dice to remove all digits. Ruta Lee was on hand to cheer contestants on.

Nearly two years after its first cancellation, the show got a revival with modified rules. Now nine digits from 1 to 9 lined up in three columns on the board, with at least one column able to be "cleared" by a high roll of the dice (e.g., a column with numbers 2, 4, and 6 could be cleared with the roll of 12, since they totaled that amount). Any column with all three numbers removed won a contestant the prize(s) underneath it, with one prize added to a column for each round no contestant won, up to a maximum of five prizes per column. Other rules remained intact, and the top prize in the bonus round was $10,000.

The show also aired in a nighttime weekly syndicated version in 1974–75 with Trebek hosting and Elaine Stewart rolling the dice, and in syndication again in 1987 with Wink Martindale as host.

•HIT MAN
Game; Color
January 3, 1983–April 1, 1983

NBC Mon.–Fri. 11:30 a.m.–Noon (1/3/83–4/1/83)

Host: *Peter Tomarken*

This game show violated the twin principles of its genre by being both monotonous and confusing. The first round had three players watch a seemingly interminable (actually, it ran about three minutes) photomontage with dry narration about a particular subject, then answer questions about details had which popped up in the piece. Each correct answer won a contestant a gremlinlike figure called a "hit man." The first two contestants to amass six "hit men" played another drawn-out memory round. This time when answering questions, however, they faced the previous day's winner and his or her six "hit men," and a correct answer by a player removed a "hit man" from another contestant's column. If possible, this part of the competition was even more irritating to watch than the previous round. The contestant who survived with at least one "hit man" in this round went into a bonus round to win up to $10,000. All the erratic and often boring activity made this anything but a hit, man, and it went off after 13 weeks.

HOCKEY—See *NHL Game of the Week.*

HOLD 'ER NEWT
Children's; B&W
September 11, 1950–May 17, 1952

ABC Mon.–Fri. 5:30–5:45 p.m. (9/11/50–10/13/50)
ABC Sat. 10:30–11 a.m. (1/26/52–5/17/52)

Voice Specialist/Puppeteer: *Don Tennant*

In this short-lived puppet show from WENR Chicago, Newt was the proprietor of a country store whose various misadventures with pal Mr. Nosegay formed the crux of each show. In addition to his onscreen work, Don Tennant created and wrote the show plus co-produced it with Les Weinrott. It was seen in Chicago nightly as early as June 1950. It returned briefly in 1952 for three shows which alternated weekly with *Hollywood Junior Circus.*

HOLLYWOOD BACKSTAGE—See *Ern Westmore Show, The.*

HOLLYWOOD JUNIOR CIRCUS
Children's; B&W
March 11, 1951–March 1, 1952

NBC Sun. 5:30–6 p.m. (3/11/51–8/26/51)
ABC Sat. 10:30–11 a.m. (9/8/51–3/1/52)

Regulars: *Art Jacobson (as ringmaster; 1951), Paul Barnes (as ringmaster Billy Booker; 1951–52), Carl Marx (as Buffo the Clown; 1951), George Cisar (as Buffo the Clown; 1951–52), Max Bronstein (as Zero the Midget), the Bruce Chase Orchestra*

The "Hollywood" in the title of this Chicago production, which alternated weekly on NBC with *The Magic Slate,* referred to its sponsor, Hollywood Candy Company. When the show moved to ABC in the fall of 1951, it got a new ringmaster. Zero the Midget did commercials for the advertiser between circus acts. The set had children in the bleachers being interviewed with the performers. The show alternated weekly with several other series during its run except from October 27, 1951–January 27, 1952, when it appeared every week.

•HOLLYWOOD SQUARES, THE

Game; Color
October 17, 1966–June 20, 1980

NBC Mon.–Fri. 11:30 a.m.–Noon (10/17/66–10/1/76)
NBC Mon.–Fri. 10:30–11 a.m. (10/4/76–9/29/78)
NBC Mon.–Fri. 1–1:30 p.m. (10/2/78–3/2/79)
NBC Mon.–Fri. 10:30–11 a.m. (3/5/79–6/20/80)

Host: *Peter Marshall*

Regulars: *Rose Marie, Cliff Arquette (as Charley Weaver; October 1966–April 1972, January 1973–October 1974), Wally Cox (October 1966–February 1973), Abby Dalton (October 1966–November 1970), Morey Amsterdam (October 1966–September 1968), Paul Lynde (May 1968–August 1979), George Gobel (April 1972–June 1980)*

Semiregulars: *Jan Murray (1967–73), Kaye Ballard (1967–68), Nanette Fabray (1968–71), Vincent Price (1970–76), Karen Valentine (1970–77), John Davidson (1973–74), Charo (1974–75), Sandy Duncan (1974–75), Roddy McDowall (1974–75), Joan Rivers (1975–76)*

TV's longest-running daytime celebrity panel game was played out in the most unlikely of sets—a 17-foot-tall tic-tac-toe board containing approximately 3,500 cubic feet. It also possessed nine stars, each within a square. To win a square, one of two players had to decide whether a star's answer to a question was correct. A wrong choice let the opponent win the square. Contestants alternated in picking the stars, and the first player to connect three squares horizontally, vertically, or diagonally, or win five out of nine squares if none of the former was possible, won the game.

The first player to win two games won a match, with each game worth $200. Contestants who won five matches not only claimed $2,000 but a car and various other merchandise. Each day's first game included a "Secret Square": If a contestant picked the celebrity in that square, and made the right call on the star's answer, he or she could win a bonanza of prizes, including a fur by Dicker and Dicker of Beverly Hills (and modeled by a female star), and luxury apparel items from the Spiegel catalog from Chicago.

All these rules were secondary to why most people watched *Squares* for 14 seasons—the comic quips by celebrities known as "zingers" given to answer the show's questions. The zingers became so popular they were used in at least two books and one record album in the 1970s. However, they were mostly given to the celebrities prior to taping to use on the show, which the show noted in its indecipherable disclaimer, "The areas of questions designed for each celebrity and possible bluff answers are discussed with each celebrity in advance. In the course of their briefing, actual questions and answers may be given or discerned by the celebrities."

GEORGE C. SCOTT

In 1974 George C. Scott and his then-wife Trish Van Devere (right) made their debut on The Hollywood Squares *to the delight of host Peter Marshall (left).*

The regulars' styles of jokes, and their location on the board, became fairly consistent. Top middle square Rose Marie was sex-starved and desperate (to one male contestant who said, "I'll try Rose Marie," she remarked coquettishly, "Yeah, why *don't* you try Rose Marie?"), while lower right corner square Cliff Arquette mined old-timer humor from his Charley Weaver character (asked once what the peak of a certain fruit was, he said, "Peter, I haven't had a peak in 20 years!"). Arquette had a near-fatal heart attack on April 24, 1972 that kept him off for a few months. George Gobel replaced him temporarily in the same laid-back groove, then permanently following Arquette's death in 1974. Wally Cox died during the show's run in 1972. Two other original panelists, Morey Amsterdam and Abby Dalton, had left a few years earlier.

But the undisputed jewel of the show was its center square—Paul Lynde. Lynde guested on the show's second week (October 24–29, 1966), then made increasingly frequent appearances until he became a regular by 1968. Who else but Lynde, when asked "True or false: A Detroit housewife was awarded $275,000 by a jury because she doesn't feel a thing when she kisses her husband?" would respond, "Does Charo live in Detroit? Good for you, Charo." His many-faceted comic persona on the show was unique for television, and he could be humorously wicked (Marshall: "Eddie Fisher recently said, 'I'm sorry. I'm sorry for them both.' Who was he referring to?" Lynde: "His fans.") or bizarrely kinky (Marshall: "True or false: The famous philosopher Plato believed that at the beginning, each person was created part man and part woman?" Lynde: "Right on, Plato!"). Lynde was so popular that there were two weeks in July 1979 where he was the only regular kept in place when the rest of the board was filled with soap opera stars. The decision to replace him the same year was ill-advised, as his popularity was not fading, and the show survived less than a year without him.

Of course, hundreds of other stars did *Squares*, including such unlikely participants as George C. Scott, Betty Grable, Pat Boone, and even Big Bird and Oscar the Grouch. Those who appeared for at least two consecutive years in at least one-fifth to one-half of a calendar year's shows (Karen Valentine was in the latter group) are listed above as semiregulars. Some of them appeared on the show in other years on a lighter schedule, and those years are not listed.

The following people made at least six weekly appearances in a calendar year on the show (years in which they did so are given): Glenn Ford (1967); Zsa Zsa Gabor (1967); Ruta Lee (1967–68); Marty Allen (1967–77); Judy Carne (1968); Jim Backus (1968–70); Bill Bixby (1968, 1973); Gypsy Rose Lee (1968–69); Jack Cassidy (1969); Stu Gilliam (1969–70); Arte Johnson (1969, 1971, 1975); Harvey Korman (1969, 1973–78); Mickey Rooney (1970); Lily Tomlin (1970); JoAnne Worley (1970); Suzanne Pleshette (1970–72); Virginia Graham (1971); Burt Reynolds (1971); Joey Bishop (1972); Kent McCord (1972); Ernest Borgnine (1973); Demond Wilson (1973–74); Rich Little (1973–75); McLean Stevenson (1973–78); Florence Henderson (1974–77); David Brenner (1975); Robert Fuller (1975–77); Jimmie Walker (1975–79); John Byner (1976); Marcia Wallace (1976); Bill and Susan Seaforth Hayes (1976–77); Earl Holliman (1976–78); Wayland and Madame (1976–80); Diahann Carroll (1978); David Doyle (1978); Steve Landesberg (1978–79); Bernie Kopell (1979); Fred Willard (1979); and Tom Poston (1979).

Apart from its daytime run, *Hollywood Squares* ran in a nighttime syndicated version from 1971–81, going from once a week to—eventually—nightly status. NBC also ran a Friday night edition from January 12–September 13, 1968, and the next year spun off a Saturday morning entry for children (see *Storybook Squares, The*). All these versions had basically the same regulars as listed above. The show was revived in 1982–84 on NBC daytime as part of *The Match Game–Hollywood Squares Hour* (q.v.), then returned in a new syndicated version from 1986–89 with John Davidson as host and Joan Rivers, JM J. Bullock, and Shadoe Stevens as regulars. And in 1995 comedienne Roseanne announced plans to air yet another rendition in syndication titled *Planet Hollywood Squares* in honor of the celebrity restaurant chain.

HOLLYWOOD TODAY WITH SHEILAH GRAHAM

Informational; B&W
January 3, 1955–August 19, 1955

NBC Mon.–Fri. 10:45–11 a.m. (1/3/55–8/19/55)

Host: *Sheilah Graham*

Longtime celebrity columnist Sheilah Graham interviewed guests on this daily series.

HOLLYWOOD'S TALKING

Game; Color
March 26, 1973–June 22, 1973

CBS Mon.–Fri. 3:30–4 p.m. (3/26/73–6/22/73)

Host: *Geoff Edwards*

Hollywood's Talking used approximately 19 celebrities per show in snippets in which a trio of contestants competed to be the first to identify what topic the stars were discussing. Correct answers in the first third of the piece netted $150, $100 for the first two parts and $50 before it ended. The first to reach $250 played a bonus clip-identification round worth up to $2,000.

HOME

Informational; B&W and Color
March 1, 1954–August 9, 1957

NBC Mon.–Fri. 11 a.m.–Noon (3/1/54–12/28/56)
NBC Mon.–Fri. 10–11 a.m. (12/31/56–8/9/57)

Hosts: *Arlene Francis, Hugh Downs*

Regulars/"Editors": *Dr. Leona Baumgartern (infant care), Dr. Rose Franzblau (psychology), Poppy Cannon (food; March 1954), Eve Hunter (fashions), Estelle Parsons (special projects), Will Peigelbock (home improvement), Katherine Kinne (food; at least 1954), Jack Fuller (special projects; at least 1955), Natalie Core (grooming; at least 1955), Dorsey Connors (Chicago reporter; at least 1955), Nancyanne Graham (home decorating; at least 1955), Dr. Ashley Montagu (family matters; at least 1955), Esther Von Wagoner Tufty, a.k.a. "the Duchess" (Washington, D.C. reporter; at least 1955), Gloria Brown (at least 1955), John Cameron Swayze (travel; at least 1956), Sydney Smith (home decorating)*

Home was the third element of NBC executive Sylvester "Pat" Weaver's planned specialty shows for home audiences, the others being *Today* and the late night *Tonight Show*. Why those two properties were still running in 1996 while *Home* failed rather quickly probably says more about the insecure programming decisions in the NBC daytime department in the 1950s than it does about this series, which was well received critically and had a fairly substantial following. Its format of offering useful advice for the viewer from a variety of experts has been run into the ground by a score of daytime shows since, with many sorely lacking the inventiveness shown here.

Fran Allison was actually the first choice to host the show, but NBC refused to meet her contractual demands and Arlene Francis won the job instead. Hugh Downs, formerly used mostly as an announcer, became Francis's on-air foil. The show attempted to have a mascot à la J. Fred Muggs on *Today* with the Bannister Baby, an infant in diapers seen in daily activities on film, but Baby was never a hit. The lineup of "editors" dispensing information had its own share of problems, including a fair amount of turnover. For example, Poppy Cannon, food columnist for *House Beautiful* magazine, was replaced by Katherine Kinne after only a month; others in various specialities left or were dropped, and others were added, depending on what topics the show wanted to emphasize. (See the Regulars list to connect the talent with their field of expertise.)

By 1955 *Home* was airing in color for the last 15 minutes of each show and started visiting a few cities on the road, including Chicago, Milwaukee, and San Francisco. On October 10 of that year, the show did what is believed to be TV's first ship-to-shore remote telecast from a boat on Lake Erie five miles from Cleveland. The next year, John Cameron Swayze started a half-hour weekly travel feature. Later, on April 1, 1957, the show tried to attract a bigger audience with a five-minute daily "Coffee Break" musical segment featuring weekly guest artists. Also notable was a filmed interview Francis did with poet Carl Sandburg on July 25, 1957. Sandburg indicated his dissatisfaction with her medium, but also stated, "You are not what is wrong with television."

Home, however, was finishing second to CBS in the ratings and had high costs and sponsorship problems, and NBC canceled the show not long after Sandburg's interview and replaced it with *The Arlene Francis Show* (q.v.). The concept had a brief revival on the NBC radio series *Monitor* on September 11, 1965, with Francis again serving as host of the segment.

•HOME SHOW, THE
Informational; Color
January 18, 1988–April 8, 1994

ABC Mon.–Fri. 11:30 a.m–Noon (1/18/88–9/16/88)
ABC Mon.–Fri. 11 a.m.–Noon (9/19/88–9/30/88)
ABC Mon.–Fri. 11:30 a.m.–Noon (10/3/88–1/13/89)
ABC Mon.–Fri. 11 a.m.–Noon (1/16/89–7/12/91)
ABC Mon.–Fri. 11 a.m.-12:30 p.m. (7/15/91–9/18/92)
ABC Mon.–Fri. 11 a.m.–Noon (9/21/92–4/8/94)

Host: *Robb Weller (1988–89), Sandy Hill (1988), Gary Collins (1989–94), Dana Fleming (1990–91), Beth Ruyak (1991–92), Sarah Purcell (1992–94)*

Why ABC kept this unremarkable advice and guest interview show for women on the air for more than six years despite lackluster ratings (*The Price Is Right* on CBS always swamped

it) is almost as hard to figure out as it was to try to keep up with the show's hosts. Originally Robb Weller and Sandy Hill helmed the show. After Hill left by mutual agreement with the producers, Weller hosted until being replaced by Gary Collins in 1989. By April 1990 Dana Fleming had joined Collins as co-host. Beth Ruyak replaced Fleming when the show went to 90 minutes, a big surprise for network watchers, since ABC reportedly had planned to replace it or at least slice it to a half hour (most stations still carried it for only a half hour or an hour). Sarah Purcell was the final hostess once it shrank back to 60 minutes. The show aired on tape from Los Angeles.

HOMEMAKER'S EXCHANGE
Informational; B&W
October 10, 1949–January 25, 1952

CBS Mon.–Fri. 4–4:30 p.m. (10/10/49–1/25/52)

Hostess: *Louise Leslie*

One of CBS's earliest daytime shows, *Homemaker's Exchange* was an unpretentious time killer offering household and cooking tips. CBS tried to encourage advertisers to participate by saying they could demonstrate their products live on the show. It was sponsored by Nash Cars and was seen on at least 12 stations, a rather wide distribution at the time.

HONEYMOON RACE, THE
Game; Color
July 17, 1967–December 1, 1967

ABC Mon.–Fri. 11–11:30 a.m. (7/17/67–12/1/67)

Host: *Bill Malone*

Meshing nicely in theme with ABC's other games at the time (*The Dating Game* and *The Newlywed Game), The Honeymoon Race* had three newlywed duos compete in a scavenger hunt of five items hidden in a mall in Hollywood, Florida. However, unlike its successor *Supermarket Sweep,* the couples used electric scooters rather than shopping carts to locate their booty. Another loser game show, *Temptation,* replaced this in 1968.

•HONG KONG PHOOEY
Cartoon; Color
September 7, 1974–September 5, 1981

ABC Sat. 9–9:30 a.m. (9/7/74–8/30/75)
ABC Sat. 8–8:30 a.m. (9/6/75–9/4/76)
NBC Sat. 8–8:30 a.m. (2/4/78–9/2/78)
NBC Sat. 11:30 a.m.–Noon (5/23/81–9/5/81)

Voices:

Hong Kong Phooey	Scatman Crothers
Sgt. Flint	Joe E. Ross
Rosemary	Kathi Gori
Spot	Don Messick

What superhero was a dog who changed into a black mask and robe in a file cabinet before emerging to fight off evildoers throughout the land? Hong Kong Phooey, of course. Phooey, with his faithful cat Spot and somewhat clumsy vehicle Phooeymobile, used kung fu techniques to capture his foes. In civilian life, our hero disguised himself as janitor alter ego Penrod Pooch and hung out with the goofy-sounding Sgt. Flint (there were ample occasions for actor Joe E. Ross's character to make the patented "Ooo, ooo!" sounds also used by Botch in *Help! It's the Hair Bear Bunch*) and dizzy nasal-voiced switchboard operator Rosemary. Penrod/Hong Kong kept most of the action going by making frequent humorous asides to the audience and consulting his handbook of kung fu tricks.

NBC reran the series in 1978 and 1981. Additionally, it ran its repeats as part of *Godzilla* (q.v.) from 1980–81.

HOPALONG CASSIDY
Western; B&W
March 13, 1949–September 24, 1950

NBC Sun. 2:30–3 p.m. (3/13/49–4/3/49)
NBC Sun. 5:30–6 p.m. (4/17/49–6/26/49)
NBC Sun. 5:30–6 p.m. (1/8/50–9/24/50)

Cast:
Hopalong Cassidy   *Bill Boyd*

Who would have thought that an unexceptional collection of old shoot-em-ups from the 1930s and 1940s would become the TV sensation of the late 1940s and 1950s? Bill Boyd certainly thought so. He bought up all TV rights to his Hopalong Cassidy movies, based very loosely on stories written by Clarence E. Mulford, in the hopes that these rather unremarkable 54 films could become a hit in the new medium. It was a wise move.

The first activity on the films came in September 1948, when NBC Television Features Service announced it had the TV rights to 35 Hopalong Cassidy westerns to syndicate for three years under a $100,000 contract. By December 1948, the network's New York station WNBT had begun airing some of them Sundays from 5:45–7 p.m.

But in 1949 the films went to NBC under General Foods' sponsorship, where they became an instant hit despite chronological oddities. For example, the first movie, made in 1935, which told how Hoppy got his name (from a limp after he was shot in the leg), did not air until January 22, 1950. The films also had rather rudimentary plots, which simply had Hopalong, dressed in an all-black outfit and usually joined by one of several sidekicks, stop bad guys; there was very little character development or decent dialogue. These potential limitations, however, did not bother children, who were Boyd's principal audience, and Hopalong mania grew big within a few months.

By the end of 1949, Boyd had struck deals for a new recording contract, radio show, and newspaper comic strip. Surprisingly, Bill Boyd resisted capitalizing on his newfound fame at first. He told *Variety* in its June 15, 1949 issue that he did not plan to make any new Hopalong Cassidy films because they would look cheap compared to the early ones,

and that he planned to do a western travelogue series instead. As Hoppy's popularity reached a fever pitch over the next few months, that idea was dropped.

In November 1950 NBC purchased the exclusive rights to all *Hopalong Cassidy* films, most of which had already aired at least four times on television. Worried about overexposure, General Foods ended its contract with the show in the spring of 1951, but NBC kept the program in syndication. In 1952–53, Boyd filmed 52 new TV shows to add in circulation. These films, with Edgar Buchanan as sidekick Red Connors, were Boyd's last appearances as Hopalong Cassidy before a camera.

The Hopalong Cassidy radio show ran on Mutual in 1950 and on CBS from 1950–52. The TV series was much rerun during the 1950s but faded in the 1960s as a welter of other, more sophisticated westerns emerged. However, *Variety* reported in June 1966 that there was one station, KJEO in Fresno, California, that had been rerunning the series since June 8, 1953. But when Boyd died in 1972, so did most TV exposure of a series that had once been the top filmed show on television.

HOPPITY HOOPER—See Adventures of Hoppity Hooper, The.

•HORIZONS
Informational; B&W
January 6, 1952–May 11, 1952

ABC Sun. 1–1:30 p.m. (1/6/52–5/11/52)

Each week on *Horizons*, a different Columbia University professor lectured on the future of a topic (e.g., the Communist Party of America, women's rights, race relations) to 5 to 10 students. After speaking at least half the show, the teacher yielded the floor to students' questions. The show, which had no sponsors or commercials (known as a *sustaining* program), ended with voice-over descriptions of each student's academic interests and achievements. It also aired on ABC Sunday nights occasionally from December 2, 1951–June 29, 1952.

HORSE RACES
Sports; B&W
April 18, 1953–February 27, 1960

CBS Sat. 4–4:30 p.m. (4/18/53–8/1/53)
CBS Sat. 5–5:30 p.m. (8/8/53–8/29/53)
NBC Sat. 4:30–5 p.m. (1/18/58–2/27/60; winter months only)

Announcers: *Fred Capossola (1958–60), Chris Schenkel (1958–59), Tommy Roberts (1960)*

In 1953, Gillette sponsored a series of horse races on CBS and contributed a purebred Hackney pony for auction to the highest bidder, with all money raised going to the Damon Runyon Fund for cancer research. A less ambitious slate of races from the tracks in Hialeah, Florida, aired in the late 1950s under the same name. See also *NBC Takes You to the Races.*

HOT DOG
Children's; Color
September 12, 1970–September 4, 1971
NBC Sat. Noon–12:30 p.m. (9/12/70–9/4/71)
Hosts: *Woody Allen, Jonathan Winters, Joanne Worley*
Music: *Ed Bogas, the Youngbloods*
Creator/Producer/Writer/Director: *Frank Buxton*

Premiering as a Saturday morning special on NBC March 28, 1970, with all the daytime cast except Tom Smothers in place of Jonathan Winters, *Hot Dog* was another in a long line of children's series which tried to be entertaining and educational but failed to gather enough viewers to sustain it. The collection of mini-documentaries sprang from the mind of former *Discovery* host Frank Buxton, who said the inspiration for the show's theme—learning the origins of items—came from visiting factories while he was touring cities as a comedian in the mid-1960s. He covered 70 different subjects in 13 shows, ranging from what makes people snore to how does toothpaste get inside the tube to, yes, how hot dogs are made, and filmed his three comic hosts doing commentaries on the subjects wherever they were working.

Filling out the program was music from the then-popular group the Youngbloods ("Get Together") and animation from the Yellow Ball Workshop in Lexington, Massachusetts. The show's title was the name of Buxton's office in Burlingame, California.

•HOT HERO SANDWICH
Children's; Color
November 3, 1979–April 5, 1980
NBC Sat. Noon–1 p.m. (11/3/79–4/5/80)
Regulars: *L. Michael Craig, Vicky Dawson, Denny Dillon, Matt McCoy, Nan-Lynn Nelson, Paul O'Keefe, Jason Smith Wrick, Dr. Tom Cottle*

Hot Hero Sandwich had interviews with celebrities like Olivia Newton-John discussing her feelings about religion interspersed with skits set at the Hot Hero Sandwich Cafe. Seven actors ranging in age from 16 to 19 appeared on the show, and Harvard psychologist Dr. Thomas Cottle asked in-studio children their feelings about the issues raised.

•HOT POTATO
Game; Color
January 23, 1984–June 29, 1984
NBC Mon.–Fri. Noon–12:30 p.m. (1/23/84–6/29/84)
Host: *Bill Cullen*

The last network game show hosted by veteran Bill Cullen, *Hot Potato* initially had two trios of similarly designated

people (e.g., three flight attendants) compete in identifying any of the seven responses people had made most often to a survey question (e.g., "What was the greatest movie of all time?") or coming up with a fact (e.g., the names of celebrities who appeared most often on the cover of *TV Guide*). An incorrect response meant the other team got to guess. The team that had given the most correct answers by the end of the round won it, and two rounds won gave a team $1,000 and the chance to play a similar game in the bonus round for an additional $5,000.

In a sure sign of desperation to increase ratings, the teams became led by one celebrity and two contestants on April 18, 1984, when the show was retitled *Celebrity Hot Potato.* Among those appearing were Milton Berle.

HOT SEAT
Game; Color
July 12, 1976–October 22, 1976
ABC Mon.–Fri. Noon–12:30 p.m. (7/12/76–10/22/76)
Host: *Jim Peck*

Two married couples played, with one mate having to predict how the other would respond to a question. An "emotional response" electrode (which worked sort of like a lie detector) measured the other mate's reaction. Three questions were posed, worth $100, $200, and $400, and the couple with the most money at the end could play a bonus round for additional booty.

HOT STOVE LEAGUE—See *Laraine Day Show, The.*

HOT STREAK—See *Bruce Forsyth's Hot Streak.*

HOT WHEELS
Cartoon; Color
September 6, 1969–September 4, 1971
ABC Sat. 10–10:30 a.m. (9/6/69–9/5/70)
ABC Sat. 11–11:30 a.m. (9/12/70–9/4/71)
Voices:

Jack Wheeler/Doc Warren	*Bob Arbogast*
Janet Martin	*Melinda Casey*
Mickey Barnes/Kip Chogi	*Albert Brooks*
Tank Mallory/Dexter Carter	*Casey Kasem*
Ardeth Pratt	*Susan Davis*
Mother O'Hare	*Nora Marlowe*
Mike Wheeler	*Michael Rye*

Metro City High School student Jack "Rabbit" Wheeler was known as the best car driver in his town, as well as the leader of a racing club called the Hot Wheels. He was the son of former racing champ Mike Wheeler, who had retired after an auto accident and who worried about Jack's hobby. Jack had a love interest in Janet Martin and an enjoyable group of club members, including Mickey Barnes, the apprentice mechanic; Ardeth, Mickey's love interest; Kip, the African ambassador's son; and Tank Mallory, the mechanic at Mike

Wheeler's Motors. Doc Warren was a veteran mechanic who belonged to the Hot Wheels Club as a honorary member and mentor. The club hung out at Mother's soda shop, operated by Mother O'Hara. Dexter Carter, banned from the club due to his reckless behavior, led Dexter's Demons, a rival car club. Each show typically climaxed in a wild race in which the Hot Wheels won, but lest the kids got the wrong idea, plenty of educational driving tips were dispensed at the end.

The story lines of *Hot Wheels*, however, were irrelevant to the real impact the show had on TV cartoons. *Hot Wheels* was based on a product by sponsor Mattel Toys, and the Federal Communications Commission demanded that its 57-second opening and references to the title and lines of makes of cars be counted as commercial time. Basically, the FCC ruled that the whole show was a commercial for the toy cars rather than an entertainment program. This crackdown on blatant commercial promotion by a cartoon was unprecedented (for an earlier example of a series that used commercial products as part of the show, see *Linus the Lionhearted*), and the ruling in effect until 1983, when a new lineup in the FCC ended the restrictions. The series had a partial revival in 1991–92 on the Family Channel cable channel with a cartoon called *Heroes on Hot Wheels*.

HOTEL COSMOPOLITAN
Dramatic Anthology; B&W
August 19, 1957–April 11, 1958

CBS Mon.–Fri. Noon–12:15 p.m. (8/19/57–4/11/58)

Cast:

Donald Woods	*Himself*
The house detective	*Henderson Forsythe*

Hotel Cosmopolitan, the last 15-minute network daily series to debut in the 1950s, was to premiere in late July 1957, but early production problems forced it back a few weeks. Also lost in the delay was actor Chester Morris, who was to be the host and narrator. Taking his place was Donald Woods, who commented about the goings-on during the day's show from his chair in the lobby of the Cosmopolitan, a spiffy New York City hotel. After eight months of unremarkable stories, CBS condemned this property to expand *Love of Life*, which followed it at 12:15 p.m., to 30 minutes.

HOUNDCATS, THE
Cartoon; Color
September 9, 1972–September 1, 1973

NBC Sat. 9:30–10 a.m. (9/9/72–12/16/72)
NBC Sat. 8–8:30 a.m. (12/23/72–9/1/73)

Voices:

Stutz	*Daws Butler*
Muscle Mutt	*Aldo Ray*
Rhubarb	*Arte Johnson*
Puttypuss	*Joe Besser*
Dingdong	*Stu Gilliam*

The Houndcats were not all felines (Muscle Mutt and Dingdong were in fact dogs), but they did not let that fact stand in their way of being a crack espionage team à la the CBS nighttime adventure *Mission: Impossible* (1967–73), the show's obvious inspiration. In fact, each member had an analog on *Mission*. Their leader was Stutz (Jim Phelps on *Mission*), who enlisted the help of Muscle Mutt the strongman (Willie), Rhubarb the electronic genius (Barney), Puttypuss the master of disguise (Rollin Hand) and Dingdong the stuntdog (OK, the one exception, maybe put in to avoid a lawsuit). They rode a flivver named Sparkplug to their adventures, and like *Mission* they received background information via tapes which self-destructed in five seconds. They defeated their enemies in every episode, but could not vanish *Scooby-Doo, Where Are You?* or *Bugs Bunny*, which aired opposite them on CBS during their two slots in 1972–73.

•HOUR MAGAZINE
Talk; Color
Summer 1980–December 1988

Syndicated 60 minutes daily beginning September 1980

Regulars: *Gary Collins, Pat Mitchell (1980–83), Bonnie Strauss (1983–85)*

Gary Collins, the bland star of several forgettable short-lived nighttime TV series like *The Iron Horse* and *The Sixth Sense* in the 1960s and 1970s, started a new career as a bland talk show host in this long-running program. It came in the aftermath of *Everyday* (q.v.). When it flopped, Group W asked women what they wanted to see in a daily TV series, and *Hour Magazine* was the result.

Sitting in a set styled as a plush living room, Gary conducted interviews and introduced taped investigations by Pat Mitchell, who left in March 1983 and was replaced by Bonnie Strauss. Most information dispensed on the show was slanted toward housewives in a low-key manner, with advice on mental and physical health, exercise, dieting, cooking, and finances.

When Strauss left in 1985, the show made a distinct shift to feature more celebrities, who now joined Collins in participating in the segments throughout the day's shows. Some big names got involved with the program this way, including Nancy Reagan, America's first lady, who co-hosted for a week in May 1984; Jane Fonda, who spent much of the show hawking her exercise videos; Jane Wyman; Danny DeVito; and others. Perhaps the most notorious (and least worthy) co-host was Fawn Hall, who came to the series fresh from a rash of publicity about her actions as secretary to Col. Oliver North during the Iran-Contra affair.

By the end of the decade, Collins and company lost the ratings race to the more issue-oriented fare of Phil Donahue and Oprah Winfrey, and the series went off the air. But Collins returned as steadfast a host as ever (see *The Home Show*).

HOUSE ON HIGH STREET, THE
Dramatic Anthology; B&W
September 28, 1959–February 5, 1960
NBC Mon.–Fri. 4–4:30 p.m. (9/28/59–2/5/60)

Cast:

John Collier	Philip Abbott
Dr. Harris B. Peck	Himself
Judge James Gehrig	Himself

NBC was so sold on this series that it ordered 13 weeks of shows before scheduling it or getting a sponsor. However, when the series arrived in 1959, its opposition (*American Bandstand* on ABC, *The Brighter Day* and *The Secret Storm* on CBS) did so much better in the ratings that taping another 13 weeks was out of the question. As with most NBC daily anthologies of the 1950s, it acted out tales over the course of several days. The difference was that several characters reappeared, including probation officer John Collier, who, in the course of each drama, interviewed both victims and perpetrators in examining the relevant social issues. Collier also discussed the situations with two professionals in real life who played themselves, Judge James Gehrig and psychiatrist Dr. Harris B. Peck. The initial story was a four-day series on a male juvenile delinquent. Later installments included one about a 15-year-old girl picked up at a gangster's apartment, who has an alcoholic father and neurotic mother and whom authorities tell to get help, and a story about a young girl who attacks her mom with a knife.

HOUSE PARTY—See *Art Linkletter's House Party.*

HOW DO YOU RATE?
Game; B&W
March 31, 1958–June 26, 1958
CBS Mon.–Thu. 10:30–11 a.m. (3/31/58–6/26/58)

Host: *Tom Reddy*

Tester: *Dr. Robert Goldenson*

Psychology professor Dr. Robert Goldenson of Hunter College in New York City tested players' aptitude in this New York–based game, with the high scorer of a test getting at least $150 and a low scorer $25. It was replaced rather suddenly with *Play Your Hunch* when a sponsor fell through due to low ratings. CBS promised the show would get an 8 rating, but it averaged a mere 3.4 instead. Ironically, Dr. Goldenson was a cousin of ABC President Leonard Goldenson.

HOW DOES YOUR GARDEN GROW?
Informational; B&W
July 22, 1951–September 9, 1951
NBC Sun. 5–5:30 p.m. (7/22/51–8/19/51)
NBC Sun. 3:30–4 p.m. (8/26/51–9/9/51)

Host: *John Ott Jr.*

John Ott Jr. was a banker turned horticulturalist, and his series aired locally in Chicago before going on NBC. Here he doubled as cinematographer doing time-lapse photography of plants. On this short-lived show, Ott also dispensed gardening tips.

HOW TO SURVIVE A MARRIAGE
Soap Opera; Color
January 7, 1974–April 18, 1975
NBC Mon.–Fri. 3:30–4 p.m. (1/7/74–4/18/75)

Cast:

Larry Kirby (1974)	Michael Landrum
Larry Kirby (1974)	Ken Kercheval
Larry Kirby (1975 at least)	Michael Hawkins
Chris Kirby	Jennifer Harmon
Lori Kirby (1974 at least)	Suzanne Davidson
Lori Kirby (1975 at least)	Cathy Greene
Sandra Henderson (1974 at least)	Lynn Lowry
Dr. Julie Franklin (1974)	Rosemary Prinz
Dr. Tony DeAngelo (1974)	George Welbes
Monica Courtland	Joan Copeland
Terry Courtland	Peter Brandon
Fran Bachman	Fran Brill
David Bachman (1974)	Allan Miller
Rachel Bachman	Elissa Leeds
Moe Bachman	Albert Ottenheimer
Peter Willis (1974)	Steve Elmore
Peter Willis (1974–75)	Berkeley Harris
Joan Willis	Tricia O'Neil
Dr. Max Cooper (1975)	James Shannon
Maria McGhee	Lauren White
Johnny McGhee	Armand Assante
Alexander Kronos (1974 at least)	Brad Davis
Joshua Browne	F. Murray Abraham
Susan Pritchett, R.N. (1975)	Veleka Gray

How to Survive a Marriage was launched with a much-hyped hour and a half opener featuring the first "nude" (implied only, since the bodies were under covers) bedroom scene on daytime television. The scene was between Larry Kirby and his mistress Sandra Henderson, though Larry had had sex earlier with his wife of 12 years, Chris. Larry decided to leave Chris and daughter Lori for Sandra, but he reaped bitter consequences, since Lori was hit by a car while he was bedding Sandra. (The debut generated 150 negative calls to NBC's Boston affiliate alone.) Later on, Larry realized he loved his family, but his mother-in-law Monica hated him and did everything to discourage a reconciliation between Larry and Chris. It was not until the end of the run when Chris, having been shocked out of her drinking problem when her negligence at home led to Lori's being hurt, recognized that she still cared for Larry and not her boyfriend Dr. Max Cooper. Likewise, Larry's patient treatment of Lori convinced Monica that he was worthy of a second chance.

Other characters started out one way, but metamorphosed into people who wouldn't have been at home in the previous story lines. Feminist Dr. Julie Franklin, who had counseled Lori on how she could and should become independent, decided her life would be complete by getting married to Dr. DeAngelo. Peter Willis, the male chauvinist pig who flirted with the ladies while wife Joan sought solace in alcohol, somehow transformed into being everybody's confidante whose big problem was having a wife who did not want a baby. (The story line twisted again and ended with the two having a baby, but not before the pregnancy was threatened by German measles, which, it turned out, Joan didn't have after all.) And just why did the thrice-wed Monica (Chris's mother) turn mother figure and adopt a critically ill man abandoned by his gangster stepfather?

One element, however, was so consistent that it became an in-joke among the show's staff. Anyone leaving the show invariably had his or her character "transferred to Detroit," as was the case for Michael Landrum when he was written out as Larry. That was a better fate than what happened when Allen Miller had to leave unexpectedly in the summer of 1974. His character David went into bankruptcy, then had a heart attack and died, leaving behind his grieving wife Fran.

How to Survive a Marriage was the ultimate "relevant" soap effort of the 1970s, from its self-help title to its preoccupation with sex. Unfortunately, the series suffered all the potential disadvantages of that approach, with long, drawn-out, superficial psychotherapy discussions and stock recitations of "women's lib" dogma taking precedence over good old-fashioned storytelling. Viewers stuck by the easier-to-take competition, *Match Game* on CBS and *One Life to Live* on ABC.

HOWARD COSELL'S SPORTS MAGAZINE

Sports; Color
January 7, 1972–April 27, 1975

ABC Sat. 5:15–5:30 p.m. (at least 1973; winter months)
ABC Sat. 3:15–3:30 p.m. (1974–75; January–April only)

Host: *Howard Cosell*

Howard Cosell, the man who had an opinion on everything in sports and let you know it whether you wanted to hear it or not, hosted this sports spot typically seen before *The American Sportsman* in the mid-1970s.

HOWARD MILLER SHOW, THE—See *Club 60.*

•HOWDY DOODY

Children's; B&W and Color
December 27, 1947–September 24, 1960

NBC Sat. 5–6 p.m. (12/27/47–1/31/48)
NBC Various days 5:30–6 p.m. and Saturdays 5–6 p.m. (2/5/48–8/14/48)
NBC Mon.–Fri. 5:30–6 p.m. (8/16/48–6/1/56)
NBC Sat. 10–10:30 a.m. (6/16/56–9/24/60)

Regulars: *"Buffalo" Bob Smith, Bob Keeshan (as Clarabell; 1948–52), Bill LeCornec (1949–60), Dayton Allen (1949–52),*

Judy Tyler (as Princess Summerfall Winterspring; 1951–53), Robert A. "Nick" Nicholson (as Clarabell and others; 1952–60), Allen Swift (1953–56), Gina Ginardi (1954–55), Gabby Hayes (1954–55), Lowell Thomas Jr. (1955–56), Alene Dalton (as the Story Princess; 1955–56), Marti Barris (as Peppi Mint; 1959–60)

Puppeteers: *Frank Paris (1947–48), Rhoda Mann (1947–52), Rufus Rose (1952–60), Lee Carney (1952–60)*

"Say kids! What time is it?"

"It's Howdy Doody time" was the proper answer, as any TV fan of the 1940s and 1950s who said this along with the Peanut Gallery could tell you. *Howdy Doody* was the daytime show that hooked millions of baby-boomers on the new medium, one designed specifically for them. *Howdy Doody* was not the first daytime network TV show for children (for that honor, see *Small Fry Club*), but it was the first to become a hit, and at more than 12 years, one of the longest-running kids shows ever.

Buffalo Bob and Clarabell lie amid the puppets on Howdy Doody *while the people controlling the strings stand aloft.*

In the mid-1940s, Martin Stone, producer of the radio hit *Author Meets the Critics,* was asked to do a TV children's show. Stone thought of Bob Smith, the Buffalo Bob of *The Triple B Ranch* show on NBC radio, which featured a moronic character who exclaimed "Howdy doody!" and Smith agreed to try a TV show while keeping his radio show. With writer Eddie Kean, Smith fashioned the lyrics to "It's Howdy Doody Time," sung to the tune of "Ta-ra-ra Boom-dee-ay," then drafted Frank Paris to serve as puppeteer along with his assistant Rhoda Mann, who would handle the Howdy Doody doll. The result debuted under the title *Puppet Playhouse,* and, though no one knew it at the time, Smith and company had given birth to a pop culture classic.

The star of Howdy Doody *stands between fellow puppets Phineas T. Bluster (left) and Dilly Dally.*

The opener garnered terrific audience response and a rave from *Variety* ("It's the type of show that could be responsible for the sale of a lot of sets," enthused the reviewer). Smith did about 20 minutes of repartee with a voice in a box claiming to be Howdy Doody, as Paris did not finish the character in time for the debut. There were also some minor guest acts and the airing of a Ben Turpin film short (the first film of what would air through 1955 as the Old Time Movie segment). The show expanded with this basic formula of live and filmed slapstick to two, three, and then five days a week, with Smith referring to the group of 35 to 40 children seen in the studio audience as the Peanut Gallery. In January 1948 Howdy, a lantern-jawed, fright-wigged cowboy who interacted with other puppets, was unveiled. The other big move during the first few

Buffalo Bob Smith, Howdy Doody, and Clarabell, from left to right, stand in front of the Peanut Gallery as the latter celebrates a decade of Howdy Doody.

months was making Bob Keeshan, an NBC page who kept the studio audience under control, into Clarabell the mute clown in a zebra suit. Clarabell talked by blowing a right horn for yes and a left horn for no, and generally acted like an overgrown child. He drew considerable giggles from the Peanut Gallery for his liberal use of a seltzer bottle, which he squirted at Buffalo Bob almost every show.

But no one laughed in May 1948 when Paris asked for merchandising rights for his doll. NBC refused, claiming that it had a copyright on the character's name, so Paris went to New York independent TV station WPIX for a show in which the doll was rechristened Peter Pixie. Pixie bombed, but the new, friendlier-looking Howdy, who could even use a phone and play a piano, was a hit after having undergone "plastic surgery" in June. The show's popularity grew even more during the successful "Howdy Doody for President of the Kids" campaign that summer, in which Howdy foiled his devilish opponent Mr. X's plot to steal the world's only Swiss cheese hole puncher. The campaign was so popular it drew 58,000 requests for campaign buttons among viewers.

Such activities in turn drew considerable advertiser interest. By July 1948 the series had its first sponsor, Polaroid, which

sold more than 150 "Magic Pictures" in conjunction with the series. Soon *Howdy Doody* was chock full of sponsors and had begun marketing its own products as well (though the show drew the line at merchandising Howdy Doody mouthwash). By December 1948, Hooper ratings for New York City placed *Howdy Doody* sixth among all shows, ahead of such nighttime programs as *Kraft Television Theatre* and *Break the Bank.*

But if anyone had any doubts of the show's appeal, they were wiped away on October 25, 1948, when a personal appearance by Buffalo Bob and Howdy Doody at Macy's in New York prompted the largest turnout ever at that department store. Three weeks after that visit, the store reported selling 10,000 Howdy Doody dolls.

Howdy's popularity widened in 1949, and the show's production became more elaborate. Some changes were superficial (the title was now officially *Howdy Doody*); others, such as setting the puppets in a town called Doodyville rather than a circus, were more important. And many new, long-running puppets joined the mix—Howdy's blowhard foe Phineas T. Bluster; fidgety Dilly Dally, initially Bluster's lackey; Flubadub, Howdy's pet composed of various parts of other animals; and, most memorably, Inspector John J. Fadoozle, America's Number One (Boing!) Private Eye. The show hired Bill LeCornec to do Dilly Dally's voice and Dayton Allen to do the others. Both men soon came on camera as well. Allen did Ugly Sam the wrestler, Pierre the chef, Sir Archibald the explorer, and Lanky Lou the cowhand. LeCornec did Oil Well Willie the prospector, Dr. Singasong, and Chief Thunderthud of the Ooragnak tribe. Chief Thunderthud was a rival to Chief Featherman, played by Bob Keeshan, but he proved to be more popular, especially given his catch phrase of "Kowa-bonga!"

Later on that year, on June 23, there was an impressive TV first created by a split screen shot where Buffalo Bob sat in New York and talked to Howdy while the latter was in Chicago. All the while the ratings remained the highest of any show before 6 p.m., prompting columnist Walter Winchell to dub the show as "the Milton Berle of the lollipop set."

In 1950 NBC decided that the show needed a feminine character, to appeal more to girls in the audience. The result was a puppet named Princess Summerfall Winterspring of the Tinka Tonka tribe. On October 22, 1951, the puppet became a real-life character, and actress Judy Tyler was a hit in the part until she left two years later for a burgeoning career. (Tragically, Tyler died in a car accident in 1957 at age 23.) The addition of Tyler went smoothly for the cast, but when Smith hired Bob Nicholson in 1952 to write songs, do puppetry, act the new character of Cornelius J. "Corny" Cobb the storekeeper, and learn the character of Clarabell, it was too much for some. Near the end of 1952, Allen, Keeshan, LeCornec, and Mann requested a bigger part of the show's merchandising and they either quit or were fired; versions differ. LeCornec later rejoined the show; the others did not.

Doodyville found itself in 1953 with a new Clarabell (Nicholson), new puppeteers, and a new Corny Cobb (Allen Swift, who assumed the voices Dayton Allen had done). Swift also did a few new characters like Chief Thunderchicken, Monsieur Fontainebleau the artist, and the voice of Captain Windy Scuttlebutt. But no new female characters appeared, and when Tyler left they tried to fill her spot with Papoose Gina Runningwater (Gina Ginardi), but the character did not click.

The show faced its biggest crisis on September 8, 1954, when Smith suffered a heart attack. Occasional guest Gabby Hayes and Ted Brown as Bison Bill substituted for him, while Smith was said to be off on a secret mission (Allen Swift assumed Howdy's voice). Smith recuperated enough to come back via remotes from his home by January 17, 1955; meanwhile a new Clarabell had emerged (Nicholson was tired of the role). On September 12, 1955, Smith returned to the studio and the show added color permanently (color had been used occasionally since 1953). Added that same

day were a travelogue hosted by Lowell Thomas Jr. called "Flight to Adventure," appearances by the Story Princess, played by Alene Dalton, and a new puppet, Heidi Doody (Howdy's sister, voiced by Dalton)—all part of an effort to fight the new *Mickey Mouse Club* opposite the show on ABC. The effort failed. The lavish competition sucked away kid viewers, and within a year Howdy Doody moved to Saturdays, where it added *Gumby* (q.v.) cartoons as a segment for a time.

On Saturdays the show went to videotape and added many new puppets, a new girl named Peppi Mint, and even a chimp named Kokomo Jr., but Howdy's glory days were gone. A 10th anniversary show on December 28, 1957 basked in past glories, with three kids from the first Peanut Gallery appearing. Sponsors began losing interest, and when Nabisco promised to co-sponsor *The Shari Lewis Show* while Howdy got no advertisers, NBC had to cancel. On the show's last (and 2,343rd) show, Clarabell provided a touching ending by finally speaking the words, "Goodbye, kids."

Howdy Doody was not seen again until the 1970s, when a nostalgia boom propelled Buffalo Bob to do the show on college campuses. On September 12, 1972, NBC aired an hour-long nighttime special "Howdy Doody and Friends," which featured Buffalo Bob and Lew Anderson and introduced the network's fall Saturday morning lineup. Four years later, a syndicated revival of the show included Smith, Dayton Allen, LeCornec, Anderson, Nicholson, and a few new players. The revival failed, but *Howdy Doody* and its impact on kids in the 1950s are an integral part of the heritage of 20th-century America.

For an excellent, detailed history of the show, see *Say Kids! What Time Is It?* by Stephen Davis (Little, Brown, 1987).

HOW'S YOUR MOTHER-IN-LAW?
Game; Color
December 4, 1967–March 1, 1968
ABC Mon.–Fri. 11:30 a.m.–Noon (12/4/67–3/1/68)
Host: *Wink Martindale*

Yet another obnoxious Chuck Barris Production, this show featured married men who appeared on stage to make derogatory claims about their mothers-in-law and three celebrity "defense attorneys" who stood up for the women's honor. Deciding who among the several mothers-in-law featured on that day's show was the least shrewish and thus deserving of the $100 top prize was a "bachelor jury" of five unmarried men and women each. It was about as funny as any mother-in-law joke you could hear from a loser comic.

HUDSON BROTHERS RAZZLE DAZZLE SHOW, THE
Comedy Variety; Color
September 7, 1974–April 3, 1977
CBS Sat. 11:30 a.m.–Noon (9/7/74–8/30/75)
CBS Sun. 9–9:30 a.m. (9/12/76–4/3/77)

Regulars: *The Hudson Brothers (Bill, Mark, and Brett, oldest to youngest), Stephanie Edwards, Ronny Graham, Rod Hull (and his emu puppet), Katie McClure, Gary Owens*

Produced by the same company that did the nighttime CBS hit *The Sonny and Cher Show* (1970–74), *The Hudson Brothers* debuted as a summer nighttime series from July 31–August 28, 1974. The taped Toronto-based production then transferred with much of its cast to the Saturday morning schedule due to the believed appeal of variety shows to children. It had the same comic "bumpers" Sonny and Cher did between light songs by the Hudson trio, who really were related, and goofy sketches (for example, Rod Hull had a hand-puppet emu, which attacked any cast member who made fun of it). But despite the quick pace of it all, this series lasted only one season, with repeats running from 1976–77.

HULK HOGAN'S ROCK 'N' WRESTLING
Cartoon; Color
September 14, 1985–June 13, 1987

CBS Sat. 10–11 a.m. (9/14/85–9/6/86)
CBS Sat. Noon–1 p.m. (9/13/86–6/13/87)

Voices:

Hulk Hogan	Brad Garrett
"Mean" Gene Okerlund	Neil Ross
Rowdy Roddy Piper	Charlie Adler
Captain Lou Albano	George DiCenzo
The Iron Sheik	Aron Kincaid
Andre the Giant	Ronald A. Feinberg
Moolah/Richter	Jodi Carlisle
Junkyard Dog	James Avery
Jimmy "Superfly" Snuka	Lewis Arquette
Tito Santana	Joey Pento
Big John Studd	Chuck Licini
Mr. Fuji	Ernest Harada
Hillbilly Jim	Pat Fraley

Regulars: *Hulk Hogan, "Mean" Gene Okerlund*

Hulk Hogan, born Terry Bollea, a muscular blonde with a droopy mustache, was perhaps the biggest superstar of the inexplicable mid-1980s fad for the World Wrestling Federation (WWF), a group whose "sport" was seen often on weekends in syndication at the time. In this, his only network series, he hosted cartoon vignettes involving him and his fellow competitors against assorted baddies, plus music videos featuring them in live-action performances (yes, there was even an album featuring the WWF singing, if that's the verb, such rock classics as "Land of 1,000 Dances"). Joining him in the live-action portion was WWF announcer Gene Okerlund, who despite his nickname was the most mild-mannered person on the show. All the cartoon characters were wrestlers representing various specialties or stereotypes with the exception of Gene, including token female grapplers Moolah and Richter.

•HYPERNAUTS
Sci-Fi; Color
March 2, 1996–May 4, 1996

ABC Sat. 10–10:30 a.m. (3/2/96–5/4/96)

Cast:

Sharkey (Ricardo Alvarez)	Marc Brandon Daniel
Ace (Russell Antonov)	Glenn Herman
Max (Noriko Matsudo)	Heidi Lucas
Kulai	Carrie Dobro

Produced in association with Greengrass Productions, a division of ABC, *Hypernauts* was a visually impressive science fiction adventure yarn set sometime in the future wherein three teenage cadets from the Academy of Galactic Explorations found themselves having to defend their home planet Earth against alien invaders, the Triiad. One of its members, Paiyin the Traitor, had helped destroy the planet Pyrus. Kulai, a leathery, sex-neutral survivor of that attack, befriended the cadets in an attempt to seek revenge for the damage. The space crew included Sharkey the computer genius, Max the somewhat introverted group explorer, and Ace the occasionally overreacting pilot. Their ship was the Star Ranger 7, and its computer was named Horten.

INN NEWS—MIDDAY EDITION—See *Independent Network News—Midday Edition.*

I AM THE GREATEST: THE ADVENTURES OF MUHAMMAD ALI
Cartoon; Color
September 10, 1977–September 2, 1978

NBC Sat. 10:30–11 a.m. (9/10/77–1/28/78)
NBC Sat. 7:30–8 a.m. (2/11/78–9/2/78)

Voices:

Muhammad Ali	Himself
Frank Bannister	Himself
Nicky	Patrice Carmichael
Damon	Casey Carmichael

The first TV cartoon based on a single real-life athlete (*The Harlem Globetrotters* debuted seven years earlier), *I am the Greatest* focused on flamboyant heavyweight boxing champion Muhammad Ali. Although it used the voice of Ali, replete with his weighty statements, and the fighter's real-life public relations agent Frank Bannister, it would be a stretch to call it even semiautobiographical. Designed to appeal to kids, it had Ali participating in contrived adventures with his niece Nicky and nephew Damon, and used the typical hackneyed TV cartoon approach combining weak comedy and jumbled action.

I COVER TIMES SQUARE

Drama; B&W
January 20, 1951–October 13, 1951
ABC Sat. 12:30–1 p.m. (1/20/51–10/13/51)
Cast:
Johnny Warren   *Harold Huber*

I Cover Times Square aired first as an episode of the nighttime NBC anthology *Chevrolet Tele-Theatre* on December 26, 1949. It became an ABC nighttime series on October 5, 1950, then moved to Saturday afternoons at the start of 1951. Character actor Harold Huber played Johnny Warren, a muckraking newspaper columnist who uncovered underworld activity in New York City. Huber also produced the show, which alternated weekly with *The Faith Baldwin Theatre of Romance* beginning in April 1951 until its cancellation six months later.

I'LL BET

Game; Color
March 29, 1965–September 24, 1965
NBC Mon.–Fri. 12:30–12:55 p.m. (3/29/65–9/24/65)
Host: *Jack Narz*

On this quiz entry, celebrities and their spouses (on the debut, Mr. and Mrs. Bob Barker versus Laraine Day and her husband) played for winnings which went to charity. One member of each couple took turns in listening to a question asked on a special telephone and then wagering from 25 to 100 points on whether his or her spouse could answer the question correctly. For a correct prediction, the couple received the amount of points wagered. The first team to reach 200 points received $200 and played for another $200.

The show was revived in 1969 and syndicated as *It's Your Bet*. It went through four hosts in as many years—Hal March, Dick Gautier, Tom Kennedy, and by 1972, Lyle Waggoner.

I'LL BUY THAT

Game; B&W
June 15, 1953–July 2, 1954
CBS Various periods, starting with Mon.–Fri. 11–11:30 a.m. and ending Fri. 11–11:30 a.m.(6/15/53–7/2/54))
Host: *Mike Wallace*
Regulars: *Vanessa Brown, Audrey Meadows, Albert Moorehead, Hans Conreid (6/14/53–3/2/54), Ernie Kovacs (3/5/54–7/2/54)*

Four celebrity panelists on this game show could ask up to 30 questions about an item submitted by a guest, but there was a catch. Each "no" answer generated by a panelist's query awarded the guest $5. Contestants who managed to stump the panel could triple their winnings by answering three questions right. Items used for this guessing game ranged from a shillelagh to long underwear. Comedian Ernie Kovacs joined actresses Vanessa Brown and Audrey Meadows and bridge expert Albert Moorehead on the panel

nine months into its run as a replacement for actor Hans Conreid. This show was marked by several schedule changes in its one-year run, including one period when it aired Tuesdays and Thursdays from 2–2:30 p.m.

•I'M TELLING

Game; Color
September 12, 1987– September 3, 1988
NBC Sat. 12:30–1 p.m. (9/12/87–9/3/88)
Host: *Laurie Faso*

In this unfortunate for-children ripoff of *The Newlywed Game* (a ripoff so blatant that even *Newlywed* producer Chuck Barris filed a $5 million lawsuit again the show's production company), three pairs of brothers and sisters tried to predict each other's answers to personal questions while their sibling was offstage. As with *Newlywed*, participants were encouraged to give embarrassing responses and get angry with each other for wrong replies. The show's main difference was that the prizes at stake were higher—a $1,000 savings bond and a chance to play the Pick-a-Prize Arcade to win more than $5,000 in merchandise. Such high stakes for so trivial and exploitative an activity guaranteed *I'm Telling* a spot on the list of worst daytime shows ever. The only interesting aspect is that Laurie Faso, formerly host of the well-regarded *Marlo and the Magic Movie Machine* (q.v.), debased himself with this fiasco.

IN THE PARK

Children's; B&W
December 9, 1951–May 31, 1953
CBS Sun. 11:30 a.m.–Noon (12/9/51–5/25/52)
CBS Sun. Noon–12:30 p.m. (6/1/52–10/12/52)
CBS Sun. 11:45 a.m.–12:15 p.m. (10/19/52–1/11/53)
CBS Sun. Noon–12:30 p.m. (1/18/53–5/31/53)
Regulars: *Bill Sears, Paul Ritts, Mary Holliday*

This Philadelphia-based program had Paul Ritts, director of *Big Top* (q.v.), serving as puppeteer to such characters as pontificating Sir Geoffrey the Giraffe, whining Albert the Chipmunk, primping Magnolia the Ostrich, and Calvin the Crow, who sounded like Jimmy Durante. (Calvin, incidentally, may be the only children's puppet on daytime television who smoked cigarettes.) Actor Bill Sears sat on a bench as he talked to these zoo creatures about their stories and feelings. Mary Holliday was another puppeteer along with Ritts (she voiced Magnolia), and both of them wrote for the show.

•IN THE ZONE

Sports; Color
June 1, 1996–
Fox Sat. Noon–12:30 p.m. (6/1/96–)
Regulars: *Richard MacGregor, Valarie Rae Miller, Mike Simmrin, Zack Ward*

Just as NBC created *NBA Inside Stuff* in 1990 to promote professional basketball watching among children, Fox Sports attempted to do the same for "America's game" in this series produced in association with Major League Baseball. But while the former series opted for adult hosts from inside a studio, *In the Zone* had four youthful-looking regulars who made wisecracks and trivial small talk while introducing several features. "On Deck" previewed the day's attractions. "Away from the Plate" featured a player talking about his life in and out of the stadium (it was 20-year-old Seattle Mariners shortstop Alex Rodriguez on the debut). "Inside Pitch" gave viewers advice on how to play the game. "The Hot Corner" examined trends or people affecting pro baseball. "In a Pickle" showcased bloopers, complete with sound effects. The most interactive feature was "Cyberbase," wherein one viewer's baseball fantasies could be fulfilled by writing a request to Fox or even sending the request to the network via the Internet.

Consistent with Fox's view that baseball's ratings were hurt by coverage as drawn out as the games sometimes were, this series jazzed up its presentations with weird camera angles, jackhammer editing, and flashy graphics. Likewise, there was no interviewer seen or heard during the features, making it look as if the presenter was talking directly to the camera. It was flashy and glitzy and probably offended traditionalists, but even baseball lovers could not accuse Fox of making a boring program.

IN WHICH WE LIVE
News Documentary; Color
May 3, 1970–June 28, 1970

NBC Sun. 5:30–6 p.m. (5/3/70–6/28/70)

Host: *Edwin Newman*

In Which We Live examined ecology, featuring reports dealing with such topics as DDT, radon gas in uranium mines, and threats posed by the SST aircraft, the Alaskan pipeline, and overpopulation. Paul Simon's song "America" played at the close of each telecast.

•INCH HIGH PRIVATE EYE
Cartoon; Color
September 8, 1973–August 31, 1974

NBC Sat. 8:30–9 a.m. (9/8/73–12/29/73)
NBC Sat. 9:30–10 a.m. (1/5/74–8/31/74)

Voices:

Inch High	*Lennie Weinrib*
Lori	*Kathy Gori*
Gator	*Bob Lutell*
Mr. Finkerton	*John Stephenson*
Braveheart	*Don Messick*

Were it not for the fact that he was smaller than a thumb, investigator Inch High could have easily been mistaken for Agent Maxwell Smart of *Get Smart!* fame. Like the live-action Don Adams character of the prime-time sitcom

which ran on NBC and CBS from 1965–70, Inch had a small frame, spoke in a pinched nasal tone, and had a bumbling style of fighting crime. But he handled his height with relative ingenuity (he dialed a rotary phone using his feet in the holes, for example), and had effective help from his niece Lori. Others on the show were Gator, Lori's Gomer Pyle–type boyfriend and Inch's aide; Braveheart, Inch's St. Bernard; and Mr. Finkerton, who was head of the agency which employed Inch and who sounded like Joe Flynn. This series went into development originally for ABC in 1971.

•INCREDIBLE HULK/AMAZING SPIDER-MAN HOUR, THE
Cartoon; Color
September 19, 1982–September 7, 1985

NBC Sat. 11 a.m.–Noon (9/19/82–9/10/83)
NBC Sat. 11:30 a.m.–12:30 p.m. (9/17/83–9/8/84)
NBC Sat. Noon–1 p.m. (12/15/84–9/7/85)

Narrator: *Stan Lee*

Two of Marvel Comics' best-known characters combined forces for two seasons following one season of *Spider-Man* (see for credits and story line). The Spider-Man segments (two per show) were repeats, while the Incredible Hulk segments (one per show) were new adventures. Based loosely on the live-action CBS nighttime series of the same name which aired from March 10, 1978–June 2, 1982, *The Incredible Hulk* had Dr. Bruce Banner attempting to control a condition that caused him to be transformed, whenever he got angry, into a ripped, bulging green being known as the Incredible Hulk. His adventures in trying to cure his condition, and the use of his powers in defeating criminals, were the basis for the cartoon.

The cartoon differed from the nighttime show (in which Bill Bixby played Banner and Lou Ferrigno played the Hulk) in its explanation of the Hulk's origins and in the regulars. The cartoon Dr. Banner experimented with gamma rays at a western test site accidentally invaded by Rick Jones, a drifter in a Jeep. Banner saved Rick, but another scientist, Dr. Carlston, sabotaged the project and exposed Bruce to the rays. Carlston turned out to be a robot controlled by the insectlike alien Number One, who commanded a spider-shaped spaceship, and the Incredible Hulk defeated them both, with only Rick knowing who the Hulk really was. Assisting them was Dr. Betty Ross, who worked on Army projects and helped the men without knowing about Banner's alter ego.

Other attributes of the Hulk not found in the nighttime show were incredible jumping powers, giving the cartoon Hulk the ability to leap high and long, and the capacity for gravelly speech. A final difference was the presence of Stan Lee, creator of the comic character and TV cartoon, serving as narrator.

Three months after its original cancellation, the show returned in December 1984 for a few months as *The Incredible Hulk* without the Spider-Man sequences. A syndicated 1966 cartoon, *The Incredible Hulk,* also aired with a different cast.

The UPN network aired a new version Sunday mornings in the fall of 1996, with Lou Ferrigno, the nighttime Hulk from 1978–82, supplying the green guy's voice.

•INDEPENDENT NETWORK NEWS—MIDDAY EDITION
News; Color
October 1981–1986

Syndicated 30 minutes daily beginning October 1981

Anchors: *Claire Carter, Marvin Scott*

Independent Network News began June 9, 1980 as an arrangement which allowed some 30 nonnetwork commercial TV stations the chance to have a network-type nightly newscast thanks to the then relatively new process of feeding the program using a communications satellite. Fifteen months after its debut, a daytime version aired in most markets between 11:30 a.m. and 2 p.m. Eastern Standard Time with a different set of anchors (Steve Besh, Pat Harper, and Bill Jorgensen did the honors at nighttime). Both shows came from WPIX New York and summarized current events with live and taped reports. The main addition was "Spotlight," a five-minute interview segment with a personality from the entertainment field. The show was also known as *INN News—Midday Edition.*

INNER FLAME, THE—See *Portia Faces Life.*

INSIDE LOOK—See *Major League Baseball: An Inside Look.*

INSIDE PHOTOPLAY
Talk; B&W
January 12, 1949–March 4, 1949

DuMont Mon.–Fri. 2:30–3 p.m. (1/12/49–3/4/49)

Hostess: *Wendy Barrie*

Inside Photoplay began on WABD New York on November 1, 1948 from 4:15–4:45 p.m. Like its namesake, *Photoplay* magazine, the show emphasized movie coverage, and the debut included a profile of Rita Hayworth, a quiz segment, and a guest segment with *Photoplay* editor Adele Fletcher. When it reached network status, *Newsweek* reported that "Miss Barrie dispensed equal shares of Hollywood gossip, feminine fiddle-faddle and sugarcoated vituperation on her show amid occasional talks with guests whom she called variously 'Sweetie,' 'Pet,' and 'Dearie.'" After moving the show to nighttime TV for various runs through 1950, Barrie later returned to daytime locally for her own show on WABD in 1955.

INSIDE POLITICS
Public Affairs; B&W
September 9, 1962–November 4, 1962

ABC Sun. 1:30–2 p.m. (9/9/62–11/4/62)

Hosts: *Bill Lawrence, John Rolfson*

Inside Politics examined issues affecting the congressional races in 1962. Hosts Bill Lawrence and John Rolfson were reporters based in Washington, D.C. who introduced reports filed by various correspondents across America.

INSIDE STUFF—See *NBA Inside Stuff.*

•INSIGHT
Religious Anthology; B&W and Color
1960–1991

Syndicated 30 minutes weekly beginning Fall 1960

Host/Creator/Executive Producer: *Father Ellwood E. "Bud" Kieser*

Insight was one of TV's longest-running and most star-studded syndicated religious series. Its first season had Father Kieser, a tall (6 feet 6 inches) Paulist priest who had been chaplain of the UCLA Medical Center, delivering lectures on morality. Feeling this approach was static, he decided in 1961 he would host "theological conflict" dramas, often involving social issues, using Hollywood actors, and keep his on-camera appearance to less than three minutes. It was a radical idea, for the actors and offstage personnel would be required to donate their services, as stations were to receive free tapes of the show. But players on and offstage did come, and the results were a huge success despite the fact that the costs limited production to a range of only 5 to 14 new programs a year.

Some stories were based on fact, such as the story of Bishop Frank Ford, played by Raymond Massey, who was held in a Communist jail on charges of spying for America, and many showcased an array of well-known talent. One 1967 telecast, for example, had Barry Sullivan, Martin Milner, Howard Morris, Celeste Holm, Harold Gould, and Ted Cassidy, among other performers, with Arthur Hiller directing. Other top names who appeared over the years included Dorothy Malone and Bob Newhart (as God!), and one impressive 1977 offering featured Ed Asner, Carol Burnett, and Walter Matthau. TV veterans Robert Lansing and Efrem Zimbalist Jr. thought they did some of their best work in the medium on this series.

"A lot of people in the entertainment community do not look at *Insight* as 'religious,'" Kieser said in an interview in *Emmy* magazine in 1983. "Then again, if they're theologically sophisticated, they know it is religious, because at the deepest level it is."

With more than a quarter century of original dramas, *Insight* became the longest-running anthology series on national television. After production ended, Kieser concentrated on his Humanitas Awards, which he began in the mid-1970s to give monetary rewards to writers of nighttime network shows communicating "enriching values" to viewers.

•INSPECTOR GADGET
Cartoon; Color
November 2, 1991–August 29, 1992

CBS Sat. Noon–12:30 a.m. (11/2/91–8/29/92)

Voices:

Inspector Gadget	*Don Adams*
Penny	*Cree Summers Francks*
Brain/Dr. Claw/Madcat	*Frank Welker*
Chief Quimby	*Maurice LaMarche*

Also: *Don Francks, Dan Hennessey, Greg Duffell, Jeri Cradden, Melleny Brown*

Inspector Gadget was a gangly motorized detective in a trench coat and gloves who used apparatuses from his body to nab wrongdoers, and had such strange talents as the ability to extend his arms and inflate his body. In many ways the inspector was reminiscent of Agent Maxwell Smart, the character Don Adams played on the 1960s comedy favorite *Get Smart!* Gadget's niece Penny and pet dog Brain assisted Gadget, though they were often smarter than his bumbling tactics. A recurring enemy was the unseen Dr. Claw, who managed to escape before the end of each episode along with his pet Madcat, named in honor of Claw's group MAD (Mean and Dirty). Chief Quimby delivered each show's mission to Gadget. Also seen frequently was the inspector's somewhat cumbersome Gadgetmobile.

Inspector Gadget was in production originally for syndication in 1983–85. The show aired in repeats on the Nickelodeon cable channel from October 5, 1987 through 1992, with its last season overlapping the few months when CBS reran it as

well. On December 4, 1992, Don Adams voiced the character one more time on the NBC nighttime special "Inspector Gadget Saves Christmas."

INTERNATIONAL CHAMPIONSHIP BOXING
Sports; Color
January 29, 1978–March 29, 1981
ABC Sun. 3:15–4 or 4:30 p.m. (1/29/78–3/29/81; winters only)
Announcers: *Keith Jackson, Howard Cosell (1978–80)*

Amateur pugilists from America competed with others in their weight classes from foreign countries in this series taped at various locales in the United States.

IREENE WICKER—See *Singing Lady, The.*

•ISIS
Adventure; Color
September 17, 1977–September 2, 1978
CBS Sat. 1–1:30 p.m. (9/17/75–10/8/77)
CBS Sat. Noon–12:30 p.m. (10/15/77–1/12/78)
CBS Sat. 11:30 a.m.–Noon (1/19/78–9/2/78)

Joanna Cameron became the spirit of Egyptian goddess Isis *in this children's show.*

Regulars:

Andrea Thomas/Isis	*Joanna Cameron*
Rick Mason (1975–77)	*Brian Cutler*
Renee Carroll (1975–77)	*Ronalda Douglas*
Cindy Lee (1977–78)	*Joanna Pang*
Dr. Barnes (1977–78)	*Albert Reed*

High school teacher Andrea Thomas had a secret power she gained after discovering a golden amulet on an archaeological dig in Egypt. She found that when she said "Oh mighty Isis!" and showed the amulet, she was transformed into the ancient goddess Isis. As Isis, she flew in a white tunic with her arms turned out by her side rather than out in front like most superheroes, but despite the atypical arm position, she still managed to help right triumph over wrong and impart a moral lesson for the audience. Her pet crow was Tut. Somehow students Renee and Cindy and fellow school employees Rick and Dr. Barnes never connected her with her magical alter ego, despite the fact that both Andrea and Isis were stunning and intelligent brunette beauties.

The character first appeared in 1975–77 as part of *The Shazam!/Isis Hour* (q.v.), then became a separate series which was officially titled *The Secrets of Isis* and which offered new adventures. Isis reappeared in cartoon form in 1978 as part of *Tarzan and the Super 7* (q.v.).

ISSUES AND ANSWERS
News Interview; B&W and Color
November 27, 1960–November 8, 1981

ABC Sun. 1:30–2 p.m. (11/27/60–3/26/61)
ABC Sun. 4:30–5 p.m. (4/9/61–9/3/61)
ABC Sun. 3–3:30 p.m. (11/19/61–12/31/61)
ABC Sun. 4–4:30 p.m. (1/14/62–9/2/62)
ABC Sun. 2–2:30 p.m. (9/30/62–10/21/62)
ABC Sun. 3–3:30 p.m. (10/28/62–1/6/63)
ABC Sun. 1:30–2 p.m. (1/13/63–12/29/75)
ABC Sun. Noon–12:30 p.m. (1/11/76–11/8/81)

Regular: *Bob Clark (1975 at least)*

Creator/producer Peggy Whedon sold this long-running news show to ABC as that network's counterpart to CBS's *Face the Nation* and NBC's *Meet the Press,* but unlike those shows, *Issues and Answers* had no permanent host. Two ABC reporters questioned one newsmaker per show, with Senator Paul Douglas (D-Illinois) being the first guest. By the mid-1960s, nonpolitical types like Maurice Chevalier were occasionally making appearances.

Probably the series' biggest event was a special one-hour pre–California primary debate on Saturday, June 1, 1968, between Democratic presidential candidates Eugene McCarthy and Robert Kennedy. Four days after the show, in the wake of a celebration of his primary victory, Kennedy was assassinated.

In 1975 Bob Clark, a 10-year ABC News congressional reporter, became chief correspondent and permanent panelist on the show for a time. Barbara Walters later served the same

duties occasionally in the late 1970s. After more than two decades, *Issues and Answers* went off the air in favor of a new show, *This Week with David Brinkley.*

IT COULD BE YOU
Game; B&W and Color
June 4, 1956–December 29, 1961

NBC Mon.–Fri. 12:30–1 p.m. (6/4/56–10/7/60)
NBC Mon.–Fri. 12:30–12:55 p.m. (10/10/60–12/29/61)

Host: *Bill Leyden*
Announcer/Assistant: *Wendell Niles*
Producer: *Ralph Edwards*

It Could Be You was similar to producer Ralph Edwards's NBC nighttime series *This Is Your Life* (1952–61), though it was done with civilians instead of celebrities, was performed more

Bill Leyden hosted It Could Be You *in 1956.*

quickly, and had a more varied format. Each day at least one unknowing guest met three people from his or her past and had to identify them as part of a "reunion quiz," and other guests received unexpected surprises. Usually 10 to 15 people became participants each day, each of whom were picked out after a camera zoomed in on their faces in the audience and Wendell Niles announced, "It could be you, _____!"

On the debut, a firefighter was congratulated by people he had rescued, and a woman who had been a tomboy as a child got back her baseball mitt and other items from her youth. On a later show, twins who had long been separated were reunited. *It Could Be You* was based in Hollywood, and celebrities (like Bob Hope, who was seen during the first week) sometimes popped up as part of the surprise for a contestant. Announcer Wendell Niles assisted host Bill Leyden on the air occasionally. Leyden also sent a gift each day to a home viewer.

NBC received an average of 1,000 letters weekly suggesting participants for the show, and more than 1,000 people appeared on the show within the first four months of its run. A staff of 16 worked diligently on each segment, and often an episode which took only a minute on air required 15 manhours to set up, get the unsuspecting persons to the studio, and put them into a seat where the camera could capture them.

It Could Be You also aired on NBC as a nighttime series for various periods from July 2, 1958–September 27, 1961 with the same cast.

IT PAYS TO BE MARRIED
Game; B&W
July 4, 1955–October 28, 1955
NBC Mon.–Fri. 3:30–4 p.m. (7/4/55–10/28/55)
Host: *Bill Goodwin*

This show ran two years on NBC radio before coming to television. Three wedded couples chatted with the host about their courtship before playing the game. Stories featured might be tear-jerking (a husband who overcame near-fatal tuberculosis, and a nurse who fell in love with her patient, a paraplegic soldier) or simply unusual (a college girl who found the man she wanted to wed marching in a parade, prompting her to chase after him in the procession, and a couple who were professional babysitters). Husbands and wives received one question each to answer, and the couple answering their questions in the shortest total amount of time won a top daily jackpot of $350.

IT TAKES TWO
Game; Color
March 31, 1969–July 31, 1970
NBC Mon.–Fri. 10–10:25 a.m. (3/31/69–7/31/70)
Host: *Vin Scully*

On this Hollywood-based offering three celebrity couples (on the debut week it was Richard Long, Shelly Berman,

and Mike Connors and their wives) examined various situations that involved guessing a number, for example, the combined weight of an elephant and a Playboy bunny model. For each couple, both husband and wife came up with a number, and the two numbers were averaged. A member of the studio audience picked the couple he or she felt had the response closest to the correct number, and if right, he or she won a prize. A year after the show began, audience members could win a new car if they picked the right answer four times in a row. The show's more successful replacement was *Dinah's Place.*

IT'S A HIT
Game; B&W
June 1, 1957–September 21, 1957
CBS Sat. 11:30 a.m.–Noon (6/1/57–9/21/57)
Host/Producer: *Happy Felton*

It's a Hit was a children's game that aired in New York City as early as 1950 before coming to CBS. Competing youth from two teams swung at a baseball attached to a special shaft (to prevent anyone in the studio from being hit, one presumes!), then answered questions to "get on base." Each question's value was based on what a scoreboard said the youngster's swing was worth, ranging from foul ball to home run. Teams won points on "hits" and "runs" for correct answers. Happy Felton served as host and "umpire."

By August 17, 1957, there was a "commissioner" who ruled on the acceptability of the answers, and big-league players like Willie Mays and Don Drysdale served as "managers" for each team. Feminists, take note: This series even allowed girls to swing the bat.

IT'S A PROBLEM
Discussion; B&W
February 25, 1952–October 13, 1952
NBC Mon.–Fri. 12:30–1 p.m. (2/25/52–3/7/52)
NBC Mon.–Fri. 11:30 a.m.–Noon (3/10/52–10/13/52)
Host: *Ben Grauer*
Moderators: *Fanny Hurst, Helen Parkhurst (2/52–8/52), Alice Thompson (8/52–10/52)*

A trio of experts discussed everyday living difficulties in this show, including some rather provocative issues for the time (menopause, segregated housing, teenage sex, etc.). Authors Helen Parkhurst and Fannie Hurst alternated as moderators of the panel, with Hurst handling Tuesdays and Thursdays. The show's original title was *What's the Problem,* and it ran daily from 10:30–11 a.m. on WNBT New York starting October 1951. When NBC installed *It's in the Bag* in that time slot in January 1952, WNBT refused to carry it, and continued to air the local show. Eventually *It's a Problem* went on the network in a later time slot. Alice Thompson, editor-publisher of *Seventeen* magazine, succeeded Parkhurst in August.

IT'S ANYBODY'S GUESS
Game; Color
June 13, 1977–September 30, 1977

NBC Mon.–Fri. 11:30 a.m.–Noon (6/13/77–9/30/77)

Host: *Monty Hall*

Taking a cue from *Family Feud*, *It's Anybody Guess* had two contestants predict whether or not five members of the studio audience would be able to give the show's selected answer to a question with multiple answers. A correct prediction earned the contestant two points. A contestant could make a prediction using only three audience members, but in that case a correct prediction earned only one point. The first contestant with five points played a bonus round where he or she received $300 for every time he or she gave an answer to a questions that was not one of the two possibilities selected by the show's producers. If none of the five panelists gave one of the two preselected answers either, the contestant received a new car.

IT'S FUN TO KNOW
Children's; B&W
April 23, 1951–June 22, 1951

CBS Mon.–Fri. 4:30–5 p.m. (4/23/51–6/22/51)

Host: *Dorothy Engel Clark*

It's Fun to Know was a rather dry, boring classroom presentation of information designed for children ages 9–13, with themes for each day. For example, Monday, subtitled "The World and You," dealt with current events and history, and Wednesday, subtitled "Why?" dealt with science. The show posed no threat to *The Kate Smith Hour* on NBC and perished after two months.

IT'S HAPPENING
Music; Color
January 6, 1968–September 20, 1969

ABC Sat. 1:30–2 p.m. (1/6/68–9/7/68)
ABC Mon.–Fri. 1:30–1:55 p.m. (7/15/68–10/25/68)
ABC Sat. 1:30–2 p.m. (1/4/69–9/20/69)

Regulars: *Mark Lindsay, Paul Revere, Kathy Orloff (1968), Keith Rogers (1968)*

Producer: *Dick Clark*

Titled *Happening '68* in its Saturday slot, *It's Happening* was the second daytime show from Dick Clark Productions to use Paul Revere and the Raiders; the first was *Where the Action Is* (q.v.). The format was similar to *Action*, with the main difference being that guests and the studio audience were on a soundstage rather than on location. In the summer of 1968 the show expanded to six days a week, and the opener on July 15 had such unlikely "happening" guests as Joey Bishop, Regis Philbin, Don Adams, and Don Rickles. Kathy Orloff provided gossip, and model Keith Rogers handled the "Style Faire" segment in the daily shows, which fared poorly against *As the World Turns* on CBS. After a layoff in the fall of 1968 due to *NCAA Football*, the show returned in 1969 in the time slot following the show whose success it could only hope to emulate, *American Bandstand*.

IT'S IN THE BAG
Game; B&W
November 16, 1950–February 15, 1952

DuMont Thu. 1:30–2 p.m. (11/16/50–7/5/51)
NBC Mon.–Fri. 10:30–11 a.m. (1/14/52–2/15/52)

Regulars: *Win Elliot (1950–51), Don Russell (at least May 1951–1952), the Jesters, Florence Morris (1950–probably 1951), Arlene James (1952)*

Based on a radio game show, *It's in the Bag* posed questions to two female contestants (three on NBC), who got items in a paper bag, taken from a grocery-store set, each time they gave a correct answer. Between the question sessions by Win Elliot and later Don Russell came music from singer Florence Morris (replaced by Arlene James on NBC) and the Jesters, a quartet led by Red Latham. An early contest for home viewers involved awarding a $100 war bond to whoever came up with the best name for the show's fictional grocery store.

When it switched networks, *It's in the Bag* did not air on NBC's New York affiliate, which preferred its local show *It's Your Problem*. That series eventually superseded *It's in the Bag* on the network schedule.

•IT'S PUNKY BREWSTER
Cartoon; Color
September 14, 1985–September 2, 1989

NBC Sat. 10:30–11 a.m. (9/14/85–10/18/86)
NBC Sat. 11:30 a.m.–Noon (10/25/86–9/5/87)
NBC Sat. Noon–12:30 p.m. (10/29/88–9/2/89)

Voices:

Penelope "Punky" Brewster	Soleil Moon-Frye
Cherie Johnson	Herself
Margaux Kramer	Ami Foster
Allen Anderson	Casey Ellison
Henry Warnimont	George Gaynes
Glomer	Frank Welker

In its original incarnation, *Punky Brewster* was a critically reviled, low-rated sitcom that NBC aired Sunday nights from September 16, 1984–September 7, 1986 against CBS's hit *60 Minutes*. But it had a faithful core audience of children, so NBC had no problem in adding a cartoon adaptation using most of the nighttime cast. As with the sitcom, it featured Punky Brewster, an agreeable elementary-age child with pigtails who took part in occasional misadventures with her pals Cherie, Margaux, and Allen. Her guardian, Henry Warnimont, was somewhat past middle age, and she had a pet dog named Brandon (supposedly in honor of NBC President Brandon Tartikoff). All the actors from the sitcom voiced their characters on the cartoon, but Glomer, a gopherlike creature found in an enchanted village at the end of a rainbow, was new. Glomer had somewhat out-of-control magical abilities which he used to let Punky and company visit other lands. *It's Punky Brewster* ran for two years in original episodes and then in repeats from 1988–89.

IT'S TIME FOR ERNIE—See *Ernie Kovacs Show, The.*

J

•JABBERJAW
Cartoon; Color
September 11, 1976–September 3, 1978

ABC Sat. 9–9:30 a.m. (9/11/76–11/27/76)
ABC Sat. 8:30–9 a.m. (12/4/76–9/3/77)
ABC Sun. 10:30–11 a.m. (9/11/77–9/3/78)

Cast:

Jabberjaw	Frank Welker
Biff	Tommy Cook
Shelly	Pat Paris
Bubbles	Julie McWhirter
Clam-Head	Barry Gordon

In this obvious knockoff of the 1975 hit movie *Jaws*, *Jabberjaw* featured a shark living 100 years in the future with a motley crew of teenage pals in an underwater world. He served as drummer for the teenagers' rock band, the Neptunes, which was also comprised of guitarist Biff, the nominal leader; tambourine player Shelly, the narcissist; pianist Bubbles, an airhead à la Gracie Burns; and cellist Clam-Head, the Shaggy-type character (see *Scooby Doo, Where Are You?*). Jabberjaw and the gang rode in the Aquacar to their concert dates and invariably got caught up with criminals who pursued them unsuccessfully in chase scenes to the background beat of bubblegum rock. Jabberjaw constantly whined, "I don't get no respect!" but he hardly deserved it, as his actions and speech patterns were such a blatant copy of Curly Howard of the Three Stooges that the late comic's estate probably could have sued successfully for theft of intellectual property. The 1977–78 season consisted of repeats.

•JACK LA LANNE
Exercise; B&W and Color
1956–1970; 1982

Syndicated 30 minutes daily beginning 1956

Host: *Jack La Lanne*

One of TV's longest-running exercise shows, *Jack La Lanne* began as a local San Francisco show in 1951 before going national five years later when he moved it to Los Angeles. Dressed in a tight-fitting dark gray gym suit, La Lanne often used a chair in doing his exercises, and regularly hawked his

line of products and gym stores on the show. Typically, La Lanne barked out his instructions, including saying to children who were watching, "OK, kiddies, go get mama." Dave Bacal played the organ music offstage which accompanied La Lanne's instructions. After the show ended, La Lanne prepped 195 new shows for syndication in 1982, then popped up occasionally on various TV shows, including an infomercial and a commercial for America Online in the 1990s.

•JACK PAAR SHOW
Variety; B&W
November 13, 1953–May 25, 1956

CBS Fri. 10–11 a.m. (11/13/53–7/2/54)
CBS Mon.–Fri. 1–1:30 p.m. (7/4/55–5/25/56)

Regulars: *Jack Paar, Betty Clooney (11/13/53–1954 at least), Clark Dennis (11/13/53 at least), Pupi Campo (11/13/53 at least), Edie Adams (1955–56 at least), Jack Haskell (1955–56 at least), Jose Melis and Trio (1954–56)*

Jack Paar tried radio in 1947 (with a different eponymous show on NBC), then movies before finally finding his niche as a television personality of the 1950s. He first hosted two nighttime game shows (*Up to Paar* in 1952 and *Bank on the Stars* in 1953) before getting his own daytime TV show. On its debut Paar told his audience about how he had moved to his new base of New York City after seven years in Hollywood, then delivered a monologue about his wife and about Randy, his daughter. Clooney and Dennis were vocalists, while Campo did some sketches with Paar as well as conducting and playing with his orchestra. A regular segment was "Advice to America," where Paar answered supposed letters to the editor.

After six months Paar moved his show to nighttime on CBS from July 17–September 4, 1954, while also serving part of that time as host of *The Morning Show*. He transferred his cast from *The Morning Show* when he received another daytime series in 1955. The Independence Day opener had a takeoff on *This Is Your Life*, as well as comedy sketches, including one in which Davy Crockett was being interviewed at an unemployment office, plus monologues and music. Paar continued the format through the next year, but real success for him in television came when he took over as host of *The Tonight Show* on NBC late night from July 29, 1957–March 30, 1962. He then hosted a nighttime NBC variety show from September 21, 1962–September 10, 1965, after which he more or less retired from show business.

•JACKPOT
Game; Color
January 7, 1974–September 26, 1975

NBC Mon.–Fri. Noon–12:30 p.m. (1/7/74–7/4/75)
NBC Mon.–Fri. 12:30–1 p.m. (7/7/75–9/26/75)

Host: *Geoff Edwards*

Jackpot holds the record for a network game show featuring the most contestants. Fifteen players sat on three rows of seats (six on top, five in the middle, and four on the bottom) while another contestant on a podium called their individual placement numbers. Each called player revealed a cash amount and a riddle the contestant on the podium had to answer to remain at the position. A correct response added the riddle's cash amount to the pot for the podium contestant and let that player continue his or her questioning. Podium players could win the money in the pot by calling the number of the player with the riddle whose money amount was "Jackpot." A correct answer to that riddle split the money in the pot between the questioner and the podium player. An incorrect answer at any point forced the podium player to switch positions with the questioner, with the latter continuing to build the current pot using the remaining uncalled players. The only exception was if the question missed was the "Jackpot" one, in which case the pot was emptied and the 15 seated players received a new round of riddles.

An extra feature was the "Super Jackpot," which involved a target number which could be attained by answering riddles with certain cash amounts whose total matched the target number. Once that match occurred, a player could try to find the "Jackpot" riddle and answer it to win the "Super Jackpot," which could be up to $50,000. The level for just the "Jackpot" payoffs usually was no more than a few thousand dollars. Players competed for a full working week and received their week's total winnings on Fridays.

After a so-so showing as a network offering, *Jackpot* reappeared on the USA Cable channel from September 30, 1985–December 30, 1988 with Mike Darrow as host. In 1989 a new version aired in syndication with Geoff Edwards back as moderator.

•JACKSON FIVE, THE
Cartoon; Color
September 11, 1971–September 1, 1973

ABC Sat. 9:30–10 a.m. (9/11/71–9/2/72)
ABC Sat. 8:30–9 a.m. (9/9/72–9/1/73)

Voices:
The Jackson Five (Michael, Jackie,
    Tito, Jermaine, and David)   *Themselves*

The popular Jackson Five soul recording group, coming off four consecutive Number One pop hits in 1970 ("I Want You Back," "ABC," "The Love You Save," and "I'll Be There"), became the second musical group after the Beatles to be used as the basis for a Saturday morning cartoon series. Like its predecessor, it was nothing more than a series of fictional comic misadventures, this time involving the young quintet of brothers from Gary, Indiana, with the use of at least one song per show (one visually dazzling sequence was the one for "ABC," an appropriate effort given which network was airing the show). The second season consisted of repeats. The cable channel MTV also

aired repeats for a period in the mid-1980s in the wake of Michael Jackson's massive popularity as a solo singer.

JAMAICA RACES—See *NBC Takes You to the Races.*

JAMBO
Children's; Color
September 6, 1969–September 4, 1971

NBC Sat. 11:30 a.m.–Noon (9/6/69–12/20/69)
NBC Sat. Noon–12:30 p.m. (1/3/70–9/5/70)
NBC Sat. 12:30–1 p.m. (9/12/70–9/4/71)

Host: *Marshall Thompson*

Jambo is Swahili for "hello," or "greetings." This series showed films of animals in the wild. Host Marshall Thompson had starred on the CBS animal adventure nighttime series *Daktari* from January 11, 1966–January 15, 1969, and one of his simian co-stars on that show, Judy the chimp, served as a regular on this program as well.

JAMES PIKE
Religious; B&W
October 9, 1955–May 15, 1960

ABC Sun. 1:30–2 p.m. (10/9/55–12/11/55)
ABC Sun. 4–4:30 p.m. (12/18/55–5/27/56)
ABC Sun. 5–5:30 p.m. (11/11/56–6/9/57)
ABC Sun. 3:30–4 p.m. (10/6/57–12/29/57)
ABC Sun. Noon–12:30 p.m. (10/26/58–6/14/59)
ABC Sun. 12:30–1 p.m. (10/11/59–5/15/60)

Host: *Rev. James A. Pike*

Dean, and later Bishop, James Pike was one of the most thought-provoking and controversial religious figures on television. He began in the Episcopal ministry in 1942, becoming an ordained deacon in 1944 and a priest in 1946. In 1952 the Very Reverend Dr. Pike became Dean of the Cathedral of St. John the Divine in New York City, the post he held when his series began. Pike interviewed guests about modern moral issues. His wife Ester offered her input in roughly two out of every three shows, and his teenage daughter Cathy turned up when the topic was specifically geared to young people. But the show was not just a family affair, nor was it limited to nonsecular issues. Pike liked to invite nontheologian celebrities he considered to be "great thinkers," such as writers Erle Stanley Gardner and Aldous Huxley and Nobel Prize-winning scientist Dr. Linus Pauling to his discussions, giving the show a grittier tone than most others in the genre. In fact, one 1959 show on suicide was too graphic for ABC and did not air.

In the fall of 1958 Pike went to a new post, as the fifth California bishop of the Protestant Episcopal Church, but his public support for liberal attitudes involving civil rights for minorities, women, and homosexuals did not sit well with the church hierarchy. In the fall of 1960 ABC decided to do a new religion series (see *Directions*), and dropped *James Pike*. Pike's growing dissatisfaction with conventional religion culminated in 1966 when his teenage son committed suicide and Pike used mediums to try to contact the boy. He left his post as bishop the same year. Three years later, Pike traveled to Israel, and in September 1969, he died while on a desert trek. Pike was only 56 at the time of his death.

JAN MURRAY SHOW, THE

Game; Color

September 5, 1960–September 28, 1962

NBC Mon.–Fri. 2–2:30 p.m. (9/5/60–12/29/61)

NBC Mon.–Fri. 2–2:25 p.m. (1/2/62–9/28/62)

Regulars: *Jan Murray, Maureen Arthur, Morgan Schmitter, Milton DeLugg and His Orchestra*

The Jan Murray Show, the eponymous title of which was a rarity for a game show, began with two players selecting prizes they wanted as part of their "charge account" for the game. Each contestant then received his or her own bingo-style grid of four squares down and across and decided where to place 16 different scrambled letters as host Jan Murray announced them, with the object being to make as many three- and four-letter words as possible. Morgan Schmitter, a Columbia University professor of English and comparative literature, kept score and judged the veracity of the answers, with correct three-letter words earning $10 each and four-letter words earning $25 each, for the player's account. Unlike most game shows, even the loser could "buy" the prizes he or she had specified at the start of the game, using the money raised in the game (the winner got the chance to play another game).

Between game segments, Maureen Arthur served as a combination model, singer, comedienne, and impersonator of Marilyn Monroe. The show was also known by its subtitle *Charge Account.*

•JANE WHITNEY SHOW, THE

Talk; Color

January 17, 1994–October 7, 1994

NBC Mon.–Fri. 11 a.m.–Noon (1/17/94–10/7/94)

Host: *Jane Whitney*

Pert blonde ex-Philadelphia news anchor Jane Whitney arrived on NBC as an Oprah clone following a somewhat convoluted production history. Her show began in nightly syndication in March of 1992; it was taped in Boston and aired under the title *Night Talk with Jane Whitney.* By June 1992, retitled *The Jane Whitney Show* and examining just one subject per show, the program began taping in New York. Although it was now aimed more at a daytime audience, most stations still aired the show late at night. Following its syndication cancellation in December 1993, it moved to NBC for an eight-month run.

•JASON OF STAR COMMAND

Science Fiction; Color

September 15, 1979–September 5, 1981

CBS Sat. Noon–12:30 p.m. (9/15/79–12/29/79)

CBS Sun. 8:30–9 a.m. (1/6/80–3/8/81)

CBS Sat. 1–1:30 p.m. (3/14/81–9/5/81)

Cast:

Jason	*Craig Littler*
Commander Canarvin (1978–79)	*James Doohan*
Commander Stone (1979–81)	*John Russell*
Nicole Davidoff (1978–79)	*Susan O'Hanlin*
Dr. E. J. Parsafoot	*Charlie Dell*
Dragos	*Sid Haig*
Samantha (1979–81)	*Tamara Dobson*

Jason of Star Command first blasted off as a live-action segment on *Tarzan and the Super Seven* from 1978–79 before spending two years as a separate show. It was something of a throwback to the space series of the 1950s, although there were a few modern touches, the most notable of which was the casting of James Doohan, formerly Engineer Scott on *Star Trek,* as the first commander of *The Starfire.* The show's real focal point, though, was Jason, the intrepid, handsome member of Star Command, a law enforcement agency for the galaxy 200 years in the future. His friend was the shapely Nicole Davidoff, replaced by Samantha in 1979, while Dr. Parsafoot was a bushy-browed inventor. Their regular nemesis was Dragos, a towering, bearded figure.

Due to high production costs (about $200,000 per episode) only 12 shows were produced for the 1979–81 run, even though some footage was recycled from *Space Academy* (q.v.).

•JEANNIE

Cartoon; Color

September 8, 1973–August 30, 1975

CBS Sat. 10:30–11 a.m. (9/8/73–8/31/74)

CBS Sat. 9–9:30 a.m. (9/7/74–8/30/75)

Voices:

Jeannie	*Julie McWhirter*
Corry Anders	*Mark Hamill*
Babu	*Joe Besser*
Henry Glopp	*Bob Hastings*
Mrs. Anders	*Janet Waldo*

Three years after going to rerun heaven, the sitcom *I Dream of Jeannie,* aired on NBC nighttime from September 16, 1965–September 1, 1970, received a revival in cartoon form using none of the original actors. Here Jeannie, a genie in a bottle, had as her "master" surfer Corry Anders, who released her from being trapped by removing the top of the bottle when he found it on the beach. In turn, Jeannie and Babu, her inept fellow genie, pledged to serve Corry's wishes, often with unintentionally disastrous consequences (on one episode things were so jumbled that Jeannie had to reverse everything that had happened by going backward in time).

Jeannie whipped her ponytail for magic, while Babu gestured and uttered, "Yabble dabble" to do his work. Henry, Corry's fellow student at Century High School, knew of the situation but told no one else, including Corry's unsuspecting mother Mrs. Anders. The second season consisted of repeats.

•JENNY JONES SHOW, THE
Talk; Color
1991–

Syndicated 60 minutes daily beginning September 1991

Hostess: *Jenny Jones*

Comedian Jenny Jones dropped her nightclub act to be another Oprah Winfrey clone in a show based in Oprah's home TV city, Chicago. After one season as a light celebrity-oriented entry, the series became a standard-issue 1990s-style collection of outrageous situations and guests making bizarre claims, but it outdid its competitors in an unfortunate taping during its run. On March 6, 1995, the topic was "Secret Admirers," and guest Scott Amedure confessed that the object of his hidden affection was his friend Jonathan Schmitz. Three days later Schmitz, who claimed the show deceived him by saying his secret admirer would be a woman, was charged with killing Amedure. After the incident, Jones insisted that Schmitz knew it could be a man and expressed regret over the situation. The show never aired, but the controversy prompted talk about how tawdry and pathetic the genre had become, and sparked a lawsuit against the show. Nevertheless, in the mid-1990s *The Jenny Jones Show* was still in production and was still a top-rated offering.

•JEOPARDY!
Game; Color
March 30, 1964–March 2, 1979

NBC Mon.–Fri. 11:30 a.m.–Noon (3/30/64–9/24/65)
NBC Mon.–Fri. Noon–12:30 p.m. (9/27/65–1/4/74)
NBC Mon.–Fri. 10:30–11 a.m. (1/7/74–6/28/74)
NBC Mon.–Fri. 1:30–2 p.m. (7/1/74–1/3/75)
NBC Mon.–Fri. 10:30–11 a.m. (10/2/78–1/5/79)
NBC Mon.–Fri. Noon–12:30 p.m. (1/8/79–3/2/79)

Host: *Art Fleming*

In 1993 *TV Guide* proclaimed this series to be TV's all-time best game show, and it would be hard to disagree. Unlike most examples of the genre, *Jeopardy!* contestants were not either foolishly overexuberant or dull, the host was not frenetic or pandering, and the game was not laden with gimmicks. Three players came on camera one by one at the start of the show, followed by the host who revealed a board with five columns of categories. Each column contained five hidden "answers" relevant to the category in the amounts of $10, $20, $30, $40, and $50. The first contestant to hit a buzzer after the answer was revealed had to give the proper response in question form (for example, category: Hail to the Chief; answer: Surveyed parts of the

Shenandoah Valley in Virginia; correct question: "Who was George Washington?") to win that answer's money amount. A wrong response meant that amount was subtracted from a player's score, hence the "jeopardy" part of the game. (It also earned the player a civil "No, sorry," response from Art Fleming, perhaps the most sincere-sounding game show host ever on television.) The "last correct questioner" controlled which category and dollar amount would be revealed. After all the answers had been revealed or time ran out, players took part in the Double Jeopardy round, where dollar amounts doubled. There was also one "daily double" answer in the first round, as well as two in the second round, on which players could bet any or all of their previous earnings.

At the end of the show came Final Jeopardy, where a category was revealed and players bet any or all of their winnings before a commercial, then received an answer

Art Fleming served as emcee of Jeopardy *from 1964–75 and 1978–79.*

and had to write the correct question within a short period (behind some of producer Merv Griffin's "think music") to win the money they had bet. The highest money earner received his or her earnings and came back the next day.

Jeopardy! ran successfully for a decade or so in its noontime slot on the East Coast before NBC executives made the stupid move of tinkering with its location in 1974, causing audience share to drop, and the show to be canceled within a year. There was a syndicated version of the show from 1974–75 with Fleming as host.

In 1977 CBS announced plans to revive the show, but the series did not come back until two years later on NBC. That version had an elimination feature whereby only the two top scorers played Double Jeopardy. The winner of that round played Super Jeopardy, a bingo-style bonus where to win $5,000 one had to answer five questions in a row horizontally, vertically, or diagonally from five categories on the board. That incarnation lasted less than half a year.

In 1984, following well-received cameos by Fleming doing *Jeopardy!* in the movie *Airplane II* and in the weird Al Yankovic music spoof "I Lost on Jeopardy," Merv Griffin Productions revived the game as a nightly syndicated offering sold in tandem with the hit *Wheel of Fortune* (q.v.). Here Alex Trebek hosted, and a new board with electronic monitors and cash values 10 times the amount of the original appeared. The rules were the same as the 1964–75 version, including Final Jeopardy. The revival was a huge success and spawned an ABC nighttime series from June 16–September 8, 1990 called *Super Jeopardy!* in which winners from the revival competed for a $250,000 grand prize. As of this writing, the syndicated series remains in production.

•JERRY FALWELL
Religious; Color
1971–

Syndicated 30 minutes weekly beginning 1971

Host: *The Rev. Jerry Falwell*

The Rev. Jerry Falwell had a relatively anonymous syndicated religious series in the 1970s before he became a major force in right-wing politics in the 1980s. He founded his main religious post, Thomas Road Baptist Church in Lynchburg, Virginia, in 1956, and later established the Christian-based Liberty Baptist College there. He began appearing on local television in 1957 on a show titled *The Old-Time Gospel Hour,* which became the original name for the syndicated series 14 years later. But he really made no waves until June 1979, when he founded the Moral Majority, a coalition calling for implementation of strongly conservative religious values by government. The win of Ronald Reagan as President and several conservative Republicans in the U.S. Senate in 1980 gave his group increased attention, and Falwell received as much TV exposure on secular news and talk shows as he did from his own series.

Despite the free publicity, Falwell never sought election for any government office. That was perhaps surprising, but critics were even more surprised when he announced the dissolution of the Moral Majority in June 1989. Before that, he took over *The PTL Club* (q.v.) briefly in 1987 following the fall of the Bakkers. Falwell continued preaching as a major televangelist into the 1990s without garnering as much publicity as he had during the previous decade, but obvious disgust at all things liberal continued to permeate his sermons. What Fallwell may do next is anyone's guess.

JERRY LESTER SHOW, THE
Variety; B&W
September 28, 1953–May 14, 1954
ABC Mon.–Fri. 3–4 p.m. (9/28/53–5/14/54)

Regulars: *Jerry Lester, Leon Belasco, Kathy Collin, Lorenzo Fuller, Ellie Russell, the Buddy Weed Orchestra*

This unspectacular effort was another of ABC's daytime disasters in the early 1950s. It starred comedian Jerry Lester, formerly host of NBC's pioneering late night series *Broadway Open House* from 1950–51, along with violinist Leon Belasco and three little-known singers as regulars. Lester gave the impression on air he did not care much for the series. On its debut he joked, "When this show gets a rating, we'll move to another network." Neither occurred, and Lester was seen only infrequently on television after this series.

•JERRY SPRINGER
Talk; Color
1991–

Syndicated 60 minutes daily beginning September 1991

Host: *Jerry Springer*

Jerry Springer was the quintessential "sleaze" talk show of the 1990s, though it did not start out that way. Mild-mannered and bespectacled, the middle-aged Springer, whose style and looks were reminiscent of a serious Wally Cox, served as a councilman and mayor of Cincinnati in the 1970s, then went into TV reporting on that city's WLWT from 1982 until starting his talk show, in Chicago, nearly a decade later. At first the program was a junior-league *Donahue,* but by its third year, sporting a rowdy reactive studio audience in Chicago, *Jerry Springer* had become a loud, raucous affair with provocative show titles along the lines of "My In-Laws Hate You!" and guests who came across as belligerent, ignorant, or both as they explained their feelings. Springer himself often did nothing to control the frequent verbal and occasionally physical outbursts of anger, preferring instead to let them run their course until stagehands had to intercede. After questions from him and the audience to guests, Springer offered his own thoughts about the day's topic in a relatively meek wrap-up, followed by an enthusiastic close featuring the audience whipping itself into a frenzy and shots of them cheering for Jerry.

In the mid-1990s, with criticism of the talk show genre reaching a fever pitch among some politicians and viewers, Springer defended his program steadfastly while enjoying okay but not great ratings. "We get 3,000 to 4,000 phone calls a day at an 800 number—both suggestions for shows and people who want to be on," he told James Brady in *Parade* magazine in 1996. "Our producers are told, 'Pick out the ones that are the most outrageous but also truthful.' It has to be truthful and interesting and, for our show, it must be outrageous. If it's normal living, that's not what our show is all about." Let the viewer beware.

JET JACKSON, FLYING COMMANDO—See *Captain Midnight*.

•JETSONS, THE
Cartoon; Color
September 21, 1963–April 2, 1983

ABC Sat. 10:30–11 a.m. (9/21/63–4/18/64)
CBS Sat. 11:30 a.m.–Noon (9/26/64–9/18/65)
NBC Sat. 9–9:30 a.m. (10/2/65–9/3/66)
NBC Sat. 11:30 a.m.–Noon (9/10/66–9/2/67)
CBS Sat. 8–8:30 a.m. (9/13/69–9/5/70)
CBS Sat. 1:30–2 p.m. (9/12/70–9/4/71)
NBC Sat. 12:30–1 p.m. (9/11/71–12/25/71)
NBC Sat. 10–10:30 a.m. (1/8/72–9/2/72)

NBC Sat. 8:30–9 a.m. (9/9/72–12/16/72)
NBC Sat. 9–9:30 a.m. (12/23/72–9/1/73)
NBC Sat. Noon–12:30 p.m. (9/8/73–8/30/75)
NBC Sat. Noon–12:30 p.m. (10/25/75–9/4/76)
NBC Sat. Various half hours between 11:30 a.m. and 1 p.m. (2/3/79–9/5/81)
NBC Sat. Noon–12:30 p.m. (9/18/82–4/2/83)

Voices:

George Jetson	*George O'Hanlon*
Jane Jetson	*Penny Singleton*
Judy Jetson	*Janet Waldo*
Elroy Jetson	*Daws Butler*
Astro	*Don Messick*
Cosmo G. Spacely	*Mel Blanc*

Producers: *William Hanna and Joseph Barbera*

The Jetsons is the nighttime cartoon show having the highest number of repeats on Saturday morning network television. It aired first on ABC nighttime from September 23, 1962–September 8, 1963, when it flopped against *Walt Disney's Wonderful World of Color* on NBC. Nevertheless, that season's 24 episodes provided a collection that would remain almost constantly in reruns over the next 20 years.

The cartoon's central family was similar to many 1960s sitcom families, with a rather bumbling dad (George), a devoted wife who was a bit of a spendthrift (Jane), a free-spirited teenage daughter (Judy), and an inquisitive son

The Jetsons *were, from left, Judy, George, Jane, Elroy, and Astro.*

(beanie-wearing Elroy). What made *The Jetsons* stand out was its view of the 21st century—which the family inhabited—as an automated heaven. The Jetsons lived amid the clouds in a towering apartment complex replete with automatically opening doors and buttons that could be pushed to receive nearly every imaginable convenience, from food to personal hygiene products. Astro the family dog took walks on a conveyer belt outside the apartment. And in the memorable opening sequence, George drove a bubble car to take Elroy to Little Dipper School, Judy to Orbit High, and Jane to a shopper's paradise, after which he drove to his workplace, where the car converted into an attaché case. Cosmo G. Spacely was George's blustering, diminutive boss at Spacely Space Sprockets. Seen occasionally was Rosie, voiced by Jean VanderPyl, the Jetsons' robot maid who constantly apologized for her unintentional mishaps.

In 1985, Hanna-Barbera Productions created 41 new episodes of the series to allow the program to run 13 weeks daily of original shows in syndication. Frank Welker voiced the character of Orbity, a gremlin space elf pet, and most of the cast returned for the series. They did the same in 1988 for a home video entitled *The Jetsons Meet the Flintstones,* wherein characters from two of Hanna-Barbera's, and TV's, most successful cartoon series met for the first time thanks to a time machine which Elroy built. In 1990 came *Jetsons: The Movie* with the voices of O'Hanlon, Singleton, Blanc, and Butler (Butler died in 1988, and O'Hanlon and Blanc both died in 1989). It was a critical and commercial flop. However, plans for a live action film adaptation of the series were announced in 1996.

JIM HENSON'S ANIMAL SHOW WITH STINKY AND JAKE—See *Cubhouse.*

JIM HENSON'S DOG CITY—See *Dog City.*

JIM HENSON'S FRAGGLE ROCK—See *Fraggle Rock.*

JIM HENSON'S MUPPET BABIES—See *Muppet Babies.*

JIM LEE'S WILDC.A.T.S—See *WildC.A.T.S.*

JIMMY DEAN SHOW, THE
Musical Variety; B&W
April 8, 1957–June 26, 1959

CBS Mon.–Fri. 7–7:45 a.m. (4/8/57–9/27/57)
CBS Mon.–Fri. 7–7:45 a.m. and Sat. Noon–1 p.m. (9/28/57–12/14/57)
CBS Sat. Noon–1 p.m. (12/21/57–8/30/58)
CBS Mon.–Fri. 2–2:30 p.m. (9/15/58–6/26/59)

Regulars: *Jimmy Dean, Alec Houston, Billie Graves (1957 at least), Dick Flood (1957 at least), the Texas Wildcats (1957 at least), Herbie Jones (9/15/58 at least), the Double Daters (9/15/58–10/13/58), the Noteworthies (10/13/58 at least), the Joel Harron Orchestra (9/15/58 at least)*

Before making his mark as a pop/country artist ("Big Bad John" was a hit in 1961) and lending his name to a line of pork products, Jimmy Dean spent much of the 1950s trying to make a name for himself on television. In 1956 Dean and his musical group the Texas Wildcats starred in a weekly syndicated series called *Town and Country Time,* available in 52 15-minute shows or 26 half-hour shows. The following year the same bunch came to CBS early morning (some stations aired kinescopes in the afternoon) with a few new regulars, such as ventriloquist Alec Houston and his dummy Elmer, and mostly musical guests, such as Andy Williams and the Fontane Sisters. From June 22–September 14, 1957, this Washington, D.C.–based show aired six days a week, plus Saturday nights on CBS.

By September 1958 Dean was in New York City with an almost new cast including guitarist Herbie Jones and the male-female singing quartet the Double Daters (replaced in October by the Noteworthies, a three-man, two-woman vocal/instrumental quintet). One of the last guests was country singer Patsy Cline on June 8, 1959. Dean later did an ABC nighttime show from September 19, 1963–April 1, 1966. But apart from his TV commercials for Jimmy Dean sausages, hams, etc., his TV appearances have been rare since then.

JIMMY SWAGGART
Religious; Color
1977–

Syndicated 30 minutes daily and 60 minutes weekly beginning 1977

Host: *The Rev. Jimmy Swaggart*

One of several televangelists caught up in a scandal in the 1980s, the Rev. Jimmy Swaggart proved to be as controversial a headline maker as his rambunctious cousin, rock 'n' roll legend Jerry Lee Lewis. He built his religious following in Baton Rouge, Louisiana, with a Bible college, even though he had never finished high school. His ministry expanded successfully in national syndication during the 1980s, and stations could use his hour-long Sunday sermon show and/or his daily half-hour show, which featured interpretations of the scripture and had the official title of *A Study in the Word.* But in the late 1980s, his popularity stopped increasing, then dropped dramatically, thanks to his involvement in some highly publicized events.

In 1987 Swaggart had a hand in revealing the adulterous activities of Rev. Marvin Gorman, a local New Orleans TV preacher, and Jim Bakker of *The PTL Club* (q.v.). Swaggert vociferously denounced both men's doings and placed himself on the moral high ground. Asked to comment in *TV Guide* in August 1987 on the current scandals bothering Bakker et al., he said, "I don't care how many doctorates you have! When you make the wrong choice, you fail!" These words, and other statements, would come back to haunt him.

Reverend Gorman refused to go down without a fight, and retaliated by obtaining photos of Swaggert going into motel rooms with a New Orleans prostitute named Debra Jo Murphree. Faced with the evidence, Swaggart, tears streaming down his face, told his stunned congregation in February 1988, "I have sinned against you." Many followers took his apology at face value, while more jaded observers mocked it, most hilariously Robin Williams in a spoof on the Academy Awards show. To add insult to injury, Murphree discussed her activities on talk shows like *Donahue* and appeared naked in a *Penthouse* photo spread, where she was represented reenacting certain activities while a male model representing Swaggart looked on. Officials with the Assemblies of God denomination in which Swaggart preached were appalled by the publicity and ordered him to step down from office.

In late 1988 Swaggart, who had been off the air for only three months, returned to his TV pulpit. Fewer affiliates carried the show, however, and when Swaggart announced a few years later that he had had another adulterous tryst (this time blaming it on the devil), both stations and true believers continued to dwindle. As of this writing, his series still airs in a few markets.

•JOAN RIVERS SHOW, THE
Talk; Color
1969; Fall 1989–Spring 1994

Syndicated 30 minutes daily beginning March 1969 and 60 minutes daily beginning September 1989

Host: *Joan Rivers*

Comedienne Joan Rivers had two separate daytime talk shows at wildly divergent points in her up-and-down career. The 1969 series, officially titled *That Show with Joan Rivers*, featured her as a rising comic talent hot off gigs on *The Tonight Show* and *The Ed Sullivan Show.* She performed a monologue at the start of the show, then had a celebrity guest join her in examining another guest whose occupation or hobby was the focus of the day's show. Actor James Earl Jones, for example, appeared in a mock argument with Joan on a show featuring a psychotherapist expert on marital fights. Johnny Carson, whose late night show gave Joan her big break, also guested.

It was Joan's relationship with Carson which led to her next daytime show 20 years later. In 1986, after three years of being permanent guest hostess of *The Tonight Show,* she took an offer by the then-fledgling Fox network to host a late-night program against Carson. It bombed after a year, and not long afterward her husband committed suicide. After a fruitless two-year period of activity where her main work was serving as the center square of the syndicated *Hollywood Squares,* she returned to daytime in a show that was, as her prior effort had been, based in New York City. As before, she did a monologue and featured celebrity guests, but as time wore on the show added a gossip report from a daily rotating group of correspondents and featured more theme shows on controversial topics. The show was sent to stations live via satellite beginning April 30, 1990.

Two months later, Rivers won her first Emmy for her work and accepted it with an emotional speech.

As Rivers's ratings in the fall of 1993 plummeted, the show changed itself into a home shopping series similar to the ones proliferating on cable, with guests coming by to hawk their products to home viewers. *Can We Shop?,* which debuted in January 1994, was a total flop, and the show had wrapped production by that summer. Rivers went back to a performing career, including a Tony-nominated performance on Broadway as Lenny Bruce's mother and a 1994 TV movie about her tumultuous life.

JOE DiMAGGIO SHOW, THE
Children's; B&W
September 23, 1950–December 16, 1950

NBC Sat. 5:30–5:45 p.m. (9/23/50–12/16/50)

Regulars: *Joe DiMaggio, Jack Barry*

In this early filmed show, the great New York Yankees slugger Joe DiMaggio talked, on a clubhouse set, with an audience of about 10 children and introduced clips from sports newsreels. DiMaggio also introduced a weekly guest athlete whom the kids interviewed; teammate Phil Rizzuto was in the opener. Jack Barry served as co-host (or "manager") and producer of the series, the same tasks he did on a somewhat different show with the same title which aired on CBS radio in 1949. Incidentally, Barry told *Variety* that his contract with DiMaggio called for all of the show's films to be destroyed following their first run on television to protect DiMaggio's right to accept movie acting offers.

JOE GARAGIOLA'S MEMORY GAME
Game; Color
February 15, 1971–July 30, 1971

NBC Mon.–Fri. 1:30–2 p.m. (2/15/71–7/30/71)

Host: *Joe Garagiola*

Joe Garagiola's Memory Game was one of several shows NBC used unsuccessfully in the late 1960s and early 1970s to establish a foothold against *As the World Turns* on CBS and *Let's Make a Deal* on ABC. A quintet of players received $50 each and had 25 seconds to study some questions and their answers to be used throughout each day's game at the start of this show. NBC baseball announcer and *Today* show regular Joe Garagiola then began asking questions, and the player in control had the option of answering them or passing them to another player by calling out his or her number. The obstacle facing the contestant in control was the possibility that a buzzer would force them to answer the question immediately. The value of each question was $5, and that sum was added to a player's pot if right or subtracted if wrong. Contestants played until the end of each show, with the high scorer declared the winner.

Joe Garagiola's Memory Game was one of only two daily series to debut on the networks in 1971. The other was its replacement, *Three on a Match,* which was the first show on NBC's 1:30–2 p.m. time slot to last more than a year there following the move of *Let's Make a Deal* to ABC in 1968. An interesting note is that Merv Griffin, whose New York City production company created the series when he was in Hollywood, asked that his name be removed from the final product.

•JOHN AND LEEZA FROM HOLLYWOOD
Talk; Color
June 14, 1993–January 14, 1994
NBC Mon.–Fri. 10–11 a.m. (6/14/93–1/14/94)
Hosts: *John Tesh, Leeza Gibbons*

Regis and Kathie Lee—er, John Tesh and Leeza Gibbons—hosted this rather gushy celebrity-laden attraction which included satellite interviews. Los Angeles entertainment reporter Sam Rubin occasionally contributed some gossip as well. The fawning over guests like Sherman Hemsley and Isabel Sanford from a reunion of *The Jeffersons* seemed condescending for John and Leeza, both of whom had a somewhat harder edge as anchors on the syndicated nightly show *Entertainment Tonight,* and Tesh seemed especially out of place. NBC decided to replace the show with the issues-oriented *Leeza* (q.v.), with Gibbons hosting. Tesh had his own daily show on NBC earlier (see *One on One with John Tesh*).

•JOHN DAVIDSON SHOW, THE
Talk; Color
Spring 1980–Late 1981
Syndicated daily 60 or 90 minutes beginning June 1980
Host: *John Davidson*

Boyishly handsome actor-singer John Davidson was Group W Productions' pick to replace the long-running *Mike Douglas Show* (q.v.) as a talk show host designed to attract women ages 18–49, but he ended up going off the air the same time as Douglas, who got a new syndicator once Group W dropped him. Davidson, who had been a constant guest on all talk shows including Mike Douglas and had a contract to host *The Tonight Show* for two weeks each year at the time, used the same approach as Douglas, keeping the patter light with celebrity guests and a weekly co-host (actress Linda Gray in the debut), singing a few songs, and talking with the audience occasionally. As with the Douglas entry, stations could run the show for 90 minutes or in an edited hour-long format.

JOHNNY CARSON SHOW, THE
Variety; B&W
May 28, 1956–September 28, 1956
CBS Mon.–Fri. 2–2:30 p.m. (5/28/56–9/28/56)
Regulars: *Johnny Carson, Laurie Carroll, Pete Hanley, Glenn Turnbull, the Cal Gooden Orchestra*

After getting his first prime-time variety show on CBS on June 30, 1955—and seeing it disappear on March 29, 1956 against *Lux Video Theatre* on NBC—Johnny Carson received another opportunity. The show offered odd guests, offbeat props, and a recurring sketch where Johnny answers questions humorously while wearing a mortarboard. Other recurring features were "Happy Household Hints" and "Carson's Correspondence Etiquette Clinic," both send-ups of daytime TV show advice segments for women. Singers Laurie Carroll and Pete Hanley and dancer Glenn Turnbull rounded out the entertainment.

Despite good critical notices, Carson suffered the same fate that his heir apparent, David Letterman, endured in daytime nearly a quarter century later, and probably for the same reason: He was too hip to attract the fifties housewife audience. "This show deserves a sponsor," said a reviewer for *Billboard.* But it never got one. After dropping Carson from its daytime schedule, CBS put him under a five-year contract but could not develop a suitable property for him, with the result being that Carson ended up back on daytime as host of a more successful show, *Who Do You Trust?* (q.v.).

JOHNNY DUGAN SHOW, THE
Variety; B&W
May 19, 1952–September 5, 1952
NBC Mon.–Fri. 3:30–4 p.m. (5/19/52–9/5/52)
Regulars: *Johnny Dugan, Arch Presby, Barbara Logan*

This was an unspectacular musical variety show from Hollywood with a studio audience starring little-known vocalist Johnny Dugan, with Arch Presby as his sidekick and Barbara Logan as a singer.

JOHNNY JOHNSTON SHOW, THE
Variety; B&W
January 22, 1951–February 9, 1951
CBS Mon.–Fri. 2:45–3:30 p.m. (1/22/51–2/9/51)
Regulars: *Johnny Johnston, Rosemary Clooney, Hal Loman and Joan Fields, the Bernie Leighton Orchestra*

This served, or rather was supposed to serve, as a temporary fill-in for *The Robert Q. Lewis Show* as CBS attempted to negotiate with the star of that series, who was unhappy at the time with the shuffling and reduction of his show on the daily schedule. Lewis regulars—singer Rosemary Clooney, dancers Loman and Fields, and the Bernie Leighton Orchestra—joined vocalist Johnny Johnston on the show, but it was gone after three weeks.

JOHNNY OLSEN'S RUMPUS ROOM
Variety; B&W
January 12, 1949–July 4, 1952
DuMont Mon.–Fri. Various half hours between 10 a.m. and 1:30 p.m. (1/12/49–7/4/52)
Host: *Johnny Olsen*

Johnny Olsen's Rumpus Room *had the host and his wife Penny, seen at top, lead an annual children's charity drive before Christmas involving all stations airing the show.*

Johnny Olsen's Rumpus Room originally aired as a prime-time special on DuMont's New York station WABD on August 6, 1946, after having started on radio. It arrived on DuMont more than two years later, with Olsen offering his studio audience the chance to play musical identification games to win merchandise such as washing machines.

Like most DuMont series, the show had few affiliates to carry it (two stations in the fall of 1950, and only five as of April 1951). It moved around the schedule quite frequently, disappearing from the network after a three-year run in 1952. The show remained on WABD daily 12:30–1 p.m. through at least the fall of 1953.

JOHNS HOPKINS FILE 7
Discussion; B&W
September 12, 1954–September 18, 1960

DuMont Sun. 1–1:30 p.m. (9/12/54–3/6/55)
ABC Sun. 3:30–4 p.m. (11/11/56–6/8/57)
ABC Sun. 3–3:30 p.m. (10/6/57–6/1/58)
ABC Sun. 4–4:30 p.m. (6/8/58–8/31/58)
ABC Sun. 11:30 a.m.–Noon (10/19/58–10/4/59)
ABC Sun. Noon–12:30 p.m. or 12:30–1 p.m. (10/11/59–9/18/60)
Host/Co-Producer: *Lynn Poole*

Johns Hopkins University of Baltimore, Maryland had its own informational TV series in roughly the first decade of network television. It started in nighttime on CBS as *The Johns Hopkins Science Review* on December 31, 1948 for a five-month run, then returned on DuMont on October 3, 1950 for four years before going to Sunday afternoons on the network. After DuMont virtually went out of networking in the spring of 1955, the show went to ABC locally on Saturdays 11–11:30 a.m. in April 1955, then onto the ABC network a year and a half later under the title *Johns Hopkins File 7*.

Although shows were ostensibly devoted to current research at the university in the humanities, in the arts, and in science, shows on science dominated the daytime run. Presentations included studies on prehistoric life and its origin, atomic physics, and brainwashing techniques. The show celebrated its 10th anniversary on television in 1958 with members of the faculty predicting advances in their fields over the next decade. Adding a special touch at the start of each season was a brief talk by Johns Hopkins President Dr. Milton S. Eisenhower. Host and co-producer Lynn Poole was also public relations director for Johns Hopkins.

JOHNSON AND FRIENDS—See *Cubhouse*.

•JOKER'S WILD, THE
Game; Color
September 4, 1972–June 13, 1975
CBS Mon.–Fri. 10–10:30 a.m. (9/4/72–6/13/75)
Host: *Jack Barry*

The Joker's Wild was a half-quiz and half-luck game show. The luck part came from the spin generated by one of the two alternating players pulling a lever. The action sent three windows resembling those of a slot machine into a blur until stopping on one of five categories for the game, or on the Joker, a wild card which could be used to represent any of the categories. Each category or Joker per slot was worth $50 ($100 if in two slots, $200 if in three slots). The payoff amount depended on the category the contestant picked and the contestant's answer (if correct, the contestant won the money up for grabs; if wrong, the other player could guess). However, any player who spun three Jokers could win $500 for a correct answer to any category. The other player had to spin the same amount in order to at least tie the game, as $500 was the target goal. The winner went to a bonus round in which he or she might spin various amounts ranging from $20 to $200 or "the devil." A contestant could stop at any time and keep the winnings, but anyone who reached $1,000 without spinning the devil kept the cash, plus a prize. Players competed until defeated.

Director Ira Skutch in his 1989 memoirs claimed that Jack Barry worked with Goodson-Todman Productions for a period and developed this game during his tenure. Barry made the pilot for CBS in 1968; it took four years to sell. It was Barry's first TV appearance on screen since his involvement with the quiz show scandals of the 1950s. The show fared better as a long-running syndicated nighttime series from 1976 to 1986, with Barry hosting until his unexpected death in 1984 (Bill Cullen replaced him through 1986). Barry also hosted a syndicated children's version called *Joker! Joker! Joker!* from 1979–81. In 1990 *The Joker's Wild* returned in a failed syndicated revival hosted by Pat Finn.

• JONNY QUEST
Cartoon; Color
September 9, 1967–September 6, 1981

CBS Sat. 12:30–1 p.m. (9/9/67–9/6/69)
CBS Sat. 1:30–2 p.m. (9/13/69–9/5/70)
ABC Sun. 10–10:30 a.m. (9/13/70–9/5/71)
ABC Sat. Noon–12:30 p.m. (9/11/71–9/9/72)
NBC Sat. Noon–12:30 p.m. (9/8/79–11/3/79)
NBC Sat. 11:30 a.m.–Noon (4/12/80–9/20/80)
NBC Sat. Noon–12:30 p.m. (9/27/80–9/6/81)

Voices:

Jonny Quest	Tim Matheson
Dr. Benton Quest (early shows only)	John Stephenson
Dr. Benton Quest/Bandit	Don Messick
Hadji	Danny Bravo
Roger "Race" Bannon	Mike Road

Producers: *William Hanna and Joseph Barbera*

Jonny Quest was runner-up to *The Jetsons* among 1960s cartoons which flopped in nighttime but prospered in daytime network reruns in the 1970s and 1980s. It first ran on ABC nighttime from September 18, 1964–September 9, 1965. Two years later it returned on CBS Saturday afternoons and ran in daytime for five years, then turned up again in 1979, lasting until 1981.

The object of all this repeat attention was a fairly standard adventure series, a rarity among TV cartoons during its debut season. Jonny was the prepubescent son of Dr. Benton Quest, a scientist in search of the unusual throughout the world. Jonny, his pet bulldog Bandit, and his turban-wearing friend from India Hadji tagged along with Dr. Quest in an airplane piloted by Race Bannon as they met some fantastic nefarious creatures while Dr. Quest did investigative research. In their original 26 episodes Jonny and his troupe came across a werewolf, an invisible giant, a crazed general building a missile base, and "the Turu," a large flying dinosaur.

In addition to the runs listed, *Jonny Quest* appeared in 1978 as part of *The Godzilla Show* (q.v.). In 1987 Hanna-Barbera Productions released 13 new Jonny Quest cartoons with only Don Messick returning to voice his characters. A decade later, the Turner Company announced plans for another update titled *The Real Adventures of Jonny Quest* to air in the fall of 1996 simultaneously on the cable channels TBS, TNT, and the Cartoon Network.

• JOSIE AND THE PUSSYCATS
Cartoon; Color
September 12, 1970–September 4, 1976

CBS Sat. 10–10:30 a.m. (9/12/70–9/4/71)
CBS Sat. 11:30 a.m.–Noon (9/11/71–9/2/72)
CBS Sat. 10:30–11 a.m. (9/9/72–9/1/73)
CBS Sat. 11:30 a.m.–Noon (9/8/73–8/31/74)
NBC Sat. Noon–12:30 p.m. (9/6/75–10/18/75)
NBC Sat. 8:30–9 a.m. (10/25/75–9/4/76)

Voices:

Josie	Janet Waldo
Melody	Jackie Joseph
Valerie	Barbara Pariot
Alexandra Cabot	Sherry Alberoni
Alan	Jerry Dexter
Alexander Cabot III	Casey Kasem
Sebastian/Bleep (1972–74)	Don Messick

Singing Voices: *Cathy Douglas, Patricia Holloway, Cherie Moore (Cheryl Ladd)*

Josie and the Pussycats was the group name of a trio of young female singers on tour who performed in skin-tight feline outfits which included an adorable pair of ears. Josie, the redheaded lead singer of the band, played tambourine. Alexandra (a cross between Veronica of *The Archies* and Cruella De Vil from the Walt Disney animated film *101 Dalmations*), a member of the tour group, hated the attention lavished on Josie and tried constantly to undermine her. Alexandra's brother Alexander, the group's manager, liked Josie but was cowardly in his actions. Alan was the brawny, handsome blond friend who also liked Josie, much to Alexandra's chagrin. The Pussycats were Melody the giggly blonde and Valerie the down-to-earth token black member. Sebastian was Alexandra's snickering cat.

On September 9, 1972 the show revised its story line and became *Josie and the Pussycats in Outer Space*. While posing for press photos at a rocket launching pad, Alexandra accidentally shoved the group into the missile at the time of takeoff. The spaceship took them to another inhabited planet where they dealt with various unusual species while attempting to return home. A new regular companion of the group was Bleep, a cute space alien that looked like a fluffy duck and spoke only its own name. Melody loved the creature and treated it like a pet.

Josie and the Pussycats was a major Saturday morning hit of the early 1970s, following in the comedy and bubblegum music mold of *The Archies (q.v.)*. Their records did not hit the music charts like those of the Archies, however, and several of them were relegated to the lowly status of mail-in prizes on the backs of Kellogg's cereals. (One of the vocalists, Cherie Moore, later changed her professional name to Cheryl Ladd and became an actress on ABC's nighttime late 1970s hit *Charlie's Angels*, in addition to having a short-lived solo singing career.) CBS did have Janet Waldo (as Josie) narrate its *In the Know* minute-long informational Saturday morning segments from 1970–71 before CBS newsman Christopher Glenn took over the job for the rest of the decade under the title *In the News*. After the show ended its CBS run, NBC repeated the series a year later for a season.

•JOURNEY TO THE CENTER OF THE EARTH
Cartoon; Color
September 9, 1967–August 30, 1969

ABC Sat. 10:30–11 a.m. (9/9/67–9/7/68)
ABC Sat. 11–11:30 a.m. (9/14/68–8/30/69)

Voices:

Professor Lindenbrook/Count	
Saccnuson	*Ted Knight*
Alec McEwen/Lars/Torg	*Pat Harrington, Jr.*
Cindy Lindenbrook	*Jane Webb*

The first TV cartoon series based on a Jules Verne novel (*Around the World in 80 Days* arrived in 1972), this was a loose adaptation of the 1865 book, which also appeared as a movie in 1959 starring Pat Boone. Professor Lindenbrook took his niece Cindy and her classmate Alec on an expedition through caverns with the group's brawny blonde guide Lars. Calamity struck when the evil Count, a descendent of the explorer who found that the route they were traveling led to the middle of the world, sealed off the entrance in an effort to prevent them from returning to the surface. The Count's manservant Tors helped in trying to stop Lindenbrook's group in 17 shows, all of which had cliffhanger endings. Adding a lighter touch to the menacing chases through the caves was Cindy's pet duck, Gertrude.

Though producers Lou Scheimer and Norm Prescott boasted in *Variety* that the series used writers who also crafted such live-action nighttime TV shows as *Daktari* and *Star Trek*, there was little in the scripting that made this cartoon any better than others seen at the time. By 1994, *Journey to the Center of the Earth* had reappeared on Saturday mornings in reruns on the Sci-Fi cable channel.

•JUDGE, THE
Dramatic Anthology; Color
1986–1993

Syndicated 30 minutes daily beginning September 1986

Regular: *Bob Shield (as Judge Robert Franklin)*

Based on a weekly access series seen on WBNS Columbus, Ohio, from 1967–79, *The Judge* provided fictionalized accounts of civil trials presided over by mature Judge Robert Franklin, who felt compelled to add his own morals and

opinions whenever necessary. As in other daytime court shows, such as *Divorce Court*, the sides were represented by actors.

JUDY SPLINTERS
Children's; B&W
October 3, 1949–June 30, 1950

NBC Mon.–Fri. 5:15–5:30 p.m. (10/3/49–6/30/50)

Hostess: *Shirley Dinsdale*

Ventriloquist Shirley Dinsdale and her dummy Judy Splinters were an early TV act favorite. Dinsdale appeared as early as 1947 on KTLA Hollywood, where she hosted a Thursday night show called *Kiddie Party*. Two years later she was in New York City, bringing her act to NBC's audience before *Howdy Doody* for a time. The recurring theme of her routine was Judy's machinations to get Miss Dinsdale married. Prior to the daytime run, *Judy Splinters* aired on NBC from Chicago as a nightly replacement for *Kukla, Fran and Ollie* from June 13–August 5, 1949.

•JUNIOR ALMOST ANYTHING GOES
Children's; Color
September 11, 1976–September 4, 1977

ABC Sat. Noon–12:30 p.m. (9/11/76–1/8/77)
ABC Sun. 10:30–11 a.m. (1/16/77–9/4/77)

Host: *Soupy Sales*

Commentator: *"Fast Eddie" Alexander*

Almost Anything Goes, a mid-1970s series that tried hard but never really caught on, aired on ABC nighttime from July 31, 1975–April 10, 1976, went on the network Saturday morning in a version using kids from 1976–77, then came back again in syndication in the fall of 1977, this time using celebrities under the title *All Star Almost Anything Goes*. It was nothing more than a competition with games designed to make players look goofy, messy, or both. Any contestant who did not want the chance to fall into a big bucket of water should have stayed away from this series. Different groups of children played each week on three teams divided by color (red, white, and blue). Soupy Sales kept tally of the scores, while "Fast Eddie" Alexander gave the play-by-play for the often yucky events.

JUNIOR HI-JINX
Children's; B&W
March 2, 1952–May 25, 1952

CBS Sun. 12:15–12:30 p.m. (3/2/52–5/25/52)

Host/Puppeteer: *Warren Wright*

A Philadelphia-based offering, where it had aired locally on WCAU for nearly two years before going network, this obscure series told of the adventures of puppet Willie the Worm trying to get a college education. The 1920s black-and-white theatrical cartoon shorts "Aesop's Fables" aired between the live-action sketches.

JUNIOR PRESS CONFERENCE
Public Affairs; B&W
November 23, 1952–November 20, 1960

ABC Sun. 11:30–Noon (11/23/52–1/25/53)
ABC Sun. 9:30–10 a.m. or 10–10:30 a.m.
   (4/12/53–7/12/53)
ABC Sat. 11:30 a.m.–Noon (1/22/55–7/2/55)
ABC Sun. 1–1:30 p.m. (10/9/55–12/11/55)
ABC Sun. 4:30–5 p.m. (12/18/55–9/2/56)
ABC Sun. 4–4:30 p.m. (9/9/56–6/9/57)
ABC Sun. 5–5:30 p.m. (6/23/57–9/29/57)
ABC Sun. 2:30–3 p.m. (10/6/57–12/29/57)
ABC Sun. 1:30–2 p.m. (1/5/58–10/12/58)
ABC Sun. 1–1:30 p.m. (10/19/58–9/4/60)
ABC Sun. 1:30–2 p.m. (9/11/60–11/20/60)

Hostess/Producer: *Ruth Geri Hagy*

ABC's answer to NBC's *Youth Wants to Know* (q.v.) aired live from WFIL Philadelphia, where Hagy was women's club editor of the *Evening Bulletin* newspaper. It featured four college reporters interviewing figures in current events. After a year in daytime, ABC moved the show to Monday nights from October 5, 1953–December 13, 1954 before returning to Sunday mornings under the title *College Press Conference,* which it adopted in October 1954. It was retitled again in 1957 as *College News Conference* before ending its run.

JUNIOR RODEO
Children's; B&W
November 15, 1952–December 13, 1952

ABC Sat. 11:30 a.m.–Noon (11/15/52–12/13/52)

Host/Singer: *Bob Atcher*

Regular: *Valerie Alberts*

An obscure, short-lived entry for the kiddies from Chicago, *Junior Rodeo* was a western-style attraction with songs and contests for children in the studio audience.

•JUST MEN!
Game; Color
January 3, 1983–April 1, 1983

NBC Mon.–Fri. Noon–12:30 p.m. (1/3/83–4/1/83)

Hostess: *Betty White*

Betty White, who seemed to appear on every game show needing a celebrity from the 1950s through the 1980s, took her only shot as a hostess in the genre in this undeservedly short-lived effort. *Just Men!* featured seven male celebrities who during each round of the day's game had a hidden answer to a yes or no question. Two women contestants tried to guess how each man had responded by quizzing them for one minute, each using questions provided by the show's writers. After a minute had elapsed, the first contestant had to guess a celebrity's answer, and a match won her a car key held by the performer. After the first round of questioning, an incorrect guess gave the contestant's opponent control of

the celebrity's key. The player with the most keys at the end of the day won the game and had to choose which of her keys could start a car seen onstage. Contestants could play on the show for up to seven days or until they won the car.

A typical segment had White asking, "Do you enjoy finger painting?" while the men engaged in the activity. Guests on the first week of shows were Steve Sax (the most frequently seen celebrity, appearing on three weeks of shows), Jeff Altman, Leif Garrett, David Hasselhoff, Tim Reid, Josh Taylor, and Dick Van Patten, who alternated daily with his son Nels. Betty was bright and personable, as always, and the game moved briskly, but the competition of *Family Feud* on ABC proved to be too much, and the show ended after 13 weeks.

JUVENILE JURY
Children's; B&W
September 16, 1951–March 27, 1955

NBC Sun. 3:30–4 p.m. (9/16/51–12/31/51)
NBC Sun. 4:30–5 p.m. (1/6/52–3/16/52)
NBC Sun. 3:30–4 p.m. (12/14/52–1/25/53)
CBS Sun. 4–4:30 p.m. (10/11/53–4/4/54)
NBC Sun. 4–4:30 p.m. (1/2/55–3/27/55)

Host: *Jack Barry*

A transfer from radio, where it aired from 1946–51 on Mutual and 1952–53 on NBC, *Juvenile Jury* first came to network television on NBC nighttime on April 3, 1947. It left the air after a three-month run, but returned four years later as the summer replacement for *The Milton Berle Show,* then went into Sunday afternoons that fall, where it remained for four years, though it also had some nighttime runs during that period. Five kids from ages 3–12 gave individual answers to questions like "How does an airplane work?" Their comments could be insightful, funny, or sometimes even both. No panelist remained long enough on the show to be considered a regular. Jack Barry also produced the series and hosted a 1970 syndicated revival.

KALEIDOSCOPE
Documentary/Various; B&W
November 2, 1958–May 17, 1959

NBC Sun. 5–6 p.m. (11/2/58–5/17/59)

Host: *Charles Van Doren*

Officially titled *NBC Kaleidoscope,* this loosely formatted series had a roughly even split of shows from the network's news and entertainment divisions. Many programs featured a profile of a single subject, with topics from the Rockettes at Radio City Music Hall to new and controversial eavesdropping procedures. There were also some nondocumentary presentations, such as

"Projection '59," where Frank McGee anchored a review of the top stories of 1958 with 10 other NBC reporters who also offered their predictions for 1959, and "The Third Commandment," a pilot for a projected drama series based on the Ten Commandments, written by Ben Hecht and starring Arthur Kennedy and Anne Francis. *Kaleidoscope* alternated weekly with *Omnibus*.

KARATE KID, THE
Cartoon; Color
September 9, 1989–September 1, 1990

NBC Sat. 9:30–10 a.m. (9/9/89–9/1/90)

Voices:

Daniel	Joe Dedio
Miyagi Yakuga	Robert Ito
Taki	Janice Kawaye

Based loosely on the 1984 motion picture of the same name with Ralph Macchio as Daniel and Pat Morita as Miyagi, *The Karate Kid* cartoon came after two movie sequels. In this one-season cartoon, Daniel was a New Jerseyite having a hard time after being transplanted to California until his mystical Asian mentor Miyagi taught him the sport of karate. Miyagi had another student named Taki (not seen in the movies) who teamed with them to search for a magical shrine located on Okinawa Island.

•KATE SMITH HOUR, THE
Variety; B&W
September 25, 1950–June 18, 1954

NBC Mon.–Fri. 4–5 p.m. (9/25/50–6/5/53; off summers)
NBC Mon.–Fri. 3–4 p.m. (9/21/53–6/18/54)

Regulars: *Kate Smith, Ted Collins, Dorothy Daye, the Jack Allison Singers (1950–51 at least), the John Butler Ballet Group (1950–51 at least), the Jack Miller Orchestra, Peg Lynch (1950–52), Al Bunce (1950–52), Alene Dalton (1953–54), Jeff Clark (1953–54), Jimmy Nelson (1953–54), the Katydids [Joan Gilbert, Betsy Holland, Rita Noble, Michele Burke] (1953), Delores Dahl (at least 1953–54), the Kateds (at least 1953–54), the Showtimers (at least 1953–54)*

Theme: *"When the Moon Comes Over the Mountain," by Howard Johnson and Harry Woods*

One of early daytime network TV's grandest and biggest hits was *The Kate Smith Hour.* "Big" certainly applied to its star, in many senses. Kate Smith was a 235-pound vocalist whose contralto made her one of the most popular singers of the first half of the 20th century. She popularized "God Bless America," among other tunes. She was also incredibly successful as a nighttime radio personality, on NBC in 1930, CBS from 1931 to 1947, and ABC from 1949 to 1950. She was just as widely appreciated on daytime TV as she had been during her radio heyday until a combination of factors ended her television career earlier than most would have predicted.

Smith was adept at singing, dancing, and comedy, and at carrying out small talk with her audience at home and in the studio, but from the start the show had much more to offer viewers. There was "The Private Lives of Ethel and Albert," a 15-minute segment with Peg Lynch and Al Bunce, which debuted October 6, 1950 and later spun off as the nighttime TV series *Ethel and Albert* from 1953–56. Dorothy Daye narrated a fashion segment. Also seen at various times were ventriloquist Jimmy Nelson, singer Jeff Clark, the Katydids female singing quartet, the Kateds dance trio, and the Showtimers singing trio (the latter two threesomes each consisted of two males and one female). There were plenty of guests too, including the McGuire Sisters on their network TV debut.

Other segments popping up for periods on the show were a travelogue with dance and music featuring folk singer Oscar Brand as a "wandering minstrel" (it debuted May 14, 1951); interviews with "Sons and Daughters of Favorite Show People," such as George M. Cohan Jr. (December 6, 1951); "The House in the Garden," based on *Fairmeadows U.S.A.* (q.v.; September 1952); a weekly 15-minute drama sketch featuring such actors as Chester Morris and John Carradine (January 5, 1953); "The Story Princess," with Alene Dalton, a performer from KDYL Salt Lake City, Utah, who came to New York to tell tales for children once a month (January 1953); "Talent Showcase," a half-hour weekly segment with unknown professional acts making their TV debuts and competing to win $500 (April 24, 1953); "Tales of Morpheus," half-hour dramatizations of people's dreams with John Newland as the eerie narrator Morpheus (May 22, 1953); and "The World of Mr. Sweeney," a 10-minute weekly spot with Charles Ruggles, Glenn Walken, and Helen Wagner (October 14, 1953). The latter became a daytime series in 1954 under the same name.

But the most important and constant regular element apart from Kate was her manager Ted Collins. Beside being the series' co-producer, Collins also served as an interviewer. His "The Cracker Barrel" interview segments with politicos began accidentally one day in April 1950 when Kate couldn't manage a costume change in time to get on air. Collins's interviews became the show's longest-running non-Kate feature, and he even got some scoops, such as when Republican Sen. Robert Taft announced he was running for president in 1952. By 1953, Collins was also hosting "International Forum," where four college students discussed current issues.

By November 1950, the show boasted an impressive rating of 18.5, the first network daytime TV show to measure in double digits. It was also one of the most expensive daytime shows, costing $13,000 per day and involving a staff of 91 people. But more important to NBC than the costs was the growing audience. In the spring of 1951, Smith's rating reached 25.2 and more than 10 million viewers a week were watching, almost double the audience for most other daytime network TV series. Sponsors responded in droves, and in the fall of 1951 *Variety* announced that Smith had tied with

CBS's Arthur Godfrey as the top commercial personality in broadcasting, bringing NBC some $12 million yearly in gross revenues with her TV and radio shows. However, when NBC placed a nighttime version of her show against Godfrey from September 19, 1951–June 11, 1952, it bombed.

Nevertheless, Kate gave the impression of relishing her work as a daytime powerhouse. Once when a boom mike poked into camera range, she joked, "Let's not have any of that sloppy nighttime TV work." She had less to joke about by January 1954, when the show ranked 25th in daytime behind such losers as *The Bennetts* and *Three Steps to Heaven* following a switch in time slots. That was of course troublesome, but the network reportedly was more upset with Collins's refusal to have Smith make personal identifications for products of the show's sponsors, a policy that did nothing to win or hold advertisers.

In March 1954, NBC announced it would cancel the show. No other daytime variety show since has matched it

in ambition or prestige. Smith herself returned in a nighttime CBS show in 1960, then made occasional guest appearances through the 1970s until illness curtailed her activities. She died in 1986.

KAY WESTFALL SHOW, THE—See *Oh, Kay!*

KELLOGG'S PRESENTS THE BANANA SPLITS ADVENTURE HOUR—See *Banana Splits Adventure Hour, The.*

KID 'N' PLAY
Cartoon; Color
September 8, 1990–September 7, 1991
NBC Sat. 10–10:30 a.m. (9/8/90–9/7/91)

Shown here are famous singer Kate Smith, star of the The Kate Smith Hour, *and her manager Ted Collins, who did interviews on the show and was also co-producer.*

Hosts:

Christopher Martin ("Kid")	*Himself*
Christopher Reid ("Play")	*Himself*

Voices: *Jack Angel, Tommy Davidson, Cree Summer Francks, Alaina Reed Hall, J. D. Hall, Dorian Harewood, Chris Hooks, Martin Lawrence, Dawnn Lewis, Danny Mann, Brian Mitchell, Umberto Ortiz, Rain Pryor*

Rap artists Kid 'n' Play found themselves converted into cartoon form along with their manager Herbie in this short-lived effort. Also showing up were Play's sister Marika, who was a teenage backup singer for the duo along with Lela and Downtown Patty, Kid's sister Terry, and the bullies Acorn and Pitbull. Kid 'n' Play appeared in live segments between the cartoon adventures but did not voice their characters.

•KID POWER

Cartoon; Color
September 16, 1972–September 1, 1974

ABC Sat. 11:30 a.m.–Noon (9/16/72–9/1/73)
ABC Sun. 10–10:30 a.m. (9/9/73–9/1/74)

Voices:

Oliver	*Jay Silverheels Jr.*
Ralph	*Gary Shapiro*
Wellington	*Charles Kennedy Jr.*
Nipper	*John Gardiner*
Jerry	*Allan Melvin*
Connie	*Carey Wong*
Sybil	*Michele Johnson*
Diz	*Jeff Thomas*
Albert	*Greg Thomas*

Cartoonist Morrie Turner transferred his "Wee Pals" newspaper strip, which he started in 1965, into this well-meaning multicultural series. The cast included Oliver, a portly protagonist with glasses often threatened by meanie Ralph; Sybil, a black fortune teller; Connie, a tomboy; Wellington, a shaggy-haired lad with a pet parrot named Polly; Jerry, a Jewish boy; and George, a Chinese chum. All of them were members of the Rainbow Club, and tried to promote racial and social harmony despite their own occasional internal squabbles.

The show had a nighttime preview on ABC August 24, 1972. Despite the advance publicity, *Kid Power* never reached a huge audience, and spent its second season airing only reruns.

KID SUPER POWER HOUR WITH SHAZAM, THE

Cartoon/Variety; Color
September 12, 1981–September 11, 1982

NBC Sat. 9:30–10:30 a.m. (9/12/81–9/11/82)

Cast:

Captain California	*Christopher Hensel*
Gorgeous Gal	*Becky Perle*
Dirty Trixie	*Maylo McCaslin*
Misty Magic	*Jere Fields*
Rex Ruthless	*John Berwick*
Weatherman	*Jim Greenleaf*
Punk Rock	*Johnny Venocour*
Billy Batson/Shazam (voice only)	*Burr Middleton*
Mary Freeman/Mary Marvel (voice only)	*Erika Scheimer*
Freddy Freeman/Captain Marvel Jr. (voice only)	*Barry Gordon*
Uncle Dudley Batson/Tawky Tawny (voice only)	*Alan Oppenheimer*
Narrator	*Norm Prescott*

This odd combination of live-action sketches and cartoons featured a rock 'n' roll septet whose "members" (actually actors) served as hosts and performers and provided the voices for "Hero High," a cartoon segment featuring the characters in their teenage years. The other cartoon on the show was "Shazam," featuring the familiar Saturday morning superhero (see the series under the same name for details on the 1970s live-action version). Here Captain Marvel was joined by two other members of his superhero "family" (Billy's sister Mary and Marvel's "foster child" Freddy) to battle wrongdoers. Scam artist Uncle Dudley tried to convince others that he was as strong as his kin, while Tawky Tawny was a tiger who assisted Captain Marvel. Most kid viewers thought the show neither "super" nor a "power hour," and it ended after a season.

KID TALK

Children's; Color
January 23, 1972–September 17, 1972

CBS Sun. 5–5:30 p.m. (1/23/72–9/17/72)

Host: *Bill Adler*

Regulars: *Nellie Henderson (age 12), Mona Tera (age 8), Alan Winston (age 12), Andy Yamamoto (age 10)*

In this creation four children interviewed celebrities, such as Greg Morris and George Plimpton. The series did not run on the five stations owned and operated by CBS, including those in New York City and Los Angeles, because those stations had a policy of airing public service shows during that time period. Independent stations in those markets aired the show instead. The series began in syndication in 1970.

KIDD VIDEO

Children's; Color
September 15, 1984–December 26, 1987

NBC Sat. 11–11:30 a.m. (9/15/84–9/7/85)
NBC Sat. 11:30 a.m.–Noon (9/14/85–9/6/86)
NBC Sat. 12:30–1 p.m. (9/13/86–4/4/87)
CBS Sat. 12:30–1 p.m. (9/19/87–12/26/87)

Cast:

Kidd Video	*Bryan Scott*
Ash	*Steve Alterman*

Whiz	*Robbie Rist*
Carla	*Gabrielle Bennett*
Glitter	*Cathy Cavadini*
Master Blaster	*Peter Renaday*
Fat Cat (voice only)	*Marshall Efron*
She Lion (voice only)	*Susan Silo*
Cool Kitty (voice only)	*Robert Towers*

Kidd Video exploited the popularity of music videos in a story line combining live action and cartoons. Four actors played Kidd, Ash, Whiz, and Carla, a rock quartet which disappeared into another world known as "The Flip Side" and became cartoon characters. In that world, evil Master Blaster and his henchmen Fat Cat, She Lion, and Cool Kitty, known collectively as the Copy Cats, attempted to steal the group's sound. Glitter, a friend of Kidd's, helped the group avert this potential disaster. A pulsating mix of videos of current rock hits helped give this entry a rather contemporary feel for a Saturday morning show. The CBS shows were reruns.

•KIDS AND COMPANY
Children; B&W
September 5, 1951–May 2, 1953

DuMont Sat. 11–11:30 a.m. (9/1/51–6/9/52)
DuMont Sat. 11:30 a.m.–Noon (8/9/52–5/2/53)

Regulars: *Johnny Olsen, Ham Fisher (1951), Al Greiner (1951), Bill Wirges (1952–53)*

The novelty of this talent series was that in conjunction with the U.S. Junior Chamber of Commerce, each show rewarded a "Kid of the Week" for public service, with the honoree receiving a citation and prizes. On June 9, 1952, the show named Jimmy Carrick of Pittsburgh its "Kid of the Year" for garnering 8,000 pints for blood banks on a cross-country month-long tour. Four to five children guested per show, and 8-year-old Leslie Uggams made an early TV appearance on the debut singing solo, with guest Johnny Desmond. All participating performers received Helbros watches for appearing.

Johnny Olsen hosted the festivities, while Al Greiner was its organist and musical director. Before the end of its first season Greiner had been replaced by Bill Wirges, cartoonist Ham Fisher had left as co-host, and Mona the Red Goose, a puppet named in honor of sponsor Red Goose Shoes, had become Olsen's sidekick.

•KIDS ARE PEOPLE TOO
Children's; Color
September 17, 1978–November 7, 1982

ABC Sun. 10–11:30 a.m. (9/17/78–8/31/80)
ABC Sun. 10:30–11:30 a.m. (9/7/80–9/5/82)
ABC Sun. 9:30–10:30 a.m. (9/12/82–11/7/82)

Host: *Bob McAllister (1978–79), Michael Young (1979–81), Randy Hamilton (1981–82)*

A departure from most network fare for children, *Kids Are People Too* was an interview show which offered a fair split between informative guests like Ralph Nader (on the debut), and entertaining ones such as the Captain and Tennille, Ethel Merman, Eddie Money, and Christopher Reeve. Both the host and the predominately youthful audience had a chance to ask questions of visitors to the program. Another segment in 1978–79 was "Dear Alex and Annie," where actors Bing Bingham (Alex) and Donna Drake (Annie) answered viewers' letters with songs. ABC encouraged its owned and operated stations to install two separate 13-minute segments within the show with local material.

The show came from New York City in its first year, then moved production to Hollywood in its second season before returning to Gotham in the fall of 1980. That same autumn the show shrank to 60 minutes and dropped the local cut-ins. Meanwhile, youthful (age 25) Michael Young had replaced the more mature Bob McAllister as host, but Young was in turn dropped in favor of another youthful actor, Randy Hamilton, in 1981. The show ended production in 1982, and reruns aired briefly in the fall of that year before leaving the air.

KIDS FROM C.A.P.E.R., THE
Children's; Color
September 11, 1976–September 3, 1977

NBC Sat. Noon–12:30 p.m. (9/11/76–11/20/76)
NBC Sat. 12:30–1 p.m. (4/16/77–9/3/77)

Cast:

P.T.	*Steve Bonimo*
Bugs	*Cosie Costa*
Doc	*John Lansing*
Doomsday	*Biff Warren*
Chief Vinton	*Robert Emhardt*
Klintsinger	*Robert Lussier*

A quartet of boys made up C.A.P.E.R. (Civilian Authority for the Protection of Everyone, Regardless), a crime-fighting unit featured in this loser of a sitcom. Between occasional song segments, all the kids reported to Chief Vinton of the 927th police district. Klintsinger, a reporter for the local paper in the town of Northeast Southwestern, often tailed the group in order to get a scoop. He was about the only person who seemed to care what C.A.P.E.R. did; NBC dropped the show after two months, with repeats airing in the summer of 1977.

KIDS KAPERS
Cartoons; B&W
October 19, 1952–January 25, 1953

ABC Sun. Noon–12:15 p.m. (10/19/52–1/25/53)

Kids Kapers was a collection of assorted cartoons first released theatrically before appearing on television. No record exists of the exact cartoon content of the series.

•KIDSWORLD
Children's; Color
1976–1985

Syndicated 30 minutes weekly beginning October 1976

In this widely seen informational series, various children between the ages of 7 and 12 shared hosting duties for at least eight segments per program on features showcasing unique or interesting youth across America, plus an interview with a celebrity. Three young guests reported each week.

KILLY STYLE, THE
Sports; Color
January 5, 1969–March 29, 1970

CBS Sun. 5–5:30 p.m. (1/5/69–4/20/69)
CBS Sun. 4:30–5 p.m. (2/1/70–3/29/70)

Regulars: *Jean-Claude Killy, Bob Landers (1969), Gil Stratton Jr. (1970), Doug Pfeiffer (1970)*

French skier Jean-Claude Killy became internationally known when he won three gold medals in the 1968 Olympics, in the triple crown of the downhill, slalom, and giant slalom events. For two winter seasons after that triumph, he starred in a television series spotlighting his talents. On the debut he performed the spectacular feat of skiing down an active volcano on New Zealand's North Island while Bob Landers narrated the activity.

In 1970 the show changed its title—to *The Killy Challenge*—and its format. Each week four challengers went through two elimination heats to determine a winner who would face Killy in a downhill race for a prize of $10,000. Killy took a handicap ranging from 0.5 to 3.2 seconds in the race, and if he beat his challenger, the latter received a consolation prize of $2,500. Filmed at various resorts in America, it had Gil Stratton Jr. and magazine editor Doug Pfeiffer serve as commentators.

KING AND ODIE, THE—The syndicated title for *King Leonardo and His Short Subjects* (q.v.).

•KING KONG
Cartoon; Color
September 10, 1966–August 31, 1969

ABC Sat. 10–10:30 a.m. (9/10/66–9/2/67)
ABC Sat. 11–11:30 a.m. (9/9/67–9/7/68)
ABC Sun. 10:30–11 a.m. (9/15/68–8/31/69)

Voice:
Bobby Bond   Billie Richards

Also: *Carl Banas, Susan Conway, John Drainie, Alf Scopp, Paul Scoles*

Bearing scant resemblance to the 1933 movie classic of the same name, *King Kong* told of an ape 10 times as big as a man who was the pet of Bobby Bond on Mondo Island in the South Seas. Bobby's dad was a science foundation

professor studying the island. Sue was Bobby's sister. They all united in each episode to halt some human trying to harm the island or Kong, but unlike the film, Kong never killed anyone and only defended himself.

The show's other segment was the much more inspired, genuinely funny spy spoof "Tom of T.H.U.M.B." (Tiny Humans Underground Military Bureau). As the prologue explained, Tom was an average member of the U.S. Intelligence maintenance department wounded in the line of duty (he fell down the stairs into a lab). As pilot Swingin' Jack tried to save him, both of them were shrunk accidentally by a ray, or as the introduction put it, "They gave their height for their country." Tom and Jack reported to grumpy Chief Homer J. Chief at the Pentagon to fight the doings of the evil empire M.A.D. (Maladjusted, Anti-Social and Darn Mean). This segment ran between two "King Kong" episodes.

The cartoon actually debuted with an hour-long preview on ABC nighttime September 6, 1966. It was produced in Japan.

•KING LEONARDO AND HIS SHORT SUBJECTS
Cartoon; Color
October 15, 1960–September 28, 1963

NBC Sat. 10:30–11 a.m. (10/15/60–9/28/63)

Voices:

King Leonardo/Biggy Rat	Jackson Beck
Odie Colognie/Itchy Brother/	
Tooter Turtle	Allen Swift
Wizard the Lizard	Sandy Becker
The Hunter	Kenny Delmar
The Fox	Ben Stone

In the African province of Bongoland, the cross-eyed King Leonardo the Lion found his rule opposed by shifty-eyed, cigar-smoking Biggy Rat, who wanted to install Itchy Brother, the king's beatnik kin, as his puppet on the throne. But Odie Colognie, a skunk faithful to King Leonardo, managed to help prevent Biggy and Itchy's nefarious plans from succeeding. Other segments were "Tooter Turtle" and "The Hunter." The former embarked on adventures to exotic places via magic from Mr. Wizard the Lizard, who then narrated the adventure. Tooter always ended up in a danger from which he could not escape and asked the lizard for help, with the latter saying, "Drizzle drazzle druzzle drome, time for this one to come home" to end the episode. The Hunter was a confused private-eye bloodhound reminiscent of Kenny Delmar's Senator character on radio, right down to his "That's a joke, son!" catchphrase, who haphazardly trailed but always caught the cunning Fox, who had a handlebar moustache. Parts of this show were repeated on *Tennessee Tuxedo* (q.v.).

•KISSYFUR
Cartoon; Color
September 13, 1986–August 25, 1990

NBC Sat. 8–8:30 a.m. (9/13/86–9/5/87)
NBC Sat. 8–8:30 a.m. (9/10/88–9/2/89)
NBC Sat. 12:30–1 p.m. (9/9/89–3/3/90)
NBC Sat. 8–8:30 a.m. (3/10/90–8/25/90)

Voices:

Kissyfur (1986–87)	R. J. Williams
Kissyfur (1987–88)	Max Meier
Gus	Edmund Gilbert
Beehonie/Miss Emmy Lou/Toot (1987–88)	Russi Taylor
Lennie/Charles Warthog	Lennie Weinrib
Stuckey/Floyd	Stuart M. Rosen
Toot (1986–87)	Devon Feldman
Duane	Neil Ross
Jolene	Terence McGovern
Uncle Shelby	Frank Welker

Kissyfur first aired as a 30-minute special on NBC nighttime December 22, 1985, and the pilot was a rather depressing affair for the first few minutes. Kissyfur and his father Gus performed joylessly as clown bears in a circus act following the death of Kissyfur's mom. Unhappy with their situation, Gus took advantage when a train transporting them to another show jumped its tracks and sent their car into a ravine. The two went down the river and arrived at the swamp village of Paddlecab, where the tone lightened considerably. Kissyfur found friendship with fellow animal classmates Stuckey the porcupine, Beehonie the bunny, Toot the beaver, and Duane the pig. The one drawback was Lonnie the hog, a bully who called Kissyfur "Sissyface" and generally showed little respect for his classmate. Gus kept himself active by building a treehouse and paddle boat for his family and romancing Miss Emmy Lou, a fellow bear and school teacher for the kids.

Other village folk were Shelby the turtle and Charles the belligerent pig, the latter serving as sort of a mayor for the area. They all stood on guard against Floyd and Jolene, the vicious yet often befuddled alligators ready to chew them to bits should they fall into the swamp. Their stories ran on NBC for three years, taking a break from 1987–88.

KITTY FOYLE

Soap Opera; B&W
January 13, 1958–June 27, 1958

NBC Mon.–Fri. 2:30–3 p.m. (1/13/58–6/27/58)

Cast:

Kitty Foyle	Kathleen Murray
Ed Foyle	Bob Hastings
Mack Foyle	Larry Robinson
Pop Foyle	Ralph Dunn
Sophie Foyle	Kay Medford
Stacylea Balla	Marie Worsham
Molly Scharf	Judy Lewis
Wyn Stafford	William Redfield
Olivia Stafford	Valerie Cossart
Flip Martin	Conard Fowkes
Nick Amsted	Lee Bergere
Rosie Rittenhouse	Les Damon

One of the radio soap opera transplants that never really thrived in its new soil was *Kitty Foyle,* which aired on CBS from 1942–44 with Julie Stevens in the lead. It followed the 1940 movie of the same title which won Gingers Rogers the Oscar for best actress in the lead role. The source for all the adaptations was a novel by Christopher Morley.

The TV version of *Kitty Foyle* was unique in that the titular character did not appear immediately. Kitty first popped up on February 10, by which time viewers had become accustomed to her simple yet troubled family, which lived in Philadelphia. She arrived from college ready to go to her freshman dance with Flip Martin, but found her beloved Pop ill and her brothers Ed and Mack acting like strangers. Ed, who was jailed at one point, discovered some peace with his marriage to Sophie before the end of the run. Unfortunately, Mack borrowed cash from a loan shark. Kitty had her own problems, mostly in the romantic field. Deciding not to go back to school, she ditched Flip for Wyn Strafford, who naturally did his soap opera best by falling for Stacylea, a society hound. Then when Nick Amsted revealed his interest in Kitty— surprise!—Wyn decided he wanted her too. Molly was Kitty's friend (played by Patty Duke as a girl, in flashbacks).

Kitty Foyle had other soap staples in its subplots, like dead bodies and secret schemes, but it never challenged *Art Linkletter's House Party* on CBS. By all accounts the show had a lousy debut that it never rose above. As a review in *Billboard* put it, "Judgment as to acting is very difficult when writing is so poor. . . . This show needs sharp improvement quickly."

KNOCKOUT

Game; Color
October 3, 1977–April 21, 1978

NBC Mon.–Fri. 11:30 a.m.–Noon (10/3/77–4/21/78)

Host: *Arte Johnson*

This number from Ralph Edwards Productions had a trio of players try to be the first to spell "Knockout" by identifying the one element not belonging among a quartet of words or phrases. Each identification earned a contestant one letter, who could then earn another letter by telling the relationship among the remaining three elements, or try to win two extra letters by challenging another contestant to do the same. There was a catch in the second option in that the challenged player could get the two letters instead of the challenger if he or she made a correct identification. The game winner then played a two-tiered bonus round where on the first level he or she tried to guess the topic connecting three clues revealed one at a time. A correct guess was worth $500 on the first clue, $300 after two clues, and $100 after three clues. Correct identification on any level led to a chance to win 10 times that amount by playing the same game but getting only one clue to name the category.

KORG: 70,000 B.C.
Children's; Color
September 7, 1974–August 31, 1975

ABC Sat. 10:30–11 a.m. (9/7/74–1/25/75)
ABC Sun. 10:30–11 a.m. (2/2/75–8/31/75)

Cast:

Korg	Jim Malinda
Mara	Naomi Pollack
Bok	Bill Ewing
Tone	Christopher Man
Tor	Charles Morteo
Ree	Janelle Pransky

Narrator: *Burgess Meredith*

A no-name cast (narrator notwithstanding), dubious concept, and bad scheduling (it aired right after shows with similar settings, *Land of the Lost* on NBC and *Valley of the Dinosaurs* on CBS) helped sink this Stone Age drama for kids. The adventures of the show's prehistoric family—parents Korg and Mara, their oldest boy, Bok, and three other siblings, Tone, Tor, and Ree—were uniformly dull, despite the fact that the American Museum of Natural History in New York and the Los Angeles County Museum of Natural History served as resource consultants to the series.

KOVACS ON THE CORNER—See *Ernie Kovacs.*

•KROFFT SUPERSHOW, THE
Children's; Color
September 11, 1976–September 2, 1978

ABC Sat. 10:30 a.m.–Noon (9/11/76–11/27/76)
ABC Sat. 10:30–11:30 a.m. (12/4/76–9/3/77)
ABC Sat. 11 a.m.–Noon (9/10/77–7/1/78)
ABC Sat. 11:30 a.m.–12:30 p.m. (7/8/78–9/2/78)

Cast:

Kaptain Kool	Michael Lembeck
Superchick	Debbie Clinger
Turkey	Mickey McMeel
Nashville	Louise Duart
Flatbush	Bert Sommer
Wonderbug (voice only)	Frank Welker
Bobby Buntrock	David Levy
Susan	Carol Anne Seflinger
C.C.	John Anthony Bailey
Dr. Shrinker (1976–77)	Jay Robinson
Hugo (1976–77)	Billy Barty
Brad (1976–77)	Ted Eccles
B.J. (1976–77)	Susan Lawrence
Gordie (1976–77)	Jeff McKay
Lori/Electra Woman (1976–77)	Deidre Hall
Judy/Dyna Girl (1976–77)	Judy Strangis
Professor Frank Heflin (1976–77)	Norman Alden
Magic Mongo (1977–78)	Lennie Weinrib
Donald Connelly (1977–78)	Paul Hinckley
Lorraine (1977–78)	Helaine Lembeck
Kristy (1977–78)	Robin Dearden

It might be said of *The Krofft Supershow* that it was representative of both the peak (at least in terms of airtime) and the decline of Sid and Marty Krofft Productions (*H.R. Pufnstuf, Land of the Lost*) for Saturday morning television in the 1970s. ABC gave the Kroffts a 90-minute slot which they filled with an extravaganza of several acts. Hosting and doing comedy sketches were the bright polyester-wearing Kaptain Kool and the Kongs (Superchick, Turkey, Nashville, and Flatbush). Their skits were taped at the World of Sid and Marty Krofft, a then-new indoor amusement park at the Omni International structure in Atlanta.

Between the bits were four Hollywood segments. "Wonderbug" had an interracial trio of teens (Bobby, Susan, and C.C.) who rode a broken-down dune buggy called Schlep Car which in times of humorous complications could be transformed into a gleaming, powerful four-wheeler by squeezing its horn. Dr. Shrinker was "an evil man with an evil mind," according to the theme song, who used a ray to reduce the size of another trio of teens (Brad, B.J., and Gordie) to a few inches. The three managed to escape from the scientist's lair, leading Dr. Shrinker and his diminutive sidekick Hugo on a quest for the "shrinkies." Condensed repeats of *The Lost Saucer* (q.v.) also aired.

But the most elaborate segment was "Electra Woman and Dyna Girl," where two reporters for *Newsmaker* magazine secretly fought crime as Electra Woman and Dyna Girl. They drove a triangular three-wheeled dune buggy and used electrical beams received on a wrist apparatus. Professor Heflin aided them as he manned the Crimescope Computer. Among recurring fantastic villains on the cliffhanger episodes were the Sorcerer (played by Michael Constantine) and the Pharaoh (Peter Mark Richman), each using at least one henchman.

Within three months of the debut, *The Krofft Supershow* lost half an hour of programming, cutting *The Lost Saucer* repeats and some sketches in the process. The show's second season had a fairly major overhaul, with only "Wonderbug" remaining unchanged. The still-youthful Kaptain Kool and the Kongs now did their routines before a largely juvenile audience in Hollywood, following the financial folly and eventual closing of the World of Sid and Marty Krofft. There were two new segments—"Magic Mongo," about an inept genie who used his powers to help his cowardly master Donald impress his pals Lorraine and Kristy on the beach, and *Bigfoot and Wildboy* (q.v.).

The changes did not encourage ABC to take another year with the show. However, NBC was desperate enough in 1978 to accept another, far worse rendition of the show, at first titled *The Krofft Superstar Hour*. (See *Bay City Rollers Show, The* for more details.)

•KUKLA, FRAN AND OLLIE

Puppet; B&W

August 24, 1952–June 22, 1962

NBC Sun. 4–4:30 p.m. (8/24/52–12/13/53; off summer of 1953)

NBC Sun. 3:30–4 p.m. (12/20/53–6/13/54)

NBC Mon.–Fri. 5–5:05 p.m. (9/25/61–6/22/62)

Regulars: *Burr Tillstrom, Fran Allison, the Jack Fascinato Orchestra (1952–54)*

If any children's series designed for television can be termed a "classic," *Kukla, Fran and Ollie* deserves that distinction. First seen on television in 1939, the series began locally in Chicago on October 13, 1947 before going onto NBC's Midwest TV network nightly beginning November 29, 1948. Four years later it came to daytime television.

A capsule description makes the show sound unspectacular: An actress (Fran Allison) appeared in front of a puppet stage to talk spontaneously to a cast of characters. But it was those characters, as delineated by puppeteer Burr Tillstrom, that made the show special. The stars were Kukla, a somewhat whiny semi-introvert, and Ollie (Oliver J. Dragon), a lovable one-fanged creature, but other unique personalities came and went at various points of each show, including Beulah Witch, buck-toothed, rumpled Fletcher Rabbit, and Cecil Bill (who said only something like "tooie"), and others. The chemistry and clever conversation between Allison and all the characters were a delight, and virtually no other TV puppet show has been as seamlessly put together as *Kukla, Fran and Ollie.*

The Sunday afternoon shows added a studio audience and pianist Jack Fascinato as musical director of his 12-piece orchestra. Hugh Downs, then just a Chicago TV personality, was the announcer. Fran and the puppets effortlessly wove in ads for sponsor RCA Victor in each week's show in their ad-libbed story lines; they also sang some songs.

Popping up from behind the stage of Kukla, Fran and Ollie *is puppeteer Burr Tillstrom, with Kukla to the left of him and Ollie on his right, and their pal Fran Allison.*

After two years, the series left daytime for a nightly slot on ABC from September 6, 1954–August 30, 1957. Then after four years with no network exposure, NBC offered a five-minute late afternoon slot where Fran appeared only weekly. A new featured character was the oh-so-proper Mrs. Buff-Orpington. The show's odd location (most series its length were seen in the last five minutes of every half hour, not the first) doomed its chances for success. In 1962, 65 extra shows were made to add to the 130 repeats for daily syndication in 1962.

Starting in 1967, the troupe hosted the long-running *CBS Children's Film Festival* (q.v.), and there was a series on public television from 1969–71. A syndicated weekly half-hour version in September 1975 generated little interest during its 39-show run. Tillstrom's death in 1985 ended any hopes of a revival.

The wit of *Kukla, Fran and Ollie* produced such notable admirers as authors Robert E. Sherwood, John Steinbeck, and Thorton Wilder. It was a true rarity, a TV production so unusual, with such stellar talent, that no one could produce even an inferior knockoff. One anonymous ex–NBC vice president made a telling comment about the program's fate to *TV Guide* in 1970. Asked why the show had had only limited TV exposure since the 1950s, he said, "It may have been too good."

KWICKY KOALA SHOW, THE

Cartoon; Color
September 12, 1981–August 28, 1982

CBS Sat. 8–8:30 a.m. (9/12/81–11/28/81)
CBS Sat. 1–1:30 p.m. (12/5/81–8/28/82)

Voices:

Kwicky Koala/Rawhide Clyde	*Robert Allen Ogle*
Wilfred Wolf	*John Stephenson*
Dirty Dawg	*Frank Welker*
Ratso	*Marshall Efron*
Officer Bullhorn	*Matthew Faison*
Crazy Claws	*Jim McGeorge*
Bristletooth	*Peter Cullen*
George Bungle/Ranger Rangerfield	*Michael Bell*
Joey Bungle	*Allan Melvin*

A throwback to the multiple-segment cartoons which dominated Saturday mornings in the 1960s, *The Kwicky Koala Show* had as its centerpiece an adorable bear from the land down under. Kwicky Koala did not always live up to his name (for one thing, he talked slowly), but his wits were quick enough to outsmart his nemesis Wilfred Wolf. Seen in other adventures were "Dirty Dawg," who, with his pal Ratso in their garbage dump home base, concocted schemes against Bullhorn the cop; "Crazy Claws," a wildcat who used wordplay to protect himself from Rawhide Clyde and Bristletooth the dog (likewise, the latter two were the quarry of wimpy Ranger Rangerfield); and "the Bungle Brothers," two dogs attempting to get

their big break as stars. The series was created by the great movie cartoon director Tex Avery in 1980, but his death that year resulted in a delay and slight restructuring of the property.

LADIES CHOICE

Game; B&W
June 8, 1953–September 25, 1953

NBC Mon.–Fri. 4:30–5 p.m. (6/8/53–9/25/53)

Host: *Johnny Dugan*

Done in cooperation with the Federation of Women's Clubs, whose members selected the show's talent, *Ladies Choice* was a typical 1950s audience-participation show. Johnny Dugan sang occasionally in addition to introducing guests and calling home viewers to ask them to guess a person in a "spinning picture" using some mystery limericks as a clue. It aired from Los Angeles.

LADIES DATE

Game; B&W
October 13, 1952–July 31, 1953

DuMont Mon.–Fri. 1–1:30 p.m. (10/13/52–7/31/53)

Host/Producer: *Bruce Mayer*

Singer: *Bob Hund*

Airing from WABD New York with Bruce Mayer, who had previously done a similar show in Detroit, this series spotlighted a woman's organization each day amid the games, stunts, and prizes for the in-studio audience that were the usual stock in trade for daytime shows of the period. Mayer returned when the show aired locally on WABD starting September 14, 1953 with the same format but without Bob Hund.

LADIES DAY

Variety; B&W
November 12, 1948–June 3, 1949

CBS Fri. 1:30–2 p.m., later Mon./Wed./Fri. 1–1:30 p.m. (11/12/48–4/15/49)
CBS Mon.–Fri. Noon–12:30 p.m. (4/18/49–6/3/49)

Regulars: *Warren Hull, Tom Mahoney, Sunny Raye, Andy Sanella's Quintet*

This standard-issue variety show hosted by Warren Hull had Tom Mahoney as Hull's sidekick. Also featured were female vocalist Sunny Raye, music by Andy Sanella's Quintet, guests, and stunts involving three housewives in the audience. In 1949 it became known as *The Warren Hull Show.*

•LAMP UNTO MY FEET
Religious; B&W and Color
November 21, 1948–January 21, 1979

CBS Sun. Various half hours between 3 and 6 p.m.
(11/21/48–12/27/53)
CBS Sun. 10–10:30 a.m. (1/3/54–1/21/79; off summers of
1954, 1976–78)

Host: *Dr. Lyman Bryson (1949–59 at least), Bill Leonard
(1954), Dr. George Crothers (1960–63 at least)*

Billed on its debut as a program designed to promote
understanding of different religious faiths, *Lamp Unto My
Feet* began its impressive run by presenting children's stories
as told at the Riverside Church of New York. However, this
documentary-style approach soon gave way to experimental
theater-in-the-round presentations due to a limited budget
and no sponsorship. Within that framework, the first
half hour of *Lamp Unto My Feet* dramatized and explored
ethical and religious issues ranging from racial and religious
intolerance to labor disputes, and that segment was usually
followed by a discussion between Dr. Bryson and a visiting
theologian, although sometimes the guest was from the
secular world. For example, in 1958 playwrights Carson
McCullers and N. Richard Nash made their TV debuts to
discuss their feelings in a three-part series, "Religion and
the Arts."

The series eventually became fluid enough to allow
ballets and dances to be used instead of dramas to express
opinions and issues. As with other religious series, it made
room for several up-and-coming actors to make early TV
appearances (James Earl Jones, for example) and also induced
a few seasoned veterans, such as Mercedes McCambridge,
to take the plunge.

After more than 30 years on air, the series ended in
January 1979 (along with the similarly long-lasting *Look
Up and Live* and *Camera Three*) because only 26 affiliates
were carrying the show. The network replaced it with *For
Our Times* (q.v.).

•LANCELOT LINK, SECRET CHIMP
Sitcom; Color
September 12, 1970–September 2, 1972

ABC Sat. 9–10 a.m. (9/12/70–9/4/71)
ABC Sat. 12:30–1 p.m. (9/11/71–9/2/72)

Voices: *Dayton Allen, Mel Blanc (1970–71), Joan Gerber,
Steven Hoffman, Bernie Kopell, Malachi Throne*

This all-ape (except for Henry the orangutan) extravaganza
was a spoof of spy adventures using simians in place of
humans. The good guys were from APE (Agency to Prevent
Evil) and had Lancelot Link and Marta Hairi work on behalf
of Commander Darwin. A chimp named Tonga was in charge
of the evil operation CHUMP (Criminal Headquarters for
Underworld Master Plan) along with such baddies as Baron
von Butcher and his sidekick Creto, the blond bewigged

Duchess, Dr. Strangemind, Wang Fu, and Ali AssaSeen.
Breaking up the action in the first season were Daffy Duck
cartoons (thus the appearance of Mel Blanc in the listing
above) and performances by the Evolution Revolution, an
all-chimp rock combo. Besides providing a voice, Malachi
Throne also served as narrator of the tales.

•LAND OF THE LOST
Adventure; Color
September 7, 1974–September 3, 1994

NBC Sat. 10–10:30 a.m. (9/7/74–9/4/76)
NBC Sat. 11–11:30 a.m. (9/11/76–11/20/76)
NBC Sat. Noon–12:30 p.m. (11/27/76–9/3/77)
NBC Sat. Noon–12:30 p.m. (2/4/78–9/2/78)
CBS Sat. 11:30 a.m.–Noon (6/22/85–9/7/85)
CBS Sat. Noon–12:30 p.m. (9/14/85–12/28/85)
CBS Sat. 11:30 a.m.–Noon (6/20/87–9/5/87)
ABC Sat. 8:30–9 a.m. (9/7/91–1/30/93)
ABC Sat. 11–11:30 a.m. (2/6/93–5/22/93)
ABC Sat. 10–10:30 a.m. (5/29/93–9/11/93)
ABC Sat. 11:30 a.m.–Noon (9/18/93–11/13/93)
ABC Sat. 10:30–11:30 a.m. (two shows; 5/7/94–9/3/94)

Cast:

Ranger Rick Marshall (1974–76)	*Spencer Milligan*
Will Marshall (1974–78)	*Wesley Eure*
Holly Marshall (1974–78)	*Kathy Coleman*
Uncle Jack Marshall (1976–78)	*Ron Harper*
Cha-ka the child simian (1974–78)	*Phillip Paley*
Sa (1974–78)	*Sharon Baird*
Ta (1974–78)	*Joe Giambalva*
Tom Porter (1991–93)	*Timothy Bottoms*
Annie Porter (1991–93)	*Jennifer Drugan*
Kevin Porter (1991–93)	*Robert Gavin*
Tasha (costumed actor; 1991–93)	*Ed Gale*
Tasha (voice; 1991–93)	*Danny Mann*
Christa (1991–93)	*Shannon Day*
Stink (1991–93)	*Bobby Porter*
Shung (1991–93)	*Tom Allard*

On the first episode of *Land of the Lost,* forest ranger
Rick Marshall and his children Will and Holly were
enjoying a day of rafting when they suddenly went over
a cliff into a strange land that resembled the Earth when
dinosaurs were king. However, their real nemeses were
not dinosaurs, but Sleestaks, hissing, human-sized lizards.
Helping them avoid these creatures were the friendly half-
ape, half-human species called the Pakunis, of which Cha-
Ka, Sa, and Ta were members. In 1976 Will and Holly's
Uncle Jack fell through a time vortex while dad Rick
disappeared back into the future, but otherwise the format
remained the same, with everyone trying to get back to
the present day. NBC reran the series in 1978, as did CBS
briefly in 1985 and 1987.

In 1991 a revived *Land of the Lost* surfaced with a
different family, this one consisting of Tom Porter, his

teenage son Kevin, and his daughter Annie, who sported some prominent eyeglasses and a ponytail. Their encounter with the prehistoric world came when their jeep fell into a crevice during an earthquake, dropping them onto a planet with three moons and dinosaurs of all kinds. Annie "adopted" one friendly baby dinosaur as her pet, called her Tasha, and brought her back to live with the family in their treehouse. As with the first incarnation, the Sleestaks were the group's principal threat, only now they spoke English; Shung was the evil leader of the Sleestaks. Also seen some was Christa, another human who had apparently fallen onto the planet from Earth while a child, though she had no memory of her past. Stink was her primate pal.

The 1990s series was filmed, while the 1970s version was taped. The use of film gave the stop-action photography in the dinosaur sequences a more realistic look, as did extensive use of outdoor shooting. Both series were productions of Sid and Marty Krofft. In the summer of 1994 repeats of the 1990s series aired back-to-back before going to the Nickelodeon cable channel.

LARAINE DAY SHOW, THE
Talk/Variety; B&W
May 5, 1951–August 18, 1951

ABC Sat. 1–1:30 p.m. (5/5/51–8/18/51)

Host: *Laraine Day*

Announcer: *Ruth Woodner*

On this series Laraine Day interviewed guests (Barbara Britton, Fannie Hurst, and Constance Moore appeared on the debut), and Ruth Woodner was her sidekick and commercial announcer. The show was preempted nine times during the summer of 1951 by a warmup show she did for the New York Giants baseball games on Gotham independent station WPIX.

This series should not be confused with another Day did that was seen on Saturday afternoons in some markets in 1951, originally titled *Hot Stove League*. That was a 15-minute weekly syndicated series she co-hosted with ex-baseball player Leo Durocher, her husband at the time, in which they interviewed a guest connected with baseball. That series remained in production through 1952, but was retitled *Double Play with Durocher and Day*. Day also hosted a similar Thursday night show on ABC, called *Daydreaming with Laraine*, from May 17–July 19, 1951.

LAS VEGAS GAMBIT—See *Gambit*.

LASSIE'S RESCUE RANGERS
Cartoon; Color
September 8, 1973–August 30, 1975

ABC Sat. 10–10:30 a.m. (9/8/73–8/31/74)
ABC Sun. 10:30–11 a.m. (9/8/74–1/26/75)
ABC Sat. 10:30–11 a.m. (2/1/75–8/30/75)

Voices:

Ben Turner/Narrator	*Ted Knight*
Laura Turner	*Jane Webb*
Ben Turner Jr./Gene Fox	*Hal Harvey*
Susan Turner	*Lane Scheimer*
Jackie Turner	*Keith Sutherland*

Lassie, the famous collie first seen in movies in 1942's *Lassie Come Home* and even heard on a radio series on ABC in 1947 and NBC in 1948–50 (with Earl Keen providing the barks and yelps), had his biggest success in television. His live-action series ran on CBS from 1954–71 and then three years more in syndication, overlapping with the start of this cartoon adaptation. Here Lassie served as part of the Forest Force, a rescue team that protected Thunder Mountain National Park and its creatures (who had their own safety group, the Rescue Rangers, led by Lassie and composed of eight other animals ranging from Groucho the owl to Toothless the mountain lion). The Turner family was part of the force, and Ben Jr. was the young boy who bonded with Lassie the most. Gene was a native American and Ben Jr.'s friend. The show's second season was all repeats.

LAST WORD, THE
Discussion; B&W
January 5, 1957–October 18, 1959

CBS Sun. 2:30–3 p.m. (1/5/57–3/31/57)
CBS Sun. 3:30–4 p.m. (1/5/58–2/23/58)
CBS Sun. 5–5:30 p.m. (6/1/58–9/21/58)
CBS Sun. 3–3:30 p.m. (1/18/59–3/15/59)
CBS Sun. Noon–12:30 p.m. (3/29/59–4/19/59)
CBS Sun. 5–5:30 p.m. (7/5/59–10/18/59)

Regulars: *Dr. Bergen Evans, John Mason Brown*

This discussion show was about discussion itself, or rather words and phrases used in discussion. Each week a panel of regulars and usually two other guests met to review what should and should not be considered proper in the English language. For example, the show ruled that the phrase "It is me" is acceptable English, and even that "Ain't I?" was allowable as a contraction for "Am I not?" Among the regulars, host Dr. Evans thought that colloquialisms such as "you all" were fine, but he loathed clichés, while continuing panelist John Mason Brown characterized himself as a "word conservative."

Guests ranged from writers Truman Capote, S. J. Perelman, and Emily Kimbrough to performers Olivia de Havilland, June Lockhart, and Mary Margaret McBride. Even Groucho Marx visited in a raucous session on January 27, 1958 (he called Dr. Evans "Bergie"). By the summer of 1958 it became one of the first TV series to go to videotape when it started recording shows on Fridays because panelists did not like coming in the studio on a Sunday afternoon.

Twice during its run—the summer of 1957 and again from March to May 1958—the show left its afternoon slot for a CBS Sunday at 6 p.m. airing.

This 1959 panel of The Last Word *consisted of, from left, host Dr. Bergen Evans, film critic Arthur Knight, actress June Havoc, and regular John Mason Brown.*

•LAVERNE AND SHIRLEY

Cartoon; Color
October 10, 1981–September 3, 1983

ABC Sat. 9:30–10 a.m. (10/10/81–9/18/82)
ABC Sat. 10–11 a.m. (9/25/82–1/1/83)
ABC Sat. 11 a.m.–Noon (1/8/83–9/3/83)

Voices:

Laverne De Fazio	Penny Marshall
Shirley Feeney (1981–82)	Cindy Williams
Shirley Feeney (1982–83)	Lynn Marie Stewart
Sgt. Turnbuckle (1981)	Ken Mars
Sgt. Squealy	Ron Palillo
Mork (1982–83)	Robin Williams
Mindy McConnell (1982–83)	Pam Dawber
Fred McConnell (1982–83)	Conrad Janis
Mr. Caruthers (1982–83)	Stanley Jones
Eugene (1982–83)	Shavar Ross
Hamilton (1982–83)	Mark Taylor
Orson (1982–83)	Ralph James
Arthur "the Fonz" Fonzarelli	
(1982–83)	Henry Winkler
Mr. Cool/Doing (both 1982–83)	Frank Welker

The first season of the cartoon form of *Laverne and Shirley* was fairly similar to the ABC nighttime sitcom (1976–83), at least in tone. Laverne (a crass, loudmouthed New York City type) and Shirley (her saccharinely sweet friend) left the Schotz Brewery in Milwaukee for a more challenging world as privates in the U.S. Army under tough Sgt. Turnbuckle and later the "hog with an attitude" Sgt. Squealy.

In 1982 the show expanded to be *The Mork and Mindy/Laverne and Shirley/Fonz Hour*. The basic premise of the Laverne and Shirley story lines was the same, but now joining them in the service was Fonzie (who had dated Laverne on the *Happy Days* nighttime show) and his dog Mr. Cool (see *Fonz and the Happy Days Gang* for more details), and Lynn Marie Stewart replaced Cindy Williams, who had by that time also left the nighttime show. As for the first title feature, it was a fairly faithful recreation of the 1978–82 ABC nighttime sitcom *Mork and Mindy* in terms of its cast. Demented alien Mork enrolled at Mount Mount High on Earth, following the urgings of Orson, his leader on the planet Ork, to learn more about teenage life. His adolescent schoolmates there were Eugene and Hamilton, and his pet was the six-legged Doing. Mindy, the daughter of music enthusiast Fred McConnell, was still his pal. Those recreating their nighttime roles in voice were Robin Williams, Pam Dawber, Conrad Janis, Shavar Ross, and Ralph James.

•LAZERTAG ACADEMY
Cartoon; Color
September 13, 1986–August 22, 1987

NBC Sat. Noon–12:30 p.m. (9/13/86–8/22/87)

Voices:

Jamie Jaren	Noelle Harding
Draxel Drear	Brooker Bradshaw
Beth Jaren	Christina MacGregor
Tom Jaren	Billy Jacoby
Nicky Jaren	R. J. Williams
Andrew Jaren/Skugg	Frank Welker
Charlie/Skugg	Pat Fraley
Genna Jaren	Tress MacNeille
Professor Olanga	Sid McCoy

LazerTag Academy world champion Jamie Jaren left the year 3010 to help rescue her ancestors, teenagers Tom and Beth and toddler Nicky, from the clutches of criminal Draxl Drear and his genetically engineered werewolflike accomplices, the Skuggs. The Skuggs' starship had crashed into the Atlantic Ocean decades earlier, but Professor Olanga revived them from suspended animation and they went back in time to 1987 to destroy Beth, who created the starlight gun and star sensor worn by Jamie to stun others and move items and other actions done commonly in 3010. While their battles received scant notice from the Jarens' parents, Andrew and Genna, who accepted Jamie as a foreign exchange student, next-door neighbor Charlie was much more snoopy and irritating, believing that Jamie was an alien. Another complication was that Drear was a relative of Jamie's and able to use her powers at times. However, Beth and Tom adapted and learned how to use some of Jamie's powers in their fights. Jamie updated Professor Olanga on her status each week. Ralphie was the Jarens' sheepdog.

The cartoon was based on the arcade game LazerTag, which was a lot easier to understand and, judging by the series' lack of success, apparently easier to enjoy too.

LEARN TO DRAW—See *You Are An Artist.*

•LEAVE IT TO THE GIRLS
Discussion; B&W and Color
1958; 1962–63; 1971; 1981–82

Syndicated 30 and 55 minutes weekly and daily beginning 1958

Hosts: *Nancy Connors (1958), Maggie McNellis (1962–63), Al Hamel (1971), Stephanie Edwards (1981–82)*

Regulars (1962–63): *Patricia Bright, Rita Hayes, Sue Oakland*

Leave It to the Girls aired on Mutual radio from 1945 to 1949, and appeared on television in several incarnations. Its debut was on a special local simulcast on W6AXAO Los Angeles on July 2, 1948 from 3–3:30 p.m. with Mike Frankovitch as moderator and Binnie Barnes, Constance Bennett, Robin Chandler, and Ann Rutherford as panelists.

The show went into syndication first as a weekly offering with a rotating panel led by Nancy Connors. Four years later came the next installment, this one a daily 55-minute version with regulars Patricia Bright, Rita Hayes, and Sue Oakland. In 1971 a daily half-hour version called *Mantrap* appeared under the auspices of Al Hamel–Dick Clark Productions from Vancouver, British Columbia, Canada. Here three women grilled the male guest. Seen occasionally on the panel were Phyllis Kirk, Sue Lyon, and Carol Wayne.

The last version came out in 1981 under the enlightened title of *Leave It to the Women.* It had more leeway than the previous versions to air potentially controversial issues, covering such topics as male strippers and X-rated movies, but the basic format was the same: a panel of women grilled one male guest about a cause he was representing, often with snide, condescending comments. Like *Mantrap,* it aired daily for half an hour and had recurring albeit rotating panelists, who included June Lockhart and Della Reese.

•LEEZA
Talk; Color
January 17, 1994–

NBC Mon.–Fri. 11 a.m.–Noon (1/17/94–10/13/95)
NBC Mon.–Fri. 10 a.m.–Noon (two shows daily; 10/16/95–3/1/96)
NBC Mon.–Fri. 11 a.m.–Noon (3/4/96–)

Host: *Leeza Gibbons*

Leeza Gibbons, the co-host of *John and Leeza from Hollywood,* went solo after six months and hosted a harder-hitting talk show examining one issue a day with a studio audience. As it proved to be successful, in the summer of 1995 Gibbons officially ended her ties with the nightly syndicated *Entertainment Tonight* to concentrate on this show. A few months later, the series became the first network talk show to air twice a day when NBC canceled its critically drubbed *The Other Side,* then reverted to once daily when *Real Life* debuted in March 1996.

LET'S GO TO THE RACES—See *Championship Bowling.*

•LET'S MAKE A DEAL
Game; Color
December 30, 1963–January 11, 1991

NBC Mon.–Fri. 2–2:25 p.m. (12/30/63–6/26/64)
NBC Mon.–Fri. 1:30–1:55 p.m. (6/29/64–9/29/67)
NBC Mon.–Fri. 1:30–2 p.m. (10/2/67–12/27/68)
ABC Mon.–Fri. 1:30–2 p.m. (12/30/68–7/9/76)
NBC Mon.–Fri. 10–10:30 a.m. (7/9/90–1/11/91)

Regulars: *Monty Hall, Wendell Niles (1963–64), Jay Stewart (1964–76), Carol Merrill (1963–76), Bob Hilton (1990)*

The costumes, the prizes (both clunky and fancy), the barkerlike style of Monty Hall—if there ever was a game show that created a carnival atmosphere, *Let's Make a Deal* was it. No real intelligence was needed, only the ability to attract Monty's attention to play fast-moving guessing games in a shot to win cash, merchandise, and ultimately a shot at the "Big Deal of the Day" hidden behind one of three doors. It was loud and frenetic, but millions loved the show, and it became one of TV's biggest daytime hits.

The program hadn't started out that way. Originally, prospective contestants were supposed to bring some knickknack to trade with Monty for a chance at prizes, hence the show's title. The costumes made their appearance a few months after the show began, when a few eager types tried to catch Hall's eye by wearing them, and the trend mushroomed; some would-be participants even wore placards expressing their intentions. (By the end of the 1960s, costumes became standard for any contestant picked from the audience.)

But back to the show. The hidden items ran from modest to elaborate prizes to "zonks," worthless items like oversized prop furniture. But even zonks, of which the show gave away an estimated 10,000 during its run in the 1960s and 1970s, had to be honored as prizes per network rules, so most contestants signed a certificate of forfeiture and

received another prize in the place of the zonk they had won, including such respectable items as a stereo or television. The players who fared best in the day's five to six contests could trade what they won for a chance at the "Big Deal of the Day," where each player picked one of three doors where model Carol Merrill stood. Generally, what was behind the doors was worth more than what they had earned in the regular game. After this segment ended, Hall went back to wheeling and dealing in the show's last few minutes, telling audience members things like he'd pay them $50 for each silver dollar they had on their person. Announcer Jay Stewart appeared on hand often as part of Hall's elaborate schemes (or, if you prefer, con games).

Let's Make a Deal proved to be the first successful competition NBC mounted against the daytime CBS Goliath *As the World Turns*. But just when it was reaching its peak in late 1968, the network erred in negotiations with Hall, the show's co-producer, and he left for ABC in the same time

Monty Hall, host/regular of Let's Make a Deal *in the early 1960s, seen with some of the wildly dressed audience members who hoped to attract his attention and get a spot on the show.*

slot. The switch in networks cost NBC greatly, both literally and figuratively. The network lost approximately $100 million in revenues with the show's disappearance, and its momentary lead over CBS in daytime in 1968 vanished so completely that the network fell into third behind ABC for a time in 1969. And NBC never really had a viable successor to *Let's Make a Deal* until it expanded *Days of Our Lives* to an hour in 1975.

NBC tried *Let's Make a Deal* in a nighttime slot from May to September 1967, but decided against giving the show that slot permanently, so the program jumped to ABC. ABC installed it on its lineup February 1969 through August 1971, after which the show went into nightly syndication until 1976. After short-lived syndicated revivals in 1980 and 1984, the series returned to NBC daytime in 1990 taped at the Disney/MGM Studios near Orlando, Florida. Bob Hilton hosted at first, but the network wanted Hall, and he had regained the reins by October. After its short run, Hall kept the show going by using TV commercials to invite viewers to play the game via phone. Some salesmen don't know when to stop.

LET'S PLAY POST OFFICE

Game; Color
September 27, 1965–July 1, 1966
NBC Mon.–Fri. 12:30–12:55 p.m. (9/27/65–7/1/66)

Host: *Don Morrow*

A trio of players read letters supposedly authored by a celebrity, and each contestant tried to be the first to identify who "wrote" them. A quicker answer meant more money. Among the names invoked on the debut were Sitting Bull and Barbra Streisand.

LET'S TAKE A TRIP

Children's; B&W
April 17, 1955–February 23, 1958
CBS Sun. 3:30–4 p.m. (4/17/55–6/26/55)
CBS Sun. 5:30–6 p.m. (7/21/55–12/25/55)
CBS Sun. Noon–12:30 p.m. (1/8/56–2/23/58)

Regulars: *Sonny Fox, Pud Flanagan (4/17/55–4/28/57), Ginger MacManus (4/17/55–4/28/57), Joan Terrace (4/21/57–2/23/58), Jimmy Walsh (4/21/57–2/23/58)*

Sonny Fox took two children around New York City and outside the area each week on this children's informational series. When the show started, he made excursions with Pud, 10, and Ginger, 9, to such places as a bakery, a dairy farm, an aircraft carrier, a firehouse, and even Ebbets Field to meet the Brooklyn Dodgers baseball team. Two notable visits were to Independence, Missouri, on June 30, 1956, when ex-president Harry Truman guided the children on a tour of his library (it was taped three days in advance of the air date), and to Connecticut on July 21, 1956 to see Katharine Hepburn and Alfred Drake rehearsing a production of "Much Ado About Nothing."

In 1957 Pud and Ginger were nearing their teens, and the series got two new kids, 8-year-old Joan Terrace and 9-year-old Jimmy Walsh. Lack of a sponsor caused CBS to drop the show a year later.

LETTERS TO LAUGH-IN

Game; Color
September 29, 1969–December 26, 1969
NBC Mon.–Fri. 4–4:30 p.m. (9/29/69–12/26/69)

Host: *Gary Owens*

The strength of the show business phenomenon that was *Laugh-In*, NBC's huge Monday night comedy hit that ran from 1968 to 1973, was such that it spawned the first—and likely the only—game show to be spun off from a variety series. Four stars, two of whom usually were *Laugh-In* regulars, read jokes behind podiums shaped like mailboxes on a set resembling *Laugh-In's* psychedelic color bursts. Jokes were scored on a scale of zero to 100, with the highest joke getting a prize, and the lowest joke earning the writer a trip to "beautiful downtown Burbank," as one of *Laugh-In's* many catchphrases went. Among the *Laugh-In* personnel appearing in addition to Gary Owens (he acted as the bombastic announcer on the nighttime show) were hosts Dan Rowan and Dick Martin, Ruth Buzzi, Teresa Graves, Alan Sues, and Jo Anne Worley.

LIBERACE SHOW, THE

Musical Variety; B&W
October 13, 1958–April 10, 1959
ABC Mon.–Fri. 1–1:30 p.m. (10/13/58–4/10/59)

Regulars: *Liberace, Dick Roman, Marilynn Lovell, the Gordon Robinson Orchestra*

Liberace (pronounced "lih-bur-RAH-chee") established his huge following by becoming a flamboyant presence on television. Everything about his shows was glittering and gaudy, from his outrageous outfits to the candelabra on his grand piano. He first appeared on an early evening show on NBC from July 1–August 28, 1952, then an even more popular syndicated show produced in the years from 1953 to 1955 and much rerun in years after that. By 1955 he and his brother George, Liberace's onetime bandleader, had 300 fan clubs in North America, and repeats of his show aired twice daily on WPIX in New York City as well as more than 200 stations across America. In 1958 some films were on their 11th runs, and in New York City he ran six times a week.

Given all that, ABC no doubt thought it had a surefire hit when Liberace started a new show from Hollywood in 1958. Along with baritone Dick Roman and assistant Marilynn Lovell, the show featured music from a guest "girl of the month." And what other popular pianist but Liberace would play a mix of the classics along with "Volare," "'S Wonderful," and "The Purple People Eater" on his TV show's debut? Surprisingly, given expectations, the ratings were low, and sponsors stayed away, forcing cancellation of the show after just six months. Liberace did just one more TV show a decade later, a summer series produced in London and seen on CBS Tuesday nights from July 15–September 16, 1969.

•LIDSVILLE
Sitcom; Color
September 11, 1971–August 31, 1974

ABC Sat. 10:30–11 a.m. (9/11/71–9/2/72)
ABC Sat. 12:30–1 p.m. (9/9/72–9/1/73)
NBC Sat. 8–8:30 a.m. (9/8/73–8/31/74)

Cast:

Horatio J. Hoodoo	*Charles Nelson Reilly*
Weenie the Genie	*Billie Hayes*
Mark	*Butch Patrick*

Voices: *Joan Gerber, Walker Edmiston, Lennie Weinrib*

Costumed Actors: *Sharon Baird, Joy Campbell, Jerry Maren, Angelo Rossito, Felix Silla, Hommy Stewart, Van Stewart, the Hermine Midgets*

When teenager Mark went to a magician's dressing room, he saw the magician's hat enlarge. Intrigued, he looked into the hat but fell in it down to Lidsville, where life-sized caps lived. Evil magician Hoodoo thought Mark was a spy for the good hats and imprisoned him with Weenie the Genie. When Mark got the magic ring which housed Weenie, she helped him escape and became his servant. Then a dozen good hats, including Colonel the pith helmet, Big Mother Wheels the motorcycle helmet, Hiram the straw hat, and Boomer the football helmet, befriended Mark and tried to help him get home while fighting Hoodoo. Hoodoo, who shot bombs from his fingers and had a top hat he converted into a hovercraft, had help from four bad hats. He also had a house inhabited by a dumb rabbit aide, talking furniture, and even a "hat band." Obviously, puns abounded on this program.

Though the theme song said Mark's arrival at Lidsville was in a park, a sign advertising magician "Merlo the Great" (also played by Charles Nelson Reilly but without Hoodoo's red hair and goatee and green face) indicated the opening was filmed at Six Flags Over Texas. Mark claimed he was from Jackson City, but gave no state. The series was created and produced by Sid and Marty Krofft, and the elaborately costumed puppets were created and executed by Krofft Productions. Sid Krofft also co-wrote the theme song. The videotaped show aired repeats from 1972–74.

LIFE WITH LINKLETTER—See *Art Linkletter's House Party.*

•LIFE WITH LOUIE
Cartoon; Color
September 9, 1995–

Fox Sat. 11:30 a.m.–Noon (9/9/95–)

Voice:

Louie Anderson/Mr. Anderson	*Louie Anderson*

For 8-year-old Louie Anderson, life growing up in the Midwest as one of seven kids was no picnic. His war veteran father, who was almost always grumpy, was given to expounding on his war years in a crabby voice. In addition, Louie had to care for his little brother Tommy, the baby of the family. Louie consoled himself by fooling his brother at every turn (he tried to convince Tommy he was adopted), trying to lighten up his dad unsuccessfully via "fun" activities like fishing, and mooning over his unrequited love Jeannie Harper. The series was a semiautobiographical account from stand-up comedian Louie Anderson, its creator and executive producer, albeit with the accent on humor. It was adapted from a special seen on Fox Saturday morning December 24, 1994.

LIFE WITH SNARKY PARKER
Children's; B&W
September 11, 1950–October 13, 1950

CBS Mon.–Fri. 5:15–5:30 p.m. (9/11/50–10/13/50)

Puppeteers: *Bil and Cora Baird*

Voices: *Frank Fazakas, Frank Sullivan*

Narrator: *Slugger Ryan*

Snarky Parker's life in Hot Rock was typical for a TV sheriff in the wild west. He hung out at the local saloon (the Bent Elbow), had a love interest (the town's schoolmarm), and fought for justice against a perennial enemy (Ronald Rodent). Need we reveal who always won the fights between Snarky and Ronald? This puppet show ran mostly in the early evening on CBS from January 9-August 30, 1950 before switching to a late daytime slot before cancellation. It preceded another puppet show, *Lucky Pup* (q.v.).

LIFE WITH UNCLE JOHNNY COONS—See *Uncle Johnny Coons Show, The.*

•LIFESTYLES OF THE RICH AND FAMOUS
Magazine; Color
April 7, 1986–May 29, 1987

ABC Mon.–Fri. 11–11:30 a.m. (4/7/86–5/29/87)

Host/Producer/Co-Writer: *Robin Leach*

Narrator: *Les Marshak*

Depending on one's viewpoint, the 1980s phenomenon *Lifestyles of the Rich and Famous* was either an innocent look at how the upper crust lives and what it buys, or a crass celebration of capitalism and greed. Begun as a syndicated special in August 1983, it became a weekly syndicated series the following year, prompting this network daytime version of original shows and repeats for a time.

The show was nothing more than a lush-looking videotaped documentary, showing the stars at home with their various objets d'art or on vacation at some posh getaway. At least once during Les Marchak's calm narration of each segment, pudgy former gossip columnist Robin Leach felt compelled to interject some statements as if they were the pronouncements of God. (As Dana Carvey mockingly put it in his impersonation of Leach on *Saturday Night Live* at the time, "I'm Robin Leach, I'm yelling, and I don't know WHY!") The show always ended with Leach bidding his viewers "champagne wishes and caviar dreams," which later served as the title of the show's theme song in the 1990s when sung by Dionne Warwick.

On June 16, 1986, the series was retitled *Fame, Fortune and Romance* with a slight revamp in format to favor celebrity profiles, and Sophia Loren, Clint Eastwood, and Raquel Welch were all on the debut. However, there was still an occasional detour into a place or item chock full of luxury, like a visit to St. Tropez. This version ran two weeks before reverting back to *Lifestyles of the Rich and Famous*, then continued in the time slot on September 8, 1986 through the end of the run. The show had a fair number of repeats leavened into its brief run.

Besides the daytime run, ABC also aired this series weeknights at midnight from July 21–September 19, 1986. The show has continued running in syndication to the present, with actress Shari Belafonte joining Leach as co-host briefly in 1994. By 1996, the show's title had been shortened to *Lifestyles*.

LINUS THE LIONHEARTED

Cartoon; Color
September 26, 1964–August 31, 1969

CBS Sat. 11–11:30 a.m. (9/26/64–9/18/65)
CBS Sat. 10:30–11 a.m. (9/25/65–2/19/66)
CBS Sat. 12:30–1 p.m. (2/26/66–9/3/66)
ABC Sun. 9:30–10 a.m. (9/25/66–12/25/66)
ABC Sun. 10–10:30 a.m. (1/1/67–8/31/69)

Voices:

Linus	Sheldon Leonard
Sascha Grouse/Dinny	
Kangaroo/Rory Raccoon	Carl Reiner
The Giant	Jonathan Winters
Billie Bird/So-Hi	Ed Graham
Granny Goodwitch	Ruth Buzzi

Theme: *Johnny Mann*

Linus the Lionhearted featured characters originally introduced for a line of cereals from the Post company. Headlining the show was Linus the Lion, who was king of a land of animals which included such subjects as Billie Bird, Sascha Grouse, and Dinny Kangaroo. Linus had one adventure per show starring himself and another with the rest of the cast. They included, in separate adventures each week, Sugar Bear, who tried to get a free meal from Granny Goodwitch; Rory Raccoon, who guarded a cornfield; Lovable Yours Truly, a postman who saved dogs from the clutches of dastardly silent movie star Richard Harry Nearly; and So-Hi, a Chinese boy who told fables.

Producer Ed Graham, who also voiced Billie Bird the Mockingbird, said he managed to get Sheldon Leonard, Carl Reiner, and Jonathan Winters to work for salary on the cartoon because they were old pals. Winters was especially enjoyable as the club-wielding Chinese Giant who spouted exclamations like "Jumping Buddha!" The recording booth had Winters miked all the time to tape any spontaneous comic bits the actor devised. Other guest comedians who did voices on the show included the married duo of Jerry Stiller and Anne Meara.

When this cartoon took a beating in the ratings in 1965–66 against *The Beatles* on ABC, *Variety* reported that CBS was "jazzing up" the show, but did not specify what the changes were to be. In any event, CBS canceled it and ABC reran its two years of shows through 1969, by which time Sugar Bear was about the only character still seen on Post cereal boxes.

•LION KING'S TIMON AND PUMBAA, THE

Cartoon; Color
September 16, 1995–

CBS Sat. 8:30–9 a.m. (9/16/95–)

Voices:

Timon	Nathan Lane
Pumbaa	Ernie Sabella

Theme: *"Hakuna Matata," music by Elton John, lyrics by Tim Rice*

Like *The Little Mermaid*, this CBS cartoon was based on a successful Disney animated feature, in this case 1994's *The Lion King*. In both the film and TV series the diminutive Timon was an intelligent yet irritable and irresponsible meerkat who bonded with the more conscientious Pumbaa the warthog. As their main daily concern was that of getting bugs to eat, they clearly followed their mantra of "hakuna matata," or "no worries," when it came to living. Their comic misadventures took place both in and out of the forest jungle, and both the humor and the animation were several notches above the usual Saturday morning fare.

Between the two Timon and Pumbaa segments on each show was one segment on "Rafiki Fables," centered on a tree-dwelling monkey who granted one wish to a visiting animal that usually ended up teaching that creature a lesson in life. As with Timon and Pumbaa, Rafiki was a character first seen in *The Lion King* movie, as was the show's theme, an Oscar nominee for Best Song which lost to another *Lion King* tune, "Can You Feel the Love Tonight?"

LISA HOWARD—See ABC Midday Report.

LITTLE CLOWNS OF HAPPYTOWN

Cartoon; Color
September 26, 1987–July 16, 1988

ABC Sat. 8:30–9 a.m. (9/26/87–1/23/88)
ABC Sat. 8–8:30 a.m. (1/30/88–7/16/88)

Voices: *Charlie Adler, Susan Blu, Danny Cooksey, Pat Fraley, Ellen Gerstell, Howard Morris, Ron Palillo, Josh Rodine, Frank Welker*

The residents of Itty Bitty City, also known as Happytown, were miniature clowns designed to spread happiness throughout the world. This cute cartoon was designed for preschool viewers. Of some interest is the fact that writer Norman Cousins, whose philosophy that "laughter is the best medicine" helped him overcome disease, was a series consultant.

•LITTLE MERMAID, THE
Cartoon; Color
September 13, 1992–September 2, 1995

CBS Sat. 8:30–9 a.m. (9/18/92–8/27/94)
CBS Sat. 8–8:30 a.m. (9/3/94–9/2/95)

Voices:

Ariel, the Little Mermaid	*Jodi Benson*
Sebastian the Crab	*Samuel E. Wright*
Flounder	*Edan Gross*
Triton	*Kenneth Mars*
Various	*Frank Welker*

Based on the 1989 hit Disney full-length cartoon musical of the same name, which in turn was derived from Hans Christian Anderson's fairy tale, *The Little Mermaid* presented gentle stories of the sea lass Ariel in the time before the film was set, when she was a teenager. Sebastian was her cowardly crab chum, while Flounder was a more adventurous yellow youngster. The trio often managed to get into messes, but using their brains and respect for one another typically got things straightened out before the end of each show. Triton was Ariel's wise, bearded dad.

The cartoon was quite a faithful adaptation of the Disney movie, using many of the same voices (Benson and Wright) and similar artwork and music. The show's theme, "Under the Sea" by Alan Menken, had won the Oscar for Best Song in 1990. The series should not be confused with a ripoff cartoon syndicated in 1991 titled officially *Saban's Adventures of the Little Mermaid Fantasy.*

LITTLE RASCALS/RICHIE RICH SHOW, THE—See Richie Rich Show, The.

LITTLE ROSEY
Cartoon; Color
September 8, 1990–August 13, 1991

ABC Sat. Noon–12:30 p.m. (9/8/90–8/13/91)

Voices:

Roseanne	*Kathleen Laskey*

Little Rosey took ABC's top nighttime star at the time, comedienne Roseanne of the sitcom of the same name which started in 1988, and transformed her into a tyke with a devilish grin. Joining her in various scenarios were her friend Buddy, her sister Tess, and her brother Tater.

LITTLE SHOP
Cartoon; Color
September 7, 1991–September 5, 1992

Fox Sat. 10–10:30 a.m. (9/7/91–10/19/91)
Fox Sat. 10:30–11 a.m. (10/26/91–9/5/92)

Voices: *Harvey Atkins, David Huban, Tamar Lee, Roland "Buddy" Lewis, Marlo Vola*

Given the lineage of this bizarre story line (the 1961 cult movie *The Little Shop of Horrors* became the inspiration for a 1982 off-Broadway musical of the same name which later became another movie), devotees were probably not surprised to see a cartoon adaptation appear. Although Roger Corman, director of the 1961 film, served as creative consultant, the cartoon bore little resemblance to his movie other than the main characters of Audrey Jr., a man-eating talking plant; its caretaker at the greenhouse, Seymour Krelborn; and Seymour's girlfriend, Audrey. Seymour and Audrey, adults originally, now were lovesick teens who had to contend with a neighborhood creep aptly named Paine and Audrey's dad Mushnick. As in the musical, the characters thought nothing of breaking into song during part of each week's episodes— in fact, Audrey Jr. now seemed more rapper than man-eater.

The emphasis was on learning little lessons each week rather than sustaining the freakish atmosphere of the previous versions, which may be why this show lasted only one year. The show was promoted as having at least six musical numbers per episode.

LITTLE WIZARDS
Cartoon; Color
September 26, 1987–September 3, 1988

ABC Sat. 10–10:30 a.m. (9/26/87–1/23/88)
ABC Sat. 9:30–10 a.m. (1/30/88–7/16/88)
ABC Sat. 8–8:30 a.m. (7/23/88–9/3/88)

Voices: *Charlie Adler, Joey Camen, Peter Cullen, Katie Leigh, Danny Mann, Scott Menville, Amber Souza, Frank Welker*

Finger-sized Boo, Bump, and Winkle assisted Prince Dexter, a human of normal height, in the latter's quest to regain his kingdom, which had been usurped by his evil Uncle Renwick. This show originally ran a half hour after another show featuring diminutive creatures, *Little Clowns of Happytown.*

•LITTLES, THE
Cartoon; Color
September 10, 1983–September 6, 1986

ABC Sat. 10:30–11 a.m. (9/10/83–9/1/84)
ABC Sat. 11:30 a.m.–Noon (9/8/84–2/22/86)
ABC Sat. 8:30–9 a.m. (3/1/86–9/6/86)

Voices:

Henry Bigg	*Jimmy E. Keegan*
Mr. George Bigg/Dinky Little	*Robert David Hall*
Mrs. Bigg	*Laurel Page*
Lucy Little	*Bettina Bush*

Tom Little	*Donavan Freberg*
Slick	*Patrick Fraley*
Ashley	*B. J. Ward*
Grandpa Little	*Alvy Moore*

The Littles were a tribe of people similar to elves without magic. They had pointy ears and tails, measured one inch to every foot of human size in height, and lived behind the walls of people's house. An ingenious lot, they used sardine cans for beds and an inverted baby bottle for a shower. The family included children Lucy and Tom, wise Grandpa, and goofy aviator cousin Dinky. Their pal Henry Bigg, the son of Mr. and Mrs. Bigg, saved them from other humans who would have exploited them. Stories were promoted by ABC as emphasizing loyalty, friendship, and caring.

The source of the program was John Peterson's children's books about the Littles, which began in 1967 and had sold 5 million copies by the time the TV installments started. Many of the characters and actors voicing them appeared in the 1983 feature film *Here Come the Littles*.

LIVE WITH REGIS AND KATHIE LEE—See *Regis Philbin Show, The*.

LOIS AND LOOIE
Children's; B&W
October 16, 1950–June 15, 1951

ABC Mon.–Fri. 5–5:15 p.m. (10/16/50–2/10/51)
ABC Mon.–Fri. 5–5:15 p.m. (5/14/51–6/15/51)

Hostess/Cartoonist: *Lois Fisher*

Lois Fisher was a children's performer seen on Chicago TV stations as early as 1944. Looie was her creation, a male cartoon character whose stories were told and drawn by Fisher on the show along with Starbaby the horse and Poco the toy dog. They all appeared briefly on this series from WENR Chicago. Fisher later used other juvenile literature as source material for her stories, including Margaret E. Morcomb's *Red Feather* and its two sequels. This practice, according to *Publishers Weekly*, "has been successfully using children's books on the air and stimulating sales in book stores." It did not prevent network cancellation, however.

LONE RANGER, THE
Cartoon; Color
September 10, 1966–September 6, 1969

CBS Sat. 11:30 a.m.–Noon (9/10/66–9/2/67)
CBS Sat. 1–1:30 p.m. (9/9/67–9/7/68)
CBS Sat. 1:30–2 p.m. (9/14/68–9/6/69)

Voices:

The Lone Ranger	*Michael Rye*
Tonto	*Shep Menken*

One of the most enduring media creations of the 20th century, *The Lone Ranger* began as a local Detroit radio show on WXYZ on January 30, 1933. In 1934, the original became the basis for a Mutual radio network version that lasted until 1942, when it went to ABC for another 13 years (ending on May 27, 1955). On television it had a long run from September 15, 1949–September 12, 1957 on ABC Thursday nights, and was seen in weekend repeats on CBS, NBC, and ABC from June 1953–September 1961, with Clayton Moore as the Ranger most of the time and Jay Silverheels as Tonto.

All versions were true to George W. Trendle's creation of a Texas ranger in the Old West ambushed and then brought back to health by an Indian named Tonto. Dropping his birth name of John Reid, he donned a mask and became the Lone Ranger and made Tonto his "kemo sabe" (faithful friend) as they fought for justice. The ranger's horse was Silver (as in the familiar cry, "Hi-yo, Silver, away!"), while Tonto's was Scout. Their familiar theme was the bouncy "William Tell Overture."

When *The Lone Ranger* became a cartoon in 1966, there were different voices for the Ranger and Tonto, and the adventures went much more quickly—at the rate of three villains per show. Most were not the evil varmints seen in the earlier renditions but rather campy cads like the Black Widow (voiced by no less than Agnes Moorehead) and the Puppetmaster. Frankly, the legend was much better served by a hilarious Jeno's Pizza commercial from Stan Freberg running at the same time in which Moore and Silverheels reprised their roles. The Lone Ranger later reappeared in another cartoon from 1980–82 as a supporting act (see *Tarzan*).

LOOK HERE
Talk; B&W
September 15, 1957–April 4, 1958

NBC Sun. 3:30–4 p.m. (9/15/57–4/4/58)

Host: *Martin Agronsky*

NBC's answer to Edward R. Murrow's *Person to Person* on CBS nighttime was this live interview show which usually came from the guest's home or workplace. In addition to discussing interviewees' work and personal life, Martin Agronsky delved into their opinions on current issues. Guests from entertainment predominated, including Benny Goodman, Jack Webb, Rod Serling, Leonard Bernstein, and Anthony Perkins, but some political leaders took part too, including the Rev. Martin Luther King Jr., Sen. John F. Kennedy, and Cuban president Fulgencio Batista. Batista's appearance marked the first live Cuba-to-United States transmission. However, *Look Here*'s most publicized potential guests, Marilyn Monroe and then-husband Arthur Miller, never made it on air.

LOOK UP AND LIVE
Religious; B&W and Color
January 3, 1954–January 21, 1979

CBS Sun. 10:30–11 a.m. (1/3/54–1/21/79; off summers of 1954, 1974, 1975, and 1978)

Host: *Merv Griffin (1955), Dr. William Hamilton (1964)*

Produced by CBS News' Public Affairs Department in cooperation with the National Council of Churches of Christ, *Look Up and Live* was CBS's companion religious series to *Lamp Unto My Feet,* which preceded it on Sunday mornings. The two series were virtually interchangeable, as both presented dramas, discussions, and performances that were all related in some way to religious beliefs and concerns.

Among the highlights were "The Theology of Jazz" with the Dave Brubeck Quartet supplying music and the Rev. Lawrence McMaster of the Oxford (Pennsylvania) Presbyterian Church discussing how jazz and religion let an individual explore himself fully (August 28, 1955); "No Man is an Island," a drama about two ex-Army pals, one Caucasian and one African-American, who want to attend the same church (July 21, 1957); Mahalia Jackson singing (December 15, 1957); a five-part series in 1959 on "Contemporary Theatre and Religion" which featured Larry Kert and Carol Lawrence from the original Broadway cast of *West Side Story* doing songs and scenes from the show; another series in 1961 titled "As Seen from the Stage" showing plays by Edward Albee ("The Sandbox") and Jean-Paul Sartre ("The Flies"); the 18th-anniversary celebration with folk singer Pete Seeger leading traditional spirituals at the Shaker Museum in Old Chatham, New York (November 20, 1966); and many assorted documentaries, including footage CBS News shot in Africa for several shows in 1966.

A year after the show's debut, Merv Griffin, of future talk show fame, became the unlikely host, and he was followed almost a decade later by Dr. William Hamilton, theology professor at Colgate-Rochester Divinity School. The show used mostly unknowns in its dramas, but such familiar names as Siobhan McKenna and Theodore Bikel did appear occasionally. It ran for more than 25 years until CBS replaced it with *Sunday Morning* (q.v.).

LOOK YOUR BEST
Fashion; B&W
September 18, 1950–November 3, 1950

CBS Mon. and Fri. 3:30–4 p.m. (10/16/50–11/3/50)

Host: *Richard Willis*

Look Your Best, sponsored by International Latex, was a beauty hints show similar to *Meet Your Cover Girl,* which ran in its time slot on Tuesdays and Thursdays. Host Richard Willis also wrote for the show, which was replaced by the similar *Fashion Magic.*

•LOST SAUCER, THE
Sitcom; Color
September 6, 1975–September 4, 1976

ABC Sat. 9:30–10 a.m. (9/6/75–2/14/76)
ABC Noon–12:30 p.m. (2/21/76–9/4/76)

Cast:
Fi	Ruth Buzzi
Fum	Jim Nabors
Alice	Alice Playten
Jerry	Jarrod Johnson
Dorse (costumed character)	Larry Larson

Set in the 25th century, *The Lost Saucer* told of a pair of humanoid aliens named Fi and Fum who inadvertently landed on 20th-century Earth and got youngster Jerry and his babysitter Alice on board their space vehicle. Fi and Fum's various misadventures in returning the duo to their proper home and time formed the crux of this series. Dorse was Fi and Fum's resident pet, a combination of—surprise—a dog's body and a horse's head.

The Lost Saucer reappeared after cancellation as an element in *The Krofft Supershow* in 1976–77. When it was its own series, few viewers probably realized that actress Alice Playten also sang ABC's "Funshine Saturday" song promoting its 1975 fall lineup.

LOVE IS A MANY SPLENDORED THING
Soap; Color
September 18, 1967–March 23, 1973

CBS Mon.–Fri. 2–2:30 p.m. (9/18/67–9/1/72)
CBS Mon.–Fri. 3–3:30 p.m. (9/4/72–3/23/73)

Cast:
Mia Elliott (1967–68)	Nancy Hsueh
Paul Bradley (1967)	Nicholas Pryor
Dr. Jim Abbott (1967–68)	Robert Milli
Dr. Jim Abbott (1972–73)	Ron Hale
Helen Elliott Donnelly (1967)	Grace Albertson
Helen Elliott Donnelly (1968–73)	Gloria Hoye
Iris Donnelly Garrison (1967–70)	Leslie Charleson
Iris Donnelly Garrison (1971–73)	Bibi Besch
Laura Donnelly (1967–70)	Donna Mills
Laura Donnelly (1970–71)	Veleka Gray
Laura Donnelly (1972–73)	Barbara Stanger
Lt. Tom Donnelly (1967–69)	Robert Burr
Lt. Tom Donnelly (1969–73)	Albert Stratton
Ricky Donnelly	Shawn Campbell
Phillip Elliott (1967)	Len Wayland
Mark Elliott (1968)	Sam Wade
Mark Elliott (1969–70)	David Birney
Mark Elliott (1970–71)	Michael Hawkins
Mark Elliott (1972–73)	Tom Fuccello
Dr. Will Donnelly (1968–73)	Judson Laire
Spence Garrison (1968)	Michael Hanrahan
Spence Garrison (1968–72)	Ed Power
Spence Garrison (1973)	Brett Halsey
Dr. Peter Chernak (1969–70)	Paul Michael Glaser
Dr. Peter Chernak (1970)	Michael Zaslow
Dr. Peter Chernak (1970–73)	Vincent Bagetta
Angel Allison Chernak (1969–73)	Suzie Kay Stone
Dr. Ellis, psychiatrist (1969, 1971–72)	Robert Drew
Nancy Garrison (1969)	Susan Browning
Dr. Betsy Chernak Taylor (1970–73)	Andrea Marcovicci

Lily Chernak Donnelly (1970–73)	Diana Douglas
Martha Donelly (a.k.a. Julie Richards; 1970–71)	Beverlee McKinsey
Jim Whitman (1970)	Berkeley Harris
Sen. Alfred Preston (1971–72)	Don Gantry
Marion Hiller (1971–72)	Constance Towers
Dr. Sanford Hiller (at least 1971)	Stephen Joyce
Jean Garrison (at least 1971)	Jane Manning
Sam Watson (at least 1971)	James Bruge
Celia Winter (1972–73)	Abigail Kellogg
Joe Taylor (1972–73)	Leon Russom
Walter Travis (c. 1971)	John Carpenter

Love is a Many Splendored Thing was a sequel to, not a re-creation of, the 1955 movie of the same name starring William Holden, which was in turn based on the 1952 autobiography *A Many Splendored Thing* by an anonymous author. The TV adaptation was a pet project of CBS daytime president Fred Silverman, who saw to it that the show got to use the movie's Oscar-winning title theme by Sammy Fain and Paul Francis Webster, and have accompaniment by 12 musicians rather than the stock-in-trade organ used for dramatic bridges at the time. It was his bid to reclaim the 2 p.m. time period after *The Newlywed Game* on ABC and *Days of Our Lives* on NBC overtook *Password.*

The soap featured two eyebrow-raising stories for that period, the first being that of Mia Elliott, the Eurasian daughter of a dead Korean War soldier, who emigrated to San Francisco from Hong Kong and fell in love with Paul Bradley and then Dr. Jim Abbott. The other major story involved Laura Donnelly, a nun who fought romantic feelings for her sister Iris's boyfriend Mark Elliott, the son of Mia's Aunt Helen and Uncle Philip Elliott. Interracial romance and a tug-of-war between spiritual and carnal desires were not what viewers wanted to see, CBS daytime president Fred Silverman told creator Irna Phillips. She disagreed, and, in a harsh reaction typical of Phillips during such arguments, left the show.

Mia's story line ended messily by having her find that Dr. Abbott had performed an illegal abortion which killed a woman. That knowledge repelled Mia and made her leave town, while Dr. Abbott found himself facing a criminal investigation into his work. He ended up taking a job out of town. Laura's story continued, albeit without her nun's habit. She and Iris fought vigorously for the love of Mark, much to the displeasure of their father Dr. Will Donnelly. Mark's mom Helen had no fondness for Iris, finding her too flighty, and was no doubt gratified when Mark wed Laura instead. Iris made a play for Dr. Abbott, of all people, then started seeing a candidate for the Senate named Spence Garrison, whose only drawback was that he had a manipulative wife named Nancy who refused to divorce him. Complicating matters further was that when Spence and Iris went on a plane to Lake Tahoe for a romantic getaway, it crashed, leaving Iris blind.

Iris, despite (perhaps because of) her new condition, proved to be a noble sort in 1969, urging Laura and Mark to stay married when Mark cheated during their marriage. Their situation took on a whole new dynamic when Iris, cured of her blindness by Dr. Chernak, found herself pregnant by Mark after he had forced himself on her in a drunken stupor one night, believing her to be Laura. Iris eventually confessed to her now-husband Spence that their daughter was not his, a fact which crushed him initially but didn't destroy his campaign for Senate against incumbent Alfred E. Preston. Preston, incidentally, was a puppet for the rich Walter Travis, and Walter's ex-employee Joe Taylor was the one who tried to embarrass Spence about the latter's situation.

Laura and Mark had reunited by 1971, but, learning they could not conceive children, argued over whether to adopt a baby or a troubled 6-year-old girl that Laura favored. Then Laura tried to adopt Iris's child by Mark, and she even worked with the newly returned Dr. Jim Abbott to prove that Iris was unfit as a mother. Eventually, Laura and Mark adopted a different child, and Iris and Spence stayed together. Meanwhile Mark's mother Helen and Laura's brother Tom had remarried, Helen's husband Philip having died years before. Tom, who had a son named Ricky, had faced considerable grief the year before when his believed-to-be-deceased wife Martha, now called Julie Richards, popped up alive with a boyfriend, Jim Whitman. Jim was murdered and Tom was believed the culprit until it was found that Martha/Julie had done the deed accidentally.

Also in 1971, Dr. Sanford Hiller, married to Marion Hiller, fell in love with Betsy, Dr. Peter Chernak's sister. However, Betsy loved paraplegic Vietnam War veteran Sam Watson, then moved in with Joe Taylor. Lily, Betsy and Peter's mom, married Dr. Will Donnelly the following year.

Love is a Many Splendored Thing fared decently in the ratings until Procter & Gamble, in a questionable move, forced CBS to air all its soaps in one continuous block and moved this entry back an hour, where it flopped against *Another World* on NBC and *General Hospital* on ABC. Surprisingly, it managed to wrap up almost all of its story lines during the final two weeks on the air despite being notified of the cancellation in early February. The final sequence had Betsy Chernak marry Joe Taylor, followed by actor Judson Laire stepping out of character as Dr. Donnelly to thank the audience for their support over the years. Would that more shows would end that way . . . .

•LOVE OF LIFE

Soap Opera; B&W and Color
September 24, 1951–February 1, 1980

CBS Mon.–Fri. 12:15–12:30 p.m. (9/24/51–4/11/58)
CBS Mon.–Fri. Noon–12:30 p.m. (4/14/58–9/28/62)
CBS Mon.–Fri. Noon–12:25 p.m. (10/1/62–9/5/69)
CBS Mon.–Fri. 11:30 a.m.–Noon (9/8/69–3/23/73)
CBS Mon.–Fri. 11:30–11:55 a.m. (3/26/73–4/20/79)
CBS Mon.–Fri. 4–4:30 p.m. (4/23/79–2/1/80)

Cast:

Vanessa Dale (9/24/51–11/18/55)	Peggy McCay
Vanessa Dale (11/21/55–4/59)/	
Ellie Crown (1951)	Bonnie Bartlett
Vanessa Dale (4/59–2/1/80)	Audrey Peters
Meg Dale (1951–58)	Jean McBride
Meg Dale (1974–80)	Tudi Wiggins
Sarah Dale (1951–60)	Jane Rose
Sarah Dale (1968–78)/Althea	
Raven (1954–57)	Joanna Roos
Sarah Dale (1979–80)	Valerie Cossart
Will Dale (1951–53)	Edwin Jerome
Charlie Harper (1951–53)	Paul Potter
Charlie Harper (1953)	John Graham
Ben "Beanie" Harper (1951–57)	Dennis Parnell
Ben "Beanie" Harper (1957–58)	Tommy White
Ben Harper (1974–76)	Christopher Reeve
Ben Harper (1976–80)	Chandler Hill Harben
Ellie Crown (1951–55)	Hildy Parks
Ellie Crown (1955–56)	Mary K. Wells
Ellie Crown (1956)	Bethel Leslie
Paul Raven (1951–58)	Richard Coogan
Paul Raven (a.k.a. Matt Corby;	
1970–72)	Robert Burr
Miles Pardee (1951)	Joe Allen, Jr.
Evans Baker (1951–57 at least)	Ronald Long
Mrs. Rivers the housekeeper	
(1951 at least)	Marie Kenney
Warren Nash (1952–53 at least)	Grant Richards
Marty (1952–53 at least)	Earl Montgomery
Hal Craig (1953–57)	Steven Gethers
Matt Slocum (1953–54)	Burt French
Collie Jordan (c. 1954–55)	Carl Betz
Judith Lodge Raven (1954–57)	Virginia Robinson
Tammy Forrest (1956–57)	Scottie McGregor
Tammy Forrest (1956–70)	Ann Loring
Jack Andrews (1958)	Donald Symington
Tom Craythorne (1958)	Lauren Gilbert
Noel Penn (1958)	Gene Peterson
Bruce Sterling (1959–80)	Ron Tomme
Alan Sterling (1959–64)	Jim Bayer
Alan Sterling (1964–65)	Dan Ferrone
Alan Sterling (1965–67)	Dennis Cooney
Alan Sterling (1969–70)	John Fink
Barbara Sterling (1959–61)	Nina Reader
Barbara Sterling (1961–65;	
1970)	Lee Lawson
Barbara Sterling (1965–71)	Zina Bethune
Vivian Carlson (1959)	Eleanor Wilson
Vivian Carlson (1959–71)	Helen Dumas
Henry Carlson (1959–61)	Tom Shirley
Henry Carlson (1961–71)	Jack Stamberger
Dr. Tony Vento (1959–65)	Ron Jackson
Dr. Tony Vento (1965)	Jordan Charney
Cindy Craythorne (at least 1959)	Kimetha Laurie
Link Porter (1960–66)	Gene Pellegrini
Maggie Porter (1960–62)/Kay	
Logan (1962–63)	Joan Copeland
Rick Latimer (1960–66)	Paul Savior
Rick Latimer (1966–70)	Michael Ebert
Rick Latimer (1970–72)	Edward Moore
Rick Latimer (1972–78)	Jerry Lacy
Ginny Crandall (1960)	Barbara Barrie
Sandy Porter (1961–67)	Bonnie Bedelia
Julie Murano (1962–65)	Jessica Walter
Julie Murano (1965)	Jane Manning
Guy Latimer (1962–63)	John Straub
Connie Loomis (1962–65)	Chris Chase
Philip Holden (1963–65)	David Rounds
Glenn Hamilton (1963)	Bert Convy
Ace Hubbard (1964)	Jed Allan
Jonas Falk (1965)	Ben Piazza
Jonas Falk (1965–66)	Roy Scheider
Mickey Krakauer (1965–68)	Alan Feinstein
Hank Latimer (1965)	Justin Sterling
Hank Latimer (1970–78)	David Carlton Stambaugh
Tess Krakauer (1966–73)	Toni Bull Bua
Anna Krakauer (1966–67)	Jocelyn Brando
Charles Lamont (1966)	Stan Watt
Charles Lamont (1966–78)	Jonathan Moore
Diana Lamont (1966–76)	Diane Rousseau
Alex Caldwell (1966–71)	Fred Stewart
Alex Caldwell (1971–)	Charles White
Jason Ferris (1966–67)	Robert Alda
Sharon Ferris (1966–67)	Eileen Letchworth
Hester Ferris (1966–67)	Marie Masters
Bill Prentiss (1967–72)	Gene Bua
Toni Prentiss Davis (1967–68)	Frances Sternhagen
Toni Prentiss Davis (1969)	Louise Larabee
John Randolph (1967)	Barton Stone
John Randolph (1967–70)	Byron Sanders
Kate Swanson (1967–69)	Leonie Norton
Kate Swanson (1969–75)	Sally Stark
Beatrice Swanson (1968–75)	Jane Hoffman
Joe Bond (1968–70)	Lincoln Kirkpatrick
Rita Bond (1968–70)	Darlene Cotton
Monica Nelson (1968–70)	Beverly Todd
Link Morrison (1969–70)	George Kane
Link Morrison (1970–72)	John Gabriel
Dr. Jennifer Stark (1969–71)	Joan Bassie
Richard Rollins (1969–71)	Lawrence Weber
Jamie Rollins (1969–71)	Donald Warfield
Jamie Rollins (1970–76)	Ray Wise
Sally Bridgeman Rollins	
(1969–73)	Catherine Bacon
Clair Bridgeman (1969 at least)	Renee Roy
Ed Bridgeman (1969)	Hugh Franklin
Dr. Dan Phillips (1970–74)	Drew Snyder
Vinnie Phillips (1970)	Beatrice Straight
Vinnie Phillips (1970–74)	Nancy Marchand
Loretta Allen (1970–72)	Janet DuBois
Daisy Allen (1970–71)	Irene Cara

Daisy Allen (1971)
Dr. Joe Corelli (1971)
Dr. Joe Corelli (1971–73)
Judith Cole (1971–72)
Stacy Corby (1971–72)
Arden Dellacorte (1971)
Johnny Prentiss (1972–78)
Nurse Candy Lowe (1972–73)
Nurse Candy Lowe (1973–74)
Dr. Lloyd Phillips (1972–73)
Betsy Crawford (1973–77)
Betsy Crawford (1978–80)
Arlene Lovett (1974–80)
Carrie Johnson (1974–80)
Caroline Aleata (1974–76)
Caroline Aleata (1976–78)
Felicia Fleming (1974–77)
Dr. Ted Chandler (1974–75)
David Hart (1974–75)
Jeff Hart (1974)
Ray Slater (1975–80)
Eddie Aleata (1975–78)
Dr. Tom Crawford (1976–79)
Dr. Tom Crawford (1979–80)
Dr. Joe Cusak (1976–78)
Ian Russell (1976–77)
Bambi Brewster (1977–80)
Mia Marriott (1977–80)
Dr. Andrew Marriott (1977)
Dr. Andrew Marriott (1977–80)
Andy Marriott (1977–78)
Dory Patton (1977–78)
Wendy Hayes (1977–78)
Elliott Lang (1978–80)
Wesley Osborne III (1979–80)
Dr. Leann Wilson (1979–80)
Steve Harbach (1979–80)
Amy Russell (1979–80)
Professor Timothy McCauley
(1979–80)

Sharon Brown
Paul Michael Glaser
Tony LoBianco
Marsha Mason
Cindy Grover
Geraldine Brooks
Trip Randall
Nancy McKay
Season Hubley
Douglass Watson
Elizabeth Kemp
Margo McKenna
Birgitta Tolksdorf
Peg Murray
Deborah Courtney
Roxanne Gregory
Pamela Lincoln
Keith Charles
Brian Farrell
Charles Baxter
Lloyd Battista
John Aniston
Richard K. Weber
Mark Pinter
Peter Brouwer
Michael Allinson
Ann McCarthy
Veleka Gray
Richard Higgs
Ron Harper
Christian Marlowe
Sherry Rooney
Elaine Grove
Ted LePlat
Woody Brown
Mary Ann Johnson
Paul Craggs
Dana Delany

Shepperd Strudwick

Host/Commercial Announcer: Dan Hancock (1952–53 at least)

Love of Life changed several principal characters and actors, time slots, locales, you name it, in its run of over 28 years, yet remained fairly consistent in its resolve to be an "old-fashioned soap," where good was good and bad was bad, and characters were delineated more in black and white than in shades of gray. Overseeing this throughout the transitions was director Larry Auerbach, who was with the show from its first to its last day. In the show's early days, it was Auerbach who insisted that all the commercials be put at the beginning and end of the program, leaving the middle part for the drama. And there was plenty of that.

Will and Sarah Dale of fictional Barrowsville, New York, had two grown daughters living in New York City, virtuous Van and amoral Meg. Meg was married to rich Charlie Harper, and they had a son, Beanie. Meg's disinterest in doing things positively meant that she was the black sheep of an otherwise decent family, but she cared little, as she was involved in a passionate fling with flashy mobster Miles Pardee. When Meg was unjustly convicted of murdering Miles Pardee, she had lawyer Evans Baker clear her along with the help of her sister Van and Van's boyfriend, FBI agent Paul Raven. During this period Charlie, fed up with Meg's antics, divorced her and aptly quipped, "Meg is the greatest actress in the world, on or off stage."

As for Van, she continued to see Paul Raven in 1953, while working at a travel agency in New York, where the evil Warren Nash tried to steal $15,000 from under her and Marty the bookkeeper's nose, with the help of Meg, also working at the agency. After this incident, Van left New York and her supportive roommate Ellie Crown to pursue her romance with Paul, who went into law practice with Collie Jordan in Barrowsville. They ended up marrying in 1954 with the approval of his mother Althea and adopting the somewhat irascible 6-year-old Carol. Then, to her shock, Van learned that Paul had been married before, to newcomer in town Judith Lodge, and that Carol was their child, a fact that Paul claimed not to have known. The insane Judith fought Van and Paul for Carol's custody, but Judith was subsequently found dead when Sarah's house burned down. Van was tried for the murder, but it turned out that Paul's brother Ben Raven had done the deed.

Also during 1955–56, fugitive gangster Hal Craig threatened Carol when she saw him kill his twin brother, causing her to become mute. Carol did not speak again until Craig was caught and confessed to the crime. She and her grandmother Althea left town and disappeared from the show forever, while Van and Paul relocated from Barrowsville back to New York City.

Meanwhile, Meg had been dating Matt Slocum, another sleazeball, and then Hal Craig, who ran a halfway house and let Meg operate a nightclub. Van suspected Hal of shady dealings, but Hal told her to butt out of his affairs. After Hal was convicted, Meg went to New York City and wed con man Jack Andrews. A suspicious Paul went to Mexico, to check out Jack's claims of real estate investments there, but his plane crashed and Paul was presumed dead. While Van grieved, Meg also found herself without a husband too because Jack left town with her money.

Much of this activity happened in 1958, a busy year as the show went to 30 minutes daily. After Meg divorced Jack, she wed Tom Craythorne with the knowledge that she was carrying Jack's baby. Jack returned to blackmail Tom for $25,000, but fellow gang members later killed Jack for money. When it was proved that Tom was not the baby's father, Meg left town with Beanie. At the same time, Van learned that TV producer Noel Penn wanted to use her rather than alcoholic Tammy Forrest as star of his new show. Needless to say, Tammy was not thrilled, but grew to like Van when the latter helped her kick the drinking habit.

The appeal of New York City finally ended for Van when she met Bruce Sterling, a teacher at Winfield prep school in Rosehill, New York. She wed him in 1959 and moved to Rosehill to be with his grown family, daughter Barbara and son Alan, who were treated by Bruce's in-laws Henry and Vivian Carlson almost as if they were the Carlson's own. (Interestingly, when actress Bonnie Bartlett left her role as Van due to a salary dispute, Audrey Peters assumed it and made her debut going down the aisle to marry Bruce!) These characters dominated the show during the 1960s.

Vivian was resentful of Van joining the family, as was Barbara, since Van blabbed to Bruce about Barbara planning to elope with Dr. Tony Vento. While Bruce was recuperating from injuries he had sustained trying to stop rapist Glenn Hamilton from attacking Sandy Porter, Barbara insinuated to him that Van was being unfaithful, which nearly caused a divorce. However, some real infidelity occurred when Bruce was seduced by his secretary, Ginny Crandall. She used Bruce to obtain a patented formula Henry Carlson had which the latter's

unscrupulous rival Guy Latimer wanted to force Henry to sell to him. Bruce managed to expose Latimer's plot, but Van found out about his affair too, and left to live with his son Alan.

Meanwhile, Sandy Porter's parents Maggie and Link came to town and became friends with the Sterlings. The terminally ill Maggie hoped that the then-separated Van would marry Link after her death, but in 1962, when Maggie Porter died, her twin sister Kay (played by the same actress) tried to seduce Link instead. However, Link decided to marry Van's old actress pal Tammy Forrest and stayed with her until he died of cancer in 1966.

Van and Bruce eventually reunited, but they were aghast as Barbara decided to wed Rick Latimer, son of convicted felon Guy Latimer. The new duo ended up separated even before Barbara gave birth to their son Hank, and Rick successfully sued Barbara for custody of the child.

Love of Life *had as its main story a battle of wills between sisters Vanessa Sterling (at left, played by Audrey Peters) and Meg Hart (Tudi Wiggins), seen here in a 1976 shot.*

Others popping up in the 1960s were the philandering Jason Ferris, his disturbed wife Sharon, and their daughter Hester; pharmacist Alex Caldwell, who married Van's mother Sarah (Will Dale died in 1953); Rita and Joe Bond, the token black couple; and Charles and Diana Lamont, the Sterlings' next-door neighbors. Charles's son Bill Prentiss wed Tess Krakauer, who found themselves enmeshed in many of the plots of the late 1960s. Sally Bridgeman, a fellow college student of Bill's, fell in love with him and then took drugs when he rejected her. Another drug addict, Jamie Rollins, fell in love with Sally, but they sobered up when they learned of the damage they were doing to other people because of their habit. But Sally was confused in her feelings when she learned that her mother Clair was in love with Jamie's married dad Richard. Sally and Jamie did marry, but she ended up running away from him, and by the mid-1970s Jamie had embarked on an adulterous affair with the older Diana Lamont. Charles then divorced Diana and wed Felicia Flemming.

Also in the late 1960s, Tess and Bill had domestic problems due to her immaturity, which led to a divorce from Bill and a marriage to rich John Randolph. Tess then dropped John and remarried Bill, but unfortunately, John was found dead shortly thereafter, and so both of them were under a cloud of suspicion until Jamie's father Richard, of all people, was found to be the murderer.

What was most intriguing about Tess and Bill's trial was their defending lawyer Matt Corby, who turned out to be none other than Van's presumed dead husband Paul Raven suffering from amnesia. Paul slowly regained his memory, and Van was tempted to marry him again thanks to yet another dalliance by Bruce with Dr. Jennifer Stark. Sadly, she discovered that Paul had been married previously. His daughter by the earlier marriage, Stacy Corby, showed up, but his wife was found murdered, and in 1972 Matt/Paul was found guilty of the crime, eventually dying in a prison riot. Stacy became Van's ward, and Van eventually remarried Bruce.

While Bruce and Van's children had left the story at this point, their ex-son-in-law Rick Latimer remained a key figure. He had a love triangle with singer Kate Swanson and Dr. Dan Phillips, with the latter two marrying and having a child despite the machinations of Dan's jealous nurse Candy Lowe. Then Dr. Phillips and his daughter died in a car accident, and Kate wed Dr. Ted Chandler, who was treating Charles Lamont for his impotency with wife Diana. They left town in 1974, by which time Bill Prentiss had died of the fictional leukocytemia, Dr. Joe Corelli had become infatuated with Bill's widow Tess, and Tess had gone away after being exonerated for the murder of a criminal.

Also in 1974, with the show's popularity having dropped drastically since the 1950s and 1960s, when it was one of the top 10 daytime series, *Love of Life* made a return to its plot line roots by reintroducing Meg into the drama under the pretext of Meg's mom Sarah being near death and wanting to see Meg one last time. Meg, conniving as ever, brought her son Beanie, now called Ben, with her, and their arrival was preceded by the appearance of her daughter Cal. Cal's father and Meg's ex-husband, Eddie Aleata, arrived a few months later, making moves first on Van and then Felicia Lamont. Eddie's adulterous affair with the latter ended with Felicia's death following the birth of their child. Sarah recovered, and the new family members became focal points in the drama. Meg wed Rosehill Mayor Jeff Hart, another amoral person, while Jeff's son David fell in love with Cal until Jeff attempted to rape her, causing David to kill his father, after which he was committed to a mental hospital.

And as for Ben, he proved to be just as venal as his mother in adulthood. He made doctored photos of Bruce which helped Jeff defeat Bruce in his run for mayor of Rosehill, then inherited a fortune from his mother for marrying Betsy Crawford. Unbeknownst to them, Ben already was wed to Arlene Lovett. Arlene, who played piano at a club owned by Meg and Rick Latimer, was willing to pretend not to be Ben's wife if it meant she could pocket the money his mom promised him if he married Betsy Crawford. The only other person who knew about the situation, Arlene's mom Carrie, was too timid to tell Betsy because she was afraid of what it might do to her friend.

Entanglements between all these characters continued to grow in complexity. Meg tried to prevent a romance between her amour Rick and Cal by telling David Hart to leave his sanitarium and return to her. When David saw Rick and Cal together, he assumed incorrectly that an affair was underway and set fire to the club where Arlene played. David saved Arlene from the fire, and fell in love with her, but he had to acknowledge during a subsequent trial that he and not Rick had burned the club. David went back to the mental home, and Cal, who learned of her mother's plot, did manage to marry Rick despite her mother's continual efforts to thwart the union. Cal and Rick then left town with Rick's son Hank.

David's attorney during the trial, Jamie Rollins, discovered Ben and Arlene's secret marriage, and in an effort to stop Jamie's new wife Ben took compromising photos making it look like Jamie and Arlene were having an affair. Ben sent the photos to Jamie's live-in lover Diana Lamont, who eventually left him and became a nun. But Ben could no longer hide the truth; he confessed his bigamy and went to jail, leaving Betsy to give birth without him and leave town. Arlene was not charged for her part in the bigamous marriage, but had to endure her mom Carrie falling in love with her boyfriend—Betsy's brother Dr. Tom Crawford. Complicating matters for Arlene was that she had to work for pimp Ray Slater to pay for her mom's medical bills, which led to her being followed by rich client Ian Russell. Arlene was incorrectly suspected of Russell's murder, and Tom Crawford, discovering that Arlene had borne a child by Russell, refused to marry her. Arlene wed instead the reformed Ray Slater.

Arlene's ex-hubby Ben, released from prison, became the surrogate son of Dr. Andrew Marriott and his wife Mia after fearing that he had accidentally killed their child. Naturally, Ben began having an affair with Mia. Andrew later separated from Mia, and Bruce, worried he might die of aplastic anemia, tried to fix him up with his wife Van. When the disease went into remission, Bruce and Van bought a house owned by Professor Timothy McCauley, who married Van's mother Sarah. But Ben and Mia were not to have the smooth sailing enjoyed by a couple like Bruce and Van, as Ben found himself attracted again to the returning Betsy despite the fact she was wed to Elliott Lang.

Others popping up in the late 1970s were Bambi Brewster, the nutso abused girl who became a ward under Arlene and Ray; Lynn Henderson, a teen alcoholic who became a ward of Van and Bruce; Dr. Joe Cusack, who treated Lynn before dying in a car accident; Andy Marriott, Andrew's son who romanced therapist Mary Jane Owens; Dory Patten, a lawyer who married Eddie Aleata and left town with him; Wes Osborne, another young newcomer; and Amy Russell, a student who surprised Bruce by informing him she was his illegitimate daughter.

None of these new characters really perked up the show, which had been unsteady in the ratings ever since it moved into its late morning slot. Then in 1979, when CBS moved it to 4 p.m. daily, some affiliates dropped the show and ratings drooped, causing the network to shelve it in favor of reruns of *One Day at a Time*. The producers, claiming they did not have enough time to do the necessary rewrites and holding out hope that another network or syndicator would take the series, left some story lines unresolved.

On the show's final week, Van battled allegations that she and Steve were having an affair, and Mia testified in court on Meg's attempt to bribe her to testify in Ben's favor during the latter's trial for battery on Betsy. Bruce, now an attorney, defended Ben from the false accusation. Then Betsy fainted at the trial, and during the last scene, observers said that Betsy's physical condition was so poor that she would probably die. For longtime viewers who had invested nearly 30 years in the show, the disappearance of Van, Meg, Bruce, and the rest without explanation must have felt like a betrayal. It was certainly a sad coda to one of TV's longest-running series.

LOVE REPORT, THE
Informational; Color
June 18, 1984–July 27, 1984

ABC Mon.–Fri. 11–11:30 a.m. (6/18/84–7/27/84)

Hosts: *Chuck Henry, Tawny Schneider*

The wide world of romance—its techniques and its impact on people—was the subject of this program. The series originally ran as a test pilot the week of April 2–6, 1984, at 11 a.m., when it attracted some notoriety with the April 4 show in which squeaky clean singer John Davidson confessed to an affair he had during his first marriage. Nothing in the rest of its run proved so dramatic, and so *The Love Report* went off after six weeks in the summer of 1984.

LOVE STORY—See *Welcome Travelers.*

LOVERS AND FRIENDS—See *For Richer, For Poorer.*

•LOVING
Soap Opera; Color
June 26, 1983–

ABC Mon.–Fri. 11:30 a.m.–Noon (6/26/83–10/5/84)
ABC Mon.–Fri. 12:30–1 p.m. (10/8/84–)

Cast:

Cabot Alden (1983–92, 1995 at least)	*Wesley Addy*
Isabelle Alden (1983)	*Meg Mundy*
Isabelle Alden (1983–87, 1995 at least)	*Augusta Dabney*
Isabelle Alden (at least 1991–92)	*Celeste Holm*
Isabelle Alden (1992 at least)	*Patricia Barry*
Curtis Alden (1983–85, 1995 at least)	*Christopher Marcantel*
Curtis Alden (1985–86)	*Linden Ashley*
Curtis Alden (1986–87)	*Burke Moses*
Roger Forbes (1983)	*John Shearin*
Roger Forbes (1983–84)	*Peter Brown*
Ann Alden Forbes (1983–84)	*Shannon Eubanks*
Ann Alden Forbes (1984–87 at least)	*Callan White*
Jack Forbes (1983–)	*Perry Stephens*
Lorna Forbes (1983–86)	*Susan Walters*
Lorna Forbes (1986–87)	*O'Hara Parker*
Rose Donovan (1983–84)	*Teri Keane*
Rose Donovan (1984–87)	*Dorothy Stinnette*
Patrick Donovan (1983–84)	*Noah Keen*
Patrick Donovan (1984–85)	*George L. Smith*
Douglas Donovan (1983–84)	*Bryan Cranston*
Douglas Donovan (1985–86)	*Victor Bevine*
Stacey Donovan (1983–95)	*Lauren-Marie Taylor*
Mike Donovan (1983–85)	*James Kibard*
Garth Slater (1983)	*John Cunningham*
Lily Slater (1983–84)	*Jennifer Ashe*
Lily Slater (1987–88 at least)	*Britt Helfer*
June Slater (1983–84)	*Ann Williams*
Billy Bristow (1983–84)	*Tom Ligon*
Rita Mae Bristow (1983–85)	*Pamela Blair*
Merrill Vochek (1983–84)	*Patricia Kalember*
Father Jim Vochek (1983–87 at least)	*Peter Davies*
Noreen Vochek (1983–84)	*Marilyn McIntyre*
Noreen Vochek (1985)	*Elizabeth Burr*
Tony Perelli (1983)	*Peter Radon*
Tony Perelli (1984–85)	*Richard McWilliams*
Ava Rescott (1984)	*Patty Lotz*
Ava Rescott (1984–at least 1987)	*Roya Megnot*
Ava (at least 1993–95)	*Lisa Peluso*
Lt. Art Hindman (1984, 1986–87 at least)	*John Danelle*
Shana Sloane (1984–88 at least, 1993 at least)	*Susan Keith*

Dane Hammond (1984–86)	Anthony Herrera
Gwyneth Alden (1984–87 at least, 1992–95)	Christine Tudor
Gwyneth Alden (1989–92)	Elizabeth Savage
Trisha Alden (1984–93)	Noelle Beck
Kate Rescott (1984–)	Nada Rowand
Keith Lane (1984–86)/Jonathan Matalaine (1984–85)	John O'Hurley
Colby Cantrell (1984–85)	Pamela Bowen
Cecilia Thompson (1985)	Rebecca Staab
Cecilia Thompson (1985–86)	Alice Haining
Cecilia Thompson (1986–87)	Colleen Dion
Rebekka Beecham (1985–86)	Jane Powell
Judd Beecham (1985)	Dan Doby
Judd Beecham (1986)	Neil Zevnik
Linc Beecham (1985)	Phil MacGregor
Linc Beecham (1985–86)	Brian Robert Taylor
Tug Watley (1985–86)	Brett Porter
Sherri Watley (1985)	Susan Wands
Sherri Watley (1985–86)	Deidre O'Connell
Lotty Bates (1986–87 at least)	Judith Hoag
Zack Conway (1986–87)	John Gabriel
Kelly Conway (1986–87)	Kathleen Fisk
Rob Carpenter (1986–87)	Timothy Owen
Eban Japes (1986–87)	Matthew Cowles
Nick Dinatos (1986–87)	Jeff Gendelman
Jenny Baylor (1986–87)	Mary Lynn Blanks
Hunter Beldon (1986)	Jeff Trachta
Alex Masters (1987–)	Randolph Mantooth
Alex Masters (1991 at least)	Robert Dubac
Clay Alden (1991 at least)	James Horan
Clay Alden (1991–92)	Larkin Malloy
Clay Alden (1992–95)	Dennis Parlato
Ned Bates (1987–)	Luke Perry
April Hathaway (1987–)	Alexandra Wilson
Rick Stewart (1987–)	Ron Nummi
Marty Edison (1987–)	Isabel Glasser
Diane Winston (1987–)	Jacqueline Courtney
Dan Hollister (1987–)	Mark Pinter
Egypt (1988–91)	Linda Cook
Jeff Hartman (1988)	Scott Feraco
Jeff Hartman (1988)	Michael Maguire
Jeff Hartman (1988–89 at least)	Richard Steinmetz
Todd Jones (1989)	Stan Albers
Todd Jones (1989–90 at least)	Todd McDurmont
Trucker McKenzie (1989–95)	Robert Tyler
Rocky (1989–90 at least)	Rena Sofer
Louie Slavinski (1990–93)	Bernard Barrow
Kate Rescott (1990–91 at least)	Nada Rowand
Rio (1990 at least)	Rick Telles
Norma the waitress (at least 1990–at least 1991)	Ilene Kristen
Paul the paraplegic (at least 1991)	Joe Breen
Allison Rescott (at least 1991– at least 1992)	Laura Sisk
Staige Prince, snotty sorority girl (at least 1992)	Eden Atwood
Jeremy Hunter/Gilbert (1992–95)	Jean LeClerc
Cooper Alden (at least 1992–95)	Michael Weatherly
Ceara (1992 at least)	Genie Francis
Tess Wilder (1993–)	Catherine Hickland
Buck Huston the bartender (1993–)	Philip Brown
Faison (1993)	Anders T. Hove
Dr. Angie Hubbard (1994–)	Debbie Morgan
Casey Bowman, reformed cokehead (1992–95)	Paul Anthony Stewart
Steffi Brewster (at least 1994–95)	Amelia Heinle Weatherly
Dinah Lee (at least 1994–)	Jessica Collins
Jacob Johnson (1995–)	Darnell Williams
Sydney Chase (1995–96)	Morgan Fairchild
Azure C. (at least 1996–)	Carlotta Chang
Bernardo Castro (at least 1996–)	Philip Anthony

Loving was the albatross of ABC's daytime schedule of the 1980s and 1990s, being the lowest-rated network soap throughout most of its run. Why it survived more than a decade with little audience or critical support was probably due to the faith the network had in its creator, Agnes Nixon. Nixon said she did the series for several reasons: She wondered if she could create another success almost a decade and a half after fashioning *All My Children;* she wanted to do a half-hour series; and she wanted to do a show with a college as its focal point. To assist her, ABC gave the show a nighttime debut as a $3 million filmed TV movie the day before its daytime run commenced.

As befitted its title, *Loving* initially emphasized romance of a rather generic sort. It had the clichéd contrast between the rich but troubled Aldens (long-wed Cabot and Isabelle, their daughter Ann, and grandson Curtis) and Forbeses (Roger and his children Jack and Lorna), and the poor but noble Donovans (Rose and Patrick and their children Mike, Douglas, and Stacey). All were connected in some way to Alden University in Corinth on the upper East Coast. Cabot was chairman of the board and grandson of the university's founder, Roger was its new president, Patrick the head of campus security, Douglas a professor, and Jack, Lorna, and Stacey were students. Other university-connected characters included Dean Garth Slater, married to June and father of Lily, and athletic department chair Billy Bristow, wed to Rita Mae.

Ann Alden's marriage to Roger Forbes was troubled, thanks to his interest in WCN news anchor Merrill Vochek. Meanwhile Merrill's sister Noreen, a nurse, and her brother, Father Jim Vochek, had their own challenges. Noreen's husband Mike Donovan attempted to come to terms with his status as a bitter veteran of the Vietnam War, while the priest struggled with his romantic impulses. Amid these and other stories, *Loving* attracted the most attention in its first year for a bit of guest casting. In December 1983 Englebert Humperdinck played himself as an old pal of Douglas Donovan's giving a benefit for the Alden University theater.

Trying to woo a young crowd, Loving *debuted in 1983 with this youthful cast. Clockwise from top are Lauren-Marie Taylor (as Stacey Donovan), Susan Walters (Lorna Forbes), Chris Marcantel (Curtis Alden), Jennifer Ashe (Lily Slater), and Perry Stephens (Jack Forbes).*

Roger's reported death in a plane crash was followed by a reduction in the Donovan and Forbes families' involvement on the show in favor of the Aldens. Ann wed Dane Hammond, the natural father of Jack Forbes. Jack, who had been fond of Lily Slater, an incest victim, then dated Stacey Donovan, only to find himself in a failed marriage with Ava Rescott when she became pregnant by him. (Actually, Ava faked her pregnancy with a pillow while convincing her expecting sister Kate to pretend that her baby was Ava's.) Stacey also canceled her later engagement to Tony Perelli when it was revealed that he had impregnated Lorna. (To complicate things even further for ardent fans, actress Susan Walters,

who played Lorna, later in real life wed actor Linden Ashley, who played Lorna's cousin Curtis.)

In 1986, Zack Conway was the defense lawyer for Lorna Forbes, who was charged with murdering Zona Beecham. That same year Steve and Trisha eloped and went on the lam from Spider. And Trisha Alden, upset by Steve's marriage to ex-punk Cecilia Thompson, changed her debutante looks and fell under the spell of Nick Dinatos, a slick casino manager. Also, ex-prisoner Lotty Bates worked with fellow former con Eban Japes. Hunter Beldon was a creepy drug dealer. The year ended with Father Jim marrying Shana Sloane while the latter was under amnesia.

In 1987 Trisha romanced and wed the poor Steve Sowolsky. Also, the always unpredictable Ava, divorced from Curtis Alden, went after tycoon Clay Alden, newly divorced from resident bitch Gwyneth. Gwyneth, in turn, reached out for the son she had given up at birth while being an executive head of a division in Alden Enterprises. Diane Winston was a classy madam.

As *Loving* trudged along in the late 1980s and early 1990s, no story line really stirred a chord in viewers—not Gwyneth Alden competing with her daughter Trisha Sowolsky for the affections of new TV producer Jeff Hartman in 1988, or the love of Todd Jones for courageous coed Rocky in 1989, or the oddball romance of trash collector Louie Slavinski with cancer patient Kate Rescott in 1990. (Kate, a grandmother, ran for public office in 1992 while Louie retired and dealt with impotency after prostate surgery.) There was some tension caused by the ups and downs with Trucker and Trisha, who divorced in 1992, plus the "killing off" of patriarch Cabot along with Alex and Egypt in 1991. But none of this did much to reinvigorate *Loving*, which was so desperate by the summer of 1992 that it wrote in a ghost story that summer. It even, unbelievably, fired veteran actress Celeste Holm, who played matriarch Isabelle.

Characters from other ABC soaps started popping into Corinth. In 1993 Genie Francis visited as her *All My Children* character Ceara, joining fellow refugee Jeremy Hunter. He gained the attention of Ava Rescott, and a former *General Hospital* psychopath named Faison terrorized the duo. In 1994 Jeremy was imprisoned by his evil twin brother Gilbert, who fell in love with Ava. Then Jeremy got freed, and fell in love with Ava until he ended up dying. That same year, Ally Rescott planned to wed while her fiancée Cooper Alden made love to Tess Wilder. Also, Shana and Leo planned to wed, and teen model Steffi Brewster fell in love with Cooper. Another exiled *All My Children* character, Dr. Angie Hubbard, arrived in town and developed an attraction to Jacob Johnson, who resembled her old husband Jessie (actor Darnell Williams played both parts).

In July 1995, *Loving,* still a cellar dweller, resorted to having a serial killer murder much of the cast, including virtually the whole Alden clan of Cabot, Isabelle, Curtis, Clay, Gwyneth, and Isabelle. Ava, understandably worried, left town, and Jeremy also perished. About 12 cast members survived as the show revamped itself into *The City* on November 13, 1995. The action was relocated to New York's SoHo neighborhood, and characters included Buck the bartender, who simply changed taverns, and his ex-love Tess.

The refurbished show included a "name" star (Morgan Fairchild, playing her umpteenth bitch as vicious communications mogul Sydney Chase), flashy camera work, and taping (it was transferred from videotape to film

and edited quickly) and much location shooting. In 1996, they ran a shocker story line, when model Azure C. was revealed to be a transsexual, to the dismay of her boyfriend Bernardo Castro. But the show remained the lowest-rated soap on air, and ABC announced a cancellation date of March 1997.

LUCILLE RIVERS SHOW—FASHIONS IN SEWING, THE
Instructional; Color
June 1969–1974

Syndicated 10 minutes daily beginning 1969

Hostess: *Lucille Rivers*

Veteran TV seamstress Lucille Rivers gave housewives hints on how to handle sewing problems in this popular syndicated entry of the early 1970s, when it aired on 120 stations in America. Rivers had appeared in the medium on local shows in New York in the early 1950s and on *Home* in the mid-1950s discussing her field, which followed years of lecturing and writing for *McCall's* magazine plus owning her own custom dressmaking shop in the Big Apple. One of the last TV series to run only 10 minutes, the program was retitled *The New Lucille Rivers Show* in 1973.

LUCKY PARTNERS
Game; B&W
June 30, 1958–August 22, 1958

NBC Mon.–Fri. 2–2:30 p.m. (6/30/58–8/22/58)

Host: *Carl Cordell*

This quickly on and off game (it lasted a mere eight weeks) had its studio audience and home viewers play bingo using serial numbers on dollar bills and questions answered by two contestants on stage. To play the game, participants wrote the letters "L-U-C-K-Y" in place of "BINGO" at the top of their cards, and under each letter wrote the last five serial numbers of one of their dollar bills. Anyone getting bingo using this process turned in the dollar with the winning serial number, making that person eligible for a grand prize ranging from a car to a "Queen's Ransom of Jewels."

LUCKY PUP
Puppets; B&W
September 11, 1950–June 23, 1951

CBS Mon.–Fri. 5–5:15 p.m. (9/11/50–6/23/51)

Narrator: *Doris Brown*

Puppeteers: *Hope and Murey Bunin*

This early puppet show, which began August 23, 1948, spent much of its run as an early evening entry on CBS from Mondays through Saturdays from January 1949 until its cancellation in 1951. However, in the fall of 1950 it went into a late afternoon slot for one season. Stories centered on Lucky Pup, a pooch with a $5 million inheritance, and his pal, Jolo the Clown. Their rivals were evil but bumbling Foodini the magician and his stooge Pinhead, who came to dominate the action on most of the shows.

CBS got rid of the series supposedly because network executives did not want any puppet shows. NBC considered reviving *Lucky Pup* Sundays from 12:30–1 p.m., but instead the show was reincarnated in a different form on ABC (see *Foodini the Great*).

LUNCH WITH SOUPY SALES—See *Soupy Sales Show, The.*

M

M & M CANDY CARNIVAL, THE—See *Grand Chance Roundup.*

MADELINE
Cartoon; Color
September 9, 1995–October 21, 1995
ABC Sat. 8–8:30 a.m. (9/9/95–10/21/95)

Based on the memorable 1940 book by Ludwig Bemelmans, *Madeline* told the story of a delightfully adventuresome young redhead who went to private school in Paris, along with 11 other, more regimented girls. Their teacher Miss Clavell, a nun, tolerated Madeline's antics fairly well, since she knew they relieved some of the stresses the other children faced and never meant to hurt anyone. In the network series, Madeline's adventures included Pepito and his fellow attendees at a nearby boys' school.

Madeline had been around several years before coming to ABC. The first episode, made by DIC in 1988, was narrated by Christopher Plummer. It aired on the Family Channel in 1993, but in 1995 it flopped and was replaced by *The New Adventures of Winnie the Pooh* (q.v.).

MAGAZINE
News/Informational; Color
October 6, 1977–September 3, 1981
CBS Thu. 10–11 a.m. monthly (10/6/77–9/7/78)
CBS Thu. 10:30–11:30 a.m. monthly (10/2/78–4/5/79)
CBS Thu. 10–11 a.m. monthly (5/3/79–9/3/81)
Anchor/"Editor": *Sharron Lovejoy*

This daytime news feature offering began as a pilot on May 2, 1974 with Sylvia Chase and Charles Kuralt as hosts. It then aired as specials roughly every two months with Chase and either Hughes Rudd or Charles Osgood as co-host until the March 31, 1976 telecast, when Chase began hosting solo. When Sharron Lovejoy took over on October 19, 1976, the program started putting the month's name in front of the show's name. A year later, it assumed a regular pattern, airing the first of each month. Among its stories were profiles of famous folk like Erma Bombeck, Joan Rivers, Phil Donahue, Glenda Jackson, and Bob Barker (whose *Price Is Right* usually ran in *Magazine*'s time period),

and reports on incest, cults, teenage suicides, amniocentesis, and care for the terminally ill.

MAGIC ADVENTURES OF MUMFIE, THE—See *Cubhouse.*

MAGIC CIRCUS—See *Magic Land of Allakazam, The.*

•MAGIC CLOWN, THE
Children's; B&W
January 14, 1951–July 13, 1952
NBC Sun. 11:30–11:45 a.m. (1/14/51–7/13/52)
Regulars: *Zovella (1951–52), Richard DuBois (1952), Mimi Walters (1952)*
Organist/Musical Director: *Jack Ward*

This official title of this series was *Bonomo's Presents the Magic Clown*, in honor of sponsor Bonomo's Turkish Taffy. Even by early TV advertising standards, Bonomo's promotional saturation in this series was excessive, going so far as to have kids in the audience wear fezzes, sing about the company in the show's theme song (to the tune of "The Farmer in the Dell"), and shout "Bonomo" as the secret word to tricks done by a man in a clown's costume. The Magic Clown (exuberant Zovella at first, replaced by folksier Richard DuBois and his assistant Mimi Walters) also did feats with Laffy, a mute, fez-wearing hand puppet. Magic equipment came from Lou Tannen's Magic Shop in New York City. Although it was filmed, a look at the abrupt closings on the surviving copies suggests that timing was not a top priority.

The Magic Clown aired locally on WNBT New York first on September 11, 1949 on Sunday mornings. It remained a local show in New York through the mid-1960s. A 1970 syndicated daily revival had the Amazing Randi perform tricks available in 60 six-minute episodes or 20 half-hour shows.

MAGIC LAND OF ALLAKAZAM, THE
Children's; B&W
October 1, 1960–December 12, 1964
CBS Sat. 11–11:30 a.m. (10/1/60–9/22/62)
ABC Sat. 12:30–1 p.m. (12/29/62–12/28/63)
ABC Sat. 10:30–11 a.m. (4/25/64–9/5/64)
ABC Sat. 1–1:30 p.m. (9/12/64–12/12/64)
Regulars: *Mark Wilson, Nini Darnell, Mike Wilson, Bev Bergeron (as Rebo the Mixed-Up Clown), Chuck Burns (as Periwinkle), Bob Turner (as Emilio the King; 1962–63)*

Magician Mark Wilson played a circus ringmaster in this fantasy with a story line which employed his family on camera. His wife Nini and son Mike played themselves as assistants to Mark. They were all citizens of Allakazam, as were Rebo the Clown and Periwinkle the Loyal Subject. There were some comic sketches between the illusions and levitations. Regular animals seen were Basil the Baffling Bunny, Bernard the Biggest Bunny in the Business, Charles the Charming Chicken, Deborah the Darling Duck, Doris the Daring Dove, Gertrude the Glamorous Guinea Pig, and Harriet the Harmonious Hamster.

In 1962 the show, which had been videotaped before a studio audience from Hollywood, went to ABC on film and added Emilio the wicked magician. It also dropped the occasional Hanna-Barbera cartoons of such characters as Yogi Bear, which it had used between acts in the first season. Wilson, who was the show's executive producer, later displayed his magical talents on semirevivals of this series in syndication, *Magic Circus* from 1971–73 and *The Magic World of Mark Wilson* in 1977.

MAGIC MIDWAY
Children's; B&W
September 22, 1962–March 16, 1963
NBC Sat. 11:30 a.m.–Noon (9/22/62–3/16/63)
Regulars: *Claude Kirchner, Douglas Anderson (as Mr. Pocus), Bill Bailey (as Boom Boom), Paul Kiley (as Coo Coo), Bonnie Lee Glier, Lou Stein and the Circus 7 Jazz Band*

Taped in New York City, this circus show had Douglas Anderson, Bill Bailey, and Paul Dooley play clowns, while Bonnie Lee Glier was the baton twirler and pianist Lou Stein led a combo which featured Dick Hyman at the electric organ. Ringmaster Claude Kirchner and Bill Bailey probably felt most at home in this offering due to their experiences on 1950s circus shows (Kirchner had been ringmaster on *Super Circus;* Bailey was a clown on *The M & M Candy Carnival*). The show was also known as *Marx Magic Midway* in honor of its sponsor Marx Toys.

MAGIC OF MARK WILSON, THE—See *Magic Land of Allakazam, The.*

MAGIC RANCH, THE
Children's; B&W
September 30, 1961–December 23, 1961
ABC Sat. 11:30 a.m.–Noon (9/30/61–12/23/61)
Host: *Don Alan*

Feats of prestidigitation and other tricks by generally obscure guests made up most of this show, although Don Alan performed magic too. Filmed in Park Ridge, Illinois, it followed *On Your Mark.*

MAGIC SLATE, THE
Children's; B&W
January 21, 1951–July 8, 1951
NBC Sun. 5:30–6 p.m. (1/21/51–7/8/51)

Presentations from the Goodman Children's Theater of Chicago under the direction of Charlotte Corpening made up the offerings for *The Magic Slate*. Most of the talent was

unknown. Its debut tale was "Aladdin" starring Vi Berwick and Norman Gottschalk. Peter Pan Peanut Butter was the sponsor. The show alternated weekly with *Hollywood Junior Circus*. It first ran on NBC Fridays at 8 p.m. from June 2–August 25, 1950, alternating weekly there with *The Quiz Kids*.

MAGILLA GORILLA
Cartoon; Color
January 1, 1966–September 2, 1967
ABC Sun. 11:30 a.m.–Noon (1/1/66–12/31/66)
ABC Sun. 12:30–1 p.m. (1/7/67–9/2/67)
Voices:

Magilla Gorilla/Punkin Puss	*Allan Melvin*
Mr. Peebles/Mush Mouse	*Howard Morris*
Ogee	*Jean VanderPyl*
Ricochet Rabbit	*Don Messick*
Droopalong Coyote	*Mel Blanc*

Magilla Gorilla, first seen in syndication in 1964, had three main components. The headliner involved a simian whom pet store Mr. Peebles tried desperately to pawn off to customers (or, as the theme song put it, "We've got a gorilla for sale . . ."). A recurring character was a girl called Ogee who wanted to be Magilla's owner, and he wanted to be her pet, but circumstances continued to keep them apart. Also seen were Mush Mouse, a hillbilly rat who feuded with Punkin Puss, and Ricochet Rabbit, the sheriff, who was assisted by his deputy Droopalong Coyote. The latter element sometimes appeared on *Peter Potamus*, which aired after *Magilla*, and in turn *Peter's* "Breezly and Sneezly" showed up on *Magilla* frequently.

Although few would argue that *Magilla Gorilla* was one of Hanna-Barbera's better cartoons, it did receive an award in 1964 given by the Volunteers of America in the category of children shows "in the best tradition of wholesome American humor." A total of 26 shows were produced.

•MAGNIFICENT MARBLE MACHINE, THE
Game; Color
July 7, 1975–June 11, 1976
NBC Mon.–Fri. Noon–12:30 p.m. (7/7/75–6/11/76)
Host: *Art James*

Has there ever been a bigger pinball machine than the gargantuan one created for this monument to set design excess in the game show world of the 1970s? To operate the "Magnificent Marble Machine," which measured 4,800 square feet (50 feet high!) a celebrity-contestant duo had to press huge plungers and oversized handle controls in an effort to light up seven bumpers, each representing a prize, within 60 seconds without losing the ball at play, thus meriting a bonus "gold ball" to rack up additional points within another minute. If the duo racked up at least 15,000 points in the two plays, the contestant won a car or other top prize.

But to get the chance to play this gizmo, the duo had to take on a similar pair in a mystery phrase identification contest whereby hints rolled out on a screen like a Broadway marquee and then the spaces for the mystery subject did the same underneath the hint. The spaces had one letter revealed from left to right until one team correctly identified the subject. Five correct identifications won a team the opportunity to play pinball.

Despite the popularity of pinball machines at the time, the show was not the hit NBC had hoped, and in 1976 the format changed so that players were now all celebrities competing on behalf of selected members of the studio audience. That old trick did not win viewers either, and *The Magnificent Marble Machine,* together with its continued high production costs, died after one year. The concept, however, did surface once more, in an unusual context: In the 1979 theatrical movie *The China Syndrome,* a clip of Joan Rivers playing the Marble Machine aired just before a scene showing Jane Fonda reporting on a cover-up of a nuclear accident.

MAJOR DELL CONWAY OF THE FLYING TIGERS
Adventure; B&W
July 29, 1951–March 2, 1952

DuMont Sun. 12:30–1 p.m. (7/29/51–3/2/52)

Cast:

Maj. Dell Conway	*Ed Peck*
Caribou Jones	*Bern Hoffman*

The Flying Tigers was the real-life name of a World War II squadron whose ex-members, including Major Dell Conway, formed an airline by the same name after the war. When it became a series, the show detailed fictional exploits of airline pilot Dell and his pal Caribou Jones in various locales around the world, always working for the good old U.S.A. and pitted against various nefarious types. A typical plot was the one aired on September 2, 1951, set in Calcutta, where Frank Silvera played the priest of the temple of Kalee while Dell and Caribou worked to recover the stolen jewel of Ashtar.

The series started on DuMont Saturdays at 6:30 p.m. from April 7–May 26, 1951. Before the end of that run, actor Eric Fleming had left the show and Ed Peck had assumed the role of Maj. Conway, but Bern Hoffman remained the only Caribou. Gen Genovese, another World War II veteran, was producer of both versions. In 1957 *Billboard* announced that Genovese was preparing a new version of the series, but there is no record that such a program ever saw daylight.

MAJOR LEAGUE BASEBALL—See *Baseball Game of the Week.*

MAKE A FACE
Game; B&W
October 2, 1961–December 22, 1962

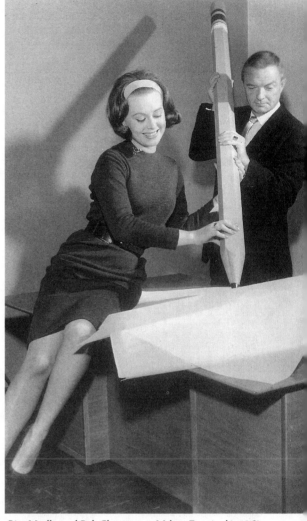

Rita Mueller and Bob Clayton try to Make a Face *in this 1962 promotional shot.*

ABC Mon.–Fri. 12:30–1 p.m. (10/2/61–3/30/62)
ABC Sat. 11–11:30 a.m. (9/29/62–12/22/62)

Host: *Bob Clayton*

Assistant: *Rita Mueller*

Two contestants had to "make a face" using segments of a celebrity's head shot seen on the belts of three rotating drums. A contestant could align the segments properly if he or she called out the right numbers to stop the segments. The object was to become the first to identify the person. Following an unsuccessful daily run, ABC gave this creation another shot and another slot—for children on Saturday mornings—but it bombed there as well.

•MAKE A WISH
Children's; Color
September 12, 1971–September 5, 1976
ABC Sun. 11:30 a.m.–Noon (9/12/71–9/5/76)

Host/Narrator: *Tom Chapin*

Make a Wish explored two topics per show via a sprightly mix of animation, films, and a song by host Tom Chapin, who also wrote many of the show's tunes and played his guitar while singing them. ABC replaced this with another five-year series for children; see *Animals, Animals, Animals.*

MAMA
Situation Comedy; B&W
December 16, 1956–March 17, 1957
CBS Sun. 5–5:30 p.m. (12/16/56–3/17/57)

Cast:

Marta Hansen (Mama)	*Peggy Wood*
Lars Hansen (Papa)	*Judson Laire*
Nels	*Dick Van Patten*
Katrin	*Rosemary Rice*
Dagmar	*Toni Campbell*
Aunt Jenny	*Ruth Gates*
Uncle Gunnar Gunnerson	*Carl Frank*
Aunt Trina Gunnerson	*Alice Frost*
T. R. Ryan	*Kevin Coughlin*

One of the first series to return to the air due to viewer protest was *Mama*, which spent most of its TV life on CBS Fridays at 8 p.m. from July 1, 1949–July 27, 1956. When CBS canceled it in 1956, producer Carol Irwin made a public plea for viewers to send in their protests, which was no doubt responsible for some of the 175,000 letters which poured into the network to keep *Mama* going. One church congregation alone submitted 5,000 protest letters. The show went off not due to low ratings, but because its sponsor Maxwell House learned that the same people had been watching for seven years and thus the show was not attracting any new buyers for Maxwell House products. Despite this immediate lack of a sponsor, CBS found a spot for the show on late Sunday afternoons, as all the nighttime slots on the network had advertisers, and gave it an ultimately unsuccessful four-month run.

The show remained essentially the same as it had been on nighttime, with the only casting change being 13-year-old Toni Campbell replacing Robin Morgan as youngest child Dagmar. Based on Kathryn Forbes's autobiographical novel *Remember Mama*, which was made into a hit play in 1944 and a hit movie in 1948, it told the stories of the Norwegian immigrant family the Hansens, supposedly from middle child Katrin's eyes. As "she" said in the show's opening narration while looking over the family album, "I remember my brother Nels, and my little sister Dagmar, and of course Papa. But most of all, I remember Mama."

Mama was the warm, sweet matriarch who balanced old-world values with new customs as the family adjusted to a different way of life in San Francisco during the first half of the 20th century. Beside looking after her family, she also gave comfort to her older sister Jenny and younger sister Trina, the latter wed to Gunnar Gunnerson. The show's humor, not to mention appeal, arose through warmth and story line complexities, not random one-liners. The stories on the Sunday shows focused on the family's plight in World War II, with Nels in the Army preparing to go overseas and Katrin a newlywed.

The problem with the series' unchanging audience remained valid on Sundays, with very few new viewers tuning into the program, so CBS canceled it after 10 shows. An additional 16 shows filmed but not aired on CBS were included when the 10 shows went into reruns in syndication in the fall of 1957.

•MAN OF THE WEEK
Interview; B&W
August 26, 1951–October 10, 1954
CBS Sun. 5–5:30 p.m. (8/26/51–4/13/52)
CBS Sun. 3:30–4 p.m. (2/1/53–5/10/53)
CBS Sun. 4:30–5 p.m. (5/17/53–6/21/53)
CBS Sun. 5:30–6 p.m. (6/28/53–10/4/53)
CBS Sun. 3:30–4 p.m. or 4–4:30 p.m. (10/11/53–6/27/54)
CBS Sun. 5–5:30 p.m. (8/29/54–10/10/54)

Host: *George Allen (1951–52), Ron Cochran (1953–54)*

Man of the Week initially had four guests, typically two Democrats and two Republicans, in a roundtable discussion. One of the guests received special focus as the source of much of the conversation and thus was the "man of the week." George Allen created and served as the first moderator of the Washington, D.C.–based series (for the earliest programs, there was no moderator). When the show returned in 1953, CBS's Washington, D.C., reporter Ron Cochran hosted from New York City, discussing timely concerns with three guest reporters and a guest "man of the week" at a roundtable. As before, the show had no sponsor. Between its daytime runs, the series aired on CBS early Sunday evenings during 1952–53 and 1954.

MAN ON THE STREET
Talk; B&W
January 12, 1949–April 13, 1951
DuMont Mon.–Fri. 12:15–12:30 p.m. or 1:30–1:45 p.m. (1/12/49–4/13/51)

This self-descriptive offering of interviews with passersby in Manhattan was one of the first shows on DuMont's daily lineup. During its first few months it was known as *Sidewalks of New York*, and toward the end of the run in 1951, as *Sidewalk Interviews.*

MANTRAP—See *Leave It to the Girls.*

MARGARET JOHNSON SHOW, THE
Musical Variety; B&W
February 7, 1949–June 2, 1950

DuMont Mon.–Fri. 10–10:15 a.m. (2/7/49–2/11/49)
DuMont Mon.–Fri. 10:15–10:30 a.m. (2/14/49–12/9/49)
DuMont Mon.–Fri. 1:45–2 p.m. (12/12/49–6/2/50)

Hostess: *Margaret Johnson*

This brief musical interlude featured obscure singer Margaret Johnson.

MARLENE SANDERS WITH THE NEWS WITH THE WOMAN'S TOUCH—See *ABC News.*

MARLO AND THE MAGIC MOVIE MACHINE
Children's; Color
1977–1980

Syndicated 60 and 30 minutes weekly beginning April 1977

Cast:

Marlo Higgins	Laurie Faso
The machine (voice only)	Mert Koplin

Originating from WCAU Philadelphia, *Marlo and the Magic Movie Machine* featured the doings of Marlo, an operations whiz who watched old films shown in the basement of Leo Dullo's computer company. Marlo and the machine supplying the movies also engaged in repartee. The clips ranged from instructional to frivolous, but most children's critics felt that, overall, the show was quite good and useful. Besides providing the voice of the machine, Mert Koplin also wrote for the series.

Executive Producer Sanford Fisher whipped up the concept in 1976 for CBS-owned-and-operated stations by finding out about a film archive called the Corporation for Entertainment and Learning which contained some 11 million feet of film back to 1893. The show began as an hour offering but went to 30 minutes in April 1978 to entice more affiliates into carrying the show. The move was successful enough to allow Marlo and his machine to show movies for two more seasons.

•MARSHA WARFIELD
Talk; Color
March 26, 1990–January 25, 1991

NBC Mon.–Fri. 11:30 a.m.–Noon (3/26/90–1/25/91)

Host: *Marsha Warfield*

On a set designed to look like an apartment complete with a play basket and backboard, actress Marsha Warfield, then starring on the NBC nighttime sitcom *Night Court,* invited two or three celebrity guests to discuss the day's issue in a light manner, complete with a humorous monologue from Warfield introducing the topic. Among those talking and being asked questions from the studio audience were actress Jeanne Cooper from *The Young and the Restless,* TV producer Garry Marshall, and comedian Jim J. Bullock. The show aired from Los Angeles.

•MARSHALL EFRON'S ILLUSTRATED, SIMPLIFIED AND PAINLESS SUNDAY SCHOOL
Religious; Color
February 2, 1973–August 16, 1987

CBS Sun. 10–10:30 a.m. or 10:30–11 a.m. (2/2/73–8/25/74)
CBS Sun. Various times, usually 10:30–11 a.m. (7/6/75–8/28/77; summers only)
CBS Sun. 8:30–9 a.m. (7/20/86–8/31/86)
CBS Sun. 11–11:30 a.m. (7/5/87–8/16/87)

Regulars: *Marshall Efron, Alfa-Betty Olson*

The oddest network TV religious show had to be this series, which was offbeat if not irreverent in its dramatizations and teachings of the Gospel. Marshall Efron, who resembled an obese Ernie Kovacs, starred in sketches he wrote, playing everything from all of the Three Wise Men coming to see the baby Jesus to an illusionist explaining the miracle of the five loaves and two fishes that fed 5,000 people. Joining him occasionally on screen was Alfa-Betty Olson.

Efron taped the episodes in 1974 and 1975. A former English teacher at UCLA, he had done some minor work in show business, including some satiric commentaries on *The CBS Morning News,* before embarking on his own show, which was seen in rather irregular time slots during its run on CBS. A decade after its original erratic run, CBS repeated the show in the summers of 1986 and 1987, with the 1986 set of repeats running as part of *For Our Times* (q.v.).

•MARSUPILAMI
Cartoon; Color
September 18, 1992–September 3, 1994

CBS Sat. 11:30 a.m.–Noon (9/18/92–9/4/93)
CBS Sat. 8–8:30 a.m. (9/18/93–9/3/94)

Voices: *Jim Cummings, Steve Mackall, Frank Welker, Jeff Bennett (1992–93), Roger Bumpass (1992–93), Terry McGovern (1992–93), Marcia Wallace (1992–93), Rene Auberjonois (1993–94), Dan Castellaneta (1993–94), Tress MacNeille (1993–94), Danny Mann (1993–94), Samuel E. Wright (1993–94)*

Marsupilami, a character created in a 1950s Belgian comic strip, went from being support to star after the first season of this cartoon creation from Walt Disney TV Animation. From 1992–93 the series was titled *Raw Toonage* and had various Disney characters hosting an anthology. In addition to a segment spoofing TV shows and commercials, called "Totally Tasteless Videos," the show had two main components. The aforementioned Marsupilami was a spotted "wacky jungle critter," identified as a Houbster but resembling a cheetah, who used his 25-foot tail to help him out of jams or just entertain himself. His pal was Maurice the ape, who unlike Marsupilami did not talk. Their recurring opponent was Norman, a rough-hewn, burly blue-collar type, and the episodes took place in an unspecified jungle. Marsupilami's happy exclamation was "Houba!" (pronounced "hoo-bah").

The other element seen from 1992–93 was "He's Bonkers," featuring fired cartoon star Bonkers D. Bobcat trying to adjust from his former pampered life to that of a delivery boy. That character starred in his own syndicated daily cartoon in 1993 called *Bonkers;* on *Bonkers* Bobcat's career, after he was forced out of W. W. Wacky Studios in Toon Town, consisted of fighting crime with 12-year veteran patrolman Lucky Piquel, a partnership that began when Bonkers inadvertently helped the latter in saving the life of Donald Duck. Guest spots by Donald and other famous Disney characters, plus Bonkers's wacky demeanor, gave the cartoon the same flavor as the hit 1988 film *Who Framed Roger Rabbit?* Jim Cummings voiced both Bonkers and the fat, perturbed Piquel, who resembled Oliver Hardy, while Earl Boen voiced their Chief Kennifkey.

When the CBS series became simply *Marsupilami* in the fall of 1993, new segments featuring Sebastian the Crab from *The Little Mermaid* (q.v.) replaced the Bonkers featurettes. Sebastian, voiced by Samuel E. Wright, played the concierge at an underwater hotel, joined by Chef Louie, voiced by Rene Auberjonois. Another announced segment was "Snookums and Meat," about a dog and a cat, but it may not have appeared. As for Marsupilami, he continued, as merrily madcap as ever, in roughly five-minute shorts.

MARX MAGIC MIDWAY—See *Magic Midway.*

MARY HARTLINE SHOW, THE
Children's; B&W
February 12, 1951–June 15, 1951

ABC Mon.–Fri. 5–5:15 p.m. (2/12/51–3/2/51)
ABC Mon./Wed./Fri. 5–5:15 p.m. (3/5/51–4/13/51)
ABC Mon.–Fri. 5–5:15 p.m. (4/16/51–6/15/51)

Regulars: *Mary Hartline, Chet Roble*

Mary Hartline, the baton twirler on *Super Circus,* had aired her own series on WENR Chicago since 1950 before this show appeared briefly on ABC. Children in the studio sang and played contests with Mary and Chet to win dolls, clothes, and toys, and home viewers might get a "surprise" call from Hartline, who asked them a song question, with a correct answer winning a small prize. Chet also accompanied Mary's singing on the piano. In the middle of this show's short run it alternated daily with another children's series, *Ozmoe.*

•MASK, THE
Cartoon; Color
August 12, 1995–

CBS Sat. 10–10:30 a.m. (8/12/95–)

Voice:

Stanley Ipkiss/The Mask	*Rob Paulsen*

The 1994 film of the same title, based on an underground comic book, became the first of three Saturday morning cartoons during 1995–96 adapted from a movie starring

comedian Jim Carrey (for the other two, see *Ace Ventura: Pet Detective* and *Dumb and Dumber*). Stanley was a nebbish who found that a green 11th-century mask he wore on his face took control of his personality and made him a wacky, comic sort who was also invulnerable to pain. His girlfriend Peggy and pet hound Milo joined him as he attempted to curb crime via his alter ego in the community of Edge City.

•MASKED RIDER, THE
Cartoon; Color
September 16, 1995–

Fox Sat. 9–9:30 a.m. (9/16/95–10/28/95)
Fox Sat. 9:30–10 a.m. (11/4/95–4/13/96)
Fox Sat. 8:30–9 a.m. (4/27/96–6/8/96)
Fox Sat. 8–8:30 a.m. (6/15/96–)

Cast:

The Masked Rider/Dex	*T. J. Roberts*
Molly Stewart	*Rheannon Jo Slover*
Albee Stewart	*Ashton McArn II*
Hal Stewart	*David Stenstrom*
Barbara Stewart	*Candace Camille Bender*
Count Dregon	*Ken Ring*
Nefaria	*Jennifer Tung*
Ferbus (voice and puppeteer)	*Paul Pistore*
Patsy	*Libby Letlow*
Herbie	*Matt Bates*
Combat Chopper (voice only)	*Jason Narvy*
Magno (voice only)	*Wendee Lee*

The Masked Rider was a prince on the distant planet Edenoi who escaped to Earth via powers given to him by his grandfather, the king of Edenoi. He came to save the planet from his evil uncle, Count Dregon. Dregon, with his Insectivores, planned to enslave Earth as he had enslaved Edenoi. When the Masked Rider crash-landed on the lawn of the Stewart family in the town of Leawood, parents Hal and Barbara "adopted" him as a teenager named Dex, just as they had done previously with their children Molly and Albert. While they kept his heritage a secret, Molly and Albert did some hiding of their own by sheltering Dex's alien pal named Ferbus, as their father was allergic to fur and would not have kept the animal in the house. Ferbus added comic relief, as did next-door neighbor Patsy, who hated Molly and forced nerdy Herbie to conspire in plots—invariably botched—to get back at her.

But make no mistake, this show's emphasis was on cheesy, mindlessly violent action. As Dregon and his shifty aide Nefaria sent creepy warriors to Earth to establish his army of darkness, Dex fought them with martial arts moves with assistance from his "electra saber" plus his talking vehicles Combat Chopper, a motorcycle, and Magno, an automobile. And after two or three of these fights, the show spent the last minute or so on the usual token lesson in good behavior. Hypocrisy was apparently not on the list of proscribed behaviors in Edenoi society.

Those elements, plus a no-name cast and vaguely Asian villains, let observant viewers know that *The Masked Rider* was another Saban Production in the manner of *Mighty Morphin Power Rangers* (q.v.). This time the Japanese footage came from characters created by Shotaro Ishinomori, and the series was a co-production of Toei Company, Ltd. and Bugboy Productions, Inc. The show's biggest surprise was that the Tel Aviv Symphony Orchestra conducted by Udi Harpaz provided a rousing musical score.

•MATCH GAME, THE
Game; Color
December 31, 1962–July 12, 1991
NBC Mon.–Fri. 4–4:25 p.m. (12/31/62–9/20/69)
CBS Mon.–Fri. 3:30–4 p.m. (7/2/73–8/15/75)
CBS Mon.–Fri. 3–3:30 p.m. (8/18/75–11/28/75)
CBS Mon.–Fri. 3:30–4 p.m. (12/1/75–11/4/77)
CBS Mon.–Fri. 11–11:30 a.m. (11/7/77–12/16/77)
CBS Mon.–Fri. 4–4:30 p.m. (12/19/77–4/20/79)
ABC Mon.–Fri. Noon–12:30 p.m. (7/16/90–7/12/91)

Host: *Gene Rayburn (1962–79), Ross Shafer (1990–91)*

Regulars: *Richard Dawson (July 1973–August 1978), Charles Nelson Reilly (September 1973–April 1979; 1990–91), Brett Somers (September 1973–April 1979)*

Semiregulars: *Betty White (September 1973–March 1979), Fannie Flagg (December 1973–March 1979)*

Match Game had two long runs, with two distinctly different formats. On the first version two teams of two contestants and a celebrity each had to respond to such tame requests as "Name a city in Europe" or "Name a game played on grass." Each matching answer made by the teammates was worth $25, and the first team to reach $100 won the right to play "Audience Match," where each match with a participating audience member won $50.

The second, more popular version (it was the #1 daytime program in the spring of 1974) was named *Match Game '73–'79*, with the second part of the title based on what year it was. Now two players competed to match six celebrities in coming up with the "correct" responses to sentences booby-trapped to elicit double entendres (e.g., typical answers were "boobs" for a noun and "tinkle" for a verb). Each player picked one question for the celebrities to answer, and any celebrities that player did not match in the first round played the same game for a second round. After two rounds, the player with the most matches played a bonus game, unless there was a tie, in which case another round was played.

In the bonus, "Super Match," the audience was surveyed and the three most popular survey responses to a phrase like "Horse _____" were worth $500 (most popular of the three), $250, and $100. A match at any level let the contestant play for 10 times the amount by calling on one celebrity to match with, using another phrase. By 1978 the show was using a money wheel, allowing for more variation among celebrities and money amounts. This segment was often good for laughs,

with perhaps the loudest laughs evoked by the player who, when asked to complete the phrase, "Cuckoo _____," said "Cuckoo, Fran and Ollie."

Regulars on the panel, composed of two tiers with three stars apiece, were gravel-voiced actress Brett Somers on the top middle seat, fey Charles Nelson Reilly in the top right seat, and debonair Richard Dawson in the bottom middle seat. Both Somers and Reilly appeared first during the week of July 9–13, 1973, but they did not become regulars until the fall. Around that time, Betty White and Fannie Flagg started occupying the lower right end chair roughly once a month for most of the rest of the run in the 1970s. The panel typically was half male and half female. The only regular to drop out before the end was Dawson, who became a success on his own in 1976 hosting *Family Feud*.

The game received a revival in 1990 with youthful Ross Shafer replacing previous host Gene Rayburn. The format was the same as the 1970s except that the two contestants got $50 per match in the main game, then each played "Match Up" with one celebrity in 30 seconds as the star tried to pick what the contestant selected as answers to phrases, for $50 in the first round and $100 in the second.

Besides these incarnations, the game ran in nighttime syndication as *Match Game P.M.* from 1975–82 and had a partial revival in *The Match Game/Hollywood Squares Hour* (q.v.).

MATCH GAME/HOLLYWOOD SQUARES HOUR, THE
Game; Color
October 31, 1983–July 27, 1984
NBC Mon.–Fri. 3–4 p.m. (10/31/83–7/27/84)

Hosts: *Gene Rayburn, Jon "Bowzer" Bauman*

This revival of two favorite celebrity comedy game shows of the 1970s competed unsuccessfully with *General Hospital* on ABC and *Guiding Light* on CBS. The formats of each game remained the same, with the exception that *The Match Game* portion now had an extra tier of three celebrities, who worked the second half hour of the show doing *The Hollywood Squares* game. Additionally, Gene Rayburn appeared on the panel during the *Squares* portion, while toothy co-host Jon Bauman, late of the 1950s revival group Sha Na Na, took the spot for the *Match Game*. The show made an intentional decision to avoid hiring regulars from the past series, which could explain its failure, as previous fans were left wondering where Rose Marie, Charles Nelson Reilly, and others had gone.

MATINEE IN NEW YORK
Variety; B&W
June 9, 1952–September 5, 1952
NBC Mon.–Fri. 4–5 p.m. (6/9/52–9/5/52)

Regulars: *Robin Chandler, Bill Goodwin, Caroline Burke, Ted Collins, Bill Cullen*

This summer replacement for *The Kate Smith Hour* probably reminded viewers of that show and several other earlier daytime entries. Robin Chandler and Bill Goodwin introduced segments of varying formats, including revivals of the quiz *Winner Take All* (q.v.) led by Bill Cullen and *Vacation Wonderlands* (q.v.) with Caroline Burke hosting and producing. Guest interviews and cooking demonstrations were also featured. *Matinee in New York* was produced by Ted Collins, from *The Kate Smith Hour,* who also transferred his "Cracker Barrel" interview segment from that show.

MATINEE THEATER
Dramatic Anthology; Color
October 31, 1955–June 27, 1958
NBC Mon.–Fri. 3–4 p.m. (10/31/55–6/27/58)
Host: *John Conte*

Matinee Theater was the most elaborate live drama ever done on television. Airing from NBC's Burbank studios, the show used new and veteran writers, including some scripts from the *Kraft, Philco,* and *Goodyear* nighttime TV anthology series, to generate its daily offerings. NBC's preshow publicity boasted that it cost $100,000 a week to produce and used some 4,000 actors and 20 directors per year. The large operation somehow generated decent ratings and sponsorships for a few years. In 1956 it won an Emmy for Best Contribution to Daytime Programming.

The new-live-show-each-day idea sounds like folly in the world of videotaped daytime TV today, but it somehow worked. Crews rehearsed for the next day's show while the current program went out live on air, with a heavy curtain dividing the two operations. The show also employed a female director (a rarity then) named Livia Granito, who admitted to *TV Guide* that the demands of the series were such that "on each show you die a thousand deaths."

The notables who acted on the show included Sir Cedric Hardwicke, Roddy McDowall, Geraldine Page, and Margaret Truman. John Drew Barrymore acted at least six times plus directed one show. Sarah Churchill portrayed her grandmother in *The Remarkable Mr. Jerome,* written by her cousin Anita Leslie, and then acted in her father Winston Churchill's play *Savrola* on October 31, 1956, only one of at least 10 appearances. Eddie Cantor made his TV dramatic debut in *George Has a Birthday* on June 23, 1956. Wendy Hiller made her American TV debut in *Ann Veronica* on July 29, 1957. And Vincent Price, Judith Evelyn, and Leo G. Carroll recreated their Broadway roles for a production of *Angel Street* on May 9, 1958.

There was also a young actress who managed the impressive feat of landing three starring roles in the first seven shows. Her name was Angie Dickinson. Personable host John Conte himself acted on at least eight programs.

The program ended after more than 660 shows because ratings declined somewhat in 1958 (*American Bandstand* and *Who Do You Trust?* came on ABC then), and the show attracted few sponsors. By its cancellation, it had used 7,000 actors, built 4,200 sets, and gone through 15,000 costumes. Conte, who told *TV Guide* that hosting the series was "by far the most important thing I've ever done," started a campaign with his wife Ruth to keep the show on the air called the Fund for the Preservation of *Matinee Theatre,* but despite 10,000 letters of support they found no takers. *Matinee Theatre* was relegated to enthusiasts' TV nostalgia, although 26 episodes filmed in 13-show batches in 1956 and 1957 were syndicated as *Cameo Theater.*

•MATTY'S FUNDAY FUNNIES
Cartoons; Color
October 11, 1959–September 18, 1960
ABC Sun. 5–5:30 p.m. (10/11/59–9/18/60)
Voice of Matty: *Cecil Roy*

Matty's Funday Funnies played cartoons of Casper, Little Audrey, Baby Huey, Herman, and Katnip, and others first seen in theaters from Paramount Pictures. Characters Matty and Sisterbelle introduced the cartoons for sponsor Mattel Toy Company and provided the show with its only new animation. ABC transferred the series to the early evening from September 30, 1960–December 29, 1962, during which time it had a major transformation. In January 1962 it began airing new cartoons of Beany and Cecil, and became *Matty's Funnies with Beany and Cecil.* In April 1962 it became just *Beany and Cecil,* a title it kept when it moved to Saturday mornings in 1963. (For more details, see *Beany and Cecil.*)

MAURICE EVANS PRESENTS—See *Hallmark Hall of Fame.*

•MAURY POVICH SHOW, THE
Talk; Color
1990–
Syndicated 60 minutes daily beginning September 1990
Host: *Maury Povich*

Maury Povich, a reporter known for hosting the syndicated nightly tabloid *A Current Affair* and for being the husband of CBS reporter Connie Chung, decided to follow Phil Donahue's footsteps in this long-running but unexceptional talk show featuring questions from the audience. It aired from New York.

MCDUFF, THE TALKING DOG
Sitcom; Color
September 11, 1976–November 20, 1976
NBC Sat. 10–10:30 a.m. (9/11/76–11/20/76)
Cast:

McDuff *(voice)*	*Jack Lester*
Dr. Calvin Campbell	*Walter Willson*
Amos Ferguson	*Gordon Jump*
Mrs. Osgood	*Monty Margetts*

Squeaky	*Johnnie Collins III*
Kimmy	*Michelle Stacy*

Combine *Topper* and *Mr. Ed* and you get a rough version of *McDuff the Talking Dog*. Veterinarian Dr. Calvin Campbell found himself in the odd position of being the only human who could see or talk to McDuff, the 100-year-old spirit of an English sheepdog who inhabited his home, a situation which sparked considerable suspicions in his nosy neighbor Amos Ferguson. McDuff never seemed to mind the complications he caused, probably because he liked speaking to Dr. Campbell and to other animal species too. Calvin's maid was Mrs. Osgood, while Amos Ferguson's nephew was Squeaky.

MEATBALLS AND SPAGHETTI
Cartoon; Color
September 18, 1982–September 10, 1983

CBS Sat. 11:30 a.m.–Noon (9/18/82–1/29/83)
CBS Sat. 9–9:30 a.m. (2/5/83–9/10/83)

Voices: *Jack Angel, Wally Burr, Phillip Clarke, Peter Cullen, Ronald Gans, Barry Gordon, David Hall, Sally Julian, Morgan Lofting, Ron Masak, Bill Ratner, Ronnie Schell, Marilyn Schreffler, Hal Smith, Frank Welker, Paul Winchell*

In this production from ex–network programming whiz Fred Silverman's Intermedia Entertainment, Meatballs was an obese rock star, an apparent homage to the bombastic popular singer Meatloaf, and Spaghetti was his stringy wife. Joining them in two episodes per show, along with original songs, were Clyde, Meatball's assistant, and Woofer, their dog. *Variety*'s assessment was "No try at music here, or even much comedy either. It's without any socially redeeming value."

MEDICAL HORIZONS
Documentary; B&W
September 9, 1956–June 9, 1957

ABC Sun. 4:30–5 p.m. (9/9/56–6/9/57)

Host/Narrator: *Don Goddard*

Medical Horizons went on location to find out the latest advances in scientific care and treatment in the health field. On October 14, 1956, for example, the series aired a live report from the New London, Connecticut, Navy submarine base on how U.S. Navy research scientists simulate conditions to determine how submarine crews and divers can survive the dangers of the sea. Other shows included procedures for premature babies at Baltimore's Sinai Hospital and studies on menopause's effects at the Medical College of Georgia.

Produced in cooperation with the American Medical Association, the show's sponsor was CIBA Pharmaceutical Products. The series first aired on ABC Mondays at 9:30 p.m. from September 12, 1955–March 5, 1956, with Quincy Howe hosting for the first month and Don Goddard thereafter.

MEET BETTY FURNESS
Interview; B&W
January 2, 1953–June 25, 1953

CBS Fri. 10:45–11 a.m. (1/2/53–6/25/53)

Hostess: *Betty Furness*

Meet Betty Furness was one of several short shows CBS used in 1953 to cover Arthur Godfrey's absences Friday. It starred then-popular commercial speaker Betty Furness talking with celebrity guests like composer Richard Rodgers. Her sponsor was Westinghouse, of course.

MEET ME AT THE ZOO
Informational; B&W
January 10, 1953–May 30, 1953

CBS Sat. 1–1:30 p.m. (1/10/53–5/30/53)

Regulars: *Jack Whitaker, Freeman Shelly, Roger Connant*

Airing live from the Philadelphia Zoo, this weekly show hosted by local personality Jack Whitaker featured visits to zoo director Freeman Shelly and some area children. CBS replaced this with the more popular reruns of *The Lone Ranger*.

MEET THE MASTERS
Documentary; B&W
February 24, 1952–December 14, 1952

NBC Sun. 5:30–6 p.m. (2/24/52–12/14/52; off summer)

Meet the Masters consisted mainly of short films made in 1951 for movie theaters, profiling such world-class musicians as Artur Rubinstein (on the debut) and Marian Anderson (on the second show). It alternated weekly with, of all things, *Sky King*.

•MEET THE PRESS
Public Affairs; B&W and Color
February 26, 1950–

NBC Sun. 4:30–5 p.m. or 5–5:30 p.m. (2/26/50–9/24/50)
NBC Sun. 4–4:30 p.m. (10/1/50–5/18/52; off summer 1951)
NBC Sun. 1–1:30 p.m. (9/19/65–9/13/70)
NBC Sun. 12:30–1 p.m. (9/20/70–9/14/75)
NBC Sun. Noon–12:30 p.m. (fall season); 12:30–1 p.m. (January–August) (9/21/75–9/13/87)
NBC Sun. 9:30–10 a.m. (9/20/87–9/13/92)
NBC Sun. 9–10 a.m. (9/20/92–)

Regulars: *Martha Rountree (1950–52), Lawrence Spivak (1950–75), Bill Monroe (1975–86), Marvin Kalb (1984–87), Chris Wallace (1987–88), Garrick Utley (1988–91), Tim Russert (1992–)*

The granddaddy of all TV newsmaker interview shows, not to mention the longest-running show on television, was *Meet the Press*, which began on radio in 1945 and started its TV run on November 6, 1947, going to NBC beginning

November 20, 1947. Coming over from radio with the show were its co-creators Lawrence Spivak and Martha Rountree. Rountree continued to serve as host, and Spivak was a somewhat hard-nosed panelist who interrogated a guest, usually from the political world, about current concerns. Joining Spivak were three guest journalists each week, a format that lasted for the next 45 years.

When Spivak bought out Martha Rountree's interest in the show in 1953, she left as moderator and Ned Brooks replaced her. As in the past, Spivak served as moderator occasionally when needed. He completely took over the duties from Brooks when the show went to Sunday afternoons exclusively in 1965, following a few brief runs in the early 1950s (the show had aired mostly on NBC Sundays at 6 p.m. in its first 18 years on air). After Spivak retired in late 1975, a succession of NBC News reporters replaced him as host. The longest-running of these was Spivak's immediate successor Bill Monroe, who had stepped down by the fall of 1984, when the show was subtitled *Decision '84* and written to focus on political races through December. The new host was Marvin Kalb, occasionally assisted by Roger Mudd. Monroe remained on the show with a letters-to-the-editor segment until retiring in February 1986 after 25 years with NBC News. Kalb left in May 1987 to work at Harvard University, and Chris Wallace and then Garrick Utley replaced him.

The show's questionings generated a number of exclusives, such as Thomas Dewey's 1950 announcement that he would not seek a third nomination as Republican candidate for president; a rare TV guest shot by ex-President Herbert Hoover in 1955; and a special hour discussion in 1968 with Secretary of State Dean Rusk and Defense Secretary Robert McNamara about the Vietnam War. If they were not on the show, politicos usually knew about it. Both Harry Truman and Dwight Eisenhower were said to be avid viewers during the 1950s. Other exclusives included being the first news show to air in color in 1954, and the first to have a live satellite interview.

Several politicians made repeat appearances. In its first quarter century on television, the guest seen most often was Hubert Humphrey, who appeared 22 times. By the mid-1990s Senator Bob Dole had surpassed Humphrey, appearing more than three times as often. The show has had more than 1,000 guests interviewed, including Presidents Gerald Ford and Bill Clinton on its 30th and 45th anniversaries on television in 1977 and 1992, respectively.

At the start of 1992 NBC News Tim Russert assumed hosting duties from Garrick Utley, who had also hosted the Sunday edition of *Today*, which led into *Meet the Press* from 1988–92, and shortly thereafter the program was revamped into an hour-long concoction in the manner of its successful competitor *This Week with David Brinkley*. Now Russert and one or two other reporters asked a guest questions, followed by a discussion about the guest and what the guest had said, and other issues, by the reporters and a brief clip of a vintage *Meet the Press* episode from

Meet the Press *had ex-President Herbert Hoover as a guest in the 1950s. Host Lawrence E. Spivak stands next to him.*

years earlier. The format clicked, and by 1996 the show appeared to be on its way to celebrating an unprecedented 50 years on television, longer than any other series ever.

MEET THE PROFESSOR
Educational; B&W
February 5, 1961–June 9, 1963

ABC Sun. Noon–12:30 p.m. (2/5/61–5/14/61)
ABC Sun. 2:30–3 p.m. (1/7/62–7/1/62)
ABC Sun. 1:30–2 p.m. (11/11/62–6/9/63)

Host: *Dr. Harold Taylor (1961)*

Meet the Professor profiled an educator in action at the college or university where he or she worked as part of the early 1960s TV trend toward more highbrow commercial programming. Not all programs had intellectual pretensions, however. One installment featured dancer Pearl Primus doing the twist on the February 11, 1962 edition, with Dr. Ethel Anpelfels, a New York University professor of anthropology, as host. The show was taped in 1961 with ex–Sarah Lawrence College president Dr. Harold Taylor hosting, then filmed with no regulars thereafter.

MEET THE VEEP

Discussion; B&W

February 1, 1953–March 29, 1953

NBC Sun. 5:30–5:45 p.m. (2/1/53–3/29/53)

Host: *Earl Godwin*

Interviewee: *Alben W. Barkley*

Washington, D.C., correspondent Earl Godwin reviewed current issues with Alben Barkley, the U.S. Vice President (or "veep") under Harry Truman in this series live from the nation's capital. Barkley told *Variety* that the latest "Veep," Richard Nixon, had suggested the show's title and even sent the first telegram of best wishes for the show. A few guests also appeared, including Bob Hope on March 8. The show continued on NBC Tuesdays at 10:45 p.m. from June 30–August 25, 1953.

MEET YOUR CONGRESS

Public Affairs; B&W

March 13, 1949–June 19, 1949

NBC Sun. 4:30–5 p.m. (3/13/49–6/19/49)

Host: *Blair Moody*

Former Senator Blair Moody of Michigan hosted this Washington, D.C.–based news show where a duo of Democratic congressmen faced off with a Republican Congressional twosome in a discussion of current topics. After its NBC run, the show went into syndication until DuMont picked it up from July 8, 1953–July 4, 1954 as a nighttime show.

MEET YOUR COVER GIRL

Fashions; B&W

October 24, 1950–November 1, 1951

CBS Tue./Thu. or Tue./Wed. 3:30–4 p.m.
  (10/24/50–12/27/50)

CBS Wed. 3:30–4 p.m. (1/3/51–5/30/51)

CBS Thu. 3:30–4 p.m. (6/7/51–11/1/51)

Host: *Robin Chandler*

Interviews with fashion authorities and Manhattan models were the emphasis on *Meet Your Cover Girl*, though the show had an occasional dramatic interlude, such as the one in which a guest enacted her decision to come to America. There was no sponsor for the New York–based show, which shared a time slot with several other daily shows during its run, most notably *Fashion Magic*.

MEL TORME SHOW, THE

Variety; Color and B&W

September 17, 1951–August 21, 1952

CBS Mon.–Fri. 4:30–5 p.m. (9/17/51–10/26/51)

CBS Mon.–Fri. 3:30–4 p.m. (11/5/51–1/11/52)

CBS Tue./Thu. 3:30–4 p.m. (1/14/52–8/21/52)

Regulars: *Mel Torme, Peggy King (September 1951–October 1951), Ellen Martin (September 1951–October 1951), Kaye*

Ballard (at least November 1951–August 1952), the Mellowlarks (at least November 1951–August 1952), Al Pellegrini, with the Red Norvo Trio (September 1951–October 1951), with the Terry Gibbs Combo (at least November 1951–August 1952)

This tunefest led by great scat vocalist Mel Torme was one of the few shows CBS aired in its experimental color format in the fall of 1951 before reverting to black and white. Besides Torme, the regulars included vocalist Ellen Martin, dancer Peggy King, comedienne Kaye Ballard (in the first of several regular TV roles), and Al Pellegrini, who conducted the Red Norvo Trio and then the Terry Gibbs Combo.

MEMORY GAME—See *Joe Garagiola's Memory Game.*

•MERV GRIFFIN SHOW, THE

Talk; Color

October 1, 1962–March 29, 1983

NBC Mon.–Fri. 2–2:55 p.m. (10/1/62–3/29/63)

Host: *Merv Griffin*

Merv Griffin was best known (if he was known at all) as a passable singer and game show host (e.g., *Play Your Hunch*) when he got his NBC daytime show after getting positive response for his guest hosting of *The Tonight Show* during the period between Jack Paar's departure and Johnny Carson's arrival. Among the network show's writers were Dick Cavett and Pat McCormick, both of whom also worked on *The Tonight Show* under Carson. But despite their efforts and decent reviews, Merv went off after six months, unable to beat *Password* and *Art Linkletter's House Party* on CBS.

Griffin revived his series in syndication in the spring of 1965 with such unlikely guests as Brigitte Bardot and John Lennon. He became known for "theme" shows unifying his guests, such as a tribute to a movie and its participants, and for singing a few songs before sitting down to introduce stars and chat with them. The show did so well that the William Morris Agency offered Griffin the chance to do a similar show late nights on CBS, which led to a run there from August 18, 1969–February 11, 1972.

David Frost was tabbed as Griffin's replacement in syndication. Frost, an Englishman seen occasionally in America in the 1960s, had a high-profile tenure as host. In 1970 alone, he got such top name guests as Johnny Carson, Jackie Gleason, Sophia Loren (in her talk show debut), and the then-married Richard Burton and Elizabeth Taylor. He also coerced Arthur Godfrey and Harve Presnell to announce that they had vasectomies. But despite such successes and reasonable ratings, when Griffin and CBS parted ways in 1972 following arguments between Griffin and programming head Fred Silverman about the show's approach (it always finished second to Johnny Carson),

Griffin got the nod to return to hosting this show, and Frost was knocked out.

Griffin's daytime talk show lasted another 14 years, long enough to outlive his competitors Mike Douglas and Dinah Shore, among others. On September 4, 1981 he went to delivering his show on satellite in a daily hour format. But the show's approach, involving a celebrity-heavy format which reportedly allowed Griffin to interview more than 25,000 guests, was out of favor by the time it ended, (*Donahue* and other talk shows of that ilk were gaining in popularity), and no program like *The Merv Griffin Show* has been as successful since. Griffin became a very successful businessman, and is now retired.

•MICKEY MOUSE CLUB, THE
Children's; B&W
October 3, 1955–September 25, 1959

ABC Mon.–Fri. 5–6 p.m. (10/3/55–9/27/57)
ABC Mon.–Fri. 5:30–6 p.m. (9/30/57–9/25/59)

Hosts: *Jimmie Dodd, Roy Williams*

The Mouseketeers: *Sharon Baird, Bobby Burgess, Lonnie Burr, Tommy Cole, Annette Funicello, Darlene Gillespie, Carl O'Brien ("Cubby"), Karen Pendleton, Doreen Tracey, Dennis Day (1955–57), Nancy Abbate (1955–56), Billie Jean Beanblossom (1955–56), Johnny Crawford (1955–56), Dickie Dodd (1955–56), Mary Espinosa (1955–56), Judy Harriet (1955–56), John Lee Johann (1955–56), Bonni Lou Kern (1955–56), Mary Sartori (1955–56), Bronson Scott (1955–56), Michael Smith (1955–56), Ronnie Steiner (1955–56), Mark Sutherland (1955–56), Don Underhill (1955–56), Paul Peterson (1955), Tim Rooney (1955), Mickey Rooney, Jr. (1955), Cheryl Holdridge (1956–59), Sherry Allen (1956–57), Eileen Diamond (1956–57), Charley Laney (1956–57), Larry Larsen (1956–57), Jay-Jay Solari (1956–57), Margene Storey (1956–57), Don Agrati (Don Grady; 1957–59), Bonnie Lynn Fields (1957–59), Linda Hughes (1957–59), Lynn Ready (1957–59)*

Serial Performers: *Tim Considine, David Stollery, Roy Barcroft, Tommy Kirk*

Walt Disney spent an estimated $1.125 million on this classic children's show of the 1950s, but the dividends, both for him and for daytime television, were huge. The ambitious production formed the foundation on which ABC built its daytime lineup, and had the show failed, there is a distinct possibility that ABC's might never have established the toehold that allowed the network's daily schedule to be competitive with NBC and CBS. ABC's alliance with Walt Disney, which began with the nighttime anthology *Disneyland* in 1954, also benefited the movie company immensely, giving Disney a chance to promote its California theme park and develop new franchises for promotions, most notably the "mouse ears" cap the performers wore. The best result, though, remains the shows themselves, which are as great entertainment today as they were some 40 years ago.

The biggest star of The Mickey Mouse Club *was Annette Funicello, seen here second from left. The other cast members with Annette are, from left, Mouseketeers Eileen Diamond and Cubby O'Brien, and "Big Mooseketeer" Roy Williams, a Disney animator.*

The show boasted of 21 separate elements which comprised its first 260 hours of shows. (To save expenses, only 20 weeks of shows were shot in the first year, so some shows were repeated twice.) Included in the mix were films on "What I Want to Be" (Alvy Moore was host/companion to Pat Morrow and Duncan Richardson in the adventures); "Meet the _____" (shark hunter, rodeo driver, etc.); "I'm No Fool" (safety tips hosted by cartoon character Jiminy Cricket from the classic 1940 film *Pinocchio);* "The Mickey Mouse Newsreel," which consumed the first 15 minutes of three shows each week; and a daily Mickey Mouse cartoon from 1929–49. Each day's show also had a special themed event, which in order from Mondays through Fridays were "Fun with Music Day," "Guest Star Day," "Anything Can Happen Day," "Circus Day," and "Talent Roundup Day."

Involved in all the latter as participants or hosts for the segments were the group of talented children who formed the Mouseketeers. (There were 27 of them initially, but this number had been reduced to half that amount by the last two seasons.) The kids who stood out from the others in some way generally had the longest runs on the show, such as Bobby Burgess, the toothy tall dancer who took his legs to ABC's nighttime *Lawrence Welk Show* as a regular in the 1960s and 1970s, and "Cubby" O'Brien, the chubby drummer.

But the one everyone remembers is Annette Funicello, who received the most fan mail, perhaps in part because of her burgeoning figure. Annette appeared in a few serials on the show in addition to her performances with the rest of the troupe, and Walt Disney was so impressed with her abilities that he encouraged her to act full-time (first on Disney's ABC nighttime series *Zorro* in 1958–59) and begin a successful recording career (with the hit single "Tall Paul"). Both careers lasted far into the 1960s for her and made her the best-known Mouseketeer outside the show.

Besides the ones involving Annette, other major serials seen involved the junior detectives from the world of books, the Hardy Boys, played by Tommy Kirk and Tim Considine, and cowhands-in-training Spin and Marty, with Considine again, David Stollery as his pal Marty, and Roy Barcroft as their mentor. In fact, the child talent on the show was so impressive that adults must have found it reassuring to see two of their own get into the action. Roy Williams was a Disney animator known familiarly as "The Big Mooseketeer," while Jimmie Dodd was the boyishly handsome unofficial head of the gang who wrote many of the show's songs and sang lead on most of them, including the catchy theme song which opened and closed each show ("Who's the leader of the club that's made for you and me?/M-I-C, K-E-Y, M-O-U-S-E!").

It all moved effortlessly on film and paid off beautifully in the ratings for a time. The show had zoomed to first place in daytime by the end of 1955, pulling more than twice the audience than second-place finisher *Arthur Godfrey Time*

The 1956 cast of The Mickey Mouse Club.

plus reaching more adults than most of the other daytime network shows. But while it proved successful in knocking *Howdy Doody* out of competition, *The Mickey Mouse Club* had a far worse time when NBC ran repeats of *I Married Joan* in the fall of 1956. On September 30, 1957, the show shortened to 30 minutes and ran only three times a week; on Tuesdays and Thursdays repeats of serials on the show aired under the title *Adventure Time*. Two years later it went off the air.

In 1977, eighteen years after cancellation and two years after the show ran in repeats in syndication, *The New Mickey Mouse Club* debuted. The daily syndicated offering, in color on videotape, was much heralded but not successful. An oddity of the show was that two of its members, Julie Piekarski and Lisa Whelchel, later starred on the NBC nighttime sitcom *The Facts of Life.*

A new *Mickey Mouse Club* debuted on cable's The Disney Channel on April 24, 1989, without the mouse ears but with a lot of music and comic sketches. The series, videotaped at the Disney/MGM studios in Orlando, Florida, was in production until 1994 but continued to air in repeats at least two years after that.

MID-DAY CHAPEL—See Morning Chapel.

MID-DAY NEWS
News; B&W
September 3, 1951–September 21, 1951
CBS Mon.–Fri. 12:15–12:30 p.m. (9/3/51–9/21/51)
Anchors: *Dorothy Doan, John Schafer*

A program CBS aired three weeks until *Love of Life* debuted, *Mid-Day News* had a male and female sit side by side updating stories. But Dorothy Doan, a feature writer for the International News Service covering the United Nations, did "women's stories" while John Schafer delivered hard news and stood before a map to illustrate reports from across the world. Film clips came from Telenews.

MIDWESTERN HAYRIDE
Musical Variety; B&W
January 26, 1952–June 8, 1952
NBC Sat. Noon–1 p.m. (1/26/52–3/29/52)
NBC Sun. 3–4 p.m. (5/4/52–6/8/52)
Host: *Bill Thall*

One of TV's longest-running country music shows hailed not from Nashville but from the unlikely base of Cincinnati, Ohio. *Midwestern Hayride* began airing on WLW radio in 1939 as *Boone County Jamboree*, then became a half-hour video entry under its new title on WLW-TV on February 13, 1948 with Bill Thall as host. It came onto NBC Saturdays at 9–10 p.m. on June 16, 1951, then went into daytime in early 1952 and returned to various nighttime slots on NBC summers from 1952–56 (except for 1953) and on ABC summers from 1957–58. In the summer of

1959, it went back to NBC, and ended that fall, on September 6. Sometimes it ran as a half-hour show. The hosts changed a fair amount (Thall lasted from 1951–54 only), and during the 1950s most of the talent shown consisted of guest acts.

Midwestern Hayride continued running in syndication in the 1960s, both in hour and half-hour versions weekly. In August 1969 it began airing in a new youth-oriented format. Dean Richards, who had hosted since the last network version in 1959, was demoted to music director in favor of 28-year-old country singer Henson Cargill as host. It also aired under different titles in some locations, such as *Country Hayride* or simply *Hayride*. In 1970 Cargill left as host and Kenny Price, a performer on the show since 1953, replaced him. The show then ran only on stations owned by the Avco Corporation, most of which were in Ohio, until its cancellation in September 1972.

MIGHTY HEROES, THE
Cartoon; Color
October 29, 1966–September 2, 1967
CBS Sat. 9–9:30 a.m. (10/29/66–9/2/67)
Voices: *Herschel Bernardi, Lionel Wilson*

Cuckoo Man, Diaper Man, Rope Man, Strong Man, and Tornado Man—they were hardly the *Super Friends* (q.v.), but they somehow triumphed over their opponents despite the less than intimidating powers suggested by their names. This superhero spoof replacement for the venerable *Mighty Mouse Playhouse* came from that show's executive producer Bill Weiss and production company CBS Terrytoons. However, the real brains behind the enterprise was its creator and director Ralph Bakshi. After its one-season run it was syndicated with *Mighty Mouse Playhouse.*

•MIGHTY MORPHIN POWER RANGERS
Children's; Color
August 28, 1993–

Fox Sat. 11:30 a.m.–Noon (8/28/93–1/1/94)
Fox Sat. 8:30–9 a.m. (1/8/94–6/25/94)
Fox Sat. 8:30–9 a.m. (8/27/94–1/28/95)
Fox Sat. 8–8:30 a.m. (2/4/95–3/11/95)
Fox Sat. 8:30–9 a.m. (3/18/95–10/28/95)
Fox Sat. 9–9:30 a.m. (11/4/95–)

Cast:

Tommy (Green, later White, Ranger)	*Jason David Frank*
Kimberly (Pink Ranger; 1993–96)	*Amy Jo Johnson*
Billy (Blue Ranger; 1993–96)	*David Yost*
Zack (Black Ranger; 1993–94)	*Walter Jones*
Jason (Red Ranger; 1993–94)	*Austin St. John*
Trini (Yellow Ranger; 1993–94)	*Thuy Trang*
Aisha (Yellow Ranger; 1994–96)	*Karen Ashley*

Bulk	Paul Schrier
Skull	Jason Narvy
Rita Repulsa (voice only; 1993–94)	Barbara Goodson
Goldar (voice only; 1993–96)	Kerrigan Mahan
Squatt (voice only; 1993–96)	Michael J. Sorich
Baboo (voice only; 1993–96)	Colin Phillips
Adam (Black, later Green Ranger; 1994–)	Johnny Yong Bosch
Rocky (Red, later Blue Ranger; 1994–)	Steve Cardenas
Tonya (Yellow Ranger; 1996–)	Nakia Burrise
Kat (Pink Ranger; 1996–)	Catherine Sutherland

Every generation of TV viewers seems to have one show which kids love and parents hate, and in the 1990s that show was *Mighty Morphin Power Rangers*. Five stereotypical teenagers (originally, handsome Jason, troubled Tommy, trendy Kimberly, wise Asian Trini, and somewhat nerdy Billy) went to school in the town of Angel Grove, whose residents never suspected that when evil sorceress Rita Repulsa or her boss Lord Zedd sent alien creatures to attack Earth, the quintet transformed into the Power Rangers, colorfully attired karate experts with helmets who fought the intruders. They also could become dinosaurs or speedy aircraft, and if ultimate power was necessary to defeat the foes, they combined to become a gigantic robotlike entity called a Megazord. Baboo, Goldar, and Squatt were Rita's underlings, who began to work for Lord Zedd directly when he tired of her inability to stop the Rangers and took over operations in the fall of 1994. While not working as Rangers under the directions of Zordon at Command Center, the five kids could be seen at school, dealing with the envious comic duo of Angel Grove students Bulk and Skull, who considered themselves crime fighters in their own right.

What drove adults up the wall about the show was its emphasis on elaborate, violent fight sequences with reptilian creatures, souped up with raucous background rock music. The only way the Rangers knew how to handle an opponent was to beat it senseless until it died or vanished. Americans were not alone in objecting to the violence. Scandanavian nations banned the show from airing after three boys, fans of the program, beat a little girl unconscious.

Fox Children's Network President Margaret Loesch admitted she had some qualms about the show as well, but as she told *TV Guide* in 1995, "Our staff psychologist, Dr. Helen Boehm, has made me feel a lot better about *Power Rangers*—not that I felt bad about it. . . . Helen says that children love to be swept away, and that this is what *Power Rangers* does."

Actually, what might have "swept away" those older viewers who did not object to the mayhem was its campy look and feel. Producer Haim Saban based the show on a Japanese program variously translated as *Zyu Rangers, Galaxy Rangers,* and *Dai Rangers* produced by Toci Company, Ltd., with the original concept by Saburo Yatsude. Using footage of the Power Rangers from that show was fine, as their faces were covered, but much of the film was grainy and cheap-looking, and Rita in particular looked horribly dubbed, with her words and mouth movements rarely matching. No wonder it took him nearly a decade to sell the concept.

In 1994 the show's success spread as it went from five to six days a week, and new Power Rangers entered to replace some of the actors who wanted more money. The departing Power Rangers were written out by saying they had gone to a peace conference in Switzerland(!), while the new ones assumed their roles. Tommy was now the head good guy. In the summer of 1995 came *Mighty Morphin Power Rangers: The Movie,* which got nowhere near the attention of the TV series despite being higher budgeted and loaded with better special effects.

On April 20, 1996, the Saturday show got another overhaul and was retitled *Power Rangers ZEO*. New adversaries were King Mondo, Queen Machina, and Prince Sprocket of the Machine Empire, who wiped out Zedd and his crew and led invasions with their robotish Cogs. The two new Rangers were Tanya and Kat, and returning Rangers had new uniforms and powers. Tommy was now the Red Ranger, with the power of the Phoenix; Adam was the Green Ranger, with the strength of Taurus the bull; and Rocky was the Blue Ranger, with the power of the Sphinx. Got all that?

While *Power Rangers ZEO* aired on Saturdays, Fox reran old episodes in the afternoon. Fox announced the show would run only daily in the fall of 1996, even though the show remained a popular if controversial top audience getter for the network on Saturdays.

•MIGHTY MOUSE PLAYHOUSE, THE
Cartoons; Color
December 10, 1955–December 26, 1992

CBS Sat. 11–11:30 a.m. (12/10/55–3/17/56)
CBS Sat. 10:30–11 a.m. (3/24/56–9/24/60)
CBS Sat. 11:30 a.m.–Noon (10/1/60–12/31/60)
CBS Sat. 12:30–1 p.m. (1/7/61–4/8/61)
CBS Sat. 10:30–11 a.m. (4/15/61–9/18/65)
CBS Sat. 10–10:30 a.m. (9/25/65–9/3/66)
CBS Sat. 9–9:30 a.m. (9/10/66–10/22/66)
CBS Sat. 8–9 a.m. (9/8/79–8/30/80)
CBS Sat. 8–8:30 a.m. (9/6/80–3/7/81)
CBS Sun. 8–8:30 a.m. (3/15/81–9/12/82)
CBS Sat. 10:30–11 a.m. (9/19/87–9/10/88)
CBS Sat. Noon–12:30 p.m. (9/17/88–10/22/88)
CBS Sat. 11–11:30 a.m. (10/29/88–12/31/88)
CBS Sat. Noon–12:30 p.m. (1/7/89–9/2/89)
Fox Sat. 11–11:30 a.m. (11/14/92–12/26/92)

Voices:

Mighty Mouse/Narrator (1955–66)	Tom Morrison
Gandy Goose/Sourpuss (1955–66)	Arthur Kay

Mighty Mouse/Oil Can Harry
   (1979–82)   *Alan Oppenheimer*
Pearl Pureheart (1979–82)   *Diane Pershing*
Heckle/Jeckle/Quackula (1979–82)   *Frank Welker*
Theodore H. Bear (1979–82)   *Norm Prescott*

Also (1987–89): *Dana Hill, Beau Weaver, Patrick Pinney, Maggie Roswell*

"Here I come to save the day!" With that magnificent operatic delivery, sung by Roy Halee, Mighty Mouse signaled his arrival on each show of the first version of this enduring Saturday cartoon. The 1955–66 version was basically just a compilation of theatrical cartoons by Terrytoons featuring a muscular rodent who arrived in the nick of time to save Pearl Pureheart and others from the machinations of Powerful Puss (in the early cartoons) or Oilcan Harry. Supporting cartoon shorts appearing in the shows were ones featuring such types as Gandy Goose and Dinky Duck, plus a few occasional one-shot creations.

The Mighty Mouse Playhouse was mighty indeed on Saturday mornings in the late 1950s and early 1960s, often ending up as the top-rated network show in that time period. *Billboard* reported in 1956 that the show had higher ratings than any other network daytime series including *The Mickey Mouse Club,* with a mind-boggling 70.8 share of the audience, easily swamping NBC's competition of *The Children's Corner.* After 11 years, a new cartoon from its creators was tried as its replacement, but failed to do well (see *Mighty Heroes*). Thereafter Mighty Mouse was banished to repeats on local stations and was little mentioned except by Andy Kaufman in a wonderful pantomime to the show's theme song on *Saturday Night Live* in 1975.

In 1979 the cartoon received a three-year revival titled *The New Adventures of Mighty Mouse and Heckle and Jeckle.* The mouse now spoke in couplets during his adventures in outer space (no opera), and the other two title characters continued to be the wisecracking magpies they had been on the earlier *Heckle and Jeckle* (q.v.). A new character with his own segment was the vampire duck Quackula, who was never popular with viewers and vanished when the series went to a half hour for its last two seasons.

Five years after the first revival's cancellation came *Mighty Mouse: The New Adventures,* produced by Ralph Bakshi, who had worked on some of the last Mighty Mouse cartoons of the 1960s. Now Mighty had a Clark Kent equivalent in the form of his everyday persona Mike the Mouse, who worked on the assembly line at Pearl Pureheart's factory, and stories were on the wacky side, even to the point of making fun of Mighty's own legacy.

But the one show most people remember from this edition was one they probably only heard about—a first-season episode in which Mighty Mouse regained his powers by inhaling flowers, which the Rev. Donald Wildmon's group the American Family Association charged was representing him inhaling cocaine! Though the controversy

amused some (Johnny Carson wondered on *The Tonight Show* why someone had not asked earlier what drugs made Daffy Duck talk the way he did), the flowers segment was cut. The series ran one more season before cancellation, mixing in a few adult concerns like W-2 forms without any complaints from Wildmon. The shows on Fox in 1992 were repeats that ran when *X-Men* was having a temporary production problem.

•MIGHTY ORBOTS, THE
Cartoon; Color
September 8, 1984–August 31, 1985
ABC Sat. 9–9:30 a.m. (9/8/84–8/31/85)

Voices:

Rob   *Barry Gordon*
Dia   *Jennifer Darling*
Tor/Umbra   *Bill Martin*
Bort   *Jim MacGeorge*
Bo   *Sherry Alberoni*
Boo   *Julie Bennett*
Crunch/Rondu   *Don Messick*
Ohno   *Noelle North*
Narrator   *Gary Owens*

For a typical toy-based cartoon of the 1980s, *The Mighty Orbots* stood out due to the names attached to it. No less than former network programming wizard Fred Silverman served as an executive producer, and veteran actor and voiceover artist Howard Morris served as voice director. Unfortunately, their contributions did not help the show to become any more than a routine effort.

The stories focused on a group of patrollers for the United Planets for Galactic Control in the 23rd century. The lead members were Rob and Dia, who were romantically involved as well, and their five robot comrades known as Orbots, who could combine to make one oversized robot, or rather Orbot. As the theme song put it, "They're joining together to fight for what's right everywhere." The Orbots were strongman Tor, childlike Bort, fun-loving gals Bo and Boo, and moronic Crunch. Rob commanded the oversized hybrid Orbot along with diminutive driver Ohno. Rondu was their commander contact on Earth. Their recurring foe Umbra attempted to destroy Earth, but failed to do so in the 13 episodes made for this show.

MIKE AND BUFF
Talk; Color and B&W
August 20, 1951–February 27, 1953
CBS Mon.–Fri. 10:30–11 a.m. (8/20/51–10/26/51)
CBS Mon.–Fri. 3–3:30 p.m. (11/5/51–2/1/52)
CBS Mon.–Fri. 2:45–3:30 p.m. (2/4/52–8/29/52)
CBS Mon.–Fri. 3:15–4 p.m. (9/1/52–12/26/52)
CBS Mon.–Fri. 2:30–2:45 p.m. (12/29/52–1/30/53)
CBS Mon.–Fri. 3–3:30 p.m. (2/2/53–2/27/53)

Hosts: *Mike Wallace, Buff Cobb*

Incredible as it may seem, daytime viewers in 1951 could get a double dose of Mike Wallace and his then-wife Buff Cobb, who hosted this unexceptional chat show as well as *All Around the Town* on Monday, Wednesday, and Friday afternoons. During its first time slot the show was titled *Two Sleepy People* and aired in CBS's experimental color system. Then it went into the afternoon as *All Around the Town* moved into nighttime. Wallace later did another daily series in 1953, *I'll Buy That.*

•MIKE AND MATY
Talk; Color
April 11, 1994–June 7, 1996

ABC Mon.–Fri. 11 a.m.–Noon (4/11/94–6/7/96)

Hosts: *Michael Burger, Maty Monfort*

Young, personable Michael Burger and Maty Monfort were ABC's umpteenth unsuccessful effort to program against *The Price Is Right* on CBS. It supplanted *The Home Show,* which it resembled somewhat with its advice for homemakers,

although it did tend to lean more toward celebrity interviews. The show was replaced by the similar *Caryl & Marilyn: Real Friends.*

•MIKE DOUGLAS SHOW, THE
Talk; B&W and Color
1961–1982

Syndicated 90 and 60 minutes beginning August 1963

Host: *Mike Douglas*

The top daytime talk show for much of the 1960s and 1970s was *The Mike Douglas Show,* an easy-to-take hour (90 minutes in some markets) of celebrity guests and songs by the former big band singer (among the many tunes done by Douglas was Kay Kyser's #1 hit "Old Buttermilk Sky" in the 1940s). The show developed when Westinghouse, owning many of the stations that were part of the old

The Mike Douglas Show *celebrated its 18th anniversary with, from left, Don Rickles, Mike, Mike's wife Genevieve, Dick Van Dyke, Mariette Hartley, and Tony Orlando.*

DuMont network, decided in 1961 to have a talk show at the Cleveland affiliate to compete against another local show. The director was Forest "Woody" Fraser, who had worked with Douglas on the network daytime show *Club 60* (q.v.). Fraser recalled Douglas and convinced the latter, then eking out a living as a lounge singer in California, to audition for the show. The result won over executives and the local audience, and grew wider in circulation after a few years.

Douglas debuted on KYW Cleveland on December 11, 1961 on a daily 1–2:30 p.m. show. On August 5, 1963, the show became part of the Westinghouse station lineup on affiliates from Boston to San Francisco, but it did not break the key New York market until February 1965. By that time the show had its basic elements down pat—a guest co-host for the week (June Allyson on the New York premiere), interviews with other stars, and a song or two by Douglas, who broke talk show tradition by not sitting behind a desk. The combination clicked with viewers and most critics, and in 1967 Douglas won the first individual Emmy for Achievement in Daytime Programming.

Douglas remained a top daytime attraction for the next decade, taping more than 4,000 programs. Some of his most interesting shows included a surprise reunion of Lucille Ball and her *I Love Lucy* co-star Vivian Vance in 1968; a guest visit by fellow daytime talk competitor Merv Griffin in 1968; a collection of six movie Tarzans, including Jim Pierce, Johnny Weissmuller, Jack Mahoney, Denny Miller, Gordon Scott, and Buster Crabbe, all clad in loincloths, in 1975; a duet by Cher with her ex-husband Sonny Bono when she co-hosted for a week in 1979 (the tacky tune chosen was "United We Stand"); and perhaps his biggest exclusive of all, the first TV interview with Prince Rainier and Princess Grace at their palace in Monaco in 1979. Another top moment was a rare talk show visit by Paul Newman in 1975, but that was with substitute host David Steinberg, as Douglas was recovering from an appendectomy at the time.

Douglas moved his show from Cleveland to Philadelphia in the fall of 1965. In 1978 Douglas, by then earning $2.2 million annually, signed a four-year contract with Group W Productions requiring him to move the show from Philadelphia to Los Angeles, ostensibly for better guest selection. Two years later the company dumped him for another host (see *The John Davidson Show*). Douglas landed another syndicator, but the show went downhill in the ratings, and in drastic maneuvers in late 1981 Douglas fired a third of his staff and closed his Los Angeles studio operation in what was supposed to be a temporary change. The new show, titled *The Mike Douglas Entertainment Hour,* had Douglas hosting a daily variety format on the road, but with no interviews. These changes didn't help ratings, and by early 1982 the show had ended its two-decade run. Douglas went on to host *Mike Douglas People Now* briefly on the Cable News Network (CNN) until January 3, 1983, then virtually vanished from television except for infomercials.

MILTON THE MONSTER

Cartoon; Color

October 9, 1965–September 8, 1968

ABC Sat. 12:30–1 p.m. (10/9/65–12/24/66)
ABC Sat. 11:30 a.m.–Noon (1/7/67–9/2/67)
ABC Sun. 9:30–10 a.m. (9/10/67–9/8/68)

Voices:

Milton the Monster	*Bob McFadden*
Professor Weirdo/Fearless Fly/Stuffy Durma/Bradley Brinkley/ Flukey Luke/Chester Penguin	*Dayton Allen*
Count Kook/Muggy Doo/Two Feathers	*Larry Best*
Penny Penguin/Flora Fly	*Beverly Arnold*
Beulah Penguin	*Hettie Galen*

Milton, a flat-topped creature resembling a dopier looking version of Frankenstein's monster, liked nothing better than to eat and party at Horrible Hill, Transylvania. He was created by Professor Weirdo and his sidekick Count Kook, but turned out so docile that they rejected him, as did his fellow Transylvanian monsters. The professor and count tried to get Milton out of the castle, but failed miserably despite his klutziness.

Five supporting segments rotated on the show. "Fearless Fly" was the alter ego of Hyram, who went into a matchbox to change into his hero costume. His glasses activated energy in his head that he could use to fight enemies. Flora was his girlfriend. Another segment featured cowboy "Flukey Luke," who rode his horse Pronto and had Native American Two Feathers help him try to stop the machinations of Spider Webb. In "Penny Penguin," the title bird acted like Dennis the Menace in unintentionally terrorizing her parents Chester and Beulah. "Muggy Doo" was a crafty cat con man. And on "Stuffy Durma," sort of a *Beverly Hillbillies* knockoff, a bum who inherited a mansion got into comic situations because his actions, despite the help of his Henry Higgins–like adviser Bradley Brinkley, always betrayed his roots in poverty.

As with most cartoons, all episodes after the first season were repeats.

MIND YOUR MANNERS

Informational; B&W

June 24, 1951–March 9, 1952

NBC Sun. 12:15–12:45 p.m. (6/24/51–9/30/51)
NBC Sun. 12:30–1 p.m. (10/7/51–3/9/52)

Host: *Allen Ludden*

Mind Your Manners aired on local television in Hartford, Connecticut, and as an NBC radio show on Saturday mornings before it became a network TV series airing live from New York City. Questions submitted by viewers under age 20 were answered by their peers, with prizes awarded to viewers whose questions were read on the air. The show also dispensed etiquette tips.

•MINDREADERS
Game; Color
August 13, 1979–January 11, 1980
NBC Mon.–Fri. Noon–12:30 p.m. (8/13/79–1/11/80)
Host: *Dick Martin*

Mindreaders is of note chiefly because it was the last game show bearing the imprint of Mark Goodson–Bill Todman Productions, Todman having died in late 1979. It had a quartet of boys compete for a week against the same number of girls; both teams had a celebrity captain. The captains tried to guess the response of their teammates to a subjective question asked by the host. Each right answer was worth $50, but a wrong response gave $50 to the other team, and the captain who was wrong had to guess how his or her had teammates voted on the question. The first team to win $300 played a bonus game of trying to guess how many of a "jury" of five men and women from the studio audience had responded to three questions. An exact guess won the team $500 per question, while being within two either way netted $200. After the questions, the amounts won were totaled and multiplied by 10 to be played for the "Celebrity Turnabout" round, where a majority of team members tried to predict the reaction of their celebrity captain to a yes-no question.

MISS SUSAN
Soap Opera; B&W
March 12, 1951–December 28, 1951
NBC Mon.–Fri. 3–3:15 p.m. (3/12/51–12/28/51)
Cast:

Susan Martin	Susan Peters
Bill Carter	Mark Roberts
Laura the housekeeper	Helen Ray
Mrs. Peck	Kathryn Grill

Also: *Gerry Lock, Jon Lormer, Robert McQueeney, Natalie Priest*

The first NBC TV series to originate from Philadelphia, *Miss Susan* was a tearjerker about a lawyer with paralyzed legs who returned to her hometown of Martinsville, Ohio, with her nurse and companion in tow. When they arrived, they learned that Laura, the family housekeeper, had been charged with theft. "Laura can't be a thief—or can she?" the narrator dramatically intoned at the end of the debut. Few viewers seemed to care, nor were they much interested in the prime story line—Susan's dealing with her love for Bill Carter while considering how her condition would affect their relationship.

There has been some doubt over whether low ratings actually prompted this show's cancellation. *Billboard* reported in September 1951 that Peters, an actual paraplegic since 1945, was in poor health (the actress died in 1952 at age 31 due to pneumonia and chronic kidney problems). However, its sponsor Colgate said the reason it dropped the show for *The Big Payoff* was because it felt game shows were more in demand on daytime television. Whatever the reason for the cancellation, not many people felt the show's disappearance was a big loss for television.

MISSING LINKS
Game; Color
September 9, 1963–December 25, 1964
NBC Mon.–Fri. 11:30 a.m.–Noon (9/9/63–3/27/64)
ABC Mon.–Fri. 11:30 a.m.–Noon (3/30/64–12/25/64)
Host: *Ed MacMahon (1963–64), Dick Clark (1964)*

On *Missing Links* a player had to choose one of three celebrities on a rotating panel and bet on their ability to guess the missing words in a story. During Ed McMahon's tenure, players tried to guess the words left out of speeches by guests like the man who caught Roger Maris's 61st home run. It was taped in New York City at this time.

When ABC brought the show over on the same time slot after six months, it installed Dick Clark as host (an appropriate decision, given Ed MacMahon's position as Johnny Carson's sidekick on *The Tonight Show* on NBC at the time). Unfortunately, NBC replaced the show with *Jeopardy*, which was a much bigger audience draw, so *Missing Links* became a missing series after Christmas 1964.

MISSION MAGIC
Cartoon; Color
September 8, 1973–August 31, 1974
ABC Sat. 11:30 a.m.–Noon (9/8/73–8/31/74)
Voices:

Rick Springfield	Himself
Miss Tickle	Erika Scheimer
Kim/Carol	Lola Fisher
Harvey/Socks/Tolamy/Tut Tut	Howard Morris
Franklin/Vinnie	Lane Scheimer

Here each week rock singer Rick Springfield, joined by his pet owl Tolamy, contacted high school teacher Miss Tickle with a magic gramophone about a concern in a fantasy world that required the help of her sextet of students who formed the Adventurers Club. Miss Tickle (a pun; get it?) rounded up her pupils and her cat Tut Tut, and drew a magic circle which became a portal through which club members and Springfield passed on the way to adventure. Springfield, who in real life was an aspiring singer from Australia and who had an American hit, "Speak to the Sky," in 1972, also contributed one song per show, sung by the cartoon Rick. The cartoon character, with its flowing hair, somewhat resembled the human singer, although it is doubtful that the rock singer wore a sweatshirt with a lightning bolt on it. Running against two other teenybopper music cartoons (*Butch Cassidy and the Sundance Kids* on NBC and *Josie and the Pussycats* on CBS), this mission ended after a year.

MISSUS GOES A-SHOPPING, THE
Game; B&W
May 5, 1948–January 12, 1949
CBS Wed. 1:30–2 p.m., later Thu. 1–1:30 p.m.
(5/5/48–1/12/49)

Host: *John Reed King (1948), Bud Collyer (November 1948), Warren Hull (December 1948–1949)*

One of the pioneers of TV game shows, *The Missus Goes A-Shopping* was seen unsponsored from August 3, 1944–January 8, 1946 on WCBS New York, going off because its host John Reed King wanted more time to do two other local TV shows. It then reappeared on WCBS November 19, 1947, with four sponsors paying its $900 weekly facility cost, before going on the network on 1948. King supervised activities from various New York City supermarkets with the help of Jimmy Brown, who played his assistant "Uncle Jim." Typical of the contests for viewers was an April 1948 feature called "Mr. Who," where a jigsaw puzzle with the photo of a prominent reporter had a few pieces revealed at a time; in addition, a "jingle riddle" containing a clue to the identity was aired each week. Viewers had to write the answer on the back of sponsors Sweetheart Soap, Bab-O cleaner, and Mueller's macaroni products, plus write in 25 words or less a statement on what changes television had brought to the entrant's home.

On November 17, 1948, the show was retitled *This Is the Missus;* the new emphasis was on women doing various stunts. Bud Collyer took over as "host" (playing a grocery store operator) for a few weeks, but was replaced by Warren Hull before the end of the year. Please note that the starting date is an educated guess based on when CBS started network programming and had not been confirmed at press time.

MRS. ROOSEVELT MEETS THE PUBLIC—See *Today with Mrs. Roosevelt.*

•MISTER ED
Sitcom; B&W
September 12, 1965–September 4, 1966
CBS Sun. 5–5:30 p.m. (9/12/65–9/4/66)

Cast:

Wilbur Post	Alan Young
Carol Post	Connie Hines
Mr. Ed (voice only)	Allan "Rocky" Lane

"A horse is a horse, of course, of course . . ." went part of the memorable theme song of this memorably silly show. But Mr. Ed was no ordinary equine, because he could talk, or at least he talked to his owner Wilbur Post. As a consequence, Wilbur bonded with the horse while his wife Carol regarded the animal more skeptically. Steadfast in his love for Mr. Ed, Wilbur invariably rescued the horse from whatever predicament he got into, while making sure Ed's vocal abilities remained a secret as well.

The premise of this sitcom could be traced back to short stories published in the late 1930s in *The Saturday Evening Post, Argosy, Esquire,* and *Liberty* magazines. Producer Arthur Lubin remembered them and tried unsuccessfully to woo comedian Alan Young into doing a TV series in 1954 and 1957. Finally Young relented, and the result first aired in syndication in January 1961. Its success led CBS to add it to early Sunday evenings on October 1, 1961, and the network carried the show in various slots through September 8, 1965 before airing it late Sunday afternoons during the final season.

During the nighttime run, the Posts had two sets of neighbors, Roger and Kay Addison from 1961–63 (played by Larry Keating and Edna Skinner, respectively), and Gordon and Winnie Kirkwood (Leon Ames and Florence MacMichael) from 1963–65. Among its many guest stars was Mae West, who made two rare TV acting shots as herself in 1964 and 1965. In one, Mr. Ed showed up on her doorstep and offered to be her pet, impressed that she pampered her animals with bubble baths.

The voice of Mr. Ed remained a mystery for much of its run until it was revealed that ex–Western star Rocky Lane provided it. As for the equine, Mr. Ed's trainer Lester Hilton said he found the 8-year-old horse within four miles of his home in the San Fernando Valley.

TV Guide reported that Alan Young had planned to leave the show at the end of the 1965–66 season because it was longer aired at night, but Young, in his autobiography *Mister Ed and Me,* claimed that CBS was solely responsible for the cancellation. In any event, the show was one of the most popular black-and-white series seen in reruns in the 1970s, and its popularity continued in the 1980s and 1990s, with frequent appearances on the cable channels Nickelodeon (as part of the Nick at Nite lineup), and by 1996, Nick at Nite's TV Land.

MR. I MAGINATION
Children's; B&W
April 19, 1952–June 28, 1952
CBS Sat. 1–1:30 p.m. (4/19/52–6/28/52)

Regulars: *Paul Tripp, Ruth Enders, Joe Silver, Ted Tiller*

Mr. I Magination took his viewers on a magical train ride at the start of each show. It began locally in New York City on April 24, 1949, then went on CBS Sunday evenings from May 29, 1949–April 13, 1952 before spending its last two months on Saturday afternoons. Host Paul Tripp played an engineer of a train which could take a guest child to Imaginationland, which like Disneyland was divided into fantasy sectors, like Inventorsville, Seaport City, and "I Wish I Were" Town where the child could "stop off" and take part in a dramatized adventure. For the daytime debut, Mr. I Magination took his young ward Clifford Sales to Hannibal, Missouri, during Mark Twain's heyday, with Sales playing Huck Finn and Joe Silver his angry dad.

Given the state of TV art at the time, the show required much creativity by its personnel to pull the scenes off. After the first year on air, Tripp estimated his troupe had portrayed more than 400 roles, with each actor doing an average of three parts per show. Ruth Enders, for example, played at various times Tom Thumb's mother, Queen Victoria, a tattooed woman, Jenny Lind, and a tightrope walker. Besides his hosting and acting work, Tripp also created and wrote most of the show's scenarios.

MR. MAGIC AND J.J.
Variety; B&W
April 12, 1950–October 13, 1950

ABC Wed.-Sat. 5–5:15 p.m. (4/12/50–9/9/50)
ABC Mon.-Fri. 5–5:15 p.m. (9/11/50–10/13/50)

Host: *Norman Jensen*

Mr. Magic and J.J., which originated from New York, ran on independent station WPIX starting on July 16, 1949; ABC networked the show in the spring of 1950. Twenty-three-year-old magician Norman Jensen starred and did tricks along with his hand puppet, a rabbit named J.J. Carrots.

MR. MAGOO—See *What's New, Mr. Magoo?*

MISTER MAYOR
Children's; B&W
September 26, 1964–September 18, 1965

CBS Sat. 8–9 a.m. (9/26/64–9/18/65)

Cast:
Mister Mayor	Bob Keeshan
Miss Melissa/Aunt Maude/	
Mother Homan	Jane Connell
Dudley Dudley/Herman Homan	Bill McCutcheon
Cornelius the Clown/Rollo the	
Hippo/Father Homan	Cosmo Allegretti

A replacement for the Saturday edition of *Captain Kangaroo*, *Mister Mayor* was a live-from-New York fantasy about a town and its odd residents, who engaged in skits designed to teach children the day's theme. Jane Connell was music teacher Miss Melissa, baseball fanatic Aunt Maude, and the confused Mother Homan. Bill McCutcheon played school custodian Dudley Dudley, Mother Homan's equally baffled child Herman, and even a plastic statue. Cosmo Allegretti was in costume as Cornelius and Rollo.

Though this series has largely been forgotten, at one point Bob Keeshan toyed with the idea of replacing *Captain Kangaroo* with *Mister Mayor*. The reason for contemplating such a move was Keeshan's disputes with Hollywood agent Mitchell Hamilburg, a joint owner of the latter show, who was threatening to oust Keeshan from the Captain's role. Keeshan, who owned *Mister Mayor* outright, would face no such action if it became a daily series. But a strong protest from the National Association for Better Radio and Television, which told CBS that *Mister Mayor* was "distinctly inferior" to *Captain Kangaroo*, helped to scotch the plan, and Keeshan

remained as the Captain, including three years as successor to Mister Mayor on Saturday mornings.

MR. PIPER—See *Pip the Piper.*

MISTER T
Cartoon; Color
September 17, 1983–September 6, 1986

NBC Sat. 11–11:30 a.m. (9/17/83–9/8/84)
NBC Sat. 11:30 a.m.–Noon (9/15/84–9/7/85)
NBC Sat. Noon–12:30 p.m. (9/14/85–9/6/86)

Voices:
Mr. T	Himself
Robin	Amy Linker
Kim	Siu Ming Carson
Spike	Teddy S. Field III
Woody	Phillip LaMarr
Jeff	Shawn Lieber
Miss Bisby	Takayo Fischer

While starring as B.A. on the NBC nighttime hit *The A-Team*, ex-bodyguard and one-time Rocky foe Mr. T got his own cartoon series playing himself as an operator of the gym where teenagers Robin, Kim, Spike, Woody, and Jeff worked out. Somehow this bunch, including Mr. T's dog Dozer, managed to stumble onto and solve a different mystery every week. At the end of each episode, Mr. T. delivered the requisite homily presumably designed to foster socially responsible behavior.

MR. WIZARD—See *Watch Mr. Wizard.*

•MOBY DICK AND THE MIGHTY MIGHTOR
Cartoon; Color
September 9, 1967–September 6, 1969

CBS Sat. 11–11:30 a.m. (9/9/67–9/7/68)
CBS Sat. 1–1:30 p.m. (9/14/68–9/6/69)

Voices:
Tom	Bobby Resnick
Tubb	Barry Balkin
Scooby	Don Messick
Mightor	Paul Stewart
Tor	Bobby Diamond
Pondo/Tog	John Stephenson
Sheena	Patsy Garrett
Li'l Rock	Norma McMillan

There was no "Call me Ishmael" nonsense for this Hanna-Barbera concoction. No, here the lead character of Moby the great white whale, created by Herman Melville in 1851 for the novel *Moby Dick* and utterly debased here, took care of two orphaned children, Tom and Tubb, protecting them from such dangers as white sharks in the sea. Scooby was their seal pal.

In a separate segment, prehistoric teenager Tor had the ability to raise a club given to him by an old hermit, thereby transforming himself into the Mighty Mightor to fight crime and turning his pet dinosaur Tog into a dragon. Mightor usually saved Tor's sister Sheena from disaster. Pondo was his dad, and L'il Rock his brother. Both Tor and Moby Dick disappeared when CBS rid itself of superhero cartoons in the fall of 1969.

MODERN ROMANCES
Dramatic Anthology; B&W
October 4, 1954–September 19, 1958

NBC Mon.–Fri. 4:45–5 p.m. (10/4/54–12/31/56)
NBC Mon.–Fri. 4:15–4:30 p.m. (1/3/56–6/29/56)
NBC Mon.–Fri. 4:45–5 p.m. (7/2/56–9/19/58)

Host/Narrator/"Story Editor": *Martha Scott (10/4/54–11/29/57), Mel Brandt (12/2/57–3/29/58)*

Based on an obscure NBC radio series from 1936 later transferred to ABC, *Modern Romances* featured stories running from one to several episodes on themes generally involving a love story, but there were exceptions. For example, on March 21, 1955 the show offered a Rod Serling story titled "A Long Time Till Dawn," about a wife who seeks refuge from her criminal husband in the country. Actor Roscoe Karns reprised his lead role from the 1950–54 DuMont prime time drama *Rocky King, Inside Detective* from February 6–10, 1956. And during the week of May 14–18, 1956, a present-day version of *Macbeth* aired. Actors on the series were generally unknowns such as June Dayton, Dean Harens, Ross Martin, and William Prince.

When actress Martha Scott left the show to make a movie, her role was assumed by actor Mel Brandt for nearly four months, followed by weekly guest hosts. The latter included such unlikely personalities as Buffalo Bob Smith of *Howdy Doody* fame and dance instructor Kathryn Murray. The show's cancellation marked the end of 15-minute daily shows on NBC.

MOMENT OF TRUTH
Soap Opera; B&W
January 4, 1965–November 5, 1965

NBC Mon.–Fri. 2–2:30 p.m. (1/4/65–11/5/65)

Cast:

Dr. Robert Wallace	*Douglass Watson*
Nancy Wallace	*Louise King*
Johnny Wallace	*Michael Dodds*
Sheila Wallace	*Barbara Pierce*
Wilma Leeds	*Lynn Gorman*
Walter Leeds	*Robert Goodier*
Carol Williams	*Toby Tarnow*
Jack Williams	*Stephen Levy*
Dr. Russell Wingate	*Ivor Barry*
Monique Wingate	*Fernande Giroux*
Vince Conway	*Peter Donat*
Barbara Harris	*Mira Pawluk*
Linda Harris	*Anna Hagan*
Lila	*Sandra Scott*
Diane	*Anne Campbell*
Eric	*John Horton*
Dexter	*Chris Wiggins*

Moment of Truth was the only network soap opera taped in Canada (specifically Toronto), and its use of a few scenes taped outdoors was also a rarity at the time. It starred American actor Douglass Watson as Dr. Robert Wallace, a psychology professor at an unidentified university in the Midwest. In addition to teaching, Wallace served as counselor to some characters, such as Wilma Leeds, who was in a strained marriage with Walter Leeds and had an even touchier relationship with son-in-law Jack Williams, and as an adversary to others, such as his daughter Sheila, who blamed him for her brother Johnny's illness early in the run. He also endured a job suspension, a murder charge, and frequent arguments with wife Nancy. His colleague Dr. Russell Wingate had his own woes too, with a failing marriage to Monique that included bitter words exchanged during several dinners with the Wallaces. Monique later got together with Dexter.

Adding to this unpleasant mix were Vince Conway, who had a secret marriage he revealed in May which naturally ended in divorce in September; Barbara Harris, a teenage runaway upset with the world around her; Linda Harris, Barbara's mother, who had the hots for Vince; Nancy's sister Lila; Lila's daughter Diane, who saw Jack briefly; and Diane's boyfriend Eric, who proposed to her before the series ended, after just 10 months on the air.

MONCHICHIS
Cartoon; Color
September 10, 1983–September 1, 1984

ABC Sat. 9–9:30 a.m. (9/10/83–1/7/84)
ABC Sat. 8–8:30 a.m. (1/14/84–9/1/84)

Voices:

Moncho	*Robert Morse*
Kyla	*Laurel Page*
Tootoo	*Ellen Gerstell*
Patchitt	*Frank Welker*
Thumkii	*Hank Saroyan*
Horrg	*Sidney Miller*
Wizzar	*Frank Nelson*
Snogs	*Bob Arbogast*
Shreeker/Snitchitt/Gonker	*Peter Cullen*
Yabbot/Fassit/Scumgor	*Laurie Faso*

Based on a line of dolls, the Monchichis were simian denizens of a tree world called Monchia under the guidance of a wizard named Wizzar. They all fought the Grumplins of Grumplor and the latter's head man Horrg.

MONEYMAZE, THE
Game; Color
December 23, 1974–July 4, 1975

ABC Mon.–Fri. 4–4:30 p.m. (12/23/74–7/4/75)

Host: *Nick Clooney*

The question-and-answer round for the two competing couples on *The Moneymaze* was just a prelude to the main event for the winning duo. The lucky twosome had 15 seconds to find a prize in a maze using partitions. In the bonus round, the couple had a minute for one partner to touch up to five boxes in the maze. The payoff amount began at $1 for the first box and increased tenfold each time until touching the fifth box won $10,000. This segment had one member of the couple on an observation deck giving directions to his or her spouse about how to get through the panels.

•MONSTER SQUAD

Sitcom; Color

September 11, 1976–September 3, 1977

NBC Sat. 10:30–11 a.m. (9/11/76–9/3/77)

Cast:

Walter	*Fred Grandy*
Frankenstein monster	*Michael Lane*
Dracula	*Henry Polic II*
Bruce Wolfman	*Buck Kartalian*

Walter, a teenage caretaker of a museum, found that replicas of Count Dracula, the Frankenstein monster, and the Wolf Man came to life when his computer's vibrations hit them. The horrific trio banded together with Walter and his computer to form the Monster Squad, a unit dedicated to fighting crimes caused by humans. Among the really weird villains they faced in this show was one dressed as a man on one side of his body and a woman on the other side, played by character actor Vito Scotti, who tried to combine two of the museum monsters into one being.

•MONTEL WILLIAMS SHOW, THE

Talk; Color

1992–

Syndicated 60 minutes daily beginning September 1992

Host: *Montel Williams*

Bald, tall Montel Williams was an ex–Navy intelligence officer in his mid-thirties who lectured to youth for three years before entering the talk show world in July 1991 for a trial run that became a regular series a year later. His authoritative but calm approach in examining controversial guests set him apart from the rest of the interview set. By 1996 Williams was branching out as an actor, starring in the short-lived CBS nighttime drama *Matt Waters*, and he has said he will continue to pursue an acting career along with doing this program.

MORGAN BEATTY

News; B&W

January 19, 1952–February 23, 1952

NBC Sat. 5:45–6 p.m. (1/19/52–2/23/52)

Anchor: *Morgan Beatty*

Washington, D.C., correspondent Morgan Beatty delivered a weekend wrapup of current events from his home base in this short-lived series.

MORK AND MINDY/LAVERNE AND SHIRLEY/FONZ HOUR, THE—See *Laverne and Shirley.*

MORNING COURT—See *Day in Court.*

MORNING NEWS

News; B&W

January 7, 1952–July 2, 1954

CBS Mon.–Fri. Various 15-, 30-, and 45-minute slots from 9:45–10:30 a.m. (1/7/52–7/2/54)

Regulars: *Harry Marble (1952), Charles Collingwood (1952–53 at least), Dorothy Doan (1/7/52–8/29/52), Jim Fidler, Claude Mahoney*

Starting in early 1952, CBS installed a daily news show before *Arthur Godfrey Time* four days a week and expanded it to cover the latter's absence Friday. Harry Marble and Dorothy Doan gave the news from New York City, while Jim Fidler dispensed weather forecasts from Washington, D.C. Charles Collingwood had replaced Marble by the summer, and by late August Dorothy Doan resigned from CBS to be replaced by Washington correspondent Claude Mahoney. The show continued in various slots, usually either leading into or replacing *Arthur Godfrey Time.* (For later efforts of daily news on CBS, see *The Morning Show, CBS Morning News,* and *CBS News.*)

MORNING PROGRAM, THE—See *CBS Morning News.*

MORNING SHOW, THE

News/Information; B&W

March 15, 1954–April 5, 1957

CBS Mon.–Fri. 7–9 a.m. (3/15/54–9/30/55)

CBS Mon.–Fri. 7–8 a.m. (10/3/55–4/5/57)

Regulars: *Walter Cronkite (1954–55 at least), Jack Paar (1954–55), Charles Collingwood (1954–55 at least), Winston Burdett (1954 at least), Bil and Cora Baird (1954), Carol Reed (1954 at least), Estelle Parsons (1954 at least), John Peter (1954 at least), Jim McKay (1954 at least), Pupi Campo (3/15/54–5/11/55), Jose Melis (3/15/54–5/11/55), Betty Clooney (3/15/54–5/11/55), Michel Allard (1954 at least), Elsa Maxwell (1954 at least), Edie Adams (1955 at least), John Henry Faulk (1955), Merv Griffin (1955), Sandy Stewart (1955), Dick Van Dyke (1955–56), Paul Killiam (1955), the Norman Paris Trio (1955), Jimmy Nelson (1955), Ginger Stanley (1955), Deborah Douglas (1955 at least), Will Rogers Jr. (2/20/56–4/5/57), Ned Calmer (2/20/56–4/5/57), Pamela Good (2/20/56–4/5/57)*

CBS's first effort to compete with *Today* set a precedent for the network in that it would be the first of many failures in that time period over the next 40 years. The initial emphasis was on hard news, with Walter Cronkite serving as host and Charles Collingwood and Winston Burdett alternating in giving a five-minute newscast at the end of every half hour. Carol Reed gave the weather, John Peter demonstrated gadgets, and Estelle Parsons delivered feature reports, and by May 1954 Jim McKay had joined the show as a sportscaster. However, as a sop to children who watched *Today* to see J. Fred Muggs the chimp, Cronkite also had to do commercials and converse with the Baird puppets Charlemane the Lion, a disk jockey, and Humphrey the Houn' Dog—an assignment which may have been what prompted Cronkite to leave. Cronkite was replaced by the more entertainment-inclined Jack Paar on August 16, 1954, who brought his troupe of Jose Melis, Pupi Campo, and Betty Clooney from his daytime TV show.

Not long after Jack Paar's ascension, Bil and Cora Baird were abruptly fired and replaced by French singer Michel Allard and "society editor" Elsa Maxwell. There were other

turnovers, including a change which had Edie Adams replacing Betty Clooney. Rumor had it that Clooney left because she wanted to marry the also departing Pupi Campo as soon as he got a divorce (they did marry), but Paar said the real reason was he wanted to use Edie again, as he had in his earlier daytime show. In any case, no new names were added, as talent expenses were the main reason the show cost CBS $1 million in the first year of operations.

When Paar left for his own show in July 1955, John Henry Faulk took over as host; Collingwood, the only original cast member, stayed as newscaster. The new batch of regulars were singers Merv Griffin and Sandy Stewart and the Norman Paris Trio. Dick Van Dyke appeared Mondays, Wednesdays, and Fridays to tell children's stories, and also went on weekend trips to Paris, Havana, and Mexico City to get footage for the show. On Tuesdays and Thursdays Paul Killiam introduced some old-time movies. Another gimmick was the use of Katie the Goat as a mascot. Also in 1955, Mrs. Myrt Power, a winner in the category of baseball for the CBS nighttime game show *The $64,000 Question,* showed up to cover the World Series for the program.

CBS dropped Faulk as the host after a few weeks due to blacklisting pressures (Faulk later sued for lost work revenues and won in a landmark court case). Dick Van Dyke assumed

The Morning Show *in 1954 had as regulars, from left, Charles Collingwood, Bil and Cora Baird and their puppets, and host Walter Cronkite.*

host duties on July 18 while continuing to do his "Story Corner" for children, and the following day ventriloquist Jimmy Nelson started appearing Tuesdays and Thursdays. But changeovers continued; newsman Charles Collingwood left in September 1955 to be replaced by former host Walter Cronkite, who in turn left at the end of 1955. Deborah Douglas had become the weathercaster by the time Cronkite rejoined the show, and they, along with Van Dyke, were about the only regulars.

On February 29, 1956, the show was retitled *Good Morning!* and featured Will Rogers Jr. as host, Ned Calmer as newscaster, and Pamela Good as weathercaster. Also new was its producer Jim Fleming, who had been anchor on *Today* during its first year. For three weeks in 1956 Ginger Stanley did the weather in an underwater tank, indicating conditions on a transparent map of America. But none of the new elements seemed to click, so after three years CBS gave up the effort, and did not program before 8 a.m. again until 1965 (see *The CBS Morning News*).

MORNING STAR
Soap Opera; Color
September 27, 1965–July 1, 1966

NBC Mon.–Fri. 11–11:30 a.m. (9/27/65–7/1/66)

Cast:

Katy Elliott (1965)	Shary Marshall
Katy Elliott (1966)	Elizabeth Perry
Bill Riley	Edward Mallory
Jan Elliott	Adrienne Ellis
Ed Elliott	Ed Prentiss
Aunt Millie Elliott	Shelia Bromley
Joan Mitchell	Betty Lou Gerson
Liz Mitchell	Nina Roman
Gregory Ross	Burt Douglas
Ann Burton	Olive Dunbar
Joe Bernie	Norman Burton
Eric Manning	Ron Jackson
Dana Manning	Betsy Jones Moreland
Stan Manning (first)	John Dehner
Stan Manning (second)	John Stephenson
Eve Blake	Floy Dean
Dr. Tim Blake	William Arvin
Grace Allison	Phyllis Hill

After her fiancé Gregory Ross was killed in an accident, ambitious fashion designer Katy Elliott left the small town of Springvale, Connecticut, to pursue her career in New York City. This did not sit very well with her possessive 16-year-old sister Jan. Ann Burton tried to persuade Jan to let Katy move, but an emotional Jan locked herself in her room for a time. When Jan finally went to see Katy in the Big Apple, she refused to leave. Adding to that mess, Katy's father Ed, a judge, fell victim to an extortion plot hatched by Joe Bernie. And even Aunt Millie felt she had to butt into Katy's new life. Given all these intrusions, plus Katy's flashbacks to Gregory, viewers could only

marvel at how boyfriend Bill Riley managed to cope with all the obstacles and still love her.

While Katy contended with all of her headaches, Katy's new roommate Joan Mitchell had plenty on her plate too. Among Joan's problems was her daughter Liz, who lied about her involvement with a hit-and-run accident. Others seen were the Manning and Blake families.

The "morning star" in the title referred to the sun. The show was anything but a morning star in the ratings in its 11 a.m. time slot, however, as has been true with most soap operas telecast before lunch. Or, as an obviously enlightened anonymous source told *Variety* at the time, "Those Nielsen dames don't start feeling sorry for themselves until noon."

MOTHER GOOSE AND GRIMM
Cartoon; Color
September 14, 1991–March 20, 1993

CBS Sat. 8:30–9 a.m. (9/14/91–9/5/92)
CBS Sat. 12:30–1 p.m. (9/19/92–3/20/93)

Voices: *Charlie Brill, Mitzi McCall, Greg Burton, Gregg Berger*

An adaptation of the daily comic strip of the same name by Mike Peters, *Mother Goose and Grimm* told of a woman, Mother Goose, and her souped-up yellow dog Grimm, nicknamed Grimmy, who was inordinately fascinated with gadgets in the house. Others on the show were Thorp the mean bulldog and Attila the meaner feline. In 1992–93 the show was retitled *Grimmy*.

MOTHER'S DAY
Game; B&W
October 13, 1958–January 2, 1959

ABC Mon.–Fri. 12:30–1 p.m. (10/13/58–1/2/59)

Host: *Dick Van Dyke*

Assistant: *Dotty Mack*

Three housewives participated in contests to see who would be named "Mother of the Day" on this New York–based program, the only daytime series hosted by Dick Van Dyke apart from *The Morning Show*. Among the games were guessing how many slices of ham could be cut to make a half pound and figuring out which had fewer calories, half a broiled chicken or six ounces of lean beef.

MOTOR MOUSE AND AUTO CAT
Cartoon; Color
September 12, 1970–September 4, 1971

ABC Sat. 8:30–9 a.m. (9/12/70–12/26/70)
ABC Sat. Noon–12:30 p.m. (1/2/71–9/4/71)

Voices:

Motor Mouse	Dick Curtis
Auto Cat/Lambsy	Marty Ingels
Mildew Wolf	Paul Lynde

Motor Mouse and Auto Cat, a spin-off of the 1969–70 edition of *Cattanooga Cats,* contained the latter's segment "It's the Wolf." The lead cartoon resembled a modified *Tom and Jerry* with oversized tabby Auto Cat chasing speedster Motor Mouse in car races, and as always, the rodent was ever-resourceful in outwitting the vain feline. In the other segment, cute little Lambsy found himself shouting "It's the wool-uff! It's the wool-uff!" as Mildew Wolf tried in vain to claim the former for his own.

MUGGSY

Drama; Color
September 11, 1976–April 2, 1977

NBC Sat. 12:30–1 p.m. (9/11/76–4/2/77)

Cast:

Margaret "Muggsy" Malloy	Sarah McDonnell
Nick Malloy	Ben Masters
Clytemnestra	Star-Shemah
Li'l Man	Danny Cooper
Gus Gardician	Paul Michael

Muggsy played like a never-ending—and never-upbeat—children's special. The title character lived in an unidentified large city (it was taped in Bridgeport, Connecticut) with her stepbrother in a truck behind Gus's gas station. He struggled to make ends meet as a cabbie while she and her black pals Clytemnestra and Li'l Man faced such problems as drug abuse, vandalism, and the death of parents.

•MUPPET BABIES

Cartoon; Color
September 15, 1984–September 7, 1992

CBS Sat. 9–9:30 a.m. (9/15/84–9/7/85)
CBS Sat. 9–10 a.m. (9/14/85–9/12/87)
CBS Sat. 8:30–10 a.m. (9/19/87–9/10/88)
CBS Sat. 9–10 a.m. (9/17/88–9/9/89)
CBS Sat. 8:30–9:30 a.m. (9/16/89–12/30/89)
CBS Sat. 9–10 a.m. (1/6/90–9/1/90)
CBS Sat. 8–9 a.m. (9/8/90–9/7/91)
CBS Sat. Noon–12:30 p.m. (9/14/91–9/28/91)
CBS Sat. 8–8:30 a.m. (10/5/91–9/7/92)

Voices:

Kermit/Beaker/Skeeter (later shows)	Frank Welker
Miss Piggy	Laurie O'Brien
Fozzie/Scooter	Greg Berg
Rowlf	Katie Leigh
Gonzo	Russi Taylor
Animal/Bunsen/Skeeter (earlier shows all)	Howie Mandel
Animal/Bunsen (later shows both)	Dave Coulier
Nanny	Barbara Billingsley

Jim Henson's wonderful creations the Muppets had appeared in nearly every entertainment medium except for a cartoon when this Emmy-winning series started. An unusual (for Saturday mornings) mixture of cartoons and occasional film

and tape inserts, the show featured imaginative stories about personable Kermit the Frog, his vain lovesick sidekick Miss Piggy, and the rest of the crew, set when they were toddlers in a nursery run by Nanny, seen only from the legs down. The story lines were inspired by history, fiction (including fairy tales), movies, television shows (including *The Twilight Zone* in one enjoyable spoof)—pretty much anything which struck the writers. Occasionally film or tape footage was worked into part of the show, such as a clip of Johnny Carson on *The Tonight Show* appearing to introduce Miss Piggy as a guest. Though none of the original "Muppeteers" supplied the voices on the cartoon, other actors mimicked them beautifully, and co–executive producer Jim Henson made sure their signature characteristics remained intact, like Rowlf the bear's piano playing and Animal's demented, gibberish talking. The only new character on the show was Skeeter, Skooter's sister.

Muppet Babies started as a half-hour show, then went to an hour in 1985, when it was retitled *Jim Henson's Muppets, Babies and Monsters.* The show kept that title for a season, then went back to the old title for an hour in 1986, then 90 minutes in 1987, and back to an hour in 1988 until the end of the run. In 1990 it added long-time favorites Statler and Waldorf (the grumpy old commentators), Janice, Dr. Teeth, and the Muppet Band. Two years later, the show ended its impressive eight-year run on CBS.

MUSIC BINGO

Game; B&W
December 5, 1958–January 1, 1960

ABC Mon.–Fri. 2:30–3 p.m. (12/5/58–4/10/59)
ABC Mon.–Fri. 1–1:30 p.m. (4/13/59–1/1/60)

Host: *Johnny Gilbert*

On *Music Bingo* a male and a female competed in seeing who could be the first to ring a bell and identify a song. A correct guess let the contestant put his or her symbol, either a sharp or flat, on a bingo board, with the goal being to be the first to arrange five in a line and win $500 (the runner-up got $50 for each symbol on his or her board). Winners played until defeated. Airing from New York City, this ran on NBC Thursdays at 10:30 p.m. from May 29–September 11, 1958 before going to ABC daytime.

MUSICAL CHAIRS

Game; Color
June 16, 1975–October 31, 1975

CBS Mon.–Fri. 4–4:30 p.m. (6/16/75–10/31/75)

Host: *Adam Wade*

Musical impresario Don Kirshner was co–executive producer of this wanna-be-hip knockoff of *Name That Tune.* A quartet of players heard parts of songs sung by guest performers, who stopped singing in the middle of the song, and then had to choose which lyrics, from three available choices, came next. After a few rounds of increasing payoffs starting at $50, an elimination period had the lowest-scoring contestants removed from view by having their "musical chair" pulled back behind a panel. The remaining player won the day's competition.

Guest singers on this New York–based series were mostly little-known talent, although a number of actors on CBS soap operas at the time, such as Michael Nouri, Mary Stuart, and Don Stewart, appeared. The most familiar names to turn up were Lou Rawls, the Spinners, the Stylistics, and, for some odd reason, children's performer Shari Lewis. Host Adam Wade had in fact been a moderately successful vocalist in the early 1960s, with such *Billboard* chart hits as "The Writing on the Wall" and "Take Good Care of Her."

MUTUAL OF OMAHA'S WILD KINGDOM—See *Wild Kingdom.*

•MY FAVORITE MARTIANS
Cartoon; Color
September 8, 1973–August 30, 1975

CBS Sat. 10–10:30 a.m. (9/8/73–8/31/74)
CBS Sun. 9–9:30 a.m. (9/8/74–1/12/75)
CBS Sat. 8–8:30 a.m. (1/18/75–8/30/75)

Voices:
Uncle Martin	Jonathan Harris
Tim O'Hara/Bill Brennan/Oakie Doakie	Howard Morris
Brad Brennan/Andy (Andromeda)	Lane Scheimer
Katy O'Hara/Lorelei Brown	Jane Webb

Based on the CBS nighttime sitcom *My Favorite Martian* (1963–66), this cartoon featured two aliens from Mars with antennae sprouting from the tops of their heads and their pet dog Oakie Doakie. They arrived on Earth in the company of newsman Tim O'Hara and his niece Katy, who protected the aliens by pretending that the older, male alien was Katy's Uncle Martin and that the other one was Andy, Martin's nephew (his real name was Andromeda). With all these new relatives popping up at the O'Hara household, private eye Bill Brennan and his son Brad knew something was amiss, but never could determine exactly what it was. Lorelei Brown was Tim's daft landlady who had the hots for suave, brainy Uncle Martin. The second season consisted of repeats.

•MY PET MONSTER
Cartoon; Color
September 12, 1987–September 3, 1988

ABC Sat. 9–9:30 a.m. (9/12/87–9/3/88)

Voices:
Monster	Jeff McGibbon
Max	Sunny Besen Thrasher
Chuckie	Stuart Stone
Jill	Alyson Court
Beastur	Dan Hennessey

The title creature was actually a rather cuddly blue biped with a pink face and spotted nose whose main horrific practice was eating garbage. Known by his generic name, Monster befriended Max, a blond kid who had bought Monster as a toy, only to find out that he could transform the toy into a talking, sentient being. Max's sister Jill and pal Chuckie often found themselves getting into misadventures with Max and Monster, or, as Jill called the latter, "Monsey." Most of these involved Beastur from Monster's native home of Monsterland, who wanted to capture the exile from Max and crew. Beastur, who looked like the overgrown Tasmanian devil (see *Taz-Mania*) and sounded like the Cookie Monster from public TV's *Sesame Street,* used a Dimensional Door to go to and from the human world.

NASL SOCCER—See *Soccer.*

•NBA BASKETBALL
Sports; B&W and Color
December 12, 1953–

DuMont Sat. 3 p.m.–Conclusion (12/12/53–3/27/54)
NBC Sat. Various times between 2 and 6 p.m. (11/27/54–4/7/62; winter months only)
ABC Sun. 2–4 p.m. (1/3/65–5/6/73; winter months only)
CBS Sun. Various times between 1 and 5:30 p.m. (10/20/73–6/10/90; winter months only)
NBC Sun. Various times between 1 and 7 p.m. (1/27/91–; winter months only)

Announcers: *Marty Glickman (1954–55, 1961 at least), Jack Gregson (1955–56 at least), Lindsay Nelson (1954–56 at least), Curt Gowdy (1956 and 1958–59 at least), Bud Palmer (1961 at least), Chris Schenkel (1965 and 1973 at least), Bob Cousy (1965 at least), Bill Russell (play-by-play; 1971–83), Keith Jackson (1973 at least on ABC), Pat Summerall (play-by-play; 1973 at least on CBS), Elgin Baylor (analyst; at least 1973–74), Oscar Robertson (1975), Jerry West (analyst; at least 1975), Mendy Rudolph (1976–77), Brent Musberger (play-by-play; at least 1977–89), Tim Ryan (at least 1978–), Hot Rod Hundley (at least 1973–74 and 1980–81), Rick Barry (analyst; 1974 at least–1981), Gary Bender (play-by-play; at least 1980–at least 1986), Pat O'Brien (at least 1983–at least 1985), Tommy Heinsohn (1983–88), Dick Stockton (play-by-play; at least 1981–82, 1984–85, and 1987–88), Billy Cunningham (1986–88), Tim Brant (play-by-play; 1987 at least), Bill Raftery (analyst; at least 1989), Hubie Brown (analyst; at least 1986–87 and 1989), Marv Albert (1991–), Bob Costas (1991), Dick Enberg (1991–), Mike Fratello (at least 1991–92), Steve Jones (at least 1991), Matt Guokas (analyst; at least 1993–), Ervin "Magic" Johnson (analyst; at least 1993), Hannah Storm (sideline reporter; at least 1993–)*

When the National Basketball Association made its daytime network debut on DuMont after being created in 1946, it was a ratings hit, but the network could not clear 18 weekends for it in 1954 because of NFL football games scheduled for the period, so NBC aired NBA basketball for eight years, until deciding to go with a sports anthology show during the winter years (see *NBC Sports in Action*). After two years off the networks, the game returned on ABC on Sundays, where it remained a decent but not overwhelming audience attraction. This was reflected by the money for TV rights given the sport. ABC's second three-year contract for the league (1967–70), for example, cost it only $3 million. In contrast, for just the 1969–70 season alone, CBS paid $22 million for *NFL Football*, and NBC paid $16.5 million for *Baseball Game of the Week*.

When the show moved to CBS, the analyst position kept changing each season, from ex–L.A. Laker Elgin Baylor (who was replaced by Golden State Warrior Jerry West in April 1974 following his team's elimination in the playoffs because CBS felt Baylor was too low-key) to Oscar Robertson to Mendy Rudolph (an NBA referee for 23 years). In 1978 *Sports Illustrated* denounced the series for having too many sportscasters and lousy pregame and halftime shows (among the latter were "HORSE" shooting game contests), which at least in the first season were handled by Hot Rod Hundley. By 1983 Pat O'Brien was serving as host of the halftime shows, and ex-Celtics player and coach Tom Heinsohn became an analyst with Dick Stockton as his partner.

In 1990, after NBA basketball had been on CBS for 17 years, NBC obtained rights to the league and made it a ratings contender thanks to the popularity of such stars as Michael Jordan and heavy promotion by the network. *NBA on NBC* started with Marv Albert and Bob Costas alternating doing play-by-play, but soon Costas was doing the pregame show *NBA Showtime* (q.v.), and Dick Enberg replaced Costas. Analysis was provided by Mike Fratello and Steve Jones the first season, then by 1992 Fratello and the returning Marv Albert. The league will continue on NBC through at least 1998.

•NBA INSIDE STUFF

Sports; Color
October 27, 1990–

NBC Sat. Noon–12:30 or 12:30–1 p.m. (10/27/90–; summers off)

Hosts: *Ahmad Rashad, Julie Moran (1990–91), Willow Bay (1991–)*

To hype professional basketball's appeal to young viewers (and sell the league into giving it broadcast rights), NBC aired this feature-oriented collage of player profiles and light league information, accompanied by rapid shots, usually in action, of players and/or interviewers, heavy use of rock and rap music, and promotional cameos by celebrities in and out of the NBA. A regular installment was "Rewind,"

a collection of highlights of the previous week's games. The hosts occasionally taped features outside the studio in addition to introducing the segments. By 1995 the series was airing year-round.

•NBA SHOWTIME

Sports; Color
October 13, 1990–

NBC Sun. 12:30–1 p.m. (10/13/90–; summers off)

Regulars: *Bob Costas, Pat Riley (1990–91), Bob Ferry (1990–92), Peter Vecsey (1990–at least 1992), Bill Walton (1993–), Julius Erving (1992–93 at least)*

This pregame show to NBC's NBA coverage in the 1990s first featured ex–Los Angeles Laker and ex–New York Knicks coach Pat Riley, who later became coach of the Miami Heat.

NBC BANDSTAND

Musical Variety; B&W
July 30, 1956–November 2, 1956

NBC Mon.–Fri. 10:30–11 a.m. (7/30/56–11/2/56)

Host: *Bert Parks*

The main attraction of *NBC Bandstand*, which was simulcast on NBC radio albeit in a longer two-hour format, was the presentation of numbers performed by a different guest orchestra or group each week, such as Les Elgart, Guy Lombardo, Johnny Mercer, and the Four Lads, in a café-style setting from New York. Audience interviews, comedy sketches, and jokes submitted by viewers composed the rest of the mix.

NBC Bandstand ran unsuccessfully against *Arthur Godfrey Time*, so some raised their eyebrows when the former show booked ex-Godfreyites Archie Bleyer, Frank Parker, and Julius LaRosa. "It's no planned campaign," Bert Parks told *TV Guide*. "We just like these people." Sure, Bert. Parks left the radio show by March 1957, but the show continued to air at least a year after that.

NBC COMICS

Cartoons; B&W
September 18, 1950–March 30, 1951

NBC Mon.–Fri. 5–5:15 p.m. (9/18/50–3/30/51)

Voices: *Bob Bruce, Pat McGeeham, Howard McNear, Lurene Tuttle*

The story behind *NBC Comics* is as episodic as the standard comic book adventure tales it presented on air. In 1947 *Billboard* reported on no less than two production firms calling themselves Telecomics which announced plans to use nonanimated drawings to tell stories. The one which finally made it to the air two years later in syndication under the title *Telecomics* featured the voices of Bill Grey, Jack Kirkwood, and Lillian Leigh in daily 15-minute shows. Each show consisted of four three-minute episodes, with the quartet comprised of "Brother Goose," "Rick Rack,

Special Agent," "Sa-Lih," an Arabian Nights novelty cartoon, and "Joey and Jug," two circus clowns.

When NBC bought the property a year later, it used unidentified live talent off-screen to do voices and sound effects on new segments. The result was a disaster, according to a *Billboard* review, which read, "The dialogue often seemed to have no relation to the drawings and, at times, the whole thing took on the eerie aspect of a comic strip *Strange Interlude*. It was even harder to 'tell the players without a program' when the producers economized via long shots of several characters in silhouette." The regular cartoons on NBC were "Kid Champion," about boxer Eddie Hale; "Danny March," about a private eye; "Johnny and Mr. Do-Right," about a boy and his dog, respectively, who dispensed helpful advice like "Always cover your mouth before coughing or sneezing"; and "Space Barton," about a civil war on a distant planet.

NBC EXPERIMENT IN TELEVISION—See *Experiment in Television*.

NBC GRANDSTAND—See *Grandstand*.

NBC KALEIDOSCOPE—See *Kaleidoscope*.

NBC MATINEE THEATRE—See *Matinee Theatre*.

•NBC NEWS
News; B&W and Color
October 10, 1960–December 31, 1976

NBC Mon.–Fri. 12:55–1 p.m. (10/10/60–9/29/61)
NBC Mon.–Fri. 12:55–1 p.m. and 4:55–5 p.m.
 (10/2/61–12/29/61)
NBC Mon.–Fri. 12:55–1 p.m., 2:25–3 p.m., and 4:55–5
 p.m. (1/2/62–9/28/62)
NBC Mon.–Fri. 10:25–10:30 a.m., 12:55–1 p.m., 2:55–3
 p.m., and 4:55–5 p.m. (10/1/62–12/28/62)
NBC Mon.–Fri. 10:25–10:30 a.m., 12:55–1 p.m., 2:55–3
 p.m., and 4:25–4:30 p.m. (12/31/62–3/29/63)
NBC Mon.–Fri. 10:25–10:30 a.m., 12:55–1 p.m.,
 2:25–2:30 p.m., and 4:25–4:30 p.m.(4/1/63–6/26/64)
NBC Mon.–Fri. 10:55–11 a.m., 12:55–1 p.m., 1:55–2
 p.m., and 4:25–4:30 p.m. (6/29/64–9/24/65)
NBC Mon.–Fri. 10:25–10:30 a.m., 12:55–1 p.m., 1:55–2
 p.m., and 4:25–4:30 p.m. (9/27/65–9/29/67)
NBC Mon.–Fri. 10:25–10:30 a.m., 12:55–1 p.m., and
 4:25–4:30 p.m. (10/2/67–9/20/69)
NBC Mon.–Fri. 10:25–10:30 a.m. and 12:55–1 p.m.
 (9/23/69–7/31/70)
NBC Mon.–Fri. 12:55–1 p.m. (8/3/70–12/31/76)

Anchors Included: *Sander Vanocur (for 4:55–5 p.m. 1961–63; 4:25–4:30 p.m. 1963–64 at least; 10:25–10:30 a.m. at least early 1967), Ray Scherer (for 12:55–1 p.m. 1961–62 at least), Floyd Kalber (for 2:55–3 p.m. 1961–63; 2:25–2:30 p.m. 1963–64 at least), Edwin Newman (for*

10:25–10:30 a.m. 1962–at least 1965; 12:55–1 p.m. at least 1967 and 1975), Nancy Dickerson (for 1:55–2 p.m. 1966 at least–1967; 10:25–10:30 a.m. at least 1968)

During the 1960s, NBC's daily news updates aired more frequently than those of any other networks—up to four times as often from 1962 to 1967. Most reports came from New York City, but during the early and mid-1960s they came from other points, such as Washington, D.C. (Sander Vanocur and Ray Scherer) and Chicago (Floyd Kalber).

•NBC NEWS AT SUNRISE
News; Color
August 1, 1983–

NBC Mon.–Fri. 6–7 a.m. (8/1/83–3/13/87)
NBC Mon.–Fri. 6:30–7 a.m. (3/16/87–9/16/88)
NBC Mon.–Fri. 6–7 a.m. (9/19/88–)

Regulars: *Connie Chung (anchor; 1983–March 1986), Bill Macatee (sports; 1983–84 at least), Joe Witte (weather), Jimmy Cefalo (sports; 1985–86 at least), Bob Jamieson (1986–January 1987), Deborah Norville (1987–89), John Palmer (1989–90), Faith Daniels (June 1990–91), Ann Curry (1991–)*

When it began as a replacement for *Early Today* (q.v.), *NBC News at Sunrise* offered the first regular network news anchoring job for ex–CBS reporter Connie Chung. Bob Jamieson began substituting for Chung in October 1985 and became her permanent replacement five months later when she moved into nighttime reporting. On January 5, 1987, 28-year-old Deborah Norville took over hosting duties from Jamieson, who stayed on earlier mornings with *Before Hours* (q.v.), and started substitute hosting on *Today.* Within two years, on September 5, 1989, she had switched positions with John Palmer and begun doing the news on *Today* while he moved back to anchor *NBC News at Sunrise.*

In June 1990 Faith Daniels, ex-newscaster on *The CBS Morning News,* assumed Palmer's seat during his time away from the network (he left temporarily following the change, which was regarded as a demotion, but later returned as a reporter). Her tenure lasted less than a year—in 1991 she became host of the daily show *A Closer Look* (q.v.)—and Ann Curry took over for the next few years.

NBC OPERA THEATRE
Opera; B&W and Color
October 19, 1952–April 21, 1957

NBC Sun. and Sat. Various times monthly
 (10/19/52–4/21/57; off summers)

Conductor: *Peter Herman Adler*

NBC Opera Theatre was one of the network's top "class" cultural offerings of the 1950s. Its one constant performing element amid elaborate productions was Peter Herman Adler as conductor of the Symphony of the Air and resident artistic director. After airing some presentations on weeknights from 11 p.m. to midnight in 1951–52, the series debuted in daytime with composer Benjamin Britten's *Billy Budd* starring baritone Theodor Uppman, who had sung the lead in the show's three-hour debut in London a year earlier. Later productions included *Trouble in Tahiti,* with Leonard Bernstein as composer, librettist, and guest conductor (November 16, 1952); *The Taming of the Shrew* starring John Raitt (March 13, 1954); *Tosca,* with the lead sung by Leontyne Price, marking the first time on television that a black woman had done opera (January 23, 1955); *Griffelkin,* a world premiere opera (November 6, 1955); a two-hour English version of *Madame Butterfly* (December 4, 1955); and *Amahl and the Night Visitors* (December 25, 1955). The latter became an annual tradition of the program following its debut in 1951 (see *Hallmark Hall of Fame).*

Perhaps the most spectacular of all the shows was an American version of *War and Peace* by Sergei Prokofiev and his librettist wife Mira Mendelssohn. It aired January 13, 1957 from 1:30–5 p.m. with a cast of more than 60 performers.

Executive Producer Samuel Chotzinoff said he cast roles for looks as much as vocal talent, which explains why in the May 8, 1954 production of *Salome,* John Cassavetes played John the Baptist while an offstage baritone sang his part (Sal Mineo also appeared in the show). It could also explain the unbelievable casting of Wally Cox, Charlotte Rae, Ross Martin, Robert Culp, and Nancy Wickwire in the February 27, 1955 production of Moliere's *Le Bourgeois Gentilhomme.*

In 1957, the show was retitled *NBC Opera Company* and ran as specials through 1964. Most shows aired live from New York.

NBC SATURDAY NEWS
News; B&W
November 25, 1950–December 30, 1950
NBC Sat. 5:15–5:30 p.m. (11/25/50–12/30/50)

NBC offered this short news update oddly scheduled just before the kiddie-oriented *Joe DiMaggio Show.* This series was NBC's last weekend news show until a new Saturday telecast began at 6 p.m. on October 1961.

NBC SATURDAY PROM—See *Saturday Prom.*

NBC SPORTS IN ACTION
Sports; Color
January 12, 1963–June 5, 1966
NBC Sat. 3:30–5 p.m. (1/12/63–4/6/63)
NBC Sat. 4:30–6 p.m. (1/4/64–4/11/64)
NBC Sat. 5:30–6 p.m. (4/18/64–9/5/64)
NBC Sat. 1–1:30 p.m. (9/12/64–12/26/64)
NBC Sun. 4–5 p.m. (1/17/65–5/16/65)
NBC Sat. 5:30–6 p.m. (10/23/65–12/18/65)
NBC Sun. 4–5 p.m. (1/9/66–6/5/66)

Host: *Bud Palmer (1963–64), Jim Simpson (1965–66), Bill Cullen (1966)*

NBC tried several different titles and time slots for its imitation of *ABC's Wide World of Sports* in the 1960s. First it was *Sports International* with Bud Palmer as executive producer as well as host of one event per show—for example, boxing in Thailand and bullfighting in Spain—each filmed a few months in advance with his commentary added. Then NBC News took control of the series in the fall of 1963 and changed its name to *NBC Sports Special;* this incarnation included three live and taped events per show, all of which took place outside the United States. It continued running in 1964 in a shortened format, going from 90 to 30 minutes.

In 1965 the series received its third and final title of *NBC Sports in Action.* The renamed show's debut had ski jumping in Oberstdorf, Germany, and swamp buggy racing at Naples, Florida. For the summer of 1965 (May 23–September 5), the show moved to Sundays from 6:30–7:30 p.m. before returning to daytime. In 1966 game show host Bill Cullen served as co-host with Jim Simpson and performed such duties as color commentator for the world drag racing finals in Tulsa, Oklahoma (on the debut).

NBC SPORTSWORLD—See *SportsWorld.*

NBC TAKES YOU TO THE RACES
Sports; B&W
April 2, 1949–August 4, 1951
NBC Sat. 3:30–4:30 or 5 p.m. (4/2/49–8/4/51; summers only)

Regulars: *Clem McCarthy (1949, 1951 at least), Bill Stern (1949 at least), Sammy Renick (1949 at least)*

This early network coverage of horse racing, shot in New York City, made extensive use of the then-recent Zoomar lens, which helped to keep most of the horses in focus from start to finish as they raced around the track. Longtime radio sportscasters McCarthy and Stern announced the races while ex-jockey Renick interviewed participants trackside during the first season at least, when the show also was known as *Jamaica Races.*

NBC TELEVISION OPERA THEATRE—See *NBC Opera Theatre.*

NBC TELEVISION RELIGIOUS PROGRAM
Religious; B&W and Color
October 7, 1951–July 19, 1970
NBC Sun. 1–1:30 p.m. (10/7/51–5/25/52)
NBC Sun. 1:30–2 p.m. (6/1/52–9/8/68; temporary relocations to other Sunday afternoon slots in the summers of 1955–59)
NBC Sun. 12:30–1 p.m. (9/15/68–12/22/68)
NBC Sun. 1:30–2 p.m. (1/5/69–9/7/69)
NBC Sun. 12:30–1 p.m. (9/14/69–1/4/70)
NBC Sun. 1:30–2 p.m. (1/11/70–7/19/70)

NBC Television Religious Program was a catchall title for three rotating series—*Frontiers of Faith, The Eternal Light,* and *The Catholic Hour.* Each explained the beliefs and activities of a major religious denomination (Protestant, Jewish, and Catholic, respectively) for nearly two decades of dramas, documentaries, and discussions. Two of the series were holdovers from NBC radio—*The Eternal Light* began in 1946, and *The Catholic Hour* went back to 1930. The airtime devoted to each was based on the demographics of religion in America, so *Frontiers of Faith* aired six months of the year, *The Catholic Hour* four months, and *The Eternal Light* two months. (Originally it was a rotating six-week cycle, with three shows for *Frontiers of Faith,* two for *The Catholic Hour,* and one for *The Eternal Light.*)

Frontiers of Faith, sponsored by the National Council of Churches of Christ, had guests ranging from the Archbishop of Canterbury to James Baldwin, with shows examining a wide range of topics, for example, sadism in paperback books. Some top name actors appeared, such as E. G. Marshall and Maureen Stapleton (as an Israeli poet). The Rev. Eugene Carson Blake appeared on it as early as 1954. *Time* magazine reported that a 1963–64 offering, courses on the Old Testament led by Lutheran theologian the Rev. Dr. Hagen Staack, were popular with viewers.

The Eternal Light was handled by the Jewish Theological Seminary. The series did an early dramatization of "The Diary of Anne Frank" on November 16, 1952. One whimsical drama seen frequently in the 1960s was "Home for Passover," an early starring role for Gene Wilder.

The Catholic Hour had perhaps the grandest shows of all. One four-part series in Rome in January 1958, narrated by Norman Rose, climaxed with an audience with Pope Pius XII, a feat which took seven weeks of production to achieve. The series had a few other significant four-part documentaries, such as "Reflections USA," narrated by Michael Constantine in May 1960, about the claimed moral decay in America and what Catholics should be doing in response to it, and "America and Communism," narrated by Tim O'Connor from May 13–June 3, 1962. On April 18, 1954 it also became the first TV religious show to broadcast in color.

In the late 1960s, however, it was *The Catholic Hour* that generated the most controversy. In 1968 the Jesuit-based magazine *America* wrote that the show had ratings half the size of what they had been 10 years earlier and cited programming decisions made by the National Council of Catholic Men (NCCM), which ran the series, as the culprit. "The bold documentaries and clear expository talk programs of NCCM's illustrious past have been largely displaced by posturing thesis plays that deal with outre problems or pseudo-problems, usually with the dramatic values loaded against the institutional Church," noted the periodical. "The style of these programs is sometimes smirkish and 'in'-jokish; and its handling of issues is almost uniformly unsubtle and pretentious. Scripts sound like a liberal arts sophomore's unsolicited screenplay—artsy-crafty and

stereotypical. The acting is an embarrassment." Perhaps prompted by this criticism, *The Catholic Hour* was retitled *Guideline* in 1969 and only featured interviews with episcopal headliners.

NBC canceled the series in 1970, ostensibly to increase viewer interest by having future segments air as specials on Sunday afternoons. The specials continued through at least 1983 but received much less critical and public notice than the series had.

•NCAA BASKETBALL
Sports; B&W and Color
January 4, 1950–

CBS Sat. 2 or 2:30-Conclusion (1/4/50–3/1/52; winter months only)
CBS Sat. 3–4 p.m. (12/11/54–3/5/55)
CBS Sat. 3–4:45 p.m. (12/3/55–3/24/56)
NBC Sat. 2:30–4:30 p.m. (12/13/58–3/7/59)
ABC Sat. 2–4 p.m. (1/7/60–3/11/61; January–March only)
NBC Sat. 2–6 p.m. (two games weekly; 11/29/75–3/10/90 ; winter months only)
CBS Sat. Various times (1/16/82–; winter months only)
ABC Sun. Various times (2/9/92–; winter months only)

Regulars: *Jim McManus (1950 at least), Mel Allen (1950 at least), Vin Scully (1950–51 at least), Jack Drees (1954–56, 1958–59), Bill Herlow (1955–56), Bud Palmer (1955–56 at least), Chris Schenkel (1955–56 at least), Lindsey Nelson (1958–59), Curt Gowdy (1960 at least), Bob Neal (1960 at least), Billy Packer (analyst; 1975–), Marv Albert (at least 1977–), Tom Hawkins (at least 1977–), Russ Porter (at least 1977–), Al McGuire (analyst; 1977–), Dick Enberg (play-by-play; at least 1976–), Bob Costas (1980–), Gary Bender (at least 1981–84), Rick Barry (at least 1981–84), Bill Russell (at least 1981–84), Brent Musberger (play-by-play; at least 1984–89 CBS, 1991–, ABC), Dick Vitale (1986–), Jim Lampley (CBS; at least 1987–), Tim Brant (play-by-play CBS; at least 1987–), Keith Jackson (at least 1992), Jim Valvano (1991–92, ABC), Jim Nantz (1991–, CBS)*

College basketball received occasional exposure on network weekend television during the 1950s, although college football received much more coverage. The sport arrived on the networks in 1949 when Mel Allen stopped calling college football games for CBS and moved to Madison Square Garden to check out the court action. Also, CBS aired six Navy games from Annapolis by WMAR Baltimore with Jim McManus in the 1950–51 season, when Navy was the featured home team. CBS did not resume showing NCAA basketball until it showed highlights of Big Ten games in 1954–55 and then full games of that conference the following season. Jack Drees, an ex–University of Iowa hoopster, did the play-by-play, and Big Ten official Bill Herlow provided color in 1955.

A two-year drought in coverage ended in 1959 with NBC covering a wider slate than CBS had in 1955–56; there was then another year's layoff, followed by ABC picking up the action in 1960. Then, except for specials or highlights shown on sports anthology shows, the networks didn't cover university hoop action until 14 years later, in 1975.

Leading NBC's coverage was the duo of Billy Packer and Al McGuire. Packer was an ex–Wake Forest guard and McGuire was ex-coach of Marquette. The duo, joined by Dick Enberg from 1978–81, was split when Packer went to do analysis on CBS with Gary Bender in 1981. Brent Musberger had started doing play-by-play for CBS by 1984. By 1985–89, the lead analysis teams were Al McGuire–Dick Enberg on NBC and Billy Packer–Brent Musberger on CBS. When the games made it to ABC after being exclusively on CBS for two years, Brent Musberger joined ex-coach Jim Valvano and Dick Vitale in calling them. Vitale became known for his own brand of hyperbolic lingo. He coined descriptive terms, then referred to them by initials ("PTP" meant "Prime Time Player," for example), and when he was really excited he'd throw in "Baby!" The more staid CBS stayed with the less bombastic pairing of Billy Packer and Jim Nantz into the mid-1990s.

•NCAA FOOTBALL

Sports; B&W and Color
November 3, 1946–

NBC Various afternoons and times (11/3/46–11/30/46)
NBC Sat. 2 p.m.–Conclusion (10/4/47–11/27/51; fall months only)
DuMont Sat. 2:15 p.m.–Conclusion (10/16/48–11/20/48)
CBS Sat. 2 p.m.–Conclusion (10/16/48–11/29/52; fall months only)
ABC Sat. 2 p.m.–Conclusion (9/30/50–11/25/50)
NBC Sat. Various times (9/20/52–12/29/52)
NBC Sat. 3:30–Conclusion (9/19/53–12/5/53)
ABC Sat. 1:45–Conclusion (9/18/54–11/4/54)
NBC Sat. 3:15–Conclusion (9/17/55–11/19/55)
CBS Sat. 2 p.m.–Conclusion (9/24/55–11/12/55)
NBC Sat. 1:45 p.m.–Conclusion (10/1/55–11/28/59; fall months only)
ABC Sat. 2–5 p.m. (9/17/60–12/2/61; fall months only)
CBS Sat. 2 p.m.–Conclusion (9/15/62–12/14/63; fall months only)
NBC Sat. 1:30 or 2 p.m.–Conclusion (9/12/64–12/4/65; fall months only)
ABC Sat. Various times between Noon and 6 p.m. (9/17/66–; fall months only)
CBS Sat. Various times between Noon and 6 p.m. (9/8/82–12/10/83; fall months only)
CBS Sat. Various times between Noon and 7 p.m. (9/15/84–12/8/90; fall months only)

Announcers: *Bob Stanton (1946, 1951 at least), Bill Slater (1948 at least), Mel Allen (1948, 1951–54 at least), Marty Glickman (1949 at least), Red Barber (1950, 1963 at least), Bill Stern (1951, 1954 at least), Russ Hodges (1951–53, 1955 at least), Ted Husing (1951 at least), Joe Hasel (1951 at least),*

Mal Stevens (1951–52 at least), Connie Desmond (1951 at least), Jim Britt (1951 at least), Jim Simpson (1952, 1962–63 at least), Dick Kazmaier (1952–53), Bill Henry (1952), Harold "Red" Grange (1952–53, 1955–59 at least), Lindsey Nelson (1953–59, 1962–65, 1982–85 at least), Bud Palmer (1953), Tom Harmon (1954 at least), Jack Drees (1954, 1970 at least), Bob Cooke (1955), Bob Neal (1954–55), Bud Wilkinson (at least 1956, 1965–66, and 1971–74), Terry Brennan (at least 1956 and 1962–65), Curt Gowdy (at least 1960–61), Paul Christman (at least 1960–61), Fred Mazurek (1964), Keith Jackson (1966–), Chris Schenkel (at least 1971–74), Steve Davis (analysis; 1971–84 at least), Duffy Daugherty (ex-Michigan State coach; at least 1973–74), Jim Lampley (1977–86), Tim Brant (about 1981–86), Beano Cook (at least 1982–85), Frank Broyles (analysis; at least 1982), Brent Musberger (1982–88), Pat O'Brien (1982–at least 1988), Ara Parseghian (1982–at least 1987), Pat Haden (analyst; at least 1982–89), Gary Bender (play-by-play; 1982–85), Verne Lundquist (play-by-play; 1982–86 at least), Frank Herzog (play-by-play; 1982–), Dennis Franklin (analyst; 1982–83), Brian Dowling (analyst; 1982–83), Jack Snow (analyst; at least 1984), Scott Hunter (analyst; at least 1984), Al Michaels (at least 1985), Jim Nantz (1985–90), Doug Flutie (1985–), Bob Griese (at least 1987–), Greg Gumbel (at least 1989), Andrea Joyce (at least 1990)

The dawn of regular network daytime programming—not to mention that of sports shows—came in 1946 when NBC, after years of carrying college football games locally on WNBT New York, relayed five contests from WPTZ in Philadelphia to New York in November in what is believed to be the first regular TV network affiliation contract. Most of these home-game contests featuring either Army or the University of Pennsylvania were sponsored between quarters by Goodyear in New York and Atlantic Refineries in Philadelphia. The exception was the Army-Navy game on November 30, 1946, which was sponsored by Gillette; that contest was also aired on a special hookup to Washington, D.C.

By the time the last of these games was shot, producer Burke Crotty had developed techniques for covering football which set the precedent for the next half-century—concentrating on the ball's location rather than showing all activity on the gridiron, and using cameras located at the press box, 50-yard line, and other areas to get different perspectives of the action.

In 1947, NBC carried four Navy games from Baltimore on its New York–Philadelphia–Baltimore–Schenectady network. (NBC also covered pro football regularly for the first time; see *NFL Football 1947–55.*) The schedule expanded to start in September the following year, with Bill Slater covering the eastern games and the INS-Telenews service providing scores of other contests during each show. Then in 1949, NBC started covering as many as four different regional games, including old favorite the University of Pennsylvania, whose university president Harold Stassen did a fireside chat during intermission.

Other networks had begun to cover their own specific college games by this time. In 1948, CBS used Mel Allen to describe the action at Columbia University contests (Marty Glickman took over for Allen in 1949). CBS then covered Army, Navy, and Columbia games with Red Barber in 1950. In 1948, DuMont joined CBS and NBC in covering more than one college during the season, then went to featuring Notre Dame in 1949–50 (see *Notre Dame Football* for details). Then when ABC started featuring University of Pennsylvania games in 1950, all four networks were competing Saturdays to show college football games—a situation which the NCAA didn't like, due to potential overexposure causing attendance at games to drop. This resulted in only CBS and NBC covering the games in 1951 and 1952.

In 1951, CBS used ex–Yale football coach Mal Stevens and baseball announcer Connie Desmond to handle its new color football games, which received a rave from *Variety*. NBC just had black and white, with Jim Britt doing play-by-play and Bob Stanton commentating. In 1952, CBS went back to black and white to cover *Armed Services Football* in 1952, with Jim Simpson announcing and Red Grange commentating along with some work by Mal Stevens, while NBC had Mel Allen do play-by-play and Bill Henry color.

NBC got sole coverage rights of games in 1953 with the team of Mel Allen and Lindsey Nelson, plus Bud Palmer and Red Grange doing pregame coverage and Russ Hodges and Dick Kazmaier giving a rundown of scores. The following year, the games went back on two networks. ABC had 13 NCAA football games on a record number of stations (156, to be exact), but DuMont's coverage surpassed ABC's, airing 57 games between September 26 and December 12, 1954, with as many as five games, from different regions, being shown in one afternoon. ABC's show had Tom Harmon and Jack Drees doing play-by-play and Bill Stern doing color plus pre- and postgame duties.

As a result of ABC's inability to find national advertisers on its lineup in 1954 (it lost $1 million that year), plus the dissolution of DuMont, NBC and CBS got control of the games in 1955. NBC telecast three games in 1955 in color, and installed Lindsey Nelson and Red Grange as announcers and Russ Hodges and *New York Herald Tribune* sports editor Bob Cooke as postgame score announcer. In 1956, NBC got sole control of the games through 1959, and Nelson and Grange remained as announcers through that period.

ABC's control of the games from 1960–61 was highlighted by the debut of the use of instant replay on a game on November 23, 1961. In 1962, CBS took over and brought along Lindsey Nelson, adding Terry Brennan as analyst and Jim Simpson as a sideline reporter, and starting around that time various other personalities, including Mel Allen, Bill Fleming, and Johnny Lujack, served as announcers of regional contests. NBC got rights again in 1964, then the show went back to ABC in 1966 for 15 years of exclusive rights.

ABC managed to make several reforms in the games. Tired of having to carry a slate of games composed the previous winter (which meant that viewers had to watch some games where both teams had losing records instead of seeing more exciting contests), ABC received a "wild card" bonus in 1968, allowing it to pick one extra game for a doubleheader that had not been previously scheduled. By 1971, the NCAA was picking only the first six games of each season, and ABC then picked up the ones it wanted to show on a week-by-week basis. The lead announcer was Keith Jackson, whose catchphrase was "Whoa, Nellie!"

At first ABC carried this series at a loss, mainly to please affiliates located in areas with no professional football teams, but by 1969 *NCAA Football* had grown to the point where 226 stations were carrying it—the highest clearance of any network series. Given this success, other networks became interested in getting a piece of the action, and in 1982 CBS succeeded. Lindsey Nelson, Gary Bender, Frank Herzog, and Vern Lundquist provided play-by-play in regional action, while ex-quarterbacks Pat Haden, Steve Davis (formerly of ABC), Brian Dowling, and Dennis Franklin gave analysis, with Bender and Haden being the lead announcing duo (it was Lundquist and Haden by 1986). Jack Snow and Scott Hunter replaced Dowling and Franklin after two seasons. Brent Musburger, Pat O'Brien, and Ara Parseghian gave halftime reports. By the late 1980s Jim Nantz was the top announcer for CBS.

Meanwhile, ABC added Keith Broyles as analyst and Beano Cook doing halftime reports and wrapup. In 1981 Jim Lampley hosted ABC's pregame and halftime shows, some with Beano Cook and, in 1985, with ex-quarterback Doug Flutie. In 1989 Bob Griese and Keith Jackson became the lead duo for ABC.

In 1990 ABC got four years of College Football Association games to mix with its Pac-10 and Big Ten games, which it needed because CBS had had the rights since 1986, getting better ratings because it could air contests with top teams like Notre Dame, Miami, and Nebraska. In 1990 Andrea Joyce replaced Greg Gumbel as host of the pregame show on CBS, but that job did not last long because ABC's contract precluded further coverage by the network through at least 1995. (See also *Notre Dame Football*.)

NFL (1947–55)
Sports; B&W
October 4, 1947–December 11, 1955

NBC Sun. 1:50 or 2:15 p.m.–Conclusion (10/4/47–11/23/47)
ABC Sun. 2 p.m.–Conclusion (9/19/48–12/17/50; fall months only)
DuMont Sun. 2 p.m.–Conclusion (10/7/51–12/11/55; fall months only)
ABC Sun. 2 p.m.–Conclusion (10/5/52–12/11/55; fall months only)

Announcers: *Bob Stanton (1947 at least), Arthur Daly (1947 at least), Red Grange (1949, 1952, and 1954 at least), Joe Hasel (1949 at least), Harry Wismer (1949 and 1952–54 at least), Jim Gibbons (1949 and 1954 at least), Bill Stern (1953–54 at least), Bill Fay (1954 at least), Bill Malone (1954 at least), Chris Schenkel (1954 at least)*

Though games of the National Football League (NFL) had become the top-rated TV weekend attraction by the 1960s, they had a rather rocky start of it in the first decade or so on television thanks to occasional network competition and a lack of national games. The first series began in 1947, when NBC installed the first regular series of pro football games on its schedule. Pabst Beer was the sponsor, and games aired in New York, Philadelphia, Washington, D.C., and Schenectady, New York. Generally it featured the home games of the New York Giants, with NBC announcer Bob Stanton joined by sportswriter Arthur Daly in describing the action.

By 1949 ABC had gained control of the games, with the proviso that it would not show them in the local market from which the game emanated. Red Grange, the former "Galloping Ghost" of football, did play-by-play and Joe Hasel did color, and the team of Harry Wismer and Jim Gibbons occasionally put in an appearance. Grange remained as announcer in covering the Chicago Bears and the Cardinals in 1952, while Harry Wismer covered the New York Giants the same year.

A year earlier, DuMont had started to cover 26 NFL games on a 27-station lineup. DuMont continued to have NFL rights from 1953 to 1955, but had to use some CBS and NBC stations to carry the games. In 1953 the network had nine different commentators for its slate of national and regional games, with Harry Wismer the main one for the New York Giants games. The show also generated some of the network's highest ratings, as it aired in 108 markets. In 1954 Chris Schenkel did much of the play-by-play.

During the same period, ABC also had pro football, and in 1953 Bill Stern did pregame shows for that network. In 1954, ABC aired the games of the Chicago Bears and the then–Chicago Cardinals; either Red Grange or Bill Fay, sports editor for *Collier's* magazine, did commentary and either Bill Stern or Harry Wismer did play-by-play. (Viewers in the South and East got 12 Washington Redskins games covered by Jim Gibbons, sports director of WMAL Washington, with Bill Malone adding commentary.)

Finally, with the collapse of the DuMont network in 1955, rights to NFL games went to only one network. (See the next entry for more details.)

NFL (CBS AND FOX)
Sports; B&W and Color
September 9, 1956–

CBS Sun. 2 p.m.–Conclusion (9/9/56–12/27/64; fall months only)
NBC Sun. 2 p.m.–Conclusion (?/?/60–12/17/61; fall months only)

CBS Sun. 1:30 p.m. or 2 p.m.–Conclusion (9/12/65–12/28/69; fall months only)
CBS Sun. 1 p.m.–Conclusion (10/4/70–1/23/94; fall months only)
Fox Sun. 1 p.m.–Conclusion (9/4/94–; fall months only)

Announcers: *Red Grange (1956–57 at least), Jim Gibbons (1956–58 at least), Ed Gallaher (1958), Chris Schenkel (1956–60 at least), Lindsey Nelson (play-by-play; 1960–61, 1966–at least 1981), Frankie Albert (1960–61), Pat Summerall (analyst, then play-by-play; 1961–), Ray Scott (play-by-play; at least 1959–at least 1972), Jack Buck (play-by-play; at least 1968–87), Tom Brookshier (analyst; 1964–at least 1986), Frank Glieber (play-by-play; at least 1968–84), Don Criqui (play-by-play; at least 1968–78), Jack Whitaker (play-by-play; at least 1968–70), Frank Gifford (at least 1968–69), Paul Christman (at least 1968–69), Jack Drees (play-by-play; at least 1968), George Connor (analyst; at least 1968), Chuck Thompson (at least 1968), Lenny Moore (at least 1968), Eddie LeBaron (at least 1968), John Sauer (analyst; at least 1968), Irv Cross (analyst; at least 1972–73, 1980–81, 1990–91), Jim Morse (analyst; at least 1972), Alex Hawkins (analyst; at least 1972–at least 1977), Gary Bender (play-by-play; 1974–80 and 1986 at least), Jane Chastain (1974), Al Michaels (play-by-play; 1975 at least), Sonny Jurgenson (analyst; 1975 at least), Hank Stram (analyst; 1975, 1980, and 1985–86 at least), Vin Scully (play-by-play; 1975–81), Nick Buoniconti (analyst; 1976–79 at least), Tim Ryan (play-by-play; 1977–86 at least), George Allen (analyst; 1978–81 at least), John Madden (analyst; 1979–), Curt Gowdy (play-by-play; 1979–80), Roger Staubach (analyst; 1980–83 at least), Johnny Morris (play-by-play; 1981–82 and 1986 at least), "Mean" Joe Greene (1982), Wayne Walker (play-by-play; 1982–83 and 1986 at least), Jim Kelly (1982 at least), John Dockery (1982 and 1985 at least), Dick Stockton (play-by-play; 1982–84 and 1986 at least), Dick Vermeil (play-by-play; 1983–), Charlie Waters (analyst; 1983 at least), Drew Pearson (analyst; 1983 at least–1984), Terry Bradshaw (analyst; 1984–89), Verne Lundquist (play-by-play; at least 1984–), Dan Dierdorf (play-by-play 1985; analyst 1986), Jean Fugett (analyst; 1985), Jim Hill (1985 at least), Tim Brant (play-by-play; at least 1987–88), Ken Stabler (at least 1987–88), Joe Theisman (analyst; 1987–88), Jim Lampley (play-by-play; 1987–), Merlin Olsen (at least 1991), Brad Nessler (1990–91). Gary Bender (1990–91), Jim Henderson (1990–), Sean McDonough (1991–), Jim Nantz (1991–94), Joe Buck (play-by-play; at least 1994–), Kenny Albert (at least 1994–), Thom Brennaman (at least 1994–), Mat Millen (at least 1995–)*

In 1956 the bulk of NFL games came to rest largely with one network—CBS—and stayed there for 38 years. Though it was the only network showing the games in the late 1950s, CBS did not have an exclusive league package in the early years due to legal rulings, so in 1960 NBC, which lost control of NCAA football to ABC, set up its own deal for two seasons with Lindsey Nelson and Frankie Albert in the booth. But after that, it was all CBS through 1994, although NBC later got a piece of the action; see *NFL (NBC)*.

Perhaps the one name most associated with the CBS years is Pat Summerall, who joined Chris Schenkel in 1962 after Summerall retired from being the New York Giants placekicker. Summerall lasted more than a third of a century in the broadcast booth, and his fame as a commentator will certainly outlast people's memories of him as a placekicker. In 1975 the show's lead team became Summerall and Tom Brookshier, a combo which lasted until 1981 when John Madden supplanted Brookshier. The Madden-Summerall duo became the preeminent football announcing duo for the next 15 years.

For the first 12 years, CBS continued the tradition of allowing home team announcers to cover regional games in the regular season, but by 1968 was using eight regular pairs instead to cover games (Scott-Christman, Whitaker-Gifford, Drees-Connor, Nelson-Brookshier, Thompson-Moore, Buck-Summerall, Glieber-LeBaron, and Criqui-Sauer). Some of these announcers stuck around into the 1970s, albeit not in the same configurations. In 1974 CBS even became the first to allow a woman to cover the game from the booth, but negative reaction to Jane Chastain limited her career to that one season, and no female has covered football for a network, except from the sidelines. Most of the matchups into the 1990s consisted of a sportscaster teamed with an ex-pro, such as Verne Lundquist with Terry Bradshaw in 1984 or Jim Lampley with Ken Stabler in 1987.

In 1994 Fox shocked CBS and most of the sports world when it outbid that network for rights to the game, thus ending CBS's reign. Cynics snickered at what flashy Fox would do to the game (the Mighty Morphin Power Rangers giving sideline reports, perhaps?), but the network actually did an admirable job, deciding to keep established veteran announcers Pat Summerall and John Madden as the lead team while adding flourishes which enhanced the game, particularly the use of graphics in the corner of the screen which let the viewer know at all times the current game's score, quarter, and amount of time left in the quarter. However, most observers believe that CBS wants to get NFL football back at any price, so Fox's current success may be irrelevant when bidding for rights comes up again in the late 1990s.

NFL (NBC)
Sports; Color
September 20, 1970–

NBC Sun. 1–4 p.m. or 1–7 p.m. (9/20/70–)

Regulars: *Charlie Jones (play-by-play; 1970–89 at least), Paul Maguire (analyst; 1971–79 and at least 1992–), Curt Gowdy (at least 1971–78), Al DeRogatis (at least 1971), Jim Simpson (at least 1971), Kyle Rote (analyst; at least 1971), Tim Ryan (play-by-play; at least 1975–76), Lee Leonard (at least 1976), Len Dawson (analyst; at least 1975–76), Jimmy Johnson*

(analyst; at least 1977), Andy Russell (analyst; at least 1977), Don Criqui (at least 1979–at least 1992), Bob Costas (1980–83 at least), Ahmad Rashad (1983 at least), Bob Trumpy (analyst; at least 1983–84 and 1988–), Bob Griese (analyst; 1983 at least), Harvey Martin (analyst; 1984 at least), Merlin Olsen (analyst; at least 1985–at least 1989), Dick Enberg (play-by-play; at least 1985–), Jimmy Cefalo (analyst; at least 1985–at least 1988), Paul Zimmerman (at least 1985–), Bill Walsh (analyst; 1989 at least–1991), Marv Albert (at least 1977–78, 1983, 1988, and 1994–), Joe Namath (at least 1988–), Todd Christensen (analyst; at least 1990), Chris Collinsworth (analyst; at least 1990 and 1995–), Jim Laslavic (analyst; at least 1990), Jim Lampley (play-by-play; at least 1992–), Pat McGuire (at least 1995–)

NBC's coverage of the NFL was a logical extension of its coverage of the league's former competitor, *AFL Football* (q.v.). There were some carryovers from that league, most notably Curt Gowdy, but a wider range of games meant a larger number of sportscasters being used. Apart from Gowdy, Charlie Jones and Paul Maguire were the most frequently heard announcers in the 1970s. However, there was one game where no one was heard. On December 20, 1980, NBC ran a game using only using information from the public address system and updates from Bryant Gumbel between halves and timeouts. The experiment was not a success, and announcers remained a part of NBC's coverage.

In 1985 Paul Zimmerman became a new third man in the booth for one of the secondary coverage teams, while Dick Enberg and Merlin Olsen were the lead announcers. NBC split Enberg and Olsen in 1989, pairing Enberg with former San Francisco 49ers coach Bill Walsh and Olsen with Charlie Jones. When Walsh left in 1992, Bob Trumpy teamed with Enberg.

NFL ACTION
Sports; Color
May 18, 1969–March 12, 1972

CBS Sun. 4:30–5 p.m. (5/18/69–9/7/69)
CBS Sun. 4:30–5 p.m. (5/24/70–9/6/70)
CBS Sun. 4:30–5 p.m. (1/23/72–3/12/72)

Host: *Pat Summerall (1969), John Facenda (1970, 1972)*

NFL Action began as a syndicated half-hour weekly series in 1967 hosted by Frank Gifford. Titled officially *National Football League Action*, it aired during the off-season period and included rare sideline footage and comments made during telecasts of various games. When it came to CBS, that network's longtime NFL sportscaster Pat Summerall became host, while local sportscasters associated with the team or player being profiled that week did the narration. The following year, John Facenda, a sportscaster with CBS's Philadelphia TV station WCAU, took over both hosting and narrating duties for the 1970s shows.

This series was produced by NFL Films, which also produced the syndicated half-hour *NFL Game of the Week* at the same time. Between its last two runs on CBS, *NFL Action* ran on ABC Wednesdays from 10:30–11 p.m. from May 12–September 8, 1971. After 1972, the show continued in production for syndication through at least 1975.

NFL COUNTDOWN TO KICKOFF
Sports; B&W
September 12, 1964–December 3, 1966

CBS Sat. 4–5 p.m. (9/12/64–12/3/66;
    September–December only)

Host: *Tom Harmon (1964–65), Frank Gifford (1966)*

NFL Countdown to Kickoff was both a review of the previous Sunday's National Football League games and a preview of the next day's games, with the latter involving interviews with coaches, players, and scouts. It began as a studio effort, but in 1966 it began rotating among NFL cities, originating in a different city each week to spotlight local teams and announcers. (An odd touch that same year was having Frank Gifford interview Jackie Gleason to get the latter's picks on that week's games.)

•NFL '77–'86/LIVE
Sports; Color
September 25, 1977–

NBC Sun. 12:30–1 p.m. (9/25/77–; fall months only)

Regulars: *Bryant Gumbel (1977–81), Larry Merchant (1977–78), Lee Leonard (1977 at least), Pete Axthelm (1979–85), Len Berman (1982–83), Dave Marash (at least 1983), Bill Macatee (at least 1983–84), Don Criqui (1984 at least),, Bob Costas (1984–92), John Brodie (1984 at least), Ahmad Rashad (at least 1983, 1985–88, and 1994), Larry King (1985), Frank Deford (at least 1986), Paul Maguire (at least 1986–87), Bob Trumpy (at least 1987), Jimmy Cefalo (at least 1987), Gayle Gardner (at least 1988), O. J. Simpson (1989–93), Ralph Wiley (1989), Bobby Beathard (1989), Will McDonough (1990–), Bill Parcells (1991–92 at least), Joe Gibbs (at least 1993–), Mike Ditka (1993–), Jim Lampley (1993), Greg Gumbel (1994–), Jim Gray (1994–), Hannah Storm (1994–), Joe Montana (1995)*

Following the lead of CBS's *The NFL Today*, NBC introduced *NFL '77* as a pregame studio show offering previews of that day's contests in the American Football Conference and interviews with players and coaches. Early hosts were Larry Merchant, Bryant Gumbel, Len Berman, and Bob Costas, with a few other sportscasters joining them by the early 1980s. A major overhaul in this New York City–based show took place in 1986: NBC added a studio audience, *Sports Illustrated* reporter Frank Deford gave commentaries, and Paul Maguire replaced Pete Axthelm as analyst/handicapper.

The changeover met with little popular or critical acclaim, and the show went back to its old format in 1987, when it was retitled *NFL Live*. In 1989 all the regulars save Bob Costas were dropped and replaced with O. J. Simpson

(as sideline reporter), *Sports Illustrated* writer Ralph Wiley, and ex–Washington Redskins general manager Bobby Beathard, and thereafter turnover on the show became regular for the next few seasons. Wiley and Beathard were gone by 1990, when Will McDonough became the new analyst. Later, ex–NFL coaches Bill Parcells, Joe Gibbs, and Mike Ditka added commentary, and Jim Lampley assumed hosting chores after Costas ended his nine years at the helm. In 1994 Greg Gumbel became host, moving from CBS's *NFL Today* along with reporter Jim Gray. Ahmad Rashad moved to the studio to join the two along with Ditka and Gibbs, and Hannah Storm replaced O. J. Simpson, who at the time was a murder suspect. The arrival of ex–San Francisco 49ers quarterback Joe Montana to the team in 1995 was intensely promoted, but Montana's lackluster performance meant the next season would have yet another change in the lineup.

•NFL SUNDAY
Sports; Color
September 9, 1994–

Fox Sun. Noon–1 p.m. (9/9/94–; fall months only)

Regulars: *Jim Brown, Terry Bradshaw, Howie Long, Jimmy Johnson (1994–95)*

When Fox got the rights to do NFL football, it unveiled network TV's first one-hour pregame show, borrowing some elements from *NFL Today* on CBS (regulars Jim Brown and Terry Bradshaw), and adding some new ones, including ex-player Howie Long and ex–Dallas Cowboys coach Jimmy Johnson. Most of it, though, was the same format as *NFL Today*, featuring reviews and previews of games, interviews with coaches and players, and stories related to NFL action, interspersed with barbs and wisecracks from the regulars. Johnson left at the end of 1995 to become coach of the Miami Dolphins.

•NFL TODAY, THE
Sports; Color
October 4, 1970–January 23, 1994

CBS Sun. 12:30–1 p.m. (10/4/70–1/23/94; fall months
    only)

Regulars: *Carole Howey (1970), Elinor Kaine (1971 at least), Jack Whitaker (at least 1971–75), Pat Summerall (at least 1971–72), Brent Musburger (1974–89), Irv Cross (1975–89), Phyllis George (1975–77, 1980–84), Lee Leonard (at least 1975), Jimmy "the Greek" Snyder (1976–87), Jayne Kennedy (1978–79), Charlsie Cantey (1983), Wil McDonough (at least 1986–89), Dick Butkus (1988–89), Greg Gumbel (1990–93), Terry Bradshaw (1990–93), Pat O'Brien (at least 1990), Lesley Visser (at least 1990), James Brown (at least 1993), Jim Gray (at least 1993)*

CBS had a pregame show as part of its National League Sunday contests from 1957–69. During this period it was a rather run-of-the-mill 15-minute preview of the day's

In 1995 NFL Sunday *on Fox featured, from left, Jim Brown,
Terry Bradshaw, Howie Long, and Jimmy Johnson.*

football games with various hosts, including Frank Gifford,
Red Grange, Red Scott, Tommy Harmon, Chris Schenkel,
and Johnny Lujack. But in 1970 CBS installed *The NFL
Today* as a separate half-hour introductory show with live
updates from the stadiums with announcers reporting, to
the main studio in New York, on the upcoming contests.

In the 1970s the show attempted to broaden its appeal
to women by including them as regulars, although the
attempts were usually condescending and sometimes
disastrous. First the producers tried actress Carole Howey,
formerly the Winston Girl in TV ads of the 1960s, as a
reporter. The following season Elinor Kaine took over
Howey's role, and also made game predictions. Kaine was
a more legitimate spokesperson for the game than Howey,
as she was the first female football columnist. But the
show moved away from serious female reportage when it
decided to add former Miss America Phyllis George in
1975, then went even further downhill by replacing George

with actress Jayne Kennedy, who knew even less about
the game. Kennedy was fired after a contract dispute, and
George returned as third banana. Horse racing expert
Charlsie Cantey replaced her briefly in 1983 when George
went on maternity leave.

The most controversial member of the team, however,
was Jimmy "the Greek" Snyder, who offered opinions on the
outcomes of the day's matchups. Some thought he encouraged
illegal betting on the games, which he denied, saying he
gave no point spreads. He had a harder time defending
himself on January 15, 1988, after he aired his views on
black athletes to a TV reporter, views which many found
racist. For example, he said that if blacks took over coaching,
"there's not going to be anything left for white people. I
mean, all the players are black. The only thing the whites
control is the coaching jobs." CBS canned him shortly
thereafter, and ex-footballer Dick Butkus replaced him.

When CBS fired Brent Musberger in the spring of 1990,
Greg Gumbel became the new host of the show and it
cleaned house, dropping 14-year veteran Irv Cross back to

game analysis and firing Dick Butkus and Wil McDonough (McDonough subsequently went to NBC). Joining Gumble were Terry Bradshaw, Pat O'Brien, and Lesley Visser and a new set and graphics.

NHL GAME OF THE WEEK
Sports; B&W and Color
January 5, 1957–

CBS Sat. 2–5:30 p.m. (1/5/57–3/9/57)
CBS Sat. 3–5 p.m. (11/2/57–3/22/58)
CBS Sat. 2–4:30 p.m. (10/18/58–3/21/59)
CBS Sat. 2–4:30 p.m. (1/9/60–3/19/60)
CBS Sun. 2–4:30 p.m. (1/28/68–5/4/68)
CBS Sun. 2:30–5 p.m. (1/12/69–5/4/69)
CBS Sun. 2–4:30 p.m. (1/11/70–5/7/72; winter months only)
NBC Sun. 3–5:30 p.m. (1/7/73–5/8/73)
NBC Sun. 2–4:30 p.m. (1/27/74–4/28/74)
NBC Sun. 4–6:30 p.m. (1/5/75–5/18/75)
Fox Sun. 3–6 p.m. (4/2/95–; spring months only)

Regulars: *Fred Cusick (1957–60), Bud Palmer (1957–59), Bryan McFarlane (1960, 1973–75), Jim Gordon (1968, 1971–72), Stu Nahan (1968), Dan Kelly (1969–72), Bill Mazer (1969–70), Bobby Hull (1969), Tim Ryan (1973–75), Ted Lindsay (1973–75), Ronnie Schell (as voice of "Peter Puck"; 1974 at least), James Brown (1995–), Dave Maloney (in-studio analyst; 1996 at least), Mike Emrick (announcer; 1996 at least), John Davidson (analyst; 1996 at least)*

The National Hockey League has had sporadic airings as a regular network attraction. The sport has never been as popular in the United States as it is in Canada, where hockey has long been a Saturday evening attraction. CBS was the first to try, in 1957. Bud Palmer called the action for games in New York City, Boston, Detroit, and Chicago, while Fred Cusick did a segment giving the rules of the game between the first and second periods. After three unimpressive years, toward the end of which Bryan McFarlane replaced Palmer, the network gave up on hockey for seven years.

In 1967 CBS signed a two-year, $3.6 million contract with the NHL, feeling that the league's recent expansion adding six new teams—Los Angeles, Minneapolis–St. Paul, Oakland, Philadelphia, Pittsburgh, and St. Louis—would make televised hockey action more popular in America. It didn't, as many CBS affiliates, particularly those in the South, did not carry the games. (CBS did not help itself by airing boring contests with the expansion teams and using only four cameramen to cover the action. In Canada, where hockey is as much a passion as a pastime, the Canadian Broadcasting Corporation used six cameras.) In 1970, CBS paid $1.5 million in a new contract but failed to reap a profit due to a lack of interest from sponsors, who were not impressed by the ratings. However, by 1971–72 the show began to become a decent audience winner, and in 1973 NBC bid successfully for the rights to the game, bringing substantial changes in the process.

To answer critics of the televised game who said it was too complicated for a novice to follow, NBC devised the animated character of Peter Puck, who gave instructions concerning the more complicated rules between periods of the game. The network also relied on the insight of Canadian native Tim Ryan for play-by-play and ex–Detroit Red Wings player Ted Lindsay for analysis. According to *Sports Illustrated*, the network solved one problem others had faced—the near-continuous action per period—by giving officials a mild shock in cummerbunds they wore to dramatize the need to call a timeout for commercials.

NBC tried to get some mileage out of its coverage, but the unimpressive first-year ratings continued to fall, and by 1975 audience share was a mere 11, way behind the competition (*NBA Basketball* on CBS had more than twice the audience and *ABC's Wide World of Sports* had more than three times as many viewers). NBC valiantly tried to encourage viewership with some nighttime games in 1973 and 1974, but those did little to boost popularity, and clearances were poor. In 1974, 38 stations declined to carry the game, and when that number grew to 61 in 1975 (most stations opting out were in Southern markets, where hockey was a particularly bad draw, including Houston, Memphis, and Birmingham, Alabama), the network decided not to continue showing the sport on a regular basis the following year.

Hockey then had little exposure again apart from the playoffs until the Fox network signed a five-year, $150-million deal with the league in 1994. Typical of its efforts to jazz up TV coverage of sports, the network added special effects which gave a blue glow to the puck, making it easier for the home viewer to follow, and used the upper left corner to give the time and score constantly, as it did with NFL football. Most of the games were regional ones, but James Brown served as studio host. Ratings remained unspectacular, but Fox was confident it could turn the game into a winning TV attraction by the dawn of the 21st century.

NPSL SOCCER—See *Soccer*.

NAME DROPPERS, THE
Game; Color
September 29, 1969–March 27, 1970

NBC Mon.–Fri. 12:30–12:55 p.m. (9/29/69–12/26/69)
NBC Mon.–Fri. 4–4:30 p.m. (12/29/69–3/27/70)

Hosts: *Al Lohman and Roger Barkley*

Los Angeles radio comedy duo Lohman and Barkley hosted this elaborate, *To Tell the Truth*–style contest involving 20 contestants from the studio audience and three celebrities. Three "name droppers" recounted stories telling how they were in some way connected to each of the celebrities. Two of the three were lying, and the 20 contestants had to vote on which of the "name droppers" was actually related to the celebrities. Each incorrect guess earned the name dropper

$10. The studio contestant with the most correct guesses at the end of the week won $1,000. Each day two contestants also were eligible for merchandise.

NAME THAT TUNE
Game; Color
July 29, 1974–June 10, 1977
NBC Mon.–Fri. 10–10:30 a.m. (7/29/74–1/3/75)
NBC Mon.–Fri. Noon–12:30 p.m. (1/3/77–6/10/77)
Regulars: *Dennis James (1974–75), Bob Alberti (1974–75), Tom Kennedy (1977), Stan Worth (1977)*

NBC tried twice in the 1970s to make 1950s game show warhorse *Name That Tune* into a hit but failed both times. It first came on the network in nighttime from July 6, 1953–June 14, 1954, then went to CBS from September 2, 1954–October 19, 1959. Hosts during those years were Red Benson, Bill Cullen, and George DeWitt.

When the show was revived for the 1970s by Ralph Edwards as executive producer (Harry Salter helmed the 1950s version), it featured the standard identification of a tune with as few notes as possible that the game used earlier, as well as some additions. There was the "Money Tree," where one contestant tried to pull down all the dollar bills hanging from a wire rack before the other guessed a certain number of tunes, and the "Money Wheel," where one could win several hundred dollars for naming a tune depending on where the wheel landed. In "Bid a Note" the host gave a brief description of the upcoming song, and a contestant "bid" the number of notes (the first bid had to be from 3 to 7) he or she would supposedly need to identify the tune. The other contestant either made a lower bid or challenged the first contestant to name the tune. If the second contestant's bid was lower, the first contestant could bid again or challenge, and so on. The winner after all these contests played the "Golden Medley," in which seven songs had to be identified within half a minute. Contestants could win up to $2,000 a day for five days before having to leave the show.

Name That Tune made its belated daytime debut with Dennis James as host and Bob Alberti the musical conductor in 1974, when it began a successful nighttime run in syndication. When *Name That Tune* returned for a second try two years later, its host was Tom Kennedy, who hosted the syndicated version until 1981, and Stan Worth led the band. Three years later, *The New $100,000 Name That Tune* (so-named since 1976, when it started giving out a grand prize of that amount) came into syndication with Jim Lange as host. It lasted a year.

•NAME YOUR ADVENTURE
Documentary; Color
September 12, 1992–September 2, 1995
NBC Sat. 11:30 a.m.–Noon (9/12/92–9/4/93)
NBC Sat. 10–10:30 a.m. (9/11/93–9/2/95)
Host: *Mario Lopez*

While acting as Slater on *Saved by the Bell* on NBC Saturday mornings in 1992–93, Mario Lopez had time left over to monopolize another half hour on the schedule to host this updated *Let's Take a Trip.* He took young viewers and weekly guests with him to various out-of-the-ordinary destinations, including the FBI Academy, the circus, and the last American rain forest, among others. A highlight was a show first aired January 29, 1994, on which 17-year-old Vietnamese refugee and American honors student Khahn Pham toured the White House with her idol, Clinton's press secretary Dee Dee Myers. President Bill Clinton also made an appearance.

NATION'S FUTURE, THE
Public Affairs; B&W
October 15, 1961–June 3, 1962
NBC Sun. 5–6 p.m. (10/15/61–6/3/62)
Host: *Edwin Newman*

Each installment of *The Nation's Future* posed a question which one guest supported and the other attacked depending on their viewpoint. The first question in daytime was "The Administration's Domestic Record: Success or Failure?" with HEW Secretary Abraham Ribicoff of the Kennedy administration claiming victory and Senate Minority Leader Everett M. Dirksen dissenting. The series aired roughly once a month in place of *Wisdom* and *Outlook,* and it originally ran on NBC Saturdays 9:30–10:30 p.m. from November 12, 1960–September 16, 1961, with John K. M. McCaffery as host through May 27, 1961.

NATIONAL BOWLING CHAMPIONS—See *Bowling Stars.*

NATIONAL GEOGRAPHIC REALLY WILD ANIMALS
Documentary; Color
September 16, 1995–
CBS Sat. 12:30–1 p.m. (9/16/95–)
Narrator: *Dudley Moore (as Spin the Globe)*

National Geographic magazine had been producing nature specials for television as early as 1964 on CBS, but it was not until 30 years later that it made a show specifically for children. This series, produced in 1993 and available on home video the following year, explained the lives of creatures from other countries to American children between the ages of 4 and 10. An animated character named Spin the Globe, which had arms protruding from its revolving Earth, added occasionally humorous but always informative narration. There also were a few interviews with experts, like Dr. Jane Goodall on chimpanzees, and songs especially for the program written and sung by Janis Liebhart and Alan Day. But the real attraction, as it was for any National Geographic TV show, was the spectacular footage of animals in their natural habitats.

NATIONAL LEAGUE FOOTBALL GAMES—See *NFL.*

NATIONAL PROFESSIONAL SOCCER LEAGUE—See Soccer.

NATURE OF THINGS, THE
Informational; B&W
May 22, 1949–March 28, 1954

NBC Sun. 5–5:15 p.m. (5/22/49–5/29/49)
NBC Sat. 5:30–5:45 p.m. (2/3/51–2/23/52; off summer)
NBC Sun. 1:15–1:30 p.m. (6/8/52–9/21/52)
NBC Sun. 12:45–1 p.m. (9/28/52–10/19/52)
NBC Sun. 3:15–3:30 p.m. (10/4/53–3/28/54)

Host: *Dr. Roy K. Marshall*

Airing from WPTZ Philadelphia, this entertaining science series offered programs on such varied topics as atomic energy, the fourth dimension, the human eye, and clocks. A typical example was a program on which scientist Dr. Marshall showed how a solution of dry ice and acetone at about 100 degrees Fahrenheit below zero made liquid mercury into metal, a piece of solder into a coil spring, and a rose frost-bitten. The series also aired in nighttime before and between its daytime runs from February 5, 1948–August 29, 1952.

Though not a ratings blockbuster, *The Nature of Things* was an agreeable time filler until it suddenly ended after six years on air. NBC gave no official reason, but it is known that Dr. Marshall pleaded no contest on July 1, 1954 to charges of sending obscene literature through the mails to teenage girls. He received five years' probation on the condition that he enter a state hospital for treatment. Dr. Marshall did no other network TV shows.

NAVY BASKETBALL—See College Basketball.

NEEDLE SHOP
Informational; B&W
January 12, 1949–February 18, 1949

DuMont Mon.–Fri. 3–3:15 p.m. (1/12/49–2/18/49)

Hostess: *Alice Burrows*

Alice Burrows dispensed sewing and decorating hints on this early DuMont effort, which first aired locally on WABD New York on November 1, 1948 from 2:30–2:45 p.m. The show later returned on WABD in late 1949 with Betty Hargan as Alice Burrows's assistant.

NEIGHBORS, THE
Game; Color
December 29, 1975–April 9, 1976

ABC Mon.–Fri. 2:30–3 p.m. (12/29/75–4/9/76)

Host: *Regis Philbin*

The Neighbors was a tacky daytime entry on which women used their knowledge of gossip about people on their block to win money (and despite what you may think, it was not a Chuck Barris Production, but one from Steve Carruthers

instead). In the first round, to win $25, two neighbors competed in matching a juicy tidbit with the person it was supposed to be about—either of them, or one of three other neighbors. In the next round, a player could win $100 by listening to a piece of gossip, then guessing which neighbor had said it. Most players came from the Los Angeles suburbs. This airing of dirty laundry did not distract viewers of *The Doctors* on NBC or *Guiding Light* on CBS, and it was gone within five months.

NEVER TOO YOUNG
Soap Opera; B&W
September 27, 1965–June 24, 1966

ABC Mon.–Fri. 4–4:30 p.m. (9/27/65–3/25/66)
ABC Mon.–Fri. 4–4:25 p.m. (3/28/66–6/24/66)

Cast:

Alfie	*David Watson*
Barbara	*Pat Connolly*
Chet	*Tony Dow*
Frank	*John Lupton*
Jo-Jo	*Tommy Rettig*
Joy	*Robin Grace*
Rhoda	*Patrice Wymore*
Tad	*Michael Blodgett*
Tim	*Dack Rambo*

ABC's attempt to attract the teenage market was this offbeat soap entry which had guest stars like Marvin Gaye, Johnny Rivers, and the Ramsey Lewis Trio stop by occasionally to sing at the local cafe hangout. The adolescents who starred included Chet, a race car driver who dated other girls to make his steady girl, Joy, jealous; Tad, a football player who faced a career-threatening injury; and Barbara, who upset her boyfriend Alfie by her meddlesome efforts to help him further his ambitions. Frank and Rhoda, the prime adults involved in the group, had their own unsteady relationship. The stories were supposed to take place in Malibu, but a Hollywood studio lot filled with sand provided what beach atmosphere there was.

NEW . . . , THE—See the following titles:
American Bandstand
Archie Show
Battlestars
Beatles
Card Sharks
Casper the Friendly Ghost
Divorce Court
Fantastic Four
Fat Albert and the Cosby Kids
Flintstone Comedy Show
High Rollers
Howdy Doody
Lucille Rivers Show
Mickey Mouse Club
Pink Panther

Price Is Right
Scooby-Doo
Tom and Jerry

NEW ADVENTURES OF . . . , THE—See the following titles:

Batman
Casper the Friendly Ghost
Madeline
Mighty Mouse Playhouse
Superman

•NEW ADVENTURES OF FLASH GORDON, THE

Cartoon; Color
September 22, 1979–September 10, 1983

NBC Sat. 11–11:30 a.m. (9/22/79–12/1/79)
NBC Sat. 11:30 a.m.–Noon (12/8/79–12/29/79)
NBC Sat. 12:30–1 p.m. (4/12/80–9/20/80)
NBC Sat. 12:30–1 p.m. (9/18/82–9/10/83)

Voices:

Dale Arden	Diane Pershing
Flash Gordon/Prince Barin	Robert Ridgely
King Thun	Ted Cassidy
King Vultan	Allan Melvin
Ming the Merciless/Dr. Hans Zarkov	Alan Oppenheimer

Flash Gordon, the hoary science fiction star of the 1930s in comics and movie serials, tried two media comebacks—one in 1979 and one in 1980—but both failed. The 1980 attempt was a live-action movie starring Sam J. Jones, who proved to be no Buster Crabbe (the 1930s film star). The other was this serialized NBC cartoon adventure in which our hero, accompanied by wise scientist Dr. Zarkov and love interest Dale Arden, fought the evil ruler Ming the Merciless and his robot army after they landed on his planet Mongo. Supporting them were the aliens King Thun, a somewhat humanoid ruler of the Lion People; Prince Barin, a Robin Hood look-alike and leader of Aboria; and King Vultan, head of the Hawkmen. NBC canceled the series in 1980, but reran it in 1982–83.

Flash Gordon also appeared in 1952 in a now-forgotten syndicated TV series produced in Europe with Steve Holland in the lead. And in an obscure 1986 syndicated cartoon titled *Defenders of the Earth*, Flash Gordon's son Rick fought Ming.

•NEW ADVENTURES OF GILLIGAN, THE

Cartoon; Color
September 7, 1974–September 4, 1977

ABC Sat. 9:30–10 a.m. (9/7/74–8/30/75)
ABC Sat. 10–10:30 a.m. (9/6/75–2/14/76)
ABC Sat. 9:30–10 a.m. (2/21/76–9/4/76)
ABC Sun. 10:30–11 a.m. (9/12/76–1/9/77)
ABC Sun. 11–11:30 a.m. (1/16/77–9/4/77)

Voices:

Gilligan	Bob Denver
Ginger Grant/Mary Ann Summers	Jane Webb
Lovey Howell	Natalie Schafer
Professor Roy Hinkley	Russell Johnson
Skipper (Jonas Grumby)	Alan Hale
Thurston Howell III	Jim Backus

When it ran on CBS in prime time from September 26, 1964–September 4, 1967, probably no one expected *Gilligan's Island* to become a big hit in repeats on local stations in the late 1960s and early 1970s. But the juvenile-market sitcom did just that, and in 1974 ABC attempted to mine this success with an animated recreation of the series. It used all voices of the original cast except for Tina Louise (Ginger) and Dawn Wells (Mary Ann), who were voiced by one woman who listed herself as "Jane Edwards" for the Mary Ann role. It's hard to imagine any TV viewer not familiar with the cast, but as the familiar theme song redone for the cartoon told viewers, it consisted of first mate Gilligan, his overweight buddy the Skipper, the pompous millionaire and his wife (Thurston and Lovey), the movie star (Ginger), the Professor, and Mary Ann, the common girl and probably the only cast member with a lick of sense. The plots were fairly similar. Most episodes had Gilligan fouling up in some way, often screwing up plans to get off the island, but the others seemed only to shrug it off rather than respond logically, by killing Gilligan. The only new character in *New Adventures* was Stubby, Gilligan's pet monkey.

After the successful cartoon run, the castaways reappeared in TV movies on NBC prime time in 1978, 1979, and 1981, with the full cast except Tina Louise. The series that will not die returned yet another time in animation form in 1982 (see *Gilligan's Planet*).

•NEW ADVENTURES OF WINNIE THE POOH

Cartoon; Color
September 10, 1988–

ABC Sat. 8:30–9:30 a.m. (9/10/88–9/2/89)
ABC Sat. 8–8:30 a.m. (9/8/90–1/30/93)
ABC Sat. Noon–12:30 p.m. (2/6/93–9/4/93)
ABC Sat. 8–8:30 a.m. (10/28/95–)

Voices:

Christopher Robin	Tim Hoskins
Eeyore	Peter Cullen
Gopher	Michael Gough
Kanga/Mom	Patty Parris
Owl	Hal Smith
Piglet	John Fiedler
Rabbit	Ken Sansom
Roo	Nicholas Melody
Tigger (1988–89)	Paul Winchell
Winnie the Pooh/Tigger (1989–)	Jim Cummings

The memorable denizens of Hundred Acre Woods, a magical forest created by author A. A. Milne in the 1920s with Pooh bear as its central character, received the Walt Disney treatment in three high-quality animated theatrical shorts from 1966–73 before the same studio used similar artwork in this 1988 series. Winnie the Pooh was a bear with "pale fawn fluff" for brains who loved honey (or, as the label on his jar of the stuff at home read, "hunny") and would do almost anything to get some. Pooh's childlike determination to make sure that every situation turned out well for him and his forest friends led him often to scratch his head and say, "Think, think, think" or "Oh, bother!" He was the beloved and amiable companion of a host of various woodland personalities, including peppy Tigger the tiger, timid Piglet, downbeat Eeyore the donkey, wise and somewhat pedantic Owl, and slurring Gopher. But he had perhaps his closest relationship with sole human regular, young Christopher Robin, who loved the "silly old bear," as he put it, despite the jams he and others often faced.

Each show typically had two episodes, with Robin in one of them, and the emphasis was on gentle humor, an approach that won it two Emmys for Best Children's Program. After its first season, the show joined another cartoon for 1989–90 (see *Gummi Bears),* then ran for three more years with a few new cartoons added in the mix. It returned in reruns in 1995 after *Madeline* (q.v.) bombed in the ratings after less than two months.

Pooh and his friends had appeared on television before 1988. Winnie the Pooh cartoons aired as TV specials beginning in 1970, and Pooh's first regular TV appearance was on a 1983 series for cable's Disney Channel called *Welcome to Pooh Corner.* The videotaped program featured costumed actors on indoor sets, and the only voice which appeared on the later cartoon series was that of Paul Winchell as Tigger. The channel continued to run this series weekday mornings into 1996, by which time it repeated the cartoon series daily as well.

NEW KIDS ON THE BLOCK, THE
Cartoon; Color
September 8, 1990–August 31, 1991

ABC Sat. 10:30–11 a.m. (9/8/90–7/27/91)
ABC Sat. 12:30–1 p.m. (8/3/91–8/31/91)

Voices:

Jonathan Knight	*Matt E. Mixer*
Jordan Knight	*Loren Lester*
Joe McIntyre	*Scott Menville*
Dick Scott	*Dave Fennoy*
Donnie Wahlberg	*David Coburn*
Danny Wood	*Brian Mitchell*

The teen sensations of 1989–91 (but a bane to most people not in their teens), the New Kids on the Block were a quintet of handsome pubescent boys from Boston who followed the path trod by the superior Jackson Five by amassing

a few number one hits on the *Billboard* Hot 100, like "Hanging Tough" and "Step By Step," before becoming an ABC cartoon. Like the Jacksons, Donnie, Jordan, Joe, Danny, and Jonathan (Jordan's younger brother) got into misadventures, which they straightened out by the end of each episode, plus performed a song or two. Group manager Dick Scott appeared as a character while also serving as one of the producers of this series. Other characters seen included Nikko, the group's pet dog, and Biscuit, or "B-Man," a bodyguard who protected the group from overzealous teenyboppers.

The "real" New Kids popped up in recorded bits on the show, such as the one showing them in concert doing "This One's for the Children," aired as part of a prime-time Christmas special on December 14, 1990. (Dick Scott, who approved all the cartoon's story lines, told *TV Guide* that his group could not provide their voices on the show because "it's too complicated.") But try as they might, the series garnered few fans outside the group's base of young girls below college age, and those demographics deterred so many advertisers that ABC had to can the show after a year. The group itself basically disbanded after 1992.

•NEW LOVE, AMERICAN STYLE, THE
Comic Anthology; Color
December 23, 1985–August 15, 1986

ABC Mon.–Fri. 11:30 a.m.–Noon (12/23/85–8/15/86)

Love, American Style was basically a collection of low-key filmed sketches which dealt in some manner with people in love. When ABC decided to revive the property, which ran on the network in nighttime September 26, 1969–January 11, 1974 and in daily repeats from 1971–74, it kept the same format, which used assorted celebrity guests, but now the playlets were videotaped rather than filmed. Basically, the series was a slightly modified version of the earlier show, though it dropped the familiar upbeat theme song sung by the Cowsills and ended each bit with a flurry of red valentines on screen rather than closing with a valentine-shaped freeze frame. But given that the show ran unsuccessfully against *The Price Is Right* on CBS, nobody really cared what about it was old and what was new.

NEW REVUE, THE
Variety; Color
January 8, 1954–June 18, 1954

CBS Fri. 5:30–6 p.m. (1/8/54–6/18/54)

Regulars: *Mike Wallace, Helene Ellis, Harrison Muller, Toni Southern, the Honeydreamers, the Norman Paris Trio*

One of the rare CBS 1950s color shows that did not promote that network's ill-fated color system was *The New Revue,* hosted by future investigative reporter Mike Wallace. Its regulars included dancers Ellis and Muller and music from the Honeydreamers and the Norman Paris Trio. Among the guest talent seen were Kaye Ballard and Janis Paige.

NEW SHMOO, THE

Cartoon; Color

September 22, 1979–December 1, 1979

NBC Sat. 10:30–11 a.m. (9/22/79–12/1/79)

Voices:

The Shmoo	*Frank Welker*
Nita	*Delores Cantu-Primo*
Billy Joe	*Chuck McCann*
Mickey	*Bill Idleson*

The Shmoo was probably new to most of his potential audience in 1979, since he was based on a character who had previously surfaced only in cartoonist Al Capp's "Li'l Abner" comic strip back in 1948. He was a pear-shaped entity who in this incarnation chased monsters with the assistance of a trio of novice reporters for Mighty Mysteries Comics. After bombing quickly, this show was absorbed into part of *The Flintstones Comedy Show* for the remainder of the 1979–80 season.

NEW YORK TIMES YOUTH FORUM, THE

Discussion; B&W

September 14, 1952–June 12, 1954

DuMont Sun. 5–6 p.m. (9/14/52–9/28/52)
DuMont Sat. 5:30–6:30 p.m. (10/2/53–6/12/54)

Moderator: *Dorothy Gordon*

The New York Times Youth Forum began in radio on WQXR New York in April 1943 with Dorothy Gordon as moderator. When it came to television, the radio show repeated the soundtrack of the TV show. A panel of teenagers discussed one topic per show with a celebrity or newsmaker in the first half, then an audience of adolescents asked the guest questions. Appearing on the first network show was General Carlos Romulo, the United Nations representative from the Philippines.

After June 1954, the show ran locally on WABD from October 3, 1954–June 15, 1958, then switched to WRCA as *The Dorothy Gordon Youth Forum*, where it remained as a fixture until May 11, 1970, the day Gordon died.

•NEWLYWED GAME, THE

Game; B&W and Color

July 11, 1966–December 20, 1974

ABC Mon.–Fri. 2–2:30 p.m. (7/11/66–12/20/74)

Host: *Bob Eubanks*

The Newlywed Game was a strained exercise wherein four recently married couples responded to queries designed to provoke double entendres and general titillation. While the same-sex members of each of the pairs waited offstage, their companions gave responses to match when they rejoined them. The couple's answers and reactions to, and disagreements over, questions like "What is your wife's pet name for you?" and "Who among your wife's girlfriends do you find most

exciting?" often caused the audience to hoot and howl. The original respondents held their answers, written in black ink on large white cards, face down on their laps, and invariably once on each show a player whose spouse answered wrong hit him or her over the head with the card. The first round had 5 points per question, the second had 10 points per question (there were four questions shown to the onstage spouses in this round, but one of them was saved for the final round), and the final round's question was worth 25 points. Winners received modest prizes like furniture.

Shortly after it debuted in 1966, *The Newlywed Game* became the first show to beat *Password* in the ratings. It remained ensconced in the same time slot throughout its network run, although rival *Days of Our Lives* on NBC usually topped it. ABC also added a nighttime version from January 7, 1967–August 30, 1971.

Bob Eubanks, who occasionally feigned being naive to provoke couples into making even bigger fools of themselves, virtually made a career out of this series. He hosted syndicated revivals of the series from 1977–80 and from 1985–88. Comedian Paul Rodriguez replaced him as host during the final season from 1988–89. In 1996 plans were announced to revive the show with *The Dating Game* in syndication under the title *The Dating/Newlywed Hour.*

NEWS GAL

Drama; B&W

October 20, 1951–October 27, 1951

ABC Sat. Noon–12:30 (10/20/51–10/27/51)

Cast:

Harriet Hildebrand	*Betty Furness*

Betty Furness portrayed reporter Harriet Hildebrand, "a sob sister for a press service" (*Variety*'s words) in this short-lived, critically drubbed drama. The show aired just twice between the cancellation of *Two Girls Named Smith* and the debut of *Betty Crocker*, then moved to ABC Sundays 7:30–8 p.m. from November 4–December 9, 1951, under the title *Byline.*

NICK KENNY SHOW, THE

Variety; B&W

March 22, 1952–May 17, 1952

NBC Sat. 3:45–4 p.m. (3/22/52–5/17/52)

Host: *Nick Kenny*

New York Daily Mirror columnist and erstwhile songwriter and poet Nick Kenny showed off his talents in this leisurely paced offering, supplemented with a few occasional guests. The show first ran on NBC late night (after 11 p.m.) from July 18, 1951–January 1, 1952.

Kenny did his first TV show on June 20, 1949 on independent station WPIX in New York. After the network run, Kenny came back in a thrice-weekly five-minute show on WABD New York on October 24, 1955, which by April 1956 had moved to Mondays from 11:15–11:30 p.m.

NOONTIME NEWS—See *Twelve O'Clock Headlines.*

NORTH AMERICAN SOCCER LEAGUE—See *Soccer.*

•NOT FOR WOMEN ONLY
Discussion; Color
1968–1979

Syndicated daily 30 minutes beginning July 1972

Host: *Barbara Walters (1972–76), Dr. Frank Field (1976–79), Polly Bergen (1976–77), Lynn Redgrave (1977–79)*

A panel of four experts discussed serious topical interests for anywhere from one day to a week on the ironically titled *Not for Women Only.* The title was ironic because the show had begun locally on WNBC New York under the title *For Women Only;* it was then hosted by *Today* architecture critic Aline Saarinen and aired after *Today* on that station. There also was a 15-minute series syndicated daily in 1953 under the same title with Amy Sedell as hostess and narrator. In 1971 another *Today* regular, Barbara Walters, took over for Saarinen when the latter became Paris bureau chief for NBC News, and the following year *Not for Women Only* began a successful run in syndication.

In 1976, with Walters having left *Today* for *The ABC Evening News,* the show replaced her with male and female co-hosts Dr. Frank Field and actress Polly Bergen. Bergen ended her stint on the show in January 1977, and English actress Lynn Redgrave replaced her for the remainder of the run.

NOTRE DAME FOOTBALL GAMES, THE
Sports; B&W and Color
September 24, 1949–

DuMont Sat. 2–4 p.m. (9/24/49–11/11/50; fall months only)
NBC Sat. 1 or 1:30 p.m.–Conclusion (9/7/91–; fall months only)

Announcers: *Mel Allen (1949–50), Jim Britt (1949–50), Dick Enberg (1991), Bill Walsh (1991), Tom Hammond (1992), Cris Collinsworth (1992)*

Among the various college football series which aired on the networks before the NCAA consolidated the games in 1956, one stood out from the crowd in special appeal. Powerhouse Notre Dame proved to be a perfect pick thanks to its popularity at the time and South Bend, Indiana, location, which made it easy for Chicago affiliates to carry the program. Beginning September 25, 1948, the ABC Midwest TV network consisting of Buffalo, Chicago, Cleveland, Detroit, Milwaukee, St. Louis, and Toledo telecast four of the school's home games from Chicago. The technology at the time allowed the contests to air only regionally.

In 1949 DuMont announced it would air all Notre Dame home games live on 16 stations in the East and Midwest, which made it the first full home schedule of football games seen on a network. On some stations games aired on film the following day due to a lack of cable connections. The network's Notre Dame coverage the following year had such avid fans that many stations took it over college games offered by the other networks at the same time. For six football games that season, the network had to substitute games from the Big 9 Division. Announcer Mel Allen had covered Columbia University's home football games for CBS the three previous seasons.

From September 27–November 29, 1953, ABC aired the university's games as an edited film Sunday nights from 7:45–9 p.m. with Harry Wismer and Ford Bond doing play-by-play. Later in the 1950s, the football games were taped for syndication and usually aired Sundays, the day after the competitions.

Nearly three decades later, with the NCAA's ability to limit coverage of college football curtailed by several court rulings, NBC brought back Notre Dame games as a regular feature with Bill Walsh as analyst and Dick Enberg doing play-by-play. The following year they were replaced in those positions by Chris Collinsworth and Tom Hammond, respectively. Thereafter, NBC preferred to use no regular announcers for the games.

NOTRE DAME SATURDAY
Sports; Color
September 7, 1991–November 9, 1991

NBC Sat. 1–1:30 p.m. (9/7/91–11/9/91)

Hosts: *Ahmad Rashad, Gayle Gardner*

This pregame show for NBC's first season of *Notre Dame Football Games* (q.v.) included a review of the week's college football scene and a preview of that day's contest.

NOW AND THEN
Informational; B&W
August 1, 1954–June 26, 1955

CBS Sun. 3–3:30 p.m. (8/1/54–9/5/54)
CBS Sun. 3–3:30 p.m. (1/16/55–6/26/55)

Host: *Dr. Frank Baxter*

University of Southern California professor of English literature Dr. Frank Baxter lectured on his field of expertise in this "egghead" series seen after *Face the Nation.*

•NOW YOU SEE IT
Game; Color
April 1, 1974–July 14, 1989

CBS Mon.–Fri. 11–11:30 a.m. (4/1/74–6/13/75)
CBS Mon.–Fri. 10:30–11 a.m. (4/3/89–7/14/89)

Host: *Jack Narz (1974–75), Chuck Henry (1989)*

Now You See It was a word search game. The first round had two pairs of players compete to be the first to locate words hidden in the puzzle by calling out the line and row number where the word started. The team which managed to do this most successfully after the first round split and played against each other, with that round's winner then taking on the previous day's winner to see who would make the bonus round. In the bonus round, the champ had to find 10 words in 60 seconds from a maze. Each word was worth $100, and if all 10 were found, a contestant won at least $5,000.

Fourteen years after its initial run, *Now You See It* returned to the CBS lineup with duos consisting of one contestant and one celebrity competing to find words. It lasted 15 weeks.

NUMBER PLEASE

Game; B&W

January 31, 1961–December 29, 1961

ABC Mon.–Fri. 12:30–1 p.m. (1/31/61–9/29/61)
ABC Mon.–Fri. 2–2:30 p.m. (10/2/61–12/29/61)

Host: *Bud Collyer*

Number Please was basically the game Hangman with digits used instead of letters. Two players alternated in calling out numbers on a board on his or her row of 20 spaces to see what letter was under the blank space beneath that number. Gradually a phrase involving a prize was revealed, and the first contestant to identify the phrase before all letters were revealed won the prize. Winners could continue to play more rounds for additional prizes and a $500 check.

Bud Collyer hosted the show three days after the cancellation of the other Mark Goodson–Bill Todman Production he oversaw, *Beat the Clock*. Goodson and Todman had sold this series to CBS in 1959 for a guaranteed daytime run of at least 26 weeks, but feeling uncertain about its potential, they stopped it from going on the network at that time.

NURSES, THE

Soap Opera; B&W

September 27, 1965–March 31, 1967

ABC Mon.–Fri. 2–2:30 p.m. (9/27/65–3/25/66)
ABC Mon.–Fri. 3:30–4 p.m. (3/28/66–3/31/67)

Cast:

Liz Thorpe, R.N.	Mary Fickett
Gail Lucas, R.N.	Melinda Plank
Donna Steele, R.N.	Carol Gainer
Pat Steele	Sally Gracie
Jake Steele	Richard McMurray
Mike	Darryl Wells
Martha	Joan Wetmore
Brenda McLeod (1965)	Patricia Hyland
Hugh "Mac" McLeod	Arthur Franz
Jamie McLeod	Judson Laire
Dr. John Crager	Nat Polen
Dr. Paul Fuller	Paul Stevens
Sandy Fergin	Mimi Turque
Ken Alexander (1965)	Nicholas Pryor

The Nurses brought only the setting, lead characters, and title of a nighttime CBS drama which aired September 27, 1962–September 7, 1965 to ABC daytime (that program became *The Doctors and the Nurses* in September 1964). Mary Fickett and Melinda Plank assumed the respective roles of veteran nurse Liz Thorpe and newcomer Gail Lucas at Alden Hospital in New York City, and their plights were far more tumultuous than the problems faced by the characters on CBS, although a mentor-student relationship remained.

On the early episodes, Gail planned to marry Ken Alexander (they called off the wedding in December 1965). Meanwhile, her pal, student nurse Donna Steele, had a witch of a mom in Pat, although dad Jake was not so bad. Donna and Gail found they had much in common, including Liz's maternal feelings for them. For example, Liz forbade Donna to see Mike, who was suspected of criminal activities by the police, and Mike's mother Martha put similar restrictions on him. Mixed in with this troubled staff were Brenda McLeod, a matriarch who faced several illnesses before dying three months after the debut; Jamie McLeod, who shared special memories with Liz; Dr. Paul Fuller, a psychiatrist who assisted Liz and dated Gail after her relationship with Ken faltered; Sandy Fergin, Gail's roommate; and Dr. John Crager.

Despite theoretically ideal scheduling (the show followed *General Hospital* from 1966–67), the daytime *Nurses* never generated enough enthusiasm to dent *The Edge of Night* on CBS and *You Don't Say* on NBC. ABC replaced it with *Dark Shadows*.

OBJECT IS, THE

Game; B&W

December 30, 1963–March 27, 1964

ABC Mon.–Fri. 11:30 a.m.–Noon (12/30/63–3/27/64)

Host: *Dick Clark*

Notable mainly as the first daytime game show hosted by Dick Clark (*American Bandstand* ended its Monday–Friday run on ABC a few months before this began), *The Object Is* employed a trio each of celebrities and contestants (two stars and contestants by the end of the run) trying to identify celebrities by giving as clues objects associated in some way with the personalities. The contestant winning the main game played a bonus round with one celebrity. Interestingly, the series' NBC competition, *Missing Links,* became its successor on ABC—with Dick Clark as the new host.

•ODDBALL COUPLE, THE
Cartoon; Color
September 9, 1975–September 3, 1977

ABC Sat. 11:30 a.m.–Noon (9/6/75–9/4/76)
ABC Sun. 11–11:30 a.m. (9/12/76–1/9/77)
ABC Sat. Noon–12:30 p.m. (1/15/77–9/3/77)

Voices:

Spiffy	Frank Nelson
Fleabag	Paul Winchell
Goldie	Joan Gerber

Two months after *The Odd Couple* ended five seasons as an ABC nighttime sitcom, this cartoon variant of the popular show (originally a Broadway comedy by Neil Simon) popped up on the network. Spiffy (the Felix Unger type) was a prissy feline who roomed with Fleabag (the Oscar Madison knockoff), a slobbish dog. Goldie was their secretary.

ODYSSEY
Children's; B&W
January 6, 1957–June 16, 1957

CBS Sun. 4–5 p.m. (1/6/57–3/24/57)
CBS Sun. 5–6 p.m. (4/14/57–6/16/57)

Host/Narrator: *Charles Collingwood*

Produced in cooperation with the American Association of Museums, this program for the teenage market concentrated on examining one historical event or cultural phenomenon per show, from the Stone Age to the Atomic Age. It employed both documentaries and dramatizations for such topics as the Salem witch trials of 1692, life in the Middle Ages, a look at modern art with guest Vincent Price, the 103rd birthday celebration of the great fictional sleuth Sherlock Holmes, and a review of 60 years of comic strips with artists Milton Caniff, Al Capp, Walt Kelly, Bill Mauldin, and Alan Saunders. Most shows were filmed, but a few were live.

OF ALL THINGS
Variety; B&W
July 23, 1956–August 24, 1956

CBS Mon.–Thu. 10–10:30 a.m. and Fri. 10–11:30 a.m. (7/23/56–8/24/56)

Cast: *Faye Emerson, Ilene Woods, Jack Haskell*

This unexceptional summer replacement for *The Garry Moore Show* had songs from Ilene Woods and Jack Haskell introduced by Faye Emerson. Like Moore's show, it went to 90 minutes Fridays to fill the slot left by the absence of *The Arthur Godfrey Show* following it, which didn't air on Fridays.

OH, KAY!
Variety; B&W
February 24, 1951–August 18, 1951

ABC Sat. 11–11:30 a.m. (2/24/51–8/18/51)

Regulars: *Kay Westfall, Jim Dimitri, Mary Ellen White, David LeWinter*

One of the more unusual network Saturday morning shows, *Oh, Kay!* was a live-from-Chicago variety series with a story line. Using an apartment setting, it had singer Kay Westfall as hostess joined by vocalist Jim Dimitri, pianist David LeWinter, and Mary Ellen White as Kay's "roommate." Between songs and the plot, Kay interviewed guests. *Oh, Kay!* alternated weekly with *The Faith Baldwin Theatre of Romance.*

•OKAY MOTHER
Game/Talk; B&W
December 12, 1949–July 6, 1951

DuMont Mon.–Fri. 1–1:30 p.m. (12/12/49–7/6/51)

Host: *Dennis James*

When early TV announcer Dennis James covered wrestling matches for DuMont in the late 1940s, he used the phrase, "Okay, Mother, that's a . . ." to describe holds to female viewers, who were presumably ignorant of the finer points of wrestling. The saying became the title of his daily TV series on WABD's pioneering daytime schedule on November 1, 1948, which went network a year later. Appropriately, the mostly female audience often yelled out "Okay, Dennis!" to attract the host's attention.

The show mixed games and discussions. For the former, audience members gave James a line which he had to provide a rhyming match for; if he failed, they won a prize, and a few of them were randomly selected by James to answer a "Mothergram," a quatrain about a mystery topic, for bigger awards. Then James acted out a domestic situation on "Problem Playhouse" and got audience members' reactions to the dilemma. James also talked with visiting authorities on family life and celebrities. Among the latter were Virginia Payne, radio's Ma Perkins (November 1, 1948); silent film star Constance Talmadge in her TV debut (December 9, 1949); and Dr. Allen B. DuMont, celebrating the show's network anniversary (December 12, 1950). James also read a letter from a home viewer he picked to represent the "Mother of the Day."

In 1950 *Variety* announced that James was to do a spoken-word album for Decca based on *Okay Mother.* After the show ended a year later, James did other daytime variety and game shows through the 1960s, including *The Dennis James Show* (q.v.).

OMNIBUS
Cultural/Various; B&W
November 8, 1952–April 16, 1961

CBS Sun. 4:30–6 p.m. (11/8/52–5/3/53)
CBS Sun. 5–6:30 p.m. (10/4/53–4/1/56; off summers)
NBC Sun. 4–5:30 p.m. (10/20/57–5/4/58)
NBC Sun. 4–5 p.m. (10/26/58–5/10/59)
NBC Sun. 5–6 p.m. (11/3/60–4/16/61)

Host: *Alistair Cooke*

Omnibus was the highbrow series against which all other TV anthology shows of the 1950s were judged. (It was also held up as a standard in later decades, but to a lesser degree.) Every element of it emanated class and high quality, from the dignified but not arch comments by host Alistair Cooke to the ambitious and wide-ranging slate of presentations. It was all backed by money from the Ford Foundation, and so was presented without advertisements, a rarity for a commercial show on a network.

Omnibus episodes were varied, ranging from those consisting of several different playlets and discussions to full 90-minute plays. In its first season alone it featured five films on the life of Abraham Lincoln (played by Royal Dano) as well a production of *La Bohème* commissioned especially for the show by the New York Metropolitan Opera. A show on December 28, 1952, used clips from Walt Disney's *Peter Pan* to show how animated cartoons were created, aired a filmed discussion with William Faulkner, and showed Leopold Stokowski giving a tour of an art gallery. You were just as likely to watch adaptations of plays, by, say, William Saroyan, Eugene Ionseco, or Samuel Beckett, as you were to see a documentary, like the three-part series on "American Trial by Jury" hosted by famed attorney Joseph Welch. Regardless of the content, the emphasis was always on giving viewers food for the mind rather than on simply filling up time as so many other series did.

Some *Omnibus* highlights include *Lord Byron's Love Letter,* a one-act Tennessee Williams play starring Ethel Barrymore in her TV dramatic debut (March 29, 1953); Fred Allen (and his Allen's Alley characters) reading and reenacting parts of his autobiography *Treadmill to Oblivion* (October 17, 1954); a production of the Greek classic *The Iliad* (April 3, 1955); *Salome,* starring Eartha Kitt with Patricia Neal and Martin Landau (December 18, 1955); Helen Hayes in a recreation of her starring role in the 1952 play *Mrs. McThing* (March 1958); and Gene Kelly in his TV debut in "Dancing: A Man's Game" with Edward Villella (December 21, 1958). Among other top names appearing on the series were Peter Ustinov (at least three performances), Eva Marie Saint, E. G. Marshall, Richard Kiley, Joseph Campanella, Ed Asner (an early TV appearance in 1958), and even one show with the comic duo of Mike Nichols and Elaine May.

The lofty reputation of *Omnibus* should not be overstated, however. Not all the efforts met with overwhelming critical approval, and some participants had doubts about their merits as well. As the production staff attempted to pare down Johann Strauss's *Die Fledermaus* to 62 minutes of music for the February 1, 1953 telecast, Metropolitan Opera tenor Charles Kullman, playing the male lead of Eisenstein, wailed to a *Variety* reporter, "What is this, a Shakespearean drama? I don't sing anymore, I just talk!" That particular attempt may indeed have been misguided, but considering how few TV series went to the trouble of even trying do what *Omnibus* did, one can easily forgive the occasional misfires.

Omnibus had a three-year run on Sunday afternoons on CBS, then aired from October 7, 1956–March 31, 1957 on ABC Sunday evenings. It returned to Sunday afternoons in the fall of 1957 on NBC, alternating with *Wide Wide World* in 1957–58 and then *Kaleidoscope* in 1958–59 in an hour format. Following a brief resumption in the fall of 1960 alternating with *Celebrity Golf,* it ended in 1961 after 166 shows. Some repeats were syndicated in half-hour form in 1956 under the title *Under the Sun,* with William Saroyan as host.

The program had two short-lived attempts as nighttime revivals on ABC, one as a series of specials from 1980–81 with various hosts and the other a special on May 26, 1988 hosted by Beverly Sills.

ON THE GO
Newsmagazine; B&W
April 27, 1959–July 8, 1960
CBS Mon.–Fri. 10–10:30 a.m. (4/27/59–11/13/59)
CBS Mon.–Fri. 10:30–11 a.m. (11/16/59–7/8/60)
Host: *Jack Linkletter*

Nearly a decade before Charles Kuralt began his "On the Road" segments for CBS News, the same network had a series using the exact theme, albeit on a smaller scale. *On the Go* had Jack Linkletter roam most of California (with some out-of-state side trips to locales like Las Vegas, Nevada) for unique sights and sounds. After five months of using four vehicles to get to locations, Linkletter and a crew of 11 rode in a $300,000, 20-ton, 40-foot-long Video Supercruiser, which held two videotape recording studios, four cameras able to tape up to 50 hours, and a 50-kilowatt generator. Most stories were on the lighter side, but CBS did censor a tape featuring a school for stripteasers.

For video enthusiasts wanting a copy of this program, good luck. In order to cut costs, the producers erased 200 shows (about $1 million worth of work) in the winter of 1960 to reuse the videotapes. There is no record of how many show tapes were left unaltered.

ON THE LINE WITH BOB CONSIDINE
News; B&W
January 21, 1951–January 5, 1952
NBC Sat. 5:45–6 p.m. (1/21/51–1/5/52)
Host: *Bob Considine*

INS syndicated news columnist Bob Considine started his "On the Line" column in papers in 1933, then transferred it to radio before coming to television in 1951. Here he gave an informal recap of the latest headlines and interviewed guests like Secretary of the Navy Francis Matthews and perennial Republican presidential candidate Harold Stassen. Following months on late Saturday afternoons, it moved to Tuesday nights, where it stayed from January 8, 1952–January 19, 1954, then switched to ABC Sunday nights from July 11–August 29, 1954.

After the TV series ended, the radio version continued daily on ABC through 1968, then moved to be part of NBC radio's *Monitor* series. By 1971 the show had become a nightly five-minute segment on the Mutual radio network. Considine was still reporting and doing his newspaper column when he died on September 25, 1975.

ON YOUR ACCOUNT

Game; B&W and Color
June 8, 1953–March 30, 1956

NBC Mon.–Fri. 4–4:30 p.m. (6/8/53–9/25/53)
NBC Mon.–Fri. 4:30–5 p.m. (9/28/53–7/2/54)
CBS Mon.–Fri. 4:30–5 p.m. (7/5/54–3/30/56)

Host: *Win Elliot (6/8/53–10/1/54), Dennis James (10/4/54–3/30/56)*

On Your Account offered those wanting to raise money for a good cause a chance to do so via a round of questions. Contestants answered questions worth $10 to $40 each, and each correct answer added the money attached to the question to that day's jackpot. The studio audience voted on which of each day's players should get a chance to answer the final question and claim the jackpot if correct.

In the fall of 1954, following a switch of networks, the show restricted competition for its bank accounts to servicemen only. By the next year the "good cause" angle was deemphasized, and higher amounts for questions ($25 to $100) and a bigger jackpot ($1,500 plus merchandise) were offered. The show was replaced by *The Edge of Night*.

ON YOUR MARK

Children's; B&W
September 23, 1961–December 30, 1961

ABC Sat. 11–11:30 a.m. (9/23/61–12/30/61)

Host/Executive Producer: *Sonny Fox*

On Your Mark had a trio of kids ages 9 to 13 compete for prizes in contests involving skills needed for each show's career objective. The debut, for example, involved games related to becoming an astronaut. This New York–based show was the first ABC program to air before noon Saturdays since *The Uncle Al Show* in 1959.

ONE IN A MILLION

Game; B&W
April 10, 1967–June 16, 1967

ABC Mon.–Fri. 11:30 a.m.–Noon (4/10/67–6/16/67)

Host: *Danny O'Neil*

This Merv Griffin production was a run-of-the-mill quiz where a player had to guess whether four panelists were lying about their careers. Each correct guess gave the player more clues to determine who the "prime panelist" was (the one who was "one in a million" in a category). A player successful in that mission received $250 per game, and two games were played per show. It aired from New York.

•ONE LIFE TO LIVE

Soap Opera; Color
July 15, 1968–

ABC Mon.–Fri. 3:30–4 p.m. (7/15/68–7/23/76)
ABC Mon.–Fri. 2:30–3:15 p.m. (7/26/76–1/13/78)
ABC Mon.–Fri. 2–3 p.m. (1/16/78–)

Cast:

Victoria Lord (1968–70)	*Gillian Spencer*
Victoria Lord (1970)	*Joanne Dorian*
Victoria Lord (1971–)	*Erika Slezak*
Victor Lord (1968–74)	*Ernest Graves*
Victor Lord (1974–76)	*Shepperd Strudwick*
Victor Lord (1985)	*Tom O'Rourke*
Victor Lord (1987)	*Les Tremayne*
Meredith Lord (1968–69)	*Trish Van Devere*
Meredith Lord (1969–73, 1987)	*Lynn Benesch*
Dr. Larry Wolek (1968)	*Paul Tulley*
Dr. Larry Wolek (1969)	*James Storm*
Dr. Larry Wolek (1969–)	*Michael Storm*
Anna Wolek (1968–77)	*Doris Belack*
Anna Wolek (1977–78)	*Kathleen Maguire*
Anna Wolek (1978–82)	*Phyllis Behar*
Vince Wolek (1968–75, 1987)	*Antony Ponzini*
Vince Wolek (1975–77)	*Jordan Charney*
Vince Wolek (1977–81)	*Michael Ingram*
Joe Riley (1968–70, 1972–79, 1986–87)/Thomas Dennison (1986–87 at least)	*Lee Patterson*
Eileen Riley (1968–72)	*Patricia Roe*
Eileen Riley (1972–76)	*Alice Hirson*
Dr. Jim Craig (1968–69)	*Robert Milli*
Dr. Jim Craig (1969–81)	*Nat Polen*
Carla Gray (1968–81, 1983–85)	*Ellen Holly*
Sadie Gray (1968–86)	*Lillian Hayman*
Sadie Gray (1971, temporary replacement)	*Esther Rolle*
Dr. Marcus Polk (1968)	*Donald Moffat*
Dr. Marcus Polk (1969–74)	*Norman Rose*
Dr. Marcus Polk (1985–86, 1987)	*James Douglas*
Dave Siegel (1968–72)	*Allan Miller*
Nurse Karen Martin Wolek (1968–70)	*Niki Flacks*
Lt. Ted/Jack Neal (1968–70)	*Jack Crowder*
Lt. Ted/Jack Neal (1969, temporary replacement)	*Lon Sutton*
Dr. Price Trainor (1968)	*Thurman Scott*
Dr. Price Trainor (1968–70)	*Peter DeAnda*
Cathy Craig (1969)	*Catherine Burns*
Cathy Craig (1969–71)	*Amy Levitt*
Cathy Craig (1971–72)	*Jane Alice Brandon*
Cathy Craig (1972–76)	*Dorrie Kavanaugh*
Cathy Craig (1976–78)	*Jennifer Harmon*
Julie Siegel (1969–74)	*Lee Warrick*
Julie Siegel (1974–76)	*Leonie Norton*
Bert Skelly (1969)	*Wayne Jones*

Bert Skelly (1969–72)
Tom Edwards (1969–71)
Millie Parks (1969–70)
Steve Burke (1970–75)
Jack Lawson (1970–72)
Jack Lawson (1972–73)
Tim Siegel (1970–71)
Tim Siegel (1975–76)
Marcy Wade (1970–71)
Dr. Mark Toland (1971–75)
Ed Hall (1972–89)
Wanda Webb (1972–76,
    1980–at least 1993)
Wanda Webb (1977–79)
Dr. Dorian Cramer (1973–77)
Dr. Dorian Cramer (1977–79)
Dr. Dorian Cramer (1979–87,
    1993–)
Dr. Dorian Cramer (1987–93)
Melinda Cramer (1973–74)
Melinda Cramer (1977–81, 1983)
Melinda Cramer (1987–)
Joshua Hall (1973–76)
Joshua Hall (1977)
Joshua Hall (1985–86)
Hubcap (1973–74)
Danny Wolek (1974–76)
Danny Wolek (1976–79)
Danny Wolek (1983–84)
Danny Wolek (1983, 1985)
Danny Wolek (1984)
Danny Wolek (1986)
Ben Farmer (1974–75)
Susan Barry (1974–75)
Matt McAllister (1974–75)
John Douglas (1974–75)
Rachel Wilson (1974)
Jenny Wolek (1975–78)
Jenny Wolek (1978–86)
Tony Lord (1975–77)
Tony Lord (1977–79, 1987)
Tony Lord (1981–83)
Patricia Ashley (1975–83)/
    Maggie Ashley (1979)
Brad Vernon (1976–78)
Brad Vernon (1978–86)
Dr. Will Vernon (1976–77)
Dr. Will Vernon (1977)
Dr. Will Vernon (1977–84)
Samantha Vernon (1976–81)
Samantha Vernon (1979;
    temporary replacement)
Samantha Vernon (1981–84)
Karen Wolek (1976–77)
Karen Wolek (1977–83)
Dr. Peter Jansen (1976–79, 1987)

Herb Davis
Joe Gallison
Millee Taggart
Bernard Grant
David Snell
Jack Ryland
William Cox
Tom Berenger
Francesca James
Tommy Lee Jones
Al Freeman Jr.

Marilyn Chris
Lee Lawson
Nancy Pinkerton
Claire Malis

Robin Strasser
Elaine Princi
Patricia Pearcy
Jane Badler
Sharon Gabet
Laurence Fishburne
Todd Davis
Guy Davis
Scott Jacoby
Neail Holland
Eddie Moran
Steven Culp
Timothy Owen
Ted Demers
Joshua Cox
Rod Browning
Lisa Richards
Vance Jefferis
Donald Madden
Nancy Barrett
Katherine Glass
Brynn Thayer
George Reinholt
Phillip MacHale
Chip Lucia

Jacqueline Courtney
Jameson Parker
Steve Fletcher
Farley Granger
Bernie McInerney
Anthony George
Julie Montgomery

Susan Keith
Dorian LoPinto
Kathryn Breech
Judith Light
Jeffrey David Pomerantz

Dr. Peter Jansen (1980)
Dr. Peter Jansen (1980–82)
Brian Kendall (1976–78)
Naomi Vernon (1976–77)
Lana McClain (1976–77)
Marco Dane (1977–86, 1989)
Rebecca Lee Abbott (1977–78)
Rebecca Lee Abbott (1979–86)
Richard Abbott (1977–78)
Richard Abbott (1980)
Richard Abbott (1980–81)
Richard Abbott (1986)
Paul Kendall (1977–79)
Talbot Huddleston (1977–78)
Tina Clayton (1978–81, 1985–90)
Tina Clayton (1984)
Tina Clayton (1985)
Tina Clayton (1990–93 at least)
Tina Clayton (at least 1994–)
Herb Callison (1978–)
Edwina Lewis (1978–85)
Ina Hopkins (1978–84)
Nancy Snyder (1978–83)
Dr. Jack Scott (1978–80)
Gretel Cummings (1978–80)
Paul Martin (1978–79, 1982)
Adam Brewster (1978–79)
Greg Huddleston (1978–79)
Adele Huddleston (1978–79)
Dick Grant (1978, 1983)
Asa Buchanan (1979–)
Clint Buchanan (1979–)
Bo Buchanan (1979–86, 1987–)
Chuck Wilson (1979–87 at least)
Mimi King (1979–82, 1985–86)
Dr. Ivan Kipling (1979–82, 1985)
Faith Kipling (1979–80)
Mick Gordon (1979–80)
Fran Gordon (1979)
Fran Gordon (1980)
Lt. Rafe Garrison (1980–88
    at least)
Johnny Drummond (1980–84)
Chip Warren (1980, 1981, 1983)
Marcello Salta (1980–82)
Olympia Buchanan (1980–81)
Ted Clayton (1980–81)
Ted Clayton (1981)
Cassie Callison (1981–83)
Cassie Callison (1983–86)
Cassie Callison (1986–88 at least)
Cassie Callison (1991–)
Lucinda Schenk (1981–84)
Steve Piermont (1981)
Steve Piermont (1981–82)
Delilah Ralston (1982–)

Robert Burton
Denny Albee
Stephen Austin
Teri Keane
Jacklyn Zeman
Gerald Anthony
Jill Voight
Mary Gordon Murray
Luke Reilly
Keith Langsdale
Robert Gribbon
Jeffrey Byron
Tom Fuccello
Byron Sanders
Andrea Evans
Kelli Maroney
Marsha Clark
Karen Witter
Krista Tesreau
Anthony Call
Margaret Klenck
Sally Gracie
Katrina Karr
Arthur Burghardt
Linda Dano
William Mooney
John Mansfield
Paul Joynt
Lori March
A. C. Weary
Philip Carey
Clint Richie
Robert S. Woods
Jeremy Slate
Kristen Meadows
Jack Betts
Mary Linda Rapeleye
James McDonnell
Barbara Britton
Willi Burke

Ken Meeker
Wayne Massey
Sammy Davis, Jr.
Stephen Schnetzer
Taina Elg
Keith Charles
Mark Goddard
Cusi Cram
Ava Haddad
Holly Gagnier
Laura Bonarrigo
Arlene Dahl
Richard K. Weber
Robert Desiderio
Shelly Burch

Gary Corelli (1982–85)	Jeff Fahey	Cyndy London (1987–88 at least)	Cynthia Vance
Drew Ralston (1982–83)	Matthew Ashford	Lee Halpern (1987–88)	Janet Zarish
Laurel Chapin (1983–85)	Janice Lynde	Virgil/Gilbert Lange (1987–88	
David Reynolds (1983–86)	Michael Zaslow	at least)	John Fiedler
Simon Warfield (1983–84)	Tim Hart	Geoffrey McGrath (1987–88	
Alec Lowndes (1983–84)	Roger Hill	at least)	Don Fischer
Courtney Wright (1983–84)	Phylicia Ayers-Allen (Rashad)	Donald LaMarr (1987–88 at least)	Jared Martin
		Renee Devine (1987–89 at least)	Phyllis Newman
Anthony Makana (1983–84)	Nicolas Coster	Renee Devine (at least 1992–)	Patricia Elliott
Maxie McDermott (1983–84)	Christine Ebersole	Sarah Gordon (1987–88 at least)	Jensen Buchanan
Didi O'Neill (1984–87)	Barbara Truetelaar	Sarah Gordon (1991–92)	Grace Phillips
Alex Crown (1984–85)/Sloan		Rob Coronal (at least 1988)	Mark Arnold
Carpenter (1993–95)	Roy Thinnes	Joanna Leighton (at least)	Roma Downey
Rob Conoral (1984–86)	Ted Marcoux	Megan (1988–92)	Jessica Tuck
Connie O'Neill (1984–85)	Liz Keifer	Jack (1989–90 at least)	Jim Wlcek
Connie O'Neill (1985–86)	Terry Donahue	Spring Skye (at least 1989)	Sharon Schlarth
Joy O'Neill (1984–85)	Kristen Vigard	Gabrielle (at least 1990)	Fiona Hutchinson
Joy O'Neill (1985–86)	Julie Ann Johnson	Prince Raymond (at least 1990)	Robert Westenberg
Harry O'Neill (1984)	Arlen Dean Snyder	Carlo Hesser (1990–93)/	
Harry O'Neill (1984–85)	Frank Converse	Mortimer Bern (1993)	Thom Christopher
Trent Chapin (1984–85)	David Beecroft	Charlotte Hesser, bad girl	
Michelle Boudin (1984–85)	Dana Barron	(1990–91 at least)	Audrey Landers
Jinx Rollins (1984–85)	Elizabeth Burrelle	Hunter Guthrie, a director	
Aristotle Descamedes (1984–85)	Steven Hill	(1990–91 at least)	Leonard Stabb
Brian Beckett (1984–85)	Grainger Hines	Jake Harrison (at least 1990)	Joe Lando
Ken Romak (1984–85)	Dean Hamilton	Troy Nichols (1991–93 at least)	Terry Alexander
Jesse Wilde (1984–85)	John Vickery	Jason Webb (1991–93 at least)	Mark Brettschneider
Jack Simmons (1985–87 at least)	Michael Callan	Sheila Price (at least	
Tracy James (1985–87)	Kristen Allen	1991–at least 1993)	Valarie Pettiford
Pete O'Neill (1985–87)	James O'Sullivan	Lee Ann (at least 1991–at	
Pamela Stuart, a teacher (1985–87)	Christine Jones	least 1992)	Yasmine Bleeth
Mitchell Laurence (1985–87)	Roscoe Born	Alex Olanov (1991–)	Tonja Walker
Michael James Woodward		D.A. Hank "the Cannon"	
(1985–86)	Grant Goodeve	Gannon (1992–)	Nathan Purdee
Lisa Barron (1985–86)	Laura Carrington	Nora Gannon (1992–)	Hillary Bailey Smith
Gulietta (1985–86)	Fabiano Udenio	Rev. Andrew Carpenter (1992–)	Wortham Krimmer
Clover Wilde (1985–86)	Pamela Shoemaker	Billy Douglas (at least 1992)	Ryan Phillipe
Cord Roberts (1986–)	John Loprieno	Rick Mitchell (at least 1992)	Joe Fisko
Mari Lynn Dennison (1986–88		Joey Buchanan (at least 1991–93)	Chris McKenna
at least)	Tammy Amerson	Luna Moody, New Age guru	
Jon Russell (1986–87 at least)	John Martin	(at least 1991–)	Susan Batten
Elizabeth Sanders (1986–87		Jessica Buchanan (at least 1991–)	Erin Torpey
at least)	Lois Kibbee	Rodi (1992 at least)	Latanya Richardson
Kate Sanders (1986–87 at least)	Marcia Cross	Marty Saybrooke (1992–)	Susan Haskell
Jamie Sanders (1986–87 at least)	Mark Philpot	Todd Lord (1993–)	Roger Howarth
Judith Sanders (1986–87)	Louise Sorel	Rebecca (at least 1994–)	Reiko Aylesworth
Charles Sanders (1986–87)	Peter Brown	Blair Manning (at least 1995–)	Kassie Wesley
Maria Roberts (1986–87)	BarBara Luna	Christian Vega (1995–)	Yorlin Madera
Allison Perkins (1986–87)	Barbara Garrick	Antonio Vega, ex-con and	
Rick Gardner (1986–87)	Richard Grieco	gang leader (1995–)	Kamar De Los Reyes
Max Holden (1987–89 at			
least, 1992–)	James De Paiva		
Max Holden (1990–91)	Nicholas Walker		
Steve Holden (1987–88 at least)	Russ Anderson		
Gabrielle Medina (1987–89			
at least)	Fiona Hutchison		

After writing for nine years on *Guiding Light* and two years on *Another World*, Agnes Nixon left soap packager Procter & Gamble to be an independent packager. Her first sell involved Philadelphia families living on opposite sides of the track under the title *Between Heaven and Hell*. ABC bought it and settled on the less lurid name of *One Life to Live,* and its success paved the way for future soaps by the ABC-Nixon combination, including *All My Children* and *Loving.*

When it debuted, the show was set in the fictional Philadelphia suburb of Llanview, where Victoria Lord, also known as Vicki, was connected to most of the other main characters. She was the daughter of newspaper mogul Victor Lord, who demanded so much out of her that she developed a second personality, "Nikki Smith," a rather sluttish barfly type, completely different from Vicki. Naturally, this behavior baffled her boyfriend, reporter Joe Riley, until psychiatrist Dr. Marcus Polk cured her—only temporarily, as it turned out. But after marrying Joe, Vicki was faced with tragedy when he was reported dead, and she wed executive Steven Burke, who beat a murder rap (he was accused of killing Marcy Wade). As with all soap car-crash victims, Joe turned out only to have amnesia, and he had an affair with waitress Wanda Webb until he was hospitalized and his real identity was revealed. Poor Vicki had a difficult choice, but she divorced Steven so she could return to being Joe's bride.

Vicki's younger sister Meredith wed Dr. Larry Wolek, a man whom Victor Lord did not approve of for a son-in-law. Larry was a struggling doctor who earlier had been forced into marriage by devious Nurse Karen Martin, and Meredith had been engaged to Tom Edwards before meeting Larry. Meredith had a difficult pregnancy, and only one of her twins survived, Danny Wolek. The suffering engendered by her various maladies caused Meredith to fall into such extreme grief that famed psychiatrist Dr. Joyce Brothers, playing herself in guest spots in 1972, became Meredith's counselor. Later a robbery resulted in Meredith's death. Meanwhile, Larry's brother Vince, a former paramour of "Nikki's" and fiancé of Millie Parks, married Wanda Webb, while his sister Anna wed Dr. James Craig and became stepmother to his drug-addicted daughter Cathy. In 1970 the show recorded scenes on location of actual drug addicts and recovering addicts in therapy sessions at New York City's Odyssey House, where Cathy and her dad came for family treatment.

Dr. Craig had earlier had an affair with his secretary Carla Gray, a light-skinned African-American who denied her racial origins to the point of ignoring her mother Sadie, though that did not stop her from dating Dr. Pryce Trainor. But when she wed black Lt. Ed Hall, she finally acknowledged her heritage, and they adopted and tried to reform the troubled youth Joshua West.

Joe Riley's sister Eileen and her Jewish husband Dave Siegel raised Timmy and Julie, the latter rescued from a misguided fling with Jack Lawson by Dr. Mark Toland. Julie's marriage to Mark suffered because she was a cold fish, so he found his sexual outlet with newcomer Dr. Dorian Cramer, who lived with her mentally ill sister Melinda, who knew about the affair. Dorian was to become a pivotal player in Llanview for the next few decades.

In the mid-1970s there was an influx of new characters and dramatic developments. Terminally ill Rachel Wilson begged Dr. Larry Wolek to commit euthanasia on her over the objections of her husband Ben Farmer, who hadn't given up on quack cures. When Rachel was found dead of an overdose, Larry was convicted of the crime; but Dorian and Mark later acknowledged they had done the deed, which led to Dorian being fired. Dorian's sister Melinda broke down and was put in a sanitarium, and Mark fled town. Mark later came back and plotted with Dorian to blackmail Vicki until Mark was found dead. Tim Siegel confessed to the murder, but as she was dying, alcoholic nurse Susan Barry revealed that she had killed Mark accidentally in a struggle.

Mark had been threatening Vicki with the knowledge that Joe Riley was the father of Cathy Craig's daughter Megan, who died in an accident. Dorian then told Joe the truth, and he left Vicki. Dorian also wormed her way into the affections of Dorian's father Victor, who was recuperating from a heart attack and dealing with the arrival of his rebellious illegitimate son Tony Harris Lord.

Eileen, who became a drug addict after her husband Dave died, begged her son Timmy not to see Jenny Wolek. But it was Karen Wolek who caused the show's greatest drama. On March 6, 1979, in an intense performance by actress Judith Light, Karen broke down on the witness stand under Herb Callison's interrogation and revealed she was a housewife hooker, in order to exonerate Vicki Riley, who was on trial for the murder of Marco Dane. (Karen knew that one of her clients, Talbot Huddleston, was the real murderer. In another twist, however, it turned out that Talbot had actually killed Marco's look-alike brother, Marlo, and Marco then assumed Marlo's identity.)

In the early to mid-1980s the Buchanan family from Texas arrived and began to dominate the plots. Vicki married Clint, Bo romanced Pat and Delilah, and grumpy, shifty Asa generally tried to bully his way around everyone and everything. Also making an impact was Vicki's mischievous half-sister Tina, who bought her hunky husband Cord a Caribbean island to impress him. Tina had the most incredible adventures of all during the 1980s, including being presumed dead, going down a waterfall in South America, bearing her baby among the tribespeople who had saved her, and finally fleeing to Venice, where she pretended to be a nun to infiltrate a convent, in an effort to get her infant back!

Among the others who arrived in the mid- to late 1980s were Joe Riley's twin brother Thomas Dennison (both played by Lee Patterson); rebel ski jock Rick Gardner; Lee Halpern, a murder victim; Charles Sanders III, who was involved with Maria Roberts; Renee Divine, an ex–Las Vegas madam; Kate Sanders, a woman who planned to wed Cord until Tina returned alive; and Sarah Gordon, Clint's therapist, who had an affair with his cousin Rafe Garretson. Among the main love triangles, Gabrielle was obsessed with Max while wed to his brother Steve, and Joanna Leighton bothered her old flame Rob Coronal, who was Cassie's ex-husband but still had the hots for her and her aunt Melinda Kramer.

The most important residents of Llanview on One Life to Live *in 1976 were, clockwise from top left, Dr. Peter Janssen (played by Jeffrey Pomerantz), Anna Craig (Doris Belack), Dr. Jim Craig (Nat Polen), Jenny Wolek (Kathy Glass), Dorian Lord (Nancy Pinkerton), Dr. Will Vernon (Farley Granger), Vicki Riley (Erika Slezak), and Joe Riley (Lee Patterson).*

In the late 1980s the show began to be marked by extravagantly bizarre plots. In 1986 there was Devil's Claw Island and the mad Colonel Dimitri, who planned to sell an anti–missile control system to foreign powers. The next year Vicki's marriage collapsed and she developed a potentially fatal brain aneurysm which caused amnesia. The operation on the aneurysm caused her to start seeing dead town residents in a heavenlike world. Then in 1988 the show featured flashbacks to the western world of Buchanan City 100 years earlier, which originated in the mind of Clint, who had received a blow to the head. Most of the cast played their ancestors (for example, Erika Slezak played her great grandmother Virginia Fletcher), but there were some new faces, like a saloon queen played by Loyita Chapel.

Continuing in this fantastical vein, in 1988–89 came *Fraternity Row,* a soap within the soap wherein Megan the actress played sisters Roxanne and Ruby while having the hots for the show's producer Max, whose previous experience was being a cowhand in Argentina. (Jack, the other star, had previously been a mechanic.) Megan also had to deal with the return of Marco Dane and the rivalry from Spring Skye. But the topper of them all had to be the ridiculous "Eterna the lost underground city" in early 1989, wherein Vicki discovered a daughter she never knew she had, among other silly developments.

In 1989 Bo was framed for murder while his wayward cousin Austin romanced Bo's sweetie Sarah. Also, Gabrielle switched Brenda's baby, which had undergone radiation poisoning in the womb and was delivered prematurely by C-section while Brenda was comatose, and Tina became determined to find the crown jewels of Mendorra even though it might hurt her and Cord. Renee Devine, an ex-madam and Asa's lover, made her appearance.

The following year featured the horny antics of Max and Gabrielle and Carlo Hesser's drug dealing. In 1991 lawyer turned police commissioner and widower Troy Nichols went nuts for Sheila Price, Bo wed Cassie after being stalked by crazy Alex Olanov (who then fell in love with fellow villain Carlo Hesser), and the Llanfair mansion burned down with Max, Lee Ann, and Jessica inside.

The show began to dabble in more socially relevant themes in 1992 thanks to the ideas of producer Linda Gottlieb. There was Dorian's intense affair with young long-haired blond rebel Jason Webb, a victim of abuse. Megan went into a coma from lupus and died onscreen (a rarity in the soap world). Billy Douglas, a high school senior, struggled with his homosexuality amid rumors that the Rev. Andrew Carpenter was gay (he wasn't; in fact, he slept with Cassie Buchanan). Billy met Rick Mitchell on Christmas Eve that year and the two started dating.

In 1993 the surprise was that actor Thom Christopher, whose character Carlo had supposedly been murdered, came back playing jewel expert Mortimer Bern. The next year Vicki had an affair with Sloan Carpenter while Clint was gone, and Bo Buchanan and Nora Gannon became a hot item. Nora, whose ex-hubby was black attorney Hank Gannon, survived blindness and a stalker. Also hot were Max and nutty Luna, and Asa and Alex.

The next year, Vicki lost her homophobic hubby Sloan to cancer, and some new personalities emerged—Tommy, a teenager, and Jean Randolph, a socialite. Vicki also found her son having an affair with Dorian. Fourteen-year-old Jessica Buchanan became interested in Christian Vega, a boy from East Llanview, the lower-class side of town, and ex-rapist Todd Lord left town after marrying Blair Manning. Todd had by 1994 redeemed himself by saving three people, including his former rape victim Marty Saybrooke, and survived several attempts on his life. But his "redemption" remained controversial, even for the actor playing him, who did not like the idea of a rapist becoming a hero. At press time, however, the character and actor returned to the show.

But the biggest shocker was Victoria's learning that it was her other personality, Nikki, who had killed her father Victor in 1976, not Dorian, as Victoria had long suspected. And if you think that meant that Dorian and Vicki would reconcile after more than two decades of enmity, then you obviously need a crash course in TV soap operas.

ONE MAN'S FAMILY
Soap Opera; B&W
March 1, 1954–April 1, 1955

NBC Mon.–Fri. 10:30–10:45 a.m. (3/1/54–7/2/54)
NBC Mon.–Fri. 3–3:15 p.m. (7/5/54–8/27/54)
NBC Mon.–Fri. 3:30–3:45 p.m. (8/30/54–4/1/55)

Cast:

Henry Barbour	Theodore van Eltz
Fanny Barbour	Mary Adams
Hazel Barbour	Linda Leighton
Jack Barbour	Martin Dean
Clifford Barbour	James Lee
Paul Barbour	Russell Thorson
Claudia Barbour	Anne Whitfield
Johnny Roberts	Jack Edwards
Johnny MacPherson	Glen Vernon
Joe Yarbrough	Roy Engel
Beth Holly	Lois Hall
Bill Herbert	Les Tremayne
Dr. Fred Thompson (1955)	Emerson Treacy

One Man's Family first came to television on NBC nighttime from November 4, 1949–June 21, 1952. Two years later the network tried it as a daytime serial with even less success. The failure of both was rather shocking, given the series' long run (May 13, 1932–May 8, 1959) on NBC radio, where its fans considered it an audio classic. Both TV failures might have due to the fact that producers inexplicably decided viewers needed to see the story reenacted from the start rather than picked up from the current radio story.

All versions revolved around Henry Barbour, a rather stuffy, old-fashioned broker, his wife Fanny, and their children (in descending chronological order) Paul, Hazel, fraternal twins Claudia and Cliff, and Jack, all living in the Sea Cliff section of San Francisco. In the 1954 version, Claudia figured prominently in the story lines. Her husband Johnny Roberts, along with Joe Yarbrough, spent much of 1954 fighting for the "Nationalists" in an Asian country, while Claudia had to wrestle with her own conflicts over dating seaman Johnny MacPherson, a romance which did not thrill stodgy Henry. Claudia's dilemma with the two Johnnies ended with her hubby and Joe returning home safely before the former died in an accident, leaving her free to wed MacPherson. Less problematic were the romance between Bill Herbert and Hazel, which began in October and culminated in a wedding before the series ended, and the steady relationship between Beth Holly and Paul.

Some of the daytime series regulars had been involved in the other renditions of *One Man's Family*. Russell Thorson (Paul) and Les Tremayne (Bill) played the same characters in the 1949–52 TV show, while Anne Whitfield had the oddest crossover of all—she played Penelope, the daughter of her TV character, on the radio program. And going the opposite direction, Thorson and Mary Adams (Fanny) assumed their TV roles on radio in 1955 and 1956 respectively.

In 1965 sponsor General Foods made an abortive effort to relaunch the show as a daily serial on NBC. However, NBC tried another entry instead—*Days of Our Lives*.

ONE OF A KIND
Documentary; B&W
January 12, 1964–March 29, 1964

CBS Sun. 4–5 p.m. (1/12/64–3/29/64)

Host: *Harry Reasoner*

Promoted as promising unique approaches to such subjects as the arts and sciences, *One of a Kind* usually consisted of documentaries done in conjunction with CBS News and various universities and their faculties, such as a comparison of two generations of Ohio State graduates. A notable exception was the debut, "A Bird's-Eye View of America," which was shot from a helicopter. Its writer and producer Andy Rooney later used the same technique for his wry essays on the CBS prime-time newsmagazine *60 Minutes.*

•ONE ON ONE WITH JOHN TESH
Talk; Color
September 9, 1991–June 12, 1992

NBC Mon.–Fri. 11–11:30 a.m. (9/9/91–11/1/91)
NBC Mon.–Fri. 11:30 a.m.–Noon (11/4/91–6/12/92)

Host: *John Tesh*

As its name implied, *One on One with John Tesh* had the tall anchor of the syndicated nightly informational series *Entertainment Tonight* interview a star at his or her home or on location; there were two segments per show. Guests on the debut were actresses Twiggy and Marcy Walker. Occasionally contributing interviews were correspondents Sandie Newton, Jill Rappaport, and Jennifer Valoppi. Surprisingly, NBC News produced this light fare.

After the cancellation of this short-lived show, John Tesh had a variegated daytime career with NBC. He joined *Entertainment Tonight* colleague Leeza Gibbons to do *John and Leeza from Hollywood* (q.v.) in 1992, then found himself removed from the job as it became a solo talk show for his co-host (see *Leeza*). He left *Entertainment Tonight* on May 1996 after 12 years there to concentrate on a musical career.

OPEN HEARING
Discussion; B&W
January 7, 1951–September 4, 1960

CBS Sun. 5–5:30 p.m. (1/7/51–6/24/51)
ABC Sun. 5:30–6 p.m. (4/21/57–9/15/57)
ABC Sun. 3–3:30 p.m. (10/19/58–9/4/60)

Host: *Walter Cronkite (1951), John Secondari (1957–60)*

Two similar series aired under the title *Open Hearing* in the 1950s. The first series also ran briefly on Sunday nights in the summers of 1950 (when Bill Shadel was host) and 1951, and also was titled *The Facts We Face.* It featured examinations of a current topic of note via discussions and guest interviews. The 1957–60 show was done along

similar lines but was a bit more ambitious in scope (for example, a special hour-long show on June 16, 1957 examining "Segregation and the South" featured the Rev. Martin Luther King Jr. as a guest). Between its daytime runs, this series also popped up for various periods on the ABC nighttime lineup between February 3, 1957 and September 28, 1958.

•OPRAH WINFREY SHOW, THE
Talk; Color
1985–

Syndicated 60 minutes daily beginning September 1986

Host: *Oprah Winfrey*

The top talk show of the late 1980s and 1990s, *The Oprah Winfrey Show* became a pop culture phenomenon by taking the intelligent audience participation style of *Donahue* and adding a host with fresh insight, honesty, and opinions on how audience members could improve their lives. The show can trace its roots to 1983, when Winfrey, who had been a local news personality in Baltimore for seven years, became a talk show co-host. She switched to Chicago to host *A.M. Chicago* and beat out *Donahue* in the ratings within a few weeks. The series became *The Oprah Winfrey Show* in 1985 and went into syndication the following year, where its ascendancy to the top of the national ratings scene was rapid. (Ironically, Oprah had done a Baltimore talk show earlier called *People Are Talking*, which was syndicated unsuccessfully to 13 stations before folding.)

Typically each show dealt with an emotional issue affecting women—spousal abuse, child rearing, and so on. Unlike other competitors in the 1990s, she discussed these issues in a nonexploitive manner. Oprah did not shy away from sharing her own personal battles, from her ongoing struggle to control her weight (weighing in at one point at 220 pounds, she appeared to have it under control by 1994) to her tearful admission on a show taped January 13, 1995 that she had used crack cocaine in her twenties.

Winfrey had become a multimillionaire by the time she was 32 because her company, Harpo Productions, owned the show. By 1995 she was clearing more than $70 million yearly from her series, thanks to its large distribution (it aired on 117 foreign countries) and the fact that she owned the studio where it was shot and as well as other properties. In the mid-1990s, *Forbes* magazine estimated her earnings after taxes at $340 million, putting her among the top 70 richest women in America, and noted, "If she stays popular and with the show, Winfrey's well on her way to becoming America's first black billionaire." With a contract extending her through 1997 at least and her continued domination of the ratings, plus a movie deal with Disney, she will more than likely reach that goal before the end of the century.

The star of The Oprah Winfrey Show *as she looked in the late 1980s.*

ORIGINAL AMATEUR HOUR, THE

Talent Competition; B&W and Color
October 2, 1960–September 27, 1970

CBS Sun. 5–5:30 p.m. (10/2/60–6/11/61)
CBS Sun. 5:30–6 p.m. (6/18/61–9/17/61)
CBS Sun. 5–5:30 p.m. (9/24/61–6/17/62)
CBS Sun. 5:30–6 p.m. (6/24/62–9/16/62)
CBS Sun. 5–5:30 p.m. (9/23/62–6/16/63)
CBS Sun. 5:30–6 p.m. (6/23/63–9/27/70)

Host: *Ted Mack*

What can you say about a talent contest which Ann-Margret lost when she was 16 to a man who made music by blowing a leaf; a talent show which didn't even accept Elvis Presley, who was to be one the greatest musical talents of the time, as a contestant? *The Original Amateur Hour* often lived up to its title during its incredible 35-year run on national

broadcasting by favoring the odd and corny over artists who had true potential for making it in the entertainment industry. For every Frank Sinatra, Jack Carter, and Paul Winchell "discovered" by the series, there were at least a dozen other wanna-bes who tried to win (and even won!) by using animal performers or playing with spoons, bananas, eggbeaters, and other paraphernalia.

The series did begin as a rather respected contest for newcomers when it debuted on radio in 1934 as *Major Bowes' Original Amateur Hour* hosted by Major Ed Bowes. After his death in 194? the show disappeared for two years, then was revived by Bowes's protégé as a weekly nighttime TV series on DuMont from January 18, 1948–September 25, 1949. It then made the rounds of all the networks, on NBC from October 4, 1949–September 11, 1954; ABC from October 30, 1955–June 23, 1957; back on NBC from July 1, 1957–October 4, 1958; CBS from May 1, 1959–October 9, 1959; back on ABC from March 7, 1960–September 26, 1960; and from there to a decade on CBS Sunday afternoons.

Each show presented several acts with one declared the winner by getting the highest number of votes via postcards from the viewing audience. There was also an annual competition among previous winners to be the National Amateur Champion of the Year. The best-known participant in the annual event during the 1960s was actor Raul Julia.

Despite the dubious "talents" of some winners, the lure of potential celebrity was enough to inspire more than 750,000 people to audition for the TV series, even though less than 5 percent of the applicants ever got on the show. *TV Guide* claimed in 1956 that only 500 *Original Amateur Hour* participants went on to professional entertainment careers. When one considers they had been on the same show that let a man play "Yankee Doodle Dandy" while banging a mallet on his head, perhaps that statistic is not so surprising.

The show returned briefly on cable's Family Channel on January 26, 1992 as *The New Original Amateur Hour,* with Willard Scott as host.

•OSMONDS, THE
Cartoon; Color
September 9, 1972–September 1, 1974

ABC Sat. 9–9:30 a.m. (9/9/72–9/1/73)
ABC Sun. 10:30–11 a.m. (9/9/73–9/1/74)

Voices:

The Osmonds (Donny, Jimmy, Merrill, Wayne, Alan, Jay)	Themselves
Fuji, their dog	Paul Frees

Just as the Osmonds slavishly imitated the Jackson 5 to hit the music charts in 1971 with the hit "One Bad Apple," so did this ABC cartoon series imitate *The Jackson 5ive* hit only one season later—in a time slot following the Jacksons at that! Every element of the production could be called copycat, from the installation of the Osmonds' songs in the flimsy plots (something about the Osmonds being on a global tour for the U.S. Music Committee, a concept which must have appalled any rock critic) to the admittedly occasionally enjoyable comic interplay between the Mormon siblings. The second season consisted only of repeats. By the time the show ended, the Osmonds were losing their place on the music charts while Donny's solo success continued, eventually leading to his prime-time variety show with Osmond sister Marie on ABC from January 16, 1976–May 6, 1979, on which other family members, including the brothers, often appeared.

•OTHER SIDE, THE
Talk; Color
October 10, 1994–October 13, 1995

NBC Mon.–Fri. 11 a.m.–Noon (10/10/94–10/13/95)

Host: *Dr. Will Miller (1994–95), Dana Fleming (1995)*

Interested in learning how to talk to deceased family members? Want to hear about people's experiences with UFOs? Then this would have been just the tacky talk show for you. Its obsession with the supernatural and its apparent unwillingness to debunk any tale of the so-called "other side," no matter how illogical, made this series reviled by critics, and by July 1995 even original host Dr. Will Miller, better known as the "TV psychologist," who gave humorous analyses of reruns on the Nickelodeon cable channel's "Nick at Nite" feature (e.g., Darren, on *Bewitched,* must have been crazy not to let his wife use her powers for convenience), got so fed up with the format that he departed. NBC replaced it after a year with repeats of its morning companion show *Leeza* (q.v.).

OUR FIVE DAUGHTERS
Soap Opera; B&W and Color
January 6, 1962–September 28, 1962

NBC Mon.–Fri. 3:30–4 p.m. (1/6/62–9/28/62)

Cast:

Helen Lee	Esther Ralston
Jim Lee	Michael Keene
Mary Lee Weldon	Wynne Miller
Marjorie ("Margie") Lee	Iris Joyce
Barbara Lee	Patricia Allison
Jane Lee	Nuella Dierking
Anne Lee	Jacqueline Courtney
Don Weldon	Ben Hayes
Bob Purdon	William Tabbert
Pat Nichols	Edward Griffith
Uncle Charlie	Robert W. Stewart
Cynthia Dodd	Joan Anderson
Ed Lawson	Michael Higgins

Our Five Daughters began in tragedy as Jim Lee, father of a quintet of ladies, was hospitalized in the first episode, causing much grief for his wife and brood. He came home to recuperate on the January 15 show, by which time viewers had learned that Helen was his wife, Mary was married and pregnant, and Anne was the baby daughter. All of Jim's offspring managed to antagonize him by getting in some sort of trouble during the series' eight-month run. Jane had problems with Don, while Mary had run-ins with Bob. Barbara rejected a proposal in favor of a job, and teenager Anne had the typical adolescent problems with dating Pat. The daughters did not get to have all the fun, however; at one point Jim found himself having to testify at a trial. Helen served as the rock of the family, and appropriately the show ended on an upbeat note with her celebrating her birthday.

Among the other characters were Uncle Charlie, who helped the Lees cope with some crises, and Ed Lawson, a family friend. The show aired live at least through April 1962.

OUT ON THE FARM WITH EDDY ARNOLD
News/Information; B&W
July 11, 1954–November 21, 1954

NBC Sun. 5–6 p.m. (7/11/54–8/29/54)
NBC Sun. 4–4:30 p.m. (10/3/54–11/21/54)

Regulars: *Eddy Arnold (7/11/54–9/54), Clint Youle, William Landmeier, Lloyd Burlingham (7/11/54–8/29/54), the Mid-States Four (7/11/54–8/29/54)*

One of the rare network series to address agricultural issues exclusively, *Out on the Farm with Eddy Arnold* used the 160-acre farm of the six-member Landmeier family in Cloverdale, Illinois, as its home base, employing a camera mounted on a jeep to do live pickups on every point of the property. Country vocalist and host Eddy Arnold interviewed the Landmeiers about their farm, sang a few tunes, and introduced weatherman Clint Youle, farm commentator Lloyd Burlingham, and barbershop quartet the Mid-States Four. Youle, a weatherman for WNBQ Chicago, became the sole host when the show returned on October 3, and the only other regular then was William Landmeier, patriarch of his family.

OUTLOOK
News Analysis; B&W
April 1, 1956–January 7, 1962

NBC Sun. 5:30–6 p.m. (4/1/56–9/9/56)
NBC Sun. 3–3:30 p.m. (10/29/56–3/24/57)
NBC Sun. 5:30–6 p.m. (3/31/57–12/15/57)
NBC Sun. 5:30–6 p.m. (10/11/59–1/7/62; summers off)

Host: *Chet Huntley*

Offbeat or nonpublicized news events were the initial purview of *Outlook*, which began six months before Chet Huntley became co-anchor with David Brinkley of NBC's nightly news reports. Huntley delivered the headline news while NBC correspondents contributed various features. The debut examined the difficulties of disposing of nuclear waste, Sen. James Eastland's opposition to integration, and the lives of members of Congress after leaving office. Tellingly, the latter report came from Brinkley.

By June 1957, one of several subsequent changes in format had already been made—some commentaries by Marya Mannes were added for a time. Huntley himself went into editorializing on September 29, 1957 when he spoke against racial segregation in Little Rock, Arkansas. In December 1957 the show moved to Sunday evenings and focused on one issue per show. It had been retitled *Chet Huntley Reporting* by the fall of 1958 and went back to general news coverage, although occasional one-issue shows cropped up thereafter.

In the fall of 1959 it moved back to late Sunday afternoons under the title *Time: Present—Chet Huntley Reporting*. On September 25, 1960, the title reverted to *Chet Huntley Reporting*. It moved a year later from Sunday afternoons to prime time, ending its run on June 18, 1963.

OVERSEAS PRESS CLUB
Public Affairs; B&W
October 2, 1949–June 25, 1950

CBS Sun. 5–5:30 p.m. (10/2/49–6/25/50)

Host: *Quincy Howe*

Members of the Overseas Press Club of America discussed current events in this entry from New York. A similar series, titled *Press Correspondents Panel*, had been seen on CBS Sundays from 6–6:30 p.m. in April and May 1949.

OZMOE
Children's; B&W
March 6, 1951–April 12, 1951

ABC Tue./Thu. 5–5:15 p.m. (3/6/51–4/12/51)

Voices: *Bradley Bolke, Jan Kindler, Eleanor Russell, Alan Stapleton, Jack Urbant*

On this puppet show Ozmoe was a monkey and Rhoderick Dhon't was his leprechaun pal. They and Misty Waters the mermaid, Horatio the caterpillar, and Throckmorton a sea serpent, among others, had twice weekly adventures in Studio Z, the storeroom of the sub-subbasement at ABC. It alternated daily with *The Mary Hartline Show*.

PDQ—See Baffle.

•PTL CLUB, THE
Religious; Color
1976–87

Syndicated 60 minutes daily beginning 1976

Regulars: *Jim Bakker, Tammy Faye Bakker, Jerry Falwell (1987)*

The TV show which sparked the so-called "televangelist" scandals of the late 1980s was *The PTL Club*. According to backers, PTL stood for "Praise the Lord" or "People That Love," but detractors, who thought the show's hosts engaged in shady business practices, liked to joke that the initials meant "Pass the Loot." It was also perhaps the most uninhibited religious show on television, more along the lines of *The Merv Griffin Show* than *Lamp Unto My Feet*, with its grinning host Jim Bakker singing and introducing a host of Christian guests who talked not only about their belief in God but other interests as well, often joking and singing during the segments. As a result, *The PTL Club* was one of the most popular programs of its kind until Bakker's dealings came to light, more than a decade after it was first aired.

Jim Bakker and his wife Tammy Faye set up their show near the North Carolina–South Carolina border in 1976 south of Charlotte, North Carolina. They were believers in the Pentecostal faith, which included the practice of speaking in tongues under the influence of God. But unlike other evangelists, their proselytizing was low-key on their show, and their talk show set was rather lavish and comfortable compared to the austere ones often seen in other religious series. As its popularity grew, the Bakkers found themselves playing host to other top Christian names as guests, including Pat Boone and Chuck Colson.

But amid their success, a local newspaper, *The Charlotte Observer,* began to take a closer look at the Bakkers' conspicuous wealth and the theme park they had developed around their studio called Heritage U.S.A., which included a hotel, water park, and other attractions. The paper alleged that the donations the Bakkers claimed would benefit their studio and the park were in fact being diverted to their own personal use. None of this could be confirmed immediately, and the Bakkers often condemned *The Charlotte Observer* on the air, the only time—apart from praying of course—they seemed to get truly serious.

Then the paper learned that a secretary named Jessica Hahn had had an affair with Bakker and been paid off to keep quiet about it. Furthermore, the "lifetime partnerships" the show offered to viewers who paid $1,000 apiece for the opportunity for unlimited access to Heritage U.S.A. were not being honored but used instead for covering personal expenses of the Bakkers. As a result of the disclosures, Jim Bakker lost control of his empire and faced court charges while Jerry Falwell, whom some viewers saw as a competitor rather than friend to the Bakkers, took over the reins as host, vowing to clear up the financial mess (PTL was some $70 million in debt) as PTL's new chairman. He did so at the expense of the show, which without Jim Bakker at the helm lost its appeal and went off quickly.

Not directly implicated in the scandal was Bakker's co-host Tammy Faye, who wore as much heavy makeup as a kabuki performer but whose eternally perky, bubbly personality seemed genuine. When the story broke, Tammy Faye became the butt of many jokes and comic impersonations, but she stood by Jim when he went to jail in 1989, convicted of fraud and conspiracy. After a few years she divorced him, and vowed to get on with her life, although many wondered what talents she had that might enable her to do that.

Incredibly, Tammy Faye got a chance to make a comeback in January 1996 with the daily syndicated talk show *The JM J. and Tammy Show* co-starring JM J. Bullock, but she had left the show by March, claiming too much stress on the job. Some observers said that stress had nothing to do with her departure, but rather that stations had complained about her lack of polish as an interviewer and wanted her out of the low-rated effort. By that time Jim was out of jail and trying to rebuild his shattered career, but few people, including his former supporters, seemed to care. Jim Bakker and Tammy Faye both penned autobiographies telling their own sides of the stories, which came out in the fall of 1996.

PAC-MAN/RUBIK THE AMAZING CUBE HOUR, THE
Cartoon; Color
September 25, 1982–August 31, 1985

ABC Sat. 9:30–10 a.m. (9/25/82–9/3/83)
ABC Sat. 9:30–10:30 a.m. (9/10/83–9/1/84)
ABC Sat. 10–10:30 a.m. (4/27/85–8/31/85; Rubik only)

Voices:

Pac-Man	*Marty Ingels*
Ms. Pepper Pac-Man	*Barbara Minkus*
Baby Pac	*Russi Taylor*
Chomp Chomp	*Frank Welker*
Sour Puss	*Peter Cullen*
Mezmaron	*Alan Lurie*
Blinky/Pinky	*Chuck McCann*
Inky	*Barry Gordon*
Clyde	*Neilson Ross*
Sue	*Susan Silo*
Super-Pac (1983–84)	*Lorenzo Music*
Pac-Jr. (1983–84)	*Daryl Hickman*
Rubik the Amazing Cube (1983–85)	*Ron Palillo*
Carlos Rodriguez (1983–85)	*Michael Saucedo*
Reynaldo Rodriguez/Ruby Rodriguez (1983–85)	*Michael Bell*
Lisa Rodriguez (1983–85)	*Jennifer Fajardo*
Marla Rodriguez (1983–85)	*Angela Moya*

Pac-Man, the yellow orb video game creature who scored points when he ate wafers and blue blobs, was something of a pop culture icon by the time this series debuted, having even inspired a top 10 record by one-hit wonder duo Buckner and Garcia ("Pac-Man Fever"). Wearing a hat on his head, Pac and his family (Ms. Pac-Man, Baby Pac, dog Chomp Chomp, and cat Sour Puss) lived in the Power Forest, where the forest's wafers, the source of power for Pac and crew, were the object of desire for the evil Mezmaron. Mezmaron enlisted Inky, Blinky, Pinky, Sue, and Clyde as his goons to attack the land, forcing Pac to chomp at them and make them disappear. Some additional relatives of Pac got their own adventure in the second season of the show.

Also in its second year, the series added the adventures of Rubik the Amazing Cube, based on a faddishly popular toy of the early 1980s where one had to manipulate pieces of a multicolored cube until each of the six sides was uniformly a different color. The cartoon Rubik was a talking cube in the service of children Carlos, Lisa, and Reynaldo Rodriguez (he was more their friend than pet, since they did have a dog). Out of alignment, Rubik could not speak or move, but lined up properly, he could fly and change shape to help the Rodriguezes. Following the cancellation of the series at the end of the season, Rubik only reappeared in reruns in 1985. Pac-Man was also seen in 1982–83 as a segment of *Richie Rich* (q.v.).

PADDY THE PELICAN
Children's; B&W
September 11, 1950–October 13, 1950

ABC Mon.–Fri. 5:15–5:30 p.m. (9/11/50–10/13/50)

Regular: *Frances Desmond (as Pam)*
Voices: *Ray Suber*

Puppeteer: *Helen York*

Cartoonist: *Sam Singer*

Paddy the Pelican mixed drawings, puppetry, and live action to tell the story of a bird and his adventure with his human pal Pam. Although Paddy was a puppet who acted as narrator, he was seen flying during adventures via cartoons drawn by Sam Singer, who was also the show's creator and producer. The show, which aired from WENR Chicago, was a daily entry seen 6:45–7 p.m. locally at least as early as February 1950.

PANDAMONIUM
Cartoon; Color
September 18, 1982–September 10, 1983

CBS Sat. 11–11:30 a.m. (9/18/82–10/23/82)
CBS Sat. 8:30–9 a.m. (10/30/82–9/10/83)

Voices:

Algernon	Walker Edmiston
Chesty	Jesse White
Timothy	Cliff Norton
Peter Darrow	Neilson Ross
Peggy Darrow	Katie Leigh
Mondraggorr	William Woodson
Amanda Panda	Julie McWhirter

When Peter Darrow looked into the heavens one night with his telescope, he had no idea what he was about to witness. Mondraggorr, a creature who planned to gain omnipotence with a magic Pyramid of Power, was dismayed to find the pyramid rebelling against his control, shattering, and falling down to Earth. Seeing the explosion, Peter and his sister Peggy, both adolescents, went to track down a piece of the fallen pyramid and ran into a hapless trio of talking pandas who joined the children in a race against Mondraggorr to see who could put the pyramid back together first and restore its power. Although the pandas were hindered somewhat by their personality quirks, they could unite and become "Poppapanda," a being that could stall some of the bad magic Mondraggorr used on unsuspecting Earthlings in his quest. This creation was the brainchild of ex–CBS President Fred Silverman's Intermedia Entertainment.

PANHANDLE PETE AND JENNIFER
Children's; B&W
September 18, 1950–June 28, 1951

NBC Mon.–Fri. 5:15–5:30 p.m. (9/18/50–12/8/50)
NBC Tues./Thu. 5:15–5:30 p.m. (12/11/50–6/28/51)

Regulars: *Johnny Coons (as Panhandle Pete), Jennifer Holt, Bill Newton, Adele Scott*

Panhandle Pete was a cowboy storyteller whose yarns were illustrated by Bill Newton as he related them to young Jennifer Holt on a ranch setting in this Chicago production. When Holt took four weeks off April 1951

for a delayed honeymoon, Barbara Sims was her temporary replacement. Adele Scott was the organist. The producer of this show was Stephan Hatos, who gained some recognition later when he joined with Monty Hall in the 1960s to create *Let's Make a Deal.*

When Quaker Oats dropped sponsorship of the show in favor of *Gabby Hayes,* it went to twice-a-week status, alternating with the latter series. Despite winning the Motion Picture Daily Award as the most outstanding children's TV series in 1951, the series ended after a season's run.

PANTOMIME QUIZ
Game; B&W
May 18, 1959–October 9, 1959

ABC Mon.–Fri. 12:30–1 p.m. (5/18/59–10/9/59)

Host: *Mike Stokey*

TV's most successful charades show first appeared in 1939, then began on a regular basis locally in Los Angeles in 1947. *Billboard's* review at the time was right on the money: "From the standpoint of original material and spontaneity, *Pantomime Quiz* should enjoy a large and profitable tele life." It did indeed, running in the nighttime from 1949 to 1951 on CBS, 1952 on NBC, 1952 to 1953 on CBS, 1953 to 1954 on DuMont, 1954 on CBS, 1955 on ABC, 1955 to 1957 on CBS, and 1958 to 1959 on ABC, usually but not always as a summer replacement series. In 1959 a ratings-starved ABC gave the series its only daytime slot, replacing *Play Your Hunch.*

The series, which was one of the first daytime videotaped shows on ABC, used the same rules as the nighttime version then airing on Monday nights. Two celebrity quartets competed in trying to identify four to five phrases, titles, etc., per show in the least amount of time using gestures only and no talking (two minutes was the limit for each item being pantomimed). Carol Burnett, Merv Griffin, Howard Morris, Cliff Norton, Dick Van Dyke, and Gretchen Wyler appeared frequently on the daytime show.

After the daytime run, the show reappeared on CBS Monday nights from September 17, 1962–September 16, 1963 as *Stump the Stars.* In 1969 it had a syndicated revival under the latter title with Roger C. Carmel, Deanna Lund, and Dick Patterson as the home team. Back in the early 1950s, 13 segments of the nighttime show were filmed and syndicated as well.

PAPA BEAR'S NEWSREEL
Films; B&W
April 27, 1952–October 26, 1952

ABC Sun. Noon–12:15 p.m. (4/27/52–10/26/52)

Host/Narrator: *Frank Bear*

Pre-1948 newsreels with stories and information geared to children aired on this obscure program from Chicago.

PARADISE BAY
Soap Opera; Color
September 27, 1965–July 1, 1966

NBC Mon.–Fri. 11:30 a.m.–Noon (9/27/65–7/1/66)

Cast:

Jeff Morgan	Keith Andes
Mary Morgan	Marion Ross
Kitty Morgan	Heather North
Duke Spaulding	Dennis Cole
Lucy Spaulding	June Dayton
Walter Montgomery	Walter Brooke
Charlotte Baxter	Paulle Clarke
Carlotta Chavez	Alice Reinheart
Fred Morgan	Steven Mines
Estelle Kimball	K. T. Stevens
Chuck Lucas	Craig Curtis
Judge Grayson	Frank M. Thomas
Judge Ellis	Mona Bruns

Both this series and *Morning Star,* which aired before it, started and ended on the same day and were produced in Hollywood. Paradise Bay was a fictional town on the Southern California coast somewhere between Los Angeles and the Mexican border. Its chief family consisted of local radio station manager Jeff Morgan, his nosy busybody wife Mary, and their teenage daughter Kitty, a would-be rock 'n' roll musician appearing in a group called the Moonglows. By the first episode they found themselves entwined with Duke Spaulding, son of the prominent Lucy Spaulding, who had been dating Sally Baxter. When Sally showed up dead on the seashore on the debut, Duke became the prime suspect and local editor Walter Montgomery vilified him in his newspaper. Naturally, this being a soap, this resulted in inflamed passions, an extended trial with a wrong suspect, and . . . you get the picture.

This in-house production for NBC went off after ABC premiered *The Dating Game* as its competition.

PARENT'S TIME
Informational; B&W
July 18, 1955–October 7, 1955

NBC Mon.–Fri. 10:30–10:45 p.m. (7/18/55–10/7/55)

Host: *Dr. Francis Horwich*

Dr. Frances Horwich, the teacher on *Ding Dong School,* followed her series in the summer of 1955 with this program for adult viewers.

•PARTRIDGE FAMILY: 2200 A.D.
Cartoon; Color
September 7, 1974–March 8, 1975

CBS Sat. 9:30–10 a.m. (9/7/74–3/8/75)

Voices:

Connie Partridge	Joan Gerber
Keith Partridge	Chuck McClendon
Reuben Kincaid	David Madden
Laurie Partridge	Susan Dey
Danny Partridge	Danny Bonaduce
Tracy Partridge	Suzanne Crough
Christopher Partridge	Brian Forster
Veenie	Frank Welker
Marion	Julie McWhirter

That singing troupe of kids and their widowed mother known as the Partridge Family first appeared on an ABC nighttime sitcom from September 25 1970–August 31, 1974, and even had an improbable Grammy nomination in 1970 for Best New Artist. When they moved into Saturday mornings in 1974, all the cast except leads Shirley Jones and her heartthrob stepson David Cassidy (as wavy-haired Keith—oooh!) supplied their characters' voices (those two were about the only members of the TV show to provide singing voices on the group's albums). Now set nearly 50 years in the future, mama Connie (Shirley in the original) and her clan of kids (in descending age, they were lead singer Keith, pianist Laurie, guitarist and general imp Danny, drummer Chris, and tambourine shaker Tracy) toured planets rather than cities and faced comic complications with science fiction motifs, such as Keith suddenly shrinking in size. As before, Reuben Kincaid was their fretful manager. New additions were their friends Veenie, a teenage male from Venus, and Marion, a teenage girl from Mars.

The whole Partridge Family concept was based on a real-life group called the Cowsills, whose chief claim to TV fame is that they were the first rock 'n' roll group to appear on *Today* (they made their TV debut there on September 24, 1965). But the group's appeal was virtually dead by the time it appeared in cartoon form, and when another animated series reviving a nighttime show, *The New Adventures of Gilligan* on ABC, thrashed the 21st-century Partridges in the ratings, CBS canned the program, not waiting until the end of the season.

•PASS THE BUCK
Game; Color
April 3, 1978–June 30, 1978

CBS Mon.–Fri. 10–10:30 a.m. (4/3/78–6/30/78)

Host: *Bill Cullen*

The game behind *Pass the Buck* was a variant of the more successful Bob Stewart Production *The $25,000 Pyramid.* Here four players had to list elements fitting under a category announced by Bill Cullen (e.g., "things associated with Abraham Lincoln"). A correct response added $25 to the initial $100 kitty, and an incorrect response knocked a player out of contention. The one player left after this elimination round played a four-tiered board, reminiscent of that on *Pyramid,* which went from four hidden spaces at the bottom to one at the top. To win this bonus round's prize of $5,000, a contestant either had to list all elements hidden as answers for that tier's question (e.g., "name a tourist attraction in New York City"), or get one answer right on every level. A player who failed in this task had to compete again against the same three other players for another shot at the bonus round.

•PASSWORD

Game; B&W and Color
October 2, 1961–March 24, 1989

CBS Mon.–Fri. 2–2:30 p.m. (10/2/61–9/15/67)
ABC Mon.–Fri. 4–4:30 p.m. (4/5/71–9/3/71)
ABC Mon.–Fri. 12:30–1 p.m. (9/6/71–3/17/72)
ABC Mon.–Fri. Noon–12:30 p.m. (3/20/72–6/27/75)
NBC Mon.–Fri. 12:30–1 p.m. (1/8/79–3/2/79)
NBC Mon.–Fri. Noon–12:30 p.m. (3/5/79–8/10/79)
NBC Mon.–Fri. 12:30–1 p.m. (8/13/79–8/1/80)
NBC Mon.–Fri. 11:30 a.m.–Noon (8/4/80–10/23/81)
NBC Mon.–Fri. Noon–12:30 p.m. (10/26/81–3/26/82)
NBC Mon.–Fri. Noon–12:30 p.m. (9/24/84–3/24/89)

Host: *Allen Ludden (1961–67, 1971–75, 1979–80), Tom Kennedy (1980–82), Bert Convy (1984–89)*

A landmark game show, *Password* was the first in its genre to pair a celebrity and a contestant as players on the same team—equals rather than competitors, as in most celebrity-laden game shows of the 1950s. The simple object was that one partner of each competing pair received a word, as did the home viewer, and that partner had to give a clue to the other person using just one word, with no foreign phrases, hyphenated words, or derivations of the word allowed. The first called partner did have the option to "pass or play," doing the former if they thought the other team could not guess the word with the first clue (both sides got to hear all clues given). Teams alternated until the word was identified. A correct guess on the first clue netted 10 points, on the second 9, and so on. The first team to score 25 points got to play the "Lightning Round," where one partner had to identify five words within a minute to win $250. Players continued until defeated.

Allen Ludden, who left the presumed security of hosting *G.E. College Bowl* for this job in 1961, remarked to *TV Guide*, "A celebrity who's been on *Password* for five days comes out more of a human being than on any other vehicle. It's too fast, the pressure is too great, they can't be phony. They can't be anything but themselves." He counted Carol

Password in the 1960s featured such guests as Carolyn Jones and Peter Lawford, shown here flanking longtime host Allen Ludden.

Burnett and Darren McGavin as his favorite players, while Lucille Ball, Anthony Perkins, James Stewart, and Danny Thomas were listed as fans (they not only watched, but often played). But the person most identified with the show had to be Betty White, who came on as a contestant on its third week and eventually wed Allen Ludden. She would be the most frequent competitor on the game through the end of the 1980s.

Password proved to be the first hit to carry the large audience CBS had overflowing at 2 p.m. daily from *As the World Turns,* and it ran for six years in that slot. After *The Newlywed Game* passed it in the ratings in 1967 and the show was canceled, CBS syndicated reruns of the series, a rarity for a game show. The network also ran the series for various stretches in nighttime from January 2, 1962–May 22, 1967. The game reappeared on ABC in 1971, when it was the first Mark Goodson–Bill Todman game show produced in Hollywood, but otherwise the format remained the same for three years.

On November 18, 1974, the program became *Password All-Stars,* with six celebrities alternating play during each week in an elimination process to name a top winner. Three months later it returned with noncelebrity contestants, as well as a few changes, including the option of trying to go for double points by saying your partner could get the password with one clue. Also of note during that period was that during the week of March 31–April 4, 1975, Betty White hosted the show while Ludden played as a panelist.

In 1979 NBC revived the property under the title *Password Plus.* Here contestants had only four chances to guess a word, but could do so largely with the old restrictions removed (except for using more than one word or part of the word). A successful identification put the word on a board to serve as a clue to another password which had to be identified by the receiving player to win the game. Up to five clues were played per game, with the first player to identify the mystery topic winning $100 for his or her team in the first two games and $200 in the third or possibly fourth game. It took at least $400 for a team to go on and play "Alphabetics," where one player gave the other one-word clues to 10 words whose first letters were arranged alphabetically; the time limit was one minute. Correct identification of all 10 awarded the player $5,000. Players continued until defeated.

Allen Ludden returned as host of the new format but had to leave the show in October 1980 due to illness (he died a few months later). Tom Kennedy hosted the show until 1982. It was brought back again by NBC two years later under the title *Super Password.* The format was the same as that of *Password Plus,* but now Bert Convy was host. There was one other minor difference—viewers no longer sent in their own "passwords" in which they included bits of advice in statements which inevitably were read at the end of the show and ended with Ludden (and later Kennedy) grinning and telling the audience, "Think about it."

PAT BOONE SHOW, THE
Talk; Color
October 17, 1966–June 30, 1967

NBC Mon.–Fri. 11–11:30 a.m. (10/17/66–6/30/67)

Regulars: *Pat Boone, Adam Keefe*

"We're trying to guide Pat's career so he'll be very big in 1967," Boone's manager Jack Spina told *TV Guide* in 1957 on the eve of Pat's nighttime series on ABC which ran three years. It's doubtful that Spina thought his client doing a daytime talk show would be considered "big in 1967," but by that time Boone's singing and acting career, not to mention goody-goody image, was so out of favor that the daytime world was a viable option. With comic Adam Keefe as his sidekick, Pat tried gamely to interview such types as Edie Adams and Lorne Greene on his debut, but a walk-on by Johnny Carson reminded the public who they *really* thought did this kind of show best.

Undaunted by the show's unspectacular daytime run, *Pat Boone in Hollywood* popped up in syndication as a 90-minute late-night gabfest in September 1967, but it was no more successful. Boone went back to occasional TV acting chores and guesting on others' talk shows.

PATTERNS IN MUSIC
Music; Color
September 24, 1961–September 16, 1962

NBC Sun. 4:30–5 p.m. (9/24/61–4/8/62)
NBC Sun. 5–5:30 p.m. (4/15/62–5/27/62)
NBC Sun. 5:30–6 p.m. (6/17/62–9/16/62)

Regulars: *John Doremus, the Joseph Gallichio Orchestra*

A live time filler, *Patterns in Music* had John Doremus introduce an orchestra performing songs based on the day's theme for as long a period as there remained following the network sports presentation preceding it, which ranged anywhere from 5 to a full 30 minutes. The September debut focused on the fall season, and tunes like "Autumn Leaves" and "September Song" were played while both moving and still films were seen on the screen. Doremus also hosted the local WMAQ radio version of this Chicago-based show.

PAUL DIXON SHOW, THE
Variety; B&W
February 23, 1952–April 8, 1955

ABC Mon./Wed./Fri. 11:30 a.m.–Noon (2/23/52–3/14/52)
ABC Mon.–Fri. 12:30–1 p.m. (3/17/52–5/3/52)
DuMont Mon.–Fri. 3–4 p.m. (9/29/52–4/8/55)

Regulars: *Paul Dixon, Wanda Lewis, Dotty Mack (1952), Sis Pohlkamp (1952–54)*

Paul Dixon, a midwesterner who resembled a cross between Fred Allen and Garry Moore, had a national TV career that never quite gelled into success for him outside Ohio. "Paul Baby" (his nickname) started doing radio in Cincinnati in 1945 and moved to television four years later, where he did

13 hours on local TV weekly—his daily two-hour show and a three-hour extravaganza on Wednesday nights. Part of the latter was used for a nighttime show Dixon did for ABC from August 8, 1951–September 24, 1952.

When Dixon got on ABC's daytime lineup, he was doing basically a musical pantomime series with Wanda Lewis and Dotty Mack, plus occasional interviews. Dixon then went to DuMont in the fall of 1952 in a sustained series that aired from WCPO Cincinnati beginning November 1952. By the fall of 1953 Dixon's series was the only daily show being seen on the DuMont network, and it was to be the last.

Around December 1952, Sis Pohlkamp (also known as Sis Camp) replaced Dotty Mack on the show through September 27, 1954, when the show ended its lip sync portion and started airing from New York City. Ironically, for a short time during this period his show stopped airing in Cincinnati. When the DuMont run ended, Dixon

returned to Cincinnati and had a long-running local talk/variety series. He made one last attempt to spread his fame by syndicating the show in 1973 with singers Bonnie Lou and Connie Sharp, but it bombed. A year later, on December 28, 1974, Dixon died at the age of 56.

PAUL WINCHELL AND JERRY MAHONEY
Children's Variety; B&W
November 20, 1954–April 16, 1961

NBC Sat. 10:30–11 a.m. (11/20/54–2/25/56)
NBC Sat Noon–12:30 p.m. (3/3/56–6/9/56)
ABC Sun. 5–5:30 p.m. (9/29/57–6/7/59)
ABC Sun. 4–4:30 p.m. (10/11/59–4/3/60)
ABC Sun. 4:30–5 p.m. (12/25/60–4/16/61)

The two stars of Paul Winchell and Jerry Mahoney *(Mahoney is the dummy) pose in front of their studio audience in this 1959 shot.*

Regulars: *Paul Winchell, Milton DeLugg Trio/Orchestra, Maybine Hewes (1954), Mary Ellen Taylor (1954–55), Natalie "Trudy" Trundy (October–December 1955), Carol Burnett (12/17/55–1956), Frank Fontaine (1957–59)*

Paul Winchell and his dummy Jerry Mahoney was the most frequently seen ventriloquist act on television in the 1950s and 1960s. After a series ran on NBC nighttime from September 18, 1950–May 23, 1954, he moved to daytime with a studio audience of children sitting in Jerry's clubhouse. Joining him and the dummy in sketches were singer Maybin Hewes and dancer Mary Ellen Taylor. Singer Trudy Trundy replaced Taylor a year later, then Carol Burnett replaced Trundy in her first regular TV job. Burnett played Jerry's girlfriend (!), and as she would do on later shows, she signaled to her grandmother that everything was OK for her by tugging on her ear during the routine. Paul used a few other dummies beside Jerry, including doltish Knucklehead Smith and Irving the Mouse.

After two years on Saturdays, Winchell and Jerry moved to ABC to host the Thursday night series *Circus Time* from October 4, 1956–June 27, 1957, then returned to the daytime on the same network. From 1957–61, many guests visited amid the circus and novelty acts. Winchell also gave viewers stories with morals employing his dummies called "Chips of Wisdom." It may be surprising to learn that one audience survey indicated 70 percent of his Sunday show's viewership were adults.

Before his TV success, Winchell did a short-lived variety show with his dummy on the Mutual radio network in 1943. After the ABC show ended, he started his own new show for children locally in Los Angeles in March 1963, which was syndicated as a half-hour daily program in 1964. The format was sort of a *Candid Camera* with kids. Thereafter Winchell worked primarily as a voiceover artist on several Saturday morning cartoons through the 1990s.

•PEBBLES AND BAMM BAMM
Cartoon; Color
September 11, 1971–September 4, 1976

CBS Sat. 10–10:30 a.m. (9/11/71–9/2/72)
CBS Sun. 9:30–10 a.m. (5/13/73–9/2/73)
CBS Sat Noon–12:30 p.m. (2/9/74–8/31/74)
CBS Sat. 9:30–10 a.m. (3/8/75–8/30/75)
CBS Sat. 8–8:30 a.m. (9/6/75–9/4/76)

Voices:

Pebbles Flintstone	*Sally Struthers*
Bamm Bamm Rubble	*Jay North*
Moonrock	*Lennie Weinrib*
Penny	*Mitzi McCall*
Wiggy/Cindy	*Gay Hartwig*
Fabian	*Carl Esser*
Schleprock	*Don Messick*

The fondly remembered offspring of the lead characters from *The Flintstones* (q.v.) returned as teenagers in this cartoon. Bamm Bamm was now a muscular sort who drove vivacious redhead Pebbles and other friends around town as they engaged in various misadventures. They also performed as the musical group the Bedrock Rollers, where one member played mallets on a dinosaur's teeth. The only cast member who was not part of the Bedrock Rollers was Schleprock, a depressed walking lump who seemed to jinx everyone in his path. The shows after 1972 were all repeats. (See also *Flintstones Comedy Show, The.*)

•PEE WEE'S PLAYHOUSE
Children's; Color
September 13, 1986–July 20, 1991

CBS Sat. 11–11:30 a.m. (9/13/86–10/11/86)
CBS Sat. 10–10:30 a.m. (10/18/86–9/9/89)
CBS Sat. 9:30–10 a.m. (9/16/89–12/30/89)
CBS Sat. 10–10:30 a.m. (1/6/90–9/8/90)
CBS Sat. 11:30 a.m.–Noon (9/15/90–7/20/91)

Cast:

Pee Wee	*Paul Reubens*
Dixie (early episodes)	*Johann Carlo*
Cowboy Curtis	*Laurence Fishburne*
Captain Carl (early episodes)	*Phil Hartman*
The King of Cartoons (early episodes)	*Gilbert Lewis*
The King of Cartoons (later episodes)	*William Marshall*
Reba the Mail Lady	*S. Epatha Merkerson*
Tito the Lifeguard	*Roland Rodriguez*
Miss Yvonne	*Lynne Stewart*
Mrs. Steve	*Shirley Stoler*
Opal	*Natasha Lyonne*
Elvis	*Shawn Weiss*
Cher	*Diane Yang*
Jambi/Pterri (latter voice only)	*John Paragon*
Conky/Knucklehead (voices only)	*Gregory Harrison*
Mr. Window/Salesman/Cool Cat (voices only)	*Ric Heitzman*
Globey/Fish/The Countess (voices only)	*George Michael McGrath*
Chairry/Magic Screen/Chickie Baby (voices only)	*Alison Mork*
Randy/Roger/Mr. Kite/Dirty Dog (voices only)	*Wayne White*

What can you say about a Saturday morning show that was so "hip" that none other than *Rolling Stone* magazine wrote a celebratory article on it? *Pee Wee's Playhouse* entertained viewers well past their childhood years thanks to its inventiveness and sly, somewhat campy humor. It might have run forever had it not been for its creator, co-producer, and co-writer (of the show and theme song) Paul Reubens tiring of the character and eventually creating some unwanted headlines of his own. But let's start with the series.

Pee Wee was a giggling latter-day Pinky Lee, sans lisp or bow tie, with a cropped haircut, a tight-fitting gray business suit, and a nasal voice. He started each day by greeting a wild assortment of toys and creatures living in his house, most of whom were puppets like Chairry the talking comfort seat, Globey the French-accented globe, Pterri the pterodactyl, Pee-Wee's flower bed, the talking Mr. Kite and Mr. Window, and the resident jazz combo of Cool Cat, Chickie Baby, and Dirty Dog. Pee Wee then started up Conky the robot, who divulged the secret word of the day, which, when emitted from someone's mouth, prompted the cast to scream briefly. Then came a variety of activities involving Pee Wee, ranging from his weekly wish from Jambi, a blue-headed genie in a box (Jambi's inimitable chant was "Mekka lekka hi, mekka hidy ho/Mekka lekka high, mekka johnny ho!") to a sequence in which he went inside Magic Screen to play "connect the dots" and ride in whatever vehicle the screen made for him.

A variety of people visited Pee Wee at his 1950s-style angularly constructed house, including Reba the Mail Lady, Tito the muscular lifeguard (often clad only in a bathing suit), the perfectly groomed Miss Yvonne, Cowboy Curtis, old sea salt Captain Carl, rotund Mrs. Steve, and neighborhood kids Opal, Elvis, and Cher. The arrival of the King of Cartoons, who was first introduced at the playhouse by cab driver Dixie and who showed some old-time (pre-1950s) cartoon whenever he came, was always an occasion for general excitement. The most unwelcome of the guests were Randy the puppet bully (who did, however, often end up seeing the error of his ways), and a costumed salesman whose spiel was so obnoxious that Pee Wee started screaming as soon as he saw him at the door. Added to these goings-on were excursions into stop-motion animation featuring the Dinosaur Family living in Pee Wee's wall and the food performing in the refrigerator, a weekly cartoon about an opinionated girl named Penny, an animated ant farm, and a huge hand with a face on it called Knucklehead who told knock-knock jokes.

The general reaction to this odd conglomeration was enthusiasm among all age levels. It helped that the character was introduced to many of them in movie theaters in 1985

Heh heh! It's Pee Wee's Playhouse, *with the star at home with his wild gadgets.*

in the film *Pee Wee's Big Adventure*. One audience survey found that a third of its viewers were over 18 years old, and CBS seriously considered airing the show in prime time at one point. The network did air a nighttime hour-long "Pee Wee's Playhouse Christmas Special" on December 21, 1988, which boasted a truly astounding guest list—Frankie Avalon, Charo, Cher, Annette Funicello, Zsa Zsa Gabor, Whoopi Goldberg, Magic Johnson, Little Richard, Dinah Shore, Joan Rivers, and Oprah Winfrey, among others. But the network never did give him a berth outside Saturday mornings.

Pee Wee ended each show by hopping on his scooter and blasting off to a ride outdoors. The series ending was sort of a blast-off as well, though not a pleasant one. Pee Wee and company shot their last show in January 1990, and CBS planned to stop running the show in the fall of 1991. But when actor Paul Reubens was charged with indecent exposure at an adult movie theater in Florida on July 26, 1991, CBS promptly canceled the show. Despite the fact that Reubens was not jailed because of the incident, it took several years for his career to recover; since then he has managed to come back as an actor, doing work that included a recurring role as a network stooge on the CBS nighttime sitcom *Murphy Brown* from 1995–96.

Although Reubens was the inspiration behind much of this show, it should be noted that among cast members, John Paragon was a writer for the series, Wayne White and Ric Heitzman worked on production design, and Gregory Harrison contributed to puppet and prop fabrication and design.

PENELOPE PITSTOP—See *Perils of Penelope Pitstop, The.*

PEOPLE
Interview; B&W
August 21, 1955–October 9, 1955

NBC Sun. 5–5:30 p.m. (8/21/55–10/9/55)

Host/Narrator: *Morgan Beatty*

Morgan Beatty and a few other NBC news personnel conducted brief interviews with guests filmed at their homes or workplaces; seven guests were seen on the debut alone. The show's emphasis was on human interest, such as a man who planned to raise the Monitor warship.

PEOPLE WILL TALK
Game; B&W
July 1, 1963–December 27, 1963

NBC Mon.–Fri. 2–2:25 p.m. (7/1/63–12/27/63)

Host: *Dennis James*

Executive Producers: *Merrill Heatter and Bob Quigley*

People Will Talk, scheduled for the fall of 1962, with Arthur Godfrey serving as host, was slated to be the first midseason nighttime TV series replacement for CBS. But the network did not buy the show by the January 1, 1963 deadline,

which led its producers to sell it to NBC daytime. What that network got was a game featuring the largest number of celebrities ever—15 per week! They all voted their opinions on questions given to them by Dennis James, which ran along the lines of "Should we kiss in public?" and "Should bald men wear toupees?" Each of the two contestants, having taken opposite positions, tried to find four celebrities who agreed with him or her to win the game and receive prizes. The guest celebrities were much more impressive than the idea, and they included Gene Barry, Lloyd Bridges, Broderick Crawford, Vera Miles, Connie Stevens, Gloria Swanson, and many others.

PEOPLE'S PLATFORM
Public Affairs; B&W
August 20, 1950–June 24, 1951

CBS Sun. 5:30–6 p.m. (8/20/50–6/24/51)

Host: *Charles Collingwood*

A CBS radio program from 1938–52, *People's Platform* first aired on television from August 17, 1948–August 11, 1950 on various nights on CBS before moving to its daytime slot. Charles Collingwood led invited guests in discussions on such topics as college and professional football and the effect television had on viewers. A 1951 audience survey ranked the series eighth among weekend daytime TV series, an impressive feat considering only 8 stations telecast it versus at least 20 who did so for other top series like *Zoo Parade*, but apparently this did not impress CBS enough to renew.

•PERILS OF PENELOPE PITSTOP, THE
Cartoon; Color
September 13, 1969–September 5, 1971

CBS Sat. 10–10:30 a.m. (9/13/69–2/14/70)
CBS Sat. 12:30–1 p.m. (2/21/70–9/5/70)
CBS Sun. 9:30–10 a.m. (9/13/70–9/5/71)

Voices:

Penelope Pitstop	*Janet Waldo*
Sylvester Sneekly, the Hooded Claw	*Paul Lynde*
Chug-A-Boom/Yak Yak/Bully Brothers	*Mel Blanc*
Clyde/Softie	*Paul Winchell*
Zippy/Pockets/Dum Dum/Snoozy	*Don Messick*
Narrator	*Gary Owens*

A spin-off of *Wacky Races*, *The Perils of Penelope Pitstop* spoofed clichéd movie situations of the 1920s and 1930s. Southern-accented Penelope found her life in constant jeopardy due to the devices of the dastardly Hooded Claw and his henchmen the Bully Brothers, which ranged from exploding torpedoes to hungry alligators. The Claw, who actually wore no hood but rather a purple mask and dark cape, was in reality Penelope's attorney, and he stood to get Penelope's money upon her death. Each show's plot was invariably foiled, thanks to Penelope's ingenuity and reflexes and to the help of the Ant Hill Mob, a gangster-style sextet of little men in suits. Their quick-acting leader was Clyde; the rest of the mob, including the weeping Softie, sleeping Snoozy, and chuckling Yak Yak, had their own little quirks, yet managed to overcome them to save Penelope. Their black limousine Chug-A-Boom was a tremendous asset, as it could turn into virtually any type of matter. Adding to the jokey nature of the whole enterprise was Gary Owens's typically overbaked narration. The show's second year was all repeats.

On the late 1960s game show Personality, *Larry Blyden read questions while guest stars like Marty Allen, seen in this shot, appeared on a TV monitor on film to give a reply.*

PERSONAL APPEARANCE THEATER
Dramatic Anthology; B&W
October 27, 1951–May 23, 1952

ABC Sat. 12:30–1 p.m. (10/27/51–1/12/52)
ABC Sat. 11–11:30 a.m. (1/26/52–5/23/52)

This unremarkable filmed series, which alternated weekly with *City Hospital* in the 12:30 slot, also ran in nighttime for the same dates.

PERSONALITY
Game; Color
July 3, 1967–September 26, 1969

NBC Mon.–Fri. 11–11:30 a.m. (7/3/67–9/26/69)

Host: *Larry Blyden*

A trio of celebrities, each representing either a home viewer or a member of the studio audience, played this guessing game about what other famous folk planned to say in clips, with correct answers netting $25 each. (The participants saw a clip of a celebrity being asked a question, then had to guess what the celebrity had responded.) The highest score won prizes for the viewer/audience member as well as the cash. The answers and their implications were the main appeal of the show. For example, when Robert Vaughn was asked, "What's the quickest way for a woman to reach your heart?" he replied, "Adulation toward me and total silence." Robert Morse, when asked "What's the best way to keep monogamy from being monotony?" responded, "To be honest about it? Cheat." Other top names involved included Robert Culp, Peter Falk, Sammy Davis Jr., Woody Allen, Claire Bloom, Sen. Everett Dirksen, and even Dustin Hoffman in 1968.

The show also had some fun with celebrities involved in relationships. Joan Fontaine incorrectly guessed answers from her sister Olivia DeHaviland, with whom she had one of Hollywood's most infamous feuds, and on one show Eli Wallach had a hard time trying to come up with what his wife Anne Jackson had said. But the appeal wasn't strong enough for the show to beat reruns of *The Andy Griffith Show*, so after two years NBC replaced it with *Sale of the Century.*

PETER LIND HAYES SHOW, THE
Comedy Variety; B&W
October 13, 1958–April 10, 1959

ABC Mon.–Fri. 11:30 a.m.–12:30 p.m.
  (10/13/58–4/10/59)

Regulars: *Peter Lind Hayes, John Bubbles, Don Cherry, the Four Voices, the Burt Farber Orchestra*

Peter Lind Hayes came to ABC following a three-year contract with CBS to serve as "permanent guest host" for *Arthur Godfrey Time*, and this show, one of five airing as part of ABC's pioneering "Operation Daybreak," used several ex-Godfreyites on the production, including orchestra leader

Burt Farber. The Godfrey connection didn't help ratings; the show fell far behind its competition on CBS and NBC, including *Love of Life* and *Concentration*, and went off after six months.

PETER PAN & THE PIRATES
Cartoon; Color
September 8, 1990–September 11, 1992

Fox Mon.–Fri. Various half hours (9/8/90–9/11/92)
Fox Sat. 8–8:30 a.m. (1/26/91–8/31/91)

Voices:

Captain Hook	*Tim Curry*

Also: *Chris Allport, Jack Angel, Michael Bacall, Adam Carl, Debi Derryberry, Linda Gary, Edmund Gilbert, Whitby Hartford, Tony Jay, Christina Lange, Aaron Lohr, Jack Lynch, Jason Marsden, Scott Menville, David Shaughnessy, Cree Summer, Josh Weiner, Eugene Williams, Michael Wise*

The Fox network got off to a very shaky start in programming for children with this troubled adaptation of the classic novel by James M. Barrie, whose copyright expired on December 31, 1987. Originally developed as a Saturday morning cartoon for CBS, the project ended up being a daily entry instead as part of Fox's initial schedule of daily programming for children. But the network gave the production company only a few months' lead time to make the standard minimum 65 shows for daily airing, and the compromises made to get on air by the fall of 1990 proved disastrous.

The show itself was not terrible, though hardly in a class with the 1953 animated version done by Walt Disney. It had the old crew of Peter, the boy who never grew up; Tinkerbell, his pixie assistant; and their adversary Captain Hook, who dominated the action. The show was designed to have overall appeal for older children, particularly males. But any hopes Fox had of making this Peter Pan a success were dashed when it became clear that few shows would be ready by the September airing. Ratings were horrible, not surprising given the multiple reruns seen in the first few months alone. To try and boost its appeal, Fox in early 1991 added a sixth day of broadcasts, replacing *Zazoo U.*, a series which had the unenviable distinction of being Fox's first Saturday morning casualty. The Saturday slot didn't help, and after one other daily season the cartoon quietly disappeared.

•PETER POTAMUS SHOW, THE
Cartoon; Color
January 2, 1966–December 24, 1967

ABC Sun. 10:30–11 a.m. (1/2/66–12/24/67)

Voices:

Peter Potamus/Yahooey	*Daws Butler*
So-So	*Don Messick*
Breezly	*Howard Morris*
Sneezly	*Mel Blanc*
Colonel Fusby	*John Stephenson*

Yappee/The King	*Hal Smith*
Yippee	*Doug Young*

Like its companion series *Magilla Gorilla*, this show came from syndication in 1964 to ABC with both new and repeated cartoons. Its star was a purple hippo in a safari outfit who, with his ape pal So-So, sailed along on a balloon equipped with a compass indicating time periods (past, present, and future) to which the duo traveled. They trekked from times only a few centuries past (for example, the era in which the Pilgrims came to America) to prehistoric epochs, all for laughs of course. Supporting segments were "Breezly and Sneezly," about, respectively, a weird polar bear and conniving seal who pestered Colonel Fusby on ice- and snow-covered lands, and "Yippee, Yappee and Yahooey," a threesome of palace dogs ineptly serving their beloved King.

PHIL DONAHUE SHOW, THE—See *Donahue.*

PIGGSBURG PIGS!
Cartoon; Color
September 15, 1990–August 31, 1991

Fox Sat. 10–10:30 a.m. (9/15/90–4/13/91)
Fox Sat. 10:30–11 a.m. (5/25/91–6/29/91)
Fox Sat. 10–10:30 a.m. (8/10/31–8/31/91)

In this pun-laden porcine concoction, Bo, Portley, and Pighead Bacon, all brothers, fought Rembrandt Proupork in Piggsburg, located behind a farm, and played at Newpork Beach. Other pigs seen were Proud Pork, Piggy, Pokey, and Prissy. Alliteration was apparently a biggie for this show.

PINK PANTHER AND SONS
Cartoon; Color
September 15, 1984–September 6, 1986

NBC Sat. 8:30–9 a.m. (9/15/84–12/29/84)
NBC Sat. 8–8:30 a.m. (1/5/85–1/26/85)
NBC Sat. 8:30–9 a.m. (2/2/85–9/7/85)
ABC Sat. 8–8:30 a.m. (3/1/86–9/6/86)

Voices:

Pinky	*Billy Bowles*
Panky/Punkin	*B. J. Ward*
Chatta	*Sherry Lynn*
Howl	*Marshall Efron*
Anney/Liona	*Jeanine Elias*
Finko/Rocko	*Frank Welker*
Bowlhead	*Gregg Berger*
Buckethead	*Sonny Melendrez*
Murfel	*Shane McCabe*

In this unsuccessful revival of the long-running cartoon feline, the Pink Panther returned to Saturday morning with his vocal sons Pinky, Panky, and Punkin (not triplets, but boys ranging from toddler to preadolescent). This series was a Hanna-Barbera production, as the original company of DePatie-Freleng was defunct by 1980.

•PINK PANTHER SHOW, THE

Cartoon; Color
September 6, 1969–September 1, 1979

NBC Sat. 9:30–10 a.m. (9/6/69–9/5/70)
NBC Sat. 10:30–11 a.m. (9/12/70–9/4/71)
NBC Sat. 9:30–10 a.m. (9/11/71–9/2/72)
NBC Sat. 9–9:30 a.m. (9/9/72–12/16/72)
NBC Sat. 9:30–10 a.m. (12/23/72–9/1/73)
NBC Sat. 11:30 a.m.–Noon (9/8/73–12/29/73)
NBC Sat. 10:30–11 a.m. (1/5/74–8/31/74)
NBC Sat. 11–11:30 a.m. (9/7/74–8/30/75)
NBC Sat. 9:30–10 a.m. (9/6/75–9/4/76)
NBC Sat. 8:30–10 a.m. (9/11/76–9/3/77)
NBC Sat. 10:30–11 a.m. (2/4/78–9/2/78)
ABC Sat. 11:30 a.m.–Noon (9/9/78–5/26/79)
ABC Sat Noon–12:30 p.m. (6/2/79–9/1/79)

Host (1976–77): *Lenny Schultz*

Voices:

Ant/Aardvark (1971–78)	John Byner
Inspector Clouseau (1971–78)	Pat Harrington Jr.
Misterjaws (1976–77)	Arte Johnson
Catfish the Hunter (1976–77)	Arnold Stang
Fatso (1976–77)	Don Diamond
Banjo (1976–77)	Tom Holland

Theme: *"The Pink Panther Theme," by Henry Mancini*

The Pink Panther, a 1964 movie produced by Blake Edwards and starring Peter Sellers as clumsy French Inspector Clouseau, spawned several theatrical sequels, the last of which was made in the 1980s. The title originally referred to the pantherlike image seen in a diamond when light hit the gem at a certain angle, but the NBC cartoon panther was a mute walking cat who outwitted his enemies, sometimes unintentionally. After two years, the show was retitled *The New Pink Panther Show* and now included the misadventures of Inspector Clouseau in the streets of Paris in separate segments. It also added a cartoon series seen in movie theaters since 1966, titled "The Ant and the Aardvark," which featured a resourceful red ant who sounded like Dean Martin and a bumbling, bullying blue aardvark who was a vocal dead ringer for Joey Bishop. The following year, in 1972, the show added the Paul Ritts Puppets performing between the segments.

In 1976, following several seasons when it was about the only NBC cartoon to win its time period, it became TV's first 90-minute network cartoon series under the title *The Pink Panther Laugh and a Half Hour and a Half Show.* The new additions were Lenny Schultz reading letters and jokes from home viewers, and two new cartoons—"Texas Toads," starring the hillbilly frogs Fatso and Banjo, and "Misterjaws," a nearsighted shark with a sidekick named Catfish the Hunter (get it?). The effort flopped after a season and the show went back to its old form in 1977–78. The next year, after nearly a decade on NBC, *The Pink Panther* moved to ABC in new adventures which failed to make it with viewers.

Five years later, the character was revived in quite different form (see *Pink Panther and Sons*). In 1993 the character made yet another appearance in a syndicated show, this time talking with a voice supplied by Matt Frewer, on the first TV cartoon series from Metro Goldwyn Mayer (MGM) since *Tom and Jerry* in the early 1970s.

Throughout all versions, Henry Mancini's classic theme appeared at the opening ("Da dum, da dum, da dum da dum da dum . . ."). It even gave a bouncy beat to ads for the ill-fated Pink Panther cereal brought out in the mid-1970s which turned the user's milk a different hue ("Pink Pan-ther Flakes, they're pink, . . .").

•PINKY LEE SHOW, THE

Comedy Variety; B&W and Color
January 4, 1954–June 9, 1956

NBC Mon.–Fri. 5:15–5:30 p.m. (1/4/54–1/29/54)
NBC Mon.–Fri. 5:30–6 p.m. (2/1/54–5/11/56)
NBC Sat. 10–10:30 a.m. (3/5/55–12/17/55)
NBC Sat. 10:30–11 a.m. (12/24/55–4/7/56)
NBC Sat. 10–10:30 a.m. (4/14/56–6/9/56)

Regulars: *Pinky Lee, Jimmy Brown, Molly Bee (1954–55), Betty Jane Howarth (as "Lily Chrysanthemum"; 1954–55), Jack McCoy, Mel Koontz (1955–56), Cindy Sue (1955–56), Roberta Shore (1955–56), Susabelle (1955–56), Ken Mayer (1956), Isabel Dwan (1956), Sid Fields (1956), Margie Lizst (1956), Milton Newberger (1956), Jymme Shore (1956)*

"Yoo hoo! It's me!" started the opening song to the most frenetic of all 1950s children's shows. *The Pinky Lee Show* made a comedian who had failed on a few nighttime TV series into the daytime sensation of 1954. Pinky was a lisping, mugging character in an undersized checkered coat who danced, staged, and acted in slapstick sketches and elicited big laughs from kids in the studio audience with "Game Time," where their parents competed in events like stuffing pillow cases using boxing gloves to win prizes. This all occurred as part of a rough story line involving Pinky in the show's Happy Town Circus setting. He also had guest and regular performers show off their talents (for example, 14-year-old country singer Molly Bee and 11-year-old vocalist Susabelle), and many adult critics thought this was the show's only enjoyable—or respectable—part. But Pinky's following among children proved so strong that after a year NBC gave him a sixth day on which to crack them up. His announcer was Jack McCoy.

On September 5, 1955, the daily show added new regulars when Mel Koontz joined as the lion tamer working with Pinky for "circus boss" Jimmy Brown. The show aired from a new set in Burbank, California (previously it had come from La Jolla, California), but Pinky did the same old shtick.

Nobody laughed on September 20, 1955, when Lee, doing a commercial 22 minutes into the live show from Burbank, suddenly clutched his throat and cried "Somebody help me!" before fainting. It turned out to be a sinus condition, not a heart attack as some early press reports claimed, that had felled Pinky. He returned shortly thereafter, but *The*

The Pinky Lee Show *had as regulars in 1954 Pinky and "Lily Chrysanthemum" (played by Betty Jane Howarth).*

Mickey Mouse Club on ABC arrived and stole his thunder, and Pinky's regular series vanished. Pinky did a hosting stint on *Gumby* from June to November in 1957, but after that, viewers were not to see the likes of his uninhibited loud humor until more than 30 years later on *Pee Wee's Playhouse* (q.v.).

PINPOINT BOWLING
Sports; Color
May 30, 1971–September 12, 1971
CBS Sat. 3–3:30 p.m. (5/30/71–9/12/71)
Host/Narrator/Creator/Producer: *Johnny Johnston*
Commentator: *Pat Summerall*

On this series, two bowling champions tried to make tough shots involving pins in unusual configurations. Over the course of 10 frames, each had to knock down all of a decreasing number of pins per frame. There were two matches played per week, with $2,000 going to the winner and $500 to the loser. A perfect score of 300 won $25,000. Despite its novelty, this effort failed to garner the ratings registered by *Pro Bowlers Tour* on ABC and went off quickly.

PIP THE PIPER
Children's; B&W and Color
December 25, 1960–September 22, 1962
ABC Sat/Sun 12:30–1 p.m. (12/25/60–5/28/61)
NBC Sat. 9:30–10 a.m. (6/24/61–9/22/62)

Cast:

Pip the Piper	Jack Spear
Miss Merrynote	Phyllis Spear
Mr. Leader/Professor Oompah/	
Paul the Pirate	Lucien Kaminsky

This children's fantasy series was very much a family affair. Jack Spear, a writer for the show and co-creator with Lucien Kaminsky, played one of the lead characters, Pip the Piper, and Spear's wife, Phyllis, was Miss Merrynote, his co-star. Pip, a resident of Pipertown, played lots of the musical instruments which grew on trees there, and his pal Miss Merrynote told stories, sang songs, and played games. Other characters, many played by Kaminsky, rounded out each week's story. When the show moved to NBC in the summer of 1961, it also went to color.

In the fall of 1963 a syndicated sequel from Canada called *Mr. Piper* appeared. The 39 shows, airing on the Canadian Broadcasting Corporation in black and white but in color in America, starred Alan Crofoot as Mr. Piper, who presided over four fantasy segments—"Animal Farm," "Bag of Tricks," "Port of Calls," and "Tale Times." The show got limited distribution and failed rather quickly.

•PIRATES OF DARK WATER, THE
Cartoon; Color
September 7, 1991–September 5, 1992

ABC Sat. 10:30–11 a.m. (9/7/91–9/5/92)

Voices:

Prince Ren	George Newburn
Tula	Jodi Benson
Ioz	Hector Elizondo
Niddler	Roddy McDowall

Also: Regis Cordic, Peter Cullen, Tim Curry, Dick Gautier, Allan Lurie, Dan O'Herlihy, Brock Peters, Les Tremayne, Jessica Walter, Frank Welker

This intricately plotted action-adventure entry played as an updated swashbuckler. It commenced when Prince Ren spotted a man washed ashore on his kingdom of Octopon, who turned out to be his long-estranged father King Primus. The King prophesied his son's future before dying and told him he must capture the 13 Treasures of Rule to save their land. In hot pursuit of Primus and then Ren was the evil pirate Blot, whose tactics were so vicious that the flying and talking monkey Niddler defected to join Ren. After Ren and Niddler avoided Blot's men and held on to the first treasure, a gold compass, they managed to convince profiteer Ioz to lend them his boat so they could search for the other 12 items, the locations of which would be indicated by beams from the compass. Tula, a stowaway on the boat, joined the others in their quest. But while Ren's main purpose was to save Octopon, Ioz was primarily interested in the treasures and Tula was along just for the adventure. These clashing motives often put Ren in conflict with his shipmates.

Though there were different villains for each treasure, Blot backed most of them. He preferred to stay on the deck of his ship Maelstrom and feed his enemies to a deadly eel-like creature called Constrictus. Conch, a comical type with one leg, was the most frequently seen lackey. Instilling fear into both sides was the sea-based entity Dark Water, which could swallow human beings whole as it surged and which threatened to destroy everyone.

This series had its first five episodes run as a weeklong replacement for *Peter Pan and the Pirates* on Fox from February 25–March 1, 1991 under the title *Dark Water*. However, it was ABC which picked up the series that fall for a season run. The average cost of each elaborately illustrated episode came to $500,000 versus the standard $280,000 per half hour on Saturday mornings, making it one of the pricier series to run in that period.

PLASTICMAN COMEDY-ADVENTURE SHOW, THE
Cartoon; Color
September 22, 1979–February 4, 1984

ABC Sat. 9–11 a.m. (9/22/79–12/15/79)
ABC Sat. 9–10:30 a.m. (12/22/79–9/27/80)
ABC Sat. 11:30 a.m.–Noon (10/4/80–9/5/81)
CBS Sat. 10–10:30 a.m. (11/12/83–2/4/84)

Voices:

Plasticman/Baby Plas (1980–81)	Michael Bell
Penny/The Chief	Melendy Britt
Hula-Hula	Joe Baker
Mighty Man	Peter Cullen
Yukk	Frank Welker
Rickety Rocket	Al Fann
Cosmo	Bobby Ellerbee
Splashdown	Johnny Brown
Sunstroke	John Anthony Bailey
Venus	Dee Timberlake

Wearing a tight jumpsuit and sporting nifty shades, Plasticman was no run-of-the-mill superhero. No, he had the distinction of being the most bendable one of them all, able to become any solid shape needed to defeat the criminal element. How his clothes managed to do the same was never fully explained, but since the original Plasticman had been created as a tongue-in-cheek spoof of superheros in comic books in the 1940s and was played the same way in this cartoon, few seemed to mind. Among the equally ludicrous villains doing battle with Plasticman were Carrot Man and Toy Man. Penny was Plasticman's pixieish, love-struck pilot pal. Hula-Hula, an informant for Plasticman, was Hawaiian right down to his printed shirt.

Other segments included "Mighty Man," featuring the adventures of the world's smallest superhero, whose alter ego was Brandon Brewster (Yukk was his dog); and "Rickety Rocket," a sequence in which four black teenagers working in the Far Out Detective Agency (Cosmo, Splashdown, Sunstroke, and Venus) were joined in fighting crime by a personable space missile. There also was Fossilfoot, an easygoing bear, and new adventures of *Fangface* (q.v.).

On October 4, 1980, the program was retitled *The Plasticman/Baby Plas Super Comedy Show* and dropped all segments from the first year except for "Plasticman Consumer Tips." Now not only were Plastic and Penny husband and wife, but they had a stretchable son named Baby Plas as well. Each week the entire family got involved in one adventure, while the other segment spotlighted Baby Plas exclusively. After a year's run, the series reappeared briefly in reruns on CBS from 1983–84.

PLAY YOUR HUNCH
Game; B&W and Color
June 30, 1958–September 27, 1963

CBS Mon.–Fri. 10:30–11 a.m. (6/30/58–1/2/59)
ABC Mon.–Fri. 12:30–1 p.m. (1/5/59–5/8/59)
NBC Mon.–Fri. 10:30–11 a.m. (12/7/59–9/27/63)

Host: *Merv Griffin (6/30/58–1962), Richard Hayes (1962), Gene Rayburn (10/62–11/62), Robert Q. Lewis (11/26/62–9/27/63)*

Play Your Hunch breezed through three networks in one year and four hosts in another in its five-year run as sort of a *To Tell the Truth* knockoff using items known as X, Y, and Z instead of people. However, in this game, the two competing teams were not allowed to ask questions to determine which of the items was the "right" one but instead had to make their calls based on demonstrations and visual clues. The items involved and the attempts to deduce the correct response often made for humorous games. (For example, on one show the three items were a painting done by Elizabeth Montgomery, a Picasso, and a painting made using a pair of pants, and the actress and audience were mightily amused as the teams tried to determine which was hers.) Each correct answer in a game won a point and $50 for a team. If both teams were stumped, $50 went to the people used for the X, Y, and Z item demonstrations. The first team to amass three points won the game and additional prizes.

When Merv Griffin left to host his own talk show in 1962, he was temporarily replaced by Richard Hayes. Then Gene Rayburn hosted for five weeks, but when the ratings dropped slightly, a nervous NBC, which had guaranteed the show another year on the air, forced the producers to get yet another host. At one point during its run, the show went to taping its Friday show on Thursdays after doing a live one that day. It also surfaced twice on NBC nighttime as a summer series, from April–September 1960 and from June–September 1962, both times with Griffin as host.

PLAYTIME
Puppet; B&W
November 26, 1947–March 5, 1949

NBC Wed 5–6 p.m. (11/26/47–2/18/48)
NBC Sat. 5:30–6 p.m. (11/13/48–3/5/49)

Regulars: *Agnes Birney (as Popit), Bliss Schumann (as the Guessing Girl, her assistant)*

Playtime was a pioneering children's program which aired a month before *Howdy Doody* began, yet ran nowhere near as long or generated nearly so much enthusiasm. Airing from Washington, D.C., it employed nonprofessional adults dressed in costumes who worked with children on various educational and entertainment activities, including the marionette adventures of Willy Butts, the greedy goat. Typical was the show of October 22, 1948, which had a party for 60 children from Georgetown who got to watch a "Busy Hands" craft segment, guessing games, interviews, and even news for children. It was done in cooperation with the Washington Junior League.

The show began on WNBW Washington in mid-1947 before going network for three months. It continued locally until NBC picked it up again in the fall of 1948. By February 1949 it was on the East and Midwest networks, but left at the beginning of March.

PLUCKY DUCK SHOW, THE—See *Tiny Toon Adventures.*

POLE POSITION
Cartoon; Color
September 15, 1984–August 30, 1986

CBS Sat. 10:30–11 a.m. (9/15/84–10/27/84)
CBS Sat. 10–10:30 a.m. (11/3/84–12/29/84)
CBS Sat Noon–12:30 p.m. (3/1/86–8/30/86)

Voices:

Dan Darret	*David Coburn*
Tess Darret	*Lisa Lindgren*
Daisy Darret	*Kaleena Kiff*
Roadie	*Darryl Hickman*
Wheels	*Mel Franklyn*
Dr. Zachary	*Jack Angel*
Kuma	*Marilyn Schreffler*
Teacher	*Helen Minniear*

In *Pole Position,* sort of an updated *Devlin* (q.v.), three youngsters orphaned after their parents' death in a car accident ran a stunt show. However, these kids had the help of Wheels and Roadie, computerized "vehicles of justice" which could talk to the Darrets and had their own personalities, with Wheels being the more free-spirited one. The crew also spent time busting crooks following the directives of a secret force led by the Darrets' Uncle Zach. Joining them all in their adventures was the Darrets' monkeylike feline Kuma. As with the arcade video game of the same name on which it was based, the show featured some chase sequences from a driver's-eye view.

POLITICS '62
News Analysis; B&W
September 9, 1962–November 4, 1962

ABC Sun. 1:30–2 p.m. (9/9/62–11/4/62)

Host/Reporter: *William H. Lawrence*

Politics '62 offered reports on major congressional and gubernatorial races of 1962, starting with the contest for governor of California between incumbent Democrat Edmund G. "Pat" Brown and Republican Richard Nixon. On one show, President John F. Kennedy gave his assessment of the upcoming vote.

POPEYE—See *All-New Popeye* and *Popeye and Son.*

POPEYE AND SON
Cartoon; Color
September 19, 1987–September 3, 1988

CBS Sat. 11–11:30 a.m. (9/19/87–9/3/88)

Voices:

Popeye	*Maurice LaMarche*
Popeye Jr.	*Josh Rodine*
Olive Oyl/Lizzie/Puggy	*Marilyn Schreffler*
Bluto/Wimpy	*Allan Melvin*
Tank	*David Markus*
Woody	*Penina Segall*
Dee Dee	*Kaleena Kiff*
Eugene the Jeep	*Don Messick*

The cartoon world's favorite sailor had finally settled down in this program, as Popeye and Olive were married and had a 9-year-old son Popeye, Jr. But bliss it was not, especially since Popeye's archenemy Bluto had also stayed around, and he too was wed, to a lady named Lizzie, and had a son, aptly named Tank. Both kids largely followed in the footsteps of their fathers, meaning the antagonism remained, except the younger Popeye somewhat blasphemously did not like spinach. Woody and Dee Dee were Popeye Jr.'s friends.

POPSICLE FIVE-STAR COMEDY PARTY
Children's; B&W

May 18, 1957–July 13, 1957
ABC Sat. 5:30–6 p.m. (5/18/57–7/13/57)

Regulars: *Paul Winchell, Ben Blue, Jerry Colonna, [Ole] Olsen and [Chic] Johnson, Señor Wences, Anne Martin, Bob Bean*

Popsicle Five-Star Comedy Party was a short-lived vaudeville-style show for kids with a quintet of alternating hosts beginning with Paul Winchell and running through Señor Wences (the comedy team of Olsen and Johnson of *Hellzapoppin* fame was considered one "host"). Other regulars were Anne Martin and cartoonist Bob Bean. Guest acts also appeared.

PORKY PIG SHOW, THE
Cartoon; Color
September 20, 1964–September 2, 1967

ABC Sun. 10:30–11 a.m. (9/20/64–12/20/64)
ABC Sat. 11:30 a.m.–Noon (12/26/64–12/18/65)

ABC Sat. 10–10:30 a.m. (12/25/65–9/3/66)
ABC Sun. 4–4:30 p.m. (9/25/66–12/18/66)
ABC Sat. 9:30–10 a.m. (12/31/66–9/2/67)

Voice Characterizations: *Mel Blanc*

The stuttering swine who uttered the immortal "Th-th-th-that's all, folks!" at the end of every *Looney Tunes* movie cartoon headlined his own series two years after being seen in daytime as a supporting character on *The Bugs Bunny Show.* On most of his segments Porky was either a comic foil for Daffy Duck or the unintentional terrorizer of Sylvester the Cat. Other Warner Brother characters like Foghorn Leghorn also appeared on this series, with most segments having been previously released to theaters. After its cancellation, Porky and crew went back to *The Bugs Bunny Show.*

•PORTER WAGONER SHOW, THE
Music Variety; B&W and Color
1960–1981

Syndicated 30 minutes weekly beginning 1960

Regulars: *Porter Wagoner, Norma Jean [Beasler] (1960–67), Jeannie Seely (1965–66), Dolly Parton (1967–74), Speck Rhodes*

The longest-running of a flood of syndicated country music shows seen generally on weekend afternoons since the late 1950s, *The Porter Wagoner Show* starred a tall, pompadoured singer who was pure country—hardly any of his tunes ever cracked *Billboard*'s Hot 100 pop singles chart. His original singing partner was Norma Jean, temporarily replaced by Jeannie Seely in the mid-1960s, and then Dolly Parton, who received her first national TV exposure here. Parton embarked on a highly successful solo career in 1974, in the process of which considerable ill will developed between her and Wagoner, and it was nearly two decades before they buried the hatchet.

Providing comedy between the music was Speck Rhodes, a goofy comedian who had several front teeth missing and sported a green derby and yellow checkered shirt. Speck's bits often involved him talking on an old-fashioned telephone box to his never-seen wife Sadie. But the real attractions were Wagoner and the peppy, twangy brand of country music his band performed with gusto each week. Following the cancellation of the series, Wagoner made occasional stops on the Nashville Network (TNN) cable channel into the 1990s.

•PORTIA FACES LIFE
Soap Opera; B&W
April 5, 1954–July 1, 1955

CBS Mon.–Fri. 1–1:15 p.m. (4/5/54–7/1/55)

Cast:

Portia Manning (1954)	*Frances Reid*
Portia Manning (1954–55)	*Fran Carlon*
Walter Manning (1954)	*Donald Woods*
Walter Manning (1954–55)	*Karl Swenson*

Shirley Manning (1954)
Shirley Manning (1955)
Dick "Dickie" Blake
Dorie Blake (1954)
Kathy Baker (1954)
Bill Baker (1954)
Karl Manning, Walter's
  brother (1954)
Morgan Elliott (1954)
Tony Faraday (1954–55)
Phoebe Faraday (1954–55)
Ruth Byfield (1954–55)
Rolland Teneyck "Rollie"
  Blake (1955)

Renee Jarrett
Ginger McManus
Charles Taylor
Jean Gillespie
Elizabeth York
Richard Kendrick

Patrick O'Neal
Byron Sanders
Mark Miller
Sally Gracie
Mary Fickett

William Redfield

Based to a certain degree on the radio series of the same name which ran from 1940–41 on CBS and from 1951–52 on NBC, *Portia Faces Life* came to television with a new cast and somewhat altered story line. As on radio, Portia was a dynamo both at work as an attorney and at home as a mother. On the TV debut she helped her neighbor Kathy Baker, Bill's wife, with a gambling debt that involved Kathy with a racketeer, and still found time to take interest in her children Shirley and son Dickie. Portia's husband Walter, who seemed weak-willed in comparison despite the fact that he was editor of the local paper *The Parkerstown Herald*, was often a target of the machinations of fun-loving Dorie Blake.

By March 1955 the TV show had been retitled *The Inner Flame* and Walter had been charged with murder. Matriarch Amelia Blake, grandmother of Dorie and Rollie Blake, wanted him to resign as editor before she invested her badly needed money in the paper (Amelia had bought out Bill Baker's interest in the *Herald* following his death). Amelia also wanted Dorie to live with her, causing further heartache. Amelia was an aunt to a murder victim whose wife was in love with Walter. Amelia promised to pay Walter's legal fees if that wife left town, and also told Portia to get Portia's son by a previous marriage out of town. By July the show itself had left town.

•POUND PUPPIES
Cartoon; Color
September 13, 1986–September 3, 1988

ABC Sat. 10:30–11 a.m. (9/13/86–9/5/87)
ABC Sat. 9:30–10 a.m. (9/12/87–1/23/88)
ABC Sat. 8:30–9 a.m. (1/30/88–9/3/88)

Voices:

Cooler
Whopper
Nose Marie
Bright Eyes
Howler
Holly
Katrina Stoneheart
Brattina Stoneheart
Nabbit/Cat Gut

Dan Gilvezan
B. J. Ward
Ruth Buzzi
Nancy Cartwright
Robert Morse
Ame Foster
Pat Carroll
Adrienne Alexander
Frank Welker

Based on a line of toys, *Pound Puppies* detailed the comic exploits of a quintet of canines defending their turf. Hip Cooler, fibbing Whopper, Southern belle-ish Nose Marie, eager Bright Eyes, and worrywart Howler were all pets bequeathed to 11-year-old Holly, who was able to talk to them. Their foe was a marvelous villainess in the form of next-door neighbor Katrina Stoneheart. Katrina was a cat-loving Cruella De Vil type who wanted to evict the puppies and give a home to pets like her beloved Cat Gut. Her aptly named daughter Brattina, who assisted her in efforts to eradicate the pooches, referred to her as "Mommie Dearest." Also notable were the occasional enjoyable spoofs on pop culture, such as music videos in the "Secret Agent Pup" episode. In its second season this show was retitled *All New Pound Puppies*.

POWER RANGERS ZEO—See *Mighty Morphin Power Rangers*.

PRESIDENT'S WEEK, THE
Public Affairs; B&W
October 4, 1953–March 28, 1954

NBC Sun. 12:45–1 p.m. or 3–3:15 p.m. (10/4/53–3/28/54)

Host: *Tex McCrary*

Veteran newscaster Tex McCrary led this quick recap of major recent events involving President Dwight D. Eisenhower.

PRESS CONFERENCE
Public Affairs; B&W
January 6, 1957–April 7, 1957

ABC Sun. 5:30–6 p.m. (1/6/57–4/7/57)

Host: *Martha Rountree*

Martha Rountree invited one guest per show to be interrogated by various news correspondents on this series, which generally ran in the nighttime. It first aired on NBC Wednesdays from July 4–September 26, 1956, then moved to ABC Sundays at 8:30 on October 28, 1956 before moving to Sunday afternoons briefly in 1957. It returned to the nighttime Mondays on ABC after the daytime run until July 15, 1957.

•PRESS YOUR LUCK
Game; Color
September 19, 1983–September 26, 1986

CBS Mon.–Fri. 10:30–11 a.m. (9/19/83–1/3/86)
CBS Mon.–Fri. 4–4:30 p.m. (1/6/86–9/26/86)

Host: *Peter Tomarken*

Press Your Luck was a combination of general knowledge questions and electronic gadgetry. Three players tried to be the first to provide the right answer to a question, with each correct answer earning a player three spins on the show's electronic wheel. After four questions, players then used their wheel spins to see who could amass the most money and merchandise on an electronic board, with the player with the lowest number of earned spins going first. The catch was that an animated gremlin called a whammy could be chosen by the player, causing him or her to lose all money earned to that point. Also at any time, a player could give his or her remaining spins to another player if he or she wanted to freeze at that money level and avoid possible future whammies. Two rounds of four questions and subsequent wheel spins took place each day. In the first round, the board's top prize was $1,500, and in the second it was $5,000. Four whammies eliminated a player from a game, and any whammies earned in the first round remained with the player through the second round.

The show had one winner who produced much aggravation for the production team. Michael Larson of Lebanon, Ohio, a video game enthusiast who had studied the configurations on the electronic board for six months on his television screen at home, came on the series June 8 and 11, 1984, and won more than $110,000! "His reflexes were so fast the computer had to keep giving him more turns," executive producer Bill Carruthers told *TV Guide*. "We had to split the episode into two shows. He was by far the biggest winner we've ever had." Peeved CBS executives immediately ordered a reprogramming of the computer to prevent future big winners, which indeed it did.

The pilot for *Press Your Luck* was taped in 1980 with Pat Sajak as its host. It was based on the 1977 series *Second Chance* (q.v.). When it arrived on the CBS schedule, Sajak was host of *Wheel of Fortune*, so Peter Tomarken became the moderator. This was the last show CBS programmed in its daily 4–4:30 slot before returning the period to affiliates.

•PRICE IS RIGHT, THE
Game; B&W and Color
November 26, 1956–

NBC Mon.–Fri. 10:30–11 a.m. (11/26/56–12/28/56)
NBC Mon.–Fri. 11–11:30 a.m. (12/31/56–9/6/63)
ABC Mon.–Fri. 11–11:30 a.m. (9/9/63–3/28/64)
ABC Mon.–Fri. 10:30–11 a.m. (3/31/64–12/25/64)
ABC Mon.–Fri. 11:30 a.m.–Noon (12/28/64–9/3/65)
CBS Mon.–Fri. 10:30–11 a.m. (9/4/72–3/23/73)
CBS Mon.–Fri. 3–3:30 p.m. (3/26/73–8/15/75)
CBS Mon.–Fri. 10:30–11 a.m. (8/18/75–11/28/75)
CBS Mon.–Fri. 10–11 a.m. or 10:30–11:30 a.m.
  (12/1/75–4/20/79)
CBS Mon.–Fri. 11 a.m.–Noon (4/23/79–)

Host: *Bill Cullen (1956–65), Bob Barker (1972–)*

Announcer: *Johnny Olsen (1956–85), Rod Roddy (1985–)*

The Price Is Right was that rarity of TV shows, one whose revival was infinitely more successful than its first version. The original incarnation was a big hit in the 1950s, but the show's popularity faded in the 1960s as the format wore out its welcome. A reinvented version in 1972 started slowly, then gained steam until it was the top daytime game show of the 1980s. Since 1994 *The Price Is Right* has been the only daily network game show on the air. The second

Bill Cullen models a mink coat up for bids on The Price Is Right *in 1959.*

version alone is the longest-running daytime game show, and the series is the only game show to run more than 22 years on network television.

The first edition's format was simple. Four contestants bid one at a time on various items and tried to be nearest the actual retail price without going over that amount. One could bid up to three times, or simply "freeze" the estimate at any point. Most of the items up for grabs were moderate-to-expensive merchandise, and some had hidden bonus prizes attached to them which the winner received as well.

Four times a week, people at home were encouraged to send in their best guess to claim a prize displayed in a showcase. If more than one viewer guessed the exact amount, there was a runoff question used to determine the final winner. Every Friday, the winner of the previous week's contest was announced. Within its first year, this contest averaged over 500,000 pieces of mail each week.

After nearly a year in daytime, NBC started a nighttime telecast on September 23, 1957, which cracked the top 10 ratings for the 1959–60 season. But the popularity of both installments began to wane in the early 1960s, and they moved from NBC to ABC in September 1963 after NBC refused to keep the nighttime version on the air (a similar situation occurred five years later with *Let's Make a Deal*). In 1965, the series disappeared for seven years (the nighttime edition had ended in September 1964).

CBS revived the property in 1972 under the initial title *The New Price Is Right,* and with it came a general revamping of the format. Now contestants were preselected from the studio audience as they came to the show, thus prompting Johnny Olsen to say their names one at a time and bellow, "Come on down!" The bidding on objects was abbreviated so that four players guessed only once about

Bob Barker had soap stars David Hasselhoff (left) and Terry Lester (right) appear in a special Showcase Showdown on The Price Is Right *in 1982.*

an item's cost, although if all four overbid they repeated the process. The winner then got to join Bob Barker on stage to play one of a variety of pricing games (and also got $100 if he or she guessed the item's exact price). The games generally involved guessing the numbers in the price of the merchandise at hand, matching prices with merchandise, and comparing prizes to determine which was higher or lower in cost. Three games occurred each day, and the top two scoring players participated in the Showcase Showdown, where they each received one package containing at least three prizes and had to guess the total, usually in the range of thousands of dollars.

After three years of time changes, CBS took a gamble in late 1975 and made the series the first daily hour-long game show (*Wheel of Fortune* tried that format briefly around the same time). Now there were two rounds of three games, with the contestants in each trio spinning the "money wheel" to determine who would face the other round's winner in the Showcase Showdown. The money wheel contained amounts in five-cent increments from a nickel to one dollar, and the object was to come as close to spinning one dollar within two spins without going over. Any player spinning a dollar won $1,000 and got to try one bonus spin to earn $5,000 in the two spaces adjacent to the $1 spot or $10,000 if it landed exactly on the $1 spot. The revised Showcase Showdowns were now more

elaborate, with the announcer often acting in playlets the story lines of which involved the goods. A variety of models also took part in the playlets, the longest-lasting of which was Diane Parkinson. Rod Roddy replaced Johnny Olsen as announcer in 1985 following the latter's death.

As the series became the dominant program in its 11 a.m. slot, there were several attempts to replicate its success outside daytime, but the results were disappointing. Dennis James hosted a nighttime syndicated version from 1972–76, followed by Barker for another three years. The next syndicated version popped up in 1985 with Tom Kennedy. A year later, CBS tried the show Thursday nights opposite *The Cosby Show* on NBC from August 14–September 18, 1986. The most recent effort was another nightly syndicated version in 1994 hosted by actor Doug Davidson, then playing Paul on *The Young and the Restless.*

By the way, if you thought some of the episodes seen in the early 1980s looked familiar, you were right. *The Price Is Right* was so successful at the time that it could afford to repeat some of its shows during the summers of 1981 and 1983, a practice unheard of in the first-run world of daytime game shows. But then, the success of *The Price Is Right* over five decades of programming is unparalleled as well.

PRINCETON '55
Informational; B&W
January 2, 1955–March 27, 1955
NBC Sun. 1–1:30 p.m. (1/2/55–3/27/55)

This series of lectures from Princeton University first aired on WNBT New York City Sundays from 5:30–6 p.m. for eight weeks starting April 18, 1954. When it came on the network a year later, some actors, such as Mildred Dunnock, appeared in dramatizations used for the weekly presentations. It returned as a local show titled *Princeton '56* on WRCA February 11, 1956 at 6 p.m.

•PRO BOWLERS TOUR
Sports; B&W and Color
January 6, 1962–
ABC Sat. 4:30–6 p.m. (1/6/62–4/28/62)
ABC Sat. 3:30–5 p.m. (1/12/63–4/21/84; winter months only)
ABC Sat. 3–4 p.m. (1/15/85-; winter months only)
Hosts: *Chris Schenkel, Jack Buck (1962–64), Billy Welu (1964–74), Nelson "Bo" Burton Jr. (1975–)*

In 1959, attorney Eddie Elias and 32 others joined to form The Professional Bowlers Association in Akron, Ohio, to improve bowling's image. The Association, and bowling, got a huge boost from this long-lived series, which each week had five finalists try to win a championship at various locales across the country within a 90-minute period. It really took off in 1967, when the show began a king-of-the-hill format which boosted ratings up 20 percent and set the standard practice of play for the next 30 years. Under

this system, the bowler ranked #5 played #4, then that winner played #3, and so on until the survivor met #1 in the final match.

The first two shows were taped, but then the rest were live. This added to the suspense, but not always in showcasing top performances. In its first 30 years, for example, bowlers reached a perfect 300 score to claim the top prize of a $10,000 check and a new car on only six shows. Nevertheless, the series was so popular that it often outrated the Masters golf tournament competing against it each April. The audience tended to be older and less affluent by the 1990s, making it less appealing to advertisers, but ABC has remained consistent in keeping the property on the air for a few months each year. However, in late 1996 the network announced that it would cancel the show the following year.

By dint of his tenure with the series, Chris Schenkel has become the announcer with the longest regular hosting job in sports. Among his co-analysts, the one who lasted longest was Nelson Burton Jr., the sixth all-time money winner on the PBA tour by 1980, according to *Sports Illustrated.* Apart from covering the game, all announcers typically took time to interview winners and former PBA champions during each show.

PRO FOOTBALL—See *NFL Football.*

PROFESSIONAL BOWLERS TOUR—See *Pro Bowlers Tour.*

PROFESSIONAL FOOTBALL—See *NFL Football.*

PROFESSIONAL HOCKEY—See *NHL Hockey.*

PROSTARS
Cartoon; Color
September 14, 1991–July 25, 1992
NBC Sat. 9:30–10 a.m. (9/14/91–7/25/92)

Voices:
Michael Jordan	*Dorian Harewood*
Wayne Gretsky	*Townsend Coleman*
Bo Jackson	*Dave Fennoy*
Mama	*Susan Silo*
Denise	*Diana Barrows*

Top professional athletes at the time from the world of basketball (Michael Jordan), hockey (Wayne Gretsky), and both baseball and football (Bo Jackson) headlined this adventure-oriented cartoon. The trio received word on the week's mission from their leader Mama, an inventor of many gadgets for the group. The men then left their hangout, the Man's Gym, in their specially made aircraft. Typically Mama's assistant Denise, who wanted to be a Prostars member, got caught by the villains when tagging along with the group. But Michael, Wayne, and Bo always rescued her and got the bad guys after saying, "OK, Prostars, it's game time!" and using their athletic skills along with their specially made devices. The athletes themselves appeared briefly in live-action introductions to each show and answered questions at the end of the shows.

PRYOR'S PLACE

Sitcom; Color
September 22, 1984–June 15, 1985
CBS Sat. 11:30 a.m.–Noon (9/22/84–6/15/85)

Cast:

Richard Pryor	Himself
Little Richie	Akili Prince
Wally	Cliffy Magee
Freddy	Danny Nucci
Allen	Tony Cox
Meatrack	Keland Love

Also: *The Krofft Puppets*

This well-received taped children's show was set on a street corner similar to the one where comedian Richard Pryor, the program's star, grew up. Pryor played several characters in playlets set around a single theme or moral each show. Other characters who appeared included Richard's younger self, Little Richie. Despite the show's good intentions, some did not see reformed drug user Pryor as an appropriate host for a kid's series. One who did not was Charles B. Brakefield, general manager and president of WREG Memphis, Tennessee, who announced at a CBS affiliate meeting in May 1984—without, by the way, having seen the show—that the decision to use Pryor was "disgraceful." Nevertheless, the show did win numerous awards during its only season on the air. This was a Sid and Marty Krofft production.

PUD'S PRIZE PARTY

Talent Variety; B&W
June 21, 1952–December 20, 1952
ABC Sat. 11:30 a.m.–Noon (6/21/52–12/20/52)

Host: *Todd Russell*

The competition of amateur juveniles to become "The Most Talented Child of the Week" was the main component of this show, which was staged at the Philadelphia Town Hall. Todd Russell also played games such as "Simon Says" with the studio audience, which consisted of children, and sponsor Fleer Gum laid its product-pushing on thick by having an actor playing Pud, Fleer's Dubble Bubble boy, throw out gum to the kids. (Home viewers could win prizes by winning a contest on "Why I Like Dubble Bubble" too!)

PUNKY BREWSTER—See *It's Punky Brewster.*

PUP NAMED SCOOBY DOO, A—See *Scooby Doo.*

PUPPET TELEVISION THEATRE—See *Howdy Doody.*

PUPPY'S FURTHER ADVENTURES, THE

Cartoon; Color
September 10, 1983–November 8, 1986
ABC Sat. 11–11:30 a.m. (9/10/83–9/1/84)
ABC Sat. 8–8:30 a.m. (9/8/84–11/10/84)
CBS Sat. 11:30 a.m.–Noon (9/13/86–11/8/86)

Voices:

Petey the Puppy	Billy Jacoby
Dolly	Nancy McKeon
Duke/Dash	Michael Bell
Lucky	Peter Cullen
Tommy	Tony O'Dell
Glyder	Josh Rodine
Mother	Janet Waldo
Father	John Stephenson

Petey the Puppy had one main goal in life—to find the family of humans who raised him. His human friend Dolly and fellow dogs-to-be Duke, Dash, and Lucky tried to find his master Tommy and the latter's mom and dad in 13 episodes in various locales.

The character was based on a story from Catherine Woolley, "The Puppy Who Wanted a Boy," which was first seen as an installment on *ABC Weekend Special* on May 6, 1978. Three sequels followed and were repeated over the next four years on the show, with various actors supplying Petey's voice. Petey became a supporting segment on *Scooby Doo* in 1982–83 before getting his own show, which was retitled *The Puppy's Great Adventures* in the fall of 1984 before ending later that year. CBS reran the series in 1986.

•QUEEN FOR A DAY

Game; B&W
January 3, 1956–October 2, 1964
NBC Mon.–Fri. 4:30–5 p.m. (1/3/56–6/29/56)
NBC Mon.–Fri. 4–4:45 p.m. (7/2/56–9/19/58)
NBC Mon.–Fri. 4–4:30 p.m. (9/22/58–3/27/59)
NBC Mon.–Fri. 2–2:30 p.m. (3/30/59–9/2/60)
ABC Mon.–Fri. 12:30–1 p.m. (9/28/60–11/11/60)
ABC Mon.–Fri. 3–3:30 p.m. (11/14/60–12/27/63)
ABC Mon.–Fri. 3:30–4 p.m. (12/30/63–10/2/64)

Host: *Jack Bailey*

Assistant: *Jeanne Cagney*

"What hath Sarnoff wrought?" thundered *New York Times* TV critic Jack Gould on this show's debut, referring to Robert Sarnoff, the president of NBC's parent company RCA. Sarnoff had no response, but Howard Blake, a producer for the show, did, in *Fact* magazine in 1966. "Sure, *Queen* was vulgar and sleazy and filled with bathos and bad taste,"

Blake wrote. "That was why it was so successful; it was exactly what the general public wanted."

The object of Gould's (and many others') distaste was a daily display of four or five women who tried to present themselves as the most deserving of pity to generate the all-important audience applause determining that day's "queen." Contestants telling their needs to unctuous Jack Bailey included a short-order cook with an ailing husband who wanted to become a restaurateur and a college student lacking tuition funds, but many of them told of plights so pathetic they gave the show an overall air of shameless exploitation. In the 1950s winners received a tiara and robe to wear and a bouquet of flowers, plus $1,500 worth of prizes plugged ad nauseum, and sometimes a vacation (by 1963 victors got $3,500 worth of household goods, a wardrobe, and a visit to a movie set). Occasionally women competed against each other in various categories, such as an all-grandmother contest.

Between contestants' tales of woe, there was an odd fashion segment with Jeanne Cagney, sister of movie great Jimmy Cagney, serving as commentator. Many of the models seen were young, and many, such as Nicole De Meyer, Miss Belgium of 1955, and Mitsu-ko from Japan,

were from other countries. That international flavor was presumably supposed to be enhanced when the show went to Europe in the summer of 1961 to tape a few shows.

During the early years on each weekday morning about 900 women willing to risk their dignity poured into the Moulin Rouge restaurant in Los Angeles to fill out a wish-list form to get on the show (the most popular wish as of 1957 was a washing machine). Five staff members narrowed the field to 400 possibilities after two reviews of the forms, then down to 21 candidates which Bailey reviewed to pare the list down to 8 ladies eligible for 5 slots on the day's show. Given the intense competition to get onto the show, it is not surprising that *Queen for a Day* was a ratings hit in its first few years and that NBC expanded it to an unusual (for a game show) 45-minute length to accommodate advertisers.

Queen for a Day began on the Mutual radio network on April 30, 1945 as *Queen for Today* with host Dud Williamson. By 1947 Jack Bailey was the host. The show had its first TV exposure with an experimental simulcast with the radio show on W6XAO Los Angeles at 10 a.m.

Jack Bailey stands with the winner and three other contestants on Queen for a Day.

on May 21, 1947. More shows followed, and it eventually became a regular feature on W6XAO through July 1, 1948. In 1950 *Queen for a Day* ran on that station, with the new call letters of KTSL, in a version separate from the radio show, and in 1951 it ran on KECA Los Angeles. It was simulcast with the radio show starting in 1952. At one point the show was airing on seven stations on the West Coast; six years later it went network.

In mid-1960 ABC daytime programming head Jerry Chester announced a move of the festivities to his network, which upset NBC officials, who said they had a verbal contract with producers and a written document with a five-year option to retain it on their schedule. Following an out-of-court settlement between all parties, it moved to ABC for four years. The show crowned more than 5,000 queens before it ended in 1964. A 1970 syndicated revival with Dick Curtis as host and Nancy Myers as fashion commentator was a flop.

•QUICK DRAW McGRAW
Cartoon; Color
October 28, 1963–September 3, 1966

CBS Sat. 10–10:30 a.m. (9/28/63–9/18/65)
CBS Sat. 11:30 a.m.–Noon (9/25/65–9/3/66)

Voices:

Quick Draw McGraw/Baba
   Looey et al.
Doggie Daddy   *Daws Butler*
Sagebrush Sal   *Doug Young*
                            Sally Bennett

Executive Producers: *Joseph Hanna and William Barbera*

A virtual one-man cartoon show featuring the versatile voice of Daws Butler, *Quick Draw McGraw*, which premiered in syndication in 1959, was a moderately amusing takeoff of the TV western series format that was a TV mania at the time. The star was a drawling horse engaged in maintaining justice in the Old West. When doing so, Quick Draw often assumed a saber-wielding Zorro-like counterpart called El Kabong, or at least he did whenever his mask was not at the cleaners. His sidekick Baba Looey, a burro with a sombrero on his head who was the equivalent of Pancho from *The Cisco Kid*, faithfully served with Quick Draw even though he often knew that McGraw's schemes were crazy. The duo's friends included the biscuit-loving dog Snuffles and Sagebrush Sal, a filly who was for some reason in love with McGraw. Other segments seen were "Snooper and Blabber," about a feline and a mouse, respectively, who went about spying on crimes in their trench coats; "Augie Doggie and Doggie Daddy," with the former getting advice from the latter, a Jimmy Durante sound-alike, about how to survive the rat race; and "Snagglepuss" (see *Yogi's Gang*).

The CBS shows were repeats of the program, which ended production in 1962. The series remained fairly popular in syndicated reruns into the 1990s, when it became part of the Cartoon Network's lineup.

QUIZ KIDS, THE
Game; B&W
January 20, 1952–January 11, 1953

CBS Sun. 3–3:30 p.m. (1/20/52–4/13/52)
CBS Sun. 4–4:30 p.m. (9/14/52–1/11/53)

Host: *Joe Kelly*

For any adult who wanted to feel really dumb, *The Quiz Kids* was the show to watch. Five child prodigies, mostly under the age of 8, with superior IQs answered questions submitted by viewers, with correct answers awarding points to them based on the show staff's opinion of the query's difficulty. An incorrect answer gave the home viewer who submitted it a prize. The top three highest scorers returned to the show each week, with those failing to make the grade given a second chance as a guest on a later show. Some celebrities visited the show as well, such as Adlai Stevenson on the daytime debut.

A host of children appeared on the show, with only two seen at the start of the two daytime runs on CBS, 6-year-olds Janet Ahern and Frankie Vander Ploeg. Anyone interested in learning more about the "kids" and their sometimes bittersweet life stories as grownups should read *Whatever Happened to the Quiz Kids?*, published in 1982 and written by Ruth Duskin, a one-time panelist on the show.

Begun on NBC radio on June 28, 1940 and heard on ABC and CBS as well before ending the audio version in 1953, *The Quiz Kids* came to television as a local show on WNBQ Chicago in January 1949. Two months later it went out on the NBC network at night where it remained through October 26, 1951. It returned on CBS Sunday afternoons for most of 1952, spelled by a nighttime NBC run from July through September that year, then appeared on CBS nighttime from January 17–November 8, 1953. CBS brought it back in nighttime from January 12–September 27, 1956 with Clifton Fadiman as host.

Two syndicated revivals of the show turned up in later years, with Jim McKrell as host in 1978 and actor Jonathan Prince doing the same in a modified 1990–91 version called *The Quiz Kids Challenge*. Famed TV producer Norman Lear (*All in the Family*) also hosted a rendition of the show on CBS Cable in 1981–82.

R

RAGGEDY ANN AND ANDY—See *Adventures of Raggedy Ann and Andy, The.*

RAINBOW HOUSE
Children's; B&W
January 25, 1948–May 2, 1948

DuMont Sun. 5:30–6:30 p.m. (1/25/48–5/2/48)

Host/Producer/Director: *Bob Emery*

This pioneering Sunday afternoon teenage show with audience participation aired live from WTTG Washington, D.C., to at least New York City. It started on January 18, 1948, from 6–7 p.m., then switched to a half hour earlier the following week. Bob Emery, host of *Small Fry Club*, the show that aired before this series, also oversaw this one. About 50 youths appeared weekly to discuss culture, sports, and leisure activities geared to their age group.

The series was adopted from a radio show of the same name hosted and directed by Emery which began on WNEW New York and joined the Mutual radio network in 1942.

RALPH EDWARDS SHOW, THE
Variety/Game; B&W
January 14, 1952–May 16, 1952
NBC Mon/Wed/Fri 3:30–4 p.m. (1/14/52–5/16/52)
Regulars: *Ralph Edwards, Steve Reeves, Sara Berner, Carole Richards, the Varieteers*

Ralph Edwards produced and starred in this eponymous series patterned largely after his *Truth or Consequences* program. Members of the studio audience competed in stunts to win prizes, such as a fellow who tried to earn $50 by tying balloons to his wife's hair. Carrying props and prizes was bodybuilder Steve Reeves, nearly a decade before his success in *Hercules* movies. Reeves served as pure beefcake exploitation for housewives, as he dressed in a torn shirt to show off his physique à la Marlon Brando in *A Streetcar Named Desire*. Other regulars were singer Carole Richards, the Varieteers, a three-piece instrumental combo, and Sara Berner, who did a character bit throughout the show.

The program had one stunt in its first month which literally stank. Contestants had to guess the number of pieces of fruit in a big wire crate containing 5,106 oranges. After two weeks, the oranges on top had crushed the bottom ones to a rotten, smelly pulp. Shortly thereafter, when a woman guessed 5,183 oranges, Edwards gladly declared her a winner. By that time, the show had added a "New Fathers Day" segment saluting men whose wives had just given birth and a "Fabulous Folks" interview with a news personality.

The series was to return in the fall of 1952 after a summer vacation, but NBC slated it for a morning slot where it had difficulties attracting advertisers. This forced the network to look at cheaper programs, and as a result *The Ralph Edwards Show* never returned. However, Edwards did bring *Truth or Consequences* to NBC daytime four years later.

RANGER JOE
Children's; B&W
December 3, 1950–May 25, 1952
ABC Sun. Noon–12:15 p.m. (12/3/50–2/24/52)
CBS Sun. Noon–12:15 p.m. (3/2/52–5/25/52)
Cast:

Ranger Joe	*Jessie Rogers*
Assistant	*Pee Wee Miller*
Assistant	*Monty Rosci*

This live Philadelphia-based concoction had a western adventure format that included some outside scenes despite its urban city of origination. Its name came from sponsor Ranger Joe Cereals, whose withdrawal of advertising on the show led to its cancellation.

RANGER RANCH ROUNDUP
Children's; B&W
April 16, 1950–April 23, 1950
ABC Sun. Noon–12:30 p.m. (4/16/50–4/23/50)
Host/Singer: *Boyd Heath*
Sidekick: *Floyd Buckley*

Ranger Ranch Roundup aired at least three weeks on ABC New York affiliate WJZ before going network for only two weeks before ending. It offered songs, dances, and contests for children in a western setting.

RANSOM SHERMAN SHOW, THE
Variety; B&W
October 16, 1950–January 12, 1951
NBC Mon.–Fri. 3–3:30 p.m. (10/16/50–1/12/51)
Regulars: *Ransom Sherman, Bob Graham, Nancy Wright, the Visionaires, the Art Van Damme Quintet*

Life magazine described comedian Ransom Sherman as "a bright TV light—so popular that his program will be a regular feature over NBC." That prognostication proved dreadfully wrong, as Sherman flopped both in nighttime (in an unremarkable nightly NBC summer series from July 3–August 25, 1950), and in daytime for four months. Both daytime and nighttime series came from WBKB Chicago and had singer Nancy Wright and the musical Art Van Damme Quintet as regulars. The daytime version also featured vocalist Bob Graham and the Visionaires, a singing quartet, plus how-to gags from Sherman. Lack of a sponsor killed the daily series.

RAW TOONAGE—See Marsupilami.

RAZZMATAZZ
Children's; Color
November 5, 1977–June 8, 1978
CBS Sat. 1:30–2 p.m. (11/5/77–6/8/78)
Host: *Barry Bostwick*

This once-a-month replacement for *The CBS Children's Film Festival* was produced in cooperation with *Scholastic Magazine*. The newsmagazine format concentrated on outstanding youngsters, such as a 17-year-old girl who was an apprentice railroad engineer and a 14-year-old championship female fiddler, and topics interesting to children, such as reports on how animated cartoon are made and the 1977 National Hula Hoop finals at Six Flags Over Georgia. The pilot aired April 16, 1977 with Bostwick, and it continued as an occasional weekday special through 1982 with Brian Tochi taking over as host.

REACH FOR THE STARS
Game; Color
January 2, 1967–March 31, 1967
NBC Mon.–Fri. 10–10:25 a.m. (1/2/67–3/31/67)
Host: *Bill Mazer*

Sportscaster Bill Mazer made his only foray into game show hosting with this short-lived entry. Three contestants competed to be the first to answer a question and get the chance to "reach for the stars" on the set, which contained either another question to answer or a stunt to perform. Correct answers and performances earned the players money (which was calculated down to pennies!), and each day's winner competed in the next day's show.

The idea for the series came from Merv Griffin's childhood at a theater where he played bingo. Winners got to go on stage and grab a star from the stage curtain, with the star having an amount of up to $25 listed on it as his or her prize. However, when Griffin was out of the country during preproduction on this show, his associates replaced the curtain with a cutout of a spaceship, which Merv hated. Apparently so did home viewers, as low ratings prompted NBC to replace *Reach for the Stars* with *Snap Judgment.*

READING ROOM, THE
Children's; B&W
September 22, 1962–March 16, 1963
CBS Sat. 12:30–1 p.m. (9/22/62–3/16/63)
Host: *Ned Hoopes*

Each week *Reading Room* had four children ages 8 to 12 review and discuss one book; on the debut the book was Peter Freuchen's *Whaling Boy.* The series was based in New York, but participants came from outside the city. Perhaps the most impressive show was in early 1963, when it went to Washington, D.C., to let Supreme Court Justice William O. Douglas talk with children about his book, *Exploring the Himalaya.*

•REAL GHOSTBUSTERS, THE
Cartoon; Color
September 13, 1986–September 5, 1992
ABC Sat. 10–10:30 a.m. (9/13/86–9/5/87)
ABC Sat. 10:30–11 a.m. (9/12/87–1/23/88)
ABC Sat. 10–11 a.m. (1/30/88–9/3/88)
ABC Sat. 9:30–10 a.m. (9/10/88–9/1/90)
ABC Sat. 9–10 a.m. (9/8/90–8/31/91)
ABC Sat. 10–10:30 a.m. (12/7/91–9/5/92)

Voices:

Peter Venkman (1986–87)	Lorenzo Music
Peter Venkman (1987–92)	Dave Coulier
Egon Spengler	Maurice LaMarche
Ray Stantz/Slimer	Frank Welker
Winston Zeddmore (1986–87)	Arsenio Hall
Winston Zeddmore (1987–92)	Edward L. Jones
Janine Melnitz (1986–87)	Laura Summer
Janine Melnitz (1987–92)	Kathi E. Soucie

Theme: *"Ghostbusters,"* by Ray Parker Jr.

Based on the smash 1984 movie *Ghostbusters* starring Bill Murray, this cartoon featured a quartet of ghoul-fighting guys (Peter, Egon, Ray, and Winston) who pursued their avocation in janitorial outfits replete with guns ready to stun the supernatural beings into oblivion. Slimer was their pet blob apparition with a ravenous and mischievous streak, and Janine their diligent secretary.

An immediate success, the series also went into daily syndication in 1987. On September 10, 1988, the show's title became *Slimer! and the Real Ghostbusters* and expanded to an hour, with Slimer having his (its?) own segments on quests for food and fun. The show got its first prime-time special, "The Halloween Door," a year later on October 29, 1989. For a similarly titled series often confused with this one, see *Ghost Busters.*

•REAL LIFE
Women's; Color
March 4, 1996–
NBC Mon.–Fri. 10–11 a.m. (3/4/96–)
Hosts: *Ken Taylor, Lu Hanessian*

With little fanfare, NBC launched this magazine-style series to replace repeats of *Leeza* (q.v.). It featured reports on health, money, families, and other topics primarily directed toward housewives. Its most notable feature was that one of the hosts introducing the taped reports, Ken Taylor, was the first African-American to appear on daytime in such a role.

REALLY WILD ANIMALS—See *National Geographic's Really Wild Animals.*

•REBOOT
Cartoon; Color
September 10, 1994–July 6, 1996
ABC Sat. 9:30–10 a.m. (9/10/94–7/15/95)
ABC Sat. 9:30–10:30 a.m. (two shows; 7/29/95–9/2/95)
ABC Sat. 10:30–11 a.m. (9/9/95–5/4/96)
ABC Sat. 11:30 a.m.–Noon (5/11/96–7/6/96)

Voices:

Bob ReBoot	Michael Benyaer
Dot Matrix	Kathleen Barr
Enzo (1994–95)	Jesse Moss
Enzo (1995–96)	Matthew Sinclair
Megabyte	Tony Jay
Hexadecimal	Shirley Millner
Phong, others	Michael Donovan
Slash	Phil Hayes
Hack	Gary Chalk
Mouse	Louise Vallance

ReBoot was TV's first totally computer-generated animated series, arriving a year ahead of the more publicized *Toy Story,* the first movie of its type. The plot in fact thrived on its computer heritage, using as its hero Bob ReBoot, an adolescent who came from the Internet to the city of Mainframe to defend it from viruses—i.e., invaders—specifically the giant, armored Megabyte, whose stooges were Hack and Slash, and the Medusa-like Hexadecimal. Bob's pals were Dot Matrix, the green operator of a diner, her eager younger brother Enzo, and Frisket the digital dog. Bob's best defensive tool was Glitch, a device he wore on his wrist which could do a multitude of tasks. He also received advice from the ancient Phong. Apart from impressive action sequences, the show had some comedy bits.

The cartoon used the talents of 22 computer animators and was recorded in stereo. It was produced in Vancouver, British Columbia, Canada, and aired Wednesday nights on Canada's YTV.

REBUS GAME, THE
Game; B&W
March 29, 1965–September 24, 1965
ABC Mon.–Fri. 1–1:30 p.m. (3/29/65–9/24/65)
Host: *Jack Linkletter*

Using the converse of the premise of *Concentration* crossed with *Password,* *The Rebus Game* had two duos compete in rounds where each team took turns in having one member try, using pictures, to convey a word or phrase to the other member. After six unremarkable months, ABC replaced this with reruns of *Ben Casey.*

RECITAL HALL
Music; B&W
March 1, 1952–July 17, 1955
NBC Sat. 5:30–6 p.m. (3/1/52–3/8/52)
NBC Sun. Various half hours between 2:30 and 5 p.m. (3/16/52–5/4/52)
NBC Sun. 5–5:30 p.m. (7/5/53–8/21/53)
NBC Sun. 5–5:30 p.m. (7/3/55–7/17/55)

This filmed-from-Philadelphia series (by 1953 at least) of concert soloists bounced all over the NBC schedule. The series also ran for a few weeks on NBC nighttime in the summers of 1951 (where it debuted nationally on July 1, 1951) and 1954. After its network run, *Recital Hall* reappeared as a local New York show and ran as late as 1961 on WNBC Saturdays from 10–11 p.m. with Ben Grauer as host. It was also known as *TV Recital Hall.*

RED HAND GANG, THE
Adventure; Color
September 10, 1977–January 28, 1978
NBC Sat. 12:30–1 p.m. (9/10/77–1/28/78)

Cast:
Frankie — *Matthew Laborteaux*
J.R. — *J. E. Miller*
Joanne — *Jolie Newman*
Doc — *James Bond III*
Li'l Bill — *John Brogna*

A quintet of youngsters made up the Red Hand Gang, a bunch of fledgling junior detectives who tried to solve mysteries in cliffhanger episodes. The neighborhood crew was integrated both racially (J.R. was black) and sexually (Joanne was the one in ponytails). The group's mascot was Boomer the dog.

RED ROWE SHOW, THE
Variety; B&W
November 16, 1959–July 8, 1960
CBS Mon.–Fri. 10–10:30 a.m. (11/16/59–7/8/60)
Regulars: *Red Rowe, Bill Cunningham, Peggy Taylor, the Billy Liebert Orchestra*

CBS may have had visions of another Arthur Godfrey for its daytime lineup with this series, but there was no mistaking Red Rowe for the Old Redhead. Red was a familiar Los Angeles TV personality, having starred on KNXT's *Panorama Pacific* show from 1953–57, and then hosted the daily hour series *Red Rowe's Get Together* on KNXT (the CBS affiliate) in 1956 and the 8:30–10:30 a.m. daily *Red Rowe's Panorama* on KTLA in 1958. But along with obscure singers Bill Cunningham and Peggy Taylor on CBS, Red just did not have what it takes to make it nationally. His show died against *Dough-Re-Mi* on NBC.

•REGIS PHILBIN SHOW, THE
Talk/Interview; Color
November 30, 1981–April 9, 1982
NBC Mon.–Fri. 10–10:30 a.m. (11/30/81–4/9/82)
Regulars: *Regis Philbin, Mary Hart (12/7/81–4/9/82)*

From a 1989 telecast of *The Golden Girls:*
ROSE (BETTY WHITE): *I just found out I'm the most boring person alive.*
SOPHIA (ESTELLE GETTY): *Did something happen to Regis Philbin?*

Poor Regis (or Reege, as later cohort Kathie Lee Gifford would say). His history of short-lived talk shows both locally (Los Angeles and New York) and nationally (host for a 90-minute syndicated late-night series in 1964–65, co-host on ABC's late night entry *The Joey Bishop Show* from 1967–69), plus a reputation for being somewhat less than an exciting personality, made him sort of an industry joke, and series like this did not help. Philbin did the basic talk routine consisting of amiable chatter with stars, cooking hints, and other inconsequential time fillers. His co-host for the first week was Sarah Purcell, his former sidekick at *AM Los Angeles.* The addition of perky Mary

Hart (in her first national TV role before co-hosting the syndicated hit *Entertainment Tonight)* as co-host didn't help the program stand out, nor did the lack of a studio audience at the New York City–based production. Within five months NBC had replaced the series with repeats of *Diff'rent Strokes.*

However, as it turned out, Philbin got the last laugh. In May 1982 he began hosting *Regis Philbin Celebrity Healthstyles* on the Health Network (later to become the Lifetime channel), which lasted six years. By the end of that run, he had begun co-hosting the most successful venture of his career. *Live with Regis and Kathie Lee* modified the standard talk show format by having him and co-host Kathie Lee Gifford, wife of sportscaster Frank Gifford, talking and laughing about themselves, their families, and friends, and even their young producer Michael Gelman, for at least the first third of each show. Regis and Kathie Lee started as a local talk show duo on WABC New York in 1985 before going into syndication in the fall of 1989 (the "live" part referred to those East Coast stations that could get the show on satellite when it ran on air from 9–10 a.m. in New York). The show was still going strong in 1996, by which time Philbin had published his autobiography, which generated a number of laughs at the expense of his former critics.

RELUCTANT DRAGON AND MR. TOAD, THE

Cartoon; Color
September 12, 1970–September 17, 1972

ABC Sat. 8–8:30 p.m. (9/12/70–12/26/70)
ABC Sun. 10–10:30 p.m. (9/12/71–9/17/72)

Voices: *Carl Banas, Donna Miller, Claude Rae, Paul Soles*

Kenneth Graham's 1907 novel *The Wind in the Willows* provided the principal characters in this short-lived cartoon. Each week there were two segments of Tobias the reluctant dragon, who was scared of daisies and palled around with Sir Malcolm Giles, and one segment featuring J. Thaddeus Toad, a playboy who hung out with introverted Mole, extroverted Water Rat, and philosophical recluse Badger. The show was an instant flop; ABC canned it midway through its first season and aired reruns in 1971–72.

REMEMBER THIS DATE

Game; B&W
November 14, 1950–June 28, 1951

NBC Tue./Thu. 3:30–4 p.m. (11/14/50–6/28/51)

Regulars: *Bill Stern, Mary Denny, Jet MacDonald, Murray Ross*

In this quiz show, host Bill Stern gave at least four players hints about famous events or people connected with that date's broadcast in the past. Mary Denny was his aide, and Jet MacDonald gave song clues along with organist Murray Ross. The show had no sponsor.

REPORT CARD

Public Affairs; B&W
October 30, 1955–November 27, 1955

CBS Sun. 2:30–3 p.m. (10/30/55–11/27/55)

Moderator: *Dr. Lyman Bryson*

As preparation for an upcoming White House Conference on Education, CBS offered this five-part panel discussion series from New York City in 1955. It had several guests with connections to the world of education critiquing the current state of school systems in America.

RETURN TO PEYTON PLACE

Soap Opera; Color
April 3, 1972–January 4, 1974

NBC Mon.–Fri. 3:30–4 p.m. (4/3/72–1/4/74)

Cast:

Allison Mackenzie (1972–73)	Katherine Glass
Allison Mackenzie (1973–74)	Pamela Shoop
Constance Mackenzie (1972)	Bettye Ackerman
Constance Mackenzie (1972–74)	Susan Brown
Elliot Carson	Warren Stevens
Eli Carson	Frank Ferguson*
Betty Anderson (1972–73)	Julie Parrish
Betty Anderson (1973–74)	Lynn Loring
Rodney Harrington (1972)	Lawrence Casey
Rodney Harrington (1972–74)	Yale Summers
Leslie Harrington (1972)	Frank Maxwell
Leslie Harrington (1972–73)	Stacy Harris
Norman Harrington	Ron Russell
Rita Jacks Harrington	Patricia Morrow*
Ada Jacks (1972–73)	Evelyn Scott*
Dr. Michael Rossi	Guy Stockwell
Selena Cross Rossi	Margaret Mason
Steven Cord	Joseph Gallison
Hannah Cord	Mary K. Wells
Martin Peyton (September 1972–73)	John Hoyt
Benny Tate (1972–73)/Jason Tate (1973)	Ben Andrews
Zoe Tate (1972–73)	Lesley Woods
D. B. Bentley (1973–74)	Mary Frann
Ann Howard (1973)	Susan Oliver*

*Was seen as same character in *Peyton Place* TV series.

Nearly three years after the cancellation of the hit ABC nighttime soap opera *Peyton Place* (1964–69), based in turn on the best-selling book by Grace Metalious, this far less successful follow-up came on NBC's daily schedule. It included some returning members of the nighttime show, including Patricia Morrow, who had told *TV Guide* in 1971, "I was never crazy about show business, but after I got to be one of the stars of *Peyton Place,* I really started hating it. The whole thing. All of it. Being an actress, I began hating television. I started getting sick and tired of what I was becoming. I lost myself." Apparently she found herself in time to go back to her old role.

The series spent its first year using some of the earlier show's plots. For example, Constance Mackenzie remarried Allison's dad Elliot Carson (Eli's son), and Norman Harrington waited on tables while his wife Rita Jacks (Ada's daughter) ran the local tavern. Other stories differed somewhat. Betty Anderson was pregnant by first husband Steven Cord although she was now married to Rodney Harrington, his half-brother. (Rodney also was Norman's brother and Leslie's son.) The Constance-Elliot marriage was troubled due to persistent arguments, pushing Constance into the arms of Dr. Rossi, whose wife Selena Cross, not seen in the nighttime version, was also his nurse. And Martin Peyton, descendent of the town's founders, appeared even though he had died in the original.

The show's central heroine had all new adventures. On *Peyton Place* Allison Mackenzie (Constance and Elliott's daughter) disappeared in 1966 when actress Mia Farrow left the show. Here, on the April 19, 1972 episode, Allison came home on the eve of Rodney and Betty's marriage, elusive about where she had been. This concerned Betty, given Rodney's love for Allison in the past. But Allison had bigger problems to handle. She married Benny Tate, but his evil twin Jason took his place and hooked her on drugs. Benny eventually rose from his deathbed to murder Jason. Yet on January 21, 1973, in a special nighttime show (probably the first for a daytime soap opera), poor Allison was found guilty of murder, prompting more misery until the actual murderer was found.

In retrospect, the main problem for *Return to Peyton Place* (besides the cast turnover, a rather large one given the show's short run) was the producers' uncertainty over whether to replicate, replace, or continue story lines from the earlier show. They tried all three approaches, but none satisfied weary viewers, who favored *One Life to Live* on ABC and *Match Game* on CBS.

In later years, some of the nighttime cast reunited in two TV movies, *Murder in Peyton Place* in 1977 and *Peyton Place: The Next Generation* in 1985. In 1979 came plans for a new syndicated version of *Peyton Place* focusing on another generation of townsfolk and starring Adam West of *Batman* fame, but it did not materialize.

RETURN TO THE PLANET OF THE APES
Cartoon; Color
September 6, 1975–September 4, 1976
NBC Sat. 11–11:30 a.m. (9/6/75–9/4/76)
Voices:

Bill Hudson/Dr. Zaius	Richard Blackburn
Jeff Carter	Austin Stoker
Judy Franklin/Nova	Claudette Nivens
General Urko	Henry Corden
Cornelius	Edwin Mills

In 1973 *Mad* magazine spoofed a seemingly endless movie series in a sequence titled "The Milking of *The Planet of the Apes*." Little did they know that they hadn't seen the last of efforts to milk the success of this sci-fi story line involving a future Earth run by orangutans and other hairy primates which first surfaced as a novel by Pierre Boulle and a 1968 movie titled *Planet of the Apes*. Following high ratings for the TV showings of the sequels (there were five *Apes* movies through 1973), CBS put *Planet of the Apes* on its Friday night schedule, where it ran from September 13–December 27, 1974. But that was not the end of the simian saga, as NBC made it into a Saturday morning cartoon entry the next year.

The animated retelling was set in the year 3810, nearly 1,000 years after the date given in earlier renditions. There were two new passengers in this adventure—youngsters Jeff and Judy, who crash-landed with astronaut Bill in an area where Dr. Zaius was the scientific leader of the planet, as he was the original series. And as in the movies, General Urko was the military commander. The other characters were Cornelius and Nova, young chimp buddies and rough counterparts to Jeff and Judy.

•RHYME AND REASON
Game; Color
July 7, 1975–July 9, 1976
ABC Mon.–Fri. 2:30–3 p.m. (7/7/75–12/1/75)
ABC Mon.–Fri. 1:30–2 p.m. (12/29/75–7/9/76)
Regulars: *Bob Eubanks, Nipsey Russell*

"*Match Game* with rhymes" is an apt summation of this rather derivative comedy panel show. Two contestants wrote three possible answers for a couplet with the last part blank, read by host Bob Eubanks, and picked one from a sextet of celebrities to try to match his or her answers. The first player with three matches could win $5,000 in a bonus game if he or she could get three rhyming words for a couplet from a celebrity within a half-minute.

Nipsey Russell, whose talent as a quick-witted poet on shows like *Match Game* made him a popular game show guest, was the only regular panelist (as well as the basic reason why the show got on the ABC schedule). Other frequent guests were Charlie Brill, Jamie Farr, Pat Harrington Jr., Shari Lewis, Mitzi McCall, Jaye P. Morgan, and JoAnne Worley.

RICHARD HARKNESS NEWS REVIEW
News; B&W
January 7, 1952–March 7, 1952
NBC Mon.–Fri. 11:45 a.m.–Noon (1/7/52–3/7/52)
Host/Anchor: *Richard Harkness*

NBC News reporter Richard Harkness hosted this daily report from his home base of Washington, D.C. The show featured a special "behind the scenes" news profile three times a week in addition to the announcement of headlines. Debuting one week before *Today*, this was NBC's first news program to air before 5 p.m. weekdays.

•RICHARD SIMMONS SHOW, THE

Exercise; Color
1980–1984

Syndicated daily 30 minutes beginning September 1980

Host: *Richard Simmons*

There was no confusing this workout series with Jack LaLanne. Richard Simmons was a flamboyant, peppy, curly-haired sprite who encouraged his studio audience (and presumably home audience) of obese, out-of-shape women to exercise and eat right through a combination of dramatizations, proselytizing, cooking recipes, and even calm, direct talking into the camera. He could relate to their fears about the process, having undergone a crash diet on which he lost 112 pounds (his slight, 5-foot 7-inch frame once carried 268 pounds), but which caused him lose his hair and necessitated transplants. This show followed Simmons's success with his Beverly Hills restaurant and exercise studio.

Each show had a theme illustrated by Richard in a short comic sketch at the opening, with Richard playing such recurring characters as Sister Mary Lo-Cal or Reverend Pound. The segment then cut to an upbeat introduction showing Richard and participants in action, including Richard dressed as an angel monitoring people's purchases at supermarkets (!) and Richard exiting his sporty car with a vanity plate reading YRUFATT (get it?). After some light exercises and interviews with guests, Richard always ended with a hearty "God bless you, we'll see you real soon!"

Simmons's overenergetic style wore down viewers within four years. However, he did reappear briefly as host of the syndicated home shopping show *Value Television* in 1987, then kept his career going steadily into the 1990s with assorted business projects (most prominent among these being the "Deal-A-Meal" mail order weight loss program and "Sweating to the Oldies" videos and CDs), and multiple, often self-deprecating appearances on talk shows, where his outrageousness left even David Letterman and Jay Leno temporarily speechless.

•RICHIE RICH SHOW, THE

Cartoon; Color
September 8, 1980–December 27, 1986

ABC Sat. 9:30–10:30 a.m. (9/8/80–9/5/81)
ABC Sat. 10–11 a.m. (9/12/81–9/18/82)
ABC Sat. 8:30–9:30 a.m. (9/25/82–9/3/83)
ABC Sat. 8:30–9 a.m. (9/10/83–9/1/84)
CBS Sat. 11:30 a.m.–Noon (11/7/86–12/27/86)

Voices:

Richie Rich	*Sparky Marcus*
Freckles	*Christian Hoff*
Gloria	*Nancy Cartwright*
Mr. Rich/Cadbury the Butler	*Stan Jones*
Mrs. Rich/Irona the Maid	*Joan Gerber*
Professor Keenbean	*Bill Callaway*
Dollar	*Frank Welker*
Alfalfa/Porky/Woim (all 1982–84)	*Julie Dees*
Spanky (1982–84)	*Scott Menville*
Darla (1982–84)	*Patty Maloney*
Butch/Waldo (both 1982–84)	*B. J. Ward*
Buckwheat (1982–84)	*Shavar Ross*
Pete the Pup/Officer Ed (both 1982–84)	*Peter Cullen*

Richie Rich, "the richest kid in the world," had been a character in Harvey comic books for nearly 20 years by the time he finally made it to animation form. Despite the implications of his name, Richie was actually a rather unspoiled child who preferred to hang out with his redhead friend Freckles and girlfriend Gloria and interact with the staff, including Professor Keenbean, head of the Rich Science Center and developer of many eccentric inventions. Richie's adorable dalmatian was Dollar.

Between Richie's stories, the series had some adventures of *Scooby Doo* (q.v.) in its first two years. In 1982–83 Richie shared billing in *The Pac-Man/Little Rascals/Richie Rich Show*, with the addition of *Pac-Man* (q.v.) and an animated version of the *Our Gang* comedy shorts of the 1930s. All the mischief makers came back, from gawky crooner Alfalfa to rotund nominal leader Sparky, but they proved to be no match for the shorts still being rerun in several markets at that time. From 1983–84 the series became *The Little Rascals/Richie Rich Show*, then in 1986 CBS showed repeats briefly under the title *Richie Rich*.

A live-action version of the character appeared in a theatrical movie titled *Richie Rich* in 1994 with Macauley Culkin as the lead character. In the fall of 1996 another cartoon version of the show aired in syndication.

RICK MORANIS IN GRAVEDALE HIGH

Cartoon; Color
September 8, 1990–September 7, 1991

NBC Sat. 9:30–10 a.m. (9/8/90–11/17/90)
NBC Sat. 8:30–9 a.m. (11/24/90–1/19/91)
NBC Sat. 9:30–10 a.m. (1/26/91–9/7/91)

Voice:

Mr. Schneider	*Rick Moranis*

At Gravedale High, normal human Mr. Schneider had the unenviable task of having to teach the basics to adolescent monsters Sid, Cleofatra, the invisible J. P. Blanche, Frankentyke, the vampirish Vinnie Stoker, Gill Waterman, and Duzer, among others. Ms. Crone was headmistress. This was an in-house production by NBC.

•RICKI LAKE

Talk; Color
1993–

Syndicated 60 minutes daily beginning September 1993

Hostess: *Ricki Lake*

A seemingly unlikely contender for the talk show throne held by Oprah Winfrey since the late 1980s was Ricki Lake, although she had, like Winfrey, fought obesity. The twenty-something Lake had had a rather lukewarm acting career consisting primarily of parts in movies directed by John Waters (*Hairspray, Cry Baby*) before becoming the leader of a talk show geared to a younger crowd, with the emphasis being on problems with relationships. Her audience was enthusiastic, had strong opinions about every topic, and cheered on their host at the end of the show with the chant, "Go, Ricki/Go, Ricki/Go, Ricki/Go, Ricki, Go!" Hardly intellectual, but Ricki was going for a mass audience, and she got within challenging distance of Oprah after a year and a half on air, and still found time to continue her acting career.

RIDERS IN THE SKY
Children's; Color
September 14, 1991–August 29, 1992

CBS Sat. 8–8:30 a.m. (9/14/91–9/28/91)
CBS Sat. Noon–12:30 p.m. (10/5/91–10/26/91)
CBS Sat. 12:30–1 p.m. (11/2/91–8/29/92)

Regulars: *Woody Paul, Ranger Doug, Too Slim*

CBS programmers must have had flashbacks of the days when *Fury* rode Saturday mornings when they added this lightweight western-style attraction for children. The Riders in the Sky was a singing cowboy trio seen at Harmony Ranch on this show, which also featured puppets, clay animation, and sketches with guest stars like Florence Henderson. Previously the group was best known for their appearances on The Nashville Network (TNN) cable channel, where they returned after this show's cancellation.

RIMBA'S ISLAND—See *Cubhouse.*

•ROAD OF LIFE, THE
Soap Opera; B&W
December 13, 1954–July 1, 1955

CBS Mon.–Fri. 1:15–1:30 p.m. (12/13/54–7/1/55)

Cast:

Dr. Jim Brent	Don McLaughlin
Jocelyn McLeod Brent	Virginia Dwyer
John "Butch" Brent	Bill Lipton
Malcolm Overton	Harry Holcombe
Sybil Overton Fuller	Barbara Becker
Conrad Overton	Charles Dingle
Aunt Reggie Ellis	Dorothy Sands
Francie Brent	Elizabeth Lawrence
Lil Monet	Elspeth Eric
Armand Monet	Michael Kane
Pearl Snow	Hollis Irving

Narrator: *Nelson Case*

A radio hit from September 13, 1937–January 2, 1959, on NBC for the first 17 years and then CBS for the remainder,

The Road of Life moved to television with story line, and most of its cast, intact (it aired daily immediately after the radio version ended). Surgeon Dr. Brent, his third wife Jocelyn, and adopted son John were nice guys surrounded by losers from Jocelyn's well-to-do family. Her foster father Malcolm Overton bickered constantly with his relative Conrad over how to raise grandson John. Meanwhile, Conrad's daughter Sybil, who harbored the hots for Jim, tried to keep Jocelyn from becoming Jim's wife. She also belittled her mother Ada; attempted to get her husband Mr. Fuller, missing in a plane crash for more than a year, declared dead so that she could claim sole custody of her daughter Constance; and generally was a bitch even when confined to a wheelchair. None of this bothered Conrad, who called his daughter "Bunny" and generally egged her on.

The whole lot of them disappeared within seven months. This failure might seem surprising, given the radio version's popularity, until one takes into account the small number of affiliates in the 1950s that cleared the 1–1:30 p.m. daily time slot for CBS programming.

•ROAD RUNNER SHOW, THE
Cartoon; Color
September 10, 1966–September 2, 1972

CBS Sat. Noon–12:30 p.m. (9/10/66–9/2/67)
CBS Sat. 1:30–2 p.m. (9/9/67–9/7/68)
ABC Sat. 8:30–9 a.m. (9/11/71–9/2/72)

Vocal Characterizations: *Mel Blanc*

The Road Runner has been a supporting act on *The Bugs Bunny Show* for almost thirty years, but he was only a solo star for three. The cartoons, produced by Warner Brothers in the 1950s and 1960s, had the speedy bird chased constantly on highways throughout the American Southwest desert by Wile E. Coyote, a self-proclaimed "supergenius" with an IQ of 207. The Coyote used elaborate Rube Goldberg contraptions in efforts to snag his quarry, often employing inventions from the Ajax and Acme companies, but they usually backfired and got Wile instead. Generally the only dialogue heard in each episode was the "Beep, beep!" emitted by the Road Runner at the end of each failed attempt by the Coyote to capture the fowl. One memorable feature was the humorous Latinesque derivatives used to identify the characters at the start of each segment (e.g., the Road Runner once was "Speedipus Rex," while the Coyote was "Famishus-Famishus"). Some other Warner cartoons appeared on the show as well.

Before and after the run in their own series, the Road Runner and Coyote had been popular characters. Why didn't they last longer on their own? Stupid scheduling. On CBS, the show ran against its progeny *The Bugs Bunny Show*, seen on ABC. And for its run on ABC, network officials put the show in the same time slot where it had aired with Bugs on CBS the previous season. Wile himself couldn't have botched things up any worse.

ROAD TO REALITY, THE

Soap Opera Anthology; B&W
October 17, 1960–March 31, 1961

ABC Mon.–Fri. 2:30–3 p.m. (10/17/60–3/31/61)

Cast:

Dr. Lewis	John Beal
Vic	Robert Drew
Joan	Judith Braun
Harry	Salem Ludwig
Margaret	Eugenia Rawls
Rosalind (1960)	Robin Howard
Lee (12/15/60–1961)	James Dimitri
Chris (12/20/60–1961)	Kay Doubleday

The Road to Reality was an interesting drama involving the problems besetting five or six people in fictional group therapy sessions. Using tapes made by a New York psychoanalyst with his patients' consent as the basis for scripts, the show presented such characters as marriage-phobic Vic, frigid yet desperate-for-love Joan, perfectionist Harry, and unhappily married mother Margaret discussing their neuroses with Dr. Lewis and each other. Later additions were Lee, an occasionally nasty man who hated his mother, and Chris, who had problems with "acting a way a woman should act." At least one group member, Rosalind, overcame her fear of her father and left the group before the end of the show's run.

Dr. Edward Ziman, president of the Association of Medical Group Psychoanalysts, wrote in *TV Guide* that his organization endorsed the program because it "comes as close as possible to the portrayal of actual case histories as well as response to treatment" by psychoanalysts. In fact, some psychiatric training centers asked for copies of the show's scripts to use in teaching group psychoanalysis. The series was taped in New York City.

•ROBERT Q. LEWIS SHOW, THE

Variety; B&W
October 16, 1950–May 25, 1956

CBS Mon.–Fri. 2:30–3:30 p.m. (10/16/50–12/1/50)
CBS Mon.–Fri. 2:45–3:30 p.m. (12/4/50–1/19/51)
CBS Mon./Wed./Fri. 2–2:30 p.m. (1/11/54–7/3/54)
CBS Mon.–Fri. 2–2:30 p.m. (7/6/54–5/25/56)

Regulars: *Robert Q. Lewis, Rosemary Clooney (1950–51), Tony Craig (1950), the Daydreamers (1950), Hal Lohman and Joan Fields (1950–51), the Bernie Leighton Orchestra (1950–51), Earl Wrightson (1954–56), Lois Hunt (1954–56), the Chordettes (1954–55), Jaye P. Morgan (1954–55), Jan Arden (1954 at least), Don Liberto (1954 at least), Betty Clooney (1955–56), Judy Johnson (1955–56), Merv Griffin (1955–56), the Ray Block Orchestra (1954–56)*

Bespectacled comedian Robert Q. Lewis had a good deal of exposure on network television in the 1950s without gaining much substantial success. He made his TV debut as a substitute host on the nighttime *The Arthur Godfrey Show*

on February 23, 1949, then got a regular 15-minute eponymous talk show on CBS nighttime from July 16, 1950–January 7, 1951. His own daytime show, titled *Robert Q.'s Matinee*, began three months after his nighttime series started. Besides Robert's droll quips, it featured singing from Rosemary Clooney, Tony Craig, and the Daydreamers, the latter a quartet composed of three men and one woman. Loman and Fields were a dance team.

In December 1950 CBS aired *The First 100 Years* daily from 2:30–2:45 p.m., taking the first 15 minutes of Robert's show. Then CBS announced that *Bride and Groom* would run Tuesdays and Thursdays at 3:15–3:30 p.m. by January 1951. Upset with his shrinking time slot, Lewis left the series, which limped along only a few weeks afterward (see *Johnny Johnston Show, The*).

In 1954, apparently having patched things up with CBS, Lewis returned to the network's daytime lineup with a series that alternated daily with *Double or Nothing* its first six months. It featured a larger cast with dancer/choreographer

This early shot of The Robert Q. Lewis Show *was taken on the set in 1950.*

Don Liberto and singers Jan Arden, the Chordettes, Lois Hunt, Jaye P. Morgan, and Earl Wrightson. All but Liberto appeared on Lewis's Saturday morning show on CBS radio as well. When Morgan left a year later, she was replaced by Betty Clooney, whose sister Rosemary was a regular on Lewis's earlier daytimer. By September 1955 the Chordettes had been dropped and Merv Griffin added, and Earl Wrightson and Lois Hunt had gone from daily to twice-weekly appearances to save costs. But despite these changes and an impressive guest list (e.g., Sammy Davis Jr., Jackie Gleason, Debbie Reynolds, Shelley Winters), the show's ratings failed to rise and it ended after two years.

Afterword, Lewis hosted a few other series, mainly game shows. In 1961 he told *TV Guide* he no longer had a TV variety series because "my relaxed, easygoing format just went out of vogue." He continued working in the medium (for example, he was a frequent substitute host for Bud Collyer on the daytime *To Tell the Truth* from 1963–65), but after the late 1960s his appearances became rare.

ROCKY AND HIS FRIENDS—See *Bullwinkle Show, The.*

ROD BROWN OF THE ROCKET RANGERS
Adventure; B&W
April 18, 1953–May 29, 1954

CBS Sat. 11:30 a.m.–Noon (4/18/53–5/29/54)

Cast:

Rod Brown	Cliff Robertson
Frank Boyle	Bruce Hall
Wilbur Wormser (Wormsey)	Jack Weston
Commander Swift	John Boruff

Making the universe safe in the 2100s was the mission for the Rocket Rangers, a group whose home was Omega Base and whose spaceship was the Beta. Rod Brown was the group leader, Frank Boyle and Commander Swift were co-pilots for many of the adventures, and Wormsey was a bespectacled comrade. The debut had Brown go to Jupiter to rescue a rocket carrying plans for a spaceship which could move quicker than light.

In 1953 *Variety* reported that owners of *Tom Corbett, Space Cadet* had filed a lawsuit against this show on infringement charges, a suit which was settled out of court in four months. *TV Guide*'s opinion of the show was probably accurate: "It's a cut-and-dried preposition with little or no attempt to be educational, informative or even entertaining. Unless violence per se is considered entertaining in these enlightened days of child guidance."

ROLLER DERBY
Sports; B&W
November 27, 1951–March 22, 1959

CBS Sat. 3–5:30 p.m. (11/27/51–5/17/52)
ABC Sun. 4–5 p.m. (1/24/54–5/16/54)
ABC Sun. 2:30–4 p.m. (12/29/57–5/18/58)
ABC Sun. 3:30–4:30 p.m.(10/12/58–3/22/59)

Announcers: *Ken Nydell (1954, 1957–59 at least), Ken Gurian (1954 at least), Pat Dillon (1958–59 at least)*

The Roller Derby, a sporting attraction in existence since 1935, came to daytime network television at three different times in the 1950s, all airing from New York City. These and most later versions featured two sexually segregated sextets competing in separate contests to score points going around a roller-skating rink while seemingly beating the daylights out of any competitors getting in their way.

After 1954, the show disappeared for a few years as the New York team took a tour in Europe, with bruisers like Gerry Murray and Midge "Toughie" Brasuhn being crowd favorites. Its return in the late 1950s brought with it the unique attraction of a mother-son membership on one team (Gerry and Mike Paul of the New York Chiefs). But the 1957–58 version had a rather low clearance rate (less than 50 ABC affiliates carried it), and by 1959 the series had gone back into syndication, where it has been seen off and on ever since.

•ROLONDA
Talk; Color
1993–

Syndicated 60 minutes daily beginning January 1994

Host: *Rolonda Watts*

She was enthusiastic and black, but as she told everybody, she was NOT OPRAH WINFREY! Rolonda Watts was another in a seemingly endless line of talk show hosts in the mid-1990s featuring guests aptly tagged by *Variety* as "nuts and sluts." A newscaster on ABC's New York affiliate WABC since at least 1987, her biggest TV credit prior to her talk show was as reporter and then weekend anchor for the syndicated nightly tabloid TV series *Inside Edition* in 1993. In 1994 her show replaced Les Brown, a black motivational speaker who failed to win big audiences when his daily talk series debuted in the fall of 1993. In several markets *Rolonda* aired late at night in addition to afternoon spots.

•ROMAN HOLIDAYS
Cartoon; Color
September 9, 1972–September 1, 1973

NBC Sat. 10–10:30 a.m. (9/9/72–12/16/72)
NBC Sat. 8:30–9 a.m. (12/23/72–9/1/73)

Voices:

Gus Holiday	Dave Willock
Laurie Holiday	Shirley Mitchell
Precocia Holiday	Pam Ferdin
Happius "Happy" Holiday	Stanley Livingston
Mr. Evictus	Dom DeLuise
Mr. Tycoonius	Hal Smith
Herman	Hal Peary
Henrietta	Janet Waldo
Groovia	Judy Strangis
Brutus	Daws Butler

The lives of Gus Holiday, his wife Laurie, and children Precocia and Happius, who lived at the Venus DiMilo Arms Apartments in Italy in the year A.D. 63, seemed to have plenty of 20th-century complications. There was the overbearing landlord Mr. Evictus, for example, and Gus's demanding boss at Forum Construction Company, Mr. Tycoonius. They found comfort and solace to a certain extent with their pals Herman and Henrietta, Happy's steady girl Groovia, and Brutus the family lion. This domestic sitcom cartoon from Hanna-Barbera Productions was nowhere near as funny—or successful—as its obvious inspirations, *The Flintstones* and *The Jetsons*.

•ROMPER ROOM
Children's; B&W and Color
February 1953–1991

Syndicated 30 and 60 minutes daily beginning 1954

Time magazine called it "the world's largest classroom," and during its heyday in the 1960s and 1970s *Romper Room* seemed to be just that. It was actually a franchise rather than a national production. Stations that bought *Romper Room* received rights to use their own female emcees and get merchandise and materials representing the show, such as a grinning jack-in-the-box holding a slate with the series' title. Between games and activities using *Romper Room* products, kids at home and in the studio (usually six 5-year-olds) received lessons in good behavior from the hostesses, who used "Mr. Do Bee," a smiling yellow jacket, as an example ("Mr. Do Bee says we should look both ways before crossing the street.") Every show ended with the hostess looking into her "Magic Mirror" and greeting the home viewers she "saw" that day ("I see Jackie and Karen and, oh, there's Bobby, too.")

Bert Claster first created the program for WBAL-TV in Baltimore, using his wife, Nancy Claster, as hostess "Miss Nancy," and within a year CBS wanted the series for its lineup. The Clasters nixed that in favor of a far more lucrative franchise setup, but the concept really did not fare well until 1957, when 22 stations tried it. By 1963, 119 stations had their own Romper Rooms, each led by a college-graduate hostess who had taken an intensive one-week training course led by Nancy Claster. Nancy gave up her hosting job in 1963 but continued her duties as trainer, and by the end of the show's run had trained over 500 women. The Clasters marketed other syndicated series by the 1960s as well, none as successful as *Romper Room.*

The show celebrated its 1,000th broadcast in January 1980, but the decade proved to be a difficult one for the show as stations found it more convenient to buy shows already produced. In 1981 stations that did not want to set up their own operations could take a syndicated version with "Miss Molly McCloskey" as hostess and Sally Claster Gelbard (Bert and Nancy's daughter) as co-executive producer with her husband. This version got a fair amount of exposure, but the FCC's 1984 decision to adopt a more laissez-faire attitude toward children's programming (that is, it ceased to require that stations do decent children's programs) cut into the number of outlets for *Romper Room,* a selling point of which was its "decency." The show's last production gasp came in April 1991, when stations received 85 episodes available for daily or weekly showings in a revised format. Still, its 38-year run as a children's show is impressive, and has been surpassed only by *Bozo the Clown* (q.v.).

•ROOTIE KAZOOTIE
Children's; B&W
October 13, 1951–May 16, 1953

NBC Sat. Noon–12:30 p.m. (10/13/51–12/29/51)
NBC Sat. 10–10:30 a.m. (1/5/52–4/5/52)
NBC Sat. 5:30–6 p.m. (4/12/52–10/25/52)
ABC Sat. 10:30–11 a.m. (1/3/53–5/16/53)

Cast:

Todd Russell, the "Chief Rooter"	Himself
Rootie Kazootie/El Squeeko/Polka Dottie (voices only)	Naomi Lewis
Little Nipper/Gala-Poochie Pup/ Poison Zoomack (voices only)	Frank Milano
Mr. Deetle Dootle (1951)	John Schoeopperle
Mr. Deetle Dootle (1952–53)	John Vee

Puppeteers: *Paul Ashley, Michael King, Frank Milano*
Musical Director: *Milton Kaye*

This fondly remembered children's show debuted on NBC's New York affiliate WNBT October 14, 1950, and ran Saturdays 11:30 a.m.–Noon. Host "Big" Todd Russell (as Rootie liked to call him) interacted with puppet Rootie Tootie, who played the Kazootie musical instrument and had a girlfriend called Polka Dottie and a dog named Little Nipper. (Later, when RCA stopped advertising on the show, Little Nipper became Gala Poochie Pup.) Rootie's mustachioed foe Poison Zoomack, who wore a top hat, was always trying to steal Rootie's Kazootie. The only other human regular beside Russell was the mute, somewhat dense cop Mr. Dootle, who assisted Russell and Rootie in skits and the question-and-answer session titled "Quiz-A-Rootie" where children from the studio audience could win prizes.

On December 9, 1950, the show changed Rootie's last name to Kazootie to avoid confusion with Tootsie Roll candy, which was not a sponsor. Ten months later the series went on NBC. Two months after its network cancellation, on December 22, 1952, the show began airing weekdays on WNBT from 6–6:15 p.m., and a month later began a run on ABC Saturdays. It continued locally after its ABC run through May 7, 1954.

•ROSIE O'DONNELL SHOW, THE
Talk; Color
1996–

Syndicated 60 minutes daily beginning June 1996
Regulars: *Rosie O'Donnell, John McDonald*

The best series to hit daytime television by far in 1996 was *The Rosie O'Donnell Show*, starring the chubby thirty-something comedienne previously seen mostly in movies and other people's talk shows. Hers was a celebrity-driven program in the style of Mike Douglas, who coincidentally was an early guest, with Rosie emphasizing comedy and effervescence over the exploitation offered by other daytime talkies. Apparently the dearth of such programming had been lamented by daytime viewers, as Rosie soon became the second-most popular daily hostess after the almighty Oprah in the ratings.

Each show had a member of the studio audience announce the day's guests and signal bandleader John McDonald to "Hit it!" as the theme played. After that Rosie came out, bantered for a bit with John, and then told jokes, with the last one taped to her desk. After the jokes she talked with two to four guests. (The ones on the debut were Susan Lucci and George Clooney.) Nothing extraordinary took place, but Rosie was consistently funny and pleasant to everyone, a welcome change from most everything else on the air. By the fall of 1996, *The Rosie O'Donnell Show* had become such a hit that Rosie made it to the cover of *Newsweek* magazine. Nice guys can finish first.

ROUNDUP USA—See Campaign Roundup.

RUBIK, THE AMAZING CUBE—See *The Pac-Man/Rubik the Amazing Cube Hour.*

•RUDE DOG AND THE DWEEBS
Cartoon; Color
September 16, 1989–September 8, 1990

CBS Sat. 11:30 a.m.–Noon (9/16/89–12/30/89)
CBS Sat. 11:30 a.m.–Noon (6/9/90–9/8/90)

Voices:
Rude Dog	Rob Paulsen
Caboose/Seymour/Rot	Frank Welker
Winston/Herman	Peter Cullen
Kibble/Gloria	Ellen Gerstell
Reggie	Mendi Segal
Barney	Dave Coulier
Satch	Jim Cummings
Tweek	Hank Sorayan

The denizens of auto repair shops are not all the same. Take the motley crew of Rude Dog and the Dweebs. Rude Dog was a hip, Sylvester Stallone-ish canine who drove a 1956 Cadillac that was as hot a pink as one of Rude Dog's eyes and ears (his other eye and ear was green, as were his teeth). He ran the shop with the help of a variety of other pooches he affectionately termed the Dweebs, including the stuttering Caboose, oh-so-proper Winston, Jack Nicholson-esque Reggie, Southern-drawling Barney, Ed Wynn-ish Satch, and friendly Chihuahua Tweek. Opposing these characters in various misadventures (two per show) was Seymour, a vicious cat whose assistant was Rot. A considerable amount of activity took place at Rude Dog's rather lavish auto shop.

Ruff and Reddy's *host Jimmy Blaine greets his cartoon pals Ruff (right) and Reddy (left).*

•RUFF AND REDDY
Cartoon; B&W and Color
December 14, 1957–September 26, 1964

NBC Sat. 10:30–11 a.m. (12/4/57–10/8/60)
NBC Sat. 9:30–10 a.m. (9/29/62–9/26/64)

Host: *Jimmy Blaine (1957–60), Bob Cottle (as Captain Bob; 1962–64)*

Voices:
Ruff	Don Messick
Reddy	Daws Butler
Narrator	John Stephenson

When MGM liquidated its cartoon department in 1957, animators William Hanna and Joseph Barbera opened their own studio. Their first of many successful Saturday morning cartoons was *Ruff and Reddy*, featuring humorous four-minute serialized adventures of Ruff, a smart cat with a bow tie, and his pal Reddy, a somewhat lamebrained dog who sounded like the prototype for Huckleberry Hound. The first 13 shows had them being abducted by aliens. Between skits with puppets involving the host, some cartoons seen earlier in Columbia theaters also aired. The cartoons airing from 1962–64 were all repeats.

RUMPUS ROOM—See *Johnny Olsen's Rumpus Room.*

RUN, JOE, RUN
Adventure; Color
September 7, 1974–September 4, 1976

NBC Sat. 9:30–10 a.m. (9/7/74–8/30/75)
NBC Sat. 10:30–11 a.m. (9/6/75–9/4/76)

Cast:

Sgt. William Corey (1974–75)	*Arch Whiting*
Josh McCoy (1975–76)	*Chad States*

Narrator: *Paul Frees*

Joe was a German shepherd on the lam, wrongly charged with attacking its master. As a guard dog for the Army, he faced prosecution and the likelihood of being put to sleep, so he ran away. Seeking to help clear him was Sgt. William Corey, who believed in Joe's innocence. During the second season, Sgt. Corey was ordered back to his post, and Josh McCoy, a mountaineer, joined Joe in his travels. The part of Joe was played by a dog named Heinrich of Midvale.

•RUNAROUND

Game; Color

September 9, 1972–September 1, 1973

NBC Sat. 11:30 a.m.–Noon (9/9/72–9/1/73)

Host: *Paul Winchell*

Nine children competed in *Runaround*. They watched presentations on stage and then the host asked them a question related to the skits. Three large vertical rectangles offered possible answers to each question, and contestants had to "run around" to the platform in front of the rectangle they believed had the correct response. Children choosing the right answer received a token and continued to play, while those who were wrong had to wait in a penalty box for an unspecified period before playing again. The player with the most tokens at the end of the game won prizes. This series let ventriloquist Paul Winchell do a brief routine with his dummies Jerry Mahoney and Knucklehead Smiff about midway through each show.

RUNNING THE HALLS

Sitcom; Color

September 11, 1993–September 3, 1994

NBC Sat. 11:30 a.m.–Noon (9/11/93–9/3/94)

Cast:

Andy McBain	*Richard Hayes*
Holliday Friedman	*Laurie Fortier*
David Reese	*Trevor Lissauer*
Molloy Simpson	*Lackey Bevis*
Miles Taylor	*Craig Kirkwood*
Nikki	*Senta Moses*
Miss Gilman	*Pamela Bowen*
Mark "the Shark" Stark	*Richard Speight*

Obviously designed to emulate the success of *Saved By the Bell*, this sitcom featured three boys and three girls at Middlefield Academy, a co-ed boarding school. Andy McBain was the conniving lead in love with Holliday Friedman, and his rival was David Reese, who was in love with Molloy Simpson. Watching them and the others with a suspicious eye was headmistress Miss Gilman and her student informant Mark "the Shark" Stark.

RUTH LYONS 50 CLUB

Talk; B&W

October 1, 1951–September 5, 1952

NBC Mon.–Fri. Noon–12:30 p.m. (10/1/51–9/5/52)

Regulars: *Ruth Lyons, Willie Thall, Dick Noel, the Bert Farber Orchestra*

Ruth Lyons was a broadcasting legend in her home base of Cincinnati, and probably could have become a national TV star had it not been for circumstances unrelated to ratings surrounding her series on NBC. She began her first program on WKRC Cincinnati in 1931, then came over to radio station WLW in 1942 to start *The Ruth Lyons 50 Club*. Among the up-and-coming talent who appeared on her radio shows were Doris Day and Rosemary Clooney.

She moved her series to WLW-TV on September 1949. The title reflected the format: 50 women had lunch during the program while Ruth aired her opinions in a casual yet outspoken manner, talked with guests, played games like musical chairs, and joked with studio personnel. On radio the show emanated from a downtown hotel, but television required using a downtown studio with catered food for lunch. As WLW was part of the Crosley Broadcasting Company, the show aired in Dayton and Columbus, Ohio, as well.

In the fall of 1951 Ruth made her network debut with her sidekick Bill Thall, singer Dick Noel, and guests Dave Garroway and Burgess Meredith. She needed the star power, as her slot was the first time on weekdays that all four networks (including DuMont) were competing against each other. The highlight of her network season probably was a five-day plea for contributions to the American Red Cross flood relief fund which netted $20,800.

In 1952, Lyons finished second in her slot, and NBC offered the show another year. The network, however, wanted her to do the show from New York City for a half hour, while local advertisers wanted her to do a full daily hour series, but in Cincinnati only. Ruth chose the latter, turning NBC down. Other network offers came later, but Lyons refused them also because, as she told *The Saturday Evening Post* in 1957, "I can make as much money here, and there are fewer headaches. I'm primarily a businesswoman, not a girl trying to get her name in lights."

The local show eventually expanded to 90 minutes. On January 27, 1967, Lyons, then nearing 60, stepped down from leading her show in favor of her sidekick Bob Braun, who replaced Willie Thall in 1957. Braun hosted the show under the title *The 50–50 Club* until 1982, when it became *Braun & Co.* and went into daily syndication as an hour show. The show ended on September 14, 1984, closing a major chapter in Midwestern broadcasting.

RUTH WINCHELL

Musical Variety; B&W

January 12, 1949–March 4, 1949

DuMont Mon.–Fri. 12:45–1 p.m. (1/12/49–3/4/49)

Hostess: *Ruth Winchell*

Pianist and accordionist Ruth Winchell (apparently not related to ventriloquist Paul Winchell) entertained the housewives in this inaugural DuMont daily show.

•RYAN'S HOPE

Soap Opera; Color
July 7, 1975–January 13, 1989

ABC Mon.–Fri. 1–1:30 p.m. (7/7/75–12/31/76)
ABC Mon.–Fri. 12:30–1 p.m. (1/3/77–10/5/84)
ABC Mon.–Fri. Noon–12:30 p.m. (10/8/84–1/13/89)

Cast:

Johnny Ryan	Bernard Barrow
Maeve Ryan	Helen Gallagher
Mary Ryan Fenelli (1975–77, 1983)/Maura (1986)	Kate Mulgrew
Mary Ryan Fenelli (1978)	Mary Carney
Mary Ryan Fenelli (1978–79)	Kathleen Tolan
Mary Ryan Fenelli (1979)	Nicolette Goulet
Frank Ryan (1975–76)	Michael Hawkins
Frank Ryan (1976–78)	Andrew Robinson
Frank Ryan (1978–81)	Daniel Hugh-Kelly
Frank Ryan (1983–85)	Geoffrey Pierson
Frank Ryan (1985–89)	John Sanderford
Dr. Pat Ryan (1975–78, 1983–89)	Malcolm Groome
Dr. Pat Ryan (1978–79)	John Blazo
Dr. Pat Ryan (1979)	Robert Finoccoli
Dr. Pat Ryan (1982–83)	Patrick James Clarke
Siobhan Ryan (1978–80)	Sarah Felder
Siobhan Ryan (1981–82)	Ann Gillespie
Siobhan Ryan (1982–86)	Marg Helgenberger
Siobhan Ryan (1986–87)	Carrell Myers
Delia Reid (1975–78, 1982–83, 1986–89)	Ilene Kristen
Delia Reid (1979)	Robyn Millan
Delia Reid (1979–82)	Randall Edwards
Bob Reid (1975–84)	Earl Hindman
Little John Ryan (1975–85)	Jadrian Steele
Little John Ryan (1985)	Tim Shew
John Reid Ryan (1985–89)	Jason Adams
Jack Fenelli	Michael Levin
Ryan Fenelli (1979–80)	Kerry McNamara
Ryan Fenelli (1980–84)	Jenny Rebecca Dweir
Ryan Fenelli (1985–89)	Yasmine Bleeth
Dr. Ed Coleridge (1975–76)	Frank Latimore
Jillian Coleridge (1975–87)	Nancy Addison
Dr. Roger Coleridge	Ron Hale
Dr. Faith Coleridge (1975–76)	Faith Catlin
Dr. Faith Coleridge (1976)	Nancy Barrett
Dr. Faith Coleridge (1976–78)	Catherine Hicks
Dr. Faith Coleridge (1978–83)	Karen Morris-Gowdy
Dr. Bucky Carter (1975–78)	Justin Deas
Dr. Seneca Beaulac (1975–85)	John Gabriel
Dr. Nell Beaulac (1975–76)	Diana van der Vlis
Marguerite Beaulac (1976)	Gale Sondergaard
Marguerite Beaulac (1976)	Anne Revere
Sister Mary Joel (1975)	Sylvia Sidney
Sister Mary Joel (1976)	Nancy Coleman
Sister Mary Joel (1977–78)	Natalie Priest
Sister Mary Joel (1982)	Jacqueline Brooks
Sister Mary Joel (1984–87)	Pauline Flanagan
Sister Mary Joel (1988–89)	Rosemary Prinz
Dr. Marshall Westheimer (1975–83)	William Kiehl
Dr. Clem Moultrie (1975–83)	Hannibal Penney Jr.
Nick Szabo (1975–76)	Michael Fairman
Reenie Szabo (1976)	Julia Barr
Ramona Gonzalez (1975–76)	Rosalinda Guerra
Cathleen Ryan Thompson (1976, 1978)	Nancy Reardon
Art Thompson (1978)	Gregory Abels
Sam Crowell (1976)	Dennis Jay Higgins
Tom Desmond (1977–79)	Thomas MacGreevy
Rae Woodard (1977–84)	Louise Shaffer
Bill Woodard (1977–78)	Wesley Addy
Dave Feldman (1977–79)	Joseph Leon
Alicia Nieves (1977–78)	Ana Alicia
Angel Nieves (1977–78)	Jose Aleman
Joe Novak (1979–80)	Richard Muenz
Joe Novak (1981–83, 198)	Roscoe Born
Joe Novak (1983–84)	Michael Hennessy
Joe Novak (1986–87)	Walt Willey
Tiso Novotny (1979–80)	Dan Clarke
Kevin McGuinness (1979–84)	Malachy McCourt
Wes Leonard (1979–83)	David Rasche
Annie Colleary (1979–81)	Pauline Flanagan
Ken George Jones (1980)	Trent Jones
Kimberly Harris (1980–81, 1982–83)	Kelli Maroney
Michael Pavel (1980–81)	Michael Corbett
Barry Ryan (1980–81)	Richard Backus
Lilly Darnell (1980)	Christine Ebersole
Lilly Darnell (1980)	Kathryn Dowling
Rose Melina (1980–81)	Rose Alaio
Elizabeth Jane Ryan (1981–82)	Maureen Garrett
Barbara Wilde (1981–82)	Judith Barcroft
Sgt. Jim Speed (1981–82)	Mackenzie Allen
Orson Burns (1981)	Nicolas Surovy
Orson Burns (1981–82)	Robert Desiderio
Aristotle Benedict-White (1981–82)	Gordon Thompson
Ox Knowles (1982)	Will Patton
Mitch Bronsky (1982)	James Sloyan
Hollis "Kirk" Kirkland III (1982–83)	Peter Haskell
Catsy Kirkland (1982–83)	Christine Jones
Amanda Kirkland (1982–83)	Mary Page Keller
Amanda Kirkland (1983)	Ariane Munker
Leigh Kirkland (1983–85, 1988 at least)	Felicity La Fortune
Sydney Price (1983–85)	Robin Greer
Charlotte Greer (1983)	Judith Chapman
Bess Shelby (1983–87)	Gloria DeHaven
Maggie Shelby (1983–88)	Cali Timmins

Lt. Bill Hyde (1983–85)	David Sederholm
Rick Hyde (1984–87)	Grant Show
Jacqueline Novak (1983–87)	Gerit Quealy
Max Dubujak (1984–87)	Daniel Pilon
Laslo Novotny (1984–85, 1987)	Fred Burstein
Policeman Ken Graham (1984–85)	Corbin Bernsen
Dave Greenberg (1984–85)	Scott Holmes
Pru Shepherd (1984–85)	Traci Lin
Katie Thompson (1984)	Lauren O'Bryan
Katie Thompson (1984–85)	Julia Campbell
Matthew Crane (1984–85)	Harve Presnell
Charles Whitehall (1984–85)	David O'Brien
Dakota Smith (1985–89)	Christopher Durham
Devlin Kowalski (1985–87)	Leslie Easterbrook
Melinda Weaver Ryan (1985–87)	Nancy Valen
Gabrielle Dubujak/Chessy Blake	
(1985)	Susan Scannell
Chantal Dubujak (1985)	Marisa Paven
D. J. LaSalle (1985)	Christian Slater
Dr. Evan Cooper (1986–87 at least)	Irving Allen Lee
Chris Hannold (1986–87 at least)	Lydia Hannibal
Hower Dowd (1986–87 at least)	Keith Charles
Mark D'Angelo (1986–87 at least)	Peter Love
Concetta D'Angelo (1987–87	
at least)	Lois Robbins
Diana Douglas (1986)	Tracey Ross
Ben Shelby (1987–89)	James Wlcek
Zena Brown (1987–88 at least)	Tichina Arnold
Emily Hall (1987–88 at least)	Cynthia Dozier
Nancy Don Louis (1987 at least)	Maria Pitillo
Lizzie Ransome (1987–89)	Catherine Larson

A rarity among soaps in that it was set in a real town (New York City) with an "ethnic" family, *Ryan's Hope* lasted more than 13 years. It focused on bar owner Johnny Ryan and his wife Maeve, and the efforts of their five children to adapt to the mores of the times while struggling to follow their parents' Roman Catholic faith. In the first five years all the Ryans predominated in the story line except for the happily married Cathleen, seen only briefly. The main plots involved the intricate interaction between the Ryans and the Coleridge family, headed by widower Dr. Ed Coleridge, whose children were Jill, Roger (also a doctor), and Faith.

At the outset Ed treated city council candidate Frank Ryan for a fractured skull and broken neck sustained on the stairs at Riverside Hospital. He survived amid word that his wife Delia had done the dirty deed because she found out he was sleeping with Jill. A flighty soul, Delia went back to being the faithful wife to Frank but cheated on her own with Roger, Jill's brother. Frank found out and divorced her.

Delia then tried to get Frank's brother Pat to marry her (she had dated Pat before wedding Frank) by announcing that she was pregnant with his child, but in fact the father was Roger, whom Delia ended up marrying. In this marriage Delia proved to be faithful and resourceful, even becoming owner of the Crystal Palace restaurant. But Roger began

seeing Rae Woodard, who inherited her husband William's empire on his death in 1978. Roger divorced Delia but did not get his hands on Rae's new riches because, you see . . . . (More details to come.)

Ed Coleridge loved Dr. Nell Beaulac, who was separated at the time from her husband Seneca. But Seneca learned that Nell was terminally ill, and when aneurysms burst in her brain, making it necessary that she be put on life support, Seneca disconnected the machine with her consent. Seneca faced criminal charges because of these actions, but Jill defended him so successfully that he earned only a week in jail. However, their romance was nipped in the bud by her continued attraction to Frank. Unfortunately, Jill learned that she was pregnant with Seneca's child, and so did Frank, who demanded that she give Seneca full custody of the baby if she wanted to wed him. She declined, so they broke up.

The fancy-free Frank found an enthusiastic supporter for his run to be a U.S. Senator in Rae. Jillian, convinced she had no chance with Frank, married Seneca, but when their child Edmond died in a gas explosion, she planned to leave Seneca and start anew elsewhere. A chance meeting with Frank changed that, however, and the two renewed their love. This irked Rae so much that she forced Frank to leave his seat under charges of impropriety, but he stood by Jill and even worked together with her in a law firm.

Meanwhile Faith Coleridge was in love with Pat, and Pat's fellow intern Bucky Carter wanted Faith. Pat found Faith possessive and dropped her. Faith then found herself being chased by Kenneth Castle, a stalker type whose actions were so terrifying that Ed, her dad, tried to capture him. Sadly, Ed was killed when he fell off Faith's roof while chasing Kenneth.

A rather happy love story involved Mary Ryan and Jack Fenelli, a reporter trying to dig up the dirt on her brother Frank. They lived together, much to her parents' chagrin, then argued over her working relationship with boss Sam Crowell at Channel R before finally marrying. They divorced later due to misunderstandings, but Mary's pal Tom Desmond (who had an unhappy marriage with Faith) got them back together, and in 1977 they had their "second" honeymoon in Ireland, which the show taped on location, making *Ryan's Hope* the first serial to tape outside America. Later they had a daughter, Ryan Fenelli.

A new Ryan added to the stew in 1978 was Siobhan, considered to be an iconoclast by the rest of the family, who first found herself interested in Jack Fenelli, who resisted her, and then Joe Novak, a fisherman with mob connections. The latter attraction led to terrible consequences. Joe's uncle Tiso Novotny was not happy with Mary's reports on the mob (Mary was a TV reporter), and he retaliated by sabotaging her automobile, causing a car crash in which she was killed. A bereft Jack and Johnny tried to prove that Tiso had caused the accident, and Tiso died soon after Siobhan and Joe's wedding. Joe had found Mary's assassin, but he also inherited Tiso's title, which disgusted even Siobhan to the point where she left him.

All these stories benefited from strong performances and beautiful writing from series creators Claire Labine and Paul Avila Mayer, who won Emmys for their work from 1977–80. However, the soap did have a few nagging problems which detracted from its success. Constant turnover among the four Ryan children, Delia, and family friend Sister Mary Joel made it difficult for the audience to identify with them (there were a mind-boggling 27 different performers who played the roles regularly). Also problematic were the thefts of a few movie story lines. The worst was in 1980, when Delia met a Central Park ape called Prince Albert (played by a costumed actor), who escaped from his cage and carried Delia around New York à la Fay Wray–King Kong before being felled by a tranquilizer gun. Hoo boy.

In the early 1980s the serial began to repeat plots, always a sign of wear. For one, Jill pulled the plug to end the life of terminal cancer patient Ken George Jones, just as Seneca had done with his wife years earlier, and Jill, like Seneca, was exonerated. This followed yet another separation between Jill and Frank as she romanced Jones while Frank saw the ever-hapless Faith. When Jill and Frank reconciled yet again, Faith became a sot.

Another loser at love, Rae Woodard, suffered anguish when she and her illegitimate daughter Kimberly Harris

both unwittingly slept with reporter Michael Pavel. Kim tried to break it off by wedding Seneca but kept seeing Michael. When enraged mom Rae spotted one tryst, there was a three-way struggle over a gun, and a shot rang out, killing Michael. It turned out that a gangster had actually killed Michael, but the publicity of the incident led to Seneca divorcing Kim and her leaving town even though she carried his baby.

Other mob involvement surfaced when Siobhan returned home to work as a police officer and fell back in love with Joe Novak, now managing Delia's restaurant. Joe's work in organized crime led to a cooling of the affair, and he found himself competing for her hand with detective Mitch Bronsky, who in turn was the object of affection of a sobered-up Faith. As for Joe's boss Delia, she now fancied Barry Ryan, Johnny's nephew, whose unfaithfulness to her with ingenue Lilly Darnell led Delia to run him over. Incredibly, Delia avoided a trial in the incident. Seneca

The central characters on Ryan's Hope *in 1987 were, clockwise from top left, Pat (played by Malcolm Groome), Siobhan (Carrell Myers), Dakota (Christopher Durham), Jill (Nancy Addison), Frank (John Sanderford), Jack (Michael Levin), Ryan (Yasmine Bleeth), Maeve (Helen Gallagher), Johnny (Bernard Barrow), Johnno (Jason Adams), and Delia (Ilene Kristen).*

then romanced Barbara Wilde, a soap opera star (!), but that fell apart too.

A fellow Ryan relative, Johnny's niece Elizabeth, came in 1981 and worked at Rae's newspaper as a reporter while falling for Roger Coleridge. Just one thing hindered it—her marriage to Ox Knowles, which she tried unsuccessfully to resolve before leaving town. Since he was handsome and conniving, Delia naturally went after Ox next.

In 1982 the Ryans found themselves taking a back seat in the drama to Hollis Kirkland, who, with his daughter Amanda and wife Catsy, dominated the show's action for a while. Amanda had the hots for her therapist Pat Ryan, while Hollis found his love for ex-flame Rae still burned. In fact, Hollis was the father of Rae's daughter Kimberly, and she returned to become part of the new main family in town. Kirk and Catsy ended up staying married, but they left town, and the Ryans returned to prominence. Not coincidentally, this happened concurrent with Avila and Mayer returning as head writers of the show after more than a year's absence.

John and Maeve received a meaty, novel story line in which they reminisced about their departed daughter Mary, with Kate Mulgrew returning in their flashbacks. They and others then found that Jill was only a half-sister to Frank and Ed, as her real mother, Bess Shelby, came into town with her other daughter Maggie. Maggie dated Pat Ryan but then, in a questionable plot device, ended up marrying Roger two years after their original courtship, during which he had nearly raped her.

In the mid-1980s came an influx of adolescent Ryans—Katie, Cathleen's 18-year-old daughter; a suddenly teenage Ryan Fenelli, who eloped with hunky cop Rick Hyde despite being underage; and another surprise, post-pubescent John Reid, who in six months went from being 10-year-old Little John to 19-year-old single dad Johnno! The biggest shock for the family, and many of the show's fans, was the arrival of Dakota Smith, who, John told Maeve, was his illegitimate son from an earlier affair. Maeve eventually accepted Dakota, but not all the audience did, as he went from nursing an amnesia victim Jillian who fell in love with him to dealing with Delia's lust for him (was there ever a male Ryan whom Delia did *not* want?).

Around the same time a new crime syndicate emerged. Naturally Siobhan had to wed its leader Max Dubujak. When he died in 1987, she went back to Joe Novak for the umpteenth time, then decided to leave town. Jillian also departed at that time, supposedly to visit her mother in Australia, following another reconciliation with Frank, whose ardor for her dimmed any hope Assistant D.A. Diana Douglas had of snagging him.

In other romantic complications, Jack got involved with Devlin Kowalski, while his married daughter Ryan found that her newspaper editor Mark D'Angelo wanted more than reports from her. And Pat finally found a wife in Melinda Weaver following disastrous romances with Maggie Shelby and Gabrielle Dubajak. (The latter died in 1985, but a

mysterious double named Chessy Blake appeared in town a few months later.)

New plot twists in 1987 included the Ryans acting as foster parents for Zena, a challenging, streetwise, illiterate teenager, and Delia trying to keep Ben and Lizzie apart with the help of newcomer Nancy Don Louis. The main featured triangle to emerge, however, was between Ben, Lizzie, and Lizzie's new husband John Ryan. There was also the shocking revelation for Jack Fenelli that longtime pal Sister Mary Joel was actually his natural mother.

But none of that, or the return of Leigh Kirkland as a newspaper publisher, could save the series, which had been at the bottom of the ratings since 1984, when many ABC affiliates in the East preempted it for local news. Though still finely acted and written, *Ryan's Hope* found itself with no network or syndication takers at the start of 1989, so it went out with class, as Maeve sang "Danny Boy" a bit more emotionally than she normally did at every St. Patrick's Day celebration at Ryan's Bar.

S.S. TELE-CRUISE
Musical Variety; B&W
April 28, 1951–June 2, 1951
ABC Sat. 9–10:45 a.m. (4/28/51–6/2/51)

Regulars: *Jack Steck (as Cap'n Jack), Bon Bon, Eddie Roecker, Carol Wynne, the Dave Appell Trio, the Crewman, the Thomas Cannon Ballet*

Airing from Philadelphia, this variety show with a nautical theme included as regulars several vocalists (including African-American former big band singer Bon Bon) and a few guests. It aired during ABC's abortive attempts in the early 1950s to launch a competitive Saturday morning schedule.

•SABRINA THE TEEN-AGE WITCH
Cartoon; Color
September 12, 1970–January 28, 1978
CBS Sat. 9–10 a.m. (9/12/70–9/4/71)
CBS Sat. 11–11:30 a.m. (9/1/71–9/2/72)
CBS Sat. 8:30–9 a.m. (9/9/72–9/1/73)
CBS Sat. 8:30–9 a.m. (2/1/74–8/31/74)
NBC Sat. 9:30–10 a.m. (11/12/77–1/28/78)
Voices:
Sabrina/Aunt Hilda/Aunt Zelda   Jane Webb

First seen as a regular on *The Archies* in 1969–70, blond sorceress Sabrina struck out on her own and headlined a series first titled *Sabrina and the Groovie Goolies* from 1970–71. The latter characters, seen in separate segments, had their own spin-off in 1971 (see *Groovie Goolies*), while Sabrina stayed on her own the rest of her run. Sabrina was very much a Cinderella-like character living in the 20th century, as she resided in a house with her unattractive aunts Hilda and Zelda and cousin Ambrose, a warlock. While she felt free to use her powers privately, for example, to activate a vacuum cleaner to suck up dirt on its own, she tried valiantly but not always successfully to avoid having her talents or those of the rest of her family used on acquaintances or strangers, often with comic results. Salem was Sabrina's pet tabby. The character first appeared in *Archie* comics.

After two years solo, Sabrina resurfaced in reruns in the spring of 1974 and on NBC as a midseason replacment titled *Sabrina, Super Witch.* On April 7, 1996, the character received an unlikely revival in a Showtime cable channel TV movie starring Melissa Joan Hart in the title role, which impressed ABC enough to make the show a series for its nighttime lineup in the fall of 1996.

•SALE OF THE CENTURY
Game; Color
September 29, 1969–March 24, 1989

NBC Mon.–Fri. 11–11:30 a.m. (9/29/69–7/13/73)
NBC Mon.–Fri. 10:30–11 a.m. (1/3/83–1/2/87)
NBC Mon.–Fri. 10–10:30 a.m. (1/5/87–3/24/89)

Regulars: *Jack Kelly (1969–71), Joe Garagiola (1971–73), Jim Perry (1983–89), Sally Julian (1983), Lee Menning (1983–84), Summer Bartholomew (1984–89)*

When *Sale of the Century* began in 1969, three contestants started with $25 each and gained $5 for every right answer to a question (a wrong one subtracted $5). The question asking was often interrupted by attempts to persuade the contestant with the most money to buy a prize at 10 percent or even less of its original value, sometimes with another gift added as an incentive. The winner could use the day's tally to buy more expensive items at cut rates (e.g., a $2,995 mink coat for $129) or return the next day to try to win again, add that day's amount to the tally, and claim prizes of larger value. A "Win-a-Bargain" segment appeared starting in November 1971 wherein a home viewer could win the same lower-priced item that a contestant on the show bought if that viewer's postcard was selected on the show.

After its network run ended, the show went into production for syndication through 1974. Then producer Reg Grundy took the series to Australia, where it became a long-running hit. Noting the success of the property, NBC brought it back in 1983 with Jim Perry as host and Sally Julian as his assistant. Julian was later replaced by Lee Menning and then, on December 31, 1984, by former Miss America Summer Bartholomew, who stayed till the end of the run. The format was pretty much the same as before, though gift prizes were more expensive and each contestant started with $20. Another innovation was the "Fame Game" board, which a contestant could play if he or she was the first to identify a celebrity from a mini-biography read by Perry. The board had the faces of nine stars, behind three

of which was additional spending money in the amounts of $10, $15, and $25. As before, the day's winner could return to try and win six prizes of increasing value, which now included a car and a jackpot of $50,000 which increased $1,000 every day it was not won. The bonus game changed a few times before the series ended in 1989.

•SALLY JESSY RAPHAEL
Talk; Color
1984–

Syndicated 30 and 60 minutes daily beginning 1984
Host: *Sally Jessy Raphael*

Sally Jessy Raphael was in her forties and had a full résumé when she hit the talk show world in 1984. She started doing talk radio in Puerto Rico in 1961, then was hired and fired at least 18 times during the next two decades or so before scoring a success with a daily radio show on WMCA New York City in the 1970s. That led to this successful syndicated daytime show which was packaged and promoted by the same company which handled *Donahue* (in fact, the show aired after *Donahue* in many markets). A petite blonde sporting prominent red-rimmed glasses, Sally was an early proponent of the "shock talk" genre of shows, with topics like male prostitutes and strippers, designed more to exploit the participants than to enlighten the audience. She continued in business for more than a decade despite having a few personal problems with her family which brought unwanted publicity to her, including a daughter's suicide, and was still a top contender as of 1996.

SAM LEVENSON SHOW, THE
Talk; B&W
April 27, 1959–September 25, 1959

CBS Mon.–Fri. 10:30–11 a.m. (4/27/59–9/25/59)
Host: *Sam Levenson*

Humorist Sam Levenson assumed Arthur Godfrey's time slot when the latter left his morning show for chest surgery in 1959. After a short monologue, Levensen interviewed guests, who were predominantly comedians, including Morey Amsterdam, Phil Baker, and Martha Raye. One of the show's writers was Andy Rooney.

SAMSON AND GOLIATH
Cartoon; Color
September 9, 1967–August 31, 1968

NBC Sat. 10:30–11 a.m. (9/9/67–8/31/68)
Voices:
Samson   *Tim Matheson*
Also: *Daws Butler, Don Messick, John Stephenson*

A boy named Sam got superpowers by rubbing together bracelets he wore and saying "I need Samson power!" It transformed him and his dog Goliath into the ancient hero of yore and a lion, respectively. Samson was as beefy as ever, while Goliath the lion could fly and shoot lasers from his eyes; both needed all their skills to combat the weird variety of fantastic foes they faced. *The Space Kiddettes,* previously seen on their own series in 1966–67, were a supporting segment. On April 6, 1968, the show was retitled *Young Samson,* but the ratings did not increase notably.

SANDY KOUFAX

Sports; Color

April 15, 1967–September 14, 1968

NBC Sat. 2–2:15 p.m. (4/15/67–9/14/68; summers only)

Host: *Sandy Koufax*

Ex–Los Angeles Dodger pitching great Sandy Koufax helmed a pregame baseball show before *Baseball Game of the Week* for two summers. He interviewed guests and met with other NBC announcers to preview the day's game.

•SANTA BARBARA

Soap; Color

July 30, 1984–January 15, 1993

NBC Mon.–Fri. 3–4 p.m. (7/30/84–1/15/93)

Cast:

Minx Lockridge (1984–87)	*Dame Judith Anderson*
Minx Lockridge (1987–93)	*Janis Paige*
Lionel Lockridge (1984–92)	*Nicolas Coster*
Augusta Lockridge (1984–86, 1988–91)	
Laken Lockridge (1984–85)	*Louise Sorel*
Laken Lockridge (1987–8?)	*Julie Ronnie*
Laken Lockridge (198?–91)	*Susan Marie Snyder*
Warren Lockridge (1984–86)	*Shell Danielson*
Warren Lockridge (1986–87)	*John Allen Nelson*
Warren Lockridge (1992–93)	*Scott Jenkins*
C. C. Capwell (1984)	*Jack Wagner*
C. C. Capwell (1984)	*Peter Mark Richman*
C. C. Capwell (1984–86)	*Paul Burke*
C. C. Capwell (1986–93)	*Charles Bateman*
Mason Capwell (1984–89)	*Jed Allan*
Mason Capwell (1989–91)	*Lane Davies*
Mason Capwell (1991–93)	*Terry Lester*
Kelly Capwell (1984–88)	*Gordon Thompson*
Kelly Capwell (1988–89)	*Robin Wright*
Kelly Capwell (1989–at least 1991)	*Kimberly MacArthur*
Kelly Capwell (199?–93)	*Carrington Garland*
Eden Capwell (1984–9?)	*Eileen Davidson*
Sophia Capwell (1984)	*Marcy Walker*
Sophia Capwell (1984–93)	*Rosemary Forsyth*
Ted Capwell (1984–89)	*Judith McConnell*
Ted Capwell (1991–93)	*Todd McKee*
Channing Capwell Jr. (1984–85)	*Michael Brainard*
Rosa Andrade	*Robert Wilson*
Santana Andrade (1984)	*Margarita Cardova*
Santana Andrade (1985)	*Ava Lazar*
Santana Andrade (1985–87, 1989)	*Margaret Michaels*
	Gina Gallego

Santana Andrade (1991–92)	*Wanda de Jesus*
Danny Andrade (1984–86)	*Rupert Ravens*
Gina Demott (1984–85)	*Linda Gibboney*
Gina Demott (1985–93)	*Robin Mattson*
Peter Flint (1984–85)	*Stephen Meadows*
Joe Perkins (1984)	*Dane Witherspoon*
Joe Perkins (1984–85)	*Mark Arnold*
Marisa Perkins (1984–86)	*Valorie Armstrong*
Amy Perkins (1984–86)	*Kelly Sherman*
Cruz Castillo (1984–92)	*A. Martinez*
Brick Wallace (1984–87)	*Richard Eden*
Ginger Jones (1984–85)	*Paula Kelly*
Julia Wainwright (1985–93)	*Nancy Grahn*
Michael "Pearl" Bradford III (1985–87)	*Robert Thaler*
Mary Duvall (1985–86)	*Harley Kozak*
Nick Hartley (1985–86)	*David Haskell*
Dylan Hartley (1985–86)	*Page Moseley*
Kirk Cranston Lee (1985–86, 1990)	*Joseph Bottoms*
Kirk Cranston Lee (1986)	*Robert Newman*
J. (Jack) Stanford Lee (1985)	*Joel Crothers*
Christy Duvall (1985)	*Tricia Cast*
Jake Morton (1986–89)	*Rick Edwards*
Hayley Benson Capwell (1986–88)	*Stacy Edwards*
Victoria "Tori" Lane (1986–88)	*Kristen Meadows*
Jeffrey Conrad (1986–88)	*Ross Kettle*
Caroline Wilson (1986–87)	*Lenore Kasdorf*
Madeline Capwell Laurent (1986–87)	*Terry Davis*
Courtney Capwell (1986–87)	*Julia Campbell*
Brian Bedford (1986–87)	*Kyle Secor*
Alice Jackson (1986–87)	*Marie-Alise Recasner*
Gus Jackson (1986–87)	*David Fonteno*
Paul Whitney (1986–87)	*Stoney Jackson*
Jane Wilson (1986–87)	*Jane Sibbett*
Lily Light, a.k.a "Angel" (1986–87)	*Lynn Clark*
Dr. Scott Clark (1987–89)	*Vincent Irizarry*
T. J. Daniels (1987–89)	*Chip Mayer*
Pamela Capwell (1987)	*Shirley Ann Field*
Pamela Capwell (1988, 1991)	*Marj Dusay*
Cain Garver (1987–88)	*Scott Jaeck*
Bunny Tagliatti/Bonnie (1988–89)	*Joe Marinelli*
Father Mike Donnelly (1988–91)	*Frank Runyeon*
Dr. Arthur Donnelly (1988–89)	*Jon Cypher*
Keith Timmons (1988–90)	*Justin Deas*
Keith Timmons (1990–91)	*John Novak*
Dr. Zack Kelton (1988–89)/ D.A. Ethan Asher (1989–90)	*Leigh McCloskey*
Heather Donnelly (1988–89)	*Jane Rogers*
Robert Barr/Quinn Armitage (1989–91)	*Roscoe Born*
Craig Hunt (1989–91)	*John Callahan*
Laura Simmons Asher (1989–90)	*Christopher Norris*
Ric Castillo (1989–90)	*Peter Love*
Celeste DiNapoli (1989)	*Signy Coleman*

Lisa DiNapoli (1989)	Tawny Kitaen
Greg Hughes (1989)	Paul Johansson
Mac Blake (1989)	Steve Bond
Cassandra "Cassie" Benedict	
(1990–92)	Karen Moncrieff
Dash Nichols (1990–91)	Timothy Gibbs
Amado Gonzalez (1990–91)	Rawley Valverde
Angela Raymond (1991–93)	Nina Arvesan
Suzanne Collier (1991–93)	Terri Garber
Katrina Ruyker (1991–93)	Maria Ellingsen
Jodie Walker (1992–93)	Kim Zimmer
B. J. Walker (1992–93)	Sydney Penny
Reese Walker (1992–93)	Forry Smith
Skyler Gates (1992)	Stephen Nichols

Santa Barbara was NBC's last bid to compete against *General Hospital* on ABC and *Guiding Light* on CBS. The show's early going was rough, and included numerous changeovers in cast. Four actors played the pivotal role of C. C. Capwell within the first two years alone, for example (it could have been five, but the original choice of Lloyd Bochner did not pan out, requiring Peter Mark Richman and Paul Burke to serve as temporary replacements). The biggest controversy, however, arose in 1987 when NBC took creative control away from the show's producers, Jerome and Bridget Dobson, who spent three years trying to get it back. Perhaps in part because of these problems, *Santa Barbara* never really threatened the competition at any time during its 8¹/2-year run, though it did win three consecutive Outstanding Daytime Drama Emmys through 1990.

Set in the upscale California town of the same name, *Santa Barbara* featured a name star in Dame Judith Anderson as bitchy matriarch Minx Lockridge, the domineering mother of Lionel Lockridge and his scheming wife Augusta and grandmother to Lionel and Augusta's children Warren and Laken. Their family had close connections to the Capwells, overseen by the suspicious C.C. (short for Channing Creighton), his unbalanced second wife, Sophia, and their children, Mason, Kelly, Ted, and Eden. A fifth child, Channing Capwell Jr., appeared in flashbacks during the first year, as someone had murdered him in 1979 (five years before the ostensible beginning of the action) following a dispute he had with Joe Perkins, Kelly's fiancé. Perkins reappeared at the start of the serial freed from jail and claiming innocence as Kelly prepared to marry Peter Flint. It turned out that Sophia, who remarried C.C., had mistakenly killed Channing, but she did not go to prison. In 1985, Peter killed Joe before he died, as did the rather uninvolving initial story line.

Other, better-developed characters took over the spotlight later in 1985. There was the long-running romance of blond Eden, a TV news anchor, and her dark, handsome lover, lawman Cruz Castillo. He came to town to investigate Joe's murder but stayed with Eden despite numerous calamities before they wed in 1988. These included her marriage to Kirk Cranston, the son of J. Stanford Lee, who tried to kill Eden and Cruz; the efforts of Cruz's ex-girlfriend Tori Lane

to win her old flame back by seducing him and giving birth to their son; and Eden's supposed death in a helicopter crash while disturbed Vietnam War veteran Cain Garver held her hostage. Also fascinating was Mason, a lush who felt his dad did not love him but who nevertheless came up with plenty of dry comments on the goings-on around him, including his own troubled relationships with ex-nun Mary DuVall and then Tori Lane. (The manner of Mary's death— a "C" from the rooftop of the Capwell hotel fell and crushed her—struck some viewers as blackly funny and some as an example of poor taste, and prompted many to speculate on its possible symbolic significance.)

But the wildest character had to be crazed vixen Gina DeMott, Lord love her, who was C.C.'s estranged wife. Gina had adopted Brandon, the product of an affair between the late Channing Jr. and Santana Andrade, a member of the lower-class family working for the Capwells, and tried to keep Santana, who wed C.C. and gained temporary custody of Brandon, off base by such tactics as switching Brandon's allergy pills. She also dated Mason and Dr. Scott Clark and never gave up trying to sway C.C. Gina's wacky escapades— including a hilarious contest with Keith Timmons on *Wheel of Fortune* in 1988 that included a guest shot by Vanna White, and a wild wedding to Keith in Las Vegas on Christmas Day 1990—defined the warped sense of humor that permeated *Santa Barbara* during the late 1980s.

Other Capwells also figured prominently during the first few years of the show's run. Kelly planned to wed Nick Hartley, but her affair with his jealous brother Dylan led to the latter's accidental death. Kelly was charged with his death, and landed in a sanitarium, where she stayed until cleared. She then wed Jeffrey Conrad. Her later loves were Cruz's brother Ric Castillo and Robert Barr, whose twin brother Quinn Armitage impersonated him after his death. Sophia Capwell had a son during her affair with Lionel Lockridge when she was engaged to C.C., Brick Wallace, who learned he was switched at birth by grandma Minx so that he would not be raised by a Capwell. Amy Perkins, Joe's sister, wed Brick but was later killed in an explosion. Brick then left town with Jane Wilson. Pamela Capwell, C.C.'s first wife, who was supposed to be dead, returned in an unsuccessful bid to get C.C. back but ended up marrying C.C.'s business rival Jeffrey Conrad. And Ted Capwell, first in love with Laken Lockridge, wed Hayley Benson, Gina's niece, but when she was raped, their marriage unraveled. C.C.'s nieces Courtney and Madeline also arrived for a time.

By contrast, the Lockridges seemed positively sedate. Sure, Augusta separated from Lionel, who then wed Jane Wilson's mother Caroline, and Warren became a gambling addict, but these events paled next to more exotic story lines, including the appearance of Angel the fake teenage evangelist, who was Gina's illegitimate daughter and whom Mason claimed saved his life; an interracial love triangle between Alice Jackson, Pearl Bradford, and Paul Whitney; and, in 1988, the emergence of some weird alternate personalities. Among the latter was Mason's other personality Sonny

Lionel Lockridge (played by Nicholas Coster) and his wife Augusta try to escape an earthquake in this location shot on Santa Barbara.

Sprockett, whom his girlfriend, attorney Julia Wainwright, found living in Las Vegas, and Bunny Tigliatti, a transvestite involved with the mob who rented all of Gina's rooms when Gina made the former Lockridge mansion into a bed-and-breakfast inn. Whew!

Also seen in the late 1980s were T. J. Daniels, who charmed both Sophia and Kelly despite his criminal activities; Dr. Arthur Donnelly, who meddled with his children's lives; and Dr. Zack Kelton, a gynecologist who was the "Video Rapist" who attacked several women in town including Eden. Mason and Julia had a few ups and downs due to Mason's personality problems, and Mason saw old flame Gina briefly, and Julia dated environmentalist Dash Nichols, but by the end of the show's run they were still together and expecting a child. In fact, the love between Julia and Mason, and between Eden and Cruz, was about the only constant in the intricate mix of new characters and twists that dominated in 1990, and the following year series creators Bridget and Jerome Dobson, having regained control of the show, returned to make sense of the mess.

The Dobsons' 1991 plots included Pamela Capwell's return as a buffer between her son Mason and ex-husband C.C., and a plot where Warren, accused of the murder of Amado Gonzalez and a murder attempt on Mason, jumped bail and went to the Soviet Union to emerge as a hero. Warren's adventures prompted the first-ever shooting of on-location footage of an American soap opera in Russia. Warren also was revealed not to be Lionel's son, prompting Augusta to leave town a second time, and Minx found out that Cassie, Warren's love, was the daughter she had given up at birth.

But the Dobsons showed they had not forgotten their talent for writing high camp. The highlight in that regard had to be the Christmas Eve episode where Gina, having earlier robbed C.C.'s semen from a sperm bank to get pregnant following the dissolution of her marriage to Keith, gave birth in a veterinary hospital after taking a dog she had hit with her car there for treatment!

Yet ratings did not go up appreciably, and a story line which had Eden going through multiple personalities, including those of Sophia and Channing Jr., before leaving Cruz and the town, was a major bomb with critics and viewers. NBC kicked the Dobsons out again at the start of 1992, precipitating a huge decline in the show's ratings until it hit bottom, becoming the lowest-rated soap. The unexciting stories included C.C. splitting with Santana following a brief reunion, Kelly Capwell temporarily romancing Skyler Gates, Angela Raymond pining for Warren, and Lionel marrying Gina, of all people. Two particularly weak plot lines were the one in which Julia and Mason endured a tiresome mystery connected to a haunted house named Ballymoor, and the one in which Cruz the cop suddenly got weak-willed and fled the country after taking the fall for a crime that his daughter B.J., the product of a much-earlier union with ex-cop Jodie Walker, had committed. (B.J. ended up marrying Warren the following year.)

In October 1992 NBC announced the cancellation of *Santa Barbara* despite its continuing international popularity. (The show aired in 48 countries, making it the world's most watched serial, and was a particular favorite in France, where it aired in the nighttime.) The ending in early 1993, which didn't feature the return of a single familiar face, offered no solace to the fans, however. In fact it may have boasted one of the worst closeouts in TV history: The final shot was of executive producer Paul Rauch stepping into the spotlight on a bare soundstage and rubbing out his cigarette butt! That was tackier than anything this show, which was to be sorely missed, had presented during its run of more than eight years. NBC returned the hour to affiliates for local programming.

SANTO BUGITO

Cartoon; Color
September 16, 1995–

CBS Sat. 11:30 a.m.–Noon (9/16/95–9/23/95)
CBS Sat. 10:30–11 a.m. (9/30/95–11/18/95)
CBS Sat. 11:30 a.m.–Noon (11/25/95–5/11/96)
CBS Sat. 8–8:30 a.m. (5/18/96–)

Santo Bugito was the address where Carmen and Paco de la Antchez ran a restaurant for their fellow insects in America near Mexico. Among the show's voice-over actors was Joan van Ark.

SATURDAY AT THE ZOO—See *Sunday at the Bronx Zoo.*

SATURDAY MORNING VIDEOS

Music; Color
September 8, 1990–August 29, 1992

NBC Sat. Noon–1 p.m. (9/8/90–9/7/91)
NBC Sat. Noon–12:30 p.m. (9/14/91–10/21/91)
NBC Sat. Noon–12:30 p.m. (7/11/92–8/29/92)

Saturday Morning Videos presented mostly rock videos of currently popular tunes, plus interviews with some artists, news about the music world, and a weekly countdown of the top 10 songs, all geared for a young audience. Among the various guest hosts were the cast of *Saved By the Bell* on September 15, 1990, and the rock act the Nelsons, twins Gunnar and Matthew, on January 5, 1991. The show also was known as *Saturday Videos.*

SATURDAY PROM

Musical Variety; B&W
October 15, 1960–April 1, 1961

NBC Sat. 5:30–6 p.m. (10/15/60–4/1/61)

Regulars: *Merv Griffin, the Saturday Prom Seven (11/5/60–4/1/61)*

Former big band singer Merv Griffin hosted this *American Bandstand* clone, which distinguished itself by featuring a "band of the month." The Saturday Prom Seven, a teenage instrumental group, joined the activities a few weeks after the debut.

Although the opening guest lineup was pretty lame (Anita Bryant, Conway Twitty, and Johnny and the Hurricanes), later shows did present a solid overview of popular music acts circa 1961. Guests included Bobby Vee, Tony Bennett, Neil Sedaka, Brook Benton, Fats Domino, Sam Cooke, the Bill Black Combo, Brian Hyland, and Dion.

SATURDAY SPORTS SHOWCASE

Sports Anthology; Color
April 7, 1990–September 15, 1990

NBC Sat. 4–6 p.m. (4/7/90–9/15/90)

When it lost the rights to telecast the *Baseball Game of the Week* to CBS after 24 years, NBC installed this collection of various contests to compete for ratings. The grab bag ranged from the Wimbledon tennis tournament and the PGA Seniors golf championship to rebroadcasts of classic events such as Muhammad Ali and George Foreman boxing in the "Thriller in Manila."

SATURDAY SUPERCADE

Cartoon; Color
September 17, 1983–August 24, 1985

CBS Sat. 8:30–9:30 a.m. (9/17/83–9/8/84)
CBS Sat. 9:30–10:30 a.m. (9/15/84–10/27/84)
CBS Sat. 10:30–11:30 a.m. (11/3/84–12/29/84)
CBS Sat. Noon–1 p.m. (1/5/85–3/23/85)
CBS Sat. 12:30–1:30 p.m. (3/30/85–8/24/85)

Voices:

Donkey Kong	*Soupy Sales*
Donkey Kong Jr./Q*Dad/Coilee	
Snake/Ugg/Wrongway/Monkey	
Biz Gang (1984–85)	*Frank Welker*
Mario	*Peter Cullen*
Pauline	*Judy Strangis*
Bones	*Bart Braverman*
Q*Bert	*Billy Bowles*
Q*Tee/Q*Val	*Robbie Lee*
Q*Bertha/Q*Mom/Viper	*Julie McWhirter Dees*
Frogger (1983–84)	*Bob Sarlatte*
Fanny Frog (1983–84)	*B. J. Ward*
Shellshock Turtle ("Shelly";	
1983–84)/Sidney (1984–85)	*Marvin Kaplan*
Tex (1983–84)	*Ted Field Sr.*

Mac (1983–84)	*Alan Dinehart*
Pitfall Harry (1983–84)	*Robert Ridgely*
Rhonda (1983–84)	*Noelle North*
Quick Claws (1983–84)	*Ken Mars*
Space Ace (1984–85)	*Jim Piper*
Kimberly (1984–85)	*Nancy Cartwright*
Space Marshall Vaughn (1984–85)	*Peter Renaday*
Commander Borf/Mr. Friendly	
(both 1984–85)	*Arthur Burghardt*
Katy (1984–85)	*Mea Martineau*
Joey (1984–85)	*David Mendenhall*

For kids who could not get enough of their favorite video games at the local arcade, CBS came up with *Saturday Supercade.* For two seasons the show offered five segments of different characters, with the only ones seen both seasons being "Donkey Kong," "Donkey Kong Jr.," and "Q*Bert." "Donkey Kong" told of a likable, trouble-prone large ape who ran away from the circus and was eluding recapture by Mario the carpenter and Mario's niece Pauline. A separate but related segment had Donkey Kong Jr. also looking for his dad, with the help of his pal Bones, and finding time to assist children along the way. And in "Q*Bert," the snorkel-nosed title character and his family tried to fend off attacks by Coilee Snake and the latter's stooges, Ugh, Viper, and Wrongway.

In 1983–84, the other two segments seen were "Frogger" and "Pitfall Harry." Frogger and pals Fanny Frog and Shelly Turtle, reporters for the *Swamp Gazette,* went after bad guys, with some help from animals and adults, and Harry, with his 10-year-old niece Rhoda and cowardly pet mountain lion Quick Claws, went to various lands to find hidden treasures. They were replaced in 1984–85 by "Space Ace," actually a video rather than arcade game with a Buck Rogers–like astronaut who with his main squeeze Kimberly fought Commander Borf, and "Kangaroo," about three animals of the title species (Katy, Joey, and Sidney) who defended their zoo from the naughty antics of the Monkey Biz Gang. They all disappeared after two years, with the only exception being a reappearance of Mario the carpenter as Super Mario in a cartoon six years later (see *Captain N).*

SATURDAY SUPERSTAR MOVIE—See ABC Saturday Superstar Movie, The.

SATURDAY VIDEOS—See Saturday Morning Videos.

•SAVED BY THE BELL
Sitcom; Color
August 30, 1989–

NBC Sat. 11:30 a.m.–Noon (8/30/89–9/1/90)
NBC Sat. 11–11:30 a.m. (9/8/90–9/7/91)
NBC Sat. 11 a.m.–Noon (two shows; 9/14/91–7/25/92)
NBC Sat. 10–10:30 a.m. and 11 a.m.–Noon (three shows; 8/1/92–9/5/92)

NBC Sat. 10–10:30 a.m. and 11–11:30 a.m. (two shows; 9/12/92–11/7/92)
NBC Sat. 10–10:30 a.m. and 11 a.m.–Noon (three shows; 11/14/92–9/4/93)
NBC Sat. 11–11:30 a.m. (9/11/93–9/3/94)
NBC Sat. 10:30–11:30 a.m. (two shows; 9/17/94–9/2/95)
NBC Sat. 10–10:30 and 11–11:30 a.m. (9/9/95–)

Cast:

Zack Morris (1989–93)	*Mark-Paul Gosselaar*
A. C. Slater (1989–93)	*Mario Lopez*
Samuel "Screech" Powers	
(1989–93, 1994–)	*Dustin Diamond*
Kelly Kaposki (1989–93)	*Tiffani-Amber Thiessen*
Jessie Spano (1989–93)	*Elizabeth Berkley*
Lisa Turtle (1989–93)	*Lark Voorhies*
Principal Richard Belding	*Dennis Haskins*
Tommy "Tommy D" DeLuca	
(1993–)	*Jonathan Angel*
Rachel Meyers (1993–)	*Sarah Lancaster*
Megan Jones (1993–95)	*Bianca Lawson*
Lindsay Warner (1993–94)	*Natalie Cigliuti*
Scott Erickson (1993–94)	*Robert Sutherland Telfer*
Vicki Needleman (1993–94)	*Bonnie Russavage*
Barton "Weasel" Wyzell (1993–94)	*Isaac Lidsky*
Brian Keller (1994–95)	*Christian Oliver*
Bobby Wilson (1994–95)	*Spankee Rodgers*
Ryan Parker (1995–)	*Richard Lee Jackson*
R. J. "Hollywood" Collins (1995–)	*Salim Grant*
Maria Lopez (1995–)	*Samantha Becker*

This improbably popular "teencom" was the first live-action Saturday morning series to last more than a year on NBC since *Land of the Lost* in 1977. The show debuted on NBC as a nighttime special on August 28, 1989, two days before its regular run, but its roots could be traced to a nighttime NBC special seen July 11, 1987 called *Good Morning, Miss Bliss.* The special became a series with the same name on cable's Disney Channel in 1988 with Hayley Mills as the title teacher, and the characters Zack, Screech, Lisa, and Principal Belding also appeared. As with later versions, it was produced by Peter Engler Productions in association with NBC Productions, marking the first time a commercial network produced programming for a national cable service.

When the show moved to NBC, blond lothario Zack became its lead character. Zack stopped the action to address the camera and tell where he stood in some scheme—concocted to benefit himself or help him win the hand of his love Kelly, a petite brunette babe. He often found himself at odds with fellow student Slater, a dark and handsome Latin wrestler who nicknamed Zack "preppie." Among the females, Jessie was an intelligent, statuesque beauty, and Lisa was the resident clotheshorse. For some reason this group also tolerated the inane comments and bumbling of Screech, a curly-haired geek with a torch for Lisa. Mr. Belding vacillated between being confidante and adversary of the group, depending on that week's circumstances. Their home base was Bayside High School in Palisades, California, whose mascot was the Tigers and whose school radio station was KKTY-FM 98.6.

If it all sounds like a warmed-over update of *The Archies* (q.v.), that's how it played, but viewership was so strong that on November 27, 1992, NBC aired a prime-time TV movie in which the cast went to Hawaii, and then mounted a regular nighttime TV series called *Saved By the Bell: The College Years* from 1993–94 which followed Gosselaar, Lopez, and Diamond after their graduation in the spring of 1993. That series flopped, proving that even though the series was by now a top hit in repeats in daily syndication, it lacked the appeal for older adults to make it a contender past 6 p.m.

But *Saved By the Bell: The New Class,* as the Saturday series was titled in September 1993, continued with a new set of students. Taking part in the curriculum were Tommy the somewhat dense greaser, Rachel the blonde, and others who were basically reincarnations of the types of characters seen on the earlier version. This class proved less than endearing, so most of them were dropped in 1994 in favor of a few new students and the return of Screech, hapless as ever, as Mr. Belding's gullible assistant. By this time, *Variety* reported, the series was airing in 52 countries. In 1995 Ryan, Maria, and R.J. (a black student) transferred to Bayside from rival Valley High, as had Scott Erickson earlier, but easily blended into the group. More additions were set as the show prepared for an eighth season in the fall of 1996, confounding critics and even some fans.

SAWYER VIEWS HOLLYWOOD
Variety; B&W
April 14, 1951–September 8, 1951

ABC Sat. 11:45 a.m.–Noon (4/14/51–6/23/51)
ABC Sat. 5 or 5:30 a.m. (7/28/51–9/8/51)

Host: *Hal Sawyer*

Sawyer Views Hollywood employed obscure acts from Los Angeles as its source of guests, such as the May 21 lineup of comedian Stanley Adams and singer Dotty O'Brien. Originally titled *Hal in Hollywood,* this switched to ABC Fridays 10–10:30 p.m. from June 29–August 31, 1951 before running concurrently briefly with another edition late Saturday afternoons.

SAY WHEN
Game; B&W and Color
January 2, 1961–March 25, 1965

NBC Mon.–Fri. 10–10:30 a.m. (1/2/61–9/28/62)
NBC Mon.–Fri. 10–10:25 a.m. (10/1/62–6/26/64)
NBC Mon.–Fri. Noon–12:30 a.m. (6/29/64–3/25/65)

Host: *Art James*

Two players tried to choose up to $2,000 worth of merchandise from four possible prizes, without going over that amount,

in this modestly successful game show, a knockoff by Mark Goodson–Bill Todman Productions of the company's *The Price Is Right* (which aired on NBC a half hour later daily through 1963). A unique element of the show, evident by October 1961, had each program begin with a "Joke of the Day" submitted by a viewer. Any contribution used on the air won the writer a Polaroid camera, and at least 12,000 letters came to the show each week to vie for the honor.

SCARY SCOOBY FUNNIES—See *Scooby-Doo, Where Are You?*

•SCATTERGORIES
Game; Color
January 18, 1993–June 11, 1993

NBC Mon.–Fri. 12:30–1 p.m. (1/18/93–6/11/93)

Host: *Dick Clark*

In this game, a topic was revealed along with a letter of the alphabet to two sexually segregated quartets, and one team had 15 seconds to provide as many items as possible relevant to the topic that started with that letter. The team then tried to get extra answers from four of five of the day's celebrities, who had been videotaped giving their answers. Duplications meant the team lost a point. The high-scoring team after two rounds (each team played once per round) won $500 and played a bonus for up to $4,000 similar to the earlier game. At press time, this represented the last game show to air on NBC.

SCIENCE ALL-STARS
Informational; B&W
January 12, 1964–April 25, 1965

ABC Sun. 4:30–5 p.m. (1/12/64–4/26/64)
ABC Sun. 5–5:30 p.m. (1/10/65–4/25/65)

Host: *Don Morrow*

A 15-year-old with a homemade rat maze and a 12-year-old with a computer made from scratch hardly sound like national TV material, but ABC thought they could be and put them and other children discussing their science projects on this show. Taped in New York, *Science All-Stars* interviewed more than 4,000 children as potential participants, most of them winners of the National Science Fair. Three kids appeared per show.

•SCOOBY-DOO, WHERE ARE YOU?
Cartoon; Color
September 13, 1969–September 4, 1993

CBS Sat. 10:30–11 a.m. (9/13/69–9/5/70)
CBS Sat. Noon–12:30 p.m. (9/12/70–9/4/71)
CBS Sat. 8:30–9 a.m. (9/11/71–9/2/72)
CBS Sat. 9:30–10:30 a.m. (9/9/72–9/1/73)
CBS Sat. 9–10 a.m. (9/8/73–8/31/74)
CBS Sat. 8:30–9 a.m. (9/7/74–1/11/75)
CBS Sat. 10–10:30 a.m. (1/18/75–8/30/75)

CBS Sat. 9:30–10 a.m. (9/6/75–8/7/76)
ABC Sat. 9:30–10:30 a.m. (9/11/76–11/27/76)
ABC Sat. 9–10:30 a.m. (12/4/76–9/3/77)
ABC Sat. 9–11 a.m. (9/10/77–7/1/78)
ABC Sat. 9:30–11:30 a.m. (7/8/78–9/2/78)
ABC Sat. 8–8:30 a.m. and 10–11:30 a.m.
  (9/9/78–10/28/78)
ABC Sat. 8–9:30 a.m. (11/4/78–5/26/79)
ABC Sat. 8:30–10 a.m. (6/2/79–9/8/79)
ABC Sat. 11:30 a.m.–Noon (9/22/79–12/8/79)
ABC Sat. 10:30–11:30 a.m. (12/15/79–9/27/80)
ABC Sat. 11:30 a.m.–Noon (6/21/80–9/27/80)
ABC Sat. 9–10 a.m. and 10–10:30 a.m. (10/4/80–11/1/80)
ABC Sat. 9:30–10:30 a.m. (11/8/80–9/5/81)
ABC Sat. 10–11 a.m. (9/12/81–9/18/82)
ABC Sat. 11 a.m.–Noon (9/25/82–1/1/83)
ABC Sat. 10–11 a.m. (1/8/83–9/3/83)
ABC Sat. 8–8:30 a.m. and 11:30 a.m.–Noon
  (9/10/83–1/7/84)
ABC Sat. 9–9:30 a.m. and 11:30 a.m.–Noon
  (1/14/84–9/1/84)
ABC Sat. 11–11:30 a.m. (9/8/84–10/13/84)
ABC Sat. 10:30–11:30 a.m. (two shows; 10/20/84–11/2/85)
ABC Sat. 8–8:30 a.m. and 11–11:30 a.m.
  (11/9/85–2/22/86)
ABC Sat. 10–10:30 a.m. (3/1/86–9/6/86)
ABC Sat. 10:30–11 a.m. (9/10/88–9/2/89)
ABC Sat. 8–8:30 a.m. (9/9/89–9/1/90)
ABC Sat. 12:30–1 p.m. (9/8/90–8/3/91)
ABC Sat. 10:30–11 a.m. (8/10/91–8/31/91)
ABC Sat. Noon–12:30 p.m. (9/12/92–1/30/93)
ABC Sat. 8–8:30 a.m. (2/6/93–9/4/93)

Voices:

Scooby-Doo/Scrappy-Doo (1982–86)	Don Messick
Shaggy	Casey Kasem
Freddy (1969–85)	Frank Welker
Freddy (1988–93)	Carl Stevens
Daphne (1969–86)	Heather North
Daphne (1988–93)	Kellie Martin
Velma (1969–79)	Nichole Jaffe
Velma (1979–85)	Pat Stevens
Velma (1988–93)	Christina Lange
Scooby-Dum (1976–77)	Daws Butler
Scrappy-Doo (1979–80)	Lennie Weinrib
Vincent Van Ghoul (1985–86)	Vincent Price
Flim Flam (1985–86)	Susan Blu
Weird (1985–86)	Arte Johnson
Bogel (1985–86)	Howard Morris
Red Herring (1988–93)	Scott Menville

Who would have thought that of all the cartoon characters created for television, the one with the longest run on the networks would feature a simpering Great Dane? Scooby-Doo, who got caught in strange and fantastic situations with his nominal master Shaggy, had a cute giggle, and ate "Scooby snacks" in exchange for sniffing for clues, became Saturday morning's favorite dog, When it finally ended its run, *Scooby-Doo, Where Are You?* had lasted nearly a quarter century and gone through what seems like an infinite variety of formats. Along the way Scooby-Doo gained various relatives who joined him in mysteries, met top-name guest stars, and starred in the first two-hour daytime network series with continuing characters. As the pooch himself might exclaim in happiness, "Scooby dooby doo!"

Scooby first gained prominence as the pet of four teenagers who rode in a van called the Mystery Machine, an apt name given that they stumbled into crimes being committed in eerie locales each week. Shaggy was the jittery beatnik with a goatee who said "Yikes!" a lot. He loved food but managed to stay thin. He also was Scooby's closest buddy, as evidenced by the innumerable times the dog croaked, "Right, 'Raggy!" Others with them were blond hunk Freddy, the driver; Daphne, the constant damsel in distress with wavy hair; and Velma, the somewhat homely egghead with eyeglasses who cracked most of the mysteries. Each show invariably had the criminal dress up as a ghost, mummy, or other kind of supernatural being in an effort to scare away the kids, with Scooby and Shaggy acting the most frightened. Somewhere along the way the group had a chase scene with the haunt of the week, which was backed up by some groovy bubblegum tunes. And when the villain was nabbed, he always claimed he could have gotten away with his plans had it not been for those darn kids getting in the way.

After two seasons of original shows, this format lasted in repeats until 1976. The exception were the years from 1972–74, when it became *The New Scooby-Doo Comedy Movies* and guests such as Mama Cass Elliot, the Globetrotters, Sonny and Cher, and Tim Conway, all providing their own voices, joined the kids in solving mysteries. In the fall of 1976 Scooby moved to ABC and starred in a new hour series, *The Scooby-Doo/Dynomutt Show* (see *Dynomutt* for details on that show and character), where the dog and teens participated in new episodes. Scooby's doltish cousin Scooby-Dum joined them for that season.

The next season, Scooby got yet another half-hour on ABC in the 90-minute extravaganza *Scooby's All-Star Laff-A-Lympics,* which ran through 1980, airing under the shortened title of *Scooby's All-Stars* in 1978–79. This show incorporated nearly every major Hanna-Barbera character seen on television over the last two decades in a wild competition between the Scooby Doobies, led by guess who and featuring then recent or current characters like Grape Ape and Speed Buggy; the Yogi Yahooeys, led by Huckleberry Hound and featuring mostly 1950s and 1960s characters; and the Really Rottens, led by Dastardly and Muttley and a passle of crooked types. Listing the whole cast of characters would take up too many pages, but the voiceover artists who worked regularly on the show, in addition to the ones listed above, included Mel Blanc, Bob Holt, and John Stephenson.

ABC was so high on Scooby during this period it also reran *Scooby-Doo, Where are You?* in the fall of 1978, then

The cast of Scooby-Doo *in the 1980s included, from left, Scrappy-Doo, Velma, Scooby-Doo, Shaggy, Daphne, and Freddy.*

the following fall installed *Scooby and Scrappy-Doo* along with *Laff-a-Lympics* for two years. Scrappy, as his name implied, was a diminutive cousin of Scooby's, who was as cocksure as his relative was cowardly, sometimes inappropriately so. Then in 1980 the Great Dane took supporting billing on *The Richie Rich/Scooby-Doo Show* (q.v.), gaining top credit only for reruns seen briefly in 1981 titled *Scooby-Doo Classics*.

In 1982 came the *Scooby and Scrappy-Doo/Puppy's New Adventures Hour* (see *The Puppy's New Adventures* for details on that) for a year, then just *Scooby and Scrappy-Doo*. Then in 1983–84 there was the addition of another bunch of reruns titled *The Best of Scooby-Doo*, which ran at first at 8 a.m. and then assumed the *Scooby and Scrappy-Doo* 11:30 slot in January 1984 while the latter aired separately that season. In 1984–85 there was *The New Scooby-Doo Mysteries*, which had new adventures and kept Scrappy-Doo in the mix, and *Scary Scooby Funnies*, a new name for old reruns which aired directly after the former for a season starting in October 1984.

The 1985–86 season brought another substantial overhaul in the property, when the dog starred in *The 13 Ghosts of Scooby-Doo*. Now Scooby, Shaggy, Scrappy, and a modified Daphne were joined by 9-year-old Flim Flam in fighting sometimes creepy (creepy, at least, for a Saturday morning cartoon) sorcery. Helping their campaign was

caped warlock Vincent Van Ghoul, with the voice and countenance of horror film great Vincent Price. Though they thwarted all comers, for some reason comic henchmen Weird and Bogel escaped their clutches. Also seen that season was another rerun collection titled *Scooby's Mystery Funhouse*, which first ran directly after *13 Ghosts* until November 1985, when it began airing at 8 a.m. In March 1986 Scooby appeared only in *Laff-a-Lympics* reruns.

After two years' hiatus, *A Pup Named Scooby-Doo* appeared in the fall of 1988. The original gang was back, but now they were preadolescents on the prowl for excitement. The big joke for adults was the recurring character Red Herring, whom the kids constantly suspected of committing crimes each show. That cartoon ran in original productions during the first two years only, with the rest of the run in repeats.

When Scooby finally left the air in 1993, he had been on the networks longer than any other cartoon character except Bugs Bunny. And given the show's continuing popularity in repeats on the Cartoon Network cable channel, it would not be out of the question for the networks to mount yet another revival. All of which shows that Scooby has led anything but a dog's life.

SCOUTING IN ACTION
Documentary; B&W
March 24, 1951–March 7, 1953

ABC Sat. 10:30–10:45 a.m. (3/24/51–4/21/51)
ABC Sat. 10:45–11 a.m. (4/28/51–6/23/51)
ABC Sun. 4:15–4:30 p.m. (6/24/51–12/16/51)
ABC Sat. 10:45–11 a.m. (6/7/52–12/27/52)
ABC Sat. 10:15–10:30 a.m. (1/3/53–3/7/53)

Scouting in Action featured films done in cooperation with the Boy Scouts of America.

•SCRABBLE
Game; Color
July 2, 1984–June 11, 1993

NBC Mon.–Fri. 11:30 a.m.–Noon (7/2/84–9/4/87)
NBC Mon.–Fri. 12:30–1 p.m. (9/7/87–3/24/89)
NBC Mon.–Fri. 10–10:30 a.m. (3/27/89–3/23/90)
NBC Mon.–Fri. Noon–12:30 p.m. (1/18/93–6/11/93)

Host: *Chuck Woolery*

On this show based on the popular board game, two contestants received a cryptic clue and the correct number of letters to a mystery word on an electronic board. The challenging contestant selected two numbered tiles to use, each containing a letter, and chose one of the letters to see if it was part of the mystery word. If the letter chosen was *not* in the word, it became a "stopper," that contestant lost control, and the other contestant picked two tiles. When two "stoppers" had been used, missing letters appeared one at a time until one of the contestants correctly identified the word. Each letter picked before the two stoppers appeared added $25 to the pot. The first player to guess three words right played the Scrabble Sprint against the reigning champ to guess three identical words choosing one letter from two available at the time. Winning this sprint five times won you $20,000. After nearly a six-year run, the show returned briefly in 1993 as one of the last game shows to date to air on NBC.

SCRAPBOOK JUNIOR EDITION
Children's; B&W
November 7, 1948–May 22, 1949

CBS Sun. 5:30–6 p.m. (11/7/48–2/13/49)
CBS Sun. 5–5:30 p.m. (2/20/49–4/17/49)
CBS Sun. 5:30–6 p.m. (4/24/49–5/22/49)

Host: *Scotty MacGregor*

Assistant: *Jini Boyd O'Connor (1948–49), Patricia White (1949)*

This early and now forgotten children's show was an interactive entry inviting viewers to send information about their activities to share with others in the TV audience— kind of a video equivalent of show and tell. The show started as a local New York City show in October 1947, then went onto the CBS network Sundays at 6–6:30 p.m.

starting June 27, 1948 before moving to the late afternoon slots for a few months.

SEALAB 2020
Cartoon; Color
September 9, 1972–September 1, 1973

NBC Sat. 11–11:30 a.m. (9/9/72–9/1/73)

Voices:

Dr. Paul Williams	*Ross Martin*
Bobby Murphy	*Josh Albee*
Sally Murphy	*Pamelyn Ferdin*
Captain Mike Murphy	*John Stephenson*
Sparks	*Bill Callaway*
Hal	*Jerry Dexter*
Gail	*Ann Jillian*
Ed	*Ron Pinckard*
Mrs. Thomas	*Olga James*
Jamie	*Gary Shapiro*

The Sealab was an underwater laboratory where 250 people, including children, lived. Its leading scientist was oceanographer and Chinook Indian Dr. Paul Williams, a Ph.D. who studied the undersea world assisted by aquanauts Hal, Gail, and Ed, and radio dispatcher Sparks. Complicating their work were the Murphys, who had been sailing above the sea until their ship sank and they were saved by Sealab. Children Bobby and Sally and their pet sea turtles typically got involved in many of the plots. The cartoon originally went into development for CBS in 1971 with plans to set the adventures only 30 years into the future.

SEARCH, THE
Documentary; B&W
October 17, 1954–April 24, 1955

CBS Sun. 4:30–5 p.m. (10/17/54–4/24/55)

Host: *Charles Romaine*

The Search examined 26 American university research centers as part of, as a press release put it, "a search for truth . . . but also a search that leads us down strange new pathways to greater understanding and better living for all." The debut showed work on stuttering done at the University of Iowa by Dr. Wendell Johnson's speech clinic. There was also a two-part program on psychiatric treatment at Tulane University, and a survey of what had been learned on previous shows. CBS reporter Don Hollenbeck appeared posthumously on a December show after his suicide on June 22, 1954.

Work on *The Search* began in 1952 with plans to do dramatic reenactments along with news reports. But, as producer Irving Gitlin told *TV Guide*, "We discovered that you have to shoot straight drama or straight documentary. You can't successfully combine the two. So we threw out all the film and started over again."

Following its daytime run, *The Search* moved to Tuesday nights on CBS where it ran through September 1955. It was repeated on Sundays from 6–6:30 p.m. from June–October 1958. Plans were announced later for a sequel to the series, but it never came to pass.

SEARCH AND RESCUE: THE ALPHA TEAM
Adventure; Color
September 10, 1977–January 28, 1978

NBC Sat. 11:30 a.m.–Noon (9/10/77–1/28/78)

Cast:

Dr. Bob Donell	Michael J. Reynolds
Katy Donell	Doann Cavin
Jim Donell	Michael Tough
Dr. Liz Warren	Helen Shaver

A co-production with Canada's CTV, which aired the show Tuesday nights, *Search and Rescue* told the story of widower Dr. Bob Donnell and his two teenage children working with veterinarian Liz Warren on the world's first (and fictional) rescue squad for endangered animals. The Donells lived and worked on the Alpha Ranch. This drama fared so poorly in America that NBC aired only 13 out of 26 shows shot.

SEARCH FOR BEAUTY, THE—See *Ern Westmore Show, The.*

SEARCH FOR TOMORROW
Soap Opera; B&W and Color
September 3, 1951–December 26, 1986

CBS Mon.–Fri. 12:30–12:45 p.m. (9/3/51–9/6/68)
CBS Mon.–Fri. 12:30–1 p.m. (9/9/68–6/5/81)
CBS Mon.–Fri. 2:30–3 p.m. (6/8/81–3/26/82)
NBC Mon.–Fri. 12:30–1 p.m. (3/29/82–12/26/86)

Cast:

Joanne Gardner	Mary Stuart
Stu Bergman	Larry Haines
Marge Bergman (1951–71)	Melba Rae
Patti Barron (1951–61)	Lynn Loring
Patti Barron (1961)	Nancy Pinkerton
Patti Barron (1961–64)	Abigail Kellogg
Patti Barron (1964–65)	Patricia Harty
Patti Barron (1965)	Gretchen Walther
Patti Barron (1965–66)	Melissa Murphy
Patti Barron (1967)	Trish Van Devere
Patti Barron (1967–69)	Melinda Plank
Patti Barron (1969–75)	Leigh Lassen
Patti Barron (1976–77)	Tina Sloan
Patti Barron (1985–86)	Jacqueline Schultz
Janet Bergman (1951–56)	Ellen Spencer
Janet Bergman (1956–61)	Sandy Robinson
Janet Bergman (1961–65)	Fran Sharon
Janet Bergman (1965–66)	Nancy Franklin
Janet Bergman (1971)	Marian Hailey
Janet Bergman (1971–82)	Millee Taggart
Irene Barron (1951–54, 1960–61)	Bess Johnson

Victor Barron (1951–54)	Cliff Hall
Keith Barron (1951–52)	Johnny Sylvester
Louise Barron (1951–52)	Sara Anderson
Dr. Ned Hilton (1951–54)	Coe Norton
Arthur Tate (1952–68)	Terry O'Sullivan
Arthur Tate (temporary replacement; 1955–56)	Karl Weber
Nathan Walsh (1953)	David Orrick
Nathan Walsh (1954–58)	George Petrie
Nathan Walsh (1959)	Frank Overton
Nathan Walsh (1959)	Richard Derr
Nathan Walsh (1959–60)	Mark Lenard
Rose Peterson (1953–54)	Lee Grant
Rose Peterson (1954–55)	Nita Talbot
Rose Peterson (1955–56)	Constance Ford
Wilbur Peterson (1953–55)	Don Knotts
Mortimer Higbee (1953–55)	Ian Martin
Hazel/Sue Tate (1953–54)	Mary Patton
Jim Wilcox (1953)	Les Damon
John Eddy (1953)	Earl Hammond
Eunice Gardner (1957–61)	Marion Brash
Eunice Gardner (1966–76)	Ann Williams
Frank Gardner (1957)	Harry Holcombe
Frank Gardner (1957–58)	Eric Dressler
Allison Simmons (1958–59)	Nina Reader
Allison Simmons (1959–65)	Anne Pearson
Jessie Bergman (1958–59)	Joanna Roos
Jessie Bergman (1959–60)	Nydia Westman
Cornelia Simmons (1958–60)	Doris Dalton
Rex Twining (1958–59)	Laurence Hugo
Bud Gardner (1959–60)	Tony Ray
Bud Gardner (1960)	Anthony Cannon
Bud Gardner (1960–61)	George Maharis
Pearl March (1959)	Isabel Price
Pearl March (1959–60)	Sylvia Field
Harriet Baxter (1959–60)	Vicki Viola
Dr. Dan Walton (1960–61)/Dr. Everett Moore (1962–64)	Martin E. Brooks
Dr. Dan Walton (1961–63)	Philip Abbott
Dr. Dan Walton (1971–72)	Ron Husmann
Fred Metcalf (1961–64)	Tom Carlin
Fred Metcalf (1964)	Donald Madden
Fred Metcalf (1965–66)	David O'Brien
Agnes Metcalf (1961–64)	Katherine Meskill
Marion Gill (1962–64)	Jane McArthur
Isabel Moore (1962–64)	Lenka Peterson
Dr. Brad Campbell (1962–64)	George Kane
Monica Bergman (1962)	Barbara Baxley
Jimmy Bergman (1962)	Peter Lazar
Dr. Len Whiting (1964–72, 1976)	Dino Narizzano
Dr. Len Whiting (1974)	Jeffrey David Pomerantz
Dr. Bob Rogers (1965–79)	Carl Low
Andrea Whiting (1965–67)	Virginia Gilmore
Andrea Whiting (1967)	Lesley Woods
Andrea Whiting (1968–72)	Joan Copeland

Sam Reynolds (1965–70)
Sam Reynolds (1971–72)
Sam Reynolds (1972)
Dr. Nick Hunter (1965)
Dr. Nick Hunter (1965–67, 1972–73)
Dr. Nick Hunter (1968)
Dr. Nick Hunter (1968)
Emily Rogers (1966–67)
Emily Rogers (1967–68)
Emily Rogers (1972–73)
Cal Foster (1966–68)
Doug Martin (1967–74)
Walter Haskins (1967)
Walter Haskins (1967–68)
Tom Bergman (1968–71)
Tom Bergman (1973–77)
Tom Bergman (1977–78)
Tom Bergman (1981–83)
Tom Bergman (1983)
Ellie Harper (1968–81)
Scott Phillips (1969–77)
Scott Phillips (1977–78)
Erik Leshinsky (1969–77)
Lauri Leshinsky (1969–73)
Ida Weston (1969–72)
Dr. Peter Murphy (1969–71)
Magda Leshinsky (1969–70)
Grace Bolton (1969–70)
Dr. Tony Vincente (1970–75)
Dr. Tony Vincente (1972)
Dr. Tony Vincente (1973)
Marcy Vincente (1970–71)
Claire Hart (1970–71)
Dick Hart (1970–71)
Liza Walton (1971)
Liza Walton (1971–74)
Liza Walton (1974–77)
Liza Walton (1977–78)
Liza Walton (1978–85)
Liza Walton (1985–86)
Kathy Parker (1971–78, 1983–84)
Kathy Parker (1979–82)
Dr. Gary Walton (1971–73)
Dr. Gary Walton (1973–74)
Dr. Gary Walton (1976–78)
Bruce Carson (1971–73)
Bruce Carson (1973)
Bruce Carson (1973–74)
Bruce Carson (1974–75)
Bruce Carson (1975–78)
Dr. Wade Collins (1971–77)
Helen Collins (1971–72)
William Collins (1971–72)
Karl Devlin (1972–73)

Robert Mandan
George Gaynes
Roy Shuman
Burr DeBenning

Ken Kercheval
Stephen Joyce
Terry Logan
Pamela Murphy
Louise Shaffer
Kathryn Walker
Colgate Salisbury
Ken Harvey
Ernest Graves
Douglass Watson
Peter Broderick
Ray Bellaran
John James
Mitch Litrofsky
Robert LuPone
Billie Lou Watt
Peter Simon
Peter Ratray
Christopher Lowe
Kelly Wood
Vera Allen
Charles Siebert
Lilia Skala
Jill Clayburgh
Anthony George
Lawrence Weber
Robert Loggia
Jeanne Carson
Peggy Whitton
Michael Zaslow
Denise Nickerson
Kathleen Beller
Meg Bennett
Hope Busby
Sherry Mathis
Louan Gideon

Courtney Sherman
Nicolette Goulet
Tommy Norden
John Driver
Richard Lohman
Robby Benson
Michael Maitland
Gary Tomlin
Steve Nisbet
Joel Higgins
John Cunningham
Natalie Schafer
Ralph Clanton
David Ford

Marian Malin (1972–73)
John Wyatt (1973–79)
Dr. Carolyn Hanley Walton (1973–74)
Dr. Carolyn Hanley Walton (1976–80)
Jennifer Pace (1973)
Jennifer Pace (1973–77)
Melissa Hayley (1973)
Dr. Matt Weldon (1973)
Stephanie Wilkins Wyatt (1974–84)
Stephanie Wilkins Wyatt (1984–86)
Wendy Wilkins (1974–77)
Wendy Wilkins (1977–86)
David Wilkins (1974–75)
Hal Conrad (1974)
Hal Conrad (1974–75)
Ralph Haywood (1974)
Ralph Haywood (1976)
Danny Walton (1975–77)
Danny Walton (1983)
Danny Walton (1985–86)
Steve Kaslo (1975–78)
Amy Kaslo (1975)
Amy Kaslo (1975–78)
Walter Pace (1975)
Walter Pace (1976)
Walter Pace (1976–77)
Susan "Suzi" Martin (1976–79)
Susan "Suzi" Martin (1981–83)
Susan "Suzi" Martin (1983–84)
David Sutton (1976–77)
Gail Caldwell (1976–77)
Meredith Hartford (1977–78)
Dr. Greg Hartford (1977–78)
Donna Davis (1977–78)
Kylie Halliday (1977–78)
Chance Halliday (1977–78)
Sunny Adamson (1978–86)
Martin Tourneur (1978–84)
Travis Sentell (1978–84)
Ted Adamson (1978)
Ted Adamson (1978–82)
Mignon Sentell (1978–79, 1981)
Nick D'Antoni (1978–79)
Mark D'Antoni (1978–79)
Laine Adamson (1978–79)
Gen. Roger Tourneur (1978–79)
Lee Sentell (1979–82)
Cissie Mitchell Sentell (1979–82)
Beau Mitchell (1979–80)
Prince Antonio Stradella (1979–80)
Renata Corelli Sutton (1979–80)

Pat Stanley
Val Dufour

Gayle Pines

Marilyn McIntyre
Robin Eisenman
Morgan Fairchild
Linda Bove
Robert Phelps

Marie Cheatham

Louise Shaffer
Andrea McArdle
Lisa Peluso
Dale Robinette
Ben Hammer
Vince O'Brien
James O'Sullivan
Drew Snyder
Neil Billingsley
Cain Devore
John Loprieno
Michael Nouri
Pamela Miller
Anne Wyndham
Wayne Tippit
Edward Glover
Tom Klunis
Stacey Moran
Cynthia Gibb
Elizabeth Swackhamer
Lewis Arlt
Sherry Rooney
Tina Orr
Robert Rockwell
Leslie Ray
Lisa Buck
George Shannon
Marcia McCabe
John Aniston
Rod Arrants
Malachi Throne
Wayne Tippit
Anita Keal
Jerry Lanning
Christopher Goutman
Megan Bagot
William Robertson
Douglas Stevenson
Patsy Pease
Danny Goldring

Robert Desiderio
Sonia Petrovna

Dr. Winston Kyle (1979–80)
Dr. Jamie Larsen (1979–80)
Tod Adamson (1979)
Brian Emerson (1980)
Brian Emerson (1981)
Brian Emerson (1981–83)
Brian Emerson (1983–84)
Spencer Langley (1980–81)
Garth Taper (1980–81)
Dr. Max Taper (1980–81)
Dane Taylor (1981–83)
Aja Doyan (1982–83)
Warren Carter (1982–85)
Steve Kendall (1982–83)
Steve Kendall (1985)
Kristen Carter (1982–84)
Ringo Altman (1982–84)
Jenny Deacon (1982–83)
Keith McNeil (1982–83)
Andie McNeil (1982–83)
Michael Kendall (1982–83)
Lloyd Kendall (1983–85)
Lloyd Kendall (1985–86)
Lloyd Kendall (1986)
Hogan McCleary (1983–86)
Vargas (1983–84)
Jack Benton (1983–84)
Rhonda Sue Huckaby (1983–84)
Dr. Barbara Moreno (1983)
Josh Moreno (1983)
Josh Moreno (1983)
Det. John Colton (1983)
Ruby Ashford (1983)
Cagney McCleary (1984–86)
Rebecca "T. R." Kendall
    (1984–86)
Chase Kendall (1984–85)
Chase Kendall (1985–86)
Kate McCleary (1984–85)
Kate McCleary (1986)
Adair McCleary (1984–85)
Adair McCleary (1985)
Alec Kendall (1984–85)
Kentucky Bluebird (1984–85)
Brett Hamilton III (1984–85)
Big Bigelowe (1984–85)
Justine Calvert (1984–85)
Andrew Ryder (1985–86)
Bela Garody (1985)
Bela Garody (1985–86)
Evie Stone (1985–86)
Evie Stone (1986)
Estelle Kendall (1985–86)
Quinn McCleary (1985–86)
Wilma Holliday (1986)
Matt McCleary (1986)

Nicholas Courtland
Patricia Estrin
Kevin Bacon
Paul Joynt
Larry Joshua
Gene Pietragallo
Jay Acovone
Timothy Patrick Murphy
David Gautreaux
Don Chastain
Marcus Smythe
Susan Monts
Michael Corbett
Philip Brown
Steve Lundquist
Susan Scannell
Larry Fleischman
Linda Gibboney
Craig Augustine
Stacey Glick
Tom Sullivan
Peter Haskell
Joe Lambie
Robert Reed
David Forsyth
John Glover
Patrick James Clarke
Tina Johnson
Olympia Dukakis
Josh Freund
Damion Scheller
Tom Wright
Michelle Phillips
Matthew Ashford

Jane Krakowski
Kevin Conroy
Robert Wilson
Jo Henderson
Maeve McGuire
Page Hannah
Susan Carey-Lamm
Robert Curtis Brown
Will Patton
Brett Porter
Malachy McCourt
Leslie Stevens
Adam Storke
Paul Espel
Lee Godart
Colleen Dion
Joanna Going
Domini Blyther
Jeffrey Meek
Anita Gillette
Patrick Tovatt

Search for Tomorrow could have been subtitled "The Joanne Gardner Barron Tate Vincente Tourneur Story," for that character; certainly Mary Stuart, the actress portraying her, set the tone for the show's 35-year run. In many ways Joanne was much like a radio soap opera heroine, remaining strong and supporting her friends while enduring terrible suffering in her life. But she also had time for lighter moments with her longtime friend Stu Bergman, who was first seen in December 1951 and stayed until the end of the run, and, by the 1970s, a chance to break out in song occasionally. The combination worked for viewers for at least 30 years, as the show was the top-rated soap from 1952–55, stayed near the top through the 1960s, and remained a serious contender until CBS, in a dispute with sponsor Procter & Gamble, canceled it in 1982. The show limped along four more years on NBC, but never returned to its glory days.

The series opened with Joanne, also known as Jo, married to Keith Barron with a 6-year-old daughter named Patti. Keith's father Victor argued often with Keith over the latter's preference for photography over Victor's contracting business. The actual argument was that Victor thought Keith was a weak man. Even more judgmental was Keith's mom Irene, who actively disliked Jo. The only support the young couple had came from Keith's sister Louise, Dr. Ned Hilton, and the Bergmans—Stu, his wife Marge, and their daughter Janet.

When Keith died unexpectedly in 1952, Jo found herself being romanced unsuccessfully by Dr. Hilton while fighting Irene's plots to harm her. Irene had Jim Wilcox and his partner John Eddy do her dirty work, without Victor's knowledge, but at the same time Victor was investigating Wilcox and Eddy. Irene tried to get custody of Patti, then kidnapped the child, but Jo got her back. Jo kept afloat financially during this time while working as a nurse for the hospital in the town of Henderson, and while there she met Arthur Tate. Arthur gave her love, but a new set of complications, in addition to those caused by Irene's machinations, cropped up.

In 1953–55, when Jo teamed with Stu to run a lodge called the Motor Haven, the mob, led by Mortimer Higbee, tried to use it as a base for selling drugs. To take control of the inn, they first tried to convince Arthur he was still married to his presumed dead wife Hazel by using Hazel's twin sister Sue to impersonate her sibling, who really was dead. Arthur's lawyer pal Nathan Walsh learned of the ruse and devised a plan to disorient Sue, which unfortunately ended with her murder. While solving that crime, Arthur got shot, became an invalid, and had to be convinced by Jo that he should marry her, which they did in 1955. By that time, the syndicate had concocted a second plot to take over the inn, and this one involved having Rose Peabody and her mute brother Wilbur stay as guests. But Rose proved too weak-willed to frame Jo and Stu, and Wilbur found that he could speak again once had overcome the psychosomatic condition causing his muteness.

New problems for Jo in the mid-1950s came from her family rather than the mob. Arthur received a financial boost to operate the Motor Haven from his aunt Cornelia Simmons, who hated Jo. Then Jo's sister Eunice and her father Frank Gardner came to stay with the Tates, with the former seducing Arthur and causing much stress. Even a story line involving Jo's giving birth to a boy named Duncan Eric in 1956, which was timed to coincide with Mary Stuart's actual pregnancy and delivery, turned ugly. As Stuart later told *TV Guide,* "They [the producers] made him the victim in an auto accident. If that wasn't sufficiently gruesome, they had him undergo a brain operation before he died. And he was the same age as our real son. Ugh!"

Things had gotten quite complicated by 1958. Rex Twining, a man married to Cornelia, found himself drawn to Eunice. Then Cornelia was found dead and Eunice and Rex were the chief suspects until Cornelia's daughter Allison discovered that Harriet Baxter, her mother's maid, was the murderer. Rex and Eunice wed and left for Puerto Rico, while Frank married and moved out as well. But there was no relief for Jo, because now her daughter Patti was an adolescent with a host of her own problems.

During the late 1950s and early 1960s, Patti's woes included paralysis of her legs, which ended abruptly when she was able to surprise an armed attacker by standing, and two affairs with older, married men. The second of these, with Dr. Everett Moore, led to pregnancy. But following her miscarriage and Everett's wife Isabel committing suicide, Patti gave up on love for a time. Her pal Janet Bergman got involved with Bud Gardner, Jo's handsome, orphaned 17-year-old juvenile delinquent cousin, after he toyed with Allison Simmons. Bud married Janet and fathered her child Chuck (later forgotten by the show), but his rebel spirit never stopped. He took off to Chicago to race cars but supposedly died when a truck in which he had hitched a ride crashed. A grieving Janet wed Dr. Dan Walton, but much to her horror, Bud turned up alive and angry. Janet returned to Bud despite being still in love with Dan, but after Bud died accidentally, she was able to marry Dan, this time for real. Allison Simmons was as unlucky as her pals in love, marrying Fred Metcalf, a weak alcoholic smothered by his insufferable mother Agnes Metcalf.

Another alcoholic was Arthur Tate, who eventually died of a heart attack. Jo's friend Dr. Bob Rogers got her a job as librarian at Henderson Hospital, where she learned that businessman Sam Reynolds had taken over her late husband's enterprises, an act which had precipitated his death. Sam became captivated by Jo despite her hostility and eventually won her over, but she subsequently learned that Sam was separated from his wife Andrea Whiting Reynolds, a woman so domineering she got her maiden name to be used as the last name of her and Sam's son Len Whiting. Len, an intern training to be a doctor, fell in love with Patti, but unfortunately he shared with her a lack of self-esteem.

Andrea became so desperate to prevent Sam and Jo from marrying that she tried to kill him but ended up accidentally poisoning herself. Sam went on trial for attempted murder of Andrea, yet it was Andrea who confessed sins to the jury, including neglect that had led to the death of Len's twin

brother. As Andrea received counseling, Len went through his own trauma caused by the revelations and left Patti and his job. An affair in 1969 with Grace Bolton, a woman who had a brain tumor, led to a pregnancy ending in Grace's death but the child's survival. By that time Len had wed Patti. Patti had another miscarriage, and she became so distraught that Len and Jo convinced her to adopt Grace's son, but without telling her of his lineage. (Long-time viewers might have wondered whether the Jo of the 1950s would have done the same thing.)

By this time it was the late 1960s, and Jo's sister Eunice had come back from Puerto Rico, having divorced Rex Twining and wed Doug Martin, with whom she had a daughter named Suzi. Doug's illegitimate son Scott Phillips ended his marriage to Lauri Lawson to wed Kathy Parker. Kathy hated children to the point of aborting her and Scott's child, but after they were married, Scott convinced a reluctant Kathy to adopt Lauri's child, Eric Leshinsky. Their problems would worsen by the mid-1970s.

Jo began the 1970s happily wed to Sam, but as usual tragedy gummed up the works. Sam was reported missing in Africa on business, and Jo was in a car crash, which left her blind. While being treated by Dr. Tony Vincente, Jo learned that Sam had been officially declared dead. She got over her grief by working in a center for troubled youth with Dr. Vincente, which eventually led to romance even though Tony was married to Marcy Vincente. But when Tony learned Marcy was faking her paralysis (sound familiar?), he divorced her. Then just as Tony and Jo got engaged—ta da!—Sam returned alive, and this fresh conflict caused Jo to suffer psychosomatic blindness. Sam had changed—he was now deeply disturbed—and he eventually kidnapped Jo, but a couple stumbled on the cabin he was keeping Jo in and killed Sam. After straightening out the ensuing mess, Jo and Tony finally wed in 1972.

Jo's old buddy Stu Bergman had had more than his fair share of grief by this time, as his beloved wife Marge had died (as did actress Melba Rae in 1971). He found love and a new wife in his maid Ellie Harper, who helped him raise his son Tommy. Sadly, his daughter Janet's husband Dan also died, making her a single parent to their kids Liza and Gary until she wed psychiatrist Dr. Wade Collins. Like her mom, Liza would have troubled relationships for most of the 1970s, including ones with Bruce Carson, whose guardian was Jo, and Steve Kaslo, who was dying of leukemia.

Jo's sister Eunice found herself working as a freelancer on a magazine that had been bought by newcomer lawyer John Wyatt, a job her husband Doug did not appreciate. Eunice developed her own qualms about the work when the magazine's previous owner Karl Devlin went psychotic and tried to kill her. Doug saved Eunice but became temporarily paralyzed and forced Eunice to divorce him, and the lonely lady took John Wyatt up on his offer of marriage. Doug's life got even worse when, after recovering from the paralysis, he became the victim of a hit-and-run accident, caused by none other than Len Whiting, and became a quadriplegic.

An upset Eunice moved close by so she could help Doug. The helpless Doug asked his son Scott to commit euthanasia on him, but the person who did so was not Scott, but Scott's lover Jennifer Pace, who would cause much trouble in the 1970s. Len was forgiven for his part in Doug's hit-and-run accident after he stopped Jennifer's evil partner Hal Conrad, who tried to kill Doug, and Len left town with his wife Patti. Earlier, the couple had weathered an attempt by Dr. Bob Rogers's daughter Emily Hunter to destroy their marriage. Emily later died in a fire, and her death led to a reconciliation between Len and his mother Andrea.

Other major events on the show revolved around Henderson Hospital. In 1973 deaf Melissa Hayley wed Dr. Matt Weldon, a friend of Jo and Tony's. A year later, Tony cheated on Jo with nurse Stephanie Wilkins, his old flame who claimed that her daughter Wendy Wilkins was his child. Tony believed Stephanie and even left Jo to be closer to the child, but when Stephanie's ex-husband Dave Wilkins proved to Tony that he was Wendy's real father, Tony suffered a heart attack and left Stephanie. A second heart attack killed Tony, and Jo became a widow for the third time.

A few other romantic entanglements hit the skids in the mid-1970s. When Jennifer Pace went to jail, she found out that her affair with Scott had left her pregnant, so Kathy left Scott. Out on probation, Jennifer found that Scott was still carrying a torch for Kathy and argued with him repeatedly about it. Scott developed a drinking problem that was exacerbated when an accident caused Jennifer to miscarry and also left her with scars that required plastic surgery. Scott eventually left Jennifer and saved Kathy from death, after which the two remarried. But sadly, Scott and Kathy's difficulties continued when she slept with David Sutton and became pregnant by him, which led Scott to start drinking again. Scott and Kathy got divorced again, and Kathy married Garth Taper, who died in a car crash in 1981.

Scott's ex-lover Jennifer continued her bitchy ways by sleeping with Eunice's husband John Wyatt and, working with her conniving pal Stephanie Wilkins, convincing John that she was being stalked. When John learned of the ruse, he left Jennifer and she went psycho, killing Eunice and trying to frame John for the crime. Jennifer was caught and sent to a facility for mental patients, but Stephanie, who had married Jennifer's father Walter Pace, now found herself attracted to John.

Stephanie's love life was complicated because she had been seeing David Sutton, a U.S. Marshal who was guarding a gangster set to testify in court, and John was now infatuated with his late wife's sister, Jo. Jo had by this time survived a gunshot wound caused by men who were actually after Sutton's gangster, but her affections now lay with Dr. Greg Hartford. However, Dr. Hartford's daughter Meredith was jealous of Jo, and refused to connect with her, and so Jo was left alone once more.

Stephanie wed John, but she also plotted with evil construction worker Ted Adamson to acquire the Hartford House, a new inn run by Jo and Stu. This led to escalating battles between Ted and John, which ended with John's accidental death during a struggle with Ted. John's stepdaughter Suzi came to live with Jo.

By the late 1970s, Jo's ward Bruce had his own romantic mess. After a fling with Jennifer, of all people, he became obsessed with Amy Kaslo, the sister of Liza's husband Steve. When she gave birth to their daughter, she agreed to live with him, but not have sex with him. A depressed Bruce had an affair with Gail Caldwell, after which he and Amy tried to act like a true married couple.

By then, Amy's sister-in-law Liza was having a much rougher time. Her husband Steve died and her stepfather Wade Collins was killed by kidnappers. Her mom Janet planned to wed Ted Adamson until Dr. Jamie Larsen blackmailed him into marriage instead; eventually Janet, Ted, and Jamie all left town. As for Liza, she moved in with Ted's daughter Laine and tried to make a movie using a song of Steve's. While doing so she met Travis Tourneur Sentell, who became her lover and savior over the next few years as they embarked on exotic adventures. Liza found herself the target of several would-be murderers, including Mignon Sentell, the mother of Travis, and Nick D'Antoni, a mobster stopped by Travis and Nick's brother Marc. During one of their excursions, Travis learned he had a half-sister in Italy named Renata Corelli, who wed David Sutton but was later killed in a fire.

The person responsible for the fire was Martin Tourneur, Travis's flamboyant bachelor uncle, who had somehow charmed Jo into marrying him, though his incessant gambling and drinking later caused her to divorce him. Other people related to Travis came to Henderson, and he and Liza began to dominate the story line. His estranged father Rusty, a mobster, tried to get Travis to marry Rusty's ward Aja Doyan, only to end up killed by Aja. And Lee Sentell, a cousin to Travis, fell in love with Ted Adamson's other daughter Sunny despite the fact that he had impregnated waitress Cissie Mitchell. Cissie gave her baby up for adoption, and the baby was adopted by Liza and Travis, who knew nothing of its lineage. Lee remained torn between Sunny, who was temporarily imprisoned in Jamaica by crazed Dr. Winston Kyle, and Cissie, who eventually got her child back. Lee finally decided to leave town and reconnect with Cissie and their daughter, while Sunny endured a failed relationship with Dane Taylor and a date rape by co-worker Jack Benton before finding apparent happiness through an engagement to Bela Garody.

The big news in the early 1980s was not the plot of the series, but its fall in the ratings and subsequent rescheduling. When the show dropped from a 26 share to 22, CBS switched it from 12:30 to 2:30 p.m. in 1981. The network insisted on keeping it there, preferring *The Young and the Restless* to air in the 12:30 slot. Procter & Gamble wanted *Search for Tomorrow* back in the earlier slot, so switched the show to NBC's sagging daytime schedule in 1982. This change caused a further ratings decline, and as a result the show went through numerous writers, producers, and cast additions in an unsuccessful effort at rejuvenation.

In 1982 cast members of Search for Tomorrow *(from left, John Aniston, Mary Stuart, Susan Monts, and Lisa Peluso) encouraged viewers to follow its switch to NBC from CBS. Unfortunately, many did not.*

Some of the changes involved the older set, like Stu Bergman's romance with Dr. Barbara Moreno, mother of the introverted Josh Moreno, after his wife Ellie deserted him, and Jo's kidnapping by Vargas. Others involved the love lives of Jo's niece Suzi and Stephanie's daughter Wendy. Wendy first fell in love with con artist Spence Langley and then with struggling Keith McNeil. Suzi loved blinded boxer Brian Emerson, but he ended their relationship and led her into seeing the cad Warren Carter. Warren's sister Kristen was impregnated by Brian and forced him to wed her even though she had secretly miscarried, while Warren went on to an extramarital affair with Wendy, now married to Keith.

Other new characters included Kristen's second husband, detective John Colton; fraternal twins Alec and Chase Kendall; their brother Steve; their father, communications magnate Lloyd Kendall; and Lloyd's lover, widow Ruby Ashford. (It was impressive enough that the show got ex–Mamas and Papas singer Michelle Phillips to play Ruby, but originally Cher was to play the role!) The show also did its first live episode since 1968 in 1983, claiming that the day's tape was missing, but

many suspected it was a publicity stunt designed to mimic a similar situation in the recent hit movie *Tootsie.*

The soap made more drastic maneuvers in 1984. Longtime romantic lead Travis died, and his widow Liza became attracted to new scientist Cord Windsor, who turned out to be a Tourneur who tried to sabotage the Tourneur Instruments' prototypes for government planes. Liza was also interested in oddly named Kentucky Bluebird, a suspected spy. And Suzi set a new record for short pregnancies even by soap opera standards when she found out in mid-March that she was pregnant and somehow ended up giving birth within two months. Still, the most publicity the show got that year was when Mary Stuart donated the ruffled apron she had worn on the first shows to the Smithsonian Institute.

The show meandered into 1985 with such run-of-the-mill story lines as T. R. Kendall and her lover Andrew Ryder becoming involved in a circus, and Steve Kendall returning to Henderson to work on his brother's newspaper as a sportswriter. The only real excitement came when Jo's daughter Patti came back to her mom, divorced from Len yet looking younger than the 40 years she should have been based on the show's original outline.

In 1986 the McCleary brothers took center stage as Patti helped Hogan McCleary solve Stephanie's murder in January, then had a love triangle with him and his fiancée Liza. Later, the Hogan brothers went to Ireland to track a villain and unravel their dad's death, which had taken place 21 years earlier.

But Jo and Stu still occasionally managed to take center stage on the show. In February a flood forced everyone in Henderson to live in the same makeshift apartment that the duo managed, with the Kendalls occupying the plush duplex (15 new fancy sets were built for the show). Stu also found romance with Wilma the nightclub singer, while both of them lied about themselves to impress each other. And the two spent an episode in September reminiscing about their pasts while clips from shows dating to the 1950s ran as part of a 35th anniversary special.

There was not, however, to be a 36th anniversary show, as *Search for Tomorrow* had fallen to the bottom of the soap ratings. Instead, there was a grand sendoff at the end of 1986, with several characters getting either "happy endings" or returning to see Patti marry Hogan. At the end of the event, Stu asked Jo, "What is it, Jo? What are you searching for?" and she said, "Tomorrow, and I can't wait!" Then, in a separate taped piece, Mary Stuart thanked her fans for their love and devotion before the screen went to black and more than three decades of drama and trauma faded from the airwaves.

SECOND CHANCE
Game; Color
March 7, 1977–July 15, 1977
ABC Mon.–Fri. Noon–12:30 p.m. (3/7/77–7/15/77)

Host: *Jim Peck*

Three contestants answered three questions, while being shown three possible answers, to win point for spins on an electronic board. The object was to collect the most money and merchandise on spots on the board without landing on a devil, which forfeited all wins. Four devils eliminated a player. (For a revised version of this series, see *Press Your Luck.*)

SECRET FILES OF CAPTAIN VIDEO, THE—See *Captain Video.*

SECRET LIVES OF WALDO KITTY, THE
Cartoon; Color
September 6, 1975–September 4, 1976
NBC Sat. 9–9:30 a.m. (9/6/75–9/4/76)

Voices:

Waldo Kitty	*Howard Morris*
Felicia	*Jane Webb*
Tyrone	*Allen Melvin*

Meek Waldo Kitty found himself intimidated by Tyrone the bullying bulldog and perplexed by his girlfriend Felicia, a female tabby. All were shown in live-action shots of cats and dogs at the start of the show, going into animation to display the fantasies Waldo had of controlling the other animals in various superhero incarnations, all parodies of human ones

(e.g., Catman). The show's biggest fantasy had to have been NBC running this for a year and thinking it could outrate *Bugs Bunny* on CBS.

The overt inspiration for this series was the saga of Walter Mitty, a meek comic character created by author James Thurber whose alter egos in daydreams did what Mitty wished he could do in real life. On December 30, 1975, Samuel Goldwyn Productions and Thurber's widow Helen W. Thurber filed a $500,000 copyright infringement suit against the cartoon, charging it with "debasing, distorting and diluting the quality and reputation of the story by James Thurber," as well as the character and film adaptation of the story by the Goldwyn company. It is not known whether the suit was settled before the cartoon went off the air, but it should be noted that the property continued in syndication as part of *Groovie Goolies and Friends* under the title *The New Adventures of Waldo Kitty.*

SECRET SQUIRREL, THE—See *Atom Ant/Secret Squirrel Show, The.*

•SECRET STORM, THE
Soap Opera; B&W and Color
February 1, 1954–February 8, 1974
CBS Mon.–Fri. 4:15–4:30 p.m. (2/1/54–6/15/62)
CBS Mon.–Fri. 4–4:30 p.m. (6/18/62–9/6/68)
CBS Mon.–Fri. 3–3:30 p.m. (9/9/68–9/1/72)
CBS Mon.–Fri. 3:30–4 p.m. (9/4/72–3/23/73)
CBS Mon.–Fri. 4–4:30 p.m. (3/26/73–2/8/74)

Cast:

Peter Ames (1954–62)	*Peter Hobbs*
Peter Ames (1962–64)	*Cec Linder*
Peter Ames (1964–66)	*Ward Costello*
Peter Ames (1966–68)	*Lawrence Weber*
Susan Ames (1954–56)	*Jean Mowry*
Susan Ames (1956–57)	*Rachel Taylor*
Susan Ames (1958)	*Norma Moore*
Susan Ames (1958–64)	*Mary Foskett*
Susan Ames (1964)	*Frances Helm*
Susan Ames (1964–68, 1969–71)	*Judy Lewis*
Susan Ames (1968–69)	*Mary McGregor*
Jerry Ames (1954)	*Dick Trask*
Jerry Ames (1954)	*Robert Morse*
Jerry Ames (1954–57)	*Warren Berlinger*
Jerry Ames (1957–59)	*Ken Gerard*
Jerry Ames (1959–65)	*Wayne Tippit*
Jerry Ames (1965–66)	*Peter White*
Jerry Ames (1968–69)	*Stephen Bolster*
Amy Ames (1954–58, 1960–71, 1973–74)	*Jada Rowland*
Amy Ames (1958–60)	*Beverly Lunsford*
Amy Ames (1971–73)	*Lynne Adams*
Pauline Rysdale (1954–70)	*Haila Stoddard*
Grace Tyrell (1954–69)	*Marjorie Gateson*
Grace Tyrell (1969)	*Margaret Barker*

Grace Tyrell (1970–72)	Eleanor Phelps	Ken Stevens (1968–69)	Gordon Gray
Judge J. T. Tyrell (1954)	Russell Hicks	Ken Stevens (1969–71)	Joel Crothers
Jane Edwards (1954, 1958)	Marylyn Monk	Jill Stevens (1968)	Irene Bundle
Jane Edwards (1955)	Barbara Joyce	Jill Stevens (1968–69, 1972)	Audrey Johnstone
Jane Edwards (1955–56)	Virginia Dwyer	Jill Stevens (1969–70)	Barbara Rodell
Bruce Edwards (1955)	Biff McGuire	Nick Kane (1968–70)/Dr.	
Bruce Edwards (1955–56)	Ed Bryce	Brian Neeves (1973–74)	Keith Charles
Alan Dunbar (1957–66)	James Vickery	Wilfred Hollister (1968–69)	Barnard Hughes
Alan Dunbar (1971)	Liam Sullivan	Wilfred Hollister (1969)	Alexander Clark
Myra Lake (1958)	Joan Hotchkis	Judge Sam Stevens (1968–69)	Terry O'Sullivan
Myra Lake (1959–63)	June Graham	Joan Borman (1968–69)	Christina Crawford
Ezra Lake (1958)	Wendell Phillips	Mrs. Borman (1968)	Elspeth Eric
Ezra Lake (1959–63)	Don McHenry	Archie Borman (1968)	Ken Kercheval
Joe Sullivan (1960)	James Broderick	Tom Kane (1968)	Coe Norton
Joe Sullivan (1960–61)	Frank Sutton	Laurie Hollister (1969)	Linda DeCoff
Bryan Fuller (1958–59)	Carl King	Laurie Hollister (1970–74)	Stephanie Braxton
Jeff Nichols (1960–61)	James Pritchett	Lisa Britton (1969)	Diane Dell
Nancy Hewlett (1961 at least)	Jane McArthur	Lisa Britton (1970)	Terry Falls
Kip Rysdale (1962)	Don Galloway	Lisa Britton (1972–74)	Judy Safran
Kip Rysdale (1963–64)	David O'Brien	Dr. Ian Northcote/Owen	
Kip Rysdale (1964–68)	Edward Griffith	Northcote (both 1969–71)	Gordon Rigsby
Arthur Rysdale (1962)	Lester Rawlins	Dr. Ian Northcote (1972–73)	Alexander Scourby
Arthur Rysdale (1962–64)	John Baragrey	Kevin Kincaid (1970–71)	Dennis Cooney
Arthur Rysdale (1966–67)	Frank Schofield	Kevin Kincaid (1971–74)	David Ackroyd
Kate Lodge Ames (1962)	Polly Childs	Aggie Parsons (1970–71)	Jane Rose
Nina DiFrancisco (c. 1963)	Nita Talbot	Hugh Clayborn (1970)	Peter MacLean
Valerie Hill (1964–71)	Lori March	R. B. Keefer (1970)	Troy Donahue
Paul Britton (1964, 1968–69)	Nicolas Coster	Mary Lou Northcote (1970)	Clarice Blackburn
Paul Britton (1964–65)	Jed Allan	Dan Kincaid (1971–74)	Bernard Barrow
Paul Britton (1965–66)	Edward Kemmer	Joanna Morrison (1971–72)	Audrey Landers
Paul Britton (1966–67)	Ryan MacDonald	Joanna Morrison (1972–74)	Ellen Barber
Paul Britton (1969–70)	Conard Fowkes	Kitty Styles (1971)	Diana Millay
Paul Britton (1970)	Linden Chiles	Kitty Styles (1971–72)	Diane Ladd
Ann Wicker (1965)	Diana Muldaur	D.A. Ursula Winthrope	
Chuck Bannister (1965)	John Cunningham	(1971–72)	Jacqueline Brooks
Dr. Tony Porter (1966–68)	Arlen Dean Snyder	Cory Boucher (1971)	Terry Kiser
Wendy Porter (1966)	Rita McLaughlin	Sean Childers (1971)	James Storm
Wendy Porter (1966–68)	Julie Mannix	Dr. Brian Neeves (1972–73)	Jeffrey David Pomerantz
Janet Hill (1966–67)	Bibi Besch	Rev. Mark Reddin (1972–74)	David Gale
Hope Ames (1966)	Pamela Raymond	Robert Landers (1972–74)	Dan Hamilton
Brooke Lawrence (1966)	Julie Wilson	Monsignor Quinn (c. 1972)	Sydney Walker
George Bennett (1966)	Dan Frazer	Stace Reddin (1973–74)	Gary Sandy
Marian Bennett (1966)	Gloria Hoye	Jessie Reddin (1973–74)	Frances Sternhagen
Frank Carver (1967–68)	Laurence Luckinbill	Doreen Post (1973–74)	Linda Purl
Frank Carver (1971)	Jack Ryland	Niele Neeves (1973–74)	Betsy von Furstenberg
Frank Carver (1972)	Robert Loggia		
Bob Hill (1967)	Roy Scheider		
Bob Hill (1967–68)	Justin McDonough		
Bob Hill (1969)	Edward Winter		
Erik Fulda (1967–68)	George Reinholt		
Mary Lou Carver (1967–68)	Joanna Miles		
Charles Clemens (1967–68 at least)	Jeffrey Lynn		
Belle Clemens (1968–74)	Marla Adams		
Nola Hollister (1968–69)	Rita Morley		
Nola Hollister (1969–70)	Rosemary Murphy		
Nola Hollister (1971)	Mary K. Wells		

This long-running serial dealt with "the secret storm" of emotions within people and with their relationships, chiefly the Ames family of Woodbridge, New York. A top attraction on CBS for 15 years despite considerable changes among leading cast members, it took a downturn in the early 1970s, when the network took control of its writing and producing. As the soap lagged in third place behind *Another World* on NBC and *General Hospital* on ABC, some drastic changes occurred, but they failed to generate the old ratings and the series ended after more than 20 years on air.

On the debut Pauline Rysdale was arguing with her dad Judge Tyrell not to give his son-in-law Peter Ames the presidency of the family department store, a position which Tyrell had held. Pauline's reason was a selfish one—she still loved Peter as much as she had 20 years earlier, before he left her for her sister. Then word came that Peter's wife Ellen was in a serious car wreck. Ellen died before the end of the first week, plunging Peter into a depression and propelling his children into other reactions. Oldest daughter Susan tried to assume her mother's role as family protector, while son Jerry vowed revenge on the man whose car hit Ellen and ended up having to go to a reform school. Nine-year-old Amy had a hard time digesting everybody's problems. Also taking news of Ellen's death hard was Judge Tyrell, who passed out and had to be revived by his wife Grace. Grace comforted her son-in-law's family too, but crafty Pauline had marriage to Peter on her mind all the time she was doing her altruistic bits for the Ameses, a fact which Susan readily noticed and opposed.

But Pauline found she had a real competitor for Peter's affections in his new maid Jane Edwards, mother of David Edwards. As Peter and Jane planned for a wedding, Pauline hit paydirt when she discovered Jane's presumed dead husband Bruce was in fact alive. Bruce came to Woodbridge and later really did die in a plane crash, but his arrival disrupted Jane's relationship with Peter, and she left town empty-handed. Bruce's mom Mother Edwards showed up as well for a time.

In 1957 Pauline appeared to have the field clear to marry Peter, but she was struck by a temporary blindness, which of course preoccupied her. Meanwhile that same year, Grace tried to learn why ex-bullfighter Alan Dunbar was following Pauline and Amy. Her suspicions were on the money, as it turned out he did have criminal contacts, but Alan eventually went straight and married Susan. However, in 1958 Susan found herself out west preparing to have a baby by Alan, but Alan deserted her for an heiress. (Susan later gave birth to a son named Peter.) At the same time, she had to fight off the amorous moves of reporter Joe Sullivan, who eventually

Aunt Pauline (played by Haila Stoddard) attempts to seduce the unwary Peter Ames (Peter Hobbs) on The Secret Storm *in the 1950s.*

became a priest after failing to win her over. She was not as strong in resisting her own adulterous yen for Jeff Nichols, but she stopped romancing him in the early 1960s, and went back with Alan, once she learned Jeff was using her as a source for a book on the ordeals of the Ameses.

Also in 1958, Peter's assistant and rival Bryan Fuller tried to take Peter's girlfriend Myra Lake and his job as president of the Tyrell Department store, while also making a play for Pauline Harris. Nonetheless, Myra's dad Ezra liked Bryan better than Peter, but Bryan decided to go for Pauline instead. They wed, but divorced as Bryan's connections to the mob emerged. Peter married Myra in 1959, but Ezra remained unmoved by him, and they divorced. Peter finally found true love and happiness in the 1960s with Valerie Hill, which lasted until his death on a business trip in 1968.

The other Ameses had a rockier time with love in the 1960s. Jerry was the object of desire for Nancy Hewlett, but he preferred Kate Lodge. Tragedy struck when someone killed Kate after she wed Jerry, and he became the prime suspect. After Jerry was cleared of the crime, he wed Hope the painter and left the show, returning only briefly at the end of the decade. As for Susan, she found herself the victim of an adulterous affair between Alan and Ann Wicker. Alan went off to fight in Vietnam, and was reported dead, leaving Susan to follow after newspaper reporter Frank Carver. Alan later turned up alive as a demented war veteran, and when he was murdered, Susan became the top suspect; however, Frank helped clear her.

But little Amy, now a young woman, had them all beat when it came to romantic complications. When her Aunt Pauline married Arthur Rysdale, Amy became attracted to his son Kip but had to endure Kip's affair with his Spanish teacher Nina DiFrancisco, whom he accidentally killed. While Kip was serving time in jail, Amy took up with her married college professor Paul Britton and had a child by him, named Lisa. Paul offered to divorce his wife and wed Amy, but she accepted an offer of matrimony from the newly freed Kip instead. The marriage was a disaster, with Amy haunted by her feelings for Paul, and when Paul informed her he was divorced, she left Kip, taking Lisa with her, and had a few happy years with Paul.

Others who popped up in the 1960s were Brooke Lawrence, a schemer who plotted to win over the married Peter Ames but ended up dying accidentally; Charlie Clemens, who attempted to take over the local newspaper, *The Herald;* and Amy's married pals Ken and Jill Stevens. Ken left his wife and had a child with Laurie Hollister before dying, while Jill married Hugh Clayborn before they died in an airplane crash around Christmas in 1970.

In 1968 film actress Joan Crawford's daughter Christina joined the show as Joan Borman, wife of Nick Kane. "I played a neurotic young wife with a passion for mischief who developed a drinking problem when she suspected her husband of seeing other women," recounted Christina in her 1978 best-selling autobiography *Mommie Dearest,* in which she charged her adoptive mother with child abuse.

When Christina had a tumor removed from her fallopian tubes later that year, her mother, then 64, volunteered to play Joan, who was 28! CBS went for the idea as a publicity grabber, which it was, but Christina insisted her mother was drunk and terrible when she taped the three shows.

The part Crawford might have really loved to play was that of Belle Clemens, who blamed Amy for her daughter Robin's accidental death and got wicked revenge by convincing Paul to divorce Amy and marry her. This left Amy a basket case, and only after much counseling with Dr. Ian Northcote did her mental condition improve. By 1971, Northcote had married Amy's stepmother Valerie. Amy needed all her faculties after that, as she found herself attracted to Kevin Kincaid, the son of ambitious politician Dan Kincaid, whose new wife was—yep—Belle. Dan's ambition to become governor of New York was thwarted when his mob connections came to light, and he went to jail. But one of his cronies shot Kevin, leaving him an impotent paraplegic.

Now the plot really thickened. Before the shooting, Amy had lied to Kevin that she was pregnant, and now, not wanting to disappoint her already stressed husband, she decided to have herself secretly artificially inseminated (ex-husband Paul had left town altogether, although Lisa remained with Amy). Though she did not know it, the donor was her doctor, Brian Neeves. When Belle discovered the truth, she blackmailed Amy to get money for the man she wanted to be her next boyfriend, a racing car buff named Robert Landers. But in a further twist, another admirer of Robert's, Joanna Morrison, turned up, and Joanna knew that Belle's ex-husband Dan was actually Robert's father! Robert had affairs with both women, and Joanna ended up carrying his child. When he learned that secret toward the end of the show's run, he got engaged to Joanna and tried to make amends with his newly found dad Dan and brother Kevin, while Belle left them all to pursue her own singing career.

That story line was but one of a plethora that emerged in the last few years as the show desperately tried to gain audiences. Among the gimmicks were drug peddling (1960s hunk Troy Donahue played a scraggly, unrecognizable dealer named Keefer); con impersonators (Cory Boucher pretended to be Amy's illegitimate half brother Sean Childers, Jr., who had told his story to Boucher before dying, but Boucher left town because his growing love for Amy made him unable to carry out the plan); and the temptation of a priest (Laurie Hollister and Father Mark Reddin had a romance that ultimately dissolved). There was also a lot of just plain lurid, exploitative writing (Stace Reddin tried to rape his brother Mark's fiancée Laurie but fought with him and their mother Jessie, leading to the latter's accidental death by being impaled on a pitchfork). Nothing brought back many viewers, not even the 1973 return of longtime favorite Jada Rowland as Amy, who had left the series in 1971 because of fatigue and a desire to try a writing career.

With its 1973 lead-in *Match Game* performing well while *The Secret Storm* remained near the bottom of the ratings pack, CBS canceled the show. There was no reunion between Amy and her now departed brother and sister on the final show, just a reconciliation with her crippled husband Kevin, who had left her and gone to London, asking Amy to marry Dr. Reeves after learning that Reeves was Danielle's real father. Amy ended Dr. Reeves's efforts to woo her, then came home to see Kevin stand up and walk haltingly before falling. She joined him along with her kids and Valerie on the floor, a rather unconventional end to an often intense, long-lived daytime drama.

SECRETS OF ISIS, THE—See *Isis.*

•SEE IT NOW
News Analysis/Documentary; B&W
November 18, 1951–July 7, 1958

CBS Sun. 3:30–4 p.m. (11/18/51–4/13/52)
CBS Sun. 5–6 p.m. (10/7/56–7/7/58; summers off)

Host/Co-Producer: *Edward R. Murrow*

The grandfather of all TV documentaries and newsmagazines, including *60 Minutes, See It Now* was the brainchild of anchor Edward R. Murrow and co-producer Fred Friendly. An outgrowth of a radio show the two did together called *Hear It Now,* it stood apart from other TV news shows aired both then and now in its hard-hitting exploration of whatever topics were covered and in occasional editorializing by its host. *See It Now* also distinguished itself with its reliance on original filmed reports rather than material gathered from other sources, and efforts to talk with the major national figures of the day.

The show often did live remotes, such as on the debut, where a split screen showing both the Statue of Liberty in New York City and the San Francisco Bay prompted Murrow to say, "We are impressed by a medium through which a man sitting in his living room has been able for the first time to look at two oceans at once." On that same show, Eric Sevareid talked in New York City about Korean War atrocities while films of troops overseas aired. The Korean War was a heavily covered topic during *See It Now*'s first season on daytime and later years, as was Sen. Joe McCarthy, who first appeared in a film about his campaign to find Communists on December 16, 1951. Murrow was the first major newsman to take on McCarthy and his smear campaign, in a program aired on March 9, 1954, and the senator responded in a rather rambling, unimpressive manner on April 6, 1954, in another *See It Now* broadcast.

By then, *See It Now* was airing on Tuesdays at 10:30 p.m. However, with the massive success in the summer of 1955 of *The $64,000 Question,* which led into *See It Now,* CBS officials decided the slot would be better filled by a bigger audience draw and dropped the series. It returned Sunday afternoons in 1956 with a discussion of the Suez Canal difficulties and at first alternated weekly with other programs until appearing monthly by the last season. The most newsworthy show of this period was a 90-minute

telecast on December 2, 1956 titled "The Secret Life of Danny Kaye," which profiled the actor's dedicated work for UNICEF.

Following *See It Now*'s cancellation, Murrow was seen for a few years on its replacement *CBS Reports,* garnering his last loud acclaim with that series for his 1960 report "Harvest of Shame" on the sorry plight of migrant workers in America. He then went to work for the Kennedy administration for a few years before dying of cancer in 1965.

SEEKING HEART, THE
Soap Opera; B&W
July 5, 1954–December 10, 1954

CBS Mon.–Fri. 1:15–1:30 p.m. (7/5/54–12/10/54)

Cast:

Dr. John Adams	*Scott Forbes*
Grace Adams	*Dorothy Lovett*
Dr. Robinson McKay	*Flora Campbell*
The local police officer	*Chris Plummer*
The local editor	*Les Damon*
Neurotic lady	*Judith Braun*
Her playboy boyfriend	*Robert Webber*

In this short-lived serial, Dr. John Adams was a married medical criminologist who worked with Dr. McKay and found that their relationship was more than professional. In addition to the Adams-McKay plot line, which involved various colleagues who worked with them on mysteries, there was a story about a neurotic woman who was afraid of her mother and stepfather. This was the first of several shows which died in CBS's 1–1:30 p.m. daily slot in the 1950s; for others, see *Road of Life, Portia Faces Life, Jack Paar Show,* and *Stand Up and Be Counted.*

SEMINAR—See *Columbia University Seminar.*

SENATE COMMITTEE HEARING HIGHLIGHTS
Public Affairs; Color
June 19, 1966–July 31, 1966

NBC Sun. 3:30–5 p.m. (6/19/66–7/31/66)

This taped coverage of the week's Senate activity focused on one committee per show. Among those covered were the Senate Judiciary Committee, headed by Sen. Ted Kennedy (D-Massachusetts), and the Foreign Relations Committee, chaired by Sen. William J. Fulbright (D-Arkansas).

SEVEN KEYS
Game; B&W
April 3, 1961–March 27, 1964

ABC Mon.–Fri. 2:30–3 p.m. (4/3/61–3/29/63)
ABC Mon.–Fri. 11:30 a.m.–Noon (4/2/63–12/27/63)
ABC Mon.–Fri. Noon–12:30 p.m. (12/30/63–3/27/64)

Host: *Jack Narz*

Seven Keys involved contestants navigating a 70-space board to win one of seven keys needed to claim an assortment of prizes. By pressing buttons, contestants received passes, stops, bonuses, and penalties, on a gigantic lighted-up panel which stopped at a picture requiring identification. The winner could keep the key and see what prize he or she had won, or go for another game in an attempt to win more keys. It began as a local show on KTLA Hollywood on September 12, 1960, and after its network run returned to KTLA through January 15, 1965.

SEVEN LIVELY ARTS, THE
Various; B&W
November 3, 1957–February 16, 1958
CBS Sun. 5–6 p.m. (11/3/57–2/16/58)

Host: *John Crosby*

The seven lively arts in 1957, according to host John Crosby and producer John Houseman, were drama, writing, film, dance, music, graphic arts, and television. This series tried to explore them all but ended with mixed success, despite winning an Emmy for Best New Program Series of the Year. Some reviewers attacked both the show and the hosting style of Crosby, the TV critic for the New York *Herald Tribune*. For example, Terence O'Flaherty of the *San Francisco Chronicle* wrote, "I hope that brother Crosby can take it as well as dish it out." He could not. Crosby testily responded in *Newsweek*, "My fellow critics were gunning for us from the start. I wouldn't say they were jealous, but . . . ."

By all accounts the show started shakily with S. J. Perelman's "The Changing Ways of Love," a review of America since the 1920s narrated by Perelman and Mike Wallace. Perelman later mocked his on-camera work, writing in *TV Guide,* "Prior to the telecast, my wife injudiciously urged various friends and tradespeople to watch me. The morning after, I received a closing bill from our meat market, regretting that they could no longer extend us credit."

Following the debut, the program fared somewhat better with such shows as "The World of Nick Adams," a fusion of five Ernest Hemingway stories with Steven Hill and Eli Wallach; "The Revivalists," a documentary on evangelists; and "The Sound of Jazz" with Billie Holiday and Count Basie. Its last show was "Gold Rush," a ballet choreographed by Agnes DeMille with songs by Alan Jay Lerner and Frederick Loewe and performances by Beatrice Arthur and James Mitchell. But sponsors stayed away in droves, and its high costs ($100,000 per show) and iffy reputation led CBS to can it after just 10 shows. It alternated weekly with *See It Now.*

SHARI LEWIS SHOW, THE
Children's; B&W
October 1, 1960–September 28, 1963
NBC Sat. 10–10:30 a.m. (10/1/60–9/28/63)

Regulars: *Shari Lewis, Ronald Radd (as Mr. Goodfellow), Jackie Warner (as Jump Pup), Clive Russell (various roles)*

Petite puppeteer Shari Lewis starred in several local New York TV series, including *Facts 'n' Fun* (1953), *Shari and Her Friends* (1954), *Shariland* (1957), and *Hi, Mom!* (1958), before going on NBC. The show had a few regulars like Jump Pup the large dog and Mr. Goodfellow the next-door neighbor, and guests such as Tom Bosley, Ozzie Davis, and even Kukla and Ollie (without Fran), but the focus was on Shari and her hand puppets, which included the baby-talking, closed-eyed Lamb Chop, Louisiana patois–talking Hush Puppy, and goony Charlie Horse.

Lewis later appeared in a syndicated series called *The Shari Show* in 1975, then returned in 1991 with her biggest TV success, the daily public television series *Lamb Chop's Play-Along!,* which won many awards including an Emmy for best children's show. It was still airing in 1996.

•SHAZAM!
Adventure; Color
September 7, 1974–August 30, 1980
CBS Sat. 10:30–11 a.m. (9/7/74–8/30/75)
CBS Sat. 10–11 a.m. (9/6/75–10/30/76)
CBS Sat. 10:30–11 a.m. (11/6/76–2/5/77)
CBS Sat. 11–11:30 a.m. (2/12/77–9/3/77)
CBS Sat. Noon–12:30 p.m. (1/6/80–8/30/80)

Cast:

Billy Batson	*Michael Gray*
Mentor	*Les Tremayne*
Captain Marvel (1974–75)	*Jackson Bostwick*
Captain Marvel (1975–77)	*John Davey*

Traveling in a van to various locales with a silver-haired gentleman aptly named Mentor, teenager Billy Batson tried to right wrongs by describing his dilemmas with his "elders," the Greek Gods Solomon, Hercules, Atlas, Zeus, Achilles, and Mercury, all seen in animated form. The initials of the elders formed the word "Shazam!" which Billy cried out to become Captain Marvel, his muscular, crime-fighting alter ego. After Captain Marvel fixed the situation, Billy reverted to his old self and mused about the lessons learned with Mentor, although the show was typical of most superhero series in that the only thing viewers were likely to remember about each show were the action sequences.

Shazam! began as a Fawcett Comics book in the 1940s, with Fred MacMurray reportedly serving as the inspiration for the superhero's face. However, National Comics sued Fawcett on the grounds that Captain Marvel was too similar to National's Superman and had gained control of the superhero by the time this show hit Saturday mornings on CBS. Ironically, the series generated its own lawsuit when Jackson Bostwick, who had been replaced by John Davey, tried unsuccessfully in 1975 to win $790,000 in damages he said the show's production company Filmation owed him for barring him from appearing as Captain Marvel in public after he left the show.

The show spent its last two years as *The Shazam!/Isis Hour,* with the addition of *Isis* (q.v.), and was canceled in

1977. Shazam the character reappeared in cartoon form in 1982 as part of *The Kid Super Power Hour with Shazam* (q.v.). The live-action series was also repeated briefly in 1980.

•SHAZZAN!
Cartoon; Color
September 9, 1967–September 6, 1969

CBS Sat. 10–10:30 a.m. (9/9/67–9/7/68)
CBS Sat. Noon–12:30 p.m. (9/14/68–9/6/69)
Voices:

Shazzan	*Barney Phillips*
Chuck	*Jerry Dexter*
Nancy	*Janet Waldo*
Kaboobie	*Don Messick*

While scavenging off the coast of Maine, fraternal twins Chuck and Nancy found ring parts with the first and last syllables of the word "Shazzan." When they connected them, a 60-foot genie with a goatee and earrings appeared in their midst calling himself Shazzan, and they also found themselves transported back to ancient Arabian times. Shazzan offered to be their protector against other sorcerers, while Chuck and Nancy learned that they could not return to the present until they returned the ring to its rightful owner. Assisting them in their efforts were a cloak of invisibility and Kaboobie, a flying camel whose giggles would later be appropriated by *Scooby-Doo* (q.v.). Two episodes aired per show.

SHELL'S WONDERFUL WORLD OF GOLF—See *Wonderful World of Golf.*

SHENANIGANS
Game; B&W and Color
September 26, 1964–December 18, 1965

ABC Sat. 10–10:30 a.m. (9/26/64–12/18/65; off summer)
Host: *Stubby Kaye*
Assistant: *Kenny Williams*

An update of *Video Village*, this game show employed a three-dimensional board on which children competed. Each contestant had to roll two dice and do whatever the space on which he or she landed asked (a question or a stunt). Kenny Williams was the announcer and also played a cop. Originally (in 1952) *Shenanigans* was a local show on WPIX New York, with its future co-producer Bob Quigley (along with Merrill Heatter) as host. By the time it arrived on ABC, Milton Bradley had the game available for purchase in stores and was sponsoring the TV series.

•SHIRT TALES
Cartoon; Color
September 18, 1982–March 23, 1985

NBC Sat. 8:30–9 a.m. (9/18/82–9/8/84)
CBS Sat. 8–8:30 a.m. (9/15/84–3/23/85)

Voices:

Rick Raccoon	*Ronnie Schell*
Pammy Panda	*Pat Parris*
Digger Mole	*Allan Ogle*
Tyg Tiger	*Steve Schatzberg*
Bogey Orangutan	*Fred Travelena*
Mr. Dinkle	*Herb Vigran*
Kip Kangaroo (1983–85)	*Nancy Cartwright*

Based on a line of greeting cards, *Shirt Tales* involved a bunch of animals whose attire sported simple statements reflecting their feelings or inner thoughts (e.g., "Let's go!"). Originally this group was Rick the raccoon, who sounded like Edward G. Robinson; Pammy the female panda; Digger the friendly mole; Bogey the monkey, who sounded like his namesake Humphrey Bogart; and Tyg the tiger, the group's occasionally impetuous leader. Kip the kangaroo later joined, giving the group its second female. All lived in a city park under the eyes of Mr. Dinkle, its superintendent, and took part in either helping visitors or solving mysteries. For the latter, the group used the Shirt Tales' Super-Sonic Transporter, or STSST, which not only took them to various sites but also offered defense mechanisms. They also communicated via wristwatches, but don't let all these gadgets fool you, for the emphasis here was on comedy, not adventure.

SHOOT FOR THE STARS
Game; Color
January 3, 1977–September 30, 1977

NBC Mon.–Fri. Noon–12:30 p.m. (1/3/77–9/30/77)
Host: *Geoff Edwards*

Two pairs, each with a celebrity and a contestant, alternately picked one of 24 boxes to decipher clues to parts of a familiar phrase. Each box was worth a certain amount of money, which the participant got if his or her response was correct, and the first duo to reach $1,500 won the game. (For a revival of the concept a decade later, see *Double Talk.*)

SHOPPERS MATINEE
Variety; B&W
December 12, 1949–April 7, 1950

DuMont Mon.–Fri. 2–4 p.m. (12/12/49–4/7/50)
Regulars: *Sydney Smith, Minnie Jo Curtis, Gordon Dilworth, Dorothea McFarland, Fannie Engle (1949–50), Cass Franklin (a.k.a. Monica Moore; 1949–50), Susan Raye (1949–50), Don Russell (1949–50), the Jean Bartel Quartet (1949–50), Andre Baruch (1950), Phil Hanna (1950), Bill Harrington (1950), Holly Harris (1950), Bea Wain (1950), Bill Williams (1950), the Reggie Beane Trio (1950), the Cy Coleman Trio (1950), Virginia Peine (1950)*

Shoppers Matinee was DuMont's ambitious plan to program the 2–4 p.m. daily block with light entertainment, but it backfired, and instead put a serious crimp in the network's efforts to stave off competition from the larger networks.

The debut promised some 21 entertainment segments connected by a story line which had each part taking place in a store, with Minnie Jo Curtis playing a department store elevator operator bouncing from shop to shop to view the attractions. Stations received 12 one-minute spots to do their own advertising, with DuMont offering them a news bulletin during these breaks if they could not sell the spots.

This format proved cumbersome and affiliates demanded changes, so after two months the show scrapped several regulars, almost all of them vocalists, and installed just six segments per day, including an opening 15 minutes by the Cy Coleman Trio; Andre Baruch, Bea Wain, and Bill Harrington in a 15-minute spot titled "Andre and Bea at Home"; Bill Williams hosting "Welcome Mat" with Curtis and fellow holdover Dorothea McFarland plus guests in a 30-minute slot; Phil Hanna doing 15 minutes of songs; and other contributions, such as Gordon Dilworth doing folk ballads and Sydney Smith dispensing homemaking tips. By the end of February, Virginia Peine, wife of Quentin Reynolds, was hosting a 15-minute segment called "Ladies in Waiting."

By April much of the cast had left for a similar DuMont Sunday night variety series called *Starlit Time*, which ended November 28, 1950. Smith stayed behind to do guest interviews 15 minutes Mondays, Wednesdays, and Fridays and 30 minutes Tuesdays and Thursdays. But nothing could save this turkey, and its failure signaled the end of DuMont's plans to become the leader in daytime television.

SHOWDOWN
Game; Color
July 4, 1966–October 14, 1966

NBC Mon.–Fri. 11:30 a.m.–Noon (7/4/66–10/14/66)

Host: *Joe Pyne*

Musicians: *The Bantams*

The only network game show to have a rock group (the Bantams) as regulars, *Showdown* had two groups of trios playing to be the first to come up with the right answers to a series of questions. Selecting an incorrect answer from four possibilities resulted in the person who had been wrong dropping from his or her seat onto the floor. Adding to the oddness of this setup was the choice of host—Joe Pyne, who was then known as host of a confrontational late-night syndicated series. This Heatter-Quigley Productions game was replaced by another offering from the same company, one that was much more successful (see *Hollywood Squares*).

SHOWOFFS
Game; Color
June 30, 1975–December 26, 1975

ABC Mon.–Fri. Noon–12:30 p.m. (6/30/75–12/26/75)

Host: *Bobby Van*

In *Showoffs*, an update of *Pantomime Quiz*, two duos, each composed of a celebrity and a contestant, had one minute each to guess a number of charades conveyed from one

partner to another. The highest-scoring pair at the end of the show played a bonus, where the duo received $1 per correct identification in a minute, then got another 30 seconds to guess three more words. In the 30-second segment, the contestant earned 10 times the money accumulated in the first part of the bonus round if one charade was identified, 100 times if two were identified, and 1,000 times if three were identified.

SIDEWALKS OF NEW YORK—See *Man on the Street.*

SIGHTSEEING WITH THE SWAYZES—See *Watch the World.*

•SIGMUND AND THE SEA MONSTERS
Sitcom; Color
September 8, 1973–October 18, 1975

NBC Sat. 11–11:30 a.m. (9/8/73–12/29/73)
NBC Sat. 10–10:30 a.m. (1/5/74–8/31/74)
NBC Sat. 10:30–11 a.m. (9/7/74–8/30/75)
NBC Sat. 8:30–9 a.m. (9/6/75–10/18/75)

Cast:

Sigmund Ooz (costume and voice)	Billy Barty
Johnny Stuart	Johnny Whitaker
Scott Stuart	Scott Kolden
Zelda Marshall (1973–74)	Mary Wickes
Miss Eddels (1973–74)	Margaret Hamilton
Sheriff Chuck Bevins (1973–74)	Joe Higgins
Gertrude Gouch (1974–75)	Fran Ryan
Sheldon the sea genie (1974–75)	Rip Taylor

Sigmund Ooz was a multitentacled, seaweed-covered lump who ran away from his unpleasant family life and bumped into brothers Johnny and Scott Stuart on Cypress Beach, California. The Stuarts befriended Sigmund and stowed him away in their clubhouse at home, being careful to hide him from their guardian, suspicious housekeeper Zelda. But Sigmund's mean green family, which included Big Daddy, Sweet Mama, his brothers Blurp and Slurp, Great Uncle Siggy, and Prince the angry pet lobster, went to great lengths to get Ooz back so they could continue to harass him, even going so far as to invade the clubhouse at one point. All this activity aroused considerable suspicion in Zelda and in the Stuarts' nosy neighbor Miss Eddels, both of whom felt things were amiss at the clubhouse but could never prove it. Sheriff Bevins, Zelda's love interest, often got involved in the uproar caused by the Oozes and the Stuarts.

In the show's second season Zelda left and was replaced by Gertrude as the family maid. Also joining in the mayhem was Sheldon the flamboyant sea genie, who lived in miniaturized form in a shell at the clubhouse and employed his sorcery to variable effect in helping Sheldon and the Stuarts. The series was videotaped in Hollywood.

SINGING LADY, THE
Children's; B&W
August 12, 1948–March 21, 1954

ABC Tue./Thu. 5:30–6 p.m. (8/12/48–11/3/48)
ABC Sun. 11:30 a.m.–Noon (9/27/53–3/21/54)

Regulars: *Ireene Wicker, Allen Grant (1948), the Suzari Marionettes (1948)*

Ireene Wicker (she put the extra "e" in her first name on advice from a numerologist, according to *Newsweek)* was a seasoned children's performer in broadcasting when she landed her first regular TV series. On her first network radio show, on NBC in 1932, she did 15 minutes of nursery rhymes, and she remained in that medium for two decades, eventually expanding her repertoire to stories. She was a grandmother when she started her TV series.

On August 22, 1946 she appeared on a nighttime TV special on WABD New York. Two years later, ABC installed her as a regular attraction twice a week as one of its two first daytime series (the other, *Cartoon Teletales,* appeared in the same time slot Mondays and Wednesdays). It had Wicker tell stories like Oscar Wilde's "The Happy Prince" with the Suzari Marionettes acting out the events amid the piano playing of Allen Grant and a studio audience of four children. ABC moved her to Sunday evenings from November 7, 1948–August 6, 1950.

Her first cancellation was an unfortunate byproduct of the 1950s blacklist, when her name appeared in the notorious publication *Red Channels,* which accused her of supporting Communist causes. The charges proved to be false, but she only got one other chance for a network show in 1953–54 before retiring as a society matron. Wicker died in 1987 at age 86.

•SKATEBIRDS, THE
Children's; Color
September 10, 1977–January 25, 1981

CBS Sat. 9:30–10:30 a.m. (9/10/77–11/12/77)
CBS Sat. 8–9 a.m. (11/19/77–1/21/78)
CBS Sun. 8:30–9 a.m. (9/9/79–12/30/79)
CBS Sun. 8–8:30 a.m. (1/6/80–1/25/81)

Voices:

Scooter	Don Messick
Satchel	Bob Holt
Knock Knock	Lennie Weinrib
Scat Cat	Scatman Crothers
Larry	Joe Baker
Moe	Paul Winchell
Curly/PAUPS	Frank Welker
Triple-Zero	Ross Martin
Willie Sheeler	Mickey Dolenz
Dooley Lawrence	Susan Davis

Cast (live action):

Chuck Kelly	Stephen Parr
Sue Corwin	Lynn Marie Johnston
Sandy Corwin	Larry Volk
Dr. Strange	Michael Kermoyan

Hanna-Barbera plagiarized their *Banana Splits Adventure Hour* to do this show. Here the costumed hosts were a penguin (Scooter), pelican (Satchel), and woodpecker (Knock), who were chased by Scat Cat in comic bits (though they did not sing). Their sketches fell in between three cartoon components—"The Three Robotic Stooges," "Wonder Wheels" (about a motorcycle that helped adolescent newshound Willie Sheeler and his girlfriend Dooley Lawrence to solve crimes by changing into its magical alter ego Wonder Wheels), and "Woofer and Wimper." The latter was an edited version of *Clue Club* (q.v.), which also showed up when *The Three Robotic Stooges* became its own cartoon replacing this show in January 1978 (see that title for more details about the two cartoons).

And as *Banana Splits* had the live-action "Danger Island," this show had the adventure serial "Mystery Island," where scientists Chuck Kelly, Sue Corwin, and her brother Sandy tried to keep their talking robot PAUPS out of the grip of the sinister Dr. Strange. The evil doctor used a "projector beam ray" to force the trio's jet Nimbus to land on his island in an effort to capture PAUPS, a machine who was a dead ringer for the Robot on *Lost in Space.* Dr. Strange never did hold PAUPS long enough to learn its secrets, but the humans never did escape either.

After the series performed unimpressively in 1977–78, CBS brought it in edited half-hour repeats to Sundays, but without the already spun off "Woofer and Wimper" and "Three Robotic Stooges." This incarnation lasted from 1979 to 1981, which meant, astonishingly, that *The Skatebirds* had a longer network run than *The Banana Splits,* though its obvious inspiration was much more successful with the critics and public than this run-of-the-mill knockoff.

•SKELETON WARRIORS
Cartoon; Color
October 1, 1994–September 2, 1995

CBS Sat. 9:30–10 a.m. (10/1/94–11/5/94)
CBS Sat. 10:30–11 a.m. (11/12/94–2/4/95)
CBS Sat. 11:30 a.m.–Noon (2/11/95–9/2/95)

Voices: *Jeff Bennett, Phillip L. Clarke, Jennifer Hale, Danny Mann, Kevin Schon, Nathan Carlson, Michael Corbett, Tony Jay, Valery Pappas*

Just what were CBS programmers thinking when they scheduled this violent, rather nihilistic cartoon on Saturday mornings? *Skeleton Warriors* was an unappealing action-adventure offering that began when Joshua Lightstar, jealous younger brother of Justin Lightstar, negotiated with Baron Dark about use of the Lightstar Crystal, which supplied energy for the residents of Luminicity (pronounced as "luminosity"). Joshua realized too late that the evil Baron wanted the crystal all to himself. They fought, and the crystal split, plunging Luminicity into chaos and transforming the Baron into a mere skeleton, while Joshua retained a gaunt visage with a gaping mouth and eye sockets.

When Justin and his sister Jennifer Lightstar learned of the situation, they flew on their sky cycles to their Uncle Ersac, who told them that they must protect their half of the crystal and use the unique powers they received from it to be "warriors of the light" to defeat the Baron and his crew and rejoin the two halves of the crystal. He renamed Justin Prince Lightstar, as he had the fire of the crystal in his blood, and Jennifer became Talyn in honor of her new ability to fly, possibly due to the influence of her pet dove Sarafina. Uncle Ersac became known as Guardian, and Joshua, the family member who had started all the mess, accepted the name of Grimskull, which certainly reflected his looks and general mood.

Baron Dark remained a powerful, ghastly foe. His touch changed his own men into skeletons when they were going to fight the Lightstars, and they all had the ability to recombine their bones when shattered, making them tough to stop. The Baron, who sported a pair of fangs and a necklace embedded with miniature skulls, used ESP to try to brainwash Joshua into joining his side. Charming, no?

To round out this unappealing scenario, the show was crammed with many loud explosions amid tiresome plots. And just to keep everything in the proper spirit, a skull appeared to deliver the opening and closing segments of each show. No wonder most kids avoided this show like a cadaver.

SKY HAWKS
Cartoon; Color
September 6, 1969–September 4, 1971

ABC Sat. 11–11:30 a.m. (9/6/69–9/5/70)
ABC Sat. 11:30 a.m.–Noon (9/12/70–9/4/71)

Voices:

Captain Mike Wilson	*Michael Rye*
Steve Wilson/Joe Conway	*Casey Kasem*
Caroline Wilson	*Iris Rainer*
Pappy Wilson/Baron "Red" Hughes	*Dick Curtis*
Cynthia "Mugs" Hughes	*Melinda Casey*
Maggie McNalley	*Joan Gerber*
Buck Devlin	*Bob Arbogast*

Sky Hawks, Inc., was an airline service based in San Marcos Field, which was also home base for unscrupulous competitor Buck Devlin and his pilots. Operating the former was World War II veteran Captain Mike Wilson, assisted by his septuagenarian father Pappy, Mike's 17-year-old twins Steve and Caroline, and Mike's foster children, 14-year-old Baron "Red" Hughes and his 9-year-old sister Cynthia. Their airline acted alternately as a rescue service, transportation mode, and crime protection unit. Mike's love interest was Maggie McNalley, and the Sky Hawks' chief mechanic was Joe Conway.

SKY KING
Adventure; B&W
September 16, 1951–September 3, 1966

NBC Sun. 5:30–6 p.m. (9/16/51–10/26/52)
ABC Sat. 11:30 a.m.–Noon (11/8/52–9/12/53)
CBS Sat. Noon–12:30 p.m. (10/3/59–9/3/66)

Sky King starred, from left, Kirby Grant in the title role, Gloria Winters as Penny, and Ron Hagerthy as Clipper.

Cast:

Schuyler J. "Sky" King	Kirby Grant
Penny	Gloria Winters
Clipper (1951–52)	Ron Hagerthy
Bob Carey (1959–66)	Norman Ollstead
Mickey (1959–66)	Gary Hunley

Sky King ran on ABC radio from 1946 to 1950 and on Mutual from 1950 to 1954, but with a different cast. It came to television in 1951 under a $1 million deal with Derby Foods to have Peter Pan Peanut Butter sponsor it. It was set on the Flying Crown Ranch in Grover City, Arizona, where rich airplane operator Sky King served as guardian to his niece Penny and nephew Clipper. The trio often found themselves fighting no-good types via Sky's Cessna, the *Songbird.*

Actor Ron Hagerthy went into the military after the first season of 52 films were shot and reappeared only in reruns from 1959–66. In 1955–56 the show filmed 78 new shows, probably to make the package more attractive for syndication, and added a few new regulars, for a total of 130 shows.

During its years in daytime in the early 1950s it alternated weekly with *Youth Wants to Know* and then *Meet the Masters* on NBC and *Hail the Champ* on ABC. After a run of repeats on ABC nighttime from September 21, 1953–September 12, 1954, it returned to Saturday mornings in 1959 in reruns.

SLIMER AND THE REAL GHOSTBUSTERS—See *Real Ghostbusters, The.*

SMALL FRY CLUB

Children's; B&W

January 18, 1948–May 2, 1948

DuMont Sun. 5:30–6 p.m. (1/18/48)
DuMont Sun. 5–5:30 p.m. (1/25/48–5/2/48)

Host: *Bob Emery*

Bob Emery, who was something of a grandfather figure when he came to early children's television, in fact had been around a long time in broadcasting. His first radio announcing job occurred in 1921 on a Medford Hillside, Massachusetts, station. He made his TV debut in 1944, and by January 1947 he had become the program department chief for WABD. Then on March 11, 1947, on Tuesday from 7–8 p.m., Emery debuted on *Small Fry Club.* The series became a nightly series a month later, a format it would keep for the next four years.

The show aired old theatrical cartoons initially, then added drawings and stories. With virtually nothing else on TV at the time, the show soon became a big hit with early TV viewers. By the time it added a late Sunday afternoon edition in early 1948, it was seen seven days a week and had more than 3,500 still pictures of viewers submitted to be part of the show's club. A week after its Sunday debut it moved up a half hour for the rescheduling

of *Rainbow House* (q.v.), which Emery also hosted. The Sunday installment did not last long, but probably was discontinued due to time constraints on Emery rather than any sponsor or ratings problems.

The importance of *Small Fry Club* for children's programming should not be underestimated. Its success spurred NBC to develop *Howdy Doody,* for example, and demonstrated that there was a considerable, responsive audience out there for this genre of programming. But the show's cancellation, on June 15, 1951, did nothing for Emery's national presence. He moved over to Boston TV station WBZ to star in another children's show from December 1952 until his retirement on January 13, 1968.

•SMILIN' ED McCONNELL AND HIS BUSTER BROWN GANG

Children; B&W

August 11, 1951–June 28, 1958

CBS Sat. 11:30 a.m.–Noon (8/11/51–4/11/53)
ABC Sat. 10:30–11 a.m. (8/22/53–4/23/55; off summer 1954)
NBC Sat. 10:30–11 a.m. (11/23/57–12/7/57)
NBC Sat. 11:30 a.m.–Noon (12/14/57–6/28/58)

Host: *Ed McConnell (1951–55), Andy Devine (1957–58)*

Voices:

Midnight the Cat/Old	
Grandie the Piano	June Foray
Tige	Bud Tollefson
Froggy the Gremlin	Archie Presby

Cast:

Poet Algernon Archibald	
Percival Shortfellow	Alan Reed
Buster Brown	Jerry Maren
Various characters	Billy Gilbert
Various characters (1957–58)	Bill Rodriguez
Ghanga the Elephant Boy/Indian	
Little Fox	Nino Marcell
Rama, Ghanga's pal	Vito Scotti
Maharaja of Bakore, Ghanga's dad	Lou Krugman

This now-dated children's series ran on NBC radio from 1944 to 1952, then transferred to television, first on NBC Saturdays at 6:30 p.m. from August 26, 1950–May 19, 1951. Filmed in Hollywood from the start (a rarity for a 1950 network children's show), it starred bulldog-faced Ed McConnell as a teller of tales and host to puppets like Old Grandie the talking piano and animals like Midnight the Cat, who purred "Nice!" and Squeaky the mouse. To summon the best-remembered character, McConnell bellowed, "Plunk your Magic Twanger, Froggy!" and Froggy the Gremlin appeared (voiced by McConnell first, then Archie Presby) to cause big trouble for the host as well as for Billy Gilbert and Alan Reed's stuffy characters. Also seen were storyteller Uncle Fishface and Mrs. Twiddle Van Scout.

McConnell's stories often led into the show's continuing adventure segment, "Ghanga (also known as Gunga) the Jungle Boy," set in India. It told of the exploits of Ghanga, who had a pet elephant named Teela and whose pals were cowardly Rama and brave Little Fox. The other continuing element was the commercials for Buster Brown shoes, starring little person Jerry Maren as the title character.

Among the things that make this series look bad nowadays is its questionable humor—involving, for example, animals forced to pretend to play instruments and Froggie's nasty pranks (Froggie once cackled how he changed the weather in Alaska to harm Eskimos!), which the host always laughed off. Add to that the use of non-Indians in the jungle films and the excessive use of dubbed audience shots and laughter to imply that children were actually watching the show at a studio, and the result, in today's context, is more appalling than appealing.

McConnell's death on July 24, 1954 at the age of 62 forced the show's 1954–55 season to be repeats. Then Andy Devine hosted the show from August 20, 1955–December 31, 1960 under the title *Andy's Gang*. It was a local show in New York City except for the 1957–58 season, when it aired on NBC.

The title host of Smilin' Ed McConnell *prepares to read another tale to be dramatized on the show.*

SMITHSONIAN, THE

Documentary; Color
October 15, 1966–April 8, 1967
NBC Sat. 12:30–1 p.m. (10/15/66–4/8/67)
Host: *Bill Ryan*
Writer/Producer/Director: *Craig Fisher*

The Smithsonian spotlighted the national Americanmuseum's holdings by using at least one artifact as a reference point to review history or general-interest topics. The opener featured the wreck of the Spanish galleon *San Antonio*, which sank near Bermuda in 1621. After its daytime run, NBC repeated *The Smithsonian* Sundays at 6:30 p.m. from June 25–August 27, 1967. Some shows were sold to educational TV stations before they aired on NBC.

Later shows with the Smithsonian Institute's involvement were the June 13, 1971 nighttime CBS special "Search for the Goddess of Love" produced in conjunction with CBS News; three docudramas seen on CBS a few years later titled "Monsters! Mysteries or Myths" (November 25, 1974), "Flight: The Sky's the Limit" (January 31, 1975), and "The Legendary Curse of the Hope Diamond" (March 27, 1975); a monthly hour documentary on public television titled *Smithsonian World* beginning January 18, 1984 and running through the end of the decade; and six hour-long specials available in syndication starting in 1990 titled *Smithsonian Treasures*.

SMOKEY BEAR SHOW, THE

Cartoon; Color
September 6, 1969–September 12, 1971
ABC Sat. 8:30–9 a.m. (9/9/69–9/5/70)
ABC Sun. 9:30–10 a.m. (9/13/70–9/12/71)
Voices:
Smokey the Bear   Jackson Weaver
Also: *Billie Richards, Paul Soles, Carl Banas*

On November 24, 1966, cartoon producers Rankin and Bass made an NBC nighttime special with animated puppets called "The Ballad of Smokey Bear" which featured the voice of James Cagney. In 1969 ABC announced that the same producers would make a cartoon with the bear character in three seven-minute segments per week, two with an adult Smokey and one when he was a cub, followed by a conservation message at the end of each show delivered by Smokey. Though this version lacked Cagney, it did have the venerable Smokey character, created in 1943 by the U.S. government to remind the American public that "Only you can prevent forest fires." After a lackluster season of 17 original shows, the second season consisted of reruns.

•SMURFS, THE

Cartoon; Color
September 12, 1981–August 25, 1990

NBC Sat. 8:30–9:30 a.m. (9/12/81–9/11/82)
NBC Sat. 9–10:30 a.m. (9/18/82–9/5/87)
NBC Sat. 8:30–10 a.m. (9/12/87–9/3/88)
NBC Sat. 9–10 a.m. (9/10/88–9/2/89)
NBC Sat. 10–11 a.m. (9/9/89–8/25/90)

Voices:

Papa Smurf/Azrael the Cat	*Don Messick*
Gargamel	*Paul Winchell*
Hefty/Poet/Peewit (1982–90)/	
others	*Frank Welker*
Lazy/Handy/Grouchy/Johan	
(1982–90)	*Michael Bell*
Jokey/Mother Nature	*June Foray*
Greedy/Harmony	*Hamilton Camp*
Vanity	*Alan Oppenheimer*
Brainy	*Danny Goldman*
Clumsy	*Bill Callaway*
Smurfette	*Lucille Bliss*
Baby Smurf (1983–90)/Sassette	
(1985–90)	*Julie Dees*
Snappy (1985–90)	*Pat Musick*
Nat (1985–90)	*Charlie Adler*
Slouchy (1985–90)	*Noelle North*
Scruple (1986–90)	*Brenda Vaccaro*
Grandpa Smurf (1986–90)	*Jonathan Winters*

The Smurfs were a tribe of 100 dark blue people who stood just three apples tall and lived in Smurf Village. Their leader was 543-year-old Papa Smurf. Their principal foe was the wizard Gargamel, who tried to capture them for his own vile purposes. Among the most frequently seen members were Hefty, Lazy, Jokey, Handy, Grouchy, Greedy, Harmony, Vanity, Brainy, and Clumsy, all of whose personalities were signaled by their names.

Later additions to the troupe included the five Smurflings, who fell back in time and became youngsters, including Snappy, Nat, and Slouchy; Grandpa Smurf, who was distinguished by his white beard; and Scruple, a co-conspirator with Gargamel and his cat Azrael in efforts to defeat the Smurfs. In 1982 a separate installment, featuring the comic medieval adventures of Johan and his aide Peewit appeared, but it never caught on the way the Smurfs did. Though the cartoon's accent was on light comedy, it did find time in 1987 to air an anti–drug abuse episode wherein Poet Smurf became addicted after rubbing a witch's magic "orb."

The appeal of these pseudo-dwarfs to very young children was intense, and *The Smurfs* virtually dominated NBC's Saturday morning lineup in the 1980s, spawning a flurry of adorable itty bitty humanoids on network schedules (e.g., *The Gummi Bears, Little Wizards,* and *Snorks,* and so on, ad nauseam). But to others, particularly more critical adults, the show's popularity was unfortunate, especially in light of some faults. It was very sexist. Smurfette, its first female member, appeared in the first season as a creation of Gargamel's designed to fool the other Smurfs, but Papa Smurf used magic to make her a member. The only other

female to show up was Smurfling Sassette in 1985. Also irritating was the excessive use of such terms as "smurfy" and "smurfing" in the characters' conversations. And the emphasis on cuteness via the bright colors, squeaky voices, and insipid theme song was tough for anyone out of kindergarten to take after several repeated weekly showings.

Some adults obviously sided with the children, however, as the show was an Emmy winner in 1982 and 1983 as Outstanding Children's Entertainment Series. Children's positive response also kept the show at the #1 slot for Saturday mornings during those years. Fans may have been confused when an animated movie by a Belgium firm called *The Smurfs and the Magic Flute* came out in 1984, using different voices and characters. The film was not a success, but that was about the only flop connected to the Smurfs at that time. It was not until the 1989–90 season that the show really ran out of gas, prompting producers to try to jump-start it by having the Smurfs leave their land and visit various times and locations.

The characters were the brainchild of Flemish cartoonist Peyo Culliford, who created the *Schtroumphs* (loosely translated as "whatchamacallits") in 1957. The Schtrouhmphs became the easier-to-pronounce Smurfs, and by 1980 a line of the dolls had become popular as toys in America. One owner was NBC President Fred Silverman's daughter, whose enjoyment of the toy prompted Silverman to call for a cartoon series based on it. Culliford also created the Johan and Peewit characters used on the series, but ironically that duo appeared in his cartoons a decade before the Smurfs did as supporting characters.

SNAP JUDGMENT
Game; Color
April 10, 1967–March 27, 1969

NBC Mon.–Fri. 10–10:25 a.m. (4/10/67–3/27/69)

Host: *Ed McMahon*

On *Snap Judgment* two contestants wrote words as clues to other words before the show and their star partners tried to guess them, with one star getting three chances before his or her opponent could guess. If neither could, the word's letters were revealed one by one, and the first to guess then won that contest. After several rounds of alternating play, the highest-scoring contestant got to go to a bonus round where he or she could win up to $500.

In a last-ditch effort to gain viewership, the show's format changed to that of *Password* on December 23, 1968. But even with that famous format, and despite the presence of such big names as Johnny Carson and Bob Hope as guests, *Snap Judgment* never did click with audiences.

•SNORKS
Cartoon; Color
September 15, 1984–September 6, 1986

NBC Sat. 8–8:30 a.m. (9/15/84–9/6/86)

Voices:

Allstar/Elder 4	Michael Bell
Tooter/Occy	Frank Welker
Casey	B. J. Ward
Dimmy	Brian Cummings
Daffney	Nancy Cartwright
Junior Wetworth	Barry Gordon
Governor Wetworth	Frank Nelson
Elders 1, 2, 3	Peter Cullen

The Snorks were underwater creatures with bubble-sized heads and cute ways of talking. They rode seahorses and had "snorkels" (which actually were hornlike protuberances) on their heads. Most stories—which used light comedy to teach little lessons in life—centered on high school students Allstar, his girlfriend Casey, their pals Tooter, Dimmy, and Daffney, and their nemesis Junior Wetworth, whose father the Governor was a bombastic blast of hot air. Occy was Allstar's pet. Occasionally seen was "misfit" Snork Jo-Jo, who had a pet fish called Finji and worried about fitting in with the others. Like *The Smurfs*, which no doubt inspired this cartoon, it was based on the creation of a cartoonist in Belgium, in this case Freddy Monnickendam.

SOCCER

Sports; Color
April 16, 1967–June 8, 1980

CBS Sun. 2:30–4:30 p.m. (4/16/67–9/3/67)
CBS Sun. 3–5 p.m. (5/13/68–8/25/68)
CBS Sun. Various (9/14/68–9/28/68)
ABC Sat. 2:30–5 p.m. (4/7/79–7/28/79)
ABC Sun. 2–4:30 p.m. (5/18/80–6/8/80)

Regulars: *Jack Whitaker (1967–68), Danny Blanchflower (1967), Mario Machado (1968), Jim McKay (at least 1979), Paul Gardner (at least 1979), Verne Lundquist (at least 1979)*

No other major sport, including hockey, had as poor a record in getting ratings as soccer did on American television in the 20th century. The networks did not even begin airing the sport until the late 1960s, well after most other sports had been tried, and audience response was so lukewarm that soccer got very few chances on the networks. The situation was surprising, given soccer's intense popularity elsewhere, but its lack of a strong presence on the college and professional levels in comparison with football, basketball, and baseball limited its appeal among many U.S. viewers.

When the sport belatedly arrived in 1967, it was in the form of the National Professional Soccer League (NPSL), which had East and West divisions of 10 teams each, including Toronto in the West. CBS signed to cover the League rather than the competing 12-member United Soccer Association because Jack Kent Cooke, owner of the Association's Los Angeles franchise, wanted more money and a contract guaranteeing a minimum of three years of TV coverage.

By far the show's biggest spark was commentator Danny Blanchflower, a 20-year soccer veteran who had covered the

sport for the British Broadcasting Corporation before teaming up with play-by-play man Jack Whitaker on CBS. Blanchflower was so candid that when NPSL Commissioner P. K. Macker told him not to be so forthright in his opinions, Blanchflower relayed the information to the home audience!

When he was not asked back in 1968, Blanchflower wrote an article in *Sports Illustrated* defending his approach to calling soccer on television, in addition to noting his problems with CBS Sports executives. "I called it as I saw it, gave [the players] credit by their own standards, and when they made a bad pass or move I said so. It must have sounded critical to American sponsors and owners who had seldom heard a bad shot called a bad shot before. How else would the American public understand and appreciate soccer if it was not told what was good and what was bad?"

Blanchflower proved to be the least of CBS's concerns. For example, it was difficult to get referees to call "official timeouts" for commercials in a game using two 45-minute periods of continuous play. CBS switched to the North American Soccer League (NASL) in 1968 with Mario Machado replacing Blanchflower, but ended up losing $2 million in the venture and dropped the sport.

A decade later, soccer returned to television using the expanded 24-member NASL, with the New York Cosmos as the featured team on nine games shown that year. Jim McKay served as anchor and play-by-play man, Paul Gardner was analyst, and Vern Lundquist was the on-field reporter. Despite such innovations as no official timeouts for commercials in 1979, the two-year, $1.8 million contract was a bust for ABC, which gave up soccer after roughly biweekly Sunday coverage in 1979 and a five-week run in 1980. There have been no regular soccer telecasts on the networks since then.

SOMERSET

Soap Opera; Color
March 30, 1970–December 31, 1976

NBC Mon.–Fri. 4–4:30 p.m. (3/3/70–12/31/76)

Cast:

Sam Lucas (1970–73)	Jordan Charney
Lahoma Lucas (1970–73)	Ann Wedgeworth
Missy Matthews (1970)	Carol Roux
Ellen Grant	Georgann Johnson
Ben Grant (1970–74)	Edward Kemmer
David Grant (1970–74)	Ron Martin
David Grant (1975–76)	Tom Callaway
David Grant (1976)	Phillip MacHale
Rex Cooper	Paul Sparer
Tony Cooper (1970–71)	Douglas Chapin
Tony Cooper (1972–74)	Ernest Thompson
Tony Cooper (1974–76)	Barry Jenner
Jill Grant Farmer (1970–72, 1974–76)	
	Susan MacDonald
Jessica Buchanan (1970–72)	Wynne Miller

Randy Buchanan (1970–72)	Gary Sandy
Laura Delaney Cooper (1970–73)	Dorothy Stinnette
Robert Delaney (1970–72)	Nicolas Coster
Peter Delaney (1970–72)	Len Gochman
India Delaney (1970–72)	Marie Wallace
Jasper Delaney (1970)	Ralph Clanton
Pammy Davis (1970)	Pamela Toll
Gerald Davis (1970)	Walter Matthews
Ike Harding/Harry Wilson (1970)	Fred J. Scollay
Randy Buchanan (1970–72)	Gary Sandy
Dr. Stan Kurtz (1971–75)	Michael Lipton
Leo Kurtz (1971)	George Coe
Leo Kurtz (1972–73)	Gene Fanning
Mitch Farmer (1971–72)	Richard Shoberg
Ginger Kurtz Cooper (1972)	Meg Wittner
Ginger Kurtz Cooper (1972–73)	Renne Jarrett
Ginger Kurtz Cooper (1973–76)	Fawne Harriman
Julian Cannell (1972–76)	Joel Crothers
Zoe Cannell (1972–73)	Lois Smith
Andrea Moore (1972–74)	Harriet Hall
Dana Moore (1972–73)	Christopher Pennock
Emily Moore Matson (1972–73)	Lois Kibbee
Philip Matson (1972–73)	Frank Schofield
Carter Matson (1972–73)	Jay Gregory
Eve Lawrence Paisley (1973–76)	Bibi Besch
Dr. Teri Martin Kurtz (1973–76)	Gloria Hoye
Doris Hiller (1973–74)	Gretchen Wyler
Chrystal Ames (1973)	Diahn Williams
Virgil Paris (1973 at least)	Marc Alaimo
Judge Brad Bishop (c. 1973)	Allan Gifford
Tom Conway (1974)	Michael Nouri
Tom Conway (1974–76)	Ted Danson
Kate Thorton Cannell (1974–76)	Tina Sloan
Heather Lawrence Kane (1974–76)	Audrey Landers
Dr. Jerry Kane (1974–76)	James O'Sullivan
Greg Mercer (1974–76)	Gary Swanson
Mark Mercer (1974)	Stanley Grover
Edith Mercer (1974)	Judith Searle
Carrie Wheeler (1975–76)	JoBeth Williams
Ned Paisley (1975–76)	James Congdon
Victoria Paisley (1975–76)	Veleka Gray
Sarah Briskin (1976, first)	Dorothy Blackburn
Sarah Briskin (1976, second)	Molly Picon
Dale Robinson (1976)	Jameson Parker
Steve Slade (1976)	Gene Bua

From 1970–71 the official title of this, the first daytime soap opera spinoff, was *Another World—Somerset*, in honor of the show from which top characters Sam and his wife Lahoma Lucas plus Missy Matthews moved. Somerset, a moderately sized town said to lie about an hour's drive from *Another World*'s Bay City, had moderate interaction with characters from the other show initially, but soon stood on its own.

The star family in the early years were the Delaneys. Jasper owned the family business, and Peter, Robert, and Laura were his kids. Robert followed in his dad's footsteps unwillingly while unhappily wed to India. He fell in love with Jessica Buchanan, a nightclub singer at the Riverboat Club played by the late bandleader Glenn Miller's niece Wynne Miller, but his dad forbade him to divorce India. Jessica's brother Randy was a gambling casino operator at the Riverboat who played rough. So did its owner, Ike Harding, who was actually Harry Wilson, the man who fathered Laura Cooper's son Tony. An inquisitive Jasper found out and threatened to expose Wilson, but the latter retaliated by killing him. Harry's villainy was later revealed, and he died in a gunfight at his club. A distraught Laura went into a sanitarium.

A somewhat more stable family for a time were the Grants—Ben, who had a law practice with Sam Lucas, Ellen, and their children David and Jill. Ellen offered comfort to the children when Jill's husband Mitch Farmer and Ben both died in a plane crash in 1974. Ellen later drew their ire for dating a younger man named Dale Robinson, while Jill dated Greg Mercer.

As for the Delaneys, following Jasper's death, his sons Robert and Peter proved unwilling to assume control of Delaney Brands, so crime boss Leo Kurtz bought the company. His brother Dr. Stanley Kurtz was more noble, treating socialite Andrea Moore when she was poisoned by Zoe and marrying Dr. Teri Martin. Zoe eventually killed both Chrystal Ames, a secretary at Delaney, and her own brother Carter Matson, the latter accidentally in a last-ditch effort to get Andrea. Zoe went to an insane asylum, and Andrea's mom Emily, dad Philip Matson, and brother Dana Moore left town.

Around the same time, Sam Lucas left his law practice to become president of Delaney Brands, whose operator Leo Kurtz had aroused the suspicions of Sam's ex-partner Ben. Then Rex Cooper became paralyzed from the waist down following an "accident," and Chrystal (before her death) insinuated that she had a relationship with Sam. This caused Lahoma to leave Sam and later prompted him to return to Bay City briefly (see *Another World*). But Kurtz eventually got caught when he had associates kill plant manager Virgil Paris for raping Leo's daughter Ginger. Mark Mercer became the new plant manager, and Rex Cooper followed Sam Lucas as its president.

Meanwhile Ellen Grant had to deal with the shock that her father, Judge Brad Bishop, was retiring and marrying Eve Lawrence, a woman half his age. Eve's daughter Heather was none too thrilled with the prospect of marriage between the two either, nor was Edith Mercer, whose husband Mark had been involved with Eve years earlier. That involvement had tragic consequences when Heather, falling in love with Mark and Edith's son Greg, learned that he was actually her half-brother due to a previous affair between Eve and Mark. Judge Bishop decided not to wed Eve but went on an extended vacation with grandson David Grant for a time (David later returned). Heather went on to have a troubled marriage with the older Dr. Jerry Kane.

The core family on Somerset *in the early 1970s consisted of, from left, Rex Cooper (played by Paul Sparer), his wife Laura (Dorothy Stinnette), and their son Tony (Doug Chapin).*

In the show's last two years, Julian Cannell, Zoe's ex-husband, took center stage as its romantic lead as well as editor of the *Somerset Register* newspaper. After the murder of his second wife, Chrystal, and then a failed relationship with Eve Lawrence, Julian took another shot at marriage, this time with Kate Thorton. But Kate was impressionable, and sleazy lawyer Tom Conway's insinuations about the stability of her marriage led her to have an abortion. When bitchy Victoria Paisley told luckless Julian that Kate had aborted their child, he divorced Kate and went back to Eve. Unfortunately for him, Eve decided to wed Ned Paisley, Victoria's brother. He then tried Victoria, and that relationship actually turned out to be his best, since she mellowed considerably. One of his reporters, Carrie Wheeler, also found true love with fellow newshound Steve Slade after pursuing Greg Mercer, who was killed by a hit man.

Though it occupied the same time slot for over six years, *Somerset* was never a ratings winner. Few of its characters and stories really caught on with viewers. Even when its successful parent *Another World* preceded it

(from 1975–76), *Somerset* failed to hold on to the *Another World's* large audience. Its replacement was, of all things, *The Gong Show.*

SONIC THE HEDGEHOG
Cartoon; Color
September 18, 1993–June 3, 1995

ABC Sat. 8:30–9 a.m. (9/18/93–11/13/93)
ABC Sat. 8:30–9:30 a.m. (two shows; 11/20/93–9/3/94)
ABC Sat. 8:30–9 a.m. (9/10/94–12/3/94)
ABC Sat. 8–8:30 a.m. (12/10/94–6/3/95)

Voices:

Sonic	Jaleel White
Princess Sally	Kath Soucie

Sonic the Hedgehog seemed basically nothing more than an updated *Road Runner Show,* with the differences being that Sonic was blue, had a wisecracking mouth on him, and was fast enough in running on his two legs that he turned himself into a buzzsaw. The character, based on a video game, went on two different cartoons seen in 1993 and produced by DIC Enterprises. The daily syndicated version, titled *Adventures of Sonic the Hedgehog,* accented humor. In contrast, the ABC weekly had the lead character involved in a rather serious adventure, the effort to help Princess Sally locate her father, though Sonic did maintain his tendency to make wisecracks in his somewhat whiny voice. Their constant opponent was Dr. Robotnik.

•SOUL TRAIN
Music; Color
August 1970–

Syndicated 60 minutes weekly beginning 1971

Host/Creator/Producer: *Don Cornelius*

Soul Train, TV's longest-running showcase for rhythm and blues music, started in Chicago on August 17, 1970 locally, then went to Los Angeles for syndication in 1971. After that change, the show soon became the top showcase for R&B, with music ranging from the smooth sounds of Dionne Warwick to the raucous funk of James Brown,

That hair and that set could mean only one thing—Soul Train and its host Don Cornelius in the 1970s.

plus a few Caucasian artists able to lay down a few grooves like Elton John and K.C. and the Sunshine Band. As with *American Bandstand,* usually two acts were performed between the dancing of the studio audience to the latest hit songs, and these dancers' gyrations were imitated and admired by many viewers—*Soul Train* is credited with popularizing the Robot dance, among others. Even Fred Astaire confessed to *TV Guide* in 1978, "That show will get me going. Sometimes for a few laughs I'll get up and dance along with them."

Each show a man and woman dancer did "the Soul Train Scramble," where they could within 45 seconds win prizes if they could unscramble the title of a song playing. (Somehow they always managed to do this before time was up. Hmmm . . . .) Later, some dancers also performed on the show, such as Jody Watley, who had hits as part of the group Shalamar in the 1970s and as a solo artist in the 1980s. But the show's biggest success was when its new theme in 1974, "The Sound of Philadelphia," became a #1 hit as performed by the session group MFSB with vocals by the Three Degrees. With a few modifications, it remained the show's theme song for over 20 years.

Presiding over the festivities was deep-voiced Don Cornelius, who ended each show by wishing viewers "peace, love and soul." He also helped develop an annual syndicated special honoring artists called the *Soul Train Music Awards,* which first aired on March 23, 1987, and worked on the "Soul Train's 25th Anniversary Hall of Fame Special," which aired on CBS nighttime on November 22, 1995 and was hosted by Arsenio Hall. In the 1990s Cornelius appeared only occasionally on the show, preferring to have guest hosts instead, but his influence on the show, as well as the program's impact on the music scene, remained as strong as it had been a quarter of a century earlier.

SOUPY SALES SHOW, THE
Children's; B&W
October 3, 1959–April 1, 1961

ABC Sat. Noon–12:30 p.m. (10/3/59–4/1/61; off summer 1960)

Regulars: *Soupy Sales, Frank Natasi, Clyde Adler*

One of TV's favorite entertainers for children, Soupy Sales began doing TV shows for juveniles in the early 1950s in Cincinnati and Cleveland before finally landing a seven-year run (1953–60) in Detroit. This was followed by work in Los Angeles from 1961–64, then New York from 1964–67, then, a decade later, Hollywood. But let's go back to the beginning.

The basic format for all the shows was established in the 1950s, except for Soupy's crushed top hat, oversized bow tie, and bulky black sweater, which had disappeared by the 1960s. Frank Natasi did the voices (or sometimes just grunts) for puppets White Fang, Black Tooth, Hippie, Herby, and Pookie the Lion, while Clyde Adler handled the puppets and threw pies at Soupy. *Time* reported in 1957

The Soupy Sales Show *celebrates an anniversary in the 1950s, and the star adjusts his oversized tie to celebrate.*

that Sales had the top-rated daytime series in Detroit and attracted such guests as Duke Ellington and Ella Fitzgerald.

ABC gave Soupy his first national exposure on a nightly series running 7–7:15 p.m. from July 4–August 26, 1955. The network tried him again four years later on Saturday afternoons, by which time he had been hit in the face by over 14,000 pies, according to *Newsweek*. The series, still from Detroit, was officially titled *Lunch with Soupy Sales*. His humor here was laden with puns, such as a joke which went, "Show me a bathing beauty, and I'll show you a girl worth wading for" and a routine about a typewriter with no L's that Sales said typed "ousy," followed promptly by a pie.

Then ABC gave him a show from Hollywood January 26–April 23, 1962, which aired Fridays from 7:30–8 p.m. His greatest success, however, came in an hour-long daily show which debuted on September 7, 1964 on WNEW New York City and went into syndication the following year. By that time, Sales had been hit with nearly 20,000 pies and a cult following for his wacky humor had developed. He also had a minor hit song called "The Mouse," which he performed on *The Ed Sullivan Show*.

Flushed with success, Sales left his show in 1966 to star in the film *Birds Do It*, which flopped. He went back to doing game shows and guest shots for the rest of his TV career, save only for a short-lived syndicated revival in 1979. In the 1990s he performed mostly on a New York City radio show.

•SPACE ACADEMY
Adventure; Color
September 10, 1977–September 1, 1979

CBS Sat. 10:30–11 a.m. (9/10/77–11/12/77)
CBS Sat. 11:30 a.m.–Noon (11/19/77–1/21/78)
CBS Sat. 12:30–1 p.m. (1/28/78–9/2/78)
CBS Sat. Noon–12:30 p.m. (9/16/78–9/1/79)

Cast:

Commander Isaac Gampu	Jonathan Harris
Captain Chris Gentry	Rick Carrott
Cadet Laura Gentry	Pam Ferdin
Tee Gar Sume	Brian Tochi
Loki	Eric Greene
Adrian	Pam Cooper
Lt. Paul Jerome	Ty Henderson

The Space Academy was established in Star Year 3732 as a satellite station traveling the galaxy to teach upcoming cadets how to meet with other life forms. Its leader was 300-year-old Commander Gampu. The other regulars were mostly young adults. Lieutenant Jerome was the only human apart from Commander Gampu, who was not a cadet. Their spaceship was the *Seeker*.

Space Academy was the highest-budgeted Saturday morning TV show up to that time, costing $150,000 per episode. Designers created a four-foot-long plastic model for the space base, and Christmas lights were used to represent stars, all of which looked fairly impressive for a Saturday morning show. Scientific accuracy, though, was another matter. For example, one show had the crew pass through a black hole with nary a problem. After running one year of original shows and a second of repeats, some of the show's footage and its mascot, Peepo the small robot, reappeared in its quasi-spin-off follow-up, *Jason of Star Command* (q.v.).

SPACE CADET—See *Tom Corbett, Space Cadet.*

•SPACE GHOST AND DINO BOY
Cartoon; Color
September 10, 1966–September 3, 1977

CBS Sat. 10:30–11 a.m. (9/10/66–9/7/68)
NBC Sat. 11–11:30 a.m. (11/27/76–9/3/77)

Voices:

Space Ghost	Gary Owens
Jayce	Tim Matheson
Jan	Ginny Tyler
Blip/Bronty	Don Messick
Dino Boy	Johnny Carson
Ugh	Mike Road

Space Ghost was the first of several so-called "Weird Superheroes" which gripped Saturday morning television in the late 1960s and drew much criticism from adults. The truth is that Space was much more funny and less violent than others which followed in his wake. He deserves credit as a virtually unknown creation able to topple his competition *The Beatles* from their perch as the number one cartoon of 1965–66.

The title character was a yellow-caped, black-hooded being, not actually a dead person, who had a magic belt that made him and those around him invisible (actually it had the characters seen only in outline). His crew consisted of his teenage wards Jan and Jayce. Both wore masks, as did Blip the monkey, who joined them on the Phantom Cruiser as they outwitted attackers. Two episodes aired per show.

The show's supporting element involved Dino Boy (the actor who voiced him was not the talk show host of the same name), a modern-day child who parachuted into the Lost Valley and found himself trapped in a Neanderthal world, which of course means in TV cartoon land that dinosaurs were there too. His protector there was a caveman called Ugh, who somehow spoke English albeit primitively. Bronty was the cute brontosaurus who tagged along with the duo despite the considerable number of predators they faced.

The series is the source of at least one industry rumor surrounding Fred Silverman, known for his hands-on approach to programming. Supposedly while watching one episode when he was head of CBS programming for children, Silverman piped up after listening to a space creature and said, "Wait a minute! A Venusian would never talk like that!" Maybe this anecdote is not true, but it is beyond dispute that *Space Ghost* helped catapult CBS into the number one position on Saturday mornings from 1966 to the end of the decade, by which time *Space Ghost* was laid off in favor of more comedy-oriented shows.

Nearly a decade after its cancellation, NBC brought back the series in reruns as a midseason replacement titled *Space Ghost and Frankenstein Jr.* (see *Frankenstein Jr. and the Impossibles* for cast and details on that show). It also ran in new segments in 1981's *Space Stars* (q.v.).

After more than a decade's absence, on April 15, 1994 *Space Ghost Coast to Coast* debuted as a weekly late-night cartoon talk show with live guests on cable's Cartoon Network. Blip, Jane, and Jayce were gone (according to the Cartoon Network site on America Online, the latter two were enrolled in community college), but two ex-villains from the 1960s cartoon reappeared. Zorak, a large green insectlike extraterrestrial with an evil laugh, became the resident bandleader, and Moltar, once the feared "lord of the mighty ovens," became the show's "director." With guests like magicians Penn and Teller and some rather adult jokes, there was no confusing this *Space Ghost* with the earlier version, although the latter was airing on the Cartoon Network at the same time.

SPACE KIDDETTES
Cartoon; Color
September 10, 1966–September 2, 1967
NBC Sat. 10:30–11 a.m. (9/10/66–9/2/67)

Voices:

Scooter	Chris Allen
Snoopy	Lucille Bliss
Jenny	Janet Waldo
Countdown/Pupstar	Don Messick
Captain Skyhook/Static	Daws Butler

Operating out of a satellite clubhouse in space, Scooter, Snoopy, Jenny, and Countdown, and the group's pet Pupstar acted to defend the universe from the evil doings of Captain Skyhook and his aide Static. In an unusual move, Skyhook also narrated the episodes.

• SPACE PATROL
Adventure; B&W
September 11, 1950–February 26, 1955

ABC Mon.–Fri. 5:45–6 p.m. (9/11/50–10/13/50)
ABC Mon.–Fri. 5:15–5:30 p.m. (10/16/50–12/8/50)
ABC Sun. 4:30–5 p.m. (1/21/51–3/4/51)
ABC Sun. 4–4:30 p.m. (3/11/51–6/17/51)
ABC Sun. 4:30–5 p.m. (9/9/51–12/31/51)
ABC Sat. 11–11:30 a.m. (6/14/52–2/26/55)

Cast:

Commander Buzz Corey	Ed Kemmer
Cadet Happy	Lyn Osborn
Carol Karlyle	Virginia Hewitt
Major Robbie Robertson	Ken Mayer
Tonga (1950–53)	Nina Bara
Prince Baccarratti, the Black Falcon	Bela Kovacs

Space Patrol debuted locally on KECA Los Angeles on March 9, 1950 with Glen Denning as Commander Kit Corry. On that show viewers learned that Space Patrol was the guardian unit for the city of Terra, which was found on a manmade planet. Kit's sidekick Cadet Happy said, "Holy smokes!" a lot as they went through the speed of sound to complete their missions. That episode laid the groundwork for future adventures on the show, which fought its cheap look by including films of destruction from the U.S. Navy.

When it arrived on ABC in the fall, *Space Patrol* renamed its commander Buzz Corey. Now he and Happy worked for the United Planets of the Universe on their spaceship the *Terra* in the 30th century to fight both natural and criminal elements. Happy's pals included Major Robertson; Carol Karlyle, daughter of the United Planets' Secretary General, who often had to be rescued by Happy and company; and Tonga, an attractive ex-nemesis who mended her ways and joined the Patrol. One recurring enemy was Prince Baccarratti, played by Bela Kovacs, the show's associate producer.

In terms of believability, the series fell somewhere between its East Coast counterparts *Captain Video* (little

Commander Buzz Corey (at top, played by Ed Kemmer) adjusts the controls of a spaceship while Cadet Happy (Lyn Osborn) observes on Space Patrol.

credibility) and *Tom Corbett* (the best of the bunch). It was not always scientifically factual but strove to be, with some fancy instruments like the viewscope, a supersensitive telescope for two eyes, and other futuristic creations offering a reasonable view of what life could be like in the future. Still, the live show was hurt by a reliance on fistfights and sometimes wooden acting.

After running daily in 1950, *Space Patrol* went to weekends on ABC for the next four years, appearing in some early evening slots in the summer of 1951 and the first part of 1952 when not on daytime. It continued as a daily local show on KECA, and on the May 5, 1953 program Los Angeles viewers got to see a demonstration of 3-D television, which bombed due to a blurred picture. The series also ran on ABC radio from 1950–55. When it ended on ABC television in 1955, ABC virtually stopped broadcasting on Saturday mornings through the rest of the 1950s.

SPACE SENTINELS—See ***Young Sentinels, The.***

SPACE STARS
Cartoon; Color
September 12, 1981–September 11, 1982
NBC Sat. 10:30–11:30 a.m. (9/12/81–11/14/81)
NBC Sat. 11 a.m.–Noon (11/21/81–9/11/82)

Voices:

Astro/Gleep/Gloop	*Don Messick*
Cosmo/Blip	*Frank Welker*
Dipper	*Lennie Weinrib*
Space Ace	*Mike Bell*
Kid Comet	*Darryl Hickman*
Moleculad	*David Hubbard*
Elektra	*B. J. Ward*
Plutem	*Mike Winslow*
Uglor	*Alan Lurie*
Zandor/Tundro/Igoo/Zok	*Mike Road*
Tara	*Virginia Gregg*
Dorno	*Sparky Marcus*
Space Ghost	*Gary Owens*
Jan	*Alexandra Stewart*
Jace	*Steve Spears*
Narrator (Herculoids and Space Ghost segments)	*Keene Curtis*

Space Stars cranked out new segments of two old Hanna-Barbera series—see *The Herculoids* and *Space Ghost* for plot information—and added two new ones, "Astro and the Space Mutts" and "Teen Force." "New" is a relative term for "Astro and the Space Mutts," as it took the dog from *The Jetsons* and placed him in his childhood with pals Cosmo and Dipper as part of an intergalactic enforcement unit under the leadership of Space Ace. "Teen Force" concerned superhero teenagers Kid Comet, Moleculad, and Elektra, who fought such baddies as Uglor the terrible. The whole lot of them could not defeat Hanna-Barbera's reliable *Scooby-Doo,* which aired against them on ABC.

SPACECATS
Cartoon; Color
September 14, 1991–July 25, 1992
NBC Sat. 10:30–11 a.m. (9/14/91–10/12/91)
NBC Sat. 8–8:30 a.m. (10/19/91–7/25/92)

Voices:

DORC	*Charles Nelson Reilly*

Also: *Paul Fusco, Townsend Coleman, Pat Fraley, Rob Paulsen, Bob Ridgely*

As with *The Secret Lives of Waldo Kitty* (q.v.) 14 years earlier, *SpaceCats* began each show with live-action shots of cats. However, the felines in question supposedly lived on the planet Tryglyceride 7, where their ruler was a human known as DORC, the Disembodied Omnipotent Ruler of Cats. DORC ordered a quartet of cats to act as ambassadors to Earth, and their adventures, seen in animated form, were the crux of the show. The tabbies were Tom, Scratch, Sniff, and their Captain Catgut. Paul Fusco, one of the voices on the show, also served as creator and co–executive producer. This was one of the last cartoons to air on NBC.

•SPEED BUGGY
Cartoon; Color
September 8, 1973–January 29, 1983

CBS Sat. 11–11:30 a.m. (9/8/73–8/31/74)
CBS Sat. 8–8:30 a.m. (9/7/74–1/11/75)
CBS Sat. 8:30–9 a.m. (1/18/75–8/30/75)
ABC Sat. Noon–12:30 p.m. (9/6/75–11/18/75)
ABC Sat. 11–11:30 a.m. (11/25/75–9/4/76)
NBC Sat. 10–10:30 a.m. (11/27/76–9/3/77)
CBS Sat. 8:30–9 a.m. (1/28/78–9/2/78)
CBS Sat. 8–8:30 a.m. (9/18/82–1/29/83)

Voices:

Speed Buggy	*Mel Blanc*
Tinker	*Phil Luther Jr.*
Debbie	*Arlene Golonka*
Mark	*Mike Bell*

Mel Blanc transferred the putt-putts and other sound effects he used as the "voice" of the ancient Maxwell jalopy on Jack Benny's radio and TV shows to this routine cartoon. It was another Hanna-Barbera ripoff of its own *Scooby-Doo,* albeit with fewer supernatural influences on the crooks being chased. Speed Buggy was a Scooby-Dooish dune buggy who had a mouth in the grille and eyes in the headlights to express its personality and talk to the trio of teenagers who rode it. Tinker was the Shaggy-like mechanic who drove the dune buggy in races and bonded with Speed Buggy as his best friend. Mark was the good-looking Freddy equivalent, and Debbie the gorgeous Daphne clone.

For some reason the automobile with an attitude became a favorite with the networks, appearing on the three major networks after its initial two-year run on CBS, often as a midseason replacement, even though the show was in production for only one season. CBS even installed reruns on its fall 1982 schedule. (For details on another Saturday morning dune buggy with a personality, see the "Wonderbug" segment on *The Krofft Supershow.)*

•SPIDER-MAN
Cartoon; Color
September 9, 1967–

ABC Sat. 10–10:30 a.m. (9/9/67–8/30/69)
ABC Sun. 10:30–11 a.m. (3/22/70–9/6/70)
NBC Sat. 11:30 a.m.–Noon (9/12/81–11/14/81)
NBC Sat. 10:30–11 a.m. (11/21/81–9/11/82)
Fox Sat. 10–10:30 a.m. (2/4/95–4/13/96)
Fox Sat. 10:30–11 a.m. (4/20/96–6/8/96)
Fox Sat. 10:30–11:30 a.m (two shows; 6/15/96–7/6/96)
Fox Sat. 11–11:30 a.m. (7/13/96–)

Voices (1967–70):

Spider-Man (1967–68)	*Bernard Cowan*
Spider-Man (1968–69)	*Paul Soles*

Betty Brandt	*Peg Dixon*
Jonah Jameson	*Paul Kligman*

Voices (1981–86): *Anne Lockhart, George DiCenzo, Alan Dinehart, Jerry Dexter, Michael Evans, Walker Edmiston, Alan Young, Dennis Marks, William Woodson, John Hammer, Keye Luke, Allan Melvin, Sally Julian*

Voices (1995–):

Spider-Man	*Christopher Daniel (C. D.) Barnes*
Dr. Curt Connors	*Joseph Campanella*
Jonah Jameson	*Ed Asner*
Aunt May	*Linda Gary*
Felicia Hardy	*Jennifer Hale*
The Kingpin	*Roscoe Lee Browne*

Spider-Man has had the good fortune of almost always being on television in some form as well as in comic books. First appearing in the Marvel line in 1962, the superhero showed up on ABC five years later in a largely consistent adaptation. Working under bossy *New York Daily Bugle* editor Jonah Jameson as a photographer, Peter Parker was bitten by a spider in a lab one night, and thereafter had the traits of a spider—he could crawl up and down walls, leap high, etc. He added some innovations of his own—like a red and blue body suit and a special liquid he made which shot taut webs he could use to swing from skyscraper to skyscraper—to become his crime-fighting alter ego. Unfortunately, Jameson and others remained dubious about whether Spider-Man was a force for good, and Peter found that he often had to juggle his efforts to fight evil with the demands of his relationship with *Bugle* reporter Betty Brandt.

The first series, which had Ralph Bakshi serve as executive producer, director, and story supervisor, ran two years in original episodes, then in repeats in the summer of 1970. In the 1970s "Spidey" appeared in still cartoons on the public television educational series for children *The Electric Company,* and as a CBS short-run live-action series from April 5–May 3, 1978 on Wednesdays from 8–9 p.m. titled *The Amazing Spider-Man* and starring Nicholas Hammond.

The character returned to Saturday mornings in 1981, using a bizarre format in which the camera scanned from one panel to another, with some "panels" becoming sets on which costumed actors mimed some plot points. Now, however, Peter Parker was a college student who teamed up with two other student-superheroes, Bobby Drake/Iceman and Angelica Jones/Firestar. Betty and Jonah also returned. In the fall of 1982 the show went into repeats for two years as a supporting segment with *The Incredible Hulk* (q.v.).

Spider-Man next shot his webs over to Fox, where a few specials in November 1994 led to a continuing cartoon the following year with Stan Lee as co–executive producer. This time it was a continuing adventure with college student Peter Parker trying to control his condition, since it could now convert him, without warning, into a large "man-spider," as it did one time with his girlfriend Felicia Hardy. Dr. Curt Connors tried to reverse his condition, while an unknowing Aunt May provided Parker with love. And as usual, Spider-Man was considered an enemy and not the savior of the city thanks to Jonah Jameson of *The Daily Bugle*, who ranked him along with mob boss the Kingpin as among the town's worst undesirables. Given all this grief, why he didn't he ever just move to the country?

•SPIDER-WOMAN
Cartoon; Color
September 22, 1979–March 1, 1980
ABC Sat. 11–11:30 a.m. (9/22/79–12/8/79)
ABC Sat. 11:30 a.m.–Noon (12/15/79–3/1/80)
Voices:

Jessica Drew	*Joan Van Ark*
Jeff Hunt	*Bruce Miller*
Billy Drew	*Bryan Scott*

Justice magazine editor/publisher Jessica Drew had been bitten by a spider as a child in her dad Dr. Alexander Drew's lab and, when cured by a serum from him, found herself possessing that arachnid's abilities—and then some. She shot webs, delivered "venom blasts" to foes, possessed supersensitive hearing, and even flew. Her photographer Jeff Hunt and young nephew Billy had no inkling of her crime-fighting alter ego, which she became by twirling into a red and yellow outfit.

The synopsis sounds like a distaff *Spider-Man* with only a few minor alterations, but it prompted no lawsuits from Marvel Company because its executive producer was Stan Lee, the comic book company's founder, who created the character in the comics in 1977. Interestingly, the voice of actress Joan Van Ark had been heard the previous season on *Tarzan and the Super 7*, a cartoon series on which one of the segments was a similar production called "Webwoman." Also of note is that this was the last series produced by DePatie-Freleng Productions. The David Depatie–Friz Freleng partnership had lasted for 17 years; the best known of the DePatie-Freleng creations was probably the 1969–79 version of *The Pink Panther* (q.v.).

SPIN-OFF
Game; Color
June 16, 1975–September 5, 1975
CBS Mon.–Fri. 10–10:30 a.m. (6/16/75–9/5/75)
Host: *Jim Lange*

Two couples played poker on *Spin-Off* using five rotating electronic wheels with numbers 1–9 written on them. Their hands were based on what numbers landed on a selected spot. Payoff amounts were $50 for a pair, $75 for two pairs, $100 for three of a kind, $125 for a straight, $150 for full house, $175 for four of a kind, and $200-plus for five of a kind. The first couple to reach $250 got to play a bonus for up to $10,000 for five of a kind.

SPLIT PERSONALITY
Game; B&W
September 28, 1959–February 5, 1960
NBC Mon.–Fri. 4:30–5 p.m. (9/28/59–2/5/60)
Host: *Tom Poston*

The object in *Split Personality* was to identify a person from features which made up a composite picture. The two players each received characteristics on two blackboards, and each player decided which characteristic from his or her blackboard the opponent would get to see as a clue. Winning two games in a row earned prizes and a chance to guess the identity of another "split personality" for a grand prize. The show aired from New York.

•SPLIT SECOND
Game; Color
March 20, 1972–June 27, 1975
ABC Mon.–Fri. 12:30–1 p.m. (3/20/72–6/27/75)
Host: *Tom Kennedy*

On the first two rounds of *Split Second*, a trio of players saw three answers on a board which applied to a statement read by the host, such as "Pick one of these and tell me if it was a character in Alice in Wonderland." The first player to sound a buzzer and then pick a correct answer won at least some money, depending on how the other players responded to the remaining answers. If the first player was the only one right, he or she cleared $25. If another contestant was also correct, they received $10 each. If all three were right, each garnered $5. The payoff amounts doubled in round two. In the third round each player had to be the first to answer four or more questions correctly (the player who had won the most money in the early rounds had to answer only four), to go to the bonus game. In all rounds the players had to respond quickly; they were penalized if they took longer than a few seconds to answer.

The bonus had a player select one of five automobiles on stage and try to start them with a key given to him or her by the host. Theoretically only one car could be started when it was a contestant's first try, but this did not always work. (Once a mechanic disconnected a spark plug rather than a coil for a car, causing the selected automobile to smoke for an interminable minute. The show gave the car away anyway.) Each day that any contestant returned to the bonus, one car would be eliminated.

ABC canned this show on the same day it eliminated its lead-in, *Password*. Monty Hall, whose production company with Stefan Hatos created this series, hosted a daily syndicated version from 1986 to 1987.

SPORT BILLY
Cartoon; Color
July 31, 1982–September 11, 1982
NBC Sat. 12:30–1 p.m. (7/31/82–9/11/82)

Voices:

Sport Billy	*Lane Scheimer*
Sport Lillie/Queen Vanda	*Joyce Bulifant*
Willie/Sporticus XI	*Frank Welker*

A rare summer cartoon, *Sport Billy* came onto NBC after a brief run in syndication. An odd entry indeed, it focused on a title character who went to Earth via an order from Sporticus XI, leader of the planet Olympus, to ensure fair play in games with no interference from the crafty Queen Vanda. Accompanied by girlfriend Sport Lillie and dog Willie, alien Sport Billy used his common sense and magic powers to accomplish his mission and promote sportsmanship and physical fitness to home viewers. The series was a replacement for repeats of the better-remembered *Bullwinkle Show.*

SPORTS CHALLENGE
Game; Color
May 20, 1973–September 9, 1973

CBS Sun. 5–5:30 p.m. (5/20/73–9/9/73)

Host: *Dick Enberg*

This Los Angeles–based quizzer had two trios of celebrity athletes, with each trio representing a major league team, compete in answering questions about sports. Contestants included Don Drysdale, Joe DiMaggio, Mickey Mantle, Billy Martin, Vida Blue, Norm Cash, and Catfish Hunter. Some film clips imparted clues, and there were the invariable "most embarrassing moment" blooper shots in each show too. The winning team got prizes to benefit youth sports groups and a chance to defend their title on the next show. *Sports Challenge* began airing in syndication in January 1971 before coming to CBS in 1973, then went back into syndication with new episodes through 1979.

SPORTS ILLUSTRATED—See *CBS Sports Illustrated.*

SPORTS IN ACTION—See *NBC Sports in Action.*

SPORTS INTERNATIONAL—See *NBC Sports in Action.*

SPORTS SPECIAL—See *NBC Sports in Action.*

SPORTS SPECTACULAR—See *CBS Sports Spectacular.*

SPORTSBEAT
Sports; Color
August 16, 1981–December 15, 1985

ABC Sun. 4:30–5 p.m. monthly (8/16/81–12/27/81)
ABC Sun. 2–2:30 p.m. (2/7/82–4/25/82)
ABC Sun. 3–3:30 p.m. (5/2/82–6/13/82)
ABC Sat. 3–3:30 p.m. (1/7/84–4/21/84)
ABC Sat. 3–3:30 p.m. or 4:30–5 p.m. monthly
(5/5/84–12/22/84)
ABC Sun. Various half hours (2/24/85–12/15/85)

Host: *Howard Cosell*

This investigative look at the sports world was beleaguered by a somewhat low clearance rate (only 140 of 200 ABC affiliates carried it at one point in its run) and erratic time slots. Howard Cosell took a hard-edged approach in examining athletics-related issues ranging from financial impacts to substance abuse. The show even did a rather critical report of USFL football in 1984, which ABC, surprisingly, carried.

SPORTSMAN'S HOLIDAY
Sports; Color
June 26, 1965–August 13, 1967

NBC Sat. 5:45–6 p.m. (6/26/65–9/4/65)
NBC Sun. 5:30–6 p.m. (6/19/66–8/21/66)
NBC Sun. 5:30–6 p.m. (6/18/67–8/13/67)

Host: *Curt Gowdy*

NBC's answer to ABC's long-running *American Sportsman* was this summer series that even used the host of the latter, Curt Gowdy. Like its inspiration, it used films and guest interviews amid the outdoor activities being featured.

SPORTSWORLD
Sports; Color
January 22, 1978–

NBC Sun. 2:30–4 p.m. (1/22/78–2/26/78)
NBC Sun. 4–5:30 or 6 p.m. (3/26/78–; January–August
only each year)

Regulars: *Mike Adamle (1978–c. 1983), Dick Enberg (1978–79 at least), Len Berman (at least 1982), Bill Macatee (c. 1984–85 at least)*

SportsWorld, a replacement for *Grandstand,* was NBC's attempt to establish itself as the preeminent leader in TV sports. Beyond basic coverage of a potpourri of events, it also sought to investigate serious issues related to athletics, such as fan violence. Many of the activities covered were contests that were to be played in the 1980 Olympics and were televised to build interest in the event, but unfortunately the United States boycotted the event.

Among its presentations in the first few years were the World Belly-Flop Championship (only those weighing at least 250 pounds were allowed to compete) and non-ice sports played on ice, including softball, horse racing, and motorcycle racing. By 1981 things had improved somewhat, with the addition of a "Sports Journal" investigative segment produced by none other than Howard Cosell's daughter Hilary, but in general this was a rather unexceptional sports anthology show.

STAINED GLASS WINDOWS
Religious; B&W
November 7, 1948–December 26, 1948

ABC Sun. 5:30–6 p.m. (11/7/48–12/26/48)

This filmed program, supervised by Rev. Everett Parker of the Joint Radio-TV Commission, spent most of its run (September 26, 1948–October 16, 1949) on ABC early Sunday evenings, sometimes in a 15-minute slot. It included dramatizations and discussions on nonsecular matters.

STAN SHAW SHOW, THE
Variety; B&W
January 12, 1949–March 4, 1949

DuMont Mon.–Fri. 11 a.m.–Noon (1/12/49–3/4/49)

Host: *Stan Shaw*

Music: *The Allen Logan Trio*

This early DuMont daytimer starred musically inclined Stan Shaw in a series similar to his *Record Rendezvous* program then airing locally on WPIX New York, with a trio led by pianist Allen Logan along with a guitarist and bass fiddler backing him and his guests in assorted songs. It was seen as early as November 1948 on WABD New York.

•STAND UP AND BE COUNTED!
Game/Discussion; B&W
May 28, 1956–September 6, 1957

CBS Mon.–Fri. 1:10–1:30 p.m. (5/28/56–9/6/57)

Host: *Robert Russell*

Should an 18-year-old Golden Gloves champ turn pro? Should a widow give her 17-year-old in the service legal permission to marry? Studio audience members left their seats to stand at a rail near the stage and offered opinions on these queries to the host. The audience then voted pro or con by standing, and a computer counted them and translated the numbers into percentages. The person making the query received a week to return and hear the audience's vote plus opinions in letters from home viewers before making a decision (the show gave him or her a gift depending on the final choice). The show also offered the home viewer with the best letter on the situation, as judged by the staff, a trip to the show in New York, a car, and a tour of various cities across America.

CBS had clearance problems with this program's weekday 1:10–1:30 time slot (it followed a 10-minute news report), as it had throughout the 1950s, and when sponsorship difficulties emerged, the network canceled the series and returned the time slot back to affiliates until the 1980s.

STAR TREK
Cartoon; Color
September 8, 1973–August 30, 1975

NBC Sat. 10:30–11 a.m. (9/8/73–12/29/73)
NBC Sat. 11–11:30 a.m. (1/5/74–8/31/74)
NBC Sat. 11:30 a.m.–Noon (9/7/74–8/30/75)

Voices:

Captain James Tiberius Kirk	*William Shatner*
Mr. Spock	*Leonard Nimoy*
Dr. Leonard "Bones" McCoy	*DeForest Kelley*
Chief Engineer Montgomery Scott ("Scotty")	*James Doohan*
Lt. Sulu	*George Takei*
Lt. Uhura	*Nichelle Nichols*
Nurse Christine Chapel	*Majel Barrett*

The followers of the most successful science fiction franchise in the history of popular culture (*Star Trek*, NBC nighttime from 1966–69, in case you either were not alive or were living as a hermit at the time) spent most of the 1970s trying to resurrect the series on television. In 1972 NBC approached Roddenberry about reviving *Star Trek* as a two-hour TV movie pilot for a series, but plans fell through. The same thing happened in 1977, when Paramount planned a "fourth network" based on *Star Trek* as its head show. It finally ended up in 1979 as the first of at least six theatrical movies based on the show. All that ended up on television to reunite the

The animated version of Star Trek *gave 1970s Saturday morning viewers a chance to see new adventures, though it must be said that the characters, including (from left) Scotty, Captain Kirk, Mr. Spock, and Dr. McCoy, moved rather stiffly.*

original 1960s cast was this cartoon, using all the regulars except Lt. Pavel Chekhov (played by Walter Koenig).

As before, the show detailed the voyages of the U.S.S. Starship *Enterprise,* a large space vessel containing 430 crewmen in the 23rd century whose five-year mission, as the familiar introduction noted, was "to go where no man has gone before" and establish communication and hopefully friendly relationships with people on other planets. Captain Kirk guided the ship in its exploration, assisted by his first officer Mr. Spock, who was half human and half Vulcan. The pointy-eared Vulcans operated in a world governed by logic rather than subjective feelings, which sometimes caused conflict when Spock, Kirk, and the crew were confronted by emotion-charged issues. Doctor McCoy was the ship's physician; he was also antagonistic, usually with comic effect, toward Spock. Nurse Chapel was McCoy's assistant, Lt. Sulu was the ship's helmsman, and Lt. Uhura was its communications officer. The guiding philosophy of the *Enterprise* was to follow the Prime Directive set forth by the United Federation of Planets, the group under which the ship operated, of not interfering with the growth of other civilizations.

In an effort to be as faithful to the live-action source as possible, the cartoon brought back many of the writers and others involved in the original, including executive producer Gene Roddenberry. A few other favorite characters came back too, like the adorable but burdensome Tribbles in one episode and space con man Harry Mudd, voiced by Roger C. Carmel, in another. Some new aliens appeared as crewmen too, such as M'ress, a catlike officer.

The results, while producing adventures too complex for younger children to follow, got a great critical and popular reception, and were even approved of by *Star Trek*'s fanatic cult. As *Variety* raved, "Although this falls into the category of Saturday morning's shrunken adult programming, this science fiction remake is superior enough in animation, scoring and narrative to create an atmosphere of reality against the frenzied product all around it." The show ran for two years of original episodes, unusual for Saturday morning at the time, then went into repeats on both local stations and the Nickelodeon cable channel for the next two decades.

STATE OF THE NATION
News Discussion; B&W
February 1, 1953–May 10, 1953
CBS Sun. 4–4:30 p.m. (2/1/53–5/10/53)
Host: *Eric Sevareid (first show), Douglas Edwards*

Airing live from Washington, D.C., *State of the Nation* focused on a topical concern in America using background film and an interview with a guest, who on the debut was, appropriately, Secretary of State John Foster Dulles.

STEVE ALLEN SHOW, THE
Comedy Variety; B&W
March 26, 1951–February 22, 1952

CBS Mon.–Fri. 11:30 a.m.-12:30 p.m. (3/26/51–5/4/51)
CBS Mon.–Fri. Noon–1 p.m. (5/7/51–8/31/51)
CBS Mon.–Fri. 12:45–1:30 p.m. (9/3/51–2/22/52)
Regulars: *Steve Allen, Peggy Lee (1952)*

Steve Allen, one of the founding fathers of TV comedy and an enduring performer in the medium into the 1990s, had his first network TV series on CBS Mondays through Fridays from 7–7:30 p.m. starting Christmas Day 1950. After a three-month run the nighttime show shifted to a daily slot. The show, as would future Allen efforts, depended on its studio audience for much of the humor, as Allen ad-libbed jokes with various members in attendance between playing the piano and talking to various guests like Buster Crabbe. Peggy Lee was a regular singer on the show. Another regular was Llemuel the Llama, which was originally intended as a one-shot gag at the start of 1952 but which stayed for the rest of the run.

The main obstacle for this program in the fall of 1951 was its time period. *The Steve Allen Show* followed *Search for Tomorrow,* of all things, and suffered clearance problems because a number of stations declined to carry it (Allen had the same problem with his 1950 nighttime show). CBS wanted to have it follow *Arthur Godfrey Time* when the latter debuted in the morning in January 1952, but Procter & Gamble refused to switch sponsorship of the 1:15–1:30 p.m. portion of the show, so Steve Allen stayed put. CBS eventually canceled this series and returned the 12:45–1:30 p.m. daily slot to its affiliates until it moved *Guiding Light* to 12:45–1 p.m. in December 1952.

After this show's cancellation, Allen went into a long career of hosting talk and variety shows in prime time on the networks and syndication almost continuously for the next two decades. One of these, *The Steve Allen Show,* which was syndicated from 1968–72, was a talk show seen in daytime on many markets in 30-, 60-, or 90-minute daily form.

STEVEN SPIELBERG PRESENTS . . .—See *Animaniacs, Freakazoid!, Pinky and the Brain,* and *Tiny Toon Adventures.*

•STORYBOOK SQUARES, THE
Game; Color
January 4, 1969–August 20, 1969
NBC Sat. Noon–12:30 p.m. (1/4/69–8/20/69)
Host: *Peter Marshall*

Take *The Hollywood Squares,* have the stars dress up as fictional characters, and use children as players and you have *The Storybook Squares,* where children competed for age-appropriate prizes rather than money. Despite the short run of *The Storybook Squares,* producers of *The Hollywood Squares* revived the concept for a few weeks each year in the 1970s. Taking a break from the regular format, it used children as players, with the characters introduced on a red carpet amid much mock formality by announcer Kenny

Williams. Among the costumed celebrities over the years were William Shatner as Captain James Kirk from *Star Trek*, Bill Hayes and wife Susan Seaforth as Adam and Eve, and Paul Lynde as the Evil Queen from *Snow White and the Seven Dwarfs* (!).

•STRANGE PARADISE
Soap Opera; Color
1969–70

Syndicated daily 30 minutes beginning September 1969

Cast:

Jean Paul Desmond/Jacques Eloi Des Mondes	Colin Fox
Erica Desmond/Helena Des Mondes	Tudi Wiggins
Dr. Alison Carr	Dawn Greenhalgh
Dan Forest	Jon Granik
Raxl	Cosette Lee
Quito	Kurt Shigel
Tim Stanton	Bruce Gray
Holly Marshall	Sylvia Feigel
Elizabeth Marshall	Paisley Maxwell
Rev. Matt Dawson	Dan MacDonald
Vangie Abbott	Angela Roland

Syndicated daytime soap operas are a rarity, and efforts like *Strange Paradise* explain why. This unabashed ripoff of *Dark Shadows* copied the latter down to its picture at the mantle of an ancestor who haunted a Gothic mansion. Here it involved the 300-year-old spirit of Jacques Des Mondes, who possessed the body of his 1969 look-alike descendant Jean Paul when the latter freed him from a voodoo curse while trying to revive the corpse of his wife Erica. (A sequence on the debut intercut Jean Paul's unearthing with a diva at a local bar belting out "That Old Black Magic." Very subtle.) As luck would have it, Erica resembled Jacques's wife Helena, whom he killed, and Erica's sister, Dr. Alison Carr, also looked like Helena's sister. As Jacques attempted to seduce the investigating and nervous Dr. Carr as he had done with her look-alike in the 1600s, Erica managed to break out of her cryonic suspension in the dungeon and wreak some havoc of her own. Adding to the eerie atmosphere was Raxl the voodoo-fearing housekeeper who lived back in the 1600s, and Quito the bald, mute, hulking caretaker.

Blended uneasily into this ghastly stew were Dan Forest, Jean Paul's suspicious lawyer; Tim Stanton, a struggling artist; Holly Marshall, a beautiful blonde loved by Tim; Elizabeth Marshall, Holly's meddling mom; Reverend Dawson, who kept tabs on Holly for Elizabeth; and Vangie Abbott, who read tarot cards and offered dire predictions. All felt the effects of the occult on the Caribbean island of Maljardin, French for "garden of evil," which Jean Paul owned as part of his vast corporate holdings. The actors tried hard, but this Ottawa, Canada–based taped production went off most stations before the end of its run in 1970. Jerry Layton was executive producer and Ian Martin was the initial writer; both were veterans of *The Doctors* (q.v.),

STRAW HAT MATINEE
Variety; B&W
June 25, 1951–September 7, 1951

NBC Mon.–Fri. 4–5 p.m. (6/25/51–9/7/51)

Regulars: *Mel Martin, Rosemary Olberding, the Ernie Lee Orchestra with June Perkins*

Previously a local show in Cincinnati, *Straw Hat Matinee* consisted of four parts. It opened with a song and talk segment by the regulars. Following were a quiz hosted by Martin, where in order to win contestants had to wear a straw hat whenever any false statement was given; a country music segment with such guests as the Log Jammers and the Pine Mountain Boys; and finally an amateur performance. The series was a summer replacement for *The Kate Smith Hour.*

•STRIKE IT RICH
Game; B&W
May 7, 1951–January 3, 1958

CBS Mon.–Fri. 11:30 a.m.–Noon (5/7/51–1/3/58)

Host: *Warren Hull*

Voice of the Heart Fund/Creator/Owner/Producer: *Walt Framer*

Strike It Rich was the unfortunate model for many less successful 1950s game shows which exploited the destitute as objects for entertainment. The so-called "show with a heart" began on radio on CBS from 1947 to 1950, then went to NBC in the 1950s. In 1951 it came to television in daytime and nighttime versions, with the latter airing from July 4, 1951–January 12, 1955 on NBC. Initially the TV morning edition was taped and played on NBC radio a day after the video broadcast at 4 p.m.

To get on the program, you had to be in poor shape financially (evictees, widows, and ill or physically challenged people were favorites). Contestants received $15 (later $30) and could earn more by betting part or all of their money on each of four questions asked. The questions were simple, like "Spell purple." If they failed in their efforts, they could go to the Heart Line, where viewers phoned in donations after hearing about the players' sufferings. The original top Heart Line amount of $800 went down to $300 by 1953 because, as Walt Framer told *Newsweek*, "Go above that, and you're attracting people who are looking for money. There isn't a cause anywhere that can't use $500."

Others thought that even $300 was attracting the wrong kind of people. *Time* reported in 1954 that New York City Commissioner of Welfare Henry McCarthy ruled *Strike It Rich* needed a city license as a welfare agency due to its "public solicitation of money" and accused the program of encouraging people who needed public relief to come to Gotham. The show denied the claim, and no law agency ever charged the series with a crime, so *Strike It Rich* kept dispensing its morally dubious handouts into 1958.

Strike It Rich had host Warren Hull, right, and announcer Ralph Paul, left, introduce Nancy Walters, "The Heart Line Girl," as part of a special contest in which viewers were supposed to guess the number of sequins on Walters's dress, with the person mailing in the closest answer getting a jackpot of prizes including a new car.

In 1986 the series was revived in syndication, in title only, in a new game involving married couples. That version, hosted by Joe Garagiola, lasted less than a year.

STUMP THE STARS—See *Pantomime Quiz.*

STUMPERS
Game; Color
October 4, 1976–December 31, 1976

NBC Mon.–Fri. 11:30 a.m.–Noon (10/4/76–12/31/76)

Host: *Allen Ludden*

On *Stumpers* two celebrity-contestant pairs challenged each other by revealing three clues to a subject one at a time, with a right guess on the first clue worth 15 points, on the second clue 10 points, and on the third 5 points. A second round doubled the points, and at the end of that one the winning duo had one member try to guess 10 "stumpers" in a minute for $10,000. *Stumpers* was stumped in the ratings by *Love of Life* on CBS opposite.

SUMMER SCHOOL
Informational; B&W
June 30, 1952–August 28, 1953

CBS Mon/Wed/Fri 3:30–4 p.m. (6/30/52–8/29/52)
CBS Mon.–Fri. 4–4:30 p.m. (6/29/53–8/28/53)

Who said children waste their time watching TV shows? Why, for the summers of 1952 and 1953, kids had the fun opportunity to see educators lecture on basic subjects to 40–50 students between the ages of 9 and 12 in the Lower Merion School District in Philadelphia, plus presumably many times that amount in homes across America. There is no record of what, if any, sort of credit home viewers got from watching the show. However, some guest speakers were impressive, like Willy Ley, adviser to the U.S. government in rocket research, who addressed "Man's Conquests" in 1953.

SUMMER SEMESTER—See *Sunrise Semester.*

SUMMER SPORTS SPECTACULAR—See *CBS Sports Spectacular.*

SUNDAY
News/Information; B&W and Color
October 27, 1963–June 27, 1965

NBC Sun. 4–5 p.m. (10/27/63–6/27/65)

Regulars: *Frank Blair, Bob Abernethy (news for kids), Cleveland Amory (culture), Joe Garagiola (sports), Roy Neal (science), Edwin Newman (theater criticism), Aline Saarinen (art and architecture), Ray Scherer (news), Richard Schickel (books), William Zinsser (film and Broadway)*

This highbrow New York–based culture series, an offshoot of *The Today Show,* used some of that show's regulars (Amory and Garagiola) and had *The Today Show*'s newsman Frank Blair as its host. The debut used film and live interviews to profile the movie *Tom Jones,* discuss architect Frank Lloyd Wright's house in Bear Run, Pennsylvania, analyze the appeal of Sen. Barry Goldwater, and interview Israeli general Yigael Yadin on his book *Battles in the Bible.* A few shows, such as the one aired on the first anniversary of John F. Kennedy's assassination, dealt with only one topic. Besides the listed regulars, other frequent contributors to the series were Martin Bookspan on music and Frederic Ramsey Jr.

SUNDAY AT THE ZOO
Informational; B&W
June 11, 1950–December 23, 1950

ABC Sun. 4:30–5 p.m. (6/11/50–9/17/50)
ABC Sat. 11–11:30 a.m. (10/7/50–12/23/50)

Host: *Durward Kirby*

Regular: *William Bridges*

The Bronx Zoo and its menagerie of animals formed the background for this show. William Bridges, one of the zoo's curators, guided Durward Kirby and his TV audience through various exhibits like the Gorilla House on the opener, where Jimmy the chimp ate an ice cream pop and Andy the orangutan played with a swing and an empty beer can.

After leaving Sunday afternoons, the series returned on Saturday mornings on WJZ New York September 23, 1950 and came back on ABC two weeks later under the title *Saturday at the Zoo.* Though it lasted only three months there, it did win a postcancellation Peabody Award for best children's show (a joint award, along with *Zoo Parade*).

•SUNDAY MORNING

News; Color

January 28, 1979–

CBS Sun. 9–10:30 a.m. (1/28/79–)

Host: *Charles Kuralt (1/28/79–4/3/94), Charles Osgood (4/10/94–)*

Regulars Included: *Ray Gandolf (sports; 1979–82), Richard Threlkeld (cover story reporter; 1979–81 at least), Jeff Greenfield (media critic; 1979–82 at least), Dr. Billy Taylor (jazz pianist/composer; 1982–), Ron Powers (media critic; 1983–88), Bill Geist (comic reports; 1987–), John Leonard (media critic; 1988–).*

Sunday Morning was the TV equivalent of a Sunday morning newspaper, with various correspondents contributing stories in different areas such as the fine arts, current events, cultural activities, and the like. CBS News President Richard Salant began development of the show in 1978, and his successor William Leonard took over leadership. It had a fairly low clearance with affiliates at first because most of them did not carry the shows it replaced—*Camera Three, Light Unto My Path,* and *Look Up and Live*—but soon established itself as a favorite for those seeking a laid-back approach to news and information, as befitted its hosts Charles Kuralt and successor Charles Osgood.

The set had transparent Plexiglas panels listing the titles of the day's stories, with Kuralt sitting at an easel with his notes. Kuralt typically gave a brief update of the news, sports, and weather plus a "Milestone" of the week involving a review of some major recent story. He then introduced the day's stories, with some correspondents joining him on the set, such as bearded John Leonard, the TV reviewer for *New York* magazine who reviewed the latest offerings on the tube. After a perusal of the week's letters and a few more stories, each show ended with a lovely shot of some natural habitat and the creatures living there.

Charles Kuralt served as host of Sunday Morning *for more than a decade.*

Though *Sunday Morning* covered the gamut of the human experience, it seemed most at home with high culture. A special highlight was the April 20, 1986, show, where classical pianist Vladimir Horowitz gave his first performance in Russia since leaving the country in 1925. With this and other high-quality attractions maintaining a standard that had been set some 15 years earlier, the show remained a crown jewel in the CBS News division.

SUNDAY NEWS—See *CBS Sunday News.*

SUNDAY SPORTS SPECTACULAR—See *CBS Sports Spectacular.*

SUNDAY TODAY—See *Today.*

•SUNRISE SEMESTER
Public Affairs; B&W and Color
September 23, 1963–October 1, 1982

CBS Mon.–Fri. Various half hour between 5:30 and 7:30 a.m. (9/23/63–10/1/82)

Sunrise Semester was a long-running but fairly sparsely viewed series offering college credits to participants at home. Begun on WCBS on September 17, 1957 on Saturdays from 3:30–4 p.m., followed by a daily course starting September 23, 1957 from 6:30–7 a.m., it utilized professors from New York University to lead each semester, which consisted of two courses alternating daily each week. The first offering, "Comparative Literature 10," on modern fiction, led by Dr. Floyd Zulli Jr. from NYU's Department of Romance Languages, was an immediate hit, generating nearly 10,000 written requests about information on the course. The show's title became *Summer Semester* during that season each year, and unlike the usual setup, it offered no college credit. By 1958 it was on videotape.

Six years after its local start the show went on CBS, although the number of affiliates carrying it was low (usually less than 100 stations). Courses were $75 each, plus $5 for a study guide, for those who wanted college credits. Veteran announcer Red Barber even took a course once. *Sunrise Semester* lasted until stations began to crave even earlier morning news in the 1980s, at which point it was shoved off the air.

•SUPER CIRCUS
Variety; B&W
January 16, 1949–June 3, 1956

ABC Sun. 5–6 p.m. (1/16/49–6/3/56)

Regulars: Claude Kirchner (1949–55), Mary Hartline (1949–55), Cliff Soubier (as Cliffy; 1949–55), Bardy Patton (as Scampy; 1949–53), Sandy Dobritch (as Scampy; 1953–55), Nick Francis (as Nicky; 5/14/50–12/18/55), the Bruce Chase Orchestra (1949–55), Jerry Colonna (1955–56), Sandy Wirth (1955–56), Jerry Bergen (1955–56), the Baron Twins (1955–56), the Ralph Herman Orchestra (1955–56)

Super Circus was an ABC radio show in the 1940s before becoming a local weekly telecast in Chicago in 1948. By late 1948 the ABC Midwest TV network was airing the show Sundays from 4:30–5:30 p.m. Central Time. It became a network show at the start of 1949 and stayed on the ABC lineup thanks to its ability to accommodate its advertisers. For example, when Canada Dry came aboard as a sponsor on April 1949, the show included many plugs for it, including a contest where two kids tried to write as many words as possible with chalk on a blackboard on which the sponsor's name appeared, and displayed placards and such with the name of the sponsor on them. And when Derby Foods joined the show a month later, a barker who appeared on the main show also hawked peanut butter in commercials.

As for entertainment, six-foot-five Claude Kirchner blew his whistle often and presided over the ring where various artists appeared for children's entertainment. Acts included acrobats, dogs jumping through hoops, monkeys riding on horses, etc. Featured regulars were baton twirler Mary Hartline; Scampy, a child clown first played by the son of show producer Phil Patton until he outgrew the role; and adult clowns Cliffy and Nicky. Also seen in the 1950s was Jinx the Super Chimp. A measure of the show's popularity was a guest shot by famed clown Emmett Kelly in 1949.

On December 25, 1955, *Super Circus* relocated to New York City, and offered sketches by comedian and new ringmaster Jerry Colonna, baton twirling from 19-year-old Sandy Wirth (Miss Florida 1955), and comedy routines featuring Jerry Bergen dressed as an old-fashioned cop and clown group the Baron Twins. Ostensibly the move was made to provide better camera angles and a greater variety of acts for the circus, but despite the change,

Super Circus celebrated its third anniversary with its regulars (standing from left, Cliffy, Nicky, Mary Hartline, Scampy, and Claude Kirchner) joined by guest act Willie Necker (kneeling at left) and his dalmatians.

it was announced in 1956 that the series would locate to Miami that fall, supposedly to do more outdoor productions, if a sponsor could be found. No sponsor was forthcoming, so the top-rated *Super Circus* abruptly left the air despite having consistently beaten its CBS and NBC competition over seven years.

SUPER DAVE
Cartoon; Color
September 12, 1992–August 28, 1993

Fox Sat. 11–11:30 a.m. (9/12/92–11/7/92)
Fox Sat. 11:30 a.m.–Noon (11/14/92–8/28/93)

Voices:

"Super Dave" Osborne	Bob Einstein
Fuji	Art Irizawa

Fearless, gravel-voiced "Super Dave" Osborne, billed as "Daredevil for Hire," was the comic equivalent of Evel Knievel, willing to do a series of stunts that put his body in grave danger without blinking an eye, even though the stunts constantly went awry and mangled him. Nonetheless, he continued to ply his trade while serving as a U.S. secret agent teamed with pal Fuji, who wore large eyeglasses and a baseball cap. His archenemy was Slash Hazard. Slash, who had three jagged teeth and a buzz haircut, had been chased by Dave into a car compactor after Slash robbed a bank, and emerged from the compactor half-man, half-vehicle. A segment with Bob Einstein ended each show, where he played Super Dave doing a bungled live-action stunt (for example, Einstein got inside a 16-foot yo-yo which subsequently ran amok and rolled down a cliff). Einstein had played the character over nearly a quarter century on various variety shows on which he was a writer, producer, or guest performer, including *Redd Foxx* in 1977 and the Showtime cable channel comedy *Bizarre* from 1980–85.

•SUPER FRIENDS
Cartoon; Color
September 8, 1973–September 6, 1986

ABC Sat. 9–10 a.m. (9/8/73–8/31/74)
ABC Sat. 11 a.m.–Noon (9/7/74–8/30/75)
ABC Sat. 10–11 a.m. (2/21/76–9/4/76)
ABC Sat. 11:30 a.m.–Noon (12/4/76–9/3/77)
ABC Sat. 8–9 a.m. (9/10/77–7/1/78)
ABC Sat. 8:30–9:30 a.m. (7/8/78–9/2/78)
ABC Sat. 9–10 a.m. (9/9/78–10/28/78)
ABC Sat. 9:30–11 a.m. (11/4/78–5/26/79)
ABC Sat. 10–11:30 a.m. (6/2/79–9/15/79)
ABC Sat. 8–9 a.m (9/22/79–9/5/81)
ABC Sat. 8–8:30 a.m. (9/12/81–9/3/83)
ABC Sat. 8:30–9 a.m. (9/8/84–11/24/84)
ABC Sat. 8–9 a.m. (two shows; 12/1/84–8/31/85)
ABC Sat. 10–10:30 a.m. (9/7/85–11/2/85)
ABC Sat. 10:30–11 a.m. (11/9/85–2/22/86)
ABC Sat. 11:30 a.m.–Noon (3/1/86–9/6/86)

Voices:

Superman	*Danny Dark*
Batman (1973–83)	*Olan Soule*
Batman (1984–86)	*Adam West*
Robin	*Casey Kasem*
Wonder Woman (1973–83)	*Shannon Farnon*
Wonder Woman (1984–86)	*B. J. Ward*
Aquaman (1973–78)	*Norman Alden*
Aquaman (1978–83)	*Bill Callaway*
Marvin (1973–77)	*Frank Welker*
Wendy (1973–77)	*Sherry Alberoni*
Marvel the Wonder Dog (1973–77)	*Frank Welker*
Narrator (1973–77)	*Ted Knight*
Narrator (1977–83)	*Bill Woodson*
Zan (1977–83)	*Mike Bell*
Jayna (1977–83)	*Liberty Williams*
Black Vulcan (1978–83)	*Buster Jones*
Green Lantern/Apache Chief (1978–83)	*Mike Rye*
Firestorm (1984–86)	*Mark Taylor*
Cyborg (1984–86)	*Ernie Hudson*

Super Friends took three superheroes seen previously in their own cartoons—Superman, Batman, Aquaman—and teamed them with Wonder Woman to form the Justice League of America, the same name used by the DC Comics company on whose book series this cartoon was based. Joining them in defending the universe were young superhero wanna-bes Marvin, Wendy, and Wonder Dog, who formed the Junior Justice League.

After the show aired in repeats from 1976–77, new episodes emerged in the fall of 1977 under the title *The All-New Super Friends Hour.* What was all new were Zan and Jayna, a more mature and muscular duo than Marvin and Wendy, clad in purple tights and known as the Wonder Twins. In times when their own superpowers were needed, Zan and Jayna touched each other and shouted, "Wonder Twin powers, activate!" to assume any shape or form they thought would assist their pals. Other superheroes joined the Justice League occasionally in their adventures.

The new format remained consistent despite several changes in titles over the years—*Challenge of the Super Friends* from 1978–79, *The World's Greatest Super Friends* from 1979–80, and *The Super Friends Hour* from 1980–83. The last version consisted solely of reruns.

After a year's layoff, a new edition emerged in 1984 titled *Super Friends: The Legendary Super Powers Show* (retitled *Super Powers Team: Galactic Guardians* in the fall of 1985). Now Cyborg, a half-human, half-robot entity, and Firestorm, an intelligent teenager type, joined Superman, Batman and Robin, and Wonder Woman in fighting more out-of-this-world villainy. Other members of the old troupe disappeared, which may be why this edition lasted but two years.

•SUPER GLOBETROTTERS, THE

Cartoon; Color
September 22, 1979–May 3, 1980
NBC Sat. 10–10:30 a.m. (9/22/79–12/1/79)
NBC Sat. 8–8:30 a.m. (4/12/80–5/3/80)

Voices:

Nate Branch/Fluid Man	Scatman Crothers
Curly Neal/Sphere Man	Stu Gilliam
Twiggy Sanders/Spaghetti Man	Buster Jones
Geese Ausbie/Multi Man	John Williams
Sweet Lou Dunbar/Gizmo Man	Adam Wade
Crime Globe	Frank Welker
Narrator	Michael Rye

The Super Globetrotters was a lame revival of the basketball group that had been seen to better advantage in animated and live-action shows earlier in the 1970s (see *The Harlem Globetrotters* cartoon and *The Harlem Globetrotters Popcorn Machine*). Here a quintet of familiar Globetrotters could transform into crime fighters with fantastic powers thanks to an amulet found by Nate. Bald Curly, for example, became Sphere Man, an oversized basketball, while Nate, Twiggy, and Geese had powers similar to that of Fluid Man, Coil Man, and Multi Man, respectively, of *Frankenstein Jr. and the Impossibles* (q.v.). As for Sweet Lou Dunbar, when he became Gizmo Man, he had perhaps the biggest Afro ever seen on network television. They could fly and liked to say in unison while battling as superheroes, "Super Globetrotters, away!" Guiding them on whom to fight and what course of action to take was the megaphone-like Crime Globe. Each show typically ended with a wild basketball game. As for the series, it dribbled off the NBC schedule within three months and reappeared just briefly a few months later in repeats before ending.

SUPER MARIO BROS. SUPER SHOW!, THE—
See *Captain N and the Adventures of Super Mario Bros.*

SUPER PASSWORD—See *Password.*

SUPER POWERS TEAM: GALACTIC GUARDIANS—
See *Super Friends.*

SUPER PRESIDENT AND SPY SHADOW

Cartoon; Color
September 16, 1967–December 28, 1968
NBC Sat. 9:30–10 a.m. (9/16/67–9/14/68)
NBC Sat. 12:30–1 p.m. (9/21/68–12/28/68)

Voices:

(Super) President James Norcross	Paul Frees
Richard Vance	Daws Butler

Also: *Ted Cassidy, June Foray, Shepard Menken, Don Menken, Don Messick, Lorrie Scott, Mark Skor*

U.S. President James Norcross, thanks to a cosmic storm, could "change his molecular structure so that his body becomes any solid or gaseous substance," according to an NBC press release. He also could fly, use incredible muscular strength—just name a typical superhero trait and he had it. The chief executive somehow found time away from the White House to use his abilities to stop a variety of baddies. The show's other title character, Spy Shadow, was Detective Richard Vance, who found he had a shadow which moved and acted on its own. That was a fanciful notion, to be sure, but a lot more plausible than a Commander in Chief busting heads on the side.

SUPER SIX, THE

Cartoon; Color
September 10, 1966–September 6, 1969
NBC Sat. 9–9:30 a.m. (9/10/66–9/6/69)

Voices:

Magnet Man/Matzoriley Brother	Daws Butler
Captain Zammo/Matzoriley Brother	Paul Frees
Elevator Man	Paul Stewart
Super Scuba	Arte Johnson
Granite Man	Lynn Johnson
Super Bwoing	Charles Smith

The Super Six actually consisted of a rather bizarre quintet of superheroes. Super Service, Inc. provided for lease the superheroes Elevator Man, Granite Man, Magnet Man, Super Scuba, and Captain Zammo, who each appeared in their own adventures where their unique, if that's the word, powers came into play. In other segments, Super Bwoing was an inept hero who played guitar, and the Brothers Matzoriley were a pair of Irish-Jewish brothers involved in comic escapades set in a variety of places.

SUPER WITCH—See *Sabrina the Teen-age Witch.*

SUPERBOY—See *Superman.*

•SUPERIOR COURT

Anthology; Color
1986–1990
Syndicated 30 minutes daily beginning September 1986
Regular: *Raymond St. Jacques as the judge (1988–90)*

Superior Court presented dramatizations of various fictitious criminal and civil cases, all of them using actors as attorneys, judges, and litigants. Each show presented one case with a verdict, and the overall writing, directing, and acting were definite improvements over the herky-jerky inspiration for this show, *Divorce Court* (q.v.).

SUPERMAN

Cartoon; Color
September 10, 1966–September 9, 1989

CBS Sat. 11–11:30 a.m. (9/10/66–9/2/67)
CBS Sat. 11:30–12:30 a.m. (9/9/67–9/7/68)
CBS Sat. 10:30–11 a.m. (9/14/68–9/6/69)
CBS Sat. 1–1:30 p.m. (9/13/69–9/5/70)
CBS Sat. 8:30–9 a.m. (9/17/88–9/9/89)

Voices (1966–69):

Superman/Clark Kent	Bud Collyer
Lois Lane	Joan Alexander
Jimmy Olsen	Jack Grimes
Perry White/Superboy Narrator	Ted Knight
Superboy	Bob Hastings
Lana Lang	Janet Waldo
Superman Narrator	Jackson Beck

Voices (1988–89):

Superman/Clark Kent	Beau Weaver
Lois Lane	Ginny McSwain
Jimmy Olsen	Mark Taylor
Perry White	Stanley Ralph Ross

One of TV's anomalies is that the live-action versions of comic book icon Superman have done much better than the animated ones. Indeed, when on mentions a TV Superman, most people think only of George Reeves, who starred in the syndicated *Adventures of Superman* produced from 1951–57, or Dean Cain, who has starred in *Lois and Clark: The New Adventures of Superman* on ABC nighttime since September 12, 1993. Ironically, Superman had a longer run on Saturday mornings as one of the *Super Friends* in the 1970s than he did as headliner of his own show.

Believe it or not, there was a time when this all-American hero did not exist. Superman sprung from the minds of Jerry Siegel and Joe Shuster, who unveiled him in 1938. His background and exploits have been so detailed that they are the source of several books, so in the interest of space and avoiding repetition, let's just condense the story and say that Superman was an alien baby from the dying planet Krypton sent to Earth in a special spaceship by his elders. When the ship landed in the U.S. community of Smallville, the Kents, an elderly couple who ran a farm, adopted him and kept mum about his powers to fly, lift heavy objects, go faster than a speeding locomotive, and generally outdo every human around him. When he finally grew up, Superman, called Clark Kent by his family, went to the big town of Metropolis to work at the *Daily Planet* newspaper with diligent reporter Lois Lane and eager cub newshound Jimmy Olsen. Clark adopted a shy, almost bumbling manner around Lois, while she in turn had the hots for his alter ego Superman, seen sporting blue tights, a red cape, and a red "S" on his chest as he fought major criminals. Though he had close calls and disguised himself basically only by wearing glasses as Kent, nobody seemed to notice that Clark and Superman were the same person.

Superman gained popularity quickly, appearing in everything from serialized theatrical cartoons in the 1940s to the Broadway musical *It's a Bird, It's a Plane, It's Superman!* in 1966 shortly before the TV cartoon hit the air. The first animated version was a virtual recreation of the 1940–51 network radio show. Not only were Bud Collyer, Joan Alexander, Jack Grimes, and Jackson Beck reprising their roles, they also recorded them at the same studios in New York. The other major element in the 1960s shows consisted of the weekly adventures of Superboy growing up in Smallville with his dog Krypto and girlfriend Lana Lang.

The official title in its first season was *The New Adventures of Superman*. In 1967–68 it added another superhero and became *The Superman/Aquaman Hour* (see *Aquaman* for details of the latter). In its last season the Metropolis man lost top billing to another do-gooder as the series was titled *The Batman/Superman Hour* (see *Batman*). Then came cancellation and no action on television except for the *Super Friends* gig.

On February 29, 1988, CBS aired an hour-long prime-time tongue-in-cheek special hosted by Dana Carvey called "Superman's 50th Anniversary: A Celebration of the Man of Steel." That fall, the same network unveiled the latest version of the Metropolis man, but this one was done as straight as he had been in the 1960s. This, however, was the biggest TV failure of the lot, and it lasted only one year, probably suffering from the same complaints many were voicing about Superman the comic book character at the time—he was too invincible for his own good. That concern remained as the WB network unveiled another animated Superman in the fall of 1996 featuring Tim Daly as the lead voice and Dana Delaney as Lois Lane.

SUPERMARKET SWEEP
Game; B&W
December 20, 1965–July 14, 1967
ABC Mon.–Fri. 11–11:30 a.m. (12/20/65–7/14/67)
Host: *Bill Malone*

No other game show celebrated greed so shamelessly as *Supermarket Sweep*. Each day a trio of players answered some perfunctory questions about prices of various merchandise in that week's host supermarket to win additional time. Then came time for the "supermarket sweep," wherein each contestant received a grocery cart and grabbed as many meats, canned goods, boxes, and other items off grocery shelves (limit five of each kind per customer, please!) within a limited period of time, then had their goods tallied to determined who had the highest total. The victor in this portion got two minutes to "sweep" again for more groceries. Contestants could return to compete, and some did quite well, with a Mrs. Harold Rathson of New Jersey earning a trip to the Bahamas by winning 10 days in a row.

Despite the inherent tackiness of the project, and the fact that one contestant on the show's pilot had a heart attack while "sweeping," ABC backed this show for a year-

and-a-half run. By April 24, 1967 the show was based in Miami, and no longer toured various supermarkets, but shortly thereafter *Supermarket Sweep* was swept under the rug, being replaced by the similar *Honeymoon Race* (q.v.).

How did David Susskind, the producer of many great TV dramas of the 1950s and 1960s, including the 1966 Emmy-winning production of *Death of a Salesman*, defend being executive producer of this tripe? "We enjoy the profits from *Supermarket Sweep* because it gives us the money for other projects," he told *TV Guide*. But he later added that in spite of his title, "I have absolutely nothing to do with it."

Incredibly, the series spawned a successful revival on the Lifetime cable channel that began on February 5, 1990 and was still on air at press time. Host David Ruprecht presided over the festivities in what was a Los Angeles TV studio designed to look like a supermarket.

•SUPERSTARS, THE
Sports; Color
January 27, 1974–February 20, 1983

ABC Sun. 2–3:15 p.m. (1/27/74–3/23/75; January–March each year only)
ABC Sun. 2–3:30 p.m. (1/11/76–3/26/78; January–March each year only)
ABC Sun. 2–3:15 p.m. (1/14/79–3/29/81; January–March each year only)
ABC Sun. 2:30–3:30 p.m. (1/24/82–3/28/82)
ABC Sun. 2–3:30 p.m. (2/6/83–2/20/83)

Host: *Jim McKay (1974), Keith Jackson (1975–83)*

Begun as a special in 1973, *The Superstars* returned as a series in 1974 with 48 professional athletes competing in athletic contests in four divisions, with the top three athletes in each heat going onto the final competition. Each division winner received $10,000 plus $100 per point, with a point being earned by finishing among the top five in any individual contest. Bob Seagren, a two-time Olympic-winning pole vaulter, won over nine other athletes in the special and returned to defend his crown in 1974 against such athletes as John Havlicek, Reggie Jackson, Jean-Claude Killy, Jim Palmer, Pete Rose, and O. J. Simpson.

The competition broadened in 1975 to include women athletes. By 1977, the males were competing for more than $250,000 and the women for $122,000, and "Superteams" (members of various sports groups) were playing for $330,000. The abbreviated final season in 1983 had players vie for $15,000 for first place, $10,000 for second, and $5,000 for third. The contests ranged from weight lifting to running to hitting baseballs, with an athlete having to sit out any event judged to be in his or her specialty.

The idea for *The Superstars* came from one Dick Button, the Olympic ice skating champion from the middle of the century. He owned part of the show, which beat *NBA Basketball* on CBS and *NHL Game of the Week* on NBC in the ratings in its first few years. It ran as a winter series for nearly a decade, then ran for at least another 10 years as a special event on *ABC's Wide World of Sports*.

SURVIVAL
Informational; B&W
July 8, 1951–August 19, 1951

NBC Sun. 4–4:30 p.m. (7/8/51–8/19/51)

Narrator: *Richard Harkness*

Produced by the TV division of the Federal Civil Defense Administration, *Survival* used films, graphs, and live in-studio guests to show how the public could best handle an atomic attack. Although NBC had rights to the series' 10 kinescopes (not all of which aired), they were available for any TV station to use at the time.

SUSAN'S SHOW
Children's; B&W
May 4, 1957–January 18, 1958

CBS Sat. 11–11:30 a.m. (5/4/57–1/18/58)

Regulars: *Susan Heinkel, John Coughlin (as Caesar P. Penguin)*

Twelve-year-old Susan Heinkel was a TV veteran by the time her TV show debuted on CBS. She first appeared on the tube in her native St. Louis at age 3 in 1948. On September 10, 1956, she began hosting *Susie's Show* weekdays in Chicago at 4 p.m. Central Time, which fared so well it caught the attention of CBS for a network version that debuted eight months later. The series offered fantasy excursions on which Susan went to the land of Wonderville and interacted with Pegasus the talking table, her terrier Rusty, a flying magic stool, and a Cartoon-a-Machine which ran Terrytoon cartoons previously seen in movie theaters. Music came from an all-animal orchestra playing in Foolish Forest, including Wolfgang the bear on violin, Gregory the bunny on flute, and Caesar P. Penguin as conductor. Critics loved it, but kids preferred *Fury* on NBC, and so the series ended within a year.

•SWAMP THING
Cartoon; Color
April 20, 1991–August 3, 1991

Fox Sat. 10:30–11 a.m. (4/20/91–5/18/91)
Fox Sat. 10:30–11 a.m. (7/6/91–8/3/91)

Voices:

Swamp Thing (Swampy)	*Len Carlson*
Tomahawk	*Harvey Atkin*
Bayou Jack	*Phil Aiken*
Dr. Anton Arcane	*Don Francks*
Dr. Deemo	*Errol Slue*
Skin Man	*Gordon Masten*
Weed Killer	*Joe Matheson*

Abby Arcane	Pauline Gillis
J. T.	Richard Yearwood
Delbert	Jonathon Potts

Swamp Thing was an adaptation of the DC comic book and 1982 movie of the same name. "Swampy" was scientist Alec Holland who, due to a lab accident caused by envious, vampirelike Dr. Arcane and Arcane's henchmen Skin Man and Weed Killer, became a walking 7-foot lump of moss living in the Louisiana bayou. In his Tree Lab, Swampy tried to reverse his condition, which allowed him to grow roughly 10 times his size, while stopping Arcane's machinations. Helping him were the muscular duo of Tomahawk and Bayou Jack, Arcane's stepdaughter Abby, and teenagers J. T. and Delbert, the latter of which provided comic relief from the action-packed adventures. The cartoon's theme song "Swamp Thing" was based on the Troggs' 1960s hit "Wild Thing," but, oddly, writer Chip Taylor got no on-screen credit.

SWIFT HOME SERVICE CLUB, THE
Informational; B&W
October 10, 1947–March 26, 1948
NBC Fri 1–1:30 p.m. (10/10/47–3/26/48)

Regulars: *Tex Falkenberg, Jinx Falkenberg, Sandra Gahle, Martha Logan*

In 1947 daytime television was at a crossroads. Demand by salesmen for programming that would stimulate afternoon sales was growing, which was good, but few had the ambition to put on anything for entertainment. Finally the Swift food company took the initiative and planned a half-hour entertainment piece from New York on WNBT, which would air in the early afternoon so as not to interfere with WNBT's coverage of New York Giants baseball games, which started at 2:30 p.m. Snagging the popular radio husband-and-wife team of Tex and Jinx was a coup for the series, and it received a guaranteed 39-week contract with its first show, which aired May 16, 1947.

The debut had three segments, one with Sandra Gahle giving interior decorating tips, another with Martha Logan acting as Swift's home economist, and the last an audience participation feature with the day's guest, hat designer Walter Florell. In his segment, Florell judged three women's knowledge of hats, and the winner took home one of his creations. The program received positive reviews and continued locally that summer as the only daytime TV series in New York. On September 26 it added a feature on lost and found dogs in New York, but the following month WNBW in Washington, D.C., began carrying the show, providing it with a bare-bones network and allowing the programmers to set their sights beyond local issues.

On November 7, 1947, the lineup increased again when WPTZ Philadelphia added the show to its schedule, and in the process made Swift TV's first full-network sponsor. The show made more headlines three weeks later when film of the British royal wedding of Queen Elizabeth and Prince Philip aired on the show just 29 hours after the ceremony had taken place. The footage was taken off the face of a receiving tube in the BBC studios in London with soundtrack included, and the film was in the hands of NBC studios within 90 minutes after it arrived in La Guardia Airport—just in time to use as part of the show.

After a year of production, Swift moved the show to nighttime. When it transferred, Tex and Jinx ended their involvement because Jinx was pregnant. However, the duo did later return to daytime (see *Close-Up*). The nighttime *Swift Show* ran from April 1, 1948–August 4, 1949 on NBC Thursdays at 8:30 p.m. with Lanny Ross as host.

Despite Swift's change in time slot, it felt its initial foray into daytime programming was a success. The show managed to stay within its $1 million budget and was the first TV series to integrate film into a live show smoothly. Swift would in fact remain a sponsor on television for the next 50 years.

SWINGING COUNTRY
Musical Variety; Color
July 4, 1966–December 30, 1966
NBC Mon.–Fri. 12:30–12:55 p.m. (7/4/66–12/30/66)

Regulars: *Rusty Draper, Molly Bee, Roy Clark (July–September), Johnny Tillotson (September–December), the Swinging Countrymen, the Hometown Singers*

A rare attempt by a network to program country music daily, *Swinging Country* was taped in Hollywood under the direction of Dick Clark Productions. Male vocalist Rusty Draper hosted the hoedown while fellow country stars singer Molly Bee and fiddler Roy Clark, among others, lent musical support. In the fall singer Johnny Tillotson replaced Clark.

•SYLVESTER AND TWEETY
Cartoon; Color
September 11, 1976–September 3, 1977
CBS Sat. 8–8:30 a.m. (9/11/76–9/3/77)

Voices: *Mel Blanc, June Foray*

Following 15 years as a supporting act on *The Bugs Bunny Show,* slobbering cat Sylvester and the yellow Tweety bird got their own show for a season, which initially preceded their parent series. The recurring conflict between the two was simple: Sylvester wanted to eat the bird, and Tweety wanted to avoid the "bad old puddytat." Often aiding Tweety was the only character without a speech impediment, kindly Granny, who nevertheless could pack a mean punch when she found Sylvester was trying to con her or consume Tweety. In a few other Warner Brothers cartoons included in the package, Sylvester found himself embroiled with an escaped kangaroo he thought was an oversized mouse, or with an idiotic cat who also wanted to eat Tweety up, or with his look-alike diminutive son, who was embarrassed by his father's inability to catch food.

TV GENERAL STORE
Auction; B&W
June 14, 1953–July 12, 1953

ABC Sun. 11 a.m.–Noon (6/14/53–7/12/53)

Hosts: *Dave Clark, Judy Clark*

In this predecessor of infomercials, Dave Clark and his wife Judy offered home viewers the chance to write in or wire their requests to buy items like razor blades, steam irons, electric percolators, and housecoats. A quartet of guests checked out the merchandise on the premiere, but apparently their implied quality assurance did not entice viewers, as ABC canned the series after only six shows.

TV RECITAL HALL—See *Recital Hall*.

TV TOTS TIME
Children's; B&W
January 22, 1951–March 2, 1952

ABC Mon.–Fri. 5:15–5:30 p.m. (1/22/51–7/11/51)
ABC Sun. 4:45–5 p.m. (12/30/51–3/2/52)

TV Tots Time was first seen locally on WJZ (ABC, New York) from February 4–April 22, 1950, where it used 10 European-made puppet films as part of its presentations. When it went network briefly a few times in later months, some theatrically released cartoons were included in the mix.

TWIB 20—See *This Week in Baseball*.

TAKE A GIANT STEP
Children's; Color
September 11, 1971–September 1, 1973

NBC Sat. 10:30–11:30 a.m. (9/11/71–12/25/71)
NBC Sat. 11 a.m.–Noon (1/8/72–8/26/72)
NBC Sat. 12:30–1 p.m. (9/9/72–9/1/73)

This "do-good" entry for children was nicknamed by wags *Heinemann Street* because it was viewed as NBC Vice President of Children's Programming George Heinemann's attempt to establish the equivalent of the esteemed public TV series *Sesame Street* on his network. Each week three different teenagers hosted live from NBC studios in New York an examination of a particular theme, such as life cycles, money, beauty, etc., which included films and other explanatory materials. Each one of the hosts had to research his or her topic at least two times a week for six weeks for the show (the research was supervised), and *Scholastic Magazine* offered assistance in the making of the episodes.

Despite heavy promotions and the best of intentions, *Take a Giant Step* was a ratings disaster, at one point averaging a measly 9 share of the available audience. In September 1972

the show lost half an hour and became *Talking with a Giant*. On this new version, teenagers met with celebrity guests to talk about the latter's life experiences, but this show wasn't a success either, and it went off after a year.

TAKE ANOTHER LOOK
Sports; B&W
September 30, 1951–November 25, 1951

CBS Sun. 3–4 p.m. (9/30/51–10/7/51)
CBS Sun. 12:30–1:30 p.m. (10/14/51–11/25/51)

Hosts/Narrators: *Red Barber, Dr. Mal Stevens*

Viewers had the chance to "take another look" at films of the top NCAA game on the East Coast played the day before the Sunday broadcast. This series aired as a special on CBS on two Sundays a year before its regular scheduling in 1951, when Dr. Stevens also served as commentator for NCAA football games on CBS.

TAKE KERR—See *Galloping Gourmet, The*.

•TAKE MY ADVICE
Talk; Color
January 5, 1976–June 11, 1976

NBC Mon.–Fri. 12:30–12:55 p.m. (1/5/76–6/11/76)

Host: *Kelly Lange*

Ever wanted the opinions of celebrity couples like the Sammy Davis Jrs. or the Carroll O'Connors? *Take My Advice* gave viewers that option in its debut, with later shows continuing the pattern of having stars and their spouses offering often humorous help to viewers who submitted questions for them to answer. The show's most dubious device was airing what appeared to be a live studio audience pushing buttons to record their vote on an issue, when in actuality they were recreating an earlier audience's vote. Swamped in the ratings by *All My Children* on ABC and *Search for Tomorrow* on CBS, this show was replaced by *The Gong Show*.

TAKE TWO
Game; B&W
May 5, 1963–August 11, 1963

ABC Sun. 4:30–5 p.m. (5/5/63–8/11/63)

Host: *Don McNeill*

A rare Sunday afternoon game show, *Take Two* was a Chicago-based entry where two duos of civilians played to be the first to pair correctly two of four displayed pictures connected in some way. For example, contestants who received images of Groucho Marx, Bertrand Russell, a puppy, and Jimmy Durante had to say Marx and Durante belonged together because they were comedians. The debut had a special competition between two teams of actors, Julie Newmar and Joel Grey versus Julie Wilson and her husband.

On June 23, 1963, a special show had Don McNeill playing the game while Peter Donald and Fran Allison co-emceed. McNeill also received a tribute on the 30th anniversary of his *Breakfast Club* radio show, which had failed as a TV program in 1954. The radio show lasted five more years; *Take Two* was gone less than two months later.

•TALES FROM THE CRYPTKEEPER
Cartoon; Color
September 18, 1993–July 15, 1995

ABC Sat. 10–10:30 a.m. (9/18/93–9/3/94)
ABC Sat. 10:30–11 a.m. (9/10/94–12/3/94)
ABC Sat. 9–9:30 a.m. (12/10/94–7/15/95)

Voice:

The Cryptkeeper	*John Kassir*

Times do change. In the 1950s EC Comics had to end production of its successful but controversial line of horror books due to questionable research claiming they caused juvenile delinquency. Among these titles was one called *Tales from the Crypt*. Forty years later, following cable channel HBO's success with a nighttime live-action anthology series of the same name which began in 1989, ABC deemed it okay to present a Saturday morning cartoon version, where the emphasis on horror was downplayed but not eliminated in favor of irony. The Cryptkeeper (basically a skeleton with eyes) served as narrator/host to macabre tales, such as the one about a man who went into an amusement-park haunted house with his kin and found it really did have spooks. And although children often appeared as characters in the eerie tales, there were surprisingly few complaints filed about the series and its content.

In 1996 CBS announced plans for *Secrets of the Cryptkeeper's Haunted House*, set to debut in the fall on Saturdays at 11:30 a.m.

TALES OF THE TEXAS RANGERS
Adventure; B&W
September 3, 1955–December 18, 1958

CBS Sat. 11:30 a.m.–Noon (9/3/55–5/25/57)
ABC Sun. 5–5:30 p.m. (9/22/57–6/15/58)
ABC Thu. 5–5:30 p.m. (10/2/58–12/18/58)

Cast:

Jace Pearson	*Willard Parker*
Clay Morgan	*Harry Lauter*

Tales of the Texas Rangers might be described as a "semiwestern," in that Rangers Pearson and Morgan did their jobs of rounding up the bad guys in time periods ranging from the 1830s to the 1950s in the Lone Star State. No explanation was given for the characters' seeming immortality and imperviousness to aging as they hopped between decades doing their work. Instead, the emphasis was on rather straightforward action and adventure to appeal to children.

Running on NBC radio from 1950–52 with Joel McCrea as Jace, *Tales of the Texas Rangers* was filmed for television in October 1951 by its radio producer and owner Stacy Keach. Keach had a 90-day option for actor Craig Stevens in the lead

role, but when sponsors failed to line up in time, Keach found himself with a dormant property. (Commenting on the pilot to *TV Guide* in 1959, Stevens said, "The present *Texas Rangers* is an entirely different show.") Finally, Keach sold the concept to General Mills in April 1955, and the sponsor assigned it to Screen Gems for production. After two years and 52 shows on CBS, it was rerun on ABC for two years, ending with an early evening run from December 22, 1958–May 25, 1959.

TALKAROUND
Discussion; B&W
October 9, 1955–January 1, 1956

CBS Sun. 3–3:30 p.m. (10/9/55–1/1/56)

Hostess/Producer: *Katherine "Kathy" Copeland*

Six teenagers (in the debut, 12- to 14-year-olds) discussed one topic per show, such as parent-child relationships, on this short-lived panel series from New York City. Thirty-something ex-teacher Katherine Copeland conducted the sessions like a group therapy setup, and noted and reviewed major words and phrases used by the children in the talks by writing them on a blackboard.

TALKING WITH A GIANT—See *Take a Giant Step.*

TARZAN, LORD OF THE JUNGLE
Cartoon; Color
September 11, 1976–September 8, 1984

CBS Sat. 9:30–10 a.m. (9/11/76–10/30/76)
CBS Sat. 10–10:30 a.m. (11/6/76–9/3/77)
CBS Sat. 10:30 a.m.–Noon (9/9/78–9/1/79)
CBS Sat. 12:30–1:30 p.m. (9/15/79–2/28/81)
CBS Sat. 10–11 a.m. (3/7/81–6/13/81)
CBS Sat. 11 a.m.–Noon (6/20/81–9/5/81)
CBS Sat. 11:30 a.m.-12:30 p.m. (9/12/81–11/28/81)
CBS Sat. 8:30–9:30 a.m. (12/5/81–9/11/82)
CBS Sat. 10–10:30 a.m. (2/11/84–9/8/84)

Voices:

Tarzan	*Robert Ridgely*
Batman (1978–80)	*Adam West*
Robin (1978–80)	*Burt Ward*
Manta (1978–80)	*Joan Van Ark*
Moray (1978–80)	*Joe Stern*
Super Stretch (1978–80)	*Ty Henderson*
Micro Woman (1978–80)	*Kim Hamilton*
Kelly Webster (Webwoman)	
(1978–80)	*Linda Gary*
Hercules (1978–80)	*Bob Denison*
Isis (1978–80)	*Diane Pershing*
Merlin/Super Samurai/Sinbad	
(all 1978–80)	*Mike Bell*
The Lone Ranger (1980–82)	*William Conrad*
Tonto (1980–82)	*Ivan Naranjo*
Zorro (Don Diego) (1981–82)	*Henry Darrow*
Miguel (1981–82)	*Julio Medina*
Sgt. Gonzales (1981–82)	*Don Diamond*

Tarzan, Edgar Rice Burroughs's character who grew up with the animals in Africa, has long been a media favorite. In terms of broadcasting, *Tarzan* aired on radio in a syndicated series from 1932–35, and then on another syndicated series in 1951 that CBS picked up for a few months the following year. On television NBC aired *Tarzan* as a nighttime series with Ron Ely in the lead from 1966–68. Nearly a decade later, CBS brought the loinclothed one back to the wilds of Saturday morning television for his own cartoon.

After a year as a half-hour series, Tarzan took a supporting role in the 1977–78 season with *The Batman/Tarzan Adventure Hour* (q.v.). In 1978 he returned as a headliner with the 90-minute *Tarzan and the Super 7,* the latter consisting of superheroes "Manta and Moray" (fish teenagers), "Super Stretch and Micro Woman" (their alter egos were Chris and Christy, respectively, and they had a dog, Trouble), "Webwoman" (scientist Kelly Webster became this superheroine with her heroic side having a spider partner named Spinner), "Freedom Force" (all the characters voiced by Bob Denison, Mike Bell, and Diane Pershing), and two segments later to be series on their own, *Batman and Robin* and *Jason of Star Command* (q.v.). On September 6, 1980, the show switched titles again to *The Tarzan/Lone Ranger Adventure Hour,* and added another hero a year later to become *The Tarzan/Lone Ranger/Zorro Adventure Hour.* The Lone Ranger resembled the 1960s cartoon (q.v.), while Zorro was a modification of the California swashbuckler with his sidekick Miguel and nemesis Sgt. Gonzales. Fernando Lamas was set to do Zorro's voice but left the job, so Henry Darrow replaced him. Two years after the last incarnation's cancellation, CBS reran the original show for seven months in 1984.

•TATTLETALES
Game; Color
February 18, 1974–June 1, 1984

CBS Mon.–Fri. 4–4:30 p.m. (2/18/74–6/13/75)
CBS Mon.–Fri. 11–11:30 a.m. (6/16/75–8/8/75)
CBS Mon.–Fri. 3:30–4 p.m. (8/11/75–11/28/75)
CBS Mon.–Fri. 4–4:30 p.m. (12/1/75–11/4/77)
CBS Mon.–Fri. (12/7/77–3/31/78)
CBS Mon.–Fri. 4–4:30 p.m. (1/18/82–6/1/84)

Host: *Bert Convy*

Somewhat of a celebrity knockoff of *The Newlywed Game,* *Tattletales* had three dating or married couples, at least one of whom was a celebrity, compete in trying to match answers with their spouses to subjective questions with multiple choice answers. In the first round the husbands were backstage wearing headphones while their wives made their guesses, then the husbands' heads appeared on monitors in front of the wives facing the audience (which the women could not see) as each man gave his answer. Matches were worth $300 if only one couple agreed, $150 each for two correct couples, or $100 each if all three matched. Midway through the show the couples switched positions. The duo with the most money amassed at the end of the day collected a $1,000 bonus.

Each couple represented a section of 100 audience members (red, green, and banana), who received equal amounts of the booty collected by their couple.

Tattletales had its roots in another Mark Goodson–Bill Todman Production seen in syndication from 1969–70 titled *He Said, She Said,* where four couples competed for individual audience members under the guidance of host Joe Garagiola. The couples seen on the debut of *Tattletales* were Anne Meara and Jerry Stiller, Bobby Van and Elaine Joyce, and Dick Gautier and Barbara Stuart. They all reappeared on the show several times, as did a few other celebrity couples like Betty White and Allen Ludden. After a four-year run, the series had a brief revival on CBS from 1982–84.

•TAZ-MANIA
Cartoon; Color
September 7, 1991–September 3, 1994

Fox Sat. 9:30–10 a.m. (9/7/91–11/14/92)
Fox Sat. 10:30–11 a.m. (11/21/92–9/3/94)

Voices:

Taz	Jim Cummings
Bull Gator	John Astin

The slobbering, growling Tasmanian devil had long been a favorite nemesis on *Bugs Bunny,* but it was not until 37 years after Taz's first appearance in animated shorts that he got his own series. The new program had him joined in adventures by his own family—parents Hugh and Jean, sister Molly, and infant brother Jake—while Taz worked as a bellhop in Hotel Tazmania in Australia. Other cartoon characters on the continent made guest shots, including the supposedly crafty Bull Gator, who with his pal Axel Gator fruitlessly hunted Taz. The show had several self-references and in-jokes about cartoons and their conventions, which no doubt adults in the audience enjoyed more than the children did. After years on Saturday mornings, the show aired in repeats daily on Fox in the fall of 1996.

TED MACK MATINEE
Variety; B&W
April 4, 1955–October 28, 1955

NBC Mon.–Fri. 3–3:30 p.m. (4/4/55–10/28/55)

Regulars: *Ted Mack, Dick Lee, Elise Rhodes, the Dreamboaters*

Ted Mack, host of *The Original Amateur Hour,* tried out a daytime counterpart in this new talent-oriented variety series. There were other regulars on the show, all of whom except Mack were vocalists, and special segments honoring the "Baby of the Week," "Man of the Week," and "Hero of the Week." This aired during a lull in production for *The Original Amateur Hour,* which NBC dropped on September 11, 1954 after a five-year run, but ABC picked up two days after this show ended, on October 30, 1955, for a two-year stint.

TED STEELE SHOW, THE
Variety; B&W
December 6, 1948–April 28, 1950

DuMont Mon.–Fri. 12:30–1 p.m. (12/6/48–6/3/49)
CBS Mon.–Fri. Noon–12:30 p.m. (6/6/49–7/9/49)
CBS Mon.–Fri. 5–5:30 p.m. (10/10/49–12/9/49)
CBS Mon.–Fri. 5–5:15 p.m. (12/12/49–4/28/50)

Host: *Ted Steele*

Ted Steele, a musician and disk jockey on WMCA radio in New York City, was already doing a daily show on DuMont's New York affiliate WABD from 5–5:15 p.m. when his network series debuted (it first aired locally, on November 1, 1948 from 12:15–12:45 a.m.). This, plus his radio work, gave the busy Steele a total of 22 hours of broadcasting each week. He transferred to CBS nighttime on July 11, 1949, then started a new daily show there three months later. On all shows Steele sang, played piano, and read viewer mail.

By April 1950, Steele was doing a local variety show on WPIX Saturdays from 2:30–5:30 p.m., which along with

The Ted Steele Show, *from the 1950s, was one of the most popular early daily variety shows.*

his daily shows and other work gave him a weekly tally of more than 32 hours. He transferred his daily show to WPIX on May 1, 1950, with *Ted Steele Matinee* running for an impressive 2¹/₂ hours daily through July 1954, then to WOR through at least 1958.

TEEN WOLF
Cartoon; Color
September 13, 1986–September 2, 1989

CBS Sat. 10:30–11 a.m. (9/13/86–9/12/87)
CBS Sat. 11:30 a.m.–Noon (9/19/87–12/26/87)
CBS Sat. Noon–12:30 p.m. (1/2/88–8/27/88)
CBS Sat. 11:30 a.m.–Noon (10/29/88–9/2/89)

Voices:

Scott Howard/Teen Wolf	Townsend Coleman
Boof	Jeannie Elias
Grandma Howard/Mrs. Sesslick	June Foray
Grandpa Howard	Stacy Keach Sr.
Harold	James Hampton
Styles	Donny Most
Mick	Craig Schaffer
Chuck	Will Ryan

A blah 1985 movie comedy starring Michael J. Fox as the title character somehow merited this cartoon version a year later. *Teen Wolf* was what the title said, a pubescent who involuntarily transformed into a hairy creature. But although Scott Howard was one of a whole family of werewolves in the town of Wolverton, including his Grandma, Grandpa, dad Harold, and little sister Lupe, he tried to keep his condition a secret from outsiders. Only his pals Styles and Boof knew that the change happened when Scott was angry or exposed to a full moon. His chief antagonist was Mick the star high school athlete, who vied with Scott for the hand of Pam. Mrs. Sesslick was the prying next-door neighbor who knew all about Scott and, with her clumsy reporter son Waldo, unsuccessfully attempted to expose him.

•TEENAGE MUTANT NINJA TURTLES
Cartoon; Color
September 8, 1990–

CBS Sat. 10–11 a.m. (9/8/90–9/11/93)
CBS Sat. 10:30–11:30 a.m. (9/18/93–11/20/93)
CBS Sat. 10–11 a.m. (11/27/93–2/26/94)
CBS Sat. 10:30–11:30 a.m. (3/5/94–3/26/94)
CBS Sat. 10–11 a.m. (4/2/94–9/10/94)
CBS Sat. 10:30–11 a.m. (9/17/94–11/5/94)
CBS Sat. 9:30–10 a.m. (11/12/94–9/10/95)
CBS Sat. 9:30–10 and 11:30 a.m.–Noon (two shows;
   9/17/95–11/18/95)
CBS Sat. 9:30–10 and 10:30–11 a.m. (two shows;
   11/25/95–1/13/96)
CBS Sat. 9:30–10 a.m. (1/20/96–2/10/96)
CBS Sat. 8–8:30 and 9:30–10 a.m. (two shows;
   2/17/96–5/11/96)
CBS Sat. 9:30–10 a.m. (5/18/96–)

Voices:

Leonardo	Cam Clarke
Michaelangelo	Townsend Coleman
Donatello	Barry Gordon
Raphael	Rob Paulsen
Shredder	James Avery
Krang	Pat Fraley
April O'Neil	Renae Jacobs
Splinter	Peter Renaday
Irma	Jennifer Darling

This immensely popular creation began as a cult comic book in 1983, came to television first in syndication in 1987, became a hit live-action movie in 1989, then made a debut as a prime-time special on CBS a day before it started a successful Saturday morning run. It was the phenomenon known as the Teenage Mutant Ninja Turtles, four pizza-loving superheroes who were CBS's biggest sensation on Saturdays in the 1990s. Leonardo was leader and swordsman, Michaelangelo was a prankster who did karate, Raphael was a jokester who used a dagger, and Donatello was a technical whiz who used a staff. They learned their defensive talents from Splinter the rat, and he helped guide them, along with April O'Neil, a TV reporter. Their constant foe was Shredder, whose evil superior was Krang. Irma was a ditzy co-worker of April's.

The characters also starred in a prime-time special, "Planet of the Turtleoids," on August 31, 1991. All versions were set in New York City, and none of the versions other than the comic book took the crime fighting too seriously, preferring a little levity and humor among the quartet both on and off the job.

•TEKNOMAN

Cartoon; Color
September 10, 1995–

UPN Sun. 10:30–11 a.m. (9/10/95–)

Voice:
Slade/Teknoman — Bob Bergen

Teknoman was yet another cartoon whose scenario had Earth's fate hinging on the success or failure of a few intrepid warriors. The leader was Teknoman, a being with impenetrable armor and various superpowers, including flying, who was the alter ego of an Earth native named Slade. Slade was part of a spaceship flying in the year 2087 to combat the evil Darkon, a foreboding entity living in the underground on the dark side of Earth's moon who commanded various foreign creatures to attack the planet and/or Teknoman. Human shipmates aiding Slade/Teknoman and his battles with Darkon in the violence-laden serialized adventures included Commander Jameson, Star, Ringo, Mac, and young computer whiz Dana.

TELE-COMICS—See NBC Comics.

TELEVISION SHOPPER—See Your Television Shopper.

TEMPTATION

Game; Color
December 4, 1967–March 1, 1968

ABC Mon.–Fri. 11–11:25 a.m. (12/4/67–3/1/68)

Host: *Art James*

Art James told three contestants about a trio of merchandise showcases which they could select on each round of this show. Contestants got to keep any showcase that the others had not also chosen. Although it claimed to offer the most merchandise of any game show then on the air (more than $50,000 a week), *Temptation* did little to tempt viewers of *Personality* on NBC to watch it.

$10,000 PYRAMID—See The $25,000 Pyramid.

•TENNESSEE ERNIE FORD SHOW, THE

Variety; B&W
January 3, 1955–March 26, 1965

NBC Mon.–Fri. Noon–12:30 p.m. (1/3/55–6/1/56)
NBC Mon.–Fri. 2:30–3 p.m. (6/4/56–6/28/57)
ABC Mon.–Fri. 11–11:30 a.m. (4/2/62–11/16/62)
ABC Mon.–Fri. Noon–12:30 p.m. (11/19/62–12/27/63)
ABC Mon.–Fri. 1–1:30 p.m. (12/30/63–3/27/64)
ABC Mon.–Fri. 12:30–1 p.m. (3/30/64–12/25/64)
ABC Mon.–Fri. 1–1:30 p.m. (12/28/64–3/26/65)

Regulars: *Tennessee Ernie Ford, Molly Bee (1955 at least), Doris Drew (1955 at least), Skip Farrell (1955 at least), Anita Gordon (1962–65), Hank [Jones] and Dean [Kay] (1962 at least), Jim Lange (1962–65), Dick Noel (1962 at least), Cathie Taylor (1964–65), the Jack Fascinato Orchestra*

Tennessee Ernie Ford was a rising country star who broke into the popular music scene with "Sixteen Tons" in 1955, the same year he started his first daytime show. The debut was a bungled affair, but not through any fault of Ernie's; someone at NBC accidentally transmitted *Uncle Archie*, a children's show from KRCA Hollywood, for the first 90 seconds before correcting the error. Those who stuck past that gaffe and watched the show regularly saw that Ernie and Molly Bee, Doris Drew, and Skip Farrell did a lot of singing, while orchestra leader Jack Fascinato took out time to do a few sketches.

Besides his vocalizing, Ernie made quite an impression with his colorful vocabulary (when one guest accidentally stepped on his lines, Ernie quipped, "You tossed me from the buggy 'fore I finished riding.") His popularity expanded so fast that NBC gave him a nighttime series on October 4, 1956 titled *The Ford Show* (not after Ernie, but for sponsor Ford Motor Company), which ran five years. He left daytime in 1957 saying he needed more time for his nighttime show.

Ford returned to daytime five years later with a series in which he taped six shows three days a week in his home in San Francisco. This time music came from Anita Gordon, Dick Noel, and the young folk-pop duo Hank and Dean. Jim Lange, later the host of *The Dating Game*, served as announcer and on-air foil. As usual, each show ended with a hymn by

Performing on the debut of The Tennessee Ernie Ford Show *were, from left, Skip Farrell, Doris Drew, Tennessee Ernie, and Molly Bee.*

Ernie and the regulars. Despite having the highest number of stations airing an ABC daytime series in 1962 (more than 150), the ratings were so-so. On October 12, 1964, the show was retitled *Hello, Peapickers*. In an attempt to lure viewers, this incarnation sported a new homey set for more interviews, and featured singer Cathie Taylor, but the strategy failed and the series went off six months later.

Ford did some fairly popular nighttime TV specials through the rest of the 1960s. He then appeared only infrequently on the medium before his death in 1991.

•TENNESSEE TUXEDO AND HIS TALES
Cartoon; Color
September 28, 1963–December 18, 1966

CBS Sat. 9:30–10 a.m. (9/28/63–9/3/66)
ABC Sun. 4:30–5 p.m. (9/18/66–12/18/66)

Cast:

Tennessee Tuxedo	Don Adams
Chumley	Bradley Bolke
Mr. Phineas J. Whoopie	Larry Storch
Yak/Baldy/Commander McBragg	Kenny Delmar

Don Adams used the same pinched voice he would employ later on the NBC nighttime sitcom *Get Smart* for the lead in

this cartoon, a penguin wearing a porkpie hat. Chumley was a slow-witted walrus who typically got involved in various dilemmas with his pal Tennessee. Unable to come up with answers to questions like "How do we start a newspaper?," the duo escaped Megopolis Zoo and visited Mr. Whoopie for advice, which he dispensed on an expanding animated chalkboard he called 3DBB. The answers typically were informative, but the accent was on comedy. Fellow zoo denizens Yak the steer and Baldy the eagle also got involved in the activities, as did irritable zoo curator Stanley Livingston, who often yelled at Tennessee, and his idiotic right-hand man Flunkey. Also seen as a continuing segment was "The World of Commander McBragg," about a stuffy statesman who recounted his world travels in often exaggerated fashion. Other segments on the show were repeats from *King Leonardo and His Short Subjects* (q.v.). After three years on CBS, ABC reran the series in the fall of 1966.

TEX AND JINX—See *Close-Up.*

•TEXAS
Soap Opera; Color
August 4, 1980–December 31, 1982

NBC Mon.–Fri. 3–4 p.m. (8/4/80–4/23/82)
NBC Mon.–Fri. 11 a.m.–Noon (4/26/82–12/31/82)

Cast:

Iris Carrington (1980–81)	Beverlee McKinsey
Alex Wheeler (1980–81)	Bert Kramer
Dennis Carrington (1980–81)	Jim Poyner
Eliot Carrington	Daniel Davis
Reena Cook	Carla Borelli
Justin Marshall	Jerry Lanning
Paige Marshall	Lisby Larson
Ginny Marshall	Barbara Rucker
Kate Marshall	Josephine Nichols
Ryan Connor	Philip Clark
Elena Dekker	Caryn Richmond
Rikki Dekker	Randy Hamilton
Victoria Bellman	Elizabeth Allen
Striker Bellman (1980–81)	Robert Gerringer
Striker Bellman (1981–82)	Clifton James
Billy Joe Wright	John McCafferty
Nita Wright	Ellen Maxted
Vivien Gorrow, the Wheeler maid	Gretchen Oehler
Dr. Kevin Cook (1980–81)	Lee Patterson
Mike Marshall (1980)/Barrett Marshall (1981)	Stephen Newman
Jeb Hampton (1980–81)	Ken Shriner
Princess Jasmin Cehdi (1980)	Donna Cyrus
Sheik Cehdi (1980)	Mitch Gred
Col. Ahmed Al Hassin (1980)	Maher Boutros
Grant Wheeler (1981–82)	Donald May
John Brady (1981–82)	James Rebhorn
Bernie Stokes (1981–82)	Michael Medeiros
Ashley Linden (1981–82)	Pamela K. Long
Gregory Linden (1981–82)	Damion Scheller

Allison Linden (1981–82)   Elizabeth Berridge
Allison Linden (1982)   Terri Garber
T. J. Canfield (1981–82)   David Forsyth
Brette Wheeler (1981–82)   Harley Kozak
Mark Wheeler (1981–82)   Ernie Garrett
Mark Wheeler (1982)   Michael Woods
Bubba Wadsworth (1981–82)   Stephen Joyce
Phil Roberts (1981–82)   Berkeley Harris
Ruby Wright (1981–82)   Dianne Thompson Neil
Lurleen Harper (1981–82)   Tina Johnson
Beau Baker (1981–82)   Robert Burton
Miles Renquist (1981–82)   Philip English
Mr. Hannibal (1981–82)   Richard Young
Mildred Canfield (1982)   Lori March
Burton Canfield (1982)   Donald Crabtree
Burton Canfield (1982)   Lawrence Weber
Judith Wheeler (1982)   Sharon Acker
Rev. Hunt Weston (1982)   Michael Longfield
Doris Hodges (1982)   Mary Pat Gleason
Stella Stanton (1982)   Virginia Graham
Mavis Cobb (1982)   Dody Goodman

The second spinoff from *Another World* (for the other, see *Somerset*), *Texas* received considerable hoopla as NBC's effort to stanch the ratings damage caused by its competition at 3 p.m., *General Hospital* on ABC and *Guiding Light* on CBS. The main transplant from *Another World* was Iris Carrington, who had spent at least five years giving Rachel grief for loving her father Mac before striking out for the Lone Star State. Other characters joining her in the switch were Iris's son Dennis, Dr. Kevin Cook, Reena Cook, and Victoria Bellman.

The obvious influence for the show's format was the CBS series *Dallas,* then the top hit on nighttime television, and the daytime show's attempts to recreate the Texas lifestyle were prodigious. Toasting the series at a 1980 debut in New York City, Texas Lt. Governor William Hobby told *TV Guide* he was impressed by the venture. "They filmed a lot in Houston, and the murals at their Brooklyn studio look realistic to me," he said.

Unfortunately, the program's plots were nowhere near as inventive as its settings. The powers that be made the same strategic blunder that CBS did when it moved Eileen Fulton's character of Lisa from *As the World Turns* into a mellowed role subordinate to the other action on the 1965 prime-time soap *Our Private World.* Here Beverly McKinsey's Iris showed only flashes of her old viperish self as she became chummy with Alex Wheeler, a lover from nearly a quarter century before, following a move to Houston to be near her only son Dennis Carrington. There also was the underdone Arabian-flavored intrigue with Princess and Sheik Cehdi, which showcased bad accents with a boring plot that interested virtually no one.

Iris and her situation took center stage early on as she told Alex her big secret that Dennis was really his son, not ex-husband Eliot Carrington's. Eliot, learning of this, popped up in town to try to kill Alex during the latter's wedding to Iris. Alex later was murdered when he discovered mob activities

in his oil business, and a grieving Iris broke down when at one point it appeared Eliot was getting together with Paige Marshall, an ex-porno queen and wife of Dennis. She ended up leaving town with her newly divorced son, while Alex's brother Grant took over the family oil business. (Iris did return to *Another World* years later, albeit played by a different actress.)

Other Houston-based characters were Justin Marshall, who held Alex responsible for causing his rival oil tycoon dad Mike's suicide; Barrett Marshall, Justin's brother and a look-alike for Alex, who returned from Vietnam where he had been declared missing in action only to find that wife Ginny Marshall was pregnant by Ryan Connor (she lost her child in a tussle with Barrett, prompting him to seek therapy, which was soon followed by Ryan's death); and Reena, the show's resident Erica Kane, who left an unhappy marriage to Dr. Kevin Cook for Max Dekker, who later died in an explosion.

Reena found herself central to several later plots. Her mother Vicky Bellman, livid over learning that her attorney husband Striker was a bigamist who had another family in Mexico, went on to have a doomed relationship with Hunt Weston, a priest. Meanwhile, Reena got involved in a love triangle with Justin Marshall, who was married to Ashley Linden, and Justin's employer Grant Wheeler. Justin broke up with his wife, who had her own secret in that her 10-year-old cousin Gregory, who lived with her and her sister Allison Linden, really was her son by T. J. Canfield. T. J.'s parents Burton and Mildred Canfield disapproved of Ashley and T. J.'s romance, and with T. J.'s love for Paige Marshall it seemed that his interest for Ashley was history. Indeed, he did not challenge her for custody of Gregory when Justin showed renewed love for Ashley.

Meanwhile, Billy Joe Wright, an ex-con who had raped Dawn Marshall, somehow avoided prison and married Nita Wright, then dated Elena Dekker, Max's sister, after Nina divorced him. Grant Wheeler meddled with his kids Lacey, Brette (who was dating Elena's brother Rikki Dekker), and Mark. Mark began seeing Ruby Wright, Billy Joe's sister, but his ex-wife Judith tried to woo him away. Lurleen Harper, Ruby's pal, saved the life of wounded tour guide Joel Walker, and then married him. Mark chose Ruby over Allison Linden. Brette and Rikki broke up when he got a job in California. And Judith divorced Grant so he could marry Reena.

None of these typical soap melodramas could make up for the show's continuing problem—bad time slots. After finishing third in the afternoon, NBC tried airing it before noon, traditionally a poor period for soaps, and watched helplessly as only 84 percent of affiliates decided to carry it, making ratings worse than they had been the first year. NBC tried no more soaps in that slot after canceling *Texas.*

THAT SHOW—See Joan Rivers Show, The.

THAT'S O'TOOLE
Sitcom; B&W
March 13, 1949–June 5, 1949
ABC Sun. 4:45–5 p.m. (3/13/49–6/5/49)

Cast:

Tinker O'Toole	Arthur Peterson
His wife	Norma Ransome
His wife's sister	Pat Dunlap

An early live network series from Chicago, *That's O'Toole* featured the misadventures of a handyman, his scatterbrained wife, and his sister-in-law, a publisher's representative. On the debut the trio lassoed an author to do a book on woodworking, which he found to be more trying than he had imagined. The show's sponsor, the Delta Manufacturing Company of Detroit, did not follow the pattern, current at the time, of plugging the company's tools in the series, but kept that aspect separate in commercials done by the show's announcer Ed Prentiss. When Delta ended its sponsorship, *That's O'Toole* went off the air.

THERE'S ONE IN EVERY FAMILY
Game; B&W
September 29, 1952–June 12, 1953

CBS Mon.–Fri. 11–11:30 a.m. (9/29/52–11/7/52)
CBS Mon.–Sat 11–11:30 a.m. (11/10/52–2/7/53)
CBS Mon.–Wed/Fri./Sat. 11–11:30 a.m. (2/9/53–6/12/53)

Host: *John Reed King (9/29/52–3/6/53), Mike Wallace (11/15/52–3/7/53), Dean Miller (3/9/53–6/12/53)*

Billed as a showcase for "outstandingly different family members," *There's One in Every Family* employed such contestants as a boy who wanted to fly to the moon and a woman who had served as "big sister" to several homesick servicemen. These people competed in generating the most studio audience support via applause and by winning money for their dreams by a question-and-answer session. On November 15, 1952 this show added a sixth day per week of broadcasts, which shrank back to five in February 1953 when *The Bill Cullen Show* debuted. Mike Wallace hosted the Saturday edition. When it started airing from Los Angeles on March 9, 1953, Dean Miller assumed hosting duties for all the shows each week.

THESE ARE MY CHILDREN
Soap Opera; B&W
January 31, 1949–February 25, 1949

NBC Mon.–Fri. 5–5:15 p.m. (1/31/49–2/25/49)

Cast:

Mrs. Henehan	Alma Platts
John Henehan	George Kluge
Jean Henehan	Joan Arlt
Patricia Henehan	Jane Brooksmith
Penny Henehan	Martha McClain
Aunt Kitty Henehan	Margaret Heneghan
Katherine Carter	Eloise Kummer

The first—and also shortest-lived—daytime network TV soap opera was *These Are My Children.* Created by veteran radio (and later television) writer-producer Irna Phillips, who said she was writing the series with a slant to both a TV and radio audience, this live Chicago-based melodrama was supposed to focus on family life in the postwar era. It focused on the Henehan family, whose mother ran a boarding house. John was the weak son, Jean his spendthrift wife, Patricia the selfish daughter, and Katherine the good boarder. The show's reviews were generally negative, with *Variety* stating that "this type of hausfrau fodder will have extremely hard sledding on the medium. . . . Acting of any of the principals won't win any awards."

The given explanation of why the show ended after just two months was that AT&T announced that as of May 1, 1949, the eastbound coaxial cable from Chicago could not be used to transmit programs. But *Billboard* reported that NBC executives privately were not happy with the quality of the series and preferred to do more on the East Coast. At the same time, the high production costs of *These Are My Children* prevented it from becoming a local show once the network dropped it, thus sealing its cancellation.

THESE ARE THE DAYS
Cartoon; Color
September 7, 1974–September 5, 1976

ABC Sat. Noon–12:30 p.m. (9/7/74–8/30/75)
ABC Sun. 11–11:30 a.m. (9/7/75–9/5/76)

Cast:

Martha Day	June Lockhart
Grandpa Day	Henry Jones
Kathy Day	Pamelyn Ferdin
Danny Day	Jackie Haley
Ben Day	Andrew Parks
Homer	Frank Cady

The Days were a clan living in the early 1900s in a world whose artwork was inspired by 1930s movie techniques and atmosphere, according to co-producer Joseph Barbera. Barbera told *Variety,* "It's like a lithograph come to life," but most reviewers thought it more like a knockoff come to life of the CBS nighttime Depression drama *The Waltons.* Martha Day was a widow living in Elmsville with her three kids and Grandpa, the operator of the Day General Store. This old-fashioned entry failed after a season and ran in repeats in 1976.

THINK PINK PANTHER SHOW, THE—See *Pink Panther, The.*

13 GHOSTS OF SCOOBY-DOO, THE—See *Scooby-Doo, Where Are You?*

•30 MINUTES
News; Color
September 16, 1978–August 28, 1982

CBS Sat. 1:30–2 p.m. (9/16/78–8/28/82; off summer of 1979)

Regulars: *Christopher Glenn, Betsy Aaron (1978–80), Betty Ann Bowser (1980–82), Patricia McGuire*

This hard-hitting magazine documentary series for youth was every bit as aggressive and thorough as its source of inspiration, CBS's long-running nighttime hit *60 Minutes* (1968–). Reporters pulled no punches in being frank with controversial issues. Among the topics covered were life for teenagers in prison, censorship of a high school play performance, drug addiction, teenage homosexuality, anorexia nervosa, school vandalism, runaways, and children of alcoholic parents. Some lighter features did pop up, like a behind-the-scenes visit to *Mad* magazine and a profile of singing idol Shaun Cassidy. Another regular feature starred Patricia McGuire, Assistant Director of the Street Law Program in Washington, D.C. "Who's Right?" had McGuire explain answers to tricky legal questions such as "Can principals search students' lockers?" The series, which was taped in New York City, lasted four years despite unimpressive ratings.

THIS IS NBC NEWS
News; B&W
July 2, 1961–March 24, 1963

NBC Sun. 5:30–6 p.m. (7/2/61–9/3/61)
NBC Sun. 4:30–5 p.m. (10/14/62–12/23/62)
NBC Sun. 3–3:30 p.m. (1/6/63–3/24/63)

Host: *Edwin Newman (1961), Martin Agronsky (1962–63)*

This Is NBC News spotlighted reports from less-seen NBC foreign correspondents, including live, taped, and filmed interviews and stories. Occasionally it had an entire newscast devoted to one topic, from a look at the Berlin Crisis to Venezuelan President Romulo Betancourt's visit to America. After its first season, the series aired on NBC Sundays at 6:30 p.m. from June 3–September 16, 1962, with Ray Scherer, as anchor before returning to daytime with its third host.

THIS IS THE MISSUS—See *Missus Goes A-Shopping, The.*

•THIS WEEK IN BASEBALL
Sports; Color
1977–

Syndicated 30 minutes weekly beginning Summer 1977

Narrator: *Mel Allen (1977–95), Warner Fusselle (1996–)*

This long-running series recapped the highlights of major league baseball games each week, plus had a few interviews with players, coaches, announcers, and others associated with the sport. It aired during the summers only. In 1996 it was retitled *TWIB 20*, honoring its 20th season of coverage by using its initials. Sadly, Mel Allen, one of the game's greatest announcers, had to leave the show before that time due to illness. Allen died on June 16, 1996. Warner Fusselle was his replacement.

THIS WEEK IN SPORTS—See *General Sports Time.*

•THIS WEEK WITH DAVID BRINKLEY
News Discussion; Color
November 15, 1981–

ABC Sun. 11:30 a.m.–12:30 p.m. (11/15/81–9/5/82)
ABC Sun. 10:30–11:30 a.m. (9/12/82–)

Regulars: *David Brinkley, Sam Donaldson, George Will, Cokie Roberts (1992–)*

The one show which revolutionized the TV news panel discussion format was *This Week with David Brinkley*, a series born out of frustration on the part of both Brinkley, its future host, and Roone Arledge, who became producer. Arledge had thought most Sunday morning talk shows were dinosaurs and planned to cancel ABC'S long-running but staid *Issues and Answers*. Brinkley was fed up with what he felt was interference in the NBC News division by then–NBC News President William Small and left his network after more than a quarter century of service. He was intrigued by Arledge's idea to refashion weekend informational series, and this was the successful result.

This Week with David Brinkley *featured the formidable trio of (from left) George Will, David Brinkley, and Sam Donaldson.*

Each show, based in Washington, D.C., began with a short news update from Brinkley. Then a lead-in report (initially done by Jim Wooten, later by other ABC correspondents) gave an overview of that day's topic. After a commercial, Brinkley, ABC White House correspondent Sam Donaldson, and conservative columnist George Will interrogated that week's guests for roughly a third of the hour. Then Brinkley, Donaldson, Will, and a guest spent the last part of the show in a free-for-all dialogue about the week's news, with Donaldson and Will often getting in some good verbal jabs at each other. Cokie Roberts, who first guested in 1988, became the permanent third member four years later. Brinkley closed each show with a wry observation, usually involving some government stupidity.

Though its debut was a little rocky (David Stockman, budget director for President Reagan, backed out of his set appearance), this series soon became known as a leading newsmaker, on the basis of the opinions and facts it brought out from its guests. It was here, for example, that ex-Senator John Tower on February 26, 1989, went all out for his unsuccessful bid to be appointed Secretary of Defense by saying he would quit his reported habit of drinking if nominated. In August 1996 Brinkley announced he planned to retire from the show by the start of 1997, with Sam Donaldson and Cokie Roberts set to replace him as co-anchors.

THOSE ENDEARING YOUNG CHARMS
Sitcom; B&W
December 30, 1951–January 6, 1952
NBC Sun. 5:30–6 p.m. (12/30/51–1/6/52)

Cast:

Ralph Charm	Maurice Copeland
Abbe Charm	Betty Arnold
Clem Charm	Gerald Garvey
Connie Charm	Pat Matthews
Uncle Duff	Clarence Hartzell

The Charms were a New England family running a household gadgets mail-order business whose misadventures made up the crux of each week's story. After a two-week run, this live sitcom from Chicago moved into Sunday evenings briefly in March 1952, then permanently on Tuesday and Thursday evenings in May 1952 before ending on June 17, 1952. By the nighttime airings, Fern Persons had replaced Betty Arnold as Abbe and Charon Follett had replaced Pat Matthews as Connie.

THREE FOR THE MONEY
Game; Color
September 29, 1975–November 28, 1975
NBC Mon.–Fri. 12:30–12:55 p.m. (9/29/75–11/28/75)
Host: *Dick Enberg*

Two trios, each led by a celebrity, competed at the same time to identify items. Each team could challenge the other team at $100 per person for a maximum of $300 per question in the contests. After time was called in this round, the leading team went to a bonus identification round which increased $1,000 day each day of that week it was not solved.

•THREE ON A MATCH
Game; Color
August 2, 1971–June 28, 1974
NBC Mon.–Fri. 1:30–2 p.m. (8/2/71–6/28/74)
Host: *Bill Cullen*

Three categories were revealed and a trio of contestants bid from one to four on the number of questions they thought they could get right in each category. The highest bidder for each category answered yes-no questions for the amount he or she had bid to try to win 10 times the total number of questions bid by the players. The first player to amass $150 had enough money to buy $20, $30, and $40 squares on another board, where the money amounts appeared in three columns divided by four rows of colors (blue, green, red, and yellow). The player tried to match three prizes. If successful, that player faced two new challengers; otherwise, he or she faced a new round with the contestants from the earlier game. The show changed its format slightly and increased its prize money on April 23, 1973, but those moves didn't help it beat the competition, *As the World Turns* and *Let's Make a Deal.*

•THREE ROBONIC STOOGES, THE
Cartoon; Color
January 28, 1978–September 6, 1981
CBS Sat. 8–8:30 a.m. (1/28/78–9/2/78)
CBS Sun. 8–8:30 a.m. (9/9/79–12/30/79)
CBS Sun. 8–8:30 a.m. (9/7/80–3/8/81)
CBS Sun. 8:30–9 a.m. (3/15/81–9/6/81)

Voices:

Curly	Frank Welker
Larry	Joe Baker
Moe	Paul Winchell
Triple Zero	Ross Martin

The most famous (or infamous, if you prefer) slapstick comedy team in motion pictures provided the framework for a gimmicky cartoon first seen on *The Skatebirds* (q.v.) in 1977. Curly (the fat bald one with weird sounds and body movements), Larry (the frizzy-haired finicky one), and Moe (the supposedly smart one with a page-boy haircut) worked as crime busters for easily irritated Triple Zero. The android trio often ended up crashing into each other while solving crimes, resulting in a pile of discombobulated joints and springs, but they somehow succeeded in bringing the bad guys to justice. This cartoon, although mildly successful, could not match the immense popularity of the original Stooges' 1930s and 1940s black-and-white films on local TV stations. Also airing during the show were "Woofer and Wimper, Dog Detectives," abbreviated repeats of *Clue Club* (q.v.).

THREE STEPS TO HEAVEN
Soap Opera; B&W and Color
August 3, 1953–December 31, 1954

NBC Mon.–Fri. 11:30–11:45 a.m. (8/3/53–12/26/54)
NBC Mon.–Fri. 10:45–11 a.m. (3/1/54–12/31/54)

Cast:

Mary Jane "Poco" Thurmond (1953 at least)	Phyllis Hill
Mary Jane "Poco" Thurmond (1954 at least)	Diana Douglas
Mary Jane "Poco" Thurmond (by October 1954)	Kathleen Maguire
Bill Morgan (1953–54)	Walter Brooke
Bill Morgan (1959–)	Gene Blakely
Bill Morgan (1954)	Mark Roberts
Vince Bannister	John Marley
Barry Thurmond	Roger Sullivan
Jennifer Alden (at least 1954)	Lori March
Alice Trent (at least 1954)	Laurie Vendig
Jason Cleve (at least 1954)	Lauren Gilbert
Nan Waring (at least 1954)	Beth Douglas
Beth Waring (at least 1954)	Madeline Belgard

This show's title referred to the three steps up to the balcony of Poco's tenement slum in New York City, where one could see the sky and escape the garbage below. Poco certainly needed this optimistic outlook, as she found plenty of dilemmas in her efforts to become a model and carry on a romance with Bill Morgan. Bill was a writer who liked to help people. On the debut he aided a frightened woman married to an evil psychiatrist with underworld connections. Such altruism impressed Poco, who eventually married Bill despite many obstacles.

Among other characters, Jason, Nan, and Jennifer (formerly a competitor for Bill's affections) were pals of Poco's. Vince was a gangster who harassed Poco a lot. NBC telecast at least one show, on March 23, 1954, in color.

THREE STOOGES, THE—See *Three Robonic Stooges, The*

•THUNDARR THE BARBARIAN
Cartoon; Color
October 4, 1980–September 8, 1984

ABC Sat. 10:30–11 a.m. (10/4/80–9/5/81)
ABC Sat. 11:30 a.m.–Noon (9/12/81–2/6/82)
ABC Sat. 8:30–9 a.m. (2/13/82–9/18/82)
NBC Sat. Noon–12:30 p.m. (4/9/83–9/10/83)
NBC Sat. 12:30–1 p.m. (9/17/83–9/8/84)

Voices:

Thundarr	Robert Ridgely
Ariel	Nellie Bellflower
Ookla the Mok	Henry Corden

The opening narration on *Thundarr the Barbarian* stated that in 1994, a runaway planet had hurtled between Earth and its moon, "unleashing cosmic destruction. Man's civilization is cast in ruin." Then 2,000 years later, Earth was reborn in a strange new savage world. Breaking away from it was Thundarr, a blond Adonis who fought for justice along with Ariel and Ookla the Mok. Ariel was the stepdaughter of a wizard who gave Thundarr the Sun Sword, which resembled a conventional sabre when strapped on him, but which in use provided an energy ray capable of destroying anything in its path. Ookla was an apelike mutant pal. Together the trio fought everything from mummies to witches to keep order on the planet they loved. The NBC shows were repeats.

THUNDER
Children's; Color
September 10, 1977–September 2, 1978

NBC Sat. 11–11:30 a.m. (9/10/77–9/2/78)

Cast:

Anne Prescott	Melissa Converse
Bill Prescott	Clint Ritchie
Cindy Prescott	Melora Hardin
Willie Williams	Justin Randi

Eight-year-old Cindy lived on a ranch in the Southwest with her rancher dad Bill and her mom Anne, a veterinarian; Willie, a young neighbor who rode a cookie-eating mule called Cupcake, was her best pal. Thunder was the black stallion Cindy rode.

THUNDERBIRDS
Children's; Color
July 2, 1994–August 20, 1994

Fox Sat. 9:30–10 a.m. (7/2/94–7/30/94)
Fox Sat. 8:30–9 a.m. (8/6/94–8/20/94)

Voices:

Jeff Tracy	Peter Dyneley
John Tracy	Ray Barrett
Gordon Tracy, various others	David Grahan
Lady Penelope	Sylvia Anderson
Tin-Tin	Christine Finn
Virgil Tracy	Jeremy Wilkin
Scott Tracy	Shane Rimmer
Alan Tracy	Matt Zimmerman

One of Great Britain's most enduring children's science fiction shows, *Thunderbirds* concentrated on the exploits of millionaire Jeff Tracy and his five sons fighting fantastic foes with their elaborate aircraft 100 years in the future. The shows seen on Fox were edited from the hour-long editions aired on the British Broadcasting Corporation. Previously *Thunderbirds* aired in America in syndication in 1966, and the supermarionation technique used to animate the puppets in the adventures were seen on NBC from 1963–65 on *Fireball XL-5* (q.v.).

•TIC TAC DOUGH
Game; B&W and Color
July 30, 1956–September 1, 1978

NBC Mon.–Fri. Noon–12:30 p.m. (7/30/56–10/30/59)
CBS Mon.–Fri. 10–10:30 a.m. (7/3/78–9/1/78)

Host: *Jack Barry, Gene Rayburn, Bill Wendell (10/58–10/30/59), Wink Martindale (1978)*

Tic Tac Dough had two players compete in a tic-tac-toe game on a wall by selecting a category contained in one of the nine squares on the board and answering that question correctly to put an "X" or "O" mark on it, depending on what side he or she was on. Three in a row horizontally, diagonally, or vertically won $100 in the 1950s version ($100 extra to a person answering the center square correctly in any game), upped to $300 per box and $500 for the center square in 1978. There was a bonus game for the 1978 incarnation, which used video monitors instead of a wall, where a winner tried to uncover three X's or O's hidden in a row for various money amounts which could be lost if he or she uncovered the box with a dragon behind it.

Earnings on the series often were large. *Time* reported that the 1950s daytime version's biggest winner was Air Force Lieutenant James Astrue, who in November 1958 started using his 70 days of accumulated leave at McGuire Air Force Base in New Jersey to go to Manhattan on alternate weeks for the show's taping schedule. He won at least $137,800 before his leave was all used up, in March 1959.

However, the series fell under the same cloud of suspicion that hung over other big-money game shows in the quiz show scandals of the late 1950s, especially because its producers Jack Barry and Dan Enright were connected to the biggest offender, the nighttime series *Twenty-One*. In fact, one contestant, Richard K. Clark, filed suit against the producers and NBC for $540,000, for damage to his reputation. He claimed to have won $22,500 on *Tic Tac Dough* legitimately against a contestant who was given assistance.

Jack Barry, co-creator of the series, hosted it until his busy schedule forced him to drop it. When the show was revived in 1978 by Barry without the rigging, Wink Martindale was host. Martindale continued to do the chore in a highly successful syndicated version of the show through 1985, then Jim Caldwell replaced him through 1986. Patrick Wayne hosted a new version in syndication in 1990.

•TICK, THE
Cartoon; Color
September 10, 1994–April 13, 1996

Fox Sat. 11:30 am.–Noon (9/10/94–9/17/94)
Fox Sat. 10:30–11 a.m. (9/24/94–12/9/95)
Fox Sat. 11–11:30 a.m. (12/16/95–4/13/96)

Voices:

The Tick	Townsend Coleman
Arthur (1994–95)	Mickey Dolenz
Arthur (1995–96)	Rob Paulsen

As he himself recalled his origins in the opening episode, the Tick was a blue, 400-pound, 7-foot-tall superhero looking for a city to defend. He competed at a superhero convention

in Reno, Nevada, and pleaded for employment, which resulted in his going to a burg known simply as "The City." There he met Arthur, a meek ex-accountant wearing a pale purple moth outfit with an eye mask. Sensing Arthur's desire for adventure, the Tick deemed him his official sidekick, and together they fought such outlandish opponents as Chairface Chippendale, who lived up to his name.

This campy sendup of the superhero genre won a cult following and helped Fox reign as number one in Saturday morning children's programming in the mid-1990s. Ben Edlund created the character in 1993 and also co-wrote several episodes.

TIME FOR COLOR
Various; Color
June 28, 1954–August 9, 1954

CBS Mon. 5–5:30 p.m. (6/28/54–8/9/54)

Time for Color was CBS's rare venture outside black-and-white programming in the mid-1950s, and seems to have been done more to test the potential use of color than to produce interesting programming. It debuted with what was billed as the first presentation of a color film on TV, in this case a 16mm Gene Autry western made especially for the program. Most later programs were easily forgotten westerns or documentaries.

TIME FOR US, A
Soap Opera; B&W
December 28, 1964–December 16, 1966

ABC Mon.–Fri. 2–2:30 p.m. (12/28/64–6/25/65)
ABC Mon.–Fri. 2:30–2:55 p.m. (6/28/65–12/16/66)

Cast:

Al Skerba/Driscoll	Roy Poole
Martha Skerba/Driscoll	Lenka Peterson
Linda Skerba (1964–February 1965)	Barbara Rodell
Linda Skerba (March–June 1965)	Jane Elliot
Linda Driscoll (June 1965– c. October 1965)	Joanna Miles
Linda Driscoll (November 1965–)	Beret Arcaya
Jane Skerba (1964–c. February 1965)	Margaret Ladd
Jane Skerba/Driscoll (c. May 1965–1966)	Beverly Hayes
Craig Reynolds (1964–February 1965)	Frank Schofield
Roxanne Reynolds	Maggie Hayes
Steve Reynolds (1964–June 1965)	Gordon Gray
Steve Reynolds (June 1965–1966)	Tom Fielding
Jason Farrell	Walter Coy
Leslie Farrell	Rita Lloyd
Kate Austen (1964–June 1965)	Kathleen Maguire
Chris Austen (1964–June 1965)	Richard Thomas
Louise Austen	Josephine Nichols
Flora Perkins (1964–65 at least)	Jacqueline Brookes

Tony Grey (1964–65)/Stan
  (late 1965)   Morgan Sterne
Doug Colton (1965 at least)   Ion Berger
Paul Davis (1965)   Conard Fowkes
Miriam Bentley   Lesley Brooks
David Simon (1965 at least)   Terry Logan

The initial story in *A Flame in the Wind* (the serial's debut title) had certain citizens in the town of Haviland trying to stop the *roman à clef* widow Kate Austen was writing. She certainly had plenty of raw material around her. For example, Craig Reynolds, a publishing executive involved in Kate's novel, left his wife Roxanne within the first three months of the show. This did not make life easier for his father-in-law Jason Farrell, who ran the troubled publishing empire and had a flirt of a wife in Leslie, or for Craig's son Steve, involved in an unrequited love for Linda Skerba, whose sister Jane in turn desired Steve. Need we add that Steve, a Yale graduate, worked for the ladies' father Al with his pal Dave Simon, who also loved Linda? Naturally, author Kate needed to get her own house in order, what with a troubled relationship with Tony Grey and a deteriorating one with the rest of the townsfolk.

On June 28, 1965, the show became *A Time For Us.* There was now more focus on youth stories, plus a few changes in the cast and surnames for the Skerbas. Linda and Jane became the protagonists, with Linda an actress in New York City in love with Paul Davis, a director, yet not willing to give up her career for marriage. Steve still loved her, but gave up and decided to see Jane. When Jane became pregnant in October 1965, she and Steve wed, even though Linda returned home unexpectedly, realizing she loved Steve.

That same month, Steve's mom Roxanne threw a six-episode party, wherein she was attracted to piano player Doug Colton, who seemed more fascinated with Roxanne's money. That detail did not go unnoticed by Steve, who remained supportive to his mom in affairs of the heart and vice versa. But, irony of ironies, Linda decided to compete with Roxanne for Doug after being rejected by Steve (Roxanne eventually married Doug). Kate and her son Chris were gone from the action, with Miriam Bentley taking Kate's place as town gossip, but Louise, Kate's mother-in-law, remained as a confidante (or more?) for Jason. Poor Martha Skerba/Driscoll seemed left out of all the fun, as she mainly served as Al's wife and support to Linda and Jane during the two years this serial ran.

TIME MACHINE
Game; Color
January 7, 1985–April 26, 1985
NBC Mon.–Fri. 10–10:30 a.m. (1/7/85–4/26/85)
Host: *John Davidson*

Time Machine initially had three contestants (then just two by February 11) compete in various question-and-answer sessions involving mostly 20th-century history and nostalgia with an emphasis on pop culture. The final round to determine the day's winner was "The Time Capsule," where four items

were submitted and contestants had to guess to which year they pertained. The one guessing the year, or coming closest, won $1,000 and played a bonus game where he or she picked the one headline out of four that referred to an event that had happened during the given year. The February 11 format change included one winner from the two competing that day taking on the winner from the day before in another year-guessing game for a new automobile and the right to return the next day.

TIME: PRESENT—CHET HUNTLEY REPORTING—See *Outlook.*

TIME TO LIVE, A
Soap Opera; B&W
July 5, 1954–December 31, 1954
NBC Mon.–Fri. 10:30–10:45 a.m. (7/5/54–12/31/54)
Cast:

Julie Byron   Pat Sully
Don Richard   Larry Kerr
Don Richard (later shows)   John Himes
Chick Buchanan   Len Wayland
Madge Byron   Viola Berwick
Greta Powers   Zohra Alton
Greta Powers (later shows)   Jeanne Jerrems
Lenore Eustice   Barbara Foley
Rudy Marion   Zachary Charles
Lt. Miles Dow   Dort Clark
Donna Sims   Muriel Monsel

Julie Byron was a proofreader who wanted to be a part-time reporter at her newspaper. She eventually got the chance and joined forces with Don Richard to uncover scandals, first involving Greta Powers, later the murder of Lenore Eustice. During the latter episode, Julie had to be convinced by Lieutenant Dow that something fishy was occurring and that her boyfriend Chick was being framed for the incident. With the help of Dow and Donna, the real killer was found, and Julie married Chick on the last show. *A Time to Live,* which aired live from Chicago, found out its time was up at the end of 1954 when it could not challenge *Arthur Godfrey Time.*

TIMON AND PUMBAA—See *Lion King's Timon and Pumbaa, The.*

•TINY TOON ADVENTURES
Cartoon; Color
September 19, 1992–September 3, 1994
Fox Sat. 10–10:30 a.m. (9/19/92–9/3/94)
Voices:

Buster Bunny (first)   Charlie Adler
Buster Bunny (second)   John Kassir
Barbara Ann "Babs" Bunny   Tress MacNeille
Plucky Duck   Joe Alaskey
Hamton Pig   Don Messick

Elmyra	Cree Summer
Shirley the Loon (Duck)	Gail Matthius
Dizzy Devil (later named Taz)	Maurice LaMarche
Montana Max	Danny Cooksey
Fifi Le Pew	Kath Soucie
Bugs Bunny/Daffy Duck/Porky	
Pig/Tweety Bird	Noel Blanc

Launched as one of the most ambitious cartoons ever produced for television, as cinema great Steven Spielberg was its executive producer, *Tiny Toon Adventures* made an odd debut as a CBS prime-time special on September 14, 1990 before its first 65 episodes went into daily syndication. When the show became a hit there, Fox added it to the Saturday lineup under the title *The Plucky Duck Show,* where it stayed until November 1992. No new episodes were produced after that time, although Fox did give the show another nighttime special on December 6, 1992, titled "It's A Wonderful Tiny Toons Christmas Special."

Basically, the series was a redo of Warner Bros. *Looney Tunes* movie shorts featuring the offspring of the original characters. Stars Babs and Buster Bunny (no relation other than same species) lived in Acme Acres along with the fellow kids of Daffy Duck (Plucky) and Porky Pig (Hamton). They studied under their elders, voiced by Mel Blanc's son Noel, at Acme Looniversity. Other characters seen included Elmyra, the perky girl who loved animals a little too much, squeezing and harming them while thinking she was giving them the love and care they needed, and Shirley the Valley Girl–type fowl. The accent was on wild, raucous slapstick designed to appeal to adults as much as to children.

•TO SAY THE LEAST
Game; Color
October 3, 1977–April 21, 1978

NBC Mon.–Fri. Noon–12:30 p.m. (10/3/77–4/21/78)

Host: Tom Kennedy

To Say the Least resembled the "Bid a Note" competition from *Name That Tune* (q.v.), but with words in a phrase rather than notes in a tune. Two teams of three, each with two celebrities, competed by having one member of each see a clue and begin removing one word at a time in it until one of the two decided the other should have his or her team try to figure out the mystery subject from the remaining words. A correct response by the other two members of the guessing team netted a point for that team; if the guess was incorrect, the other team won the point. The first team to win two points played a bonus round. In that round, both celebrity partners were offstage and unable to hear the clue, and the player eliminated all but three words of the clue for one of the celebrities to guess, then, if he or she was successful, eliminated one more word from the clue for the remaining celebrity to guess.

•TO TELL THE TRUTH
Game; B&W and Color
June 18, 1962–May 31, 1991

CBS Mon.–Fri. 3:30–3:55 p.m. (6/18/62–12/28/62)
CBS Mon.–Fri. 3–3:25 p.m. (12/31/62–9/6/68)
CBS Sun. 5–5:30 p.m. (9/11/66–10/23/66)
NBC Mon.–Fri. 11–11:30 a.m. (9/3/90–5/31/91)

Hosts: Bud Collyer (1962–68), Gordon Elliott (9/3/90–10/26/90), Lynn Swann (10/29/90–2/1/91), Alex Trebek (2/4/91–5/31/91)

Regulars: Joan Fontaine (1962–July 1965), Phyllis Newman (1962–August 1965), Barry Nelson (1962–August 1965), Orson Bean (July 1965–1968), Peggy Cass (July 1965–1968), Tom Poston (July 1965–1968), Kitty Carlisle (September 1965–1968)

The show which made the phrase, "Will the real _____ please stand up?" part of the pop culture vernacular of the 20th century, *To Tell the Truth* was nothing more than an elaborate bluffing game. A quartet of celebrities had to determine through questioning which of three contestants was actually who he or she claimed to be. Each wrong vote by the panel won money for the contestants, which was split among the three (the amounts varied during the run). The job done by the contestants usually was good enough that few panels ever all correctly identified the person who was not lying.

Finding people who were convincing liars was the biggest hurdle the show's staff faced. Producer Willie Stein told *TV Guide* in late 1966 that he figured his employees interviewed 15,000 people to get the 6,000 contestants (two-thirds of whom were imposters, of course) for the program. He also noted that the man billed as the "Fastest Draw in the World" was beaten out on air by one of the "imposters"!

Before it hit daytime, the show first ran on CBS nighttime from December 18, 1956–May 22, 1967, with a brief detour into Sunday afternoons in 1966. Bud Collyer served as host there as well, with several celebrities billed as regular panelists during its prime-time tenure.

For the daytime show, although never officially classified as "regulars," Joan Fontaine, Phyllis Newman, and Barry Nelson were seen the most frequently in the first three years (nearly half of each year's shows). Nighttime regulars Kitty Carlisle and Tom Poston did not appear, and Peggy Cass and Orson Bean made only a few appearances in 1962–63 before they became nighttime regulars in 1964. By July 1965, however, CBS wanted to improve the show's iffy ratings, so Cass, Bean, and Poston became regulars in place of Fontaine, Newman, and Nelson, and on September 27, 1965, Carlisle officially joined the troupe, making it the same as the nighttime version for the rest of its run. Other panelists seen frequently in the daytime show from 1962–65 (at least 10 weeks of appearances) were Abe Burrows, Skitch Henderson, Sally Ann Howes, Milt Kamen, Sam Levenson, Darren McGavin, Chester Morris, Ann Sheridan, and Gretchen Wyler.

After ending in 1968, *To Tell the Truth* returned in a syndicated version a year later hosted by Garry Moore with Bean, Cass, Carlisle, and Bill Cullen as the regular panel. This lasted until 1978, with Joe Garagiola replacing the retiring Moore as host during the last season. In another syndicated version in 1980, in which Cass returned as a regular and Robin Ward was host, the show ended with "One on One," a game involving an undisclosed fact about one of the imposters in that day's activities which the panel had to pick.

Nearly a decade later, the show came back but failed to click despite trying several different hosts, including Alex Trebek, who also presided over *Concentration* on NBC at the same time. The 1991 version had Kitty Carlisle appear as a frequent guest, along with a few other unlikely personalities, such as controversial talk show host Morton Downey Jr.

•TODAY

News/Information; B&W and Color
January 14, 1952–

NBC Mon.–Fri. 7–9 a.m. (1/14/52–)
NBC Sun. 8–9:30 a.m. (9/20/87–9/13/92)
NBC Sun. 8–9 a.m. (9/20/92–)
NBC Sat. 8–10 a.m. (8/1/92–)

Hosts: *Dave Garroway (1/14/52–7/14/61), John Chancellor (7/17/61–9/28/62), Hugh Downs (10/1/62–10/11/71), Barbara Walters (1964–June 1976), Frank McGee (10/14/71–4/74), Jim Hartz (7/29/74–8/26/76), Tom Brokaw (8/29/76–12/18/81), Jane Pauley (1976–12/29/89), Bryant Gumbel (1/4/82–), Deborah Norville (9/5/89–2/18/91), Katie Couric (4/4/91–)*

Newscasters: *Jim Fleming (1/14/52–3/11/53), Frank Blair (3/14/53–3/14/75), Ed Newman (7/17/61–1962), Lew Wood (3/17/75–4/78), Floyd Kalber (6/77–8/3/79), Tony Guida (1979), Chris Wallace (1/4/82–9/24/82), John Palmer (9/27/82–1991), Faith Daniels (1991–92), Margaret Larson (1992–93), Matt Lauer (1/94–)*

Weathermen: *Bob Ryan (4/78–2/80), Willard Scott (3/80–)*

Regulars: *Jack Lescoulie (1/14/52–9/2/66), Charles Van Doren (1957–59), Martin Agronsky (at least 1961), Cleveland Amory (at least 1962–at least 1967), Aline Saarinen (at least 1962–72), Richard Watts (at least 1962), Ogden Nash (at least 1962), S. J. Perelman (at least 1963–at least 1965), Judith Crist (1964–73), Joe Garagiola (1967–73, 1991–92), Brian O'Doherty (at least 1972), Gene Shalit (1973–), Betty Furness (at least 1976–92), Dr. Art Ulene (1976–92, 1995–), Betty Furness (1976–92), Phil Donahue (1979–82), Ron Hendren (1979–80, 1984), Rona Barrett (1980–81), Linda Ellerbee (1984–86), Bill Macatee (1984)*

"The Today Girls": *Estelle Parsons (1954 at least), Lee Meriwether (1956), Helen O'Connell (1956–58), Betsy Palmer (1958–59), Florence Henderson (1959–60), Beryl Pfizer (1960–61), Robbin Bain (1961), Pat Fontaine (1962–64), Maureen O'Sullivan (March 1964–September 1964)*

Sunday Regulars: *Boyd Matson (1987–88), Maria Shriver (1987–90), Garrick Utley (1987–92), Mary Alice Williams (1990–92), Al Roker (1987–89, 1992–94), Bill MacAtee (1987–88)*

Saturday and Sunday Regulars: *Scott Simon (1992–93), Jackie Nespral (1992–94), Andy Pargh (1992–), Mike Schneider (1993–95), Giselle Fernandez (1994–96), Jack Ford (1995–), Jodie Applegate (1996–), Bob Kur (1996–)*

Today came to television as a pioneer in early morning (read before 10 a.m.) programming on the networks. It ended up being the longest-running daytime show ever, heading toward 45 years on NBC in 1997, and making almost as much news on its own with its backstage and on-air rumblings and changeovers. It made the careers of some, such as Barbara Walters and Hugh Downs, and inadvertently harmed those of others, such as Dave Garroway, but the show itself seemed invincible, despite the competition it faced in the 1990s from other networks and media. Indeed, no other network show but *Today* could claim to be on seven days a week.

Created by NBC executive Pat Weaver, who later gave NBC *Home* (q.v.), the show that debuted in 1952 resembled most of what still was on the show four decades later—news and weather updates every half hour, a genial host discussing items of current interest, and cutaways to local stations at around 25 minutes on the hour to do their own 5-minute local updates. Bespectacled Dave Garroway oversaw the whole affair, ending each show by extending the palm of his hand to the camera and saying "Peace." Also seen were sidekick Jack Lescoulie and newsman Frank Blair. Garroway handled the assignment for nine years until deciding to step down after his wife's death, and attempts to make a comeback on television afterward proved fruitless. After appearing on various *Today* anniversary shows, he took his life, in 1982.

But the element most responsible for making the show a hot ticket with the public was a chimpanzee dubbed J. Fred Muggs, whose mischievous antics tickled kids and forced their parents to watch the show. In fact, when the program scored an early major exclusive on June 29, 1953, as ex-President Harry Truman visited outside the big street window where the camera occasionally ventured to get shots of New Yorkers, Truman mistook J. Fred Muggs for a human infant! The glass screen disappeared on July 7, 1958, but it reappeared in the background of the show on June 20, 1994, an effort that boosted ratings to the top as it gave viewers the chance to hold up signs in the background.

As for J. Fred Muggs, he ended up becoming monkey non grata by biting Garroway on air at different times, once on the cheek and once on a finger. When the show dropped him, Muggs's owners filed a $500,000 lawsuit against NBC and Garroway for—you guessed it—"defamation of character." Muggs never appeared in the anniversary shows for *Today*, ending up instead as a twice-daily attraction on display at Busch Gardens in Tampa, Florida, by the mid-1970s, and in the 1980s *TV Guide* named its yearly recounting of dubious achievements in Muggs's honor.

Today overcame the influence of Muggs and took a more ambitious approach to covering the world around it. By 1960 the New York City–based series had visited Chicago, San Francisco, Los Angeles, Miami, Paris, London, Rome, and Berlin. For some overseas shows, programs were taped a day in advance and sent back to America by jet.

Some controversy did bedevil the show during the 1950s, however. The worst came in 1959 when show contributor Charles Van Doren admitted having received answers ahead

Today *regulars in 1956 were, clockwise from top left, Helen O'Connell, Frank Blair, Jack Lescoulie, the immortal J. Fred Muggs the chimp, and host Dave Garroway.*

of time for questions asked of him on the game show *Twenty-One*. His success on that show had led to his job at *Today*. "What do you want me to say?" a teary-eyed Dave Garroway told his audience following the revelation and Van Doren's immediate dismissal. "I can only say I'm heartsick."

Two years later, Garroway gave another emotional statement to his audience about his departure from the show. Reporter John Chancellor assumed hosting chores and Frank Blair was boosted to sidekick, and Edwin Newman became the latest newsreader. That group never clicked with viewers, so NBC tried another combination in 1962—Chancellor and Newman were out, Blair went back to doing news, and, most importantly, Hugh Downs became host. This one worked much better.

When Downs took over as host, a new "repertory company" of regular contributors appeared, including Cleveland Amory as social critic, Aline Saarinen as art critic, Richard Watts as theater critic (he did the same for *The New York Post*), Martin Agronsky as the lead interviewer in Washington, D.C., and Ogden Nash as poet laureate. The Muppets also made several appearances in the early years. The final major addition under Downs was that of Joe Garagiola as sidekick, taking over when producers decided not to renew

Jack Lescoulie's contract after some 13 years of work on the show (Lescoulie was not seen from July 1961–July 1962 as he hosted NBC'S nighttime children's series *1, 2, 3, Go*).

The one weak element left at the start of the Downs era was "the Today Girl," a post created in the mid-1950s in an effort to inject a feminine touch in the male-dominated show. The Today Girl's chores, like reading the weather and other minor announcements, were often demeaning, and turnover was high. (The longest-running ones are listed above.) The low point for the Today Girls might have been in 1958 when Betsy Palmer enthused, "Atta girl, Minnie!" after announcing that Cleveland Indians outfielder Minnie Minoso had scored a home run. Finally, when actress Maureen O'Sullivan left after six months in 1964, calling her job "asinine" and saying, "It's not enough to sit there and smile every day with nothing to do . . . . The show is simply no place for a woman," producer Al Morgan felt compelled to drop the title and simply promote a woman who had been doing three reports a week for the show. Her name was Barbara Walters, and her intelligent reporting pieces moved her up to co-anchor status by 1965.

Other highlights of the Downs era were his rare TV interview on April 19, 1963, with actor Marlon Brando, who railed against irresponsible journalism and remarked, "It seems to me that within two or three years I am coming to the end of my acting career"; the first Japan-to-United States telecast for eight minutes via satellite on March 25, 1964; and inauguration of the format in which shows were devoted to reviewing one topic or person in the two-hour period.

On the eve of its 15th anniversary, on January 8, 1967, the series had the first of its rather infrequent nighttime specials, *Today in Britain.* Not long after that, *TV Guide* praised the series in an "As We See It" column with the following comments: "If *Today* were the only television show on the air, we believe it would pay viewers to own a set . . . . *Today* is more than a good program. It's a necessary one." The Academy of Television Arts and Sciences showed that it concurred with that opinion by bestowing on *Today* Emmys for Outstanding Achievement in Daytime Programming in 1968, 1970, and 1971.

In 1971 Downs left, and veteran newsman Frank McGee, who had little regard for Walters and limited her role somewhat, joined the show until his untimely death in 1974. Later that year Jim Hartz, the late-night news anchor on WNBC New York City, got the hosting job over other candidates Tom Brokaw and Garrick Utley because, unlike them, he had no qualms about doing commercials. Things then went along relatively smoothly until Walters left the show in 1976 for the nighttime anchor spot on ABC. Her replacement was a 25-year-old reporter from Chicago named Jane Pauley, and with Pauley's arrival came a replacement for Jim Hartz as well, his former competition: Washington, D.C., reporter Tom Brokaw.

Floyd Kalber, Pauley's former news co-anchor in Chicago, became the new newsreader in June 1977. That move demoted Lew Wood, who had replaced Frank Blair after the latter retired following 22 years on the show, to weatherman, and Wood left within a year. Wood was replaced first by Bob Ryan and then by the man who held the post the longest, Willard Scott. Scott, a 250-pound, toupee-wearing jokester, started his tradition of wishing people a happy 100th birthday when a man wrote to the show in 1981 and asked him to do so for his uncle. His antics continued into 1996, by which time he was alternating duties with former weekend weatherman and equally rotund and antic Al Roker. Meanwhile, when Kalber left in 1979, Tony Guida replaced him briefly until the decision was made to have Brokaw and Pauley read the news.

Others seen in the 1970s were Brian O'Doherty, the replacement for Saarinen as art critic (she ended her tenure doing filmed reports from Europe); health expert Dr. Art Ulene; bushy-haired movie critic Gene Shalit, who took over from Judith Crist; TV reviewer Ron Hendren; and Phil Donahue, who did a brief taped audience discussion piece.

An important new contributor emerged in 1980. Bryant Gumbel began doing sports segments three days a week on *Today* starting September 8, 1980, then a year later did his first stint as a substitute host. A few months later, he became co-anchor with Pauley when Brokaw left to do *The NBC*

The main team on Today *in the 1960s was, from left, Hugh Downs, Barbara Walters, and Frank Blair.*

Nightly News. It was a tough decade for the show, as *Good Morning America* overtook it in the ratings, but apart from having Chris Wallace and then John Palmer handle the news, the team of Gumbel, Pauley, and Willard remained steady until things really unraveled in 1989.

In February of that year, many newspapers reported on Gumbel's infamous memo criticizing virtually all of the on-air performers except Pauley (he characterized Willard as "corny" and Dr. Art Ulene as "boring," for example). Gumbel apologized on air, but the damage had already been done. Then later that year Deborah Norville, newsreader on *NBC News at Sunrise,* moved onto the show to replace John Palmer, who swapped to get Norville's old job temporarily. Then, on September 5, 1989, Norville joined Bryant and Pauley on the couch on *Today*'s opening, and rumors began flying concerning the not very convincing on-air friendship between Norville and Pauley. To many it appeared that the ultimate goal of the show's producers was to move the younger, blonde Norville into Pauley's spot. The maneuvering was so obvious that even NBC's own *Saturday Night Live* spoofed it in a parody titled *All About Deborah.*

Pauley showed how classy she was by announcing on air her decision to step down "voluntarily," as she put it, and Norville had taken over by the start of 1990. But plenty of the

Regulars on Today *in the 1980s included, clockwise from top left, Willard Scott, Gene Shalit, John Palmer, Bryant Gumbel, and Jane Pauley.*

audience still felt that Norville had wormed her way into the job, fairly or unfairly, and ratings fell. Rehiring Joe Garagiola to do sports and another blonde, Faith Daniels, to do news did not help. Then in April 1991, with Norville on maternity leave, NBC announced that Washington, D.C.–based reporter Katie Couric, who had been reporting for the show for at least a year in addition to substituting occasionally for Katie, had officially replaced Norville as hostess. She clicked, and by 1996 *Today* was topping *Good Morning America* in the ratings. That same year, Gumbel announced he planned to leave the show by 1997, giving rise to speculation that current news anchor Matt Lauer would take over his post.

The show added a weekend edition in 1987 (there was a quasi-spin-off from 1963–65; see *Sunday).* Boyd Matson and Maria Shriver were the original co-hosts, with Garrick Utley the news anchor and Al Roker the weathercaster. Regular segments were "Fast Forward" (a preview of the week's events), "What's Happening" (arts and entertainment news), and "Sunday Brunch" (chefs presenting their meals). In 1988 Utley replaced Matson, then became the sole host for a time starting January 15, 1989 when production moved from New York City to Washington, D.C., to accommodate Utley's hosting duties for *Meet the Press.* Shriver rejoined him, then left on April 8, 1990, and Mary Alice Williams replaced her. Production went back to New York City in 1992 when a Saturday edition was added, and Utley and Williams had been dropped by August.

For the new Saturday and Sunday shows, former National Public Radio reporter Scott Simon and Jackie Nespral assumed hosting duties. Simon left within the year by mutual agreement with producers that neither was what the other wanted, and ex–*Good Morning America* newscaster Mike Schneider replaced him. Schneider was gone by May 1995, with legal correspondent Jack Ford taking his place, while Nespral returned to reporting in Miami. Giselle Fernandez replaced Nespral until 1996, when Jodie Applegate took over and Bob Kur started doing the half-hour news summaries from Washington, D.C. Al Roker's departure two years earlier was covered by guest meteorologists from various NBC affiliates. Somehow surviving all the personnel changeover was jovial Andy Pargh, the "Gadget Guru" who introduced inventions each week.

TODAY IS OURS
Soap Opera; B&W
June 30, 1958–December 26, 1958

NBC Mon.–Fri. 3–3:30 p.m. (6/30/58–12/26/58)

Cast:

Laura Manning	Patricia Benoit
Karl Manning	Patrick O'Neal
Glenn Turner	Ernest Graves
Nick "Nicky" Manning	Peter Lazar
Leslie Williams Manning	Joyce Lear
Ellen Wilson	Chase Crosley
Peter Hall	John McGovern

Today Is Ours holds the distinction of being the first TV soap opera to feature a divorcée as the romantic heroine. Laura Manning, the assistant principal of Bolton Central High School, had to manage a single household with her prepubescent son Nicky. Her ex-husband Karl loved her, but Laura felt more of an attraction to architect Glenn Turner. She had to juggle her romantic life with plenty of conflicts at school and home, which ranged from a parent who tried to bribe her into giving his spoiled son passing grades to Nicky playing hooky from school. Meanwhile, Karl married New York society girl Leslie Williams, and his attention to her upset Nicky greatly. Many other subplots were woven into the story, the most prominent of which was the turbulent relationship of Ellen Wilson and Peter Hall. This series was a short-lived replacement for *Matinee Theater*.

TODAY ON THE FARM
Informational; B&W
October 1, 1960–March 11, 1961

NBC Sat. 7–7:30 a.m. (10/1/60–3/11/61)

Regulars: *Eddy Arnold, Alex Dreier, Mal Hansen, Carmelita Pope, Joe Slattery, Slim Wilson*

Six years after using Eddy Arnold as host of *Out on the Farm* (q.v.), NBC tried him for another agricultural news show based in Chicago. It included news from Alex Dreier, farm updates from Mal Hansen, weather from Joe Slattery, and women's information from Carmelita Pope. Slim Wilson joined Arnold to do an occasional song. The series was taped to allow all NBC affiliates to air it during the Saturday morning breakfast hour of 7 a.m.

TODAY WITH MRS. ROOSEVELT
Public Affairs; B&W
February 12, 1950–July 15, 1951

NBC Sun. 4–4:30 p.m. (2/12/50–5/28/50)
NBC Sun. 3:30–4 p.m. (10/1/50–7/15/51)

Hostess: *Eleanor Roosevelt*

A classy discussion series simulcast on radio, *Today with Mrs. Roosevelt* presented the former First Lady and widow of President Franklin D. Roosevelt as moderator of talks involving dignitaries. The debut, dealing with plans for the hydrogen bomb, featured none other than Dr. Albert Einstein in a newsworthy interview filmed the Friday before in which he said that the H-bomb was bad. A few of the follow-ups also made headlines. President Harry Truman requested a copy of the March 26, 1950 show featuring Democratic officials addressing foreign policy concerns (he received only a soundtrack, as there was no kinescope of the live program). The following month, the American Civil Liberties Union protested the cancellation of a show with Paul Robeson discussing "The Position of the Negro in American Life," with the release of a statement which read, "We deplore in this case what those who protested meant to accomplish, and what they did accomplish, namely the suppression of ideas repugnant to themselves."

Other less controversial guests seen were Tallulah Bankhead, Jose Ferrer, and TV critic John Crosby. The show originated from the Park Sheraton Hotel in New York, where Mrs. Roosevelt offered guests tea and bread before air time. *Newsweek* reported her set was specially brought from her old home, now the national museum at Hyde Park. Her son Elliot Roosevelt co-produced the show. After a summer hiatus when Mrs. Roosevelt went to Europe, the show had one more season under the title *Mrs. Roosevelt Meets the Public*.

•TOM AND JERRY
Cartoon; Color
September 25, 1965–September 4, 1982

CBS Sat. 11–11:30 a.m. (9/25/65–9/3/66)
CBS Sat. 1–1:30 p.m. (9/10/66–9/2/67)
CBS Sun. 9–9:30 a.m. (9/10/67–9/17/72)
ABC Sat. 8:30–9:30 a.m. (9/6/75–9/4/76)
ABC Sat. 8–9 a.m. (9/11/76–11/27/76)
ABC Sat. 8–8:30 a.m. (12/4/76–9/3/77)
CBS Sat. 8:30–9 a.m. (9/6/80–3/7/81)
CBS Sat. 8–8:30 a.m. (3/14/81–9/5/81)
CBS Sat. 12:30–1 p.m. (9/19/81–9/4/82)

Voices:

Grape Ape (1975–77)	Bob Holt
Beagle (1975–77)	Marty Ingels
Mumbly (1976–77)	Don Messick
Schnooker (1976–77)	John Stephenson

*Barney Bear/Droopy/Spike/Slick
    the Wolf (all 1980–82)*   *Frank Welker*

Tom the cat and Jerry the mouse spent 25 years on movie
screens without talking before they brought their slapstick
pantomime to Saturday morning cartoons. The duo was
unique in that they could be working against each other in
one adventure while united to fight a common enemy in
another. The 1965–72 run included repeats of their theatrical
shorts plus two other MGM movie cartoon series, "Barney
Bear" (it ran from 1948–54) and "Droopy," about a mush-
mouthed, meek bloodhound who fought Spike the bulldog
and Slick the Wolf (it ran from 1949–58).

In 1975 ABC revived the property as *The Tom and
Jerry/Grape Ape Show*, with new cartoons of the former. Grape
Ape was a 30-foot-tall simian whose dog pal was Beagle (see
The Great Grape Ape for more details). A year later it became
The Tom and Jerry/Grape Ape/Mumbly Show, with the new
character in the title referring to a private-eye dog and his
partner Schnooker. The Grape Ape spun off its own show
in December 1976, and *The Tom and Jerry/Mumbly Show*
became history on September 3, 1977.

Three years later, the new *Tom and Jerry Comedy Hour*
brought back the star animals along with new versions of
their MGM cartoon buddies Barney, Droopy, Spike, and
Slick. Most of them reappeared in yet another rendition a
decade later (see *Tom and Jerry Kids*).

•TOM AND JERRY KIDS
Cartoon; Color
September 8, 1990–October 30, 1993

Fox Sat. 9–9:30 a.m. (9/8/90–4/13/91)
Fox Sat. 9–10 a.m. (two shows; 4/20/91–8/31/91)
Fox Sat. 9–9:30 a.m. (9/7/91–10/30/93)

Voices: *Frank Welker*

The younger versions of the old cat and mouse duo became
the focal point of this cartoon, along with a host of new
characters (Wild Mouse, the Gator Brothers, Slow Poke
Antonio) and old favorites (Droopy, Spike, Slick). Frank
Welker was back to voice the old 1940s supporting characters,
with the new Droopy, seen with his soon Dripple, getting
his own show in 1993 (see *Droopy, Master Detective*). The
shows also aired daily in repeats from 1992–93.

•TOM CORBETT, SPACE CADET
Science Fiction; B&W
August 29, 1953–June 25, 1955

Dumont Sat. 11:30 a.m.–Noon (8/29/53–5/22/54)
NBC Sat. 11:30 a.m.–Noon (12/11/54–6/25/55)

Cast:

Tom Corbett	*Frankie Thomas*
Capt. Steve Strong	*Ed Bryce*
Astro the Venusian	*Al Markim*
Cadet Roger Manning	
(1953–54)	*Jan Merlin*
Cadet T. J. Thistle (1954–55)	*Jack Grimes*
Commander Arkwright	
(1953–54 at least)	*Carter Blake*
Betty (1953–54)	*Beryl Berney*
Gloria (1953–54)	*Marion Brash*
Dr. Joan Gale	*Margaret Garland*

Based on Robert A. Heinlein's novel *Space Cadet, Tom Corbett*
was one of the rare TV shows to be seen on four networks. It
debuted in a nighttime slot, thrice weekly on CBS from 6:45–7
p.m., on October 2, 1950. The show was set 400 years in the
future; humans had contacted aliens from Mars and Venus and
formed the Solar Alliance with them 100 years earlier, in 2250,
following a period of initial conflicts. The alliance established
Solar Guards as ambassadors of peace for other planets, and
the guards, who trained as space cadets, would fight only for
freedom and liberty (there were no guns in the 2350s). The
series focused on one of these trainees, the eager Tom Corbett.

Overseeing Tom's career and education was Captain
Steve Strong. Tom's fellow student and friend was the rather
endearing Astro the Venusian. These characters lasted the
show's full run. Cadet Roger Manning served as comic relief
until T. J. Thistle took his place. A new addition in 1953
was Commander Arkwright, the space school's sympathetic
leader. Dr. Gale stayed as Tom's girlfriend. They all took part
in reality-based adventures set in space.

Conferring about matters not of this earth on Tom Corbett, Space
Cadet *in 1955 are, from left, T. J. Thistle (Jack Grimes), Tom
Corbett (Frankie Thomas), and Astro the Venusian (Al Markim).*

Tom Corbett ended on CBS December 29, 1950, then started on ABC thrice weekly from 6:30–6:45 p.m. from January 1, 1951–September 26, 1952. During this period, NBC got into the act by showing old kinescopes Saturdays from 7–7:30 p.m. July 7 through September 8, 1951. The next stop, fourth network DuMont, came in the fall of 1953, and despite the year's hiatus the program had retained its hold on the public. Shortly before starting its daytime run, *Variety* announced that there were 30 firms distributing 100 products related to the series, from clothes to toys.

The series alternated for a year on Dumont with the similar (but cheaper looking and much less realistic) *Captain Video*, then returned six months later to finish its run on NBC, which outbid DuMont for the show. *Tom Corbett* also ran briefly on radio on ABC in 1952 with the TV cast in a separate series.

TOMFOOLERY
Cartoon; Color
September 12, 1970–September 4, 1971

NBC Sat. 9–9:30 a.m. (9/12/70–1/9/71)
NBC Sat. 8–8:30 a.m. (1/16/71–9/4/71)

Voices: *Peter Hawkins, Bernard Spear, the Maury Laws Singers*

Tomfoolery used the characters and plots of Edward Lear's *The Nonsense Books* and a few other "literary" pieces as the source for a hard-to-follow rapid-fire assortment of limericks, songs, and sketches. *Lancelot Link* on ABC and *Sabrina and the Groovie Goolies* on CBS smothered this effort within four months, after which NBC moved it up an hour before it died an unlamented death.

TOOTSIE HIPPODROME
Children's; B&W
February 3, 1952–January 30, 1954

ABC Sun. 12:15–12:30 p.m. (2/3/52–1/25/53)
ABC Sun. Noon–12:30 p.m. (2/1/53–6/28/53)
ABC Sat. 10–10:30 a.m. (8/29/53–1/30/54)

Hosts: *John Reed King (1952), Boyd Heath (1952–53), Whitey Carson (as Captain Tootsie; 1953–54)*
Assistant: *Mary Reynolds (1953–54)*

Children ages 5–10 competed on this talent contest for the chance to win a performing slot on *Paul Whiteman's TV Teen Club*, a nighttime ABC series begun in 1949 which coincidentally or not went off the air only two months after this series ended. The show also had some circus acts and giveaway prizes and went through three hosts, ending with Whitey Carson, who was one of the series' producers. It aired live from New York.

•TOP CAT
Cartoon; Color
October 6, 1962–May 10, 1969

ABC Sat. 11:30 a.m.–Noon (10/6/62–12/29/62)
ABC Sat. 11–11:30 a.m. (1/5/63–3/30/63)

Arnold Stang, the voice of the title character on Top Cat, *stands next to the cartoon feline, who is hugging Benny the Ball.*

NBC Sat. 9–9:30 a.m. (4/3/65–9/25/65)
NBC Sat. 11–11:30 a.m. (10/2/65–9/3/66)
NBC Sat. Noon–12:30 p.m. (9/10/66–12/31/66)
NBC Sat. Noon–12:30 p.m. (9/9/67–5/25/68)
NBC Sat. 9:30–10 a.m. (9/14/68–5/10/69)

Voices:

Top Cat ("T. C.")	Arnold Stang
Officer Dibble	Allen Jenkins
Benny the Ball	Maurice Gosfield
Choo Choo	Marvin Kaplan
Fancy-Fancy	John Stephenson
Spook/The Brain	Leo De Lyon
Various	Paul Frees

Producers/Directors: *William Hanna and Joseph Barbera*

Imagine the 1955–59 CBS nighttime sitcom *The Phil Silvers Show* (a.k.a *You'll Never Get Rich*) redone using alley cats in New York City and you will have a good idea of what this cartoon was like. Top Cat ("T. C." to his five feline cohorts) was the Sergeant Bilko equivalent, the one who masterminded the scams, including pool and pinochle games, to get the best things in life for free. His activities, especially when they involved using the police telephone on a pole in his alley, often drew the wrath of Officer Dibble, but the gullible cop was always too thoroughly fooled by T. C.'s cons to be able to capture and put the latter behind bars. His five followers had rather indistinct personalities, although Benny, the short, rotund blue cat, did seem to be his most diligent follower and the ironically named Brain had the most trouble in following orders. Interestingly, Maurice Gosfield, who voiced Benny, had a similar role in *Phil Silvers* as Private Duane Doberman.

Believe it or not, this Hanna-Barbera production attracted some major names who auditioned unsuccessfully to voice a cat, such as Herschel Bernardi, Stubby Kaye, Ken Murray, Jack Oakie, and Jesse White. Additionally, Daws Butler was set to do the voice of T. C. when other commitments forced him to withdraw.

Top Cat aired on Saturday mornings in repeats. It had only one season of original episodes which first aired on ABC Tuesdays from 8:30–9 p.m. from September 27, 1961–September 26, 1962.

TOP DOLLAR
Game; B&W
August 18, 1958–October 23, 1959
CBS Mon.–Fri. 11:30–Noon (8/18/58–10/23/59)
Regulars: *Warren Hull (8/18/58–10/31/58), Jack Narz (11/3/58–10/23/59), Dr. Bergen Evans*

The old parlor game Ghost was revised for this series, wherein a trio of players gave one letter at a time in an attempt to force the other player or players to make a word out of it and disqualify them from further rounds. Any player who felt another contestant was adding a letter that could not make a word could challenge that contestant, with Dr. Bergen Evans serving as final judge as to whether the claim was right. Each letter added was worth $100, and the one remaining contestant at the end won all the money amassed in the game. After a few months in this format, the show had contestants play Hangman instead (see *Wheel of Fortune* for information on that game).

The "top dollar" session in the program involved home viewers trying to match the first eight letters of the longest word created in the game, with the letters being converted to numbers using the arrangement of a telephone dial. Those who sent matching dollar bills won $100 each.

Top Dollar went on daytime rather suddenly to replace the scandal-plagued *Dotto* (q.v.). CBS did the series pilot in 1957, and plans were under way for the show to replace *The Garry Moore Show*, with Durward Kirby of that series as host, but they did not materialize. *Top Dollar* began airing first on CBS Saturdays at 8:30 p.m. from March 29–August 30, 1958 with Toby Reed as host. (On one memorable evening show on June 21, 1958, contestant Alice Young left the stage when she was not allowed to start a word with the letter "J"!) After a year of being unable to beat *Concentration* on NBC, the daytime version ended too.

TOP PRO GOLF—See *All-Star Golf.*

TOP 10 DANCE PARTY
Music; B&W
1955–67

Syndicated 60 minutes daily beginning September 1955

Another "franchised" series (for others, see *Bozo the Clown* and *Romper Room*), *Top 10 Dance Party* was an *American Bandstand*–type dance show for teenagers. Local stations used their own hosts and dancers from their area to move to the recorded music as part of the production. The show began in Memphis, Tennessee.

TOPPER CARTOON FUN
Cartoon; Color
September 26, 1965–December 19, 1965
ABC Sun. 4:30–5 p.m. (9/26/65–12/19/65)

This series repeated episodes of *Hoppity Hooper* and *Dudley Do-Right*. (See individual titles for voices and details.)

TRACK AND FIELD—See *AAU Track and Field.*

TREASURE HUNT
Game; B&W
August 12, 1957–December 4, 1959
NBC Mon.–Fri. 10:30–11 a.m. (8/12/57–12/4/59)
Host: *Jan Murray*
"The Pirate Girl": *Pat White (1957), Marian Stafford (1957–59)*

Treasure Hunt was basically a game of hide-and-seek for adults. Two players took part in a question-and-answer session and earned $50 for each right answer. The one with the most money at the end of the round got to pick from 30 "treasure chests" seen on stage which contained everything from worthless prizes to a check for $10,000, which increased $1,000 each week it was not found. Helping out in the festivities was "the Pirate Girl" (also the show's theme), played by Pat White until December 1957.

The show began on ABC Fridays at 9 p.m. from September 7, 1956–May 24, 1957. After three months on NBC daytime, the latter network also added an edition Tuesdays at 7:30 p.m. from December 24, 1957–June 17, 1958. Jan Murray, who created the show, also hosted the nighttime installments. The daytime edition went off the air in 1959 when advertisers pulled out, thinking it was rigged like others in the quiz show scandals even though NBC insisted it was "clean." Ironically, its replacement, *Play Your Hunch*, ran against it on CBS in 1958.

In 1973 a revival titled *The New Treasure Hunt* aired in nighttime syndication through 1976. Now hosted by Geoff Edwards, it dispensed with the game portion and concentrated solely on two contestants each day picking their own chest and getting a money amount revealed to them. The player could keep that money or tell Edwards that he or she wanted what was in the box, which now went up to a check for $25,000. Most boxes, however, contained elaborate sketches done by Edwards and various actors which led up to a contestant winning anything from a worthless gift to a car. Edwards hosted another syndicated revival of the show from 1981–82.

•TREASURE ISLE
Game; Color
December 18, 1967–December 27, 1968
ABC Mon.–Fri. 12:30–1 p.m. (12/18/67–12/27/68)

Host: *John Bartholemew Tucker*

For people who loved complicated yet stupid games, *Treasure Isle* was a mother lode. The idiocy started with the host and two married or engaged couples, one the red team and one the yellow team, entering camera range while riding boats and wearing swimsuits. They wore this unconventional TV attire because the show was set on an outdoor mock island, complete with lagoon, that took up a city block in Palm Beach Shores, Florida, in the Colonnades Beach Hotel facing the Atlantic Ocean. This, mind you, was the least confusing element of the series.

The show's first contest allotted 90 seconds for the women to break balloons and retrieve cut foam puzzle pieces from the lagoon to give to their partner on Treasure Isle (later programs had the men paddle alone in rubber rafts in the lagoon while being directed by their wives to get the pieces). Each piece returned to the island helped form a nonsense riddle, a quatrain referring to a real or fictional person. For example, "Motoring seat/Tot's spoon/Can't be beat/Goddess of moon" referred to Diana Ross and the Supremes because their hometown of Detroit was the "Motoring seat," "Tot's spoon" suggested their hit record "Baby Love," "Can't be beat" means something is supreme, and Diana is the "Goddess of moon." Got all that?

After hints from the host, one couple somehow usually succeeded in deciphering the clues and solving the riddle

Yo ho ho! Even John Bartholomew Tucker, the host of Treasure Isle, *looks a bit disgruntled on the set of this weird and not-so-wonderful game show.*

and so got to play the bonus round, a two-minute treasure hunt to locate boxes hidden on the island containing prizes, including two boxes with prizes for home viewers. Here again, some locations involved clues from the host, who seemed almost as flustered as the contestants in this final section, especially when he reviewed the booty they collected. It could have been worse; test runs had contestants use Geiger counters and metal detectors to search for "buried treasure," and planned to use a monkey to call a "lucky viewer" at home about the prizes won. The producers also paid Jordan Kline, the gadget designer for the James Bond film *Thunderball,* some $180,000 for special effects like whirlpools and tidal waves that were never used on air. This was not because they would have added to the confusion, of course, but because of the extra hazards they might have been for contestants.

Sherman Adler, head of the series' packaging company MacArthur Productions, gave *TV Guide* his assessment of the show: "If it bombs, at least we can say we dared to do it." He might also have said that he gave the world possibly the worst game show of all time.

TRIALWATCH
Informational; Color
January 28, 1991–July 26, 1991
NBC Mon.–Fri. 10–10:30 a.m. (1/28/91–7/26/91)

Hosts: *Robb Weller, Lisa Specht*

Reviews and reports of actual court cases across America formed the focus for this show, with participants often interviewed as part of the presentations. Co-host Lisa Specht was also a practicing attorney.

•TRIVIA TRAP
Game; Color
October 8, 1984–April 5, 1985
ABC Mon.–Fri. 11–11:30 a.m. (10/8/84–4/5/85)

Host: *Bob Eubanks*

Inspired no doubt by the success of the home game Trivial Pursuit, *Trivia Trap* had a basic three-on-three competition, with one trio above the age of 30 and the other below it, answering general-knowledge questions to amass $1,000 and being able to play a bonus game for a possible $10,000. Among the typical stumpers in the bonus, where contestants picked one correct answer out of four possibilities, was "Who was Burt Reynolds's first wife?"

TROLLKINS
Cartoon; Color
September 12, 1981–September 4, 1982
CBS Sat. 8:30–9 a.m. (9/12/81–11/28/81)
CBS Sat. Noon–12:30 p.m. (12/5/81–9/4/82)

Voices:

Sheriff Pudge Trollsom	Allan Oppenheimer
Pixlee Trollsom/DepuTroll	
Dolly Durkle	Jennifer Darling

Top Troll/Bogg/Flooky	Frank Welker
Grubb Trollmaine	Michael Bell
DepuTroll Flake	Marshall Efron
Mayor Lumpkin	Paul Winchell
Aphid	Hank Saroyan
Slug	Bill Callaway
Blitz Plumkin	Steve Spears

Trolltown was a burg located in a hollow tree trunk. Its itsy-bitsy populace had blue, green, and purple faces, sported items like Trollchoppers, and dropped the word "troll" into seemingly every sentence as an adjective. In other words, they were pretty much like The Smurfs. Minor differences between their world and the Smurfs' included a more sexually integrated society, an overtly comic mayor named Lumpkin, and the mayor's daughter Pixlee, who was wed to Sheriff Pudge. Ironically, the show ran against *The Smurfs*' first half hour before moving to noon and then cancellation.

TRUE STORY

Dramatic Anthology; B&W
March 16, 1957–September 9, 1961

NBC Sat. Noon–12:30 p.m. (3/16/57–9/9/61)

Hostess/Narrator: *Kathi Norris*

This live New York playhouse production was based on the long-running magazine of the same name, which in turn became a radio show on ABC from 1943–57, NBC from 1957–59 and Mutual from 1961–62 under the title *My True Story*. On TV, its novelty was that the hostess addressed the camera as if she were interviewing the participants of that day's tale. Otherwise, it was standard melodramatic fare with mostly little-known actors. The opener, with Phil Abbott and June Dayton in a potboiler about a man trying to prove his alibi for the night when his ex-girlfriend was murdered, was typical. But some top talent did appear in this series, such as Charles Grodin, Jean Stapleton, and Ruth Warrick in 1960 alone.

•TRUTH OR CONSEQUENCES

Game; B&W and Color
December 31, 1956–September 24, 1965

NBC Mon.–Fri. 11:30 a.m.–Noon (12/31/56–7/25/58)
NBC Mon.–Fri. 2–2:30 p.m. (8/25/58–3/27/59)
NBC Mon.–Fri. 4–4:30 p.m. (3/30/59–9/25/59)
NBC Mon.–Fri. Noon–12:30 p.m. (11/2/59–12/29/61)
NBC Mon.–Fri. 12:30–12:55 p.m. (1/2/62–3/26/65)
NBC Mon.–Fri. 10–10:30 a.m. (3/29/65–9/24/65)

Host: *Bob Barker*

Producer/Creator: *Ralph Edwards*

The granddaddy of all TV stunt games, *Truth or Consequences* began on CBS radio March 23, 1940, switched to NBC from 1941–50, then returned to CBS 1950–51, and finally returned to NBC from 1952–57. It made its TV debut on WNBT

New York on July 1, 1941, then had another experimental telecast on KNBH Hollywood in January 1949 before becoming a CBS nighttime series from September 7, 1950–June 7, 1951. Another nighttime version aired on NBC from May 18, 1954–September 28, 1956 and then December 13, 1957–June 6, 1958, by which time it had started a run in daytime that lasted for nearly a decade.

Each contestant invariably had to perform an out-of-the-ordinary activity as a "consequence" of not telling "the truth" about a riddle posed by the emcee. (A typical riddle went, "How many successful jumps must a successful paratrooper make?" The answer was, of course, "All of them.") Most of the situations were humorous to the audience if not the participants, but not all of them. (One setup, for example, had a man agree to spend months on a desert island without access to outside communication.) No matter what the challenge was, however, contestants usually found themselves adequately compensated by money or gifts after completing their tasks. There were also other segments, ranging from reunions of long-lost relatives to contests for the home studio audience.

Ginny Kruse, a mother of two, was an assistant to the show's producer. Kruse also served as the guinea pig in predicting contestants' reactions to the "consequences," testing such stunts as drinking water upside down or telling the difference between a bald head and a watermelon. Her expertise must have counted for something, as the show piled up an impressive daytime run of nearly nine years.

Bob Barker seemed to be the only host with the magic touch for this series, as he continued to do the same job from 1966–75 in syndication. Among nighttime network efforts, show producer Ralph Edwards (1950–51), Jack Bailey (1954–56), and Steve Dunne (1957–58) flopped. Attempted syndicated revivals by hosts Bob Hilton (1977) and Larry Anderson (1987) failed as well.

TURBO TEEN

Cartoon; Color
September 8, 1984–August 31, 1985

ABC Sat. 9:30–10 a.m. (9/8/84–8/31/85)

Voices:

Brett Matthews	
Pattie	Michael Mish
Alex	Pamela Hayden
Flip/Rusty	T. K. Carter
Eddie	Frank Welker
	Pat Fraley

Thanks to an accident at a government laboratory, sports car driver Brett Matthews found that whenever his body heat rose, he could transform himself into his automobile. He kept this a secret known only to federal officials, his girlfriend Pattie, and his pal Alex, as he used his powers to fight for good in the world against such foes as a big-wheeled truck. That's fine and dandy, but adults have got to wonder just what this guy could do for fun, anyway. The show aired segments in 3-D.

TURN TO A FRIEND
Game; B&W
October 5, 1953–December 31, 1953
ABC Mon.–Fri. 4–4:30 p.m. (10/5/53–12/31/53

Host: *Dennis James*

Three people in the audience, all in dire straits, came onstage with a pal to answer questions and win money in this adaptation of a game show previously airing on ABC radio with James as host. ABC-TV axed this at the end of 1953, the same time it canned its only other daily series, *The Ern Westmore Show*, which followed *Turn*—both due to a lack of sponsors.

$20,000 PYRAMID, THE—See $25,000 Pyramid, The.

•$25,000 PYRAMID, THE
Game; Color
March 26, 1973–July 1, 1988
CBS Mon.–Fri. 10:30–11 a.m. (3/26/73–3/29/74)
ABC Mon.–Fri. 4–4:30 p.m. (5/6/74–12/20/74)
ABC Mon.–Fri. 2–2:30 p.m. (12/23/74–1/13/78)
ABC Mon.–Fri. Noon–12:30 p.m.
CBS Mon.–Fri. 10–10:30 a.m. (9/20/82–12/31/87)
CBS Mon.–Fri. 10–10:30 a.m. (4/4/88–7/1/88)

Host: *Dick Clark*

One of television's greatest game shows, *The $25,000 Pyramid* began as *The $10,000 Pyramid* in 1973 before being upped to *The $25,000 Pyramid* on January 19, 1976 and increased $5,000 more in 1982. Created by Bob Stewart (the man who came up with *To Tell the Truth* and *Password* for Goodson-Todman Productions) it had two pairs, each with a celebrity, compete at the start of the show by alternately selecting one of six cryptically titled boxes in a pyramid formation (one at the top, two in the middle, three at the bottom). The host told the pair at play the category of seven things (originally eight) that one partner had to convey to the other within 30 seconds in any manner except using part of the word as a clue. After three rounds to use up all six boxes and let both partners play, plus a tiebreaker if needed, the team with the most identifications played the Winner's Circle. Here one partner had a minute to give only a list of elements in categories revealed by each of six boxes in the same pyramid setup as before, beginning with the three on bottom and working across from row to row up to the top. Correct identification of all six won at least $10,000 the first time. For less than six matches, the payoff was $100 per bottom box, $200 per middle box, and $300 for the top box from 1973–76, then double those amounts from 1976–80, and then $50 for the first box increasing $50 more to the last one at the top for $300 in 1982–88.

After a contestant went through the first Winner's Circle of the day, he or she competed in another qualifying game involving six subjects. In the 1970s the player had a new opponent each time and, by 1976, got to try $15,000 the second time and $20,000 every time thereafter until they won the top prize. From 1982–88 teams switched partners

on each day's show, and the one earning the most at the Winner's Circle got the opportunity to come back and play for more money the next day. A person who played the Winner's Circle twice that day went for $10,000 the first time and $25,000 the second.

The show offered a few extra incentives in the qualifying games. In the 1970s one round each day had a hidden "Big 7" where a player could win $500 for getting all seven items in that category, plus a bonus of $1,000 for anyone scoring a perfect 21 in a round with his or her partner. In the 1980s, the "Mystery 7" continued the "Big 7" tradition with the twist that no player knew what the category was, and the "7–11," where a team getting all seven right in 30 seconds for this box won $1,100.

The show was taped in New York City, which meant that Dick Clark had to commute from Hollywood to do the show. He was involved in one syndicated version of the show, *The $50,000 Pyramid* in 1981, as well, while other syndicated spin-offs included *The $25,000 Pyramid* in 1974–79 with Bill Cullen as host, and *The $100,000 Pyramid* in 1991 with John Davidson as emcee.

•TWISTED TALES OF FELIX THE CAT, THE
Cartoon; Color
September 16, 1995–
CBS Sat. 11–11:30 a.m. (9/16/95–)

Voice:
Felix   *Thom Adcox*

Felix the Cat was one of the first superstars to appear on television. Actually, it was a model of the comic strip character which showed up on experimental telecasts in 1928, at a time when the hot lights needed to transmit images across the airwaves were impossible for any human to bear. The feline's real debut in the entertainment world occurred in movie cartoons in 1922, followed by a TV series which began in production in 1958 and went into syndication in five-minute cartoons in January 1960. Here Felix used a magic bag that he could reach into and pluck out extraordinary items. He had to avoid letting this power fall prey to the cunning Professor, who coveted it and who enlisted as his henchman in efforts to steal the bag Rock Bottom, his bulldog. In less stressful moments, Felix spent time helping the Professor's egghead nephew Poindexter. All characters were voiced by Jack Mercer.

Nearly 35 years later, CBS decided the time was ripe for a revival of the property. The network had become so enthusiastic about the idea in 1994 that it developed 55 five-second "bumpers" featuring Felix to use between its cartoons that fall, as the network wanted to introduce the character to a new generation successfully yet did not have time to get it on the schedule. A year later, *The Twisted Tales of Felix the Cat* debuted in a jerky style (the characters seemed to bounce) much like that seen in the 1920s cartoons created by Otto Messmer and Joe Oriolo. This was understandable given that the new series had Oriolo's son Don as co–executive producer.

On the new cartoon Felix was seen in seven-minute segments using both his magic bag and his magic tail to defeat a variety of enemies. His tail could transform itself from a flashlight to a grappling device to a sword in the fast-moving, often inventive entries. Felix also could talk, in a childlike voice, and, as in 1994, several *Felix* bumpers appeared between segments.

TWO GIRLS NAMED SMITH
Sitcom; B&W
January 20, 1951–October 13, 1951

ABC Sat. Noon–12:30 p.m. (1/20/51–10/13/51)

Cast:

Babs Smith (1/20/51–9/22/51)	*Peggy Ann Garner*
Babs Smith (9/29/51–10/13/51)	*Marcia Henderson*
Peggy Smith	*Peggy French*

Others: *Joseph Buloff, Adelaide Klein*

Two Girls Named Smith featured two actresses named Peggy as leads in this pioneering Saturday morning sitcom. Babs was an aspiring model, while Peggy (the character) was a painter. Adelaide Klein played their landlady, while Joseph Buloff played a Bohemian poet who lived in their apartment building. Its cancellation after eight months was rather surprising. All audience surveys had the series in the top five among weekend daytime shows, and it had one of the highest distributions for any network show at the time, especially on ABC, with 53 cities carrying it. Perhaps the program's demise was connected with a lawsuit that writers of the *My Sister Eileen* radio show had against the show for copyright infringement.

2 HIP FOR TV
Children's; Color
September 10, 1988–October 22, 1988

NBC Sat. Noon–1 p.m. (9/10/88–10/22/88)

Host: *Ahmet Zappa*

Assistant: *Colin Quinn*

Obviously influenced by the MTV (Music Television) cable channel, this show featured music and rock celebrity interviews set in the basement of Ahmet Zappa, the young son of avant-garde rock musician Frank Zappa.

TWO SLEEPY PEOPLE—See *Mike and Buff.*

U

U.N. GENERAL ASSEMBLY SESSIONS
Public Affairs; B&W
November 7, 1949–December 19, 1952

CBS Mon.–Fri. 11 a.m.–1 p.m. and 3–4 p.m. (11/7/49–12/9/49)
CBS Mon.–Fri. 5:15–6 p.m. (10/16/50–12/15/50)

NBC Mon.–Fri. 11 a.m.–Noon (10/20/52–12/19/52)

Narrators (1949–50): *Lyman Bryson, Larry LeSeuer*

A personal pitch by CBS President Frank Stanton to Henry Ford II, president of Ford Motors, led to Ford's sponsorship of the daily U.N. General Assembly meetings in 1949. Ford paid coverage costs in exchange for being identified as the sponsor at the start and close of each show. The idea that a major car company would sponsor pickups of the world organization's daily business, and that a network president would encourage it to do so, appears incredible today. But CBS had time to fill in the early days of networking, and kinescopes could be used for nonconnected stations and U.N. member countries, so the series started its run. CBS and Ford offered ABC and NBC the chance to pool the network pickups, but both networks nixed the idea.

Lyman Bryson, CBS's counselor on public affairs, and reporter Larry LeSeuer served as the respective equivalents of play-by-play and color commentators, with their comments identifying foreign delegates and explaining protocol to home viewers. They also interviewed delegates between sessions, and an English translator handled speeches by foreign dignitaries.

After nearly a two-year absence, NBC brought the sessions back briefly in 1952 at the same time CBS aired a similar show in the afternoons (see *The U.N. in Action*).

U.N. IN ACTION, THE
Public Affairs; B&W
November 11, 1951–December 25, 1960

CBS Sun. 3–3:30 p.m. (11/11/51–1/6/52)
CBS Mon.–Fri. 4:30–5 p.m. (10/29/52–12/11/53; summers off)
CBS Mon./Tue./Thu. 5–5:30 p.m. and Wed./Fri. 5:15–5:30 p.m. (9/20/54–12/17/54)
CBS Sun. 11–11:30 a.m. (10/2/55–12/25/60; off January–August all years except 1957, when off June–August, and 1958, when off March–August)

Regulars: *Walter Cronkite (1951–52), Larry LeSeuer (8/17/53–12/11/53 at least), George Hicks (1955–59), Stuart Novins (1960)*

Walter Cronkite narrated what started as a weekly wrap-up called *The U.N. This Week*, consisting of kinescoped highlights of CBS's daily coverage of the United Nations General Assembly sessions. Nine months after his show ended, CBS brought it back in title only, as it covered the daily afternoon session off and on for roughly two years.

On September 25, 1955 the show went back to a weekly setup and had George Hicks report a summary of either the U.N.'s activity for that week or the organization's previous work on a specific issue. *The U.N. in Action*, as it was titled from 1955–60, went unsponsored throughout its run.

In 1957 a syndicated 15-minute weekly series titled *U.N. Review* provided coverage similar to *The U.N. in Action* under the auspices of United Nations Television. The original host was Charles Lynch of the Canadian Broadcasting Corporation;

Lynch was replaced in 1958 by ABC reporter John MacVane, who had in turn been replaced by Stanley Burke by 1961. U.N. Television produced another 15-minute syndicated weekly in 1958, *Dateline: U.N.*, with Sonny Fox as host, narrator, and interviewer. U.N. correspondent George Moushon replaced Fox in 1959 as the show expanded to 30 minutes.

To promote its message in the 1960s, the U.N. produced several ABC nighttime dramas, from 1964's "A Carol for Another Christmas" to 1966's "The Poppy Is Also a Flower," but the organization has been markedly less involved in American television since that time.

U.N. REVIEW—See *U.N. in Action, The.*

U.N. THIS WEEK, THE—See *U.N. in Action, The.*

U.S. BOXING CHAMPIONSHIPS—See *United States Boxing Championships.*

U.S. OF ARCHIE—See *Archie Show, The.*

U.S.A. VERSUS THE WORLD
Sports; Color
January 31, 1982–March 28, 1982

ABC Sun. 3–4 p.m. or 3:30–4:30 p.m. (1/31/82–3/28/82)

American amateur athletes took on foreign competitors in such sports as boxing and gymnastics on this series. There were no regular announcers, but ABC veterans Keith Jackson and Jack Whitaker did cover a few events.

•USFL FOOTBALL
Sports; Color
March 6, 1983–July 7, 1985

ABC Sun. 1:30–4:30 p.m. (3/6/83–7/10/83)
ABC Sun. 2:30–6 p.m. (2/26/84–7/8/84)
ABC Sun. 2:30–Conclusion (2/24/85–7/7/85)

Anchors: *Keith Jackson, Lynn Swann, Tim Brant (1983–84), Jim Lampley (1983), Lee Corso (1983), Lee Grosscup (1984)*

ABC paid $20 million to cover two years of what turned out to be the folly called the United States Football League. The USFL was the first major effort to compete against the National Football League since the disastrous World Football League in 1974, which failed to secure network airings, but the USFL differed in that it ran in the spring and summer rather than go directly against the NFL fall lineup. In the first season, joining veteran play-by-play man Keith Jackson as analyst in the main games was former Pittsburgh Steelers receiver Lynn Swann, with Tim Brant reporting from the sidelines, and Jim Lampley and Lee Corso doing regional activity. In 1984 Brant moved to play-by-play in the regional games, and Lee Grosscup joined him as analyst as they supplanted Lampley and Corso.

After the second season the league was a shambles. Seven ownerships fell out, and attendance was abysmal (Chicago

played at home against New Jersey on Memorial Day for a crowd officially totaling 4,307). Gimmicks designed to spark fan interest abounded; the worst of these had to be one in New Orleans, where fans were encouraged to submit their plays for that week and the team had to run one of them during a game. Commissioner Chet Simmons started telling ABC that it needed to cover more than two games a week and black out local teams to generate stadium attendance figures, comments which made the network bristle. Instead, ABC aired only one national game a week covered by Jackson and Swann in 1985, but affiliates were now wary of the league, and only 83 percent of them aired the games. The last championship game aired July 14, 1985 at 8 p.m.

When the league decided in 1985 it would go to a fall schedule to compete against the NFL the following year, ABC dropped it, citing another year of declining ratings (a 4.9 average in 1985 versus 6.4 in 1984). The USFL then tried to syndicate the series instead but found the going tough. The league virtually went out of business on July 29, 1986, when a jury found in its favor in the antitrust lawsuit brought by the USFL against the NFL, but awarded the USFL only $3, and the USFL's owners gave up trying to compete against the older league.

UNCLE AL SHOW, THE
Children's; B&W
October 25, 1958–September 19, 1959

ABC Sat. 11 a.m.–Noon (10/25/58–4/11/59)
ABC Sat. Noon–1 p.m. (4/18/59–9/19/59)

Regulars: *"Uncle" Al Lewis, Wanda Lewis (as Captain Windy), Janet Greene (as Cinderella), Larry Smith*

The human cast of The Uncle Al Show *consisted of, from left, Wanda Lewis, "Uncle" Al Lewis, Larry Smith, and Janet Greene.*

The Uncle Al Show was the longest-running local TV show with the same host (it ran with Al Lewis in Cincinnati, Ohio, from 1950–85), but it flopped as the only attraction on ABC's virtually nonexistent Saturday morning schedule of the late 1950s. Star Al Lewis told stories, played the accordion, and acted in sketches for children, often while wearing a straw hat. His wife Wanda played Captain Windy, who drew pictures and told stories. Larry Smith gave puppet shows, and Janet Greene sang. Children in the TV studio participated in some of the activities too. The show was a videotape of one of two hours that appeared weekdays on WCPO Cincinnati.

Prior to the ABC run, WCPO offered DuMont in 1952 the chance to carry Uncle Al's daily show airing 9–10 a.m. Central Time, but the network said no. After the show ended, Al and Wanda continued to work for WCPO until retiring in 1989. Uncle Al should not be confused with actor Al Lewis, who is perhaps best known as Grandpa on *The Munsters*.

UNCLE CROC'S BLOCK
Children's; Color
September 6, 1975–February 14, 1976

ABC Sat. 10:30–11:30 a.m. (9/6/75–10/18/75)
ABC Sat. Noon–12:30 p.m. (10/25/75–2/14/76)

Cast:

Uncle Croc	*Charles Nelson Reilly*
Mr. Rabbit Ears	*Alfie Wise*
Basil Bitterbottom	*Jonathan Harris*

Voices: *Alan Oppenheimer, Lennie Weinrib, Robert Ridgely, Kenneth Mars, Allan Melvin*

Uncle Croc's Block was an odd spoof of children's shows, unusual in that most of its anticipated viewers were too young to recognize (or care) that the show was intended as a parody. Uncle Croc was an exasperated host of a kiddie show who engaged in forced banter with his sidekick Mr. Rabbit Ears (both men sported costumes resembling the creatures in their names). Between their playlets aired three cartoon segments. "Fraidy Cat" featured a feline who was nervous about the fact that he was in his ninth and final life; he had to cope with the ghosts of his previous lives as well. Alan Oppenheimer voiced Fraidy, and he and Lennie Weinrib voiced most of Fraidy's former lives. "M*U*S*H," an obvious takeoff on the nighttime hit sitcom *M*A*S*H*, had mounted dog policemen with names like Bullseye, Tricky John, Cold Lips, and Colonel Flake (voiced by Robert Ridgely and Kenneth Mars) working as part of a group called Mangy Unwanted Shabby Heroes. "Wacky and Packy" told of the misadventures of two prehistoric creatures, voiced by Allan Melvin, transported to Manhattan in the 20th century.

Early ratings for *Uncle Croc's Block* caused ABC executives to treat the show with the same disdain shown by Basil Bitterbottom for Uncle Croc. The program halved its running time after a month, then went off four months later. The cartoon segments later aired in syndication as part of a package called *Groovie Goolies and Friends, The*.

UNCLE JOHNNY COONS SHOW, THE
Children's; B&W and Color
November 27, 1954–November 24, 1956

CBS Sat. 1:30–2 p.m. (11/27/54–12/3/55)
NBC Sat. 11:30 a.m.–Noon (3/3/56–11/24/56)

Host: *Johnny Coons*

Moon-faced, bespectacled Johnny Coons was a chubby radio performer who started on television in Chicago in 1949 as the title voice on *Uncle Mistletoe*, a daily puppet show on WENR. He then appeared on *Panhandle Pete and Jennifer* (q.v.), and in 1952 had his own local show called *Noontime Comics*. When he arrived on CBS, "Uncle" Johnny Coons was not too different from other "uncles" on local 1950s TV shows. He joked with his pal in ventriloquism, George Dummy, and his invisible companions Blackie the dog and Joe the giant, and played characters like cowboys and colonels. He also gave behavior tips and showed silent comedy films between his routines.

UNCLE WALDO—A syndicated title for *Hoppity Hooper* (q.v.).

UNDER THE SUN—A syndicated title for *Omnibus* (q.v.).

•UNDERDOG SHOW, THE
Cartoon; Color
October 3, 1964–September 1, 1973

NBC Sat. 10–10:30 a.m. (10/3/64–9/25/65)
NBC Sat. 10:30–11 a.m. (10/2/65–9/3/66)
CBS Sat. 9:30–10 a.m. (9/10/66–9/2/67)
CBS Sun. 9:30–10 a.m. (9/67–9/1/68)
NBC Sat. 11:30 a.m.–Noon (9/7/68–8/31/69)
NBC Sat. 12:30–1 p.m. (9/9/69–9/5/70)
NBC Sat. 8–8:30 a.m. (9/9/72–12/16/72)
NBC Sat. 10–10:30 a.m. (12/23/72–9/1/73)

Voices:

Underdog/Shoeshine Boy	*Wally Cox*
Sweet Polly Purebred	*Norma McMillan*
Running Board (1966–68)	*George S. Irving*
Ruffled Feather/Sgt. Okey Homa	
(both 1966–68)	*Sandy Becker*
Col. Kit Coyote (1966–68)	*Kenny Delmar*

Underdog was an okay ribbing of the Superman story, with meek Shoeshine Boy changing into caped crime fighter Underdog whenever his true love, TV reporter Sweet Polly Purebred, faced abduction, threats, or other ills from various nefarious types like scientist Simon Bar Sinister. The rest of the population in Washington, D.C., were too cowardly to handle the criminal elements but, as Wally Cox said in the operatic theme song and whenever changing character in a phone booth, "Have no fear—Underdog is here!" Actually, Underdog was only a smidgen more confident than Shoeshine Boy in his ability to save Polly, but somehow he managed to do the trick within two cliffhanging episodes.

No need to fear, Underdog *is here!*

Supporting segments from 1964–66 included "The Hunter," from *King Leonardo and His Short Subjects* (q.v.) and "The World of Commander McBragg," from *Tennessee Tuxedo* (q.v.). A new segment in 1966 was "Go Go Gophers," which became its own series with the same title in 1968 with "Klondike Kat" in support (see *Go Go Gophers* for details). All characters listed above after Polly Purebred were in the "Go Go Gophers." *Underdog* segments on CBS from 1966 onward were repeats. The character appeared frequently later as a balloon in the Macy's Thanksgiving Day parade in New York through the 1990s, and returned in cartoon form in commercials for Cheerios cereal in 1996.

UNITED NATIONS—See *U.N. General Assembly Sessions* and *U.N. in Action, The.*

UNITED STATES BOXING CHAMPIONSHIPS
Sports; Color
January 16, 1977–April 10, 1977
ABC Sun. Various hours between 1 and 6 p.m. alternating weekly (1/16/77–4/10/77)
Announcer: *Chris Schenkel*
Creator/Producer: *Don King*
Theme: *"Gonna Fly Now (Theme from 'Rocky')," by Bill Conti, Carol Connors, and Ayn Robbins*

This effort to exploit the ratings popularity of boxing on *ABC's Wide World of Sports* in the 1970s met with controversy, and the network aborted it. The format called for 56 pugilists

to compete in a 16–show tournament to crown a winner. But before the tournament could end, both ABC and a federal grand jury began investigating claims of fixed fights and kickbacks on the show. The network dropped the series in light of the allegations. The findings were that no fights were fixed, but several boxers received improper payments or had their records falsified. Flamboyant promoter Don King, who organized the event, was exonerated, as was ABC, but some of King's associates were found guilty of crimes in the incident. ABC came back the following year with the untainted *International Championship Boxing.*

UNIVERSITY OF PENNSYLVANIA FOOTBALL—See NCAA *Football*.

UNTAMED WORLD, THE
Nature; Color
January 4, 1969–August 30, 1969
NBC Sat. 12:30–1 p.m. (1/4/69–8/30/69)
Host/Narrator: *Philip Carey*

Co-produced with Canada's CTV network, *The Untamed World* was a breezily paced documentary presenting to viewers scenes of the animal kingdom and descriptions of its habits and anomalies. A typical show profiled bats, rhinos, hyenas, crabs, vultures, and a few other species. After a short NBC run, *The Untamed World* reappeared in syndication with new episodes through 1975.

UP TO THE MINUTE
News Magazine; Color
September 28, 1981–January 15, 1982
CBS Mon.–Fri. 4–4:30 p.m. (9/28/81–1/15/82)
Hosts: *Ed Bradley, Harry Reasoner, Morley Safer, Mike Wallace*

When discussing the careers of this series' hosts, their work on the long-running prime-time newsmagazine *60 Minutes* (1968–) immediately comes to mind, while this effort hardly rates a footnote. It was CBS's attempt to have a viable informational feature series in late afternoon, but low affiliate clearances and low ratings made it a disaster. Originally CBS wanted Candice Bergen or Marlo Thomas to host, over the objections of CBS News staffers, but the actresses wisely rejected the offer, and the *60 Minutes* crew instead alternated as weekly hosts. Mike Wallace reportedly was very reluctant to do the task. It was no matter; the show ended before he had to do more than four weeks of the show.

UPDATE
News; B&W
September 16, 1961–June 2, 1963
NBC Sat. Noon–12:30 p.m. (9/16/61–1/27/62)
NBC Sun. 5:30–6 p.m. (2/4/62–5/13/62)
NBC Sun. 5–5:30 p.m. (10/14/62–6/2/63)
Host/"On The Air Editor": *Bob Abernethy*

Update, airing live from New York City, was a newsmagazine aimed specifically at young viewers. Each show had a review of the week's news headlines, an analysis of top stories, a feature story, an interview by two students per show of prominent Americans such as Senators Everett Dirksen and Hubert Humphrey, and a "man on the street" question. The first program included a recap of the United Nations' history, a feature on President John Kennedy's Youth Fitness Program, film footage from the Mercury space capsule, and a talk with theologian Dr. Reinhold Niebuhr. After a two-year run, this type of programming largely disappeared from the networks until CBS tried it with *30 Minutes* in the late 1970s.

V

VACATION WONDERLAND
Travelogue; B&W
January 15, 1951–October 14, 1951

NBC Mon.–Fri. 3–3:30 p.m. (1/15/51–3/9/51)
NBC Mon.–Fri. 3:15–3:30 p.m. (3/12/51–5/11/51)
NBC Mon.–Fri. 3:15–3:30 p.m. (7/2/51–10/14/51)

Hosts: *Dick Joseph (through April 1951 at latest), Caroline Burke (by May 1951 at latest)*

Begun as a local show on WNBT New York in 1950, *Vacation Wonderland* went on NBC the following year. Dick Joseph, travel editor for *Esquire* magazine and president of the Travel Writers Association, talked with guests and narrated films of one tourist destination per show. Comic pianist Victor Borge guested on the February 28, 1951 show on his native Denmark. A few months later, Caroline Burke, the show's producer, became host and profiled her home state of Oregon on July 6 before the show was canceled. It reappeared as a 15-minute weekly segment again hosted and produced by Burke in the 1952 daytime show *Matinee in New York* (q.v.).

VACATIONLAND AMERICA—See *Watch the World.*

VALIANT LADY
Soap Opera; B&W
October 12, 1953–August 16, 1957

CBS Mon.–Fri. Noon–12:15 p.m. (10/12/53–8/16/57)

Cast:

Helen Emerson (1953–54)	Nancy Coleman
Helen Emerson (1954–57)	Flora Campbell
Frank Emerson (1953)	Jerome Cowan
Mickey Emerson	James Kirkwood Jr.
Diane Emerson Soames (1953–54)	Anne Pearson
Diane Emerson Soames (1954–55)	Delores Sutton
Diane Emerson Soames (1955–56)	Sue Randall
Diane Emerson Soames (1956–57)	Leila Martin
Kim Emerson (1953–54)	Lydia Reed
Kim Emerson (1954–57)	Bonnie Sawyer
Hal Soames (1954–55)	Earl Hammond
Bonnie Withers (1954–55)	Joan Lorring
Bonnie Withers (1955)	Shirley Egleston
Chris Kendall (1954–55)	Lawrence Weber
Linda Kendall (1955)	Frances Helm
David Kendall (1955)	Johnny Coleman
Margot Finchley (1954–55)	Katherine Anderson
Elliott Norris (1955)	Terry O'Sullivan
Joey Gordon (1955)	Martin Balsam
Roberta Wilcox (1956–57)	Betty Oakes
Gov. Lawrence Walker (1956–57)	John Graham
Announcer/Occasional Actor	Win Elliot

Helen Emerson (played by Flora Campbell) hugs her daughter Kim (Bonnie Sawyer) on Valiant Lady.

Valiant Lady was an in-name-only adaptation of the
NBC radio serial which ran from 1938–46 and 1951–52.
TV's "valiant lady" was Helen Emerson, a resident of the
town of Middlebury and a mother to Mickey, 19, Diane,
17, and Kim, 9. Early in the run trouble struck her
husband Frank, who had a failing heart but overworked
himself at business nonetheless to provide for his family.
He died within a few months, plunging his family into
numerous traumas.

Helen became attracted to airplane pilot Chris Kendall,
who unfortunately was married, albeit separated. Despite
that, even family friend Margot thought he was the man
for Helen. Helen stayed with him as he divorced Linda but
endured much adversity in the ensuing custody battle for
Chris and Linda's son David. While her relationship with
Chris proved not to be, Helen found true love with Governor
Walker and wed him in February 1957.

Her relationship with her kids were more problematic.
Her chief giver of grief was Diane, who whined about
wanting to go to Briarmount, an expensive college. She
ditched college plans in 1954 and eloped with Hal Soames,
a previously married man, then got infatuated with Joey
Gordon, who saved the Emerson clan when they were held
hostage by a crazed ex-lover of Helen's in 1955. Ne'er-do-
well Diane certainly was a popular character for actresses to
play (in 1955, Sue Randall beat out 60 other contenders
for the part), but despite that, the character had the show's
highest number of recasts.

Mickey was almost as bothersome for Helen. He had an
up-and-down relationship with Bonnie, who at one point
ran away to Bloomfield to escape him. He also fought some
with Elliott before gaining a fiancée in the form of Roberta
Wilcox. Kim did not mature fast enough to get her cut of
the action her brother and sister had on this show.

Valiant Lady aired live from New York. In 1955 actress
Signe Hasso guest-starred, and *Billboard* said other "name"
stars would appear on the show too, such as Shelley Winters
and Charlton Heston. There is no record of those two
celebrities turning up on the series, however.

•VALLEY OF THE DINOSAURS
Cartoon; Color
September 7, 1974–September 4, 1976

CBS Sat. 10–10:30 a.m. (9/7/74–1/11/75)
CBS Sat. 11–11:30 a.m. (1/18/75–8/30/75)
CBS Sat. Noon–12:30 p.m. (9/6/75–9/4/76)

Voices:

John Butler	Mike Road
Kim Butler	Shannon Farnon
Katie Butler	Margene Fudenna
Greg Butler	Jackie Earle Haley
Gorak	Alan Oppenheimer
Gera	Joan Gardner
Tana	Melanie Baker
Lok	Steacy Bertheau

While rafting in an uncharted section of the Amazon river,
John Butler, his wife Kim, and their kids Katie and Greg
found themselves sucked into a whirlpool that led them back
in time. They emerged from the water to find themselves
thousands of years in the prehistoric past and being helped
to survive there by a family the ages of whose members—
Gorak, Gera, Tana, and Lok—respectively paralleled the
Butlers' ages. Even the Butlers' dog Digger, who survived
the trip with the family, found an equivalent, Lok's pet
stegosaurus Glomb. If that seems improbable, consider that
almost every episode involved both families interacting
with dinosaurs when it is well known that the latter were
extinct long before the human race appeared on earth, and
you get the idea that realism was not a priority for this
passable cartoon.

For a similar (and no less goofy) prehistoric adventure
for children on Saturday mornings in 1974, see *Land of
the Lost.*

VALUE TELEVISION—See *Richard Simmons Show, The.*

VANITY FAIR
Interview; B&W
October 12, 1948–November 2, 1951

CBS Tue./Thu. 1–1:30 p.m. (10/12/48–1/8/49)
CBS Mon./Tue./Thu./Fri. 1:30–2 p.m.
 (1/12/49–4/15/49)
CBS Mon./Wed./Fri. 12:30–1 p.m. (4/18/49–7/9/49)
CBS Mon.–Fri. 5–5:30 p.m. (9/6/49–10/7/49)
CBS Mon.–Fri. 4:30–5 p.m. (10/10/49–4/28/51)
CBS Mon./Wed./Fri. 2:45–3:15 p.m. and Tue./Thu.
 2:45–3:30 p.m. (5/1/51–11/2/51)

Regulars: *Dorothy Doan, Gil Fates (1948–January 1949),
Robin Chandler (5/2/51–11/2/51)*

The first daily interview show on CBS was *Vanity Fair;*
its features were geared toward women but its attitude
was somewhat less patronizing than the attitude of other
"women's shows" at the time. Sure, viewers got fashion
shows and demonstrations of projects, but there were
also serious discussions of issues, for example, a debate
between a man and a woman over the role of women in
the military.

Dorothy Doan, women's editor for the International
News Service (INS) and writer for the show, was the show's
first hostess/"editor," joined by Gil Fates, the show's producer,
as "assistant editor." Due to previous commitments Fates
left his on-camera duties in 1949. Doan stayed as hostess,
and her levelheadedness was an asset. For example, when
Maidenform Bras became a sponsor in 1949 and company
executives were wringing their hands over how to advertise
their product, an unfazed Doan suggested she should simply
hold the bras up and tell viewers about their features as a
saleslady would. The company brass viewed Doan's solution
as "stupendous."

Dorothy Doan and Gil Fates enjoy a rest from their work on Vanity Fair *in 1949.*

In the fall of 1949 the show added a living room set to spruce up looks. On September 30 that year a special experimental color show was transmitted to communications lawyers in Washington, D.C., by CBS to encourage the FCC to adopt its color system as the standard one for television. (The regular show was only on three CBS affiliates at the time.) In 1951, the show expanded its Tuesday and Thursday shows to 45 minutes and had Robin Chandler as hostess in place of Doan, who held the job on the other days until the show ended. Chandler also hosted *Meet Your Cover Girl* Thursdays following the show.

VEGETABLE SOUP
Children's; Color
November 2, 1975–August 1, 1976

NBC Sun. 8–8:30 a.m. (11/2/75–8/1/76)

Voices:

Woody the Spoon	*Bette Midler*
Long John Spoilsport	*James Earl Jones*

The first series to be carried concurrently on public and commercial TV stations (more than 200 in all), *Vegetable Soup* offered children the chance to learn more about other cultures and appreciate diversity through multiple regular segments in each show. "Outerscope" featured profiles of minority professionals; "Real People" had ethnic actors in a soap opera; and cartoons included "Adventures in Saniland," which involved the activities of Long John Spoilsport, whom children were not to emulate, and Luther, a character who encouraged friendliness. Nonprofessional child actors appeared in skits involving minorities, and there were "man on the street" questions, films, and other attractions. But to most reviewers the show's highlight was the "Woody the Spoon" cartoon; in those segments, Bette Midler vocals dispensed recipes from different ethnic cuisines.

Vegetable Soup was the end result of a $1.58 million federal HEW grant to the N.Y. State Education Department (the latter agency produced and supplied the show). About 100 NBC affiliates aired the show on Sundays (the New York station put it on a week later on Saturdays at 7:30 a.m.), while public TV stations began running it on September 22, 1975. Educators' reactions to the show were as mixed as its format, and many thought the quality was uneven. Somebody with power somewhere down the line must have liked it, for in the fall of 1978, 39 new episodes aired, mainly in syndication.

•VERDICT IS YOURS, THE
Anthology; B&W
September 2, 1957–September 28, 1962

CBS Mon.–Fri. 3:30–4 p.m. (9/2/57–10/9/61)
CBS Mon.–Fri. 3:30–3:55 p.m. (10/12/61–6/15/62)
CBS Mon.–Fri. 11–11:30 a.m. (6/18/62–9/28/62)

Host/"Court Reporter": *Jim McKay (9/2/57–7/22/60), Bill Stout (7/25/60–6/15/62), Jack Whitaker (6/18/62–9/28/62)*

A popular and at the start unique daytime drama, *The Verdict Is Yours* was a remake of a Chicago-based prime time-show called *They Stand Accused,* which aired on CBS and DuMont sporadically from January 18, 1949–December 30, 1954, before the Frank Cooper advertising agency acquired rights to the series and sold the idea to CBS as a daily offering. Viewers saw lawsuits argued by real lawyers and presided over by real judges, with actors as plaintiffs and defendants and some members of the studio audience as the jury (those selected had to come back to the studio every day of the case). There were no scripts; all participants except the jury received a "case outline" of up to 65 pages which basically gave exposition. Other than that, there was room for improvisation by all, and some trials ran as long as nine days until the jury made its decision. The "court reporter" gave home viewers background information, including what was happening in counsels' meetings with the judge.

Cases ranged from custody suits, such as the woman on the debut who kidnapped her 6-year-old son from the family in which he lived, to murder raps. All supposedly took place in the fictional town of Overlook (population 125,000). Actors generally were unknowns or novices, including Diane Ladd in her TV debut.

But to some the real stars were the attorneys, as the highly charged situations often made them go over the top to win their side. Actor Mandel Kramer, who played a bailiff, had to physically separate lawyers at times. Nonetheless, many in the legal profession enjoyed doing the show, and in 1959 nearly 100 lawyers who had formerly been on the show formed the Overlook Bar Association, whose motto, *Veredictum Vobis,* was the series title in Latin.

The Verdict Is Yours fared well enough that CBS tried a version Thursdays at 8:30 p.m. from July 3–September 25, 1958. By that time, CBS had made the daytime show one of the first to be videotaped. In July 1960 CBS switched production from New York City to Hollywood, which prompted Jim McKay to leave as host. A switch to morning hours in 1962 led to another host and declining ratings, giving the show a final verdict of cancellation in the fall.

VERSATILE VARIETIES
Children's; B&W
January 28, 1951–July 22, 1951

CBS Sun. 11:30 a.m.–Noon (1/28/51–7/22/51)

Hostess: *Lady Iris Mountbatten*

Music: *The Mark Tower Orchestra*

Versatile Varieties made a versatile run on three networks in TV's early days. It debuted on NBC nighttime from August 26, 1949–January 19, 1951 with several different hosts introducing guest show business professionals. Next came this CBS daytime series, which was a talent show for youth hosted by Lady Iris Mountbatten, a third cousin to King

George VI of Great Britain. Its official name was *Bonny Maid Versatile Varieties* in honor of its unlikely sponsor Bonafide Mills, which made roof and floor coverings. The show and Mountbatten moved to ABC nighttime in the same format from September 21–December 14, 1951.

•VICKI!
Talk; Color
1992–1994

Syndicated 60 minutes daily beginning September 1992

Host: *Vicki Lawrence Schultz*

Former *Carol Burnett Show* sidekick and one-time million-selling singer (for 1973's "The Night the Lights Went Out in Georgia") Vicki Lawrence emceed her own show which was a hit in its first season but faded with increased competition in 1993–94. Most guests were celebrities. Her topics might be comic or serious, but they were never exploitative, which may have been her undoing in her second season, when more outrageous entries appeared. Following the show's cancellation, Lawrence wrote her autobiography using the same title.

•VICTORY AT SEA
Documentary; B&W
October 26, 1952–April 26, 1953

NBC Sun. 3–3:30 p.m. (10/26/52–4/26/53)

Narrator: *Leonard Graves*

Score: *By Richard Rodgers, performed by the NBC Symphony Orchestra under the direction of Robert Russell Bennett*

One of TV's best-known, most highly respected, and much-rerun documentaries, and the model for many subsequent documentaries, *Victory at Sea* aired 26 episodes that told of battles fought by naval craft in World War II from activity in the late 1930s through the war's aftermath. Most shows described several skirmishes, but one was devoted solely to the Allies' preparation of Operation D-Day, the invasion of Normandy in 1944. A stirring theme by famed composer Richard Rodgers, and Leonard Graves's solid narration, enhanced the project's gripping atmosphere.

The creator of the ambitious series was Henry Salomon, who based it on a book by Captain Samuel E. Morison called *History of U.S. Naval Operations, World War II.* Salomon proposed the idea to Robert Sarnoff, executive vice president of NBC and the son of RCA President David Sarnoff. The junior Sarnoff approved the concept and even made many of the Naval arrangements for the program. Saloman and series co-supervisor Daniel Jones used 60,000 feet of film shot during the war, including much unseen footage captured by the Axis forces.

The result was a ratings and critical success. It won a Peabody Award and the 1953 Emmy for Best Public Affairs Program, among other honors. Even Rodgers's score became a hit, with several albums featuring the themes hitting the top 10 on *Billboard's* Top Albums Chart in the 1950s and 1960s. And executive producer Don Hyatt told *Variety* in 1963 that virtually every U.S. naval vessel had a copy of the program. Unfortunately, Salomon never created another documentary with the breadth and impact of *Victory at Sea.*

VIDEO VILLAGE
Game; B&W
July 11, 1960–June 16, 1962
CBS Mon.–Fri. 10:30–11 a.m. (7/11/60–9/29/61)
CBS Mon.–Fri. 11–11:30 a.m. (10/2/61–6/15/62)
CBS Sat. 10–10:30 a.m. (9/30/61–6/16/62)
Regulars: *Jack Narz (7/11/60–9/60), Monty Hall (10/3/60–6/16/62), Joanne Copeland (7/11/60–3/10/61), Eileen Barton (3/13/61–6/16/62), Kenny Williams*
Producers: *Merrill Heatter and Bob Quigley*

First seen on CBS Fridays at 9 p.m. from July 1–September 16, 1960, *Video Village* had one of the most imaginative sets ever created for a TV game show. In fact, the concept may have been too elaborate, for contestants were dwarfed as they became virtual pieces on a set designed as a game board. Groups of pairs competed to go all the way through the village, with one member turning a chuck-a-luck cage to roll a die and the other moving the number shown on the die on spaces marked "Take A Chance," "Lose A Turn," "Go To Jail," and so forth in front of some colorful store facades. Along with the typical game board benefits and penalties, players could win merchandise and cash as they headed for the finish. Money won in early shows was rather skimpy (less than $100); presumably earnings increased later in the run.

Original host Jack Narz and hostess Joanne Copeland were the respective "mayor" and "assistant mayor" of Video Village, and announcer Kenny Williams was the "town crier." Monty Hall and Eileen Barton became mayor and assistant mayor later in the run, and in the final season they and Williams appeared in a children's version that aired Saturday mornings in addition to the daily run.

VIETNAM: THE WAR THIS WEEK—See *Vietnam Weekly Review, The.*

VIETNAM WEEKLY REVIEW, THE
Public Affairs; Color
April 17, 1966–July 7, 1968
NBC Sun. 5–5:30 p.m. (4/17/66–8/21/66)
NBC Sun. 2–3 p.m. (9/18/66–10/16/66)
NBC Sat. 4:30–5 p.m. (10/22/66–4/29/67)
NBC Sun. 4–4:30 p.m. (3/17/68–4/28/68)
NBC Sun. 5–5:30 p.m. (5/5/68–7/7/68)
Hosts: *Garrick Utley (4/17/66–8/14/66), Dean Brelis (8/21/66–11/12/66, 1968), Ron Nessen (11/19/66–1/28/67), Bill Ryan (2/18/67–5/6/67), Howard Tuckner (1968)*

Anyone who watched this series could sense the shift in public opinion toward the Vietnam War during the late 1960s. NBC news reporters presented updates of what had happened over the seven days before each show and offered analysis of war activity plus related events. The program gave the war's casualty

figures beginning with the May 8, 1966 telecast. Some shows departed from the usual format when the situation warranted. Two memorable examples were an hour-long special on October 2, 1966 that examined Sen. J. William Fulbright's opposition to U.S. involvement in the war despite his serving as chair of the Senate Foreign Relations Committee, and the May 13, 1967 show on boxer Muhammad Ali's refusal to join the Army due to religious objections.

Original host Garrick Utley covered the war on location 18 months before doing the series. His replacement Dean Brelis also was a NBC correspondent in Vietnam, and he had been wounded during the conflict. Ron Nessen and then Bill Ryan helmed the show before Brelis returned as co-host in 1968 with Howard Tuckner, when the show's title was *Vietnam: The War This Week.* Like Brelis and Nessen, Tuckner was injured while reporting in Vietnam, and in fact he had covered news for the show frequently in 1966–67. As if to complete the circle, Utley returned to appear in 1968 as a reporter in Vietnam.

The last few shows aired increasingly negative opinions and information about the war (for example, Brelis announced that a record 4,000 American men had become casualties and concluded that the South Vietnamese were the real losers in this "stalemate war"), but the United States would not pull out of Vietnam and surrounding countries until 1975, nearly seven years after *The Vietnam Weekly Review* went off the air.

VIN SCULLY SHOW, THE
Talk; Color
January 15, 1973–March 23, 1973
CBS Mon.–Fri. 4–4:30 p.m. (1/15/73–3/23/73)
Host: *Vin Scully*

Vin Scully, lead announcer for the Dodgers baseball franchise since it moved to Los Angeles from Brooklyn in 1955, failed as a talk show host in the Mike Douglas–Merv Griffin mold in this effort. He interviewed one guest per show, usually a celebrity like Walter Matthau, before a studio audience. Scully seemed ill at ease outside of an announcing booth, and CBS replaced his show with *The Secret Storm.*

VINCENT LOPEZ SPEAKING
Variety; B&W
January 12, 1949–March 4, 1949
DuMont Mon.–Fri. 3:15–3:30 p.m. (1/12/49–3/4/49)
Host: *Vincent Lopez*

Vincent Lopez, a familiar voice on records and radio in the 1940s, came to television as a host, interviewer, and piano player for daytime and nighttime shows on DuMont. The latter ran from March 7, 1949–July 22, 1950. Lopez returned later with a series on WCBS New York that ran on the CBS network Saturdays at 7 p.m. from February 9–March 9, 1957.

VIRGINIA GRAHAM SHOW, THE—See *Girl Talk.*

VISIT WITH . . . , A—See *Wisdom.*

•WLAF FOOTBALL

Sports; Color

March 17, 1991–May 31, 1992

ABC Sun. 1–4 p.m. (3/17/91–5/31/92; spring months only)

Announcers: Dick Vermeil, Brent Musberger (1991), Roger Twibell (1992), Jim Valvano (1992)

As if it had not learned its lesson six years earlier with *USFL Football* (q.v.), ABC gave another go to airing professional football in the spring of 1991, with disastrous results. The World League of American Football, or WLAF (or as its detractors clucked, WLAUGH), first consisted of 10 professional teams, mostly in North American cities, with others in foreign venues such as London. Unlike the USFL, the league was created as an adjunct to the NFL, but the quality of play hardly seemed as professional to viewers accustomed to that league, and there were few big names playing in it. The changes in rules from the NFL (e.g., two-point conversions allowed after field goals) likewise gave the league a gimmicky image which enticed few viewers.

In its first season Dick Vermeil served as analyst while Brent Musberger handled play-by-play. In 1992, apparently desperate to get *any* sports fans—from whatever sport—to watch the games, ABC replaced Musberger with golf analyst Roger Twibell, plus put its NCAA basketball announcer Jim Valvano on the sidelines to report any action. But the problem with this show was not the announcing, but the scheduling and the rather unpolished play among teams few people liked. While the World League continued successfully overseas and aired occasionally on cable, it vanished from network television after two lackluster years.

•WACKO

Comedy Variety; Color

September 17, 1977–September 3, 1978

CBS Sat. Noon–12:30 p.m. (9/17/77–10/8/77)

CBS Sat. 1–1:30 p.m. (10/15/77–11/12/77)

CBS Sun. 9:30–10 a.m. (11/20/77–9/3/78)

Cast: Charles Fleischer, Bo Kaprall, Julie McWhirter, Bob Comfort, Doug Cox, Millicent Crisp, Rick Kellard, the Sylvers (occasional)

Comedians Charles Fleischer, Bo Kaprall, and Julie McWhirter served loosely as hosts of this up-tempo collection of jokes, sketches, and one or two musical numbers. Each of them played themselves plus a variety of other characters both fictional and real (e.g., McWhirter as Dolly Parton), along with several supporting players and a few guests in short segments that may have been a little too witty for the show's juvenile audience to comprehend. Among the typical setups were the countdown of the week's top three worst jokes and a vaudeville-style routine where a physician bellowed in his

office, "Oh, nurse, nurse, nurse!" before making a wisecrack. There were even a few times when the musical guest (which often was the Sylvers soul group) had a taped number interrupted briefly for a quick bit. But the best recurring gag was near brilliance—a shot of one person with a bag on his or her head clapping near the back of an otherwise empty and cobweb-strewn theater following another stab at humor.

Guests on *Wacko* included Loretta Swit and Gary Owens, the latter of whom probably felt right at home with the program's obvious similarity to the late 1960s prime-time smash *Laugh-In. Wacko* first aired as a prime-time special in September 1977 promoting CBS's fall Saturday morning lineup.

•WACKY RACES

Cartoon; Color

September 14, 1968–September 5, 1970

CBS Sat. 9:30–10 a.m. (9/14/68–9/6/69)

CBS Sat. 12:30–1 p.m. (9/13/69–2/14/70)

CBS Sat. 10–10:30 a.m. (2/21/70–9/5/70)

Voices:

Dick Dastardly/Clyde/Red Max	*Paul Winchell*
Penelope Pitstop	*Janet Waldo*
Muttley/Professor Pat Pending/	
Sawtooth/Ring-A-Ding/Little	
Gruesome	*Don Messick*
Peter Perfect/Rufus Ruffcut/	
Sergeant/Rock Slug/Gravel	
Slug/Big Gruesome	*Daws Butler*
The General/Luke Bear/Blubber	
Bear	*John Stephenson*
The Anthill Mob	*Mel Blanc*
Narrator	*Dave Willock*

The Wacky Races emerged as a slapstick antidote to the violent superheros which had saturated Saturday morning cartoons in 1967–68, and it set some sort of precedent when a season after its debut it spun off not one but two other cartoons while continuing its run on the network. The main antagonists in the never-ending worldwide car race, conniving Dastardly and his snickering dog Muttley in their Mean Machine, had their own show in this series' time slot in 1969. And *Penelope Pitstop*, who drove the Compact Pussy Cat complete with her toilette, had her own show following *Dastardly and Muttley* in 1969.

The other drivers in the competition (and their cars) were Professor Pending in the Ring-A-Ding Convert-A-Car, which could talk and often stopped Dastardly and Muttley; Peter Perfect with Turbo Terrific; Rufus and Sawtooth with Buzz Wagon; the General, Sergeant, and Private Pinkley with the Army Surplus Special; Neanderthals Rock and Gravel Slug with the Boulder Mobile; Clyde and Anthill Mob with the Bulletproof Bomb; Red Max with the Crimson Haybaler; the Gruesome Twosome with the Creepy Coupe; and Luke and Blubber Bear with the Arkansas Chugabug.

Although basically a Hanna-Barbera Production, this cartoon had the unusual distinction of being co-produced with game show experts Heatter-Quigley Productions.

WAKE UP WITH THE CAPTAIN—See *Captain Kangaroo.*

WALDO KITTY—See *Secret Lives of Waldo Kitty, The.*

WARREN HULL SHOW, THE—See *Ladies Day.*

WASHINGTON CONVERSATION
Interview; B&W
February 26, 1961–September 16, 1962

CBS Sun. Noon–12:30 p.m. (2/26/61–4/23/61)
CBS Sun. 11–11:30 a.m. (4/30/61–5/14/61)
CBS Sun. 12:30–1 p.m. (10/1/61–9/16/62)

Host: *Paul Niven*

Washington Conversation served roughly as a temporary replacement for *Face the Nation* in the early 1960s. As the title implied, it featured talks on current issues with a top political figure in the District of Columbia. It aired live through May 1961, then taped for the rest of its run. Its time slot was taken over by *CBS Washington Report* (q.v.).

WASHINGTON SQUARE
Musical Variety; Color
October 21, 1956–April 21, 1957

NBC Sun. 4–5 p.m. (10/21/56–4/21/57)

Regulars: *Ray Bolger, Elaine Stritch, Rusty Draper, the Three Flames, Jo Wilder, Danziga Ilitsch (10/21/56–11/4/56), Kay Armen (11/18/56–4/21/57), Mata and Hari, Arnold Stang (voice only), the Bil and Cora Baird Puppets, the Charles Sanford Orchestra*

Washington Square *star Ray Bolger joins Elaine Stritch in song in this shot from the October 21, 1956 show.*

This live variety show with a story line starred Ray Bolger playing an entrepreneur assisting those who wanted to be part of show business while he toured Washington Square in New York City. Among the people he met were vocalist Elaine Stritch, operator of the Greenwich Village Inn nightclub; two other singing acts appearing at the Inn, Rusty Draper and the Three Flames; and the dance duo of Mata and Hari, who ran a dancing school with the help of tap dancer Sammy Daniels. There were also sets for the streets, the park, and the Washington Square Playhouse; at the latter, starlet Jo Wilder acted with guests in a dramatic skit each week. Rounding out the cast was Mama Rosa (played by Danziga Ilitsch for the first two shows, then by singer Kay Armen), a widow with six children who wanted to be an opera star, and Arnold Stang voicing a turtle puppet.

The New York–based production had the essential ingredients for a hit variety series—top stars (Bert Lahr, Bolger's co-star in the 1939 film classic *The Wizard of Oz,* was the show's debut guest, and later came Martha Raye and Jim Backus), elaborate sets, an enjoyable pace. But the biweekly scheduling seemed to limit its audience. NBC gave it a second chance as an evening entry, with prime-time specials airing on May 9, May 20, June 4, and June 13, 1957, but decided to drop it after that effort.

•WATCH MR. WIZARD
Children's; B&W
March 3, 1951–September 2, 1972

NBC Sat. 5–5:30 p.m. (3/3/51–5/26/51)
NBC Sat. 4:30–5 p.m. (4/16/55–6/25/55)
NBC Sat. 11:30 a.m.–Noon (7/2/55–12/24/55)
NBC Sat. 12:30–1 p.m. or 5:30–6 p.m. (2/4/56–3/23/57)
NBC Sun. Various half hours between 11:30 a.m. and 4:30 p.m. (4/7/57–5/15/60)
NBC Sat. Various half hours between Noon and 2:30 p.m. (6/5/60–4/11/64)
NBC Sat. 12:30–1 p.m. (4/18/64–9/5/64)
NBC Sun. 12:30–1 p.m. (10/25/64–7/4/65)
NBC Sat. Noon–12:30 p.m. (9/11/71–9/2/72)

Host/Executive Producer: *Don Herbert*

This long-running, time-slot–bouncing vintage TV instructional show on science originally came from Chicago. Designed for 8- to 13-year-olds, the series employed magnets, plastics, and other everyday household objects to make science more accessible to home viewers. Experiments ranged from floating paper to make it support a book to having a piece of balloon secured over the top of a coffee can with a rubber band and attaching a straw to it to create a mock barometer. Joining friendly Don Herbert in the activities were various juvenile actors who ad-libbed their participation with the host and were always ready to pipe up with the phrase "Gee, Mr. Wizard!" after an impressive display. After production moved to New York in 1955, the series was produced for a time in cooperation with New York University. It aired on a sustaining basis from 1956 into the 1960s.

Two months after it began in daytime, *Watch Mr. Wizard* went into NBC's early Saturday evening lineup in May 1951 and stayed there for nearly four years before returning as a Saturday or Sunday afternoon attraction. After going off NBC on Independence Day 1965, it returned on the network six years later for one season. In 1983 it reappeared as a new weekly series on the Nickelodeon cable channel titled *Mr. Wizard's World*, again with Herbert as host, and remained in production through 1991.

WATCH THE WORLD
Documentary; B&W
April 23, 1950–June 28, 1953

NBC Sun. 3:30–4 p.m. (4/23/50–6/11/50)
NBC Sun. 5–5:30 p.m. (9/10/50–9/24/50)
NBC Sun. 5:30–6 p.m. (10/1/50–2/25/51)
NBC Sun. 2–2:30 p.m. (4/1/51–6/24/51)
NBC Sun. 5:30–5:45 p.m. (4/5/53–6/28/53)

Host/Narrator: *John Cameron Swayze*
Interviewer (1950–51): *Radcliff Hall*
Regulars (1953): *Tuffie Swayze, Suzanne Swayze, John Swayze Jr.*

Produced in cooperation with the National Education Association, *Watch the World* was a magazine-style documentary for children with information about current events, history, and general interest topics. The series had roughly six stories per show presented in newsreel fashion on such subjects as copper mining in Chile, juvenile circus performers in training, and sailboating. John Cameron Swayze also served as NBC nighttime news anchor while hosting this show. Radcliff Hall interviewed guests. In July and August 1950 the show moved into Sunday nights with NBC reporter Don Goddard taking over as host for the vacationing Swayze.

Swayze hosted a similar program in 1953 titled variously *Vacationland America* or *Sightseeing with the Swayzes* and featuring films of his wife Tuffie and two children taken during weekend trips across America. The 13 shows later aired in repeats in syndication.

WAY OF THE WORLD
Dramatic Anthology;
January 3, 1955–October 7, 1955

NBC Mon.–Fri. 10:30–11 a.m. (1/3/55–7/1/55)
NBC Mon.–Fri. 4–4:15 p.m. (7/4/55–10/7/55)

Hostess: *Gloria Louis (as "Linda Porter")*

At the start of the debut of this series, "hostess" Linda Porter told the home audience her show would provide "a variety of plays reflecting the emotions and reactions of the world in which we live." In other words, it was an anthology of short-run soap opera dramas featuring stories (and stars) of the second rank at best. The first installment had an actress, played by Claudia Morgan, who was going deaf and worried how it would affect the performing team she had developed with her husband, played by Philip Reed. This story line ran from

January 3–17, 1955. Other melodramas included two bickering sisters who were forced to live together and a group of plane crash survivors who worked together and faced their fears to handle their predicament.

•WAY OUT GAMES
Children's; Color
September 11, 1976–September 4, 1977

CBS Sat. 12:30–1 p.m. (9/11/76–2/5/77)
CBS Sat. 1–1:30 p.m. (2/12/77–4/2/77)
CBS Sun. 7–7:30 a.m. (4/10/77–9/4/77)

Host: *Sonny Fox*

In *Way Out Games*, three sexually integrated sextets of young pubescents, with each group representing one state in the Unites States, competed in three rounds of games in a season-long competition for a national title. The series was taped on location outdoors at the Magic Mountain amusement park in Valencia, California, which imbued it with the aura of high production values—higher, anyway, than such previous studio-based children's game shows as *Shenanigans* and *Runaround*.

WEDDING PARTY
Game; Color
April 1, 1968–July 12, 1968

ABC Mon.–Fri. 1:30–2 p.m. (4/1/68–7/12/68)

Host: *Alan Hamel*

The simplistic format of this show must have had viewers wondering on its debut if it was a big April Fools' Day joke by ABC. The bride-to-be of an engaged couple went offstage while her fiancé picked one of three prizes on stage for her. A match by the female won them both the prize and a honeymoon trip. With that low-level contest, it's no wonder this died quickly against *As the World Turns* and *Let's Make a Deal*. Alan Hamel commuted to New York City each Thursday for two days to tape this series before returning to his native Toronto to host the Canadian Broadcasting Corporation variety show *In Person*.

WELCOME NEIGHBOR
Variety; B&W
January 12, 1949–January 28, 1949

DuMont Mon.–Fri. 10:30–11 a.m. (1/12/49–1/28/49)

This forgotten audience participation show was the second show seen on DuMont's initial daily schedule after *Johnny Olsen's Rumpus Room*. It was also the first daily DuMont show to be canceled after less than three weeks on the network.

WELCOME TRAVELERS
Interview; B&W
September 8, 1952–March 30, 1956

NBC Mon.–Fri. 3:30–4 p.m. (9/8/52–7/31/53)
NBC Mon.–Fri. 4–4:30 p.m. (8/3/53–7/2/54)
CBS Mon.–Fri. 1:30–2 p.m. (7/5/54–3/30/56)

Regulars: *Tommy Bartlett (9/8/52–5/6/55), Bob Cunningham, "Smiling" Jack Smith (5/9/55–3/30/56), Pat Meikle (5/9/55–3/30/56), John Garth (5/9/55–3/30/56)*

Welcome Travelers debuted as an ABC radio series on June 30, 1947, switched to NBC two years later, and became televised simultaneously in 1952. Co-creator Tommy Bartlett served as host and interviewer of people visiting Chicago and willing to share something about their lives with the general public. Initially the interviewees told lighthearted vignettes, but by 1954, apparently inspired by the success of *Strike It Rich*, the tales had become litanies of woe, like the 60-year-old widow forced to pay a $4,000 bill after her husband's death and the woman who had a nervous breakdown after learning of her only daughter's marriage. All guests received various gifts for sharing their stories.

Procter & Gamble gave this series an initial boost in 1952 when it decided to sponsor the series after giving up on the soap opera *The First 100 Years*. When the show switched to CBS in July 1954, its radio version was dropped. A bigger transition occurred on May 9, 1955, when the show moved to New York City and left behind Bartlett and the sorrowful stories. In their place was vocalist Jack Smith playing games with three tourists introduced by Pat Meikle. The contestants could try to answer questions correctly or guess what spot a spinning compass would land on. A final difficult question answered correctly near the end of the show allowed a contestant to enter the "Treasure Room" and claim a reward in U.S. defense bonds. John Garth played the organ in the revamped format.

Welcome Travelers *co-hosts Bob Cunningham (left) and Tommy Barlett enjoy a first anniversary cake for the show in 1953 from Jo Hoppe, Miss Chicago of 1952.*

Another addition at the time was former child actor Freddie Bartholomew, who served as the new director.

On October 31, 1955, the show had another revision. Now titled *Love Story*, it had Smith and Meikle interview couples competing for such merchandise as a car, a trip for two to Paris, and $500. However, the cost of talent on the New York version went up more than the ratings did, so by the end of 1955 CBS canceled the show and replaced it with what became a huge hit—*As the World Turns*.

WENDY BARRIE SHOW, THE—See *Inside Photoplay.*

WESTBROOK HOSPITAL—See *Faith for Today.*

WESTERN BALLADEER
Musical Variety; B&W
January 31, 1949–July 15, 1949

NBC Mon.–Fri. 5:15–5:30 p.m. (1/31/49–2/25/49)
NBC Mon./Fri. 5–5:30 p.m. (2/28/49–5/6/49)
NBC Mon./Wed./Fri. 5–5:30 p.m. and Tue./Thu. 5:15–5:30 p.m. (5/9/49–7/15/49)

This early music show with a cowboy theme preceded *Howdy Doody* on NBC's daily lineup.

WESTWIND
Adventure; Color
September 6, 1975–September 4, 1976

NBC Sat. 11:30 a.m.–Noon (9/6/75–9/4/76)

Cast:

Steve Andrews	*Van Williams*
Kate Andrews	*Niki Dantine*
Robin Andrews	*Kimberly Beck*
Tom Andrews	*Steve Burns*

The adventures of a family on a boat called Westwind anchored off Hawaii was the basis of this Saturday morning drama for children. Steve was an underwater photographer, his wife was Kate a marine biologist, and their kids Robin and Tom were practicing scuba divers. Plenty of contrived melodrama and danger in and out of water faced them in this one-year entry.

WHAT IN THE WORLD
Informational; B&W
October 7, 1951–March 26, 1955

CBS Sun. 4:30–5 p.m. (10/7/51–4/13/52)
CBS Sun. 5:30–6 p.m. (4/20/52–10/12/52)
CBS Sun. 3:30–4 p.m. (11/9/52–1/25/53)
CBS Sat. 1:30–2 p.m. (10/17/53–6/26/54)
CBS Sat. 2–2:30 p.m. (10/16/54–3/26/55)

Regulars: *Dr. Froelich Rainey, Dr. Alfred Kidder, Dr. Carleton Coon*

Begun as a local series on WCAU Philadelphia in the spring of 1951, *What in the World* had three professors examine artifacts from the University of Pennsylvania Museum in an

The panel examining artifacts in this session of What in the World *are, from left, Dr. Carlton Coon, Margo Plass, Dr. Alfred Kidder, and Dr. Froelich Rainey.*

effort to identify them, their creators, their dates of creation, and their uses. At first it was a rather dry affair, with the observers sitting on chairs, but then producers added music, maps, and special effects as they superimposed the items on a thick, foglike background, making for a more entertaining show. Objects on view ranged from a Buddha from Siam to a ceremonial mask of the Athapaskan people of the lower Yukon.

Newsweek reported in 1952 that the panelists made correct identifications almost 9 out of 10 times, and that of the 250,000 artifacts held in the museum's storerooms, 50,000 of them were different enough from others in the museum's collection to be used on air. The experts may have had an easy time, but most items frankly baffled the layman at home—and apparently at the museum, too, for on April 3, 1954, the show had to air a repeat instead of the intended broadcast because a janitor at the museum mistakenly threw out nine archaeological pieces that had been laid out for the show, believing them to be junk.

Dr. Rainey, the moderator, was the museum director, while panelists Dr. Kidder and Dr. Coon were assistant director and head of the museum's ethnology section respectively. There was at least one guest panelist per show. From February 7–September 5, 1953, the show aired early Saturday evenings on CBS. After its cancellation in 1955, it reverted to being a local show on WCAU for most of the rest of the 1950s with the same regulars.

•WHAT-A-MESS
Cartoon; Color
September 9, 1995–

ABC Sat. Noon–12:30 p.m. (9/9/95–)

Voices:

What-A-Mess	*Ryan O'Donohue*
Felicia	*Jo Ann Harris Belson*
Trash	*Joe Nipote*
Frank the narrating dog	*Frank Muir*
Duchess	*Charity James*
Mother	*Miriam Flynn*
Father	*Michael Bell*
Daughter	*Debi Derryberry*
Son	*Adam Hendershott*

What-A-Mess was an Afghan hound (real name: Prince Amir of Kinjan) who had a childlike curiosity about his world (wondering, for example, what those white flakes were that fell from the sky when it was cold). Joining him in exploring was Baldwin, a mute bird who nestled in the pooch's scraggly hair. His minor antagonists were Felicia, a condescending kitty, and Trash, the neighborhood bully guard dog with a Jack Nicholson voice. The Duchess was the mother of What-A-Mess, and they were the pet dogs of a family whose members' faces were unseen. The show was based on books by Frank Muir illustrated by Joseph Wright.

•WHAT'S NEW, MR. MAGOO?
Cartoon; Color
September 10, 1977–September 9, 1979

CBS Sat. 9–9:30 a.m. (9/10/77–10/8/77)
CBS Sat. 1–1:30 p.m. (10/15/77–11/12/77)
CBS Sun. 9–9:30 a.m. (11/19/77–8/26/78)
CBS Sun. 8–8:30 a.m. (9/10/78–9/9/79)

Voices:

Mr. Quincy Magoo	*Jim Backus*
Waldo	*Frank Welker*
McBarker	*Robert Ogle*

Jim Backus had been supplying the voice of crotchety, myopic Mr. Magoo in movie cartoon shorts since 1949 when the creation made a belated debut on Saturday morning television in the late 1970s. As in the theatrical version, Magoo acted as a guardian to his nephew Waldo, but the new cartoons added Magoo's talking pet dog McBarker, also a squinter, to the madcap misadventures. Most stories revolved around how Magoo's notoriously awful eyesight, of which he seemed blissfully unaware, contributed to unintentional, yet hilarious, near-disasters in the lives of the trio of regulars.

Besides this series, Magoo's TV appearances included four 60-second beer commercials in 1956; more than 100 five-minute cartoons produced and syndicated in 1960 under the title *Mr. Magoo;* and a nighttime NBC series titled *The Famous Adventures of Mr. Magoo,* which ran from September 19, 1964–August 7, 1965. Backus voiced all versions.

WHAT'S THE PROBLEM—See *It's a Problem.*

WHAT'S THIS SONG?
Game; Color
October 26, 1964–September 24, 1965
NBC Mon.–Fri. 10:30–10:55 a.m. (10/26/64–9/24/65)
Host: *Wink Martindale*

"*Password* with tunes" is an apt summation of this game's setup. Two duos, each with one celebrity, competed in trying to identify a piece of music. A right answer earned 20 points and had the winning duo sing or hum the first four bars of the tune for another 20 points. The other team could challenge the lyrics sung as incorrect and claim the 20 points by giving the correct words. The first team to amass 100 points got to play the "Minute Medley," a bonus game where a contestant could win $200 if his or her team could identify 10 songs within 60 seconds. Singing on the show's debut week were unlikely vocalists Beverly Garland and Lorne Greene.

What's This Song? was one of TV's oldest and longest-running local game shows, having been nominated for an Emmy back in 1949 when it aired on KTSL in Hollywood as *What's the Name of That Song?* The series first ran on the Mutual radio network under the latter title from 1944–49. After its NBC run, the program returned in 1968 as a syndicated series titled *Win with the Stars,* with Allen Ludden as host. That incarnation lasted only one year.

WHEEL OF FORTUNE
Game; B&W
October 3, 1952–December 25, 1953
CBS Fri 10–11 a.m. (10/3/52–12/25/53)
Host: *Todd Russell*

The 1950s show with this name had people identified as do-gooders as its contestants. They faced a carnival wheel with cash prizes ranging from $30 to $1,000; the number of questions that had to be answered in order to win was listed under each amount. Spins of the wheel determined which amounts the

contestants would vie for. The show was the Friday replacement for *Arthur Godfrey Time.* The series also aired on CBS Tuesdays at 8:30 p.m. from July 7–September 15, 1953.

•WHEEL OF FORTUNE
Game; Color
January 6, 1975–September 20, 1991

NBC Mon.–Fri. 10:30–11 a.m. (1/6/75–11/28/75)
NBC Mon.–Fri. 10:30–11:30 a.m. (12/1/75–1/16/76)
NBC Mon.–Fri. 11–11:30 a.m. (1/19/76–4/21/78)
NBC Mon.–Fri. 11:30 a.m.–Noon (4/24/78–8/1/80)
NBC Mon.–Fri. 11–11:30 a.m. (8/4/80–4/23/82)
NBC Mon.–Fri. 10:30–11 a.m. (4/26/82–12/31/82)
NBC Mon.–Fri. 11–11:30 a.m. (1/3/83–6/30/89)
CBS Mon.–Fri. 10:30–11 a.m. (7/3/89–1/11/91)
NBC Mon.–Fri. 10:30–11 a.m. (1/28/91–9/20/91)

Host: *Chuck Woolery (1/6/75–12/25/81), Pat Sajak (12/28/81–1/6/89), Rolf Bernischke (1/9/89–6/30/89), Bob Goen (7/3/89–9/20/91)*

Hostess/"Letter Turner": *Susan Stafford (1/6/75–10/22/82), Vanna White (12/13/82–9/20/91)*

Creator: *Merv Griffin*

Merv Griffin recalled his childhood pastime of playing Hangman in coming up with this hit, which was even more successful as a prime-time syndicated offering in the 1980s and 1990s. Three contestants took turns in spinning a horizontal wheel marked with dollar amounts in the hundreds to determine how much money was at stake for their guess of a letter in a mystery phrase (an overhead camera captured the action of the spinning wheel). Players called for consonants only; it cost them $250 to "buy a vowel." An incorrect guess meant that player turned the wheel over to the next contestant, as did landing on a "Lose a Turn" or "Bankrupt" space. For each puzzle, only the player saying the correct phrase won money from that round. From 1975–87 the winner would use the money earned to "go shopping" for prizes in a gift room, with any remainder usually put on a gift certificate (he or she also could put the remainder "on account" as cash, but if that person later landed on "Bankrupt," the money on account was lost). Shows from 1988 onward eliminated the gifts in the regular games; contestants won money only.

Starting on December 28, 1981, the player with the most money near the end of the show played a bonus round for an unknown merchandise prize. The winner had to pick five consonants and one vowel to use to solve the mystery phrase within 15 seconds. Since everyone invariably chose L, N, R, S, T, and E, later installments gave a player these letters automatically and let them pick three other consonants and another vowel. Those who did not win could return to try up to two more shows.

Beyond the game itself, *Wheel of Fortune* stood out from the rest of the pack because of the folksy demeanor of its first two hosts, ex-country singer Chuck Woolery and ex-weatherman Pat Sajak, and the pleasant runway-type model's maneuvers of "letter turners" Susan Stafford and Vanna White. As soon as it debuted it was popular enough for NBC to try it briefly as an hour entry à la *The Price Is Right* in late 1975.

In 1983 NBC sold the nighttime syndication rights for the show in exchange for extending its daytime run. That year *Wheel of Fortune* went into nighttime syndication and became a huge hit. It differed only in minor ways from the network show. For example, on NBC the top amount on one spin was $2,000; in syndication it was $5,000.

In 1989 Griffin picked Rolf Bernischke, a 34-year-old former San Diego Charger placekicker, out of a pack of some 30 hopefuls to host the daytime show following Pat Sajak's departure to do a failed nighttime TV talk show for CBS (Sajak and White continued doing the syndicated version, as they had from its start). When the show switched from NBC to CBS six months later, Bob Goen became host. The show ended its network run a year and a half later, but as of this writing remains strong in syndication.

•WHEELIE AND THE CHOPPER BUNCH
Cartoon; Color
September 7, 1974–August 30, 1975

NBC Sat. 8:30–9 a.m. (9/7/74–8/30/75)

Voices:

Wheelie/Chopper	Frank Welker
Rota Ree	Judy Strangis
Scrambles	Don Messick
Revs	Paul Winchell
High Riser	Lennie Weinrib

In this undistinguished effort from Hanna-Barbera Productions, Wheelie was a friendly automobile who had a girlfriend, fellow talking Volkswagen Rota Lee, as well as regular antagonists, the Chopper Bunch, a gang of motorcycles out to oppose him. They all crashed after a season of being clobbered in the ratings by *The Bugs Bunny Show*.

•WHERE ON EARTH IS CARMEN SANDIEGO?
Cartoon; Color
February 5, 1994–June 8, 1996

Fox Sat. 11:30 a.m.–Noon (2/5/94–9/3/94)
Fox Sat. 8:30–9 a.m. (2/4/95–3/11/95)
Fox Sat. 11:30 a.m.–Noon (3/18/95–9/2/95)
Fox Sat. 8–8:30 a.m. (9/9/95–6/8/96)

Voices:

Carmen Sandiego	Rita Moreno
The Chief	Roger Bumpass
Ivy	Jennifer Hale
Zack	Scott Menville

This cartoon was based on the Peabody Award–winning public television game show *Where in the World Is Carmen Sandiego?*, which began September 30, 1991 and was still there by 1996. On the game show, children tried to locate Carmen, a trench coat–wearing ex-agent, via geography clues and questions. The cartoon gave viewers the same task, and all were assisted by the investigative talents of Acme Detective Agency agents 18-year-old Ivy and her 14-year-old brother Zack. The Chief was a disembodied head who dispatched C-5s, or portals, to transport Ivy and Zack to various locales, along the way dispensing facts about the region in quick and humorous yet enjoyable bits. Indeed, the show struck a solid balance between entertainment and education, with home viewers asked a question before each commercial about an item mentioned in the previous segment.

WHERE THE ACTION IS
Musical Variety; B&W and Color
June 28, 1965–September 14, 1974

ABC Mon.–Fri. 2–2:30 p.m. (6/28/65–9/24/65)
ABC Mon.–Fri. 4:30–5 p.m. (9/27/65–3/31/67)
ABC Sat. Various hours between 12:30 and 2:30 p.m. monthly (7/7/73–9/14/74)

Regulars: *Steve Alaimo (1965–67), Linda Scott (1965–67), Paul Revere and the Raiders (1965–67), Jimmy Hibbard and the Action Kids (1965–67), Dick Clark (1973–74)*

Theme: *"Action," written by Tommy Boyce (1965–67)*

Roughly a year after *American Bandstand* went off its daily schedule, ABC added this Dick Clark production which had similarities to the parent show, but with far more intentional youth appeal. The main differences were that it used younger regulars and often had popular musicians lip-synching their tunes on outdoor locations. Guesting on the debut were Dee Dee Sharp and the duo of Jan and Dean.

Although all the 1960s regulars had active recording careers as artists, the group which received the biggest boost by far from the series was Paul Revere and the Raiders. Floundering for years without a hit, the group racked up such successes as "Kicks," "Hungry," and "Good Thing" during the show's first run, and it led to their participation as hosts in the series' semi-successor *It's Happening* (q.v.). Additionally, the show's theme "Action" was a top seller for Freddy Cannon in 1965.

Six years after cancellation, Dick Clark updated his show as *Action '73/'74*; it was an occasional replacement for *American Bandstand* and usually aired the last Saturday of every month. Clark left his podium on the latter show to do what *Where the Action Is* had done in the 1960s—go on location (in Malibu, California, when it was warm enough, and in Big Bear, California, in the winter months) and introduce top singing acts and a "dance of the month" before a crowd of ready-to-party teenagers. Many hit artists of the period appeared (David Essex, the Staples Singers, Bill Withers, the DeFranco Family), but the group which had the greatest exposure by far was Bo Donaldson and the Heywoods, with seven shows credited.

WHERE THE HEART IS
Soap Opera; Color
September 8, 1969–March 23, 1973

CBS Mon.–Fri. Noon–12:25 p.m. (9/8/69–3/23/73)

Cast:

Julian Hathaway	James Mitchell
Mary Hathaway	Diana Walker
Michael Hathaway	Gregory Abels
Kate Hathaway Prescott	Diana van der Vlis
Vicky Lucas Hathaway (1969–71)	Robyn Millan
Vicky Lucas Hathaway (1972)	Lisa Richards
Ed Lucas (1969)	Mark Gordon
Ed Lucas (1969–70)	Charles Cioffi
Ed Lucas (1970–73)	Joseph Mascolo
Steve Prescott (1969–70)	Laurence Luckinbill
Steve Prescott (1970–73)	Ron Harper
Dr. Joe Prescott (1970–73)	William Post Jr.
Terry Prescott (1970–71)	Douglas Ross
Terry Prescott (1971–72)	Ted LePlat
Nan Prescott (1970–72)	Katherine Meskill
Allison Archer Jessup	Louise Shaffer
Roy Archer (1969–70)	Stephen Joyce
Dr. Hugh Jessup (1970)	Rex Robbins
Dr. Hugh Jessup (1970–73)	David Cryer
Ben Jessup (1969–72)	Daniel Keyes
Christine Cameron (1969)	Terry O'Connor
Christine Cameron (1969–73)	Delphi Harrington
Stella O'Brien (1969–72)	Bibi Osterwald
Arthur Saxton (1969–71)	Bernard Kates
Tony Monroe (1969–70)	David Bailey
Ruth Monroe (1969–70)	Nancy Franklin
Earl Dana (1969–70)	Bernard Barrow
Lois Snowden (1970–72)	Jeanne Ruskin
Amy Snowden (1971–73)	Clarice Blackburn
Helen Wyatt (1970–71)	Meg Myles
Ellie Jardin (1970–71)	Zohra Lampert
Peter Jardin (1970–73)	Michael Bersell
Loretta Jardin (1971–73)	Alice Drummond
Margaret Jardin (1971)	Barbara Baxley
Margaret Jardin (1971–72)	Rue McClanahan
Liz Rainey Hathaway (1971–73)	Tracy Brooks Swope
John Rainey (1971–73)	Peter MacLean
Laura Blackburn (1971)	Marsha Mason
Adrienne Harris Rainey (1972–73)	Priscilla Pointer

This serial's main cast was introduced a month in advance on *Love of Life* before assuming the latter's time slot. And what sort of characters were they? Well, on the debut, "screwballs" was one description applied to the Hathaways. That's a charitable characterization. This central family on this series was so sexually obsessed it could have used the services of an entire psychiatric clinic.

Consider that at the outset when, as the family mourned the death of patriarch Judge Hathaway, Julian told his sister Kate that he hated his dad and added, "Freud had a few comments on the subject." Sorry, incest fans; Julian's mother was dead, preventing any sort of Oedipal fantasy from being played out. But that was about the only form of sex from which characters on *Where the Heart Is* shied away.

Julian should have worried more about his new young wife Mary and his son Michael, who were in love with each other. Before that affair could bloom, Vicky Lucas, a daughter of Ed Lucas, a man who worked for the Hathaways, became pregnant by Michael and married him. Theirs was an unpleasant marriage; after Vicky miscarried, she pushed Mary (pregnant by Julian, supposedly) down a flight of stairs. When she was committed to an insane asylum, Michael divorced her, only to marry a more sane Vicky a few years later.

Michael may have gone back to Vicky because second wife Liz Rainey was even more problematic. She became

Where the Heart Is featured as a central couple Kate Hathaway (played by Diana Van der Vlis) and Steve Prescott (Ron Harper).

pregnant in an affair with Julian and tried to make Julian's estranged wife Mary think her hubby was seeing Loretta Jardin, but eventually Mary and Julian got back together, and Liz left town. Meanwhile, Loretta's relative Ellie had romanced Steve Prescott, the man Kate loved, during a time when Steve had amnesia. Steve eventually regained his memory, married Kate, and adopted Ellie's mute son Peter when Ellie was murdered. Tragically, Peter later died in a fire.

Kate and Julian's sister Allison had her own share of woes. After divorcing Roy Archer, she married Dr. Hugh Jessup, who had an affair with Christine Cameron which resulted in a child. Observing all this activity was Stella O'Brien, a family acquaintance who was said to have moved from the soap's setting of Northcross, Connecticut, to upstate New York to care for an ill aunt when actress Bibi Osterwald left the show to star in the nighttime CBS sitcom *Bridget Loves Bernie* in 1972. The show went off the air within a year of her departure.

•WHERE'S HUDDLES
Cartoon; Color
July 11, 1971–September 5, 1971

CBS Sun. 5:30–6 p.m. (7/11/71–9/5/71)

Voices:

Ed Huddles	Cliff Norton
Bubba McCoy	Mel Blanc
Freight Train	Herb Jeffries
Claude Pertwee	Paul Lynde
Marge Huddles	Jean VanderPyl
Penny McCoy	Marie Wilson
Mad Dog Maloney	Alan Reed
Play-by-Play Announcer	Dick Enberg
Fumbles/Beverly	Don Messick

Originally airing as the summer replacement for *Hee Haw* on CBS nighttime from July 1–September 10, 1970, *Where's Huddles* returned in repeats on late Sunday afternoons the following summer. It followed the money-making schemes of Ed Huddles, quarterback for the struggling Rhinos professional football team, and his neighbor Bubba McCoy, the Rhinos' center. Mad Dog Maloney coached them, their hulking pal Freight Train, and other teammates. The action was just as challenging for Ed and Bubba back home as they contended with their wives Marge and Penny and their snooty neighbor Claude Pertwee, who considered the duo "savages." Fumbles was Ed's dog, who intimidated Pertwee's cat Beverly. Penny and Ed also had a little-seen baby daughter named Pom-Pom.

•WHERE'S WALDO?
Cartoon; Color
September 14, 1991–September 5, 1992

CBS Sat. 11:30 a.m.–Noon (9/14/91–9/5/92)

"Where's Waldo" was a series of drawings started in 1987 by Martin Handford in the United Kingdom in which viewers had to peruse an elaborately detailed drawing to locate the hidden Waldo, a tall chap dressed in a red and white striped sweater and glasses. On this series, which Handford created and co-executive-produced, children could do the same in "Where's Waldo Moments," which were interspersed between the main attraction, a story line featuring Waldo, his dog Woof, and his girlfriend Wenda, all of whom dressed alike. The crew typically visited places via a portal created by the tip of a magic cane from Waldo's friend Wizard Whitebeard, an elder comic-relief type. Their nemesis was Waldo's evil doppelganger Odlaw, who sported dark shades, a black and yellow striped shirt, and a pencil moustache. Commenting on the activity was a rather wise-guy narrator whose disdain for Odlaw was evident. The *Where's Waldo* book series kept proliferating following this program's short run, with at least 13 million copies sold.

•WHEW!
Game; Color
April 23, 1979–May 30, 1980

CBS Mon.–Fri. 10:30–11 a.m. (4/23/79–11/2/79)
CBS Mon.–Fri. 10:30–10:55 a.m. (11/5/79–5/30/80)

Host: *Tom Kennedy*

An appropriately titled game show, *Whew!* started with two contestants playing on a large game board consisting of five rows of five boxes with amounts of $10, $20, $30, $40, and $50 each, and a top row of three boxes with amounts of $200, $350, and $500. After revealing a category to both players, one went offstage while the other placed six hidden "blocks" on the board, with no more than three per row and no more than one on the top row. The offstage player returned and had a minute to scale the board by calling a box's dollar amount on each row and correcting a "blooper" behind a box on each row. Bloopers were false answers concealing the correct responses, such as Black Panther leader Eldridge Cleaver being given as *Beaver* Cleaver. However, if the box called had a block on it, the contestant had to wait five seconds before choosing another box.

If blocks or an incorrect answer prevented the player from progressing to the top quickly, he or she could yell out, "Long Shot!" to stop the action, after which the player could call one box on the top row, with a correct answer within the allotted five seconds winning the game. The only drawback was that doing so let his or her opponent place a block on that level, and if another block already existed on that row, there would only be one nonblocked box left. Players alternated positions, and the first contestant to win two games went to the bonus round.

In the bonus, the winner had a minute plus an additional second for every $100 he or she had amassed from the earlier games. The player had to answer 10 bloopers in the resulting time frame to win $25,000. The bonus-round set gave the viewer a visual bonus, as the player had to progress through 10 cutouts of villains during that round.

On November 5, 1979 the show was retitled *Celebrity Whew!* and went to 25 minutes. Each player now had a celebrity who alternated in solving rows during the regular game, and handled either the first or last five villains in the bonus.

WHISTLE STOP USA
News/Informational; B&W
September 28, 1952–November 2, 1952

CBS Sun. 3:30–4 p.m. (9/28/52–11/2/52)

Narrator: *Charles Collingwood*

CBS reporter Charles Collingwood narrated this collection of film reports on the 1952 political campaigns. The debut profiled the presidential candidate tours of Republican Dwight D. Eisenhower, the eventual winner, and Democratic challenger Adlai Stevenson, and also aired reactions to the "Checkers" speech by Richard Nixon, Eisenhower's pick for vice president. The show alternated weekly with *What in the World*.

WHISTLING WIZARD, THE
Children's; Color and B&W
October 15, 1951–September 20, 1952

CBS Mon.–Fri. 5:30–5:45 p.m. (10/15/51–10/26/51)
CBS Sat. 11–11:30 a.m. (11/3/51–9/20/52)

Regulars: *Bil Baird, Cora Baird, Franz Fazakas, Ray Hedge, Frank Sullivan*

This imaginative marionette show was the first of its kind to be presented on television in color. It began with a boy named J. P. and his gabbing horse Heathcliff being beckoned by Ting-a-Ling the firefly to search in the Land of Beyond for "the Whistling Wizard." The Wiz turned out to be a leprechaun named Dooley, who joined J. P. and Heathcliff in adventures which often were adaptations of famous stories or events in history. Regularly trying to spoil their fun along the way was the evil Spider Lady, who chanted the name of film director Elia Kazan to invoke her black powers. The show featured a fair number of such in-jokes, including one episode where two singing fleas were named after bandleaders Skitch Henderson and Mitch Miller. Charlemane the lion helped in hosting the show.

Controlling the string-and-glove-operated puppets was the husband-and-wife team of Bil and Cora Baird. Bil also produced the show, played the guitar for background music, and provided the voices for the Whistling Wizard and Charlemane, while Cora provided the voices for J. P. and the Spider Lady. The other regulars voiced an assortment of characters, including Franz Fazakas as Heathcliff.

The show was serialized when it ran daily for three weeks opposite *Howdy Doody*, then had two-parters when it became a weekly show. When it ran daily, it was one of a few shows CBS broadcast in its experimental color system in 1951 (the weekly shows were black and white). CBS canned it in 1952 due to high production costs.

WHO DO YOU TRUST?
Game; B&W
September 30, 1957–December 27, 1963

ABC Mon.–Fri. 4:30–5 p.m. (9/30/57–11/15/57)
ABC Mon.–Fri. 3:30–4 p.m. (11/18/57–12/27/63)

Regulars: *Johnny Carson (9/30/57–9/7/62), Woody Woodbury (9/10/62–12/27/63), Del Sharbutt (9/30/57–11/15/57, 9/10/62–12/27/63), Bill Nimmo (11/18/57–1958), Todd Russell (1958), Ed McMahon (10/13/58–9/7/62)*

We have America's greatest ventriloquist to thank for inadvertently boosting the career of America's greatest talk show host. When the CBS nighttime program *Do You Trust Your Wife?* (the daytime show's first title through July 1958), which ran from January 3, 1956–March 26, 1957, was set to become an ABC series in the fall of 1957, its emcee Edgar Bergen said he would host the daytime show only if there was a nighttime slot for it as well. ABC did not agree to that condition, and instead Johnny Carson obtained a release from his exclusive contract with CBS to do the program. Carson's success with *Who Do You Trust?* eventually made him attractive to NBC executives who were looking for a successor to Jack Paar as host of *The Tonight Show* and the result is history: In 1962 Carson began his 30-year reign as king of late-night television.

The format of *Who Do You Trust?* was basically the same as the nighttime version. Couples displayed their odd hobbies or backgrounds, then had the husband decide on each of three questions whether he or his wife would answer the query. The first question was worth $25, the second $50, and the third $75. After two couples finished the process, the highest-scoring duo challenged the previous day's winning couple to name the most items in a category, with the top prize being $500 (later $1,000) per show. Eric and Helena Gude, the holdover winners from the nighttime series, competed in the first afternoon show.

The main distinguishing element of the daytime show was that Carson, unlike Bergen, actively participated with the contestants in whatever their interests involved. If that meant having to drive a motorized soapbox derby car which could crash into the set (and did), so be it. This freewheeling demeanor was to become part of the trademark Carson persona.

While Carson's attitude did draw audiences, so did some solid scheduling. In late 1957 ABC put the series in the middle of *American Bandstand* to bring up its ratings and improve its selling situation. It worked; by 1958 *Billboard* reported both shows were 50 percent sponsored. In the same year, Carson gained his best sidekick when Ed McMahon became the announcer/assistant. Carson and McMahon ended up having one of network television's longest-running professional on-air partnerships—nearly 35 years.

Carson's ascension to *The Tonight Show* was widely watched, but few cared for his successors on *Who Do You Trust?*, comedian Woody Woodbury and Del Sharbutt (the original Carson sidekick). The show died not long after a year of Woodbury's hosting. As Jay Leno found out in the 1990s, it was anything but easy to follow Carson.

WHO, WHAT OR WHERE GAME, THE
Game; Color
December 29, 1969–January 4, 1974

NBC Mon.–Fri. 12:30–12:55 p.m. (12/29/69–1/4/74)

Host: *Art James*

Taped in New York City, this game had a trio of contestants face off in a competition involving three elements of an unknown subject. Each contestant started with $150 and could bid up to $50 on saying whether he or she could identify the who, what, or where of the subject from a clue given by the host. Contestants who wanted the same element (e.g., two wanting to guess who) could face an auction where the $50 ceiling was lifted and the highest bidder won the right to answer the question. Like *Jeopardy!*, the show ended with a final question where contestants could risk all of their money to win and earn the right to compete the following day.

•WIDE WIDE WORLD
Informational; B&W
October 16, 1955–June 8, 1958

NBC Sun. 4–5:30 p.m. (10/16/55–6/8/58; off summers)

Host: *Dave Garroway*

Wide Wide World, one of the most ambitious of the series that broadcast live technical pickups, emerged from a show on the nighttime NBC series *Producers Showcase* on June 27, 1955. Using 40 cameras and 12 mobile vans, it showcased remotes shot over a 32,000-mile panorama, from the New York City skyline to Mexico, Canada, and points in between (Iowa, Colorado, Utah, Oregon, and Washington, D.C.). When it came to Sundays four months later, its scope was no less ambitious; on the debut, live shots of New York City, San Francisco, Dallas, St. Louis, and the Grand Canyon were tied in with a look at autumn outdoors. David Garroway told viewers on that show that it had 73 cameras, 41,000 miles of telephone lines, and 1,800 technicians at its disposal.

Six weeks of preparation time were necessary for each and every broadcast. Timing was of the essence in making the live-pickup technique work, and often Garroway found himself ad-libbing to cover problems. "Every show is a nerve-wracking ordeal, because there are about 300 word and music cues in each script," Garroway told *The Saturday Evening Post.* "If one cue is missed by five seconds, a chain reaction is started that jams up subsequent scenes." About a quarter of the first season's planned pictures had some sort of technical snafu. The scariest near-miss might have been the one caused by a cameraman in Florida shooting underwater ballet sequences, who missed his cue by two minutes, putting six girls who were holding their breaths under water, waiting for filming to begin, in serious jeopardy.

Nevertheless, viewers were fascinated by this live 90-minute assortment of segments from locales in the United States (by the end of the run, every state had appeared at least once) and abroad, and *Wide Wide World* became the top-rated Sunday afternoon show in the 1950s. Among the firsts on this show were the first live shot broadcast from an overseas country to America, in this case from Havana, Cuba (November 13, 1955); the first TV signals from the Caribbean island of Bimini

(January 29, 1956); the first live telecast from Europe, in this case London (September 16, 1956); and the first live shot of the river gorge and bottom of the Grand Canyon (April 14, 1957). Other notable shows included a closeup of a baby's birth (March 4, 1956), and "The Fabulous Infant," a review of TV's first decade of network broadcasts with guests Gracie Allen, Milton Berle, Perry Como, and Ernie Kovacs (November 10, 1957).

The series appeared on two out of every four Sundays in the 1955–56 season, alternating with *Hallmark Hall of Fame* and *NBC Opera Theater.* In 1956–57 it alternated with *Washington Square* and reruns of the prime time-series *Topper,* and in 1957–58 it alternated with *Omnibus.* It ended abruptly in 1958 because production costs became too high to entice sponsors to cover the amount.

WIDE WORLD OF SPORTS—See ABC's *Wide World of Sports.*

•WILD KINGDOM
Nature Documentary; Color
January 6, 1963–April 16, 1967

NBC Sun. 3:30–4 p.m. (1/6/63–3/31/63)
NBC Sun. 5–5:30 p.m. (10/20/63–4/16/67; off summers)

Regulars: *Marlin Perkins, Jim Fowler*

TV's longest-running nature documentary series had the official title of *Mutual of Omaha's Wild Kingdom* in honor of its sponsor. Marlin Perkins, former star of *Zoo Parade* (q.v.), was host and Jim Fowler was assistant from the start, when the show had some material from the St. Louis Zoo (where Perkins was director) and some from rural parts of America. Eventually, however, most footage used was shot overseas, much of it from Africa, and it was this show that gave many Americans their first look at exotic flora and fauna from other continents. The scenery looked inviting to viewers, but Perkins and Fowler often faced danger and endured pain on location. During filming on the first two years alone, for example, a tiger bit Perkins's wrist and a chimp smacked Fowler in the head. Less eventful were the filmed Mutual of Omaha commercials in which Perkins served as spokesman.

After four years on Sunday afternoons, during which time it won Emmys for Achievement in Daytime Programming in 1966 and 1967, *Wild Kingdom* ran on Sunday evenings on NBC from January 7, 1968–April 11, 1971. Thereafter, new shows were created for syndication through 1988, with Fowler replacing an ill Perkins as host in 1985 (Perkins died in 1986), and Peter Eros as the new assistant.

WILD WEST C.O.W.-BOYS OF MOO MESA
Cartoon; Color
September 12, 1992–September 3, 1994

ABC Sat. 9–9:30 a.m. (9/12/92–1/30/93)
ABC Sat. 8:30–9 a.m. (2/6/93–11/13/93)
ABC Sat. 11:30 a.m.–Noon (11/20/93–9/3/94)

Voices: *Jeff Bennett, Troy Davidson, Bill Farmer, Pat Fraley, Michael Horse, Charity James, Kay Lenz, Danny Mann, Joe Piscopo, Neil Ross*

"It's like no other Western you've ever seen," trumpeted the ads. No kidding. A comet that crash-landed in the territory of Moo Mesa resulted in desert animals there becoming humanoid natives. The good guys, who became known as the C.O.W. (Code Of the West)-Boys, were led by bull Marshal Moo Montana and his deputies Tenderfoot and Dakota Dude, with an occasional assist from free agent Cowlorado Kid. They fought the Wild Wild Bullies and the Gila Hooligans. Others seen were Miss Lilly, Calamity Kate, goofy Sheriff Terribull, and corrupt Mayor Bulloney.

ABC Children's Entertainment President Jennie Trias told *TV Guide* in 1995 how she and the show's producers attempted to play down or eliminate violence on this odd oater: "So one deputy had no weapon at all; he could only use brute strength. One had a lariat. And the marshal had a gun, but he only used it when absolutely necessary, and the gun shot 'marshal stars.'" With this mixed bag of "nonviolent" fighting power, it's no wonder *Wild West C.O.W.-Boys* was little seen after its two-year run.

•WILDC.A.T.S

Cartoon; Color
October 1, 1994–September 2, 1995

CBS Sat. 10–10:30 a.m. (10/1/94–2/4/95)
CBS Sat. 11–11:30 a.m. (2/11/95–9/2/95)

Voices:

Grifter	Colin O'Meara
Zealot	Roscoe Handford
Voodoo	Ruth Marshall
WarBlade	Dean McDermott
Maul	Paul Mota
Spartan	Rod Wilson
Lord Helspont	Maurice Dean Wint
Jacob Marlowe	Sean McCann
Void	Janet-Laine Green
Dockwell	Dennis Akiyama

WildC.A.T.S involved six freedom fighters on Earth in a centuries-long battle against evil in the galaxy. Fighting for good was the human Grifter, nicknamed "the G-Man," and five aliens called Kherubim (pronounced "care-a-bim") warriors—Zealot, Grifter's girlfriend; Voodoo, another female; Maul, a hulking green entity; and WarBlade and Spartan. Their base of operations in the 20th century was the skyscraper headquarters of Halo Enterprise, whose boss Jacob Marlowe gave orders to the sextet and narrated the show's introductions. Opposing them was Lord Helspont, a humanoid with a smoldering skull who led the Daemonites, gargoylish aliens who could control others' minds. Loud, violent battle scenes, spectacular hardware, and a roaring rock soundtrack characterized all episodes. In the last original show before the summer rerun cycle, the WildC.A.T.S rid the galaxy of Helspont and the Daemonites,

vanquishing the latter even after they thought they had gained ultimate control from an orb of pure evil.

The C.A.T. in the title's stood for "Covert Action Teams." The show's official title was *Jim Lee's WildC.A.T.S* in honor of its co–executive producer and co-creator (Lee created the characters in a comic book with Brandon Choi).

WILDFIRE

Cartoon; Color
September 13, 1986–September 5, 1987

CBS Sat. 8:30–9 a.m. (9/13/86–9/5/87)

Voices:

Wildfire	John Vernon
Princess Sara	Georgi Irene
Diabolyn	Jessica Walter
Dorin	Bobby Jacoby
Brutus	Susan Blu
Alvinar	Rene Auberjonois
Dweedle	Billy Barty
John	David Ackroyd
Ellen	Lilly Moon

Wildfire was a horse who saved the baby Princess Sara from certain doom at the hands of the evil witch Diabolyn, who ultimately gained control of Sara's home planet, Dar-Shan. Twelve years later, the grown princess used her magical stallion and help from Dorin, a boy, Brutus, an uncoordinated equine, and Alvinar, a farmer, to combat Diabolyn. John, Sara's father, and his friend Ellen offered moral support for their ongoing fight. Dweedle was Diabolyn's bumbling sidekick.

WILDLIFE ADVENTURES—See *Animal World.*

WILL THE REAL JERRY LEWIS PLEASE SIT DOWN?

Cartoon; Color
September 12, 1970–September 2, 1972

ABC Sat. 10–10:30 a.m. (9/12/70–9/4/71)
ABC Sat. 8–8:30 a.m. (9/11/71–9/2/72)

Voices:

Jerry Lewis	David L. Lander
Rhonda/Geraldine Lewis	Jane Webb
Various	Howard Morris

In 1963 *The Jerry Lewis Show,* a jumbled talk-variety effort, was a massive Saturday night disaster for ABC and left its star vowing never to return to the medium. Seven years later, the network and the comic decided to let bygones be bygones as ABC accepted this cartoon created by, but not using the voice of, Lewis. Lewis did do show development and function as a script consultant, but according to *Variety* he declined the voiceover work because he felt some mimics did his younger voice better than he did in 1970!

The series had Lewis as a temp with the Odd Job Employment Agency who took different occupations with each episode, from a valet to a spy, and always with disastrous consequences. Seen occasionally were Jerry's girlfriend Rhonda and sister Geraldine. Howard Morris voiced Jerry's agency boss Mr. Blunderbuss plus a multitude of other characters, many of which were inspired by Lewis's movies of the 1950s and 1960s.

•WIN, LOSE OR DRAW
Game; Color
September 7, 1987–September 1, 1989
NBC Mon.–Fri. 11:30 a.m.–Noon (9/7/87–9/1/89)

Hostess: *Vicki Lawrence (Schultz)*

Executive Producers: *Burt Reynolds, Bert Convy*

This game show was created by actor Burt Reynolds in 1972 as a pastime for his celebrity pals (Betty White, Dom DeLuise, etc.). However, he did not develop the game for television with his partner, actor Bert Convy, until July 1986 when he realized what a financial success it could be. A moderately popular offering, it went onto network daytime and nighttime syndication simultaneously in September 1987, with Convy hosting the latter for two years followed by Robb Weller in its last (1989–90) season. A children's version titled *Teen Win, Lose or Draw* also aired in 1989 on cable's Disney Channel with Marc Price as host.

All versions used a model of Reynolds's living room as its set, with two sexually segregated teams of a pair of celebrities and one contestant sitting on plush white sofas as turns alternated. Following the announcement of a round's category, a member of one team had a minute to draw clues using a pen on a large white tablet in the middle of the room without writing words or symbols to identify a mystery noun or phrase related to the category. All team members had to draw clues at least once, and the team with the most correct identifications played a bonus round where one member had 90 seconds to draw as many subjects as possible for the other two to identify. A nice contrast to the amateurs' efforts were the professionally drawn caricatures used to introduce the guest celebrities each week.

Actress Vicki Lawrence, the first woman to host a daytime game show since Betty White on *Just Men!*, had begun using her married name as her professional one by the last year of the network series run. A few guest celebrities substituted for her on some weeks, including Sally Struthers. Besides producing, Reynolds also appeared a few times as a player.

WIN WITH THE STARS—See *What's This Song?*

WINCHELL AND MAHONEY—See *Paul Winchell and Jerry Mahoney Show, The.*

WINDOW ON WASHINGTON
Documentary; B&W
January 18, 1953–July 12, 1953
NBC Sun. 5:45–6 p.m. (1/18/53–7/12/53)

Narrator: *Bill Henry*

Bill Henry served as the voiceover "guide" to a weekly film about Washington, D.C., and the events going on in the

nation's capital, such as the route of Dwight D. Eisenhower's inaugural parade on the debut. The title came from the show's opening set, which featured a picture window looking out over the Capitol building.

WINDOW SHOPPING
Game; B&W
April 2, 1962–June 29, 1962
ABC Mon.–Fri. 12:30–1 p.m. (4/2/62–6/29/62)

Regulars: *Bob Kennedy, Professor William Wood*

This game of recall let a trio of players view a photo for 15 seconds, then take turns describing some detail of the picture, earning points with each correct revelation. An incorrect response eliminated a player , until only one of them was left. The winner then viewed a "window" of merchandise totaling $2,000 to $3,000 for as many seconds as points they had amassed in the elimination round. Winners received whatever items they described and could win the entire contents of the "window" if one of the prizes they named was in an envelope they picked. Professor William Wood of the Columbia University School of Journalism judged the veracity of the answers.

•WINKY DINK AND YOU
Children's; B&W
October 10, 1953–April 27, 1957
CBS Sat. 11–11:30 a.m. (10/10/53–8/28/54)
CBS Sat. 10:30–11 a.m. (9/4/54–2/26/55)
CBS Sat. 11–11:30 a.m. (3/5/55–9/17/55)
CBS Sat. 10:30–11 a.m. (9/24/55–3/17/56)
CBS Sat. 11–11:30 a.m. (3/24/56–4/27/57)
CBS Sun. Noon–12:30 p.m. (9/26/54–1/1/56)

Regulars: *Jack Barry, Mae Questel (as voice only of Winky Dink), Dayton Allen (1954–57)*

This fondly remembered 1950s children's show—perhaps the first example of "interactive television"—was a departure for its producers, game show magnates Jack Barry and Dan Enright. Barry hosted the affair, which starred a cartoon boy named Winky Dink. Winky was a giggly imp who sported an oversized head with a blonde hairdo in the shape of a star. He often found himself in predicaments which required the help of home viewers, who drew the required pictures on their TV screens to save him. Some misadventures involved his dog Woofer, voiced by Dayton Allen. Allen also played the live-action character of comically trouble-prone Mr. Bungle, who did skits with Barry. A few segments only had Barry to narrate the action and deliver coloring instructions for various characters.

To participate in the drawing exercises, home viewers paid 50 cents for each kit containing black, green, yellow, and red crayons, an erasing cloth, and clear acetate for them to put over their TV screens to draw on. *Billboard* reported in 1954 that viewers bought 4,000 kits during the show's first month, followed by sales averaging 30,000 kits weekly. Within its first year, the series had sold 1,250,000 kits. Kids probably did not feel constrained by the limited size of their "canvas," as Barry confined crayon strokes to the middle of the screen.

The show ran on Saturdays and Sundays from 1954–55. In 1969 Barry and Enright revived the property briefly with a series of new color five-minute *Winky Dink* cartoons in syndication. Barry also announced plans for a new version to air on the Disney cable channel in 1987, but this did not come to fruition.

WINNER TAKE ALL
Game; B&W
February 12, 1951–April 25, 1952

CBS Mon./Wed./Fri. 2:45–3:30 p.m. and Tue./Thu. 2:45–3:15 p.m. (2/12/51–4/20/51)
NBC Mon.–Fri. 10:30–11 a.m. (2/27/52–4/25/52)

Regulars: *Barry Gray (1951), Bill Cullen (1952), Jerry Austen (1951), Howard Malone (1951), Betty Jane Watson (1951), the Bernard Leighton Orchestra*

The first TV game show for Mark Goodson and Bill Todman, *Winner Take All* had its origins as a CBS radio show in 1946. It became a CBS nighttime show from June 15, 1948–October 3, 1950, with Bud Collyer as host. Four months later it came to daytime in a version revamped from its question-and-answer format. Barry Gray hosted the show, which now had contestants guess answers with clues provided in sketches. Jerry Austen and Betty Jane Watson were vocalists, and Howard Malone was a tap dancer. They and Gray all participated in skits. The show ran 45 minutes three days a week and 30 minutes Tuesdays and Thursdays to make room for *Bride and Groom.*

After a two-month daytime run, *Winner Take All* had its last show on CBS. NBC revived the show for another unsuccessful two-month stay in 1952, this time with Bill Cullen as host using the nighttime format. Two months after that cancellation, the show made its final appearance as a segment of *Matinee in New York* (q.v.), again with Cullen as host.

WINNIE THE POOH—See New Adventures of Winnie the Pooh, The.

WINNING STREAK
Game; Color
July 1, 1974–January 3, 1975

NBC Mon.–Fri. 10:30–11 a.m. (7/1/74–1/3/75)

Host: *Bill Cullen*

On *Winning Streak,* two players faced a board with a category and 16 letters. Contestants picked a letter and could win the hidden points associated with it by giving a correct answer to a question related to the category by using the first letter of a word provided by the host as the first letter in the answer. The first player to reach or pass a preselected total of points got to play a previous game winner in a bonus match where they alternated in picking up to 12 hidden letters to use in one

word. Giving an incorrect word resulted in the other player winning money attached to each letter, plus the opportunity to face future challengers.

This series was notable in that it replaced a long-running game show (*Jeopardy*) and in turn went off the air in favor of another hit (*Wheel of Fortune*). Bill Cullen reappeared three months later in daytime with another word game packaged by this show's company, Bob Stewart Productions (see *Blankety Blanks*).

WISDOM
Documentary; B&W and Color
January 1, 1956–April 1, 1962

NBC Sun. 2–2:30 p.m. (1/1/56–1/29/56)
NBC Sun. 2:30–3 p.m. (9/15/57–3/30/58)
NBC Sun. 2–2:30 p.m. (2/28/59–5/10/59) [times varied in May]
NBC Sun. 5–5:30 p.m. (9/17/61–4/1/62)

Occasional Interviewer/Producer (1956–58): *Robert D. Graff*

Wisdom was the brainchild of NBC President Sylvester "Pat" Weaver, who in the early 1950s wanted the network to profile 50 celebrated artistic, religious, and political leaders above the age of 65. NBC produced 19 interviews and aired them mostly as specials from May 18, 1952 (with British philosopher Bertrand Russell) until September 23, 1956 under the titles *Conversations with Elder Wise Men* or *Conversations with Distinguished Persons.* Five profiles, on theologian Paul J. Tillich, cellist Pablo Casals, French artist Marcel Duchamp, Irish dramatist Sean O'Casey, and Indian Prime Minister Jawaharlal Nehru, aired weekly in January 1956.

A year later, NBC inaugurated a new series of seven interviews in color and aired them with earlier specials under the title *Wisdom.* "A Visit with Pablo Picasso" was the debut show, with the 76-year-old artist painting, sculpting, and drawing, but not talking. After a one-season run, 12 new shows appeared in 1959.

For all the shows, the interviews were shot at the residence of the guest of honor over a period of two or three days. "We keep after them until they say yes," Robert Graff told *Newsweek* of the series' subjects. However, Albert Einstein and T. S. Eliot never did say yes.

In 1960 *TV Guide* reported that NBC executives were considering a follow-up titled *Entertainment Wisdom,* which would feature shows on mature celebrities such as a "Jimmy Durante Piano Recital" or "Marlene Dietrich Singing Lili Marlene." The project never got off the ground. However, NBC did repeat the series in 1961–62 and aired four new specials from September 19–November 14, 1965 before the concept died.

•WISH KID STARRING MACAULEY CULKIN
Cartoon; Color
September 14, 1991–September 5, 1992

NBC Sat. 10–10:30 a.m. (9/14/91–7/25/92)
NBC Sat. 10:30–11 a.m. (8/1/92–9/5/92)

Voices:

Nick McClary	*Macauley Culkin*
Peggy McClary	*Quinn Culkin*

Others: *Paul de la Rosa, Paul Haddad, Marilyn Lightstone, Judy Marshak, James Rankin, Andrew Sabiston, Stuart Stone*

Given the massive success of the 1990 movie *Home Alone,* in which Macauley Culkin starred as a child who defended his house against would-be criminals through elaborate and comical defenses, one would have thought that a cartoon with Culkin the next year would use the same setup as its model. Instead, "Mac" voiced Nick, a boy whose magical glove granted him one wish a week, like a pet dinosaur. His friend Darryl Singletary was the only other person who knew about the magical glove and found himself invariably mixed up in the chaos that ensued following each wish. Enmeshed in these comic complications were Nick's baby sister Peggy (voiced by Culkin's actual younger sister Quinn), his reporter/photographer father, his real-estate agent mother, and Frankie Dutweiler, the resident bully. As with the old ABC nighttime sitcom *Bewitched,* with which this cartoon shared a certain similarity, there was a suspicious neighbor, Mrs. Opal, who witnessed the magic in disbelief as she never could verify the odd happenings to others. Slobber was Nick's cute dog.

Wish Kid originally was developed for the fledgling Fox lineup before it appeared as the last cartoon seen on NBC's Saturday lineup. Fox reportedly had plans to rework the cartoon for a second season, but dropped the idea.

WIZARD OF ODDS, THE
Game; Color
July 17, 1973–June 28, 1974

NBC Mon.–Fri. 11–11:30 a.m. (7/17/73–6/28/74)

Host: *Alex Trebek*

A trio of contestants spent three rounds trying to identify as many mystery personalities as possible based on clues from the host, and after three rounds the two top scorers got to play for a merchandise prize by playing one of several games used on this series that were based on statistical data. Two interesting notes are that one of the show's producers was Alan Thicke, in one of his first American television jobs, and host Alex Trebek starred in the program's replacement, *High Rollers.*

WIZARD OF OZ, THE
Cartoon; Color
September 8, 1990–September 6, 1991

ABC Sat. 8:30–9 a.m. (9/8/90–9/6/91)

Voices: *Charlie Adler, Liz Georges, David Lodge, Tress MacNeille, Alan Oppenheimer, Hal Rayle, B. J. Ward, Frank Welker*

The astonishing popularity of *The Wizard of Oz,* the 1939 movie classic starring Judy Garland that since 1956 has been TV's most often repeated film, is probably the main reason that animated versions of L. Frank Baum's turn-of-the-century classic and its sequels have not been very successful. A 1961

syndicated version titled *Tales of the Wizard of Oz* did not generate much enthusiasm, nor did a 1974 movie sequel called *Journey Back to Oz* (with Liza Minnelli assuming the voice for her mother's role) and a 1990–92 series on the HBO pay cable service titled *Wonderful Wizard of Oz.* The ABC version followed the movie story line fairly faithfully, with native Kansas farm girl Dorothy, her dog Toto, the Scarecrow, the Tin Man, and the Cowardly Lion up against the machinations of the Wicked Witch of the West. Even some Munchkins appeared. The series was syndicated in repeats in 1992 as part of a daily package of other original cartoons titled *Amazin' Adventures.*

WOLF ROCK TV
Cartoon; Color
September 8, 1984–September 30, 1984

ABC Sat. 10:30–11 a.m. (9/8/84–9/30/84)

Voices:

Wolfman Jack	*Himself*
Mr. Morris	*Jason Bernard*
Sunny	*Siu Ming Carson*
Ricky	*Robert Vega*
Sara	*Noelle North*
Bopper	*Frank Welker*

This short-lived cartoon had veteran radio deejay Wolfman Jack as mentor to three teenagers at his TV station in charge of showing rock videos, much to the chagrin of station manager Mr. Morris. Bopper was a bird who hung around the pubescent trio. Among the elements also seen in the cartoon were "Wolf Rock News" and "The Rock 'n' Roll Museum." Two to four real music videos and artist interviews per episode popped up between the action, no doubt a contribution from the show's co-producer, Dick Clark. The show ran in repeats in syndication with *Kidd Video* under the title *Wolf Rock Power Hour.*

WOMAN TO REMEMBER, A
Soap Opera; B&W
February 21, 1949–April 28, 1949

DuMont Mon.–Fri. 3–3:15 p.m. or 11:45 a.m.–Noon
  (2/21/49–4/28/49)

Cast:

Christine Baker	*Patricia Wheel*
Steve Hammond	*John Raby*
Carol Winstead	*Joan Catlin*
Bessie Thatcher	*Ruth McDevitt*
Charley Anderson	*Frankie Thomas*

DuMont's only daytime soap opera, *A Woman to Remember,,* focused on the dilemmas facing Christine Baker, a star of radio serials who found her world in real life threatened by professional and social rival Carol Winstead. Christine's boyfriend was Steve, and Bessie and Charley were her confidantes. After two months in daytime, the show moved to weeknights on DuMont for two more months and ended on July 15, 1949.

WOMAN WITH A PAST

Soap Opera; B&W
February 1, 1954–July 2, 1954

CBS Mon.–Fri. 4–4:15 p.m. (2/1/54–7/2/54)

Cast:

Lynn Sherwood	Constance Ford
Diane Sherwood (early)	Felice Camargo
Diane Sherwood (later)	Barbara Myers
Steve Rockwell	Gene Lyons
Sylvia Rockwell (2/54–5/54)	Mary Sinclair
Sylvia Rockwell (5/54–7/54)	Geraldine Brooks
Gwen	Jean Stapleton
Pegs	Ann Hegira

Also: *John Ridgely, Bram Nossen, Geoffrey Lumb, Beverly Roberts, Dennis Harrison, Lila Skala, Kathleen Comegys, Jay Barney, Marta Linden, Maurice Burke, John Conte*

The woman with a past in this show was Lynn Sherwood, a dress designer in New York City whose big secret was that her 7-year-old daughter Diane was illegitimate. Her rival Sylvia Rockwell attempted to use that information and some other machinations to keep Lynn from winning the affections of Sylvia's in-name-only husband Steve. Keeping an eye out on the activities of both were friends Gwen and Pegs, the latter being Lynn's schoolteacher sister. In April 1954 Lynn opened her own shop to allow the show to stage fashion exhibits for home viewers.

Even for a daytime soap opera, which typically had a lot of personnel changes, the turnover among regulars during this show's five-month run was high. Those listed under "also" popped up for brief periods throughout the run. There are no records as to what their characters' names were.

WOMEN'S CLUB, THE

Talk; B&W
December 24, 1951–August 1, 1952

DuMont Noon–12:15 p.m. (12/24/51–8/1/52)

Hostess: *Julann Caffrey*

This obscure interview show, devoted to parent-child relationships, for some reason had hostess and actress Julann Caffrey address guests from a rostrum rather than sit down next to them, as was customary. A show with the same title spotlighting organizations in which women play a prominent role ran on WABD New York in late 1948.

WOMEN'S MAJOR LEAGUE BOWLING

Sports; B&W
January 11, 1959–April 18, 1959

NBC Sat. 5–5:30 p.m. (1/11/59–4/18/59)

Announcers: *Jack Buck, Fred Wolf*

Thirteen games filmed in Coral Gables, Florida, made up the action seen on *Women's Major League Bowling.* Each week's winner received money and a mink coat and the chance to defend her title the next week. The sponsor, appropriately, was Brunswick.

WONDERFUL WORLD OF GOLF

Sports; B&W and Color
January 7, 1962–February 28, 1970

CBS Sun. 4–5 p.m. (1/7/62–3/18/62)
NBC Sun. 4–5 p.m. (1/20/63–3/29/64; spring months only)
ABC Sun. 4–5 p.m. (1/17/65–3/28/65)
NBC Sat. 5–6 p.m. (1/8/66–2/28/70; spring months only)

Hosts: *Gene Sarazen, George Rogers*

Officially titled *Shell's Wonderful World of Golf,* this series lived up to its international moniker for most of its run by having one American golfer competing each week against a player from another country, where the show was being recorded. The format changed on January 4, 1969, when the series became an 18-man elimination tournament with a top prize of $20,000 for the winner. The show left CBS after one season for NBC because the latter accommodated sponsor Shell Oil's desire for the show to be in color. The series won an Emmy in 1966 for Achievement in Sports Programs.

•WOODY WOODPECKER SHOW, THE

Cartoon; Color
October 3, 1957–September 3, 1977

ABC Thu. 5–5:30 p.m. (10/3/57–9/25/58)
NBC Sat. 8:30–9 a.m. (9/12/70–1/9/71)
NBC Sat. 9–9:30 a.m. (1/16/71–9/4/71)
NBC Sat. 8:30–9 a.m. (9/11/71–1/1/72)
NBC Sat. 9–9:30 a.m. (1/8/72–9/2/72)
NBC Sat. 8–8:30 a.m. (9/11/76–9/3/77)

Host: *Walter Lantz (1957–58)*

Voices: *Grace Stafford, Daws Butler, Walter Tetley, June Foray, Paul Frees*

As millions of children did for two decades, the star of The Woody Woodpecker Show *checks the time to see if his show is on the air.*

Woody Woodpecker ("Ha-ha-ha-HA-ha!"), the most mischievous bird in the cartoon world, came to network television in short but memorable runs in the 1950s and 1970s. In 1957–58, Walter Lantz hosted the series à la Walt Disney from his office. Three theatrical cartoon shorts aired per show featuring Woody, a sometimes obnoxious, hypertensive troublemaker, and other characters like Wally Walrus, Andy Panda, and Oswald the Rabbit.

The show zoomed to the top of the daytime ratings during its first year, in 1957, and was soon being carried by 166 stations, up from the original 101. Lantz told *Billboard* that more than 9,000 feet of film had been shot for the series for new characters like Chilly Willy the penguin. The 1957–58 shows used roughly 120 cartoons, but about 25 sequences of Woody's antics on movie screens featuring such scenes as drunken horses and Woody having a nervous breakdown failed to make it on air due to concerns about their impact on children.

In 1970–72 NBC revived the property with post-1948 cartoons of Woody and other Walter Lantz creations first seen in movie theaters, such as Inspector Willoughby, Maw and Paw, Sugarfoot, and "Foolish Fables." In 1976–77 NBC used those cartoons with other more recent theatrical cartoons like "The Beary Family."

By the way, the unlikely source of Woody's voice was a woman. Her name was Grace Stafford, and she just happened to be Mrs. Walter Lantz.

WORD FOR WORD
Game; Color
September 30, 1963–October 23, 1964

NBC Mon.–Fri. 10:30–11 a.m. (9/30/63–6/26/64)
NBC Mon.–Fri. 10:30–10:55 a.m. (6/29/64–10/23/64)

Host: *Merv Griffin*

Officially titled *Merv Griffin's Word for Word*, this game had two players try to make as many words as possible using letters from one main word, with the winner of two games going on to play a bonus for extra winnings. Merv Griffin, whose production company handled this series, went on to launch his eponymous long-running syndicated talk show shortly after *Word for Word's* cancellation.

•WORDPLAY
Game; Color
December 29, 1986–September 4, 1987

NBC Mon.–Fri. 12:30–1 p.m. (12/29/86–9/4/87)

Host: *Tom Kennedy*

Wordplay's main claim to fame is that it replaced *Search for Tomorrow* after a 35-year run. *Wordplay* was not nearly so fortunate, as this basic update of *Call My Bluff* lasted less than a year. Two players alternated in choosing one of nine words on a board. Three guest celebrities each offered their own definitions for the picked word, with only one being correct. (Generally at least three words were easy to identify.)

A player identifying the right definition won a hidden dollar amount attached to the word. The highest-scoring contestant after six words were picked played an end game where the object was to connect a 24-square board (six columns of four boxes) from one side to another in 45 seconds for $5,000. This was done by guessing the word suggested by two definitions revealed in a box and thus claiming the box. An incorrect guess led to a block and forced a player to go to an adjacent box in order to continue. If unsuccessful in the bonus, the contestant could try up to two more days for a total prize of $10,000, following a successful defense of their post in the regular game.

WORDS AND MUSIC
Game; Color
September 28, 1970–February 12, 1971

NBC Mon.–Fri. 1:30–2 p.m. (9/28/70–2/12/71)

Regulars: *Wink Martindale, Peggy Connelly, Katie Gran, Pat Henderson, Bob Marlo, Don Minter*

Creator/Music Director: *Jack Quigley*

The only game show to debut in daytime in 1970 (the first calendar year since the 1940s in which just one game show was introduced), *Words and Music* had a trio of players compete in a contest involving a board with 16 squares. Each square had a clue to a word in the lyrics of a song to be sung on that day's show. Contestants heard tunes one by one and could win money by matching a word in the song's lyrics with the correct square. Players went through four rounds, with money amounts increasing each round, and the high scorer tried to get three consecutive wins for a new automobile. Wink Martindale, who had his own hit on *Billboard's* Hot 100 chart in 1959 ("Deck of Cards"), hosted the affair, with five unknown vocalists singing the tunes.

WORLD APART, A
Soap Opera; Color
March 30, 1970–June 25, 1971

ABC Mon.–Fri. 12:30–1 p.m. (3/30/70–6/25/71)

Cast:

Betty Kahlman Barry (1970 at least)	Elizabeth Lawrence
Betty Kahlman Barry	Augusta Dabney
Patrice Kahlman	Susan Sarandon
Chris Kahlman	Matthew Cowles
Russell Barry	William Prince
T. D. Drinkard	Tom Ligon
Meg Johns	Anna Minot
Dr. Ed Sims	James Noble
Adrian Sims	Kathleen Maguire
Becky Sims	Erin Connor
Dr. John Carr	Robert Gentry
Jack Condon	Stephen Elliott
Nancy Condon	Susan Sullivan
Oliver Harrell	David Birney

Bud Whitman (c. 1971)   Kevin Conway
Julie Stark (c. 1971)   Dorothy Lyman
Matt Hampton (c. 1971)   Clifton Davis
Olivia Hampton (1971)   Jane White
Linda Peters (1971)   Heather MacRae
Dr. Neil Stevens (1971)   Albert Paulsen

If Irna Phillips could create *As the World Turns* for CBS and *Another World* for NBC, why couldn't she have *A World Apart* on ABC? Actually, Irna served as story editor on the soap, while her adopted daughter Katherine was listed as creator. But the autobiographical scenario suggested heavy input on Irna's part. The title supposedly referred to how unmarried Betty Kahlman's work as writer of soap operas kept her "a world apart" from her daughter Patrice and son Chris, both adopted. But Irna gave *Variety* a different explanation: "It's indeed a world apart that we live in. Race is separated from race, parents are alienated from children—and we hope to sew it up a little in *A World Apart*."

Beside her familial conflict offstage, Betty Kahlman found herself consoled at work by her attorney T. D. Drinkard and associate writer Meg Johns. She also saw her friends the Sims endure their own troubles with their daughter Becky and her hippie pals Bud Whitman and Julie Stark. Other regulars, many of them youthful, included the Hamptons, the token blacks, and Oliver Harrell, played by David Birney following his departure from *Love Is a Many Splendored Thing* over a salary dispute.

Recalling her role as Patrice to *TV Guide* in 1988, Susan Sarandon said, "I loved it. I was the girl everything happened to . . . . I aged from like 17 to 20 in a year. My boyfriend was this terrorist who was dying of mercury poisoning. I also had a nervous breakdown and became a nurses' aide—all in about a month. And then I got pregnant—after unbuttoning *one button* of my nurses' uniform."

WORLD AT HOME, THE
Informational; Color
August 22, 1955–September 9, 1955

NBC Mon.–Fri. 10:45–11 a.m. (8/22/55–9/9/55)

Hostess: *Arlene Francis*

Preceding its originator series *Home*, *The World at Home* was an interview show designed to give housewives a closer look at current events in the world. The debut had three Chinese exchange students talking about their government's efforts to deport them. With Francis as host and Hugh Downs as announcer, this show came off looking more like a miniaturized version of *Home* than a truly different series, and it soon went off the air.

WORLD CHAMPIONSHIP GOLF
Sports; B&W
October 18, 1959–June 26, 1960

NBC Sun. 5–6 p.m. (10/18/59–6/26/60)

Regulars: *Bob Crosby, Chick Harbert, Dutch Harrison*

The largest purse in professional golf's history up to the time ($171,000) was the drawing card for this competition. *World Championship Golf* featured 32 players with the Professional Golf Association (PGA) in a filmed season-long tournament. A player winning the first round claimed $1,500 and could go on to win $2,500 in the second round, $3,500 in the quarterfinals, and $5,000 in the semifinals. For the final round, two players faced off in 36 holes on two shows for the chance to win $25,000 (the loser claimed $10,000). A player won $12,500 for any hole-in-one. And like *All-Star Golf* on ABC, which aired the same season on Saturdays, *World Championship Golf* gave home viewers a one-minute lesson per show in how to play the game.

Bandleader Bob Crosby hosted and Chick Harbert and Dutch Harrison were pro golf players who served as referees for the series. The show's short run (one season) may have been partly due to ill-conceived camera work. In a letter to *TV Guide*, Richard Bartell of Hollywood, who claimed 36 years' experience in the movie industry and even more than that in playing golf, wrote that the series' cameramen should "focus on the ball, club and body of the golfer instead of showing the golfer's head, the gallery and surrounding trees and countryside."

WORLD CHAMPIONSHIP TENNIS
Sports; Color
February 24, 1974–May 23, 1976

NBC Sun. 4:30–6:30 p.m. (2/24/74–5/12/74)
NBC Sun. 2–4 p.m. (2/23/75–5/11/75)
NBC Sun. 1:30–3:30 p.m. (2/15/76–5/23/76)

Announcers: *Bud Collins, Jim Simpson (1974), Dan Rowan (1975)*

Billionaire Lamar Hunt helped create this perennial springtime tennis tournament, which began in 1974 with three different circuits (Red, Green, and Blue) of internationally integrated players vying for a top prize of $10,000 in each tour. The top two finishers in each circuit and the two next-highest point winners from all three groups met in May for a first-place prize of $50,000. In 1975 the show went celebrity-crazy, with comedian Dan Rowan of *Laugh-In* fame joining Bud Collins in the announcing booth for some odd reason for a few telecasts beginning March 16. Stars like George Peppard and Clint Eastwood also participated in the competition, which unlike 1974 included taped as well as live games. The last season eschewed Hollywood in favor of Collins doing live best-of-five sets with two pros per show from Keauhou-Kona, Hawaii.

WORLD INVITATIONAL TENNIS CLASSIC
Sports; Color
April 14, 1974–July 23, 1978

ABC Sun. 3:30–4:30 p.m. (4/14/74–7/11/76; April–June or July only)
ABC Sun. 2:30–4 p.m. (5/1/77–6/12/77)
ABC Sun. 2–3:30 p.m. (5/21/78–7/23/78)

Announcers: *Chris Schenkel, Pancho Gonzalez, Butch Buchholz (1975), Billie Jean King (1976), Andrea Kirby (1978)*

Eight of the world's top male and female professional tennis players took part in this annual spring tournament for the chance to win a high stake of money as the top prize ($135,000 in the first season alone). Billie Jean King took part in the tournament during its first year and was a commentator in the third year.

WORLD IS YOURS, THE
Nature; Color
June 26, 1951–August 31, 1951
CBS Mon.–Fri. 4:30–5 p.m. (6/26/51–8/31/51)
Host: *Ivan Sanderson*
Assistant: *Patty Painter*

This obscure program has the honor of being TV's first regularly scheduled color series; it represented CBS's short-lived try at using the process in 1951 (which no one with a regular black-and-white set could get unless they had an adapter). The show featured educational information about the outdoors and its creatures dispensed by naturalist Ivan Sanderson.

WORLD LEAGUE OF AMERICAN FOOTBALL—See WLAF Football.

WORLD NEWS ROUNDUP—See CBS Sunday News.

WORLD NEWS THIS MORNING—See ABC World News This Morning.

WORLD OF IDEAS, THE
Informational; B&W
January 18, 1959–May 3, 1959
CBS Sun. 3:30–4 p.m. (1/18/59–5/3/59)
Moderator: *Dr. Charles Frankel*

The World of Ideas was a New York City–based symposium analyzing how people arrive at their conclusions, as well as the significance of decisions based on those conclusions. Some 40 people addressed topics like the debut's "Is Censorship of the Arts Ever Justified?" Moderator Dr. Charles Frankel was chairman of the Philosophy Department at Columbia University.

WORLD OF MR. SWEENEY, THE
Comedy-Drama; B&W
October 4, 1954–December 31, 1955
NBC Mon.–Fri. 4:30–4:15 p.m. (10/4/54–12/31/55)
Cast:

Cicero P. Sweeney	*Charles Ruggles*
Marge Franklin (10/4/54–11/4/55)	*Helen Wagner*
Kippie Franklin (10/4/54–11/4/55)	*Glenn Walken*
Liz Thompson (11/7/55–12/31/55)	*Helen Warnow*
Timmy Thompson (11/7/55–12/31/55)	*Jimmy Baird*
Sue Thompson (11/7/55–12/31/55)	*Susan Odin*

The World of Mr. Sweeney began as a sketch on *The Kate Smith Show* on October 14, 1953, then became a thrice-weekly nighttime show on NBC on June 30, 1954 before switching to daytime within a few months. Throughout its run it featured the activities that surrounded easygoing Cicero P. Sweeney, manager of a general store in the village of Mapleton, who interacted with his daughter Marge and her adorable son Kippie, dispensing wise advice along the way. Typical stories involved gossip when Cicero's son-in-law was seen with an attractive young lady and Cicero's decision to join a birdwatchers' society. Fans of *The Andy Griffith Show* should take special note of the October 11, 1954 telecast in which a character called Sheriff Barney Fife investigated a wave of locks being picked in town.

On November 7, 1955, Cicero became acquainted with the Thompsons (his daughter Liz and her kids Sue and Timmy) on the California branch of his family tree. The show also moved production from New York to Hollywood that day, but the series ended within two months. Nearly a year later, *TV Guide* reported that a new filmed version of the series was under preparation, but no record of such a program actually airing exists.

WORLD OF SPORTS ILLUSTRATED, THE—See CBS Sports Illustrated.

WORLD SERIES OF AUTO RACING
Sports; Color
January 4, 1978–March 29, 1980
ABC Sat. 2–3 or 2:30–3:30 p.m. (1/4/78–3/29/80; winters only)
Announcers: *Jackie Stewart, Al Michaels, Chris Economaki*

Identically prepared cars competed in this gimmicky contest. For example, in January 1979 the show had three exclusive preliminary events for different divisions of car racing—NASCAR, USAC, and Grand Prix. Also in March of that year, two separate finals were held, one for road racing and one for oval track competition.

WORLD'S GREATEST SUPER FRIENDS, THE—See Super Friends.

WRESTLING—See Championship Wrestling from Hollywood;

WUZZLES, THE
Cartoon; Color
September 14, 1985–September 5, 1987
CBS Sat. 8:30–9 a.m. (9/14/85–4/19/86)
CBS Sat. 8–8:30 a.m. (4/26/86–9/6/86)
ABC Sat. 8–8:30 a.m. (9/13/86–9/5/87)

Voices:

Eleroo/Girafbra	*Henry Gibson*
Hoppopotamus	*Jo Anne Worley*
Rhinokey/Croc/Pack Cat	*Alan Oppenheimer*
Moosel/Brat	*Bill Scott*
Bumblelion/Flizard	*Brian Cummings*
Butterbear	*Kathy Helppie*
Mrs. Pedigree	*Tress MacNeille*
Narrator	*Stan Freberg*

As their character names implied, the Wuzzles were a group of animals consisting of parts of two species (e.g., Eleroo was part pachyderm and part kangaroo). They all lived on Wuz Island, and despite having no contact with the rest of the world, their emotions often mimicked human emotions and their weekly activities mirrored the conventions of human society. The series' second season on ABC consisted of repeats.

• X-MEN

Cartoon; Color
October 31, 1992–June 8, 1996

Fox Sat. 11:30 a.m.–Noon (10/31/92–11/7/92)
Fox Sat. 11–11:30 a.m.(1/2/93–12/9/95)
Fox Sat. 10:30–11 a.m. (12/16/95–4/13/96)
Fox Sat. 11–11:30 a.m. (4/20/96–6/8/96)

Voice Director: *Dan Hennessey*

Based on the Marvel Comic book which began in 1963, *X-Men* featured the exploits of superheroic mutants who worked for the good of mankind on Earth in spite of being rejected and feared by the public. Calm, bald Professor Charles Xavier led the crew of eight, whom he named after himself. "Professor X," who himself had the ability to transmit thoughts telepathically and read minds, convinced the mutants to practice their powers at his School of the Gifted. The lore behind the action was that all mutants had become aware of their powers while teenagers, and as the hulking but all-knowing X-Man, the Beast, succinctly put it, their mutations came from "Gamma rays, pollution, ozone depletion . . . television."

Other X-Men were Cyclops (Scott Summers), the nominal head of missions, who stored solar energy which he used to shoot beams from his glasses; Wolverine, also known as Logan, a prowling loner with elongated claws; Rogue, a combative female who absorbed others' strengths for her powers; Gambit (Remy LeBeau), a suave Cajun who could charge objects to explode; Storm, "Mistress of the Elements"; and Morph, a constantly transmogrifying imp. Jean Grey, Professor X's aide, possessed telekinetic and telepathic powers.

The premiere introduced the latest addition to the group, the adolescent Jubilee (born Jubilation Lee), who had the electromagnetic power to blast others away. She was abducted by robots working for the Mutant Control Agency, a private organization "occasionally supported by the government" which tried to suppress the X-Men. After the X-Men freed Jubilee, she joined them in their adventures against fantastic foes, while they tried in vain to convince fellow humans that they deserved fair treatment.

X-Men was an immediate success, leading Fox to the top of the Saturday morning market by the mid-1990s and leaving the audience wondering why the rather intelligently written cartoon had not appeared sooner (a syndicated pilot did appear in 1988 with a somewhat different cast). No individual credits were given for continuing characters in the multitude of actors listed at the end of each show, but Dan Hennessey did provide at least one voice in addition to being vocal director. The show had its pilot debut as a two-part special on October 31 and November 7, 1992 before debuting in early 1993.

YO YO BEARS, THE—The syndicated title for *Help! It's the Hair Bear Bunch* (q.v.)

YO, YOGI!
Cartoon; Color
September 14, 1991–July 25, 1992

NBC Sat. 8:30–9 a.m. (9/14/91–7/25/92)

Voices:

Yogi Bear	*Greg Burson*
Boo Boo	*Don Messick*

On this go-round, the veteran bear and his diminutive pal Boo Boo were depicted in their teenage years roaming around Jellystone Mall with several other Hanna-Barbera favorites, from Huckleberry Hound to Snagglepuss to Dastardly and Muttley. To combat unimpressive ratings, the show added one part in 3-D starting January 25, 1992, making glasses available for viewing the segment via mail order from sponsor Rice Krispies cereal, but the extra dimension resulted in no substantial change in viewership. (For more character information, see *Yogi's Gang.*)

YOGI BEAR—See *Yo, Yogi!; Yogi's Gang; Yogi's Space Race.*

YOGI'S GANG
Cartoon; Color
September 8, 1973–August 30, 1975

ABC Sat. 8:30–9 a.m. (9/8/73–8/31/74)
ABC Sat. 8–8:30 a.m. (9/7/74–8/30/75)

Voices:

Yogi Bear/Quick Draw McGraw/	
Huckleberry Hound/Snagglepuss/Augie	
Doggie/Wally Gator/Peter Potamus	*Daws Butler*
Boo Boo/Ranger John Smith/Touche	
Turtle/Squiddly/Diddly/Atom Ant	*Don Messick*

Doggie Daddy	John Stephenson
Secret Squirrel	Mel Blanc
Magilla Gorilla	Allan Melvin
Paw Rugg	Henry Corden

While his claim of being "smarter than the average bear" may be in dispute, there is no doubt than Yogi Bear is one of the most popular and venerable TV cartoon characters. First seen on the syndicated *Huckleberry Hound* in 1958, Yogi got his own syndicated series in 1961 featuring pranks he played on visitors to Jellystone Park with the sometimes reluctant participation of his diminutive partner Boo Boo. Ranger Smith tried to put a stop to their efforts but usually ended up looking like a fool in the process. (Ironically, there was a Ranger Denny Smith who worked at the real-life Yellowstone Park. He liked the attention he got, telling *TV Guide* that "Yogi's fans are all pleasant people.")

Other segments on the show were "Snagglepuss," a cowardly, lisping lion whose catch phrase was "Exit, stage left!" whenever potential disaster was near (he appeared earlier on *Quick Draw McGraw),* and "Yakky Doodle," a hard-to-understand yellow duck voiced by Jimmy Weldon who enlisted the help of his protective pal Chopper the bulldog, voiced by Vance Colvig, in dire circumstances. The cartoons continued in production through 1962, after which Yakky Doodle and Chopper did not appear in new Hanna-Barbera productions.

Hey Boo Boo! It's me, Yogi Bear, star of Yogi's Gang, Yogi's Space Race, *and much more!*

Twelve years later, Yogi and other Hanna-Barbera characters belatedly came to the Saturday morning network schedule aboard an ark which hovered above the ground before landing in areas where they were needed to right social wrongs. Among the foes they encountered were the grungy, cigar-chomping Mr. Smog and the lie-spouting Mr. Fibber. Yogi was the ostensible leader of the series, which consisted of repeats in its second season.

After another Saturday morning show (see *Yogi's Space Race), Yogi's Treasure Hunt* appeared in syndication in 1985. Yogi now was co-captain with Ranger Smith, and Boo Boo was first mate, of the S.S. *Jelly Roger,* a vessel they used for fortune hunting along with a host of other Hanna-Barbera veterans of the 1960s. In the crew were Augie and Doggie Daddy as navigators, Top Cat as treasure master, Snooper and Blabbermouse as security heads, and Snagglepuss as the cook.

In 1988 the final round of new syndicated episodes reverted to the *Yogi Bear* title and featured only Yogi, Boo Boo, and Ranger Smith in their old stomping ground of Jellystone Park. Greg Burson assumed Yogi's voice following Daws Butler's death, and did Yogi again in 1991 for a third network series, *Yo, Yogi!* (q.v.). By that time, Yogi was the corporate symbol for a nationwide conglomerate of RV campgrounds called Jellystone Park. Previously, he had made his mark by starring in his own feature film (*Hey There, It's Yogi Bear,* in 1964) and by being the subject of a top 10 novelty song on *Billboard's* Hot 100 chart (the Ivy Three's "Yogi," in 1960). Yogi may not be smarter than the average bear, but he has certainly become better known than one.

YOGI'S SPACE RACE
Cartoon; Color
September 9, 1978–March 3, 1979

NBC Sat. 8–9:30 a.m. (9/9/78–10/28/78)
NBC Sat. 8–8:30 a.m. and 11 a.m.–Noon (11/4/78–1/27/79)
NBC Sat. 8–8:30 a.m. (2/3/79–3/3/79)

Voices:

Yogi Bear/Huckleberry Hound	Daws Butler
Scarebear	Joe Besser
Quack-Up	Mel Blanc
Captain Snerdley	John Stephenson
Jabberjaw/Captain Good/Clean Cat/Phantom Phink/Sinister Sludge/Buford/Nugget Nose	Frank Welker
Woody	Dave Landsburg
Cindy Mae/Rita	Pat Parris
Wendy	Marilyn Shreffler
Sheriff	Henry Corden
Narrator	Gary Owens

NBC attempted to capture the same success ABC had with *Scooby's All-Star Laff-A-Lympics* in 1977–78 by launching its own 90-minute extravaganza with Hanna-Barbera cartoons, but the result was disastrous. Yogi Bear, who was on *Laff-A-Lympics,* now found himself in a space race through the galaxy, but with a new sidekick, the easily intimidated Scarebear, in place of Boo Boo. Opposing them were such baddies as Phantom Phink and Sinister Sludge. In subordinate segments were "The Buford Files," "The Galloping Ghost," and "The Galaxy Goofups." In the latter, Yogi, Scarebear, and their pals Huckleberry Hound and Quack-Up (a duck) acted as outer space patrolmen under the leadership of Captain Snerdley.

This cartoon could have been nicknamed "The Incredible Shrinking Series." By November 1978 it lost a half hour when *The Galaxy Goofups* spun off on its own. Then in February 1979 *Buford and the Galloping Ghost* became a separate series, leaving the parent series only 30 minutes long. *Yogi's Space Race* lasted only a month after the second spinoff, assuming the 8 a.m. time slot of *The Galaxy Goofups* when the latter ended on January 27, 1979. (For more details, see *Buford and the Galloping Ghost.)*

YOGI'S TREASURE HUNT—See *Yogi's Gang.*

YOU ARE THERE
Drama; Color
September 11, 1971–May 13, 1973

CBS Sat. 12:30–1 p.m. (9/11/71–9/2/72)
CBS Sun. 5–5:30 p.m. (1/28/73–5/13/73)

Host: *Walter Cronkite*

Critics who complain that the distinction between TV news and entertainment has recently become blurred have obviously forgotten this series, a pioneer in marrying the two genres. It started on radio in 1947 as *CBS Is There,* with host John Daly taking listeners back in time with network correspondents "covering" such events as Julius Caesar's assassination. Actors played the principals in each event. Retitled *You Are There* in 1948, it ran until 1950 on radio, then returned on CBS-TV early Sunday evenings from February 1, 1953–October 13, 1957 with Walter Cronkite as host until reappearing here in a version designed for children.

Apart from the supposed juvenile-market angle, the 1971 revival remained quite faithful to the earlier renditions in terms of weaving historical facts with fictional details to dramatize sometimes complex situations. The show had a prime-time preview on September 8, 1971 with "G. Wood" playing Woodrow Wilson in a World War I crisis in "Ordeal of a President." Other, more familiar actors who followed were Geraldine Brooks (as Amelia Earhart), E. G. Marshall (as John Adams), and Colleen Dewhurst (as Susan B. Anthony). CBS correspondents who appeared included Hughes Rudd and Gary Shepard.

Some argue that the show's real star was Cronkite, who spoke the series' classic lines. For the opening, Cronkite gave the event's time and place before saying, "All things are as they were then, except you are there"; at the conclusion, he said, "What sort of day was it? A day like all days, filled with those events that alter and illuminate our times—and you were there." The segments remained when CBS reran the 1971–72 version in early 1973.

YOU DON'T SAY
Game; Color
April 1, 1963–November 26, 1975

NBC Mon.–Fri. 3:30–4 p.m. (4/1/63–9/26/69)
ABC Mon.–Fri. 4–4:30 p.m. (7/7/75–11/26/75)

Host: *Tom Kennedy*

Two duos, each composed of a contestant and a celebrity, competed in this guessing game involving a famous person, place, or thing. One member of each duo learned of the item to be identified and had to convey a clue to their partner by using a sentence with the last word blank (the part "you don't say"). The missing word was a clue to the famous noun under consideration. A correct answer won a point for the duo. Team members alternated giving clues until one duo had three points, which let the noncelebrity winner play a similar game using sentence clues on an electronic board. That contestant could win $500 on the first clue, $200 on the second, and $100 on the third.

The game's format sounded vaguely familiar to that of *Password,* whose production company of Mark Goodson and Bill Todman sued Ralph Andrews for copyright infringement. Goodson and Todman lost, but *You Don't Say* had to change its stage layout so that Tom Kennedy stood on the left of the players rather than between the players as did Allen Ludden on *Password.* Apart from that minor controversy, the series ran successfully for more than six years in its first incarnation (seven if one counts its start as a local show in Los Angeles in 1962 with Jack Barry as host). Tom Kennedy also hosted a NBC nighttime run from January 7–May 5, 1964, and the 1975 revival.

The revival had four guest celebrities giving clues to two contestants, with answers worth $200 on the first clue, $150 on the second, and $100 on the third. The first player to amass $500 faced a bonus round where earnings could double with right answers to a maximum of five clues. A 1978 syndicated version had Jim Peck as host.

•YOUNG AND THE RESTLESS, THE
Soap Opera; Color
March 26, 1973–

CBS Mon.–Fri. Noon–12:30 p.m. (3/26/73–2/1/80)
CBS Mon.–Fri. 1–2 p.m. (2/4/80–6/5/81)
CBS Mon.–Fri. 12:30–1:30 p.m. (6/8/81–)

Cast:

Jill Foster Abbott (1973–80, 1983–87)	*Brenda Dickson*
Jill Foster Abbott (1980)	*Bond Gideon*
Jill Foster Abbott (1980–83)	*Deborah Adair*
Jill Foster Abbott (1987–)	*Jess Walton*
Liz Foster (1973–86)	*Julianna McCarthy*
Dr. Snapper Foster (1973–75)	*William Gray Espy*
Dr. Snapper Foster (1975–82)	*David Hasselhoff*
Greg Foster (1973–76)	*James Houghton*
Greg Foster (1976–77)	*Brian Kerwin*

Greg Foster (1977–81)
Greg Foster (1981–82)
Stuart Brooks (1973–83)
Jennifer Brooks (1973–77)
Chris Brooks (1973–78, 1984)
Chris Brooks (1979–82)
Lauralee Brooks (1973–82, 1984)
Leslie Brooks (1973–77)
Leslie Brooks (1977–82, 1984)
Peggy Brooks (1973–81, 1984)
Peggy Brooks (1979, temporary
    replacement)
Kay Chancellor
Phillip Chancellor (1973–74)
Phillip Chancellor (1974–75)
Brad Eliot (1973–78)
Sally McGuire (1973–74, 1981–82)
Nurse Barbara Anderson (1973–75)
Pierre Rolland (1973–74)
George Curtis (1973)
Brock Reynolds (1974–80, 1984–86)
Maestro Fautsch (1974–85)
Jed Andrews (1974–75)
Gwen Sherman (1974–75)
Jeff (1974)/Dr. Steven Lassiter
    (1987–88 at least)
Marianne Rolland (1974)
Sam Powers (1974–75)
Joann Curtis (1975–78)
Jack Curtis (1975–77)
Dr. Bruce Henderson (1975)
Dr. Bruce Henderson (1975–76)
Dr. Mark Henderson (1975–76)
Bill Foster (1975–76)
Lance Prentiss (1975–80)
Lance Prentiss (1981–82)
Vanessa Prentiss (1976–80)
Ron Becker (1976–77, 1984)
Derek Thurston (1977–80, 1984)
Nancy Becker (1977–78)
Karen Becker (1977–78)
Nikki Reed (1978–79)
Nikki Reed (1979–)
Dr. Casey Reed (1978–81,
    1984–87)
Lucas Prentiss (1978–82)
Paul Williams (1979–)
April Stevens (1979)
April Stevens (1979–82, 199?)
Jonas (1979–81)
Suzanne Lynch (1979–80)
Nick Reed (1979)/Rex Sterling
    (1987–94)
John Abbott (1980–82)
John Abbott (1982–)
Victor Newman (1980–)

Wings Hauser
Howard McGillin
Robert Colbert
Dorothy Green
Trish Stewart
Lynne Topping
Jaime Lyn Bauer
Janice Lynde
Victoria Mallory
Pamela Peters

Patricia Everly
Jeanne Cooper
John Considine
Donnelly Rhodes
Tom Hallick
Lee Crawford
Deidre Hall
Robert Clary
Anthony Geary
Beau Kayzer
Karl Bruck
Tom Selleck
Jennifer Leak

Rod Arrants
Lilyan Chauvin
Barry Cahill
Kay Heberle
Anthony Herrera
Robert Clarke
Paul Stevens
Steve Carlson
Charles Gray
John McCook
Dennis Cole
K. T. Stevens
Dick DeCoit
Joe LaDue
Cathy Carricaburu
Brandi Tucker
Erica Hope
Melody Thomas

Roberta Leighton
Tom Ligon
Doug Davidson
Janet Wood
Cynthia Eilbacher
Jerry Lacy
Ellen Weston

Quinn Redeker
Brett Halsey
Jerry Douglas
Eric Braeden

Julia Newman (1980–84, 1986–8)
Douglas Austin (1980–85, 1987–)
Eve Howard (1980–84, 1993–94)
Mary Williams (1980–)
Carl Williams (1980–8?)
Patty Williams (1980)
Patty Williams (1980–83)
Patty Williams (1983–84)
Steve Williams (1980)
Dorothy Stevens (1980–82)
Wayne Stevens (1980–82)
Rose DeVille (1980, 1986–87)
Michael Scott (1980–81)
Filipe Ramirez (1980–81)
Danny Romalotti (1981–93,
    1994–)
Andy Richards (1981–87)
Kevin Bancroft (1981–83)
Allison Bancroft (1981–83)
Jerry Cashman (1981–82)
Robert Laurence (1981–82)
Jack Abbott (1980–89)
Jack Abbott (1989–)
Ashley Abbott (1982–89)
Ashley Abbott (1989–95)
Traci Abbott (1982–92)
Gina Roma(lotti) (1982–)
Esther Valentine, Kay Chancellor's
    maid (1982–)
Mamie Johnson (1982–)
Mamie Johnson (19 -95)
Frank Lewis (1982–85)
Diane Jenkins (1982–84, 1986)
Brian Forbes (1982–83)
Cindy Lake (1982–83)
Earl Bancroft (1982–83)
Lauren Fenmore (1983–95)
Cricket Blair (1983–)
Carole Robbins (1983–88 at least)
Dina Abbott (1983–86, 1996)
Amy Lewis (1983–8?)
Joe Blair (1983–87)
Neil Fenmore (1983–86)
Jazz Jackson (1983–86)
Tim Sullivan (1983–85, 1986–87)
Marc Mergeron (1983–84, 1987)
Eric Garrison (1983–85)
Rick Darrows (1983–84)
Rebecca the cult leader (1983)/
    Dana Nielsen (1987 at least)
Dr. Sharon Reaves/Ruby the
    manicurist (both 1983)
JoAnna Manning (1984–88)
Shawn Garrett (1984–86)
Lindsey Wells (1984–86)
Tyrone Jackson (1984–86)

Meg Bennett
Michael Evans
Margaret Mason
Carolyn Conwell
Brett Hadley
Tammy Taylor
Lillibet Stern
Andrea Evans
David Winn
Melinda Cordell
William Long Jr.
Darlene Conley
Nicholas Benedict
Victor Mohica

Michael Damian
Steve Ford
Christopher Holder
Lynn Wood
John Gibson
Peter Brown
Terry Lester
Peter Bergman
Eileen Davidson
Brenda Epperson
Beth Maitland
Patty Weaver

Kate Linder
Marguerite Ray
Veronica Redd Forrest
Brock Peters
Alex Donnelley
Jay Kerr
DeAnna Robbins
Mark Tapscott
Tracey E. Bregman
Lauralee Bell
Christopher Templeton
Marla Adams
Stephanie E. Williams
Joe Denos
James Storm
Jon St. Elwood
Scott Palmer
Frank M. Bernard
Brian Matthews
Randy Holland

Cindy Fisher

Veleka Gray
Susan Seaforth Hayes
Grant Cramer
Lauren Koslow
Phil Morris

Brent Davis (1984)
Brent Davis (1984–85)
Joseph Anthony (1984–85)
Boobsie Caswell (1984–85)
Jared Markson (1984–85)
Cora Miller (1984)
Brad Carlton (1985–96)
Nathan Hastings (1985–92)
Matt Miller (1985–87)
Michael Crawford (1985–87)
Alana Anthony (1985)
Nina Webster (1986–)
Phillip Chancellor Jr. (1986–89)
Faren O'Connor (1986–87)
Evan Sanderson (1986–87)
Ellen Winters (1986–87)
David Kimble (1987–91)
Leanna Randolph (1987–92)
Jessica Blair (1987–88 at least)
Skip Evans the photographer
    (1987–88 at least)
Dr. Scott Grainger (1988–93)
Cassandra Rawlins (1988–91)
George Rawlins (1988–89 at least)
Dr. Jim Grainger (1989 at least)
Daryl Stuart (1989–90 at least)
Olivia Barber (1990–)
Drucilla Barber (1990–)
Nurse Sheila Carter (1990–92)
John Silva (1990 at least–)
Clint Radisson (1990 at least)
Victoria Newman (1991–)
Flo Webster (1991–)
Ryan McNeil (1991–)
Neil Winters (1991–)
Cole Howard (1993–)
Hope Adams Newman (1993–)
Nick Newman (1994–)
Phyllis Summers (1994–)
Malcolm (1994–)
Keemo Volien (1994–95)
Luan Volien Abbott (1994–96)
Marilyn (1994 at least)

Jim McMullan
Bert Kramer
Logan Ramsey
Joy Garrett
Linwood Dalton
Dorothy McGuire
Don Diamont
Nathan Purdee
Robert Parucha
Colby Chester
Amy Gibson
Tricia Cast
Thom Bierdz
Colleen Casey
John Shearin
Jennifer Karr
Michael Corbett
Barbara Crampton
Rebecca Sweet

Todd Curtis
Peter Barton
Nina Arveson
Jonathan Farwell
John Philip Law
Ken Olandt
Tonya Lee Williams
Victoria Rowell
Kimberlin Brown
John Castellanos
James Michael Gregary
Heather Tom
Sharon Farrell
Scott Reeves
Kristoff St. John
J. Eddie Peck
Signy Coleman
Joshua Morrow
Michelle Stafford
Shemar Moore
Philip Moon
Elizabeth Sung
Diana Barton

The most popular daytime soap opera of the 1990s was *The Young and the Restless,* which had been emphasizing both elements of its title for two decades during its rising popularity. Ironically, the cast member with the longest tenure has been Jeanne Cooper, an actress who was already middle-aged at the show's start in 1973 but who was looking just fine nearly a quarter century later. She survived through several changeovers in core families involved in the show and an impressive display of beautiful male and female actors in plots which, it should not be forgotten, often emphasized important social issues from weight concerns to sexual problems. And even people who did not like the show had to admit it had a catchy

theme song, which became a hit in 1976 when released in a single titled "Nadia's Theme" (Olympic gymnast Nadia Comaneci performed to it that year).

The setup in the early years was quite simple, revolving around one well-to-do family. Stuart Brooks, owner of the *Genoa City Chronicle* (at first Genoa City was located in "the upper Midwest," but later it became officially set in Wisconsin), and his wife Jennifer had four daughters. One of them, introverted concert pianist Leslie, romanced a distraught, mysterious stranger named Brad Eliot, who came to work for Stuart following his son's death during an operation he performed on him in Chicago (the child was a product of his affair with Nurse Barbara Anderson). Their love survived her breakdown and his confession of his previous life, but a brain tumor which Brad kept hidden from Leslie led to their eventual separation. Leslie went on with her singing career.

The big romance during the early years involved another Brooks daughter, Chris, with poor medical student Snapper Foster. Because Stuart opposed Snapper and Chris did not want premarital relations, Snapper decided to have sex with Sally McGuire, a waitress at a nightclub run by Pierre Rouland. When Sally was carrying Snapper's child (she had become pregnant on purpose in an attempt to win Snapper from Chris), Snapper rejected her, but a noble Pierre married her despite his sister Marianne's efforts to thwart this move. Then a mugger killed Pierre just before Sally had the baby, and Marianne told everyone who the father was. But Sally left town alone with her child, for the now-married Snapper and Chris had endured a far harder test of their love earlier, when Chris had been raped by George Curtis but, after a brief separation as Chris went to "find herself" in life, had returned to a happy married life with Snapper.

It was Snapper's hairdresser sister Jill who provided *The Young and the Restless* with its longest-running story line, the never-ending feud she had with socialite Katherine "Kay" Chancellor. Befriended by Kay, she began working at the latter's mansion when she discovered that Phillip Chancellor loved her rather than his alcoholic wife. Phillip divorced Kay and planned to marry Jill when an increasingly manipulative Kay, who had been seeing her young stableboy Jeff, drove him and herself off a cliff. On his deathbed, Phillip wed Jill and bequeathed his estate to her. But Kay had the marriage annulled and remained Phillip's main heir. Jill had one trump card to play, however; she gave birth to Phillip's son whom she named in his honor.

Meanwhile, another Brooks daughter, Lauri, tried to break up Brad and Leslie, then wrote a roman à clef titled *Naked at Dawn* about her affair in Paris with Brock Reynolds, Kay's son and Phillip's stepson. Following that fling Brock had become a born-again Christian who pressed Kay unsuccessfully into stopping her campaign of hate against Jill. Lauri, however, romanced several men in ill-fated relationships, including Jed Andrews. The worst choice had to have been Mark Henderson, whose father Dr. Bruce Henderson was actually Lauri's natural father, making them half-brother and sister. This produced enmity between Lauri and her mom Jennifer that dissipated only when the latter faced a mastectomy.

The Young and the Restless *featured intense competition between Jill Foster (left, played by Brenda Dickson) and Kay Chancellor (Jeanne Cooper) over various men in their lives. In 1978 they fought for the affections of Derek Thurston (Joe La Due).*

The last Brooks daughter, Peggy, fell in love with her college teacher Jack Curtis until learning about his wife Joann's struggle with obesity, which led Peggy, after she had married him, to convince him to go back to Joann. But her nobility was tested to the breaking point when Ron Becker raped her and was acquitted of the crime. When Ron's wife Nancy learned he really had raped Peggy, she had a breakdown and then fought for custody of her daughter Nancy before leaving town.

The other two main characters of the early years were Jill's mother Liz and other brother Greg, a law student. Greg bombed out romantically, loving first his sister-in-law Chris and then client Gwen Sherman, who he learned was a hooker. Greg eventually rescued Gwen from that life, only to see her become a nun! Liz's dilemma was that her estranged husband Bill was returning to Genoa City terminally ill while she was engaged to Sam Powers. She dropped Sam, out of compassion for her cancer-ridden husband, then pulled the plug on him, suffering a mild stroke in the process. Greg successfully defended his brother Snapper on charges that he had killed Bill, while Liz avoided prosecution and found a new husband in Stuart Brooks following Jennifer's death. Stuart had wed Jill before marrying Liz because Jill had claimed falsely that she was carrying his child, but when he discovered the truth, he divorced Jill.

Toward the end of the 1970s a stampede of new characters emerged to interact with the old core favorites. Some were failed lovers of Kay Chancellor, who had even had a quasi-affair with Joann Curtis, which ended quickly due to negative audience reaction to the lesbian story line. There was ambitious hairdresser Derek Thurston, whom Kay stole from rival Jill,

only to face his crazed ex-wife Suzane Lynch, who gave Kay chocolates laced with mind-altering drugs that sent her to a mental hospital. Kay was able to fake her own death following a fire at the hospital, and she then pretended to be a ghost to terrorize Suzanne, plus spoil Jill's marriage to Stuart Brooks. She returned to Derek, and they went on a second honeymoon cruise, where she found herself approached by two other men. Her old rich flame Douglas Austin's passes at her were misinterpreted by both Derek and the exotic Filipe Ramirez, so when Kay arrived at the mainland she found herself without a man.

Then there were the complications involving Leslie and Lauri with the Prentiss boys. Leslie dated bon vivant Lance Prentiss briefly before he became more interested in her sultry sister. When Leslie learned that she was pregnant, Lance's seafaring brother Lucas married her. Then Leslie had a mental breakdown after Lauri told her she knew about her whole situation, and an amnesiac Leslie wound up at Jonas's Bar, where Jonas himself was smitten by her. After recovering her memory, Leslie decided she wanted neither man, and after a failed second try with Lance and a doomed romance with married lawyer Robert Laurence, Leslie left Genoa City for good.

Lauri held on to Lance despite the efforts of his vindictive mother Vanessa, who nearly got away with framing Lauri for her suicide staged as a murder in an elaborate scheme. But Lance left Lauri when she unwisely gave control of Prentiss Industries to Victor Newman, a newcomer running Kay Chancellor's empire. When Victor decided he wanted to marry Lauri and returned control of Prentiss Industries to her as a prewedding gift, she left him at the altar, gave the documents back to Lance, and left town.

Victor, an aloof man capable of displaying both intense devotion and intense hatred, was a story all by himself. His wife, model Julia Newman, found herself facing the hatred when she had a tryst with photographer Michael Scott and became pregnant. Thinking that Michael was the father (and feeling sure that he was not, as he had undergone a vasectomy, which Julia did not know about), Victor set about torturing Michael in his private chamber in the basement. But Julia discovered this ghastly activity, and in trying to rescue Michael she fell down the stairs, causing a miscarriage. When Victor learned that he really had been the father of Julia's fetus, as his vasectomy had been not performed properly, he was grief-stricken. He meekly agreed to divorce Julia, who left Genoa City with Michael.

Victor then became victim—of a scheme cooked up by his ex-girlfriend Eve Howard, who claimed that he had fathered her son, Charles. Eve planned an bizarre and ultimately unsuccessful method of killing Victor, which ended with her being locked up at the nuthouse. Then Victor blossomed into a loving sort when he was smitten with stripper Nikki Reed. Nikki's first marriage was a by-product of an attempt by her perverted father Nick to molest her the way he earlier molested her sister, Dr. Casey Reed. She killed Nick in self-defense, and Greg Foster married her after clearing her name in court. But

Greg found Nikki too much of a sprite, and she moved on to wed Kevin Bancroft while getting increasingly warm with Victor. She eventually became pregnant by Victor, gave birth to their daughter Victoria, and after having narrowly avoided an attempt on her life by Brian Forbes, she and Victor wed in a lavish ceremony which was completed despite an attempt on their lives by Eve Howard and which marked the return and last appearance of many of the 1970s characters, including all of the Brooks daughters.

Indeed, by the early 1980s, the Brooks were history, as were most of the Fosters. Snapper and Chris, for one, left on a happy note after weathering the return of Sally McGuire and her son by Snapper named Chuckie. The sole Foster remaining in town was Jill, who first dated bartender Andy Richards, then, after going to work for Jabot Cosmetics, vacillated between wealthy respected businessman John Abbott and his blond son Jack. She eventually decided that John had more to offer and wed him.

Jack then moved on Patty Williams, whose cop father Carl, mother Mary, and brothers Paul and Steve remained suspicious of the Abbott scion. The relationship did dissolve, due to Jack cheating on Patty with model Diane Jenkins, who ended up marrying and divorcing Andy Richards. Patty used a gun to try to kill Jack but only wounded him; they subsequently divorced. Yet this incident hardly qualified her as the black sheep of the family. Paul had her beat easily, having transmitted VD to one-time girlfriend Nikki Reed, impregnating April Stevens and then competing with Greg Foster for her love, and dating ex-prostitute Cindy Lake. He reformed somewhat in the mid-1980s when he and Andy Richards teamed up to start a detective firm.

Around that time, Jill had had sex with Jack one night in a lodge retreat which came back to haunt them both as pictures of the event were taken by fellow Jabot employee Lindsey Wells. Lindsey wanted to marry Jack herself, and in an effort to get the photos, he tried to fool her into believing she *had* married him, but the ruse didn't work. By 1986 Jill's old foe Kay had learned of the pictures and used several unsuccessful methods to get John to view them (even sending them to him at work as puzzle pieces!) before showing him slides of the affair with Jack's face obliterated per the latter's request. Nonetheless, John realized who it was, threw Jack out of the house, and was planning to do the same with Jill when he suffered a stroke. After recovering, he divorced Jill, but she managed to keep her job and get a nice settlement from John when she threatened to publish a tell-all tome.

Jill's activities elicited little sympathy from her stepdaughters Ashley and Traci Abbott and the family maid, Mamie Johnson, who also had mixed feelings when John's estranged wife Dina returned to make amends to everyone. Ashley had perhaps the hardest time, enduring failed romances with Dina's French-accented stepson Marc, bland Eric Garrison, and Victor Newman's hunky brother Matt Miller. Then Ashley went bonkers upon learning that dying alcoholic Brent Davis was really her father and that she had been conceived during an affair between Dina and Brent. She became an amnesiac,

then returned to her senses when a concerned Victor Newman brought her back to his ranch, by which time Dina had split from Genoa City. At this point, Ashley had been seeing Victor while her brother Jack had been seeing Nikki.

As for Traci, she had to deal with her overweight condition while falling in love with the resident heartthrob, babyface singer Danny Romalotti, whose ex-con sister Gina performed as a lounge act with the stage name of Gina Roma. Patty wanted Danny too, but seeing that Traci had a stronger hold on him, she left town. A new rival for Danny emerged in Lauren Fenmore, a real trickster. Traci had support from Amy Lewis, daughter of police investigator Frank Lewis, and Gina, who hated Lauren for destroying her engagement to Lauren's dad Neil by revealing Gina's criminal past.

Meanwhile, Kay Chancellor, whose disastrous relationships in the early 1980s included Nikki's one-time male stripper partner Jerry "Cash" Cashman and Earle Bancroft, Kevin's father and husband to snooty cold fish Allison Bancroft, finally married Danny and Gina's father Rex Sterling after he had been released from prison and reunited with his children.

In 1984 Danny married Traci even though she was carrying Tim's baby. The two later divorced, and although Traci still wanted Tim she instead had another unproductive marriage, this time with hunky Brad Carlton, then left town. Danny went on to wed young Jabot model Cricket Blair after winning her away from Philip Chancellor Jr., Jill's illegitimate son, who later died in a car crash, and Dr. Scott Grainger, who turned out to be Cricket's half-brother. (She also endured a nasty date rape incident with Daryl Stuart in 1989.) In a further twist, Scott wed Danny's old flame wanna-be Lauren Fenmore before he died and she moved onto *The Bold and the Beautiful* (see that entry for more details about her and her whacked-out nemesis Nurse Sheila Carter, who stole Lauren's baby in 1991).

Before becoming Scott's wife, Lauren had wed Paul Williams, but that marriage was undone by her own chicanery (she once got a nude photo of him published in a magazine). Paul's detective partner Andy Richards left town after romancing singer Faren O'Connor. Paul had dated teacher Dana Nielsen (played by Davidson's real-life wife Cindy Fisher) in 1987, then in 1989 found himself attracted to the exotic Cassandra Rawlins, whose dying husband George tried to frame him. Later his ex-flame April returned and he helped her fight against her abusive husband, but that relationship faltered too.

By 1987, the love quadrangle of Jack, Nikki, Victor, and Ashley had disintegrated. Jack was thrown out of his father's house when John learned he had slept with Jill; he was then tried for Jill's attempted murder, and worked in a shelter on Skid Row. He also vied with his dad for the hand of Ellen Winters. Meanwhile, Ashley had already aborted Victor's baby and separated from him for a while; however, Victor was ready to marry her and leave Nikki, until Nikki revealed she had a terminal illness. Nikki survived, and in 1989 started dating Dr. Jim Grainger, Scott's father. She ended up marrying Jack in the 1990s, but when they lost their baby, the marriage ended. As for Victor, he wed psychotic Leanna Randolph. Leanna was a former patient of Dr. Steven Lassiter, and loathed him because he had treated, then married, Ashley (Lassiter died shortly after the wedding). Leanna also published an unauthorized biography of Victor titled *Ruthless*.

Throughout all this, Jill was as active as ever. In 1987 she rebuffed photographer Skip Evans, who later married Jack's loyal secretary Carol, then courted a few more suitors before, incredibly, she remarried John Abbott. In 1995 John had an affair with his black maid Mamie after finding Jill had cheated on him (wow!), but Jill bought Mamie out and she went away. Even the return of John's ex-wife Dina in 1996 did not break up the marriage, though it kept Jill off guard.

In the early 1990s the show went through a few shabby story lines before getting back on track. One of the loser plots had Rex Sterling duped in a con that involved having his wife Kay replaced by a double, earthy waitress Marge, also played by Jeanne Cooper. (Rex later died, leaving Kay a lonely woman.) Another had Jill's secretary David try to kill Nina Webster before being crushed in a trash compactor. Faring better was Nina; she romanced and eventually married Jabot executive Ryan McNeil, who had previously been forced into marrying Victoria, Victor and Nikki's teenage daughter. (Nina had earlier been married to Philip Chancellor and had given birth to his son before Chancellor's death.) Ryan's departure scarcely bothered Victoria, as she became attracted to aspiring author Cole Howard. Unfortunately, her mother also lusted after Cole, but he favored Victoria, and the two of them went on to marry after learning he was

not the product of an affair his mother Eve claimed to have had with her father Victor.

The mid-1990s saw the emergence of some really bizarre twists. In 1994, for example, Cricket got the tragic news that Danny had an affair with deranged groupie Phyllis while on tour in *Joseph and the Amazing Technicolor Dreamcoat* that resulted in a child, leading him to attempt to divorce Cricket and "do the right thing" and marry Phyllis, even though she tried to kill Paul, who was now having an affair with Cricket! And Victor left home after disappointing everyone, wandered into a romance at a Kansas farm with a blind woman named Hope Adams, was declared dead, and turned out not to be dead. His return and subsequent marriage to Hope left everyone agog, as did news that Jack's Vietnamese girlfriend Luan and their son Keemo Volien had also hit town. Like all of Jack's relationships, this one ended rather abruptly in 1996 when Luan died of some odd, unnamed disease.

Also in the mid-1990s, Jabot model Drucilla Barber, high on flu medication, had sex with Malcolm, the brother of her husband Neil Winters, but somehow this seemed of little

The Young and the Restless *celebrated 10 years on the air with cast members (clockwise from top left) Terry Lester (as Jack Abbott), Jay Kerr (Brian Forbes), Christopher Holder (Kevin Bancroft), Steven Ford (Andy Richards), Michael Damian (Danny Romalotti), Julianna McCarthy (Liz Foster), and John Denos (Joe Blair). Michael Damian was the only one left when the show celebrated its 20th anniversary in 1993.*

import given the rest of the show's intrigues. Olivia, Drucilla's sister, found that her husband Nathan was HIV-positive after sleeping with another woman. And Nick Newman, Nikki and Victor's son, was accused of murder. The only person who seemed to be having fun was Phyllis Summers, who was involved in an affair where she was using her psychiatrist to help her be declared sane and gain custody of her child with Danny. Maybe the shrink's professional incompetence in dealing with Phyllis was symbolic of the character defects that were continuing to screw up Genoa City's young and restless residents in the late 1990s.

YOUNG DR. MALONE

Soap Opera; B&W and Color
December 29, 1958–March 29, 1963

NBC Mon.–Fri. 3–3:30 p.m. (12/29/58–9/28/62)
NBC Mon.–Fri. 3:30–4 p.m. (10/1/62–3/29/63)

Cast:

Dr. Jerry Malone	William Prince
Tracey Bannister Malone (1958–59)	Virginia Dwyer
Tracey Bannister Malone (1959–63)	Augusta Dabney
Dr. David Malone	John Connell
Jill Malone Renfrew (1958–59)	Kathleen Widdoes
Jill Malone Renfrew (1959–62)	Freda Holloway
Jill Malone Renfrew (1962–63)	Sarah Hardy
Clare Bannister Steele	Lesley Woods
Emory Bannister (1959–61)	Judson Laire
Lionel Steele (1959–63)	Martin Blaine
Lisha Steele (1959–60)	Zina Bethune
Lisha Steele (1960)	Michele Tuttle
Lisha Steele (1960–61)	Susan Hallaran
Lisha Steele (1962)	Patty McCormack
Faye Bannister Koda (1959–61)	Lenka Peterson
Faye Bannister Koda (1961–63)	Chase Crosley
Dr. Stefan Koda (1959–63)	Michael Ingram
Dr. Ted Powell (1959–63)	Peter Brandon
Peter Brooks (1959)	Robert Lansing
Phyllis Brooks (1959)	Barbara O'Neill
Jody Baker (1959–60)	Stephen Bolster
Dorothy Ferris (1960)	Liz Gardner
Dorothy Ferris (1960)	Florence Mitchell
Eve Dunbar (1960–63)	Loretta Leversee
Deirdre "Dee Dee" Bannister (1960–63)	Elizabeth St. Clair
Pete Ferris (1960)	Luke Halpin
Gig Houseman Malone (1961–62)	Diana Hyland
Mrs. Lillian Houseman (1961)	Elizabeth Watts
Larry Renfrew (1961–62)	Dick Van Patten
Harold Cranston (1961–63)	William Post Jr.
Dr. Matt Steele (1961)	Eddie Jones
Dr. Matt Steele (1961)	Franklyn Spodak
Dr. Matt Steele (1962–63)	Nicolas Coster
Miss Fisher (1962)	Betty Sinclair
Erica Brandt (1962–63)	Ann Williams
Lt. Flagler (1962–63)	William Smithers
Natalie (1962–63)	Joan Wetmore

This TV adaptation of the long-running radio serial of the same name (heard on NBC at first and then CBS from 1939–60) transferred only the principal characters' names and the credits of Irna Phillips as creator and Julian Funt as writer. Set at Valley Hospital in Denison, Maryland, its title character was Dr. David Malone, son of Dr. Jerry Malone (whom one observer described as "the most generous, gifted doctor to ever put on rubber gloves") and Jerry's wife Tracey. David struggled to follow his respected father's footsteps with a successful career and marriage, but it was not easy. During the show's run he found himself either in love with or loved by Dorothy Ferris, Eve Dunbar, and Gig Houseman, finally marrying the latter. His parents disapproved of Gig, though, and if that was not enough heartache, he was put on trial for murder after the suspicious death of Lillian Houseman, Gig's mom. David was, however, exonerated and managed to continue his career.

The show's real star in terms of activity was Clare Bannister Steele, who rivaled Lisa on *As the World Turns* for overall chicanery on a soap opera at the time. She became Tracey's stepmother-in-law when she wed Emory Bannister, and devoted considerable effort to driving a wedge between Jerry and Tracey. She also belittled Tracey's sister, and Emory's other daughter, Faye. By 1960 Clare was cheating on Emory with Lionel Steele. Clare and Lionel intimidated Emory to the point at which he threatened Clare, and the devilish duo used his action to put him through a messy court trial. After Emory died in January 1961, Clare and Lionel began an off-and-on relationship which lasted through the end of the show's run and included marriage, jealousy, deception, and other soap opera staples. It was hardly a surprise that Lionel's daughter Lisha, witnessing her parents' behavior, felt she was living in a world of scheming adults.

But there was more to Clare's story than a search for love. In 1961 she lost sight first in one eye (due to thrombosis) and then in the other (due to hysteria), but her vision returned. Judged insane later that year, she returned to Denison in 1962 and stayed with Dee Dee, the only woman patient enough to keep a relationship going with Dr. Ted Powell (he tried in 1960 to break up David's romance with Dorothy, among other noble deeds). But she never really mellowed and continued to cause trouble for her former daughters-in-law.

Meanwhile, Dr. Jerry Malone ran into a few roadblocks of his own. He faced a malpractice suit in October 1960 for his care of Pete, a chronically ill child. Helping his defense was Dr. Eileen Seaton, who nursed an unrequited love for the doctor who had helped her survive a run-in the previous year with the evil Peter Brooks. Interestingly, actor Robert Lansing played Brooks opposite his then-wife Emily McLaughlin, who played Dr. Seaton. And playing Jerry and Tracey Malone were real-life couple William Prince and Augusta Dabney.

The Malones of Young Dr. Malone *were, clockwise from top left, Dr. David Malone (played by John Connell), Jill (in 1959–62, Freda Holloway), Tracey (in 1959–63, Augusta Dabney), and Dr. Jerry Malone (William Prince).*

Other doctors were Stefan Koda, who wed Faye in February 1962 after a challenging courtship, and Matt Steele, who found himself a suspect in yet another extended trial in 1962–63, this time for the death of wheelchair-bound Larry Renfrew following surgery that was supposed to make him able to walk again. Renfrew was wed to David Malone's sister Jill, who had failed in a relationship earlier with Jody Baker, and both she and Dr. Steele had to rely on lawyer Harold Cranston's defense work to pull them out (Cranston had defended several other characters in earlier episodes).

Young Dr. Malone wound up its 4½ year run with good news. Jerry, ill during Jill's trial, recuperated from a hospital stay and saw his daughter freed, while son David agreed to run a pediatric clinic with Erica Brandt. NBC replaced the series with the long-running game show *You Don't Say.*

YOUNG MARRIEDS, THE

Soap Opera; B&W
October 5, 1964–March 25, 1966
ABC Mon.–Fri. 3:30–4 p.m. (10/5/64–3/25/66)

Cast:

Walter Reynolds	Michael Mikler
Ann Reynolds (1964)	Lee Meriwether
Ann Reynolds (c. 1964–66)	Susan Brown
Dr. Dan Garrett	Paul Picerni
Susan Garrett	Peggy McCay
Matt Crane/Stevens (1964, 1965–66)	Scott Graham
Matt Crane/Stevens (1964–65)	Charles Grodin
Liz Forsyth Stevens	Floy Dean
Irene Forsyth (1964)	Irene Hervey
Irene Forsyth (1965)	Constance Moore
Mady Stevens (1964–65)	Maria Palmer
Phil Sterling (1965)	Ted Knight
Jerry Karr	Pat Rossen
Lena Karr Gilroy	Norma Connolly
Roy Gilroy	Barry Russo
Jill McComb (March–July 1965)	Betty Connor
Jill McComb (July 1965–66)	Brenda Benet
Jimmy (1965)	Ken Metcalf
Buzz Korman (1965–66)	Les Brown Jr.
Mr. Korman (1965–66)	Frank Maxwell
Mrs. Korman (1965–66)	Maxine Stuart
Carol West (1965–66)	Susan Seaforth Hayes
Aunt Alex (1965)	Irene Tedrow
Gillespie (1965–66)	Robert Hogan

Supposedly set in the suburbs of the same town as *General Hospital,* which preceded it daily, *The Young Marrieds* concentrated on several newlyweds and their early marital difficulties. The most volatile were the bickering Reynolds. Ann was jealous of husband Walter's work with models Jill and Carol and desired more from the world, from money to self-worth ("I want a purpose in life," she once said). The two began divorce proceedings in June 1965, and Walter started seeing Carol. But when the show ended, a guilty Walter was standing on a cliff contemplating suicide, though producers had planned for him to be saved by Carol's devotion and then return to Ann.

Then there were Liz and Matt, who had to deal with their mothers' interference with their courtship and marriage. Matt, for example, fretted that he owed his job at Forsyth Industries to his mother-in-law Irene's machinations. (In his 1989 autobiography *It Would Be So Nice If You Weren't Here,* Charles Grodin, who played Matt in 1964–65, recalled that he and Ted Knight, who played his boss, regularly broke up laughing while taping their roles and had a hard time completing lines.) The other main couple was the Garretts, who eventually fought to take custody of Jerry Karr (Susan's son) away from Lena and Roy.

Others entangled in the melodrama were Jimmy and Buzz, who found themselves sentenced for misdeeds to the chagrin of Buzz's parents, the Kormans; Gillespie, a lawyer helping Buzz who ended up romancing Jill; and Aunt Alex.

YOUNG SENTINELS, THE

Cartoon; Color
September 10, 1977–September 2, 1978
NBC Sat. 9–9:30 a.m. (9/10/77–1/28/78)
NBC Sat. 11:30 a.m.–Noon (2/4/78–9/2/78)

Voices:

Hercules/Sentinel One	*George DiCenzo*
Astrea	*Dee Timberlake*
Mercury	*Evan Kim*
M.O. (Maintenance Operator)	*Ross Hagen*

A trio from outer space disguised as teenagers came to Earth to protect the planet with their unique abilities. There was Hercules, the appropriately named strongman of the group; Astrea, the one who could transform herself into any physical object; and Mercury, the creature who moved at the speed of light. For their missions, they followed directions from their alien leader Sentinel One, who imbued them with their skills; they were helped in their adventures by M.O., a robot. This series had been retitled *Space Sentinels* by 1978.

YOUNG SET, THE

Interview; B&W
September 6, 1965–December 17, 1965
ABC Mon.–Fri. 11 a.m.–Noon (9/6/65–12/17/65)

Hostess: *Phyllis Kirk*

This New York–based talk show typically featured at least three people under the age of 35 discussing a common interest. (The moderator, actress Phyllis Kirk, was 39 at the time.) The debut featured a conversation with offspring of celebrities, including Richard Burton's daughter Sybil Burton, Charlie Chaplin's son Sydney Chaplin, Dorothy Kilgallen's daughter Jill Grossman, and Rex Harrison's son Noel Harrison.

YOUR FIRST IMPRESSION

Game; Color
January 2, 1962–June 26, 1964
NBC Mon.–Fri. Noon–12:30 p.m. (1/2/62–6/26/64)

Regulars: *Bill Leyden, Dennis James, George Kirgo (1962–January 1963)*

Free association in the manner of *To Tell the Truth* was the name of this game. A panel of three celebrities attempted, through question-and-answer rounds and their "first impressions," to identify a guest from among five possibilities. Two panelists were regulars in the first year, Dennis James and comedy writer George Kirgo. James continued as a regular in 1963 even while hosting *People Will Talk* on the NBC daytime schedule 90 minutes after *Your First Impression* aired.

Additionally, a few celebrities spent extended weeks on the panel as well, such as Betty White in December 1962–January 1963 and Jayne Meadows in January 1963. A most unusual guest panelist was Richard Nixon in 1962, when he was running for California's gubernatorial seat.

Although it was a Monty Hall production, its creator and associate producer was Nat Ligerman, a laundrette operator in New York City who told Hall about his concept in 1958. CBS had first dibs but let its option drop, resulting in an audition for NBC, which bought the show. Hall guest hosted the show from August 13–17, 1962.

YOUR NUMBER'S UP

Game; Color
September 23, 1985–December 20, 1985
NBC Mon.–Fri. 10–10:30 a.m. (9/23/85–12/20/85)

Host: *Nipsey Russell*
Assistant: *Lee Menning*

This game began with an electronic wheel spinning under three contestants. The wheel left numbers from zero to nine under two contestants; the contestant with no number chose one of two phrases, and the two "numbered" contestants vied to be the first to guess what some initials in the phrase stood for. A correct answer won a point, and five points won a game.

Meanwhile, the number under a contestant who guessed correctly became part of that day's number lineup in chronological order. Using the digits, the studio audience and viewers tried to match the last four digits of their phone numbers to a board containing the numbers from the contestant who had answered correctly. Those doing so were eligible to win a prize as well. This form of home participation was not enough to keep the show from ending after three months.

YOUR PET PARADE

Children's; B&W
March 18, 1951–September 2, 1951
ABC Sun. 4:30–5 p.m. (3/18/51–9/2/51)

Host: *Jack Gregson*

Three or four kids each week had their pets compete in this New York–based show, with winner getting prizes and a year's supply of sponsor Ralston Purina's pet food. The set even had the Ralston checkerboard theme throughout it. A footnote: Shortly after this series ended, a writer named Frances Fradin filed a $100,000 federal lawsuit against ABC and Ralston Purina, claiming that she had presented the show's concept to ABC in January 1950 and that ABC had given the idea to Ralston and put it on the air without crediting her.

YOUR SURPRISE PACKAGE

Game; B&W
March 13, 1961–February 23, 1962
CBS Mon.–Fri. 11:30 a.m.–Noon (3/13/61–9/29/61)
CBS Mon.–Fri. 11:30–11:55 a.m. (10/2/61–2/23/62)

Host: *George Fenneman*

A trio of contestants asked questions about the "surprise package" hidden behind them on stage but visible to the home viewer. Players received a maximum of five clues about the collection, and between getting each clue contestants could ask questions. Each question asked by a contestant cost him or her some money from their initial kitty, whose total amount was equal to the value of the "surprise package," thus encouraging them to get the right answer early. The most expensive prize on the debut was a stereo hi-fi set.

The Hollywood-based *Your Surprise Package* replaced *The Clear Horizon* in 1961. When it ended in 1962, its replacement was a new version of *The Clear Horizon*. Some surprise.

YOUR SURPRISE STORE
Game; B&W
May 12, 1952–June 27, 1952

CBS Mon.–Thu. 10:45–11:15 a.m. & Fri 10:30–11 a.m.
  (5/12/52–5/23/62)
CBS Mon.–Thu. 10:30–11:15 a.m. & Fri 10:30–11 a.m.
  (5/26/52–6/27/52)

Host: *Lew Parker*

Assistant: *Jacqueline Susann*

A precursor to *Let's Make a Deal, Your Surprise Store* had contestants bring items on stage to swap for unknown prizes ranging from shoelaces to jewelry. Before the exchange occurred, players had to answer a question or perform a stunt to get the prize. Persons who answered two questions right and performed a stunt properly won a "super prize." Lew Parker went on to be the TV dad of Marlo Thomas on *That Girl*, while Jacqueline Susann became the bestselling author of trashy novels like *Valley of the Dolls*.

YOU'RE PUTTING ME ON
Game; Color
June 30, 1969–December 26, 1969

NBC Mon.–Fri. 1:30–2 p.m. (6/30/69–12/26/69)

Regulars: *Bill Leyden (6/30/69–9/26/69), Larry Blyden, Peggy Cass, Bill Cullen*

When *You're Putting Me On* started, it had three celebrity players—Larry Blyden, Peggy Cass, and Bill Cullen—paired with three other stars each week in name identification contests. The first required participants to identify other personalities by roundabout comparison clues—for example, Anita Ekberg described in terms of an ice cream sundae (double dip—get it?) and Bette Davis as overstuffed furniture (?!). Next came the "quickie" round, where one member of each duo gave a speedy description of a well-known person or character which their partner had to guess within a few seconds (e.g., "I leap over the tallest building" was the clue for Superman). Celebrities making multiple guest appearances were Jack Cassidy, Joan Fontaine, Anne Meara, Alejandro Rey, Burt Reynolds, William Shatner, Brenda Vaccaro, and Vivian Vance.

The show originally was a pilot taped for CBS in 1967. It had an unusual cast change in late September, when performer Blyden replaced Bill Leyden as host. Neither the show nor Leyden lasted long after that; *You're Putting Me*

On was off the air before 1970, and Leyden died on March 11 of that year at age 47.

YOURS FOR A SONG
Game; B&W
December 4, 1961–March 29, 1963

ABC Mon.–Fri. 11:30 a.m.–Noon (12/4/61–3/29/63)

Host: *Bert Parks*

Music Director: *Ted Rapf*

A fill-in-the-blanks game using music, *Yours for a Song* had two players try to identify missing words to lines of familiar lyrics. For each word recalled, contestants received $20. The winner after two rounds faced a new challenger. For each song's final chorus, Parks told the audience to sing using the words printed on screen, à la the popular nighttime musical series of the time, *Sing Along with Mitch*. Songs typically were old standards like "My Blue Heaven," "Toot Toot Tootsie Goodbye," and "Winter Wonderland."

The music game scenario was familiar to both Parks, who hosted the nighttime *Stop the Music* from 1949–56, and producer Harry Salter, who produced the prime-time *Name That Tune* (q.v.) in the 1950s. The show actually began on ABC Tuesdays at 9:30 p.m. from November 14, 1961–September 18, 1962.

YOUTH TAKES A STAND
Public Affairs; B&W
October 11, 1953–April 2, 1955

CBS Sun. 3:30–4 p.m. (10/11/53–1/10/54)
CBS Sun. 3–3:30 p.m. (1/17/54–3/28/54)
CBS Sun. 4:30–5 p.m. (4/4/54–6/27/54)
CBS Sun. 5:30–6 p.m. (7/4/54–10/10/54)
CBS Sat. 2:30–3 p.m. (10/16/54–4/2/55)

Host: *Allen Jackson (1953–54), Jim McKay (1954–55)*

CBS's answer to *Youth Wants to Know* had a quartet of students from a different high school or junior college each week asking a guest CBS correspondent about the top news stories of the week. The show started on prime time on August 18, 1953 with its co-producer Marc Cramer as host, but by the time it arrived on Sunday afternoons a month later, Alan Jackson had replaced Cramer. Jim McKay succeeded Jackson on April 25, 1954.

•YOUTH WANTS TO KNOW
Public Affairs; B&W
December 8, 1951–October 12, 1958

NBC Sat. 5–5:30 p.m. (12/8/51–5/24/52)
NBC Sun. 1–1:30 p.m. (9/28/52–12/26/54)
NBC Sun. Various half hours between 2:30 and 5 p.m.
  (1/2/55–8/31/58)
NBC Sun. 5:30–6 p.m. (9/7/58–10/12/58)

Host: *Theodore Granik (1951–54), Stephen McCormick (1954–58)*

This was the longest-running of several 1950s public affairs series involving adolescents (for others, see *Junior Press Conference, The New York Times Youth Forum,* and *Youth Takes a Stand*). Theodore Granik created the show in 1930 while lining up speakers for his radio show *American Forum of the Air* and noting how his 13-year-old son Bill took an interest in the process and asked intelligent questions of the speakers set for that show. That inspired him to create a format where one politician met each week, in a press conference setting, with young people ranging in age from 16–19 asking questions of the guest. Members of the American Legion selected some 50 high school and junior college students from the Washington, D.C., area for the show. Granik picked out interrogators from the audience and moderated discussions until he left as host, though he continued as producer.

Guests ranged from Sen. Howard Taft in 1951 to ex-President Harry Truman in 1958. By 1957 nonpolitical types had begun appearing often, such as comedian Jerry Lewis, actor Burt Lancaster, and movie producer Mike Todd. Most found they needed to be quick-witted with the younger set, who had no inhibitions in asking tough questions or telling a wordy politico to stop the filibustering. A measure of the show's reputation is that German Chancellor Konrad Adenauer appeared on it during a U.S. visit while rejecting offers from *Face the Nation* and *Meet the Press.* The show also achieved a unique distinction when host McCormick and 12 panelists played themselves in the 1958 movie comedy *Miss Casey Jones,* where Doris Day's character appeared before them explaining her opposition to an evil railroad owner played by Ernie Kovacs.

But the extracurricular activity did not win over NBC, which ended a seven-year network run that began Saturday evenings on September 8, 1951 under the title *The American Youth Forum.* When it moved to Saturday afternoons, it aired Sundays at noon on kinescopes in New York City. In January 1952 it was renamed *Youth Wants to Know,* and returned to NBC in the nighttime in the summers of 1952 and 1954 in addition to its regular Sunday afternoon shows.

A syndicated version of *Youth Wants to Know* began on March 1959 with Granik hosting a monthly offering in Washington, D.C. The series moved production to New York in 1962 and continued with other hosts through at least 1967.

Z

ZAZOO U.
Cartoon; Color
September 8, 1990–August 31, 1991

Fox Sat. 8:30–9 a.m. (9/8/90–10/6/90)
Fox Sat. 8–8:30 a.m. (10/13/90–8/31/91)

Fox promoted *Zazoo U.* as a "new *Sesame Street*–like series with offbeat animal characters who teach valuable lessons to

kids," according to *Variety.* Students included Boink, Tess, Grizzle, and Bully. The cartoon was the first one canceled by Fox on its initial Saturday morning lineup, though the network repeated it through the summer of 1991.

ZOO PARADE
Educational; B&W and Color
May 28, 1950–September 1, 1957

NBC Sun. 4:30–5 p.m. (5/28/50–12/23/51)
NBC Sun. 5–5:30 p.m. (12/30/51–11/16/52)
NBC Sun. 4:30–5 p.m. (11/23/52–10/2/55)
NBC Sun. 3:30–4 p.m. (10/9/55–6/16/57)
NBC Sun. 4:30–5 p.m. (6/23/57–9/1/57)

Regulars: *Marlin Perkins, Jim Hurlbut*

Marlin Perkins became a nationally known, and much parodied, animal expert thanks to the groundwork laid by this long-running show. Using a living room set, it showcased animals from Chicago's Lincoln Park Zoo, where Perkins had served as director since 1944 (he had his first industry job nearly 20 years earlier as a hedge trimmer at the St. Louis Zoo). Perkins used this format as early as 1945 on local television in the Windy City, then turned it into a local series in 1949 called *Lincoln Park Zoo,* which went to NBC in 1950.

Perkins and his assistant Jim Hurlbut screened the animals to find the ones that would be the least camera-shy and most entertaining on air, such as Sinbad the gorilla and Fuad the small fox, but Hurlbut and Perkins were not infallible.

Marlin Perkins tickles a capybara, on Zoo Parade.

On April Fools' Day in 1951 a rattlesnake bit Perkins during a dress rehearsal, requiring a 16-day hospital stay, and the on-air substitute that day faced an angry elephant which threw him onto a bale of hay.

In July and August 1955 Perkins and Hurlbut went on a South African safari and shot color footage for the show which first aired on December 18, 1955. Also in the fall of 1955, the program aired from locations outside the studio (New Orleans, Philadelphia, Dallas, Detroit, Milwaukee, etc.). The series ended two years later, but Perkins returned in 1963 with the even more successful *Wild Kingdom*.

•ZOOBILEE ZOO
Children; Color
1986

Syndicated 30 minutes daily beginning September 1986

Cast:

Mayor Ben	*Ben Vereen*
Bill Der Beaver	*Michael Sheehan*
Lookout Bear	*Michael Moynahan*
Whazzat Kangaroo	*Louise Vallance*
Van Go Lion	*Forrest Gardner*
Bravo Fox	*Gary Schwartz*
Talkatoo Cockatoo	*Karen Hartman*

Zoobilee Zoo sought to teach preschoolers simple activities with rhymes, songs, and other forms of communication using actors made up as animals. Mayor Ben, a leopard, was host of each episode and had only nominal involvement with the other characters in the story lines. The creatures included Bill Der Beaver, an inventor; Whazzat Kangaroo, a pianist; Van Go Lion, an artist; and Bravo Fox, an Ed Wynn–type entertainer. With its colorful set, which looked more like a village than a zoo, and makeup which did a realistic job of getting the actors to resemble animals, this videotaped series was one of the best children's shows to air on commercial television in the 1980s.

ZOORAMA
Educational; B&W
April 18, 1965–September 26, 1965

CBS Sun. 5–5:30 p.m. (4/18/65–9/26/65)

Host: *Bob Dale*

The San Diego Zoo, considered one of the finest animal-exhibiting facilities in the world, was where *Zoorama* profiled groups or species of creatures in three segments per show. Executive Producer George Stantis told *TV Guide* that Bob Dale's role was that of "the guy from the sticks who knows nothing and asks the curator to explain everything." One wonders if Dale was in character during a taping where he had his coat torn off by a gorilla.

Zoorama was a local show on KFMB San Diego for a decade before airing on CBS (a few reruns did appear on New York and Los Angeles stations in the fall of 1963), and continued as a local offering through the 1960s. It was offered in syndication from 1968–71. Joan Embery, an employee with the zoo, plugged *Zoorama* on national TV, starting in the early 1970s and continuing through the 1990s, with appearances on *The Tonight Show Starring Johnny Carson* and other talk shows during which she displayed some of the zoo's animals.

DAYTIME RERUNS OF NIGHTTIME AND SYNDICATED SERIES

In February 1951, ABC inauspiciously launched the first nighttime series to show repeats in daytime when it reran the first season of *Dick Tracy* on Saturday mornings through April 1951. A few other cases of reruns hit the weekend period over the next few years, with *The Lone Ranger* being the first to have original episodes air on one network in nighttime (ABC) and daytime repeats on another (CBS). Then in 1956, NBC inaugurated a series known as *Comedy Time,* which showed filmed programs like *I Married Joan* five days a week. The network probably was inspired by reports in trade papers about the strong ratings local stations were enjoying in 1955 "stripping" repeats of such shows as *My Little Margie* and *Amos 'n' Andy. I Married Joan* in fact knocked down its competition *The Mickey Mouse Club,* but the network did not have rights for long to repeat the show and purchased instead some of its other canceled series like *It's a Great Life, It's Always Jan,* and *So This Is Hollywood* to fill out the period. They were just as unappealing and unsuccessful in daytime as they had been at night. But ABC developed some counterprogramming of its own and brought in old episodes of network and syndicated children's shows like *The Adventures of Superman* and *The Buccaneers* at 5 p.m. daily in 1957, where they fared quite well.

What really put daytime reruns on the map was the January 5, 1959 daily debut of *I Love Lucy. I Love Lucy* proved to be just as popular in reruns as it had been when it was the top nighttime sitcom of the 1950s, and the show set several records: the show with the longest run in repeats on a network daily ($7^1/2$ years), the first program to air in repeats only at night (from 1955–61) and then in daytime, and the only series to be repeated all seven days of the week by a network (in the summer of 1960, when it aired before noon Mondays through Saturdays and Sundays from 10–10:30 p.m. in last-season repeats under the title *Lucy in Connecticut).*

Lucy's success prompted ABC to add repeats to its sagging daytime lineup in 1959, beginning with *The Gale Storm Show* and followed with *The Restless Gun* and *The Bob Cummings Show.* Late in 1959, the game show scandals prompted cancellations of several programs believed to be rigged (*Top Dollar* and *The Big Payoff),* and their replacements were repeats of *December Bride* and *The Millionaire.* The rush to rerun was on and dominated much of the programming

of the 1960s on all three networks, not only weekdays but also weekends, and sitcoms were found to be the most appealing form to show over again and again. In fact, from the fall of 1965 to the fall of 1969 the CBS morning lineup from 10 a.m. to noon consisted solely of comedy repeats. But though these shows brought decent ratings, they never appeared at the top of the listings.

In an article in *Variety* that appeared on October 29, 1969, CBS executives announced that the network had lost interest in nighttime TV show reruns because contracts to repeat such programs as *Here's Lucy, Gomer Pyle,* and *Family Affair* were long-term deals that cost approximately $5 million per show if five years' worth of episodes were to be repeated. Beside the rising costs, the shows typically attracted more children than women viewers, making them less desirable for advertisers. It took a few years for this change in programming to take place—indeed, CBS reserved the 10–11:30 a.m. block for comedy repeats through the fall of 1972—but by that time, for the reasons the article listed, the glow for reruns was off all the networks, completely for the weekends and almost totally in the daytime. In 1973 the only reruns one could find were *The Brady Bunch* and *Love American Style* on ABC. For the next two decades the networks did occasionally install reruns daily, usually as a temporary plug to fill gaps in the schedule, and rarely did they air more than an hour's worth during each network's daytime lineup.

In 1993 *Designing Women* became the last nighttime show to date to be repeated in the daytime. It will probably retain that distinction because the networks are finding it harder than ever to convince affiliates to carry their daily programming, and some station operators wonder why they should show repeats when they can air the same type of programming without having to bump local advertisers for the network's sponsors.

Listed below alphabetically are all of the network and syndicated programs which aired in the nighttime before running in repeats on the networks in daytime, either daily or on weekends. Also included are umbrella titles for several series run under a certain banner. Due to space limitations, their runs in nighttime and daytime are not listed, but they all definitely aired on the network in reruns in daytime at one time between 1951 and 1993.

Abbott and Costello Show, The
Adventure Time (umbrella title)
Adventures of Rin Tin Tin, The
Adventures of Sir Lancelot, The
Adventures of Robin Hood, The
Adventures of Superman, The
Adventures of Wild Bill Hickok, The
Alice
All in the Family
Andy Griffith Show, The
Angie
Annie Oakley

Ben Casey
Benson
Beverly Hillbillies, The
Bewitched
Blondie (1957 version)
Bob Cummings Show, The
Brady Bunch, The
Broken Arrow
Buccaneers, The
Buckskin
Buffalo Billy Jr.

Candid Camera
Celebrity Game, The
Chico & the Man
Chips
Circus Boy
Comedy Circus
Comedy Theater (umbrella title)
Comedy Time (umbrella title)

Danny Thomas Show
Dear Phoebe
December Bride
Dennis the Menace
Designing Women
Dick Tracy
Dick Van Dyke Show, The
Diff'rent Strokes
Donna Reed

Facts of Life, The
Family Affair
Family Ties
Father Knows Best
Fibber McGee & Molly
Fireside Theater
Fugitive, The
Full House
Fun at Five (umbrella title)

Gale Storm Show, The
Golden Girls, The
Gomer Pyle
Growing Pains

Happy Days
Here's Lucy

I Love Lucy
I Married Joan
It's a Great Life
It's Always Jan

Jack Benny
Jeffersons, The
Junior Crossroads

Lash of the West
Lassie
Laverne & Shirley
Lone Ranger, The
Loretta Young Show, The
Love, American Style
Love Boat, The
Lucy Show, The

M*A*S*H
Mark Saber
Millionaire, The
Mr. Belvedere
Monkees

Morning Playhouse (daytime
    title for Schlitz Playhouse
    of Stars)
My Friend Flicka
My Three Sons

NBC News Encore

One Day at a Time
Our Miss Brooks

Perfect Strangers
Pete and Gladys

Range Rider, The
Real McCoys, The
Restless Gun, The
Roomies
Roy Rogers Show, The

Sanford and Son
Saturday Playhouse (daytime title
    for Schlitz Playhouse of Stars)
Sergeant Preston of the Yukon
Silver Spoons
So This Is Hollywood
Soap Box Theater

Texan, The
That Girl
Thin Man
Three's Company
Three's a Crowd
Too Close for Comfort
Topper
227

Wagon Train
Webster
Who's the Boss?

Yancy Derringer

LONGEST RUNNING DAYTIME NETWORK TV SERIES

Note: The shows are listed as of August 1996, with generic series of specific sports and news not included. Their daytime runs are the only ones counted, which is why the longest running network TV series of all time, *Meet the Press,* is not ranked in first place, as it ran in nighttime from 1947–49 and 1952–65. Any gap of at least a year between appearances is not counted in the total either, but noted in the calculations for the show's tenure in the list.

1. *The Today Show*—NBC, January 14, 1952–. Total run: 44 years 7 months

2. *Guiding Light*—CBS, June 30, 1952–. Total run: 44 years 2 months

3. *As the World Turns*—CBS, May 2, 1956–. Total run: 40 years 3 months

4. *Face the Nation*—CBS, November 7, 1954–September 1960, September 1963–. Total run: 38 years 9 months

5. *ABC's Wide World of Sports*—ABC, April 29, 1961–. Total run: 35 years 4 months

6. *Search for Tomorrow*—CBS and NBC, September 3, 1951–December 26, 1986. Total run: 35 years 3 months

7. *Pro Bowlers Tour*—ABC, January 6, 1962–. Total run: 34 years 7 months

8. *Bugs Bunny Show*—ABC and CBS, April 7, 1962–. Total run: 34 years 4 months

9. *General Hospital*—ABC, April 1, 1963–. Total run: 33 years 4 months

10. *Meet the Press*—NBC, February 26, 1950–May 1952, September 1965–. Total run: 33 years 2 months

11. *CBS Morning News*—CBS, September 2, 1963–. Total run: 32 years 11 months

12. *The Price Is Right*—NBC, ABC, and CBS, November 26, 1956–September 1965, September 1972–. Total run: 32 years 9 months

13. *Another World*—NBC, May 4, 1964–. Total run: 32 years 3 months

14. *CBS Sports Spectacular*—CBS, January 3, 1960–August 1967, January 1973–. Total run: 31 years 4 months

15. *Days of Our Lives*—NBC, November 8, 1965–. Total run: 30 years 9 months

16. *Lamp Unto My Feet*—CBS, November 21, 1948–January 21, 1979. Total run: 30 years 2 months

17. *American Bandstand*—ABC, August 5, 1957–September 5, 1987. Total run: 30 years 1 month

18. *Captain Kangaroo*—CBS, October 3, 1955–December 8, 1984. Total run: 29 years 2 months

19. *The Edge of Night*—CBS and ABC, May 2, 1956–December 28, 1984. Total run: 28 years 7 months

20. *Love of Life*—CBS, September 24, 1951–February 1, 1980. Total run: 28 years 5 months

21. *One Life to Live*—ABC, July 15, 1968–. Total run: 28 years 1 month

22. *All My Children*—ABC, January 5, 1970–. Total run: 26 years 7 months

23. *Look Up and Live*—CBS, January 3, 1954–January 21, 1979. Total run: 25 years

24. *The Young and the Restless*—CBS, March 26, 1973–. Total run: 23 years 5 months

25. *Directions*—ABC, November 13, 1960–March 25, 1984. Total run: 23 years 4 months

26. *Camera Three*—CBS, January 22, 1956–January 21, 1979. Total run: 23 years

27. *Concentration*—NBC, July 26, 1958–March 1973, May 1987–December 31, 1993–. Total run: 21 years 3 months

28. *Issues and Answers*—ABC, November 27, 1960–November 8, 1981. Total run: 21 years

29. *Scooby-Doo*—CBS and ABC, September 13, 1969–September 1986, September 1988–August 1991, September 1992–September 4, 1993. Total run: 20 years 11 months

30. *Good Morning America*—ABC, November 3, 1975–. Total run: 20 years 9 months

31. *The Secret Storm*—CBS, February 1, 1954–February 8, 1954. Total run: 20 years

32. *The Doctors*—NBC, April 1, 1963–December 31, 1982. Total run: 19 years 9 months

33. *The ABC Weekend Special*—ABC, January 29, 1977–. Total run: 19 years 7 months

34. *The American Sportsman*—ABC, January 31, 1965–June 24, 1984. Total run: 19 years 5 months

35. *Sunrise Semester*—CBS, September 23, 1963–October 1, 1982. Total run: 19 years 1 month

36. *NBC-TV Religious Program*—NBC, October 7, 1951–July 19, 1970. Total run: 18 years 9 months

37. *Art Linkletter's House Party*—CBS and NBC, September 1, 1952–September 25, 1970. Total run: 18 years

38. *Password*—CBS, ABC, and NBC, October 1961–September 1967, March 1971–June 1975, January 1979–March 1982, September 1984–March 1989. Total run: 17 years 9 months

39. *Sunday Morning*—CBS, January 28, 1979–. Total run: 17 years 7 months

40. *Wheel of Fortune*—NBC and CBS, January 7, 1975–September 20, 1991. Total run: 16 years 8 months

41. *This Week with David Brinkley*—ABC, November 15, 1981–. Total run: 14 years 9 months

42. *The Jetsons*—ABC, CBS, and NBC, September 21, 1963–September 1967, September 1969–September 1976, February 1979–September 1981, September 1982–April 2, 1983. Total run: 14 years 2 months

43. *The Bullwinkle Show*—ABC and NBC, November 19, 1959–September 1961, September 1962–September 1973, September 1981–July 24, 1982. Total run: 13 years 8 months

44. *The Hollywood Squares*—NBC, October 17, 1966–June 20, 1980. Total run: 13 years 7 months

45. *Ryan's Hope*—ABC, July 7, 1975–January 13, 1989. Total run: 13 years 6 months

46. *The Match Game*—NBC, CBS, and ABC, December 31, 1962–September 1969, July 1973–April 1979, July 1990–July 12, 1991. Total run: 13 years 5 months

47. *Loving*—ABC, June 27, 1983–. Total run: 13 years 2 months

48. *Family Feud*—ABC and CBS, July 12, 1976–June 1985, June 1988–September 3, 1993. Total run: 13 years 2 months

49. *Let's Make a Deal*—NBC and ABC, December 30, 1963–July 1976, July 1990–January 11, 1991. Total run: 13 years 1 month

50. *The $10,000 Pyramid*—CBS and ABC, March 26, 1973–June 1980, September 1982–July 1, 1988. Total run: 13 years 1 month

APPENDIX C

BIBLIOGRAPHY

BOOKS

Brooks, Tim, and Earle Marsh. *The Complete Directory to Prime Time Network and Cable Shows, 1946–Present,* 6th ed. New York: Ballantine, 1995.

Buxton, Frank, and Bill Owen. *The Big Broadcast.* New York: Viking, 1972.

Castleman, Harry, and Walter J. Podrazik. *The TV Schedule Book.* New York: McGraw-Hill, 1984.

Davis, Stephen. *Say Kids! What Time Is It?* Boston: Little, Brown, 1987.

Dunning, John. *Tune In Yesterday: The Ultimate Encyclopedia of Old-Time Radio 1925–1976.* Englewood Cliffs, N.J.: Prentice-Hall, 1976.

Einstein, Daniel. *Special Edition: A Guide to Network Television Documentary Series and Special News Reports, 1955–1979.* Metuchen, N.J.: Scarecrow, 1987.

Erickson, Hal. *Television Cartoon Shows: An Illustrated Encyclopedia, 1949 Through 1993.* Jefferson, N.C.: 1995.

Grossman, Gary H. *Saturday Morning TV.* New York: Dell, 1981.

Kessler, Judy. *Inside Today: The Battle for the Morning.* New York: Villard, 1992.

LaGuardia, Robert. *From Ma Perkins to Mary Hartman: The Illustrated History of Soap Operas.* New York: Ballantine, 1977.

LaGuardia, Robert. *Soap World.* New York: Arbor House, 1983.

LaGuardia, Robert. *The Wonderful World of TV Soap Operas.* New York: Ballantine, 1974.

Lenburg, Jeff. *The Encyclopedia of Animated Cartoons.* New York: Facts on File, 1991.

McNeil, Alex. *Total Television: A Comprehensive Guide to Programming from 1948 to the Present,* 3rd ed. New York: Penguin, 1991.

Perry, Dick. *Not Just a Sound: The Story of WLW.* Englewood Cliffs, N.J.: Prentice-Hall, 1971.

Poll, Julie. *As the World Turns: The Complete Family Scrapbook.* Los Angeles: General Publishing, 1996.

Schemering, Christopher. *The Soap Opera Encyclopedia.* New York: Ballantine Books, 1985 (revised 1987).

Schwartz, David, Steve Ryan, and Fred Wostbrock. *The Encyclopedia of TV Game Shows,* 2nd ed. New York: Facts on File, 1995.

Scott, Kathryn Leigh, and Jim Pierson, eds. *Dark Shadows Almanac.* Beverly Hills: Pomegranate Press, 1995.

Series, Serials and Packages. New York: Broadcast Information Bureau, 1978.

Skutch, Ira. *Ira Skutch: I Remember Television: A Memoir.* Metuchen, N.J.: Scarecrow, 1989.

Smith, Curt. *Voices of the Game, Updated Edition.* New York: Simon and Schuster, 1992.

Terrace, Vincent. *Television 1970-1980.* San Diego: A.S. Barnes, 1981.

Terrace, Vincent. *Encyclopedia of Television Series, Pilots and Specials 1937–1973.* New York: Zoetrope, 1986.

Waggett, Gerald T. *The Soap Opera Book of Lists.* New York: HarperCollins, 1996.

Waldron, Robert. *The Bold and the Beautiful: A Tenth Anniversary Celebration.* New York: HarperCollins, 1996.

Warner, Gary. *All My Children: The Complete Family Scrapbook.* Los Angeles: General Publishing, 1994.

Warner, Gary. *General Hospital: The Complete Scrapbook.* Los Angeles: General Publishing, 1995.

Woolery, George W. *Children's Television: The First Thirty-Five Years.* Metuchen, N.J.: Scarecrow, 1983 (Part I) and 1985 (Part II).

Zenka, Lorraine. *Days of Our Lives: The Complete Family Album.* New York: HarperCollins, 1995.

PERIODICALS

Billboard. 1946–1958 (ended television coverage on February 17, 1958).

The New York Times. 1948–60.

TV Guide. 1954–1996.

Variety. 1946–1996.

INDEX